W9-ANI-806

Index

TO THE

Prerogative Wills of Ireland,

1536–1810.

Index

TO THE

Prerogative Wills of Ireland,

1536–1810.

EDITED BY

SIR ARTHUR VICARS, F.S.A.,

ULSTER KING OF ARMS.

Genealogical Publishing Co., Inc.

Baltimore

Originally Published in Dublin, 1897
Reprinted by Genealogical Publishing Co., Inc.
Baltimore, 1967, 1989, 1997
Library of Congress Catalogue Card Number 67-29834
International Standard Book Number 0-8063-0361-1
Made in the United States of America

PREFACE.

AMONGST the various sources of information open to the genealogist, it is generally admitted that Wills occupy the most important place. From a testamentary document, it is often possible to obtain particulars of three or four generations of a family, besides a general insight into the extent of civilization and social position of our ancestors. Not only can we see the autograph of the testator, but often ascertain the armorial bearings of the family, since it was customary in former days for testators not only to sign, but also to seal, their wills.

By means of the armorial bearings on seals attached to wills one often obtains important clues to family descent—not to speak of the value of information about lands and residences, places of burial, and other useful matter mentioned in such documents.

The wills in Ireland may be said to consist of two classes, Prerogative and Diocesan. Those proved in the Prerogative Court are the most important, containing, as they do, testamentary devises from all parts of Ireland, and generally referring to the more important members of the community. They commence in 1536, and continue to 1858.

Before 1857, wills used to be proved in the Consistorial Court, that is, the Court of the Bishop or Ordinary, within whose diocese or jurisdiction the testator dwelt ; but if there were effects to the value of £5 (called *bona notabilia*), in two or more dioceses, the will had to be proved in the Prerogative Court of the Archbishop of Armagh, Primate of all Ireland, which was the Supreme Court in matters of which the ecclesiastical jurisdiction had cognisance.

b

The right of appointing a Judge or Commissary of the Prerogative Court in Ireland was originally vested in the Crown.
By Letters Patent of 20 James I., the Archbishop of Armagh and
his successors were appointed the Judges of the Court, and later
were empowered (Letters Patent, 20 Charles I.) to appoint a
Commissary of the Prerogative Court, instead of being obliged,
as formerly, to act in person.

By the Act 7 & 8 George IV., c. 44, the office. of Judge of the
Court of Faculties, which dealt with Ecclesiastical causes, was
consolidated with that of Judge of the Prerogative Court.

The jurisdiction of the various Consistorial Courts in Ireland
was confined to dealing with the assets of deceased persons
who were domiciled in the Diocese, and who had no personal
estate in any other Diocese in the Kingdom ; and in the case of
a person dying out of Ireland, who left personal estate in only
one Diocese, the Consistorial Court of that Diocese had jurisdiction over such estate.

Up to 1816 the Court of Prerogative used to be held in the
private residence of the judge, and sometimes in the Chapter
Room of S. Patrick's Cathedral, and the original wills and
records were not kept in any certain or secure custody, no proper
building having been provided for these purposes.

Owing chiefly to the efforts of Dr. Radcliff, who was appointed
Judge of the Court in 1816, the Court of Prerogative was established in Henrietta-street, Dublin, and the original wills and
other records were then transferred there, where they remained
until removed to the Public Record Office, their present de-
pository.

By the Court of Probate Act, 1857 (20 & 21 Vict. c. 77),
the jurisdiction of the antient Ecclesiastical Courts, and of the
few surviving courts of exempt jurisdiction, was abolished,
and transferred to the Probate Court, constituted a separate
Division of the High Court by the Judicature Act, 1873 ; and
further amalgamated with the Queen's Bench Division, a par-
ticular Judge being assigned to deal with testamentary matters,
under the Judicature Act, 1897.

Not till the year 1810, when the Irish Record Commission

began its labours, did any index to these wills exist, nor was it possible for the public to consult them before that date without considerable difficulty. Amongst the most useful works undertaken by that body was the arrangement and classification of the Wills of Ireland.

This work was in a large measure carried out by Sir William Betham, Ulster King-of-Arms, who superintended the alphabetical indexing of the Prerogative Wills, and at the same time, with his own hand, took genealogical notes from each will, forming them into chart pedigrees. These latter invaluable records are included among the collections of that indefatigable genealogist, and are now deposited in the Office of Arms, Dublin Castle. An idea of the magnitude of the work may be gathered when it is stated that they are contained in 34 folio volumes, and are accompanied by an elaborate Index of Alliances.

Through the courtesy of the Deputy Keeper of the Public Records of Ireland, Dr. J. J. Digges La Touche, who procured the necessary permission of the Master of the Rolls, the Indexes compiled under the supervision and direction of Sir William Betham, Ulster King-of-Arms, were placed at my service.

Although arranged on the slip system, similar to that adopted in the British Museum Catalogue, the lexicographical order was but loosely adhered to, and it became necessary to largely recast the Index, while, to ensure accuracy, constant reference had to be made to the original wills in the Public Record Office.

Owing to the variations which occur in the form and the spelling of many names, it has been thought advisable to add cross-references where they seem desirable, in order to afford aid to the less experienced searcher; though no competent genealogist will fail to consult every likely orthographical rendering of the name of which he is in quest. For a similar reason, cross-references have been given to the surnames of bishops, whose wills are generally indexed under the name of their See.

In cases where wills were proved in England, only copies of the originals will be found in Ireland, and this is denoted in the Index.

A separate Index to the Alliances and Aliases mentioned in the wills (and given in large type in the main Index) is added at the end, where will also be found a Catalogue of some one hundred wills, called the Hawkins Collection, reprinted from the Fourteenth Report of the Deputy Keeper of the Public Records in Ireland.

As the number of wills proved in the Prerogative Court increased considerably after the commencement of the present century, it was thought better not to continue the Index beyond the year 1810 (which is the year in which a break in the series is recognised in the Public Record Office), especially as the later wills are of comparatively small utility for genealogical purposes.

The complete classification of the wills of Ireland in public custody is as follows:—

I. Prerogative Wills, 1536–1858, deposited in the Public Record Office.

II. Diocesan Wills, 1536–1858, deposited in the Public Record Office.*

III. A limited number of unproved wills dealing with Real Property only, recorded from the year 1708, at the Registry of Deeds, Henrietta-street.

IV. Wills from the Inquisitions (Henry VIII. to George I.); an excerpt of which, with an Index Nominum, is in the Public Record Office.

V. A few very early wills in the Royal Irish Academy, and in Trinity College Library.†

As wills belonging to members of the same families as those mentioned in the Index to the Prerogative Wills are likely to be found among the Diocesan Wills, it has been thought advis-

---

* An Index to the Dublin Diocesan Wills and Grants is printed in the Appendix to the XXVIth Report of the Deputy Keeper of the P.R.O. of Ireland.

† The latter are in course of publication by Mr. Henry F. Berry, M.A., of the P.R.O., under the auspices of the Royal Society of Antiquaries of Ireland, under the title of " The Register of the Diocese of Dublin in the times of Archbishops Tregury and Walton, 1467–1483," from a MS. in Trinity College, Dublin.

able to give a table showing in what dioceses the various Irish counties are situated, which will be found at the end of this volume.

For further information regarding the depositories of Irish Wills and other particulars concerning them, I would refer to the chapter on " Irish Genealogy " in an excellent little handbook entitled " A Supplement to ' How to write the History of a Family,' " by W. P. W. Phillimore, 8vo, London, 1896.

While thanking the subscribers to this Index for their public-spirited support, I feel I ought to apologize to them for the delay in its publication, which, in a great measure, was due to the necessity of obtaining a sufficient number of subscribers before going to press.

In conclusion I must not forget to acknowledge the kind help which I have received from the Deputy Keeper of the Public Records and his courteous assistants ; nor to record my indebtedness to Mr. Edmund Fry, Honorary Secretary to the British Record Society, for valuable hints, and to Mr. Arthur Samuels, Q.C., LL.D., for information concerning the history of the Ecclesiastical Courts of Ireland ; and last, and not least, to the great help afforded by my assistant, Mr. Frank S. Marsh, of the Office of Arms, who, with remarkable perseverance and accuracy, has prepared for press, and corrected the proofs of, the greater portion of the Index. In a work of the kind, perfection is scarcely to be expected, but I feel that any reputation for accuracy which this work may obtain is, in a great measure, due to his painstaking assistance.

If I have by the publication of this Index in any way assisted the researches of my brother genealogists, I shall feel amply rewarded ; and it is to be hoped that at no distant date an Index to the Diocesan Wills of Ireland may be published.

ARTHUR VICARS, Ulster.

Office of Arms,
Dublin Castle,
November, 1897.

CONTENTS.

INDEX

TO

PREROGATIVE WILLS OF IRELAND.

————◆————

B

1746 **Ackland**, Dudley, Dublin, esq.
1709 **Acourt**, Alice, Dublin, widow
1699 **Acson**, Christian, Chester, widow
1767 **Acteson**, Elizabeth, Waterford, widow
1801 ,, Mary
1804 ,, William, Glenhouse, co. Waterford, gent.
1656 **Acton**, Edward, son of Edward Acton, Loughill, co. Longford, gent. [**V**. 298
1765 ,, James, Athlone, gent.
1716 ,, John, Dublin, felt maker
1780 ,, Mary, Athlone, co. Westmeath, merchant
1689 ,, Richard, D.D., vice-provost, Trinity College, Dublin
1736 ,, Richard, Longford, King's County, gent.
1750 ,, Thomas, Dublin, esq.
1755 ,, William, Athlone, co. Westmeath, gent. (This will revoked).
1779 ,, William, Dublin, esq. [gent.
1787 **Adair**, Arthur, Parkgate, co. Antrim,
1711 ,, Charles, cornet in gen. Pearce's regiment of dragoons
1688 ,, Elinor, Clonbroney, co. Longford, widow [low, esq.
1786 ,, Foster, Hollybrooke, co. Wick-
1751 ,, James, Crow-street, Dublin
1747 ,, Jane, Hollybrooke, co. Wicklow, widow
1800 ,, dame Jane
1760 ,, John, Dublin, esq. [esq.
1809 ,, John, Rath, Queen's County,
1767 ,, Patrick, London, merchant (Copy)
1656 ,, sir Robert, Ballymena, co. Antrim
1737 ,, Robert, Dublin, esq.
1791 ,, Robert, Stratford-place, Middlesex, esq. (Copy)
1792 ,, Thomas, Stradbally, Queen's County
1666 ,, William, Ballimena, co. Antrim, esq. (2 probates).
1746 ,, William, Belfast, formerly of London, merchant
1774 ,, William, of Rath, Queen's County, gent.
1797 ,, William, Dublin, esq.
1799 ,, William, Ballymenesla, dio. Connor
1699 **Adaire**, Michael, Dublin, merchant tailor
1755 ,, Thomas, Clonterry, Queen's County, gent.
1712 ,, William, Litter, King's County, esq.

1769 **Adam**, James, Granard, co. Longford
1761 ,, John, Granard, co. Longford, shopkeeper
1806 ,, John, South Cumberland-street
1790 **Adams**, Abigail, Ennis, co. Clare, widow
1756 ,, Allen, Carronary
1806 ,, the rev. Arthur Noble, Shercock-house, co. Cavan
1766 ,, Anthony, Aclare, co. Meath, gent.
1805 ,, Cosby, Dorset-street, Dublin, esq.
1716 ,, Daniel, Knockmonebeg, co. Cork
1656 ,, Edward, Doneraile [**VI**. 60
1809 ,, Edward, Drumkirk, co. Tyrone
1749 ,, Elizabeth
1773 ,, Elizabeth, Dublin, widow
1802 ,, Elizabeth, Dromgoon, widow
1680 ,, Francis, Boardstown, co. Westmeath, esq.
1798 ,, Francis, Rathconnell
1811 ,, Francis, Doohat, co. Fermanagh, farmer
1775 ,, George, Heathstown, co. Meath, esq.
1787 ,, Henry Humphrey, Dublin, gent.
1799 ,, James, Tullydoey, co. Tyrone
1809 ,, Jas., Coronary, co. Cavan, esq.
1715 ,, John, Portna, co. Londonderry, esq.
1809 ,, John, city of Dublin, painter
1773 ,, Joseph, Ennis, co. Clare, gent.
1784 ,, Laurence, Dublin, tailor.
1802 ,, Michael, Charleville, co. Cork, esq.
1801 ,, Owen, Richmond
1778 ,, Prudence, Miltown, co. Cork, widow
1725 ,, Randall, Gore, Kent, esq. (Copy)
1749 ,, Randall, major in gen. Otway's regiment of foot
1753 ,, Randal, Dublin, esq.
1774 ,, Richard, Dublin, grocer
1789 ,, Richard, city of Cork, esq.
1790 ,, Richard, Shercock House, co. Cavan, esq.
1729 ,, Robert, Heathstown, co. Meath, gent.
1733 ,, Robert, Granard, co. Longford, merchant
1792 ,, Robert, surgeon in Bombay (Copy)
1806 ,, Robert, town of Galway, merchant
1762 ,, Roger, Shandrum, co. Cork, gent.

1789 **Adams**, Roger, Jones-sq., city of Cork
1791 ,, Samuel, city of Cork, esq.
1799 ,, Samuel, Linnen Hall-st., Dubl.
1753 ,, Sarah, Coleraine, co. Derry, widow
1810 ,, Stewart, Mecklenburgh-st., esq.
1660 ,, Thomas, Kilkenny, esq.
1757 ,, William, Killue, co. Clare, gent.
1758 ,, William, Royal Hospital, Dublin, gent.
1802 ,, William, city of Dublin, toy merchant
[See ADDAMES.]
1764 **Adamson**, Benjamin, Moate, co. Westmeath
1747 ,, Charles, Cloneyhegan, co. Westmeath, farmer
1782 ,, George, Cloneyegan, co. Westmeath, gent.
1779 ,, James, Capell-street, publican
1641 ,, John, city of Chester, innholder
1749 ,, John, Dublin, alderman
1768 ,, Joseph, Clara, King's County
1784 ,, Josiah, New Abby, co. Kildare, brewer
1781 ,, Mary, Dublin, widow
1781 ,, Rebecca, city of Bath, widow
1771 ,, Robert, Moate, co. Westmeath, shopkeeper [widow
1768 ,, Sarah, Moate, co. Westmeath,
1795 ,, Thomas, Dublin, merchant
1807 ,, Thomas, Moate
1792 ,, William Gustavus, Nahod, co. Westmeath, esq.
[See ADOMSON.]
1753 **Adcock**, Mary, Castle-street, Dublin, confectioner
1634 **Addames**, Thomas, St. Thomas-street, dyer
1651 **Adderley**, Thomas, Inishanane, co. Cork, esq. [esq.
1791 ,, Thomas, Inishannon, co. Cork,
1719 **Adderly**, Francis, Drumkeen, near Bandon, co. Cork, esq. (Ex.)
1691 ,, Thomas, Enishonane, co. Cork, esq. (Ex.)
1616 **Addies**, Thomas, Portmarnock, co. Dublin, gent.
1790 **Addis**, Anne, Dublin, widow
1773 ,, Fenton, Summerhill, co. Cork, esq.
1655 ,, John, Frampton, Gloucestershire, yeoman
1742 ,, John, Cork, merchant
[See ADDIES.]
1675 **Addison**, George, Aghadromdoney, co. Monaghan, gent.
1776 ,, Nicholas, captain in 52nd regiment at Boston

1771 **Addy**, Mary, Atherdee, co. Louth
1691 **Adkison**, George, Crum, co. Fermanagh, yeoman
1633 **Adkynsonn**, Peter, Donore, suburbs of Dublin, chapman
[See ATKINSON.]
1789 **Adlercron**, Elizabeth, Dub., widow
1766 ,, John, lieut.-gen. and colonel 39th regiment of foot
1782 ,, John, city of Dublin, esq.
1794 ,, Meliora, Newtown, co. Dublin, widow
1780 ,, William Hargrave
1641 **Adney**, Robert, Dublin
1762 **Adomson**, William, Ballinagalsey, King's County, farmer
1647 **Adrians**, Daniel, Dublin, merchant
1794 **Adrien**, Elizabeth, Dublin, widow
1770 ,, Paul, Dublin, merchant
1805 ,, William, Thomas-st., Dublin, chandler
1759 **Agar**, Alice, Dublin, widow
1789 ,, rev. Charles
1746 ,, Henry, Gowran, co. Kilkenny
1733 ,, Jas., Gowran, co. Kilkenny, esq.
1769 ,, James, Ringwood, co. Kilkenny, esq.
1797 ,, hon. and rev. John Ellis
1785 ,, Lavinia
1714 ,, Peter, Gowran, co. Kilkenny, esq.
1660 **Aggas**, Thomas, Castlelost, co. Westmeath, gent.
1668 **Agharen**, captain Owen, Rochestown, co. Cork
1698 **Aghmooty**, Arthur, Ballykenny
1710 ,, Jane, wife of Arthur Aghmooty
[See AHMUTY.]
1779 **Agitt**, Elizabeth, Dublin, widow
1784 **Agnew**, James, Larne, co. Antrim, merchant
1799 ,, Jane, Mossvale, co. Down, widow
1781 ,, captain John, Longford, co. Longford
1725 ,, Patrick, Kilwaughter, co. Antrim, gent.
1776 ,, William, Kilwaghter, co. Antrim, esq.
1785 ,, William, lieut.-col. 24th regt. of foot
1709 **Aherin**, Maurice, captain in brigadier Whetham's regiment
1794 **Ahmuty**, Arthur, Harley-street, Middlesex, esq.
1796 ,, Arthur, Harley-street, Middlesex, esq. (Copy)
1810 ,, James, Kilmore, co. Roscommon
1791 ,, Robert, Dublin, merchant

1766 **Ahmuty**, Samuel, Brienstown, co. Longford, esq.
1787 ,, Sarah
1802 ,, Thomas, city of Bath, esq. (Copy)
1778 ,, Townly, Dublin, merchant [See AGHMOOTY.]
1806 **Aigoin**, Anna Maria, Dublin
1806 ,, Elizabeth, city of Dublin
1727 ,, John, Dublin, merchant
1742 ,, John, Dublin, merchant. (Not proved)
1777 ,, Margaret, Dublin, spinster
1781 **Aikin**, Jane, Cullin, co. Meath, widow
1784 ,, John, Dublin, attorney [See AITKIN.]
1804 **Aikman**, Sarah, Trim, co. Meath, widow
1790 ,, William, Firrmount, co. Meath, gent.   [gent.
1608 **Ailmer**, Nicholas, Killen, co. Meath, [See AYLMER.]
1593 **Ailward**, Peter, of Fathlegg, esq., and of Waterford, alderman
1626 **Ailwarde**, sir Richd., of Fathlegge, knight [See AYLWARD.]
Ainsworth [See AYNSWORTH.]
1690 **Aitkin**, Patrick, Belfast, merchant
1685 ,, Thomas, Belfast, merchant [See AIKIN.]
1758 **Aitkinson**, Abraham, Mountmelick, Queen's County, shopkeeper [See ATKINSON.]
1734 **Akie**, Wm., Feagh, co. Tyrone, esq.
1710 **Alan**, John, Anyisse, par. Tullycorbet, co. Monaghan, farmer [See ALLEN.]
1681 **Aland**, Henry, Waterford, esq.
1683 ,, Henry, Waterford, esq.
1691 ,, Jonathan, Dublin, esq.
1756 **Albert**, Barnaby, Dublin, silkweaver
1720 **Albin**, James, Rogerstown, co. Meath, yeoman
1735 **Albrittan**, Thomas, major in col. Thos. Howard's regt. of foot
1747 **Alcock**, rev. Alex., dean of Lismore
1788 ,, Alexander, archdeacon of Lismore, Waterford city
1741 ,, Anthony, Bruel, co. Kildare, farmer
1804 ,, Anthony, Cloughanagaun
1699 ,, Catherine, Athlone, widow
1798 ,, Katharine, Dublin, widow
1697 ,, Caesar, Cornamagh, co. Westmeath
1748 ,, rev. George, rector and vicar of Clonenagh and Cloneheen, diocese of Leighlin

1756 **Alcock**, George, Derrien, co. Cork, gent.
1768 ,, George, Fonstown, co. Kildare, gent.
1788 ,, George, Dublin, alderman
1780 ,, Henry, St. Martin's Castle, city of Waterford, clerk of the House of Commons
1784 ,, Henry, Nymphall, co. Waterford, esq.
1713 ,, Jane, Dublin, widow
1769 ,, John, D.D., dean of Ferns
1797 ,, John Dormer, major 47th regt. of foot
1799 ,, sir John, city of Waterford
1769 ,, Jonathan, Roberts-st., Dublin, silkweaver
1776 ,, Martha, Rockingham, co. Wicklow, widow
1805 ,, Mary, Dunlavin, co. Wicklow, widow
1798 ,, Maskelyne, Roughgrove, co. Cork, esq.
1727 ,, Simon, Dublin, gent.
1731 ,, Thomas, Rathsilla, co. Kildare
1753 ,, Thomas, Tunstown, co. Kildare, farmer
1777 ,, Thomas, Waterford, gent.
1705 ,, William, Dublin, esq.
1717 ,, William, Dublin, gent.
1779 ,, William, Waterford city, esq.
1808 ,, William, Spring House, co. Wexford
1721 **Alcocke**, Charles, Clonmel, co. Tipperary, esq.
1809 **Alcorn**, Robert, Back-lane, Dublin, leather seller
1805 **Aldborough**, rt. hon. Edward, earl of
1778 ,, John, earl of (Large)
1802 ,, right hon. Martha, countess dowager of
1810 **Alder**, Charles, Island of Madeira (Copy)
1811 ,, Finlay, Arran-quay, Dublin, timber merchant
1764 ,, John, Dublin, esq.
1800 ,, John, Dublin, timber merchant
1766 ,, Margaret, Dublin, spinster
1796 ,, William, Dubl., timber mercht.
1638 **Aldersey**, Randall, Dublin, esq. (Copy)
1686 ,, Randall, Dublin, esq.
1792 **Alderson**, Joseph, captain in the service of the East India Company (Copy)
1810 **Aldrich**, Agnes Maria (wife of C. Aldrich)
1682 ,, William, rector of Drumgoon, co. Cavan
1745 ,, William, Dublin, alderman

1789 **Aldworth**, Boyle, Newmarkett, co. Cork, esq.
1805 ,, Mary, Little Island, spinster
1707 ,, Richard, Stanlakes, Wilts, esq. (Copy)
1776 ,, Richard, Newmarkett, co. Cork, esq.
1619 **Aleen**, Anne, *alias* **Lawless,** widow
1627 **Alen**, sir Thomas, Alenscourt, kt. and bart.
[See ALLEN.]
1760 **Alexander**, Andrew, Poolbeg-street, Dublin, mariner
1803 ,, Andrew, Newtown Limavady, co. Londonderry, esq.
1809 ,, Andrew, Moss Ville, co. Tyrone, clerk
1716 ,, Edmond, Dublin, gent.
1630 ,, Francis, Dublin, gent.
1794 ,, George, Knockchroghery, co. Roscommon.
1786 ,, James, Newtownlimavady, co. Derry, merchant
1791 ,, James, Harristown, King's County, esq.
1670 ,, sir Jerome, knt., 2nd jus. Com. Pleas (Ex.)
1690 ,, captain John, Londonderry
1771 ,, John, New Ross, co. Wexford, merchant
1786 ,, John, Newtownlimavady, Derry
1801 ,, John, Strabane, co. Tyrone, painter
1803 ,, John, Knockroghry, co. Roscommon, merchant
1726 ,, Richard James, late of Dublin, now of Mawdlins, co. Meath
1799 ,, Richard, Roscommon, co. Rosc.
1770 ,, Robert, Londonderry, mercht.
1788 ,, William, Dublin, merchant.
1792 ,, William, Mary's-abbey, Dubl.
1795 ,, Wlliam, Cateaton-street, London, merchant (Copy)
1649 **Alfry**, Beatrix, Dublin, widow
1810 **Algeo**, Lewis, Glenboy, co. Leitrim, esq.
1773 **Allan**, Robt., capt. 120th regt. foot
1703 ,, Thomas, Ballyrighan, co. Longford
[See ALLEN.]
1741 **Allason**, Elinor, Dublin, spinster
1768 ,, Gilbert, Dublin, noty. pub.
1753 ,, Samuel, Dublin, gent.
1783 ,, Sarah, Dublin, widow
1800 **Allebgone**, William, Stillorgan, farmer
1776 **Allen**, Alexander, Dunover, co. Down, esq.
1784 ,, Alexander, Kingston, Jamaica, merchant

1672 **Allen**, Alice, Dundalk, co. Louth, widow.
1720 ,, Alice, late of Dublin and now of Kilballyowen, co. Limerick
1809 ,, rev. Andrew, rector of Killcevan
1754 ,, Ann, Dublin
1744 ,, Anthony, Dublin, grocer
1750 ,, Anthony, Dublin, merchant
1752 ,, Anthony, Pollardstown, co. Carlow, esq.
1771 ,, Anthony, Dubl., woollen draper
1802 ,, Archibald, Strabane
1792 ,, Aylmer, Cork, burgess
1804 ,, Christr., city of Cork, burgess
1771 ,, Deborah, New Ross, widow
1757 ,, hon. Dorothy, Dublin, widow
1791 ,, Edmond, Riverview, co. Cavan, esq.
1635 ,, Edward, Glaslough, co. Mon., gent.
1788 ,, Elizabeth, Coleraine, co. Derry, widow
1759 ,, Frances
1762 ,, hon. Frances, Dublin, widow
1606 ,, George, Newcastle, co. Wicklow, gent.
1787 ,, George, Bettyville, co. Cork
1744 ,, Hannah, *alias* **Maddocks,** wife of Stephen Allen
1797 ,, Helen, Ballimoney, co. Antrim, widow
1761 ,, Henry, New Ross, co. Wexford, gent.
1768 ,, Higatt, New Ross, co. Wexford, tanner
1672 ,, James, Barnstable, Devon
1787 ,, James, Castledobbs, co. Antrim, linen draper.
1758 ,, Jane, Dublin, spinster
1641 ,, John, Dublin, bricklayer
1669 ,, John, St. Bride's parish, Dublin, gent.
1698 ,, John, Limerick, gent.
1723 ,, John, Dublin, cooper
1726 ,, John, lord viscount of the kingdom of Ireland (Copy)
1741 ,, John, Dublin, yeoman
1745 ,, John, lord viscount
1754 ,, John, lord viscount
1763 ,, John, Allensgrove, co. Kilkenny, gent.
1789 ,, John, Baltinglass
1806 ,, John, Johnstown, co. Wexford, farmer [esq.
1807 ,, John, Sackville-street, Dublin,
1808 ,, John, formerly of Dublin, late of Grenane, co. Wicklow.
1742 ,, Joshua, lord viscount
1809 ,, Kyrle, Cashenure, co. Cork, gent.

1694 **Allen**, Margaret, Monaghan, widow
1758 ,, Margaret, lady, viscountess dowager.
1805 ,, Martha, Ranelagh, co. Dublin, widow
1666 ,, dame Mary, Lutterelstown, co. Dublin, widow
1667 ,, Mary, Dublin, widow (Exemp)
1672 ,, Mary, *alias* **Fitzgerald**, *alias* **Swiloge**, Newtown, Moyaghy, co. Meath, widow
1709 ,, Mary, lady, widow of sir Josh. Allen, knt.
1762 ,, Mary, Dublin, widow
1772 ,, Mary, Dublin, spinster
1796 ,, Mary, Dublin, spinster
1637 ,, Mathew, Dublin, esq. [**IV**. 250
1748 ,, Michael, Ratharigid, co. Kild.
1805 ,, Michael, Lr. Coomb, co. Dubl.
1666 ,, Patrick, Dublin, gent. (Ex.)
1723 ,, Patk., St. Wolstan or Allenscourt, co. Kildare, esq.
1742 ,, Patrick, Ratoath, co. Meath
1758 ,, Patrick, Dublin, gent.
1663 ,, Ralph, Dublin, gent.
1703 ,, Richard, Dublin, baker
1726 ,, Richard, Monaghan, esq.
1745 ,, Richard, Dublin, merchant
1745 ,, Richard, hon., Dublin, esq.
1782 ,, Richard, Cloomore, co. Roscommon, farmer
1799 ,, Richard, Dublin, gent.
1800 ,, hon. Richard
1811 ,, Richard, Killmir, co. Meath, esq.
1634 ,, Robert, Lisneshanny, co. Cav., gent.
1710 ,, Robert, Garranmore, parish of Lr. Ormond, co. Tipperary
1741 ,, Robert, Dublin, esq.
1744 ,, Robert, Innishargie, co. Down.
1764 ,, Robert, Ballymena, co. Antrim
1782 ,, Robert, Ironmonger-lane, city London, merchant (Copy)
1742 ,, Samuel, co. Clare, clothier
1808 ,, Sarah, Bride-street, Dublin, linen draper
1655 ,, Stephen, Dubl., soldier [**V**. 142
1678 ,, Stephen, Killowning, co. Tip., gent.
1677 ,, Thos., Dubl., mercht. [**XII**. 257
1742 ,, Thomas, Dublin, carpenter
1782 ,, Thomas, Elbow-lane, Dublin, grocer
1782 ,, Thomas, city Dubl., silkweaver
1810 ,, Thomas, Race Course, Baltinglass, co. Wicklow
1772 ,, sir Timothy, Dublin, knt.
1785 ,, Timothy, Richmond, Virginia, America (Copy)

1592 **Allen**, William, Thomas-street, Dubl., saddler
1741 ,, Wm., Maryborough, Queen's County, farmer
1749 ,, William, Kildrought or Cellbridge, co. Kild., innkeeper
1775 ,, Wm., Kilmarnock, Scotland, now of Dublin, merchant
1799 ,, William, Shandrum, co. **Cork**, gent.
1804 ,, Wm., Cookstown, co. Tyrone
1806 ,, William, city Cork, shipwright
[See ALAN, ALLAN, ALLEYN, ALEN, ALLIN, ALLYN.]
1738 **Allenett**, rev. Maturine, junr., fellow, T.C.D.
1788 **Alley**, Anne, Donamore, Queen's County, widow
1786 ,, Gabriel, city Limerick, mercht.
1792 ,, George, Parliament-st., Dubl., gun-maker
1775 ,, John, Montrath-street, Dublin, merchant
1728 ,, Mary, Cork, widow
1693 ,, Thos., Rathcormick, co. Cork
1783 ,, Thomas (the elder), Limerick city, gent.
1790 ,, Thomas, Limerick, chandler
1800 **Alleyn**, Charles, Ballyacky, co. Cork, gent.
1665 ,, Edward, Twomonohan, co. Leitrim, esq.
[See ALLEN.]
1715 **Allibou**, Job, London, esq.
1654 **Alliboud**, George, St. James' par., co. Dublin, gent. [**V**. 38
1800 **Alliburn**, William, Stillorgan, co. Dublin, farmer
1767 **Allin**, Elizabeth, Cork, widow
1761 ,, John, Cork, clothier
1786 ,, John, Youghal, co. Cork, merchant
1789 ,, Samuel, co. Cork, merchant
[See ALLEN.]
1765 **Allingham**, Edward, Portnasun, farmer
1782 ,, Edwd., Ballyshannon, co. Don., merchant
1797 ,, Evenna, Ballyshannon, co. Don., spinster
1772 ,, John, Ballyshannon, co. Down, merchant
1809 ,, Robert, Portnason, co. Donegal, gent.
1788 **Allinson**, John, Retreat, co. Wexford, esq.
1750 ,, Joseph, Dublin, clothier
1628 **Allon**, Henry, Oghterard, co. Kild., gent.
1772 **Alloway**, Benjn., Dublin, mercht.

1780 **Alloway**, Sarah, Marrowbone-lane, Dubl.
1766 ,, William, Dublin, merchant
1635 **Allyn**, John, *alias* **Greene**, Brehon, King's County, gent. [See ALLEN.]
1793 **Alment**, John, Prussia-st., optician
1708 **Alnutt**, Thomas, par. St. Martin-in-the-Fields, Middlesex, esq. (Copy)
1683 **Alsop**, Grace, Upper Coomb, co. Dublin
1637 ,, William, Donoure, co. Dublin, yeoman
1805 **Alt**, John, Banagher, gent.
1776 **Altamont**, John, earl of (Large)
1781 ,, Peter, earl of
1808 **Ambrose**, Elizabeth S., inhabitant of Frankenberg
1732 ,, Garret, Dublin, gent. (Not proved)
1783 ,, John, Erleston, Hampshire (Copy)
1731 ,, Michael, Dublin, brewer
1672 ,, Thomas, Dublin, staymaker
1715 ,, William, Caledon, co. Tyrone
1732 ,, William, Ambrose Hall, co. Dublin, esq.
1679 **Amirant**, Mary, Killeniefe, co. Tipperary, spinster
1729 **Amory**, Elizabeth, Dublin, widow
1629 ,, Gabriel, mariner
1713 ,, Robert, Island of Antigua, planter (Copy)
1667 ,, Thomas, Galy, co. Kerry, esq.
1728 ,, Thos., Bunratty, co. Clare, esq.
1768 **Amphlet**, Thomas, Dublin, joiner
1696 **Amye**, Anne, Edenderry, King's County, spinster
1803 **Ancell**, Samuel, Dublin, esq.
1733 **Anderson**, Alexander, Gracedieu, co. Waterford, esq.
1805 ,, Alexander, paymaster of the Tyrone militia
1772 ,, Anne, Dublin, widow
1774 ,, Anstace, Fethard, co. Tipperary, widow
1714 ,, rev. Arthur, Rower, co. Kilkenny, LL.D.
1786 ,, Catherine, Dublin city
1762 ,, Elizabeth, Dublin, spinster
1808 ,, Elizabeth, Abbey-street, Dubl., widow
1774 ,, Forster, Coote Hill, co. Cavan, apothecary
1741 ,, Francis, Dublin, gent.
1659 ,, Geo., Dubl., mercht. [**VIII**. 41
1729 ,, Gregory, Dublin, distiller
1784 ,, Hanagh
1772 ,, Henry, Coleman, co. Tip., gent.

1790 **Anderson**, Henry, Dunbell, co. Kilk., esq.
1799 ,, Henry
1748 ,, Hugh, Derrinine, King's County
1706 ,, Jas., Belfast, co. Antrim, gent.
1763 ,, James, Dublin, hosier
1635 ,, John, Dublin, gent. [**IV**. 153
1696 ,, John, Chester, aldn. (Copy)
1743 ,, John, Dublin, apothecary
1762 ,, John, Dublin, M.D.
1791 ,, John, Dolphin's Barn-lane, silk manufacturer
1797 ,, John, lieut. in 56th regt. of foot
1805 ,, John, Love-lane, co. Dublin, linen printer
1746 ,, Mary, Derrinine, King's County
1773 ,, Paris, co. Tipperary, clerk
1754 ,, Rachael (Copy)
1790 ,, Richd, Kilternan, co. Dub., esq.
1697 ,, Robert, Glenavy, co. Antrim, farmer
1751 ,, Robert, Island Bridge, co. Dublin, millwright
1793 ,, Robt., Newry, co. Down, gent.
1797 ,, Robert, Ard, King's County, farmer
1758 ,, Samuel
1786 ,, Samuel, city Armagh, mercht.
1804 ,, Samuel Jas. Bd., Cullinagh, Queen's County, gent.
1775 ,, Sarah, Dublin, widow of Dr. John A.
1729 ,, Thomas, Cloncannon, King's County, gent.
1676 ,, William, Belfast, merchant
1747 ,, William, Stoneybatter, Dublin
1748 ,, William, Dublin, staymaker
1784 ,, William the elder, Mulletornan, co. Monaghan, farmer
1788 ,, William, Dublin, gent.
1808 ,, William, Foxhall, co. Tipp., esq.
1723 **Andoe**, Francis, Rahallin, co. Meath, farmer
1788 ,, John, High-street, Dublin, woollen draper
1787 ,, Mathew, Broguestown, co. Kildare, farmer
1693 **Andrew**, James, Newtown, par. St. Margaret, co. Dublin, farmer
1701 ,, Jas., Manonstown, co. Meath, farmer
1691 ,, Richard, Newtown, Dunsaghly, co. Dublin, farmer
1634 **Andrewe**, Constance, widow of Hen. Andrewe, Dublin, esq.
1634 ,, Henry, Dublin, esq.
1634 ,, Ptk., Flemingstown, co. Meath, farmer
1710 **Andrewes**, John, Limerick, gent.

1782 **Andrews**, Alice, Kellyman, co. Tyrone, widow
1797 ,, Arabella, Clifton, Gloucester, widow
1725 ,, Bartholomew, Dublin, distiller
1733 ,, Bridgeman, Lecrue, co. Clare, gent.
1735 ,, Catherine, Dublin, widow
1775 ,, Catherine, Dublin, widow
1692 ,, Christopher, Athlone, gent.
1760 ,, Christopher, Kennetstown, co. Meath, farmer
1801 ,, Edward, Park, co. Cork, esq.
1749 ,, Elizabeth, widow of rev. John A., Kilkenny
1796 ,, Elizabeth, Dublin, widow
1708 ,, Fras., Cornekerne, co. Antrim, esq.
1774 ,, Francis, prov. Trin. Coll., Dub.
1791 ,, Hannah, Ranelagh-road, co. Dublin, widow
1746 ,, rev. Hanover, par. Seaford, co. Down, clk.
1701 ,, Henry, Clogh, co. Antrim
1745 ,, Ignatius, Dublin, chandler
1806 ,, James, Little Rath, co. Dublin
1769 ,, John, Tallow, co. Waterford, gent.
1808 ,, John, Comber, co. Down, esq.
1746 ,, Mary, Dublin, widow
1779 ,, Mary, Dublin, widow
1770 ,, Maunsel, Millbrook, co. Tipp., esq.
1768 ,, Maurice, Dublin, merchant
1808 ,, Michael, Rathmines, co. Dub.
1741 ,, Nich., Dublin, woollen draper
1755 ,, Nich., Dublin, woollen draper
1786 ,, Patrick, Lr. Abbey-street, Dub., baker
1799 ,, Patrick, Sallypark, co. Dublin, gent.
1702 ,, Peter, Ballybreedy, co. Cork, gent.
1724 ,, Richd., Tallow, co. Waterford, esq.
1725 ,, Richd., Tallow, co. Waterford, gent.
1637 ,, Samuel, gent.
1763 ,, Samuel, sir John Rogerson's-quay, Dublin, vintner
1744 ,, Thomas, Dublin, baker
1780 ,, Thos., Ranelagh-rd., co. Dub.
1668 ,, William, Finglas
1682 ,, William, Camolin, co. Wexford, gent.
1703 ,, William, Hollywood Rath, co. Dublin, farmer
1730 ,, rev. Wm., Kilkenny, clk., LL.D.
1750 ,, William, Lr. Coomb, co. Dub., weaver

1759 **Andrews**, William, Dublin, grocer
1783 ,, rev. William, rector, Clonfecle, co. Tyrone
1809 ,, William, Castle-street, Dublin, woollen draper
1638 **Androsse**, or **Andrew** Clement, par. Lismore
1799 **Angier**, Elizabeth, Dublin, spinster [See AUNGIER.]
1768 **Anglesey**, Anne, countess of
1686 ,, sir Arthur Annesley, earl of, Lt., Mt. Norris, and viscount Valentia (Copy)
1737 ,, Arthur, earl of (Copy)
1698 ,, Elizabeth, countess dowager of (Copy)
1711 ,, James, earl of (Copy)
1711 ,, John, earl of (Copy)
1777 ,, Juliana, countess dowager
1759 ,, Richard, earl of (Large)
1803 **Anketell**, Ellen, Dingle
1638 ,, John, Newmarket, co. Cork, esq.
1762 ,, John, Newcastle, co. Limerick, gent.
1784 **Anketill**, Richd., Limerick city, M.D.
1782 ,, Roger, Dornamuck, co. Mon., gent.
1784 **Annaly**, rt. hon. John, lord baron
1793 ,, lord baron of Tennelick
1805 **Annan**, Charles, Enniskillen, co. Fermanagh
1660 **Annandale**, James, earl of, viscount of Annan, lord Murray, and Lochmabene (Copy)
1802 **Annesley**, Ann, Dublin, widow
1706 ,, Arthur, par. St. James, Westminster, gent. (Copy)
1786 ,, Arthur, Lincoln's Inn Fields, Middlesex (Copy)
1795 ,, Arthur, Dublin, merchant
1741 ,, Charity, Dublin, spinster
1701 ,, captain Charles, of sir Henry Bellasis' regt. of foot (Ex.)
1747 ,, Charles, Dublin, Esq.
1769 ,, Elinor, Waterpark, co. Clare, widow
1709 ,, Francis, Ballyshannon, co. Kildare, esq.
1742 ,, Francis, Waterford, merchant
1750 ,, Francis, par. St. Giles, Middlesex, esq. (Copy)
1751 ,, Francis, Ballysax, co. Kildare, esq.
1803 ,, rt. hon. Francis Chas., earl of
1752 ,, George, Dublin, gent.
1695 ,, John, Ballyshannon, co. Kild., esq.
1780 ,, honorable Marcus
1766 ,, rev. Maurice, Waterpark, co. Clare, clk.

1800 **Annesley,** Philip, Portobello, co. Dublin, staymaker
1752 ,, rev. Richard, Kilmore, co. Galway, clk. [gent.
1796 ,, Richd., Rahavell, co. Wicklow,
1720 ,, Samuel, St. Andrew's parish, Dublin, esq.
1756 ,, Sarah, Dublin, spinster
1803 ,, William, Oughill, co. Wicklow
1796 **Annesly,** Grace, widow
1720 ,, John, Ballysax, co. Kild., esq.
1789 **Ansdell,** Samuel, Dublin, gent.
1809 **Ansley,** Thomas, Arklow, co. Wicklow, shopkeeper
1771 **Anslow,** John, Cushcallow, King's County, farmer
1795 **Anster,** John, Charleville, co. Cork
1726 ,, Martin, Charleville, co. Cork, merchant
1765 **Anthony,** John, Ballymahon, co. Longford, miller
1801 ,, Thomas, formerly of College-green, Dublin
1792 **Antisell,** Thos., Birr, King's County, gent.
1794 **Antrim,** rt. hon. Catherine, countess dowager
1802 ,, Letitia, dow. marchioness of (Copy)
1791 ,, Randall Wm., marquis of (Large)
1761 **Antrobus,** rev. Geo., Dubl., clk.
1761 ,, John, Dublin, Dr. in divinity
1680 ,, William, Athlone, innkeeper
1741 **Anyon,** Jonathan, co. Dublin, linen weaver
1730 ,, Simon, Dublin, gent.
1631 **Apfull,** John
1631 **Aphugh,** Ambrose, Carlingford, esq.
1597 ,, Richard or Rys
1804 **Apjohn,** Elizabeth, city of Limerick, spinster
1655 ,, John, city of Limerick, soldier, [**V.** 169
1802 ,, Margaret, Dublin, spinster
1782 ,, Michael, Limerick city, gent.
1788 ,, Susanna, Limerick city, widow
1760 ,, William, Limerick, saddler
1791 ,, William, Middle Temple, gent. [See ABJOHN.]
1792 **Aplen,** Nicholas, Wicklow, gent.
1659 ,, Richard, Londonderry, gent.
1745 ,, Roger, belonging to His Majesty's ship 'Victory.'
1712 **Arabin,** Bartholomew, Dublin, esq.
1732 ,, Jane Renee, widow of Barthw. Arabin, Dublin, esq.
1780 ,, Jane Mary, widow
1757 ,, John, col. of the 59th regt. foot
1802 ,, Judith, Dublin, widow

1674 **Arble,** William, soldier
1736 **Arbuckle,** Jas., Belfast, co. Antrim, merchant
1746 ,, Jas., Dubl., M.D. (Large will) [See Bundle, 1747.]
1743 ,, Priscilla, Belfast, widow (Not proved)
1752 ,, Priscilla, Belfast, widow
1798 **Arbuthnot,** John, Rockfleet Castle, co. Mayo
1776 **Arcedeckne,** Nicholas, Gortnamona, co. Galway, esq.
1675 ,, Redmond, Clonturskirt, co. Galway, gent.
1724 **Arcedikne,** Redmond, Carrowmore, co. Galway, gent.
1765 **Archbold,** Anne, Kilkenny, widow
1771 ,, Catherine, Dublin
1784 ,, Dorothea, Arran-quay Nunnery, widow
1784 ,, Emilia, Dublin, widow
1775 ,, Gerald, Naas, co. Kild., grocer
1695 ,, Gerard, Eadstown, co. Kildare, gent.
1763 ,, Gerard, Donode, co. Kildare, gent.
1755 ,, Gregory, lieut. in the elector of Mentz' service
1631 ,, Jas., Rathmecloge, co. Wick., gent.
1767 ,, James, Baldwinstown
1795 ,, James, city of Dublin, gent.
1801 ,, James
1716 ,, Joan, daughter of James Archbold, Collens, co. Kildare
1726 ,, Joan
1773 ,, John, Dublin, gent.
1782 ,, John, Blackrath, co. Kildare
1789 ,, John, Dublin city
1781 ,, Margaret, Blackrath, co. Kildare, spinster
1742 ,, Mary, *alias* **Byrne,** widow
1780 ,, Michael, Davidstown, co. Kildare, esq.
1776 ,, Pierce, Usher's-quay, Dublin, merchant
1792 ,, Pierce, Drogheda, merchant
1711 ,, Pierse, Knockanegrough, Queen's County, esq.
1704 ,, Richard, Dublin, Dr. of physic
1767 ,, Richard, Lisburn, co. Antrim, esq.
1737 ,, Robert, Davidstown, co. Kildare, esq.
1763 ,, Thomas, captain in 47th regt. of foot
1779 ,, Thomas, Kevan-street, Dublin, merchant
1753 ,, William, Davidstown, co. Kildare, esq.

1608 **Archbold**, William, *alias* **Asspoll**, Kinlestown, co. Wick., esq.
1629 **Archbolde**, Walter, Tymolin, co. Kildare, esq.
1726 **Archbould**, Anthony, Dublin, victu- aller
1796 **Archdall**, Anna Maria, Dubl., wid.
1772   ,,   Henrietta, Summer-hill, widow
1703   ,,   John, Dublin, merchant
1787   ,,   John, Dorset-street, Dubl., esq.
1791   ,,   rev. Mervyn, Dublin, clk.
1763   ,,   Nicholas, Mt. Eccles, co. Dub- lin, esq.
1792   ,,   Sarah, Great George's-street, Dublin, widow
1751   ,,   William, Dublin, assay master
1739 **Archdeacon**, Domk., Cork, mercht.
1686   ,,   Hen.,Ballym'Daniel,co.Kerry, gent.
1774   ,,   Henry, Cork, gent.
1796   ,,   Jas., Kildromin, co. Limerick, gent.
1804 **Archdeaken**, Thos., Dorset-street, Dublin, gent.
1733 **Archdekin**, James, Michael's-lane, Dublin, tailor
1719   ,,   John, senr., Kilkenny, mercht.
1768   ,,   Mathias, Kilkenny, gent.
1617   ,,   *als.* **McOdo**, Richard, Baven- more, co. Kilkenny
1798   ,,   Richard, Kells, co. Kilkenny
1780 **Archdikion**, Mary
       [See ARCEDECKNE.]
1769 **Archer**, Anne, King-street, Ox., Dublin, widow
1735   ,,   Arthur, Drumnagh, co. Dublin, gent.
1737   ,,   Arthur, Drumnagh, co. Dublin, gent.
1749   ,,   Benjamin, Dublin, merchant
1796   ,,   Benjamin, Fairview, co. Dubl.
1797   ,,   Clement, city of Dublin, M.D.
1800   ,,   Edward,   Henrietta-street, Middlesex (Copy)
1782   ,,   Elinor, Queen-street, Dublin
1656   ,,   Elisha, corporal to major Red- mond's troop   [VI. 3
1763   ,,   Elizabeth, Dubl., wid. (Large)
1767   ,,   Elizabeth, co. Wicklow, wid.
1808   ,,   Fras., city of Dublin.
1736   ,,   Hannagh, Drumna, co. Dublin widow
1730   ,,   Henry, Enniscorthy, co. Wex- ford, merchant
1758   ,,   Jane, Ash-street, co. city of Dublin, widow
1617   ,,   John Fitz Walter, Kilkenny, merchant
1642   ,,   John, Chequer-lane, Dublin, carpenter

1663 **Archer**, John, Ballyean, co. Wex., gent.
1738   ,,   John, Dublin, gent.   [esq.
1792   ,,   Joseph, Killymon, co.Wicklow,
1733   ,,   Mark, Limerick, merchant
1686   ,,   Patrick, Riverstown, co.Meath, esq.
1777   ,,   Richard, Cork, merchant
1733   ,,   Robert, Dublin, gent.
1773   ,,   Robt.,Paradise-row,Dubl.,esq.
1754   ,,   Sampson, Strabane, co. Tyrone
1663   ,,   Thomas, Kilkenny, esq.
1605   ,,   Walter, Kilkenny, gent.
1625   ,,   Walter, Kilkenny, esq.
1629   ,,   Walter, Ballyne, co. Tyrone, gent.
1752   ,,   William, Dublin, glazier
1752 **Archibald**, William, Belfast, co. Antrim, merchant
       [See ARCHBOLD.]
1655 **Ardagh**, John Richardson, bishop of   [V. 192
1746 **Ardesoif**, Dinah, Dublin, widow
1638 **Ardfert**, William Steeres, bishop of
1661   ,,   Thos., earl of, and Lord Crom- well
1687 **Ardglass**, Vere Essex, earl of
1676 **Ariskin**, lieut. William
1730 **Arkwright**, Henry, Dublin, esq.
1792 **Arland**, Elizabeth, Ranelagh, co. Dublin, spinster
1585 **Armagh**, Thomas Lancaster, arch- bishop of
       [See Dublin Collection.]
1613   ,,   Henry Usher, lord primate
1624   ,,   Christopher Hampton, arch- bishop of
1663   ,,   John Bramhall, archbishop of
1679   ,,   James Margetsen, archbishop of (Ex.)
1702   ,,   Dr. Michael Boyle, archbp. of
1713   ,,   Dr. Narcissus Marsh,archbp.of
1724   ,,   Dr. Thos. Lindsay, archb. of
1742   ,,   Dr. Hugh Boulter, archbp. of
1765   ,,   George Stone, archbishop of
1795   ,,   most rev. Richard Robinson, archbishop of
1800   ,,   most rev. William Newcome, archbishop of
1775 **Armar**, Mary, Castle Coote, co. Fer- managh, widow
1707   ,,   rev. William, Ballybrittan, co. Antrim, archdn. of Connor
1776 **Armestead**, Elizabeth
1810 **Armitage**, James, city of Dublin
1766   ,,   Robert, Liverpool, esq.
1731   ,,   Stephen, Atherdee, co. Louth
1799   ,,   Stephen, Dublin, gent.
1701   ,,   Timothy (the elder), Atherdee, co. Louth, esq.

1790 **Armstead,** Elizabeth
1785 ,, Jane, city of Cork, spinster
1771 ,, John, Cork, merchant
1783 ,, Sarah, Cork, widow
1792 ,, Sarah, Mallow, co. Cork
1783 **Armstrong,** Abigail, Belfast, co. Antrim, widow
1793 ,, Alexander, Belfast, merchant
1793 ,, Alexander, Dublin, merchant
1747 ,, Alice, Dublin, widow
1717 ,, Andrew, Ballicumber, King's County, farmer
1723 ,, Andrew, Mauristown, co. Kildare, esq.
1764 ,, Andrew, lieut. 83rd regt. foot
1785 ,, Andrew, Dublin, merchant
1786 ,, Andrew, Gallen, King's County, esq.
1789 ,, Andrew, Castle Armstrong, King's County, esq.
1802 ,, Andrew, Clara, King's County
1807 ,, Andrew, Castle Garden, King's County, esq.
1780 ,, Anna Maria, widow
1806 ,, Anne, Boyle, co. Rosc., widow
1759 ,, Archibald, Ashgrove, King's County, esq.
1694 ,, dame Catherine, par. St. Jas., Westm., widow (Copy)
1809 ,, Catherine Isabella (Copy)
1731 ,, Charles, Mountarmstrong, co. Kildare, esq.
1799 ,, Christr., Fochery, co. Leitrim
1770 ,, David, Marlough, co. Donegal, gent.
1808 ,, Deborah, city of Dublin
1745 ,, Edmond, Gillan, King's County, esq.
1747 ,, Rev. Edmond, Killaloe, co. Galway, clk.
1769 ,, Edward, Kilmacud
1800 ,, Edward, Buncraggy, co. Clare, esq.
1776 ,, Elizabeth, Birr, King's County, widow
1807 ,, George, Parliament-st., Dublin, lace man.
1768 ,, Henry, Dublin, gent.
1748 ,, Isabella, Killeely, co. Galway, widow
1743 ,, James, Dublin, staymaker
1753 ,, Jas., Cootehill, co. Cavan, gent.
1755 ,, James, Ennis, co. Clare, gent.
1762 ,, James, Richhill, co. Armagh, innkeeper
1781 ,, James, Lisgool, co. Fermanagh, esq.
1797 ,, James, Killeshandra, co. Cavan
1801 ,, rev. James, vicar of Tannagh, co. Sligo

1810 **Armstrong,** James, city of Dublin, attorney-at-law
1811 ,, James, Roper's-rest, co. Dublin, cotton dyer
1704 ,, John, lieut., earl Donegal's regt. of foot
1738 ,, John, Carrighill, co. Dublin, gent.
1745 ,, John, Strabane, co. Tyrone, merchant
1777 ,, John, Dublin, silkweaver
1782 ,, rev. John, Kingswell, co. Tipperary, clk.
1785 ,, John, King-street, Stephen's-green, Dublin
1786 ,, John, Clones, co. Monaghan, gent.
1791 ,, John, Mount Heaton, King's County, esq.
1797 ,, John, Bellview, King's County, esq.
1804 ,, John, Edergol, co. Fermanagh
1806 ,, John, Boyle, co. Roscommon, surgeon
1807 ,, John, Drumralla, co. Fermanagh, esq.
1758 ,, Margaret, Dublin, widow
1808 ,, Margaret, city of Dublin, widow
1793 ,, Mary O'Callaghan, Bath, widow
1790 ,, Nenon, lieut. and qr.-master, royal regt. of artillery
1749 ,, Rebecca, *alias* **Henzey**
1747 ,, Richard, Dublin, merchant
1790 ,, Richard
1776 ,, · Robert, Belfast, co. Antrim, merchant
1791 ,, rev. Robert Carew, Ten Acres, King's County, clk.
1797 ,, Robert, Hackwood, co. Cavan, esq.
1797 ,, Robert, Erey, co. Meath, gent.
1808 ,, Robert, Dublin, apothecary
1742 ,, Susanna, Dublin, spinster
1662 ,, sir Thomas, knt., Dublin
1763 ,, Thomas, Ennis, co. Clare
1767 ,, Thomas, Clones, co. Monaghan
1776 ,, Thomas, Castle Balfour, co. Fermanagh
1783 ,, Thomas, Aungier-street, Dub., esq.
1795 ,, Thomas, capt. 8th regt. of foot
1806 ,, Thomas, city of Dublin
1767 ,, Warneford, Ballycumber, King's County, esq.
1727 ,, Wm., Endrene, King's County, gent.
1742 ,, William, Duncannon Fort, co. Wexford
1758 ,, William, Irvey [gent.
1778 ,, Wm.. Killbrackin, co. Leitrim,

1790 **Armstrong**, Wm., Cherrybrook, co. Leitrim, gent.
1810 ,, William, High-street, Dublin, seedsman
1654 **Arnold**, capt. Clement, col. Sankey's regt.
1801 ,, Elizabeth, Dublin city, widow
1584 ,, Francis, Patrick-street, tailor [I. 25
1758 ,, John, the elder, Dublin, gent.
1790 ,, Richard, Dublin, distiller
1756 **Arnoldi**, Anne, Annsborough, co. Kildare, widow
1710 **Arnoldie**, Richard, Dublin, gent.
1654 **Arnott**, Hercules, Wickham, Buckingham, esq. (Copy)
1803 ,, Hugh, cornet and surgeon 14th regt. light dragoons
1773 **Arran**, Arthur Gore, earl of
1809 ,, right hon. Arthur Saunders, earl of
1759 ,, Charles, earl of (Large)
1687 ,, Richard, earl of (Copy)
1802 **Arrell**, Sarah, King-street, widow
1593 **Arseteken**, James, Kilkenny, merchant (Copy)
1591 **Arstaken**, *alias* **Nycodie**, Catherine, co. Kilkenny [I. 67
1765 **Arther**, John, Dubl., gent. (Large)
1627 **Arthor**, Stephen, Limerick, mercht.
1797 **Arthur**, Alexander, Belfast, co. Antrim, gent.
1686 ,, Bennett, Cabragh, co. Dublin, gent.
1750 ,, Bridget, living at Fosse, France
1652 ,, Catherine, widow
1691 ,, Dymphna, Dublin, widow
1651 ,, Edward, Dublin, alderman
1799 ,, Elinor, Dublin, spinster
1666 ,, John, par. St. Bride, Dublin, gent. (Copy)
1666 ,, John Fitz Robert, Dublin, gent. (Copy)
1795 ,, John, Ennis, co. Clare, esq.
1791 ,, Margaret, Dublin city, widow
1791 ,, Mary Anne
1799 ,, Mary, Limerick city, widow
1788 ,, Michael, Limerick city, gent.
1609 ,, Patrick, Limerick, alderman
1675 ,, Patk., Chainanna, co. Limerick, gent.
1800 ,, Patrick, Newtownperry, Lib. of Limerick, merchant
1686 ,, Rachael, Meehan, co. Armagh, widow
1649 ,, Robert, Dublin, alderman
1674 ,, Thomas, Dublin, M.D. (Ex.)
1729 ,, Thomas Fitz Francis, Limerick
1762 ,, Thomas, *vide* **Piers**, Ballyquin, co. Clare, gent.

1765 **Arthur**, Thomas, Limerick, merchant
1762 ,, Walter, Ennis, co. Clare, gent.
1662 ,, William Fitzpatrick, Limerick, merchant
1788 **Arthure**, Bartholomew, Ennis, co. Clare, gent.
1752 ,, Benedict, Seafield, co. Dublin, esq.
1756 ,, Edward, Dublin, gent.
1617 ,, George, Dublin, merchant
1608 ,, John, Dublin, alderman
1733 ,, John, Great Cabragh, co. Dub., esq.
1757 ,, John, Seafield, co. Dublin, esq.
1705 ,, Robt., Hacketstown, co. Dub., esq.
1635 ,, Thos. Fitz Dominick, Limerick, merchant
1607 ,, Thomas Fitz Daniel, Limerick, merchant
1710 ,, Thomas, Dublin, linen draper
1775 ,, Thomas, Dublin, esq.
1625 **Artoure**, Andrew, Limerick, mercht.
1726 **Arundell**, Richard, Sanherne, Cornwall, esq. (Copy)
1675 ,, Robert, Dublin, alderman
1632 **Ash**, dame Eliz., Trim, widow of sir Thos. A., knt. [IV. 2
1796 ,, George, Ashbrook, Liberties of Derry, esq.
1662 ,, John, rector Killeagh, diocese of Cloyne
1684 ,, John, Corneren, Liberties of Derry, gent.
1751 ,, Jonathan, Ashgrove, co. Tipperary, esq.
1597 ,, Laurence, Naas, co. Kildare (Copy)
1673 ,, Richard, Dublin, gent. (Ex.) [See ASHE.]
1759 **Ashbrook**, Elizabeth, lady viscountess (Copy)
1780 ,, William, lord viscount
1752 **Ashbrooke**, Henry, lord viscount
1746 **Ashburner**, John, Dublin, gent.
1796 ,, Mary, Dublin, widow
1744 ,, Richd., Dub., mercht. (Large)
1770 **Ashbury**, Jane, Dublin, widow
1754 ,, Richard, Dublin, gent.
1744 **Ashe**, Cairnes, Kinsale, co. Cork, esq.
1809 ,, Catherine, Kevin's-port, Dublin, spinster
1656 ,, Clement, Purcell's Inch, co. Kilkenny, gent.
1716 ,, Rev. Dillon, D.D.
1761 ,, Edward, Waterford, gent.
1639 ,, Elizabeth, late wife to sir Thos. Ashe, knt. (Copy)

1810 **Ashe**, Elizabeth, city of Cork, widow
1628 ,, Henry, Dublin, merchant
1743 ,, Jane, Drumcondra, co. Dublin, widow
1714 ,, John, Nurney, co. Kild., gent.
1675 ,, Jonathan, Killoquirk, co. Tipperary, esq. (Ex.)
1781 ,, Jonathan, Cork, mercht., but in Haverford West, S. Wales.
1803 ,, Jonathan, Ashville, nr. Limk., esq.
1789 ,, Lovett, city of Dublin, esq.
1717 ,, Martha, Dublin, widow
1665 ,, Nicholas, Moyrath, co. Meath, gent.
1632 ,, Richard, Dublin, merchant
1727 ,, Richard, Ashefield, co. Meath. esq.
1762 ,, Richard, Dublin
1764 ,, Richd., Dubl., Spanish leather dresser
1805 ,, Richard, Sunday Hill, co. Cork, esq.
1718 ,, St. George, bishop of Derry
1750 ,, Sarah, Kinsale, wid. of Cairnes Ashe, esq.
1708 ,, Thos., Barlbrough, Derby, now of Dublin, esq.
1722 ,, Thomas, St. John's, co. Meath, esq.
1741 ,, Thomas Moone, co. Kild., esq.
1682 ,, William, Ashfield, co. Meath, esq.
[See AYSH, ASH.]
1770 **Ashenhurst**, Edwd., Harryville, co. Kilkenny, major of horse carbineers
1665 ,, Peter, Dublin, gent.
1802 ,, William, Leabeg, co. Wicklow
1787 **Ashly**, Anne, Dublin, widow
1788 **Ashmore**, Samuel, Belfast, co. Antrim, merchant
1776 **Ashmur**, James, Loughgall, co. Armagh
1801 ,, Jas., Newry, co. Armagh, esq.
1783 **Ashton**, Joshua, formerly of Dublin, chandler
1759 ,, Isaac, Cavan-street, co. Dubl.
1790 ,, Jeremiah, Harold's Cross, near Dublin
1741 ,, John, Kilconnimore, co. Tipp.
1720 ,, Margaret, *alias* **Wilmott**, Dublin, spinster
1693 ,, Mary, Lambeth, Surrey, widow (Copy)
1758 ,, Peter, Ballinguile, co. city Limerick, farmer
1694 ,, Thomas, St. Thomas - street, Dublin, gardener

1680 **Ashurst**, Henry, London, merchant tailor
1690 ,, John, Dublin, merchant
1722 ,, sir Wm., London, knt. (Copy)
1803 **Ashworth**, Thomas, Donnybrook, co. Dublin, esq.
1661 **Aske**, Thos., Thurles, co. Tipperary, esq. (Copy)
1797 **Askin**, Christopher, Pimlico, dyer
1583 **Aspoll**, Redmond, Corbally, co. Dublin, gent.
1608 **Asspoll**, or **Archbold**, Wm., Kinlestown, co. Wicklow, esq.
1782 **Aston**, Chas., Atherdee, co. Louth, gent.
1747 ,, Edward, Dublin, M.D.
1713 ,, Henry, Dublin, esq.
1765 ,, Thomas, Drogheda, esq.
1748 ,, Tichborne, Beaulieu, co. Louth, esq.
1671 ,, sir William, Richardstown, co. Louth, knt.
1737 ,, William, East Aston, co. Wicklow, gent.   [esq.
1744 ,, William, Beaulieu, co. Louth,
1769 ,, Wm., co. Louth, but of Rathbone-Place, Middlesex, esq. (Copy)
1694 **Astwood**, Nathanl., Dublin, weaver
1791 **Atcheson**, John, Derry, merchant
1744 **Atchison**, Francis, Belfast, co. Antrim, innkeeper
[See ACHESON.]
1807 **Atfield**, Elizabeth, city of Bath, widow (Copy)
1767 ,, Hull, Dublin, esq.
1772 ,, Mary, Waterford, widow
1778 **Athenleck**, William, Cullenswood, co. Dublin, esq.
1750 **Athenry**, Francis, lord baron
1731 **Atherton**, Ellen, Cole's-alley, Lib. of Thomas-court, Dublin, widow
1690 ,, Fras., Dub., ironmonger (Copy)
1690 ,, Thomas, Dublin, merchant
1808 **Athy**, Edward Lynch, Rinvill, co. Galway, esq.
1773 ,, Oliver, Dublin, D.M.
1774 ,, Philip Lynch, Rinville, co. Galway.
1789 **Atkin**, Gore, Rossard, co. Wexford, gent.
1708 ,, John, Youghal, co. Cork, alderman (Large)
1765 ,, John Thomas, Cork, clk.
1786 ,, John Thomas, Leadintown, co. Cork, esq.
1807 ,, Samuel, town of Wexford
1741 ,, rev. Walter, Leadentown, co. Cork, clk.

1795 **Atkin**, Walter, Windsor, co. Cork, esq.
1730 ,, William, Coolnacloughfinny, co. Cork, gent.
1725 **Atkins**, Charles, Dublin, gent.
1798 ,, Jane, Waterpark, co. Cork, widow
1754 ,, Mary, Dublin, widow
1789 ,, Ringrose, Prospect Hill, co. Cork, esq.
1682 ,, Robert, Dubl., carpenter (Ex.)
1766 ,, Robert, Cork, esq.
1786 ,, Robert St. Leger
1695 ,, sir Thomas, Dublin, knt.
1605 ,, Ursula, Dublin
1656 ,, William, Youghal, co. Cork, merchant
1764 **Atkinson**, Aaron, Big Butter-lane, Dublin
1809 ,, Abraham, Ballymackanollon, co. Down
1664 ,, Anthony, Cangort, King's Co., gent. (1661)
1686 ,, Anthony, Ardinwood, co. Westmeath, tailor   [esq.
1744 ,, Anthony, Cangort, King's Co.,
1790 ,, Anthony, city of Dublin, esq.
1686 ,, Charles, Cangort, King's Co., gent.
1743 ,, Charles, Dublin, merchant
1766 ,, Charles, Dublin, gent.
1780 ,, Charles, Cangort, King's Co., esq.
1682 ,, Edward, Kilmore, co. Armagh, carpenter
1772 ,, Geo., Beleek, co. Mayo, gent.
1776 ,, George, Marymount, King's County, esq.
1784 ,, George, Dundalk, co. Louth, gent.
1804 ,, Guy, Lisburn, co. Antrim
1789 ,, Henry, Ashgrove, co. Armagh, gent.
1722 ,, James, Newry, schoolmaster
1762 ,, Jas., Newry, co. Down, mercht.
1759 ,, Jane, Drogheda, widow
1736 ,, John, Drogheda, merchant
1775 ,, John, Francis-street, Dublin, weaver
1790 ,, John, Dublin, esq.
1797 ,, Joseph, Keighlogues, co. Kildare, gent.
1705 ,, Margaret, Dublin, widow
1748 ,, Mary, *alias* **Guy**, widow of Anthony Atkinson, esq.
1673 ,, Ralph, Dublin, clothworker
1786 ,, Richard, city of Dublin, dyer
1661 ,, Robert, Glenavy, co. Antrim
1763 ,, Robert, Maghreagh, co. Down, merchant

1777 **Atkinson**, Sarah, spinster
1692 ,, Stephen, Limerick, innkeeper
1659 ,, Thomas, Dublin, gent.
        [See ADKISON, ADKYNSONN, AITKINSON.]
1705 **Atkison**, Thomas, Limerick, innkeeper
1748 ,, Thomas, Tullamore, King's County
1810 ,, Thomas, brev.-maj., 4th gn. batt.
1769 ,, William, Forgny, co Longford
1773 ,, Wm., Rahins, co. Mayo, gent.
1802 ,, Wm., Pimlico, co. Dub., clothier
1626 **Atkynson**, Anthony, Island, King's County, esq.
1801 **Atteridge**, Thos., Killybegs, mercht.
1743 **Atwell**, Thos., Dublin, linen draper
1687 **Atwood**, John, Dublin, tailor
1706 **Aubin**, Elias, French refugee, at present in city Cork
1733 **Aubrespy**, David, Dublin, gent.
1685 **Auchenleck**, Jas., Kilweetan, rector of Cleenish
1803 ,, Wm., Cuttagh, co. Fermanagh
1754 **Auchinleck**, Alex., Drogheda, esq.
1796 ,, Hugh, Dublin, attorney-at-law
1811 ,, Margaret, Hardwicke-st., Dub., widow
1769 ,, William, Strabane, co. Tyrone, merchant
1727 **Auchmuty**, Charles, Dub., mercht.
1794 ,, Clemina, Fosterstown, co. Meath, widow
1788 ,, Forbes, Fosterstown, co. Meath, esq.
1775 ,, Isabella, Bellmont, Westmeath, spinster
1726 ,, John, Newtown, co. Longford, esq.   [clk.
1792 ,, John, Fosterstown, co. Meath,
1759 ,, Richard, Dublin, esq.
        [See AGHMOOTY.]
1757 **Audivert**, John, Dublin, gent.
1630 **Augier**, Elizabeth, Dublin, spinster
1630 **Auly**, *alias* **Namona**, John, Waterford
1632 **Aungier**, Francis, lord baron of Longford, master of the rolls, and privy councillor
1639 ,, Francis
1657 ,, Gerald, lord baron of Longford [**VI.** 129
1692 ,, John, Drome Derrick, co. Cavan, clk.
        [See ANGIER.]
1794 **Austen**, Elizabeth, Dublin, widow
1808 ,, Ellen
1798 ,, Matthew, Phibsborough, co. Dublin, farmer

1792 **Austen**, Robert, D.D., archdeacon, Cork
1780 ,, dame Susanna
1740 ,, Thomas, Dublin, popish priest
1792 ,, Thomas, Ballyboghill, co. Dub., farmer   [of Man
1780 ,, Thomas Bowes, Douglas, Isle
1765 ,, William, esq., one of the masters in Chancery
1798 ,, William, Inkenny, Sth. Liberty of Cork, esq.
1762 **Austin**, Elizabeth, Cork, widow
1807 ,, Elizabeth, widow
1737 ,, Honoretta, Great Britain-street, Dublin, widow
1807 ,, Jane, city Dublin, spinster
1761 ,, Joseph, Cork, alderman
1623 ,, Nicholas, Stamollen, co. Meath, farmer
1650 ,, Nicholas, Stamollin, co. Meath, farmer
1680 ,, Richard, Stamullen, co. Meath, farmer
1728 ,, Richard, Corballis, co. Meath, farmer
1771 ,, Richard, Drogheda, merchant
1718 ,, Samuel, Waterford, alderman
1762 ,, Thomas, Inskinny, Sth. Liberty of Cork, esq. (Large)
1635 **Auston**, St. John's, by Athy, co. Kildare, maltster
[See AUSTEN, AUSTIN.]
1723 **Averall**, Adam, Larganagoose, co. Londonderry, gent.
[See AVREILL.]
1718 **Averell**, Henry, Toberhead, co. Derry, gent.
1720 ,, Nichs., Coleraine, co. Londonderry, merchant
1683 **Avery**, Samuel, London, alderman
1806 **Avonmore**, rt. hon. Barry, ld. visct.
1695 **Avreill**, John, Larganaguse, co. Derry, gent.
[See AVERALL.]
1683 **Awbrey**, William, Stephen-street, Dublin, gent.
1596 **Awdley**, captain John, Athlone
1660 **Aylett**, Richard, Killenowt, co. Cavan, esq.
1702 **Ayleway**, Robert, Mount Rawdon, co. Wicklow, esq.
1650 **Aylmer**, Alexander
1748 ,, dame Alice, *alias* **Lyster**
1755 ,, sir Andrew, Balrath, co. Meath, bart.
1650 ,, Anne, relict of Alexander
1808 ,, Anne, Newman, co. Meath, widow
1682 ,, Bartholomew, Kilcock, co. Kildare, gent.

1682 **Aylmer**, Bartholomew, Dundalk, co. Louth, gent.
1795 ,, Betty, Haverford West, South Wales (Copy)
1747 ,, dame Catherine, widow of sir Andrew Aylmer, bart.
1772 ,, Charles, Grangemore, co. Kildare, esq.
1801 ,, Charles, Painstown, co. Kildare
1791 ,, dame Dorothea, Dublin, widow
1597 ,, Edward, Killrue, co. Meath, gent.
1744 ,, Elizabeth, Lyons, co. Kildare, spinster
1797 ,, dame Elizabeth, widow
1742 ,, Ellis, Dublin, widow
1794 ,, sir Fitzgerald, Danadei, co. Kildare, bart.
1730 ,, Garrett
1730 ,, Geo., Lyons, co. Kildare, esq.
1662 ,, Gerald, Balrath, co. Meath, esq.
1729 ,, Gerald, Lyons, co. Kildare, esq.
1736 ,, sir Gerald, Danadei, co. Kildare, bart.   [bart.
1745 ,, sir Gerald, Balrath, co. Meath,
1651 ,, James, Dolardstown, co. Meath, esq.
1668 ,, James, Dublin, esq.
1765 ,, James, Seneschallstown, co. Meath, gent.
1797 ,, James Dean, of Dublin, esq.
1799 ,, James, Gillardstown
1808 ,, Jas., Navan, co. Meath, mercht.
1705 ,, John, Ballycanon, co. Kildare, gent.
1714 ,, sir John, Balrath, co. Meath, bart.
1654 ,, Mabel, *alias* **Barnewall** [V. 36
1776 ,, sir Mathew, Dublin, bart.
1739 ,, Patrick, Dublin, esq.
1665 ,, Peter, Dublin, gent.
1717 ,, Richard, Ballynefagh, co. Kildare, gent.
1746 ,, Richard, Cloncurry
1746 ,, Richard, Shenchalstown, co. Meath, gent.
1761 ,, Richard, formerly of Rathmore, co. Kildare, now of Chapelizod, co. Dublin, esq.
1779 ,, Richard, Usher's Island, Dub., esq.
1795 ,, Richard, Senschalstown, co. Meath, esq.
1738 ,, Robert, Painstown, co. Kildare, gent.
1682 ,, Thos., Lyons, co. Kildare, esq.
1687 ,, Thomas, Dublin, esq.
1737 ,, Valentine, Lyons, co. Kildare, gent.

1660 **Aylmer**, Wm., Buskagh, co. Tipperary, gent.
   [See AILMER.]
1765 **Aylward**, Barbara, widow of John A., Ballynagar, co. Galway, esq.
1778 ,, Catherine, Dublin, widow
1797 ,, Edmond, Knockmoylan, co. Kilkenny, farmer
1756 ,, John French, Ballynegar, co. Galway, esq.
1772 ,, John, Dublin, grocer   [nist
1784 ,, Judith, Dublin, widow, tobacco-
1783 ,, Lucy, Galway town, spinster
1755 ,, Michael, Lisdurrow, co. Galway, esq.
1756 ,, Nicholas, Shankill, co. Kilkenny, esq.
1783 ,, Nugent, Ballynagare, co. Galway, esq.
1739 ,, Patrick, Dublin, linen draper
1769 ,, Patrick, Dublin, gent.
1792 ,, Peter, Shankill, co. Kilk., esq.
1803 ,, Peter, late His Majesty's royal independent invalids
1777 ,, Sarah, King-street, Oxm., Dublin, widow
1749 ,, Thomas, Dublin, gent.
   [See AILWARD.]
1783 **Aynsworth**, James, Strangford, co. Down, esq.   [spinster
1765 ,, Rebecca, Strangford, co. Down,
1754 **Ayres**, Daniel, Plunkett-st., Dub.
1751 ,, John, Kilmurry, co. Wicklow
1734 ,, Robert, Tullamore, King's County, tallow chandler
1776 ,, Thomas, Ballinawley
1690 ,, William, Kilkenny, gent. (Ex.)
1774 ,, William, Dublin, merchant
1601 **Aysh**, Alson, Naas, widow (Copy)
   [See ASHE.]

—— B ——

1723 **Babe**, Ann, *alias* **Ley**, Dublin, spinster
1759 ,, Charlotte, widow of Geo. Babe, Dublin, esq.
1680 ,, George, late of Dublin, gent.
1747 ,, George, Dublin, gent.
1775 ,, rev. George, Dublin, clk.
1805 ,, George, Newry, co. Down
1715 ,, Jas., Dundalk, co. Louth, gent.
1709 ,, John, Darver, co. Louth, esq.
1789 ,, Ralph, Newry, co. Down, merchant
1786 **Babington**, George, city of Londonderry, gent.
1754 ,, Hannah, Droomkeen, co. Kerry; widow

1768 **Babington**, Humphry, Rosapena, co. Donegal, gent.
1780 ,, Mathew, Sligo (town)
1751 ,, Thomas, Dublin, gent.
1692 ,, Uriah, Dublin, esq.
1724 ,, Uriah, Drumkeen, co. Kerry, esq.
1736 ,, Wm., Strabane, co. Tyrone, esq.
1746 ,, William, Castleconway, co. Kerry, esq.
1745 **Bachan**, Peter, Dublin, merchant
1807 **Backas**, Thomas, city of Waterford, esq.
1806 **Bacon**, Anna, Mountmellick, Queen's County
1772 ,, Benjamin, Glebe Hall, co. Londonderry, D.D.
1708 ,, Dorothy, Rathkeney, co. Tipperary, widow
1791 ,, rev. Edward, Clonmel, co. Tip.
1752 ,, James, Glynn, co. Wexford
1753 ,, Jane, Camolin, co. Wexford, widow
1776 ,, Mary, widow of Dr. Ben. Bacon
1746 ,, Robert, par. Tamlaghtfinlagan, co. Derry
1798 ,, Thomas, Dublin, tailor
1680 ,, William, Rathkeaney, co. Tipperary, gent.
1688 ,, William, Ballyshonage, co. Wexford, gent.
1763 ,, William, Cornmarket, Dublin, merchant
1792 ,, Wm., Mountmellick, Queen's County, esq.
1602 **Bacstar**, Thomas, Ireland, yeoman
   [See BAXTER.]
1715 **Badcock**, Joseph, Dublin, joiner
1694 **Baddeley**, John, Dublin, chandler
1694 ,, Mary, widow of John Baddeley
1803 **Badge**, Thos., Dublin, soap boiler
1656 **Badger**, Roger, Knockaniker, co. Roscommon, gent. [V. 211
1642 ,, William, Dublin, merchant
1744 **Badham**, Brittridge, Rockfield, co. Cork, esq.
1797 ,, William Leslie
1655 **Badhams**, William, soldier [V. 166
1661 **Badley**, Walter, Ballicroge, co. Catherlagh   [maker
1652 **Badnege**, Daniel, Dublin, caster-
1802 **Bagenal**, Beauchamp, Monybeg, co. Carlow, esq. (Large)
1745 ,, Walter, Bagenall, co. Carlow, esq.
   [See BIGNILL.]
1726 **Bagge**, rev. John, parish St. Ann, co. Essex in Virginia, clk.
1772 ,, John, Monea, co. Waterford, gent.

1719 **Bagge**, Leonard, Kilbree, co. Waterford, esq.
1709 ,, Wm., Gortnegras or Crossfield, co. Cork, esq.
1735 **Baggott**, Elinor, Dublin, widow [See BAGOT.]
1793 **Baggs**, Harriett, Youghal
1795 ,, Henry, Sandville, co. Cork
1764 ,, Isham, Dublin, esq.
1781 ,, James, Lismore, co. Waterford, esq.
1766 ,, Mary, widow
1768 ,, Mary, Dublin, spinster
1742 ,, Richard, Lismore, co. Waterford, esq. [See BEGG.]
1731 **Bagnall**, Ann, Dunleckney, co. Carlow, widow
1713 ,, Nicholas, Place Newith, shire of Anglesey, esq.
1773 ,, Richard, Hawkinstown, co. Meath, gent.
1749 **Bagnell**, Edward, Shanrehen, co. Tipperary, esq.
1607 **Bagnoll**, Nicholas, Ballymone, co. Carlow, esq.
1801 **Bagot**, Cordelia, Ballymore, spinster
1680 ,, Jas., Rathjordan, co. Limerick, gent.
1754 ,, John, Nurney, co. Kildare, esq.
1760 ,, John, Ard, King's County, esq.
1804 ,, John Cuff, formerly of Ballymoe, late of Westminster
1718 ,, Mark, Dublin, esq.
1759 ,, Mark, Newtown O'More, co. Kildare, esq.
1738 ,, Milo, Kilcowsey, King's Co., esq.
1766 ,, Milo, Dublin (Not proved)
1806 ,, Sophia, Dublin city, widow
1787 ,, Thomas, Dublin, esq.
1804 ,, William, Dublin city, esq.
1786 **Bagott**, Catherine, spinster
1792 ,, John, Castle Bagott, co. Dublin, esq.
1801 ,, John Lloyd, Ballymoe, co. Galway, esq. [See BAGGOTT.]
1763 **Bagshaw**, Samuel, Ford, Derby, esq., colonel, 93rd foot
1765 ,, Thomas, William-street, Dublin, flax dresser
1739 **Bagwell**, Ann, widow
1754 ,, John, Clonmel, co. Tipperary, merchant
1785 ,, John, Kilmore, co. Tip., esq.
1765 ,, Mary, Cork, widow
1760 ,, Phineas, Cork, merchant
1756 ,, William, Clonmel, co. Tipperary, esq.

1723 **Bailey**, Jane, widow
1777 **Bailie**, Andrew Thomas, Newry, co. Down, merchant
1809 ,, Andrew, Dundalk, co. Louth, ironmonger
1753 ,, Anne, Richmond Buildings, Soho-square (Copy)
1780 ,, Anne, Dublin, widow
1778 ,, Edward, Toy, co. Down, esq.
1778 ,, Elizabeth, Clough, co. Down, widow
1770 ,, James, Clough, co. Down, esq.
1744 ,, John, M.D. (Copy)
1810 ,, John, Clonaleenan, co. Louth, gent.
1801 ,, Simon, Mount Bailie, co. Louth
1772 ,, Sophia, New Ross, co. Wexford, spinster
1750 ,, William, Dernasier, co. Tyrone, gent.
1798 ,, Wm., Killanagh, co. Monaghan
1716 **Bailley**, Archibald, Dublin, tailor
1810 **Baillie**, Anne, Granby-row, Dublin, widow
1772 ,, Francis, Portarlington, Queen's County, esq. [gent.
1785 ,, Hamilton, King-street, Dublin,
1773 ,, Hans, Dublin, alderman
1787 ,, James, Inishargie, co. Down, esq.
1781 ,, Jane, Ann-st., Dublin, widow
1795 ,, Catherine, Ryves Castle, co. Limerick, spinster
1804 ,, Richard, Sherwood Park, co. Carlow
1808 ,, Robert, Tipperary town
1788 ,, Sarah, Dublin, widow
1785 ,, William, Lurganmore, county Monaghan, gent.
1797 **Bailly**, Thos., Rahenanicka, Queen's County, gent.
1759 **Baily**, Ann, Southampton (town and county), widow
1803 ,, Everina, Newtownbutler, co. Fermanagh, widow
1666 ,, Penelope, Gortman, co. Cavan, widow (Copy)
1735 ,, Rebecca, Dublin, widow
1650 ,, Robert, colonel
1764 ,, Wm., Kilfinane, co. Limerick [See BAYLY.]
1759 **Bainbridge**, George, Dublin
1800 ,, George, Dublin, watchmaker
1689 **Bainbrigge**, Edward, Fethard, co. Tipperary, clk.
1690 ,, Richard, Clonmel, chandler
1710 **Baird**, John, Dublin, merchant
1715 ,, Robt., St. Johnstown, co. Donegal, gent. [See BEARD.]

C

1755	**Baisley**, Anne, Ricketstown, co. Carlow, widow
1737	,,	Diana, Ricketstown, co. Carlow, widow
1694	,,	Euseby, Ballyoliver, co. Carlow, esq.
1711	,,	Eusebey, Ricketstown, co. Carlow, esq.
1741	,,	Wm., Ricketstown, co. Carlow, esq.
1681	**Baker**, Benjamin, Miltown, Queen's County, esq.
		[See EXEMP., 1682]
1694	,,	Catherine, Shanagarry, county Cork, spinster
1683	,,	Edwd., Coombe, Dubl., courier
1734	,,	Edward, Newtown, co. Dublin, gent.
1792	,,	Elizabeth, Cork, widow
1736	,,	Francis, Dublin, and Richardstown, co. Louth, apothecary
1638	,,	George, Dublin, gent. **[IV.** 345
1679	,,	George, Waterford, clk.
1733	,,	Geo., Athy, co. Kild., clothier
1799	,,	George, city of Cork, cooper
1644	,,	Godfrey, Coleraine, alderman
1788	,,	Godfrey, city of Cork, esq.
1663	,,	Henry, Castle Eve, co. Kilkenny, esq.
1746	,,	Henry, Rathculbiss, co. Kilkenny, esq.
1686	,,	Jas., Miltown, Queen's County, gent.
1709	,,	Jas., Miltown, Queen's County, gent.
1798	,,	James, Ballymoreen
1626	,,	John, Culmore, co. Derry, esq.
1752	,,	John, Cork, vintner
1795	,,	John, city of Cork, gent.
1640	,,	Joice, Dublin, widow of Thos Baker, gent.
1744	,,	Lilias, *alias* **Watson**, Drumcondra, widow
1766	,,	Marcy, Mayfield, co. Tipperary, widow
1755	,,	Margaret, *alias* **Bruster**, Dublin, widow
1809	,,	Margaret, Stephen-st., Dublin, widow
1767	,,	Mary, Little Grange, co. Wicklow, widow
1793	,,	Mary, Grange, co. Wicklow, widow
1795	,,	Mary Ann, Ballydavid
1809	,,	Mathew
1789	,,	Paul, Cork, merchant
1797	,,	Peter, Cork city, gent.
1780	,,	Richard, Wicklow town, gent.
1711	,,	Robert
1801	,,	Robert, Kilkenny city

1720	**Baker**, Samuel, Dublin, tallow chandler
1784	,,	Samuel, esq.
1716	,,	Thomas, Newtown, co. Dublin, esq.
1748	,,	Thomas, Dublin, alderman
1759	,,	Thomas, Cashel, co. Tipperary, gent.
1789	,,	Thomas, Ballymoreen, co. Tipperary, esq.
1798	,,	Thomas, Royal Navy
1740	,,	Walter, Ballyvire, co. Tipperary, gent.
1669	,,	William, Whitehouse, Rathfarnham, gent.
1699	,,	William, London, vintner
1756	,,	William, Maplestown, co. Carlow, gent.
1808	,,	William, Lismacue, co. Tipperary, esq. (Large)
1711	**Balbridge**, Thomas, Tamlaghtduff. co. Londonderry
1795	**Baldwin**, Alice, Cork, widow
1736	,,	Arthur, Dublin, esq.
1765	,,	sir Bridges, Dublin (styled on the will, of B. B., esq.)
1730	,,	Charles, Dublin, esq.
1749	,,	rev Charles, Dublin, clk.
1751	,,	Elizabeth, Dublin, spinster
1778	,,	Elizabeth, wife of Joseph B., Castlecuffe, Queen's County
1769	,,	dame Frances, widow of sir Bridges B. (Large Will)
1809	,,	Grace, city of Dublin
1756	,,	Henry, Mountmellick, Queen's County, apothecary
1770	,,	Henry, Curravoidy, co. Cork, esq.
1809	,,	James, Macroom, co. Cork, esq.
1698	,,	John (senior), Shinrone, King's County, esq.
1699	,,	John, Coroghlanty, King's County, esq. (Exemp.)
1797	,,	John, Dysert, Queen's County, gent.
1748	,,	Jonathan, Summerhill, Queen's County, gent.
1758	,,	Joseph, Desart, Queen's Co., gent.
1768	,,	Lucy, Dublin, spinster
1749	,,	Mary, wife to Charles B., Dublin, esq.
1787	,,	Mary, Dublin, spinster
1666	,,	Richard, Dublin, gent.
1743	,,	rev. Richard, prebendary of Kilbrittan
1758	,,	Richard, D.D., provost Trinity College, Dublin
1768	,,	Richard, Dublin, esq.
1795	,,	Richard, Dublin, esq.

1689	**Baley,**	Elizabeth, Rathkilmore, co. Meath, widow [See BAYLY.]
1760	**Balfe,**	Andrew, Cloghreagh, co. Meath, gent.
1762	,,	Anne, Dublin, widow
1762	,,	Anne, Glanvalla, co. Roscommon, widow
1733	,,	Elinor, Dublin, widow
1587	,,	John, Kilmartin
1765	,,	John, Nobber, co. Meath
1779	,,	John, Kells, co. Meath
1727	,,	Patk., Cregg, co. Meath, gent.
1757	,,	Richd., Goat alley, Dub., gent.
1755	,,	Robert
1804	,,	Walter, Heathfield, co. Roscommon, esq.
1759	**Balfour,**	capt. Alexander, Chelsea, Middlesex (Copy)
1741	,,	Anne, *alias* **Townley,** *alias* **Percy,** Dublin, widow
1742	,,	Arthur, Dublin, esq.
1788	,,	Blaney, Townley Hall, co. Louth, esq. (Large)
1801	,,	Elizabeth, city of Londonderry
1747	,,	Isabella, Dublin, spinster
1636	,,	James, esq., son and heir of sir James Balfour, knt., late baron of Clanawley, decd. (Copy)
1786	,,	Thoms, city of Derry, mariner
1782	,,	Toomes
1660	,,	sir William, Westminster, Middlesex, knt. (Copy)
1721	,,	sir William, Westminster, Middlesex, knt.
1739	,,	William, Castle B., co. Fermanagh, esq.
1758	,,	William, son of lieut. Jere. B., Culdrum, co. Donegal
1759	,,	William Townley, Beamore, co. Meath, esq.
1740	**Ball,**	Abraham, Darver, co. Louth, esq.
1668	,,	Benjamin, Dublin
1744	,,	Benjamin, Dublin, carpenter
1724	,,	Blagrave
1776	,,	Catherine, *alias* **Fitzsimons,** Dublin, widow
1758	,,	Charles, Dublin, clk.
1626	,,	Edward, Bridge-street, Dublin
1651	,,	Elizabeth, Dublin, spinster
1662	,,	Elizabeth, St. Margaret's par., Westm., widow
1753	,,	Florinda, Kilbline, co. Kilkenny, widow [esq.
1760	,,	George, Mountball, Drogheda,
1754	,,	Grace, Dublin, spinster
1742	,,	Henry, Youghal, co. Cork, alderman

1640	**Ball,**	Jas., Baldrum, co. Dub., gent.
1787	,,	James, adjutant East Kent militia, esq.
1761	,,	Jane, widow
1597	,,	John, Dublin, esq. [**I.** 95
1608	,,	John, Baldroman, co. Dublin
1665	,,	John, Kilkenny, merchant
1685	,,	John, Dublin, merchant
1705	,,	John, Loughross, co. Armagh, esq.
1755	,,	John, Dublin, saddler
1755	,,	John, Dublin, esq.
1764	,,	John, Frederick-street, Dublin, esq.
1799	,,	rev. John, Altanagh, Queen's County
1804	,,	John, Eccles-street, Dublin
1810	,,	John, Saucerstown. co. Dublin, farmer
1795	,,	Jonathan, Dub., cabinet maker
1650	,,	Margaret, *alias* **Barry,** widow
1665	,,	Margaret, *alias* **Barry,** widow [**IX.** 19
1758	,,	Martha, Dublin, widow
1763	,,	Mildred, Dublin
1610	,,	Nicholas, Dublin, alderman
1652	,,	Nicholas, Lundrestown, co. Meath, gent. [**IV.** 191
1800	,,	Phillipa, Seapark, co. Wicklow, widow
1661	,,	Richard, Westminster, Middlesex, victualler (Copy)
1666	,,	Richard, late capt.-lieut. to sir Thomas Armstrong
1635	,,	Robert, Dublin, alderman
1761	,,	Robert
1778	,,	Robert, Ballsgrove, county of town of Drogheda, esq.
1777	,,	rev. Sterne, Drogheda, clk.
1659	,,	Thomas, soldier [**VII.** 182
1692	,,	Thomas, Glassdroman, co. Armagh, esq. (Exemp.)
1800	,,	Thomas, Seapark, co. Wicklow, esq.
1649	,,	captain William, Dublin
1792	,,	William, Rathmines-road, co. Dublin, esq.
1702	**Ballance,**	William, Dublin, tailor
1715	**Ballard,**	Benj., only son of William B., Cork, gent.
1725	,,	Charity, Smithfield, Dublin, widow
1619	**Balle,**	*alias* **Luttrell,** Begure, widow (Imperfect)
1668	**Ballow,**	Henry, London, merchant (Copy)
1669	**Ballus,**	Constantine, Dublin, gent.
1632	**Baltimore,**	sir George Calvert, knt., lord baron

1639 **Baltinglass**, Anne, viscountess, widow of Thos., visct. B.
1778 ,, John, lord baron (Large)
1637 ,, Thomas, viscount, Roper's Rest, privy councillor   [**IV.** 218
1753 **Bamber**, Dorothy, Dublin, spinster
1672 ,, John, gent., late of Dublin, merchant
1732 ,, Richard, Dublin, esq.
1788 ,, Richard Brown, Belmont, co. Down
1781 **Bambrick**, Catherine, Dub., widow
1803 ,, Henry, Janeville, co. Kild., esq.
1793 ,, John, Maidenhead, Queen's County, esq.
1781 **Bambruck**, Catherine, Dub., widow
1807 **Bamfylde**, sir Richard W., Poltimore, Devon, bart. (Copy)
1754 **Banan**, Andrew, Loaghanstown, co. Louth
1766 ,, Andrew, Killely, co. Louth, farmer
        [See BANON.]
1676 **Banckes**, Nicholas, Dubl., pewterer
        [See BANKES.]
1744 **Bancons**, Henrietta Barbier, Dubl., widow
1733 ,, Isace, Cork, merchant
1722 ,, Jeremiah, Dublin, esq.
1592 **Banester**, Thomas, Kilbrye, county Waterford, gent.
1660 **Banfield**, Edward, Rathood, county Meath, gent.
1762 ,, Francis, Carune, co. Cork, gent.
1771 ,, John, Dublin, brazier
1790 ,, Mary, Killincarrick
1763 ,, William, formerly of Tulliglass, now of Carhue, co. Cork, gent.
1793 **Bangor**, Anne, lady
1781 ,, Bernard, lord baron
1674 **Bankes**, Dorcas, Waterford, widow
1767 ,, John, Atherdee, co. Louth, gent.
1742 ,, Mary, *alias* **Fielding**.
1682 ,, Richd., clk., rector of Delgany, co. Wicklow
1730 ,, Richard, Eyre Court, co. Galway, clk.
1746 ,, Thomas, Belfast, esq.
1746 ,, Thomas, Dublin, coachmaker
1755 ,, Thomas, Belfast, merchant
1712 ,, Wm., Whitehall, Middlesex, gent.
        [See BANCKES, BANKS.]
1718 **Bankhead**, Hugh, par. of Killotin, co. Londonderry, farmer
1718 ,, James, Coleraine, merchant
1790 **Banks**, Adam, Limerick, mercht.
1808 ,, Anne, Limerick city, widow

1747 **Banks**, capt. John, in col. Leighton's regiment of foot
1658 ,, Ralph, Kilkenny, pewterer
        [**VII.** 55
1777 ,, Samuel, Atherdee, co. Louth, gent.
        [See BANCKES.]
1690 **Bannister**, Robert, St. Catherine's, co. Dublin, gent.
1804 **Banon**, Edward, Meares' Court, co. Westmeath, esq.
1767 ,, Thomas, Meares' Court, co. Westmeath, farmer
        [See BANAN.]
1684 **Baptista**, Anthony, Dublin, wine cooper
1809 **Barber**, Bridget, Glasnevin, co. Dublin, widow
1789 ,, John, Golden-lane, Dublin, cabinet maker
1679 ,, Philip, clk., chanter of St. Patrick's, Dublin
1786 ,, Rebecca, Dublin, widow
1791 ,, Rupert, Dublin, merchant
1786 ,, Thos., Dublin, cabinet maker
1787 ,, Thomas, Dublin, watchmaker
        [See BARBOR.]
1724 **Barbick**, William, Dublin, gent.
1698 **Barbier**, John, Dublin, merchant
1783 **Barbor**, Constantine, Dr. in physic
1808 ,, Thos., Longford, co. Longford, gent.
1751 **Barboult**, Abraham, Dublin, watchmaker
1755 **Barbut**, Isace, Dublin, merchant
1805 **Barclay**, Charlotte M., Ballyshannon, co. Donegal
1664 ,, Gavin, chanter of St. Patrick's, Cashel
1780 ,, George, Drumbo, co. Donegal
1807 ,, George, Dublin, apothecary
1701 ,, Jas., Court Nichola. co. Longford
1753 ,, John, Dublin, merchant
1769 ,, John, Dublin, merchant
1771 ,, Joseph, Ballybossey, co. Don., gent.
1779 ,, Robert, Strabane, co. Tyrone
1783 ,, Robt., Ballyshannon, co. Don., merchant
        [See BERKELEY.]
1760 **Barcroft**, Ambrose, Dublin, mercht.
1740 ,, Elizabeth, Ballitore, co. Kildare, widow
1673 ,, Henry, parish of St. Andrew, Undershaft, London, gent.
1724 ,, John, Arkhill, Kildare, farmer
1784 ,, Joseph, South Earl-st., Dublin, merchant   [esq.
1670 ,, Robt., Westminster, Middlesex,

1785 **Bardin**, James, Great Booter-lane, Dublin, gent.
1776 ,, Peter, Dublin, gent.
1783 ,, Benjamin, Arbour Hill, gent. (Large)
1629 **Bardon**, John, Lymehouse, Middlesex, mariner
1723 ,, John, Ringsend, near Dublin, mariner
1661 **Bardwell**, John, citizen and grocer of London
1639 **Barefote** or **Berfoot**, Walter, Lisfynyn Bridge, co. Waterford
1674 **Baret**, Gyles, gent., riding in Duke of Ormond's troop
1670 ,, John, Dublin
[See BARRETT.]
1696 **Bargany**, lord John, of Scotland (Exemp.)
1785 **Barkah**, Bryan, Tyhallon, county Monaghan
1806 **Barker**, Alexander (Copy)
1715 ,, Bernard, Dublin, upholsterer
1811 ,, Charlotte, Rathmines, co. Dublin, spinster
1702 ,, dame Elizabeth, wife of sir W. B. (Large)
1768 ,, Elizabeth, Waterford
1770 ,, Elizabeth, Dublin, spinster
1708 ,, Francis, Waterford, alderman
1773 ,, Francis, Waterford city, esq.
1683 ,, George, Dublin, vintner
1723 ,, George, lieutenant in sir John Jacobb's regt. of foot
1800 ,, James, lt.-col. 2nd regt. foot
1759 ,, John, Blackall, co. Kildare, gent.
1774 ,, John, Blackhall, co. Kildare, gent.
1771 ,, Jonathan, Dubl., land surveyor
1762 ,, Margery, Blackhall, co. Kildare, spinster
1712 ,, Philip, Dublin, tanner
1801 ,, Rainsford, Dublin, attorney
1687 ,, Richard, Ballinteige, co. Kild.
1769 ,, Samuel, Waterford, esq.
1734 ,, Simon, Butterhill, co. Wicklow, farrier
1793 ,, Simon, Moon, co. Kild., farmer
1801 ,, Thomas, Eagle Hill, co. Carlow
1629 ,, William, Dublin, esq.
1689 ,, William, Dublin, upholder
1719 ,, sir William, Cureaghmore, co. Limerick, bart. (A later will proved in 1742)
1742 ,, sir William, London, bart.
1765 ,, Wm., Tylfarris, co. Wicklow, gent.
1770 ,, sir William, Kilcooley, co. Tipperary, bart.

1776 **Barker**, rev. William, dean of Raphoe
1789 ,, William, Waterford, alderman
1584 **Barloe**, James, Dublin [I. 22
1798 **Barlow**, Aethemia, Drogheda, widow
1775 ,, Arthur
1727 ,, Elizabeth, Dublin, widow
1668 ,, Henry, Manchester, Lancashire, chapman [XIV. 197
1735 ,, Jacobb, Dublin, esq.
1716 ,, sir James, Dublin, knt.
1760 ,, James, Drogheda, esq.
1690 ,, John, Patrick-street, Dublin, brewer
1701 ,, Sir John, Minwear, Pembroke, bart.
1742 ,, John, Aghnamallagh, county Monaghan, esq.
1744 ,, John, Aghnamallagh, county Monaghan, esq.
1752 ,, John, Newhall or Gurtnafallen, gent.
1783 ,, John, Dublin, esq.
1808 ,, rev. John, Dundalk, co. Louth, clk.
1743 ,, Joshua, Dublin, merchant
1766 ,, Leonard, Dublin, gent.
1726 ,, Lewis, Ballinafirragh, co.Westmeath, gent.
1730 ,, Martha, widow of Lewis B.
1690 ,, Mary, Dublin, widow
1753 ,, Mary, Newgrove, co. Monaghan, widow
1746 ,, Ralph, Aghnamallagh, county Monaghan, gent.
1702 ,, Richard
1758 ,, Robt., Crossna, co. Roscommon
1745 ,, Thomas, Nadinea, King's Co., farmer
1726 ,, William, Dublin, esq.
1615 **Barlowe**, Richard, parson of the Lyons, dio. Kildare
1811 **Barnard**, Andrew, Cape of Good Hope
1782 ,, Anne, Dublin, widow
1660 ,, Francis, the elder, Castlemaghoun, co. Cork, gent.
1723 ,, Francis, Monard North, sub. of Cork, gent.
1793 ,, rev. Hen., Maghera, co. Derry, LL.D.
1780 ,, Hudson, Carlow town, esq.
1672 ,, Thomas, Lambeth, Surrey, and citizen and fletcher of London (Exemp.)
1683 ,, William, Dublin.
[See BERNARD.]
1678 **Barnardiston**, Nathaniel, London, merchant

1669 **Barne**, Thomas, par. of Erith, Kent
1755 **Barnes**, Alice, Dunover, co Meath, widow
1772 ,, Anthony, Boyle, co. Roscommon, gent.
1782 ,, Anthony, Dublin, gent.
1794 ,, Bartholomew, Park, co. Carlow, esq.
1763 ,, Caleb, Mahonstown, co. Meath, gent.
1730 ,, Diana, Grange, co. Kilkenny, widow
1756 ,, Esther, Kilconenmore, co. Tipperary, widow
1681 ,, Gabriel, Honiton, Devon, merchant (Copy)
1732 ,, Geo., Donore or Donorer, co. Meath, gent.
1745 ,, George, Blackhorse-lane, co. Dublin, gardener
1784 ,, Helen, widow
1730 ,, Humphrey, Brourath, co. Meath
1764 ,, James, Parkhill
1774 ,, Joanna, New Ross, co. Wexford, spinster
1707 ,, John, Dublin, gent.
1751 ,, Jonathan, Kilconinmore, co. Tipperary, gent.
1767 ,, Joseph, Edenderry, King's Co.
1800 ,, Joseph, Edenderry, King's Co., shopkeeper
1601 ,, Nicholas, Dublin, mariner
1684 ,, Thomas, Grange, co. Kilkenny, gent.
1710 ,, Thomas, Grange, co. Kilkenny, gent.
1722 ,, Thomas, Killculleeheene, Lib. of Waterford, farmer
1741 ,, Thos., Rathclanbracken, King's County, farmer
1799 ,, Thomas, Dublin, esq.
1806 ,, Thomas, Meath-row, Dublin
1672 ,, Toby, capt. (exemp.) (original delivered in 1682 to sir H. Ponsonby)
1793 **Barnesley**, Richard, Lisburn, co. Antrim, merchant
1753 **Barnett**, Hugh, Belfast, co. Antrim, merchant
1754 ,, Job, Dublin, upholder
1801 ,, Robert, Montpelier, suburbs of Dublin, gent.
[See BARRETT.]
1745 **Barnewall**, Alex., Dubl., hosier
1789 ,, Alicia, city of Paris
1692 ,, Aminet, *als.* **Plunkett**, Blackhall, co. Louth, widow.
1803 ,, Bartholomew, Boyne Lodge, co. Meath, esq.
1760 ,, Bridgett, Dublin, spinster

1618 **Barnewall**, Catherine, *als.* **Finglass**, Skydow, co. Dublin
1745 ,, Catherine, Dublin, widow
1622 ,, Christopher, Newtown, co. Dublin, gent.
1661 ,, Christopher, Grasdue, co. Dublin, gent.
1674 ,, Christopher, Shankill, esq.
1693 ,, Christopher, Athronan, county Meath, gent.
1802 ,, Christopher, Wimbleton, co. Dublin, esq.
1749 ,, Edward, Inns-quay, Dublin, merchant
1726 ,, Elizabeth, Dublin, spinster
1781 ,, Elizabeth, called lady Trimleston (See BUNDLE, T.)
1757 ,, Ellis, Dublin, widow
1758 ,, Frances, Dublin, spinster
1663 ,, George, Newtown, co. Meath, gent.
1686 ,, George, Dublin
1735 ,, sir George, Dublin, bart.
1775 ,, hon. George, par. St. George, Hanover-square
1617 ,, James, Balrath, co. Meath, gent.
1666 ,, James, Archestown, gent.
1692 ,, James, Roskerne, Queen's Co., gent.
1729 ,, James, Lusk, co. Dublin, gent.
1765 ,, James, Mullingar
1774 ,, Johanna, widow of George B., of Killarrow, co. Westmeath
1589 ,, John, Lispoppell, co. Dublin, gent.
1602 ,, John, Muneton, co. Meath
1746 ,, John, commonly called lord B., Trimleston
1766 ,, John, Dublin, apothecary
1770 ,, John, Kilroe, Co. Meath
1782 ,, hon. Joseph, Dublin
1676 ,, Mable, Trimblestown, county Meath, spinster
1750 ,, Mary, Dublin, spinster
1771 ,, Mary, commonly called lady dowager Trimlestown
1705 ,, Mathew, Bremore, co. Dublin, gent.
1784 ,, hon. Mathias, Dublin
1731 ,, Michael, Dublin, dealer
1735 ,, Nicholas, Clanmore, King's County, esq.
1805 ,, Nicholas, Dunmucky, co. Dublin, esq.
1627 ,, Patrick, Shankill, co. Dublin, esq.
1630 ,, Patrick, Dunboyne, yeoman
1702 ,, sir Patrick, Newcastle, co. Meath, bart.

1595 **Barnewall,** Peter, Lispopple, co. Dublin, gent.
1617 ,, Robt., Robertstown, co. Meath, gent.
1690 ,, Robert, Rolstown, co. Meath, esq.
1741 ,, Robert, Moyrath, co. Westmeath, gent.
1720 ,, Silvester, Clonegall, co. Carlow, merchant
1587 ,, Symon, Kilbrue, co. Meath, gent.
1668 ,, Thos., Bodine, co. Meath, gent.
1808 **Barnier,** Claudius, Cullins, co. Dublin, chandler
1784 **Barnwell,** George, Newmarket-on-the-Comb, tanner
1788 **Baron,** Francis, Dublin, merchant.
1701 ,, John, Portaferry, co. Down, merchant
1808 ,, Sarah, Coombe, co. Dublin, widow
1800 ,, William, Lakin, co. Tipperary, esq.
[See BARRON.]
1743 **Barr,** Charles, Cork, skinner
1766 ,, John, Monaghan, merchant
1599 **Barran,** Edward (description, &c., illegible)
1588 ,, John, Dublin, merchant
1649 ,, John, water bailiff, Dublin city
[See BARRON].
1743 **Barrat,** James, Philipstown, King's County, carpenter
[See BARRETT.]
1776 **Barre,** Peter, Cullenswood, co. Dublin, esq.
1685 **Barret,** dame Barb. *als.* **St. Leger,** Haymarket, London, widow of Heyward St. Leger
1599 ,, Nicholas
1729 ,, Samuel, Castletown, co. Carlow
1742 ,, Stephen, Dublin, staymaker
1674 ,, sir William, Castlemore, co. Cork, bart. (Exemp.)
1730 **Barrett,** Anne, Dublin, widow
1792 ,, Anne, Ballyduff, co. Carlow
1794 ,, Anne, Dublin, spinster
1764 ,, Cecilia, Dublin, widow
1786 ,, Charles, Loughrea, co. Galway, gent.
1800 ,, Dominick, Dublin, esq.
1757 ,, Dorothy, Rapo, co. Mayo
1758 ,, Edmond, Tonemore, co. Cork, gent.
1763 ,, Edmond, Towermore, co. Cork, merchant
1783 ,, Edmond
1783 ,, Edmond, Curlogh, co. Cork, farmer

1723 **Barrett,** Edward, Dublin, silversmith
1760 ,, Edward, Cork, merchant
1773 ,, Elizabeth, Carrowkeel, King's County
1809 ,, Elizabeth, Dublin City, widow
1732 ,, Jacob, Park, co. Carlow
1709 ,, James, Sligo, merchant
1772 ,, James, Dublin, woollen draper
1630 ,, John, Fitz Andrew, Inchcurry, co. Cork, gent.
1702 ,, John, Dublin, victualler
1764 ,, John
1774 ,, John, Coolowen, North Lib. of Cork
1797 ,, John, Galway, gent.
1811 ,, rev. Marcus, Maynooth, co. Kildare
1752 ,, Mary Anne, Dublin, spinster
1765 ,, Miles, Tullamore, King's County, miller
1792 ,, Richard, Ballyduff, co. Carlow
1810 ,, Samuel P., city of Dublin, attorney-at-law
1766 ,, Thomas, Curbagh, co. Cork, farmer
1785 ,, Thomas Mt. B., co. Mayo (late of Dublin), gent.
1780 ,, Tobias, Killala, co. Mayo
1763 ,, Walter, Dublin, gent.
1767 ,, William, Sligo, esq.
1785 ,, William, Castle Clake, co. Tipperary, esq.
1803 ,, William, Enniscorthy, co. Wexford, gent.
[See BARRATT, BARET, BARRET, BARROT.]
1622 **Barrick,** John, New Ross, co Wexford, merchant
1788 **Barrington,** Alexander, Barretstown, co. Kildare, gent.
1733 ,, Benjamin, Limerick, alderman
1748 ,, Benjamin, Dublin, esq.
1749 ,, Catherine, Dublin, spinster
1687 ,, Christr., Loghteoge, Queen's County
1753 ,, Elizabeth, Dublin, spinster
1774 ,, Elizabeth, Dublin, spinster
1762 ,, Jane, late of Barretstown, now of Baldonnell, co. Dublin
1784 ,, John Thomas, Thomas-street, Dublin, tallow chandler
1743 ,, Joshua, St. Patrick's, Liberty of Dublin
1753 ,, Margaret, the elder, Dub., widow
1796 ,, Mary, Hillbrook, co. Dublin, widow
1668 ,, captain Nicholas, Killone, Queen's County [ford
1770 ,, Nicholas, Lambstown, co. Wex-

1753 **Barrington**, Samuel, Ennis, co. Clare, esq.
1754 ,, Wheeler, Dublin, esq.
1788 ,, William, Queen's County
1622 **Barron**, Laurence, Clonmel, mercht.
1798 ,, Michael, Waterford city, dyer
1784 ,, Nicholas, Cork, priest
1623 ,, William, Stradbally, co. Waterford, gent.
1680 ,, William, Dublin, merchant
[See BARON, BARRAN.]
1569 **Barros**, Thomas, Dublin, baker
1720 **Barrot**, John, Dublin, perfumer
[See BARRETT.]
1691 **Barrow**, Deliverance, esq. (officer in the army)
1792 ,, John, Inistioge, co. Kilkenny, gent.
1809 ,, John, adjt., Londonderry militia
1748 ,, Mary, Lurgan, co. Armagh
1653 ,, Thos., Dublin, gent. [**V.** 300
1785 **Barry**, Catherine, Dublin, widow
1750 ,, Chas., Newtown, co. Louth, esq.
1768 ,, Charles, Kilcairne, co. Meath, gent.
1747 ,, Christopher, Dublin, victualler
1747 ,, Clement, Saggard, co. Dublin, esq.
1632 ,, David Fitz Richard, Great Isle, co. Cork, gent.
1744 ,, hon. David John   [gent.
1744 ,, David, Whitestown, co. Dublin,
1802 ,, David, Kanturk, co. Cork
1648 ,, Edmond, Rashee, co. Antrim, esq. (Exemp. of.)
1800 ,, Edmond, Charleville, co. Cork
1776 ,, Sir Edward, bart., M.D.
1729 ,, Elinor
1729 ,, Elizabeth, Dublin, widow
1740 ,, Elizabeth, Dublin, widow
1743 ,, Elizabeth, Loughcrew, co. Meath, widow
1751 ,, Elizabeth, Dublin, widow
1747 ,, Frances, Dublin, widow
1802 ,, Frances, Dublin, widow
1770 ,, Francis, Tinegarrah, co. Cork, now of co. Dublin
1799 ,, Garret, city of Cork, woollen draper
1799 ,, Garret, Leamlara, co. Cork, esq.
1783 ,, Garrett, Dublin, merchant
1796 ,, Gaynor, Bean, co. Dublin, esq.
1751 ,, Henry, lord baron Santry
1739 ,, Hobart, New-street, Dub., esq.
1598 ,, James, Dublin, alderman
1716 ,, James, co. Cork, esq.
1727 ,, James, Dublin, esq.
1728 ,, James, Dublin, clk.
1743 ,, James, Dublin, esq.
1752 ,, James, Carrigleagh, co. Cork

1768 **Barry**, James, Dublin, gent.
1772 ,, James, Ballymena, co. Antrim
1787 ,, James, South King-st., Dublin
1802 ,, James, Hugh Smith, esq. (Large)
1802 ,, James, Youghal, co. Cork, merchant
1803 ,, James, Castlelyons, co. Cork, attorney
1804 ,, James, Desert, co. Cork
1777 ,, John, Ballyglissane, co. Cork
1782 ,, John, Ballyshoneen, co. Cork
1793 ,, John, Ballinoonare, co. Cork, esq.
1794 ,, rev. John, D.D., dean of Elphin
1796 ,, John, Dublin, gent.
1791 ,, Joseph, Mallow, co. Cork, physician
1767 ,, Margaret, Dublin, spinster
1750 ,, Mary, Rathcormick, co. Cork, spinster
1758 ,, Mary, Dublin
1790 ,, Mary
1802 ,, Mary, Kanturk, co. Cork, widow
1695 ,, Mathew, Dublin, esq.
1745 ,, Michael, Rathrush, co. Carlow, gent.
1748 ,, Michael, Farnane, co. Limerick, gent.
1750 ,, Michl., Donnybrook, co. Dub., gent.
1786 ,, sir Nath., Dub., bart. (Large)
1730 ,, Paul, Dublin, esq.
1755 ,, Paul, Greencastle, co. Down, esq.
1762 ,, Paul, Greencastle, co. Down, gent.
1774 ,, Rebecca, Bath, co. Limerick, widow
1690 ,, Redmond, Rathcormick, co. Cork, esq.
1739 ,, Redmond, Ballyclough, co. Cork, esq.
1741 ,, Redmond, Ballyclough, co. Cork, esq.
1750 ,, Redmond, Rathcormac, co. Cork, esq. (Copy)
1790 ,, Redmond
1649 ,, Richard, Dublin, alderman (Copy)
1678 ,, Richard, Dublin, esq.
1686 ,, Richd., Fortall, King's County, esq. (Ex.)
1699 ,, Richard, Dublin, gent.
1714 ,, Richd., Tobberbonny, co. Dub., esq. (Ex.)
1732 ,, Richard, Kilcarne, co. Meath, gent.
1795 ,, rev. Richard, Leighsbrook, co. Meath, clk.

1799 **Barry**, Richards, Mitchelstown, co. Cork, innholder
1733 ,, Robert, Jamaica, mercht., now in Cork
1793 ,, Robert, Hume-street, Dublin, counsellor-at-law. (Probate cancelled, and other will proved 1795)
1795 ,, Robert
1740 ,, Samuel, Ballycreggane, co. Tipperary, gent.
1777 ,, Spranger, King-street, par. St. Paul, Covent-garden, esq.
1605 ,, Thomas, Dublin
1660 ,, Thomas, trooper **[VIII.** 101
1727 ,, Thomas, Dublin, gent.
1761 ,, Thos., the elder, Mallow-lane, Cork, merchant
1779 ,, Thomas, Tinnegara, co. Cork, gent.
1785 ,, Thomas, Walker's-alley, Dub., dealer
1745 ,, Walter, Newtown, co. Carlow
1695 ,, William, Ternonfechan, co. Louth, clk.
1745 ,, rev. William, Dublin, clk.
1755 ,, William, Duke-street, Dublin, victualler
1764 ,, William, Ellistown, co. Dublin, gent.
[See BARYE, BARRE.]
1744 **Barrymore**, Catherine, countess dowager
1747 ,, James, earl of (Large)
1752 ,, James, earl of
1792 ,, Margaret, countess dowager (Copy)
1807 **Barter**, Benjamin, Armagh. co. Cork, esq.
1787 ,, Thomas, Dublin, gent.
1672 **Bartlett**, captain John, Leary-hill, Liberties of Dublin
1770 ,, Richard, Dublin, gent.
1801 **Bartley**, Geo., M.D., town of Monaghan, [widow
1803 ,, Margaret, Barrack-st., Dublin,
1761 **Bartly**, Eugene, Dublin, gent.
1772 **Barton**, Anthony
1794 ,, Barbara, Dublin, widow
1650 ,, Edward, Dublin, merchant
1739 ,, Edward, Lurgan, co. Armagh, linen draper
1801 ,, Edward, Springhill, co. Tyrone
1786 ,, Elinor, Lisburn, co. Antrim, spinster
1747 ,, Elizabeth, Lurgan, co. Armagh, widow
1656 ,, George, lieut. of foot **[V.** 225
1750 ,, George, Gosslingtonstown, co. Kilkenny, gent.

1790 **Barton**, George, Dublin, gold-beater
1763 ,, Henry, Dublin, apothecary
1676 ,, Isaac, London, esq. (Ex.)
1718 ,, John, D.D., dean of Ardagh
1759 ,, John, Springtown, co. Ferman.
1766 ,, John, Leixlip, brewer
1808 ,, Joseph
1733 ,, Mary, Dublin, widow
1787 ,, Mary, Ormond-quay, widow
1724 ,, Robt., Irishtown, co. Kilkenny, esq.
1768 ,, Robert, Pettico, co. Donegal
1810 ,, Sarah
1805 ,, Susanna, Forkill, co. Armagh, widow
1744 ,, rev. Thos., Gowle, co. Wicklow, clk.
1781 ,, Thomas, the Palu of the Chartrous of the suburbs of Bordeaux, in France
1722 ,, Wm., Thomastown, co. Louth, esq.
1787 ,, William, Eustace-st., Dublin, merchant
1794 ,, Wm., Bordeaux, France, esq.
1780 **Bartram**, Henry, Mallow, co. Cork, clothier
1747 **Barwick**, Edward, Cork, merchant
1774 ,, Duke, Lisnecrive, co. Longford, gent.
1774 ,, Elizabeth, Movia, co. Down, widow
1581 **Barye**, Thos., Dubl., mercht. **[I.** 7
1782 **Bashford**, James, Belfast, mercht.
1783 **Basil**, Edmund, Newhouse, Buckinghamshire, esq. (Large will. Copy)
1735 ,, Martin Caulfield, of Wiltons, Buckinghamshire, esq. (Copy)
1694 ,, William, heretofore of Lincoln's Inn, Middlesex, esq. (Copy)
1655 **Baskervile**, Mary **[V.** 154
1598 **Basnet**, William
1768 **Bass**, Francis, Dublin, linen draper
1746 ,, John, Ballyarter, co. Wicklow
1648 **Basset**, Alexander, Loughreigh, co. Galway, tailor
1640 ,, sir Arthur, Belfast, knt.
1669 ,, Richard, Cork, alderman
1746 **Bassett**, Richard, esq.
1773 **Bastable**, Arthur, Castlemagner, co. Cork, gent.
1728 ,, Chas., Castlemagner, co. Cork, gent.
1794 ,, Daniel, Kanturk, co. Cork, apothecary
1808 ,, John, city of Cork, gent.

1725 **Bate**, George, esq., lieut.-governor of Charlesfort, co. Cork
1732 ,, John Dunbar, Dublin, gent.
1728 ,, Mary, Kinsale, widow
1641 ,, Thomas, Gyll Abbey, co. city Cork, merchant
1668 ,, Thomas, Dublin, gent.
1784 ,, Thomas, Dublin
1684 **Bateman**, Anne, Youghal, widow of Robert B., Ferrypoint, co. Waterford, gent.
1758 ,, Catherine, widow (Copy)
1782 ,, Elizabeth, Cork city, widow
1789 ,, George
1809 ,, G. Brook, Allavilla,
1719 ,, John, Killeen, co. Kerry, esq. (Large. Ex.)
1738 ,, John, Maherahinch, co. Down, gent.
1661 ,, Robert, London, haberdasher
1801 ,, Robert, Moira
1754 ,, Rowland, Killeen, co. Kerry, esq.
1803 ,, Rowland, Oak Park, co. Kerry, esq.
1726 ,, Susanna, Coleraine, widow
1801 **Bates**, Alexander, Dublin, mercht.
1796 ,, David, Summerhill
1659 ,, Nathaniel, Oxmantown, Dublin [VIII. 5
1805 ,, Thomas
1794 ,, William, Waterford, alderman
1776 **Bateson**, Elizabeth, city of Bath, spinster
1767 ,, Richard, Londonderry, mercht.
1768 ,, Richard, 3rd son of Richard B., Londonderry, esq.
1792 ,, Thos., Orangefield, co. Down, esq.
1798 ,, Thomas, city of Derry, esq.
1764 **Bath**, Anne, Newtown Mt. Kennedy, co. Wicklow, widow
1744 ,, Christopher, Charles-st., Dublin, gent.
1673 ,, Margt., House of Drumconragh
1782 ,, Mary, Dublin, widow
1758 ,, Mathias, Rosemarry-lane, Dublin
1643 ,, Patrick, Dublin, tailor
1675 ,, Peter, Dublin, merchant
1693 ,, Peter, Hearne, son and heir of James Bath, Drumconragh, co. Dublin, esq. deceased
1608 **Bathe**, Edwd., Drogheda, alderman
1630 ,, sir John, knt. (Ex.)
1686 ,, sir Peter, Athcarne, co. Meath, bart. (Ex.)
1584 ,, Richard, Colpe, co. Meath
1621 ,, Robert, Lea, Queen's County, gent.

1599 **Bathe**, Wm., second justice of the Common Pleas
1676 ,, William, Rath, co. Meath, gent.
1723 **Batho**, Hugh, Dublin, gent.
1661 **Bathoe**, Edwd., Patrick-street, near Dublin, merchant
1691 **Bathurst**, Elizabeth, Boulton, co. Kildare, widow
1676 ,, Henry, gent., recorder of Cork and Kinsale, and His Majesty's attorney for province of Munster (Ex.)
1805 ,, Matthew, Summerhill, co. Dublin, esq. (Large)
1666 ,, Samuel, Dublin, esq.
1784 ,, William, Nicholastown, county Kildare
1780 **Batt**, Benjamin, New Ross, co. Wexford, esq.
1745 ,, Jane, Taghmon, co. Wexford, widow
1809 ,, Jane, city of Dublin, widow
1811 ,, Jane, New Ross, co. Wexford
1780 ,, Joseph, Grange, co. Wexford, farmer
1800 ,, Joyce, town of Wexford, widow
1767 ,, Narcissus, Dunleer, clk.
1790 ,, Robert, formerly captain in the 18th regt. of foot
1776 ,, Samuel, Rathneddan, co. Wexford, gent.
1789 ,, rev. Wm., Callon, co. Louth, clk.
1773 **Battaley**, William
1714 **Batteley**, Saml., Bury St. Edmonds, Suffolk, esq.
1724 **Battell**, John, quarter-master in Lord Shannon's regt. of carbineers
1723 **Battely**, Charles, Westminster
1661 **Batten**, Worsley, Drogheda, esq.
1771 **Batter**, Samuel, Kilcock, co. Kildare, gent.
1708 ,, Thomas, Aghaboe, King's Co., farmer
1745 ,, William, Dublin, gent.
1757 **Battersby**, Charles, Philipstown, co. Meath, gent.
1803 ,, John, Leakefield, co. Meath, esq.
1785 ,, Robert, Bobsville, co. Meath, esq.
1790 ,, Wm., Smithstown, co. Meath, esq.
1743 **Batterton**, Laurence, Clonegall, co. Cather., merchant
1794 **Battier**, John Gaspard, the elder, Dublin, gent.
1670 **Batty**, Edward, Clonmel, gent.
1781 ,, Espine, Ballyhealy, co. Westmeath, esq.

1782 **Batty**, rev. John, Timolin, co. Kildare, clk.
1722 ,, Thos., Killogh, co. Tipperary
1793 **Batwell**, Andrew, Fortland, county Cork, gent.
1757 ,, Ann, Dublin, widow
1753 ,, Lallum, Dublin, gent.
1808 ,, Sarah, Mallow, co. Cork, spr.
1669 **Baudry**, John, Roen, mercht. (Ex.)
1794 **Baugh**, Launcelot, lieut.-general of His Majesty's forces
1601 **Baulch**, Nicholas, Haden, Somersetshire, soldier
1710 **Bauldry**, Paul, professor of sacred history in Utrecht
1761 **Bauman**, John, Hyde Park, co. Wexford, gent.
1650 **Baurd** or **Bird**, Emanuel, Dublin
1728 ,, Margaret, Dublin, widow
1618 **Baxter**, Edward, Plymouth, Devon, merchant,
1736 ,, Elizabeth, Dublin, widow
1757 ,, Elizabeth, Dublin, spinster
1757 ,, Jas., Newmills, co. Monaghan
1757 ,, John, Dublin, apothecary
1751 ,, Robert, Crossgare, co. Down
1656 ,, Thomas, Londonderry [**V**. 292
1692 ,, William, London, clothworker (Copy)
1749 ,, William, Dublin, linen weaver
1753 ,, William, Dublin, wigmaker [See BACSTAR.]
1734 **Bay**, William, Inishrush, co. Derry, gent. (Ex.)
1793 **Bayle**, Agnes, housekeeper to bishop of Clogher
1721 **Baylee**, Henry, Loghgurr, county Limerick, esq. [rick, esq.
1809 ,, Henry, Loughgurr, co. Lime-
1800 ,, Jane
1774 ,, Sexton, Limerick, alderman
1747 ,, Susanna, Loughgurr, co. Limerick, widow
1775 **Bayley**, Catherine, Dublin, widow
1802 ,, Catherine, Dorset-st., Dublin, widow
1785 ,, Edward, archdeacon of Dublin
1751 ,, Eleanor, Gowran, co. Kilkenny, widow
1719 ,, James, Dublin, gent.
1685 ,, John, Kilkea, co. Kildare, gent.
1753 ,, John, Dublin, gent.
1758 ,, John, Little Green, Dubl., gent.
1778 ,, Thomas, Dublin, esq.
1747 **Baylie**, Chas., Ovidstown, co. Kildare, gent.
1797 ,, Pery, city of Limerick, gent.
1635 ,, Wm., London, merchant tailor
1782 ,, William, Cork, gent. [See BAYLY.]

1754 **Baylis**, James, Dublin, gent.
1770 ,, John, Enniscorthy, co. Wexford, gent.
1804 ,, John, lieutenant-colonel, 35th regt.
1789 **Bayly**, Anna Lucinda, Dublin, spr.
1788 ,, Catherine, Prior's Wood, co. Dublin
1797 ,, Clayton, Gowran, co. Kilkenny, esq.
1742 ,, sir Edward, Tinny Park, co. Wicklow, bart.
1797 ,, Elizabeth, Dublin, widow
1766 ,, Henry, Limerick, esq.
1709 ,, John, Ballynacloghy, co. Tipperary, esq.
1712 ,, John, Dublin, goldbeater
1733 ,, John, Debsborough, co. Tipperary
1740 ,, John, Omeath, co. Louth, gent.
1745 ,, John, Gowran, co. Kilkenny, esq.
1781 ,, John, Gowran, co. Kilkenny, esq.
1795 ,, John, esq.
1797 ,, John, Debsborough, co. Tipperary, esq.
1799 ,, John, vicar of Clonmacnoise, King's County, clk.
1769 ,, Joseph, Dublin, esq.
1804 ,, Jos., Killafert, King's County, gent.
1747 ,, Lambart, Dublin, esq.
1798 ,, Lucinda
1808 ,, Rebecca, wife of John Madder Bayly
1765 ,, Richard, major in sir Robert Hamilton's regiment of foot
1788 ,, Richard, Dublin, public notary
1784 ,, Robert Clayton
1784 ,, rev. Samuel, rector of Kilmore, co. Monaghan
1784 ,, Susanna, Ballitore, co. Kildare, widow
1733 ,, Thomas, Kilneerott, co. Cavan, gent.
1777 ,, Thomas, Newtownbarry, co. Wexford, esq.
1782 ,, Thos., Smallford, co. Kildare [See BAILEY, BAILIE, BAILLEY, BAILLIE, BAILLY, BAILY, BAYLE, BAYLEE, BAYLEY, BAYLIE, BAYLY.]
1739 **Bayne**, Elizabeth, widow
1734 **Bayze**, John, officer on Irish establ. of Dublin
1705 **Bazin**, Germain, the elder, London, merchant (Copy)
1752 **Beach**, Mark, Dublin, gent.
1770 **Beachan**, Patrick, Panestown, co. Kildare, farmer

1789 **Beaghan**, John, Cornmarket, Dubl.
1683 ,, Peter, Dublin, esq. (Ex.)
1694 ,, Peter, Dublin, esq.
1788 ,, William, Watling-st., Dublin, skinner
1785 **Beahan**, James, Dublin, gent.
1798 ,, Thomas, Dublin, livery stable owner
[See BEAGHAN.]
1773 **Beale**, George, Cork, merchant
1803 ,, George, Drumgood, co. Wexford, gent.
1759 ,, John, Mountmellick, Queen's County, merchant
1710 ,, Joshua, Mountmellick, Queen's County, merchant
1762 ,, Joshua, Cork, merchant
1773 ,, Joshua, Mountmellick, Queen's County, merchant
1782 ,, Samuel, Cork, merchant
1761 ,, Thomas, Cork, merchant
1797 **Bealy**, Alexander, Killinanagh, co. Monaghan
1603 **Beame**, Patrick, Maston, co. Dublin, cottier [widow
1792 **Beamish**, Alice, Mallow, co. Cork,
1809 ,, Mary, Lissierimmeen, co. Cork, spinster
1772 ,, William, Cork, esq.
1796 **Beamsly**, Anne, Dublin, widow
1729 **Bean**, John, Dublin, clothier
1767 ,, Martin, Meath-street, Dublin, merchant
1724 **Bearcroft**, John, Arkhill, co. Kildare, farmer
1732 **Beard**, Ann, Ballyroan, Queen's County
1807 ,, Catherine, city of Dublin, spr.
1634 ,, Hugh, Dublin, merchant
1808 ,, John, Dublin, carpenter
1738 ,, Philip, Ballyroan, Queen's County, esq.
1664 **Bearde**, Thomas, Dublin, gent.
[See BAIRD.]
1787 **Beare**, Elizabeth, Cork, widow
1784 ,, John, Cork, merchant
1809 ,, Joseph, town of Carlow
1771 ,, Richard, vicar-general of the diocese of Cork
1788 **Beasley**, Edmond, Prussia-street, co. Dublin, esq.
1792 ,, Edmond, Henry-street, Dublin, grocer
1764 ,, Elizabeth, Dublin, widow
1803 ,, Jeffrey, Cork, cooper
1736 ,, Joseph, Dublin, merchant
1794 ,, Richard, Chamber-street, Dublin, clothier
1784 ,, Thomas, Britain-street, Dublin, merchant

1807 **Beasley**, Thos., the elder, New Market, co. Dublin, clothier
1794 **Beasly**, Mary, Prussia-street, Dublin, widow
1765 ,, William, Chamber-st., Dublin
1726 **Beathom**, John, Dublin, mariner
1805 **Beattie**, James, York-st., Coyentgarden (Copy)
1729 **Beatty**, lieut. Claud, Coolaherty, co. Longford
1794 ,, Edward, Dublin, merchant
1790 ,, Elizabeth, Lylo, co. Armagh, widow
1799 ,, Elizabeth, Dublin, widow
1781 ,, Francis, Mary's-abbey, Dublin, tailor
1738 ,, Henry, Dublin, apothecary
1784 ,, James, Clones, co. Monaghan
1805 ,, James, Kevin-st., co. Dublin, publican
1807 ,, Jas., Dublin, barrister-at-law
1759 ,, John, Monaghan, esq.
1789 ,, Margaret, West Arran-street, Dublin
1769 ,, Robert, Springtown, co. Longford, gent.
1780 ,, Robert, the elder, Mullinahinch, co. Fermanagh, gent.
1805 ,, Robert, Moydow, co. Longford
1796 ,, Ross, Clones, co. Monaghan
[See BEATTIE, BEATTY, BEATY, BEATYE, BETTY.]
1728 **Beaty**, Francis, bombardier
1681 **Beatye**, John, Ferinsire, parish of Killeshandra, co. Cavan
1796 **Beauchamp**, Ann
1744 ,, Benjamin, Corris, co. Carlow, esq.
1744 ,, John, Ballyloughan, co. Carlow, esq.
1776 ,, Richard, Narrowmore, co. Kildare, clk.
1776 **Beauchant**, Samuel, Portarlington, Queen's County, merchant.
1803 **Beauman**, John, Hyde Park, co. Wexford
1811 ,, Michael, capt. in the Madras artillery
1765 **Beaumont**, Thomas, Summerhill, co. Dublin, gent.
1777 ,, Thomasin, Dublin, widow
1805 **Beauvier**, Gregory, city of Dublin
1721 **Becher**, John, Dublin, gent.
1790 ,, John, Hollybrook, co. Cork, esq.
1772 ,, Lionel, Sherkin, co. Cork, esq.
1779 ,, Michl., Creagh, co. Cork, esq.
1656 ,, Phane, quar.-master-gen. of all the forces under command of the Lord Lieut. [**V.** 280

1709 **Becher,** Thomas, Sherkin, co. Cork, esq. (Large.)
1754 ,, Thomas, Creagh, co. Cork, esq. [See BEECHER.]
1799 **Beck,** Anne, Dublin, spinster
1692 ,, John, Londonderry, gent.
1700 ,, John, Long Grange, co. Wexford
1700 ,, John, Long Grange, co. Wexford, mercht. [**XVIII.** 249
1801 ,, Sarah, Dublin, spinster
1685 **Becket,** Anne, Dublin, widow
1672 ,, Randall, Dublin, gent.
1696 ,, Thomas, late of Dublin, now of London, gent.
1560 ,, Walter, Winetavern-street
1775 ,, William, Lisdornan, co. Meath, esq.
1805 **Beckett,** Mary, city of Dublin
1626 **Beckwith,** Leonard, Kildrought, co. Dublin, minister
1795 **Bective,** Thomas, earl, knight of St. Patrick (Large)
1683 **Bedel,** Ambrose, Carne, co. Cavan, esq.
1789 **Bedford,** rev. Thomas, rector of Clandevadoge
1674 **Bedrough,** Thomas, Monycoghlan, Queen's County, gent.
1626 **Bee,** James, Dublin, ald. [**I.** 107
1741 **Beeby,** Nathaniel, Dublin, tallow chandler
1790 ,, William, Dublin, merchant
1797 ,, William, Dublin, merchant
1654 **Beech,** Richd., Uttoxeter, Staffordshire, a trooper in lord H. Cromwell's regt. [**V.** 43
1786 **Beecher,** Anne, city of Cork, spr.
1787 ,, Henry, Creagh, co. Cork, esq.
1762 ,, John Townshend, Ann Grove, co. Cork, esq.
1726 ,, Michael, Aghadown, co, Cork, esq. [See BECHER.]
1797 **Beere,** Ann, Ballybay, co. Tipperary, widow
1799 ,, George, Camden-st., Dublin
1729 ,, Hercules, Ballyboe, co. Tipperary
1741 ,, Hercules, Clonmel, co. Tipperary, gent.
1800 ,, John, Ballyholane, co. Tipperary
1757 ,, Richard, Newcastle, co. Tipperary, farmer
1808 ,, Susanna, Camden-st., Dublin, widow
1774 ,, William, formerly of Ballyboy, co. Tipperary, but of Dromana, co. Waterford

1805 **Beers,** Jas., Edenderry, co. Down, esq.
1802 ,, William, Ballygrean, co. Down, gent.
1747 **Beetham,** John, Liberty of Thomascourt, co. Dub., schoolmaster
1772 **Beevin,** Henry, Camas, co. Limerick, esq.
1729 ,, Thos., junr., Camas, co. Limerick, gent.
1661 **Begg,** David, Dublin, alderman
1790 ,, Francis, Dublin, gent.
1769 ,, John, Dublin, merchant
1793 ,, John, Dublin, tallow chandler
1810 ,, John, lieutenant in the Imperial service
1741 ,, Mary, *alias* **Byrne,** Hartown, co. Meath, widow
1788 ,, Mary, Dublin, widow
1582 ,, Mathew, Boraneston, gent.
1801 ,, Nicholas, Dublin, baker
1779 ,, Patrick, Ballycannon, co. Kildare, farmer [See BAGGE, BAGGS, BIGGS.]
1769 **Beggs,** Thomas, Pill-lane, Dublin, merchant
1735 **Beilby,** Michael, London, mercht. (Copy)
1764 **Belcher,** Jas., Glasnevin, co. Dub., esq.
1798 ,, William, Kells
1792 **Belchier,** William, Lombard-street, banker (Copy)
1756 **Bell,** Andrew, Ardleny, co. Cavan, gent.
1807 ,, Andrew, Cottage, co. Cavan
1658 ,, capt. Arthur, Kilkenny, esq.
1795 ,, David, Ballyrotty, co. Down
1721 ,, Edward, Ballyboy, King's Co., farmer
1732 ,, Edward, Dublin, gent.
1799 ,, Gamaliel, Bellbrook, Queen's County
1759 ,, capt. George, Dublin
1761 ,, George, Francis-street, woollen draper
1802 ,, George, Douglas, Isle of Man
1809 ,, George, Killanure, co. Cavan, esq.
1786 ,, Henry, Lisburn, co. Antrim, linen draper
1793 ,, Hugh, Charles-street, Dublin
1801 ,, Isaac, late deceased
1808 ,, Jacob, senr., Frummery
1745 ,, James, Dublin, shoemaker
1810 ,, James, Coolock, co. Dublin, schoolmaster
1696 ,, John, Mullenteen, co. Tyrone, gent. [chant
1714 ,, John, Belfast, co. Antrim, mer-

1754	**Bell**, John, Dublin, wigmaker
1757	,, John, Dublin, gent. (Not proved)
1772	,, John, Balligilane, Queen's Co.
1776	,, John, Werburgh-street, Dublin, merchant
1778	,, John, Crevagh, co. Tyrone, esq.
1786	,, John, Killinure, co. Cavan, gent.
1792	,, John, Lagaroe, county Tyrone, farmer
1807	,, John, Creevy, co. Longfd., esq.
1676	,, Leonard, *alias* **Reynold**, Dublin, gent.
1759	,, Lyndon, Streamstown, county Mayo, esq.
1761	,, Mat., Streamstown, co. Mayo
1691	,, Michael, Killeeke, co. Dublin, farmer
1631	,, Robert, Dublin, gent.
1670	,, Robt., Ringsend, near Dublin, rope maker
1746	,, Robert, Lisburn, co. Antrim, merchant
1790	,, Robert, Ormond-quay, broker
1809	,, Robert
1781	,, Rotherain, Dublin, glazier
1694	,, Samuel, Dublin, esq.
1760	,, Susanna, widow of Robert B., Lisburn, co. Antrim
1686	,, Thos., Cloncleafe, co. Limerick, gent.
1713	,, Thomas, Newmarkett, Lib. of Donore, carpenter
1793	,, Thomas, Priestnewtown, co. Wicklow, farmer
1743	,, Wm., Ballykillaugheen, Queen's County, farmer
1784	,, Wm., Dublin, merchant tailor
1786	,, Wm., Ballykilleheen, Queen's County, gent.
1711	**Bellament**, Richard, earl of (Copy)
1802	**Bellamont**, right hon. Charles, earl of (Large)
1666	**Bellam** , Michael, Tallogh, county Waterford, innholder
1678	**Bellars**, Jonathan, Dublin, mercht.
1696	**Bellas**, Robert, Dublin, coachman
1713	**Bellasyse**, Susanna, lady bar. Osgoodbye
1771	,, Thomas, Ennis, co. Clare, gent.
1638	**Bellew**, sir Christopher, Castletown, co. Louth, knt.
1770	,, Christopher, Mount. B., co. Galway, esq.
1807	,, Christopher K., Inner Temple, barrister (Copy)
1742	,, sir Edward, bart., Bellew Mt. or Barmeath, co. Louth
1722	,, Frances, Drogheda, widow
1767	,, Frances, widow

1771	**Bellew**, Frances, Dublin, spinster
1773	,, Francis, formerly of Island St. Chris., but of Cork
1793	,, Francis
1735	,, Hester, *alias* **Sherlock**, Dubl., widow
1642	,, James, Dublin, merchant
1689	,, James, Willistown, co. Louth, gent.
1679	,, John, Barmeath, co. Louth, esq.
1735	,, sir John, Dublin, bart.
1750	,, sir John, Barmeath, co. Louth, bart.
1771	,, John, lord baron of Duleek
1801	,, Laurence, Dundalk, co. Louth, mariner
1784	,, Lucy, Arran-quay, Dublin, spr.
1788	,, Lucy, Dublin, widow
1768	,, Luke, Choniack, merchant
1772	,, Margaret, Castle Martyr, co. Cork
1797	,, Michael, Mt. Bellew
1614	,, Nicholas, Clongowswood, gent.
1729	,, Patk., Thomastown, co. Louth. gent.
1755	,, Patrick, Cook-street, Dublin, cooper
1789	,, Patrick, Dublin, esq.
1695	,, Richd., Stammeane, co. Meath.
1715	,, Richard, lord baron Duleek
1733	,, Robt., Tullydonnell, co. Louth, gent.
1734	,, Thomas, Ballyowen, co. Dublin, esq.
1794	,, Thomas, Drogheda, merchant
1662	**Bellewe**, Arthur, Dublin, gent.
1687	,, Edward, Dublin, merchant
1606	,, James, Dublin, alderman
1600	,, sir John, Bellewestown. county Meath, knt.
1627	,, sir John, Castletown, co. Louth, knt.
1699	,, Mary, lady baroness dowager, Duleek (Ex.)
1598	,, Patk., Drogheda (Imperfect)
1599	,, Patrick, of the Westone of the Nall, co. Dublin, gent.
1800	**Bellingham**, Alan, Dublin, esq. (Large)
1796	,, Allen, Castle B., co. Louth, esq.
1759	,, Anne, Castle B., co. Louth, spr.
1672	,, sir Danl., Dubl., knt. and bart.
1677	,, Henry, Garnonstowne, county Louth, esq.
1755	,, Henry, Castle B., co. Louth, esq.
1699	,, sir Richd., Dublier, co. Dublin, bart.

1721 **Bellingham**, Thomas, Castle B., co. Louth, esq.

1728 **Bellings**, Garrett, Dublin, linen draper

1692 ,, Henry, The Bay, co. Dublin, gent.

1656 ,, Oliver, Catherlogh, merchant, [**V.** 266

1729 ,, sir Richard, knt. (Copy)

1603 ,, Thos., Bealingston, co. Dublin, gent.

1631 **Bellot**, Luce, Waterford, widow

1788 **Bellwood**, Bridget, Coles-lane Market, Dublin, widow

1744 ,, Francis

1802 **Belmore**, right hon. Armar, earl (Large)

1700 **Beloche**, Martha, widow of Mr. de Laballe, mas. surgeon

1729 **Belpe**, John Jestasete, Dublin, M.D.

1792 **Belton**, Robert, Colerain, King's County, linen manufacturer

1774 **Belvedere**, Robert, earl of

1721 **Ben**, Peter, Tinoran, co. Wicklow, gent. [See BENN.]

1676 **Bence**, sir Alex., Dublin, knt. (Ex.)

1695 ,, John, London, esq. (Copy)

1703 **Bengen**, Jas., Talloagh, co. Waterford, gent.

1773 ,, Thos., Glinane, co. Cork, gent.

1804 **Benison**, Daniel, city of Dubl., gent.

1802 ,, Joseph, Mountpleasant, county Cavan [See BENSON.]

1764 **Benn**, Alice, Killinure, co. Wicklow, widow of Peter B.

1795 ,, Elizabeth, Spittlefields, Dublin, widow

1789 ,, John, Raheen, co. Limerick, gent. [See BEN.]

1785 **Benner**, John, Kilquane, co. Kerry, farmer

1792 **Bennet**, John, one of the justices of King's Bench

1793 ,, John, Quarryhill, co. Limerick, gent.

1799 ,, Mary, *alias* **Touchstone**

1788 ,, Samuel, of Drury-lane, London, tallow chandler (Copy)

1708 ,, Thomas, of Dublin, tanner

1736 **Bennett**, Benjamin, Inch, co. Kildare, gent.

1754 ,, Chas., Ballinahinch, co. Limerick, gent.

1680 ,, Christopher, Dublin, alderman

1743 ,, David, Dublin, gent.

1791 ,, Edwd., Kilkibbin, co. Wexford

1749 ,, Elizabeth, Cork, widow

1768 **Bennett**, Elizabeth, Cork, widow

1788 ,, Elizabeth, city of Cork, widow (Copy)

1666 ,, Ellen, Dublin, widow

1589 ,, Fitz-Nicholas Richard, New Ross, co. Wexford, mercht.

1627 ,, Francis

1722 ,, Francis, Cork, gent.

1800 ,, Francis, Thomastown, King's County, esq.

1738 ,, George, Dublin, tailor

1753 ,, Geo., Clownish, co. Monaghan, gent.

1705 ,, Hannah, Dublin, widow

1792 ,, Hugh, Bashelstown, co. Limerick, gent.

1742 ,, Jas., Dublin, mercht. (Large will)

1810 ,, James, city of Dublin, M.D.

1695 ,, Jane, Cork, widow (Ex.)

1741 ,, John, Dublin

1746 ,, John, Belfast, linen draper

1762 ,, John, Inch, co. Kildare, gent.

1809 ,, John, Rockspring, Lib. of Cork, esq.

1810 ,, John, Old Court, co. Kildare, landholder

1767 ,, Joseph, esq., recorder of Cork

1747 ,, Martin, parish of Drumlane, co. Cavan

1806 ,, Mary Anne, city of Cork, spr.

1655 ,, Nicholas, trooper. [**V.** 224

1783 ,, Nicholas, Eyre Court, co. Galway

1752 ,, Philip, Hillbrook, co. Cork, gent.

1659 ,, Robert, Dublin, alderman [**VIII.** 32

1729 ,, Robert, Dublin, merchant

1780 ,, Samuel, Ballinstona, co. Limerick, esq.

1807 ,, Samuel, Ballincallow, co. Limerick, esq.

1804 ,, Susanna, city of Cork, widow

1778 ,, Thomas, Ballyloughan, co. Carlow, esq.

1795 ,, Thomas, Thomastown, King's County, esq. (Large)

1715 ,, William, Dublin, merchant [See BISSETT.]

1684 **Bennis**, Andrew, Balliemulcashel, co. Clare, gent.

1623 ,, John, Dublin, alderman

1802 ,, John, Dublin, gent.

1769 ,, Richard, Dublin, merchant

1803 ,, Thomas, esq., one of the coroners of the city of Dublin

1752 **Benson**, Alice

1771 ,, rev. Arthur, rector of Langfield, diocese of Derry

1699 **Benson**, Basil, Stranarlar, co. Done-
          gal, gent.
1690   ,,   Dorothy, Dublin, widow (late
                of Cockermouth), deceased
1696   ,,   George, Dublin, vintner
1789   ,,   Hamilton, Derry, merchant
1776   ,,   John, Cork, merchant
1753   ,,   Mary, Maghera, co. London-
                derry, widow
1785   ,,   Mary, Fairview, co. Armagh,
                widow
1737   ,,   Michael, Dublin, gent.
1772   ,,   Richard, Dublin, esq.
1772   ,,   Samuel, Randsford-st., Dublin,
                velvet weaver
1631   ,,   Thomas, Bandon-bridge, co.
                Cork, merchant
1715   ,,   Thomas, archd. of Kildare
1784   ,,   rev. Thomas, Dublin, doctor in
                divinity
1804   ,,   Thomas, city of Dublin, grocer
1765   ,,   William, earl of Stokenewing-
                ton, Middlesex, esq.
1765   ,,   William (one of the auditors of
                His Majesty's imprests), esq.
                [See BENISON.]
1647 **Bent**, Henry, Dublin, brewer
1663   ,,   William, Lindridge, Leicester-
                shire, gent.
1783 **Bentinck**, lady Margaret, Hague,
                widow
1809 **Bentley**, Anne, city of Dublin,
                spinster.
1809   ,,   Anne, city of Dublin, widow
1769   ,,   John Simon, Killaderry, co.
                Clare
1769   ,,   Mary, Killaderry, co. Clare,
                widow
1764   ,,   Richard, co. Dublin, weaver
1686   ,,   Robert, Leixlip, co. Kildare,
                innholder
1735   ,,   Robert, Dublin, merchant
1631 **Bently**, Elizabeth, *als.* **Treyforde**,
                widow
1739   ,,   John, Dublin, gent.
1661   ,,   Michael (a soldier), gent.
1629   ,,   Robert, Banbury, Oxford, gent.
1797 **Benyon**, Richard, Gildea Hall,
                Essex, esq.
1794 **Bere**, Peter, Maynooth, co. Kildare,
                esq.
1732 **Beresford**, Arabella Maria, Dublin,
                spinster
1730   ,,   Araminta, Kilrue, co. Meath,
                spinster
1701   ,,   dame Catherine, Dublin, widow
1805   ,,   right hon. John
1798   ,,   Marcus, esq.
1687   ,,   Mary, Castlenorton, co. Antrim,
                widow

1682 **Beresford**, sir Randal, Coleraine,
                bart. (Copy)
1651 } ,,   Tristram, the elder, Coleraine,
1666 }   esq.   [**XIII.** 248
1674   ,,   sir Tristram, Coleraine, bart.
1701   ,,   sir Tristram, Coleraine, co.
                Londonderry and Bally-
                gawley, co. Tyrone, bart.
1708   ,,   Tristram, Coleraine, esq.
                [See BERISFORD.]
Berfoot see BAREFOTE.
1757 **Berford**, George, Ballymurry, co.
                Roscommon, gent.
1633   ,,   John, Kilroe, co. Meath, agent
1800   ,,   John, Dublin, merchant
1639   ,,   Nicholas, Scurlockstown, co.
                Meath, gent.
1662   ,,   Richard, Blanchardstown, co.
                Dublin, esq.
1748   ,,   Richard, Huntstown, co. Dub-
                lin, gent.
1797   ,,   Susanna, Dublin, spinster
1802 **Bergin**, Daniel, Kildare, gent.
1797   ,,   John, Ballyduff, King's County,
                farmer
1805   ,,   John, city of Kilkenny, mercht.
1765   ,,   Pierse, Thomas-street, Dublin,
                dealer
1766   ,,   Thomas, Fordam's-alley, Dub-
                lin, weaver
1751 **Beringuier**, Mary, co. Dublin, wid.
1661 **Berisford**, Michael, Coleraine
                (Copy)
                [See BERESFORD.]
1737 **Berkley**, Nicholas, Sallymills, co.
                Dublin, farmer
1799 **Berkeley**, Anne
1728   ,,   Dorothea, Glasnevin, co. Dub-
                lin, widow
1691   ,,   Henry, LL.D., master in chan-
                cery
1678   ,,   John, lord baron of Stratton
                and privy councillor (Copy)
1758   ,,   Mary
1764   ,,   Maurice, Scart, co. Wexford,
                clerk
1787   ,,   Robert, Ballincurra, co. Cork,
                D.D.
1723 **Berkely**, Digby, Ardriston, co. Car-
                low, esq.
1778   ,,   Ralph, Scarteen, co. Cork, gent.
1757   ,,   Rowland, Newmarket, co. Cork,
                gent.
1788 **Berkley**, Anne, widow
1731   ,,   Anthony, Dublin, alderman
1694   ,,   Edward, Dublin, gent.
1782   ,,   Hugh, Dublin, gent.
1660   ,,   Mathew, Chester, ironmonger
1703   ,,   Rowland, Killeniffe, co. Tippe-
                rary, esq.

1806 **Berkly**, Richard
    [See BARCLAY, BERKLEY, &c.]
1636 **Berkhead**, Robert
1802 **Berks**, Joseph, Hawarden, Flint-
    shire, gent. (Copy)
1753 **Bermingham**, Barnaby, Dublin.
1619 ,, Edward, Carrick, co. Kildare,
    gent.
1661 ,, Edward, Grange, co. Kildare,
    esq.
1710 ,, Edward, Grange, co. Kildare,
    esq.
1795 ,, Edward, Kilfylan, King's
    County, esq.
1717 ,, Elizabeth, Dublin, widow
1737 ,, Elizabeth, Gragaroote, co. Kil-
    dare, widow and farmer
1748 ,, Garret, Johnstown-bridge, co.
    Kildare
1768 ,, Garrett
1643 ,, George, Garrick, co. Kildare,
    gent.
1636 ,, Gerot, Grange, co. Kildare,
    gent.
1684 ,, James, Garisker, co. Kildare,
    gent.
1752 ,, Jas., Carnominane, co. Galway
1791 ,, James, Dublin, grocer
1803 ,, John, Daligan House, co. Gal-
    way, esq.
1766 ,, Mary, Smithfield, widow
1771 ,, Mathew, Finglass-road, co.
    Dublin, dealer
1801 ,, Nichs., Barbersfort, co. Galway
1799 ,, Perse R., Dublin, esq.
1809 ,, Peter, Mulruck, co. Meath,
    farmer
1786 ,, Quann, Portumna Castle, co.
    Galway
1760 ,, Richard, the younger, Roscom-
    mon town
1599 ,, Thomas, Downfurte, co. Kil-
    dare, esq.
1638 ,, Walter, Dunfert, co. Kildare,
    esq.
1749 ,, Walter, Dublin, esq.
1761 ,, Walter, Somerset House,
    Middlesex, gent.
1772 ,, Walter, Mylerstown, co. Kildare
1790 ,, Walter, Portumna Castle, co.
    Galway
1754 ,, Wm., Coombe, Dublin, weaver
    [See BIRMINGHAM.]
1782 **Bernard**, Ann, Dublin, widow
1803 ,, Frances, Dublin, spinster.
1731 ,, Francis, Dublin, esq. (one of
    the justices of the Common
    Pleas)
1791 ,, Francis, Basington Hall, Essex
    (Copy)

1782 **Bernard**, Franks, Clonmulsk, co.
    Carlow, esq.
1751 ,, George
1750 ,, Henry, major in gen. Otway's
    regiment of foot
1790 ,, James, Windsor, south Lib. of
    Cork, esq.   [esq.
1788 ,, John, Ballynegar, co. Kerry,
1789 ,, John, Carlow Town, esq.
1763 ,, Joseph, Carlow, esq.
1799 ,, Martha, Tralee, co. Kerry, spr.
1766 ,, Mary, Charleville, co. Cork,
    widow
1791 ,, Mary, Dublin, spinster
1809 ,, Mary, *alias* **Stackpoole**
1760 ,, Philip, town of Carlow, esq.
1771 ,, Richard, Fairbane, King's
    County, gent.
1774 ,, Roger, Pallace Ann, co. Cork,
    esq.
1704 ,, Thomas, the elder, Moyalloe,
    co. Cork, gent.
1744 ,, Thos., Bernard's Grove, Queen's
    County, gent.
1788 ,, Thomas, Birr, King's County,
    esq.
1798 ,, Thomas, Roseborough, co. Kil-
    dare, gent.
1807 ,, Thomas, Gayville, co. Carlow,
    esq.
1790 ,, William, Dublin, gent.
1790 ,, William, Carlow Town, esq.
    [See BARNARD.]
1771 **Bernardon**, Guston, Dublin
1747 **Bernatre**, Daniel de Boubers, **Dubl.**
1752 ,, Susanna, Dublin, widow
1786 **Berne**, Hugh, Ballygalda, co. Ros-
    common, gent.
    [See BYRNE]
1799 **Berners**, Collin, lord of Kilborry,
    N. Britain
1726 **Berniere**, John Anthony, Lisburn,
    co. Antrim, gent.
1727 **Bernstorff**, Andrew Gottlich, baron
    of, at Hanover
1740 **Berrill**, Edward, Rossnaree, co.
    Meath, farmer
1799 ,, Francis
1806 ,, James, Newgrange, co. Meath,
    farmer
1789 ,, Richd., Newgrange, co. Meath,
    gent.
1799 ,, Robt., Knouth, co. Meath, gent.
1773 **Berrin**, Thady, Lismonaghan, co.
    Fermanagh
1714 **Berry**, Henry, Clontarf, co. Dublin
1723 ,, Jane, Ballymony, King's
    County, widow
1783 ,, Jane, Dovegrove, King's
    County, widow

D

1781 **Berry,** Jonathan, Dovegrove, King's County, esq.
1626 ,, John, Dublin, gent.
1705 ,, John, Clonehone, King's County, esq.
1730 ,, John, Clonehan, King's County, esq.
1770 ,, John, Broadwood, co. Westmeath
1661 ,, Joseph, Arthurstown, co. Louth, minister of the gospel
1741 ,, Letitia, Dublin, widow
1724 ,, Mary, widow
1789 ,, Nathan, Pill-lane, Dublin, merchant
1728 ,, Robert, Dublin, gent.
1673 ,, Thomas, Castlecuffe, Queen's County, merchant
1703 ,, William, lieut. in lieut.-gen. Bellasy's regt.
1717 ,, William, late lieut.-col. of brig. Wolseley's regt. of horse
1740 **Bertie,** hon. Philip, Hayfield, Lancaster, esq. (Copy)
1723 **Bertin,** Lewis, French refugee, Dublin, merchant
1744 ,, Mary, Dublin, widow
1765 **Bertles,** Edward, Ardnagrah, co. Westmeath, esq.
1719 ,, Judith, Clonmel, co. Tipperary, widow
1741 **Bertrand,** John, Dublin, merchant
1761 ,, John, Dublin, merchant
1807 ,, Peter, Malpas-st., co. Dublin, gent.
1783 ,, Sarah Elizabeth, Dubl., widow
1635 **Berryman,** William
1758 **Besberugh,** Brabazon, earl of
1793 **Besborough,** William, earl of
1760 **Besnard,** Peter, Dublin
1778 ,, Susanna, Dublin, widow
1729 **Bessick,** Oliver, Dublin
1736 ,, Oliver, Dublin, painter
1721 **Bessiere,** John, gent.
1790 **Bessonett,** rev. Fras., Dub., LL.D.
1803 **Best,** Alice
1786 ,, Anne, Ardresten, co. Carlow, widow
1755 ,, Arundel, Bestville, co. Carlow, esq.
1769 ,, Easter, Dublin, widow
1687 ,, sir Elias, Dublin, knt.
1768 ,, Elias Caulfield, Bestville, co. Carlow, esq.
1788 ,, Elizabeth Caulfield, Clone, co. Kilkenny, widow
1700 ,, dame Jane, Dublin, widow
1750 ,, Margaret, Dublin
1663 ,, Michael, London, upholder (Copy)

1729 **Best,** Robert, Knockbeg, Queen's County, esq.
1809 ,, Robt., Warrenpoint, co. Down
1803 ,, Roger, Moy, co. Tyrone
1793 ,, Susanna, widow
1799 **Bestall,** Richard, Rathdrum, co. Wicklow, gent.
1630 **Beswick,** Arthur, Castlejordan, co. Meath, gent. [**II.** 211
1800 **Betagh,** Ann, Dublin, widow
1786 ,, Cecilia, city of Dubl., spinster
1802 ,, Chas., Dublin, timber merchant
1610 ,, Christopher, Moynaltie, co. Meath, gent.
1786 ,, Elinor, Drogheda, widow
1748 ,, Francis, Dublin, brewer
1797 ,, Henry, York-st., Dublin, gent.
1616 ,, James, Dublin, gent.
1768 ,, James, Mannin, co. Mayo
1760 ,, John, Dublin, dealer
1789 ,, John, Dublin, gent.
1723 ,, Richard, Dublin, surgeon
1811 ,, rev. Thos., city of Dubl., R. C. priest
1591 **Betaghe,** Thomas, Baleneslough, co. Clare, esq.
1590 **Bethel,** Edward
1810 ,, Gilbert, city of Dublin, public notary
1581 **Betherton,** David, Dromisken [**I.** 5
1703 **Betson,** Geo., Dublin, glassmaker
1763 ,, rev. John, Carlow, clk.
1809 **Bettesworth,** Catherine, Bellgrove, co. Dublin
1707 ,, Pet., Ballydulea, co. Cork, gent.
1648 ,, Richard, Pallas, co. Limerick, esq. (Ex.)
1779 ,, Sarah, widow
1731 **Betton,** Wriothesley, par. St. Margt., Westminster, lieut.-colonel, Royal Dragoons of Ireland (Copy)
1791 **Betts,** George, Molesworth-st., Dubl.
1658 ,, Captain Thomas, governor of Duncannon Fort [**VII.** 11
1776 ,, William, Inane, co. Tipperary
1731 **Bettson,** John, Knightstown, co. Dublin, gent.
1796 **Betty,** Charity, Dublin, widow
1802 ,, Guy, Munichan, co. Fermanagh
1790 ,, Henry, Lisburn, co. Antrim, linendraper
1793 ,, James, Drummee, co. Ferm.
1738 ,, John, Cartowne, co. Kildare [See BEATTY]
1778 **Bevan,** Anne, *alias* **Constantine,** wife of Robert Bevan
1796 ,, George, Camass, co. Limerick, gent.

1800 **Bevan**, Henry, Dublin, esq.
1801 ,, Henry, Miltown, co. Limerick
1788 ,, John, Aubrey, Waterford, merchant (Copy)
1731 ,, Joshua, Cootehill, co. Cavan, linendraper
1789 ,, Michael, Camas, co. Limerick, esq.
1751 ,, Robert, Cootehill, co. Cavan, linen draper
1729 ,, Thomas., jun., Camas, co. Limerick, gent.
1752 ,, William, Cootehill, co. Cavan, merchant
1790 **Bevans**, Benjamin, Barrack, co. Wicklow, gent.
1789 **Beven**, Robert, Dublin, gent.
[See BEVAN.]
1734 **Beveridge**, George, par. St. Giles, Middlesex, gent. (Copy)
1736 **Bevins**, Laurence, Dublin, gent.
1732 ,, Walter, Newtown, co. Kildare, farmer
[See BEVANS.]
1743 **Bewley**, Daniel, Edenderry, King's County, tanner
1758 ,, Daniel, Lazor's-hill, Dublin, merchant
1782 ,, George, Dorset-st., Dub., gent.
1765 ,, Hannah
1739 ,, Mary, Dublin, widow
1793 ,, Mary, Dublin, widow
1783 ,, Mungo, Edenderry, King's County, merchant
1778 ,, Richard, Edenderry, King's County, farmer
1730 ,, Thos., Dublin, tallow chandler
1795 ,, Thomas, city of Dublin
1656 **Bewsick**, corporal Edward   [**VI.** 4
1722 **Biard**, Noe, Dublin
[See BEARD, BAIRD.]
1734 **Bibbee**, Mary, Fleet-street, Dublin, widow
1809 **Bibby**, Elizabeth, spinster
1763 ,, James, Dublin, merchant
1765 ,, John, Courtown, co. Wexford, gent.
1775 ,, Joseph, Dublin, glass grinder
1806 ,, Mary, Fleet-street, city of Dub.
1731 ,, Thomas, Radestown, co. Kilkenny, gent.
1749 ,, Thomas, Dublin, guilder
1766 ,, William, Dublin, glass grinder
1772 **Bible**, Robert, Kilworth, co. Cork, gent.
1756 **Bickerstaff**, Catherine, Kenagh, co. Longford
1735 ,, Francis
1751 ,, John, Dublin, esq.   [esq.
1764 ,, Leonard, Kenagh, co. Longford,

1807 **Bickerstaff**, Margaret, Castletown, Queen's County, widow
1752 ,, Mary, Dublin, widow
[See BIGGAR, BIGGER.]
1740 **Bickerton**, Henry, Harwick, Essex, gent.
1787 **Bicknell**, John, city of Dublin
1806 **Biddulph**, Francis, Stradbally, Queen's County, esq.
1687 ,, sir Theo., West Combe, Kent, knt. and bt. (Copy)
1752 **Bigg**, Boleyn, Clonmel, co. Tipp., esq.
1793 **Biggar**, George, Service of East India Company (Copy)
1746 ,, Mary, Kinsale, co. Cork, widow
1771 ,, Jordan Heyland, par. St. Andrew, Undershaft, mercht.
1696 **Bigger**, Alexander, Belfast, mercht.
1778 ,, Hugh, Dublin, gent.
1801 ,, Mary, Dublin, spinster
1674 ,, Michael, Belfast, merchant
[See BICKERSTAFF.]
1810 **Biggs**, Benjamin, city of Dublin, esq.
1772 ,, Jeremiah, Bandon, clothier
1737 ,, Joseph, Londonderry, merchant
1772 ,, Jos., Bandon, co. Cork, clothier
1796 ,, Richard, Castlebiggs, co. Tipperary, esq.
1796 ,, Thomas, Belvue, co. Tipperary, esq.
[See BEGG.]   [Down
1800 **Bigham**, Gordon, Ballygilbert, co.
[See BINGHAM.]
1756 **Bignal**, Edward
1726 ,, Robert, Edenderry, King's Co., hatter
1750 **Bignell**, Joseph, Edenderry, King's County, merchant
1756 ,, Thomas, The Comb, Dublin, brewer
1750 **Bignill**, Ann, widow of John B., Mill-street, tanner
[See BIGNAL, BIGNALL, BIGNELL,]
1664 **Bigoe**, Philip, Newtown, King's Co., esq.   [**XIII.** 186
1735 **Bigos**, John, Dublin, gent.
1749 **Bijar**, Mary, Dublin, widow
1761 **Biker**, Francis, Dublin, widow
1743 ,, Robert, Dublin, weaver
1741 ,, Thomas, Dublin, weaver
[See BAKER.]
1694 **Billing**, John, Dublin, goldsmith
1759 ,, Mary, Dublin, widow
1756 ,, Robert, Dublin
1730 ,, Sarah, Dublin, spinster
1602 **Billings**, John, The Corbolles, co. Meath, gent.

1665 **Billingsley**, Elizabeth, *alias* **Wor-thell**, *alias* **Howell**, Rings-end
1708 **Billington**, dame Deborah, Dublin, widow
1703 „ sir William, Dublin, knt.
1805 **Bindon**, Anne, city Limerick, widow
1772 „ Catherine, widow
1733 „ David, Cloney, co. Clare, esq.
1765 „ Francis, Cloney, co. Clare
1644 „ Henry, Limerick, alderman
1740 „ Henry, Ennis, co. Clare, esq.
1781 „ Henry Wm., Temple, Mongert, Limerick, esq.
1740 „ Thomas, dean of Limerick
1787 **Bingham**, Cordelia, Dublin, widow
1794 „ George, Antigua, co. Mayo
1766 „ Grizell, Dublin, spinster
1744 „ right hon. Henry, New Brooke, co. Mayo, esq.
1769 „ Henry, Dublin, barrister-at-law
1790 „ Henry, Newbrook, co. Mayo, esq.
1728 „ John, Dublin, esq.
1728 „ Lettis, lady, widow of sir Henry Bingham, bart.
1778 „ Mary, Marlborough-st., Dubl.
1598 „ sir Richard, knt. (Imperfect)
       [See BIGHAM.]
1638 **Bingley**, sir John, Dublin, knt., king's counsellor-at-law
1725 „ Oliver, Birr, King's Co., gent.
1709 **Binkes**, John, Dublin, victualler
1724 „ John, Killycamin, co. Armagh
1737 „ Thos., Portadown, co. Armagh
1802 **Binks**, Anthony, Dublin, stonecutter
1786 **Binns**, Jonathan, city of Dublin, ironmonger
1784 **Binton**, Elizab., *alias* **Roberts**, *alias* **Coulson**, The Comb, Dublin
1706 **Birch**, Augustine, Ring's End, near Dublin, gent.
1748 „ Charles, Dublin, merchant
1801 „ Edward, Corville, co. Tip., esq.
1756 „ George, Dublin, gent.
1770 „ Hannah, Dublin, spinster
1755 „ John, Kilkenny, gent.
1807 „ John, captain of the 66th regt. of foot
1772 „ Mary, Kilkenny, widow
1742 „ William, Newtown, co. Meath (Dated 1742)
1776 „ rev. William, Roscrea, co. Tip.
1761 **Birchinsha**, Joseph, Lifford, county Down, clk.
1789 **Bird**, Bartholw., Drogheda, mercht.
1773 „ Elias, Raehampton, Surrey, esq.
1789 „ Elizabeth, Drogheda, widow
1761 „ Francis, Dublin, merchant

1671 **Bird**, George, Ballinrobe, co. Mayo, gent.
1754 „ Ignatius, Dublin, merchant
1713 „ James, Drogheda, merchant
1703 „ John, Bandon Bridge, co. Cork, gent.
1779 „ Josepha, spinster
1683 „ Oliver, Drogheda, merchant
1764 „ Oliver
1599 „ Philip (No date)
1680 „ Randolph, parish St. Andrew, Holborne, Middlesex, gent. (Copy)
1762 „ Roger
1650 „ Thomas, Dublin, merchant
1648 „ Walter, Dublin, cutler
1649 „ William, Dublin, cutler
1800 „ William, Birdville, King's Co., gent.
       [See BAURD, BYRD.]
1809 **Birkett**, Anne
1789 „ Henry, city of Carlisle, Cumberland
1651 **Birmingham**, Barnaby, Dublin, merchant
1792 „ Mary, Killfylan, King's Co., widow
       [See BERMINGHAM.]
1651 **Birne**, Edward, Dublin, merchant
1599 „ Gerald M'Lewis, Roscrea, co. Tipperary (No date)
1630 „ Gerald M'Lewis, Roscrea, co. Tipperary, gent. [**II.** 243
1684 „ Jas., Crevagh, co. Sligo, gent.
1629 „ Maud, *alias* **Donn**, widow (Imperfect)
1630 „ Maud, *alias* **Dunn**, widow, Dublin (Ex.)
1633 „ Patrick, Dublin, tailor
1794 „ Philip, Creggs, co. Sligo, esq.
       [See BYRNE.]
1801 **Birney**, Wm., Ballinakill, Queen's County, clk.
1740 **Birsban**, James, New Buildings, co. Tyrone
1687 **Birtt**, Richard, Limerick, chandler
1644 **Bisaker**, Richard, Dublin, currier
1796 **Bishop**, Elizabeth, city Dubl., widow (Large)
1676 „ Francis, Dublin, mercht. tailor
1805 „ Michael, Grange, co. Kilkenny
1731 „ Samuel, Ringwood, co. Kilkenny, gent.
1774 „ Terence, Dublin, vintner
1616 „ Thomas, Dublin, alderman
1809 **Bishopp**, Robert, Kinsale, co. Cork, surgeon
1737 **Biss**, John, Cork, cooper
1676 **Bissert**, John, Killibreake, county Tyrone

1782 **Bisset**, rev. Alexander, D.D.
1742 **Bissett**, Andrew, Twickenham, Middlesex, esq. (Copy) [See BENNETT.]
1715 **Bistort**, Peter, Dublin, tailor
1766 **Bitner**, Margt., Kinsale, co. Cork, widow.
1753 **Bittner**, John, Kinsale, co. Cork, innholder
1748 **Bizon**, Abraham, Dublin, merchant
1759 ,, Alice, Dublin, spinster.
1750 **Blachford**, Jas, of the Duke of Marlborough's regt. of foot.
1748 ,, rev. John, Dublin, D.D.
1728 ,, William, Lisnore, co. Cavan, esq.
1773 ,, rev. William, St. Sepulchre's, Dublin, clk.
1781 **Blachforde**, Eleanore, Dub., widow
1806 **Black**, Adam, Liverpool, Lancaster
1778 ,, Alexr., Lortmahon, co. Longford, esq.
1737 ,, David, Granshock
1809 ,, George, Glenstall, co. Antrim
1766 ,, James, Dublin, gent.
1767 ,, James, Dublin, auctioneer
1767 ,, John, Belfast, heretofore a factor in Bordeaux
1774 ,, Joseph, Tyllandoney
1800 ,, Joseph, physician, Edinburgh
1737 ,, Saml., Greggy, co. Monaghan, gent.
1796 ,, Thos. Daniel, esq., late major 13th foot
1808 ,, Thomas, city of Londonderry, ropemaker
1722 ,, William, Ballybine, co. Down, gent.
1761 **Blackall**, Andrew, Ballynascreen, co. Derry.
1701 ,, George, Dublin, alderman
1733 ,, George, Dublin, gent.
1740 ,, George, Charleville, co. Cork, apothecary
1787 ,, John, The Hill, near Loghgall, co. Antrim, esq.
1755 ,, Jonas, Barne, Tyhy, co. Limerick, gent.
1690 ,, Mary, Dublin, spinster
1791 ,, Mary, Dorset-street, Dublin
1758 ,, Robert, Sheds of Clontarf, co. Dublin, clk.
1791 ,, rev. Roger, vicar of St. Andrew's, diocese of Down
1796 ,, sir Thomas, knt. and alderman
1715 ,, Thomond, Little Rath, co. Kildare, esq.
1810 **Blackburn**, Robt., Molaghaney, co. Donegal
1673 ,, Wm., St. Patrick-st., mercht.

1708 **Blackburne**, Andrew, Carrickena, co. Roscommon, esq.
1804 ,, Anthony, city of Dublin, esq.
1775 ,, Joanna, Mooretown, spinster
1710 ,, John, Londonderry, merchant
1680 ,, Richd., Carrickdrumrousk, co. Leitrim, clk.
1761 **Blackby**, Frances Elizabeth
1802 **Blacker**, George, Drogheda
1810 ,, rev. George, vicar of Sligo
1793 ,, rev. Henry, Dublin, clk.
1736 ,, John, Rughan, county Tyrone, gent.
1775 ,, Lathum, Drogheda, esq.
1801 ,, Margaret, Drogheda, spinster
1809 ,, Mary, Castle Creagh, co. Limerick
1782 ,, Samuel, Moira, co. Down, esq.
1677 ,, Valentine, Carrick, county Armagh, esq.
1749 ,, William, Rughan, co. Tyrone, gent.
1761 **Blackerby**, Frances Elizth., widow
1759 **Blackler**, Pheasant, Athlone, now of Dublin, esq.
1801 **Blackly**, John, Dublin, merchant
1659 **Blackman**, Symon, soldier in Do. [VII. 192
1634 **Blacknall**, Richard, Ballynekill, Queen's Co., esq. [IV. 118
1718 ,, Sarah, Dublin, widow
1611 **Blackney**, George, Rickenhoe, co. Dublin, gent.
1742 ,, Jas., Ballycormick, co. Carlow, gent.
1636 ,, John, Drogheda, alderman
1810 ,, John, Graigue, co. Kilkenny
1673 ,, Stephen, Dublin, bar. surgeon
1798 **Blackny**, John
1588 ,, Thomas, Drogheda, merchant
1641 **Blackwall**, James, Firemt.-lane, co. Clare, gent.
1786 **Blackwell**, Alexander, Belfast, co. Antrim [keeper
1807 ,, Richd., city of Limerick, shop-
1807 ,, Richardson, Drogheda, gent.
1791 ,, William, Dublin, gunmaker
1685 **Blackwood**, Christopher, Dublin, merchant
1712 ,, Hanah, Dublin, widow
1755 ,, James, Dublin, esq.
1799 ,, sir John, Ballyliddy, co. Down, bart.
1810 ,, Mary, widow
1774 ,, sir Robt., Ballyleidy, co. Down, bart.
1795 ,, Townley, esq.
1724 **Bladen**, Charles, Dublin, gent.
1722 ,, Sarah, Albemarle-st., parish of St. Mar., Middlesex (Copy)

1663 **Bladen**, Wm, St. Werbourgh's par., Dublin, alderman
1667 **Bladon**, Elinor, Dublin, widow
1774 **Bladworth**, James, Dublin, painter
1732 **Blagny**, Jacob, St. Anne's, Westminster, Middlesex, esq.
1737 **Blair**, Adam, Newtown
1735 ,, Brice, Dublin, merchant
1756 ,, Bryce, Dublin, mariner
1782 ,, Eleanor, Dublin, spinster
1789 ,, Elinor, Little Forest, co. Dubl.
1786 ,, Elizabeth, Dublin, spinster
1688 ,, Hugh, Kyly, co. Londonderry, gent.
1794 ,, James, Dublin, merchant
1803 ,, John, capt. 10th regt. of foot
1804 ,, Mark Anthy., Newtown Lodge, co. Kildare, esq.
1787 ,, Patrick, Nth. Lib. of Cork, M.D.
1770 ,, Samuel, Belfast, merchant
1767 ,, Thomas, Dublin, merchant
1677 **Blaire**, John, Loghamnore, co. Antrim, gent.
1748 **Blake**, dame Agnes, widow of sir W. B., bart.
1630 ,, Andrew Fitzpatrick, Galway, alderman   [II. 238
1770 ,, Andrew, Ashford, co. Galway, esq.
1781 ,, Andrew, Ballymanagh, co. Galway, esq.
1810 ,, Andrew, Sackville-st., Dublin, M.D.
1769 ,, Anne, *alias* **Bodkin**, widow
1778 ,, Barbara, Galway, spinster
1791 ,, Bibian, Oranmore, co. Galway
1792 ,, Bridget, Galway town, widow
1801 ,, Bryan, Island of Antigua, mer.
1806 ,, Catherine, widow
1774 ,, Charity, Stephen's-gr., Dublin, widow
1769 ,, Charles, Moyne, co. Galway
1770 ,, David, col. in His Majesty's service at Bombay
1803 ,, Denis, John, capt. 98th regt.
1771 ,, Edmond, Ballegloonin, co. Galway, gent.
1776 ,, Edward, Kiltola, co. Galway, esq.
1780 ,, Elizabeth, Channell-row, Dublin, widow
1789 ,, Frances, *alias* **Bourke**
1744 ,, Francis, Dublin, esq.
1780 ,, Francis, Mace, co. Galway, esq.
1791 ,, Francis, Fitz Thomas, Galway, merchant
1808 ,, Francis, Mountjoy-square, esq.
1762 ,, George, clk.
1780 ,, Henry, Lehinch, co. Mayo, esq.
1789 ,, Henry, Ardfry, co. Galway

1807 **Blake**, Henry, Tubberpatrick, co. Wicklow, esq.
1780 ,, Ignatius, Ardfry, co. Galway, esq.
1756 ,, James, Raglass, co. Galway, gent.
1656 ,, John, lighterman
1777 ,, John, Balligloonine
1788 ,, John, Windfield, co. Galway, esq.
1788 ,, John, Ballinafad, co. Mayo
1794 ,, John, Knockatee, co. Galway
1807 ,, Jos., Ardfry, co. Galway, esq.
1624 ,, Luke, New Ross, co. Wexford, gent.
1797 ,, Mable, Galway
1766 ,, Magdalene
1785 ,, Margaret, Kilkenny city
1760 ,, Mark, Ballinafad, co. Mayo, merchant
1760 ,, Mark, Knockmore, co. Mayo
1783 ,, Mark, Milltown, co. Mayo, esq.
1794 ,, Mark, Fartimore, co. Galway
1606 ,, Martin, co. Meath and of Lispople
1749 ,, Martin, Lisaduced, co. Galway, esq.
1771 ,, Martin, Ballisnalaughny, co. Mayo, esq.
1778 ,, Martin, Balleglunin, co. Galway, gent.
1806 ,, Martin, Houndswood, co. Mayo
1765 ,, Mary, Dublin, widow
1790 ,, Maurice, city of Bath, esq.
1682 ,, Nicholas, Crumlin, co. Galway, gent.
1747 ,, Nicholas, Galway town
1737 ,, Oliver, Dublin, Esq.
1782 ,, Patrick, Drun, co. Galway, esq.
1712 ,, Peter, Corballis, co. Galway, gent.
1793 ,, Peter Bodkin, Galway town (Copy)
1747 ,, Philip, Dublin, pinmaker
1762 ,, Pierse, Loughrea, co. Galway, merchant
1624 ,, Richard, Ballie Griffine, parish of Monanimie, Señor
1663 ,, sir Richard, Ardfry, co. Galway, knt.
1735 ,, Richard, Ardfry, co. Galway, esq.
1744 ,, Richard, Newgrove, co. Galway, esq.
1769 ,, Richard, Dublin, mercht.
1796 ,, Richard, town of Galway, esq.
1801 ,, Richard, Garraeteone, co. Mayo, esq.
1616 ,, Robt. Fitz Walter Fitz Andrew, Galway, mercht.

1744 **Blake**, Robt., Ardfry, co. Galway, esq.
1760 ,, Sarah, widow
1749 ,, Stephen, Moorfield
1749 ,, sir Thomas, Summerhill, co. Galway, bart.
1766 ,, sir Ulick, bart.
1634 ,, sir Valentine, Galway, knt. and bart. [**IV**. 119
1752 ,, Valentine, formerly of London, but at Raheny, co. Dublin, merchant [esq.
1741 ,, Walter, Dunnacrene, co. Mayo,
1748 ,, sir Walter, Dublin, bart.
1758 ,, Walter, Ballinafad, co. Mayo, gent.
1797 ,, Walter, Knockatee, co. Galway
1802 ,, Walter, Ballygleeneen, co. Galway, esq.
1801 ,, William Todd, Dublin, esq.
1769 ,, Xaverius, Dunmereene, co. Mayo, esq.
1784 ,, Xaverius, Oranmore [See BLYKE.]
1788 **Blakeley**, John, King's Co., surgeon
1788 ,, John, Frankford, King's Co., miller
[See BLACKLY, BLEAKLEY, BLEAKLY.]
1811 **Blakeney**, Bury, Rochestown, co. Meath, esq.
1799 ,, Edward, Newman-street, Middlesex, esq.
1789 ,, John, Ashfield, co. Galway, esq.
1764 ,, Robert, Dublin, esq.
1789 ,, Robert, Ransford-st., Dublin, merchant
1789 ,, Thomas, Dublin, attorney
1775 **Blakeny**, Deborah, widow
1775 ,, Elizabeth, Ransford-st., Dublin, spinster
1750 ,, captain John, Distington, Cumberland (Copy)
1781 ,, John, Abbert, co. Galway, esq.
1660 ,, major Robert, Gallagh, co. Galway (delivered out in 1660)
1733 ,, Robt., Abbert, co. Galway, esq.
1763 ,, Robert, formerly of Ireland, but at Havanna, esq.
1780 ,, Simon, Tuam, co. Galway, esq.
1762 ,, Thos., Tuam, co. Galway, gent.
1762 ,, William lord (Copy)
1773 ,, William, Drogheda
1617 **Blanchvile**, Lenard, Balickwan, co. Tipperary, gent.
1692 **Blanckly**, John, Kilmainham, co. Dublin, yeoman
1789 **Bland**, Humphry, Dublin, esq.
1728 ,, John, Blandsfort, Queen's County, esq.

1790 **Bland**, John, Blandsfort
1811 ,, John, Blandsfort, Queen's County, esq.
1760 ,, Nathaniel, Dublin, LL.D.
1792 ,, Neville, Dublin, gent.
1734 **Blaney**, Cadwallader, lord baron, Monaghan
1764 ,, Charles, hon. and rev. lord baron
1630 ,, sir Edward, knt., lord Blaney, baron of Monaghan, privy councillor
1790 ,, right hon. Mary Cairnes, lady
1642 ,, Richd., Carrick, co. Monaghan, esq.
1706 ,, William, lord baron Monaghan [See BLAYNEY.]
1809 **Blangeois**, Jacque, city of Dublin, gent.
1803 **Blaquire**, James, esq.
1754 ,, Paul, Dublin, merchant
1764 **Blayney**, Charles, lord baron
1687 ,, Jane, lady dowager
1726 ,, Margaret, baroness, relict of Charles Derring, esq.
1724 ,, right hon. Mary, lady
1784 ,, William, Fleet-lane, Dublin
1804 **Bleakley**, John, Island of St. Croix (Copy)
1790 **Bleakly**, Wm., Cargan, co. Cavan [See BLAKELEY.]
1720 **Blecklin**, Christopher, Lazer's-hill, merchant
1696 **Blenerhasset**, Arthur, Sen. Fell. Trin. Coll., Dublin
1758 ,, Arthur, justice of King's Bench
1781 ,, Arthur, Tralee, co. Kerry, gent.
1790 ,, Arthur Robert, Fortfield, co. Kerry, gent.
1799 ,, Arthur, Ballyseedy, co. Kerry, esq.
1810 ,, Catherine, Blennerville, co. Kerry, widow
1696 ,, Elizabeth, Tralee, co. Kerry, widow (Copy)
1771 ,, Frances, Dublin, widow
1677 ,, Henry, Crevenish, co. Fermanagh, esq.
1676 ,, John, Ballycarty, co. Kerry, esq. (Ex.)
1677 ,, John, Ballyseedy, co. Kerry, esq.
1709 ,, John, Ballyseedy, co. Kerry, esq.
1639 ,, sir Leonard, Castlehasset, co. Fermanagh, knt.
1695 ,, Mary, Ballynagannagh, co. Limerick, widow of captain Arthur B.
1803 ,, Mary, Dublin
1713 ,, Robert, Dublin, esq.
1695 ,, Thomas, Litter, co. Kerry, esq.

1731 **Blenerhasset**, Thos., par. St. Margt., Westminster, Middlesex, clk.
1638   ,,   dame Ursula, widow
1785   ,,   William, Elmgrove, co. Kerry, esq.
1797   ,,   William, Elmgrove, co. Kerry, esq.
1624 **Blenerhayset**, sir John, knt., chief baron of Exchequer
1663 **Blenerhaysset**, Edwd., Pockthorpe and Beleek, co. Fermanagh, gent. (Ex.)
1811 **Blennerhassett**, Arthur, city of Bath, esq.
1809   ,,   Gerald, Riddlestown, co. Lime-rick, esq.
1810   ,,   Mary, I. C., par. of Walcot, Somerset (Copy)
1725 **Blesinton**, Anne, viscountess dow.
1732   ,,   Charles, lord viscount
1767   ,,   Martha, lady visct. dowager
1769   ,,   William, earl of
1718 **Blessington**, Morrogh, lord visct.
1802 **Blewett**, Patrick, late deceased
1738 **Bligh**, Anthony, lieut. in brigadier Bowles' regt.
1669   ,,   Cath., Rathmore, co. Meath, widow
1737   ,,   Elizabeth, *als.* **Napper**, Dub., . widow
1667   ,,   John, Rathmore, co. Meath, esq.
1760   ,,   Mary, spinster
1778   ,,   rev. Robert, dean of Elphin
1710   ,,   Thomas, Rathmore, co. Meath, esq.
1775   ,,   Thos., Brittas, co. Meath, esq.
1758 **Bliss**, William, Dengan, co. Meath, builder
1717 **Blocksom**, Jane, Dublin, widow
[See BLOXHAM.]
1806 **Blood**, Anne, Ennis, co. Clare, widow
1749   ,,   Charles, Ladycastle, co. Kil-dare, gent.
1750   ,,   Elizabeth, Bohersallagh, co. Clare, widow
1779   ,,   Eliz., Ennis, co. Clare, widow
1798   ,,   Elizabeth, Dublin, widow
1806   ,,   Eliz., city of Limerick, widow
1809   ,,   Frances B. (wife of Ml. Blood)
[CLIX. 61
1791   ,,   Jane, Baltiboys, co. Wicklow, widow
1799   ,,   John, Ballykilty, co. Clare, gent.
1773   ,,   Mary, Ballybarny, co. Kildare, widow
1760   ,,   Mathew, Ballikinacurra, co. Clare, gent.
1744   ,,   Neptune, Bohersallagh, co. Clare, gent.
1802   ,,   Neptune, Park, co. Clare, esq.

1802 **Blood**, Neptune, Brickhill, co. Clare
1759   ,,   Robert, Limerick, cordwainer (Not proved)
1809   ,,   Samuel, city of Dublin, glover
1731   ,,   Thos., Bohersallagh, co. Clare, gent.
1741   ,,   Thos., Corrofin, co. Clare, gent. (This will declared null and void)
1766   ,,   Thos., Ballybarny, co. Kildare, gent.
1767   ,,   Thomas, Dublin
1727   ,,   William, Dublin, merchant
1791   ,,   William, Roxton, co. Clare, esq. (Large)
1802   ,,   William, Gardiner-street, co. Dublin, attorney-at-law
1804   ,,   William, Ennis, co. Clare, gent.
1788 **Bloomer**, Edward, Dublin, publican
1793 **Bloomfield**, George, Redwood, co. Tipperary, esq. (Large)
1809   ,,   Richard, Meelicks, co. Galway, gent.
[See BLUMFIELD.]
1788 **Blosse**, sir Henry Lynch, Mote, co. Mayo, bart.
1775   ,,   sir Robert Lynch, co. Mayo, bt.
1797 **Blossett**, Eliza Dorothy, par. St. George, Hanover - square, widow
1751   ,,   Jane, *sus* De, Dublin, widow
1797   ,,   John, Dublin, esq.
1719   ,,   Paul, Dublin, esq., late col. in Brit. Maj. Service
1721   ,,   Solomon De Louche, Dub., esq
1749   ,,   Solomon, esq.
1757   ,,   Solomon Stephen, esq. (Copy)
1803   ,,   Susanna Eliz., Dub., spinster
1663 **Blount**, Charles, Clonmel, esq.
1640   ,,   Edwd., Bouletowne, co. Kildare, esq.
1640   ,,   George, Raban, co. Kildare
1677   ,,   George, Bolton, co. Kildare, esq.
1699   ,,   Saml., Lismacue, co. Tipperary, esq. (Ex.)
1759 **Blow**, James, Belfast, printer
1779 **Blowers**, Mary, Dublin
1799 **Bloxham**, Mark, Dublin, chandler
1634 **Bludworth**, Martin, Broomsgrove, Gloucestershire, merchant
1656 **Bluet**, John, Maynooth, co. Kildare
[V. 284
1758   ,,   John, Limerick, merchant
1784 **Bluett**, Catherine, Limerick, widow
1792   ,,   Patrick, Dunmore, co. Galway, M.D.
1663   ,,   William, Youghal, alderman
1737 **Blumfield**, Benjamin, Eyre Court, co. Galway

1728 **Blumfield**, Mary, St. Andrew's par., Dubl.
[See BLOOMFIELD.]
1732 **Blundell**, Ann, Dublin, widow
1650 ,, Charles, esq., captain
1808 ,, rev. Dixie, doctor in divinity
1625 ,, sir Francis, kt. and bart., vice-treasurer of Ireland
1707 ,, sir Francis, Edenderry, King's County, bart.
1806 ,, John, co. Drogheda
1811 ,, John, Preston, co. palatine of Lancaster
1785 ,, Joseph, Dublin, merchant
1650 ,, Martha, widow of captain Ch. Blundell (Copy)
1756 ,, Montague, lord visct. (Copy)
1755 ,, Ralph, Dublin, alderman
1618 ,, Richard, gent.
1775 ,, Thomas, Dublin, watchmaker
1683 ,, Winwood, Ballinrath, King's County, gent.
1783 **Blunden**, sir John, Castle B., bart.
1810 ,, John, Kilmacoliver, co. Kilkenny
1808 ,, Medhope, city of Waterford, esq.
1685 ,, Ovarington, Clanmoreney, Lib. of Kilkenny, gent.
1773 **Blunt**, Anthony the elder, Kilkenny, alderman
1603 ,, captain George, Donasse, co. Clare, esq. [gent.
1727 **Blyke**, Dudley, Kilcurley, co. Louth,
[See BLAKE.]
1739 **Blythman**, Eliz., London, widow
1739 ,, Jasper, Inner Temple, London, gent. Kildare
1803 **Boake**, Ephraim, Boakefield, co.
1724 **Board**, Joseph, Dublin, anchor smith
1750 ,, William, Glasnevin, co. Dubl., hatter
1784 **Boardman**, Constantia, co. Dublin, widow
1784 ,. Hannah, widow
1796 ,, Hannah, Jonestown, King's County, widow
1788 ,, Isaac, Dublin, merchant
1742 ,, Jos., Clonmore, King's County
1773 ,, Joseph, Jonestown, King's County, gent.
1800 ,, Jos., Cork-street, Dub., gent.
1705 ,, Robert, Nenagh, co. Tipperary, gent.
1768 ,, Robert, Parsonstown, co. Kildare, gent.
1779 ,, Robert, Clonmel, co. Tipperary
1725 ,, Thomas, Lazor's-hill, Dublin, weaver
1742 ,, Thos., Dublin, sail cloth weaver
[See BORDMAN.]

1810 **Boat**, Redmond, city of Dublin, surg.
1696 **Boate**, Gerard, Clonekeny, co. Tipperary, gent.
1704 ,, Gershon, Coolrahen, Queen's County, gent.
1744 ,, Gershon, Marystown, co. Roscommon, farmer
1681 ,, Godfrey, Dublin, esq.
1721 ,, Godfrey, justice of King's Bench
1775 **Bobbit**, David, Broadstone, co. Dublin, victualler
1741 **Boddell**, Henry, Balreask, co. Meath, farmer
1769 ,, Martha, Balresk, co. Meath, widow
1770 **Bodin**, Agnes, Galway, widow
1762 ,, Jonock, Galway, merchant
1795 **Bodkin**, Ambrose, Killorough, co. Galway, esq.
1793 ,, Anastasia
1778 ,, Andw., Tuam, co. Galway, esq.
1802 ,, Anne, Galway, spinster
1763 ,, Anthony, Galway, merchant
1796 ,, Dominick, Frasternagh, co. Galway, esq.
1771 ,, Dorothea, Limerick
1768 ,, Edmond, Kilcrony, co. Galway, esq.
1774 ,, James Fitz James, Tuam, co. Galway, gent.
1775 ,, James, Galway, gent.
1754 ,, Jane, Dublin, spinster
1778 ,, Jane
1804 ,. John, Castletown, co. Galway, esq.
1762 ,, Jonock, Galway, merchant
1793 ,, Margaret D., Dublin, widow
1779 ,, Martin, Dublin, gent.
1780 ,, Mary, Galway town, spinster
1735 ,, Michael, Dublin, merchant
1677 ,, Nicholas, Galway, merchant
1742 ,, Oliver, Carrowbane, co. Galway, gent.
1805 ,, Richard, city of Dublin, mercht.
1702 ,, Thomas, captive in city of Fes, native of Galway
1772 ,, Thomas, Moylaghbeg, co. Galway, esq.
1803 ,, Thos., town of Galway, mercht.
1630 **Bodye**, John, Cortronenagh, county Roscommon, Athlone.
1796 **Boe**, Martin, Clarendon-st., Dublin, stonecutter
1630 **Boggotts**, Edmond, Boggotstown, co. Limerick, gent.
1737 **Boggs**, Joseph, Londonderry, merchant
[See BIGGS.]
1770 **Bogle**, Jas., Castlefin, co. Donegal

1733 **Boileau**, Charles de Castlenaur, Dublin, esq.
1801 ,, Magdalen, Dublin, spinster
1767 ,, Simeon, Dublin, merchant
      Boies, see BOYS.
1737 **Boisrand**, Samuel, Dublin, esq.
1713 **Boivin**, John, Dublin, merchant
1714 ,, Mary, widow of John B., Dublin, merchant
1699 ,, Samuel, Dublin, merchant
1714 **Boju**, lieut. John, Meadstown, co. Cork
1800 **Bolan**, James, Ennis, co. Clare, gent.
1770 ,, Thomas, Ennis, co. Clare.
1769 **Boland**, James, Limerick, gent.
1789 ,, John, Dublin, gent.
1792 ,, John, Cork, esq.
1794 ,, Judith, Ricardstown, King's County, widow
1805 ,, Mary, Stephen's Green, Dublin
1681 **Bold**, Roger, Dublin, vintner
1790 **Boldock**, Clifford, Ball's Bridge, co. Dublin, gent.
1809 **Bole**, Elizabeth, Killeeney, county Longford
1779 **Boles**, Jane, Dublin
1702 ,, John, Inch Bar, Imokelly, co. Cork, esq.
1731 ,, John, Woodhouse, co. Tipperary, gent.
1752 ,, Richd., Moyge, co. Cork, gent.
1793 ,, Richard, Youghal, co. Cork, gent.
1735 ,, Saml., Middleton, co. Cork, esq.
1782 ,, Sarah, Mogealy, widow
1701 ,, Thos., Ballynecorry, co. Cork, gent. (Exemp.)
1749 ,, Thomas, Killraher, co. Cork, esq.
1780 ,, Thomas, Youghal, co. Cork, gent.
      [See BOWLES.]
1703 **Boleyn**, Jane, Drogheda, widow
1617 **Bolger**, Barnaby, dean of St. Kenny's Church, Kilkenny
1782 ,, Edward, Ballynebarly, county Wexford, esq.
1711 ,, John, Dublin, yeoman
1763 ,, Richd., Ballynebarney, co. Kilkenny, gent.
1807 ,, Thomas, city of Dublin, esq.
1804 ,, William
      [See BOULGER, BULGER.]
1635 **Bollairt** or **Bollard**, John, Dublin, merchant
1662 **Bollard**, Henry, Dublin, apothecary
                                    [IX. 50
1751 ,, Thos., Newmarket, co. Dublin, clothier

1785 **Bolster**, John, Tullorboy, co. Limerick, gent.
1792 ,, Susana, widow
            [See BOULSTER.]
1773 **Bolton**, Ann, Dublin, widow
1805 ,, Anna Maria, Charlemont-st., Dublin
1760 ,, Boyle, Carrickbagott, county Louth, gent.
1681 ,, Carroll, esq.
1796 ,, Charity, city of Derry, widow
1722 ,, Charles, Waterford, esq.
1791 ,, Chichester, Dublin, esq.
1699 ,, Cornelius, Waterford, gent.
1730 ,, Dorothy
1668 ,, Edward, Clonrusk, King's Co., esq.
1705 ,, Edward, Brazil, co. Dublin, esq. (Ex.)
1759 ,, Edwd., Brazil, co. Dublin, esq.
1811 ,, Edwd., Brazil, co. Dublin, esq.
1740 ,, Elizabeth, Drogheda, widow
1790 ,, Henry Denny, Wexford, M.D.
1759 ,, Hugh, dean of Waterford
1644 ,, James, Drogheda, esq.
1736 ,, James, Calga, co. Louth, gent.
1723 ,, John, dean of Derry
1738 ,, John, Ballyloghlane, Lib. of Dublin, esq.
1755 ,, John, Dublin, esq.
1758 ,, John, Isleland, co. Wexford, gent.
1759 ,, John, Garradine
1759 ,, John, Dublin, merchant
1793 ,, John, Waterford, esq.
1807 ,, John, Mt. Bolton, co. Waterfd.
1737 ,, Joseph, Lagore, co. Meath
1809 ,, Joseph, Dolphin's Barn, co. Dublin, gent.
1682 ,, captain Lancelot, Lisburn, co. Antrim, esq.
1755 ,, Mary
1780 ,, Mary, Britain-st., Dublin, spr.
1798 ,, Mary, Castle Bellingham, co. Louth, widow
1806 ,, Mary, city of Dublin
1715 ,, Michael, Dublin, gent.
1783 ,, Obadiah, Phenix-st., Dublin, slater
1722 ,, Penelope, Dublin, widow
1604 ,, Peter, Dublin, gent.
1787 ,, Peter, King-street, Dublin, cabinet maker
1648 ,, sir Richd., knt., ch. bar. Exch., and privy councillor
1761 ,, rev. Richard, Lagore, county Meath, clk.
1779 ,, Richard, Dromiskin, co. Louth, esq.   [esq.
1802 ,, Richd., Harcourt-st., Dublin,

1757 **Bolton**, Robert, gent.
1784 ,, Robert, town of Sligo, esq.
1735 ,, Stephen, Cashel, gent.
1774 ,, Theophilus, Grange, co. Louth, esq.
1805 ,, Theophilus, city of Dublin, esq.
1810 ,, Theophilus, Lisodiege, county Kerry, esq.
1717 ,, Thomas, Dublin, gent.
1762 ,, Thos., Lagore, co. Meath, esq.
1733 ,, William, Kilkenny, gent.
　　　　[See BOULTON.]
1810 **Bomford**, David, Gallow, co. Meath, gent.
1756 ,, Edward, Hightown, co. Westmeath
1793 ,, Isaac, Dublin, gent.
1785 ,, Jane, Dawson-street, Dublin, widow
1721 ,, Laurence, Killeglan, co. Meath, gent.
1747 ,, Laurence, Clomnaghan, county Meath, gent.
1761 ,, Laurence, Dublin, gent.
1806 ,, Stephen, Rahinstown, county Meath, esq.
1807 ,, Stephen, Gallow, co. Meath
1740 ,, Thos., Rahinstown, co. Meath, gent.
1757 ,, Thos., Clownstown, co. Meath, gent.
1803 **Bonafous**, John, Kilmolog, King's County, esq.
1747 **Bond**, Dennis, Grange, Dorsetshire, esq.
1782 ,, Dennis, Grange, Dorsetshire, esq. (Copy)
1744 ,, Edwd., Bondville, co. Armagh, esq.
1769 ,, Edwd., Tyra, co. Armagh, esq.
1744 ,, Frances, Milltown, Dunlavin, co. Dublin, farmer
1747 ,, Geo., Tyra, co. Armagh, esq.
1754 ,, Henry, Bondville, co. Armagh, esq.
1789 ,, Henry Hopkins, Bondvill, co. Armagh
1763 ,, James, Newtown Flood, co. Longford, clk.
1807 ,, James, surgeon in the East India Co.'s service
1746 ,, John, Woodfort, co. Cork, esq.
1747 ,, John, Drumsallon, co. Armagh.
1747 ,, John, Grangemore, co. Kildare
1774 ,, John, Dublin, M.D.
1795 ,, John, Ballynahelisk, co. Cork, esq.
1644 ,, Lambert, Dublin, gent.
1798 ,, Oliver
1712 ,, Sarah, Dublin, widow

1731 **Bond**, Thomas (the elder), Ballyrosheen, co. Cork
1805 ,, Thomas, Bondsglen, co. Londonderry, esq.
1811 ,, Thomas, Newtown Bond, co. Longford, esq.
1809 ,, William, Kevin-street, Dublin, coach maker
1751 **Bone**, David, Duncannon fort, co. Wexford
1787 **Bones**, John, Stafford-st., Dublin, victualler
1759 **Bonfield**, Elizabeth, Dublin, widow
1752 ,, James, Limerick, merchant
1757 ,, John, Limerick, merchant
1781 ,, Michael, Newrow, Dublin
1783 ,, Monica, St. Catherine's parish, Dublin, widow
1804 ,, Thomas, city of Limerick, esq.
1737 **Bonham**, Edward, Ballynalack, co. Westmeath, esq.
1755 ,, Francis, Dublin, esq.
1760 ,, Francis
1811 ,, Francis W., city of Bath, esq.
1781 ,, John, Dublin, esq.
1807 ,, Richard, Dublin city, esq.
1760 ,, Robert, Dublin, gent.
1798 ,, Robert, Dublin, esq.
1809 ,, Susanna, city of Dublin, widow
1724 **Bonijol**, Glandus, Dublin, mercht.
1699 **Bonnell**, James, Dublin, gent.
1754 ,, Jane, par. of Writtle, Essex, widow
1662 ,, Samuel, Dublin, gent.
1758 **De Bonneval**, Judith Julia Dumout, Portarlington, widow
1733 **Bonnevale**, Anthony Ligrone, Portarlington, Queen's County, clk.
1656 **Bonning**, Robert, Kilmore, co. Meath, clk. **[V.** 320
1712 **Bonniot**, Isace, Cork city
1744 **Bonnynge**, Frances, widow
1729 **Bonourier**, John, French refugee, Dublin
1798 **Bonynge**, Gerald, Altemira, co. Westmeath, esq.
1726 ,, John, Cabra-lane, Dub., gent.
1757 ,, John, Downings, co. Kildare. gent.
1754 ,, Joseph, Bunenagh, co. Westmeath, gent.
1797 ,, Robert, Downynges, co. Kildare, gent.
1772 **Booker**, Francis, Dubl., alderman
1668 ,, colonel John, Clonmel
1669 ,, John, Clonmel, esq., some time of London, slater (Ex.)
1749 ,, John, Dublin, looking-glass maker

1761 **Booker**, Moore, vicar of Dublin
    [See BOWKER, BUCHER.]
1785 **Bookey**, Leeson, Donishall, co.
    Wexford, gent.
1802 ,, Richard, Grangebeg, co. Kil-
    dare, esq.
1731 **Boon**, Dorothy, Dublin, widow
1688 **Boone**, John, Mount Boone, Devon-
    shire, esq. (Copy)
1688 ,, Thomas, Mount Boone, Devon-
    shire, esq. (Copy)
1708 **Boorke**, Miles, Ballylee, co. Gal-
    way, gent.
    [See BURKE.]
1783 **Boote**, Edward, Collinstown, co.
    Dublin, gent.
1744 ,, Michael, Dublin, merchant
1771 **Booth**, Catherine, Sligo, widow
1650 ,, George, Dublin, gent.
1798 ,, George, Dublin, gent.
1806 ,, George, Moate, co. Westmeath
1809 ,, George, private in 55th regt.
1709 ,, Hannah
1801 ,, Henry, Ballicommon, King's
    County, farmer
1737 ,, Humphry, Dublin, esq.
1786 ,, James, Pill-lane, Dublin, gent.
1726 ,, John, Sligo, co. Sligo, gent.
1785 ,, John, North-strand, Dublin,
    grocer
1791 ,, John, Blundelstown, co. Dublin,
    farmer
1809 ,, John, Ballinabarny, co. Wicklow
1763 ,, Joseph, Beggarsbridge, co.
    Westmeath, farmer
1792 ,, Joseph, Willowgrove, farmer
1782 ,, Margaret, *alias* **Hyndes**, Rath-
    bracken, co. Cavan, widow
1800 ,, Randall, Dubl., tinplate worker
1779 ,, Richd., Drumcarban, co. Cavan,
    gent.
1680 ,, sir Robert, knt., chief justice,
    King's Bench (Ex.)
1661 ,, Steph., Tanderagy, co. Armagh,
    gent. (Copy)
1776 ,, Thomas, Marrowbone-lane, co.
    Dublin, esq.   [gent.
1788 ,, Thos., Doughill, King's County,
1792 ,, Thomas, Rathgibbin, King's
    County, farmer
1803 ,, William, city of Dublin, mercht.
1805 **Boothman**, John, Crosscolearbour,
    co. Wicklow, farmer
1770 **Bootle**, rev. Stephen, vicar of Clo-
    nard, diocese of Meath
1674 **Bor**, Begnett, *als.* **Cusack**, widow of
    Christopher Bor, merchant
1637 ,, Christian, Dublin, merchant
1686 ,, Christian, Drynagh, co. Wex-
    ford, esq. (Ex.)

1733 **Bor**, Christian, Great Britain-lane,
    Dublin, esq. (Large will)
1782 ,, Edward, Park, co. Meath, gent.
1765 ,, Jacob, Dublin, esq.
1683 ,, John, Dublin, merchant
1741 ,, John, Dublin, esq.
1767 ,, Helena, Maria, formerly of
    Dubl., but of Hammersmith,
    Middlesex, widow
1694 ,, Margaret, Dublin, widow of
    John Bor, esq. (Ex.)
1809 **Borbidge**, Charles, Anagh, co. Wex-
    ford   [County
1712 **Bordevan**, Peter, Garrangyll, King's
1692 **Bordman**, Thomas, Brittas, co.
    Wicklow, tanner
    [See BOARDMAN.]
1647 **Borlace**, sir John, Great St. Bar-
    tholomew, London, knt.
1680 **Borne**, John, Limerick, alderman
1780 **Borough**, Richd., Limerick city, esq.
1802 **Borrelly**, Melchoir
1800 **Borringdon**, John, lord bar. (Copy)
1748 **Borrowes**, Elinor, spinster
1793 ,, George, Mountrath, merchant
1615 ,, Henry, Gilton, co. Kildare
1785 ,, John, Lisardian, co. Down,
    gent.
1709 ,, sir Kildare, Gilltown, co. Kil-
    dare, bart.
1790 ,, sir Kildare Dixon, bt. (Large)
1698 ,, lady Margaret, widow
1764 ,, dame Mary, Dublin
1764 ,, Peter, Portarlington, gent. (Not
    proved)
1682 ,, Rebecca, dame, St. Stephen's-
    green, Dublin
1651 ,, captain Richard
1691 ,, sir Walter, Giltown, co. Kil-
    dare, bart.
1785 ,, Walter Dixon, Dublin, esq.
1809 ,, William, Dublin
    [See BURROWES, BURROUGHS.]
1789 **Boshel**, John, Dublin, merchant
1765 ,, Patk., coachman to rev. Danl.
    Jackson   [LXIV. 171
1724 **De Bosteroy**, Charles Bridou
1760 **Bostock**, Thomas, Dublin, gent.
1659 **Boston**, Symon, soldier in captain
    Vyvyan's com .[VII. 184
1781 **Boswell**, Anne, Dublin, spinster
1790 ,, Catherine, Dublin, widow
1723 ,, John, Dublin, merchant
1724 ,, John, Ballycorry, co. Wicklow,
    esq.
1749 ,, John, Jun., Fellow, Trinity Col-
    lege, Dublin
1802 ,, John, Athlone, gent.
1696 ,, Joseph, Castle-street, Dublin,
    confectioner

1797 **Boswell**, Mary, Dublin, widow
1779 ,, Richard, Lazor's-hill, Dublin, painter
1760 ,, Robert, Ballycurry, co. Wicklow, esq. (Large will)
1688 **Boswood**, John, Dublin, gent.
1632 **Boteler**, Beckingham, London, esq., and Endfield, Middlesex
1683 ,, William, London, goldsmith
1759 **Bottom**, William, Crosscold Harbour, co. Wicklow, farmer
1663 **Bottomley**, William, Boston, Lincolnshire, mercht. [**IX.** 105
1716 **Bouat de la Bouterie**, Simon. Dubl., gent.
1736 **Boucaran**, William, Dubl., mercht.
1776 **Boucher**, Elizab., Eaststone House, Devon, widow (Copy)
1736 ,, Fras., Crumlin, co. Dub., gent.
1754 ,, Michael, Bolton-street, Dublin, victualler
1704 ,, Samuel, Plymouth, Devonshire, esq. (Copy)
1745 ,, Thomas
1723 **Boucherie**, John, Limerick, burgess
1768 **Bouchier**, James, Kilcullane, co. Limerick, gent.
1796 ,, James, Ardkilmartin, co. Limerick, esq.
1807 ,, James John, Baggotstown, co. Limerick, esq.
1745 ,, John, Baggotstown, co Limerick, gent.
1776 ,, John, Oakfield, North Liberty of Limerick, esq.
1789 ,, John, Elmhill, co. Clare, esq.
1720 **Bouchitière**, Charles Janore, lord of, in the province of Poictu (Copy)
1744 ,, Charles, Dublin
1754 **Boudon**, James, Dublin, gent.
1770 ,, Judith, Dublin, widow
1637 **Bough**, William, Maryborough, Queen's County
1791 **Boulger**, John, Trim, co. Meath, gent.
[See BOLGER.]
1770 **Boulster**, George, Limerick, gent.
1788 ,, John, Castle Forbes, co. Longford
1784 ,, Richard, Limerick city, saddler
[See BOLSTER.]
1692 **Boulton**, Samuel, Cove, near Cork, gent.
1732 ,, Stephen, Dublin, shipwright
[See BOLTON.]
1686 **Boumer**, Geo., Drumbegge, King's Co., gent.
1716 **Bounard**, Geo., Dublin, late servant to mr. Michael David

1800 **Bourcey**, Mathew, Foxford, co. Mayo
1716 **Bourcham**, May, Dolphin's barn, clothier
1719 **Bourchier**, Barbara, Dublin, widow
1716 ,, Charles, Dublin, esq.
1605 ,, sir George, knt., master of ordnance and privy councillor
1714 ,, Thomas, Cragg, co. Tipperary, gent.
1678 **Bourden**, John, Balleen Lodge, co. Kilkenny, esq.
1682 ,, Sarah, Balleen Lodge, co. Kilkenny, widow
1707 ,, Thomas, Suttonsrath, co. Kilkenny, gent.
1809 **Bourk**, Thomas, Redmonstown, co. Tipperary, miller
1727 ,, Walter, Dublin, joiner
1721 **Bourke**, Anne, Ballyregan, co. Kildare, widow of Walter B.
1661 ,, sir David, bart., Kilfticane, co. Limerick
1794 ,, David, Bruff, co. Limerick, gent.
1624 ,, Edmond M'Ulige, Kishiohorck, co. Limerick, gent.
1750 ,, Edmd., Caharconreff, co. Limerick.
1764 ,, Edmond
1808 ,, Edward, Cove, co. Cork, woollen draper
1799 ,, Elizabeth, *alias* **Rutledge**
1628 ,, George, Limerick, burgess
1791 ,, George, Limerick, gent.
1728 ,, Joan, Kilkenny, widow
1667 ,, sir John, Derrym'loghery, co. Galway, kt.
1690 ,, John, Kill, co. Kildare, gent.
1710 ,, John, Cahirmoyle, co. Limerick, gent.
1777 ,, Julian, Brookhill, co. Mayo, widow
1765 ,, Margaret, wife of Theo. B., Thomas-st., Dubl., mercht.
1774 ,, Mary, Curry, co. Mayo, widow
1805 ,, Michael, Springfield, co. Tipperary
1692 ,, Miles, Dublin, gent.
1783 ,, Milo, Newport, co. Tipp., esq.
1606 ,, Nicholas, Limerick, alderman
1684 ,, Nicholas, Limerick, gent.
1593 ,, Oliver, Limerick, alderman
1724 ,, Oliver, Clogheroka, co. Galway, esq.
1793 ,, Phillip, Kildare town, mercht.
1724 ,, Richard, Ballinfoola, co. Limerick, gent.
1757 ,, Richard, Drumsally, co. Limerick, esq.

1726 **Bourke**, Theobald, Palmerstown, co. Kildare, esq.
1738 ,, Theobd., Carrowkeel, co. Mayo
1747 ,, Theobald, Dublin, gent.
1773 ,, Theobald, Dublin, grocer
1779 ,, Theobald, Drogheda, gent.
1786 ,, Theobd., Knockvanie, co. Clare
1667 ,, Thomas, Dublin, esq.
1684 ,, Thomas, Limerick, gent. (Copy from dio. Cashel)
1751 ,, Thos., Thomas-st., shoemaker
1773 ,, Thomas, Dublin, grocer
1783 ,, Thomas, Limerick
1785 ,, Thomas, Carrigeen, co. Limerick, gent.
1786 ,, Thomas, Gortneskehy, co. Tipperary, farmer
1623 ,, Walter, Borres OLeagh, co. Tipperary, esq.
1627 ,, William, Garrilisse, co. Tipperary, gent.
1666 ,, William, Dublin, gent.
1752 ,, William, Cooleenee, co. Limerick, gent.
1783 ,, William, Newry, co. Down
1795 ,, William, Summerhill, co. Tipperary, gent.
1800 ,, William, Madeboy, co. Limerick, esq.
     [See BURKE.]
1726 **Bourn**, Hugh, Dublin, gent.
1772 ,, Joshua, Comb-wood, merchant
1798 **Bourne**, Daniel, St. Patrick's South Close, Dublin, gent.
1751 ,, John, Dublin
1774 ,, John, Clowncallowbeg, county Cork, esq.
1804 ,, Samuel, Westbury, co. Wells (Wiltshire ?), clothier
1776 ,, Wood, Dublin, ribbon weaver
     [See BYRNE.]
1773 **Boursiquot**, Samuel, Dublin, noty. pubc.
1701 **Boussard**, Hester, widow of John Barbier, French refugee
1724 **Bousseau**, Daniel Cristofle, Dublin, gent.
1707 **Boutaud**, Stephen, Dublin, mercht.
1627 **Bouthe**, John, Dublin, gent.
1766 **Bouvier**, James, College-st., Dubl.
1748 **De Bouvillette**, capt. John, Dubl.
1793 **Boven**, Mary, co. Cork, spinster
1710 **Bow**, Robert, Dublin, saddler
1783 **Bowden**, Deborah, Dublin, widow
1736 ,, Philip, Glasshare, co. Kilkenny, farmer
1661 **Bowdler**, John, St. Werburgh's parish, Dublin
1676 **Bowdon**, Samuel, Kiltubber, co. Westmeath, gent.

1785 **Bowdon**, Savage, lieut. in East India Company's service
1699 **Bowen**, Anne, Summerhill, co. Meath, spinster
1756 ,, Benjamin, Dublin, alderman
1726 ,, George, Derrinroe, Queen's County, esq.
1658 ,, Henry, Farghy, co. Cork, esq.
1723 ,, Henry, Kilbolane, co. Cork, esq.
1788 ,, Henry Cole, Bowen's Court, co. Cork
1781 ,, rev. Herbert, Kilbeggan, co. Westmeath
1730 ,, Howell, parish of Kilcoleman, co. Cork, esq.
1724 ,, Hugh, Mullingar, co. Wt. Meath, sen., esq.
1724 ,, Jane, *als.* **Cole**, Limerick, widow
1720 ,, John, Kilbolane, co. Cork, esq. (Large will)
1774 ,, John, Mullingar, co. Westmeath, esq.
1803 ,, John, Oakgrove, co. Cork, esq.
1716 ,, Margaret, Dublin, widow
1729 ,, Nichs., Bowensford, co. Cork, esq.
1623 ,, Robert, Balliadams, Queen's County, esq. (Probate recalled and regranted in 1627)
1627 ,, Robert, Balliadams, Queen's County [See 1623.]
1627 ,, Robert, Ballyadams, Queen's County, esq.   [**II.** 36
1762 ,, Stephens, Farrahy, co. Cork, esq.
1758 ,, Thomas the elder, Dub., gent.
1594 ,, captain William, Castle Kerrie, co. Mayo
1686 ,, William, Ballyadams, Queen's County, esq.
1763 ,, William John, Bowensford, co. Cork, clk.
1775 ,, William, Dublin, gent.
1783 **Bower**, James, Leixlip, co. Kildare
1800 **Bowerman**, Amelia, Dublin, widow
1781 ,, Henry, Coolyne, co. Cork, esq.
1771 ,, John, Prospect-hill, co. Clare, esq.
1809 ,, Richard, city of Limerick
1793 **Bowers**, John, Grageavine, co. Kilkenny, esq.
1800 ,, John, Grangenemane, co. Kilkenny
1809 ,, Martha, Owning, co. Kilkenny, widow
1735 ,, Mary, Stonehouse, co. Waterford, widow
1810 ,, Maunsell, Mount Prospect, co. Kilkenny, esq.
1802 ,, Molesworth, Wexford, gent.

1802 **Bowes,** Catherine, Mountrath, Queen's County, widow
1671 ,, Edwd., par. St. Clement Danes, Middlesex, tailor
1758 ,, John, Clincant, King's County, gent.
1767 ,, John, lord, one of the lords justices and lord High Chancellor
1777 ,, Rumsey, Bingfield, Berkshire, esq.
1804 ,, William, Mc Rath, Queen's County, carpenter
1725 **Bowin,** Peter, Dublin, merchant
1743 **Bowker,** Francis, Coolcritok [See BOOKER.]
1775 **Bowland,** Hugh, Polahoney, co. Wicklow
1761 ,, John, Sheephouse, co. Wicklow, farmer
1806 ,, Margaret, Arklow, co. Wicklow [See BOLAND.]
1803 **Bowles,** George, Mount Prospect, co. Cork, esq.
1704 ,, Jano, Dublin, widow
1749 ,, lieut.-gen. Phineas (Copy)
1799 ,, Richard, Says-place, Surrey, esq.
1760 ,, William Phineas, Dublin, esq., proved in special form in 1765
1765 ,, William Phineas, Dublin, esq. [See BOLES.]
1616 **Bowton,** John, Dublin
1694 **Bowman,** Abraham, Limerick, merchant
1751 ,, Abraham, Ballymacurragh, co. Limerick, gent.
1712 ,, Daniel, Limerick, alderman
1791 ,, Mary, *alias* **Houghton**
1757 ,, Michael, Limerick, merchant
1671 **Bowmen,** John, Ballemcrees, co. Limerick, esq., lieut.-col.
1756 **Bowyer,** Elizabeth, Dublin, widow
1745 ,, Henry, Cranary, co. Longford, esq.
1727 ,, Michael, Crannary, co. Longford, esq.
1782 ,, Robert, Dublin, esq. [See BOYER.]
1604 **Boyan,** *als.* **Bradley,** John, Maynooth, priest (Copy)
1788 **Boyce,** Richard, Ariglin, co. Cork, gent.
1797 ,, William, Gorey, co. Wexford, gent. [See BOYCE.]
1733 **Boyd,** Adam, Dublin, gent.
1803 ,, Adam, paymaster, 4th dragoon guards
1748 ,, Alexander, Waterford, esq

1794 **Boyd,** Alex., Castlebar, co. Mayo, M.D.
1804 ,, Alex., McEdwards, co. Antrim
1746 ,, Andrew, Prospect, co. Antrim, gent.
1763 ,, Andrew, Newry, merchant
1805 ,, Angel, widow
1703 ,, Ann, *alias* **Bellas,** relict of Robt. Bellas, Dublin
1782 ,, Catherine, Dublin, widow
1776 ,, Charles, Gardiner's-row, co. Dublin, esq.
1780 ,, Daniel the younger, Ballycastle, co. Antrim, esq.
1790 ,, David, Dublin, gent.
1791 ,, Ellinor, New Ross, spinster
1765 ,, Elizabeth, *alias* **Cox,** Glansinsaw, co. Kilkenny, widow
1784 ,, Francis, Dublin, yeoman
1718 ,, George, Dublin, gent.
1789 ,, George, Dublin
1746 ,, Hugh, Dublin
1766 ,, Hugh, Ballycastle, co. Antrim, esq. (Large will)
1774 ,, Hugh, Donaghadee, co. Down, esq.
1782 ,, Hugh, Ballycastle, co. Antrim, esq.
1796 ,, Hugh, Ballycastle, co. Antrim, esq.
1768 ,, James, Antrim town, linen draper [navy
1800 ,, James, lieut. in His Majesty's
1800 ,, Jane, Dublin, widow
1682 ,, Jennet, Ballinacree, co. Antrim, widow
1721 ,, John, Rathmore, gent.
1722 ,, John, Letterkenny, co. Donegal, merchant
1759 ,, John, Scaroagh, co. Down, mercht.
1764 ,, John, Letterkenny, co. Don., esq.
1771 ,, John, New Ross, gent.
1790 ,, John, Summerhill, Dublin, surgeon
1810 ,, John, Ballymacost, co. Donegal
1801 ,, Letitia, Ballymony, co. Antrim, widow
1800 ,, Margaret, *alias* **Nisbett,** Dublin, widow
1758 ,, Mary, Letterkenny, co. Don.
1786 ,, Mary, *alias* **Moore,** Ballydivity, co, Antrim, widow
1805 ,, Mary, Ballycastle, co. Londonderry
1790 ,, Patrick, Kilquade, co. Wicklow
1765 ,, Robert, Glans-saw, co. Kilkenny, esq.

1742 **Boyd**, Samuel, Carnecally, co. Down, farmer
1780 ,, Samuel, Mount Edwards, co. Antrim, gent.
1660 ,, Thomas, Portlawege, co. Down, gent.
1800 ,, Thomas, major in the army and capt. 16th regt.
1628 ,, William, Dunluce, co. Antrim, gent.
1740 ,, William, Newry, co. Down, clothier
1783 ,, William, Carrickfergus town
1791 ,, Wm., Letterkenny, co. Donegal
1800 ,, Wm., Ballycastle, co. Antrim, M.D.
1728 **Boydell**, Wm., Kells, co, Meath, innkeeper
1696 **Boyer**, Alexander, Grangemore, co. Sligo, gent.
[See BOWYER.]
1790 **Boyes**, James, Stonyford, co. Antrim, linen draper
[See BOYLE.]
1764 **Boylan**, Christopher, Dublin, baker
1750 ,, Edward, Ballynegeerah, co. Dublin, farmer
[See BOYLE.]
1801 ,, James, Clorikarin, co. Kildare, farmer
1796 ,, John, Counogh, co. Kildare, farmer
1723 ,, Nicholas, Rahalen, co. Meath, farmer
1772 ,, Nicholas, Lisdoory, co. Meath, farmer
1801 ,, Patrick, Harristown, co. Louth, farmer
1704 ,, Thomas, Timoole, barony Skreen, co. Meath, farmer
1720 ,, Thomas, Hilltown, co. Meath, farmer
1749 **Boyle**, Adam, Calrough, near Cootehill, co. Cavan
1756 ,, Arthur, Dublin, mercht.
1771 ,, Bellingham, Esq., one of the Comrs. of the Revenue
1803 ,, Celia
1744 ,, Charles, Arraghlin-bridge, co. Cork, esq.
1758 ,, Christr., Dublin, linen draper
1778 ,, Elizabeth, Dublin, spinster
1801 ,, Elizabeth, town of Galway, widow
1783 ,, Geo., Newtownbarry, co. Wexford, gent.   [Cork
1714 ,, hon. Henry, Castle Martyn, co.
1757 ,, James, Cabragh, co. Cavan
1778 ,, James, Strinagh, co. Meath, farmer

1766 **Boyle**, John, Dublin, gent.
1794 ,, John, Ballyshannon, co. Donegal
1786 ,, Margaret, Kedue, co. Cavan, spinster
1799 ,, Patrick, Booterstown, co. Dublin, gent.
1711 ,, Richard, Dublin, esq.
1692 ,, hon. Robert, Stalbridge, Dorsetshire (Copy)
1757 ,, Robt., Cavan, co. Cavan, gent.
1691 ,, William, Cork
1737 ,, William, Cork, mercht.
1788 ,, William, Belfast, co. Antrim, mercht.
1785 **Boyne**, Elizth., dowager viscountess
1802 ,, right hon. Frederick, lord visct. (Large.)
1723 ,, Gustavus, lord visct.
1746 ,, Gustavus, lord visct.
1794 ,, Michael, Oughterard, co. Kildare, farmer
1794 ,, Richard, Watling-st., Dublin, skinner
1794 **Boynham**, John, Phillipstown, King's County
1744 **Boynton**, sir Francis, bart.
1790 **Boys**, Comyn, lieut. in the East India Co.'s service
1790 ,, George, lieut. in the East India Co.'s service
1585 ,, or **Boies**, Pers, Dolandston, Meath, gent.
1781 ,, Philip, Dublin, gent.
1810 ,, Philip, French-st., Dubl., gent.
1803 ,, William, Dublin, esq.
1712 **Boyse**, Benjamin, Dublin, gent.
1724 ,, Jacob, Dublin, gent.
1775 ,, Margaret, wife of Thos. B., of Bishop's Hall, co. Kilkenny, esq.
1714 ,, Nathaniel, Dublin, esq.
1735 ,, Nathaniel, Dublin, mercht.
1792 ,, Nathaniel, vicar of Newmarket, co. Cork   [ford, esq.
1730 ,, Samuel, Cullenstown, co. Wex-
1791 ,, Thomas, Bishop's Hall, co. Kilkenny, esq.
1700 ,, William, Dublin, shoemaker
1799 ,, William, Christ Church, Surrey, surgeon (Copy)
[See BOYCE, BOYES.]
1723 **Boyton**, James, Johnstowne, co. Meath, gent.
1753 ,, Michael, Dublin, gent.
1802 **Brabazon**, Anne, Rath
1636 ,, sir Anthony, Thomas-court, Dublin, knt.
1699 ,, capt. Anthony, Kellistown, co. Louth, esq.

1724 **Brabazon**, Anthony, Creagh, co. Roscommon, esq.
1756 ,, Anthony, Beagh, co. Roscommon
1760 ,, Anthony, Carstown, co. Louth, esq. (Large will)
1805 ,, sir Anthony, Newpark, co. Mayo, knt.
1804 ,, Brabazon, Summerhill, co. Dublin, esq.
1625 ,, sir Edwd., knt., baron of Ardee
1809 ,, Edw., Tarah House, co. Meath, esq.
1779 ,, Elinor, Athlone, co. Roscommon, widow
1796 ,, Elizabeth, Wicklow town, spr.
1697 ,, George, Bell Cotton, co. Louth, gent.
1780 ,, Geo., Newpark, co. Mayo, esq.
1722 ,, Jas., Braganstown, co. Louth, gent.
1729 ,, Jas., Carrstown, co. Louth, esq.
1734 ,, James, vicar of Carbery, co. Kildare, clk.
1759 ,, Ludlow, B. Park, co. Louth, clk.
1730 ,, Ralph, Salterstown, co. Louth, gent.
1767 ,, Wallop, Rath, co. Louth, esq.
1714 ,, William, co. Louth, esq.
1741 ,, Wm., Carrogary, co. Sligo, esq.
1768 ,, Wm., Athlone, co. Roscommon, gent.
1786 ,, William, city of Dublin, esq.
1793 ,, William, Rath, co. Louth, esq.
1794 ,, hon. William, Dublin, esq.
1742 **Brabing**, Wm., Dublin, mercht.
1746 ,, William, Dublin, mercht.
1631 **Brabourne**, Hen., Norwich, maltster
1662 **Braburne**, Margery, *als.* **St. Laurence**, widow
1679 **Brachall**, Michael, co. Dublin
1678 **Brack**, John, Clanmore, co. Catherlogh, yeoman
1788 **Bracken**, Margery, Watling-street, Dublin, spr.
1684 **Bradbourne**, John, Mid. Temple, London (Copy)
1751 **Bradburn**, Edward, Rathangan, co. Kildare, innholder
1642 **Bradbury**, Anthony, St. Patrick-st., shoemaker
1800 **Braddel**, Mathew, Mallow, co. Cork, gent.
1788 ,, Michl., Croneyhone, co. Wicklow, gent.
1772 **Braddell**, George, Bullingate, co. Wicklow, esq.
1760 ,, Henry, gent.
1781 ,, John, Ballyshane, co. Carlow, gent.

1784 **Braddell**, Mary, Cronyhorn, co. Wicklow, widow [gent.
1764 ,, Michl., Carnew, co. Wicklow,
1782 ,, Wm., Dublin, woollen draper
1809 **Braddle**, Thomas, Prospect, co. Wexford, esq.
1810 **Braddish**, Elizabeth, city of Dublin
1751 **Braddock**, Elizabeth, Dublin, widow
1756 ,, Richard, Clara, King's County, mercht.
1775 ,, Thos., Newry, co. Down, merchant
1564 **Bradefeld**, Harrye
1808 **Bradfield**, James, Stokeferry, Norfolk (Copy)
1726 **Bradford**, Alex., Athy, co. Kildare, gent. (Exemp.)
1750 ,, Alex., Dublin, D.D., vicar of St. Andrew's, Dublin
1720 ,, Andrew, Athy, co. Kild., gent.
1803 ,, Frances, spinster
1769 ,, George, Dublin, gent.
1765 ,, Jas., Athy, co. Kildare, gent.
1798 ,, John, Stradbally, Queen's Co., mercht.
1756 ,, Joseph, Newmarket, co. Dublin, aledraper (*i.e.* alehouse keeper)
1810 ,, Mary, city of Dublin, spinster
1794 ,, Susanna, Dublin, spinster
1768 ,, William, Dublin, surgeon
1766 **Bradish**, Phanuel, Dublin, sword cutler
1728 ,, Wheaton, Kilkenny, gent.
1791 ,, Wheaton, Dublin, gent.
1788 ,, rev. Wm., Duleek, co. Meath, clk.
1783 **Bradley**, Abraham, stationer to His Majesty
1775 ,, Catherine, Dublin, widow
1659 ,, Francis, soldier [**VII.** 187
1673 ,, James, soldier in sir Theo. Jones' troop
1764 ,, James, Dolphin's-barn, Dublin, gent.
1705 ,, John, late purser of Her Majesty's ship ' Mary ' (Copy)
1698 ,, Robert, Dublin, gent.
1790 ,, Sarah, Dublin, widow
1783 ,, Thomas, Chamber-st., Dublin, clothier
1794 **Bradly**, Dorothy, Dublin, widow
1778 ,, Hulton, Kinsaly, co. Dublin
1807 ,, John, Knock
[See BRADLEY.]
1776 **Bradner**, John, par. of Powerscourt, co. Wicklow, farmer
1697 **Bradock**, John, Dublin, alderman
1795 **Bradshaw**, David, Ballyfreen, co. Limerick, gent.

E

1788	**Bradshaw,** George, Dublin, lime and salt manufacturer	
1756	,, James, Lurgan, co. Armagh, linen draper	
1765	,, James, Annsborough, co. Armagh, linen draper	
1745	,, Joanna, Dublin, widow	
1681	,, John, Lissebuck, co. Monaghan, tanner	
1714	,, John, Dublin, merchant	
1751	,, John, Kilnegoneeny, co. Limk.	
1797	,, John, Dublin, attorney-at-law	
1761	,, Margaret or Mary, Kilbeg, co. Tipperary	
1764	,, Paul, Sollohode, co. Tip., gent.	
1596	,, Richd., The Naas, co. Kildare	
1782	,, Richard, formerly of Cork, late of Dover-st., London, esq. (Copy)	
1792	,, Richard, Tipperary	
1752	,, Robert, Phillipstown	
1783	,, Robert, Cullen, co. Tip., esq.	
1786	,, Robert, Ballyvilode, co. Limerick, gent.	
1797	,, Robert, Longstone, co. Tip., gent.	
1808	,, Robert, Alleen, co. Tip., esq.	
1798	,, Samuel, Golden Garden, co. Tip., esq.	
1737	**Bradstock,** Rowland, Dublin, gent.	
1690	**Bradston,** Francis, Lr. Morterstown, co. Catherlow, gent.	
1773	**Bradstreet,** Dudley, Multifarnham, co. Westmeath, distiller	
1754	,, Elizabeth, Tinnescolley, county Kilkenny, widow	
1801	,, dame Elizabeth, widow	
1688	,, John, Blanchvilles Park, co. Kilkenny, esq.	
1791	,, sir Samuel, 3rd justice of the King's Bench	
1762	,, sir Simon, Kilmainhim, county Dublin, bart.	
1805	**Brady,** Anne, French-street, Dublin	
1800	,, Anthony, Dublin, brush mercht.	
1733	,, Bryan, Cluntiduffy, co. Cavan, gent	
1783	,, Catherine, *alias* **Ormsby,** *alias* **Donnellan**	
1788	,, Cornelius, Dublin, esq.	
1730	,, Elizabeth, *alias* **Thaker** (wife of John B., esq.)	
1742	,, Edmond, Dublin, brewer	
1793	,, Francis, Kilpatrick, co. W. Meath, farmer	
1801	,, Francis, Bridgefoot-st., Dublin	
1796	,, Gertrude, widow	
1770	,, Henry, Reinskea, co. Galway, gent. [gent.	
1748	,, Hugh, Kilkony, co. Galway,	

1803	**Brady,** Hugh, Limerick, esq.	
1807	,, Hugh, Dublin, Roman C. priest	
1777	,, James, Kilpatrick, farmer	
1777	,, Jas., Carrigallen, co. Leitrim	
1757	,, Jane, Thomas-street, Dublin, widow	
1788	,, Jane, Dublin, spinster	
1615	,, Jno., The Grange, husbandman	
1713	,, John, Dublin, merchant	
1733	,, John (the elder), Grange, co. Antrim, tanner	
1759	,, John, Aghuloghan, co. Cavan	
1760	,, John, Dublin, merchant	
1784	,, John, Kilwardin, co. Kildare, farmer	
1792	,, John, Muckerstaff, co. Longford, gent.	
1795	,, John, Dublin, shoemaker	
1807	,, John, Bridgefoot-st., Dublin, timber merchant	
1785	,, Owen, Watling-street, Dublin, skinner	
1771	,, Patrick, Bray, co. Kildare	
1776	,, Patk., Dubl., gent. (Large will)	
1792	,, Patrick, Smithfield, Dublin, dairyman [mercht.	
1807	,, Patrick, Vair View, co. Dublin,	
1801	,, rev. Peter, Abbey-st., Dublin,	
1777	,, Richd., Moss-st., Dubl., gent.	
1635	,, Thomas, Dublin, gent.	
1778	,, Thos., New-row, Dublin, cardmaker	
1760	,, Walter, Corglass, co. Cavan	
1741	,, William, Grange, co. Antrim, tanner	
1788	,, Wm., capt. Roy. Irish Artillery	
1791	,, William, Williamstradt, county Galway, esq.	
1757	**Brafeild,** John, Derrynahensy, co. Kilkenny, clk.	
1795	,, rev. Somerset, Dublin, clk.	
1694	**Brafield,** Alexander, Bishopstown, co. W. Meath, esq.	
1734	**Bragard,** Cyras, Clonegon, King's County, esq.	
1759	**Bragg,** Philip, lieut.-gen. and col. of foot	
1638	,, William, Kilcaugh, co. Waterford, gent.	
1680	**Bragge,** William, Dublin, gent.	
1602	**Braghall,** Thomas, Clanshellage, farmer (Copy)	
1728	**Braithwait,** Samuel, Pimlico, Dublin, clothier	
	[See **BREATHWAITE.**]	
1751	**Bramerry,** William, Dublin, linen weaver	
1741	**Bramery,** John, Coles-alley, Lib. of Thomas-court, Dublin, linen weaver	

1596 **Bran** or **Brian**, Edmond, Pheipostone, co. Dublin, farmer
1667 **Bramhall**, sir Thos., Dublin, bart.
1717 **Brannagan**, James, Athlone, innkeeper
1754 ,, James, Dublin, cooper [See BRANGAN.]
1567 **Branan**, John, Dublin, butcher
1762 **Branden**, Maurice, lord baron (Large will)
1612 ,, Margaret, *alias* **Cusack**, widow
1764 **Brandeth**, rev. John, dean of Emly
1789 **Brandon**, Ellis Agar, countess of
1803 **Brangam**, Catherine, Swords, co. Dublin, innkeeper
1800 ,, Christopher, Swords, co. Dublin, innkeeper
1811 **Brangan**, John, Killeen, co. Dublin
1640 ,, Patrick, Dublin
1595 **Brangane**, John, Dublin, mercht. [See BRANNAGAN.]
1806 **Brannon**, Frances [See BRENAN]
1759 **Brasier**, Charles, one of the younger sons of Kilner B., of Rivers, co. city of Limerick, esq.
1759 ,, Kilner, Rivers, Lib. of Limerick, esq.
1770 ,, Mary, Rivers, co. Limk., spr.
1742 **Brass**, Aris, Dublin, merchant
1794 ,, Aris, Betrete, co. Wicklow
1746 **Brassard**, Margaret, Dublin, widow
1810 **Brattan**, Mathew, lieut.-col. in East India Company's service
1713 ,, Robert, Mulligarry or Newbridge, co. Mon., gent.
1747 **Brattny**, James, Dublin, gent.
1806 **Braughall**, John, Dublin city, gent.
1807 ,, Mary, Church-st., Dubl., widow
1662 ,, Richd., Clonsillagh, co. Dublin, farmer
1707 ,, Richard, Dublin, merchant
1669 ,, Robert, Clonsillagh, gent.
1803 ,, Thos., Eccles-st., co. Dublin, merchant
1723 **Braxton**, Edwd., Grange, co. Sligo, gent.
1785 **Bray**, Elinor, Dublin, spinster
1655 ,, Francis, soldier [V. 101
1632 ,, John Fitz-John Fitz-Edmond, Clonmel, merchant
1693 ,, John, Howlingstown, co. Kilkenny, gent.
1779 ,, John, Dublin, gent.
1803 ,, Luke, Thurles, co. Tip., gent.
1763 ,, Owen, Laughlinstown, co. Dubl.
1747 ,, Robt., Portenure, co. Longford, esq.
1770 ,, Robert, Dublin, gent.
1789 ,, Robert, Dublin, gent.

1802 **Bray**, Thos., Ringsend, co. of city of Dublin
1655 **Brayrely**, Abraham, soldier [V. 209
1718 **Brazill**, Patrick, Leixlip, co. Kildare, innkeeper
1736 **Breading**, Robt., Tullamore, King's County, esq.
1729 **Bready**, John, St. Thomas-street, Dublin, yeoman
1808 **Breaky**, William, Drumskell, co. Mon.
1567 **Breanan**, John, Dublin, butcher
1761 **Breathwaite**, Geo., His Majesty's ship 'Newark' [See BRAITHWAIT.]
1729 **Bredin**, Catherine, widow
1809 ,, Christopher, Beechhill, county Cavan, esq.
1804 ,, Elizabeth, city Dublin, widow
1755 ,, Isacc, Irishmore, co. Cavan.
1762 ,, Jerome, Dublin, merchant
1781 ,, Jerome, Dorset-street, Dublin, grocer
1780 ,, John, Clancallow, co. Longford, gent.
1806 ,, Mary, Cloncullow, co. Longford, widow
1722 ,, Patrick, Drumcagh, co. Fermanagh, gent.
1741 ,, rev. Robert, Fuerty, co. Roscommon, clk.
1774 ,, Robert, Cloncallows, co. Longford, gent.
1724 ,, Susanna, Drumcagh, co. Fermanagh, spinster
1763 ,, Thos., Cloncallows, co. Longford, gent.
1759 ,, William, Dublin, merchant
1770 ,, rev. William, Cloncallows, co. Longford, clk.
1705 **Bredon**, rev. Robert, Carrick, co. Tipperary, clk.
1700 **Breedon**, Robert, Fenny Compton, Warwickshire, gent.
1699 ,, Thos., Crowetown, Northamptonshire (Copy)
1762 **Breen**, Henry, Ormond-quay, Dubl. [See BRYAN.]
1800 **Breet**, Eleanor, Crane, co. Carlow, spinster
1739 **Breghteridge**, Thos. Becket, Dublin, weaver
1749 **Breholt**, George, Wimbleton, Surrey, esq. (Copy)
1768 **Brehon**, Collins, Limerick, silversmith
1788 ,, Geo., New Ross, co. Wexford, esq.
1688 ,, Patrick, Dublin, innholder
1682 **Brenan**, Arthur, Dublin, clk.

1802	**Brenan**,	Catherine, Church-lane, Dublin
1750	,,	Daniel, Castlemarket, co. Kilk.
1768	,,	Darby, Rathgar, co. Dublin, farmer
1751	,,	Edward, Cork, chandler
1737	,,	Elizabeth, Dublin, spinster
1782	,,	Geo., Ballyragget, co. Kilkenny, farmer
1736	,,	James, Dublin, fan maker
1791	,,	Jas., Knockroe, co. Kilkenny
1725	,,	John, Crottenclogh, co. Kilkenny, gent.
1733	,,	John, Church-street, Dublin, innkeeper
1736	,,	John, Church-street, Dublin, vintner
1685	,,	Jonathan, Forgetown, Queen's County, gent.
1797	,,	Mary, *alias* **Bermingham**, Dublin, grocer
1809	,,	Michael, Harry-street, Dublin
1790	,,	Mough, Ballyeden, co. Wexford, farmer
1765	,,	Patrick, Dublin, wool comber
1799	,,	Patrick, Gurteen, Queen's Co., farmer
1803	,,	Patrick, Maryborough, Queen's Co., mercht.
1769	,,	Peter, Dublin, surgeon
1627	,,	Richard, Carrick, co. Tipperary, merchant
1753	,,	Richard, Fanaghs, co. Kildare, farmer

[See BRANNON, BRENNAN, BRENNON, BRENON.]

1751	**Brenand**,	Deborah, Dublin, widow
1688	**Brenn**,	Henry, Tulloughgory, co. Kildare, esq.
1780	**Brennan**,	Alexander, Winetavern-street, Dublin, plumber
1774	,,	Andw., Pullans, co. Monaghan
1772	,,	Ann, *alias* **Clinch**, Ballinsough, co. Meath [County
1767	,,	Catherine, Ballyhide, Queen's
1767	,,	Charles, Dublin, merchant
1809	,,	Charles, city of Kilkenny, esq.
1721	,,	Daniel, Dublin, merchant
1794	,,	Dennis, Cork, druggist
1795	,,	Elen, Iron Mills, Queen's Co.
1790	,,	Jane, Dublin, widow
1808	,,	John, Clonpiece, Queen's Co.
1783	,,	Joshua, Cole-alley, Meath-st., wool comber
1783	,,	Mary, Cole-alley, suburbs of Dublin, widow
1785	,,	Richard, Tullamore, King's Co., merchant
1767	,,	William, Dublin, innkeeper

[See BRENAN.]

1720	**Brennand**,	Joshua, London, esq., now in Dublin
1771	**Brennon**,	George, Cork, merchant [See BRENAN.]
1740	**Brenock**,	Jas., Waterfd., ale seller
1755	**Brenon**,	Grizell, Cork, widow of Edward B., merchant
1769	,,	John, Tallow, co. Waterford, gent. [See BRENAN.]
1699	**Brent**,	Thomas, Island of Jersey, esq. (Copy)
1785	**Brereton**,	Anne, Carlow town, widow
1584	,,	Arthur, Killyan and Castle Richard, co. Meath
1761	,,	Arthur, Rahinduff, Queen's County, esq
1805	,,	Arthur, Bolton-st., Dubl., gent.
1746	,,	Bowen, Rahenduff, Queen's Co., esq (Ex.)
1728	,,	Catherine, Dublin, widow
1769	,,	Edward, Carlow, gent.
1775	,,	Edward, Springmount, Queen's County, esq. (Large will)
1792	,,	Edward, Dublin, M.D.
1765	,,	Elizabeth, *alias* **Gore**, widow
1782	,,	Elizabeth
1785	,,	Frances, Springmount, Queen's County, widow
1720	,,	Geo., Carrigslaney, co. Carlow, esq. [of foot
1758	,,	Geo., capt. in col. Boles' regt.
1781	,,	Geo., Newabby, co. Kilk., esq.
1580	,,	Harrie
1673	,,	Henry, Moyle Abbey, co. Kildare, gent.
1629	,,	sir John, knt., serjeant-at-law
1701	,,	John, Dublin, gent.
1716	,,	John, Dublin, esq.
1788	,,	John, Ashgrove, King's Co., gent.
1761	,,	Mary, Dublin, spinster
1799	,,	Mary
1802	,,	Richard, Windmill, co. Kildare
1748	,,	lieut. Robt., Rahenduff, Queen's County
1764	,,	Robert, rector of Burton, co. Cork, clk.
1759	,,	Rose, Dublin, spinster
1691	,,	William, Carrigslanee, county Catherlow, esq.
1720	,,	rev. William, Limerick, clk.
1738	,,	William, Newhall, King's Co., gent.
1752	,,	William, Dublin, merchant
1794	,,	Wm., Moira, par. of St. John
1806	,,	Wm., Kilmartin, Queen's Co.
1718	**Breton**,	John, Cork, gent.
1671	**Bretsforde**,	John, Carewswood, co. Cork, gent.

1807 **Brett**, Anne, city of Dublin, widow
1773 ,, Bartholw., Drogheda, mercht.
1757 ,, Bernard, Carrowcally, co. Sligo
1748 ,, Bridget, widow
1805 ,, Daniel, Church-street, Dublin, gent.
1627 ,, Edward, Drogheda, mercht.
1737 ,, Edward, Dublin, merchant
1750 ,, Elizth., Pimlico, Lib. of Dublin, widow
1774 ,, Elinor, Birr, King's County
1640 ,, Henry, Drogheda, merchant
1672 ,, John, St. Sepulchre's parish, Middlesex, gent.
1731 ,, John, Cloode, co. Sligo, gent.
1772 ,, John, clk., doctor in divinity
1801 ,, John, North Strand, Dublin, gent.
1802 ,, John, Dublin, merchant
1810 ,, John, Downpatrick, co. Down, esq.
1765 ,, Oliver, Bullickmiron, Queen's County
1781 ,, Patrick, Dylomeid, co. Sligo
1787 ,, Richd., Francis-street, Dublin, merchant
1597 ,, Thomas, capt. and serjt.-major-general of the army
1747 ., Thomas, Dublin, merchant
1608 ,, William, Drogheda, merchant
1658 **Bretton**, Francis, of the Protector's own troop of horse (Original in Dubl. Consl. Coll.) [VII. 46 [See BRITTON.]
1683 **Brettridge**, Roger, Castlebrettridge, co. Cork, esq.
1802 **Brevitor**, Mary, Ringsend
1806 ,, Robert, Ringsend, co. Dublin, lieut. of Invalids
1773 **Brew**, Philip, Dublin, watch maker
1692 ,, William, East Acton, Middle-sex, tailor (Copy)
1685 **Brewer**, Albertus, Limerick, mer-chant
1740 **Brewster**, Elizth., wife of John B., Ballycarnan, Queen's Co.
1740 ,, sir Francis, city of Westminster, knt.
1758 ,, Samuel, Ballywilliamroe, co. Carlow, farmer
1734 ,, Wm., Shandon Park, co. Cork, gent.
1668 **Brey**, Elizabeth, *alias* **Mathews**, London, widow [See BRAY]
1684 **Brian**, P. Patrick, Grais (Gray's ?) Inn, Middlesex, esq., and of Dublin [IX. 114 [See BRYAN.]
1751 ., Thomas, esq. (Copy)

1739 **Brice**, Anastace, Dublin, widow
1742 ,, Edward, Belfast, esq.
1809 ,, Edward, Kilbroe, co. Antrim, esq. (Copy)
1672 ,, Martin, Balharry, gent.
1707 ,, Penelope, Dublin, widow
1697 ,, Randall, Lisburne, co. Antrim, esq.
1688 ,, Richard, Newtown Fermon-fechan, co. Louth, gent.
1794 **Brickell**, Frances, Carrickmacross, co. Monaghan, spinster
1762 ,, James, Carrickmacross, county Monaghan
1751 **Brickenden**, William, Dublin, gent.
1703 **Briddock**, Robert, Rorystown, co. Meath, gent.
1808 **Bride**, Patrick, city of Dublin, esq.
1785 ,, William, Dublin
1791 **Bridge**, Elizabeth, Plantation, co. Down, spinster
1809 ,, Margaret, Roscrea, co. Tippe-rary, widow
1787 ,, Timothy, Ashbury, co. Tip., esq.
1765 ,, Vizer Curtis, Roscrea, co. Tip., gent.
1763 **Bridges**, Anne, Abington, South-ampton, Hants, widow (Copy)
1702 ,, Brooke, par. of Kensington, Middlesex, esq. (Copy)
1737 ,, Brooke, parish of St. Andrew, Holborn, Middlesex, esq.
1749 ,, Catherine
1751 ,, Geo., Avington, Southampton, Hants, esq.
1712 ,, Jeremiah, Dolphin's Barn, co. Dublin, gent.
1682 ,, Richard, London, citizen and mercer (Copy)
1715 ,, Samuel, Dublin, esq.
1763 ,, Samuel, Dublin, clk., esq.
1681 ,, captain Thomas, Somerset, co. Londonderry
1774 ,, Thomas, Dublin, hosier
1717 ,, William, Tower of London, esq. (Copy)
1763 ,, William, Shramore, co. Wex-ford, esq.
1801 **Bridgeman**, Henry, Maryville, co. Clare, esq.
1658 **Bridgman**, Frances, Ballyheggan, widow
1795 ,, William, Limerick, gent.
1643 ,, Winter, Drumkevan, co. Clare, esq.
1678 **Bridgen**, Elizabeth, Stone House, co. Waterford, widow
1673 **Bridgin**, Humphry, Clonmore, co. Kilkenny, gent.

1724 **Bridou**, Charles De Bosleroy
1729 **Brien**, Dennis, Ballinhinchy, county Tipperary, gent.
1797 ,, Edward, Rathrone, co. Meath
1797 ,, Martin, Buckridges-court, Dublin, gent.
1639 ,, Mathew, Limerick, merchant
1802 ,, Mathew, Tankardstown, co. Meath
1784 ,, Michael, New-street, Dublin, carpenter
1806 ,, Patrick, Cloagh, co. Wicklow, farmer
1809 ,, Patk., Brownstown, co. Meath, farmer
[See BRYAN.]
1777 **Brierly**, Edw., Roscrea, co. Tipperary, gent.
1735 **Brigdall**, Hugh, Inch, co. Clare, gent.
1781 **Briggs**, Alice, *alias* **Hall**, Cappa, co. Galway, widow
1789 ,, Alice, Roscommon, widow
1762 ,, Benj., Castletown, co. Westmeath
1776 ,, John, Cartenomoire, co. Westmeath, gent.
1787 ,, William, Castletown, co. Westmeath, gent.
1659 **Bright**, Margaret, Londonderry, widow   [**XII.** 190
1719 **Brightwell**, Thomas, parish of St. Andrew, Holborn, Middlesex, gent.
1589 **Brinicham**, Thos., Galway, mercht.
[**I.** 63
1728 **Brindley**, Anne, Dublin, widow
1674 **Brinknell**, Ralph, St. Patrick-st., distiller
1724 **Brinley**, Benj., Dublin, mercht.
1639 **Brinnesley**, Gervas, Belturbet, co. Cavan, esq.   [cary
1664 **Brinsmead**, Saml., Dublin, apothe-
1719 **Briscoe**, Elizabeth, Dublin, widow
1762 ,, Elizabeth, Ballycowen, King's County, spr.
1736 ,, Henry, Tybraughny, co. Kilkenny, esq.
1808 ,, Henry, Tinvane, co. Tipperary, esq.
1752 ,, John, Garrynerchy, co. Kilkenny, gent.
1785 ,, John, Arden, King's Co., gent.
1797 ,, Paul, town of Trim
1759 ,, Ralph, Ralihan, King's Co., esq.
1719 ,, Temple, Dublin, esq.
1775 ,, William, Crogan, King's Co.
1681 **Brisse** or **Brissie**, Francis, Dromore, co. Donegal, esq.

1803 **Bristol**, right hon. Frederick, earl of, and bishop of Derry
1684 **Bristow**, John, Dublin, mercht.
1704 ,, Peter, col. of regt. commanded by the Earl of Donegal
1769 ,, rev. Peter, city of Bath, clk.
1745 ,, Roger, town of Antrim
1810 ,, Roger, Baggot-st., Dubl., esq.
1789 ,, Samuel, Birch-hill, co. Antrim, esq.
1809 ,, rev. William, vicar of Belfast
1617 **Britas** or **Brites**, Edward, servant to Lord Deputy St. John
1763 **Britt**, Thomas, Ballon, co. Carlow, gent.
1695 **Britten**, John, late of Coolroe, co. Wexford, now of Dublin, yeoman
1773 **Britton**, Elizabeth, Dublin, widow (1774)
1790 ,, Elizth., *alias* **Collins**, wid.
1726 ,, John, Dublin, gent. (contents of his will)
1751 ,, John, Dublin
1790 ,, Winifred, Belvedere Parish, co. Wexford
[See BRETTON, BRITTEN.]
1730 **Broadhurst**, John, Fleet-street, Dublin
1756 ,, John, Dublin, gent.
1719 ,, Joseph, Dublin, ribbon weaver
1737 ,, Joseph, Antigua, America
1707 **Broadripp**, Samuel
1747 **Brocas**, Gabriel, Dublin
1803 ,, Georgina
1770 ,, rev. Theophilus
1804 ,, rev. Theophilus
1783 **Brock**, Aungier, Battstown, co. Westmeath, esq.
1790 ,, Denis, Shean, co. Kildare
1698 ,, Edward, Dublin, carpenter
1660 ,, Elnathan, Dublin, seedsman
[**VIII.** 84
1698 ,, Mary, Dublin, widow
1786 ,, Nicholas, city of Dublin
1787 ,, Sarah, Dublin, widow
1661 **Brocket**, col. Wm., Castlepark, co. Cork, esq. (Copy)
1798 **Brocklesby**, Richd., Norfolk-street, Middlesex, M.D.
1714 ,, Thomas, Cork, clothier
1773 ,, Thos., Ballintemple, South Lib. of Cork, gent.
1751 **Brockton**, John, mariner
1804 **Broderick**, Eleanor, South King-st., Dublin, widow
1786 ,, rev. Laurence, rector of Callan, co. Kilkenny
1712 ,, sir St. John, Ballyanon, co. Cork, knt. (Large Will)

1728 **Broderick**, St. John, Middleton, co. Cork, esq
1804 ,, William, Donnybrook-road
1788 **Broders**, Wm., Dolphin's Barn-lane, farmer
1714 **Brodie**, Wm., A. M., late of Cavan, now of Dublin
1749 ,, William, major in regt. commanded by col. B. Hope
1756 **Brodigan**, Nicholas, John-street, Drogheda
1795 **Brofield**, rev. Somerset, Dubl., clk.
1756 **Brogan**, Bridget, wife of Peter B. of Athlone, surgeon
1804 ,, John, Cullen, co. Westmeath, grazier
1799 ,, Margaret, Athlone, co. Westmeath, spinster
1805 ,, Nichs., Walshestown, co. Westmeath, gent.
1707 **Brogdon**, Elizabeth, *als.* **Jackson**, Dublin, widow
1698 ,, Samuel, Glannaheltie, co. Tipperary, gent.
1677 **Broghall**, Wm., co. Dublin, farmer
1718 **Brograne**, Henry, quarter-master in brig. Croft's regt. dragoons
1682 **Bromby**, Nicholas, Newcastle, co. Limerick, gent.
1710 ,, Thomas, esq.
1617 **Brome**, William, Glassnevan, co. Dublin, gent.
1682 **Bromfield**, Humphry, Portnehinch, King's County, gent.
      [See BROOMFIELD.]
1655 **Bromidge**, Thomas, Yardley, Worcestershire   [V. 242
1750 **Bronsdon**, Mary, Blackheath, Kent, widow. (Copy)
1750 ,, Peter, Deptford, Kent, shipwright (Copy)
1800 **Brook**, Jane, Newpark, co. Antrim
1656 **Brooke**, Anne   [VI. 45
1702 ,, Arthur, Lisburne, surgeon
1737 ,, Arthur, Waterford, surgeon
1633 ,, sir Basil, knt., Donegal
1696 ,, Basil, Killodonnell, co. Donegal, esq. (Ex.)
1768 ,, Basil, formerly of Brookhill, co. Donegal, but now of Dubl.
1731 ,, Docura, Newbridge, co. Dubl., esq.
1738 ,, Edward, Dublin, esq.
1695 ,, Francis, Lisburne, co. Antrim, M.D.
1800 ,, Francis, Colebrooke, co. Fermanagh, esq.
1800 ,, Gustavus, Dublin, esq.
1671 ,, sir Henry, Donegal, knt. [esq.
1724 ,, Henry, Brookhill, co. Donegal,

1761 **Brooke**, Henry, Dublin, esq.
1786 ,, Henry, Gt. George's-st., co. Dublin, esq.
1808 ,, Henry V., co. Donegal
1649 ,, John, soldier in col. John Reynold's troop
1775 ,, John, Brocas, co. Fermanagh, gent.
1763 ,, Letitia, Dublin, widow
1696 ,, Margery, Dublin, widow
1744 ,, Oliver, London, esq.
1635 ,, Richard, New-row, Dublin, beer brewer
1731 ,, Sarah, Dublin, widow
1695 ,, Thos., Kellystown, co. Meath, esq.
1805 ,, rev. Wm., city of Dublin, clk.
1686 **Brookeing**, Richard, Dublin, gent.
1681 **Brookes**, Ann, Limerick, widow
1718 ,, Francis, Clough, co. Wexford, gent.
1684 ,, George, London, gent. (Copy)
1654 ,, John
1705 ,, John, Dublin, tanner
1710 ,, Thomas, Dublin, mercht.
1788 **Brooks**, Thomas, Palmerstown, co. Dublin
1758 ,, William, the younger, Dublin, baker
1779 **Broom**, George
1809 **Broomfield**, Scoot, Green Park, co. Down, esq.
1639 ,, Wm., Catherlogh, innholder
      [See BROMFIELD, BRUMFIELD.]
1745 **Broown**, Thomas, lieut. in brigadier Cornwallis's regt. of foot
1784 **Brophey**, John, Cornmarket, Dubl., linen draper
1785 ,, William, The Liberty, Dublin, woolcomber
1810 **Brophy**, John, High-street, Dublin, woollen draper
1790 **Broske**, Harriett, Gt. Georges's-st., Dublin, spinster
1809 **Brosnahan**, John, city of Cork, butter mercht.
1800 **Brossy**, James, Rathdangan, co. Wicklow, farmer
1701 **Broughall**, Anne, Clonsillagh, co. Dublin, widow
1784 ,, Edward, Eccles-street, Dublin
1710 ,, Thomas, Dublin, gent.
1746 **Broughton**, Charles, Dublin, esq.
1756 ,, John, Drogheda, alderman
1777 ,, Mary, relict of Robt. Broughton
1777 ,, Mary, Peter-st., Dublin, widow
1678 ;, Richard, Scribblestown, co. Dublin, esq.
1774 ,, Richard, Dublin, gent.
1777 ,, Robert, town of Galway

1738 **Broughton**, Roger, Killougea, Clough, King's County, gent.
1797 **Brouncker**, Elizabeth, Howland-st., London, widow [See BRUNKER.]
1751 **Brow**, Thomas, Blessington, co. Wicklow, farmer
1783 **Brown**, Abraham, Aughidowey, co. Derry, gent.
1775 ,, Aeils, Moore-st., Dubl., widow
1752 ,, Alexander, Dublin, merchant
1797 ,, Alexander David, Ranelagh, co. Dublin
1709 ,, Andrew, Dublin, tobacconist
1734 ,, Ann, Dublin, widow
1737 ,, Ann, Castle B., co. Kildare, spinster [XXXVII. 120
1654 ,, Anne, *als.* **Woods**, Dundalk, widow
1789 ,, Anne, Gloves, co. Galway, widow
1794 ,, Anne, Felly, co. of city of Dub., spinster
1790 ,, Anthy., Bridesheam, co. Meath
1793 ,, Anthony, Killough, co. Westmeath, esq.
1800 ,, Arthur, Gloucester-st., Dublin
1809 ,, Barbara, city of Londonderry, widow
1796 ,, Catherine, Dublin, spinster
1797 ,, Charles, Galway town
1797 ,, Christr., Galway town, mercht.
1740 ,, Daniel, Kilnecourt, Queen's County, esq.
1796 ,, Dodwell, Rahins, co. Mayo, esq.
1774 ,, Dominick, Kilticulla, co. Mayo, esq.
1777 ,, Dominick, Breafy, co. Mayo
1731 ,, Edward, city of Norwich, esq.
1773 ,, Edward, Landsdown Hill, Somersetshire, esq. (Copy)
1778 ,, rev. Edward, Brookbridge, co. Cork, clk.
1749 ,, Elizabeth, widow
1745 ,, Francis, Grangebeg, co. Kildare, gent.
1777 ,, Francis, Dublin, merchant
1737 ,, George, Neale, co. Mayo, esq.
1782 ,, hon. George, Claremont, co. Mayo, esq.
1785 ,, Hannah, Dublin, widow
1798 ,, Hannah, Summerhill, co. Dub., widow
1786 ,, Henry, Bedford-street, Dublin, gent.
1791 ,, Ignatius, city of Dublin
1710 ,, James, Drumcondra, co. Dub., yeoman
1733 ,, James Fitz Bartholomew, Galway, merchant

1742 **Brown**, James, par. St. Martin-in-the-Fields, Middlesex, tailor
1743 ,, James, Dublin, gent.
1763 ,, James, deputy storekeeper, His Majesty's stores, Dublin
1772 ,, Jas., Clonohard, co. Longford
1782 ,, James, Drumcondra, co. Dub., gent.
1782 ,, James, Limerick, merchant
1786 ,, James, city of Dublin, esq.
1792 ,, Jas., Bailyborough, co. Cavan, gent. [Cork
1797 ,, rev. Jemmell, Riverstown, co.
1712 ,, John, The Neal, co. Mayo, esq.
1732 ,, John, Kilpatrick, co. Westmeath, late of the Post, of Dublin
1734 ,, John, Clongoweswood, co. Kildare, esq. (Admon. W. Ann)
1751 ,, John, Thomas-street, Dublin, card maker
1751 ,, John, Tullamore, King's Co., gent.
1760 ,, John, Harristown, King's County
1773 ,, John, Belfast, co. Antrim, merchant
1781 ,, John, Ballynockan, co. Carlow
1791 ,, John, Dublin, grocer
1795 ,, John, Portarlington, Queen's County
1796 ,, rev. St. John, LL.D., Bandon, co. Cork
1797 ,, John, Waterford, merchant
1802 ,, John, Petershill, Belfast, esq.
1807 ,, John, city of Londonderry
1808 ,, John, Ballyraggen, co. Kildare, farmer
1809 ,, John, Jervais-st., Dub., mercht.
1811 ,, John, Mountbrown, co. Limerick, esq.
1794 ,, rev. Joshua, vicar, Castle Lyons, co. Cork
1761 ,, Julia, Galway, spinster
1764 ,, Margaret, Dublin
1765 ,, Margaret, Dublin, widow
1791 ,, Margaret, Galway, spinster
1794 ,, Margaret, Strand-st., Dublin, widow
1808 ,, Margt., wife of Joseph Brown, Dublin, merchant
1790 ,, Martin, Clonfad, co. Roscommon, gent.
1790 ,, Mary, *alias* **Robinson**, Ballymena, county Tyrone, widow
1793 ,, Mary, Galway, spinster
1797 ,, Mary, *alias* **Graydon**, Glenmore, co. Dublin, widow
1787 ,, Mathew, Burton, Pembrokeshire, S. Wales

1711	**Browne**, Joan, late of Ardagh, co. Kerry, now of Thomastown, co. Tipperary, widow	
1581	,,	John, Dublin
1616	,,	John, Dublin, merchant, Neilstown, co. Dublin
1627	,,	John Fitz Henry, Waterford
1629	,,	John, Geygostown, co. Kildare, gent.
1652	,,	John, Dublin, distiller
1665	,,	John, Dublin, gent.
1679	,,	captain John, Macetown, co. Meath
1680	,,	John, Naas, co. Kildare, gent.
1693	,,	John, Clongoeswood, co. Kildare, esq.
1704	,,	John, Dublin, gent.
1709	,,	John, Ballivaconig, co. Kerry, gent.
1727	,,	John, Mullingar, gent.
1729	,,	John, Ballynagallagh, county Limerick, gent.
1746	,,	rev. John, chancellor St. Mary's Cathedral, Limerick
1755	,,	John, Cork, revenue officer
1758	,,	rev. John, Carlow, clk.
1762	,,	John, Dublin, merchant.
1765	,,	John, Clunkelly, co. Galway, gent.
1768	,,	John, Dublin, linen weaver
1773	,,	John, Drogheda, aledraper (*i.e.* ale-house keeper)
1797	,,	John, Waterford, merchant
1803	,,	John, Maheraha, co. Down, linen draper
1806	,,	John, Merville, co. Antrim
1714	,,	Joseph, Castle Hill, co. Down, gent. [widow
1729	,,	Julia, *alias* **Bellew**, Dublin,
1742	,,	Julia, Dublin, spinster
1762	,,	Laurence, Dublin, merchant
1734	,,	Margaret, Leighlin Bridge, co. Carlow, widow
1760	,,	Margery, Galway, widow
1753	,,	Martin, Kilskeagh (Not proved)
1645	,,	dame Mary, *alias* **Plunkett**, Balanamore, co. Longford
1651	,,	Mary, Dunshaghlin, widow
1671	,,	Mary, Clonbrocke, co. Galway, widow
1721	,,	Mary, Cork, widow
1759	,,	Mathias, Dublin, silversmith
1632	,,	Michael, Dublin, merchant
1740	,,	Michael, Galway, late of Nantz, merchant [farmer
1802	,,	Michael, Skiddew, co. Dublin,
1810	,,	Michael, Rockville, co. Galway
1595	,,	Nichs., Keranstown, co. Dublin
1639	,,	Nicholas, Culchene, co. Kerry, esq. (Copy)

1670	**Browne**, Nicholas, Dublin, gent.	
1810	,,	Nicholas, Ballinabarney, co. Limerick, farmer
1754	,,	Patrick, Duke-street, Dublin
1754	,,	Peter, Kockville, co. Mayo
1670	,,	Phœbe, Limerick, widow
1766	,,	Rebecca, widow of Mathew B., Shrewl, co. Galway, esq.
1615	,,	Richard, Dublin, merchant
1642	,,	sir Richard, Ballanamore, co. Longford, bart. (Copy)
1667	,,	Richard, Dublin, gent.
1806	,,	Richard, Coolcower, co. Cork, esq.
1678	,,	Robert, Catherlogh, esq.
1769	,,	Robt., Downpatrick, co. Down
1656	,,	Roger [**V.** 262
1663	,,	sir Silvester, Dublin, bart.
1636	,,	Stephen, Ballyrenal, co. Down, gent.
1722	,,	Stephen, Dublin, gent.
1767	,,	Stephen Fitz Williams, **Castle** B., co. Kildare, esq.
1609	,,	Tamasuye, lady of Hospital
1764	,,	Temperance [Cork
1658	,,	lieut. Timothy, Roscarbery, co.
1621	,,	Thos., Clondalkin, co. Dublin
1626	,,	Thomas, Waterford, merchant
1661	,,	Thos., Kinsale, mercht. [**IX.** 32
1663	,,	Thos., esq., Hospital, co. Limk.
1677	,,	Thomas, London, esq.
1685	,,	Thomas, Gorteenroe, co. Cork, esq.
1686	,,	Thos., Hospital, co. Limerick, esq. (Ex.)
1687	,,	Thomas, Dublin, esq.
1694	,,	Thomas, Dublin, esq.
1719	,,	Thos., Charles Fort, co. Cork, esq.
1729	,,	Thomas, Cork, alderman
1730	,,	Thomas, Strabane, co. Tyrone, merchant
1759	,,	Thomas, Moyne, co. Galway
1760	,,	Thomas, Ballydonagh, co. Wicklow, esq.
1766	,,	Thomas, Athlone, co. Westmeath, merchant
1772	,,	Thomas, Dublin, gent.
1780	,,	Thomas, Newgrove, co. Clare
1802	,,	Thomas, captain, Royal Clan Alpin regt.
1803	,,	Thomas, Graigs, co. Kild., esq.
1681	,,	Tobias, Currahine, co. Cork, gent.
1753	,,	Ulick, Slane, co. Meath, gent
1733	,,	Valentine, Cork, gent.
1735	,,	Valentine, Galway, merchant
1618	,,	Walter, Kilpatrick, co. Westmeath, gent.
1623	,,	Walter, Dublin, shoemaker

1689 **Browne**, Walter, Stoneybatter, sub. of Dublin, merchant
1603 ,, Wm., Neale, co. Mayo, gent.
1681 ,, William, Weston, Montgomeryshire, esq.
1720 ,, Wm., London, mercht. (Copy)
1734 ,, William, Dublin, tobacconist
1765 ,, Wm., son to Rodk. B., late of Edinburgh
1796 **Browning**, Hercules, Summerhill, co. Clare, esq.
1772 ,, Jeffry, Youghal, co. Cork, gent.
1757 ,, Richd., Affane, co. Waterford, gent.
1719 ,, Robert, Waterford, mariner
1783 ,, Samuel, Affane, co. Waterford, gent.
1658 ,, William (the elder), Glanmorishmeen, county Wicklow, gent. [**VII**. 90
1724 ,, Wm., Oldaffane, co. Waterford
1792 ,, William (Copy)
1711 **Brownlow**, Arthur, *alias* **Chamberlaine**, B'derry, co. Armagh, esq.
1808 ,, Catherine, city Dublin, widow
1728 ,, Jas., Arbor Hill, Dublin, gent.
1683 ,, John, Dundalk, gent., corporal
1805 ,, Mary, *alias* **Whitsitt**, *alias* **Hamilton**
1739 ,, William, Brownloues, Derry, co. Armagh, esq.
1794 ,, right hon. William
1721 **Brownlowe**, Janes, relict of Arthur B., Lurgan, co. Armagh, esq.
1716 ,, John, *alias* **Chamberlaine**, Nisleiath, co. Louth
1716 ,, Standish, esq.
1660 ,, sir Wm., Brownelowes, Derry, co. Armagh, knt.
1807 **Brownly**, Grace [gent.
1803 ,, Martin, Usher's-quay, Dublin,
1757 ,, William, Dublin, apothecary
1790 **Brownrigg**, Abraham, Rahinduff, co. Wexford
1754 ,, Anna Cath., *alias* **Cross**
1763 ,, Benj., Unrigar, co. Wicklow, gent.
1790 ,, Edmond, Richmond, co. Waterford, esq.
1759 ,, George, Dublin, merchant
1723 ,, Henry, Wingfield, co. Wexford, gent.
1741 ,, Henry, Ballinglan, co. Wicklow, gent.
1795 ,, Henry, city of Dublin, esq.
1799 ,, Henry, Wingfield, co. Wexford, esq.
1800 ,, Henry, Ballywater, co. Wexford, esq.

1760 **Brownrigg**, Isabella, Dublin, widow
1805 ,, Isabella, widow
1740 ,, Jane, Wingfield, co. Wexford, widow
1792 ,, John, formerly of Jamaica, late of Dublin, esq.
1797 ,, John, Dublin, barrister-at-law
1792 ,, Lydia, Dublin, widow
1772 ,, Robt. Maghlin, Dublin, haberdasher (Not proved)
1805 ,, rev. Theobald, John Ville, co. Kilkenny
1696 ,, Thomas, Logan, co. Wexford
1750 ,, Thos., Wingfield, co. Wexford, gent.
1778 ,, Thomas, Dublin, gent.
1802 ,, Thomas, Tubberpatrick, co. Wicklow, esq.
1808 ,, Thos., Medop Hall, co. Wexfd.
1724 ,, Wm., Oldaffane, co. Waterford, esq.
1789 ,, William, Brownhill, co. Wexford, gent.
1758 **Bruce**, Jonathan, dean of Kilfenora
1744 ,, Katherine, *alias* **Stewart**, Dungannon, county Tyrone, widow
1807 ,, Rose, Dublin, widow
1755 ,, William, Dublin
1628 **Brudenell**, Edmond (the elder), Stoke Mandevile, Bucks, and Killelagh, co. Limk., esq.
1772 ,, Francis, Ballyguile, co. Limerick, gent.
1798 **Bruen**, Catherine, Dublin, spinster
1700 ,, Henry, Dublin, gent.
1796 ,, Henry, Oak Park, co. Carlow, esq.
1757 ,, Moses, Boyle
1775 **Brumfield**, Humphry, Campelone, Queen's County, farmer
1794 ,, Joseph, Iry, Queen's Co., gent. [See BROOMFIELD.]
1669 **Brumwell**, Robert, Dublin, gent.
1710 **Brun**, Peter, Dublin, periwig maker
1766 **Brunell**, Saml., Dublin, shoemaker
1707 **Brunetti**, Francis, city of Florence, at present in London (Copy)
1741 **Bruniquel**, Jane, Dublin
1783 **Brunkard**, Jane, Stephen-street, Dublin, widow
1799 **Brunker**, Ralph, Coothill, county Cavan, gent.
1808 ,, Thomas, Belgreen, co. Cavan [See BROUNCKER.]
1741 **Brunton**, Anthony, Dublin, mercht.
1773 ,, Charity, Drogheda, widow
1733 ,, Elizabeth, Dublin, widow
1757 ,, Mary, Dublin, widow
1806 ,, William, Dub., tallow chandler

1712 **Brunts**, Samuel, Mansfield, Not-
        tinghamshire, gent.
1737 **Brunyer**, James, Dublin
1760 **Brush**, John, Kilrush, co. West-
        meath, gent.
1774 ,,   Rowland, Collon, co. Louth
1801 **Bryan**, Arthur, city of Dub., mercht.
1755 ,,   Barnaby, Ballynaclough, co.
        Westmeath, esq.
1786 ,,   Bridget, Patrick-st., Kilkenny
1598 ,,   Chaplen, sir Laurence
1736 ,,   Edward, Patrick's Close, Dub.,
        weaver
1776 ,,   Edward, Hopestown, farmer
1752 ,,   Frans., Smithfield, salesmaster
                        [XLVIII. 160
1762 ,,   Garrett, Dublin, silkweaver
1787 ,,   George, Busteagah, co. Wick-
        low, farmer
1802 ,,   George, Portland-place, Mid-
        dlesex, esq.   [County
1778 ,,   Henry, Ballinasragh, King's
1799 ,,   Henry, Dublin, esq.
1794 ,,   rev. Jacob, rector of Kilrush,
        dio. of Kildare
1630 ,,   James Fitz John, Whiteswall,
        co. Kilkenny, gent.
1747 ,,   James, Ballintemple, co. Wick-
        low, gent.
1768 ,,   Jas., Ballintemple, co. Wicklow
1770 ,,   James
1804 ,,   James, Jenkinstown, co. Kil-
        kenny, esq.
1673 ,,   John, Whiteswall, co. Kilkenny
1803 ,,   John, Park-gate, co. Dublin
1765 ,,   Josiah, Church-street, Dublin,
        merchant   [low
1805 ,,   Martin, Baltinglass, co. Wick-
1758 ,,   Oliver, Lismore, co. Waterford,
        gent.
1783 ,,   Patk., Ballyvapark, co. Wicklow
1712 ,,   Pierse, Shrule, King's County,
        esq.
1777 ,,   Pierse, Jenkinstown, co. Kil-
        kenny, esq.
1625 ,,   Randall, Youghal, co. Cork,
        gent.
1638 ,,   Ralphe, Dublin, innholder
1724 ,,   Richard, mariner
1776 ,,   Robert, rector of Desertmartin,
        co. Derry
1681 ,,   Samuel, Dublin, clk. (Copy)
1746 ,,   Samuel the younger, Dublin,
        merchant
1752 ,,   Samuel, Dublin, merchant
1769 ,,   Sarah, Dublin, widow
1792 ,,   Stephen, Dublin, gent.
1748 ,,   Thomas, Dublin, cook
                        [XLIV. 151
1801 ,,   Thomas, Wicklow

1788 **Bryan**, Walter, Ashford, co. Wick-
        low, farmer
1797 ,,   William, Dublin, merchant
        [See BREEN, BRIAN, BRIEN, BRYNE.]
1629 **Bryant**, Captain Thomas, Youghal,
        co. Cork, gent.
1802 **Bryanton**, Dorothy
1755 ,,   Richd., Ballymahon, co. Long-
        ford, merchant
1693 **Bryce**, John, Dublin, merchant
1746 **Brymer**, Henry, Dublin, merchant
1720 **Bryne**, Anthony, Dublin
1679 ,,   Barnaby, Coolock, co. West-
        meath, esq.
1604 ,,   Catherine
1748 ,,   Joseph, Balnecloonagh, co.
        Westmeath, gent.
                        [See BRYAN.]
1615 **Bryver**, James, Waterford, esq.
1800 **Buchanan**, Anne, city of Cork, widow
1807 ,,   Helena Anna
1803 ,,   John, Dublin, shoemaker
1735 ,,   Nicholas, Dublin, gent.
1802 ,,   Thomas, Fermoy, co. Cork
1720 **Buchannan**, David, Royal Hospital,
        Dublin
1783 ,,   Elizabeth, widow
1695 ,,   John, Dublin, merchant
1799 ,,   John, city of Londonderry,
        attorney-at-law
1740 **Buchart**, Henry, mariner
1656 **Bucher**, John, trooper   [VI. 38
                        [See BOOKER.]
1739 **Buchinger**, Mathew (called, 'the
        little man without hands or
        feet')
1770 **Buck**, Faith, Cork, widow
1749 ,,   Mary, par. of Ringrone, co.
        Cork
1688 ,,   Thomas, Chester, ironmonger
        (Copy)
1717 **Buckely**, Richard, Dublin, brewer
                        [See BUCKLEY.]
1714 **Buckhurst**, Sibella, Dublin, widow
1743 **Buckinghamshire** and **Normandy**,
        Katherine, duchess dowager
1760 ,,   Katherine, countess dowager
1790 **Buckley**, Daniel, Blackpool, north
        sub. of Cork, clothier
1807 ,,   Daniel, Fairview, north Liberty
        of Cork
1747 ,,   Francis, par. of Powerscourt,
        co. Wicklow
1736 ,,   Henry, Dublin, notary public
1660 ,,   John, Brownsford, co. Kilkenny
                        [VIII. 181
1779 ,,   John, Old Court, co. Dublin,
        esq.
1803 ,,   John, Creemore, co. Wexford,
        gent.

1772 **Buckley**, Mary, widow
1659 ,, Oswell, of the Poddle, Dublin, tanner [**VIII.** 39
1742 ,, Thos., Pursellstown, co. Louth, gent.
[See BUCKELY, BULKELEY.]
1781 **Bucknall**, Charles, Dublin, esq.
1685 ,, Richard, Dublin, gent.
1671 **Bucknor**, John, Limerick, gent.
1700 ,, Wm., Coolefin, co. Waterford, esq.
1798 **Buckton**, Arthur, Sandymount, co. Dublin
1626 ,, Thomas, Limerick, miller
1664 **Buckworth**, Anthonie V., of Louth, and rector of Killencoole
1662 ,, Anthony, Eline, Isle of Ely, gent.
1688 ,, sir John, London, knt. (Copy)
1759 ,, John, Ballycummusk, co. Tipperary, esq.
1692 ,, Sarah, Portadown, co. Armagh, widow
1799 **Budd**, Benjamin, city of Waterford, esq.
1795 ,, Tobias, city of Waterford, gent.
1671 **Buddleston**, Edward, Kilcocke, co. Kildare
1778 **Budds**, Benjamin, Garrah, Queen's County, gent.
1723 **Budgell**, William, Dublin, esq.
1704 **Bulamor**, Elizabeth, Dublin, widow
1743 **Bulkeley**, Adrian, Dubl., merchant
1654 ,, Alice, widow of Lancelot, Archbishop of Dublin [**V.** 34
1754 ,, Ann, Rathdrum, co. Wicklow, widow
1734 ,, Jane, Dublin, widow
1699 ,, John, Dublin, esq.
1685 ,, sir Richard, Old Bawn, co. Dublin, bart.
1706 ,, Richard, Dublin, tailor
1717 ,, Richard, Dublin, brewer
1753 ,, Thomas, Dublin, clk.
1671 ,, William, Old Bawn, co. Dubl., D.D., Archdeacon of Dublin [See BUCKLEY.]
1698 **Bull**, Anne, Dublin, widow
1788 ,, Edward, Grange, Liberty of Waterford, esq.
1760 ,, Jane, Dublin, spinster
1741 ,, John, Limerick, burgess
1738 ,, Nathaniel, Grenanstown, co. Meath, esq.
1785 ,, Priscilla, city of Gloucester, spinster
1718 ,, Saml., Grenanstown, co. Meath, gent.
1771 ,, Sarah, Dublin, spinster
1745 ,, William, Dublin, gent.

1767 **Bull**, William, William-st., Dublin
1778 ,, William, George's-quay, Dubl., grocer
1747 **Bullard**, Joseph
1702 ,, Nicholas, Dublin, merchant
1734 **Bullen**, Catherine, Kilroe, co. Cork, widow
1745 ,, Edward, Old Head, co. Cork, gent.
1790 ,, rev. Richd., Corkbeg, co. Cork, clk.
1741 ,, rev. Thomas, Dublin, clk.
1755 ,, Wm., Tinnehinch, co. Wicklow, gent.
1666 **Buller**, John, colonel
1629 **Bullet**, Edmond, Dublin, gent.
1698 **Bullinbrooke**, John the elder, Galway, professor of surgery and practitioner in the science of physic
1757 **Bullingbrooke**, Hannah, Dublin, widow
1729 ,, rev. John, Castlereagh, co. Roscommon, clk.
1772 ,, Mary, Dublin, spinster
1773 ,, William, Dublin, clk.
1785 **Bullock**, Ezikiel, Greenhill, co. Down, gent.
1738 ,, Jane, Dublin, widow
1726 ,, John, Dublin, timber merchant
1682 ,, Thomas, Clonmel, gent.
1716 **Bunbury**, Benjamin, Killerick, co. Carlow, esq.
1747 ,, Benjamin, Carlow town, gent.
1766 ,, Benjamin, Kilfeacal, co. Tipperary, esq.
1792 ,, Benjamin, esq.
1810 ,, Benjamin, Johnstown, co. Kilkenny, esq.
1735 ,, Elizabeth, formerly dame Elizabeth Irwin, Dublin
1682 ,, Henry, Dublin, merchant
1742 ,, John, Cork, merchant
1766 ,, John, Mallow
1730 ,, Joseph, Johnstown, co. Cather. esq.
1769 ,, Jos., Kilfeacal, co. Tipperary, gent.
1711 ,, Mary, widow of Benjamin B., co. Carlow, esq.
1733 ,, Mathew, Kilfeacal, co. Tipperary, esq.
1776 ,, Mathew, Lismore, co. Waterford, esq.
1797 ,, Priscilla, Dublin, widow
1791 ,, Robert, Portarlington
1682 ,, Thomas, Ballyseskin, co. Wexford, clk.
1773 ,, Thos., Tip., esq.
1781 ,, Thos., Dublin, esq.

1781 **Bunbury**, Thos., Kill, co. Carlow, esq. (Large)
1791 ,, Thos., Clontarf, co. Dublin, esq.
1793 ,, Thos., Castle Martyr, co. Cork, clk.
1690 ,, Walter, Dublin, gent.
1710 ,, Wm., Lisnerragh, co. Carlow, gent.
1755 ,, Wm., Lisnevagh, co. Carlow, esq.
1776 ,, Wm., Mount William, co. Tipperary, esq.
1804 **Bunker**, John, city of Dublin [See BRUNKER.]
1672 **Bunthing**, Anthony, Ballinderry, co. Antrim, yeoman
1720 **Buntin**, John, Cole's lane, Bellowr.
1796 **Bunworth**, Elizabeth, city of Cork, spr.
1752 ,, rev. Peter
1727 ,, Richd., Newmarket, co. Cork, gent.
1756 **Burches**, rev David, Dublin, clerk
1778 ,, rev. Jones, rector of St. Marks, Dublin
1810 **Burden**, Henry, Lisburn, late of Calcutta, E. Indies
1788 ,, Robert, Lisburn, co. Antrim, linendraper
1768 **Burdet**, Arthur, Dublin, esq.
1727 ,, sir Thos., Garryhill, co. Cather, bart.
1797 **Burdett**, Arthur, Bellavilla, co. Kildare, esq. (Large)
1810 ,, Elizabeth, city of Dublin, spinster
1741 ,, George, Ballywalter, co. Tipperary, esq.
1726 ,, rev. John, dean of Clonfert
1809 ,, Robert, city of Limerick, esq.
1701 ,, Thomas, Gareahill, co. Carlow, esq.
1772 **Burdon**, Catherine, widow
1765 ,, Francis, Cloney, co. Clare, esq.
1732 ,, Wm., surgeon of His Majesty's Yacht 'Dublin'
1720 **Bureau**, John, native of Rochelle and refugee for cause of religion, now of Dublin, merchant
1700 **De Bures**, Chas. de Bethencourt, Portarlington, Queen's County, gent.
1798 **Burge**, Henry, city of Dublin
1736 **Burges**, Alice, London, widow
1732 ,, Ambrose, Ringsend, near Dublin, merchant
1668 ,, Roger, Dublin, esq.
1799 **Burgess**, Francis, Drogheda, tanner

1804 **Burgess**, Henry, Dublin, saddler
1790 ,, John, city of Armagh, esq.
1800 ,, Margt., Banbridge, co. Down, widow
1762 ,, Thomas, Coolrake, co. Kildare
1679 ,, William, Leirath, co. Kilkenny, esq.
1751 ,, William, City-quay, Dublin, anchor smith
1760 ,, William, Dublin
1794 ,, William
1761 **Burgh**, Anne
1801 ,, Anne, widow
1767 ,, Jane, Newcastle, co. Limerick, widow
1756 ,, John, Ballyline, co. Limerick, gent.
1767 ,, rev. John, clk., vicar of Donomoine, co. Monaghan
1739 ,, Richard, Drumkeen, co. Limerick, clk.
1763 ,, Richard, Dublin, esq.
1770 ,, Richard, rector of Tipperary, but in Dublin
1633 ,, Robert, Dublin, gent.
1785 ,, Robert, Bengal, East Indies (Copy)
1711 ,, Thomas, esq.
1731 ,, Thomas, Dublin, esq.
1747 ,, Thomas, Dromkeen, co. Limerick
1758 ,, Thomas, Bert, co. Kildare, esq.
1759 ,, Thomas, Old Town, co. Kildare, esq.
1810 ,, Thomas, Sackville-st., Dublin, esq.
1731 ,, William, Cullinagh, co. Limerick
1744 ,, William, Dublin, esq.
1809 ,, William, Bootham, suburbs of York, esq. (Copy)
1752 **Burgin**, Martha, the Comb, Dublin, widow
1795 **Burgoyne**, rev. Thomas, Lifford, co. Donegal
1753 **Burjand**, John, Kilmollog, King's County, esq.
1800 **Burk**, Redmond, Garrymore, co. Galway
1797 ,, Thomas, Kilkreeverily, co. Galway, gent.
1765 **Burke**, Ann, *alias* **Sap**, *alias* **Casey**, Dublin, widow
1810 ,, Anne, city of Dublin, widow
1773 ,, Anthony, Tomony, co. Galway (Not proved)
1782 ,, Bridget, *alias* **Laurence**, wid.
1801 ,, Catherine, Dublin, widow
1770 ,, Cisly, *alias* **Power**, Loughrea, co. Galway, widow

1749	**Burke**, David, Ballynaguana, co. Limerick, gent.	
1748	,, Dominick, Fartimore, co. Galway, esq.	
1785	,, Dominick, Dublin, esq.	
1686	,, sir Edmond, Garrnagh, co. Galway, bart.	
1688	,, Edmond, Inch, co. Kilkenny, esq.	
1740	,, Edmond, Birr, King's County, merchant	
1762	,, Edmond, Portumna, co. Galway, gent.	
1763	,, Edmond, Feantrim, esq.	
1786	,, Edmond, Meelick, co. Galway, esq.	
1779	,, Edward, co. of city of Dublin, weaver	
1802	,, Edward, lieut. in South Mayo Militia	
1784	,, Francis, Galway town, mercht.	
1810	,, Francis, Nenagh, co. Tipperary, gent.	
1766	,, Garrett, Dublin	
1741	,, Gerald, Dublin, esq.	
1635	,, Henry, Clogh, co. Galway, gent.	
1756	,, sir Henry, Glynske, co. Galway, bart.	
1805	,, Henry, Francis-street, Dublin, woollen draper	
1807	,, James, formerly of Ireland, late of Pennsylvania	
1795	,, Jane, Pimlico, Liberty of Dub., widow	
1798	,, Jeffrey McHugo, clk.	
1724	,, sir John, Milford, co. Galway, bart.	
1732	,, John, Cressoge, co. Wexford, gent.	
1741	,, John, Birr, King's County, merchant	
1748	,, John, Reaghan, co. Galway, esq.	
1751	,, John, Glanfosie, co. Galway, gent.	
1761	,, John, Newtown, co. Galway, gent.	
1773	,, John, Carntober, co. Galway, esq.	
1785	,, John, Glinsk, co. Galway	
1788	,, John, Tyaquin, co. Galway, esq.	
1792	,, John, Ower, co. Galway, gent.	
1794	,, John, Park, co. Galway, gent.	
1801	,, John, Kilskeagh, co. Galway, gent.	
1803	,, John, Queen-street, city of Cork, esq.	
1810	,, John, Iserclearan, co. Galway, esq.	

1743	**Burke**, Hon. Lady Letitia, Glinsk, co. Galway	
1772	,, Malachy (Not proved)	
1787	,, Margaret, Dublin, widow	
1757	,, Margery, *alias* **Brenan**, *alias* **Todderick**, Dublin, widow	
1767	,, Margery, Kilskeagh, co. Galway, widow	
1767	,, Mary, Birr, King's County, widow	
1778	,, Mary, Rincahy, co. Clare	
1789	,, Mary, Kimmage, co. Dublin, widow	
1791	,, Mary, Drogheda-st., Dublin, widow	
1795	,, Mary, Dublin, widow	
1801	,, Mary, Tuam	
1802	,, Mary, Dublin, spinster	
1740	,, Michael, Balladoogan, co. Galway, gent.	
1807	,, Michael, Usher's Island, merchant	
1811	,, Michael, Spring-garden, co. Galway, esq.	
1699	,, Miles, Clonluskert, co. Galway, esq.	
1781	,, Miles, Oranmore, co. Galway	
1810	,, Nicholas, town of Galway, merchant	
1772	,, Oliver, Palmerston, co. Mayo, esq. (Not proved)	
1756	,, Patrick, Dublin, carpenter	
1806	,, Patrick, Kanturk, co. Mayo	
1778	,, Peter, Lisheen, co. Galway, gent.	
1792	,, Peter, Carane, co. Galway, farmer	
1754	,, Redmond, Dublin	
1792	,, Redmond, Galway town, gent.	
1807	,, Redmond, Cappuarna, co. Galway, esq.	
1743	,, Richard, Clooncastle, co. Galway, esq. [gent.	
1758	,, Richard, Ganeven, co. Galway,	
1763	,, Richard, Dublin, gent.	
1768	,, Richard, formerly of Dublin, but of Corry, co. Galway	
1804	,, Richard, Loughrea, co. Galway, esq.	
1745	,, Theobald, Derrynacloghy, co. Galway, esq.	
1657	,, Thomas, Pallice, co. Galway, esq. [**VI**. 185	
1720	,, Thomas, Portumna, co. Galway, esq.	
1757	,, Thomas, Bacon, Mayo	
1758	,, Thomas, Ballydoogan, co. Galway, gent.	
1763	,, Thomas, Foxhall, co. Galway, gent.	

1764 **Burke**, hon. Thomas, Lackan, co. Roscommon, esq.
1765 ,, Thomas, High-street, Dublin, woollen draper
1776 ,, Thomas, city of Kilkenny, gent.
1782 ,, Thomas, Anglingham, co. Galway, esq.
1800 ,, Thomas John, city of Limerick, jeweller
1765 ,, Ulick, Cloncoe, co. Galway, gent.
1777 ,, Ulick, Creaghduff, co. Mayo, gent.
1791 ,, Ulick, Portumna, co. Galway, esq.
1724 ,, Walter, late of Dublin, now of Ballinpota, gent.
1768 ,, Walter, Creaghduff, co. Mayo
1792 ,, Walter, Kilemeer, co. Galway, shopkeeper
1803 ,, Walter Arcedekin, capt. 62nd regt. of foot
1808 ,, Walter, Roscrea, co. Tipperary
1756 ,, William, Thurles, co. Tipperary, merchant
1796 ,, rev. dr. William, parish priest of Athenree
1796 ,, William, Tuam, co. Galway, esq.
1804 ,, William, lieut. Galway Militia
1804 ,, William, Ower, gent.
1807 ,, William, city of Limerick
        [See BOORKE, BOURK, BOURKE, BURK.]
1753 **Burkitt**, John, Glynn, co. Wexford, farmer
1801 **Burland**, John, Loggan, co. Wexford
1783 **Burleigh**, David, Dublin city
1759 ,, Elizabeth, Dublin, widow
1754 ,, George, clk., curate of Carrickfergus
1752 ,, John, Portadown, co. Armagh, gent.
1783 ,, Langford, Arbor-hill, Dublin, gent.
1790 ,, Langford, Templepatrick, co. Antrim
1756 ,, Richard, Dublin, esq.
1803 ,, Ruth, widow
1753 ,, William, Dublin, attorney
1798 ,, William, Dublin, attorney-at-law
1700 **Burley**, Anne, Maghnamakenn, co. Tyrone
1736 ,, Edward, Dublin, brewer
        [See BURLEIGH.]
1704 **Burlington & Cork**, Charles, earl of (Copy)

1698 **Burlington**, Rd., earl of [**XVIII**. 53
1754 ,, Richard, earl of (Copy)
1656 **Burlton**, William, London, haberdasher [**V**. 234
1740 **Burn**, James, Dublin, carpenter
1741 ,, Mary, Athlone, widow
1739 ,, Mathew, Dublin, victualler
1772 ,, Richard, Waterford, brewer
1788 **Burne**, Anne
1760 ,, Edward
1717 ,, Luke, Dublin, distiller
1760 ,, Patrick, Drumskee, co. Down
1723 ,, William, Dublin, gent.
        [See BYRNE.]
1614 **Burnell**, Henry, Castleknock, esq.
1795 ,, Peter, Dublin, stucco plasterer
1664 ,, Richard, Garranes, co. Cork, esq.
1650 ,, William, Thomas-court, farmer
1783 **Burnes**, Oliver, Mill-street, Dublin, farmer
1707 **Burnet**, James, Dublin, saddler
1659 ,, Richard, M.D.
1799 ,, Wm., Pimlico, Dublin, woollen manufacturer
1752 **Burnett**, John, Dublin, upholsterer
1772 ,, Mary, Dublin, widow
1754 ,, Peter, Dublin, bricklayer
1755 ,, Rebecca, Dublin, spinster
1800 ,, Richd., Richmond, co. Dublin, seedman
1800 ,, Thomas, city of Cork, mercht.
1801 ,, William, Eyrecourt, co. Galway
1782 **Burniston**, William Hiram, Dublin
1762 **Burns**, James, Kilcock, co. Kildare, innkeeper
1778 ,, James, Hay's-court, Dublin, tailor
1789 ,, James, par. of Pancras, Middlesex, tailor (Copy)
1780 ,, Mary, Kilcock, co. Kildare, widow
        [See BYRNE.]
1694 **Burnside**, James, Mullagheloe, co. Louth, gent.
1688 **Buroloe**, Dennis, Dublin, gent.
1766 **Burr**, John, Monaghan town, merchant
1624 **Burrall**, John, Glanarvugh, co. Kerry, gent.
1776 **Burrell**, William, Portarlington, Queen's County, esq.
1708 **Burridge**, Ezekiel, Dublin, LL.D., clk.
1725 ,, Frances, Dublin, widow.
1802 **Burris**, John, Jidginstown, co. Kildare, farmer
1807 **Burroughs**, Catherine, Palace-row, Dublin, widow
1778 ,, Edmond, Dublin, pewterer

1798 **Burroughs**, Thomas
1771 ,, Wm., Dublin, gent.
1741 **Burrowes**, Alexander, Ardenwood, co. Kildare, esq.
1810 ,, Alexander, Cavan, co. Cavan, esq.
1809 ,, Angelina, widow
1773 ,, Ann, Dublin, spinster
1734 ,, Elizabeth, Dublin, widow
1675 ,, Ellinor, Ardenwood, co. Dublin, spinster
1663 ,, Henry, Ardenwood, co. Dublin, gent. [**IX**. 138
1663 ,, Henry, Ardenwood, co. Dublin, gent.
1702 ,, John, Lisadine, par. Crumline, co. Down, yeoman
1797 ,, John, Prospect, co. Dublin
1807 ,, John, Kilbride, co. Longford
1810 ,, Margery, city of Dub., spinster
1637 ,, or **Burrons**, Robert, Stradone, co. Cavan, esq.
1659 ,, Robert, soldier in major Ralph Wilson's compy.
1810 ,, Robert B., Kilmore, co. Cavan
1789 ,, Samuel, Dublin, apothecary
1679 ,, Thomas, Stradone, co. Cavan, gent.
1698 ,, Thomas, Kinsale, merchant
1777 ,, Thomas, Limerick, cordwainer
[See BORROWES, BURROUGHS.]
1740 **Burrows**, Elinor, *alias* **Davys**, wife to Alexander B., esq.
1623 ,, Geo., Dublin, yeoman
1807 ,, John, town of Carlow, gent.
1763 **Burscough**, Mathew
1682 **Burt**, Boyle, esq.
1689 ,, John, Coles-alley, Castle-street, tailor
1638 ,, Thomas, A. M., Dungarvan, preacher of God's Word
1745 **Burtchall**, Peter, parish of Kilteel, co. Kildare, farmer
1783 **Burtchell**, David the elder, Brownstown, co. Kildare, innkeeper
1716 **Burtham**, Henry, Dolphin's Barn, clothier
1765 **Burton**, Alice, Meelick, co. Clare, widow
1728 ,, Benjamin, Dublin, alderman
1771 ,, Catherine, widow of Robert B., esq.
1690 ,, Charles, Moyre, co. Clare, gent.
1775 ,, sir Charles, Dublin, bart.
1748 ,, Edward, Buncraggy, co. Clare, esq.
1714 ,, Francis, Buncraggy, co. Clare, esq. (Large will) (Ex.)
1744 ,, rt. hon. Francis, Buncraggy, co. Clare

1787 **Burton**, Francis, Dublin, esq.
1810 ,, James, Curras, co. Cork
1728 ,, John, Borris-in-Ossory, Queen's County
1737 ,, John, Meath-street, Dublin, weaver
1747 ,, rev. John, rector of Aghancon, King's County
1769 ,, John, Abbey-street, Dublin, painter
1793 ,, John, Dublin, esq
1747 ,, Martha, Dublin, widow
1737 ,, Mary, wife to Francis B., Buncraggy, co. Clare, esq.
1769 ,, Ralph, Hull Bank, Yorkshire, esq. (Copy)
1783 ,, Richard, Shinrone, King's County
1788 ,, Richard, Ballyman, co. Dub., esq.
1798 ,, Richard, Ballymeen, co. Dub., farmer
1765 ,, Robert, Dublin, esq.
1773 ,, Robert, Dublin, cooper
1712 ,, Samuel, Buncraggy, co. Clare, esq.
1733 ,, Samuel, Burton Hall, co. Car., esq.
1666 ,, Thomas, Lismacanagan, co. Cavan, esq.
1668 ,, Thomas, Estwicke, Shropshire, gent. (Copy)
1773 ,, Thomas, Dublin, esq.
1793 ,, Thos., Kilmacon, co. Kilkenny, clk.
1737 ,, Walter, Woodpark, co. Meath, esq.
1690 ,, William, Ballymoney, Queen's County, clk.
1747 ,, William, Feigh, King's County
1717 **Bury**, Anthony, co. Louth, gent.
1756 ,, rev. Anthony, Clonkelly, co. Tipperary, clk.
1783 ,, Anthony, Drogheda, mercht.
1731 ,, Faithfull, Haggardstown, co. Louth, gent.
1766 ,, Jane, Dublin, widow
1805 ,, Jane, city of Dub., spinster
1670 ,, John, Collaton, co. Devon, esq.
1722 ,, John, Shannon Grove, co. Limerick, esq.
1764 ,, John, Dublin, esq.
1769 ,, John, Cork
1801 ,, John, Rathmines, co. Dublin, gent.
1746 ,, Joseph, Dublin, esq. (see 1804)
1804 ,, Joseph, city of Dublin, esq.
1782 ,, Lucy, widow
1808 ,, Phineas, Little Island, co. Cork, esq.

1735 **Bury**, Richard, Mount Pleasant, co. Clare, esq.
1791 ,, Richd., Knockanree, co. Wicklow, gent.
1794 ,, Samuel, town of Wicklow
1746 ,, Thos., Commr. of the 'Solebay' man-of-war (Copy)
1774 ,, Thomas, Cork, esq.
1735 ,, William, Dublin
1765 ,, William, capt. in col. Worges' regt. of foot
1772 ,, William, Dublin, esq.
1731 **Bush**, rev. Thos., Edenderry. King's County, clk.
1747 **Bushby**, Mary, Edenderry, King's County, widow
1730 **Bushe**, Amyas, Kilfane, co. Kilkenny, esq.
1731 ,, Arthur, Cork, co. Dub., esq.
1761 ,, Arthur, Kilmurry, co. Kilkenny, esq.
1793 ,, Gervais Parker, esq.
1757 ,, Letitia, St. Ann's par., Dub.
1796 ,, rev. Thomas, College of Kingston, co. Cork
1750 ,, Wersopp, Derrynahinch, co. Kilkenny, esq.
1793 ,, William, city of Dub., esq.
1799 **Bushel**, William, Ballyvaughan, co. Tipperary, gent.
1691 **Bushell**, John, Ballynemore, co. Tipperary, gent.
1779 ,, Richard, co. of the city of Dub., gent.
1717 **Bushfield**, Thomas, Powderlogh, co. Meath, innkeeper
1774 **Busteed**, William, Cork, esq.
1793 ,, William, Dundanion, Sth. Lib. of Cork, gent.
1704 **Butler**, Abell, Kilkenny, esq.
1745 ,, Andrew, Castlebridge, co. Wexford, gent.
1770 ,, Anne, Dublin, widow
1772 ,, Anne, Waterford, widow
1792 ,, Anne, widow
1810 ,, Anne, Ballythomas, Queen's County, spinster
1596 ,, Bartholomew
1737 ,, Buckly, Kilkenny, esq.
1663 ,, Burgh, lieut. of sir Arthur Gore's foot company
1640 ,, Dame Catherine, Ballinacargy, co. Cavan, widow
1772 ,, Catherine, par. St. Mary-le-Bone, spinster
1807 ,, hon. Catherine O'Brien, widow
1777 ,, Charles, mate of the ship 'Polly,' Philadelphia
1786 ,, Deborah, spinster [rary, esq.
1628 ,, Edmond, Ardmaile, co. Tippe-

1636 **Butler**, Edmd.FitzRichard, Powlestown, co. Kilkenny, esq.
1681 ,, Edmond, Kilkenny, esq.
1696 ,, Edmond, Ballyragget, co. Kilkenny, esq.
1700 ,, Edmond, Monodubrecad, co. Tipperary, gent.
1707 ,, Edmond, Kinsale, co. Cork, gent.
1737 ,, Edmond, Dublin, woollen draper
1759 ,, Edmond, Newtown, Queen's County, esq.
1765 ,, Edmond, Kilroe, co. Tipperary
1778 ,, Edmond, Dublin, merchant
1785 ,, Edmond, Kilkenny city, esq.
1803 ,, Edmond, Kilkenny, esq., M.D.
1808 ,, Edmond O'Brien, Bansagh, co. Tipperary
1619 ,, Edward, Clonmel, merchant
1680 ,, Edward, Bramblestown, co. Kilkenny (Copy)
1736 ,, Edward, Dublin, gent.
1742 ,, Edward, Dublin, mariner
1750 ,, Edward, Laghane, co. Cork, gent
1752 ,, Edward, captain in the English fusiliers
1759 ,, Edward, Crumlin, co. Dublin, gent.
1767 ,, Edward, Loughrea, co. Galway, gent
1770 ,, Edward, Ballybar, co. Carlow, gent.
1793 ,, Edward, Dublin
1749 ,, Elinor, Waterford, widow
1680 ,, dame Elizabeth, wife to sir James B., knt., Lincoln's Inn [**XVIII.** 329
1700 ,, Elizabeth, lady, par. St. Andrew, Holborn, Middlesex (Copy)
1740 ,, Elizabeth, Dublin, widow
1778 ,, Elizabeth Teresa
1788 ,, Ellen, widow
1749 ,, Frances, Dublin, widow
1702 ,, Francis, Belturbet, co. Cavan, esq.
1713 ,, Francis, lieut. in col. Bowles' regt. of foot (Copy)
1767 ,, Francis, Courtnebooly, co. Kilkenny, esq.
1800 ,, Francis, Dunmanway, co. Cork, gent.
1752 ,, George, Ballyragget, co. Kilkenny, esq.
1798 ,, Gerald, city of Cashel, esq.
1679 ,, Gilbert, Tenehinch, co. Carlow, esq.
1730 ,, Grace, Dublin, widow
1782 ,, Helen, Cork, widow

1791	**Butler,**	Henry, Bryan's Castle, co. Clare, esq.	1692	**Butler,**	John, Cork
1779	,,	Hopton, Mt. Butler, King's County, gent.	1706	,,	John, Lincoln's Inn, Middlesex, esq. (Copy)
1737	,,	Hugh, Dublin, innkeeper	1725	,,	John, Westcourt, co. Kilkenny, esq.
1630	,,	James, Dowganstown, co. Carlow, gent.	1733	,,	John, Ballymont, co. Dublin, esq.
1704	,,	James, New Ross, co. Wexford, gent.	1749	,,	John, London, mercht. (Copy)
1704	,,	sir James, Lincoln's Inn, knt.	1754	,,	John, Dublin, shipwright
1711	,,	James, Rathdine, co. Carlow, gent.	1766	,,	John, Kilcash, co. Tipperary, esq.
1715	,,	James, Mullaghateny, co. Armagh, esq.	1770	,,	John, Cashel
			1772	,,	John, Ballinakill, Queen's County, merchant
1722	,,	James, Dublin, ribbon weaver.	1783	,,	John, Dublin, esq.
1723	,,	James, Castlekeal, co. Clare, esq.	1786	,,	John, Dublin, landwaiter
			1790	,,	hon. John, Dublin, esq.
1723	,,	James Dublin, esq.	1791	,,	John Judkin, Waterford city, esq.
1738	,,	James, Dublin, woollen draper.			
1738	,,	James, Dublin, gent.	1794	,,	John, Clonmel, co. Tipperary, gent.
1742	,.	James, Dublin, esq.			
1747	,,	James, Ballyragget, co. Kilkenny, esq. (This will is declared null and void, a subsequent will being proved.)	1794	,,	John, Fishamble-st., Dublin, grocer [esq.
			1795	,,	John, Arborhill, co. Tipperary,
			1657	,,	Jonathan, Bandon Bridge, co. Cork [**VI**. 231
1747	,,	James, Ballyragget, co. Kilkenny, esq.	1759	,,	Luke, Dublin, gent.
1752	,,	James, Kilmoyler, co. Tipperary, esq.	1601	,,	dame Margaret, Lackanagh, co. Kildare, widow
1754	,,	James, Dublin, carpenter.	1735	,,	dame Margaret, *alias* **Roche,** widow of sir Theo. B., counsellor-at-law
1769	,,	rev. James, Callan, co. Kilk.			
1777	,,	James, parish priest of Thurles.	1796	,,	Margaret, Dublin, widow
1780	,,	James, Kilcommon, co. Tipperary, esq.	1656	,,	Mary, Ballynakill, co. Tipp., widow [**VI**. 6
1782	,,	James, Callan, co. Kilk. esq.	1733	,,	Mary, Back-lane, Dublin, shopkeeper
1783	,,	James, Brenor, co. Kilk. gent.			
1788	,,	James, Bagshot, Hampshire, esq.	1783	,,	Mary
			1796	,,	Mary, *alias* **Mandeville.**
1791	,,	rev. James, Thurles.	1796	,,	Mary, Dublin, spinster
1798	,,	James, Millbrook, co. Clare, gent.	1737	,,	Michael, Dublin, merchant
1800	,,	James, Dublin	1762	,,	Michael, Dublin, merchant
1802	,,	James, Buckingham-st., Dub., painter and plasterer	1800	,,	Michael, Dublin, grocer
			1638	,,	Patrick, Dublin, tailor
1804	,,	James, Ballyogan	1762	,,	Peregrine, Dungarvan, co. Waterford, gent.
1804	,,	James, city of Dublin, labourer			
1805	,,	James A., formerly of Lackan, late of Clonmel	1713	,,	Perse, Moyne, co. Tipperary, gent.
1807	,,	James, Carlow, esq.	1716	,,	Perse, Urlingford, co. Kilkenny
1808	,,	James, Cross Poddle, co. Dub.	1601	,,	Peter Fitz Thomas, Old Abbey, co. Kilkenny, esq.
1706	,,	Jane, *alias* **Overend,** Dromagh, co. Cork, widow	1640	,,	Peter, Danginspiddogie, co. Kilkenny, esq. (Ex.)
1781	,,	Jane, Dublin, widow [gent.			
1601	,,	John, Ballytarsny, co. Tipp.,	1727	,,	Peter, Waterford, mariner
1629	,,	John Fitz Thomas, Shanballyduffe, co. Tipperary, gent.	1788	,,	Peter, Bunmahon, co. Clare, gent.
1663	,,	col. John, commonly called 'John for the King' (Copy)	1791	,,	Philip, Merville, co. Kildare, gent.
1668	,,	John, Ballykeefe, co. Kilkenny, gent.	1732	,,	sir Pierce, Garryhunden, co. Carlow, bart.

1630	**Butler,**	Piers, Callan, co. Kilkenny, esq.
1704	,,	Piers, par. St. Giles, Middlesex, esq.
1809	,,	Piers, Longfordpass, co. Tipp.
1793	,,	Pierse, Loughrea, co. Galway, surgeon
1655	,,	Richard, Dunleckney, co. Carlow, clk. [V. 232
1672	,,	lieut. Richard, Cootehill, co. Cavan
1705	,,	Richard, Kilkenny, gent.
1713	,,	Richard, Dublin, brewer
1714	,,	Richard, lieut. of grenadiers in col. David Creighton's regt.
1757	,,	Richard, Dublin
1758	,,	Richard, Westcourt, co. Kilk., esq.
1758	,,	Richard, Lough, co. Wexford
1759	,,	Richard, Dublin, merchant
1762	,,	Richard, Waterford, gent.
1764	,,	Richard, living with Mrs. Harman, Stephen's-Green (Not proved)
1769	,,	Richard, Jamestown, co. Tipp., gent. [esq.
1776	,,	Richard, Keylogue, co. Tipp.
1800	,,	Richard, Butler's Lodge, co. Kilkenny
1763	,,	hon. Robert, Dublin, esq.
1789	,,	Robert, Ballyragget, co. Kilkenny, esq.
1681	,,	Samuel, formerly of London, but now of Dublin, mercht.
1779	,,	Sarah, Digges-street, Dublin, widow
1799	,,	hon. Simon, Dublin, barrister-at-law
1795	,,	Sinolda, Harold's Cross, co Dublin
1638	,,	sir Stephen, Belturbet, knt. [IV. 366
1795	,,	Stephen Creagh, Dublin, esq.
1658	,,	Theobald Fitz William, Rahyn, co. Tipperary, gent.
1671	,,	Theobald, Bansigh, co. Tipp., gent.
1669	,,	Theobald, late of Lismolin, co. Tipperary, now of Ballycallen, co. Kilkenny, esq.
1701	,,	Theobald, Ballykeeffe, co. Kilkenny, gent.
1718	,,	Theobald, Derrycolony, co. Tipperary, gent.
1721	,,	sir Theobald, Dublin, Counsellor-at-Law
1724	,,	Theobald, Dublin, merchant
1765	,,	Theobald
1795	,,	Theobald, Wilford, co. Tipp., esq.

1797	**Butler,**	Theobald, Garrane, co. Tipp., esq.
1609	,,	Thomas, Ardmoile, co. Tipp., gent.
1629	,,	Thomas, Dweeninge, co. Carlow, gent.
1637	,,	Thomas, Polardstown, co. Limerick, esq.
1711	,,	Thomas, Ballinasloe, co. Galway
1738	,,	col. Thomas, Kilcash, co. Tipperary
1748	,,	Thomas, Courtnabouly, co. Kilkenny, gent.
1749	,,	Thomas, Ballyadams, Queen's County, esq.
1754	,,	hon. Thomas, esq., 2nd son of Brinsley Butler, Lord Visct. Lanesboro'
1760	,,	Thomas, Dublin, grocer
1762	,,	Thomas, Waterford, merchant
1766	,,	Thomas, Ballanvalla, co. Wicklow, gent.
1772	,,	Thomas, Garryhunden, co. Carlow, esq.
1782	,,	Thomas, Crowan, co. Tipperary, esq.
1793	,,	Thomas, Longford Pass, co. Tipperary, gent.
1795	,,	Thos., Mount Butler, co. Cork, esq
1795	,,	Thomas, city of Kilkenny, M.D.
1811	,,	Thos., Jordanstown, co. Dub.
1755	,,	Tobias, Ballinakill
1806	,,	Tobias, Forest, Queen's County
1701	,,	Walter, Garryrickin, co. Kilkenny, esq.
1717	,,	Walter, sen., Mouphin, co. Wexford, esq.
1693	,,	William, Dublin, brewer
1730	,,	William, Dublin, gent.
1735	,,	William, Rossroe, co. Clare, esq. (delivered out in 1760)
1762	,,	William, Ballyadams, Queen's County, esq.
1774	,,	William O'Brien, Bansagh, co. Tipperary, esq.
1786	,,	William, Bayswell, co. Kilkenny, esq.
1800	,,	William, Park, co. Tipperary, esq.
1802	,,	William, Lady-lane, city Waterford, esq.
1723	**Butterly,**	Christopher, Dublin, innkeeper
1781	,,	Elizabeth, Dublin
1764	,,	James, co. Dublin
1683	**Butterton,**	Jonathan, Dublin, pewterer
1773	**Buttle,**	Mary, Dublin

1676 **Buttolph,** Thomas, dean of Raphoe
1617 **Byan,** Richard, Pheposton
1714 **Byngham,** sir Henry, Castlebar, co. Mayo, bart.
1684 **Byrd,** John the elder [See BIRD.]
1713 **Byres,** Robert, Dublin, merchant
1733 **Byrn,** Charles, Drogheda, alderman
1715 ,, Christopher, Dublin, tailor
1739 ,, John, Dublin, tailor
1782 ,, Thomas
1746 **Byrne,** Alice, *alias* **Lenaghan**
1760 ,, Andrew, Athlone
1658 ,, Anne, *alias* **Bardon,** Rathroheade, co. Carlow, widow [VII. 17
1742 ,, Anne, spinster
1754 ,, Anne, *alias* **Smithson,** Dublin, widow
1782 ,, Anne, Dublin, widow
1805 ,, Anne, city of Dublin, widow
1810 ,, Anthony, Clara, co. Kilkenny, gent.
1774 ,, Bartholomew, Kilcock, co. Kildare, farmer
1783 ,, Bartholomew, Earl of Meath's Liberty, clothier
1729 ,, Bridget, Wicklow, co. Wicklow, widow
1788 ,, Bridget, Bray, co. Wicklow, spinster
1798 ,, Carbery, Dublin
1604 ,, Catherine, widow of Donogh **O'Kerewan**
1762 ,, Catherine, relict of James B., Coolnahana, co. Wexford
1728 ,, Charles, Clone, co. Wicklow, gent.
1752 ,, Charles, Dublin, merchant
1752 ,, Chas., Kilmacar, co. Kilkenny, but of Dublin, esq.
1809 ,, Charles, Harold's Cross, co. Dublin
1715 ,, Christopher, Dublin, tailor
1748 ,, Christopher, Dublin, nailer
1808 ,, Christopher, city Dublin, gent.
1784 ,, Clare, Dublin, widow
1717 ,, sir Daniel, Tymogue, Queen's County, bart.
1793 ,, Daniel, parish priest, Naas, co. Kildare
1808 ,, Daniel, Scarnaugh, co. Wexford, farmer
1773 ,, Darby, Rathrush, co. Carlow, farmer
1768 ,, David, Leighlin Bridge, co. Carlow, gent.
1729 ,, Denis, Bray, co. Dubl., farmer
1744 ,, Dennis, St. Michan's par. Dubl., popish priest

1810 **Byrne,** Dennis, Cowlowly, Queen's co., farmer
1615 ,, Denyse, Dublin, merchant
1782 ,, Dudley, Ballygalworth, co. Wexford
1624 ,, Edmond, Rathmillie, co. Carlow (Imperfect)
1744 ,, Edmond, Cournellan, co. Carl., gent.
1770 ,, Edmond, Spahill, co. Carlow
1792 ,, Edmond
1803 ,, Edmond, Cournellan, co. Carl.
1749 ,, Edward, Endhoven, Dutch Brabant, sutler
1775 ,, Edward, Kilsallaghan, co. Dublin, farmer
1784 ,, Edward, Barmeath, co. Louth
1786 ,, Edward, city of Dublin
1805 ,, Edward, North Gt. George's-street, esq.
1806 ,, Edward, Kilmurry, co. Wicklow
1777 ,, Elizabeth, Phrapper - lane, Dublin, spinster
1777 ,, Elizabeth, widow of Dudley B., Dublin, grocer
1781 ,, Elizabeth, Alardstown, co. Louth, widow
1805 ,, Elizabeth, Cournellan, co. Carlow, widow
1800 ,, Ellinor, Dublin, widow
1798 ,, Felix, Dublin, merchant
1601 ,, Felortia, Cyllmoyre, par. Wicklow (copy in Latin)
1793 ,, Frances, *alias* **Aikins,** Dublin, widow
1748 ,, Francis, New House, co. Louth, gent.
1788 ,, Francis, Kilcool, co. Wicklow, labourer
1801 ,, Francis, Dublin, linen-draper
1805 ,, Francis, town of Carlow
1714 ,, Garret, Ballymanus, co. Wicklow, gent. [farmer
1775 ,, Garret, Blackbog, co. Kildare,
1794 ,, Garret, Arklow, co. Wicklow
1768 ,, Garrett, Ballinteskin, Queen's County, farmer
1789 ,, Garrett, Elizabeth-town, North America
1806 ,, Garrett, Hacketstown, co. Carl.
1697 ,, George, Dublin, surgeon (Ex.)
1762 ,, George, Dublin
1763 ,, George, Comer's Court, co. Dublin, esq.
1769 ,, George, Dundalk, co. Louth, merchant
1737 ,, Gerald, Kilbride, co. Longford, gent.
1762 ,, Gerald, Ballysillagh, co, Kilk., gent.

1771	**Byrne**, Gerald, Prussia-street, co. Dublin, gent.
1775	,,	Gerald, Cloncurry, co. Kildare, farmer
1798	,,	Gerald, Prospect Lodge, co. Louth, gent.
1743	,,	Gregory, mariner
1793	,,	Gregory, Dublin, merchant
1782	,,	Hannah, Sallypark,, co. Dubl., widow [gent.
1762	,,	Henry, Allardstown, co. Louth,
1778	,,	Henry, Carrickmacross, co. Monaghan, merchant
1785	,,	Henry, Seatown, co. Louth, esq.
1796	,,	Henry, Mount Byrne, co. Louth, esq.
1601	,,	Hugh Fitz Teige, Ballydungan, co. Wicklow. esq.
1675	,,	Hugh, Ballynecorbeg, co. Wicklow, gent.
1765	,,	Hugh, Tollyloherny, co. Mon., gent.
1744	,,	James, Dublin, glover
1754	,.	Jas., Coulnyhorna, co. Wexford
1755	,,	James, Cornelan, co. Carlow
1762	,,	James, Dublin, merchant
1763	,,	James, Cloran, co. Tipperary
1775	,,	James, Dublin, gent.
1784	,,	James, Johnstown, co. Kildare, farmer
1795	,,	James, Athlone, co. Roscommon, merchant
1808	,,	James, paymaster, 17th dragoons (Copy)
1808	,,	James, New-street, co. Dublin, farrier
1809	,,	James, city of Dublin, esq.
1809	,,	James, Kill, co. Kildare, farmer
1776	,,	Jane, Golden-lane, Dublin, widow
1802	,,	Jane, city of Dublin, widow
1681	,,	John, Dublin, esq. (Ex.)
1741	,,	John, Dublin, esq.
1742	,,	sir John, Timogue, Queen's County, bart. (Copy)
1752	,,	John, Dublin, gent.
1753	,,	John, Stoneybatter, Dublin, breeches-maker
1760	,,	John, Phrapper-lane, Dublin, formerly brewer
1768	,,	John, Killalesh, co. Wicklow
1780	,,	John, Mullinahack, Dublin, sugar-baker
1786	,,	John, Palmerstown, co. Kildare , farmer
1793	,.	John, Knockballyboy, King's County, farmer
1795	,,	John, Kilinacree, co. Dublin
1795	.,	John, Stradbally, Queen's County, apothecary.

1798	**Byrne**, John, Rathdrum, shopkeeper
1803	,,	John, Glanely, co. Wicklow, farmer
1807	,,	John, Temple-street, co. Dubl.
1809	,,	John T., Ballymackerly, co. Roscommon
1809	,,	John, Bayswell, co. Kilkenny, farmer
1762	,,	Laughlin, Ballybrack, co. Wicklow, gent.
1759	,,	Laurence, Cork Hill, Dublin, tailor
1803	,,	Lawrence, Cronerow, co. Wicklow, farmer
1810	,,	Letitia, city of Dublin, widow
1810	,,	Loughlin, New-street, Dublin, timber merchant
1804	,,	Luke, Crueket, co. Kildare, farmer
1731	,,	Margaret, Dublin
1760	,,	Margaret, *alias* **Sherlock**, Dublin, widow
1763	,,	hon. Margaret, Dublin, widow
1763	,,	Margaret, Dublin, widow of Charles B.
1792	,,	Mark, Johnstown, co. Wicklow, gent.
1753	,,	Mary, Ormond Market, Dublin, widow
1778	,,	Mary, College-green, widow
1780	,,	Mary, Drogheda town, widow
1787	,,	Mary, Dublin, widow
1808	,,	Mary, Townsend-street, city of Dublin
1801	,,	Mathew, Redcross, co. Wicklow
1810	,,	Mathew, Tinehely, co. Wicklow
1810	,,	Matthew, Turvey
1710	,,	Michael, Carlow, gent.
1784	,,	Michael, Castlemarket, Dublin, butcher
1792	,,	Michael, Seven Churches, co. Wicklow, farmer
1755	,,	Miles, Harold's Cross, co. Dublin, dairyman
1776	,,	Morgan, Sigginstown, co. Kildare, gent.
1791	,,	Morgan, Scarnagh, co. Wexford, farmer
1774	,,	Moses, Clykeel, co. Cork, gent.
1799	,,	Nicholas, North-strand, co. Dublin
1772	,,	Owen, Dublin, merchant tailor
1764	,,	Patrick, Clonmel, co. Tipperary, innholder
1788	,,	rev. Patrick, Cronroe, co. Wick.
1790	,,	Patrick, Rainsford-street, linen manufacturer
1796	,,	Patrick, senior, Castletown, co. Louth, gent.

1801 **Byrne**, Patrick, Mountmellick, Queen's County, gent.
1802 ,, Patrick, city of Dublin, weaver
1803 ,, Patrick, Newry, co. Down, woollen draper
1811 ,, Patrick, Ardbrin, co. Down, gent.
1632 ,, Phelom M'feagh, Ballenecorra, co. Wicklow, esq.
1776 ,, Philip, Dublin, merchant
1788 ,, Phillip, Whitestown, co. Wick.
1776 ,, Pierce, Dublin, gent.
1704 ,, Redmond, Leighlin Bridge, co. Carlow, gent.
1724 ,, Redmond, Dublin, vintner
1733 ,, Richard, Athlone, co. Roscommon, merchant
1799 ,, Richard, Dublin, merchant
1802 ,, Richard   [esq.
1799 ,, Robert, Cabinteely, co. Dublin,
1748 ,, Rose, Dublin, widow
1729 ,, Samuel, Faha, co. Cork, gent.
1798 ,, Stephen, Dub., cheese monger
1808 ,, Terence, Charles-st., Dublin
1729 ,, Thos., Wicklow, co. Wicklow, gent.
1730 ,, Thos., Raggettstown, Queen's County, gent.
1754 ,, Thos., Droomeen, co. Wicklow, gent.
1760 ,, Thos., Dublin, gent.
1775 ,, Thos., Lougherrill, co. Leitrim
1798 ,, Thos., Kilboggot, co. Dublin, farmer
1800 ,, Thos., Dublin, publican
1803 ,, Thos., secretary to the House of Industry
1805 ,, Thos., Baltinglass, co. Wicklow
1806 ,, Thomas, pedlar
1809 ,, Thos., town of Wicklow, architect
1731 ,, Walter, Dublin, esq.
1699 ,, William, Dublin, surgeon
1700 ,, William, Ferglass, co. Leitrim, farmer   [gent.
1734 ,, William, Cronroe, co. Wicklow,
1768 ,, William, Dundalk, co. Louth, gent.
1792 ,, Wm., Carlow, damask weaver
1792 ,, Wm., Ballyrain, co. Wicklow, gent.
[See BERNE, BIRNE, BOURN, BOURNE, BURN, BURNE, BURNS, BYRN, BYRON.]
1786 **Byron**, Barthw., Mallow, co. Cork, shopkeeper
1699 ,, sir Edward, parish of St, Giles-in-the-Fields, Middlesex (Copy)

1679 **Byron**, capt. John, Lisburn, co. Antrim
1570 **Byrssall**, Mathew, Dublin. (Imperfect)
1788 **Byrt**, William, Belfast, co. Antrim, gent.
[See BIRTT.]
1656 **Byrtche**, John, Dublin, M.D.
[**V.** 245
1614 **Bysse**, Christopher, Dublin, esq.
1679 ,, John, esq., Ch. Bar. Exchequer
1602 ,, Robert, Dublin, gent.
1642 ,, Robert Fitz Chris., Dublin, esq.
1642 ,, Robert, Pelletstown, co. Dublin, esq.
1802 **Bytagh**, Edward, Kilgeveran, co. Galway, esq.
1602 **Bythell**, Edward.

——C——

1563 **Caane**, Brene *or* Barnaby.
[See CANE.]
1728 **Cabanel**, Nathaniel, esq.
1678 **Caddel**, James, Timoale, co. Meath, gent.
1689 ,, John, Nalle, co. Meath, esq.
1728 ,, Margaret, Dublin, widow
1581 ,, Patk., Moate, par. of Kylleghe, co. Dublin   [**V.** 1, p. 6
1651 ,, Patrick, Lissenhall, co. Dublin
1588 ,, Thomas, par. of Stamullin, co. Meath
1761 **Caddell**, David, Downpatrick, merchant
1748 ,, James, capt. in brigadier Richbell's regt. of foot
1581 ,, John, co. Meath, gent.
[**V.** 1, p. 7
1806 ,, Mary, Harold's Cross, co. Dub., widow
1732 ,, Richard, Downpatrick (not proved)
1753 ,, Thomas, Moyrath, co. Meath, gent.   [Meath, esq.
1765 ,, Thomas, Herbertstown, co.
1724 ,, Wm., Dublin, heraldic painter
1756 **Caddow**, Henry, Dublin, merchant
1774 **Caddy**, John, Tonyarragher, co. Cavan
1767 ,, rev. Joseph, Drumlane, co. Cavan, clk.
1745 **Cade**, Thomas, Dublin, hosier
1784 ,, Thomas, Willbrooke, co. Dublin, gent.
1665 **Cadogan**, Elizabeth, wid. of Wm. C., Ardbraccan, co. Meath, esq.
[**XIII.** 41

1661 **Cadogan**, Wm., Dubl., esq. (Copy)
1739   ,,   William, earl, baron of Oakley.
          (Copy)
1789 **Cadwell**, James, Saggart, co. Dub-
          lin
1638 **Caffay**, Joan, *alias* **Farrell**, widow
          of   Nicholas   C.,   Bally-
          knockan, co. Carlow
1758 **Caffery**, Patrick, Vicar-street, Dub-
          lin, merchant
1764 **Caffrey**, Bartholomew, Suttenrade,
          co. Kildare
1767   ,,   Catherine, *alias* **Short**, Sutten-
          rade, co. Kildare, widow
1781   ,,   Francis, Donadea, co. Kildare,
          farmer
1791   ,,   Thomas, Moore-street, Dublin,
          dealer
1803 **Caffry**, Elinor, Spitalfields, Dublin,
          widow
1794 **Cahally**, William, Lattytoo, co.
          Cavan.
1744 **Caher**, Thomas, lord baron
          [See CAHIR.]
1800 **Cahill**, Betty
1753   ,,   Edmond, Fossey, Queen's
          County, gent.
1764   ,,   Elizabeth,   Killinough,   co.
          Westmeath, widow
1777   ,,   Hugh, Dublin, merchant
1742   ,,   John, Youghal, co. Cork, mer-
          chant   [kenny, farmer
1792   ,,   John, Castleblundel, co. Kil-
1796   ,,   John, Dublin, chip hat manu-
          facturer
1811   ,,   John, Blackhall-parade, Dub-
          lin, attorney
1806   ,,   Joseph, Church-street, Dublin
1752   ,,   Margaret, Youghal, co. Cork
1794   ,,   Moses,   Clane,   co.   Kildare,
          gent.
1786   ,,   Patrick, Cavan, merchant
1637   ,,   Richard, Dublin, shoemaker
                              [**IV**. 240
1784   ,,   Richard, Dublin city
1810   ,,   Thomas, Sandford's Court, co.
          Kilkenny
1768   ,,   Timothy, formerly of Dublin,
          now of Templeogue, co.
          Dublin, gent.
1733   .,   William, Killylogh, co. Cork,
          gent.
1794 **Cahir**, James, lord baron
1593   ,,   sir Theo. Butler, knt., baron of
          [See CAHER.]
1705 **Caichey**, Philip, Cootehill, co.
          Cavan, tailor
1767 **Caillard**, rev. Gasper, clk.
1732 **Caillaud**, Ruben, Dublin, esq.
1791   ,,   Susana, Bath, spinster

1709 **Caillon**, Josias, Cork
1595 **Caine** *or* **Caney**, Thomas, Dublin,
          merchant
          [See CANE.]
1656 **Cairnell** *or* **Kernell**, William,
          soldier.   [**VI.** 8
1732 **Cairnes**,sir Alex., Monaghan,bart.
1722   ,,   David, Londonderry, esq.
1750   ,,   dame Frances, widow of sir
          Henry Cairnes, bart.
1801   ,,   George,   Killifaddy,   co.   Ty-
          rone, esq.
1809   ,,   Hugh, Parkmount, co. Antrim,
          esq.
1791   ,,   Jas., Killifaddy, co. Tyr., esq.
1727   ,,   John, Dublin.
1732   ,,   John, Clanmore, co. Tyrone,
          gent.
1802   ,,   John Elliot, Dungannon, co.
          Tyrone.
1745   ,,   Robert. Naas,co. Kildare,gent.
1745   ,,   Robert, Naas, co.Kildare, gent.
1706   ,,   William, Dublin, esq. (Exem.)
1739   ,,   William,   Killifaddy,   co.   Ty-
          rone, esq.
          [See CARNES.]
1791 **Calbeck**, Francis, Dublin, merchant
          [See CALDBECK.]
1792 **Calcraft**, John, Ingress, Kent, esq.
          (Copy)
1718 **Caldbeck**, Wm., Dublin, bricklayer
1803   ,,   Wm., Dublin, barrister-at-law
          [See CALBECK.]
1734 **Calder**, John, royal regt. of foot
1756 **Calderwood**, Andrew, Dublin, gent.
1783   ,,   Andrew,Ballymony,co.Antrim,
          merchant
1775   ,,   Mary, Dublin, spinster
1766   ,,   Robert, Dublin, goldsmith.
          [See CULDERWOOD.]
1722 **Caldual**, Catherine, Strabane, Tip-
          perary, widow
1796 **Caldwell**, Alicia, Dublin, spinster
1737   ,,   Andrew, Sligo, gent.
1808   ,,   Andrew, Dublin, esq. (Large)
1807   ,,   Arabella Frances, spinster
1767   ,,   Bridget, Dublin, widow
1776   ,,   Charles, Dublin, esq.
1707   ,,   Christopher, Ballyhubbock, co.
          Wicklow, esq.
1787   ,,   David
1721   ,,   Elizabeth, Dublin, spinster
1726   ,,   sir Henry, bart., Castle Cald-
          well, co. Fermanagh
1717   ,,   sir James, bart., Castle Cald-
          well, co. Fermanagh
1784   ,,   sir James, bart., Castle Cald-
          well, co Fermanagh
1640   ,,   John, Enniskillen, co. Ferman.,
          merchant

1755 **Caldwell,** John, Ballymony, co. Antrim
1779 ,, Robert, Ballycogan, co. Donegal, gent.
1741 ,, Samuel, Edenderry, King's Co.
1747 ,, Sarah, Dublin, spinster.
1670 ,, William, Curretynane, co. Armagh, esq.
1729 ,, rev. William, Delgany, co. Wicklow
　[See CALLDWELL, CALLWALL, CALLWELL.]
1802 **Caledon,** rt. hon. James, earl of (Large)
1661 **Calisto,** Adryan, Roscrea, apothecary
1797 **Callage,** Andrew, Dublin, woollen draper
1778 ,, Mary, Dublin, widow
1736 ,, Peter, Dublin, merchant
1792 ,, Peter, Dublin, merchant
1744 **Callaghan,** Ambrose, *alias* **Waller**
1742 ,, Anne, *alias* **Longueville,** widow
1786 ,, Catherine, Great Britain-street, Dublin, widow
1777 ,, Christopher, Corduff, co. Dub., farmer
1799 ,, Cornelius, Dublin, glazier
1768 ,, Dennis, Glinn, co. Cork, gent.
1778 ,, Dennis, Charles-street, Dublin, gent.
1800 ,, Edward, Castlelyons, co. Cork, gent.
1806 ,, George, city of Dublin, gent.
1800 ,, Henry, Castlelyons, co. Cork, tanner
1766 ,, James
1767 ,, James, Dublin, grocer
1801 ,, Jane, Bandon, co. Cork, widow
1762 ,, John, King-street, Stephen's-green, Dublin, gent.
1795 ,, John, Dublin, cooper
1806 ,, Margt., Ormond-market, Dub., widow
1750 ,, Mary, Clonmeen, co. Cork
1759 ,, Nicholas, Spring-garden, Dub., poulterer
1791 ,, Nicholas, Brunswick-st , Dub., distiller
1804 ,, Olivia, city of Limerick, widow
1786 ,, Patrick, Pill-lane, Dublin, chandler
1735 ,, Richard, Dublin, baker
1790 ,, Richd., Smithstown, co. Meath, farmer
1798 ,, Richard
1807 ,, Richard, Church-st., Dublin
1727 ,, Robert, Clonmeen, co. Cork, esq.

1779 **Callaghan,** Robert, Kilgobbin, co. Dublin, farmer
1801 ,, Roger, St. Finbarry's lib. of Cork, gent.
1780 ,, Thomas, Kilgobbin, co. Dubl., farmer
1776 ,, Timothy, Mallow, co. Cork, gent.
1811 ,, William, Tullow, co. Carlow, shopkeeper
1794 **Callan,** Anne, *alias* **Keane**
1785 ,, Bartholomew, Osbertstown, co. Kildare, esq.
1785 ,, Christopher, Osbertstown, cordwainer
1787 ,, Hellen, Osbertstown, co. Kildare
1763 ,, John, New-row, Dubl., mercht.
1787 ,, John, Winetavern-street, Dub., currier
1678 ,, Patk., Kilbrake, co. Monaghan
1744 ,, Patrick, Dublin, gent.
1767 ,, Patrick, Dublin, gent.
1781 ,, Robert, Dublin, merchant
1757 ,, Thos., Pimlico, Dublin, clothier
1791 ,, Thomas, Carnagarvog, co Monaghan
　[See CALLEN.]
1694 **Callanan,** Denis, Dublin, tailor
1748 ,, John, Cork, M.D.
1801 ,, Michael, Cork, apothecary
1795 ,, Peter, Cottage, co. Galway, esq.
　[See CALLNAN, CULLINAN.]
1796 **Callanane,** David, Limerick, gent.
1744 **Calldwell,** sir John, bart., Rossbeg, co. Fermanagh
　[See CALDWELL.]
1778 **Callen,** Catherine, jun., Peeltown, Isle of Man (Copy)
1773 ,, John, formerly of Peeltown, now of Drogheda
　[See CALLAN.]
1804 **Callnan,** Andrew, Dublin city
1795 ,, Catherine, *alias* **Purfield**
　[See CALLANAN.]
1725 **Callwall,** Walter, Ballynaskeagh, co. Down
　[See CALDWELL.]
1757 **Callwell,** Robert, Belfast, linen-draper
　[See CALDWELL.]
1800 **Calot,** Francis, Summerhill, Dublin
1720 **Calthorpe,** Reynolds, Elvetham, Hampshire, esq. (Copy)
1768 **Calvert,** Charles Cecil Bressan, formerly of London, now of Paris, esq.
1672 ,, Gyles, London, stationer (Copy)

1758 **Calvert**, Joseph, Dreemore, co. Tyrone
1739 ,, Judith, Dublin, spinster
1798 **Cam**, Samuel, Bradford, Wiltshire, esq. (Copy)
1725 **Camack**, John, Kilfalart, co. Down, gent.
1790 ,, John, Lurgan, co. Armagh
1726 **Camak**, *or* **Camack**, John, Park-row, co. Down, farmer
1755 ,, John, 2nd son of William C., Dublin, merchant
1733 ,, William, Dublin, merchant
1753 ,, William, Portaferry, co. Down, gent.
1792 **Cambie**, Solomon, Castletown, co. Tipperary, esq.
1745 **Cambridge**, Peter, Cork, clothier
1775 **Cameron**, Archibald, lieutenant on half pay
1733 ,, John, Dublin, gent.
1745 **Camill**, Patrick, Dublin, coachman [See CAMPBELL.]
1735 **Camocke**, capt. George (Copy)
1735 **Camoke**, Jane, *alias* **Morgan**, Dub., widow
1787 **Campbel**, David, Harold's Cross, co. Dublin, tailor
1791 ,, James, capt. 42nd regt. of foot
1795 ,, James, Charlemont-st., Dublin
1796 ,, John, Prospect, co. Donegal
1796 ,, Laurence, Dublin
1790 ,, Robert, Janeville, co. Dublin, gent.
1795 ,, rev. Thomas, D.D.
1769 **Campbell**, Andrew, Claristown, co. Louth, gent.
1729 ,, Anne, Dublin, spinster
1805 ,, Anne, Dublin, widow
1802 ,, Anthony, earl of Meath's liberty, baker
1752 ,, Bridget, St. James, Westminster, Middlesex, widow (Copy)
1764 ,, Catherine, formerly of Athlone, now of Dublin
1725 ,, Charles, Dublin, esq.
1780 ,, Charles, Ballykeigle, co. Down, gent.
1788 ,, Charles, Aughnamalla, co. Monaghan, gent.
1810 ,, Colin, city of Cork, esq.
1698 ,, David, co. Down, esq.
1781 ,, David, formerly of Dublin, merchant
1789 ,, David, Bristol, gent.
1799 ,, Drelincourt Young, Galway town, clk.
1721 ,, Dugall, capt. in col. Handasyde's regt.

1792 **Campbell**, Frans., late lieut. 13th dragoons
1741 ,, James, Dublin, merchant
1669 ,, John, Callan, co. Kilkenny, esq.
1713 ,, John, captain in lieut.-general Stewart's regt. of foot
1729 ,, John, Dublin, gent.
1734 ,, John, Dublin, grocer
1751 ,, John, Newry, co. Down, mercht.
1752 ,, John, Drumbane, co. Derry
1790 ,, John, Dublin, esq., attorney-at-law
1795 ,, rev. John, vicar of Mahereagh Cross, diocese of Clogher
1803 ,, John
1805 ,, John, Belfast, co. Antrim, esq.
1722 ,, Josias, Dublin, esq. (Large will)
1757 ,, Lettice, widow of col. Josias C.
1758 ,, Mary, Newry, co. Down, widow
1767 ,, Mary, *alias* **Haddock**, Ballinderry, co. Antrim
1788 ,, Mary, Pill-lane, Dublin
1772 ,, rev. Moses, Glack, co. Tyrone, clk.
1663 ,, Patrick, Clanboe, co. Roscommon, clerk
1720 ,, Patrick, Dublin, bookseller
1753 ,, Patrick, Clonkeen, Queen's County, farmer
1810 ,, Patrick, Ormond-quay, Dublin
1776 ,, rev. Richard, par. of Drumna, co. Armagh
1754 ,, Robert, Newtown Limavady, co. Derry, gent.
1792 ,, Samuel, city of Bath, esq.
1753 ,, Sarah, Clonkeen, Queen's County, widow
1739 ,, rev. William, Villamulloy, co. Longford, clk.
1791 ,, William, Bunna, co. Cavan, M.D.
1804 ,, William, Newry, co. Down, D.D.
1806 ,, William, Presbyterian minister, Clonmel [See CAMILL.]
1793 **Campion**, Arthur, city of Cork
1797 ,, Arthur
1807 ,, Henry, Johnstown, co. Carlow
1808 ,, John, Back-lane, Dublin, leather seller
1803 ,, Patrick, Ballyhooley, co. Cork, gent.
1761 ,, Thomas, Cork, esq.
1733 **Campsey**, Frances, Dublin, widow
1731 **Canasilhes**, Gabriel, Dublin, gent.
1742 ,, Margaret, Dublin, widow
1760 **Candler**, rev. Henry, archdeacon of Ossory

1784 **Candler,** rev. Henry, Kilkenny, LL.D.
1774 ,, John, Castlewood, Queen's County, gent.
1768 ,, Mary, Waterford, widow
1719 ,, Thomas, Callan, co. Kilkenny, esq.
1759 ,, Walsingham
1777 ,, William (Copy)
1810 **Cane,** Edward, Dublin, esq.
1789 ,, Elizabeth, Poolbeg - street, Dublin, widow
1771 ,, Grace, Marshfield, co. Kildare, widow [esq.
1794 ,, Hugh, Dowdstown, co. Kildare,
1757 ,, James, Dublin, esq.
1806 ,, James, King-street, Dublin, esq.
1802 ,, Patrick, Ballinleg, co. Kildare
1757 ,, Richard, Larabryan, co. Kildare, esq.
1799 ,, rev. Richard, Maynooth, clerk
1739 ,, William, Dublin, gent.
[See CAANE, CAINE, KANE.]
1710 **Caning,** George, Garachy, co. Londonderry, gent.
[See CANNING.]
1713 **Cann,** Thomas, Dublin, coachmaker
1783 **Cannan,** Thomas, Kilworth, co. Cork. gent.
[See CANNON.]
1749 **Canneville,** Charles, Dublin, apothecary
1799 **Cannie,** Mathew, Drumline, co. Clare, gent.
1646 **Canning,** George, Coleraine, esq.
1787 ,, Letitia, Dublin, widow
1775 ,, Mary, Dublin, spinster
1784 ,, Paul, Dublin, esq.
1644 ,, Robert, Drogheda, gent.
1775 ,, Stratford, Dublin, esq.
1787 ,, Stratford, London, merchant (Copy)
[See CANING.]
1737 **Cannon,** Alice, Dublin, spinster
1787 ,, Diana, Dublin, widow
1759 ,, Joseph, Dublin, aledraper
1803 ,, Mary, Rush, co. Dublin, widow
1792 ,, Mathew, Kilmore, co. Cavan
1802 ,, Roquier, Dublin, gent.
1788 ,, Thomas, Dublin, dealer
1809 ,, Thomas, Magaddy, co. Meath, esq.
[See CANNAN, GANNON.]
1770 **Canny,** Christian, ward of John C., Limerick, merchant
1759 ,, John, Limerick, merchant
1768 ,, John, Limerick, merchant
1780 **Canter,** James, Cantersfort, S. Lib. of Limerick, gent.
1724 ,, Richard, Limerick, gent.

1810 **Cantillon,** Thomas, Cork city, shipwright
1806 **Canton,** James, co. Dublin, weaver
1771 **Cantrell,** Elizabeth, Mountmellick, Queen's County, innholder
1686 ,, Godfrey, Schonbegg, Queen's County, farmer
1759 ,, Jos., jun., Skerry, Queen's County [County, farmer
1719 ,, Robert, Gurtnaclahy, Queen's
1756 ,, Thomas
1623 **Cantwell,** John, Mokaivike, co. Tipperary, esq.
1800 ,, Patrick, Dublin, esq.
1794 ,, Peter, Dublin, esq.
1606 ,, Thomas, Cantwell's Court, co. Kilkenny, gent.
1787 **Canvan,** James, Galway, M.D.
1800 **Capel,** Joseph, Cloghroe, co. Cork, esq.
1747 **Cappock,** Sarah, Dublin, widow [See COPPOCK.]
1659 **Capret,** Christopher, soldier [VII. 187
1791 **Carane,** John, Frankford
1810 **Carberry,** Mathew, Tubberdaly, King's County
1792 ,, Nicholas, Ballisk, co. Dublin
1733 ,, William, Saggart, co. Dublin, gent.
1758 **Carbery,** lady Anne, widow of late lord Carbery
1720 ,, Charles, Dublin
1756 ,, David, mariner belonging to the 'York'
1749 ,, George, lord baron of
1784 ,, rt. hon. George, lord baron
1805 ,, rt. hon. George, lord baron
1671 ,, John, Dublin, alderman
1720 ,, John, Dublin, gent.
1766 ,, John, Dublin, innholder
1774 ,, John, Drumcondra-lane, co. Dublin, gardener
1807 ,, rt. hon. John, baron
1788 ,, Margaret, Ballymahon, co. Longford, widow
1715 **Card,** Nathaniel, Clonmel, co. Tipperary
1805 ,, Nathaniel
1744 ,, Ralph, Dublin, esq. (Copy)
1748 ,, Ralph, Dublin, esq.
1766 ,, rev. Ralph, Dublin, clk.
1732 ,, Samuel, Dublin, merchant
1755 ,, Samuel, Dublin, esq.
1779 ,, Samuel, Haroldstown, co. Carlow, gent.
1775 ,, Sarah, Dublin, widow
1775 **Carden,** Elizabeth, Kilkenny, widow
1728 ,, John, the elder, Templemore, co. Tipperary, gent.

1767 **Carden,** John, Donore, Queen's County, esq.
1774 ,, John, Templemore, co. Tipperary (Large will)
1790 ,, John, Barnane, co. Tipperary, gent.
1734 ,, Priscilla, Templemore, co. Tipperary, widow
1788 ,, Richard Warburton, Lismore, Queen's County, clk.
1725 ,, William, Newland, co. Kildare, gent.
1759 ,, William, Ballyguides, co. Tipperary, gent.
1760 ,, William, Lismore, Queen's County, esq.
1766 ,, William, Lismore, Queen's County
1801 **Cardiff,** John, Walterstown, co. Kildare, miller
1798 ,, Joseph, Dublin, merchant
1803 ,, Matthew, Dublin, shipbuilder
1778 **Cardiffe,** Elias, High-street, Dubl., frieze merchant
1806 **Careless,** Christopher, Capel-street, Dublin, haberdasher
1784 **Carew,** Dorothy, widow
1722 ,, Lynn, Castletown, co. Waterford, gent.
1769 ,, Mark, South Liberty of Cork, gent.
1721 ,, Robt., Ballinamona, co. Waterford, esq.
1806 ,, Robert, Woodenstown, co. Tipperary
1781 ,, Shapland, Castle Boro, co. Wexford, esq.
1793 ,, Thomas, Ballinamona, Liberty of Waterford
[See CARY.]
1630 **Carewe,** John, Youghal, gent.
1668 **Carey,** Edward, Dungiven, co. Londonderry, esq.
1699 ,, Elizabeth, Ballymacpatrick, co. Cork, widow
1684 ,, James, Kilcooly, co. Tipperary, clk. [esq.
1804 ,, James, Ballymacmoy, co. Cork,
1753 ,, John, Carysville, co. Cork, esq.
1795 ,, John, Strawhall, co. Cork, esq.
1798 ,, John, Church Chapel, Dublin, priest [ford, gent.
1758 ,, Joseph, Ballynaroon, co. Water-
1789 ,, Mathew, Limerick, merchant
1737 ,, Peter, Carysville, co. Cork, esq.
1762 ,, Thomas, Cary's Lodge, co. Cork, gent.
1764 ,, William, Shanballydonagh, co. Cork, gent.
[See CARY.]

1787 **Carhampton,** Simon, earl of
1807 **Carige,** David, Dublin, gent.
1672 **Carigne,** Henry, esq. (a brief of the things contained in his will)
1774 **Carleboe,** Laurence, Dublin, cook
1786 **Carleton,** Alice, Enniskillen, co. Fermanagh
1799 ,, Anne, Dublin city, spinster
1703 ,, Chris., Dublin, esq. (exempt)
1706 ,, Chris., Londonderry, gent.
1739 ,, Christopher, Newry, co. Down, esq.
1801 ,, Conway, Belfast, co. Antrim, merchant
1695 ,, Ellen, Knockmanering, co. Tipperary, widow
1776 ,, Jas. Townsend, Dublin, paper stainer
1722 ,, John, Thomond, co. Leitrim, esq.
1730 ,, John, Darlinghill, co. Tipperary, esq.
1791 ,, John, Carlow town
1695 ,, lieut. Launcelot, Little Carleton, co. Fermanagh
1725 ,, Mary, Killeveney, co. Wicklow, widow
1806 ,, Oliver, Dublin city, esq.
1742 ,, Richd., Darlinghill, co. Tipp., esq.
1735 ,, rev. Robert, dean of Cork
1778 ,, William, Strawgowna, co. Fermanagh
1789 ,, William, parish of Blaris, co. Down
[See CARLTON.]
1792 **Carley,** James, Anne-street, Dubl., gent.
1806 **Carlile,** Christopher, Charlemont-place, co. Dublin
1787 ,, David, Newry, co. Down, gent.
1804 ,, Esther, Newry, co. Down, widow
1811 ,, rev. Francis, Bailieboro'
1774 ,, James, Newry, co. Down
1799 ,, James, Cradockstown, co. Kildare
1749 ,, John, Tullybroom, dissenting minister, Clogher parish
1778 ,, John, Belfast, co. Antrim, merchant
1784 ,, Nesbit, Springfield, co. Leitrim
1756 ,, Robert, Newry, co. Down, merchant
1771 ,, Robert, Newry, co. Down
1741 ,, William, Newry, co. Down
1741 ,, William, Newry, tanner
[See CARLISLE.]
1700 **Carlingford,** Theobald, earl of
1739 ,,   ,,   ,,

1800 **Carlisle,** James, Newry, co. Down, gent.
  [See CARLILE.]
1779 **Carlow,** William Henry, lord viscount
1779 **Carlton,** Christopher, Enniskillen, co. Fermanagh, esq.
1714 ,, Isabella, Walshtown, co. Cork, widow
  [See CARLETON.]
1806 **Carmey,** Michael, Tuam, co. Galway, farmer
1794 **Carmichael,** Andrew, Dublin, esq.
1730 ,, Colin, Dublin, gent.
1741 ,, Daniel, Moneymore, co. Derry, gent.
1776 ,, Hugh, Dublin, esq.
1788 ,, Hugh, Dublin, gent.
1744 ,, major John, Dublin
1745 ,, rev. John, Sancourt, clk.
1754 ,, John, Killeen, co. Armagh, gent.
1783 ,, John, Dublin, hosier
1764 ,, Mary, Bolton-street, Dublin, widow
1785 ,, Samuel, Grange, co. Antrim
1806 ,, Samuel, Grange, co. Antrim
1792 ,, Thomas, Dublin, gent.
1765 ,, Wm., abp. of **Dublin,** q. v.
1569 **Carmike,** Reynolde, St. John's par.
1798 **Carncross,** George, Dublin city, coachmaker
1799 ,, Hugh, Dublin, esq.
1775 ,, Joseph, Dublin, coachmaker
1701 **Carnecross,** Alexr., bp. of **Raphoe,** q. v.
1647 **Carney,** Edward, Dublin, tailor
1680 ,, Elinor, *alias* **Fleming,** widow
1709 ,, dame Lettice, widow of sir Richard C., knt.
1806 ,, Michael, Tuam, co. Galway, farmer
1761 ,, Neal, Keadow, co. Meath
1791 ,, Philip, Drogheda, merchant
1799 **Carnes,** Thomas, gold and silver lace weaver
  [See CAIRNES.]
1754 **Carolan,** Edmond, Carrickmacross
1800 ,, Elizabeth, Drogheda, widow
1787 ,, John, Carrickmacross, co. Monaghan
1666 **Caron,** Redmond, Dublin, gent.
1803 **Carothers,** James, servant to earl of Farnham
  [See CARUTHERS.]
1636 **Carpenter,** Edward, Galway, merchant
1749 ,, Hanah, Dublin, spinster
1728 ,, John, Killanean, co. Carlow, esq.

1657 **Carlingford,** Joshua, Sigginstown, co. Kildare, esq. [**VI.** 176
1703 ,, Joshua, lieut.-col. in col. Whelham's regt. of foot
1739 ,, Judith, Calverton, Bucks, spinster
1732 ,, Patrick, King-street, Oxmarket, Dublin, smith
1764 ,, Patrick, Dublin, blacksmith
1675 ,, Philip, Dublin, esq. (exemp.)
1720 ,, Philip, esq.
1703 ,, Richard, Dublin, gent.
1804 ,, Richard, Ryder's-row, Dublin, carpenter
1558 ,, Simon, Dublin
1782 ,, Thomas, Kevin-street, Dublin, slater
1786 ,, Thomas, Limerick city
1806 ,, Thomas, Ballinakill, Queen's County, apothecary
1684 ,, William, Limerick, gent.
1742 ,, rev. William, clk., rector of Calverton, Bucks (Copy)
1772 ,, William, Ballinakill, Queen's County, gent.
1794 **Carr,** Adam, Cork, mariner
1785 ,, Alice, Dublin, widow
1702 ,, Anne, London, widow
1786 ,, Anne, Dublin city, widow
1749 ,, Bridget, Dublin, widow
1739 ,, Charles, bp. of **Killaloe,** q. v.
1715 ,, Edward, Cork, gent.
1662 ,, sir George, Dublin, knight (Exemp.)
1784 ,, Hayes, Dublin
1744 ,, Mable, Ormond-quay, Dublin
1788 ,, Mary, Dublin, spinster
1750 ,, Mathew, Dublin, orange merchant
1735 ,, Morris, Ormond-market, Dublin, butcher
1778 ,, Page, Ardnindeen, co. Waterford, surgeon
1739 ,, Patrick, Loftus-lane, Dublin, butcher.
1802 ,, Richard, Cooban, Dublin
1742 ,, Robert, lieut. in gen. Otway's regiment of foot
1804 ,, Robert, city of Limerick, gent.
1720 ,, Thomas, Dublin, esq.
1784 ,, rev. Thomas, Dublin, D.D.
1800 ,, Thomas, Dublin, esq.
1803 ,, Thos., Ardnerdeen, co. Waterford, gent.
1690 ,, William, Dublin, esq.
1753 ,, William, *alias* **Buckworth,** Cashel, esq.
1799 ,, William, Parsonstown, King's County, esq.
  [See CARRE, CORR.]

1808 **Carragher**, Bryan, Cloughanmoyle, co. Louth, gent.
1784 ,, Edmond, Cool, co. Louth.
1805 ,, Patrick, Dundalk, co. Louth, innholder
1747 **Carre**, Augustus, Cork, esq. (Large will)
1779 ,, Colombine, Lee, Cork, esq.
1662 ,, John, Thurles, co. Tipperary, esq.
1692 ,, John, Dublin, gent.
      [See CARR.]
1617 **Carreghan**, Richard, Creesstown, co. Kildare
1666 **Carrick**, Anne, widow of Captain Thomas Carr, Youghal
1798 ,, Christopher, Oldtown, co. Dublin, farmer
1655 ,, Dennis, Dublin, gardener
                          [V. 78
1725 ,, Mathew, Dublin, tailor
1762 ,, Mathias, Dirty-lane, Dublin, distiller
1800 ,, Michael, Oldtown, co. Dublin, farmer
1790 ,, Philip, Red Cow, co. Dublin
1775 ,, Somerset, Hamilton, earl of
1666 ,, capt. Thomas
1735 ,, Thomas, Dublin, watchmaker
1788 ,, Walter, Dublin, gent.
      [See CRAIG.]
1738 **Carrig**, Bartle, Ringsend, co. Dublin, mariner
1683 **Carrol**, John, Garrans, King's County
1728 ,, Nicholas, Stalleen, co. Meath
1801 ,, Patrick, Little Hilltown, co. Meath, farmer
1768 **Carroll**, Alex., Dublin, esq.
1784 ,, Alex., Derrinvohala, co. Tipperary, gent.
1745 ,, Alice, Dublin, spinster
1786 ,, Anne, *alias* **Fairbrother**, Dublin, widow
1724 ,, Anthony, Lisheenboy, co. Tipperary, gent.
1797 ,, Anthony, Clony, co. Kildare, farmer
1708 ,, Bryan, Dublin, periwig maker
1724 ,, Daniel, Killieregane, co. Tipperary
1776 ,, Edward, Curragh, co. Longford, gent.
1773 ,, Ephraim, Dublin, esq.
1657 ,, Henry, Rainstoll, co. Kildare
                          [VI. 189
1752 ,, Hugh, Derrydalney, King's County, worsted comber
1762 ,, Hugh, Derrydalney, King's County, gent

1639 **Carroll**, sir James, Dublin, knt.
1712 ,, James, of the lordship of Baltinglass, co. Wicklow, esq.
1728 ,, James, Tulla, co. Tipperary, gent.
1764 ,, James, Killuny, co. Galway, esq.
1806 ,, James, Droomgoolin, co. Louth
1751 ,, John, Carlow, merchant
1783 ,, John, Glassminoge, co. Dublin, gent.
1788 ,, John, Dublin, gent.
1795 ,, John, Dublin, gent
1796 ,, John, Waterford, merchant
1796 ,, John, Dunmore, co. Galway, gent.
1796 ,, Juliana, *alias* **Connor**
1785 ,, Lydia, Dublin, widow
1671 ,, Mabrony, Devriskin, co. Tipperary, gent.
1762 ,, Mary
1808 ,, Mary, city of Dublin, widow
1807 ,, Michael, Kilfadda, co. Tipperary, esq.   [farmer
1765 ,, Neal, Larragh, co. Kildare,
1723 ,, Owen, Borris-in-Ossory, Queen's County, esq.
1766 ,, Patrick, Aston's-quay, Dublin
1788 ,, Patrick, Birr, King's County, merchant
1763 ,, Peter, Dublin, mealman
1764 ,, Rebecca, Athboy
1810 ,, Redmond, jun., Ardagh
1755 ,, Remy, Ardagh, co. Galway
1753 ,, Richard, Dublin, gent.
1754 ,, Richard, formerly of Emell, King's County, late in Lorrain, gent.
1711 ,, Robert, Emell, King's County, gent.   [dare, yeoman
1765 ,, Robert, Coghlanstown, co. Kil-
1807 ,, Robert E., Killedmona, co. Carlow
1766 ,, Sarah, Dublin, widow
1810 ,, Symon, Bow-street, Dublin
1776 ,, Thomas, Dublin, cabinetmaker
1789 ,, Thomas, Dublin, publican
1791 ,, Thomas, Castlecomer, co. Kilkenny, gent.
1704 ,, William, Anamedle, co. Tipperary, gent.
1719 ,, William, Dublin, gent.
1746 ,, William, Thurles, co. Tipperary
1789 ,, William, Bow-street, Dublin
1801 ,, William, Ballinagany, co. Tipperary
1805 ,, William, Killart, co. Kildare
1805 ,, William
      [See GORROLL.]

1795 **Carruthers,** William, cornet in 4th dragoon guards
    [See CARUTHERS.]
1658 **Carryer,** John, trooper in major Morgan's troop   **[VI.** 257
1709 **Carsan,** Benjamin, Dublin, vintner
1694 ,, James, Bishopscourt, co. Down, farmer
1722 ,, John, Dublin, brewer
1792 ,, Joseph, Pettigo, co. Donegal, gent.
1784 ,, Robert, Philadelphia, America, merchant
1748 ,, William, Dublin, gent.
    [See CARSON.]
1808 **Carshore,** James, Hollywood, merchant
1786 ,, Robert, Kilglin, co. Meath, farmer
1716 ,, Thomas, Dublin, innkeeper
1799 ,, Thomas, Hollymount, co. Mayo
1782 **Carson,** James, Dublin, esq.
1715 ,, Jane, Dublin, widow
1772 ,, John, Hillsborough, co. Down
1796 ,, Joseph, Newry, co. Down, merchant
1728 ,, Richard, New-street, Dublin, yeoman
1778 ,, Robert, Vianstown, co. Down, gent.
    [See CARSAN.]
1804 **Cartan,** Mary, Gorey, co. Wexford, spinster
1793 **Carten,** James, Poppintree, co. Dublin, farmer
    [See CARTON.]
1660 **Carter,** Anne, Grenane, widow
    [VIII. 155
1675 ,, Arthur, Lystrye, co. Kerry, lieut.
1776 ,, Arthur, Dublin, gent.
1793 ,, Brockelsby, Ballinakill, Queen's county
1806 ,, rev. Bryan, Singland, Limk., clk.
1743 ,, Charles, Palmerston, co. Dublin, gardener
1792 ,, Charles, Dublin, painter
1792 ,, Dorothea, widow
1659 ,, Edward, Dublin, esq. **[VI.** 199
1740 ,, Walter, sen., Cronihorn, co. Wicklow
1700 ,, Elizabeth, widow of Charles C., Dublin, saddler (Copy)
1805 ,, Elizabeth, Church-st., Dublin, widow
1771 ,, Francis, Dublin, fanmaker
1730 ,, George, Hackney, Middlesex (Copy)
1797 ,, Grace, Dublin, widow
1641 ,, Henry, sen., Newry, innkeeper
1790 ,, Henry Boyle, Dublin, esq.

1737 **Carter,** Jeremiah, Shinrone, King's County, farmer
1656 ,, lieut.-col. John, London
    [V. 286
1730 ,, John, Fleet-street, London
1802 ,, rev. John, Ballykilcavan, Queen's County, clk.
1785 ,, Joseph, Iron Mills, Queen's County
1800 ,, Joshua, gent.
1638 ,, Margery, Tallow, co. Waterford, widow
1770 ,, Mary, Dublin, widow
1776 ,, Mary, Dublin
1809 ,, Mary, Dublin city, widow
1766 ,, Michael, Lodge, co. Carlow, gent.
1733 ,, Nicholas, Dublin, bricklayer
1768 ,, Oliver, prebendary and vicar of Tulla
1800 ,, Patrick, Drumlease, co. Leitrim, esq.
1785 ,, Robert, Ballinakill, Queen's County, dyer
1637 ,, Thomas, Tallow, co. Waterford, burgess
1765 ,, Thomas, esq., privy councillor and secretary of state.
1765 ,, Thomas, Rathnally, co. Meath, esq.
1698 ,, William, Dublin, merchant
    [See CHARTER.]
1748 **Carthy,** Charles, Dublin, office keeper at Dublin Castle.
1740 ,, Cornelius, Gaggin, co. Cork, farmer
1733 ,, Daniel, Ballymure, co. Wicklow, gent.
1743 ,, Elizabeth, widow of major Richard Carthy
1793 ,, John, Kilmainham, co. Dublin, tanner
1790 ,, Mary, Leixlip, co. Kildare
1711 ,, Richard, Dublin, esq.
    [See CARTY.]
1779 **Cartland,** George, Ballykillen, King's County, gent.
1792 ,, George, Dublin, esq.
1713 **Carton,** David, Crooked Staff, co. Dublin, clothier
1808 ,, Thomas, Monkstown, co. Dubl.
    [See CARTAN, CARTEN, CARTY.]
1767 **Cartwright,** Caleb, Dublin, D.D.
1703 ,, Charles, Dolphin's Barn, co. Dublin, gent.
1805 ,, Edwd., Hampstead, Middlesex, esq.
1736 ,, Henry, par. of St. James, Westminster, esq. (Copy)

1636 **Cartwright**, Jeffrey, St. Patrick-st., merchant
1668 ,, Nathaniel, Dublin, felt-maker
1730 ,, Ruth Mary, Dublin, spinster
1689 ,, Thomas, bp. of **Chester**, q. v.
1805 **Carty**, Allen, Gorey, co. Wexford, gent.
1783 ,, Anne, College-green, Dublin.
1794 ,, Dennis, Birchgrove, co. Wexford, gent.
1804 ,, Dorothy, city of Waterford, widow
1772 ,, George, Redcastle, co. Down, esq.
1759 ,, Jane, Dublin, spinster
1751 ,, John, Dublin, gent.
1801 ,, John, *alias* **Crimeen**, Kinsale, co. Cork, farmer
1758 ,, Martin, cook
1808 ,, dame Mary, Tallow, co. Waterford
1780 ,, Nicholas, Fleet-street, Dublin.
1807 ,, Susanna, city of Dublin, widow
          [See CARTHY, CARTON.]
1788 **Caruthers**, James, lieutenant in the 1st regiment of horse
1803 ,, John, major 55th regt. foot
          [See CAROTHERS, CARRUTHERS, CROTHERS, CROWTHER.]
1725 **Carvile**, William, Dublin, Esq.
1670 **Carwerdine**, Thomas, Dublin, gent.
1769 **Cary**, Anne, Cork, widow
1787 ,, Anne, Artadowney, widow
1723 ,, Arthur, Coleraine, co. Derry, alderman
1670 ,, Avis, Redcastle, co. Donegal, widow
1797 ,, Deboragh, Portarlington, Queen's County, widow
1797 ,, right hon. Edward, Dublin
1718 ,, Elizabeth, Brookend, co. Tyrone, widow
1759 ,, Elizabeth, widow of George C., Redcastle, co. Donegal, esq.
1780 ,, Elizabeth, wife to Tristam C.
1804 ,, Francis, Moynalty, co. Monaghan, widow
1669 ,, George, Redcastle, co. Donegal, esq.
1749 ,, George, Dublin, esq.
1758 ,, George, surveyor of Coleraine Port
1804 ,, George, Greencastle, co. Donegal
1757 ,, Henry, Dungiven, co. Derry, esq.
1769 ,, rev. Henry, archdeacon of Killalla
1762 ,, Jane, Killowen, co. Derry, spinster

1755 **Cary**, Mary, Coleraine, co. Derry
1800 ,, Mary, *alias* **Gore**, Dubl., widow
1751 ,, Mordecai, bp. of **Killala**, q. v.
1777 ,, rev. Oliver, Munfin, co. Wexford, clk.
1672 ,, Patrick, St. Andrews, Holborn, esq. (Copy)
1739 ,, Patrick, Dublin, popish priest
1758 ,, Peter, clerk at Rasharkin, co. Antrim
1682 ,, Robert, White Castle, co. Donegal, esq.
1658 ,, dame Susan, widow of sir Patrick C., Dublin, knt.
1736 ,, Susanna, Coleraine, co. Londonderry, spinster
1662 ,, sir Thomas, Portlester, co. Meath, knt.
1676 ,, Trisham, Coleraine, esq.
1726 ,, Tristram, Raphoe, co. Donegal, gent.
1782 ,, Tristram, Bushfield, co. Donegal
1731 ,, Warren, Bristol, merchant (Copy)
1664 ,, William, London, haberdasher
          [**IX**. 218
          [See CAREW, CAREY]
1783 **Carysfort**, Elizabeth, Lady dowager (Copy)
1797 **Casan**, Henry, Kevin-street, Dublin, feather merchant
          [See CASSON.]
1784 **Casedy**, Frances, Dublin, widow
          [See CASSIDY.]
1808 **Casement**, Thomas, surgeon in the services of the East India Company
1804 **Casey**, Charles, city of Cork, esq.
1671 ,, Francis, Carcallamore, co. Clare, esq.
1769 ,, James, Ballyneety, co. Limerick, gent.
1786 ,, James, Graiguenamanagh, co. Kilkenny
1795 ,, John, the Watercourse, city of Cork, gent.
1797 ,, John, Dublin
1800 ,, John, city of Cork, cardmaker
1811 ,, John, Princes-street, Cork
1758 ,, Mary, Coomb, co. Dublin, widow   [merchant
1742 ,, Matthew, Mullingar, co. Meath,
1803 ,, Michael, Cork, woollen draper
1792 ,, Richard, Larabryan, co. Kildare, farmer
1651 ,, Robert, Dublin, gent.
1746 ,, Robert, Dublin, merchant.
1637 ,, Thomas Rathconane, co. Lim., esq.

1769 **Casey**, Thomas, Booleybeg, North Lib. of Cork, farmer.
1783 ,, Thomas, Limerick, merchant
1731 ,, William, Limerick, tobacconist
1780 ,, William, Dolphin's-barn-lane, tanner
1797 ,, William, Blossom-grove, co. Cork, gent.
[See CASIE, CASSE, CASY, CEASY.]
1624 **Cashel**, Milerus Magrath, archbishop of
1629 ,, Malcolm Hamilton, archb. of
1665 ,, Archbald Hamilton, archbp. of
1685 ,, Thomas Price, archbishop of
1726 ,, William Palliser, archbp. of
1727 ,, William Nicholson, archbp. of (lately bishop of Derry)
1729 ,, Timothy Goodwin, archbp. of
1744 ,, Theophilus Bolton, archbp. of
1752 ,, Arthur Price, archbp. of
1753 ,, John Whetcombe, archbp of
1779 ,, Michael Cox, lord archbp. of
1763 ,, Henry, Bushfield, co. Tipperary, gent.
1754 ,, James, Dublin, gent. [gent.
1731 ,, Luke, Down, co. Westmeath,
1713 ,, Nicholas, Dublin, victualler
1735 ,, Patrick, Ballynanin, co. Clare, gent.
1760 ,, Penelope, Dublin, spinster
1761 ,, Peter
1782 ,, Rebecca
1802 **Cashell**, George, Tralee, co. Kerry, esq. (Large)
1807 **Cashin**, Anne, city of Lim. spinster
1754 ,, Dorothea, Limerick, widow
1734 ,, Elizabeth, Dublin, widow
1784 ,, rev. Robert, liberty of Limerick, clk.
1660 ,, Thomas, Athy, tanner [**VIII.** 103
[See CASSON.]
1803 **Cashore**, Andrew, Strabane, co. Tyrone, merchant
1700 **Casie**, Robert, Dublin, esq.
1714 ,, Robert, Dublin, esq.
[See CASEY.]
1723 **Cassady**, Cormack, gent.
[See CASSIDY.]
1576 **Casse**, Laurence, St. John's par.
[See CASEY.]
1743 **Cassell**, Mary Anne, Dubl., widow
[See CASTLE.]
1801 **Casserly**, David, late deceased.
1651 ,, William
1779 **Cassidy**, Alexander, house steward to lord Clanwilliam
1734 ,, Barnaby, Kill, co. Westmeath, M.D.

1787 **Cassidy**, Catherine, Dublin, widow
1806 ,, David, Marylebone-street, Middlesex
1783 ,, Jane, Derry, co. Monaghan, spinster
1789 ,, Luke, Mark-street, Dublin, hatter
1809 ,, Luke, Meath-street, Dublin
1804 ,, Marcus, Newtown-avenue, co. Dublin
1775 ,, Mary, Dublin, widow
1785 ,, Maurice, College-green, Dub., confectioner
1787 ,, Michael, Glasnevin, grocer
1757 ,, Patrick, Derry, co. Monaghan, farmer [gent.
1787 ,, Patrick, Townsend-st., Dublin, [See CASSADY, CASSEDY.]
1789 **Cassin**, Alice, widow
[See CASSON.]
1710 **Cassinghurst**, Christopher, Ringsend, gunner of the "Speedwell"
1765 **Casson**, George, Dublin, merchant
1650 ,, Jane, widow of Wm. C., Donore, city and co. Dublin
1809 ,, Joseph, Harcourt-st., Dublin
1721 ,, Robert, Dublin, waterman
[See CASAN, CASHIN, CASSIN.]
1637 **Castardine**, George, Coleraine, gent.
1728 **Castel**, Alexander, Ballyhack, co. Wexford, gent.
1669 **Castell**, Constance, Stoke Newington, Middlesex, widow (Copy)
1751 ,, Edward, Ballyhack, co. Wexford, gent.
1666 ,, Michael, London, merchant (Copy)
1710 **Castle**, Anne, Painswick, Gloucestershire, spinster (Copy)
1741 ,, James, Clonmel, co. Tipperary, gent.
1750 ,, Richard, Dublin, esq.
[See CASSELL.]
1719 **Castlecomer**, Christopher, lord viscount (Copy)
1751 ,, George, lord viscount
1638 **Castleconnell**, Edwd., lord baron of
1642 **Castledine**, Rebecca
1642 ,, Richard, Farnham, co. Cavan, gent.
1746 **Castledurrow**, William, lord baron of
1720 **Castlehaven**, Elizabeth, dowager countess
1741 ,, James, lord Audley, earl of (Copy)
1778 ,, John, earl of (Copy)

1809 **Castlestewart,** right hon. Andrew
       Robert, earl of (Large)
1693 **Castleton,** George, Aghanargret,
       near Moate, co. Meath, yeo-
       man
1792 **Castro,** Peter, Dublin, cook
                        [**CXVII.** 145
1630 **Casy,** James, Rathcannon, co.
       Limerick, esq.
                        [See CASEY.]
1584 **Cateline,** Edward, London, mercht.
1637 **Catelyn,** sir Nathaniel, knt., one of
       His Majesty's serjeants-at-
       law
1665 **Cathcart,** Adam, Drumslagee, co.
       Tyrone, gent.
1735 ,,   Anne, Belcoo, co. Fermanagh,
       widow
1752 ,,   Archibald, Enniskillen, co. Fer-
       managh, esq.
1740 ,,   Carleton, son of lieut. Hugh C.,
       co. Fermanagh
1758 ,,   Carleton, Ghent, Austrian
       Netherlands, life guards-
       man.
1741 ,,   Charles, lord (Copy)
1789 ,,   Elizabeth, lady (see 1790)
1790 ,,   rt. hon. Elizabeth, lady (Copy)
1795 ,,   Ellinor, city of Dublin, widow
1730 ,,   Hugh, Claughanagh, co. Fer-
       managh, esq.
1725 ,,   Jas., Scanley, co. Fermanagh,
       clk.
1652 ,,   John, Donoughmore, co. Done-
       gal, capt.
1759 ,,   John, Cloughmills Grange, co.
       Antrim
1778 ,,   Mary, widow of col. Alexander
       Cathcart
1806 ,,   William, city of Dublin, esq.
1688 **Catherwood,** Hugh, co. Down
1766 ,,   John, Dublin, grocer
1792 ,,   John, par. St. Mary-le-bon,
       Middlesex (Copy)
1774 ,,   Margaret, Dublin, widow
1749 ,,   Robert, lieut.-col. of col. Batte-
       reau's regt.
1770 ,,   William, capt. in 73rd regt. of
       foot, òr invalids (Copy)
1737 **Caudier,** Peter, Dublin, esq.
1740 **Caufeild,** John, Wolfestown, co.
       Kildare, gent.
1732 **Caufield,** Daniel, Lanestown, co.
       Kildare, gent.
1774 **Caulfield,** rev. Adam, Dublin (By
       decree)
1755 ,,   Alice, Castlecoote, co. Rosc.
1804 ,,   rev. Caulfield, Enniskillen
1768 ,,   hon. and rev. Charles, Dublin,
       clk.

1737 **Caulfield,** Elizabeth, Ardree, co.
       Sligo, now of Dublin, widow
1712 ,,   John, Tulledowey, co. Tyrone,
       esq.
1764 ,,   John, Dublin, esq.
1771 ,,   Michael, Levittstown, co. Kil-
       dare, gent.
1747 ,,   Raphael Hunt, capt. in col.
       Folliot's regt. of foot
1789 ,,   Rebecca, Carlow town, spinster
1780 ,,   rev. doctor Robert, Sackville-
       st., Dublin
1778 ,,   St. George, Donamon, co. Gal-
       way, esq.
1811 ,,   St. George, Donamon, co. Gal-
       way, esq. (Copy)
1725 ,,   Sidney, Dublin, widow
1750 ,,   Terence, Heartwell, co. Kild.,
       gent.
1691 ,,   Thomas, Donamon, co. Gal-
       way, esq.
1747 ,,   Thomas, Donamon, co. Gal-
       way, esq.
1740 ,,   Toby, Donamon, co. Galway
1737 ,,   William, Donamon, co. Galway
       [See CAUFEILD, CAUFIELD.]
1673 **Causabon,** Thomas, Youghal, esq.
1733 **Cavallies,** Samuel, Dublin, esq.
1660 **Cavan,** Charles, earl of
                        [**VIII.** 120
1742 ,,   Richard Lambert, earl of
1674 **Cavanagh,** Darby, Ballymallow, dio.
       Leighlin
1775 ,,   Edward, High-street, Dublin,
       hatter
1808 ,,   Jacob, Pitt-street, Dublin
1789 ,,   Jas., Ballyhook, co. Wicklow,
       farmer
1777 ,,   Jane, Dunbrow, co. Dublin,
       widow
1796 ,,   Jane, *alias* **Maguire,** Dublin
1796 ,,   John, city of Limerick, shop-
       keeper
1802 ,,   John, Newtown, co. Dublin,
       farmer
1781 ,,   Kennedy, New Ross, co. Wex-
       ford, merchant
1808 ,,   Langrishe, New Ross, co. Wex-
       ford, merchant
1794 ,,   Mary, Coolmina, co. Dublin,
       spinster
1707 ,,   Murtagh, Dublin, maltster
1777 ,,   Thomas, Meath-street, Dublin,
       merchant
1795 ,,   Wentworth, New Ross, co.
       Wexford, merchant
1785 ,,   William, Three Castles, co.
       Wicklow, farmer
       [See CAVENAGH, CAVINAGH,
               KAVANAGH.]

1803 **Cave,** Elizabeth, Dublin, spinster
1775 ,, Margaret, Dublin, spinster
1793 ,, Richard, Dublin, merchant
1639 ,, Thomas, Dublin, esq.
1669 ,, Vincent, archdn. of the Boyle, dio. Elphin
1758 **Cavell,** James, Lemonstown, co. Wicklow, gent.
1752 **Cavenagh,** Dennis, Dublin, hatter
1664 ,, Edward, Dublin, gent.
1775 ,, Hugh, Grangegorman-lane, Dublin
1784 ,, Jane, Great Britain-st., Dublin, widow
1793 ,, Nathaniel, Dublin, esq. [See CAVANAGH.]
1779 **Cavendish,** Catherine, lady
1797 ,, Elizabeth, Cork, widow
1777 ,, sir Henry, Doveridge, Derbyshire, but residing in Dublin, bart., privy councillor.
1804 ,, sir Henry, city of Dublin, bart.
1747 ,, rev. James, rector of Navan
1752 ,, James, commonly called lord James C., Staley, Derbyshire (Copy)
1760 ,, John, Mallow, co. Cork
1769 **Cavinagh,** James, Graigue, co. Kilkenny, gauger [See CAVANAGH.]
1781 **Cawthorn,** George, High-st., Dub., gent.
1757 **Ceasy,** Patrick, Mullinoran, co. Westmeath, farmer [See CASEY.]
1684 **Cecil,** cornet Philip, Drummurry, co. Cavan, gent.
1779 ,, Joseph, Ballykelly, co. Tipp., farmer
1684 **Cecill,** Phil., Drummurry, co. Cavan, gent. **[XVI.** 90
1719 **Cerelly,** Thomas, Ballakelly, co. Monaghan, gent.
1707 **Chabenor,** Henry, Giltown, co. Kildare, gent.
1801 **Chabert,** Andrew, Island of St. Croix, W. Indies (Copy)
1711 **Chads,** Henry, Belfast, merchant
1673 **Chadwick,** Henry, soldier in brevet-capt. Moor's regt. of guards
1722 ,, Richard, Ballinard, co. Tipp., gent.
1771 ,, Richard, Ballinard, co. Tipp., esq. (Not proved)
1753 **Chadwicke,** Ellinor, *alias* **Gibbs,** widow [See SEDGWICK.]
1780 **Chaigneau,** Abraham, son of Peter Chaigneau
1783 ,, Charlotte, Dublin, spinster

1753 **Chaigneau,** David, Dublin, esq.
1779 ,, John, Dublin, merchant
1780 ,, John, Dublin, gent.
1724 ,, Lewis, Dublin, merchant
1797 ,, Margaret, Dublin, widow
1750 ,, Mary, Dublin, widow
1779 ,, Mary, Dublin, spinster
1767 ,, Peter, Dublin, merchant
1705 ,, Stephen, Dublin, merchant·
1779 ,, Susanna, Dublin, spinster
1781 ,, William, Dublin, esq.
1791 **Chalcraft,** Anne, city of Bath, spinster
1726 **Chalke,** Isaac, Dublin, painter, stainer, and plasterer
1752 ,, Thomas, Dublin, gent.
1676 **Challenor,** Margaret, Dubl., widow
1585 **Challoner,** Elizabeth, widow of John Challoner, principal secretary in Ireland
1680 ,, James, Drogheda, gent.
1704 ,, James, Dublin, brewer [See CHALONER.]
1632 **Chalmers,** Alexander, par. of Stains, co. Down, gent.
1765 ,, sir Chas., capt. in royal regt. of artillery (Copy)
1702 ,, David, Belfast, esq.
1681 ,, James, Belfast, merchant
1789 ,, James, Dublin, bookbinder
1725 ,, John, Belfast, merchant
1569 **Chalon,** Lewis, Dublin, merchant
1756 **Chaloner,** Anne, Steevens' hospital, widow
1671 ,, Daniel, Dubl., dancing master
1755 ,, George, steward of Steevens' hospital
1733 ,, John, Rathenree [esq.
1779 ,, John, Kingsfort, co. Meath,
1808 ,, John, Clonmel [See CHALLENOR, CHALLONER.]
1743 **Chamberlain,** Christopher, Dublin, esq.
1790 ,, Hannah, Dublin, widow
1764 ,, Lawr., Magaddy, co. Meath, farmer
1658 ,, Robert, trooper **[VI.** 296
1800 ,, Theophilus, Knockfin, Queen's County, gent.
1681 ,, Walter, Dublin, gent.
1728 ,, William, Dublin, surgeon
1804 **Chamberlaine,** Alicia, city of Dubl., widow [County
1802 ,, Eliz., Mountmellick, Queen's
1747 ,, Leonard, Dublin, wine cooper
1803 ,, Mary
1808 ,, Mathias, Toolestown, co. Kildare, gent.
1802 ,, hon. Tankervill, one of the Justices of the King's Bench

1604 **Chamberlayne,** Marcus
1626 ,,   Michael, Dublin, alderman
1673 **Chamberline,** Jane, Dublin, widow
1686 ,,   Peter, Killinetower, co. West-
          meath, gent.
1783 **Chambers,** Abraham, Totteridge,
          Hertfordshire, esq. (Copy)
1767 ,,   Alice, Drogheda, widow
1664 ,,   Edward, Dublin, merchant
1772 ,,   Hugh, Dublin, carpenter
1806 ,,   Hugh, Tullyrean, co. Down,
          esq.
1673 ,,   John, Ballingowne, co. Kerry,
          gent.
1793 ,,   John, Dublin, timber merchant
1800 ,,   John, Eccles-street, Dub., esq.
1804 ,,   John, Galway, but late of the city
          of Dublin
1674 ,,   Mary, Dublin, widow
1776 ,,   Mary, Londonderry, widow
1730 ,,   Matthew, dissenting minister of
          Plunkett-street meeting
1794 ,,   Sarah, Dublin, widow
1664 ,,   Thomas, Armagh, esq.
1714 ,,   William, Kilboyne, co. Mayo,
          gent.
1768 ,,   William, son of James C., Trim,
          co. Meath, officer of excise
1801 **Chambert,** Andrew, Island of St.
          Croix, in the West Indies,
          esq. (Copy)
1796 **Chambre,** Anna Maria
1635 ,,   Calcott, Carnow, co. Wicklow,
          esq.
1638 ,,   Calcott, Carnowe, co. Wicklow,
          esq.
1640 ,,   Calcott, jun., Carnowe, co.
          Wicklow, esq.
1786 ,,   Calcott, Athy, co. Kildare,
          gent.
1670 ,,   John, Stormonstown, co. Louth,
          esq.
1753 ,,   Mary, Dublin, widow
1696 ,,   Robert, Dublin, clk.
1804 **Chamney,** Barthw., Rathmullen, co.
          Meath, esq.
1749 ,,   Edwd., Knocklow, co. Wicklow
1794 ,,   Graves, Platin, co. Meath, esq.
1733 ,,   John, Ballard, co. Wicklow,
          gent.
1761 ,,   John, Wexford town, esq.
1768 ,,   John, Castletown, co. Wexford,
          esq.
1792 ,,   John, Drogheda, esq.
1796 ,,   John Vanhomrigh, capt. 25th
          foot
1742 ,,   Joseph, the Forge, co. Wicklow,
          esq.
1798 ,,   Joseph, Ballyraheen. co. Wick-
          low, esq.

1737 **Chamney,** Thos., Ballyshanoge, co.
          Wexford, esq.
1799 ,,   Thos., city of Dublin, esq.
1809 ,,   Thos., Ballyrokine, co. Wick-
          low, esq.
1800 **Champagne,** rev. Arthur, dean of
          Clonmacnoise
1642 **Champen,** Arthur, Christchurch-
          yard, Dublin, merchant
1671 **Champion,** John, par. St. Saviour,
          Southwark, Surrey, gent.
          (Copy)
1787 **Champion,** John Leary, Donagha-
          dee, co. Down
1725 **Champlorier,** Mark Thebaut, Dub-
          lin, gent.
1740 **Chance,** John, Baltinglass, co.
          Wicklow, gent.
1727 **Chandlee,** John, Roosk, King's
          County, yeoman
1731 ,,   Joseph, Clanmore, King's
          County
1783 ,,   Joseph, Cork city, clerk
1793 **Chandler,** John Meekins
1790 **Chandos,** James Brydges, duke of
          (Copy)
1740 **Chapel,** Mary, Armagh, widow
1707 ,,   Richard, Armagh, esq. (Ex.)
          [See CHAPPEL.]
1787 **Chapelier,** Catherine
1799 **Chapell,** Joseph, Milltown, co. Dub-
          lin, gent.
1715 **Chapelle,** Anne, Dublin, widow
1741 ,,   Peter, lieut. in col. St. Clair's
          regiment of foot
1784 **Chapellier,** Lewis, Kilkenny city,
          gent.
1655 **Chappell,** Daniel, Belturbet, co.
          Cavan   [**V.** 126
1638 ,,   Richard, Tallow, co. Water-
          ford, gent.   [gent.
1699 ,,   Richd., Proudstown, co. Meath,
1699 ,,   Thomas, Rushtown, co. Mon.
          esq.
[See CHAPEL, CHAPELL, CHAPELLE.]
1792 **Chapman,** Anne, Dublin, widow
1767 ,,   Anthony, Dublin, barber-sur-
          geon
1660 ,,   Arthur, Dublin, gardener
                    [**VIII.** 50
1779 ,,   Benjamin, Killua, co. West-
          meath, esq.
1810 ,,   sir Benjamin, St. Lucy's, co.
          Westmeath, bart.
1779 ,,   George, the younger, Kilkenny
1698 ,,   Grace, Dublin, widow
1758 ,,   Isma, Athboy, co. Meath, wid.
1788 ,,   James, par. priest, Ahascragh
1782 ,,   Joseph, Rheban, co. Kild. gent.
1787 ,,   Mary, Boulbane, co. Galway

1631 **Chapman**, Nathl., Carragoran, co. Clare, rector Traderry, dio. Kildare
1736 ,, Saml., formerly of Dublin, now of Delgany, co. Wicklow, farmer
1799 ,, Susana, Trim, widow
1685 ,, Thomas, Dublin, mariner
1734 ,, Wm., Kilua, co. Westmeath, esq.
1794 ,, sir Wm., Lowtham hall, Suffolk, bt. (Copy)
1810 ,, William, city of Dublin, timber merchant
1678 **Chareton**, John, Aghabane, co. Cavan, gent.
[See CHARLTON.]
1729 **Charlemont**, Anne, dowager visc.
1744 ,, Elizabeth, lady viscountess
1799 ,, James, earl of (Large)
1663 ,, lady Mary Caulfield, baroness of
1640 ,, William, lord Caulfield, baron of
1726 ,, William, lord viscount
1627 **Charlemount**, Tobie Caulfield, lord Caulfield, baron of
1672 ,, William, lord viscount
1759 **Charles**, Alice, Moorpark, co. Meath, widow [gent.
1743 ,, Elijah, Moorpark, co. Meath,
1788 ,, George, Kells, co. Meath
1791 ,, James, Cork-street, Dublin, tanner
1724 ,, John, Moorpark, co. Meath, esq.
1794 ,, Joseph, Rossmead, co. Westmeath, gent.
1732 ,, Peter, Dublin, merchant
1660 ,, Thomas, fort of Ballimore [VIII. 158
1801 **Charleton**, George, city Londonderry
1752 ,, Mary, Dublin, widow
1788 ,, William, Ballykelly, co. Wexford, gent.
[See CHARLTON.]
1764 **Charlevill**, Charles, earl of (Large will) [tess
1789 **Charleville**, Hester, dowager coun-
1757 **Charlton**, Andrew, Dublin, esq.
1757 ,, Elizabeth, Dublin, widow
1731 ,, Job, Killaveny, co. Wicklow, gent.
1727 ,, Richard, Dublin, merchant
1634 ,, Thos., Clownes, co. Fermanagh, merchant
1793 ,, Thos., Curratown, co. Meath
[See CHARETON, CHARLETON.]
1685 **Charnock**, Hugh, Drogheda, chandler
1719 **Charriere**, Frans (native of Switzerland), Dublin, brewer

1802 **Charter**, Samuel, Tuam, co. Galway, coach harness maker
1662 ,, Wm., the elder, Grange Trevet, co. Meath, gent.
1762 ,, William, capt. in genl. Handasyd's regt.
[See CARTER.]
1707 **Charters**, Henry, Lisburn, co. Antrim, merchant [gent.
1805 **Chartres**, John, Ennis, co. Clare,
1805 ,, Richard, of Ringsend, surveyor
1723 ,, William, Cork, esq.
1740 ,, William, Cork, esq.
1758 **Charurier**, Isaac, Dublin, mercht.
1682 **Chastelaine**, Daniel, Dublin, merchant
1637 **Chattell**, Richard, Dublin, yeoman [IV. 255
1806 **Chatterton**, sir James, city of Cork, bart.
1794 ,, Thomas, city of Cork, esq.
1726 **Chaucherie**, Clenet, Dublin
1727 ,, Sarah, Dublin, widow
1764 **Chauncey**, Charles, Newington, Middlesex, gent. (Copy)
1739 **Chaunders**, Caleb, Cloncoss, Queen's County, farmer
1695 ,, Thos., Straughnalal, Queen's County, nailer
1736 **Chauvett**, John, Dublin, merchant
1746 **Chauvin**, Martha, Dublin, widow
1765 **Chawner**, Daniel, Clonenny, co. Tipperary, farmer
1770 **Chaytor**, John, Kilmacurrow, co. Wicklow, farmer
1762 ,, Nicholas, Dublin, chandler
1803 ,, Thos., Clonmel, co. Tipperary, school master
[See CHEATOR.]
1787 **Chearnley**, Anthony, Springfield, co. Waterford, esq.
1791 ,, Richd., Saltibridge, co. Waterford, esq.
1750 **Cheator**, Christopher, Dub., dairyman
[See CHAYTOR.]
1670 **Chedle**, Judith, Dublin, widow
1741 **Cheesman**, John, Dublin, comber
1696 **Cheetham**, Ellinor, Dublin, widow
[See CHETHAM.]
1769 **Cheevers**, Barbara, Kilkenny, wid.
1779 ,, Francis, Dublin, joiner
1759 ,, Hyacinth, Cregan, co. Galway, esq.
1595 ,, John, Maston, co. Meath, esq.
1805 ,, John, Killoyne, co. Galway
1810 ,, Patrick, town of Galway, esq.
1633 ,, Thomas, St. Michan's parish, Dublin, merchant
[See CHEVERS.]

1738 **Chelar**, Peter, Waterford, gent.
1776 **Chenevix**, Daniel, major of the
        Royal Irish regiment of
        artillery
1758 ,, col. Philip, Dublin, esq.
1791 ,, Susanna, Frederick-st., Dublin,
        spinster
        [See CHEVENIX.]
1811 **Cheney**, Elizabeth, co. of the town
        of Drogheda, spinster [law
1789 ,, George, Dublin, attorney-at-
1757 ,, Henry, Collinstown, co. Kil-
        dare, gent.
1754 ,, John, Collinstown, co. Kildare,
        esq.   [gent.
1762 ,, John, Kilgoan, co. Kildare,
1735 ,, Oliver, Dublin, merchant
1776 **Cherry**, Dennis, Waterford, mer-
        chant   [widow
1784 ,, Esther, Violet hill, co. Armagh,
1804 ,, Francis Penrose, city of Water-
        ford, merchant
1791 ,, Saml., Waterford, mercht.
1779 **Cheshire**, Edward, Drogheda, esq.
1656 ,, Captain Thomas
        [See CHESTER.]
1660 **Chesman**, Mary, Ballyreny, co.
        Tyrone, widow
1766 **Chesshire**, Edward, the elder,
        Drogheda, alderman.
        [See CHESTER.]
1778 **Chester**, Catherine, Ballrunning,
        co. Dublin, spinster
1772 ,, Christopher, Dublin, mercht.
1794 ,, Miles, Drogheda, merchant
1778 ,, Richard, Chesterfield, co.Cork,
        esq.   [(Ex.)
1689 ,, Thomas Cartwright, bishop of
        [See CHESHIRE, CHESSHIRE.]
1659 **Cheswick**, Mary, *alias* dame Mary
        Leigh, Omagh, co. Tyrone,
        widow (original in Dublin
        collection)   [VII. 116
1649 **Chetham**, Mary, Dublin, widow
        [See CHEETHAM.]
1671 **Chettle**, *or* **Cettle**, William, Lis-
        more, co. Waterford, gent.
1791 **Chetwood**, Hannah Symes, Dublin,
        widow
1781 ,, Hill, Dublin, gent.
1791 **Chetwynd**, William, lord visct.
1772 **Chevenix**, rev. Phillip, Waterford,
        clk.
        [See CHENEVIX.]
1675 **Chever**, Ales., *alias* **Andrews**, *alias*
        Griffin, Drogheda, widow
1585 ,, Patrick, House of Macetone,
        co. Meath
1567 ,, Richard, par. Portrane, co.
        Dublin, husbandman

1582 **Chevers**, sir Christopher, Maceton,
        co. Meath, knt.
1805 ,, Christopher, Turlogh, co. Gal-
        way, esq.
1768 ,, Mary, Dublin, widow
1780 ,, Mary, Turlogh, co. Galway,
        widow   [esq.
1779 ,, Michael, Killyan, co. Galway,
1779 ,, Wm., Meadstown, co. Meath,
        esq.
        [See CHEEVERS, CHIVER.]
1604 **Chevyn**, Thomas
1624 **Chichester**, sir Arthur, knt., lord
        Chichester, baron, Belfast
        (Copy)
1680 ,, Edward, of the 'Unicorn' ship-
        of-war, and Prospect, co.
        Wexford, esq.
1657 ,, John, Dungannon, esq.
                            [VI. 133
1716 ,, John, Prospect, co. Wexford,
        esq.
1720 ,, John Etchingham, par. St. Jas.,
        Westminster, esq.   (Copy)
1695 **Chiffinch**, William, Whitehall, esq.
        (Copy)
1747 **Child**, Robert, Bandon, co. Cork,
        merchant
1584 **Chillam**, Patrick, Drogheda, aldn.
1633 ,, Robert, Drogheda, alderman
1763 **Chillcott**, John Congreve, Dublin,
        esq.
1673 **Chilton**, Thomas, Dublin, gent.
1714 **Chinn**, Richd., Newenham, Glouces-
        tershire, mariner (Ex)
1809 **Chinnery**, sir Broderick, bart.
                            (Large)
1755 ,, rev. Geo., Middleton, co. Cork,
        clk.
1780 ,, George, bp. of **Cloyne**, q. v.
1783 ,, Nicholas, Flintfield, co. Cork,
        esq.
1708 ,, Richard, Limerick, gent.
1787 ,, St. John, capt. in Royal Navy
1763 **Chittick**, Walter, Bath, Somerset-
        shire, esq. (Copy)
1640 **Chiver**, *or* **Chevers**, Thomas,
        Drogheda, merchant
1789 **Chivers**, Nicholas, Summerscove,
        Ree, co. Cork, boatman
1702 **Cholan**, Denis, Kilbeg, co. Wicklow,
        yeoman
1695 **Cholet**, Samuel, Sieur-de-Fetilly,
        late of Brende, near Rochelle,
        in France
1695 ,, widow of said Samuel
1701 **Cheppynge**, Mary, Rockingham,
        co. Roscommon, widow
1695 ,, Robert, Newcastle, co. Long-
        ford (Ex.)

1747 **Chouvin**, John, Dublin, peruke maker
1803 **Christee**, Alexander, Dub., gent. [See CHRISTY.]
1786 **Christell**, Mary, Monaghan, spr.
1788 **Christian**, Brabazon, Waterford city, esq.
1753 ,, rev. John, Kill, co. Kildare, clk.
1782 ,, Mary, Dublin, spinster
1709 ,, Mathew, Dublin, merchant
1678 ,, Minard, Dublin, merchant
1699 ,, Minard, Dublin, merchant
1714 ,, Minard, Waterford, esq.
1687 ,, Patk, Portnescully, co. Kilk., clk., preby. of Kilrossenty, Lismore
1721 ,, Wm., Old Grange, co. Watfd., gent.
1784 **Christie**, rev. John, Aughacollin, co. Tyrone, clk. See [CHRISTY.]
1749 **Christisan**, Bridget, Sheds of Clontarf, co. Dublin, widow
1770 **Christmas**, Elizabeth, widow
1723 ,, Richard, Waterford, esq.
1704 ,, Thomas, Waterford, merchant
1747 ,, Thomas, Whitfield, co. Waterford, esq. [ford, esq.
1749 ,, Thomas, Whitfield, co. Water-
1703 ,, rev. William, junior fellow of Trinity College, Dublin
1803 ,, William, Dublin, esq. (Large)
1793 **Christy**, Jas., Lurgan, co. Armagh
1772 ,, John, Stranmore, co. Down, linendraper [foot
1802 ,, Richard, lieut. in 89th regt. of
1769 ,, Thos., Gormanstown, gardener
1780 ,, Thomas, Moyallan, co. Down, linendraper
[See CHRISTEE, CHRISTIE.]
1755 **Chritohly**, James, Derrybawne, co. Wicklow, gent.
1795 ,, Lucy, Rathdrum, co. Wicklow, widow
1740 **Church**, Arthur, Coleraine, co. Londonderry
1810 ,, Charles, Whitehaven, Cumberland (Copy)
1790 ,, Frances, Dublin, spinster
1733 ,, George, Coleraine, co. Londonderry, gent.
1657 ,, Hester, wife to Thomas C. [VI. 166
1804 ,, Jane, formerly of Coleraine, late of Dublin, spinster
1803 ,, Matthew, Cork, merchant
1747 ,, Thomas, Drumbane, co. Londonderry
1810 ,, Walter, Killien, King's County, gent.

1753 **Chute**, Francis, Tralee, co. Kerry, esq.
1782 ,, Francis, Tulligarron, co. Kerry, esq. (Large will)
1800 ,, Rebecca, Montpelier-hill, co. Dublin, widow
1776 ,, Richd., Tullygarron, co. Kerry, esq.
1758 ,, Thomas, Cork, merchant
1773 **Civill**, Rebecca, Dublin, widow
1741 ,, William, Dublin, merchant
1804 **Civills**, Clare
1803 **Claffy**, Thomas, Broadwood, co. Westmeath
1792 **Clanbrassil**, rt. hon. Hariet, dowager countess
1661 ,, James, earl of [VIII. 198
1798 ,, James, earl of
1758 **Clanbrassill**, James, earl of
1675 **Clanbrazil**, Henry, earl of
1665 **Clancartie**, Donogh, earl of
1698 ,, Elizabeth, dowager countess of (Copy)
[See CLONCARTHY.]
1805 **Clancarty**, rt. hon. William Power Keating, earl of
1789 **Clanchy**, Catherine, city of Limerick, widow
1728 ,, George, Dublin, gent.
1779 ,, Geo., Knockish, co. Limerick, gent.
1656 ,, Roger, Furleagh, co. Waterford, yeoman [V. 227
1767 ,, Thomas, Caherconlish, co. Limerick, gent.
1801 **Clancy**, John, city of Dublin, gent.
1736 ,, Martin, Dublin, vintner
1810 ,, Patrick, Blackhall-st., Dublin, gent.
1799 ,, Roger, Tuam, co. Galway [See CLANCHY.]
1771 **Clandinen**, Andrew, Curdarren, co. Cavan, gent.
1787 **Clandinin**, James, Carran, co. Cavan, farmer
1772 **Clandining**, John, Ballymahon, co. Longford, gent. [See CLINDINING.]
1741 **Claney**, Patrick, Cadiz, Spain, merchant (Copy)
1709 **Clanmaleer**, Dorothy, lady viscountess
1722 **Clanricard**, Helena, dowager countess
1636 **Clanricard and St. Albans**, Richd. Burke, earl of (Copy)
1687 **Clanricard**, William, earl of (Ex.)
1668 **Clanricarde**, Eliz. Butler, dowager countess of
1664 ,, Richard, earl of

1728 **Clanrickard**, Michael, earl of
1806 **Clanwilliam**, rt. hon. Richard, earl of (Copy)
1684 **Clapham**, George, Mountmellick, vicar of Oregon or Rosenallis
1685 ,, John, Mountmellick, gent.
1730 ,, John, Dublin, clothier
1735 ,, John, the younger, Dublin
1616 ,, Thomas, Limerick, gent.
1791 **Clare**, Benjamin, Leixlip
1802 ,, rt. hon. John, earl of (Large)
1797 ,, Joshua, Claremont, co. Meath, gent.
1778 ,, Robert, Dublin, gent.
1650 ,, Thomas, Corn market, mercht. (Copy)
1723 **Clarendon**, Edwd., earl of (Copy)
1793 ,, Robert Villiers, Doveridge, Derbyshire
1798 **Clarges**, Anne, Dublin, spinster
1780 ,, Christopher, Dublin, esq.
1784 ,, George, Birr, King's County, esq. (Copy)
1804 **Clarina**, rt. hon. Eyre Massy, lord baron
1811 ,, rt. hon. Nathaniel William, lord baron
1795 **Clark**, rev. Alexander, Ballycastle, co. Antrim, clk.
1793 ,, Andrew, Blessington, co. Wicklow, dealer
1797 ,, Andrew, Ballinrobe, co. Mayo, gent.
1792 ,, rev. Arthur, preby. of St. Munchin's, Limerick
1764 ,, Elizabeth, Belfast, widow
1795 ,, Elizabeth, Booterstown - lane, co. Dublin, widow.
1777 ,, George, gent.
1757 ,, Jackson, Maghera, co. Londonderry, gent.
1770 ,, James, Ballymount, co. Mayo
1713 ,, John, Queen's County, gent.
1715 ,, John, Kiltubrid, King's Co., gent.
1774 ,, John, Tallow, co. Wat., gent.
1780 ,, John, Carrowbeg, co. Mayo, gent.
1786 ,, John, · Belfast, co. Antrim, linendraper
1799 ,, John, Clarkstown, co. Meath, farmer
1761 ,, Jonathan, Dublin, coachmaker
1795 ,, Mary, Portarlington, Queen's County, widow
1790 ,, Michael, Dublin, esq.
1779 ,, Midleton, Castlebar, co. Mayo, esq.
1798 ,, Page, Tallow, co. Waterford, gent.

1793 **Clark**, Rebecca, Limerick, widow
1766 ,, Richard, Dublin, painter
1746 ,, Robert, Glenmaquill, co. Londonderry, linendraper
1782 ,, rev. Robert, D. D., dean of Tuam (Copy)
1784 ,, Thomas, Ballinderry, co. Antrim, gent.
1729 ,, William, Dublin, merchant
1732 ,, William, Dublin, merchant
1767 ,, William, Croghan, co. Donegal
1772 ,, William, late of Hollymount, co. Mayo, now of Aughrim, co. Galway, gent.
1690 **Clarke**, Andrew, Dublin, merchant
1752 ,, Anne, Dublin, widow
1797 ,, Anne, Clontarf, co. Dublin, widow
1747 ,, Catherine, Dublin, spinster
1792 ,, Catherine, Dyor-street, Drogheda, spinster
1793 ,, Charles, West Passage, Cork, surveyor
1791 ,, Christopher, Dublin, watchmaker
1751 ,, Darley, Dublin, esq.
1755 ,, David, Dublin, embroiderer
1794 ,, David, Portarlington, esq.
1698 ,, Edward, the elder, Atherdee, co. Louth, merchant
1725 ,, Elizabeth, par. East Moulsey, Surrey, widow (Copy)
1748 ,, Elizabeth, wife of Gabriel C., of Dublin, merchant
1768 ,, Elizabeth, widow of Richard C. of Dublin, LL. D. (not proved)
1777 ,, Elizabeth, Dublin, spinster
1729 ,, Gabriel, Lisnalea, co. Kilkenny, gent.
1765 ,, Gabriel, Dublin
1663 ,, George, London, merchant (Copy)
1774 ,, George, Rath, King's County gent.
1807 ,, George, Tancraft, King's Co.
1727 ,, Henry, Anaghsamry, co. Armagh, esq.
1777 ,, rev. Henry, D.D., rector of Clonfecle, dio. Armagh
1706 ,, Humphry, Ballinderry, co. Antrim, gent.
1691 ,, James, Proudstown, co. Meath, esq.
1709 ,, James, par. St. Martin in the Fields, Middlesex, gent. (Copy)
1713 ,, James, Dublin, merchant
1728 ,, sir Jas., East Moulsey, Surrey, knt. (Ex.)

1746 **Clarke**, James, Athboy, co. Meath, esq.
1759 ,, James, Dublin, woollendraper.
1776 ,, James, Clontarf, co. Dublin, esq.
1747 ,, hon. Jane, relict of John C. of Portadown, co. Armagh, esq.
1770 ,, Jane
1672 ,, John, Maine, co. Meath, gent.
1689 ,, John, Lisburn, merchant
1691 ,, John, Portadown, co. Armagh, gent.
1719 ,, John, Killarney, co. Kerry, gent.
1729 ,, John, Portadown, co. Armagh, esq.
1752 ,, John, Newry, co. Down, esq.
1766 ., John, Anagh, co, Tipp., gent.
1770 ,, John, Dublin, tallow chandler
1784 ,, John, Rath, King's County
1795 ,, John, Warrenpoint, Co. Down, gent.
1795 ,, John, Drinagh, co. Wexford, esq.
1804 ,, John, co. Dublin
1807 ,, John, Kill, King's County, esq,
1791 ,, Jonathan, Portarlington, Queen's County, esq.
1811 ,, Joseph, Slutt's Inn, co. Dublin, coachmaker
1713 ,, Luke, Dublin, merchant
1753 ,, Mary, Dungarvan, co. Waterford, widow
1760 ,, Mary, Athboy, co. Meath, widow
1641 ,, Michael, Six Mile Bridge, co. Clare, maltster
1724 ,, Michael, Dublin, gent.
1774 ,, Michael, Dublin, esq.
1811 ,, Nicholas, city of Dublin, gunmaker
1797 ,, Pascal, Ballinla, King's County, gent.
1809 ,, Patrick, North King - street, Dublin, iron-founder
1804 ,, Peter, Ballinanagh, co. Cavan, gent.
1782 ,, Precious, Dublin, merchant
1727 ,, Prudence, Portadown, co. Armagh, widow
1798 ,, Ralph, Drumkeele, co. Cavan, esq.
1729 ,, Richard, Bandon Bridge, co. Cork
1774 ,, Richard, Ballybough Bridge, co. Dublin, lime-burner
1796 ,, Richard, Shangarry, co. Galway, nurseryman
1811 ,, Richard, city of Limerick, cabinet-maker
1628 ,, Robert, Dublin, gent.

1717 **Clarke**, Robert, Enniskillen, co. Fermanagh, gent.
1807 ,, Robert, Borrisoleigh, co. Tipp.
1751 ,, Samuel, Grange, co. Antrim, gent.
1753 ,, Samuel, master of the public school at Drogheda
1755 ,, lieutenant Samuel, Drogheda
1759 ,, Sarah, Dublin, widow
1729 ,, Simon, Dublin, esq.
1657 ,, Susanna, widow of John Clarke, late of Dublin [**VI**. 128
1630 ,, Thomas, Drogheda
1662 ,, Thomas, Dublin, clothier
1672 ,, Thos., Dremintian, co. Down, esq.
1752 ,, Thomas, Ardress, co. Armagh, esq.
1765 ,, Thomas Downham, Ennishsoye, co. Donegal, esq.
1775 ,, Thomas, Great Booter-lane, Dublin, gent.
1669 ,, sir William, Westminster, Middlesex, knt., Secretary at War (Copy)
1774 ,, William, Cork, burgess
1788 ,, William, Bow Church-yard, London, merchant (Copy)
1798 ,, William, Summer Island, co. Armagh
1810 ,, William, North King - street, Dublin, brewer [See CLERK.]
1781 **Clarkson**, Alice, Dublin, spinster
1766 ,, Joseph, Dublin, gent,
1711 ,, Mary, Dublin, spinster
1797 ,, Thomas, Coolharbour, co. Wicklow, gent.
1778 **Classon**, James, Rathmines, co. Dublin, gent.
1737 ,, Peter, Kevin-street, Dublin, hosier
1687 **Claughton**, Jeremy, Coleraine, par. Killowan, gent.
1703 ,, Richard, Dublin, victualler
1755 **Clausade**, John, Portarlington
1744 **Claverie**, John Augustus, Portarlington
1773 **Claxton**, Henry, Corbally, Queen's County, gent.
1760 ,, William, Corbally, Queen's County, farmer
1639 **Clayton**, Anne, Lady, Mallow, wid.
1789 ,, Bridget, Gt. Ormond-st., Middlesex, wid. (Large, Copy)
1766 ,, Catherine, widow of Bishop of Clogher
1762 ,, Courthope, par. St. Mary le bon, Middlesex (Copy)
1800 ,, Elizabeth, Dublin, widow

1750 **Clayton**, Jasper, Fernhill, Berkshire, lieutenant-general (Copy)
1726 ,, John, dean of Kildare. [esq.
1712 ,, Laurence, Mallow, co. Cork,
1696 ,, Margaret, spinster
1681 ,, Randall, Moyalloe (Mallow), co. Cork, esq.
1770 ,, Richd., lord ch. jus. of the common pleas in Ireland (Copy)
1724 ,, Robert, Dublin, esq. (Copy)
1760 ,, Robert, bp. of **Clogher**, q. v.
1663 ,, Thomas, gent. in the army
[**IX.** 85
[See CLEATON.]
1786 **Clealand**, Patrick, Ballymagee, co. Down, gent.
[See CLELAND.]
1739 **Clear**, Martella, Dub., spinster (Ex.)
1675 **Cleare**, James, Dublin, merchant
1754 ,, John, Kilburry, co. Tipp., esq.
1785 ,, John
1697 ,, Margaret, Dublin, widow
1734 ,, Richard, Dublin, merchant
1745 ,, Robert, Dublin, coachman
1737 ,, Thomas, Lawlestownemore, co. Tipperary, esq.
[See CLEAR, CLEER, CLEERE, CLERE.]
1805 **Cleary**, Daniel, Kildare
1786 ,, Jas., Killashandra, co. Cavan
1803 ,, Laurence, Cahervillaho, co. Tipperary, farmer
1809 ,, Patrick, Balline, co. Limerick, farmer [dare
1801 ,, William, Killinerue, co. Kil-
1672 **Cleaton**, Jane, Dublin, spinster
[See CLAYTON.]
1684 **Cleburne**, William, Ballycullatan, co. Tipperary, gent.
[See CLIBBORN.]
1632 **Cleer**, James, Ferns, co. Wexford, gent.
1663 **Cleere**, Edward, Waterford, merchant, now of Dublin
1703 ,, John, Lisdowny, co Kilk., gent.
[See CLEARE.]
1736 **Clegg**, Francis, Enniskillen, co. Fermanagh
1790 ,, George
1788 ,, James, Stephen-street, Dublin, staymaker
1763 ,, John, Enniskillen, co. Ferm.
1787 ,, John, Hacketstown
1789 **Clegharn**, George, Dublin, M.D.
1790 **Cleland**, David, St. Paul's par., Dublin, gent.
1777 ,, James, Newtown Ards, co. Down, gent.
1760 ,, William, Newry, co. Down, tobacconist
[See CLEALAND.]

1744 **Clement**, Hugh, Dublin, gent.
[**CLIX.** 107
1778 ,, Joseph, Carrickmacross, co. Monaghan
1769 ,, Margaret, Dublin, widow
1781 ,, Thomas, Carrickmacross, co. Monaghan, gent.
1784 ,, Thomas, Cromartin, co. Louth, esq.
1782 ,, William, M.D., vice-provost of Trinity College
1680 **Clements**, Daniel, Rakenny, co. Cavan, esq.
1797 ,, Eliza Hanah, Dublin, spinster
1809 ,, Elizabeth, Carrickfergus, co. Antrim, spinster
1746 ,, Fras. Robert, esq., Waterford
1781 ,, Hanah, Dublin, widow
1745 ,, Henry, major in colonel Johnston's regiment of foot
1767 ,, Henry, Dublin, merchant
1795 ,, Henry Theophilus, Dublin, rt. hon.
1805 ,, Jane, city of Dublin
1806 ,, John, Lucknaine Grove, par. Colerne, Wiltshire, esq.
1777 ,, Nathaniel, rt. hon., privy councillor
1692 ,, Richard, Cork, merchant
1722 ,, Robert, Dublin, esq.
1723 ,, Robert, Dublin, esq.
1728 ,, Theophilus, Dublin, esq.
1805 ,, Theophilus, Rakenny, co. Cavan, esq.
1780 ,, Thomas, Madame, co. Cork, gent.
1769 ,, William, Dub., tallow-chandler
1601 **Clere**, David, Kilkenny, clk.
1608 ,, Luke, Kilkenny, gent.
[See CLEARE.]
1640 **Clerk**, Edward, Marragh, co. Cork, clk.
1789 ,, sir Phillip Jennings, bart. (Copy)
1710 ,, Thomas, Mount Bagnell, co. Louth, esq.
[See CLARKE.]
1732 **Clerke**, Alice, Dublin, widow
1686 ,, Edmond, Newry, gent.
1658 ,, George, servant to sir Patrick Wemys, Danesfort, knt.
[**VII.** 99
1662 " Richard, Dublin, apothecary
1807 **Clermont**, rt. hon. William, earl of (Copy)
1727 **Clervaux**, Hesther, Portarlington, widow [co. Down, clk.
1700 **Clewlow**, rev. James, Killyleagh,
1809 ,, James, Saintfield, co. Down, clk. [**CLIX.** 107

1699 **Clewlowe**, James, Killyleagh, co. Down [**XVIII.** 340

1762 **Clibborn**, Abraham, Aghenergit, co. Westmeath

1770 ,, Anne, *alias* **Cappock**, Dublin

1789 ,, Barclay,Moate, co.Westmeath, esq. [Westmeath

1693 ,, George, Moate Grenoge, co.

1805 ,, George, Moate Grenoge, co. Westmeath, esq.

1805 ,, Henry, Monasterevan, co. Kildare, esq.

1783 ,, James, Moate, co. Westmeath

1763 ,, John, Moate, co. Westmeath, gent.

1728 ,, Joshua, Moate Grenoge, co. Westmeath, gent.

1773 ,, Joshua, Ballymadder, co. Wexford, esq.

1794 ,, Joshua, Moate, co.Westmeath

1786 ,, Robert, Uhulam Grove, co. Kildare

1799 ,, Robert, Dublin, merchant

1774 ,, Sarah, Moate, co. Westmeath, widow

1805 ,, Saragh, city of Dublin, widow

1803 ,, Thomas, Moate, co. Westmeath, linen manufacturer. [See CLEBURNE.]

1789 **Clifden**, James, lord Viscount

1802 ,, rt. hon. Lucia, viscountess

1725 **Cliferly**, Robert, Dublin, vintner

1803 **Cliff**, Anthony, formerly of New Ross, co. Wexford, esq.

1782 ,, Edward, Larah, co. Carlow, clergyman.

1762 **Cliffe**, Ellinor, Dungulph, co. Wexford, gent.

1691 ,, Joan, Dungulph, co. Wexford, esq. (Ex.)

1728 ,, John, New Ross, co. Wex., esq.

1761 ,, John, New Ross, co. Wex., esq.

1729 ,, Loftus, Blarney, co. Cork, esq.

1666 ,, Robert, Sand Bank, Cheshire, surgeon (Copy) [See CLUFF.]

1744 **Clifford**, Arethusa, dowager Viscountess of (Copy)

1786 ,, Catherine, Rathfarnham bridge, widow

1779 ,, Edward, lord baron

1779 ,, Elizabeth, Donalty, co. Monaghan, spinster

1804 ,, Eliz., Castle Annesley, co. Wex.

1701 ,, Knight, Dublin, gent.

1740 ,, Mary, Dublin, widow

1711 ,, Miller, Castle Annesley, co. Wexford, gent.

1796 ,, Miller, town of Wexford, esq. (Large)

1770 **Clifford**, Richard, Carrick, co. Leitrim

1785 ,, William, Castle Annesley, co. Wexford, esq. [See CLUGSTON, CLUXTON.]

1725 **Clift**, Thomas, lieut. in col. Graves' regiment of foot

1795 **Clifton**, Margaret, Dublin, widow

1785 ,, Thomas, Great Britain-street, Dublin, gent.

1771 **Clinch**, Bartholomew, Ballen, co. Meath

1775 ,, Elizabeth, Cork-st., Dublin,wid.

1744 ,, Ellis, Johnstown, co. Meath, widow

1753 ,, James, Newcastle, co. Dublin

1760 ,, John, Dublin, gent.

1782 ,, Margaret, Clindalan, co. Dublin, widow

1762 ,, Michael, Dublin, brewer

1559 ,, Nicholas, Newcastle, co. Dubl.

1609 ,, Richard, Newcastle [gent.

1761 ,, William, Kildonan, co. Dublin,

1799 **Clindining**, Alexander, minister of Westport, co. Mayo. [See CLANDINING.]

1800 **Clinton**, Alexander, Booterstown, near Dublin

1798 ,, Anne, *alias* **Taaffe**, Begstown, co. Meath, widow

1805 ,, Bartholomew, Carrickmacross, co. Monaghan

1656 ,, Jas., Clintonstown, co. Louth, esq. [**V.** 298

1764 ,, Jane, Lismany, co. Galway, widow

1799 ,, John, city of Dublin

1605 ,, Nichs., Dubl., mercht. [**I.** 110

1729 ,, Nicholas, Patrickswell - lane, Dublin, gunsmith

1751 ,, Nicholas, Dublin, esq.

1719 ,, Laurence, Dublin, merchant

1597 ,, Thomas [**I.** 96

1768 ,, Thomas, Dublin, victualler

1787 ,, William, Engine-alley, Dublin, shoemaker [Cavan

1798 **Clisdale**, John, Kilcloughan, co.

1780 **Clive**, George, Arlington - street, Middlesex, esq. (Copy)

1797 ,, George, par. St. George, Middlesex, esq. (Copy)

1672 **Clogher**, Robert Leslie, bishop of

1673 ,, James Spottiswood, bishop of

1687 ,, Roger Boyle, bishop of

1745 ,, John Stearne, bishop of

1760 ,, Robert Clayton, bishop of

1782 ,, John Garnet, lord bishop of

1796 ,, John Hotham, lord bishop of (Copy)

1797 ,, William Foster, lord bishop of

1776 **Clohesy**, Susana, widow of Darby Clohesy
1795 **Clonbrock**, rt. hon. Robert, lord baron
1805 **Cloncarthy**, rt. hon. W. P. Keating, earl of
    [See CLONCARTIE, CLONCARTY.]
1799 **Cloncurry**, rt. hon. Nicholas, lord baron
1644 **Clonfert**, Robert Dawson, bishop of (Copy)
1687 ,, Edward Wolley, bishop of
1722 ,, **and Kilmacduagh**, William Fitzgerald, bishop of
1801 ,, Mathew Young, lord bishop of
1799 **Clonie**, Dennis, Moneyhore, co. Wexford, gent.
1798 **Clonmell**, John, earl of
1808 **Clooney**, Denis, Bray
    [See CLONIE, CLUNE.]
1780 **Clopton**, Anthony, Moate, co. Westmeath, gent.
1744 **Close**, Elizab., Lisburn, co. Antrim
1738 ,, Henry, Waringstown, co. Down
1742 ,, Henry, Plantation, co. Down, farmer
1692 ,, Richard, Waringstown, co. Down
1716 ,, Richard, Waringstown, co. Down, esq.   [gent.
1701 ,, William, Patmore, co. Antrim,
1720 ,, William, Drumoe and Drumers, co. Down, gent.
1769 ,, William, Forge, co. Down, gent.
1781 ,, William, Plantation, co. Down, gent.
1757 **Closkey**, William, Smithstown, co. Meath, farmer
1756 **Closky**, John, Tuckmill, near Julianstown, co. Meath, farmer
1776 **Clossey**, Darby, Limerick, shopkeeper
1746 **Clossy**, Bartholomew, Dublin, gent.
1725 **Clotterbook**, Laurence, Derryluskan, co. Tipperary, clk.
1739 **Clotterbooke**, Richard, Derryluskan, co. Tipperary, esq.
1734 Thomas, Banaxtown, co. Tipp. esq.
    [See CLUTTERBUCK.]
1631 **Clotworthie**, sir Hugh, Antrim, knt.
1662 **Clotworthy**, Hugh, Dublin, gent.
1659 ,, James, Moneymore, co. Derry, esq.   [VIII. 19
1682 ,, Mary, widow
1633 ,, lieut. Thomas, Dungannon, gent.
1801 **Clouder**, William, York-st., Westminster, Middlesex, pocketbook maker (Copy)

1756 **Clouds**, Bartholomew, Dublin, gent.
1768 **Clough**, John, Tullamore, King's County, innholder
1742 **Clouney**, Dominick, Dublin, linendraper
1671 **Clove**, Stephen, Youghal, burgess and alderman
1675 **Clove or Clow**, Thomas, Dublin, gent.
1663 **Cloyne**, George Synge, bishop of   [XI. 108
1726 ,, Charles Crow, lord bishop of
1754 ,, George Berkeley, bp. of (Copy)
1759 ,, James Stopford, bishop of
1767 ,, Robert Johnson, bishop of (Original in Dublin collection.)
1780 ,, George Chinnery, lord bishop of
1794 ,, Richard Woodward, lord bishop (Copy)
1787 **Cluff**, James, Dublin, clothier
1753 ,, Richard, Kildress, Cookstown, co. Tyrone
    [See CLIFFE.]
1760 **Clugston**, James, Kilcullen Bridge, co. Kildare, gent.
    [See CLAXTON.]
1808 **Clune**, James, Carrigan, co. Clare, farmer
    [See CLOONEY.]
1674 **Clungeon**, Peter, Oyle Mills, co. Clare, merchant
1774 **Clutterbuck**, Richard, Bannextown, co. Tipperary
1764 ,, Samuel, Galway, esq.
1776 ,, Thomas, Galway town, esq.
1800 ,, Thomas, Kilgrogy, co. Tipperary, gent.
1805 ,, Thomas, Spafield, co. Tipp.
    [See CLOTTERBOOKE.]
1801 **Cluxton**, Baillie
    [See CLAXSTON.]
1765 **Clysdall**, Alicia, Charleville, co. Cork, widow
1700 **Coach**, Thomas, esq.
1764 **Coakley**, Abraham, Curragh, co. Cork
1784 ,, Abraham, Kanturk, co Cork, gent.
    [See COLCLOUGH.]
1810 **Coalman**, Derby, Canageen, co. Cork
    [See COLEMAN.]
1757 **Coane**, Anthony, Strabane, esq., collector   [gal, widow
1802 ,, Jane, Ballyshannon, co. Done-
1790 ,, Patience
1723 ,, Thady, Ballyshannon, co. Donegal, gent.   [Donegal
1789 ,, William, Ballyshannon, co.
    [See COYNE, QUANE.]

1802 **Coates**, Catherine, Clinen, co. Longford, spinster
1802 ,, rev. George, Castlepollard, co. Westmeath, clk.
1763 ,, Henry, Rathdrum, tanner
1770 ,, Hosea, Dublin, banker
1764 ,, Israel, Belfast, gent.
1796 ,, James, Athlone, co. Rosc., esq.
1756 ,, John, Dublin, merchant
1775 ,, John, Lismore. co. Waterford, gent.
1797 ,, John Dawson, Dublin, esq. (Large)
1805 ,, John, Rath, co.Tipp. gent.
1782 ,, Mathew, Knockanally, co. Kildare, gent.
1777 ,, Thomas, Driminure, formerly of Abbeyshrule, co. Longford
1781 ,, Thomas, Ballinefa, co. Kildare, gent. [gent.
1794 ,, Thomas, Clerkstown,co.Meath,
1810 ,, Thomas, Newbridge, co. Longford, esq.
1749 ,, William, Dublin, merchant
1766 ,, William, Knockannally, co. Kildare, gent. [ford, esq.
1789 ,, Wm., Abbeyshrule, co. Long-
1779 **Cobb**, John, par. St. Martin in the Fields, Middlesex (Copy)
1765 **Cobbe**, Chas., abp. of **Dublin**, q. v.
1799 ,, Charles, city of Bath, esq.
1809 **Cochran**, Arabella, Fownes-street, Dublin, widow
1692 ,, capt. Francis, Dublin
1807 ,, Hugh, Cornmarket, Dublin city, weigher [merchant
1760 ,, Nathaniel, Newry, co. Down,
1770 ,, Richd., Abbey-st., Dubl., tailor [See COGHRAN, CORCORAN.]
1794 **Cochrane**, Margaret, city of Bath, widow
1679 **Cock**, George, Greenwich, Kent, merchant (Copy)
1782 ,, Joseph, Dublin, cooper
1785 ,, Lucy, Dublin, widow
1762 ,, Martha, Dublin, widow
1751 ,, William, Leatherhead, Surrey (Copy)
1775 **Cockburn**, George, Dublin, esq.
1707 **Cockerill**, William, Cork, esq.
1773 **Cocking**, Ralph, rector of Raheny, co. Dublin
1732 **Cocks**, Catherine, widow of William C. of Ninch, co. Meath
1658 ,, John, Belturbet, burgess [VII. 62
1702 ,, Richard, Leigh, Wiltshire, esq. (Copy)
1728 ,, Wm., Ninch, co. Meath, gent. [See COX.]

1734 **Cocksedge**, Francis, Dublin, esq.
1768 ,, Margaret, King's Co., widow
1741 ,, William, Dublin, esq.
1711 **Cockshutt**, John, Liverpool, Lancashire (Copy) [**XXIII.** 77
1744 **Codd**, Elizabeth, Limerick, widow
1777 ,, James, Bishop-st., Dub., grocer
1779 ,, John, Clonegall, co. Carlow, shopkeeper
1739 ,, Joseph, Dub., formerly of Gainsborough in England, gent.
1789 ,, Mark, city of Cork
1743 ,, Thomas, Dublin, chandler
1736 **Coddington**, Anne, Holmpatrick, co. Dublin, widow
1728 ,, Dixie, Holmpatrick, co. Dublin, esq
1776 ,, Dixie, Queen-street, Dublin, esq.
1798 ,, Dixie, Boyne Hill, co. Meath esq.
1747 ,, Frances, Drogheda, widow
1751 ,, Henry, Ninch, co. Meath, esq.
1691 ,, John, Clenerrell, King's County, gent.
1740 ,, John, Old-Bridge, co. Meath (Large Will)
1685 ,, Nicholas, Holmpatrick, co. Dublin, esq.
1737 ,, Nicholas, Drogheda, esq.
1657 ,, William, Holmpatrick, co. Dublin, esq.
1670 ,, William, Holmpatrick, co. Dublin, gent.
1767 ,, rev. William, vicar of Magheross, co. Monaghan
1780 ,, William, Drogheda, esq.
1794 **Codington**, Dixie, Dublin, esq.
1785 ,, Mary, Oldbridge, co. Meath, widow
1802 **Cody**, John, Dublin, carpenter [See CUDDY.]
1785 **Coen**, John, Digges-street, Dublin, gent. [See COYNE.]
1784 **Cofey**, John, Birr, King's County, victualler
1596 **Coffe**, James, Saggart, miller
1762 **Coffee**, William, Aston's - quay, Dublin, mariner
1776 **Coffey**, Charles, Back-lane, Dublin, grocer
1738 **Coffie**, Barnaby, Lara, co. Westmeath, gent. [widow
1757 ,, Mary, Lara. co. Westmeath,
1745 ,, Thomas, Ballymahon
1691 **Coffy**, Casny, Lynally, King's Co., gent. (Ex.)
1703 ,, Gilbert, Bolanacaragh, King's County, gent.

1797 **Coffy,** James, Dunboyne, co. Meath, farmer
1722 ,, John, Dublin, tobacconist
1801 ,, Leslie, lieut. in the King's Co. militia
1771 ,, Mary, Summerhill, co. Dublin, widow
1692 ,, Owen, Tristernaugh, co. West-meath, gent.
1717 ,, Patrick, Dublin, gent.
1754 ,, Patrick, Dublin, carpenter
1695 ,, Thomas, Lynally, King's Co., clk.
    [See COFEY, &c.]
1717 **Cogan,** Thomas, Gervaghy, co. Down
1738 **Coghill,** James, Dublin, esq.
1700 ,, sir John, Dublin, knt., Judge of the Prerogative Court, Master in Chancery and V-genl. of Armagh
1738 ,, Marmaduke, LL.D., Chancellor of the Exchequer, and Judge of the Prerogative Court
1755 ,, Mary, Drumcondra, co. Dublin, spinster
1777 **Coghlan,** Anne, Blackheath, Kent, widow (See 1778)
1778 ,, Anne, Blackheath, Kent, widow
1809 ,, Anne, Bedford-street, Dublin, widow
1741 ,, Anthony, Kilcolgan, King's County, but of Dublin
1752 ,, Barnaby, Killinagulling, King's County
1749 ,, Cicily, Dublin, widow
1663 ,, Daniel, Feddan, King's County, gent.
1801 ,, Edward, Usher's-quay, Dublin, gent.
1775 ,, Elizabeth, Dublin, widow
1712 ,, Eugene, Coolderagh, King's County, gent.
1738 ,, Francis, Dublin, esq.
1792 ,, Francis, Mountmellick
1767 ,, George, an officer in the 63rd regiment of foot
1771 ,, George, Ennis, co. Clare, esq.
1789 ,, Henry, Waterford city
1590 ,, Sir John, knt., rector of the par. of Fuize
1705 ,, John, Garrycastle, King's Co., esq.
1709 ,, John, Bandon Bridge, co. Cork, esq.
1757 ,, John, Ardbraccan, co. Meath, esq.
1791 ,, John, Portman-square, Middlesex, esq. (Copy)
1697 ,, Joseph, Dublin, esq. (Ex.)

1765 **Coghlan,** Joseph, Banagher, King's County, gent.
1810 ,, Joseph
1757 ,, Laughlin, Ballaghanogher, King's County, gent.
1766 ,, Mary, Acrantrim, King's Co.
1808 ,, Michael, city of Dublin, timber merchant
1800 ,, Oliver, Togher, King's County, gent.
1795 ,, Owen, Rathowen, co. Carlow, gent.
1719 ,, Patrick, Bellewstown, co. Meath, gent.
1805 ,, Rebecca, formerly of Galway, late of Dublin, widow
1654 ,, Terence, Kilcolgan, King's Co.
1756 ,, Terence, Ballymahon, co. Longford, dealer
1748 ,, Thady, Moate, co. Mayo, gent.
1794 ,, Thomas, Cloghan, King's Co., esq.
1716 ,, Timothy, Ballea, co. Cork, joiner
1764 ,, William, Aghafan, co. West-meath, gent.
1772 ,, William, Youghal, co. Cork, alderman
    [See COUGHLAN, COUGLAN.]
1677 **Coghlane,** Dermitius, Limerick, esq.
1779 **Coghran,** Ellinor, Dublin, widow
1779 ,, John, Edenmore, co. Donegal, gent.
    [See COCHRAN, CORCORAN.]
1756 **Coker,** John, Broghill, co. Cork, gent.
1738 **Colbrant,** Francis, Dublin, mercht.
1655 **Colclogh,** Adam, Tintern, co. Wexford   **V.** 106
1637 **Colclough,** sir Adam, Tintern, co. Wexford, bart.
1760 ,, Adam, Crowsgrove, co. Carlow, gent.
1800 ,, Adam, Duffery Hall
1684 ,, sir Caesar, Tintern, co. Wexford, bart. (Ex.)
1726 ,, Caesar, Rosgarland, co. Wexford, esq.
1766 " Caesar, Mocorry, co. Wexford, esq.
1802 ,, Caesar, New Ross, co. Wexford, esq.
1809 ,, Charlotte, Greenfield Lodge, co. Dublin
1717 ,, John Pigott, Kilfenny, co. Limerick, esq.
1770 ,, John, St. Kierans, co. Wexford
1807 ,, John

1774 **Colclough**, Joseph, Kilmurray, co.
    Wicklow, farmer
1723 ,, Margt. Pigott, Dublin, widow
1789 ,, Margaret, Little Park, co. Car-
    low, widow
1695 ,, Robert Leigh, Tintern, co.
    Wexford, esq.
1809 ,, Thomas, Tullamore, King's Co.
1798 ,, sir Vesey, Tintern Abbey, co.
    Wexford, bart.
1805 ,, William, Dame-street, Dublin,
    vintner
    [See COAKLEY, KEILY.]
1713 **Colcock**, Isaac, Dublin, cordwainer
1716 **Cole**, dame Anne, widow of Thomas
    Whitney, Newpass, co.
    Westmeath, esq.
1779 ,, Anne, Dublin
1810 ,, Arthur, city of Dublin
1676 ,, cornet Mathew
1711 ,, dame Elizabeth, Dublin, widow
1781 ,, Danl., Naas, co. Kild., farmer
1703 ,, Francis, captain in lord Hay's
    regiment of dragoons at
    Breda (Copy)
1758 ,, Hanah, Dublin, widow
1754 ,, Jane, Dublin, widow [bart.
1691 ,, sir John, Newland, co. Dublin,
1800 ,, John, senr., Cork city, cooper
1794 ,, hon. Mariana, Dublin, spinster
1723 ,, Mary, Limerick, spinster
1773 ,, Mary, Dublin
1711 ,, sir Michael, Enniskillen, but at
    London (Copy)
1758 ,, Michael, Enniskillen, co. Fer-
    managh, esq.
1729 ,, Richard, esq., lieut.-col. in sir
    John Witherington's regt.
1730 ,, Richard, Archerstown, co. Kil-
    kenny, esq.
1670 ,, Thomas, Dublin, miller
1791 ,, Thomas, esq.
1654 ,, sir William, Enniskillen, co.
    Fermanagh, knt.
1735 ,, William Graigue, Queen's
    County, farmer
    [See COLES.]
1803 **Coleman**, Anne, Drogheda, widow
1802 ,, Bernard, Brabazon-row, co.
    Dublin, pawnbroker
1732 ,, Chas., Ballycreen, co. Wick-
    low, gent.
1759 ,, Charles, Dublin, gent.
1708 ,, Daniel, Dublin, gent.
1753 ,, Francis, Ardover
1808 ,, Francis, Dame-street, Dublin,
    silk mercer
1704 ,, Henry, Dublin, cutler
1798 ,, James, Ballyduff, co. Water-
    ford, farmer

1748 **Coleman**, Jeremiah, John's-lane, co.
    Dublin, tailor
1709 ,, John, parish St. James, West-
    minster, Middlesex, esq.
1741 ,, John, Richmond, Surrey, esq.
1769 ,, John, Drogheda, carpenter
1732 ,, Martha, Dublin, widow
1790 ,, Mary, Dublin, widow
1808 ,, Mary, Ardee, co. Louth, widow
1764 ,, Patrick, Poddle, grocer
1793 ,, Patrick, Largy, co. Meath,
    farmer
1728 ,, Richard, parish St. Clements
    Danes, tailor (Copy)
1754 ,, Richard, Dublin, innkeeper
1783 ,, Thomas, Tuam, co. Gal., gent.
1788 ,, Thos., Ballybarrack, co. Louth,
    farmer
1790 ,, William, Baltray, co. Meath,
    landholder
    [See COALMAN, COLLMAN, COLMAN.]
1781 **Coles**, Jane, Gorey, co. Wex., spr.
1779 ,, John, Dublin, gent.
1795 ,, John, South Great George's-
    street, Dublin
1798 ,, Martha, Dublin, widow
1805 ,, Philip, Newrath Bridge, co.
    Wicklow
    [See COLE.]
1799 **Colgan**, Andrew, city of Dublin,
    grocer
1799 ,, Andrew, Dubl., mathematician
1798 ,, Christopher, Dublin, grocer
1772 ,, Jas., Hartland, co. Kild., farmer
1795 ,, James, Philipstown, King's
    County, innkeeper
1800 ,, James, Tully, co. Kildare, gent.
1557 ,, Richard, Ballygory
1766 ,, Thos., Scurlogstown, co. Kild.
1757 **Colhoun**, William, Strabane, co.
    Tyrone, esq.
1754 **Colinder**, Wm., Waterford, merchant
1790 **Colles**, Anne, Dublin, widow
1785 ,, Barry, Dublin, esq.
1727 ,, Charles, Dublin
1724 ,, Chris., Dranfield, Derby, clk.
1740 ,, Dudley, Collesford, co. Sligo,
    gent.
1775 ,, Henrietta, Dublin, widow
1759 ,, John, Swords, co. Dublin, gent.
1760 ,, John, Dublin, merchant
1763 ,, Robert, Dingle, co. Kerry, tide
    surveyor
1700 ,, Wm., Carrowbeg, co. Galway,
    gent.
1729 ,, William, Lisnefulshion, co. Kil-
    kenny, gent.
1779 ,, Wm., Millmount, co. Kilkenny
    [See COLLIS.]
1698 **Collet**, George, Clonmel, skinner

1730 **Colley**, Arthur, Kilroy, Queen's County, gent.
1771 ,, Chas., Rahin, co. Kild., esq.
1709 ,, Christopher, Dublin, gent.
1768 ,, Dudley, Rahin, co. Kild., esq.
1760 ,, Elizabeth, Dublin, daughter of hon. Mr. C., Castle Carberry, co. Kildare
1743 ,, Frances, Dublin, spinster
1712 ,, Geo., Rahin, co. Kild., gent.
1683 ,, Gerard, Drogheda, apothecary
1637 ,, sir Henry, Castle Carberry, co. Kildare, knt.
1719 ,, Henry, _alias_ **Courley**, Castle Carberry, co. Kildare, esq,
1759 ,, Henry, Rahin, co. Kildare
1777 ,, John, Ballywalter, co. Wexford, gent.
1772 ,, Judith, Dublin, spinster
1764 ,, Mary, Castle Carberry, daughter of Henry C.
1784 ,, Roger, Ballnacarrig, co. Wexford, gent.
1746 ,, Sarah, Dublin, spinster
1768 ,, Thos., Killurin, King's Co., esq.
1645 ,, sir William, Edenderry, knt.
1766 ,, William, Dublin, skinner
[See COOLEY, COWLEY.]
1730 **Collier**, Enoch, Kilkenny, esq.
1772 ,, John, Dublin, merchant
1793 ,, John, Little Acton, Shropshire, gent.
1773 ,, Martha, widow
1656 ,, Nicholas, soldier [**V.** 276
1763 ,, Thomas, rector of Listerlin, dio. Ossory
[See COLLYER.]
1787 **Collin**, Anne Clare, Dublin, spinster
1771 ,, Margt., Church-st., Dub., wid.
1758 ,, Thomas, Dublin, grocer
1767 ,, Thomas, Dublin, merchant
1779 **Collins**, Andrew, par. St. Pancras, Middlesex (Copy)
1676 ,, Charles, Dublin, merchant
1753 ,, Christr., Malahide, co. Dub.
1690 ,, David, Dublin, merchant
1794 ,, Edward esq., Magherie, co. Cork,
1796 ,, Henry, Gortmacellis, co. Tipperary, gent.
1772 ,, James, Gurteen, co. Cork, gent.
1799 ,, James, Dublin, gent.
1804 ,, James, Garr, King's Co., gent.
1805 ,, James, lieutenant in the East India Co.'s Service (Ex.)
1667 ,, John, Shankill, co. Kilk., gent.
1766 ,, John, Garr, King's Co., gent.
1777 ,, John, Marlinstown, co. Westmeath, gent.

1784 **Collins**, John, Newry, co. Down
1809 ,, John, city of Cork, gent.
1811 ,, John, Loy, co. Tyr., merchant
1799 ,, Martha, Kilbeggan, co. Westmeath, spinster
1778 ,, Mary, Booterstown, co. Dublin, widow
1804 ,, Mary, Richmond, co. Dub., spr.
1770 ,, Mathew, Dublin, gunsmith
1656 ,, Patrick, trooper [**VI.** 21
1782 ,, Rachael, Dublin, widow
1648 ,, Richard, Carlingford, gent.
1682 ,, Richard, Dublin, gent.
1785 ,, Robert, Garr, King's Co., gent.
1799 ,, Robert, Usher's-quay, Dublin, merchant
1766 ,, Samuel, Dublin, ribbon weaver
1769 ,, Saml., Bristol, miniature painter
1760 ,, Terence, Summerhill, co. Dublin, gent.
1794 ,, Terence, Cashel, co. Tip., gent.
1790 ,, Thomas, gent.
1793 ,, Thos., Tralee, co. Kerry, esq.
1799 ,, Thomas, Shanacloun, co. Cork, gent.
1802 ,, Thomas, late captain in His Majesty's 11th West India regiment
1636 ,, William, Dublin, merchant
1746 ,, Wm., Carrick, co. Tip., merch.
[See CULLEN.]
1782 **Collis**, Anne, Cork-st., Dublin, wid.
1804 ,, Anne, Tralee, co. Kerry, widow
1775 ,, Arthur, Cork, gent.
1784 ,, Avis, widow [esq.
1685 ,, Chas., Magherymore, co. Sligo,
1762 ,, Edward, Barrow, co. Kerry
1805 ,, Edward, Barrow, co. Kerry
1690 ,, Elizabeth, Dublin, widow
1763 ,, Elizabeth
1785 ,, Eliz., Barrow, co. Kerry, wid.
1767 ,, George, Dublin, brassfounder
1800 ,, rev. Henry, dio. Limk., chanter
1728 ,, John, Bannagh, co. Kerry
1793 ,, John Fitzgerald, York-st., Dublin, esq.
1800 ,, John, Rockabbey, co. Limk., esq.
1785 ,, Martha, Cork city, widow
1779 ,, or **Colles**, Purefoy, Alverstoke, Hants, clk. (Copy)
1766 ,, Rev. Thomas, Monaree, co. Kerry, clk.
1790 ,, Thos., Tralee, co. Kerry, gent.
1772 ,, Rev. Wm., Tralee, co. Kerry
[See COLLES.]
1714 **Collman**, James, Cappoquin, co. Waterford, farmer
[See COLEMAN.]
1792 **Collopy**, Catherine, Limerick, wid.
1584 **Colly**, sir Henry, knt.

1703 **Colly,** Robert, Drogheda, apothecary (Copy)
1788 **Collyer,** Barbara, Belfast, wid.
1720 ,, Rev. Isaac, rector of Donoghmore, co. Donegal
1732 ,, Thomas, Belfast, esq.
[See COLLIER.]
1722 **Colman,** Anne, Grafton-st., Dublin, widow [Meath, farmer
1604 ,, Christopher, Rathalin, co.
1722 ,, George, Dublin, mariner
1560 ,, Nicholas, Dublin, merchant
1802 ,, Thomas, Dundalk, co. Louth, merchant
[See COLEMAN.]
1781 **Colombine,** Rev. Charles, LL.D.
1755 **Colt,** Rose, Dublin, widow
1793 **Colthurst,** Edward, Killegrogan, co. Cork, esq.
1681 ,, John, the elder, Cooleneshanvally, co. Cork, gent.
1756 ,, John, Cork, esq.
1776 ,, sir John Conway, Ardrum, co. Cork, bart. [Cork
1787 ,, sir John Conway, Ardrum, co.
1750 ,, Nicholas, son to Col. John C.
1751 ,, Nicholas, Cork, mariner (Copy)
1755 ,, Nichs., Ballyally, co. Cork, esq.
1795 ,, sir Nicholas Conway, Ardrum, co. Cork, bart.
[See COULTHURST.]
1774 **Colvill,** Elizabeth, Dublin, spinster
1784 ,, Jane, Dublin, widow
1686 ,, dame Margaret, Wexford, wid.
1697 ,, sir Robert, Newtown, co. Down, knt.
1746 ,, Robert, parish of St. George's, Hanover-square, Middlesex (set aside by decree of delegates; Copy)
1788 ,, Robert, Dublin, gent.
1789 ,, Robert, Youghal, co. Cork
1791 **Combe,** Hanah, Dublin, spinster
1746 **Combecrose,** Rachael, Dublin, wid.
1776 **Combs,** John, Meath-st., Dublin, linen merchant
1720 **Comby,** Catherine, Dunmoon, co. Waterford, widow
1720 ,, Wm., Dunmoon, co. Wat., gent.
1666 **Comely,** John, Dublin, gent.
1719 **Comerford,** Barbara, *alias* **Brown,** Clonmel, co. Tip., widow
1673 ,, Catherine, *alias* **Hippesley,** Callan, co. Kilkenny, widow
1679 ,, Edward, Clonmel, merchant
1596 ,, Garrett, Inchioleghan, co. Kilkenny, gent.
1644 ,, Garrett, Inchioleghan, co. Kilkenny, esq. (Copy)
1602 ,, George, Waterford, alderman

1632 **Comerford,** Henry, Polecaple, co. Tipperary, gent.
1769 ,, John, Cork, merchant
1796 ,, John, Dublin, merchant
1729 ,, Joseph, esq., lord of Anglure, living in Paris (Copy)
1687 ,, Margaret, Loughteage, Queen's County, spinster
1759 ,, Margt., Gormanstown, spinster
1640 ,, Patrick, Graigue, Modeshell, co. Tipperary, gent.
1796 ,, Patrick, city of Cork, esq.
1800 ,, Peter, city of Cork, gent.
1626 ,, Philip, Tomduff, Queen's Co., gent.
1629 ,, Richard, Danganmore, co. Kilkenny, gent. (Copy)
1637 ,, Richard, Ballybur, co. Kilkenny, esq.
[See COMERFORTHE, CUMBERFORT.]
1583 **Comerforthe,** Patrick, Dublin
1771 **Commin,** Margt., Clonmel, widow
1737 ,, William, Cork, merchant
1786 **Commisky,** Thos., Drogheda, corn merchant
[See COMERFORD.]
1723 **Commons,** Daniel, co. Dublin, labourer
1784 ,, John, Crow-st., Dublin, master tailor
[See CUMING.]
1725 **Comon,** William, Dublin, poulterer
1732 **Compton,** Mary, Dublin, widow
1732 ,, Mary, Dub., wid. (Not proved)
1740 ,, hon. Hatton, London
1809 ,, William, commander of the sloop " Lilly "
1638 **Comyn,** David, Limerick, Alderman
1638 ,, George, Ballybody, co. Tipperary, gent. **[IV.** 352
1602 ,, Nicholas
1734 ,, Nich., Moyne, co. Clare, gent.
1746 ,, Nicholas, Lisryan, co. Longford, esq.
1747 ,, James, Dublin, gent. (This will revoked, a later being proved)
1748 ,, James, Dublin, gent. (Proved in special form)
1673 ,, John Fitzchris., Limerick, ald.
1682 ,, John, Limerick, gent.
1810 ,, Laurence, Ennis, co. Clare, esq.
1798 ,, Peter, Rochestown, co. Dublin, esq.
1637 **Comyne,** Edmond, Tullaghmaine, co. Tipperary, gent. **[IV.** 270
1810 **Comyns,** Eliz., Lucan, co. Dub., wid.
1685 **Conan,** Edmond, Kilcock, co. Kildare, gent. [farmer
1684 ,, Hugh, Kilcock, co. Kildare,

1768 **Conan**, John, Bushy Park, co. Kilkenny, gent.
1602 ,, Thomas, Dublin, gent.
1728 **Conar**, Dennis, Dublin, merchant
1746 **Concanen**, Jas., Dublin, merchant
1793 **Concannon**, Andw., Dubl., merchant
1757 ,, Chas., Ballyshannon, co. Down
1766 ,, Cicily, *alias* **Ward**, widow of William C., Lurgan
1811 ,, Henry, Carronacraggy, co. Galway, esq.
1792 ,, John, Prussia-st., Dublin, gent.
1786 ,, Peter, Dundalk, surgeon
    [See CONCANEN.]
1722 **Concaret**, John, captain in Dormer's regiment of foot
1799 **Condon**, David, Ardgoulemore, co. Limerick, gent. [Cork, gent.
1766 ,, Richard, Ballintrideen, co.
1805 **Condron**, James, Bishop's Court, co. Kildare
    [See CONRAN.]
1669 **Condutt**, Robert, Dublin, distiller
1740 **Conelly**, Terence, Mass-lane, Dub. dealer and tobacconist
    [See CONNOLLY.]
1697 **Coney**, Charles, parish of St. Martin's-in-the-Fields, Middlesex (Copy)
1623 ,, Danl., parish of Dysart (Copy)
    [See COONEY.]
1766 **Congaltone**, Alex., Dublin, gent.
1600 **Congan**, Nicholas, Lecahill, Down
1809 **Congreve**, Ambrose Usher, Mount Congreve, co. Wat., esq.
1777 ,, Rev. Charles Walter, Archdeacon of Armagh (Copy)
1710 ,, John, Kilmacow, co. Kilk., clerk
1801 ,, John, Mount Congreve, co. Waterford, esq.
1801 ,, John, Landscape, co. Wat., esq.
1788 **Conilan**, Bartholomew, Tubberscanavan, co. Sligo
1773 ,, James, Tubberscanavan, co. Sligo, gent.
    [See CONNELLAN.]
1642 **Conincks**, Anthony, some time of Antwerp, now of Roscrea, merchant
1782 **Coningesby**, Rt. Hon. Lady Frances (Copy)
1741 ,, Thomas, Earl of (Copy)
1673 **Coningham**, Alexander, Londonderry, merchant
1791 ,, Anne, Cole alley, Castle-street, Dublin, spinster
1746 ,, Daniel, senr.. Dub., merchant
1746 ,, Daniel, Dublin, merchant
1688 ,, Henry, Castle Coningham, co. Donegal, esq. (Ex.)

1666 **Coningham**, James, Blarwhush, Scotland (Ex.)
1778 ,, John, formerly Lieut.-Col. 29th Foot
1802 ,, John, Londonderry, merchant
1802 ,, Simon Luttrell, Dublin, esq.
1787 ,, Wm., Pill-lane, Dub., merchant
    [See CUNINGHAM.]
1802 **Conlan**, Richard, Rathmines, co. Dublin, victualler
    [See CONNELLAN.]
1709 **Conley**, Bartholomew, parish of St. Clement Danes. Middlesex, merchant (Copy)
1808 **Conly**, Elizabeth, Drogheda, spr.
1694 ,, Luke, Drogheda, merchant
1623 ,, Patrick, Dublin, merchant
1769 ,, Patrick, Drogheda
1769 ,, Patrick, Drogheda, mariner
    [See CONOLLY.]
1759 **Conmee**, Patrick, Dublin
1783 **Conneen**, Patrick, Limerick, tanner
1793 **Connel**, Amy, Cork. widow
1783 **Connell**, Daniel, Ballynablaune, co. Kerry, gent.
1749 ,, David, north sub. of Cork, apothecary
1764 ,, Hannah, Dublin, widow of Wm. C., tailor
1800 ,, Honora, Limerick, widow
1722 ,, Hugh, Killeen, co. Long., gent.
1716 ,, James, *alias* **M'Connell**, Lower Coombe, Dublin, gent.
1720 ,, James, Kingston, Jamaica, tavern keeper (Copy)
1807 ,, James, city of Dublin, slater
1680 ,, John, Irishtown, co. Dub., gent.
1791 ,, John, south suburbs of Limk., gent.
1810 ,, John, Dublin, esq.
1789 ,, Mary, Dublin, widow
1765 ,, Michael, parish of St. James, Westminster, Middlesex, M.D. (Copy) [gent.
1747 ,, Morgan, Kilferny, co. Limk.,
1740 ,, Patrick, Cork, vintner
1749 ,, Patrick, Fanningstown, co. Kilkenny, farmer
1769 ,, Patrick, Galway, gent.
1802 ,, Patrick, Ballygurtagh, co. Meath, farmer and grazier
1777 ,, Peter, Cranary, co. Long., esq.
1778 ,, Philip, Shandrum, co. Cork, farmer
1775 ,, Rt. Hon. Lady Phillipa, parish of St. James, Middlesex, widow (Copy)
1740 ,, Richard, Dublin, gent.
1785 ,, Richard, Dublin, measurer
1748 ,, Thos., Dublin, woollen draper

1772	**Connell**, Thomas, Carrick-on-Suir, co. Tipperary, shopkeeper	
1794	,, Thomas, Nassau-street, Dubl., saddler	
1808	,, Thomas, Milltown, co. Dublin, farmer	
1808	,, Timothy, dealer	
1793	,, William, Cork, gent.	
1794	,, William, city of Kilkenny, esq.	
1809	,, Wm., Milltown, co. Dub., gent.	
1810	,, William, Linenhall-st., Dublin, merchant	
1811	,, William, Ballinaslow lodge, co. Wicklow	
	[See CONOLLY.]	
1731	**Connellan**, James	
1802	,, Jas., Loughrea, co. Gal., gent.	
1801	,, Martin, Rahasane, co. Galway	
	[See CONILAN, CONLAN.]	
1746	**Connelly**, Arthur, Dublin, potter	
1713	,, John, Morrell, co. Meath, farmer	
1768	,, Patrick, Limerick, merchant	
	[See CONOLLY.]	
1784	**Conner**, Geo., Bandon, co. Cork, esq.	
1741	,, Richard, Dublin, wine cooper	
	[See CONNOR.]	
1806	**Connery**, John, Townsend-street, Dublin, merchant	
1721	,, Joseph, Drogheda, farmer (not proved)	
1808	,, Susanna, city of Dublin, widow	
	[See CONRY.]	
1739	**Connock**, Philadelphia, widow	
1658	,, Richard, trooper in Capt. Dean's troop **[VII.** 51	
1746	**Connolley**, Henry, Dublin, merchant **[LIII.** 12 4	
1768	**Connolly**, Anne, Limk., shopkeeper	
1764	,, George, Cutpurse-row, Dublin, cordwainer	
1803	,, Henrietta	
1761	,, Sarah, Dublin, widow	
1771	,, Wm., par. of Palmerstown, co. Dub., bricklayer (not proved)	
	[See CONOLLY.]	
1763	**Connor**, Agnes, *alias* **Brown**, Beaugh, co. Galway, widow	
1730	,, Anne, Dublin, widow	
1748	,, Arthur, Talbot co., prov. of Maryland, planter (Copy)	
1747	,, Barnaby, mariner on board the " Defiance "	
1721	,, Bryan, Dublin, grocer	
1677	,, Charles, Lisheen, co. Tipperary, gent.	
1794	,, Charles, Dublin, barrister	
1705	,, Constant, Dublin, gent.	
1737	,, Danl., Bandon, co. Cork, gent.	
1762	,, Daniel, Bandon, co. Cork, esq.	

1804	**Connor**, Daniel, Ballybrickan, co. Cork.	
1785	,, Dennis, Molesworth-st., Dubl.	
1746	,, Dominick, Dublin, victualler	
1657	,, Donogh, Killien, King's Co. **[VI.** 111	
1794	,, Dorothy	
1802	,, Edwd., Mallow,co.Cork,merch.	
1761	,, Ellinor, Dublin, spinster	
1774	,, Francis, Dublin, linen draper	
1770	,, George, Ballybrickan, co. Cork, esq.	
1789	,, George, Cloyne, co. Cork, gent.	
1788	,, Henry, Waterford, clerk	
1761	,, Hugh, Garden-lane, Dublin, weaver	
1783	,, Hugh, Bachelor's-walk, Dubl., merchant	
1785	,, Hugh, Ballycooge, co. Wicklow	
1744	,, Jacob, Dublin, tape weaver	
1635	,, James, Naas, gent. **[IV.** 155	
1802	,, Jas., Brooklodge, co. Cork, esq.	
1768	,, Jane, Longford town, widow	
1809	,, Jane, Limerick, widow	
1739	,, Joan, Dublin, widow	
1713	,, John, jun., Dublin, merchant	
1722	,, John, Dublin, linen draper	
1742	,, John, Smithfield, gent.	
1746	,, John, Dublin, merchant	
1766	,, John, Clonmel, co. Tipp., gent.	
1772	,, John, Dublin, merchant	
1785	,, Rev. John, Bellistin, co. Antrim	
1808	,, John, Joseph's-lane, Dublin, vintner	
1744	,, Margaret, suburbs of Dub., wid.	
1774	,, Margaret, widow of John C., Jervis-st., Dublin, merchant	
1777	,, Margaret, spinster	
1767	,, Mary, Ellison's-lane, co. Dubl.	
1801	,, Mary, widow	
1679	,, Mathew, Dublin, gent.	
1760	,, Maurice, Donnybrook-road, co. Dublin, esq.	
1795	,, Maurice, Bail-hill, co. Kerry, gent.	
1787	,, Michael	
1788	,, Michael, Drogheda	
1809	,, Michael, city of Dublin, gent.	
1753	,, Nicholas, Galway, apothecary	
1731	,, Patrick, Dublin, linen draper	
1737	,, Patrick, Lime-st., Dublin, gent.	
1794	,, Patk., Conway, Nth.Wales,esq.	
1803	,, Patk., Cook-st., Dublin, mcht.	
1779	,, Rachael, Dublin, widow	
1745	,, Richd., Dublin, timber mercht.	
1683	,, Thady, Corbally, co. Tip., gent.	
1711	,, Thady, Dublin, saddler	
1754	,, Thomas, Dublin, gent.	
1794	,, Thomas, Gt. Britain-st., Dubl., carpenter	

1804 **Connor,** Walker, Tralee, co. Kerry, gent.
1736 ,, Wm., Clonmel, co. Tip., esq.
1755 ,, Wm., Dublin, coachman (Not proved)
1766 ,, William, Dublin, esq.
1766 ,, Wm., Mishells, co. Cork, esq.
1799 ,, William, late of the city of Bristol, esq.
[See CONNER, CONYERS.]
1806 **Connors,** Walter, Clontubrid, co. Kilkenny
1617 **Connyame,** Gerald Bane
1625 **Connye,** Samuel, Drogheda, skinner
1654 **Connynhame,** Robert, minister of Taghboyne, Co. Donegal
[See CUNINGHAM.]
1702 **Conolan,** Denis, Kilbegg, co. Wicklow, yeoman
1762 **Conolly,** Rev. Arthur, Finglas, co. Dublin, clk.
1808 ,, Arthur, Barrack-st., Dublin, lime burner
1794 ,, Bernard, Clones, co. Monaghan
1804 ,, Bryan, city of Dublin, attorney-at-law
1752 ,, Catherine, widow of the right hon. William Conolly
1782 ,, Catherine, Dublin, widow
1779 ,, Christopher, Dublin, grocer
1740 ,, Constant, Dublin, innholder
1747 ,, Edmond, Dublin, merchant
1797 ,, Edward, Dublin, linen draper
1778 ,, Ellinor, Sackville-st., Dub., wid.
1782 ,, James, Parliament-st., Dublin, shoemaker
1805 ,, John, Palmerstown, co. Dublin
1784 ,, Marcella, Dublin, widow
1730 ,, Margt., *alias* **Purfield,** Dublin
1775 ,, Patrick, Limerick, ale seller
1810 ,, Patrick, Tullamore, King's County, brewer
1800 ,, Terence, Lisgall, co. Monaghan
1751 ,, Thos., Drumcondra-lane, suburbs of Dublin
1803 ,, right hon. Thomas (Large)
1729 ,, right hon. William, Dublin
1737 ,, William, Dublin, tailor
1754 ,, right hon. William, Castletown, co. Kildare (Large)
[See CONELLY, CONLY, CONNELL, CONNELLY, CONNOLLY, &c.]
1709 **Conquest,** Richard, Ringsend, near Dublin, innkeeper
1783 **Conrahy,** Edward, Killeigh, King's County, gent.
1799 ,, Patk., Ballyhuppihaun, Queen's County, farmer
1772 **Conran,** Christopher, senr., Cork, esq.
1747 ,, James, Dublin, drover

1768 **Conran,** James, Dublin, merchant
1804 ,, Jas., Newtownhouse, co. Louth
1690 ,, John, Dublin, merchant
1616 ,, Philip, Dublin, alderman
1707 ,, William, Dublin, merchant
[See CONDRON, CONRON.]
1762 **Conron,** Carleton, Charleville, co. Cork, gent.
1761 ,, rev. Downes, Churchtown, Great Island, co. Cork
1767 ,, Hy., Chancery-lane, Dub., gent.
1730 ,, Robert, Walshstown, co. Cork, gent.
[See CONRAN.]
1771 **Conroy,** Eliz., Anne-st., Dubl., wid.
1808 ,, John, Redcross, co. Wicklow
1774 ,, Maurice, Dublin
1805 ,, Patk., Pill-lane, Dub., publican
1803 ,, Thomas, Dublin, wine merchant
1769 **Conry,** John, Dublin, esq.
1777 ,, John, Pollymount, co. Roscommon, esq.
1769 ,, Margt., Newtown Forbes, wid.
1796 ,, Thomas, Carrownskehan, co. Roscommon
[See CONNERY.]
1667 **Consedine,** captain Mathew
[See CONSTANTINE.]
1786 **Conseil,** Anne, Dublin, widow
1800 **Considen,** Joseph, Dublin, grocer and merchant
[See CONSTANTINE.]
1737 **Constable,** Alice, Loggan, co. Wexford, widow
1757 ,, Benjamin, Ballyloughlin, co. Wexford, farmer
1760 ,, Gore, Cork, ironmonger
1752 ,, Henry, Loggan, co. Wexford
1764 ,, Henry, Dublin, merchant
1781 ,, Nicholson, Beeverstown, co. Tipperary
1796 ,, Sidney, Dublin, widow
1710 ,, Thomas, Loggan, co. Wexford, farmer
1744 ,, William, Dublin, ironmonger
1772 **Constantine,** John, Ennis, co. Clare, gent.
1735 ,, Paul, Ennis, co. Clare, mercht.
1760 ,, Thomas, Carlow, gent.
1791 ,, William, Cork, merchant
[See CONSEDINE, CONSIDEN.]
1792 **Conway,** Agnes, Dublin
1739 ,, Daniel, Strabane, co. Tyrone
1796 ,, rev. doctor Dennis, Limk. city
1632 ,, and **Killullagh,** Edward, lord viscount, lord President of Privy Council
1673 ,, capt. Edwd., St. George's-lane, Dublin
1787 ,, Elizabeth, Dublin, widow

1732 **Conway**, Francis, lord baronBagley Great Britain, and Kilulta in Ireland (Large will, Ex.)
1790 ,, Francis, Dublin, gent.
1702 ,, Hugh, Castleiffe, co. Kilkenny, gent.
1791 ,, Jas., Timolin, co. Kild., glazier
1795 ,, James, Greek-st., Dublin
1804 ,, James Henry, Bath, Somerset
1770 ,, John, Dublin, carpenter
1800 ,, Margt., Summerhill, co. Dubl., widow
1785 ,, Michael, Dublin, merchant
1660 ,, Patrick, Galway, a native of Cashel
1744 ,, Patrick, Tullaghmedan
1602 ,, Robert, LL.D.
1720 ,, Thomas, New-st., Dublin
1738 ,, Thomas
1737 ,, William, Dublin, merchant
1807 ,, Wm., Killeen, co. Gal., farmer
1810 ,, Wm., southAnne-st.,Dubl.,gent
1802 **Conyers**, Charles, Rathkeale, co. Limerick, esq.
1766 ,, Edward, capt.-lieutenant in the 2nd regiment of horse
1756 ,, Odell, Castletown M'Enry, co. Limerick, esq.
1726 ,, Thomas, Catherlogh, gent. [See CONNOR.]
1809 **Conyngham**, Adam, city of Dublin, esq.
1754 ,, Alexander
1784 ,, Alexander, Dublin, esq., lieut. in Scots Greys
1668 ,, Frances or Rose, of Corncammon, wid. of Robert C., sometime of Taghboyne, clerk
1750 ,, Henry, Ballydavid, co. Donegal, gent.
1661 ,, Hugh, Bachymochy, co. Donegal, minister
1761 ,, Hugh, Dublin, gent.
1747 ,, Jane, the elder, Dublin, widow
1788 ,, Jane, Springhill, co. Derry, wid.
1775 ,, John, Bath, Somerset, esq.
1777 ,, John, capt. in 92nd regt. of foot
1738 ,, Wm., Slane, co. Meath, esq.
1766 ,, William, Dublin, gent.
1782 ,, rev. William, Letterkenny, co. Donegal, clk.
1796 ,, right hon. William, Dublin
1798 ,, right hon. William [See CUNINGHAM.]
1775 **Coogan**, Edwd., Rathmore, co. Car.
1745 ,, Michael, Dublin, tailor
1749 ,, Priscilla, Dublin, widow
1804 **Cook**, Esther, city of Dublin, widow
1762 ,, John, Reedsland, co. Meath, farmer

1772 **Coogan**, John, Dublin, alderman
1764 ,, Mary, High-st., Dublin, widow
1713 ,, Randal, Burris, co. Tip., gent.
1751 ,, William, Leatherhead, Surrey, esq. (Copy)
1793 **Cooke**, Alexander, Paradise-row, Dublin
1810 ,, Alicia, Prussia-st., co. Dublin
1660 ,, Anne, Dublin [**VIII.** 146
1679 ,, dame Anne, Dungiven, co. Londonderry, widow
1611 ,, Arthur, vicar of Dunshaughlin, co. Meath
1810 ,, Bridget, Dungarvan, co.Watfd.
1666 ,, Catherine, Dunshaughlin, co. Meath, widow
1697 ,, Catherine, Mount Kennedy, co. Wicklow, widow (Ex.)
1719 ,, Daniel, Dublin, gent.
1740 ,, Daniel, Dublin, tailor
1755 ,, Daniel, Dublin, alderman
1782 ,, Daniel, Dublin, M.D.
1797 ,, David, Ballyavill, lieutenant
1784 ,, Digby, Geashill, King's County
1715 ,, Elizabeth, Clonmel, co. Tip., widow of Peter C., gent.
1735 ,, Elizabeth, Dublin, widow
1791 ,, Elizabeth, Henry-st., Dub., wid.
1667 ,, Edwd., Dub., LL.D. [**XIII.** 127
1686 ,, Edwd.,Westminr., gent. (Copy)
1751 ,, Edward, Castletown, co. Kilkenny, esq.
1779 ,, Edward, Painstown, co. Carlow
1668 ,, George, Dublin, brewer
1727 ,, George, Fethard, co. Tip., gent.
1731 ,, George, captain in the earl of Deloraine's regiment of foot
1771 ,, George, Drom., co. Tip., gent.
1778 ,, rev. George, rector of Graigue and Ullard, dio. Leighlin
1785 ,, George, Cohita, gent.
1604 ,, Henry (Copy) [gent.
1788 ,, Hugh, Newgrove, co. Cavan,
1741 ,, James, Francis-street, Dublin, woollen draper
1756 ,, James, Kilkenny, gent.
1782 ,, James, Dublin, merchant
1807 ,, James, Milltown, co. Monaghan
1775 ,, Jane, Dublin, spinster
1642 ,, John, New-st., Dublin, brewer
1659 ,, John, soldier in capt. Vivian's company [**VII.** 183
1687 ,, John, Limerick, baker
1708 ,, John, Kiltinan, co. Tipperary, esq. (Large Will; Ex.)
1713 ,, John, Youghal, co. Cork, esq.
1733 ,, John, Cooksborough, co. Westmeath, esq.
1735 ,, John, parish Overwharton, co. Stafford in Virginia (Copy)

1749	**Cooke**, John, Dublin, gent.	
1757	,,	John, Kevin-st., Dublin, hosier
1774	,,	John, Prussia-st., co. Dub., esq.
1775	,,	John, Pointstown, co. Tip., esq.
1787	,,	John, Cordangan, co. Tip., gent.
1794	,,	John, Gortalowry, co. Tyrone, linen draper
1798	,,	John, Clonmel, co. Tip., gent.
1799	,,	John, Rathmoy, co. Tip., gent.
1807	,,	John, city of Dublin
1743	,,	Joseph, Arglin, co. Tip., gent.
1780	,,	Joseph, Tipperary town, gent.
1782	,,	rev. Joseph, St. James's-street, Dublin, clk.
1785	,,	Laurence, Clonmore, co Carlow
1703	,,	Margaret, Dublin, widow
1692	,,	Martha, Dublin (now of Liverpool), widow (Copy)
1703	,,	Martha, Dublin, widow
1771	,,	Martha, Dublin, spinster
1798	,,	Martha, Dublin, spinster
1768	,,	Mathew, Pointstown, co. Tip., gent.
1767	,,	Nathaniel
1797	,,	Nathaniel, Ringsend, Dublin, surveyor
1706	,,	Peter, Garrick, co. Tip., gent.
1711	,,	Peter, Castle Cook, co. Cork, esq. (Ex.)
1787	,,	rev. Peter, Steeven's hospital, Dublin
1707	,,	Phanuel, Garrangibbon, co. Tipperary, gent.
1733	,,	Phaniel, Clonomelehon, co. Tipperary, esq.
1801	,,	Randall, Millview, gent.
1659	,,	Richard, soldier in captain Vivyan's company [**VII**. 182
1670	,,	Richard, Dublin, alderman
1720	,,	Richard, Dublin, merchant
1747	,,	Richard, senr., Dublin, gent.
1777	,,	Richard, Leeson-st., Dub., esq.
1798	,,	Richard, Morristown, co. Kildare, esq.
1691	,,	Robert, Mygullen, co. Westmeath, esq.
1703	,,	Robert, Cappoquin, co. Waterford, gent.
1747	,,	Robert, parish St. George the Martyr, Middlesex (Copy)
1749	,,	Robert, Lodge, co. Galway, esq.
1773	,,	Robert, Kiltinane, co. Sligo, gent.
1787	,,	Robert, Cooksborough, co. Westmeath, esq. (Large)
1704	,,	Samuel, Clonmel, co. Tipperary
1745	,,	Samuel, Dublin, gent.
1758	,,	sir Samuel, Dublin, bart.
1794	,,	Sarah, Patricia, Dublin, widow
1719	,,	Susanna, Dublin, widow

1794	**Cooke,**	Theodore, city of Watfd, esq.
1663	,,	Thomas, Dunshaughlin, co. Meath, gent.
1686	,,	Thomas, New-street, brewer
1706	,,	Thomas, Cork, merchant
1726	,,	Thomas, Dublin, gent.
1737	,,	Thos., Finglas, co. Dub., gent.
1750	,,	Thos., Youghal, co. Cork, gent.
1758	,,	Thos., Aghada, co. Cork, esq.
1761	,,	Thos., Painstown, co. Car., esq.
1762	,,	Thomas, Clara, King's Co., M.D.
1767	,,	Thomas, Dublin, alderman
1798	,,	Thomas, Athlone, co. Westmeath, esq.
1810	,,	Thomas, Retreat, co. Westmeath, esq,
1639	,,	Walter, New-street, co. Dublin, chandler
1723	,,	Wm., Painstown, co. Car., esq.
1742	,,	William, Camphire, co. Watfd.
1757	,,	Wm. Porter, Dublin, merchant
1771	,,	Wm., Drumcondra, co. Dublin, esq.
1764	,,	Zachary, Tallow, co. Wat., gent. [See COOK.]
1774	**Cookman,**	Edward, Enniscorthy, co. Wexford, esq.
1760	,,	John, Enniscorthy, co. Wexford, esq.
1759	,,	Richard, Enniscorthy, co. Wexford, gent.
1750	**Cooksey**,	Frances, Kilkenny, widow
1711	**Cookshut**,	John, Liverpool, Lancashire, merchant (Copy)
1707	**Cooley**,	John, Lisheen or Lisheenreagh, co. Tipperary, gent. (Ex.)
1770	,,	John, Thomas-court, and Donore, Dublin, merchant
1803	,,	John, Mary's-lane, Dub., smith
1807	,,	Margaret, Dublin, spinster
1793	,,	Sarah, Dublin, widow
1756	,,	Thomas, Dublin, esq.
1784	,,	Thomas, Dublin, architect [See COLLEY.]
1654	**Coomes**,	Richard, New Ross
1800	**Cooney**,	Edward, Balbriggan [See CONEY.]
1597	,,	*alias* **Cold**, Gregory, Dub., gent.
1779	,,	Mary, Dublin, fruiterer
1799	,,	Patrick, Townsend-st., Dublin
1807	,,	Patk., Grange, co. Kild., farmer
1790	,,	Robt., Clare, co. Mayo, mercht.
1809	,,	Wm., Newtown Mt. Kennedy
1807	**Cooper**,	Alicia, widow of the Rt. Hon. Joshua Cooper
1799	,,	Arthur, Seafort, co. Sligo, esq.
1791	,,	Charles, Eastown, co. Wicklow farmer

1674 **Cooper,** Edmond, Widford, Essex, gent. (Copy)
1680 ,, Edward, Markry, co. Sligo, esq. (Ex.) [farmer
1743 ,, Edwd., Sragh, Queen's County,
1766 ,, Elizabeth, Dublin, widow
1711 ,, Colonel Ellis
1773 ,, Experience, formerly of Cooper's-hill, Queen's Co., now of Dublin, widow
1795 ,, Francis, formerly of Armagh, but late of Dublin, gent.
1657 ,, Geo., Dub., butcher [VI. 141
1790 ,, Henry, Birchgrove, co. Wexford, farmer
1810 ,, Henry, town of Wexford, gent.
1777 ,, Jas., Mary's-lane, Dub., gent.
1748 ,, Jane, Carlow, spinster
1747 ,, John, Drogheda, gent.
1786 ,, John, city of Dublin
1793 ,, John Thomas, Springfield, Blackhorse lane, esq.
1784 ,, Joseph, Genaugh, co. Mon.
1758 ,, Joshua Meneray (Markree ?), co. Sligo, esq.
1801 ,, Joshua, Mercury (Markree ?), co. Sligo, privy councillor
1755 ,, Mary, Carlow, widow
1763 ,, Mary, Mercury (Markree ?), co. Sligo, widow
1774 ,, Mary, Enniskillen, co. Fermanagh, widow
1723 ,, Rev. Nathaniel, Lifford, co. Donegal, clerk
1738 ,, Nathaniel, Grange, co. Kilkenny, gent.
1770 ,, Nicholas, Ballycarrigeen, co. Wicklow, farmer
1755 ,, Robert, Dublin, dairyman
1784 ,, Richard, Great Cuffe-st., Dub.
1762 ,, Samuel, Beamore, co. Meath, gent.
1755 ,, Thomas, Dublin, esq.
1759 ,, Thomas, Dublin, esq.
1773 ,, rev. Thomas, Derrybrusk, co. Fermanagh, clerk
1658 ,, William, foot soldier
1736 ,, William, Newdown, co. Westmeath, gent.
1761 ,, sir William, Dublin, Bart.
1761 ,, William, Cooper's-hill, Queen's County
1764 ,, William, Dublin, esq., councillor-at-law
1768 ,, William, formerly of Tausyfort, co. Sligo, now of Dublin, esq. (Large Will) [See COWPER.]
1681 **Coote,** Anne, Killester, co. Dublin, widow of Chidley C., esq.

1774 **Coote,** Catherine, formerly of Mount Coote, Limerick, now of Newtown, Somerset, wid.
1801 ,, Catherine
1652 ,, sir Charles, Castlecuffe, Queen's County, knt. and bart.
1661 ,, sir Charles, Castlecoote, co. Rosc., knt. and bart., President of Connaught [IX. 37
1750 ,, Charles, Cootehill, co. Cavan, esq. (Large will)
1780 ,, rev. Charles
1796 ,, rev. Chas., Dean of Kilfenora
1668 ,, Chidley, Killester, co. Dublin, esq.
1691 ,, Chidley, esq., son of Charles, 1st Earl Mountrath
1702 ,, Chidley, Kilmallock, co. Limk.
1719 ,, Chidley, Dublin, esq.
1764 ,, Chidley, Mount Coote, co. Limerick, esq.
1799 ,, sir Eyre, lieut.-general, K.C.B.
1799 ,, Guy Moore, Dublin, esq.
1806 ,, Guy Moore, city of Dublin, esq.
1765 ,, Jane, Cork, widow
1808 ,, John Oliver, lieut. in the East India Co.'s service (Copy)
1777 ,, Margaret, Dublin, widow
1779 ,, Prudence, Dublin, widow
1809 ,, Ricd., Cootehill, co. Cavan, esq.
1671 ,, Thos., Cootehill, co. Cavan, esq.
1772 ,, Thomas, Dublin, esq.
1805 **Cope,** Alice
1743 ,, Anne, Drumully, co. Arm., wid.
1636 ,, Anthony, Ballyeath, co. Armagh, esq. (Copy)
1695 ,, Anthony, Drumully, co. Armagh, esq.
1764 ,, Anthony, dean of Armagh
1791 ,, Arthur, city of Dublin, esq.
1767 ,, Catherine, Dublin, widow
1705 ,, Downham, Loughall par., co. Armagh, esq.
1715 ,, Elizabeth, Dublin, widow
1750 ,, Erasmus, Dublin, goldsmith
1728 ,, Francis, par. St. James, Westminster (Copy)
1652 ,, Geo., Knole, Warwick (Copy)
1739 ,, Geo., Monasterevan, co. Kild.
1742 ,, Henry, Dublin, esq., M.D.
1775 ,, Henry, Ship-street, Dub., esq.
1688 ,, Jane, Drumully, co. Arm., wid.
1766 ,, John, Dublin, esq. (Not proved)
1786 ,, John, Rostrevor, co. Down, esq.
1670 ,, Martha, Drumully, co. Armagh, widow
1671 ,, *alias* **Berkley,** Mary, Loughall, co. Armagh, widow
1745 ,, Mary, Christchurch-yard, co. Dublin, widow

1761 **Cope**, Mary, Dublin, widow
1776 ,, Mary, Dublin, widow
1699 ,, Richard, Siddan, co. Meath, esq., capt. in Gustavus Hamilton's regiment
1638 ,, Richard, Leighlin, co. Carlow, esq. **[IV.** 347
1753 ,, Robt., Loughall, co. Arm., esq.
1768 ,, Robert, Island Bridge, co. Dublin, esq.
1742 ,, Sarah, Drumully, co. Armagh
1740 ,, Thomas, Dublin, watchmaker
1658 ,, Walter, senr., Drumully, co. Armagh, esq. **[VII.** 154
1724 ,, Walter,Drumully,co.Arm.,esq.
1787 ,, Walter, bp. of **Ferns**, q. v.
1715 ,, William, Dublin, silk dyer
1723 ,, William, Rossmenouge, co. Wexford, esq.
1780 **Copeland**, Margaret, North Strand, co. Dublin, widow
1734 ,, William, Lower Belnagon, co. Meath, gent.
1688 **Copinger**, Dominick, Ringeulliskie, co. Cork, esq.
1752 ,, John, Dublin, esq.
1761 ,, Laurence, Dublin, merchant
1785 ,, Michael, Cork city, esq.
1743 ,, Richard, Coolnaspishy, co. Cork, gent.
1779 ,, Richard, Hawkins'-st., Dublin, brewer
1795 ,, Thomas Henry, Ballinoe, co. Cork, esq.
[See COPPINGER.]
1744 **Copley**, Anthony, Newcastle, co. Limerick, esq.
1795 ,, Anthony, Ballyclogh, co. Limerick, esq.
1758 ,, John, Cork, esq.
1793 ,, John, Cregg, co. Clare, esq.
1673 ,, Mary, *alias* **Chichester**, Dublin, widow
1736 **Copperthwait**, James, Annymullen, co. Meath, gent.
1776 **Copperthwaite**, Thos., Tycroughan, gent.
1743 **Copping**, rev. John, dean of Clogher
1765 **Coppinger**, Bridget, Dublin, widow
1624 ,, Edward, Youghal, alderman
1770 ,, Elizabeth, Ballinvolane, co. Cork, widow
1764 ,, Helen
1639 ,, John, Leixlip, priest
1747 ,, John, Ballinvolane, co. of city of Cork, esq.
1806 ,, Nichs. Fras., city of Cork, esq.
1714 ,, Robert, Dublin, esq.
1808 ,, Stephen, city of Cork, merchant
1750 ,, Thomas, city of Gottenborg

1759 **Coppinger**, Thomas, Dublin, linen-draper
1705 ,, Walter, Dublin, surgeon
[See COPINGER.]
1762 **Coppock**, John, Dublin, merchant
[See CAPPOCK.]
1805 **Corballis**, John, New-st., co. Dubl., merchant
1757 ,, Joseph, Dublin, baker
1758 ,, Richard, Stephen-st., Dublin, carpenter
[See CORBALLYS, CORBOLYS.]
1760 **Corbally**, Elias, Rathregan, co. Meath, gent.
1704 ,, Henry, Dublin, yeoman
1747 ,, Mary, Dublin, spinster
1794 ,, Mathew, Sydenham, co.Meath, esq. (Large)
1772 ,, Michael
1780 ,, Richd., Kilcomacon, co.Meath, gent.
1798 ,, Susanna,Sydenham,co.Meath, widow
1780 **Corballys**, Bridget, Cornmarket, Dublin, widow
[See CORBALLIS.]
1730 **Corbet**, Daniel, Dublin, tailor
1775 **Corbett**, rev. Francis, D.D., dean of St. Patrick's, Dublin
1791 ,, Patrick, Dublin, gent.
1769 ,, Samuel, Durrow, co. Kilk.,gent.
1721 ,, Thos., Dungannon, co. Tyrone, merchant
1780 ,, Thomas, Dublin, gent.
1804 ,, William, Clonmel, gent.
[See CORBOTT, &c.]
1739 **Corbette**, Margaret, Dublin, widow
1776 **Corbolys**, Jas., Cornmarket, Dubl., linendraper
[See CORBALLIS.]
1804 **Corbott**, Robert, Corbott-hill, co. Wexford
1792 **Corcoran**, Barthw., Dub., printer
1799 ,, Barthw., Dub., bookseller
1777 ,, Catherine, *alias* **Lawler**, Dub., widow
1802 ,, Laur., Borris, co. Carlow, gent.
1788 ,, Margaret, Dublin, spinster
1799 ,, Mary, Dublin, widow
1736 ,, Richard, Dublin, merchant
1785 ,, William, Dublin, corn factor
[See COCHRANE, COGHRAN, CORKRAN, COUGHERANE, &c.]
1597 **Core**, Nicholas
1717 **Corey**, Jane, Carrigroghan, co. of city of Cork, spinster
[See CORRY.]
1627 **Cork and Ross**, Wm. Lyon, bp. of
1678 ,, **Cloyne, and Ross**, Edward Synge, bishop of

1709 **Cork and Ross**, Dive Downes, bp. of
1735 ,, Peter Brown, bishop of
1789 ,, Isaac Mann, D.D., bishop of
1805 ,, Thos. St. Lawrance, lord bp. of
1763 ,, **and Ossory**, John, earl of
1668 ,, Richd., earl of (Large will)
1698 ,, **and Burlington**, Richard, earl of **[XVIII.** 53
1748 **Corker**, Chambre, Dublin, esq.
1790 ,, rev. Chambre, Upper Lota, co. Cork, clk.
1755 ,, Daniel, King-st., Oxmantown, Dublin, esq.
1733 ,, Edw., Ballymaloe, co. Cork, esq.
1720 ,, Esther, Dublin, widow
1772 ,, Jos., par. St. Burian, Cornwall
1790 ,, Martha, Dublin, spinster
1739 ,, Rebecca, Dublin, spinster
1765 ,, Robert, par. St. Burian, Cornwall, LL.D. (Copy)
1770 ,, Robert, par. St. Burian, Cornwall (Copy)
1772 ,, Ruth, Dublin, widow
1737 ,, Thomas, Dublin, merchant
1799 **Corkoran**, Andrew, Dub., gardener
1771 **Corkran**, Edward, Sligo, merchant
1748 ,, Francis, Sligo, merchant
1802 ,, Hannah, Sligo, widow
1731 ,, Thomas, Sligo, merchant
1754 ,, Thomas, lordship of Roscrea
1621 ,, William (Imperfect)
[See CORCORAN.]
1770 **Corkrane**, Daniel, Ballyhiland, Queen's County, farmer
1804 **Corles**, Thomas, city of Chester, merchant (Copy)
1711 **Corly**, Mary, Dublin, widow
1809 **Cormack**, Thomas, Clonmel, co. Tipperary, merchant
1746 **Cormick**, Catherine, Dublin, widow
1801 ,, Catherine, Bridge-st., Dub. city
1733 ,, James, Dublin, tailor
1739 ,, Mary, Kilkenny, widow
1780 ,, Michael, Parliament-st., Dubl., goldsmith [esq.
1780 ,, Michl., Mullinmore, co. Mayo,
1758 ,, Robert, par. priest of Carbery, dio. Kildare (See 1759)
1759 ,, Robert, par. priest of Carbery, co. Kildare (See 1758)
[See CORMACK, CORMICKE, CORMOCK]
1736 **Cormicke**, Francis, Mullinmore, co. Mayo, esq.
1737 ,, Richd., Mullinmore, co. Mayo, esq. (Unproved)
1737 **Cormier**, Danl., Lisburn, co. Antrim, gent.
1672 **Cormock**, Charles, Presbytery, St. Michan's, Dublin

1790 **Corne**, Patience
1792 **Corneille**, Daniel, Dublin, esq.
1791 ,, Edward, Dublin, esq.
1803 ,, Jane, Dublin, spinster
1792 ,, John
1787 ,, Mary, Ennis, co. Clare, widow
1803 ,, Mary, Dublin, spinster
1669 **Cornellis**, Daniel, Portsmouth, Hampshire, esq.
1745 **Corner**, John, Dublin, gent.
1714 **Cornewall**, Fras. Eastham, knt., and baron of Burford, Shropshire
1730 **Cornish**, William, Trevarick, Cornwall, gent.
1800 **Cornistine**, William, Sligo
1761 **Cornock**, Mary, Bandon, relict of Isaac C., esq.
1740 ,, Zachary, Kilcasan, co. Wexford, gent.
1691 **Cornocke**, Isaac, Cork, merchant
1752 **Cornwal**, Esther, *alias* **Hamilton**, Ramalton, widow
1779 **Cornwall**, Alexander, Lismote, co. Limerick, esq.
1793 ,, Anne, Dublin, spinster
1697 ,, Catherine, Madeybenny, co. Londonderry, widow
1806 ,, Esther, Longford, spinster
1741 ,, Francis, Ballyhisky, co. Tipperary, esq.
1786 ,, Gabriel, city of Dublin, gent.
1732 ,, John, Cornwall's Grove, co. Tyrone, gent.
1786 ,, John, Longford, co. Longford
1805 ,, John, Strokestown
1755 **Cornyn**, Dominick, surgeon of the "John" galley, Jamaica
1737 ,, Manuel, Dublin, gent.
1776 ,, Mary, Dublin, widow
1795 **Corr**, Edm., Durham, co. Rosc., esq.
1734 ,, James, Coolaghmore, co. Kilkenny, gent.
1781 ,, Jas., Ballytobin, co. Kild., esq.
1805 ,, Nicholas, Dublin, merchant
1783 ,, Pierse, Callan, co. Kilk., esq.
1803 ,, Thomas, Creggs
[See CARR.]
1778 **Corraghan**, Monica, Dublin, widow
[See CORRIGAN.]
1804 **Corrahan**, Patrick, city of Dublin, dairyman
[See CORRIGAN.]
1739 **Corran**, Manus, Greenan, co. Armagh, linendraper
1742 ,, Thos., Greenan, co. Armagh, linendraper
[See CORRIN, CURWEN.]
1709 **Correges**, John, Dublin, gent.
1774 **Corrig**, Thomas, Tully, co. Kildare, farmer

1758 **Corrigan**, John, Cooloney, co. Sligo, shopkeeper
1791 ,, Patrick, Drogheda, rope maker
[See CORRAGHAN, CORRAHAN.]
1743 **Corrin**, Joseph, Bristol, mariner
[See CORRAN.]
1744 **Corry**, Alice, Dublin, widow
1764 ,, Edmond Leslie, Dublin, esq.
1792 ,, Edward, Newry, co. Down, esq.
1752 ,, Isaac, senr., Newry, co. Down, merchant
1809 ,, Isaac, Newry, co. Down, esq.
1725 ,, Isaiah, Newtown Corry, co. Monaghan, esq.
1718 ,, James, Castlecoole, co. Fermanagh, esq.
1727 ,, John, Castlecoole, co. Fermanagh, esq. (Large will)
1786 ,, John, Fairfield, co. Mon., clerk
1807 ,, John, Newtown Butler, co. Fermanagh
1769 ,, Jos., Dawson's Grove, co. Arm.
1741 ,, Leslie, Castlecoole, co. Fermanagh, esq.
1747 ,, Mary, Rakean, co. Cavan, wid.
1740 ,, Mathew, co. Monaghan
1805 ,, Nich. Henry Walter, Drumsna, co. Leitrim
1775 ,, Ralph, Kinsale, co. Cork
1805 ,, Rebecca, widow
1777 ,, Sarah Lowry, Castlecoole, co. Fermanagh, widow
1780 ,, sir Trevor, Dantzig, Poland, bt.
1699 ,, Walter, Glen, co. Mon., esq.
1738 ,, William, Dublin, gent.
1776 ,, William, Dromory, co. Fermanagh, gent.
[See COREY, CURRIE, CURRY.]
1742 **Cory**, James, Manusmore, co. Clare, farmer
1749 **Cosby**, Anne, widow of Henry C., Stradbally, Queen's County
1674 ,, Francis, Stradbally, Queen's County, esq.
1809 ,, Phillips, Stradbally Hall, Queen's County, esq. (Copy)
1764 ,, Sidney, Poolsbridge, Queen's County, gent.
1697 ,, Walter, Tinnakill, Queen's County, gent.
1783 ,, rev. Wm., rector of Tomregan, diocese of Kilmore
1722 **Cosbye**, Arnold, Lismore, co. Cavan, esq.
[See CROSBY.]
1586 **Coserowe**, Thomas, Dublin, alderman [I. 69
1796 **Cosgrave**, Amelia, *alias* **Carroll**, Dublin, widow
1727 ,, Eliz., *alias* **Gonne**, Dubl., wid.

1775 **Cosgrave**, Henry, Dublin, gent.
1762 ,, James, Dublin, merchant
1765 ,, Jas., Antigua, West Ind. (Copy)
1597 ,, John, Little Cabra
1670 ,, Laurence, Dublin, shoe maker
1625 ,, Mary, *alias* **Barnewall**, Dubl., widow
1767 ,, Mary, co. or city of Dub., spr.
1787 ,, Michael, Dublin, merchant
1797 ,, Philip, Dublin, gent.
1781 ,, Robert
1597 ,, William, Dublin, gent.
1724 **Coskarane**, Michael, Curraleigh, co. Tipperary, yeoman
1701 **Cossart**, Daniel, Sligo, merchant
1808 ,, Elizabeth, city of Cork, widow
1773 ,, George, Dublin, gent.
1756 ,, John, Dublin, merchant
1744 ,, Peter, Cork, merchant
1784 ,, Peter, Cork, merchant
1728 **Cossens**, George, Ballymaddock, Queen's County, innkeeper
1786 **Cosslett**, Charles, Anadorn, co. Down, esq.
1719 **Costello**, Charles, gent.
1738 ,, Charles, Tobrackan, barony of Costello
1770 ,, Edmond, Dublin, esq.
1742 ,, Jas., Tallaghan, co. Mayo, gent.
1776 ,, Jane
1762 ,, Michael, Jamaica, surgeon
1778 ,, Peter, Jervis-st., Dublin, gent.
1807 ,, Phillip, Dublin, coach maker
1775 ,, Stephen, Clonfert, co. Galway, farmer
1804 ,, William, Ballyfeighan, co. Meath, farmer
1734 **Costelloe**, Anthony, Dublin, mercht.
1735 ,, Catherine, Dublin, widow
1735 ,, Dudley, Tobrackan, co. Mayo, gent.
1791 ,, James, Treensealy, co. Mayo
1742 **Costeloe**, Stephen, Dublin, gent.
1799 **Costigan**, Augustin, Dublin, patten and last maker
1790 ,, Laurence, Clonaslee, Queen's County, farmer
1754 **Costigin**, Dennis, Dublin
1792 ,, Martin, Dublin, gent.
1756 **Costikin**, Elizabeth, *alias* **Tailford**, wife to William C., farmer
1745 ,, William, Philipstown, King's County, gent.
1763 ,, Wm., Ballina, King's Co., gent.
1709 **Cottand**, Charles, major in H. M. Queen Anne's Service (Copy)
1611 **Cottel**, John, Skreen, co. Meath, esq.
1632 ,, Walter, New Ross, co. Wexford, esq.

1771 **Cotter**, Edmond (not proved)
1705 ,, sir Jas., Ballmoperry or Cotter's Lodge, co. Cork, knt.
1794 ,, James, Mill-st., co. Cork, gent.
1782 ,, Mary, Dublin, widow
1792 ,, Mary, Dublin, widow
1760 ,, Maurice, Cork, merchant
1792 ,, Sharmar, Wicklow town, widow
1768 ,, Thomas, Wicklow town, farmer
1784 **Cottingham**, Henry, Whaley Abbey, co. Wicklow, esq.
1703 ,, James, Dublin, goldsmith
1804 ,, rev. James (Large)
1762 ,, Mary, Dublin, widow
1717 **Cottnam**, Abraham, Dernoney, co. Cavan, gent.
1740 ,, Thos., Belturbet, co. Cav., gent.
1787 **Cottom**, Edwd., Waterford, mercht.
1803 **Cotton**, Catherine, city of Dublin, widow
1668 ,, Eusebius, New Ross, co. Wexford, gent.
1697 ,, Henry, Limerick, merchant
1754 ,, James, Dublin, linendraper
1744 ,, Lydia, Swordlestown, co. Kildare, widow
1722 ,, Samuel, Dublin, gent.
1740 ,, Samuel, Dublin, esq.
1736 ,, Thomas, Swordlestown, co. Kildare, farmer
1746 ,, Thomas, Swordlestown, co. Kildare, farmer
1776 ,, William, Dublin, merchant
1794 ,, William, Ship-street, Dublin, cabinet maker
1788 **Cottrell**, rev. Edward, co. Cork, clk.
1701 **Coudell**, Thos., Donard, co. Wicklow, esq. (Ex.)
1704 ,, William, Donard, co. Wicklow, gent.
1711 **Coudert**, Bernard, Dublin, merchant
1623 **Cougherane**, James, par. of Aughadowey, diocese of Derry [See CORCORAN.]
1746 **Coughlan**, David, Dublin, gent.
1804 ,, Edward, Ratoe, co. Carlow, esq.
1776 ,, Ellinor, Ballea, co. Cork, wid.
1735 ,, Jeremy, Lismore, co. Waterford, esq.
1779 ,, Joanna, *alias* **Hussey**, wife to Henry Coughlan
1781 ,, John, Dublin, merchant
1796 ,, Richard, city of Cork, gent.
1731 ,, Wm., Ballea, co. Cork, gent.
1798 **Couglan**, Ellinor, Cork, spinster [See COGHLAN.]
1759 **Coulahan**, Daniel
1712 **Coulhoun**, Elizabeth
1755 **Coulhoune**, John, Strabane

1762 **Coulsen**, John, Bellmont, co. Fermanagh, esq.
1783 **Coulson**, Henry, Nenagh, co. Tipperary, gent.
1787 ,, John, Belmont, co. Ferm., esq.
1770 ,, Joseph, Dublin, ironmonger
1784 ,, Thos., Haroldscross, co. Dubl.
1801 ,, William, Lisburn, co. Antrim, linendraper
1706 **Coulter**, Andrew, Clonmel, co. Tipperary, gent.
1796 ,, Joseph Dowdallshill, co. Louth, gent.
1801 ,, Joseph, Carnbegg, co. Louth, gent.
1660 **Coulthurst**, John, Naas [**VIII.** 102 [See COLTHURST.]
1779 **Coulton**, John, Carrick-on-Suir, co. Tipperary, apothecary
1656 ,, Richard, cornet of capt. Claypoole's troop of horse
1725 **Coupman**, John, Dublin, glover
1776 **Courcy**, John, Kilgarvan, co. Kerry, gent.
1674 **Courreagh**, William, Dublin, tanner
1728 **Court**, Wm., Dublin, peruke maker
1754 **Courtenay**, Anna, formerly of Dublin, but of Mountmellick, Queen's County, widow
1660 ,, Francis, Newcastle, co. Limk., esq. (Copy)
1791 ,, George, Middleton, Cork, gent.
1737 ,, Hercules, Kilrush, co. Westmeath, esq.
1739 ,, Mary, Dublin, formerly of Kilrush, co. Westmeath
1756 ,, Mary, Dublin, widow
1700 ,, Richard, esq., third son of sir Wm. C., Powderham Castle, Devon, bart. (Copy)
1750 ,, sir Wm., Powderham Castle, Devon, bart. (Copy)
1763 ,, William, lord visct., formerly sir William C., bart. (Copy) [See COURTNEY.]
1680 **Courthope**, sir Peter, Little Island, co. Cork, knt. (Ex.)
1685 **Couthorp**, Peter, Ballyderowne, co. Cork, gent.
1763 **Courtney**, Chas., Newry, co. Down, gent.
1788 ,, David, Ballinrobe
1783 ,, Edward, Harrymount, co. Down
1755 ,, Francis, Dublin, merchant
1783 ,, Henry, Hollyhead
1810 ,, Henry C., Newry, esq.
1789 ,, John Cooke, Dublin, attorney-at-law
1805 ,, John, Lota, Liberties of Cork
1809 ,, Joseph, Glenone, linen draper

1811 **Courtney**, Jos., Mespil Grove, Dubl.
1779   ,,   Penelope
1789   ,,   William, lord viscount   (Copy)
          [See COURTENAY.]
1788 **Courtown**, right hon. Elizabeth,
          dow. countess
1770   ,,   James, earl of,
1810   ,,   James, earl of   (Copy)
1727 **Cousser**, John Sigismond, Dublin
1707 **De Coutiers**, Augustine, lieutenant
          in col. Sankey's regt. of foot
1760   ,,   Eliz., Portarlington, Queen's
          County, widow
1751   ,,   captain Isaac, Portarlington
1804 **Coveney**, Daniel, Cork city, tailor
1700 **Covert**, Robert, Cork, gent.
1807 **Covey**, John, city of Dublin, grocer
1647 **Covill**, Archbold, sergt.-major
          [**IX**. 46
1784 **Cowan**, Andrew, Ballintaugh, co.
          Down
1791   ,,   John, Ely place, parish St.
          Andrew's, London   (Copy)
1800   ,,   Margaret, Dublin
1676   ,,   Robert   Macreymeson,   co.
          Tyrone, gent.
          [See COWEN.]
1733 **Cowdall**, Margery, Donard, co.
          Wicklow, widow
1785 **Cowden**, William, King's Mews,
          Charing Cross, esq.   (Copy)
1782 **Cowel**, Catherine, Dublin, widow
1799   ,,   John Holden, Rathangan, co.
          Kildare, esq.
1783   ,,   Thomas, Ballymore Eustace,
          co. Dublin, gent.
1768 **Cowell**, Bryan, Logadowden, co.
          Dublin, gent.
1627   ,,   Robt., Tynan, co. Armagh, esq.
1778 **Cowen**, Arthur, Dublin, gent.
1789   ,,   Jane, Dublin, widow
1811   ,,   Robert, Bailieborough, co.
          Cavan, attorney-at-law
1800   ,,   Stephen, gunner in R. Ir. Artill.
          [See COWAN.]
1736 **Cowingham**, James, Dub., merch.
1768 **Cowley**, Christian, Dublin, widow
1650   ,,   captain George, Dublin
1657   ,,   Lettice, *alias* **Shee**, widow
          [**VI**. 223
          [See COLLEY.]
1805 **Cowly**, Wm., Mt. Pleasant, co. Dub.
1741 **Cowman**, Daniel, Dublin, tallow
          chandler
1777 **Cowney**, Roger, Limerick, mercht.
1595 **Cowper**, Richard, gent.
1790   ,,   rev. Thos., Drumcliff, co, Sligo
          [See COOPER.]
1754 **Cox**, Allan, Ballyvadden, co. Wex-
          ford, esq.

1753 **Cox**, Cornelius, Dublin, merchant
1730   ,,   Elinor, Dublin, spinster
1785   ,,   Eliz., Fordham's-alley, Dublin,
          widow
1763   ,,   Ellinor, wid. of rev. Marmaduke
          C., Great Island, co. Cork
1750   ,,   Frances, Dublin, spinster
1713   ,,   Henry, Dublin, gent.
1785   ,,   Henry Shute, Shire-lane, Mid-
          dlesex, esq.
1783   ,,   Hugh, Ballynoe, co. Lim., esq.
1716   ,,   rev. Jas., archdeacon of Ferns
1770   ,,   James, Shire-lane, Middlesex,
          esq.   (Copy)
1664   ,,   Jasper, Youghal, alderman
1736   ,,   John, Mullans, co. Ant., gent.
1737   ,,   John, Kilmagulagh, co. Clare,
          gent.
1758   ,,   John Fitzmathew, Gal., burgess
1781   ,,   John, Granard, co. Longford
1795   ,,   John, Wexford, esq.
1795   ,,   John, Carrick-on-Suir, co. Tip-
          perary, gent.
1806   ,,   Joseph, lieut. in the 70th regt.
          of foot   (Copy)
1762   ,,   rev. Marmaduke, Great Island,
          near Cork
1803   ,,   Martha, Dublin, widow
1739   ,,   Mary, Dublin, widow
1779   ,,   Mathew, Dublin, gent.
1773   ,,   sir Michael, Dunmanway, co.
          Cork, bart.
1779   ,,   Michael, bp. of **Cashel**, q. v.
1701   ,,   Peter, Killimore, co. Cavan,
          yeoman   [Dublin, esq.
1767   ,,   Philip, Sligo town, but now of
1596   ,,   Richard, parson of Dysse, Nor-
          folk   (Copy)
1733   ,,   sir Richard, Dunmanway, co.
          Cork, knt. and bart.   (Ex.)
1761   ,,   Richard, Dublin, gent.
1766   ,,   sir Richard, Dunmanway, co.
          Cork, bart.
1776   ,,   Richd., Kildare-st., Dub., grocer
1790   ,,   Richard, Castletown, co. Kil-
          kenny, esq.
1718   ,,   rev. Thos., dean of Ferns, and
          vicar of St. Peter's, Drogheda
1685   ,,   Walter, Dundalk, gent.
1663   ,,   William, Donore, near Dublin,
          brewer
1736   ,,   Wm., Island Bridge, co. Dubl.,
1766   ,,   Wm., Ballynoe, co. Limerick,
          but of Cork
          [See COCKS.]
1585 **Coxe**, Edward, gent.   (proved in
          Limerick 1581, Copy)
1761   ,,   Mary, parish of St. George,
          Hanover-square, Middlesex,
          spinster   (Copy)

1793 **Coxon**, Mich., Killarney, Kerry, esq.
1803 **Coyle**, Denis, Townsend-st., Dublin, linen draper
1809 ,, Geo., North Earl-st., Dubl., esq.
1805 ,, Laurence, city of Dublin, gent.
1773 ,, Michael Gerardstown, co. Meath, farmer
1548 ,, Patk., parish of Santry, farmer
1548 ,, Richard
1809 ,, Stephen, Sherlockstown, co. Kildare, esq.
1625 ,, Wm., Geraldstown, co. Meath
1791 **Coyne**, Anne, *alias* **Eccles**, Ballyshannon, co Donegal, widow
1785 ,, Jas., Clogher, co. Rosc., gent.
1699 ,, John, Dublin, alderman (Ex.)
1752 ,, John, Lackan, co.Westm., esq.
1764 ,, Nicholas, Dublin, esq.
1625 ,, Wm., Geraldstown, co. Meath
[See COANE, COEN.]
1762 **Craddock**, John, Arklow, co. Wicklow, gent.
1713 ,, William, Belfast, co. Antrim, tide waiter
1805 **Cradock**, Ma.
1776 ,, Phillip, Ardbraccan, co. Meath, gent.
1730 **Crafford**, Alexander, island of Antigua, gent. (Copy)
1690 ,, George, Dublin, gunsmith
1686 ,, Hugh, Belfast, merchant
1658 ,, Robert, Ballysallagh, co. Down, gent. **[VII.** 71
1695 ,, Sarah, widow of George C., Dublin, gunsmith
1786 ,, Thos., Tiermoyle, co. Tip., esq.
1716 ,, William, Belfast, esq.
1723 ,, William, esq. (Copy)
[See CRAWFORD.]
1737 **Craford**, David, Belfast, gent.
1771 ,, James, Downpatrick, mercht.
1746 **Cragell**, Joseph, Dublin, joiner
1750 ,, William, Dublin, joiner
1650 **Cragges**, Geo., Thomas-court, gent.
1650 **Craggs**, Anthony, St.Thomas-court, maltster
1787 ,, Leslie, Cork city, esq.
1738 **Craghead**, Robert, Dublin, gent.
1755 **Crags**, John, Cork, gent.
[See CRAGGS.]
1772 **Craig**, Campbell, Dublin, gent.
1803 ,, David, Enniskillen, gent.
1783 ,, James, Carrickfergus, linendraper
1806 ,, James, Hammond's marsh, city of Cork, distiller
1750 ,, Jane, Newry, co. Down
1692 ,, John, par. St. Paul, Covent Garden, Middlesex, M.D. (Copy)

1752 **Craig**. John, Ballyboy, co. Mon., mercht.
1753 ,, Jos., Newry, co. Down, merch.
1681 ,, Lewis, Ricarstown in Scotland, esq. (Ex.)
1791 ,, Mary, *alias* **Filgate**
1811 ,, Peter, general in H. M. S.
1807 ,, Robert, Cork-street, Dublin
1789 ,, rev. William, Dublin, clerk
1809 ,, William, Cork, distiller
1810 ,, William, Cork, gent.
1762 ,, John, Rathbawn
[See CREAGH.]
1725 **De Cramahe**, HectorF. Chataigner
1771 **Cramer**, Ambrose, Newry, esq.
1660 ,, or **Kramer**, Balthasar, Dublin, esq.
1705 ,, Balthasar, Ballyfoyle, co. Kilkenny, esq.
1741 ,, Balthazar, John, Dublin, esq.
1802 ,, Coghill, Clontarf, co. Dublin, esq. (Large)
1723 ,, Elizabeth, widow
1730 ,, Francis, Ballybranighan, co. Longford, farmer
1790 ,, Jane, Dublin, spinster
1761 ,, John, Telogh, barony of Carbery, co. Kildare
1749 ,, Judith, Dublin, widow
1723 ,, Oliver, Ballyfoyle, co. Kilk.,esq.
1754 ,, Oliver, Carlow, gent.
1762 ,, Sarah, wife to Theo. C., Kilkenny, gent. [kenny, esq.
1684 ,, Tobias, Ballyfoyle, co. Kil-
[See CREAMER.]
1785 **Crampton**, Cath., Dublin, spinster
1758 ,, John, Dublin, clockmaker
1792 ,, John, Dublin, gent.
1792 ,, Philip, Dublin, alderman
1751 ,, Thomas, Dublin, watchmaker
[See CROMPTON.]
1771 **Crane**, Cathne., Park-st., Dub., wid.
1685 ,, Simon, Great Forest, co. Dublin, esq.
[See CREAN.]
1750 **Cranfield**, Richard, Dublin, joiner and gilder
1809 ,, Richard, Tritonville Lodge, co. Dublin
1615 **Cranford**, capt. Patrick, Tradonill, co. Donegal, esq.
1667 **Crannedge**, Humphrey, Newberry, Berkshire, butcher (Copy)
1763 **Cranny**, Nicholas, Garryduff, Queen's County
1762 **Cranston**, John, archdeacon of Clogher and rector of Tedaunet
1800 ,, rev. John, Mellfield, co. Tyr., clk.

1638 **Cranston**, Thomas, Aghrain, parish of Devenish, co. Ferm., gent.

1602 **Cranysborough**, Thomas, Waterford, merchant

1754 **Crathorn**, Jefferey, Baltinglass, co. Wicklow

1788 ,,   Jeffery, Baltinglass, co. Wicklow, gent.

1732 **Craven**, Alice, Dublin, widow
1766 ,,   Anne, Dublin, widow
1792 ,,   Arthur, Drumcashel, co. Louth
1781 ,,   Catherine, Dublin, spinster
1725 ,,   Charles, Dublin, gent.
1806 ,,   Hanah, city of Dublin, spr.
1723 ,,   Jefford, Cork, gent.
1708 ,,   John, Limerick, alderman
1790 ,,   Loughlin, Clara, Kings County, dealer
1739 ,,   Philip, Dublin, gent.
1768 ,,   rev. Robert, Ballymackey, co. Tipperary, clerk
1803 ,,   Sarah, Dublin, spinster
1670 ,,   William, Dublin, cutler
1658 **Craw**, John, Dubl., gent. [**VI.** 262
1767 **Crawford**, Alexander, Millwood, co. Fermanagh, esq.
1800 ,,   Alicia, Tullavally, co. Tyrone
1795 ,,   Andrew, Dublin, esq.
1799 ,,   Andrew, Castle Dawson, co. Derry
1698 ,,   Anne, Scurloghstown, co. Meath, widow
1766 ,,   Anne, *alias* **Nixon**, Lurganboy, co. Leitrim
1780 ,,   Anne, Dublin, widow
1802 ,,   Anne, Lyndcomb and Wyecomb, Somersetshire, widow (Copy)
1764 ,,   Charles, Newtown Stewart, co. Tyrone, esq.
1799 ,,   Charles, Newtown Stewart, co. Tyrone, esq. (Large)
1772 ,,   David, Dublin, merchant
1799 ,,   Elizabeth, Dublin, widow
1808 ,,   George, major 2nd West India regiment
1759 ,,   Gustavus, Lurganboy, co. Leitrim, gent.
1755 ,,   Henry, Millwood, co. Ferm.
1757 ,,   Henry, Dublin, esq.
1790 ,,   Henry
1777 ,,   Hugh, Carlingford, co. Louth, merchant
1770 ,,   Isabella, Legacorry, co. Mon., widow
1754 ,,   James, Enniskillen, co. Fermanagh, esq.
1786 ,,   James, Armagh, co. Tyrone
1788 ,,   James (Copy)

1769 **Crawford**, Jason, Lawrencetown, co. Meath, esq.
1660 ,,   John, Wexford   [**VIII.** 110
1803 ,,   John, Rockfield, co. Westmeath
1808 ,,   John, Lawrencetown, co. Meath
1771 ,,   Mary, *alias* **Sarsfield**, Athlone, widow
1808 ,,   Nicholas, Tullamore, Kings County, gent.
1734 ,,   Robert, Aughnacloy, co. Fermanagh, gent.
1789 ,,   Robert, Castle Dawson, co. Derry, gent.
1804 ,,   Samuel, Castle Dawson, co. Londonderry, linen draper
1707 ,,   Thomas, New Ross, co. Wex.
1792 ,,   Thos., Fermoyle, co. Tip., esq.
1679 ,,   Ursly, Kilbuck, co. Down, spr.
1634 ,,   Wm., Ballysavage or Dunegur, co. Antrim, gent. (Copy)
1735 ,,   William, Finards, co. Down
1749 ,,   William, Snow Hill, co. Fermanagh, gent.
1793 ,,   William, Larne, co. Antrim
1806 ,,   William, Ballyshannon, co. Donegal, esq.
1808 ,,   Wm., Dublin, apothecary
[See CRAFFORD, CRAFORD.]

1771 **Crawley**, Anne, widow of James C., Kilfinane, co. Limerick
1809 ,,   Christr., Callaville, co. Arm.
1768 ,,   James, Kilfinane, co. Limerick
1775 ,,   James, Dublin, shoemaker
1803 ,,   rev. Patrick
[See CROWLY.]

1797 **Cray**, Phillip, St. Clements, East Cheap, Lond., gent. (Copy)

1752 **Creagh**, Andw., St. Francis Abbey, co. Limerick
1763 ,,   Andrew, Limerick, merchant
1790 ,,   Bartholomew, Knockanees, co. Tipperary, gent.
1804 ,,   Bartholomew, Cork
1743 ,,   Charles, Ballykilty, co. Clare, gent.
1804 ,,   Eliz., Askeaton, co. Limk., spr.
1770 ,,   Ellen, Sixmilebridge, co. Clare, widow
1776 ,,   Ellinor, Limerick, widow
1789 ,,   Francis, Limerick, merchant
1674 ,,   Gabriel, Ennis, co. Clare, merchant
1726 ,,   James, Limerick, merchant
1758 ,,   James, Limerick, merchant
1765 ,,   James, senr., Limerick, merch.
1742 ,,   John Baptist, Woodfield, co. Clare, gent.
1790 ,,   John, the elder, Cork, mercht.
1792 ,,   John, Creagh Castle, co. Cork, M.D.

1793 **Creagh,** John Ricd., Abbey, co. Tipp.
1805 ,, John B., Castle Widenham, co. Cork, M.D.
1620 ,, Leonard Fitz Thos., Clonmel, burgess
1710 ,, Michael, Limerick, merchant
1764 ,, Michael, Cork, merchant
1782 ,, Michl.,Liscarroll, co. Cork,esq.
1743 ,, Patk., Bearnagilry, co. Clare, gent.
1671 ,, Pierce, Dungivigne, co. Clare, esq. (Ex.)
1810 ,, Richard, Liscarroll, co. Cork
1759 ,, Savage, Dublin, wine cooper
1754 ,, Simon, Dublin, merchant
1800 ,, Stephen Fitzpatrick, Dromon, co. Clare, gent.
1773 ,, Theobald, Kill, co. Tipp., gent.
1626 ,, Wm. Fitzmartin, Limk., merch.
1786 ,, Wm., Cork city, woollen draper
[See CARRICK, CRAIG.]
1673 **Creaghe,** Francis, Ballywolloge, co. Limerick, gent.
1628 ,, John, Kilmallock, burgess
1802 **Creamer,** rev Marmaduke, Dublin, LL.D.
[See CRAMER.]
1784 **Crean,** James, Carrareagh, co. Galway, gent.
1659 ,, Peter, Sligo, merch. [**VII.** 145
[See CRANE.]
1630 **Credland,** John, vicar of Cowlocke, near Dublin
1806 **Creed,** Edward, Cork, esq.
1747 ,, Fras., Ballygrenane, co. Limk., gent.
1805 ,, Nathaniel, Dubl., lace manufr.
1809 ,, Rebecca, Cork, widow
1804 **Creek,** Edward, Newry, co. Down, merchant
1811 **Creery,** rev. John, Tanderagee, co. Armagh
1809 ,, Wm., Ballinrobe, co. Mayo, clk.
1621 **Crehall,** Catherine, *alias* **Freeman,** Loughanstown, co. Dublin, widow
1706 **Creichton,** Abraham, Crum, co. Fermanagh, esq.
1728 ,, David, major-gen., and Master of the Royal Hospital
1755 ,, Hester, late of Crum, but of par. St. James,Westmr., wid.
1715 ,, John, Crum, co. Ferm., esq.
1731 ,, Sarah, Creichton's Grove, co. Louth, widow
1743 ,, rev. William
[See CREIGHTON.]
1694 **Creichtoune,** John, Aghalane, co. Fermanagh, esq.

1738 **Creichtowne,** John, esq.
1800 **Creighton,** Abraham, Dublin, merchant tailor [Dublin
1809 ,, hon. Abraham, Mountjoy-sq.,
1803 ,, Hamilton, city of Dublin
1702 ,, James, Crum, co. Ferm., esq.
1778 ,, Jas., Leighlinbridge, co. Carlow, gent.
1801 ,, hon. Meliora, Dublin, spinster
[See CREICHTON, CRIECHTON, CRIGHTONE, &c.]
1746 **Crellen,** Mary, Dublin, widow
1692 **Crelling,** William, Dublin, gent.
1651 **Crenan,** Patk., Stamullin, co. Meath
[See CRENNAN, CRINAN.]
1714 **Crenegan,** Samuel, Dirnegarragh, co. Westmeath, gent.
1766 **Crennan,** Wm., Smithfield, Dublin, salesmaster
[See CRENAN.]
1664 **Cressy,** Geo., Dubl., esq. [**III.** 46
1797 **Creswell,** Mary, Dublin, widow
1655 **Crewkerne,** capt. Henry, Tramplestown, co. Carlow
1683 ,, Margaret, Carlow, widow
1555 **Creffyord,** James, soldier
1595 **Cribbes,** Robert, Dublin
1705 **Crichly,** Phil., Cootehill, co. Cavan, tailor
1670 **Crichton,** John, dean of Ferns
1741 **Criechton,** Mary, Dublin, spinster
[See CREIGHTON.]
1809 **Crigan,** Alexander, Ballybogan, co. Donegal
1655 **Crightone,** David, Aghalane, co. Fermanagh, esq.
[See CREIGHTON.]
1729 **Crilly,** John, Kilcurry, co. Louth, gent.
1797 ,, Mary, city of Limerick, widow
1805 **Crinan,** George, Kinoud, co. Dubl.
[See CRENAN.]
1805 **Crinian,** Thomasin, Halpenny-hill, co. Dublin
1789 **Crinigan,** Daniel, Queen-st., Dubl., printer and cutler
1731 **Crips,** Joseph, Cahemary, co. of city of Limerick
1728 **Cripps,** Elias, Dublin, merchant
1806 **Critchly,** Abraham, Cassino, co. Wicklow, esq.
1766 ,, Henry
1684 ,, Wm., Tullagh, co. Carlow, esq.
1740 **Croasdaile,** Thomas, Clostokin, co. Galway, esq.
[See CROSDAILE.]
1676 **Crocker,** Mary
[See CROKER.]
1732 **Croft,** Alice, Dublin, widow
1714 ,, Jas., Pill-lane, Dubl., mercht.

1768 **Crofton,** Ash, Castlefish, co. Kildare
1741 ,, Henry, capt. in genl. Paget's regt. at Minorca
1806 ,, Chidley, Mohill, co. Leit., gent.
1810 ,, Curtis, Castlefish, co. Kild.,esq.
1669 ,, Duke, Dublin, gent.
1782 ,, Duke, Lurga, co. Leit., gent.
1733 ,, sir Edwd., Moate, co. Rosc., bt.
1740 ,, sir Edwd., Moate, co. Rosc.,bt.
1741 ,, Edward, Athy, co. Kildare
1745 ,, Edward, Clonard, co. Meath
1781 ,, Edward, Chancery-hill, co. Westmeath, esq.
1798 ,, Edward, Royal Hospital, esq.
1786 ,, Elizabeth, city of Cork, widow
1736 ,, Geo., Drumgrana, co. Leitrim, gent.
1796 ,, Hamilton Lowther, major 13th dragoons
1770 ,, Hanah, Dublin
1742 ,, Hen., Grange, co. Rosc., gent.
1763 ,, Hen., Longford, co. Sligo, esq.
1767 ,, Hugh, Dublin, esq.
1706 ,, James, capt. in lord Dungannon's regt. of foot
1761 ,, James, town of Sligo, gent.
1750 ,, John, esq.
1765 ,, John, Lisdom, now of Dub., esq.
1788 ,, sir Marcus Lowther, Moate, co. Roscommon, bart.
1747 ,, Margaret, Athy, co. Kild., wid.
1734 ,, Mary, Baskin, co. Dubl., wid.
1721 ,, Michl., Park, co. Meath, gent.
1802 ,, sir Morgan, Dublin, bart.
1781 ,, sir Oliver, Lissanard, co. Limerick, bart.
1768 ,, rev. Perkins, Rochfort, co. Cork
1783 ,, Philip, Queen-street, Dublin
1667 ,, Richard, Lissedcorne, co. Roscommon, esq. (Copy)
1704 ,, col. Richard
1734 ,, Theophilus, Baskin, co. Dubl., gent.
1743 ,, Thos., Mohill, co. Leitrim, esq.
1780 ,, Thomas, Merryville, King's County, esq.
1794 ,, Thos., Culvin, co Westm., esq.
1762 ,, capt. William, Dublin
1775 ,, Wm., Arbour-hill, late qr.-mr. 13th dragoons
1797 ,, Wm. Lowther, Englishtown, co. Roscommon, esq.
1804 **Crofts,** Alexander, town of Boyle
1712 ,, Christopher, Cork, esq.
1750 ,, Christopher, Dublin, hosier
1757 ,, Christopher, Velvetstown, co. Cork, gent.
1741 ,, Geo., Churchtown, co. Cork, esq.
1760 ,, George, Cork, cooper

1802 **Crofts,** George, Churchtown, co. Cork, esq.
1732 ,, James, major-gen., parish of St. James, Westminster (Copy)
1735 ,, James, Carcalla, co. Clare, but now of Dublin, esq.
1741 ,, Mary, Churchtown, co. Cork, widow
1730 ,, Philip, Cork, gent.
1705 ,, Ralph, Dublin, ribbon weaver
1725 ,, Salisbury, wife to brigadier James Crofts
1784 ,, William, Velvetstown, co. Cork, esq. (Large)
1769 **Croghan,** Alice, Leitrim, co. Roscommon, widow
1777 ,, Dennis, Roscommon, co. Roscommon, M.D. (Copy)
1801 ,, Elizabeth, Galway town, widow
1775 ,, Owen, Grange, co. Rosc., esq.
1768 ,, Wm., Drimkeelvy, co. Leitrim, gent.
1782 ,, Wm., Grange, co. Roscommon
1717 **Crohare,** John, Kilkenny, surgeon
1658 **Croke,** Amy, Dublin, widow
1797 **Croker,** Bridget, city of Cork, widow
1732 ,, Edward, Rawleighstown, co. Limerick, esq.
1771 ,, Edward, Dublin, apothecary
1759 ,, Elizabeth, Dublin, widow
1668 ,, Hugh, Ballyhamlis, co. Waterford, gent.
1684 ,, John, Ariglin Bridge, co. Cork, gent.
1750 ,, John, Dub., one of the attorneys of the Common Pleas
1751 ,, John, Ballyneguard, co. Limerick, esq.
1784 ,, John, Airhill, co. Cork
1794 ,, John, Nadrid, co. Cork, esq.
1676 ,, Mary, Londonderry, widow
1800 ,, Michael, Beaufield, co. Wexford, esq.
1726 ,, Richard, Nadrid, co. Cork, esq.
1732 ,, Ricd., north sub. of Cork, gent.
1684 ,, Thomas, Cahirkereely, co. Limerick, esq.
1704 ,, Thos., Ballyauker, co. Waterford, gent. [alderman
1718 ,, Thomas, Youghal, co. Cork,
1750 ,, Thos., Butlerstown, co. Cork, esq.
1794 ,, Thomas, city of London, lieutenant in the navy
1796 ,, Thomas, Dublin, gent.
1800 ,, Thomas, Dublin, esq. [gent.
1714 ,, Walter, Whitestown, co. Dubl.,
1757 ,, William, Dublin, cordwainer
1801 ,, Wm., Johnstown, co. Cork,esq.
[See CROCKER.]

1780 **Crolly**, Lucy, *alias* **Savage**, Ballykilbeg, co Down
1651 ,, Mathew, Dublin, shoe maker
1705 **Croly**, Cromack, Dublin, merchant
1809 ,, John, South Crig, co. Cork
1623 ,, Patrick, Dublin, shoemaker
[See CROWLEY.]
1612 **Cromall**, John, Balrothery, co. Dubl.
1728 **Cromelin**, Lewis, Lisburn, co. Ant.
[See CROMMELIN.]
1625 **Cromer**, John, Rasbeg, co. Fermanagh, gent.
1725 **Cromey**, William, Mullans, co. Ant.
1776 **Cromie**, Andrew, Dublin, merchant
1785 ,, James, Baldoyle, co. Dublin
1805 ,, James, Baldoyle, co. Dublin
1781 ,, Michael, Dublin, merchant
1723 ,, William. Dublin, merchant
[See CRUNNY.]
1737 **Crommelin**, Alexander, Lisburn, co. Antrim, gent.
1756 ,, Anne, Lisburn, co. Ant., wid.
1728 ,, Louis, Lisburn, co. Antrim
1726 ,, Samuel, Lisburn, co. Antrim
1743 ,, Samuel Lewis, Lisburn, co. Antrim, gent.
[See CROMELIN.]
1713 **Crompton**, Chas., Drogheda, merch.
1804 ,, Charlotta, town of Drogheda, spinster (Large)
1698 ,, James, Dublin, merchant
1696 ,, Thomas, Powlamalon, co. Wexford, gent.
[See CRAMPTON.]
1790 **Crone**, John, Limerick, esq.
1804 ,, Richard, Summerhill, Dublin
1802 **Cronin**, Cornelius, Cork. gent.
1756 ,, Daniel, Knocknagree, co. Cork
1786 ,, Daniel, Park, co. Kerry, esq.
[See CRONYN.]
1727 **Cronyn**, Wm., Sledy, co. Wat., gent.
1757 **Crooke**, Catherine, Dublin
1638 ,, Edmond. Dublin, stationer
1631 ,, sir Thomas, Ballimore, co. Cork, knt. and bart. (Copy)
1759 ,, William
1742 **Crookes**, Henry, Moneymore, co. Derry (will set aside in the court of delegates)
1657 ,, James, Carrickfergus, burgess [**VI**. 207
[See CROOKS.]
1724 **Crookey**, Anne, Bryanstown, co. Dublin [Londonderry, gent.
1724 **Crooks**, James, Mulkeerogh, co.
1769 ,, Thos., Vesingstown, co. Meath, farmer
1768 ,, Wm., Leixlip, co. Kild., gent.
1790 ,, Wm., Moira, co. Down, gent.
[See CROOKE, CROOKES.]

1787 **Crookshank**, George, Dublin, esq.
1719 ,, William, Dublin, innkeeper
1780 ,, William, Dublin, esq.
1678 **Crookshanks**, Thomas
1803 **Crosbie**, Agnes
1662 ,, dame Anne, *alias* **Furlong**, Dublin, widow
1759 ,, Bryan
1806 ,, dame Castiliana, Dubl. (Large)
1802 ,, Catherine Mary
1658 ,, col. David, Ardfert, co. Kerry [**VI**. 291
1717 ,, David, Ardfert, co. Kerry, esq.
1798 ,, Edwd., Finglas, co. Dubl., esq.
1804 ,, sir Edward Wm., Viewmount, co. Carlow, bart.
1800 ,, Elizabeth, Dublin, spinster
1776 ,, Frances, Dublin, widow
1783 ,, Frances, *alias* **Mager**, *alias* **Cahill**
1807 ,, Fras., Rusheen, co. Kerry, esq.
1760 ,, Hy., Truck-st., Dub., clothier
1801 ,, Henry, Dublin, woollen draper
1774 ,, Jane
1755 ,, John, Lurgan, co. Armagh
1762 ,, John, esq.
1774 ,, John, Dublin
1781 ,, Lancelot, Tubrid, co. Kerry, esq. (Large will)
1801 ,, Lucy, Dublin, spinster
1765 ,, Margaret, widow of Pierse C., Rusheen, co. Kerry, esq.
1782 ,, Mary, Dublin, widow
1762 ,, Maur., Ballykelly, co. Kerry, esq.
1809 ,, Maurice, hon. and rev.
1611 ,, Patrick, Maryborough, esq.
1663 ,, sir Pierce, Dubl., knt. and bart.
1767 ,, Pierce, Rusheen, co. Kerry, esq.
1731 ,, Thomas, Ballyheigh, co. Kerry, esq.
1748 ,, Thomas, Dublin, tailor
1638 ,, sir Walter, Maryborough, knt. and bart.
1759 ,, sir Warren, Crosbie Park, co. Wicklow, bart.
1743 ,, Wm., Tubrid, co. Kerry, esq.
1761 ,, William Francis, Dublin, esq.
1803 ,, William Arthur, Dublin, esq.
1806 **Crosdaile**, Elizabeth, widow
1753 ,, Pilkinton, Rynn, Queen's co., gent.
1749 ,, Ricd., Finmure, co. Galw., esq.
[See CROASDAILE, CROSSDAILE.]
1751 **Croses**, Isaac, Dublin
1801 **Crosley**, Daniel, Pill-lane, Dublin, brazier
1692 ,, John, Dublin, M.D.
1695 ,, sir Thomas, Ballyheigh, co. Kerry, knt.
[See CROSSLY.]

I

1804 **Cross**, Abraham, Shandy Hall, co. Cork, esq.
1810 ,, Anne, Bridge-st., Dubl., wid.
1804 ,, Benj., corpl. in 44th regt. foot
1704 ,, Epenetus, St. Dominick's, near Cork, esq.
1742 ,, James, Ballanamore, gauger
1736 ,, Jane, *alias* **Wainwright**, *alias* **Anderson**, Glasnevin, co. Dublin, widow
1787 ,, Jane, city of Cork
1734 ,, Philip Hawes, Cronody, co. Cork, esq.
1782 ,, Philip, Westfield, esq.
1743 ,, Ricd., Swadlingbar, co. Cavan, esq.
1809 ,, Ricd., city of Dubl., bookseller
1734 ,, Thomas, Dublin, wine cooper
1773 ,, Westenra, Moy, co. Tyr., gent.
1709 ,, William, Dublin, gardener
1767 ,, Wm.,Trevorhill, co.Down,gent.
1809 ,, Wm.T., Belturbet, co.Cav.,esq.
       [See CROSSE.]
1709 **Crossdaile**, Thomas, Crostoakin, co. Galway, esq.
       [See CROSDAILE.]
1776 **Crosse**, Epenetus, Broomhill, co. Cork, esq.
1656 ,, John, gent., capt.   [**V**. 346
1674 ,, Margt., Chester, widow (Copy)
1684 ,, Randolfe, parish St. Mary-le-Strand, Middlesex (Copy)
1644 ,, Silvester, Cork, merchant
1730 ,, Silvester, Dublin, esq.
1767 ,, Silvester, Passage, co. Watfd.
1749 ,, William, dean of Leighlin and rector of St. Mary's, Dublin
       [See CROSS.]
1725 **Crossly**, Aaron, heraldic painter
       [See CROSLEY.]
1728 **Crossthwait**, Wm., Dub., druggist
1751 **Crosthwaite**, Elizabeth, Dublin
1796 ,, Jos., Killart, co. Kild., farmer
1771 ,, Philip, Shanraheen, co. Kildare, farmer
1686 ,, Thomas, Cockermouth, Cumberland, mercer
1748 ,, William, Dublin, gent.
1810 **Crothers**, Hugh, city of Dublin, alderman
1777 ,, James, Ballydown, co. Down
       [See CARUTHERS.]
1746 **Crotty**, Andrew, Mountdeligo, co. Cork, gent.   [terford, esq.
1788 ,, Andrew, Ballygallane, co. Wa-
1741 ,, Anstace, Cappoquin, co.Waterford, widow
1784 ,, John. Ballygallane, co. Waterford. gent.
1801 ,, Michael, Meath-row, carpenter

1794 **Crouch**, Thomas, Grand Canal Harbour, Dublin, farmer
1782 **Crow**, Anne, Dublin, widow
1772 ,, Baldwin, Belmount, King's Co., esq.
1734 ,, Catherine, widow of Charles, lord bishop of Cloyne
1726 ,, Chas. bp. of **Cloyne**, q. v.
1782 ,, Christopher, Killashandra, co. Cavan, gent.
1772 ,, Daniel, Dublin, grocer
1718 ,, John, Dublin, collier
1740 ,, rev. John, Dublin, clk.
1798 ,, John,Chamber-st., Dubl., gent.
1777 ,, Mary, *alias* **Baldwin**, Tullamore, King's County, widow
1783 ,, Michael, Blindwell, co. Galway
1767 ,, Thomas, capt. in col. Mostyn's regt. of dragoons
1809 **Crowe**, Christopher, Hermitage, co. Fermanagh, esq.
1798 ,, rev. Dawson, Kells, co. Meath
1715 ,, Edward, Spruce Hall, co. Galway, esq.
1811 ,, Fras.,Castlebar,co. Mayo, wid.
1803 ,, Fridesweda, Dublin, widow
1808 ,, George, city of Dublin, esq.
1760 ,, Grafton, Dublin, gent.
1774 ,, James, Dublin, gent.
1747 ,, John, Dublin, esq.
1802 ,, rev. Jos., Crowefort, co. Mon.
1736 ,, Lettice, Island Bridge, co. Dublin, widow
1783 ,, Mary, Dublin, widow
1809 ,, Michael,Trin. Coll., Dubl., A.M.
1805 ,, Patk.,city of Dubl.,haberdasher
1753 ,, Rebecca, Dublin, widow
1659 ,, Richard, the elder, Paston, Norfolk, gent. [**VIII**. 30
1724 ,, Robert, Island Bridge, co. Dublin, esq.
1776 ,, Robert, Dublin, upholder
1791 ,, Robert, Dublin, upholder
1790 ,, Susanna,Prussia-st., Dub.,wid.
1801 ,, Thomas, Ennis, co Clare, esq.
1627 ,, William, Dublin, esq.
1754 ,, William, Dublin
1767 ,, rev. William, dean of Ardfert
1787 ,, William, Dublin, esq.
1747 **Crowley**, Charles, Mitchelstown,co. Cork, gent.
1780 ,, Cornelius   [farmer
1800 ,, Daniel, Ballyglass, co. Cork,
1762 ,, Humphrey, Cork, merchant
1796 ,, Humphrey, city of Cork
1657 ,, John, Carrigilyne, co. Cork
1767 ,, Margt., north sub. of Cork, wid.
1796 ,, Patrick, Bandon-road, suburbs of Cork, merchant
       [See CRAWLEY, CROLY.]

1724 **Crowther**, Joshua, Poolbeg-street, Dublin, limeburner
1734 ,, Joshua, Dublin, brewer
1758 ,, Philip, mariner belonging to the "Bristol" man-of-war [See CARUTHERS.]
1751 **Crox**, Isaac, Dublin
1668 **Croxall**, Ricd., Bracka, co. Armagh
1706 **Crozer**, John, Cavan, gent.
1807 **Crozier**, Arthur, Dunbar, co. Ferm.
1765 ,, Collin, Stramore, co. Dublin
1750 ,, John, Magheradunbar, co. Fermanagh [merchant
1752 ,, Joseph, Stramore, co. Down,
1765 ,, Samuel, Park, co. Down, gent
1809 ,, Samuel, Newry, co. Armagh
1798 ,, Sarah, Wexford town, widow
1737 ,, William, Magheradunbar, co. Fermanagh
1538 **Cruce**, Shane or Silvester, co. Dublin
1807 ,, Peter, Springtown, co. Galway
1684 **Cruchly**, Wm., Tullagh, co. Carlow, esq.
1780 **Cruise**, Andrew, Drinan, co. Dubl.
1610 ,, Christopher, Cruicetown, co. Meath, esq.
1709 ,, Christopher, Dublin, M.D.
1807 ,, Eliz., James's-st., Dublin, wid.
1807 ,, Fras., Belgard, co. Dubl., esq.
1806 ,, George, Celbridge, co. Kildare
1792 ,, James, Prospect, co. Galway
1810 ,, James, Deens, co. Meath, gent.
1805 ,, John, James's-street, Dublin
1806 ,, John, Cloncha, co. Roscommon
1807 ,, Joseph, city of Dublin
1791 ,, Laurence, Fennor, co. Meath, farmer
1795 ,, Laur., Dub. city, tallowchandler
1771 ,, Mary, Dublin, spinster
1784 ,, Mary, Watling-st., Dublin, wid.
1778 ,, Michael, Watling-st., Dublin, skinner
1772 ,, Patk., Rahood, co. Meath, gent.
1741 ,, Peter, Rahood, co. Meath, gt.
1810 ,, Robt. R., Drinan, co. Dubl., esq.
1761 ,, Valentine, Killenerk, co. Westmeath, esq.
[See CRUCE, CRUSE, CRUYSE.]
1798 **Crump**, Angelica, Dublin city
1805 ,, Christr., Ury, co. Mayo, M.D.
1775 ,, rev. George, Carlow, clk.
1737 ,, James, Dublin, merchant
1755 ,, Martha, *alias* **Campbell**, wife to rev. Westenra C.
1730 ,, rev. Richard, Carlingford, co. Louth, clerk
1735 ,, Richard, Doonanarow, co. Mayo, farmer
1701 **Crumpe**, sir Richard, Bristol, knt. (Copy)

1737 **Crumy**, Elizabeth, Manicanon, co. Antrim, widow [See CROMIE.]
1583 **Cruse**, Donaght [I. p. 20 [See CRUISE.]
1785 **Crusius**, Anne, Charterhouse-sq., London, widow (Copy)
1617 **Cruyse**, Geo. of the Nall, co. Dubl.
1617 ,, Walter, the Gralloghe, farmer [See CRUISE.]
1700 **Crymble**, Charles, Donaghadee, co. Down, gent.
1800 ,, Charles, the elder, Ballygeloch, co. Antrim, gent. (Large)
1789 ,, Edward, Clementshill, co. Antrim, esq.
1805 **Cuddewe**, Lillius, city of Dublin
1794 **Cuddy**, Alexander, L'derry city
1800 ,, Cornelius, Gortmacloy, Queen's County, M.D.
1789 ,, Elizabeth, Dublin
1808 ,, Eliz., Eccles-st., Dublin, wid. [See CODY.]
1737 **Cudmore**, Abigail, Dublin, widow
1698 ,, Edmund, Caherely, co. Limk., gent.
1789 ,, Henry, Dolphin's-barn, gent.
1792 ,, John, capt. in the East India Co.'s Service
1799 ,, Margaret, Dublin, spinster
1797 ,, Ricd., Dubl., attorney-at-law
1799 **Cuff**, Bridget, Dublin, spinster
1792 ,, Hanah
1762 ,, James, Ballinrobe, co. Mayo, esq.
1788 ,, Sarah, Dublin, widow
1803 ,, Thomas B., Dublin
1809 ,, Thomas
1797 ,, William Lowther, Englishtown, co. Roscommon, esq.
1727 **Cuffe**, Agmondisham, Desart, co. Kilkenny, esq.
1778 ,, Alice, Dublin, spinster
1797 ,, Anne
1777 ,, Catherine, Dublin, widow
1760 ,, rev. Caulfield, Wheathill, co. Fermanagh, clerk
1798 ,, Daniel, Kilmacow, co. Kilkenny, clerk
1763 ,, Denny, Sandhills, co. Carlow, now of Dub., esq. (Large)
1790 ,, Denny Baker, Sweet Lodge, co. Kilkenny, esq.
1694 ,, Francis, Dublin, esq.
1761 ,, Francis, Ballymoe, co. Galway,
1775 ,, rev. Francis, Marlboro'-street, Dublin, clerk
1678 ,, sir James, knt., Dublin
1696 ,, John, Darbystown, co. Kilkenny, esq.

1804 **Cuffe**, John, Raheen, Queen's Co., esq.
1679   ,,   Joseph, Castle Inch, co. Kilkenny, esq.
1761   ,,   Joseph, Grove, co. Tipp., esq.
1777   ,,   Jos., Blackrock, co. Dub., esq.
1799   ,,   Joseph, Athy, co. Kildare, esq.
1804   ,,   Joseph John, Dublin, esq.
1806   ,,   Luke, Dublin, coachmaker
1804   ,,   Mary, Pill-lane, Dublin, wid.
1638   ,,   Maurice, Innish, co. Clare, merchant
1767   ,,   Maurice, St. Albin's, co. Kilkenny, esq.
1744   ,,   Michael, Dublin, esq.
1764   ,,   Michael, Ballymoe, co. Roscommon, lieut. in sir David Cunningham's regt. of foot
1797   ,,   sir Richard Wheeler Denny, Leyrath, co. Kilkenny, knt.
1797   ,,   Sarah, Newtown-avenue, wid.
1770   ,,   Thomas, Dublin, esq.
1747 **Culbrath**, John, Corkiran, co. Mon.
1767 **Culcah**, John, Grangebeg, co. Westmeath, farmer
1706 **Culcheth**, Ralph, Clinakilty, co. Tipperary, esq.
1775 **Culderwood**, Mary, Dublin, spinster
         [See CALDERWOOD.]
1718 **Cullen**, Alexander
1773   ,,   Catherine, *alias* **Wemys**, *alias* **Bermingham**, Danesfort, co. Kildare, widow
1760   ,,   Daniel, Dublin, apothecary
1780   ,,   Daniel, co. Dublin, gardener
1804   ,,   David, Blackwater, co. Wex.
1785   ,,   Edward, esq.
1805   ,,   Francis N., Manor Hamilton, co. Leitrim, esq.
1729   ,,   Geo.,Thurles, co. Tipp., merch.
1804   ,,   Geo., Arran-quay, Dub., atty.
1769   ,,   James, Ballyclough, co. Wick.
1802   ,,   James, Hacketstown, co. Car.
1794   ,,   John, Dublin, gent.   [farmer
1798   ,,   Joseph, Quarryfield, co. Meath,
1796   ,,   Judith
1808   ,,   Laur., quarterm. 8th dragoons
1774   ,,   Margaret, Dublin, widow
1783   ,,   Martin, Drogheda, linen draper
1743   ,,   Mathew, Roskeen, Queen's County, M.D.
1780   ,,   Michl., Mainscourt, co. Dublin
1610   ,,   Patrick, Armagh, one of His Majesty's pensioners
1744   ,,   Patk., Skreen, co. Leitr., gent.
1775   ,,   Patrick, Skreen, co. Leitrim, esq. (Large)
1786   ,,   Patrick, Skreen, co. Leitrim
1801   ,,   Patrick, Ballinaglough, co. Wexford, clerk

1805 **Cullen**, Peter, Ballinasloe, co. Galway, innholder
1687   ,,   Richard, Naas, gent.
1781   ,,   Richd., Quarryfield, co. Meath, gent.
1787   ,,   Richard, Dublin, fanner
1720   ,,   Thomas, Marymount, Queen's co., gent.
1734   ,,   William. Lisbigney, Queen's co., gent.
         [See COLLIN, COLLINS, CULLIN, CULLON, CULLYN.]
1769 **Cullimore**, Daniel, Cork, merchant
1802   ,,   Elizabeth, New Ross, co. Wex.
1803   ,,   Isaac, Neemstown, co. Wexford, farmer (Large)
1764   ,,   Jonthn., Neemstown, co. Wex.
1802   ,,   Ruth, New Ross, co. Wexford
1806 **Cullin**, James, Mount Venus, co. Dublin, esq.
1712   ,,   Ultan, Armagh, co. Meath, gent.   [**XXIII**. 176
         [See CULLEN.]
1808 **Cullinan**, Bartholomew, Aungier-street, Dublin, grocer
1811   ,,   James, Abbey-street, grocer
         [See CALLANAN.]
1805 **Culloden**, Charles
1708 **Cullon**, Edmond, Ballygormel, Queen's County, farmer
1677   ,,   James, Dublin, esq.
1606   ,,   John, Dublin, gent.
         [See CULLEN.]
1784 **Cully**, Agnes, Newry, co. Down, widow
1654 **Cullyn**, Gabriel, co. Wicklow
         [See CULLEN.]
1650 **Culme**, Arthur, esq.
1658   ,,   Benjamin, dean of St. Patrick's, Dublin   [**VI**. 276
1648   ,,   John, Dublin, apothecary
1630   ,,   sir Hugh, knt., Cloghwater, co. Cavan (Imperfect)
1715   ,,   Margaret, Parsonstown, King's County, spinster
1662   ,,   Martha, Dublin, widow
1694   ,,   Mary, Dublin, widow
1637   ,,   Philip, St. Patrick's-close, Dublin, esq. (Codicil to his will left in England)
1646   ,,   Robt., Lond., merchant tailor
1748 **Cumberfort**, Ellen, Clonmel, co. Tipperary, widow
         [See COMERFORD.]
1775 **Cumberland**, Dennison, bp. of **Kilmore**, q. v.
1792 **Cumbra**, Hannah, Dublin, spinster
1751 **Cumin**, Mary, Caronary, co. Cavan, widow
1763 **Cumine**, Ellinor, Dublin, spinster

1756 **Cumine**, James, Ballyorgan, esq.
1753 ,, Thomas, Dublin, gent.
1724 ,, William, Dublin, apothecary
1741 **Cuming**, Hugh, Ballyleakin, King's
County, gent. [gent.
1706 ,, James, Ballywadden, co.Down,
1757 ,, John, Ballylisbreden, co. Down
1781 ,, John, Armagh, gent.
1791 ,, John, Eccles-st., Dublin, esq.
1798 ,, Juana, Dublin, widow
1733 ,, Mary, Dublin, widow
1699 ,, Thos., Lisbredin, co. Down, gt.
1772 ,, Thomas
1776 ,, William, Castlebeg, co. Down,
gent.
[See COMMONS, CUMMINS, &c.]
1714 **Cumins**, Sarah, Dublin, widow
1752 **Cummin**, George, Dublin, merchant
1777 ,, John, lieut. in the Blue Horse
1803 **Cumming**, Andw., Bull-alley, Dubl.
1713 ,, George, Dublin, tailor
1712 ,, John, Dublin, gent.
1785 **Cummins**, Jas., Corkaugh, co. Dub.
1714 **Cumpsty**, Andrew, Dublin, gent.
1724 **Cumyng**, Duncan, A.M., M.D., Dub.
1803 **Cuniff**, Hen., Kiltella, co.Galw., esq.
1757 **Cuniffe**, Bryan, Attymon, co. Galway, gent.
1753 ,, Jas., Attymon, co. Gal., M.D.
[See CUNLIFFE.]
1797 **Cuningham**, Andrew, Dubl., cabinetmaker
1750 ,, Bryan, Port, co. Leitrim, esq.
1762 ,, Chidley, Carrick, co. Leit., esq.
1789 ,, David, Belfast, esq.
1763 ,, Ellinor, Cloonmane, co. Roscommon, widow
1777 ,, Fras., Ellis-quay, Dublin, gent.
1684 ,, Geo., Killenlessery, co. Longford, esq. (Ex.)
1706 ,, Henry, Mount Charles, co.
Donegal, brig.-general
1778 ,, rev. Henry, French Park, co.
Roscommon, D.D.
1781 ,, Henry, lord viscount (Copy)
1667 ,, Jas., Ballyachon, co. Down, esq.
1778 ,, Jas., Belfast, co. Ant., mercht.
1784 ,, James, captain in general
Sinclair's regiment of foot.
1773 ,, John, Dublin, esq. (By decree)
1788 ,, Jos., Belfast, co. Antrim, gent.
1791 ,, Mary, Dublin, spinster
1791 ,, Matilda, Dublin, widow
1767 ,, Michael, Drogheda
1781 ,, Nathaniel, Leixlip, co. Kildare,
linen printer
1685 ,, Nichola, Killinlesserah, co.
Longford, widow (Ex.)
1784 ,, Redmond, Letterkenny, co.
Donegal (Large)

1701 **Cuningham**, Richard, London, late
of Scotland (Ex.)
1799 ,, Ricd., Churchill, co. Down, gt.
1800 ,, Richard, Carrick-on-Shannon,
co. Leitrim, esq.
1727 ,, Robt., capt. in Royal Fusiliers,
commanded by col. O'Hara
1691 ,, Sibella, *alias* **Graham**, widow
of Andw. C., Glasslough
1798 ,, Waddel, Belfast, esq.
1789 ,, Walter, Nth. Carolina, loyalist
1699 ,, Wm., Mohill, co. Leitrim,clerk
1767 ,, William, Tully, co. Antrim
1802 ,, William, Balaspard, co. Meath,
gent.
[See CONINGHAM, CONNYNHAME,
CONYNGHAM, CUNNINGHAM.]
1757 **Cunliffe**, Ellis, Carlow, cornet of horse
[See CUNIFFE.]
1800 **Cunneen**, Margt., city Limerick,wid.
1806 **Cunningham**, Andrew, Gt. Britain-
st., city of Dublin, merchant
1804 ,, Bryan, Port, co. Leitrim (Ex).
1769 ,, Charles, Belfast, merchant
1808 ,, John, Milltown, Kerry, mercht.
1737 ,, Mary, *alias* **Hamilton**, of
Ballygraney, co. Down
1755 ,, Mary, Brackagh, co. Armagh
1809 ,, Mary, city of Dublin, widow
1775 ,, Robert, Camashure, co. Down,
clk.
1807 ,, Thomas, Bell-hill, Wiltshire,
clerk (Copy)
1671 ,, William, Newtown Cunningham, co. Donegal, esq.
[See CONINGHAM.]
1754 **Cuolohan**, Hugh, Croghan, King's
county, gent.
1762 ,, John, Croghan, King's county
1680 **Cuppadge**, Faustin, Colermine, gt.
1709 ,, Thomas, Lambstown, co. Wexford, gent.
1793 **Cuppage**, Adam, Lurgan, co.
Armagh, linen draper
1752 ,, John,Garden-hill, co.Ant., esq.
1799 ,, John, Glenbank, co. Antrim
1809 ,, John, colonel in the service of
the East India Co.
1683 ,, Robert, Lambstown, co. Wexford, gent.
1666 ,, Stephen, Coleraine, alderman
1767 **Cuppaidge**, Anne, Dublin, spinster
[**LXVIII.** 46
1726 ,, Faustin, Dublin, esq.
1756 ,, George, Dublin, esq.
1808 ,, George, Ballybroder, Westmth.
1810 ,, James, Harolds Cross, co. Dub.
1725 ,, rev. John, Magheralin, co.
Down, clerk
1765 ,, Ricd., Moate, co. Westmeath

1798 **Cupples**, Moses, Killyree, co. Ant.
1780 ,, Samuel, Killyree, co. Antrim (proved 1771)
1780 ,, Samuel, Killyree, co. Antrim (proved 1779)
1801 ,, Thos, Newry, co. Down, M.D.
1697 **Curd**, Thomas, Grangebeg, Queen's County, esq.
1808 **Curly**, Patrick, Galway, merchant
1806 ,, Eliz., Bath Lodge, co. Galway
1735 **Curran**, John, Athy, co. Kildare, wig maker,
1770 **Curren**, Edward, Ballynebranagh, co. Carlow, gent.
1805 ,, Jacob, Kilcullen Bridge, co. Kildare
1671 **Currer**, John, Lond., grocer (Copy)
1668 ,, William, par. St. Clem. Danes, Middlesex, M.D. (Copy)
1718 **Currie**, John, senr., Dublin, linen-draper
1772 ,, William, Dublin, goldsmith [See CORRY.]
1759 **Currin**, Bernard, Dublin, gent.
1806 ,, Thomas, Mullingar, co. West-meath
1745 **Currins**, Margaret, par. of Drum-goon, co. Cavan
1780 **Curry**, John, Summerhill, Dubl., M.D.
1754 ,, Patrick, Dublin, merchant
1748 ,, William, Dublin, merchant
1810 ,, Wm., Aughnacloy, co. Tyr. [See CORRY.]
1800 **Curstis**, John, Dublin, saddler
1641 **Curtes**, Edmond, Kilmannock, co. Wexford, yeoman
1679 **Curthoise**, Humphrey, Boskel, co. Limerick
1693 **Curtis**, Christopher, Gormanstown, co. Louth, tanner
1776 ,, Edward, Dublin, apothecary
1756 ,, Frederick, Coleraine, co. Derry, mayor thereof
1751 ,, 'James, Flemington, co. Meath, farmer
1776 ,, Jas., Fishamble-st., Dub., grocer
1744 ,, Jane, Dublin, widow
1707 ,, John, Catherlogh, co. Cather-logh, esq.
1737 ,, John, Dublin, gent.
1703 ,, John, Rl. Hospital, Dubl., surg.
1775 ,, John, Mt. Hanover, co. Meath.
1673 ,, Marcus, Gormanstown, co. Meath, tanner
1758 ,, Mark, Drogheda, chandler
1797 ,, Mark, Hammondstown, co. Meath, tanner
1758 ,, Mary, Dublin, widow
1773 ,, Mary, Dublin, spinster
1780 ,, Mary

1781 **Curtis**, Patrick, Dublin, gent.
1782 ,, Patrick, St. Francis-street, Dublin, gent.
1749 ,, Peter, Flemingtown, co. Meath, tanner
1724 ,, Robt., Rl. Hosp., Dubl., surg.
1726 ,, Robert, Island-bridge, esq.
1784 ,, Robert, Summerhill, co. Dublin, gent.
1786 ,, Robert, Inane, co. Tipp., clk.
1799 ,, rev. Robert, Inane, co. Tip.
1706 ,, Thomas, Flemonstown, co. Meath, gent.
1772 ,, Thos., Cook-street, co. Dublin, tanner
1739 ,, William, Dublin, esq.
1745 ,, William, lieut. on board the "Prince Frederick" privatr.
1808 ,, Wm., James's-st., Dubl., gent. [See CURSTIS, CURTFS.]
1726 **Curwen**, Elizabeth, Chapelizod, co. Dublin, widow [See CORRAN.]
1717 **Cusack**, Adam, Rathgar, co. Dub., esq.
1804 ,, Alexander, Isle of Maghera-more, co. Antrim
1783 ,, Andrew, Rockfield, co. Ros-common, gent.
1770 ,, Anne, *alias* **Donovan**, Dublin, widow
1779 ,, Bridget, Kells, co. Meath, dealer
1793 ,, Cath., Ennis, co. Clare, widow
1772 ,, Edmond, Dublin, merchant
1772 ,, Edmond, Kilfenora, co. Clare
1719 ,, Elinor, Dublin, spinster
1774 ,, Elizabeth, Dublin, spinster
1754 ,, Edward, formerly of Dublin, but at Athboy, co. Meath, gent.
1780 ,, Edward, Dublin, esq.
1796 ,, Frances, in France, wid.
1706 ,, Francis, Killballyporter, co. Meath, gent.
1792 ,, Henry, Marlborough-st., Dub., merchant
1750 ,, James, par. priest of St. Mary's, Drogheda
1583 ,, John, Dublin, merchant
1588 ,, John, Dirlangan, co. Meath
1609 ,, John, Dublin, merchant
1719 ,, John, Kilkishine, co. Clare, esq. (Ex.)
1782 ,, John, Rathgar, co. Dubl., esq.
1777 ,, Jos., Ennis, co. Clare, merch.
1704 ,, Laurence, Dublin, gent.
1710 ,, Margt., *alias* **Proctor**, Dublin, widow
1777 ,, Marrin, *alias* **Brownly**, widow
1789 ,, Mary, Dublin, gentlewoman

1672 **Cusack**, Nicholas, Dublin, clothier
1714 ,, Patrick
1782 ,, Robert, Dublin, gent.
1610 ,, Thomas, Dublin, merchant
1746 ,, Thomas, co. Dublin, tailor
1752 ,, William, Dublin, tanner
1793 ,, Wm., Summerhill, co. Dub., gt.
1801 ,, William, city of Cork, tanner
[See CUSAKE, &c.]
1599 **Cusacke**, George, Dromolan, co. Clare, esq.
1665 ,, James, Dublin, gent.
1677 ,, Jas., Rathalron, co. Meath, esq.
1663 ,, Robt., Gerardstown, co. Meath, esq.
1673 ,, Robt., Rathgar, co. Dub., esq.
1628 **Cusak**, Edward, Lismullin
1681 **Cusake**, Adam, Rathgar, co. Dubl., esq., Jus. Com. Pleas (Ex.)
1672 ,, dame Anne, *alias* **Foorth** [esq.
1591 ,, Edward, Lismullin, co. Meath,
1688 ,, James, R. C. bishop of Meath
1637 ,, Patk., Originstown, co. Meath, gent.
1597 ,, Robert, Dublin, merchant
1722 ,, Robert, Kilballyporter, co. Meath, gent.
[See CUSACK.]
1718 **Cushin**, capt. John, Royal Hospital, Dublin
1782 **Cushing**, Ricd., Thos.-st., Dubl., gt.
1633 **Cussen**, Patrick, Dublin, gent.
1798 **Cust**, Wm., Ochill, co. Londonderry
1795 **Custis**, Edmond, New-row, Dublin, saddler
1800 ,, John, Dublin, saddler
1772 ,, Samuel, Dublin, bridle cutter
1755 **Cuthbart**, Joseph, Ballybraddagh, co. Wexford
1789 **Cuthbert**, Anne, spinster
1675 ,, Benj., Ballycarny, co. Wexford, gent. [**XIV**. 228
1783 ,, Ellinor, Cork city, widow
1779 ,, Epraim, Drogheda, clk.
1713 ,, Isaac, Dublin, serjeant-at-mace
1705 ,, John, Dublin, goldsmith
1763 ,, John, Ballygall, co. Dublin
1806 ,, John, lieut. in His Majesty's 20th regt. of foot
1700 ,, Mabel, Dublin, widow (Copy)
1786 ,, Robert, Drogheda, clk.
1693 ,, Samuel, Dublin, merchant
1785 ,, Sarah, *alias* **Minnitt**, Drogheda, widow
1789 ,, Sarah
1713 ,, Thomas, Dublin, gent.
1756 ,, Thomas, Cork
1675 ,, William, Dublin, gent. (Ex.)
1782 ,, William, Dublin, gent.
[See CUTHBART.]

1763 **Cutler**, George
1732 ,, Nicholas, Lond., merch.(Copy)
1769 **Cuttle**, Thomas, Stradrynane, co. Leitrim
1739 **Cutts**, James, Rathdrum, co. Wicklow, gent.
1709 ,, John, lord baron of Gowran (Copy)
1788 **Cuvillie**, John Baptist, Dublin

—D—

1750 **Dabsac**, Henry, Dublin
[See DABZAC.]
1679 **Dabson**, Jos., the elder, St. James's-street, Dublin, skinner
1799 **Dabzac**, Anne Louisa, Dublin
1790 ,, Henry, Rev., D.D.
1802 ,, Jane
1763 ,, Magdalene, wid. of Henry D., Dublin, esq.
[See DABSAC.]
1791 **Dace**, Mary, Dublin, widow
1789 **Dacon**, Sarah, Wicklow, spinster
1756 **D'Agar**, Constance S., Dubl., widow
1670 **Daglas**, Gawin, Dublin, mariner
[See DOUGLAS.]
1585 **Dagon**, Nicholas, Kells, gent.
1809 **Daily**, Thomas
[See DALY.]
1795 **Daker**, George, the elder, Athy, co. Kildare, esq.
1799 ,, George, Athy, co. Kildare
1723 **Dalbys**, John, Dublin, gent.
1720 **Dale**, Dennis, Mone Tower, county Wexford, gent.
1655 ,, John, Ardnamullen, gent.
1742 ,, John, Killyhevlin, co. Fer., gent.
1614 ,, Mathew, Dublin, gent.
1682 ,, Thomas, Dublin, tailor
1773 **Daley**, Charles, Callow, co. Galway
1744 ,, William, Mountain Pole, co. Meath, farmer
[See DALY.]
1639 **Dallaghan**, Hugh, Lisclooney, King's Co., gent. (Copy)
[See CALLAGHAN.]
1687 **Dallway**, John, Ballyhill, co. Ant., esq.
[See DALWAY.]
1735 **Dally**, Abel, town major of Galway, esq.
1772 ,, De Laval Henrietta, Portarlington, spinster [clothier
1767 ,, John, Brabazon-lane, Dublin,
1783 ,, Thos., Newport, co. Dub., gent.
1740 ,, William, Crookedstaff, Dublin, clothier
[See DALY.]

1782 **Dalrimple**, Thomas, Dublin, gent.
1807 **Dalrymple**, William, lieut.-gen., Chelsea Hospital. (Copy)
1802 **Daltera**, James, Cork, gent.
1658 **Dalton**, Christopher, Milton, co. Westmeath, gent.
1757 ,, Chris., Dubl., notary public
1764 ,, Christopher, Moate, co. Westmeath, merchant
1809 ,, Dominick, Cumberland-street, Dublin, esq.
1693 ,, Edmond, Dublin, wig maker
1730 ,, Edmond, Drogheda, merchant
1738 ,, Edward, Dublin, notary public
1750 ,, Edw., Deer Park, co Clare, esq.
1793 ,, Edward, Wood Park, co. Clare, esq.
1658 ,, Garrett, Derrishnakilly, co. Westmeath, gent. (Declared void)
1771 ,, Grace, Killonkert, co. Waterford, gentlewoman
1718 ,, Hugh, Dublin, merchant
1709 ,, Jas., Monoquill, co. Tip., gent.
1782 ,, Jane, Back-lane, Dublin, wid.
1774 ,, John, Athlone, esq.
1782 ,, John, Gt. Britain-st., Dublin
1794 ,, Joseph, city of Cashel
1727 ,, Isaac, Athy, co. Kildare, gent.
1716 ,, Laurence, Longford, mercht.
1804 ,, Luke, Clonsaugh, co. Dub., esq.
1776 ,, Mary
1780 ,, Mary, Dublin, spinster
1786 ,, Mary, Dublin, widow
1796 ,, Michael, Woodpark, co. Clare, esq.
1689 ,, Oliver, Miltown, co. Westmeath, esq.
1789 ,, Patrick, Dublin, gent.
1770 ,, Peter, Fisher's-lane, Dub., gent.
1785 ,, Peter, Grenanstown, co. Tipperary, esq.
1776 ,, Regina, Dublin, widow
1713 ,, Richard, Dublin, merchant
1718 ,, Richard, Dublin, now of the par. of St. Andrew, Holborn. (Extract)
1786 ,, Richard, Galway town
1603 ,, Roger, sometime Kyrkbynnsperton, Yorkshire, now of Knockmoon, co. Watfd., esq.
1721 ,, Thomas, Dublin, gent.
1722 ,, Thomas, Ballycatran, co. Limerick, gent.
1741 ,, Thomas, Mathersfort, co. Down, linendraper
1759 ,, Thomas, Monequil, co. Tipp.
1773 ,, Thomas, Killonohan, co. Limerick, esq.
1774 ,, Thomas, Dublin, gent.

1782 **Dalton**, Thomas, Ballcahane, co. Limerick, clk.
1742 ,, William, Duneel, co. Westmeath, esq.
1801 ,, William, Kilcock, co. Kildare
1797 **D'Alton**, count Edward, lieut.-gen. in Emperor's service
1800 ,, count James, major-gen. in the Imperial service
1799 ,, count Oliver, Mount D'Alton
1582 **Daltone**, Richard M'Edmond, Molynmigham
1766 **Dalway**, Anne, Bellahill, co. Antrim, spinster
1721 ,, Henry, Stewart-hall, co. Tyrone
1749 ,, Jane, Dublin, widow
1725 ,, John, Dublin, esq.
1795 ,, Marriot, Bellahill, co. Ant., esq.
1699 ,, Robert, Dublin, esq.
1765 ,, Robt., Bellahill, co. Ant., esq.
1781 ,, Robert, late captain 10th regiment of foot
[See DALLWAY.]
1762 **Daly**, Anastatia, Lismore, co. Galway, now of Dubl., spinster
1735 ,, Andrew, Port Royal, Jamaica, esq.
1743 ,, Andr., Laghill, King's co., gt.
1789 ,, Anne, Marlborough-st., Dublin
1718 ,, Anthony, Ballinahowne, co. Westmeath, gent.
1792 ,, Anthony, Hollyhill, co. Kildare
1810 ,, Anth., Lismore. co. Galw., esq.
1751 ,, Bridget, Dublin, spinster
1788 ,, rev. Bryan, Ann-street, Dublin
1747 ,, Catherine, Dublin, spinster
1778 ,, Catherine, Athlone, co. Westmeath, widow
1809 ,, Cath., Rutland-sq., Dub., wid.
1791 ,, Churchill, Dublin, gent.
1713 ,, Daniel, Dublin, gent.
1730 ,, Daniel, Cork, merchant
1783 ,, Daniel, Pottlereagh, co. Meath, miller
1769 ,, Darby, Killinore, co. Galway, now of Loughrea, gent.
1759 ,, Denis, Raford, co. Gal., esq.
1807 ,, Denis, Raford, co. Gal., esq.
1727 ,, Dennis, the elder, Carrownekelly, co. Galway, esq.
1747 ,, Dennis, Moyvaghly, co. Westmeath, gent.
1784 ,, Dennis, Castle Daly, co. Westmeath, esq.
1791 ,, Dennis, Mt. Pleasant, Galway, esq. (Set aside by decree)
1796 ,, Dennis, Mount Pleasant, co. Galway, esq. [**CXXV.** 203
1798 ,, Dennis
1806 ,, Dennis, Tokay lodge

1758	**Daly**, Edm., Freighmore, co. Meath	1759	**Daly**, Morgan, Kilcleagh, co. Meath, esq.
1768	,, Elizabeth, spinster		
1777	,, Eliz., Quansbury, co. Gal., wid.	1759	,, Nichs., Athboy, co. Meath, gt.
1791	,, Elizabeth, Dublin	1762	,, Patrick, Castlekeely, co. Kild.
1785	,, Frances, Brohall, King's co.	1789	,, Patrick, Newbridge, co. Kild.
1807	,, Frances, Dublin city, widow	1800	,, Patk., Cloghan, King's co., gt.
1754	,, George, Thomas-street, Dublin	1742	,, Peter, Dublin, gent.
1760	,, Geo., Killtullagh, co. Gal., gt.	1757	,, Peter, Quansbury, co. Gal., esq.
1808	,, Hannah, Mulhuddard, co. Dublin, widow	1793	,, Peter, Cloncha, co. Gal., esq.
		1803	,, Peter, Lismore, co. Gal., esq.
1749	,, Honora, Dublin, widow	1805	,, Peter, Streamfort, co. Galway
1767	,, Honora, Castlekeely, co. Kild., widow (Proved in 1787)	1794	,, Richard, Dunsandle
		1721	,, Robt., Calvesland, co. Kild., gt.
1787	,, Honora, Castlekeely, co. Kild.	1783	,, Thady, Knockbarron, King's co.
1782	,, Hyacinth, Dalyston, co. Galway, esq.		
		1719	,, Thomas, Kilcleagh, co. Westmeath, esq.
1759	,, Jas., Loughrea, co. Gal., gent.		
1760	,, James, Ballonan, co. Kildare, farmer	1742	,, Thomas, Dublin, tailor
		1761	,, Thomas, Monentown, co. Westmeath, gent.
1769	,, James, Dunsandle, co. Galway, esq. (Large will)	1806	,, Thomas, the elder, Cloonca, co. Galway, esq.
1789	,, James, Bolton-street, Dublin, publican	1810	,, Timothy, Griffinrath, co. Kild.
1798	,, James, Ballyshannon, co. Down, esq.	1782	,, Walter, Tonlemoma, co. Westmeath, farmer
1808	,, Jane	[See DAILY, DALEY, DALLY, DAWLEY, DEALY.]
1796	,, Jeremiah, Cork, woollen draper		
1741	,, John, Drumcondra-lane, Dublin, innkeeper	1756	**Dalyel**, Charles, Ticknevan, co. Kildare, esq.
1773	,, John, Brackland, co. Longford	1716	,, John, Ticknevan, co. Kild., esq.
1777	,, John, Mullingar, co. Westmeath, merchant	1744	**Dalyell**, James, Ticknevan, co. Kildare, esq.
1782	,, John, Dalybrook, co. Kildare	1707	,, Thomas, Ticknevan, co. Kildare, esq.
1799	,, John Michl., Dub., esq., M.D.		
1800	,, John, Clonhasten, co. Wexford, farmer	1749	,, Thomas, Ticknevan, co. Kildare, esq.
1801	,, John	1750	**Dalzell**, George, Dublin, pastry-cook
1810	,, rev. John, Newbridge, co. Kild.	1740	,, James, Dublin, linendraper
1774	,, Jos., Castle Daly, co. Meath, esq.	1783	,, William, Montgomeryfields, co. Down
1779	,, Katherine, *alias* **Blake**, Dublin, widow	1751	**Dambon**, Joseph, capt. in general Reed's regt. of foot. (Copy)
1767	,, Laughlin, Cleagh, co. Gal., esq.	1768	**Damer**, John, Shronehill, co. Tipperary, esq.
1792	,, Lawrence, Ussher's-quay, Dublin, distiller	1720	,, Joseph, Dublin, esq.
1756	,, Mary, Bridge-st., Dubl., wid.	1736	,, Joseph, Roscrea, co. Tipp., esq.
1757	,, Mary, Dublin, spinster	1755	,, Mary, Dublin, widow
1768	,, Mary, Dublin, widow	1776	**Dames**, Anne, Greenhills, King's county (wife to Thos. D.)
1785	,, Mary, Dublin, spinster		
1788	,, Mary, Carlow, gentlewoman	1810	,, Arthur, Belfield, co. Westmeath, esq.
1794	,, Mary, Dublin, spinster		
1798	,, Mary, Ballyshannon, co. Down, widow	1773	,, John, Rathmoyle, King's co.
		1703	,, Jos., Ballybeg, King's co., gt.
1803	,, Mary, *alias* **French**, Sheefin, co. Galway	1753	,, Robert, Belfield, co. Westmeath, esq.
1785	,, Margaret, Brohall, King's co.	1781	,, Thomas, Greenhills, King's co., esq.
1736	,, Michl., Brohall, King's co., gt.		
1809	,, Michael, Tokay Lodge, co. Dublin, esq. (Large)	1584	**Damporte**, Robert, Athboy, co. Meath, gent. **[VI. 243.**
1737	,, Miles, Dublin, linendraper	1657	**Danbruck**, John, trooper

1807 **Danby**, James, Wexford	1758 **Daniel**, Robert, Castle John, co. Tipperary, gent.
1626 ,, Roger, St. Mary's Abbey, Dublin, clk. [**II**. 20	1743 ,, Samuel, par. St. Martin-in-the-fields, Middlesex
1767 **Dance**, James, Dublin	1755 ,, Susana, Dublin, spinster
1723 ,, Sarah, Dublin, widow	1747 ,, Thomas, Dublin, gent.
1714 ,, Thomas, Dublin, gent.	1787 ,, rev. Thomas, Naas, co. Kildare
1747 ,, Thomas, Ballyboghill, co. Dublin, esq.	1809 ,, Townley, Dublin city, esq.
1760 ,, William	1628 ,, Wm., archbp. of **Tuam**, q. v.
1779 ,, William, Wesplestown, co. Dublin, esq.	1771 ,, Wm., Macroom, co. Cork, gent. [See DONNELL.]
1777 **Dancer**, sir Thomas, Modereany, co. Tipperary, bart.	1804 **Daniell**, Margaret, Carrickmacross, co. Monaghan
1707 **Dancey**, Paul, Rathrenoge, co. Meath, gent.	1777 ,, Stennous, Carrickmacross, co. Monaghan, gent.
1790 ,, Pockrick, Navan, Meath, esq.	1706 **Dapot**, Jean, steward of the house of his excellency lord Dowerkerk (Copy)
1767 **Dane**, Daniel, Moyvally, co. Kildare, gent.	
1742 ,, John, Killyhevlin, co. Fermanagh, gent.	1749 **D'Appremont**, Frances, Dublin, esq.
1745 ,, Paul, Lavaughey, co. Ferm.	1799 **Daragh**, Mary, Darraghville, co. Wicklow, widow
1800 ,, Paul, Killyhevlin, co. Ferm.	1769 **Darassus**, Elias, Dublin
1758 **Danevis**, Thomas, mariner on board the "Boyne" privateer	1735 ,, Elizabeth, Dublin
1740 **Daniel**, Bridges, Dublin, merchant	1803 **Darby**, Anthony
1764 ,, Cassandra, Dublin, widow	1792 ,, Damer, Dublin, merchant
1745 ,, Catherine, Coombe, co. Dublin	1802 ,, Frances
1799 ,, Coote, Naas, co. Kildare, M.D.	1786 ,, James, Stephen-st.,Dubl.,gent.
1650 ,, Dent, Dublin, wine cooper	1710 ,, John, Dublin, gent.
1754 ,, Elizabeth, Hammond-lane, Dublin, widow	1685 ,, Jonathan, Leap,King's co.,esq.
1729 ,, George, Donabate, co. Dublin, yeoman	1742 ,, Jonathan, Leap,King's co.,esq.
	1776 ,, Jonathan, Leap,King's co.,esq.
1682 ,, Henry, King's Inns, Dublin, gt.	1802 ,, Jonathan, Leap, King's co.
1738 ,, Henry, Dublin, goldsmith	1756 ,, Laurence, Dublin, grocer
1739 ,, rev. Henry, rector of Cavan-Castle, co. Antrim	1703 ,, Nicholas, Dublin, merchant
1655 ,, James, Kildare	1810 ,, Sophia, William-st., Dub., wid.
1737 ,, Jas., Francis-st., Dub., vintner	1806 ,, Susana, Leap, King's co., wid.
1775 ,, James, Carrickmacross	1810 ,, Thos., Clunanbawn, co.Westm.
1716 ,, John, Culderry, co. Meath	1746 ,, William, Dublin, gent.
1762 ,, John, preby. of Dysart, diocese of Killaloe	1785 ,, rev. William, Ballygall, co. Dublin, D.D.
1769 ,, John, Dublin, gold and silver lace weaver	[See M'DERMOTT.]
	1728 **Darcey**, Nicholas, Drogheda, gent.
1792 ,, John, Springfield, co. Mayo, gent.	1769 **Darcy**, Alexr., Dublin, wine cooper
	1798 ,, Ann, Dublin
1810 ,, John, Albridge lodge, Staffordshire, esq. (Copy)	1775 ,, Anstace, Dublin,widow of John Darcy, Galway, esq.
1804 ,, Margaret, Carrickmacross, co. Monaghan	1810 ,, Bridget, wid. of M. D., Tuam
	1801 ,, De Burgh, Dublin, esq.
1631 ,, Mary, Clonfoished, co. Galway, widow	1666 ,, Domnick, Clonvane, co. Clare, gent.
1759 ,, Mary, Dublin, widow	1728 ,, Dominick, Knockane, co.Clare, gent.
1802 ,, Michael, Belliver, co. Meath	
1739 ,, very rev. Richard,dean of Down	1804 ,, Dominick, Rockvale, co. Clare, esq.
1757 ,, Richard, vicar of Clane, co. Kildare, LL.D.	1773 ,, Chrisr., Stedalt, co. Meath, esq.
	1751 ,, Conyers,Chesterfield, co. Limk.
1796 ,, rev. Richard, Bath, clerk	1810 ,, Conyers, Ahalinny, co. Limk.
1806 ,, Richard, Armagh city, esq.	1803 ,, Elinor Howlin, Ballinahown, co. Wexford, widow
	1773 ,, Elizabeth, Dublin, widow

1786 **Darcy,** Elizabeth, Galway town, wid.
1752 ,, Frances, Rath of Grenoge, co. Meath, widow
1685 ,, Francis, Rathfarnane, co. Westmeath, gent.
1783 ,, Francis, Beamore, co. Meath
1757 ,, George, Dublin, gent.
1755 ,, Helena, Dublin, widow
1743 ,, Hyacinth, Cloonbanane, co. Mayo, gent.
1701 ,, James, the elder, Shanrath, co. Limerick, gent.
1743 ,, James, Knockaderry, co Limk., gent.
1772 ,, James, New Forest, co. Galway
1761 ,, Jane, *alias* **Lynch,** Tuam, co. Galway, widow
1732 ,, John, Milstown, co. Meath
1789 ,, John, Houndswood, co. Mayo, esq.
1798 ,, John
1636 ,, Martin, Galway, esq. (Copy)
1765 ,, Martin, late of Kiltola, co. Galway, now of Paris, esq.
1784 ,, Mary, Galway town, spinster
1809 ,, Mary
1809 ,, Mary, Dublin city, widow
1792 ,, Mathew, Tuam, co. Galway
1743 ,, Maud, daughter of Geo. Darcy, Dunmore, co. Meath
1802 ,, rev. Michael, Carrick-on-Suir, co. Tipperary, clerk
1745 ,, Nicholas, Dublin, gent.
1771 ,, Nicholas, 48th regiment
1778 ,, Nicholas, Dublin, merchant
1787 ,, Nicholas, Clonekenny, co. Wicklow, farmer
1663 ,, Oliver, Verdenstown, co. Westmeath, gent.
1673 ,, Patrick, Dublin, esq.
1756 ,, Patrick, Galway, merchant
1803 ,, Patrick, Bishop-st., Dublin, coach owner
1753 ,, Robert, Dublin, wine cooper
1765 ,, Stephen, Eyre Court, co. Galway
1801 ,, Stephen, Longford, co. Galway, esq.
1748 ,, Thomas, Ballindorrow
1787 ,, Thomas, Dublin
[See DARSYE.]
1802 **D'Arcy,** Anne, Dublin, spinster
1788 ,, George, Camden-st., Dub., gt.
1806 ,, John, Woodville, co. Galway
1793 ,, Maurice Howlin, Coolcull, co. Wexford, esq.
1775 ,, Patrick, Killtola, esq.
1779 ,, Patrick, Stedalt, co. Meath, esq.
1810 ,, Patrick, Corbally, co. Galway
1789 ,, Walter, Loughrea, co. Galway, esq.

1801 **Dardis,** Elinor, Gigginstown, co. Westmeath, spinster
1793 ,, James, Gigginstown, gent.
1802 ,, Margaret, Gigginstown, co. Westmeath, spinster
1735 **Darene,** Frans., Dublin, esq.
1760 **Dargin,** Thomas, Cork, victualler
1775 **Darley,** Edward, Dublin, merchant
1788 ,, Henry, Dublin, attorney
1796 ,, Henry, esq.
1798 ,, Henry, Dublin city, builder
1771 ,, Hugh, Dublin, gent.
1785 ,, John, Mercer-street, Dublin, stonecutter
1755 ,, Moses, Dublin, stonecutter
1743 **Darling,** Eliz., *alias* **M'Manus,** wid.
1788 ,, Job
1710 ,, Richard, Dublin, gent.
1766 ,, Richard, North-strand, Dublin, gent.
[See DARLEY.]
1805 **Darlington,** Francis, Windyharbour, carpenter
1802 ,, Rachael, *alias* **Hutchinson** (late wife to John D.)
1727 ,, Sophia Charlotte, countess of
1796 ,, Thomas, Dublin
1774 **Darlinton,** Henry, Bulford, co. Wicklow, gent.
1747 **Darneley,** Edward, earl of, and baron Clifton (Copy)
1727 ,, John, earl of
1780 ,, John, earl of (Copy)
1798 **Darquier,** James, Booterstown, co. Dublin, esq. (Copy)
1732 ,, John, Dublin, surgeon
1778 ,, William, Dublin, esq.
1797 **Darrack,** Catherine, Tralee, co. Kerry, widow
1785 **Darragh,** John, Dublin, alderman
1808 ,, John, Rathnew, co. Wicklow
1766 ,, Susana, widow
[See DARRACK.]
1744 **Darraugh,** Anthony, Dublin, merchant
1738 **Darripe,** David, Dublin, gent.
1800 **D'Arripe,** Isaac Augustice, Dublin, esq.
1603 **Darsye,** or **Dorsey,** James, mercht., mayor of Galway (Copy)
[See DARCY.]
1679 **Daton,** Walter, Waterford, gent.
1712 ,, William
1773 **Daugherty,** Judith, Londonderry, widow
[See DOUGHERTY.]
1758 **Daulhat,** Peter, Dublin, esq.
1793 ,, Peter, Greenhills, King's co., esq. [Cork, gent.
1761 **Daunt,** Achilles, Gortigrenane, co.

1785 **Daunt**, rev. Achilles, Newborough, co. Cork, clk.
1808 ,, Anne, Dublin city, spinster
1793 ,, Catherine, Dublin, widow
1786 ,, George, Dublin city, esq.
1739 ,, Henry, Fahalea, co. Cork, gent.
1741 ,, Henry, Dublin, gent.
1807 ,, Lettice, widow
1710 ,, Martha, relict of Geo. Daunt, Gortigrenane, co. Cork, esq.
1780 ,, rev. Thos., Fahalee, co. Cork, clk.
1641 **Davells,** Jouan, widow of Edward Fitzgerald, Blackhall
1729 **Davenport,** Edward, Edwardstown, co. Cavan, esq.
1657 ,, Francis
1737 ,, John, Dublin, druggist
1720 ,, Sherrington, Worville, Shropshire, esq.
1809 ,, Simon, Dorset-st., Dubl., esq.
1695 ,, Thos., Ballenecurrig, co. Cork, gent.
1732 ,, Thomas, Ennis, co. Clare, apothecary
1733 ,, Thomas, Dublin, gent. [cary
1749 ,, Thos., Ennis, co. Clare, apothe-
1754 **Davey,** Jane, Dublin, spinster
1728 ,, Joseph, Londonderry, mercht.
1755 ,, Margaret, Dublin, spinster
1727 ,, Samuel, Londonderry, mercht.
1781 ,, Samuel, Sligo, merchant
         [See DAVIS.]
1716 **David,** rev. Michael, Dubl., clk.
1746 **Davidson,** George, captain in genl. St. Clair's regt.
1784 ,, William, lieut. on board the "Vanguard." (Copy)
         [See DAVIS.]
1725 **Davie,** Jos., Orleigh, Devonshire, esq.
1764 **Davies,** Benton, Galway, apothecary
1786 ,, Dorothea, Dublin, widow
1799 ,, Francis, Loughrea, co. Galway, esq.
1723 ,, Henry, Dublin, gent.
1668 ,, John, on board the "Essex," frigate at sea. (Copy)
1706 ,, John, Islandbridge, co. Dublin, brewer
1739 ,, John, Dublin, breeches maker
1712 ,, Laurence, Enniscorthy, co. Wexford, merchant (Copy)
1770 ,, Mary, Cork, widow
1640 ,, Neville, par. St. And. Undershaft, London, mercht.
1656 ,, Rice, trooper
1736 ,, rev. Richard, clk.
1780 ,, Robert, Farthingville, co. Cork, gent.

1722 **Davies,** v. rev. Rowland, dean of Cork
1782 ,, Thomas, Newcastle, co. Galway, esq.
1795 ,, rev. Thomas, Cork city
         [See DAVIS.]
1764 **Davis,** Anna Maria
1797 ,, Anna, Dublin, widow
1797 ,, Chris., Drumocle, co. Donegal
1727 ,, David, Limerick, burgess
1753 ,, Deborah, Dublin, spinster
1726 ,, Dudley, Dublin, esq.
1778 ,, Elizabeth, *alias* **Harding**, Kilkenny city, widow
1781 ,, Elizabeth, *alias* **Welstone,** Dublin, widow
1792 ,, Elizabeth, Limerick, widow
1796 ,, Elizabeth, Limerick city
1802 ,, Elizabeth
1718 ,, George, Limerick, victualler
1763 ,, George, Dublin, butcher
1794 ,, George, Limerick city, esq.
1806 ,, George, Camden-street, co. Dublin, gent.
1800 ,, Grace, Clonmel, co. Tipperary, widow
1767 ,, Hannah, Dublin, widow
1734 ,, Henry, Lipstown, co. Kildare, farmer
1761 ,, Henry, Newport, co. Mayo
1799 ,, Henry, port surveyor of Cork
1741 ,, James, Dublin, ribbon weaver
1801 ,, James Moore, Murphystown, co. Dublin, gent.
1804 ,, James, Drogheda, esq.
1755 ,, Jane, Cullen, co. Tipperary
1763 ,, Jane, Limerick, spinster
1805 ,, Jane, Dublin city, widow
1734 ,, Jeffry, Cleggionagh, co. Roscommon, gent.
1628 ,, John, Clonshanvoyle, co. Roscommon, esq.
1659 ,, John, soldier in capt. Vivyan's company
1662 ,, John, Galway, gent.
1667 ,, John, Dublin, esq.
1750 ,, John, Dublin, merchant
1751 ,, John, Enniscorthy, co. Wexford, gent.
1781 ,, John, Belturbet, co. Cavan
1787 ,, John, Tuam, co. Galway, esq.
1806 ,, John, Dublin city
1810 ,, John, Exchequer-st., Dublin, spirit merchant
1718 ,, Joseph, Carrickfergus
1780 ,, rev. Joseph, Swords, clergyman
1788 ,, Joshua, Dublin, esq.
1766 ,, Isaac, Ballinderry, co. Antrim, farmer
1790 ,, Lucretia, *alias* **Cussack**

1724 **Davis**, Margaret, daughter of captain J. Davis, Lough, King's co.
1727 ,, Margaret, Ballinekilbeg, co. Carlow, widow
1764 ,, Margaret, Dublin, widow
1728 ,, Martha, Dublin, widow
1760 ,, Mary, widow of John Davis, Barrack-street, Dublin
1770 ,, Mary, Kilbeggan, co. Westmeath, widow
1806 ,, Mary, Sharavogue, King's co.
1806 ,, Mary, Mabbot-street, Dublin, widow
1685 ,, Mathew, Lazey-hill, Dublin, vintner
1785 ,, Moore, Booterstown, co. Dubl.
1712 ,, rev. Moses, rector of Raymoghy, co. Down, clk.
1685 ,, Nathaniel, Dublin, merchant
1704 ,, Nathl., Londonderry, mercht.
1738 ,, Paul, Dublin, gent.
1781 ,, Paul
1724 ,, Richard, Cloonbony, co. Longford, gent.
1733 ,, Richard, Littlemoortown, co. Wexford, farmer
1810 ,, Richd., Clora, co Dublin, gent.
1776 ,, Robert, Dame-street, Dublin, tinplate worker
1780 ,, Robert, Limerick city, burgess
1807 ,, Robt., Drumcondra-rd., Dub., gent.
1659 ,, Rowland, Ardnamullen, co. Meath, gent.
1792 ,, Rowland
1635 ,, Samuel, Dublin, gent.
1778 ,, Samuel, Limerick, apothecary
1660 ,, Thomas, soldier
1680 ,, Thomas, Courtstown, co. Cork, gent.
1736 ,, Thomas, Birr, King's co.
1790 ,, Thos., foreman in His Majesty's yard, Antigua
1684 ,, Tristram, Dublin, gent.
1764 ,, Walter, Hacketstown, co. Dub., coast surveyor
1660 ,, William, Ardee, dyer
1722 ,, William, Ballynekilbeg, co. Carlow, gent.
1729 ,, William, Dublin, gent.
1747 ,, William, Loughlin, co. Roscommon, gent.
1749 ,, rev. William
1761 ,, William, Dublin
1767 ,, William, Newry, co. Down, merchant
[See DAVEY, DAVIDSON, DAVIE, DAVIES, DAVISON, DAVY, DAVYE, DAVYS.]

1718 **Davison**, George, Whitechurch, Shropshire, gent.
1727 ,, George, Dublin, pewterer
1789 ,, Jocelyn, Carlow town
1705 ,, John, Dublin, gent.
1808 ,, Richard
  [See DAVIS.]
1783 **Davitt**, James, Dundalk, co. Louth, merchant
1765 **Davoran**, John, Ennis, co. Clare, gent.
1666 **Davoren**, Elizabeth, *alias* **Dutton**, Dublin, widow
1725 ,, Jas., Lisdoonvarna, co. Clare, gent.
1810 ,, rev. Michael, Cloneybeg, co. Clare, clk.
1717 **Davy**, Hugh, Londonderry, mercht.
1759 **Davey**, Margt., Youghal, co Cork
1672 **Davye**, Anne, Dublin (widow of Rous Davy, gent.)
1649 ,, or **Daie**, Nichs., Chard, Somersetshire, mercht. (Copy)
1672 ,, Rous, Kilmainham, co. Dublin, gent.
  [See DAVIS.]
1733 **Davys**, Arthur, Knocksedan, co. Dublin, esq.
1769 ,, Charles, Hampsted, co. Dubl., esq. [co. Louth
1721 ,, Elizabeth, Castlebellingham,
1736 ,, Elizabeth, Dublin (widow of Henry Davys, Carrickfergus)
1708 ,, Hy., Carrickfergus, co. Antrim, esq.
1711 ,, Henry, Dublin, gent.
1712 ,, Hercules, Dubl., esq. (Extract)
1753 ,, James, Cloomoster, co. Roscommon, gent.
1761 ,, James, Glasnevin, co. Dublin, esq.
1803 ,, James, Martinstown, co. Roscommon, esq.
1738 ,, Jane, Dublin, widow
1692 ,, sir John, Dublin, knt.
1710 ,, John, Carrickfergus, gent.
1722 ,, John, London, gent. [gent.
1743 ,, Luke, Dunmore, co. Antrim,
1690 ,, dame Mary, Dublin, widow
1773 ,, Mary, Glasnevin, co. Dublin, widow
1672 ,, sir Paul, Dublin, knt.
1718 ,, Samuel, Carrickfergus, gent.
1691 ,, Thomas, Enniskillen, co. Fermanagh
1662 ,, William, Knockballymore, co. Fermanagh, esq.
1688 ,, sir William, Dublin, knt., Ch. Jus. K. B.
  [See DAVIS.]

1694	**Dawley**, Henry, Ballydaheene, co. Cork, esq.	
	[See DALY.]	
1732	**Dawson**, Abraham, Tamnaghmore, co. Tyrone, gent.	
1784	,,	Ann, widow
1785	,,	Anne, Dublin, widow
1775	,,	Arthur, one of the Barons of Exchequer
1765	,,	Benjamin, Castletown, co. Kildare, farmer
1769	,,	Benjamin, Harold's Cross, co. Dublin, esq.
1807	,,	Dorothea, parish of St. George, co. Dublin
1774	,,	Edward, Dublin, merchant
1775	,,	Elizabeth, Dublin, spinster
1779	,,	Elizabeth, Kilkenny, widow
1804	,,	Elizabeth, Cork city (wife to R. Dawson)
1752	,,	Ellinor, Grenane, co. Tipperary, widow
1746	,,	Ephraim, Dawson's-court, Queen's co., esq.
1771	,,	Geffrey, Clonfenoge, co. Galway
1625	,,	George, Cork, merchant
1770	,,	rev. Hugh, Bamford, co. Kilk.
1737	,,	James, Ballynacourty, co. Tipperary, esq.
1790	,,	James Massy, Dublin, esq.
1776	,,	Jane, Chapelizod, co. Dublin, widow
1667	,,	John, Swaffham, Norfolk, now of Dublin, gent.
1738	,,	John, Ballneefoffy, co. Westmeath, gent.
1746	,,	John, Grenane, co. Tipperary, esq
1751	,,	John, Dublin, hosier
1764	,,	John, Dublin, merchant
1801	,,	John, Dublin, merchant
1725	,,	Joshua, Dublin, esq.
1777	,,	rev. Joshua, Dublin, clk.
1576	,,	Laurence (Imperfect)
1765	,,	Mary, Dublin, spinster
1700	,,	Richd., Woodford, Essex, gent. (Copy)
1767	,,	Richard, Dublin, esq.
1782	,,	Richard, Ardee, co. Louth, esq.
1807	,,	Richard, Dawsongrove, co. Monaghan
1644	,,	Robert, bp. of **Clonfert**, q. v.
1659	,,	Robert, drummer in captain Vivyan's company
1650	,,	Saml., Londonderry, alderman
1777	,,	Samuel, Rockcorry, co. Monaghan, gent.
1779	,,	Sarah Maria, widow
1781	,,	Sarah, Waterford, widow
1773	,,	Susana, Dublin, spinster

1710	**Dawson**, Thomas, Dublin, smith and farrier	
1727	,,	Thomas, Armagh, esq.
1727	,,	Thomas, Dublin, esq.
1729	,,	Thos., Gilford, co. Down, esq.
1732	,,	Thomas, Castle Dawson, Londonderry, esq.
1741	,,	Thomas, Ballybeg, co. Westmeath, gent.
1742	,,	Thomas, Dublin, grocer
1767	,,	rev. Thomas, Caher, co. Tipp., clk. [gent.
1768	,,	Thomas, Capel-street, Dublin,
1770	,,	Thomas, Dublin, esq
1785	,,	Thomas, Knockacroghry, co. Roscommon, gauger
1794	,,	rev. Thomas, Nenagh, co. Tipperary, clk.
1705	,,	Walter, Armagh, esq.
1718	,,	Walter, Armagh, esq.
1757	,,	Walter, Dublin, esq.
1793	,,	Walter, Lissanick, co. Monaghan, esq.
1686	,,	William, Dublin, gent.
1721	,,	William, parish St. Olaves, Southwark, merchant tailor
1746	,,	Wm., Dromore, co. Monaghan, gent.
1764	,,	William, Noghevate
1779	,,	William, Dublin, esq.
1803	,,	rev. William, Clontibret, co. Monaghan
1803	,,	rev. William, rector of Ematris, co. Monaghan
1739	**Day**, Bathsheba, Rathfarnham, co. Dublin	
1747	,,	Edwd., Lokercanan, co. Kerry, merchant
1808	,,	rev. Edward, Tralee, co. Kerry, LL.D.
1798	,,	Ellen, Cork city, widow
1781	,,	James, Youghal, co. Cork
1778	,,	Jane (widow of Keightly Day)
1771	,,	Keightly, Kevin's-port, Dublin, gent.
1753	,,	Mary, Youghal, co. Cork (wife to J. Day, merchant)
1729	,,	Robert, Dublin, merchant
1809	,,	Thomas, Tullamore, King's co., tobacconist
1767	,,	Thomas
1803	**Deacon**, Edward, Dominick-street, Dublin, grocer	
1757	,,	Elizabeth, *alias* **Clarke**, Dubl.
1674	,,	John, Youghal, alderman
1793	**Deaken**, John, Dublin, esq.	
1801	,,	Margaretta, Dublin, spinster
1745	,,	William, Dublin, gent.
1747	**Deal**, Anne, Essex-street, Dublin, hosier	

1738 **De Cresserons**, Charles, gent.
1801 **Dedrickson**, Frederick, Dublin city, merchant
1729 **Dee**, William, Dublin, esq.
1805 **Deerin**, Richard, Carlow, mercht.
1755 **Deering**, Ellinor, Dublin, widow
1754 ,, James, Dublin
1667 ,, Thos., Newtown, co. Kilkenny
1638 **Deery**, Abraham, Dundalk, mercht.
1799 ,, Christopher, Dublin, esq.
1719 ,, Peter, Dublin, gent.
1808 ,, Robert, Grotteville, co. Kildare
1788 **Deeryn**, John, Enniskillen, co. Fermanagh, mercht.
1682 **De Geer**, Laurence, lord of Osterby, commissary of the King of Sweden (Copy)
1766 **De Gennes**, Daniel, Portarlington, Queen's co., esq. (Copy)
1741 **Degge**, William, Dublin, esq.
1754 **De Grangue**, major-gen. Hy., Dub.
1794 **Degually**, Susanna, Dubl., spinster
1757 **Dehayes**, Jas., Youghal, co. Cork, esq.
1785 **Dehays**, Mary, Dublin, widow
1764 **Dejean**, Lewis, lieut.-gen.
1765 ,, Louise, widow of lieut.-gen. Lewis Dejean
1734 **Delabat**, Andrew de Bayley, Dubl., esq.
1804 **Delacour**, Gabriel, Portarlington, Queen's co., spinster
1797 **Dela Court**, Robert, Cork city, esq.
1790 **De Lacherois**, Danl., Donaghadee, co. Down, esq.
1775 ,, Samuel, Hilden, co. Antrim, esq.
1747 **Delafaye**, Martha, Dublin, widow
1638 **Delafield**, James, Derryne Shalye, co. Monaghan, esq.
1731 ,, Luke, Cloonderagh, co. Roscommon, gent.
1654 ,, Symon, Painstown, co. Meath, gent.
1806 **Delahay**, George B., Tallow, co. Waterford
1793 ,, Margt., Delamount, co. Down, widow
1803 ,, William, Tallow, co. Waterford, apothecary
1584 **Delaherd**, Laurence, Moyglare, co. Meath, esq.
1734 **Delahoid**, Rowland, Cork, alderman
1793 ,, Harmer, Cork, esq.
1674 **Delahoide**, Thomas, Drogheda, alderman
1774 **Delahoyd**, John, Drogheda, tanner
1690 ,, Patrick, Dublin, merchant
1701 ,, Thomas, Drogheda, merchant
1790 **Delahoyde**, Anne, Dublin, spinster

1780 **Delahoyde**, James, Dublin city
1761 ,, Jasper, Dublin, surgeon
1780 ,, Margaret, Dublin, widow
1796 ,, Margaret
1791 ,, rev. Patrick
1734 **De Lahue**, Wriothesly, Killee, co. Cork, esq.
1803 **Delahunt**, Dominick, Engine-alley, cotton manufacturer
1763 **Delahunty**, Richard, Dublin, shoemaker
1586 **Delahyd**, Richd., Loughshinny, gt.
1592 **Delahyde**, Michael, Beltrandye, co. Meath, gent.
1752 **Delalande**, Angelique Judith Daunis, Portarlington, wid.
1764 **De Lalande**, Francis Daulnis
1764 **Delalande**, Mary, Dublin, widow
1802 **Delamain**, William, Dublin city
1753 **Delamangottierre**, Peter Abraham Breen, Dublin
1737 **Delamar**, Barbara, late of Dublin, now of Bath, Somersetshire, widow
1734 ,, John, Dublin, esq.
1749 ,, Peter
1753 ,, Peter, Balnefid, co. Meath
1709 ,, Walter, Porterstown, co. Dub., gent.
1745 ,, Walter, Dublin, gent.
1780 **Delamaziere**, Peter, Dublin
1736 ,, Samuel, Dublin, merchant
1795 **Delamer**, George, Racline, co. Longford, gent. [See DELAMAR.]
1754 **Dela Millier**, Alexander, Hague
1738 **De Lamilliere**, Henry, capt. in lord Cavendish's regt. of foot
1740 **Delamilliere**, Susana, Dublin
1651 **Delan**, Catherine, *alias* **Farrell**, Baloge, co. Meath, widow
1679 ,, Thomas, Stamullin, co. Meath, gent.
1720 **Delane**, George, Dublin, glazier
1604 ,, Nichs., Clinteston, co. Meath, miller
1731 ,, rev. Solomon, Tipperary, clk.
1793 **Delany**, Anne, *alias* **Pattinson**, Derrygaron, Queen's co.
1739 ,, Barbara, Ballyfin, Queen's co., widow
1782 ,, Charles, Dublin, woollen draper
1735 ,, Cornelius, Dublin, clothier
1762 ,, Cornelius, Castletown, Queen's co.
1769 ,, Daniel, Kells, co. Kild., farmer
1750 ,, Dennis, Kilenagh, co. Roscommon, esq.
1780 ,, Dennis, Kilcullenbridge, co. Kildare, innkeeper

1799 **Delany**, Edward, Cork city, clk.
1753   ,,   Henry, par. St. Martin-in-the-fields, London, gunsmith (Copy)
1789   ,,   James, Mary's-lane, Dublin, publican
1790   ,,   James, Mullingar, co. Westmeath, merchant
1804   ,,   James, Turriskelly, Queen's co.
1787   ,,   John, Sheestown, co. Kilkenny
1790   ,,   John, Glasslow, King's co. (farmer)
1762   ,,   Keran, Dublin, clothier
1730   ,,   Luke, Cloopooke, Queen's co., gent.
1807   ,,   Malachy, Dublin city, esq.
1785   ,,   Mall, Ballinakill, Queen's co.
1731   ,,   Martin, Ballyfin, Queen's co., gent.
1770   ,,   Martin, Ballybrittas, Queen's co., gent.
1772   ,,   Mary, *alias* **Harris**, wife to Dennis Delany, Kilcullen Bridge, co. Kildare
1757   ,,   Patrick, Dublin, baker
1768   ,,   Patrick, D.D., dean of Down
1768   ,,   Patrick, Glengarriff, co. Cork, gent.
1747   ,,   Thady, Anabeg, Queen's co.
1808   ,,   Thos., Navan, co. Meath, gent.
1735 **Delap**, Agnes, Dublin, widow
1773   ,,   Andrew, Ray, co. Down, gent.
1767   ,,   Anne, Raan, co. Down
1805   ,,   Mary Anne, Ramelton, widow
1701   ,,   Patrick, Dublin, gent.
1789   ,,   Robert, Dublin, esq.
1763   ,,   rev. Samuel, Rawn, co. Down
1781   ,,   Samuel, Rathmelton, co. Down
1701 **Delarue**, Francis, son of col. Fras. Delarue (Copy)
1675 **Delaun**, Michl., Dublin, archdeacon
1660 **Delaune**, Henry, Gortenroe, co. Cork, esq.
1746 **De Laune**, Henry, Dublin, esq., formerly lieut.-col. of marines
1700   ,,   Gideon, Dublin, esq.
1734 **Delaval**, Angelique, formerly of London, now of Portarlington, spinster
1670 **De Lawne**, Richard, Charleville, co. Cork, gent.
1769 **Delclisor**, Gereld, Kildare, mercht.
1767 **Delgarno**, Mary
1727   ,,   rev. William, Stewartstown, co. Tyrone
1747   ,,   William, Raheen, co. Westmeath, gent.
1717 **Delisle**, Lewis Letessor, Sligo, gent.
1746   ,,   Philip, Union Park, Queen's co., gent.

1742 **Dellaney**, Elizabeth, Dublin
1753 **Delleth**, James, Castle-market, butcher
1722 **Delom**, Peter, captain
1724 **De Lon**, Mary, Dublin, widow
1741 **Delor**, Mary, Dublin
1731 **De Loraine**, Henry, earl of, visct. Hermitage, and b. of Goldy Lands, in Scotland
1805 **De Luc**, Mary, wife to John Andrew De Luc
1603 **Delvin**, sir Christopher Nugent, kt., lord baron of
1611 **Delvyn**, Mary Fitzgerald, dow. lady
1711 **Demarcon**, Lewis Duvay, Waddingstown, co. Waterford, merchant
1720 **Demestre**, John
1690 **De Mol**, John Baptister, Dub., esq.
1772 **Dempsey**, Anthony, Dublin, gent.
1732   ,,   Balaam, Dublin, coal mercht.
1760   ,,   Charles, Dublin
1810   ,,   Edmond, Ballyeen, King's co.
1770   ,,   Edmund, Stamullin, co. Meath, farmer
1803   ,,   Edward, Greatconnell, co. Kildare, farmer
1774   ,,   Felix, Kilmurry, co. Kild., gent.
1739   ,,   Francis, Fleucally, Dublin
1744   ,,   Francis, Dublin, surgeon
1701   ,,   Honora, *alias* **Brown**, Dublin, widow
1753   ,,   Henry, Longford, merchant
1784   ,,   Luke, Dublin, gent.
1638   ,,   Owen, Cloneygawny, King's co., esq.
1750   ,,   Patrick, Kilnurry, co. Kildare
1768 **Dempsy**, Anne, Carlow, widow
1764   ,,   Dominick, Mountgibboa, co. Kildare, gent.
1745   ,,   Edmond, Dublin, gent.
1802   ,,   Edward, Clonard, co. Kildare
1769   ,,   James, Grafton-street, Dublin, publican
1783   ,,   Loftus, King-st., Oxmantown, surgeon
1768   ,,   Mary, Dublin, widow
1797   ,,   Patk., Rathangan, co. Kildare, gent.
1798   ,,   Wm., Bristol city, upholsterer
1809 **Den**, Elenor, Church-street, Dubl.
1626   ,,   Fowlke, Fiddown, co. Kilk.
1752   ,,   Jane, Saggart, co. Dub., wid.
1754   ,,   Thomas, Dublin, merchant
1592 **Dengan**, John, Dublin, gent.
1759 **Denham**, John, Francis-st., Dublin, mercer
1668 **Denis**, John, Waterford, merchant
1745   ,,   rev. John, D.D., dio. of Clogher
1772   ,,   Sankey, Dublin, gent.

1749 **Denis,**rev. William, archdeacon of Lismore
1770 ,, William, Waterford, D.D. [See DENNIS.]
1693 **Denison,** John, Enniscorthy, co. Wexford, gent.
1693 ,, John, jun., Enniscorthy, co. Wexford, gent.
1737 ,, John, Dublin, gent.
1755 ,, Joseph, Dublin, clothier [See DENNISON.]
1718 **Deniston,** George, Dublin, mercht.
1739 ,, James, Maghera, co. Derry
1639 ,, Walter, Colgrayne, within the burgh of Dumbarton, Scotland, gent.
1760 ,, William, Grange, co. Tyrone, gent.
1758 **Denistone,** Jane, Usk, co. Kildare, widow [See DENNISTON.]
1789 **Denmead,** Hy., Limerick, carpenter
1783 **Dennis,** Arthur, Springvalley, co. Meath, esq.
1769 ,, Frans.,Springvalley,co.Meath, gent.
1735 ,, Geo., Springvalley, co. Meath, gent.
1757 ,, James, Cork, merchant
1743 ,, John, Cork, joiner
1806 ,, John, Dublin city, merchant
1767 ,, Robert, Drogheda
1701 ,, Samuel, Waterford, merchant [See DENIS, DENYS.]
1753 **Dennison,** Jas., *alias* **M'Donough,** Dublin
1707 ,, Richard, Clonmel, co. Tipp., gent.
1753 ,, William, Dolphin's Barn-lane, Dublin, farmer [See DENISON.]
1754 **Denniston,** Catherine, Drumall, co. Longford, widow
1791 ,, Margaret, Dublin, widow [See DENISTON.]
1779 **Denny,** Agnes, Oakpark, co. Kerry, widow
1806 ,, Anthony, Enniskillen, co. Fermanagh, esq.
1792 ,, right hon. lady Arabella
1673 ,, sir Arthur, Tralee, co. Kerry, knt.
1767 ,, Arthur, Tralee, co. Kerry, esq. (Not proved)
1695 ,, Edwd., Castle Lyons, co. Cork, esq.
1709 ,, Edwd., Tralee, co. Kerry, esq.
1775 ,, Edward, Tralee, co. Kerry
1799 ,, Edward, lieut. in the 6th dragoon guards

1728 **Denny,** John, Clonmel, co. Tipp., gent.
1678 ,, capt. Lucius, Kinsale
1678 ,, Margaret, Dublin, widow
1767 ,, Thomas, Tralee, now of Caen in Normandy, esq. (Copy)
1795 **Denroche,** Charles, Cork, merchant (Large)
1787 ,, Stephen, Cork, merchant
1749 **Dent,** John, Clontarf, co. Dub., now of Northfield, Yorkshire
1797 **Denton,** Alexander, city of Chester, M.D. (Copy)
1720 ,, Dallival, Kilkenny, gent.
1800 ,, Richard, Barrack-street, Dub.
1677 **Denys,** Michl., Dublin, sugar baker [See DENNIS.]
1678 **Deoran,** Edmond
1701 **Deoys,** Anne, Melville, co. Kilk., widow
1753 ,, Joseph, cork merchant
1711 **Deppe,** Proisy, Portarlington, esq.
1717 **Depper,** Robert, Dublin, victualler
1736 **De Prez,** Lewis, Lurgan, co. Arm., esq.
1764 **Dequaly,** Peter, Dublin, esq.
1733 **Derassus,** Elizabeth, Dub., widow
1666 **Derenzi,** Frances,*alias* **Kean,** Teencross, King's co., widow
1664 **De Renzi,** Mathew, esq.
1648 **De Renzie,** Mathew, esq. (Copy)
1784 **Derenzy,** Elinor, Whitehall, co.
1806 ,, Francis, Baltinglass, co. Wicklow [low, esq.
1634 **De Renzy,** sir Mathew or Matheo De Renzi, Dublin, knt.
1714 ,, Mathew, Strahevit, co. Wexfd., esq.
1767 ,, Mathew, Cloghbamon, co. Wexford, esq. [esq.
1795 ,, Mathew, Clobemon, co.Wexfd.,
1781 ,, Thomas, Clobemon, co. Wex., esq.
1783 **Derham,** George, Dublin, hosier
1809 ,, John, Batchelor's-walk, Dubl., merchant
1778 ,, Thomas, Dublin, merchant
1806 ,, Thomas, Dublin city
1771 **De Ribaucourt,** Mary, Dub., widow
1798 **Dering,** Anne, Dublin, widow
1760 ,, Catherine, par. St. James, co. Westminster, spr. (Copy)
1719 ,, Charles, Dublin, esq.
1779 ,, Charles, capt. 28th regt. foot
1695 ,, sir Edward, Surrenden, Kent, bart. (Copy)
1735 ,, Edward, Dublin, esq.
1774 ,, Henry, Dublin, esq.
1730 ,, Jane, *alias* **Jones,** *alias* **Lumm** [See DEERING.]

1739 **Dermody**, John, Little Island [See M'DERMOTT.]
1718 **Dermoody**, Rich., Ballybrushin, co. Kilkenny, gent.
1784 **Dermott**, Anthony, Dublin, mercht.
1741 ,, Catherine, Dublin, widow
1725 ,, Charles, Ballyglass, co. Roscommon, gent.
1727 ,, Christopher, Dublin, mercht.
1746 ,, James, Castletehin, co. Roscommon esq.
1733 ,, Owen, Portnedarragh, co. Roscommon, gent.
1617 ,, Peter, Dublin, alderman
1739 ,, Peter, Knocknish, co. Roscommon, gent.
1779 ,, Rose, Dublin, spr.
1799 **Derrick**, Elizabeth, Laughlin, co. Roscommon, spr.
1665 **Derry**, George Wild, bishop of
1681 ,, Michael Ward, bishop of
1690 ,, Ezekiel Hopkins, bishop of
1713 ,, Dr. Charles Hickman, bishop of (Copy)
1716 ,, Dr. John Hartstonge, bishop of
1718 ,, St. George Ashe (see letter A, 1718)
1734 ,, Dr. Henry Downes, bishop of
1743 ,, Dr. Thos. Rundle, bishop of
1744 ,, Dr. Carew Reynell, bishop of
1768 ,, Dr. William Bernard, bishop of
1803 ,, Frederick Augustus Hervey, bp. of (see Earl of Bristol)
1764 **Derusatt**, Andre
1777 **Desart**, rt. hon. Dorothy, dow. lady baroness
1749 ,, John, lord baron
1767 ,, John, lord baron
1804 ,, rt. hon. Otway, earl of
1768 ,, Sophia, lady baroness
1776 **Deschamps**, Susana, Drogheda, widow
1726 **Deselaux**, Norah
1704 **Desgrais**, Anne Bening, Portarlington, widow
1655 **Desley**, Edward, Dublin, carpenter [**V.** 237
1754 **Desminieres**, rev. Henry, Kilk., clk.
1638 **Desmond**, Ellinor Butler, dowager countess of
1665 **Desmyneers**, John, Enniskillen, co. Fermanagh, merchant
1689 **Des Mynieres**, Lewis, Dub., brewer
1725 **Desmyniers**, Elizabeth, Dub., wid.
1692 ,, Peter, Dublin, merchant
1751 **Desodes**, Anne, Portarlington, Queen's co., widow
1766 **Desouches**, Honora, Dublin, widow
1746 **Desoul**, Margaret, Ennis, co. Clare, widow

1711 **Despard**, Edwd., Cranagh, Queen's co., gent.
1782 ,, Francis Green, Killaghy, co. Tipperary, esq.
1717 ,, Mary, *alias* **Gray**, Cuddogh, Queen's co., widow
1741 ,, Richd., Cranagh, Queen's co., esq.
1713 ,, Wm., Cranagh, Queen's co., esq.
1720 ,, Wm., Killaghy, co. Tip., esq.
1674 **Desse**, Oliver, priest [See DEYSE.]
1699 **Destallieur**, John, esq., lord of Questebrune, and pensioned capt. of horse in lord Galway's regiment
1789 **De Esterre**, Busted, Fort St. George, East Indies
1752 ,, Henry, Rosmanaher, co. Clare, esq.
1765 ,, Henry, Rosmanaher, co. Clare, esq.
1799 ,, Norcott, Limerick city, esq.
1774 **De St. Leon**, Sarah Pollard
1736 **Desr. Mesmin**, Stephen, capt. at the Pension on Irish establisht.
1754 **Destournel**, Thos. Heatly, Dubl.
1771 **Destournell**, Daniel, Redcross, co. Wicklow, gent.
1795 **Desvoeux**, Hannah, Portarlington, Queen's co., widow
1793 ,, Marin Athbeny Vinchon, Portarlington, Queen's co., clk.
1550 **Dethyke**, John, clk., Dublin
1805 **De Veaux**, Susana, widow
1801 **Devenish**, Anne, Dubl. city, widow
1808 ,, Anne, Cork city, spinster
1702 ,, Edward, Dublin, esq.
1762 ,, Honora, Henry-street, Dublin, grocer
1692 ,, Margaret, *alias* **Jones**, *alias* **Manly**, relict of Christopher Jones
1793 ,, Silvester, Earlston, co. Galway, esq.
1792 **Devereux**, Edward, Newcross, co. Wexford, shopkeeper
1804 ,, Mathew, gent.
1762 ,, Nicholas, Bunclody, co. Wexford, esq.
1803 ,, Stephen, Dublin
1697 ,, James, Carrigmenan, co. Wexford, esq.
1794 ,, Jas., Hermitage, co. Wexford, esq.
1796 ,, James, the younger
1772 ,, John, Cork, M.D.
1789 ,, Margaret, Back-lane, Dublin, starch and blue manufact.

1797 **Devereux**, Mary, Carrickemanna, co. Wexford, widow
1763 ,, Michl.,Kilfinnane,co.Limerick, gent., now of Fountenville, Cork
1759 ,, Nicholas, Riverstown, co. Wexford, gent.
1660 ,, Paul, Baylestown, co. Wexford [VIII. 108
1735 ,, Robert, Carrigmenan, co. Wexford, esq.
1805 ,, Robert, Derrinboy, King's co., esq.
1805 ,, Stephen, lieutenant in the 82nd regiment of foot
1779 ,, Thomas,Tallow, co. Waterford, clothier
1768 ,, Walter, Banure, co. Wexford
1798 ,, Walter, Enniscorthy, co. Wexford, esq.
1804 **De Vesci**, right hon. Thomas, lord viscount
1694 **Devin**, James, Moorside, co. Meath, farmer
1797 ,, Mary, Dunleer, co. Louth, wid.
1800 ,, Patrick, Drogheda, merchant
1773 ,, Thomas, Dublin
1763 ,, William, Dublin, butcher
1802 **Devlin**, Thomas, Wilkinstown, co. Meath
1783 **Devonsher**, Abraham, Kilshanick, co. Cork, esq.
1757 ,, Elizabeth, Cork, spinster
1802 ,, John, Killshannick, co. Cork, esq.
1756 ,, Jones, Cork, merchant
1757 ,, Sarah, Cork, widow
1694 ,, Thomas, Cork, mercht. (Ex.)
1781 **Devonshire**, Cath., dow. duchess. (Copy.)
1726 ,, Christopher, Cork, merchant
1766 ,, William, duke of (Copy)
1803 **Devoy**, Daniel, Killmoary, Queen's co.
1800 ,, John, Ballyfoile, Queen's co., farmer
1807 ,, Pattick, Cloony, co. Kildare
1655 **Dewdenny**, Thomas, soldier [V. 217
1730 **D'Exauden**, Joshua Duffay, esq., Com. at Mount Prov Poitou, France
1801 **Dexter**, Christopher, Boytonrath, co. Tipperary, esq.
1654 **Dey**, Angeletta, London, wid. (prob. by Cromwell)
1701 **Deyos**, Anne, co. Kilkenny
1691 ,, George, Melville, co. Kilkenny, esq.
1747 ,, Roger, Melville, co. Kilkenny, esq.

1665 **Deyse**, Thos., Drogheda, alderman [See DESSE.]
1756 **De Zouche**, Isaac, the Coombe, co. Dublin, silkweaver
1763 **Dezouche**, Isaiah, Hanover-lane, Dublin, silkman
1752 **Diamond**, Owen, Ballydermott, co. Londonderry
1789 **Dicas**, Elizabeth, Dublin, spinster
1784 **Dick**, David, Dublin, merchant
1781 ,, rev. John, Dublin, clk.
1768 ,, Quintin, Nenagh, co. Tipperary, gent.
1802 ,, Samuel, Dublin, merchant
1656 **Dickering**, Martin, trooper [V. 337
1786 **Dickey**, Alexr., Boughan, co. Antrim
1769 ,, James, Dunmore, co. Antrim, linen draper
1775 **Dickinson**, rev. Daniel, Dublin, clk.
1777 ,, Daniel, Dublin, merchant
1777 ,, Daniel, Dublin, merchant
1758 ,, Isaac, Dublin, tanner
1792 ,, Jos., Ballyboughlan,King's co.
1797 ,, Joseph, Usher's-quay, Dublin, merchant
1791 ,, Mary, Dublin, widow
1638 ,, Thomas, Bandon Bridge, co. Cork, merchant
1658 ,, Wm., par. St. Michael Royal, London, gent.
1802 ,, William, Dublin, esq.
1750 **Dickison**, Alexr., Dubl., mercht.
1750 ,, Ephraim, Dubl., mercht.
1716 ,, John, Dublin, shopkeeper
1701 ,, Timothy, Kilkelane, co. Lim., gent.
1749 **Dicks**, Elizabeth, Cork, widow
1718 **Dickson**, Abraham, Ballybrickane, co. Cork, gent.
1740 ,, Abraham, Ballybrickane, co. Cork, gent.
1736 ,, Alexander, Dubl., victualler
1739 ,, rev. Archibald, clerk
1773 ,, Archibald
1783 ,, Archibald, Belfast, co. Antrim, gent. [draper
1795 ,, Daniel, Limerick city, woollen-
1800 ,, Frances, Waterford, widow
1746 ,, Henry, Londonderry, alderman
1738 ,, Hugh, Ballybrickane, co. Cork, esq.
1766 ,, James, Derryboyne, co. Down
1780 ,, rev. James, rector of Castle M'Adam, Dublin diocese
1802 ,, James, formerly of Ballyshannon, late of Dublin
1774 ,, John, Newry, co. Down, merchant
1790 ,, rev. John, Knockdromassel, co. Limerick, clerk

1791 **Dickson**, John, Ligadoon, co. of Limerick city, gent.
1802 ,, John, Crumlin, co. Dublin, farmer
1796 ,, Mary, Limerick city
1786 ,, Richard Moore, Rathmines-road, gent.
1706 ,, Robert, Dublin, gent.
1731 ,, Robert, Dublin, gent.
1733 ,, Thomas, Ballyshannon
1772 ,, Thomas, Ballyshannon, co. Donegal, merchant
1740 ,, William, Ballyshannon, co. Donegal, merchant
1746 ,, William, Ballyshannon, co. Donegal, merchant
1760 ,, William
1787 ,, William, Druminers, co. Down, linendraper
1796 ,, William, Ballyshannon, co. Donegal
1808 ,, William, Ballymena, co. Antrim
1810 ,, William, Navan, co. Meath, gent.
[See DIXON, DIXSON.]
1709 **Digby**, Anne, Camgort, King's co., widow
1769 ,, Benjamin, Geashill, King's co., clk.
1661 ,, Catherine, sometime of Coleshill, Warwickshire, now of Dublin, spinster
1758 ,, Edward, lord baron Geashill
1799 ,, Elizabeth
1683 ,, Essex, bishop of **Dromore**, q.v.
1810 ,, George, formerly of Dundaff, late of Mountpleasant
1794 ,, right hon. Henry, lord. (Copy)
1786 ,, John, Landenstown, co. Kildare, esq.
1805 ,, John, formerly of Cork, late of Surrey, England. (Copy)
1805 ,, Margaret, Dublin city
1795 ,, Simon, bishop of **Elphin**, q. v.
1796 ,, Simon, Leudenstown, co. Kildare, esq.
1770 ,, William, Athlone, co. Westmeath
1799 **Diggin,** Benjamin, Tullacanna, co. Wexford esq.
1696 **Diggles**, William, New-street, near Dublin, gent.
1806 **Dignam**, Peter, City-quay, Dublin, coal factor
1807 ,, Richard, Temple-street, Dubl., tanner
1801 **Dignan**, Thomas, Love-lane, Dubl., farmer
1791 ,, Timothy, Lazer's Hill, Dubl., grocer

1803 **Dignum**, Simeon, Queen's-street, Dublin, harnessmaker
1778 ,, Thomas, Carman Hall, Dublin, presser
1656 **Dikes**, Thomas, Ballyshannon, co. Donegal   [**V.** 273
1698 **Dikson**, John, par. St. Martin's-in-the-fields, Middlesex, Surrey (Copy)
1713 **Dilkes**, sir Thomas, Dublin, knt. (Copy)
1790 **Dillon**, Alley, Dublin, widow
1797 ,, Andrew, Kilkea, co. Carlow, gent.
1634 ,, Anne, lady, Dundrum, co. Dubl., widow   [**IV.** 44
1661 ,, Anne, *alias* **Ball**, wid. [**IX.** 10
1690 ,, Anne, *alias* **Bellew**, Crucerath, co. Meath, wid.
1711 ,, Anne, lady viscountess
1735 ,, Anne, Marybone-lane, near Dublin, widow
1767 ,, Anstace, Mount Bellew, co. Galway
1780 ,, Anthony, Athlone, co. Westmeath
1683 ,, Arthur, Dillonstown, co. Louth, esq.
1693 ,, Arthur, Quartertown, co. Cork, gent.
1706 ,, Arthur, Lismullin, co. Meath, esq.
1745 ,, Arthur, Lismullin, co. Meath, esq.
1772 ,, Catherine, late of Ballymahon, co. Longford, now of Dubl.
1804 ,, Catherine, town of Drogheda, also of Carlow, widow
1776 ,, Celia, Dublin, widow
1794 ,, Charlotte, lady viscountess (Copy)
1744 ,, Christy
1684 ,, Cisly, *alias* **Aylmer**, Kilkenny, co. Westmeath, widow
1775 ,, Croker, Baltidaniel, co. Cork, gent.
1804 ,, Daniel, Rathcoole, co. Dublin, innholder
1759 ,, Edgworth, Knockbrack, co. Carlow, gent.
1629 ,, Edmond, Ardnegragh, co. Westmeath, gent.
1744 ,, Edmond, Carlow town, gent.
1801 ,, Edmond, Holywell, co. Mayo, esq.
1773 ,, Edmund, Dublin, gent.
1734 ,, Edward, Dublin, gent.
1745 ,, Edward
1749 ,, Edward, Manchester, clothmaker

1804	**Dillon,**	Edward, Ballyphilip, King's co., farmer
1806	,,	Edward, Moyoore (Moyour, co. Mayo ?)
1787	,,	Eleanor, Dublin
1756	,,	Elizabeth, widow
1770	,,	Eliz., Ballinredery, Queen's co., widow
1794	,,	Ellinor, Dublin, widow
1675	,,	Frances, dow. viscountess of Castellogh and Gallen
1752	,,	Frances, visc. dow. (Copy)
1786	,,	Francis, Abbey-street, Dublin, merchant
1794	,,	Francis, Belleview, co. Dublin, thread and tape manufactr.
1730	,,	Garrett, Dublin, gent.
1671	,,	George, Quartertown, co. Cork, esq.
1746	,,	George
1629	,,	Gerald, Mayo, gent.
1737	,,	Gerald, Ballycloghduff, co. Westmeath, esq.
1782	,,	Gerald, Glasnevin, co. Dublin, gent.
1804	,,	Gerald, Coolvock, co. Westmeath
1802	,,	Hannah, Dublin, widow
1609	,,	Henry, Kentstown, co. Meath, esq.
1697	,,	Henry, Dublin, gent.
1714	,,	Henry, 2nd son of Robert D., Clonbrock, co. Galw., esq.
1716	,,	Henry, lord visct. of Castello and Gallen
1735	,,	Henry, Clonbrock, co. Galway, gent.
1772	,,	Henry, Dublin, esq. [gent.
1780	,,	Henry, Ballymadun, co. Dubl.
1782	,,	Henry, Mt. Bellew, co. Galw.
1783	,,	Henry, Ballymadun, co. Dubl., gent.
1789	,,	Henry, lord visct. (Copy)
1737	,,	Hubert, Castletown Kindalen, co. Westmeath, esq.
1754	,,	Hubert, Jervis-st., Dub., esq.
1609	,,	James, Kilkenny, co. Westm., gent.
1679	,,	James, Huntstown, co. Dublin, gent.
1711	,,	James, Rathingelduss, King's co., gent.
1745	,,	James John, gent., 2nd son of Robert D., Cappakeil, Queen's co.
1747	,,	James, Dublin, merchant
1760	,,	James, Dublin, gent.
1763	,,	James, Dublin, esq.
1779	,,	James, Merrymount, co. Carlow, esq.

1779	**Dillon,**	James, Dublin, gent.
1782	,,	James, Edward, Killeen, co. Roscommon, esq.
1799	,,	James, Lesyan, co. Mayo, esq.
1804	,,	James, Ballymahon, co. Longford, esq.
1800	,,	James, Lung, co. Mayo, esq.
1744	,,	Jane, Inch, co. Meath, wid.
1630	,,	sir John, knt., Carrickmacross, co. Monaghan
1637	,,	John, Castledillon, co. Armagh, esq.
1701	,,	John, Newtown, co. Kildare, gent. [knt.
1708	,,	sir John, Lismullin, co. Meath,
1724	,,	John, Rathcoffey, co. Kildare, gent.
1748	,,	John, Dublin, gent.
1749	,,	John, Blackhall, co. Kildare, esq.
1753	,,	John, Quartertown, co. Cork, esq.
1771	,,	John, Castlebar, co. Mayo, esq.
1782	,,	John, Capel-st., Dub., chandler
1790	,,	John, Lung, co. Mayo, esq.
1790	,,	John, Lr. Merrion-street
1795	,,	John, Ross, Queen's co.
1795	,,	John, Brown-street, Dublin, cotton printer
1797	,,	John, Dublin, merchant
1800	,,	John, Dublin, esq., but in Welbeck-st., London (Copy)
1800	,,	John Field, Dublin, chandler
1804	,,	John, Johnstown, co. Roscommon, esq.
1771	,,	Joseph
1781	,,	Joseph, Navan, co. Meath
1735	,,	Laurence, Arnaglag, co. Rosc., gent.
1592	,,	sir Lucas, Moymet, co. Meath, knt., Ch. B. Exch.
1679	,,	Luke, Dublin, esq.
1717	,,	Luke, Clonbrock, co. Galway, gent.
1740	,,	Luke, Dublin, bookseller
1773	,,	Luke, Clonbrock, co. Galway, esq.
1803	,,	Luke, Kilure, co. Galway, esq.
1713	,,	Margret, *alias* **Blake,** Ardfry, co. Galway, widow
1755	,,	Martha, *alias* **Feltham,** dau. of Chas. F., Lon., brewer
1804	,,	Martin, Nth. King-st., Dublin, gent.
1755	,,	Mary, Dublin, spr.
1756	,,	Mary, Dublin, widow
1714	,,	Mathias, Tyonan, co. Westm., gent.
1784	,,	Matthew, Leighlinbridge, co. Carlow, esq.

1610 **Dillon,** Michael, gent., son to Nathl. D., Dublin, esq.
1747 ,, Michael, Newtown, co. Kildare, gent.
1791 ,, Michl., Ballykeelan, co. Kild.
1793 ,, Michl., Ballykeelan, co. Kild.
1798 ,, Michl., Dub., woollen mercht.
1593 ,, Nathl., Dub., gent. [**I.** 94
1732 ,, Nathl., Portmore, co. Carlow, gent.
1650 ,, Patrick, Dublin
1745 ,, Patk., Knockranny, co. Rosc., esq.
1797 ,, Patrick, Newcastle, co. Limk., esq.
1634 ,, Peter, Dublin, merchant
1801 ,, Peter, par. St. George, London (Copy)
1807 ,, Peter, Castlereagh, co. Rosc.
1676 ,, Richard, Clonbrock, co. Galw., esq.
1756 ,, Richd., Ballymahon, co. Longford, mercht.
1768 ,, Richd., Ballymahon, co. Longford, esq.
1628 ,, Robert, Clonbrock, co. Galw., esq.
1634 ,, Robert, Ladyrath, co. Meath, gent.
1635 ,, Robt., Ardbraccan, co. Meath, gent.
1688 ,, Robt., Clonbrock, co. Galway, esq.
1735 ,, Robert, Dublin, esq.
1741 ,, Robt., Cappakiel, Queen's co., gent.
1803 ,, Robert, Dublin, esq.
1712 ,, Sarah, wife to Robert D., Syonan, co. Westm., gent.
1794 ,, Susanna, Clonbrock, co. Galw., spr.
1772 ,, Teresa, Dublin, widow
1736 ,, Theobald, Dublin, mercht.
1748 ,, Theobald, Dublin, gent.
1770 ,, Theobald, Lacka, co. Kildare
1778 ,, Theobald, Mullen, co. Roscommon
1606 ,, Thomas, Curraghboy, co. Roscommon, esq.
1675 ,, Thomas, viscount of Costello and Gallen (Ex.)
1722 ,, Thomas, Belgard, co. Dublin, esq.
1731 ,, Thomas, Miltown, co. Louth, gent.
,, Thomas, Kilcoleman
1746 ,, Thos., Park, co. Carlow, esq.
1757 ,, Thos., Clonbrock, co. Galway, esq.
1759 ,, esq.
1764 ,, Thomas, Dublin, M.D.

1779 **Dillon,** Thomas, Kilchreest, co. Galway
1781 ,, Thomas, Phœnix-street, Dubl., gent.
1801 ,, Tully, Loughrea, co. Galway, priest
1801 ,, Valentine, Ballymahon, co. Longford, esq.
1647 ,, Wm., Flinston, co. Meath, esq.
1654 ,,. William, Dublin, joiner
1704 ,, William
1752 ,, William, Huntingtore, co. Kilkenny, gent.
1778 ,, William, Athlone, co. Westmeath, gent.
1780 ,, William, Ballinderrin, Queen's co., esq.
1783 ,, William, Ballingarry, co. Galway, gent.
1687 **Dillworth,** John, Ballteagh, co. Armagh, yeoman
1757 **Dim,** Henry, Dublin, tailor
1743 **Dingley,** Rebecca, St. Patrick's Liberty, Dublin, spr.
1783 **Dioderici,** Joseph, Drumcondralane, co. Dublin, gent.
1677 **Dirdo,** Thomas, Gillingham, Dorsetshire, gent. (Copy)
1696 **Disborow,** Charity, Cullinwaine, King's co., widow
1655 **Disbrowe,** John, Ballinasloe
1702 ,, Nathaniel, Ellisley, Cambridgeshire (Copy)
1650 **Disnee,** Thomas, Batchelor's Leas, co. Dublin [**VI.** 303
1790 **Disney,** rev. Brabazon, Dubl., D.D.
1758 ,, Eccles, Churchtown, co. Waterford, esq.
1682 ,, George, Stebannon, co. Louth, gent.
1765 ,, Jane, Drogheda, widow
1749 ,, John, Galway town, esq.
1760 ,, Margaret, Dublin, widow
1777 ,, Moore, Dublin city (Copy)
1777 ,, Moore, Churchtown, co. Waterford, esq.
1765 ,, Rebecca, Clonmell, co. Tipperary, widow
1808 ,, Robert, Kilkenny city
1684 ,, Susana, widow of lieut. George D., Stebannon co. Louth
1754 ,, Thomas, Galway, esq.
1762 ,, Thos., Garryhunden, co. Carlow, farmer
1692 ,, William, Stebannon, co. Louth, esq.
1749 ,, William, Killough, co. Down, gent.
1738 **Ditheridge,** Elizabeth, Ruskey, co. Donegal, spinster

1768 **Divan**, Nicholas, Roestown, co.
  Louth, farmer
  [See DUANE.]
1659 **Dix**, Martin, Dublin, esq. [**VIII**. 38
1753 **Dixey**, John, Coolgreany, co. Wexford, innholder
1766 **Dixie**, Arabella, Drogheda, spinster
1746 ,, Edward, Drogheda, esq.
1786 ,, Mildmay, Drogheda, esq.
1783 **Dixon**, Anne, James's-st., Dublin,
  widow
1787 ,, Elinor, James's-street, Dublin
1685 ,, Elizabeth, Drogheda, widow
1780 ,, James, Dublin, bricklayer
1800 ,, Jane
1802 ,, Jane, Dublin, widow
1726 ,, John, Allanswood, co. Kildare,
  gent.
1784 ,, John, Kilmainham, Dublin,
  tanner
1800 ,, John
1798 ,, Joseph, Dublin, priest
1807 ,, Mary Anne, the South Liberties
  of Cork
1771 ,, rev. Philip, Tullamore, King's
  co., clk.
1684 ,, sir Richard, knt., Calverstown,
  co. Kildare
1686 ,, Richd., Carrick, co. Tipperary,
  gent.
1712 ,, Richard, Dunsink, co. Dublin,
  farmer
1810 ,, Richard, Dublin city, gent.
1695 ,, Robert, Dublin, esq.
1725 ,, Robert, Calverstown, co. Kildare, esq. (Large will)
1731 ,, Robert, Calverstown, co. Kildare, esq., 2nd serjeant-at-
  law
1750 ,, Thomas, Dublin, hosier
1666 ,, sir William, Dublin, knt.
1703 ,, William, Dublin, bricklayer
1766 ,, William, Dublin, public notary
1729 **Dixson**, Angel., widow of Mungo
  D., Dublin, slater
1747 ,, John, Derryvore, co. Armagh,
  linendraper
1710 ,, Laurence, Kiltobber, co. Meath
1745 ,, William, Dublin, gent.
1787 ,, William, Druminess, co. Down,
  linendraper
  [See DICKSON.]
1640 **Dobb**, John, Dublin, gent. (Imperfect)
1637 ,, Marmaduke, Lisnegarvie, co.
  Antrim, gent. [**VI**. 268
1621 **Dobbe**, John, Dublin, gent.
  [See DOBBS.]
1774 **Dobbin**, David, Newcastle, co. Tipperary (see 1775)

1775 **Dobbin**, David, Newcastle, co. Tipperary (see 1774)
1718 ,, James, Inishrush, co. Londonderry, gent.
1757 ,, James, Carrickfergus, M.D.
1740 ,, captain John, Dublin
1751 ,, John, Edenderry, co. Down
1718 ,, Thos., Eskeleane, co. Antrim,
  gent.
1795 ,, Thos., the elder, Armagh city
1770 ,, William, Cork, gent.
  [See DOBBYN.]
1753 **Dobbins**, Joseph, Castleyard, London, gent. (Copy)
1803 **Dobbs**, Edward Brice, Castledobbs,
  co. Antrim
1718 ,, Francis, Carrickmacross, co.
  Monaghan, esq.
1806 ,, Francis, Dublin city
1800 ,, Grace, Waterford-city, widow
1762 ,, Margaret, Dublin, widow
1775 ,, rev. Richard, Lisburn, co. Ant.,
  D.D.
1802 ,, very rev. Richd., dean of Connor
1743 **Dobby**, Dorothy, widow of major
  John D., of Duncan, co. Ant.
1794 **Dobbyn**, Andrew, city of Waterford,
  gent.
1790 ,, Elizabeth, the elder, Waterford,
  spinster
1790 ,, Margaret, the elder, Waterford,
  spinster [ney-at-law
1796 ,, Michael, Waterford city, attor-
1808 ,, Robert, Waterford city
1663 ,, William, Waterford, esq.
1721 ,, William, Waterford, merchant
1743 ,, Wm., Ballymakill, co. Waterford, esq.
1796 ,, Wm. Angeslus, sen., merchant,
  &c., in East Indies (Copy)
  [See DOBBIN.]
1792 **Dobson**, Alice, Dublin, spinster
1799 ,, Dorothea, Dublin, widow
1720 ,, Elisshal, Dundrum, co. Dublin,
  gent.
1732 ,, Elisshal, Dublin, bookseller
1733 ,, Elizabeth, Mullingar, co. Westmeath, widow
1806 ,, Eliza, Capel-street, Dublin,
  widow
1804 ,, Henry, Capel-street, Dublin
1700 ,, Isaac, Dundrum, co. Dub., esq.
1685 ,, Joseph, Dubl., merchant tailor
1788 ,, Robt., Annes Grove, co. Cork,
  esq.
1773 ,, Samuel, Dublin, glass grinder
1688 ,, Thomas, Dublin, attorney of
  Court of Exchequer
1808 ,, Thomas, Dublin city
1737 ,, William, Dublin, merchant

1758 **Docherty**, William, Coleraine, co. Londonderry, gent.
1675 **Docwra**, Anne, dowager baroness
1708 **Dod**, Paul, Galway, gent.
1797 **Dodd**, Elizabeth, Digges-st., Dublin, widow
1788 ,, Frances, spinster
1779 ,, George, Dublin, cooper
1808 ,, George, Stapolin, co. Dublin, farmer
1789 ,, Helen, widow
1790 ,, Henry, Swallowfield, Berks, esq. (Copy)
1780 ,, James, Ardagh, co. Sligo, gt.
1804 ,, James, Kinsaley, co. Dublin, farmer
1766 ,, Kingson, Kingsbrook, co. Sligo
1692 ,, Mary, Ardoyne, co. Wicklow, widow
1793 ,, Mathew, Naas, co. Kildare
1803 ,, Nichs., Brownstown, co. Dubl., farmer
1775 ,, Patrick, Thomas-street, Dubl., grocer
1788 ,, Patrick, Watling-street, Dubl., skinner
1685 ,, Paul, Galway, alderman [**XVI**. 253
1730 ,, Richard, Roberts-Walls, co. Dublin, farmer
1810 ,, Roger, lieut. Leitrim militia
1759 ,, Thomas, Dublin, baker
1775 ,, Toby, Hollymount, co. Roscommon, esq.
1781 ,, Toby, ensign 55th regt. of foot
1797 ,, William, Moyanna, Queen's co.
1741 **Doddridge**, Epaphraditus, Crooked-staff, Dublin, brewer
1749 ,, John
1746 ,, Martha, Dublin, widow
1795 **Dodgson**, Chas., bp. of **Elphin**, q.v.
1661 **Dodson**, Jane, Dundalk, widow of John D., gent.
1730 **Dodsworth**, Edward, Maryborough, Queen's co., esq.
1677 **Dodwell**, Hy., D.D., dean of Killala
1729 **Doffarell**, Eliz., *alias* **Van Nispen**, widow (Copy)
1755 **Dogherty**, Daniel, sergt. of grenadiers in col. Kennedy's regt.
1809 ,, George, Kinlough, gent.
1779 ,, James, Clones, merchant
1678 ,, John, Glenavy, co. Antrim, esq. (Copy)
1747 ,, John, Cockhill, Dublin, tailor
1789 ,, Peter, Ship-st., Dublin, grocer [See DOHERTY.]
1765 **Dogood**, Allgood, Queen-st., Dub.
1781 **D'Oher**, Isaac, the elder, Littleforest, co. Dublin, gent.

1791 **Doherty**, Abagail, Dublin, widow
1756 ,, James, Oldtown, co. Tipp., gt.
1715 ,, rev. John, Cashel, co. Tipperary, clk.
1787 ,, John, Dublin, gent.
1800 ,, John, Middleton, co. Dublin
1789 ,, Margaret, Cork, widow
1765 ,, Nichs., Outrath, co. Tipp., gt. [See DAUGHERTY, DOGHERTY, DOUGHERTY, DOUGHTY.]
1773 **Dolan**, Jas., Killakunna, co. Westmeath, farmer
1809 ,, John, Ballinagard, co. Limk.
1760 ,, Martha, Dublin, widow
1804 ,, Peter, Cornagower, co. Longford
1751 ,, Thomas, Dublin, tailor
1715 ,, William, Dublin, tailor [See DOOLAN, DOWLING.]
1751 **Doley**, Edwd., Ward's-hill, narrow weaver
1790 **D'Olier**, Isaac, Finglas, co. Dubl., gent.
1675 **Dollis**, Alexander, Dublin, mercht.
1729 **Dolon**, Dominick, Dublin, brewer
1711 ,, John de St. Sauveur, Dub., gt.
1786 **Dolphin**, George, Sprucehill, co. Tipperary, gent.
1805 ,, John, Turoe, co. Galway [way
1791 ,, Redmond, Loughrea, co. Galway
1792 ,, Redmond Joseph, Dublin
1692 **Dominick**, Christopher, Dub., M.D.
1743 ,, Christopher, Dublin, gent.
1712 **Domvile**, Bridget, Dublin, spinster
1730 ,, dame Anne, widow
1699 ,, lady Elinor, widow of sir Wm. D., knt.
1721 ,, sir Thos., Templeoge, co. Dub., bart.
1774 **Domville**, rev. Benj., formerly called B. **Barrington**, D.D.
1768 ,, sir Compton, Templeogue, co. Dublin, bart.
1634 ,, John, Dublin, gent.
1689 ,, sir Wm., knt., attorney-genl. to Chas. II. and Jas. II.
1764 ,, William, Jermyn-street, par. St. James, Middlesex, esq.
1788 **Donagh**, Charles, Pierstown, co. Meath, esq.
1774 ,, Francis, Drogheda, alderman
1721 ,, Philip, Newtown Stalaban, co. Louth, gent.
1776 ,, William, Newtown, co. Louth, gent. [See DUNCAN, M'DONAGH.]
1806 **Donagher**, James, Clooshevner, co. Galway, farmer
1808 **Donahoe**, John, Jervis-street, Dubl. [See DONOGHUE, &c.]

1776 **Donaldson**, Anne, widow
1773 ,, Archibald, Belfast, gent.
1773 ,, Elizabeth, Dublin, spinster
1762 ,, Hugh, Belfast, merchant
1775 ,, Hugh, Doumnasole, co. Antrim, gent.
1723 ,, James, Moyglive, co. Antrim, gent.
1780 ,, Jas., Castledillon, co. Antrim, esq.
1721 ,, John, Castledillon, co. Armagh, esq.
1743 ,, John, Lurgan, co. Armagh, innholder
1743 ,, John, Dublin, gent.
1756 ,, John, lieut.-col. 55th regt.
1761 ,, John, Dublin, M.D., now of Kiloroagh, co. Tyrone
1774 ,, Mary, Dublin, spinster
1748 ,, Randal
1756 ,, Richd., Possetstown, co. Meath, gent.
1748 ,, Robt., Possetstown, co. Meath, gent.
1757 ,, Robert, Dublin, gent.
1776 ,, Robert, Drumbane, co. Down, gent.
1796 ,, Sarah, Dublin, widow
1757 ,, Thomas, Faguilar
1778 ,, rev. William. par. Enniskeen, co. Cavan.
[See DONNALDSON.]
1801 **Donally**, Henry, lord baron
1758 ,, Mary, widow of William D., of Longford
1681 **Donbavand**, Nathl., Warrington, Lancashire (Copy)
1636 **Donboyne**, Margaret, dowager lady
[See DUNBOYNE.]
1786 **Dondon**, James, Limerick
1803 ,, James Michael, Limerick city
1654 **Done**, John, Dublin, chapman
[**V**. 30
1799 **Donegal**, Arthur, marquis of
1768 ,, Catherine, dowager countess of (Copy)
1695 ,, Letitia, dowager countess of
[See DONNEGALL.]
1799 **Donegan**, Jas., Charleville, apothecary
1810 ,, John, John-street, Limerick, apothecary
[See DONGAN.]
1735 **Donelan**, Anne, Dublin, widow
1782 ,, Anthony, Nutgrove, co. Galway, esq.
1746 ,, Charles, the elder, Lisenacody, co. Galway, gent.
1656 ,, Francis, Portumna, co. Galway, yeoman   [**V**. 327

1686 **Donelan**, John, Loughshinny, co. Dublin, gent.
1761 ,, John, Balleighter, co. Galway, gent.
1804 ,, Joseph, Killagh, co. Galway, esq.
1729 ,, M. Laghlin, Ballydonelan, co. Galway, esq.
1744 ,, Susana, Dublin, spinster
1805 **Donellan**, Margaret, Killswood, co. Galway
1761 ,, Sarah, *alias* **Ormsby**, Dublin, widow
1801 ,, Thomas, Limerick city, gent.
[See DONNELLAN.]
1764 **Donelly**, Henry, Navan, co. Meath
1727 **Doneraile**, Arthur, lord viscount
1751 ,, Arthur, lord viscount (Large Will, Copy)
1787 ,, St. Leger, lord viscount
1767 **Doneraille**, Hayes, lord viscount
1670 **Dongan**, Anne, Dubl., wid. (Copy)
1639 ,, Edward, Kiltaghan, co. Kildare, esq.
1636 ,, John, Curihills, co. Kildare, gt.
1663 ,, sir John, Castletown, co. Kildare, bart. (Copy)
1574 ,, Richard, Dublin (Imperfect)
1782 ,, Richard, formerly of Nantz in France, but now of Dublin
1663 ,, Thomas, Dublin, esq., Bar. Exch. (Imperfect)
1627 ,, sir Walter, Castletown Kildrought, co. Kildare, bart.
1656 ,, Wm., Killincargie, co. Wicklow   [**VI**. 9
[See DONEGAN, DONNEGAN, DUNGAN.]
1575 **Dongane**, Alsane, Dublin, spinster (Imperfect)
1753 **Donigan**, Walter, College-green, Dublin
[See DONGAN.]
1714 **Donking**, Roscarrik, Dublin, esq.
1677 **Donnagh**, Lawghling, Dublin, tailor
1666 **Donnaldson**, Alexander, Lubitavish, co. Antrim, gent
1675 ,, John, Gobban, Island Magee, co. Antrim, gent.
[See DONALDSON.]
1676 **Donnegall**, Arthur, earl of
1678 ,, Arthur, earl of
1713 ,, Arthur, earl of (Copy)
1757 ,, Arthur, earl of
[See DONEGALL.]
1801 **Donnegan**, Nicholas, Newtown, co. Meath, farmer
[See DONGAN.]
1793 **Donnelan**, Arthur, Werburgh-street, Dublin, linen draper

1801 **Donnelan**, Catherine Nixon, Artane, co. Dublin, widow
1801 ,, David Nixon, Rivensdale, co. Kildare, esq.
1798 ,, John, Milltown, co. Dublin, farmer
1778 ,, Mary, Dublin, spinster
1784 ,, Neminah Nixon, Artane, co. Dublin, esq.
1801 ,, Patrick, Island of Jamaica, planter
1790 ,, Timothy, Cartronsheehy, co. Galway, esq.
1789 ,, rev. Wm., Naas, co. Kildare [See DONNELLAN.]
1747 **Donnell**, Elizabeth, Dublin, widow
1792 ,, John, Athgarvan, co. Kildare, miller [See DANIEL.]
1792 **Donnellan**, Ann
1762 ,, Anne, par. St. George, Hanover-square (Copy)
1779 ,, Anne, Arran-quay, Dublin
1751 ,, Christopher, clerk, D.D.
1738 ,, Edmond, Streamstown, co. Westmeath, esq.
1738 ,, Gilbert, Streamstown, co.Westmeath, esq.
1778 ,, Gilbert, Cloghan, co. Roscommon, esq. (Copy)
1753 ,, Hanah, Dublin, widow
1718 ,, James, Dublin, esq.
1733 ,, James, Lattoon, co. Galway, gent.
1744 ,, John, Ballydonnellan, co. Galway, esq.
1773 ,, John, Ballydonnellan, co. Galway, esq.
1759 ,, Malachy, Ballydonnellan, co. Galway, esq.
1750 ,, Mary, Dublin, widow
1705 ,, Nehemiah, Chief Baron of the Exchequer in Ireland (Ex.)
1771 ,, Nehemiah, Caheroin, co. Galway, esq.
1772 ,, Nehemiah, Artane, co. Dublin, esq.
1777 ,, Thomas, Athenry, co. Galway
1755 ,, William, Carrowcriven, co.Galway, gent.
1767 ,, William, Sackville-lane, Dubl., ale seller [See DONELAN, DONNELAN.]
1723 **Donnelly**, James, Dublin, gent.
1753 ,, John, Dublin, merchant
1774 ,, John, Martinstown, co. Meath, farmer
1809 ,, John, Scallan, co. Tyrone
1809 ,, Myles, Longfordtown, shopkeeper

1724 **Donnelly**, Patrick, Cloghan, co. Longford, gent.
1731 ,, Patrick, Dublin, clothier
1772 ,, Peter, Tramoroe, co. Westmeath, farmer
1781 ,, Robert, Dublin, gent.
1785 **Donnely**, Arthur, Blackwater Town, co. Armagh, esq.
1787 ,, Francis, Athlone, co. Roscommon, gent.
1787 ,, John, Dublin, merchant
1784 **Donnoghue**, John, Cork, merchant [See DONOGHUE.]
1713 **Donnovan**, Anne, relict of Mortagh D., of Ballymore, co. Wexford, esq.
1743 ,, Jeremiah, Dublin, esq.
1709 ,, Jeremy, Dublin, esq.
1690 **Donoges**, Elizabeth, Dublin, widow
1566 **Donogh**, Elizabeth, St. Michan's par., Dublin, widow
1777 ,, John, Newhouse, co. Louth, gt.
1704 ,, William, Dublin, victualler
1794 **Donoghan**, Owen, Sligo, ironmonger
1714 **Donogher**, Redmond, Ballintimpan, co. Longford, esq.
1769 **Donoghoe**, Patrick, Fethard, co. Wexford, gent.
1770 ,, Patrick, the elder, Fethard, co. Wexford
1775 **Donoghu**, Stephen Ballinasloe, co. Galway, gent. (Error, Ex.)
1775 ,, Stephen, Ballinasloe, co. Galway, gent.
1774 **Donoghue**, Catherine, Rathrush, co. Carlow, widow
1757 ,, Edward, Rathrush, co. Carlow
1807 ,, William, Dublin city [See DONNOGHUE, DONOGHU, &c.]
1800 **Donoho**, James, the elder of Clonshany, King's co., farmer
1787 **Donohue**, John, Waterford city
1712 **Donovan**, Cornelius, Kilmacabe, co. Cork, gent.
1746 ,, Daniel, Dublin
1758 ,, Daniel, Dublin, merchant
1773 ,, Edward, Dublin, esq.
1808 ,, Frances, Dublin city, widow
1788 ,, Harriet, Dublin, spinster
1795 ,, Harriet, Enniscorthy, co. Wexford, spinster
1780 ,, James, the elder, of George's-quay, Dublin, merchant
1772 ,, Jeremiah, lieut. in the navy
1785 ,, Jeremiah, Castle Jane, co.Cork, esq.
1743 ,, John, Mount Tallon, co. Dubl., esq.
1802 ,, Margan, Cork, esq.
1782 ,, Mary, Dublin, widow

1794 **Donovan**, Mary, Dublin, widow
1805 ,,   Mary, St. John, co. Wexford, spinster
1733 ,,   Mathew, formerly near Ratoath, co. Meath, now of Dublin, gardener
1760 ,,   Morgan, Pouthole, co. Cork, esq.
1768 ,,   Richard, Enniscorthy, co Wexford, esq.
1781 ,,   Richard, Clonmore, co. Wexford, esq.
1597 **Donsany**, Jennett Sarsfield, dowager lady of
1745 **Donworth**, Robert, mariner
1747 ,,   Robert, Cork, gent.
1778 **Doogan**, Anne, Stonybatter, co. Dublin, widow
1711 ,,   James, Mitchelstown, co. Cork
1790 ,,   John, Indall, co. Down
1658 **Dooke**, William, Ballymacarrat, co. Down, yeoman   [**VII.** 158
1776 **Doolan**, Thomas, Portumna, co. Galway
        [See DOLAN.]
1739 **Dooling**, James, Johnstown, co. Carlow, yeoman
1756 **Doolittle**, Edward, the Coombe, mercht.
1781 ,,   Elizabeth, the Coombe, co. Dublin
1633 **Doollard**, Gerald, Kilcock, co. Kildare, gent.
1797 **Dooly**, George, town of Banagher
1786 ,,   Paul, Braganstown, co. Louth, gent.
1697 **Dopping**, Anthony, bp. of **Meath** q. v.
1742 ,,   Anthony, bp. of **Ossory**, q. v.
1794 ,,   Anthony, Lowtown, co. Westmeath, esq.
1762 ,,   Dorothea, Dublin, widow
1758 ,,   Margaret
1720 ,,   Samuel, Dublin, esq.
1794 **Doran**, Andrew, Arklow, co. Wicklow, merchant
1793 ,,   Bridget, Dublin, spinster
1808 ,,   Charles, Castlemitchell, co. Kildare, farmer
1788 ,,   Dennis, Dublin, esq.
1810 ,,   Edmond, Dublin city, esq.
1776 ,,   Edward, Watling-street, Dubl., dyer
1796 ,,   James, Dublin, shopkeeper
1803 ,,   John, Dublin, attorney
1810 ,,   John, Castlemitchell, co. Kild.
1808 ,,   Margaret, spinster
1649 ,,   Margery, Dublin, widow (Imperfect)
1756 ,,   Mary, Dublin, widow

1757 **Doran**, Mary, *alias* **Martin**, Dublin, widow
1802 ,,   Mary, Castlemitchell, co. Kild.
1802 ,,   Mary Anne, Crescent, co. Dub.
1792 ,,   Patrick, Dublin, merchant
1807 ,,   rev. Patk., Kevin-st., Dublin, clk.
1808 ,,   Patrick, son of Patrick Doran, Castlemitchell
1766 ,,   Richd., Ballymahon, co. Longford, merchant
1716 ,,   Rose
1807 ,,   Thomas, James's-street, Dublin, tanner
1799 **Dorchester**, Joseph, earl of (Copy)
1722 **Dore**, Alice, Killnockane, co. Waterford, spinster
1764 ,,   Mary, widow of Ralph D., Nuck Crack, co. Cork
1789 ,,   Ralph, Cork city, gent.
1740 ,,   Thomas, Lisnebrin, co. Cork, gent.
1726 ,,   William, Bantyre, co. Cork, gent.
1808 ,,   William, Belview, co. Cork, gent.
1758 **Dorham**, Walter, Dublin, baker
1594 **Dormer**, George, New Ross, gent.
1639 ,,   John, New Ross, co. Wexford, burgess
1638 ,,   Martin, New Ross, co. Wexford, merchant
1666 ,,   Michael, New Ross, co. Wexford, esq.
1808 **Dorman**, Francis, Mallow, co. Cork, gent.
1753 **Dornan**, Ellinor, Dublin, spinster
1694 ,,   Henry, Dublin, surgeon
1734 ,,   Mary, Dublin, widow
1722 ,,   Patk., Merchant's-quay, Dubl.
1699 **Dornant**, James, esq., Sieur des Vallecs, native of Alençon, in Normandy, now in Dublin
1725 **Dortous**, John, Dublin, esq.
1747 **Dory**, William, Balgath, co. Meath, farmer
1730 **Dosseville**, Magdalene, Dublin, spr.
1785 **Dougan**, William, Tindall, co. Down
1730 **Dougatt**, rev. Robert, precentor of St. Patrick's, Dublin
1731 **Dougharty**, William, Coleraine, merchant
1763 **Dougherty**, Andrew, New-row, Dublin, merchant
1784 ,,   Owen, Bailiborough, King's co., esq.
        [See DOHERTY.]
1746 **Doughty**, Charles, Virginia, co. Cavan

1667 **Doughty,** John, Mary's-abbey, Oxmantown, Dublin, inn-keeper
1703 ,, John, Dublin, merchant [See DOHERTY.]
1775 **Douglas,** Adam, Killenaule, co. Tipperary, gent.
1798 ,, Adam, Dublin, apothecary
1802 ,, John, Hillsborough, co. Down, shopkeeper
1741 **Douglass,** col. Charles, Brentford Butts, Middlesex (Copy)
1743 ,, James, Croyden, Surrey, esq. (Copy)
1773 ,, James, Maghralin, co. Down, merchant
1735 ,, dame Jane, widow of sir Robert D., bart.
1771 ,, John, Tullivallen, co. Armagh
1762 ,, Richardson
1733 ,, Robert, Corcasoge, co. Down, gent.
[See DAGLAS, DOWGLASS.]
1681 **Douname,** James, dean of Armagh
1683 **Douner,** Gerald, Dublin, M.D.
1679 **Dounton,** Thomas, Dublin, gent.
1795 **Douthat,** Robert, Newcastle, co. Limerick
1804 **Dover,** Dorothea S., Prussia-street, Dublin, spinster
1681 ,, Richard, clk., chanter of Christ Church, Dublin
1743 **Dowan,** Jas., Dublin, weighmaster
1808 **Dowd,** Ann, Marlinstown, co. Westmeath, widow
1803 ,, James, Drogheda
1776 ,, Michael, Ballycartlan, co. Monaghan, farmer
[See DOWDE, DOWDEN.]
1653 **Dowda,** John, Dub., alderman (Ex.)
1735 **Dowdall,** lady Ales, wife to Henry D., Athcarne, co. Meath, esq.
1735 ,, Allye, Dublin, spinster
1772 ,, Ann, Dublin, widow
1676 ,, Anne, Dublin, widow
1741 ,, Anne, Dublin, widow
1798 ,, Catherine
1721 ,, Charles, Drogheda, merchant
1640 ,, Christopher, Castledowdall, co. Louth, esq.
1625 ,, Edward, Drogheda, merchant
1626 ,, Edward, Athlumney, co. Meath, esq. [II. 53
1666 ,, Edward, Monktown, co. Meath, esq.
1739 ,, Edward, Mountown, co. Meath, esq.
1787 ,, Edward, Mullingar, co. Westmeath, gent.

1810 **Dowdall,** Edward, Dublin city
1744 ,, Elinor, widow of Mr. George Dowdall
1719 ,, Elizabeth, *alias* **Verdon,** relict of Chris. D., merchant
1755 ,, Elizabeth, Dublin, spinster
1743 ,, Fras., Drumcondra-lane, Dub., musician
1662 ,, George, Dublin, merchant (Imperfect)
1741 ,, George, Dublin, peruke maker
1797 ,, George, Ballymahon, co. Longford, gent.
1621 ,, Godfrey, Limerick, gent.
1630 ,, Godfrey, Clansharbag, co. Limerick, gent.
1574 ,, Gonett, *alias* **Talbot,** widow
1634 ,, Henry, late of Ballintober, now of Kells, co. Meath, mercht.
1664 ,, Henry, Proudstown, co. Meath, esq.
1752 ,, Henry, formerly of Athcarne, co. Meath, now of Chester, esq. (Copy)
1774 ,, Henry, Mullingar, co. Westmeath, gent.
1584 ,, sir James, Chief Justice Queen's Bench
1604 ,, James, Athboy
1746 ,, James, chairman
1613 ,, sir John, Pilltown or Ballynefoyle, co. Waterford
1624 ,, sir John, Kilfenny, co. Limerick, knt. (Copy)
1808 ,, John, Drogheda, yeoman
1593 ,, Laurence, Drogheda, merchant
1689 ,, sir Luke, Dublin, bart.
1706 ,, Margaret, Dublin, spinster
1724 ,, Mary, Gaulstown, co. Meath, spinster
1762 ,, Mary, *alias* **Byrne,** wife to Laurence D., Dubl., mercht.
1784 ,, Mary, Drogheda, widow
1807 ,, Mary, Summer-hill, co. Dubl., widow
1801 ,, Mathew, Drumcondra-lane, co. Dublin, esq.
1807 ,, Miles, Clone, co. Meath, esq.
1582 ,, Patrick, Drogheda, merchant
1629 ,, Patrick, Tymoule, co. Meath, gent. (Copy)
1721 ,, Patrick, Clonmorul, co. Meath, gent.
1740 ,, Patrick, Mullingar, co. Westmeath, merchant
1754 ,, Patrick, Dublin, peruke maker
1701 ,, rev. Richard, iron works, co. Antrim, clk.
1702 ,, rev. Richard, vicar of Drumaul
1724 ,, Richard, Dublin, gent.

1772 **Dowdall,** Richard, Dublin, gent.
1804 ,, Richd., Portarlington, Queen's co., esq.
1731 ,, Robert, Dublin, gent.
1800 ,, Robert, city of Cuta (Ceuta ?)
1648 ,, Stephen, Drogheda, alderman
1722 ,, Stephen, Gaulstown, co. Meath, gent.
1810 ,, Stephen, Elbow-lane, Dublin
1747 ,, William, esq.
      [See DOWDELL.]
1663 **Dowde,** Mary, widow of col. Edwd. Dowde, Dublin (see F.)
1629 ,, Richard, Dublin, merchant
      [See DOWD.]
1654 **Dowdell,** Elizabeth, widow
1707 ,, Henry, Athlone, co. Roscommon, esq.
1788 ,, Henry, Golden-square, Middlesex, esq. (Large copy)
      [See DOWDALL.]
1789 **Dowden,** Moore, Dublin, esq.
1794 ,, Richard, Bandon, co. Cork, linendraper
      [See DOWD.]
1682 **Dowding,** Thomas, Dublin, gent.
1804 **Dowe,** Joshua, Rusnascalp, co. Cork, gent.
1774 **Dowell,** Bryan, Killashandra, co. Cavan
1791 ,, Edmond, Gort, co. Roscommon, esq.
1795 ,, Elizabeth, Phillipstown, King's co., widow
1802 ,, Elizabeth, Inane, co. Tipperary, widow
1742 ,, John, Mantua, co. Roscommon, esq.
1755 ,, Luke, Mantua, co. Roscommon, esq.
1785 ,, Margaret, Athlone
1803 **Dowglas,** Robert, Dublin, grocer
1765 **Dowglass,** Charles, Gracehall, co. Down, esq.
1728 ,, John, capt.-lieut. in colonel Howard's regiment of foot
1696 ,, Robert, Dublin, merchant
1727 ,, Robert, Dublin, a minor
1739 ,, Thos., quarter master in brig. Nevill's regiment
1724 ,, William, Dromore, co. Down, gent.
      [See DOUGLASS.]
1682 **Dowlen,** James, Youghal, merchant
1561 **Dowlene,** Nicholas
1762 **Dowley,** Abigail, *alias* **Walfenden,** Dublin, widow
1754 ,, Marcus, Dublin, esq.
1807 ,, Patrick, Athy, co. Kildare
1782 ,, William, Dublin, merchant

1794 **Dowlin,** Elizabeth
1792 ,, Joseph, Limerick, M.D.
1743 **Dowling,** Anne, Dublin, widow
1748 ,, Dan., Newtown Skeirk, Queen's co., gent.
1774 ,, Daniel, Coleamoney, Queen's co., farmer
1786 ,, Edmond, Kilkenny city
1793 ,, Edmond, Ballagh, co. Roscom.
1700 ,, Edward, Clondalara, King's co., gent.
1809 ,, Edward, Naas, farmer
1757 ,, James, Kilkenny, victualler
1764 ,, James, Knockbarden, co. Kildare, farmer
1786 ,, James, Greek-street
1803 ,, James, Naas, co. Kildare, brewer and grocer
1797 ,, Jane, Clontarf, co. Dublin, spr.
1676 ,, John, Inchiquin, co. Kildare, gent.
1764 ,, John, Leighlinbridge, co. Carlow, merchant
1788 ,, John, Pill-lane, Dublin
1774 ,, Loughlin, Pallaghambane, co. Westmeath, farmer
1758 ,, Luke, Dublin, stationer
1758 ,, Margt., Dublin, now in Great Britain, spinster
1761 ,, Mark, Dublin, slater
1767 ,, Mary, Leighlinbridge, co. Carlow, widow
1783 ,, Mathew, Greenoge, co. Meath, gent.
1714 ,, Murtagh, Dublin, esq.
1801 ,, Patrick, Castlerod, co. Kildare
1807 ,, Peter, Nassau-street, Dublin
1747 ,, Thady
1720 ,, Thomas, Rathfeigh, co. Meath, gent.
1759 ,, Thomas, Dublin, distiller
      [See DOLAN.]
1730 **Dowlon,** Susana, Dublin, widow
1800 **Dowly,** Sylvester, Callan, co. Kilkenny, esq.
1629 **Dowlye,** Marcus, Tirvickaren, co. Clare, gent.
1695 **Down and Connor,** Samuel Foley, bishop of
1697 ,, Thos. Hackett, bishop of (Ex.)
1698 ,, Edwd. Walkington, bishop of
1720 ,, Dr. Edwd. Smith, lord bishop of
1740 ,, Dr. Fras. Hutchinson, bishop of
1783 ,, Dr. James Trail, bishop of
1667 **Down, Connor and Dromore,** Jeremy Taylor, bishop of
1786 **Downer,** Maurice, Birr, King's co., land surveyor
1749 **Downes,** Agnes, Dublin, widow
1781 ,, Anne, *alias* **Sigoe,** widow

1794 **Downes**, Anne, *alias* **Deyos**, *alias* **Bolton**, Waterford, widow
1756 ,, Catherine, Dublin, widow
1709 ,, Dive, bishop of **Cork**, q. v.
1781 ,, rev. Dives, rector of Killasher, diocese of Kilmore
1798 ,, rev. Dives, LL.D.
1807 ,, rev. Dives, D.D.
1774 ,, Dorothy, Dublin, widow
1784 ,, Edward, esq.
1707 ,, Elizabeth, wife to Dive, lord bishop of Cork and Ross
1802 ,, Gregory, Wexford, doctor of physic
1777 ,, Henrietta, Donnybrook, co. Dublin
1734 ,, Henry, bishop of **Derry**, q. v.
1808 ,, Michl., Adamstown, co. Wexford, farmer [of foot
1775 ,, Patrick, captain in the 5th regt.
1754 ,, Robert, Dublin, esq.
1763 ,, Robert, bishop of **Raphoe**, q. v.
1771 ,, Robert, late of Dublin, now of Miltown-road, Dublin, gent. (Large)
1794 ,, William, D.D., chancellor of Catherine's Church
1805 **Downey**, Agness, Galway town, wid.
1803 ,, Andrew, New-row-on-the-Poddle, skinner
1808 ,, Patk., Marlborough-st., Dubl.
1799 ,, William, Galway town, mercht. [See DOWNING.]
1721 **Downing**, Adam, Rocktown or Ballynacrag, co. Derry, esq.
1803 ,, Ann, Montgomery-st., widow
1701 ,, Cornelius, Dublin, gent.
1809 ,, Dawson, Rowesgift, co. Londonderry, esq.
1740 ,, Deborah, Kilgroggy, co. Tipperary, widow
1766 ,, Henry, Dublin, esq.
1743 ,, John, the elder, Broagh, co. Londonderry, gent.
1708 ,, Richard, Lismore, co. Waterford, gent.
1723 ,, Richard, vicar of Tubbrid, clk.
1703 ,, Thomas, Dublin, tailor
1797 ,, Thomas, Dublin, grocer [See DOWNEY.]
1629 **Downinge**, John, Ballymanagh, co. Tipperary, gent.
1699 ,, Nicholas, Drummard, co. Londonderry, esq.
1793 **Downrayl**, Elizabeth, dow. visc. of, Kilmeaden, co. Waterford [See DONERAILE.]
1810 **Downshire**, the most noble Arthur, marquis of (Copy)
1793 ,, Wills, marquis of (Large)

1659 **Downtowne**, Anthony, soldier in capt. Vivyan's com. [**VII**. 186
1676 **Dowse**, Anthony, London, haberdasher
1770 ,, Benjamin, Francis-st., Dublin, merchant
1801 ,, Margaret, Kilmolin, co. Wicklow, widow
1802 ,, Richard, Crane, co. Wexford, farmer
1789 ,, Thomas, Kilmolin, co. Wicklow, gent.
1796 **Doxey**, Benjamin, Nicholas-street, Dublin, currier
1684 ,, Hercules, Killone, Queen's co., gent.
1793 **Doyel**, Hannah, Dublin, widow
1744 **Doyle**, Andrew, Ballyboy, King's co., merchant
1796 ,, Bartholomew, Dublin, grocer and merchant
1727 ,, Catherine, *alias* **Cruise**, Aghvana, co. Wicklow, widow
1770 ,, Charles, Bramblestown, co. Kilkenny, esq.
1775 ,, Charles, Dublin, grocer
1716 ,, Daniel, Kilkenny, merchant
1773 ,, Daniel, Ballykilcavan, Queen's co., gent.
1707 ,, Denis, Ballymacar, co. Waterford, farmer
1807 ,, Denis, Patrick-street, Dublin
1743 ,, Dennis, Dublin, merchant
1747 ,, Edmond, Tomcoyle, co. Wick.
1773 ,, Edmond, Strawberry-hill, co. Dublin, gent.
1803 ,, Elinor, Waterford, widow
1810 ,, Elinor, Aclare, co. Kilkenny, spirit merchant
1778 ,, Elizabeth, St. Anne's parish, Dublin
1748 ,, Garret, mariner, belonging to the "Nassau" man-of-war
1774 ,, George, the younger, Boycetown, co. Kildare, farmer
1739 ,, Henry, Kilcasker, co. Kildare, gent.
1797 ,, James, Dublin, merchant
1803 ,, James, Woodside, co. Dublin
1807 ,, James, Ballybought, co. Dubl., farmer
1809 ,, James, Cavan-street, Dublin, grocer
1713 ,, John, Graigue, Queen's co., farmer (wanting)
1714 ,, John, Dublin, grocer
1769 ,, John, Cashel, clk.
1775 ,, John, Cavan's-port, Dublin, butcher

1798 **Doyle**, rev. John, Enniskillen, co. Fermanagh
1789 ,, Joseph, Earl-street, Dublin, merchant
1785 ,, Laurence, Dublin, dealer
1787 ,, Margaret, Dublin, widow
1732 ,, Martin, Boot-lane, Dublin, ale seller
1782 ,, Mary, Dublin, widow
1788 ,, Mathias, Dublin, brazier
1757 ,, Michael
1808 ,, Michael, Francis-street, Dubl., iron merchant
1769 ,, Miles, Newabbey, co. Kildare
1738 ,, Nicholas, Arklow, co. Wicklow
1660 ,, Patrick   [**VIII.** 110
1788 ,, Patrick
1796 ,, Patrick, Crowconaghoth, co. Meath, farmer
1798 ,, Patrick, Kevin-street, Dublin
1803 ,, Peter, Baltrasy, co. Kildare, gent.
1659 ,, Phillip, soldier in capt. Vivyan's comp.   [**VII.** 185
1643 ,, Richard, Stamullin, co. Meath, tanner
1765 ,, Richard, Dublin, merchant
1774 ,, Richard, Dublin, poulterer
1801 ,, Richard, Lemonstown, co. Wicklow
1791 ,, Russell, Camden-street, Dublin, carpenter
1751 ,, Terence, Deaneburr, co. Wicklow, farmer
1790 ,, Timothy, Aclare, co. Kilkenny, gent.
1807 ,, Timothy, Bishop-st., co. Dub., builder
1778 ,, Thomas, Dublin, plumber
1772 ,, William, Monotober, co. Kildare
1787 **Doyne**, Benjamin Burton, Altimont, co. Carlow, esq.
1773 ,, Bury, formerly of Carlow, now *audentem*, Middle Temple
1777 ,, v. rev. Charles, dean of Leighlin
1776 ,, Elizabeth, Dublin, widow
1766 ,, Hester, spinster
1763 ,, James, Dublin, esq.
1638 ,, John, Dublin, gent.
1791 ,, Mary, Dublin, widow
1749 ,, Michael, captain in brigadier Hargraves' regiment
1754 ,, Philip, Dublin, esq.
1733 ,, Robert, Dublin, esq.
1768 ,, Robt., Wells, co. Wexford, esq.
1791 ,, Robt., Wells, co. Wexford, esq.
1745 ,, Whitfield, Belgriffin, co. Dub., esq.
1808 **Draffen**, Ellis M., Dublin, gent.

1733 **Drake**, Benjamin, lieut.-col. in col. Howard's regt. of foot
1739 ,, Columb, Drakerath, co. Meath, gent.
1807 ,, Columbus, Rosistown, co. Meath, esq.
1776 ,, Darius, Waterford, esq.
1770 ,, George, Coleback, co. Wexford, gent.
1778 ,, Isabella, *alias* **Hull**, Dublin, widow
1806 ,, John, Ross, co. Wexford
1761 ,, Moses, Dublin, plumber
1805 ,, Moses, Dublin city, plumber
1789 ,, Patrick, Drakerath, co. Meath
1780 **Dralrymple**, Patrick, Milk Isle, co. Down
        [See DALRYMPLE.]
1794 **Draper**, Elizabeth, Rostrevor, co. Down, widow
1782 ,, Peter, Rostrevor, co. Down
1719 ,, William, Sligo, gent.
1750 **Draycott**, Catherine, *alias* **Wogan**, Rathcoffy, co. Kildare, widow
1694 ,, Henry, Mornantown, co. Meath, esq.
1748 ,, John, Dublin, gent.
1702 ,, Patk., Mornantown, co. Meath, esq.
1689 ,, Philip, priest
1736 **Dredge**, John, Cork, gent.
1722 **Drelincourt**, v. rev. Peter, dean of Armagh, I. U. D.
1756 ,, Mary, par. St. George, Hanover-square, Middlesex, widow (Copy)
1810 **Drew**, Alexander, Graigue, esq. (Copy)
1694 ,, Barry, Ballyduff, co. Waterford, gent.   [rick, esq.
1793 ,, Barry, Drew's-court, co. Lime-
1752 ,, Dennis, Bridge-street, Dublin
1756 ,, Francis, Drew's-court, co. Tipperary, esq.
1788 ,, Francis, Moccollop, co. Waterford, M.D.
1804 ,, Francis, Bishopstown, co. Waterford, esq.
1785 ,, George Purdon, High Park, co. Dublin, esq.
1799 ,, George, Youghal, co. Cork, esq.
1801 ,, George, late of Liverpool, esq.
1631 ,, Gilbert, Dublin, tailor
1805 ,, James
1735 ,, John, Turcullen, co. Waterford, esq.
1749 ,, John, the elder, Waterpark, co. Cork, gent.
1757 ,, John, Ballinlough, co. Kilkenny, gent.

1782 **Drew**, John, Drewslodge, co. Limerick, esq.
1787 ,, John, Summerhill, co. Meath
1807 ,, John, Tallow, co. Waterford, esq.
1711 ,, Margaret, Kilwinny, co. Waterford
1754 ,, Margaret, Kilwinny, co. Cork, widow
1756 ,, Mary, Bridge-street, Dublin, widow
1801 ,, Richard Rose, Kenton, Devonshire (Copy)
1799 ,, Ringrose, Flagmount, Lib. of Limerick, esq.
1762 ,, Robert, lieut. in general Richbell's regiment of foot
1754 ,, Ruth, Waterpark, co. Cork, spinster
1757 ,, Samuel, Scart-ne-Crohy, co. Waterford, gent.
1723 ,, Thomas, Dublin, gent.
1802 **Drinan**, Andrew, Cork, merchant
1759 **Dring**, Robert, Cork, esq.
1808 ,, Robert, Rock Grove, co. Cork, clerk
1721 ,, Simon, Cork, esq.
1781 ,, Simon, Rock Grove, co. Cork, esq. (Large)
1653 **Drinkwater**, Nathaniel
1763 **Driscoll**, Elinor, Dublin, spinster
1757 ,, Ellinor, suburbs of Limerick, widow
1750 ,, rev. Thomas, Kilkenny, clerk
1712 **Drogheda**, Alice, dowager countess of (Copy)
1735 ,, Charlotte, dowager countess of (Copy)
1759 ,, Edward, earl of
1676 ,, Henry, earl of
1714 ,, Henry, earl of
1727 ,, Henry, earl of
1726 ,, Mary, dowager countess of (Copy)
1802 **Dromgole**, Paul, Fitzwilliam-place, Dublin city
1614 **Dromgoold**, Thomas, Dubl., mer.
1751 **Dromgoole**, James, Drogheda, mer.
1740 ,, Laurence, Dublin, gent.
1809 ,, Mark
1766 ,, Michael, Drogheda, merchant
1755 ,, Nicholas, Newry, co. Down, gt.
1792 ,, Nicholas, Drogheda, merchant
1778 ,, Peter, Newry, co. Down, apothecary
1666 ,, Thomas, Dublin, merchant
1809 ,, William, Rathfarnham, co. Dublin, miller
1683 **Dromore**, Essex Digby, bishop of
1695 ,, Capel Wiseman, bishop of

1715 **Dromore**, Dr. Tobias Pullein, bishop of
1763 ,, Dr. Geo. Marlay, bishop of
1638 **Drope**, Gyles, Dublin, gent.
1758 ,, James, Ballyhaise
1774 ,, John, Cootehill, co. Cavan, gt.
1800 ,, John, Ballyhaise, co. Cavan, gt.
1754 ,, William, Ballyhaise, co. Cavan
1778 **Drought**, Alice, Cappagolan, King's co.
1730 ,, Arthur, Heath, King's co., gent.
1771 ,, Elizabeth, Birr, King's co., spinster
1801 ,, Eusebius, Bannagher, King's co., gent.
1805 ,, Frederick, Birr, King's co.
1806 ,, George, Castletown, King's co.
1781 ,, James, Ballyboy, King's co., gent.
1724 ,, John, Cappagolan, King's co., gent.
1748 ,, John, Ballyboy, King's co., gent.
1758 ,, John, Heath, King's co., esq.
1794 ,, John, Ricketstown, co. Carlow, esq.
1780 ,, John, Whigsborough, King's co., esq.
1745 ,, Mary, Cappagolan, King's co., widow
1792 ,, Mary, Power's Grove, co. Kildare, spinster
1779 ,, Phillippa, Lazer's Hill, Dublin, widow
1787 ,, Ralph, High-street, Dublin, ironmonger
1802 ,, Richard, Ballybrit, King's co., farmer
1726 ,, Robert, Park, King's co., gent.
1746 ,, Robert, Grantstown, Queen's co.
1784 ,, Robert, Ballyoran, King's co., esq.
1801 ,, Robert, Oldglass, Queen's co., gent.
1809 ,, Robert, Plunketstown, co. Kildare, clerk
1753 ,, Thomas, Plunketstown, co. Kildare
1769 ,, Thomas, Cappagolan, King's co., esq.
1782 ,, Thomas, Droughtville, esq.
1808 ,, Thomas, Cappagolan, King's co., esq.
1698 ,, William, Kilmagarvoge, co. Carlow, gent.
1751 ,, William, Commonstown, co. Kildare, farmer
1780 ,, William, Boherard, Queen's co., gent.

1793 **Drought**, William, Ricketstown, co. Carlow, gent.
1797 ,, Wm., city of Westminster, M.D.
1752 **Droz**, John Peter, minister of the Holy Gospel
1810 **Druit**, Eliza, Lurgan, widow
1773 **Druitt**, Eleanor, Dublin, widow
1770 ,, Joseph, Dublin, merchant
1750 **Drumeny**, Frances, Dublin, widow
1708 ,, John, Dublin, gent.
1779 **Drummond**, Robert, Ballymascanlan, co. Louth
1798 **Drury**, Baxter, Dublin, spinster
1798 ,, Charlotte, Dublin, spinster
1723 ,, Edward, Kingsland, co. Roscommon, esq.
1785 ,, Elizabeth, Limerick city
1778 ,, John, Limerick, merchant
1792 ,, rev. John, preby. St. John, Dublin, clerk
1777 ,, Mary, Dublin, widow
1715 ,, Robert, major of the royal Irish dragoons
1805 ,, Thomas B., Dublin city, shopkeeper
1759 **Dry**, Charles, Chamber-street, Dubl., clothier
1692 **Drysdale**, Hugh, D.D., archdeacon of Ossory
1726 ,, major Hugh, Churchill's regt. of dragoons (Copy)
1731 **Drysdall**, Griffith, Watercastle, Queen's co., gent.
1758 **Duan**, Elizabeth, Dublin, spinster
1791 **Duane**, William, friar in the Carmelite convent of Kildare [See DIVAN.]
1757 **Duany**, Francis, Dublin, surgeon
1605 **Dublin**, Adam Loftus, archbishop of, and lord chancellor
1681 ,, John Parker, archbishop of (Ex.)
1693 ,, Francis Marsh, archbishop of
1729 ,, Dr. William King, archbishop of
1765 ,, Dr. Charles Cobbe, archbishop of
1766 ,, Dr. William Carmichael, archbishop of
1771 ,, Dr. Arthur Smyth, archbishop of
1802 ,, lord archbishop of (Charles Agar)
1711 **Du Boe**, Francis, Dublin, saddler
1774 **Du Bois**, Dorothea, *alias* **Annesley**, daughter of Richard, earl of Annesley
1732 **Dubourgay**, hon. Charles, par. St. Martin-in-the-Fields, Middlesex, esq.

1784 **Ducasse**, Anne, Dublin
1729 ,, Paschal, dean of Clogher
1747 ,, Stephen, lieut. of dragoons on half pay
1734 **Duchesne**, Michael, native of Anduse in the Cevennes, now of Dublin
1804 **Duck**, Anne, Britain-lane, Dublin, widow
1658 **Duckenfield**, Francis, quar.-master in major John King's troop, **[VII.** 29
1650 ,, captain Thomas
1797 **Ducket**, Jonas, Willow Brook, co. Kildare (Large)
1739 ,, John, Newtown, co. Kildare, gent.
1781 ,, Richard, Whitestown, co. Waterford, esq.
1735 ,, Thomas, Philipstown, co. Carlow, gent.
1796 ,, Thomas, Newtown, co. Kildare, quaker
1784 **Duckett**, Wm., Phillipstown, co. Carlow, esq. (Large)
1808 ,, William, Ducketts Grove, co. Carlow, esq. (Large)
1750 **Duckworth**, William, the elder, Waterford, ropemaker
1730 **Duclos**, Anne, Dublin, widow
1768 **Ducross**, John, Dublin, apothecary
1687 **Duddell**, Richard, Loughcrew, co. Meath, clerk
1804 **Dudgeon**, Samuel, Pill-lane, Dubl., merchant
1737 ,, William, Dublin, merchant
1660 **Dudley**, Elizabeth, senr., Dublin, widow **[VIII.** 94
1638 ,, George, Killebon, Queen's co., yeoman
1660 ,, John, Castledermot, co. Kild. gent. **[VIII.** 85
1760 ,, John, Kilshane, co. Dublin, gent.
1777 ,, John, Raheny, co. Dublin, gt.
1801 ,, John, Roscrea, co. Tipperary
1794 ,, Joseph, Clonmel, co. Tipperary, miller
1757 ,, Large, Frankfort, King's co.
1808 ,, Robert, Suirville, co. Waterford
1810 ,, Robert, the younger, Clonmel, co. Tipperary
1764 ,, sir William, Heath, Yorkshire, bart. (Copy)
1749 **Duff**, Alexander, Dublin, plasterer
1715 ,, Anne, Dublin, widow
1765 ,, Anne, Arran-street, Dublin, widow
1798 ,, Anthony, Knocknatulla, co. Meath, gent.

1770 **Duff**, Bryan, Dublin, bricklayer
1805 ,, Constantine, Dublin city
1800 ,, Edward, Ballinabola, co. Kildare, farmer
1611 ,, George, Termonfeghne, co. Louth, gent.
1720 ,, George, Dublin, linen draper
1610 ,, James, New Ross, esq.
1649 ,, James, Dublin, merchant
1745 ,, John, quartermaster on board the 'Liverpool' man-of-war
1753 ,, John, Belfast, co. Antrim
1768 ,, John, Dublin, Arran-street
1771 ,, John, Dublin, linendraper
1772 ,, John, Smithfield, Dublin, baker
1808 ,, Luke, Skerries, co. Dublin, miller
1804 ,, Mary, Ballanagappak, co. Kildare, widow
1772 ,, Patrick, Bridge-street, Dublin, merchant
1803 ,, Patrick, Dublin (see 1804)
1804 ,, Patrick, Dublin, schoolmaster
1805 ,, Richard, Dublin city, baker
1756 ,, Sarah, Dublin, widow
1785 ,, Siby, widow
1624 ,, Stephen, Drogheda, alderman
1799 ,, Terence, Dublin city, tanner
[See DUFFE, DUFFEY, DUFFY.]
1664 **Duffe**, Edward, Dublin, merchant
1671 ,, Elinor, *alias* **Bathe**, Drogheda, widow
1650 ,, Elizabeth, *alias* **Taaffe** [VIII. 141
1686 ,, John, Waterford, gent.
1634 ,, Richard, Dublin, water bailiff
1700 ,, Richard, Dublin, esq.
1650 ,, Stephen, Dublin
1662 ,, Stephen, Drogheda, gent.
1670 ,, Stephen, Drogheda, gent.
1703 ,, Thady, Muckery, co. Tipperary, esq.
[See DUFF.]
1745 **Duffey**, Bryan, Dunshaughlin, co. Meath
1775 **Duffy**, Anne, Back-lane, Dublin, widow [carman
1758 ,, James, Cherry-lane, Dublin,
1789 ,, James, Staleen, co. Meath
1757 ,, Laurence, Dublin, teacher
1675 ,, Patrick, Aghnamolen, co. Mon., clk. (with another will enclosed, dated 1675, by name of Pat Duffy, bishop of Clogher) [linendraper
1755 ,, Patrick, Back-lane, Dublin,
1809 ,, Patrick
1806 ,, William, Bolton-street, Dublin city, grocer
[See DUFF.]

1711 **Dufoussat**, Pierre, refugee, near Portarlington, esq.
1793 **Dugall**, Thomas, Ballyhasky
1759 **Dugan**, Daniel
1783 ,, Mary, Cork, widow
1749 ,, Timothy, Monasterevan
1807 **Duggan**, Anne, par. of Slane
1803 ,, Elizabeth, Dublin city, spinster
1767 ,, Francis, Dublin, esq.
1768 ,, Michael, Bride's-alley, Dublin, auctioneer
1803 **Duggin**, John, Belfast, co. Antrim, revenue officer
1790 **Dughan**, Elizabeth, Sligo
1780 ,, William, Sligo town, merchant
[See DUGGAN.]
1731 **Duhart**, James, Dublin, mariner
1791 **Duhig**, Robert, Air Hill Liberties, co. Limerick, gent.
1733 **Duhigg**, Mathew, Kilcullen, co. Limerick, gent.
1796 ,, Mathew
1749 ,, Thos., Kilcullane, co. Limerick, gent.
1751 **Duhy**, Daniel, Gortneskehy, co. Tipperary, farmer
1671 **Duiegenan**, Nichs., Feltrim, gent.
[See DUIGENAN.]
1808 **Duigan**, Catherine, Thomastown, co. Kilkenny, widow
1786 ,, James, Clonereken, co. Tipp.
1800 ,, Margaret, Dublin, spinster
1805 ,, Michael, Thomastown, co. Kilkenny
1800 ,, Thomas, Dublin, tavern keeper
1798 **Duigenan**, Mary
1750 **Duigin**, Dennis, Cold Harbour, co. Wicklow, farmer
1799 ,, James, Ballyfoyle
1791 **Duignan**, Catherine, Dublin, widow
[See DUIGAN.]
1617 **Duinn**, Charles, esq., master of Chancery, LL.D.
1786 **Dukart**, Davis
1800 **Duke**, rev. Alexander, glebe house, co. Sligo, clk.
1809 ,, Anne, Branchfield, co. Sligo
1792 ,, Robert, Branchfield, co. Sligo, esq.
1551 ,, William, Kyllenaghe, co. Kild. (Imperfect)
1734 **Dulany**, Malachias, Kilkenny, popish priest
1742 **Dulehunty**, John, Dublin
1743 ,, John, Dublin, gent.
1785 **Dulhunty**, St. John
1765 ,, Terence
1808 ,, Thomas, Ennis, co. Clare, esq.
[See DELAHUNTY.]
1772 **Dullas**, William, Dublin

1792 **Dulles**, Elizabeth, Dublin, widow
1628 **Duloghere**, John, Dublin, and Dunmoylan, co. Limerick, gent. (Copy)
1746 **Dumagan**, Nicholas, Beamore, co. Meath
1777 **Dumaresq**, Anne, Dublin, widow
1737 **Dumarest**, Chas., Bonnard, par. St. Anne, Westminster (Copy)
1759 **Dumas**, Henry, Cloghereen, co. Kerry, gent.
1716 ,, capt. James, lord Stair's regt. of dragoons (Copy)
1783 ,, James
1802 **Dumphy**, William, Bennetsbridge, co. Kilkenny, gent.
1793 **Dumville**, Anne, Clonmel, co. Tipperary, widow
1810 ,, Charles, Santry House, co. Dublin, esq.
1807 ,, Henry, Clonmel, co. Tipperary, gent.
1772 ,, John, Clonmel, co. Tipperary
1785 ,, Julian, Killbalgowen, co. Wicklow
1633 **Dun**, Thomas, Lispople, co. Dublin, gent.
1763 **Dunagon**, Jane, widow of Denis D., esq., M.D.
1778 **Dunbar**, Charles, Blessington, co. Wicklow, esq.
1779 ,, George, Belfast, gent.
1799 ,, George, Belfast, co. Antrim, esq.
1802 ,, sir George, Muckram, bart. (Copy)
1807 ,, George
1724 ,, John, Ballycarney, co. Carlow, esq.
1764 ,, John, Dublin, gent.
1747 ,, Philip, Dublin, esq.
1732 ,, Richard, Chelsea Hospital, London, now at Knights, co. Dublin
1758 ,, Robert, Dublin, printer
1665 ,, Thomas, Enniskillen, co. Fermanagh, gent.
1767 ,, Thomas, Dublin, esq., major-general
1786 ,, William, the elder, Drumondoney, co. Down, gent.
1802 ,, Wm., Drumondoney, co. Down
1741 **Dunbavin**, Francis, Dub., carpenter
1624 **Dunboyne**, James, baron of, (deed of gift and declaration) [**I**. 102
1800 ,, John Butler, lord [See DONBOYNE.]
1808 **Duncan**, Agnes, widow of Robert Duncan

1740 **Duncan**, Andrew, London, surgeon
1748 ,, Ellinor, *alias* **Jackson**, Dubl., widow
1730 ,, Hugh, Middleton, co. Armagh
1717 ,, rev. Jas., Kilmore, co, Meath, clk.
1803 ,, James, Donnybrook, co. Dubl., farmer
1694 ,, John, Corndall, co. Londonderry, gent.
1703 ,, John, Donoghmore, co. Antrim, gent.
1795 ,, John, Finglas-bridge, co. Dub.
1807 ,, Robert, Lisburn, co. Antrim
1800 ,, William, Dublin, merchant [See DONAGH, DUNKIN.]
1724 **Duncannon**, William, lord viscount
1719 **Duncombe**, Thomas, Dublin, esq. [See DUNSCOMBE.]
1804 **Dundas**, Penelope Ford
1808 ,, Phil., Upper Grosvenor-street, Middlesex (Copy)
1769 **Dundass**, John, Curramore, co. Fermanagh, gent.
1657 **Dungan**, Henry, the Stoggin-green, Dublin, yeoman
1806 ,, John, Copenhagen, Denmark (Copy)
1775 ,, Patrick, Dublin, baker
1794 ,, Walter, Bridgefoot-st., Dublin, gent.
1755 ,, William, Lusk, co. Dublin, woollendraper [See DONGAN.]
1771 **Dungannon**, Arthur, lord viscount (Large will)
1707 ,, Marcus, lord viscount
1759 **Dungarvan**, Charles Boyle, lord viscount
1759 **Dunkan**, rev. Henry, clk.
1755 **Dunkin**, Anne, Enniskillen, co. Fermanagh, spinster
1792 ,, Domitia, Dublin, spinster
1766 ,, Elizabeth
1785 ,, Jane
1723 ,, Patrick, Mullincross, co. Louth, gent.
1752 ,, Rebecca, *alias* **Babbington**, *alias* **Wray**, Dublin, widow [See DUNCAN, DUNCOMBE.]
1709 **Dunlap**, James, Killirsany, co. Armagh, gent.
1805 ,, James, Daisyhill, co. Armagh [See DUNLOP.]
1805 **Dunlevy**, Alice, Dublin city
1738 **Dunlop**, Andrew, Dublin, merchant
1799 ,, Anne, Dublin, spinster
1793 ,, Elizabeth
1773 ,, Frances, Flowerhill, co. Antm. (see 175)

1775 **Dunlop**, Frances, Flowerhill, co. Antrim
1778 ,, George, Chatham Hall, co. Derry
1755 ,, Robert, Dublin, upholder [See DUNLAP.]
1757 **Dunn**, Andrew, Rathcormick, co. Cork
1781 ,, Andrew
1752 ,, Anne, Grangeford, co. Carlow
1782 ,, Arthur, Dublin, gent.
1723 ,, Barnaby, Rathleen, King's co., gent.
1786 ,, Bridget, Grangeford, co. Carlow, widow
1753 ,, Bryan, Dublin, victualler
1681 ,, Charles, Brittas, Queen's co., esq.   [dealer
1793 ,, Charles, Mullagh, co. Cavan,
1806 ,, Danl., Castlemitchell, co. Kild.
1772 ,, Denis, Dublin, grocer
1779 ,, Dominick, Mary-st., Dublin, grocer
1776 ,, Edward, Clonnaslee, Queen's co., farmer
1790 ,, Elizabeth, Dublin, spinster
1701 ,, Ellinor, *alias* **Long**, Drysoge, co. Dublin, widow
1786 ,, Esther, Dublin, widow
1804 ,, Frances, Loughrea, co. Galway, widow
1780 ,, Francis, Bolton-st., Dublin, ale seller
1801 ,, Grace, Dublin city, widow
1807 ,, Grace, Dublin city
1747 ,, Hugh, Grangeford, co. Carlow, gent.
1758 ,, James, Lisdowney, co. Kilk., gent.
1773 ,, James, Dublin, merchant
1776 ,, James, Maystown, co. Dublin, farmer
1793 ,, James, Graigue, Queen's co., merchant
1805 ,, Jas., par. of St. Thomas, Dúbl.
1810 ,, James, Dubl. city, hotel keeper
1745 ,, John, Dublin, innholder
1793 ,, John, Summerhill, co. Galway, esq.
1802 ,, John, Dolphin's Barn, co. Dub., gent.
1804 ,, John, Kilmainham, co. Dublin
1800 ,, Judith, Dolphin's Barn, co. Dublin
1722 ,, Margaret, Ballynakill, Queen's co., widow
1801 ,, Margaret, widow
1809 ,, Martha
1738 ,, Mary, Logarmarla, King's co., widow

1748 **Dunn**, dame Mary, wid. of sir Patk. D., practitioner of physic
1794 ,, Mary, Harold's Cross, co. Dub., widow
1764 ,, Mathew, Punchestown, farmer
1766 ,, Mathias, Dublin, tailor
1747 ,, Maurice, Sierass, co. Kildare
1807 ,, Michael, Rathmoyle, King's co., farmer (Unproved)
1757 ,, Murtagh, Roseberry, co. Kild.
1724 ,, Owen, Rathcoffy, co. Kildare, farmer
1713 ,, sir Patrick, Dublin, knt.
1766 ,, Patk., Mary-st., Dubl., grocer
1771 ,, Patk., Stradbally, Queen's co., shopkeeper
1775 ,, Patrick, Dublin, gent.
1800 ,, Patrick, Dublin, peruke maker
1752 ,, Richard, Dublin, farrier
1774 ,, Richard, Rathmore, co. Kild., farmer
1770 ,, Robert, Dublin, grocer
1627 ,, Thady, Dublin, shoemaker
1748 ,, Thady, Dublin, gent.
1770 ,, Thomas, Frankford, King's co.
1805 ,, Thomas, Dublin city
1784 ,, William, Dublin, esq.
1791 ,, William, Dublin, alderman
1796 ,, William, Dublin, weaver
1802 ,, William, Leggah, parish of Katharine
[See DUNNE.]
1793 **Dunnahy**, John, Cork, merchant
1808 **Dunne**, Edward, Tralee, co. Kerry, M.D.
1801 ,, James, Ballinakill, Queen's co.
1769 ,, John, Eyne, Queen's co.
1809 ,, Mary, Stradbally, Queen's co., widow
1695 ,, Thady, Classigad, King's co., gent.
1653 ,, Thos., Kells, co. Meath, gent.
1655 ,, Thomas, corporal in capt. John Salts' troop
[See DUNN.]
1786 **Dumphey**, Owen, Monasterevan, co. Kildare, dealer
1809 **Dumphy**, Bridget, widow
1792 ,, Martin, Naas, co. Kildare, vintner
1753 **Dunscombe**, George, Cork, esq.
1745 ,, Noblett, Mount Desart, co. of city of Cork, esq.
[See DUNCOMBE.]
1770 **Dunsteville**, Christ., Birr, King's co., dragoon
1633 **Dunyn**, Wm., Kildrum, co. Antrim, yeoman
1744 **Dupleackes**, George, Edenderry, King's co.

1747 **Dupleacks**, Thomas, Edenderry, King's co., esq.
1798 **Dupond**, St. John, Mallow, co. Cork, gent.
1759 **Dupre**, James, Dublin, tailor
1782 **Du Pre**, Josias, Portland - place, Middlesex, esq. (Copy)
1730 ,, Stephen, Dublin, baker
1734 **Durand**, Abraham, Dublin, gent.
1746 **Durant**, Charles Lewis, colonel in the service of the King of Sardinia (Copy)
1791 **Duras**, Edwd., Dubl., paper stamper
1711 **Durcy**, John, Coonagh, North Lib. of Limerick, gent.
1808 **Durdan**, Alexander, Dublin city
1767 **Durdin**, Ann, *alias* **Pen**, wife to Alexander D., gent.
1810 **Durham**, Barry, Culmswell, co. Kild.
1776 ,, Christopher, Church-st., Dubl., hosier
1801 ,, Frances, Prussia-st., co. Dubl., widow
1798 **Durkan**, John, Galw. town, apoth.
1775 **Duron**, Isaac, of Killmollog, King's co., gent.
1722 **Duroure**, Francis (Copy)
1709 **Dusauze**, Benoist, Dungarvan, co. Waterford, merchant.
1810 **Dutens**, Elizabeth, par. St Anne, Westminster (Copy)
1782 **Duteral**, Elizabeth, Dublin, spr.
1714 **Dutoral**, Alexr. de Bardel, Dublin, esq.
1778 **Dutton**, James Lennox, Shirbone, Gloucestershire, esq. (Large will)
1629 ,, John, Fassitmore, co. Donegal, esq.
1674 ,, John, Dublin, merchant
1688 ,, John, Dublin, merchant
1722 ,, John, Fortill, King's co., gent.
1720 ,, sir Ralph, Rathfarnham, co. Dublin, bart.
1634 ,, sir Thos., Ratheline, co. Longford, knt. and privy councillor
1719 **Duval**, Augustus, officer at the pension of Ireland
1795 **Dwen**, Edward, High-street, Dublin, hosier
1787 ,, Laurence, Tumard, co. Kildare
1790 ,, Margaret, *alias* **Ryan**, Tomard, co. Kildare
1807 **Dwenn**, Hugh, High-street, Dublin, hosier
1591 **Dwining**, John, Dublin   [I. 76
1748 **Dwyer**, Anthony, Lismolin, co. Tipperary
1786 ,, Anthony, Courneen, co. Tipperary, gent.

1796 **Dwyer**, Anthony, Dublin, esq.
1787 ,, Dennis, Ballymeety, co. Limk., gent.
1695 ,, Edmond, sen., Fanningstown, co. Limerick, gent.
1784 ,, James, Boardlays, co. Dublin
1794 ,, Jeremiah, Tipperary, attorney
1809 ,, Jeremiah, Dublin city, mercht.
1719 ,, John, Ballyadams, Queen's co., esq.
1810 ,, Richd., Horseland, co. Kildare
1721 ,, Thady, Carranahally, co. Tipperary, gent.
1761 ,, Timothy, Dublin, merchant
1788 ,, Thomas, Ennis, co. Clare, merchant
1802 ,, Thomas, Limerick, grocer
1804 **Dyas**, John, Philipburgh, co. Dub., gent.
1806 ,, Robert, Albany, State of New York (Copy) [apothecary
1810 ,, Samuel, Dorset-street, Dublin,
1775 ,, William, Kilbeg, co. Meath, gent.
1763 **Dyass**, James, Bailieborough, co. Cavan
1745 **Dyer**, Nathaniel, Dublin, shipwright [See **Dwyer**.]
1695 **Dymond**, Elizabeth, Cork, widow
1679 ,, Philip, Cork, merchant
1719 **Dynes**, William, Mullocartan, co. Antrim, gent.
1808 **Dysart**, William, Londonderry city, merchant
1676 **Dyson**, Edward, senior, Drogheda, gent.
1674 **Dysterloo**, Christiana, Amsterdam, widow   [**XII.** 313
1796 **Dyton**, Timothy, Dublin, esq.

—E—

1803 **Eades**, Christopher, Bride-st., Dub., grocer
1795 ,, Isaac, Ormond-quay, fishing tackle maker
1800 **Eager**, Ann, late of Cork, but now of Bristol, widow
1796 ,, Francis, Dublin
1793 ,, John, Clough, co. Wexford
1785 ,, Nicholas, Coolmine, co. Dubl., farmer
    [See **Egar**.]
1795 **Eagle**, George, Limerick city, esq.
1754 ,, Solomon, Hilltown, co. Meath, farmer
1790 **Eakins**, George, Newtownstewart
1745 **Eames**, Thomas, Kill, King's co., gent.

1790 **Eames**, Wm., Kilrush, co. Clare, esq.
1731 **Eanon**, Thomas, Dublin, clothier
1762 **Earbery**, Christopher, Shandangin, co. Cork, esq.
1729 ,, Mathias, Ballincollig, co. Cork, esq.
1779 ,, Mathias, Dublin, esq.
1729 ,, Nicholas, Ballincollig, co. Cork, gent.
1804 **Earl**, Daniel, Raheenagurrin, co. Wexford
1795 ,, Edwd., Knockduff, co. Wexford, farmer
1797 ,, John, Raheenagurrin, co. Wexford
1769 **Eason**, Arth., Cork, tallow chander
1777 ,, Mary, Cork, widow
1802 ,, Peter, Cork city, gent.
1730 **Eastham**, Henry, Dublin, gent.
1643 **Eastwood**, Abraham, St. Catherine's parish, clothier
1699 ,, Charles, Dublin, merchant
1740 ,, George, Dublin, merchant
1808 ,, rev. James, Castletown, co. Louth, clk.
1682 ,, John, Dublin, alderman
1790 ,, John, Castletown, co. Louth, esq.
1615 **Easworth**, Henry, Galway, tanner
1706 **Eaton**, Anne, Meath-street, Dublin, widow
1752 ,, Burley, Dublin, gent.
1796 ,, Catherine, co. Wicklow, spr.
1728 ,, Charles, Castlekelly, co. Kilkenny, esq.
1763 ,, Chas., Ardmulchan, co. Meath, gent.
1778 ,, Christopher, Coles-alley, Dubl., carpenter
1750 ,, George, Dublin, grocer
1776 ,, Letitia, widow
1755 ,, Peter, Dublin, mariner
1665 ,, Richard, servant to col. Thomas Longe
1780 ,, Richard, York-street, Dublin, gent.
1733 ,, Robert, Cashel, co. Tipperary, alderman
1698 ,, sir Simon, Dunmoylen, co. Limerick, bart. (Copy)
1701 ,, dame Susanna, relict of sir Simon E., Dunmoylen, co. Limerick, bart. (Ex.)
1668 ,, Theophilus, Dublin, esq.
[**XII.** 185
1733 ,, Thomas, Dublin, esq.
1663 ,, William, Catherlogh, gent.
1802 **Eaustace**, Ann, widow
[See EUSTACE.]

1775 **Ebbs**, Danl., Chapelizod, co. Dub., publican
1783 ,, Mary, Chapelizod, co. Dublin, widow
1762 **Eburne**, William, Cork, merchant
1764 **Eccles**, Anne, widow of Robert E., Annesville, co. Fermanagh
1756 ,, Catherine, Kinkeelin, co. Roscommon, widow
1798 ,, Charles, Dublin, gent.
1750 ,, Daniel, Fintona, co. Tyrone, esq.
1757 ,, Daniel
1794 ,, Daniel, Tallymorris, co. Fermanagh, esq.
1809 ,, Daniel, Ecclesville, co. Tyrone, esq.
1697 ,, Elizabeth, Dublin, widow (Ex.)
1771 ,, Elizabeth, Stubbins Mill, Dubl.
1680 ,, Hugh, Belfast, merchant
1761 ,, Hugh, Dublin, esq.
1809 ,, Isaac A., Cronroe, co. Wicklow, esq.
1748 ,, James, Mulloghteighe, co. Roscommon, gent.
1759 ,, James, quartermaster of horse carbineers
1773 ,, James, Dublin, gent.
1726 ,, John, Belfast
1739 ,, John, Belfast, merchant
1809 ,, John, Dorset-street, Dublin
1723 ,, Joseph, Rathmoran, co. Fermanagh, gent.
1709 ,, Joyce, wife to alderman John E., Dublin, merchant
1775 ,, Margaret, Dublin, widow
1706 ,, Mary, *alias* **Yarner**, wife to Hugh E., Dublin, esq.
1710 ,, Mary, Waterford, widow
1755 ,, Mary, *alias* **Lowry**, widow of Daniel E., Fentona, esq. (Large will)
1793 ,, Mary, Dublin, widow
1763 ,, Robert, Kilrusky, co. Fermanagh, esq.
1742 ,, William, Shanock, co. Fermanagh, gent.
[See ECKELLS, ECLES.]
1767 **Eccleston**, Edward, Dublin, watchmaker, lieutenant of marines
1762 ,, Elizabeth
1728 ,, Mary, *alias* **Barlow**, Dublin, widow
1636 ,, Tristram, Drumshallon, co. Louth, esq.
1762 ,, William, Bogtown, co. Louth, esq.   Louth, esq.
1794 ,, William, Drumshallon, co. Louth, esq.
1799 ,, William, Drumshallon, co. Louth, esq.

1805 **Echlin**, Alice
1747 ,, Ann, wife to Charles E., esq. (Ex.)
1782 ,, Anna Maria, Dublin, widow
1805 ,, Anne, Dublin city
1758 ,, Arthur, Feltrim, co.. Dublin, esq.
1754 ,, Charles, Ardquin, co. Down, esq.
1761 ,, Godfrey, esq.
1747 ,, sir Henry, Dublin, kt. and bt.
1789 ,, Henry, Clonagh, co. Kildare, esq.
1730 ,, Hugh, Dublin, carpenter
1755 ,, James, Echlin Ville, co. Down, esq. (Large)
1761 ,, Jane, Marlfield, co. Down
1771 ,, Jane, Newtown Ards, co. Down, widow
1762 ,, John, Drogheda, clk.
1764 ,, rev. John, Castletown, co. Galway, D.D.
1810 ,, rev. John, Dornanville, co. Dublin
1801 ,, Richard, Dublin, pub. notary
1657 ,, Robert, Ardquin, co. Down, esq. [**VI**. 234
1757 ,, sir Robert, Dublin, bart.
1761 ,, Robert, Newtown
          [See ECLIN.]
1689 **Eckells**, Laurence, Dublin, clothmaker
          [See ECCLES.]
1770 **Eckersall**, Anne, Dublin, spinster
1711 ,, Samuel, Dublin, gent.
1726 **Eckersley**, Charles, Ballmullmore, co. Meath, gent.
1781 **Ecles**, Henry, Lismore, co. Waterford
          [See ECCLES.]
1716 **Eclin**, Henry, New Church-street, Dublin, gent.
1756 ,, Henry, vicar of St. Catherine's, Dublin
1707 ,, Robert, Dublin, esq.
          [See ECHLIN.]
1650 **Eddys**, James, Dublin, merchant
1794 **Edgar**, Patrick, Dublin, merchant
1670 **Edge**, John, Monaghstown, co. Westmeath, gent.
1744 ,, Timothy, Dublin, apothecary
1710 **Edgeworth**, Ambrose, Edgeworthstown, co. Longfd., esq. (Ex.)
1743 ,, Ambrose, ensign in the Royal Scotch regt. of foot
1787 ,, Ann, Waterford, widow
1769 ,, Bridgman, Dublin, esq.
1724 ,, Elizabeth, Dublin, widow
1737 ,, rev. Essex, Templemichael, co. Longford, clk.

1765 **Edgeworth**, Essex, Pallasmore, co. Longford, esq.
1810 ,, Essex White (Copy)
1627 ,, Francis, Dublin, esq. [**II**. 29
1722 ,, Francis, Edgeworthstown, co. Longford, esq.
1799 ,, Francis White, Temple-street, Dublin, esq. (Large)
1719 ,, Henry, Lisard, co. Longford, esq.
1751 ,, Henry, Lisard, co. Longford, esq.
1763 ,, Henry, Cabra-lane, Dubl., esq.
1785 ,, John, Waterford city, esq.
1722 ,, Mary, Dublin, spinster
1776 ,, Mary, Dublin, widow
1791 ,, Newcomen, Kilshruly, co. Longford, esq.
1759 ,, Packington, Longwood, co. Meath, esq.
1770 ,, Richard, Edgeworthstown, co. Longford, esq. (Large will)
1727 **Edgworth**, sir John, Lisard, knt.
1768 ,, Pamela, spinster
1774 ,, Robert, Frankford, King's co.
1794 ,, Robert, Firmount, co. Longford
1802 ,, Robert, Dublin, esq.
1773 **Edie**, Wm., Killydart, co. Tyrone, esq.
1649 **Edish**, Nicholas, Dublin, merchant
1798 **Edkins**, Cornelius Donovan, Gordens-lane, Dublin, gent.
1801 ,, Elizabeth, Dublin city
1790 ,, Henry, Roper's-rest, co. Dublin, gent.
1784 ,, rev. James, Roper's-rest, co. Dublin, clk.
1802 ,, Joshua, Gordens-lane, Charlemont-street, Dublin, gent.
1677 **Edlyne**, Edmond, London, salter (Copy)
1677 ,, Thomas, par. St. Martin-in-the-Fields, London, gent. (Copy)
1648 **Edmond**, Laurence, lord baron of Limerick, co. Wexford.
1782 **Edmondson**, Andrew, Tokenhouse-yard, London, merchant
1774 ,, Ann, widow of Andrew E., Castlebar, co. Mayo, mercht.
1756 ,, William, Mountrath, Queen's co., surgeon
          [See EDMONSTONE, EDMUNSON, &c.]
1623 **Edmons**, Walter, Drogheda
1758 **Edmonston**, Samuel, Roscrea, co. Tipperary, merchant
1710 **Edmonstone**, Anna Helena, widow of Archd. E., Broad Island, co. Antrim
1711 ,, Catherine, Ballybantro, co. Antrim, widow

1791 **Edmonstone**, Charles, North Lodge, co. Antrim
[See EDMONDSON.]
1760 **Edmunds**, John, Ratra, co. Roscommon, gent.
1771 **Edmundson**, William, Mountrath, Queen's co.
1712 **Edmunson**, Wm., Feneel, Queen's co., farmer
[See EDMONDSON.]
1664 **Edsall**, Mathew, Dublin, farrier
1679 **Edwardes**, William, Londonderry, gent.
1748 **Edwards**, Abiell, Dublin, gent.
1719 ,, Anthony, Dublin, vintner
1765 ,, Anthony, Dublin, brewer
1748 ,, Cairns, Ramelton, co. Don., esq.
1769 ,, Eaton, M.D.
1796 ,, Eaton, Newtown, Liberty of Waterford
1701 ,, Edward, Castledarge, co. Tipperary, gent.
1773 ,, Edward, Grange, co. Dublin, gent.
1778 ,, Edward, Straw, co. Derry
1800 ,, Edward, Dublin, esq.
1808 ,, rev. Edward, Mount Barnard, co. Tyrone
1779 ,, Eliz., wife to Thos. Edwards, Capel-street
1783 ,, Elizabeth, Dublin, spinster
1725 ,, Francis, in parts beyond seas (Copy)
1769 ,, George, Bury-street, par. St. Catherine, London, esq. (Copy)
1675 ,, Hugh, Londonderry, merchant
1691 ,, Hugh, carter to the train of artillery at the camp
1743 ,, Hugh, Castlegore, co. Tyrone, esq.
1713 ,, James, Charlesville, co. Cork, gent.
1781 ,, James, Oldcourt, co. Wicklow
1790 ,, Jas., vestry clerk St. Andrew's par., Dublin.
1807 ,, James, Monkstown, co. Dublin, gent.
1710 ,, John, Dublin, gent.
1728 ,, John, Oldcourt, co. Wicklow, esq.
1729 ,, John, Rorington, Shropshire, esq. (Copy)
1743 ,, Mary, Kensington, Middlesex, sole daughter and heir of Fras. E., Welham, Leicestershire, esq. (Copy)
1770 ,, Osburn, Dublin, gent.
1740 ,, Oswald, Dublin, merchant

1640 **Edwards**, Richard, Dublin, tailor (Imperfct)
1671 ,, Richard, Carrickfergus
1735 ,, Richard, Dublin, esq.
1762 ,, capt. Richard, of the 83rd regt. of foot
1654 ,, Samuel, soldier in Drogheda [V. 54
1780 ,, Samuel, Golden-lane, Dublin, schoolmaster
1785 ,, Samuel, Drogheda-st., Dubl., cabinetmaker
1684 ,, Sarah (Ex.)
1675 ,, Thomas, Londonderry, gent.
1722 ,, Thomas, Castlegore, co. Tyr., esq.
1726 ,, Thomas
1754 ,, Thomas, Dublin, merchant
1761 ,, Thomas, Dublin, merchant
1778 ,, Thomas, Dublin, gent.
1767 ,, William, Northstrand, Dublin, mariner
1756 **Eeles**, capt. John
1771 ,, Robert, lately a capt. in gen. Johnstone's regt.
1767 ,, Sarah, wid. of John E., esq.
1713 ,, William, par. St. Margaret, Westminster, Middlesex, apothecary (Copy)
[See ECCLES.]
1743 **Effingham**, Francis, earl of (Copy)
1801 **Egan**, Bowes, Annagh, co. Galway
1805 ,, Carbery, Cork city
1799 ,, Constantine, Dublin, woollen draper
1760 ,, Daniel, Canturk
1736 ,, Darby, Dublin, esq.
1806 ,, Elinor, Dunblany, co. Galway, widow
1737 ,, Howard, Annameadle, co. Tipperary, esq.
1785 ,, James, Kilmurrey, co. Kildare
1803 ,, James, Dunblany, co. Galway, esq.
1754 ,, John, Dublin, gent. [gent.
1781 ,, John, Ballycane, co. Limerick,
1792 ,, John, Cooldorogh, King's co., gent.
1796 ,, John, Dunblany, co. Galway, gent.
1803 ,, John, Aughrim, co. Galway, gent.
1807 ,, John, Cork city
1810 ,, John, Dublin city, esq.
1778 ,, Mary, Dublin, spinster
1760 ,, Patrick, Kilcock, co. Kildare, maltster
1775 ,, Patrick, Dublin, carpenter
1787 ,, Patrick, Meath-street, Dublin, hatter

1808 **Egan**, Patrick, Doonis, co. Westmeath, farmer
1807 ,, Robert, Bishop-street, Dublin
1799 ,, Stephen, Galway town, M.D.
1779 ,, Thomas, Dublin, merchant
(By decree)
1759 ,, Valentine, Dublin, timber mer.
1720 ,, William, Rathgarvan, co. Kilkenny, gent.
1795 ,, Winifred, spinster
[See HAGAN.]
1772 **Egar**, John, Killarney, co. Kerry,
gent.
[See EAGER.]
1771 **Egerton**, Anne, wife to John
Egerton
1627 ,, John, dean of Kildare
1748 ,, John, mariner on board yacht
"Dublin"
1756 ,, Thomas, Drogheda
1663 ,, William, preb. of Killadrif, co.
Tipperary
1732 ,, hon. William, par. St. James,
Westminster, esq. (Copy)
1778 **Egger**, James, Ballymachan, co.
Down, mariner
1804 **Eggleso**, Peter, Stafford-st., Dubl.,
upholder
1736 **Eglin**, Mathias, Dublin, founder
1744 ,, Mathias, Dublin, brassfounder
1753 **Egmont**, Catherine, dow. countess
(Copy)
1748 ,, John, earl of (Copy)
1793 **Eife**, James, Donaghmore, co.
Meath, gent.
1779 ,, Luke, Donaghmore, co. Meath,
esq.
1760 ,, Valentine, Harlockstown, co.
Meath, gent.
1784 **Ekenhead**, Thomas, Newry, co.
Down
1776 **Ekins**, Alexander, Anglesea-st.,
Dublin, carpenter
1655 **Elcocke**, Edward, Drogheda, mer.
[**V.** 129
1606 ,, James, Drogheda, merchant
1616 ,, Nicholas, Drogheda, alderman
1801 **Elder**, Walter, Ballynaguard, Lib.
of Derry
1754 **Elesmere**, Tullamore, King's co.,
esq.
1787 **Elgee**, Charles, Dundalk, co. Louth
1734 **Eliott**, Catherine, *alias* **Keeting**,
Waterford, widow
1773 ,, Cordelia, Great Britain-street,
Dublin, widow
1783 ,, James, Smithfield, co. Down,
innkeeper
1792 ,, Laurana, Newtown, co. Louth,
widow

1805 **Eliott**, Martin, South Lib. of Cork
1736 ,, Robert, New Ross, co. Wex.,
D.D.
1769 ,, Sarah, Toomond or Sheepwalk,
co. Wicklow, widow
1665 ,, William, Dublin, innkeeper
[See ELLIOT.]
1598 **Elleis**, Thomas, dean of Kildare
1748 **Ellery**, Harriss, Kinsale, co. Cork,
gent.
1771 ,, John, Treffans, co. Meath,
farmer
1798 **Ellicott**, Honor, *alias* **Keaghry**,
Galway town, widow
1627 **Elliot**, dame Alson, Dublin, wid.
1756 ,, David, Dingle, co. Kerry
1623 ,, Edward, New Ross, gent.
1765 ,, Elizabeth, widow of Richard
E., esq.
1775 ,, George, Dublin, tailor
1755 ,, Henry, Anadroghill, co. Down
1787 ,, Isabella, Gartetrehid, co. Fer.
1773 ,, James, Dromrollagh, co. Fer.,
gent.
1729 ,, John, Lowtherstown
1747 ,, John, Ringsend, co. Dublin,
fisherman
1768 ,, John, Tomon, co. Wicklow,
brewer
1800 ,, Lucy, widow
1654 ,, Mary, widow		[**V.** 58
1751 ,, Richard, Tinneslatty, co. Kilkenny, gent.
1771 ,, Richard, Rathculbin, co. Kilkenny, esq.
1759 ,, Robert, Clonmore, co. Kilk.,
gent.
1772 ,, Robert, Killacar, co. Cavan
1787 ,, Susana, Watling-st., Dublin,
widow
1590 ,, Thomas, Balreask, co. Meath,
gent.
1629 ,, Thomas, Balreask, co. Meath,
esq.
1668 ,, Thomas, Dublin, esq.
1685 ,, Thomas, St. Patrick-st., Dubl.
gardener
1788 ,, Thomas, Carntown, co. Meath
1696 ,, William, Rathmoran, co. Ferm.
(Ex.)
[See ELIOTT.]
1785 **Ellis**, Allice, Dublin, widow
1780 ,, Arthur, Ballyheady, co. Cavan,
esq.
1781 ,, Brabazon, Wyddial, Hertfordshire
1807 ,, Dawson, Dublin city
1739 ,, Dianna, par. St. James, Westminster, Middlesex, widow
1773 ,, Edward, Dublin, esq.

1774 **Ellis,** Elizabeth, Tulliglish, co. Tyrone, widow
1789 ,, Elizabeth, Dublin, widow
1773 ,, Francis
1791 ,, Henry, Innisrush, co. Londonderry, esq.
1806 ,, Henry, co. Monaghan (Copy)
1783 ,, Hercules, Cloverville, co. Don., esq.
1772 ,, James, Dublin, shoemaker
1805 ,, James, Clonsagh, co. Dublin, farmer
1782 ,, Jane, Dunbar, co. Fermanagh
1674 ,, John, Kullaghbane, co. Arm.
1750 ,, John, par. St. James, Westminster, Middlesex, esq. (Copy, Large Will)
1755 ,, John, Londonderry, esq.
1764 ,, rev. John, Dublin, D.D., vicar of St. Catherine
1784 ,, John, Newry, co. Down, mer.
1797 ,, Joseph, Dublin, cabinetmaker
1809 ,, Margaret, Dublin city, spin.
1775 ,, Mary, Dublin, widow
1809 ,, Patrick, Kilkenny city
1756 ,, Richard, Dublin, silk weaver
1757 ,, Richard, capt. in gen. Pagett's regt. of foot
1774 ,, Richard, Monaghan town, esq.
1748 ,, Robert, Dublin, gent.
1784 ,, Robert, Drogheda
1801 ,, Sarah, Newry, co. Down, spr.
1810 ,, Sarah
1638 ,, Thos., Athlone, gent. [**IV**. 290
1744 ,, Thomas
1758 ,, Thomas, Belturbet, co. Cavan, esq.
1790 ,, Thomas, Dublin, esq.
1733 ,, Welbore, bp. of **Meath,** q.v.
1732 ,, Wm., surgeon in genl. Pearce's regiment of foot
1738 ,, William, Dublin, dyer
1748 ,, Wm., Bundoran, co. Donegal, gent.
1764 ,, rev. William, Clonykilty, co. Cork, clk.
1765 ,, Wm., Myrtle-grove, co. Cork, gent.
1776 **Ellison,** Edwd., Sohoe, co. Mayo
1794 ,, John, Ballyrate, co. Down
1774 ,, Mary, Dublin, spr.
1764 ,, William, Francis-st., Dublin, woollendraper
1779 **Ellwood,** John, Athy, co. Kildare [See ELLWOOD.]
1781 **Elly,** Samuel, New Ross, co. Wex.
1802 **Elmes,** Edwd., New Ross, co. Wexford, esq.
1793 ,, Henry, Coolherin, co. Wexford, farmer

1703 **Elmes,** John, Ballykerogbeg, co. Wexford, gent.
1801 **Elmore,** Christ., Youghal co. Cork
1662 ,, Richd., Ballyphillip, co. Wat., yeoman
1763 **Elmsby,** Francis, Cork, clothier
1639 **Elphin,** Edwd. King, lord bishop of
1686 ,, John Hodson, bp. of
1720 ,, Dr. Simon Digby, bp. of
1740 ,, Dr. Robert Howard, bp. of
1762 ,, Dr. Edwd. Synge, lord bp. of
1795 ,, right rev. Dr. Charles Dodgson, bp. of
1810 ,, right rev. John Law, lord bp. of
1723 **Elrington,** George, Dublin, gent.
1761 ,, Ralph, Dublin, gent.
1770 ,, Richard, Richmond, co. Dubl., gent.
1740 ,, William, Dublin, carpenter
1743 **Elsey,** Elizabeth, widow [gent.
1760 ,, John, Drumcondra-lane, Dubl.,
1776 **Elsmere,** Edward, Dublin, merchant
1633 **Elsworth,** Wm., Ringsend, esq.
1657 **Elsynge,** Margt., Bristol, widow [**IX.** 5
1783 **Elton,** Anth., Ormond-quay, Dubl., shoemaker
1783 ,, rev. John, Dublin, clk.
1670 **Eltonhead,** Henry, London, esq. [**XII**. 166
1569 **Elward,** Richard, Chapel Isolde
1697 **Elwes,** Jeremy, Froghing, Hertfordshire, esq. (Copy)
1736 **Elwood,** Daniel, Dublin, merchant [See ELLWOOD.]
1755 ,, Francis, Caugher, co. Roscommon, gent.
1740 ,, John, LL.D., senior fellow of Trinity College, Dublin
1692 ,, Jonas, Drogheda, alderman
1727 ,, Jos., Demallstown, co. Meath
1808 ,, rev. Joseph, vicar of Rathcoole
1806 **Ely,** the right hon. Chas. Totenham, marquis of
1783 ,, Henry, earl of
1807 ,, right hon. Jane, march. of
1773 ,, Nicholas, earl of
1770 **Emer,** Mary, Smithfield, Dub., wid.
1714 **Emerson,** Arthur, Dub., gent. (Ex.)
1804 ,, Catherine, Dublin city, widow
1728 ,, Erasmus, Paddock, Queen's co.
1804 ,, Frances, Dublin city, spr.
1774 ,, Francis, Ballysheal, co. Arm., linendraper
1759 ,, John, Wexford, gent.
1790 ,, Martha
1801 ,, Martha, Waterford city, widow
1808 ,, Mary, Dublin city, spr.
1711 ,, Timothy, Lib. of Thomas-court and Dromore, brewer

1796 **Emerson,** Thomas, Dublin city, alderman
1784 ,, Wm., Waterford city, gent.
1800 ,, Wm., Dubl., parchment manufacturer
1743 **Emett,** Christ., Tipperary town, gent.
1762 ,, William, Dublin
1794 **Emmett,** Ann Western, widow
1789 ,, Grace, Tipperary, widow
1803 ,, Robt., Cassino, co. Dub., M.D.
1806 **Emor,** Esther, Dublin city, spr.
1762 ,, James, Dublin
1762 ,, Philip, Dublin, merchant
1713 ,, Richard, Desart, co. Westmeath, gent.
1769 **Empson,** Frances, Dublin, widow
1799 ,, Thomas, Dublin city
1738 ,, William, Dublin, alderman
1761 **End,** Michael, Cork, gent.
1805 ,, Wm., Limerick city, pewterer
1797 **Enery,** Catherine, Frahan, co. Donegal, spr.
1776 ,, Dorothy, wid. of rev. Wm. E.
1756 ,, John, Bounboy, co. Cavan, esq. (Large will)
1741 ,, Patrick, Gardenhill, co. Fermanagh, gent.
1764 ,, rev. William, Killashandra, co. Cavan, clk.
1740 **Engain,** Daniel, Cork, merchant
1650 **England,** Alice
1781 ,, Ann, Ennis, co. Clare, widow
1728 ,, David, Lifford, co. Clare, gent.
1637 ,, Edmond, Limerick, merchant
1771 ,, Elizabeth, wid. of Benjamin E., Clonakenny, co. Tipperary
1759 ,, Richd., Rockmount, co. Clare, esq.
1791 ,, Richard, Limerick, merchant
1634 ,, Thomas Fitzrichard, Limerick, merchant
1792 **English,** Andrew, Little Bridge, co. Waterford
1749 ,, Arch., Oldcastle, co. Meath
1749 ,, Bartholomew, Dubl., victualler
1775 ,, Edmond, Monsborough, co. Tipperary, esq.
1747 ,, Esther, Dublin, widow
1788 ,, Honora, Carrick-on-Suir, co. Tipperary, widow
1733 ,, Jas., Mavillin, co. Arm., farmer
1731 ,, John, Grigg, co. Monaghan
1741 ,, John, Dublin, merchant
1758 ,, John, Cabra-lane, co. Dublin, merchant
1770 ,, John, formerly of Ballymeal, co. Meath, now of Dublin, bleacher
1793 ,, John, Townsend-st., Dublin, merchant

1791 **English,** Nicholas, Frederick-st., Dublin
1657 ,, Robert, soldier **[VI.** 74
1653 ,, Walter, Drumnedaine, yeoman
1763 ,, William, Ballyveelish, co. Tip., farmer
1774 ,, William, Springfield, co. Tipperary
1794 ,, Wm. Alexander, Dubl., esq.
1802 ,, Wm., Magheranesk, co. Ant. [See INGLASS.]
1769 **Ennis,** Andrew, Castlebrowne, co. Kildare, yeoman
1791 ,, Anne, Dublin, widow
1785 ,, Clare, Dublin, widow
1806 ,, Clare, Bridge-st., Dublin
1780 ,, Francis, Drogheda town
1772 ,, Garrett, Horseleap, King's co., dealer
1763 ,, James, Stonybatter, Dublin, publican
1808 ,, James, Brunswick-st., Dublin
1743 ,, John, Dublin, merchant
1763 ,, Michael, Drogheda
1789 ,, Michael, Dublin, silk manufacturer
1791 ,, rev. Michael, curate of Enniskeen, dioc. Clogher
1765 ,, Patrick, Dublin, brewer
1784 ,, Richd., Drumcondra, co. Dub.
1737 ,, Roger, St. Patrick's-close, Dub.
1754 ,, Simon, Dublin, gent.
1778 ,, Wm., Bolton-st., Dubl., grocer
1805 **Enniskillen,** right hon. William Willoughby, earl of
1707 **Ennos,** John, Claristown, co. Meath, farmer
1796 **Enraght,** Bailie, Ricketstown, co. Carlow
1765 ,, Elizabeth, Dublin, widow
1803 ,, Fras., Rathkeale, co. Limerick, attorney
1752 ,, James, Ballyclare, King's co·, esq.
1766 ,, John, Bettyville, co. Carlow, clk.
1781 ,, Mathew., Ballyanne, co. Limerick, gent.
1810 ,, Mathew, Rathkeale, co. Limerick
1808 ,, Owen, Bannagher, King's co., esq.
1803 **Ensor,** Geo., Ardress, co. Armagh, esq.
1787 ,, John, Dublin, esq.
1651 **Entwisley,** Henry, Clonmel, gent.
1651 ,, Laurence, Clonmel, gent.
1564 **Erbery,** Stephen, Dublin, gent.
1710 **Ernault,** Stephen, London, mercht. (Copy)

1772 **Erne**, Abraham, lord baron of Crom Castle, co. Fermanagh
1800 ,, Jane, dow. lady, Dublin
1795 **Erskine**, v. rev. John, dean of Cork
1795 ,, Mary, wife to dean Erskine
1744 **Erwin**, Alexander, Dublin, esq.
1756 ,, Burrowes, Kilkenny
1737 ,, Roger, capt.-lieut. in general Moyle's regt. of foot
      [See IRWIN.]
1705 **Escourre**, John (son of John E.), a pensioned officer
1795 **Esdall**, Elizabeth, Dublin, widow
1728 ,, James, Dublin, hatter
1755 ,, James, Dublin, printer
1759 ,, John, Dublin, painter
1781 ,, Samuel, Dublin, gent.
      [See ISDALL.]
1678 **Esmond**, Francis, son to William E., Johnstown, co. Wexford, decd., esq. (Copy)
1652 ,, captain Laurence, Limerick, co. Wexford
1772 ,, Thomas, Templeshannon, co. Waterford, gent.
1569 ,, sir Walter, knt.
1810 **Esmonde**, Elizabeth, Wicklow town
1799 ,, Ellis, Dublin, widow
1760 ,, sir John, Huntingdon, co. Carlow, bart.
1787 ,, rev. Laurence, Ballinkeel, co. Wexford
1738 ,, Richd., Ballyconlore, co. Wexford, esq.
1805 ,, sir Thomas, Ballinastra, co. Wexford
1769 ,, sir Walter, Cregg, co. Tipperary, bart.
1691 **Espie**, William, Maghera, co. Derry, merchant
1757 **Espinasse**, Margaret
1740 ,, Paul, Dublin, brewer
1792 ,, William, Baldoyle, co. Dublin, esq.
1744 **Espine**, rev. Joseph, prebendary of Swords
1801 **Essam**, Thomas, Dublin
1576 **Essex & Ewe**, Walter, earl of, earl marshal of Ireland, viscount Hertford and Bourchier, lord Ferrers of Chartley, Bourchier, and Louvain, kt. Garter   [v. p. I. 1
1737 **Essey**, Martin, Dublin, merchant
1743 **Essington**, Henry, Dunlavin, co. Wicklow
1746 **Este**, Charles, bp. of **Waterford**, q. v.
1730 ,, Frances, widow of Michael E., esq.

1758 **Este**, Susannah, wid. of Dr. Charles E., bishop of Waterford
1761 **Etheridge**, James, Dublin, mercht.
1720 **Etherton**, William, Dublin, joiner
1788 **Euart**, Thomas, Dublin, bookbinder
1674 **Eustace**, Alexander, Carragh, co. Kildare, gent.
1752 ,, Alexander, Craddockstown, co. Kildare, esq.
1756 ,, Alexander, Commonstown, co. Kildare, farmer
1779 ,, rev. Alexander, Swords, co. Dublin, clk.
1783 ,, Alexander, St. James's-place, Middlesex, esq. (Copy)
1809 ,, Alexander
1780 ,, Alice, Donnybrook, co. Dublin, widow
1699 ,, Alis, Cradockstown, co. Kildare, spr.
1736 ,, Andrew, Lowthstown, co. Kildare, gent.
1808 ,, Andrew, co. of Dublin city
1784 ,, Ann, Thomas-street, Dublin, widow
1809 ,, Ann, Moore-st., Dublin, widow
1711 ,, Anne, Craddockstown, co. Kildare, widow
1690 ,, Catherine, Yeomanstown, co. Kildare
1679 ,, dame Charity, widow of sir Mau. Eustace, late Lord Chancellor
1801 ,, Charles, Dublin, esq.
1756 ,, Christopher, Crookstown, co. Kildare, gent.
1597 ,, Edmond, Elwardstown, co. Dublin, gent.
1762 ,, Edward, Tinneslatty, co. Kilkenny, gent. (Copy)
1772 ,, Edward, Tinneslatty, co. Kilkenny, gent.
1809 ,, Edward, Castlemore, co. Carlow, esq.
1751 ,, Frances, Cardore town, but of St. John's Abbey, co. Kildare, spr.
1718 ,, Frans., Castlemore, co. Carlow, esq.
1742 ,, James, Dublin, gent.
1743 ,, James, Yeomanstown, co. Kildare, esq.
1790 ,, James, Knockavanna, co. Galway, gent.
1799 ,, James, Naas, co. Kildare, shopkeeper
1623 ,, John, Harristown, co. Kildare
1704 ,, sir John, Brenockstown, co. Kildare, knt.
1760 ,, John, Naas, co. Kildare

1770 **Eustace,** John, Marlbrook, co. Limerick, gent.
1802 ,, John, New Ross, co. Wexford, tallow chandler
1588 ,, Margaret, Walterstown, co. Kildare, widow [**I.** 41
1692 ,, Margt., *alias* **Keeting,** Dubl., widow
1738 ,, dame Margaret, widow
1751 ,, Margaret, Dowdingstown, co. Dublin, widow
1758 ,, Margaret, Gammonstown, co. Kildare, spr.
1775 ,, Martha, Dublin, widow
1759 ,, Mary, *alias* **Dillon**
1670 ,, sir Maur, knt., Lord Chancellor of Ireland (Copy)
1692 ,, Maurice, Rathkenagh, co. Meath, gent.
1703 ,, Maurice
1737 ,, Maurice, Dowdingstown, co. Dublin, gent.
1681 ,, Nicholas, Confy, co. Kildare, esq.
1713 ,, Nicholas, Colbinstown, co. Kildare, gent.
1638 ,, Richard, Gurtenvaughan, co. Kildare, gent.
1755 ,, Richard, Dublin, merchant
1646 ,, Robert, Dublin, joiner
1800 ,, Robt., Tullow, co. Carlow, esq.
1805 ,, Robert, Dublin city
1660 ,, Rowland, Blackhall, co. Kildare, gent.
1709 ,, Rowland, Dublin, tailor
1761 ,, Rowland, Crookstown, co. Kildare, gent.
1594 ,, Thomas Fitzrowland
1629 ,, Thomas, Dublin, tanner [**II.** 128
1732 ,, Thomas, Castlemore, co. Carlow, gent.
1746 ,, William, Craddockstown, co. Kildare, gent.
1763 ,, William, Dublin, esq. [See EAUSTACE.]
1766 **Evans,** Ambrose, Kilkenny, esq.
1803 ,, Ann, Williamstown, co. Dublin, widow
1747 ,, Anne, Dublin, widow
1787 ,, Anne, *alias* **Brewster,** Ballywilliamroe, co. Carlow
1804 ,, Anne, Exchequer-street, Dublin
1773 ,, Bartholomew, Trim, co. Meath, gent.
1729 ,, Catherine, Dublin, widow
1776 ,, Charles, Drogheda, brazier
1633 ,, David, Dublin, gent., late servant to lord viscount Montgomerie

1792 **Evans,** Edward, Kilkenny, alderman
1708 ,, Edwards, Dublin, merchant
1726 ,, Elinor, Limerick
1784 ,, Evan, Dublin, gent.
1729 ,, Frances, Dublin, widow
1659 ,, Francis, Philipstown, King's co., gent. [**VIII.** 12
1780 ,, Francis, Dublin, esq. (Large will)
1710 ,, George, the elder, Ballygrenan, co. Limerick, esq. (Ex.)
1721 ,, George, Carassy, co. Limerick, esq., Privy Councillor
1764 ,, George, Irishtown, co. Dublin, gent.
1768 ,, George, Bullgarden Hall, co. Limerick, esq. (Ex.)
1773 ,, George, Portraim, co. Dublin, esq.
1807 ,, George, Maghmore, co.Tyrone, clerk
1775 ,, Helana Maria
1770 ,, Henry, Ardra, co. Kildare, gt.
1748 ,, Hester, Dublin, widow (Copy)
1718 ,, Hugh, Ballinrobe, co. Mayo, gent.
1586 ,, John, clk., rector of Chiddingfold, Surrey
1655 ,, John, soldier in Dublin [**V.** 133
1723 ,, John, bishop of **Meath,** q. v.
1734 ,, John, Balruddery, co. Dublin, clerk
1754 ,, John, Bullgarden Hall, co.Limk.
1763 ,, John, Ashrow, co. Limerick
1765 ,, John, Waterford, painter
1781 ,, John, lieut. in 54th regt. of foot
1781 ,, John, Limerick, gent.
1802 ,, John, Dublin, gent.
1763 ,, Jonathan, Dublin, apothecary
1799 ,, Joseph, Limerick city, grocer
1775 ,, Joshua, Bridgewater, Somersetshire, gent.
1807 ,, Joshua, Johnsport, co. Meath
1729 ,, Josias, Dublin, glazier
1743 ,, Mary, Dublin, widow
1748 ,, Mary, housekeeper to James Tynte, esq.
1790 ,, Mary, Newmarket, Dublin
1738 ,, Michael, Ballinrobe, co. Mayo, gent.
1785 ,, Michael, Dublin
1723 ,, Nathaniel, Ballywilliamroe, co. Carlow, gent.
1774 ,, Nathaniel, Ballywilliamroe, gt.
1805 ,, Nicholas, Marino Crescent
1762 ,, Owen, Roscrea, co. Tipperary, farmer
1738 ,, Peter, Dublin, surgeon
1719 ,, Ralph, the elder, Dublin, bricklayer

1737 **Evans**, Ralph, Dublin, gent.
1788 ,, Ralph, Greenmount, co. Wexford, esq.
1637 ,, Rice, Dublin, maltster
1703 ,, Richard, Dublin, brewer
1749 ,, Richard, lieut. in genl. Cornwallis's regt. of marines
1754 ,, Richard, Rathmoyle, Queen's co., gent.
1784 ,, Richd.,Killadarry,co.Clare,esq.
1604)
or (,, Robert
1614)
1807 ,, Robert, Knockvillagh, co. Tip., esq.
1722 ,, Simon, Fanningstown,co.Lim., gent.
1775 ,, Sophia, Dublin, widow
1632 ,, Thomas, Dublin, alderman
1763 ,, Thomas, Dublin, chandler
1787 ,, Thomas, Carlow town,chandler
1802 ,, rev. Thomas Waller, Dunmanway, co. Cork   [esq.
1795 ,, Tyrrel, Ballinacourty,co.Limk.,
1797 ,, Walter, Archall, co. Meath, esq. (Large will)
1659 ,, William, soldier   [**VII.** 185
1742 ,, William, lieut.-gen. of His Majesty's Forces (Copy)
1795 ,, William, Ballintemple, near Cork
1798 ,, William, Dublin, merchant
1807 ,, William, Roscrea, co. Tip.
1788 **Evatt**, Abraham, Dublin, gent.
1655 ,, Blanch, Dublin, widow [**V.** 61
1810 ,, Henry, capt. in the Monaghan Militia   [esq.
1754 ,, Hmphrey, Cootehill, co. Cavan,
1759 ,, Kilner
1769 ,, Prudence, Dublin, spinster
1654 **Eveans**, David, soldier   [**V.** 53
          [See EVANS.]
1780 **Evelyn**, Elizabeth, Dublin, widow
1756 **Everard**, Benjamin, Dublin, esq.
1731 ,, Christopher, Randalstown, co. Meath, esq.
1720 ,, Easter, widow of William E.
1632 ,, Edmond, Fidert, clerk
1755 ,, Edmond, Carrigmore, co. Tip., gent.
1637 ,, Edward,Fethard,co.Tipperary, burgess
1657 ,, Henry, Clonmel, innkeeper   [**VI.** 147
1710 ,, James, Finglas, co. Dublin, gt.
1624 ,, sir John, knt., Fethard, co. Tipperary
1638 ,, John, Fethard, co. Tipperary, son and heir to Nicholas E., deceased

1764 **Everard**, John, Randalstown, co. Meath, esq.
1805 ,, John, Dublin city
1753 ,, Margaret, Kilcash, co. Tip., spinster
1795 ,, Mary Long, Thurles, co. Tip., widow
1633 ,, Nicholas, Fidert, esq.
1746 ,, sir Redmond, Fethard, now in France, bart.
1687 ,, sir Redmund, Fethard, co.Tip., bart.
1577 ,, Roger, Limerick, alderman
1720 ,, William, Newtown, co. Meath, gent.
1754 ,, William, Dublin, gent.
1799 ,, William, Youghal
1639 **Evers**,Cisly,Ballyvarden,co.Meath, gent (Copy)
1767 ,, Francis, Dublin, chandler
1706 ,, John, Drogheda, merchant
1743 ,, John, Dublin, baker
1810 ,, Michael, Larah, co. Westmeath
          [See IVERS, JEVERS.]
1762 **Eves**, Caleb, Baltrasney, co. Kildare, gent.
1771 ,, Drothy, widow of Joseph Eves
1781 ,, Hannah,widow of Joshua Eves, Killeen, King's co.
1731 ,, John, Clonmore, King's co.
1730 ,, Joseph, Edenderry, King's co.
1767 ,, Joseph, Dublin, tallow chandler
1800 ,, Mark, Baltrasy, co. Kildare
1769 ,, Mary, Edenderry, King's co.
1722 ,, Richard, Deer-park, Queen's co., farmer
1788 ,, Samuel, Edenderry, King's co.
          [See IVES.]
1789 **Evory**, James, Dublin, merchant
1679 **Ewer**,John,Bennescesy, co. Catherlogh, esq.
1687 ,, Rose, Dublin, spinster
1781 ,, Thomas, Limerick, merchant
1781 ,, William, Clounluenny,co. Tip., gent.
1699 **Ewine**, Jane, Dublin, widow
1765 **Ewing**, Alexander, Dublin, bookseller
1764 ,, George, Dublin, bookseller
1790 ,, James, Prussia-street, Dublin, gent.
1774 ,, Patrick, Dublin, merchant
1809 ,, Patrick, James's-street, Dublin
1792 ,, Robert, Barbadoes, merchant (Copy)
1776 ,, Thomas, Dublin, bookseller
1668 **Exham**, John, Dublin, esq.
1781 ,, John, Greek-street, Dublin, esq.

1771 **Exham**, Thomas, Frankford, King's co., gent.
1727 **Exshaw**, Edward, Dublin, merchant
1748 ,, Edward, Dublin, bookseller
1768 ,, Elizabeth, Galway, spinster
1746 ,, John, Dublin, merchant
1776 ,, John, Dublin, bookseller
1767 ,, Thomason, Dublin, widow
1742 **Exton**, Sarah, wife of George E., Tower-street, London, cornfactor (Copy)
1673 ,, Thomas, Dublin, gent.
1626 **Eyears**, Silvester, Cappoquin, carpenter
1732 **Eyme**, Susana, Dublin, widow
1739 **Eyre**, Edward, Galway town, esq.
1782 ,, Edward, Galway town, esq.
1698 ,, Elizabeth, widow of John E., Waterford, esq.
1757 ,, very rev. Giles, dean of Killaloe
1704 ,, capt. Henry, co. Galway
1743 ,, Jane, one of daughters of col. John E., of Eyrecourt
1761 ,, Jane, Galway, widow
1670 ,, John, Waterford, esq. [esq.
1685 ,, John, Eyre Court, co. Galway,
1742 ,, John, Woodfield, co. Galway, esq.
1745 ,, John, Eyrecourt, co. Galway, esq.
1792 ,, John, lord baron of Eyrecourt
1769 ,, Mary Anne, Dublin, widow
1778 ,, rev. Richard, D.D., rector of Brightwalten (Copy) [esq.
1780 ,, Richd., Eyrecourt, co. Galway,
1780 ,, Richard, Mount Hedges, co. Cork, esq.
1792 ,, Robert, Galway, esq.
1787 ,, Samuel Blake, Fort St. George, in India
1795 ,, Sarah, Dublin, spr.
1768 ,, Stratford, Dublin, esq.
1773 ,, Thomas, Dublin, esq. [esq.
1775 ,, Thomas, Dromoyle, King's co.,
1799 ,, Thomas, Devizes, Wilts., esq. (Copy) [esq.
1799 ,, Thomas, Eyreville, co. Galway,
1765 ,, William, captain in sir Peter Halket's regt. of foot
1707 **Eyres**, Mary, Waterford, widow
1747 ,, Rowland, Cappinown, King's co., cabinet-maker

—F—

1785 **Fabre**, Charlotte, Dublin, spr.
1721 ,, John, French refugee, Dublin
1662 **Facit**, James, corporal of the earl of Meath's troop
[See FAUCETT.]

1799 **Facon**, Ballen, Mount Stewart, co. Dublin, esq.
1801 **Fadden**, Christopher, Abbey-st., Dublin city, gent.
1729 **Fade**, Johan, captain in colonel Dubourgay's regt. of foot
1727 ,, John, Dublin, merchant
1748 ,, Joseph, Dublin, merchant
1762 ,, Jos., Anne-st., Dubl., merchant
1791 ,, Sarah, Dublin, widow
1661 **Fagan**, Alson, *alias* **Finglasse**, Dub., widow
1806 ,, Angel, Dublin city, widow
1695 ,, Anne, Dublin, widow
1605 ,, Catherine
1804 ,, Catherine, Dublin city, spr.
1806 ,, Celia, wife to James Fagan
1730 ,, Charles, Dublin, merchant
1629 ,, Eleanor, Dublin, widow
1750 ,, Elizabeth, Dublin, spr.
1785 ,, Elizabeth, Arran-quay, Dublin, widow
1789 ,, Elizabeth, Dublin, widow
1792 ,, Ellinor, Southpark, co. Roscommon, spr.
1721 ,, Hugh, Kilcarrig, co. Carlow, gent.
1808 ,, Jas., Naas, co. Kild., publican
1643 ,, John, Feltrim, co. Dublin, esq.
1683 ,, John, Waterford, merchant
1781 ,, John, Dublin, gent.
1784 ,, John, Sligo, merchant
1798 ,, John, Dublin, gent.
1750 ,, Judy, Mullingar, co. Westmeath, widow
1733 ,, Luke, Dublin, gent.
1802 ,, Mathew, Baltrassy, co. Kildare
1785 ,, Nich., Mullingar mills, miller
1754 ,, Patrick, Baronstown, co. Westmeath, farmer
1799 ,, Patrick, doctor in physic
1610 ,, Richard, Dublin, alderman
1764 ,, Sarah, *alias* **Geering**, Dub., spr.
1599 ,, Thomas, Dublin, gent. [I. 98
1742 ,, Thomas, Johnstown, co. Dubl., gent.
1753 ,, Thos., Fryanstown, co. Wickl., farmer
1786 ,, Wm., Tober, co. Westmeath, farmer
1806 ,, William, Longagar, co. Westmeath
1636 **Fagane**, Gerald Fitzwilliam, Kells, co. Meath (Copy)
1637 ,, John, Waterford, merchant
1636 ,, Wm., Kells, co. Meath, mercht.
1810 **Fahy**, Francis, Balleighler, co. Galway, esq.
1804 ,, Malachy, the elder, Dalgin, co. Mayo

1614 **Fahy**, Owen, Darr, co. Kildare
1680 ,, Wm., Ballydulgare, co. Westmeath, farmer
1802 **Fairbrother**, Isaac, Castledermot,
co. Kildare, farmer
1784 ,, Thomas, the Combe, co. Dublin
1795 ,, William, Willsborough, co.
Wicklow, esq.
1800 **Fairchild**, Thos., Kells, co. Meath,
victualler
1787 **Faircloth**, Henry, Ennis, co. Clare,
gent.
1765 ,, Thomas, Ballinacreggy, co.
Galway, gent.
1634 **Fairfax**, George, Armagh, esq.
(Original delivered out ;
copy)
1713 ,, Thomas, Dubl., major-general
1733 **Fairfield**, David, Dublin, esq.
1804 ,, Richard, Bemers-st., Middlesex (Copy)
1687 **Fairlie**, Wm., Fullivirie, co. Down,
gent.
1750 ,, William, Lisburn, co. Antrim,
gent.
[See FARLEY.]
1735 **Fairtlough**, Oliver, Drogheda, ald.
1753 ,, Oliver, Drogheda, esq.
1801 ,, Oliver, Drogheda, alderman
1804 ,, Oliver, Drogheda, esq.
1745 **Falkiner**, Caleb, Cork, merchant
1706 ,, Daniel, Dublin, merchant
1727 ,, Daniel, Dublin, merchant
1759 ,, Daniel, Dublin, alderman
1792 ,, Francis, Kilbeggan, co. Westmeath
1785 ,, Frederick, Cottage, co. Dublin,
esq.
1745 ,, John, Kevins-st., co. Dublin,
esq.
1748 ,, Mary, Dublin, widow
1766 ,, Mary, Cork, widow
1752 ,, Joseph, Dolphin's Barn
1698 ,, Richard, Dublin, clothier
1734 ,, Richard, Mount F., co. Tipperary, esq.
1786 ,, Richard, Mount Sallem, co.
Tipperary, esq.
1793 ,, Thomas Todd, Dublin, esq.
[See FAULCONER, FAULKINER,
FAULKNER.]
1810 **Falkner**, Ann, Pitt-st., Dublin, wid.
1799 ,, Danl., Abbottstown, co. Dubl.,
esq.
1777 ,, Mary, Dolphin's Barn, co. Dub.,
widow
1798 ,, sir Riggs, Annmount, co. Cork,
bart.
1801 ,, rev. Thomas, Killbeggan, co.
Westmeath

1806 **Fallon**, Ann, Hanover-st., Dublin
1807 ,, Anthony, Tuam, co. Galway
1753 ,, Bryan, Runnymead, co. Roscommon, esq.
1758 ,, Bryan, Coolgarry, barony of
Athlone, gent.
1801 ,, Catherine, Boyle, widow
1724 ,, Charles, Sligo, merchant
1771 ,, Charles, Galway, merchant
1751 ,, Christopher, Emlagh, co. Rosc.
1762 ,, Edmond, Highlake, co. Rosc.
1783 ,, Hugh, Ballyconnell
1800 ,, Hugh, Ballinasloe, co. Galway
1802 ,, James, Ashfield, co. Galway,
esq.
1809 ,, John, Clonagh, co. Rosc., esq.
1734 ,, Laurence, Coolgarry, co. Rosc.
1796 ,, Laurence, Ballinasloe, co. Galway, gent.
1771 ,, Margt., Killala town, widow
1789 ,, Margaret, widow
1756 ,, Mary, Emlagh
1757 ,, Patrick, Cloonagh, co. Roscommon, gent.
1629 ,, Peter, Athlone
1797 ,, Roger, Attironey, co. Roscommon, gent.
1733 ,, Stephen, Athlone, co. Roscommon, merchant
1759 ,, Susanna, Athlone
1744 **Falloon**, Jeremy, par. of Ballinderry,
co. Antrim, innholder
[See FALLON.]
1788 **Falls**, Alexander, Ballygawley, co.
Tyrone, distiller
1799 ,, Alexander, Newry
1763 ,, Esther, Londonderry, widow
1741 ,, William, Falses, par. of Kir-
kenedy, co. Fermanagh,
merchant
1747 **Falvey**, Cornelius, Dublin, mercht.
1793 ,, Daniel, Moynoe, co. Clare
1745 ,, John, Fahah, co. Kerry, gent.
1752 ,, John, Cork, merchant
1808 ,, John, Killarney, co. Kerry, esq.
1658 **Fancourt**, Thomas, Grantham, co.
Lincoln, clk. **[VII.** 57
1744 **Fane**, Charles, lord visct. (Copy)
1766 ,, Charles, lord visct. (Copy)
1727 ,, Elizabeth, par. St. Anne, Westminster, Middlesex, widow
(Copy)
1706 ,, Henry, Baseldon, Berkshire,
knight of the Bath (Copy)
1637 **Faninge**, Symon, Limerick, alderman
1782 **Fanner**, Laurence, Belturbet, co,
Cavan
1807 **Fannin**, Mary, Thomas-st., Dublin,
widow

1786 **Fannin**, Nicholas, John's-lane, Dublin, woollen draper
1807 ,, Patrick, Thomas-street, Dubl., innholder
1805 ,, Robert, Bride's-alley, Dublin, cabinet maker
1697 **Fanning**, Edward, Limerick, gent.
1791 ,, rev. Edward, Dublin, clk.
1742 ,, Francis, Bordeaux, now at Limerick, merchant
1789 ,, James, Dublin, clothier
1730 ,, Laurence, Ballingarry, co. Tipperary, schoolmaster
1660 ,, Nicholas, Lispopell [**VIII**. 65 [See FANNIN, FANNON.]
1770 **Fannon**, Margaret, late of Dublin, now of Bella, co. Roscommon, widow
1758 ,, Thomas, Thomas-street, Dubl., merchant
1766 **Fant**, Francis Xaverius, Dubl., gent.
1732 **Faran**, Patrick, Rush, co. Dublin, fishmonger [See FARRAN.]
1806 **Farange**, John, Dublin city, mercht.
1741 **Farcy**, Jeremiah, Plunkett-street, Dublin, grocer
1731 ,, John, lieut.-col. in col. Pocock's regiment of foot
1727 **Fargher**, Charles, Dublin, cooper
1787 **Faris**, Jane, Enniskillen, co. Fermanagh, widow
1771 ,, George, Machen, co. Cavan, gent.
1795 ,, Peter, Balinakill, co. Carlow, gent.
1785 ,, Thomas, Cavan, co. Cavan, esq.
1725 **Farjou**, David, native of Nîmes, in Languedoc, now of Dublin
1778 **Farley**, Patrick, Ballymore Eustace, co. Dublin, innholder
1708 ,, Richard, Gurtemonagh, co. Donegal, gent.
1798 ,, Robert, Limerick city, glove and breeches manufacturer
1686 ,, Thomas, Bristol, gent. [See FAIRLIE, FARRELLY.]
1749 **Farmar**, Robert, Cork, esq.
1771 **Farmer**, Hovell, Dublin, M.D.
1715 ,, Jasper, Ardevalane, co. Tipperary, esq. (Ex.)
1808 ,, Martha, Cork city, spinster
1691 ,, Richd., Ardra, co. Cork, gent.
1662 **Farneham**, John, Ballynock, co. Cork, gent.
1800 **Farnham**, Barry, earl of
1624 ,, Humphrey, Dublin, gent.
1759 ,, John, lord baron of
1775 ,, Judith, dowager lady
1779 ,, Robert, earl of

1795 **Farnham**, rt. hon. Sarah, dow. countess [See FARNEHAM.]
1797 **Farquahar**, Hester, Dublin city, spinster
1733 **Farquarson**, John, Dublin, esq.
1777 **Farquhar**, Thomas, Limerick, cordwainer
1809 **Farran**, Charles, York-st., Dublin, esq.
1788 ,, Christopher, Dublin, mariner
1778 ,, Curtis, Dublin, gent.
1808 ,, Elizabeth, Eccles-st., Dublin, spinster
1768 ,, John, Dublin, gent.
1782 ,, John, James-st., Dub., gent.
1782 ,, John, Rush, mariner
1802 ,, Stephen, Rush, co. Dublin
1786 ,, William, the elder, Dublin, merchant [See FARAN, FARREN, FEARON.]
1761 **Farren**, Thomas, Cork, alderman
1733 **Farrell**, Anne, *alias* **Beeres**, wife to James F., esq.
1770 ,, Barney
1804 ,, Bernard, Summerhill, co. Dub., publican
1704 ,, Bryan, Dublin, tailor
1748 ,, Bryan, Kill, co. Kild., yeoman
1788 ,, Catherine, Dublin
1807 ,, Catherine, Palmerstown, co. Dublin
1777 ,, Charles, Usher's-quay, Dublin, M.D.
1789 ,, Charles, Dublin
1725 ,, Christopher, Dublin, gent.
1659 ,, Connell, Ballavauter, co. Roscommon, gent. [**VII**. 21
1742 ,, Daniel, Montrath, co. Westmeath, farmer
1800 ,, Daniel, late of Slanylough
1804 ,, Daniel, Moods, co. Kildare
1762 ,, Denis, formerly of Clonlyon, co. Galway, now of Dublin
1787 ,, Denis, Rathfarnham, co. Dub., miller
1754 ,, Dennis, Dublin, stonecutter (dated 1754, but not proved)
1754 ,, Dennis, Dublin, stonecutter
1776 ,, Dominick, Waterford, mercht.
1729 ,, Edmond, Chapel Izod
1729 ,, Edward, Dublin, merchant
1751 ,, Edward, John-street, Dublin, clothworker
1770 ,, Edward, Dublin, barrister-at-law
1747 ,, Elizabeth, Dublin, spinster
1760 ,, Faghny, Dublin, merchant
1702 ,, Faughny, Dublin, vintner
1720 ,, Fergus, Dublin, gent.

1732 **Farrell**, Fergus, London, merchant (Copy)
1777 ,, Henry, Sligo, co. Sligo
1803 ,, Henry, Arran-quay, Dub., esq.
1701 ,, Ignatius, Ballboy, co. Meath, farmer
1721 ,, Jas., Lanesborough, co. Long-ford
1738 ,, James, Killmore, co. Roscom-mon, esq. (Ex.)
1743 ,, James, Dublin, silkweaver
1776 ,, James, esq.
1799 ,, James, Cornmarket, Dublin, hosier
1810 ,, James, Bride's-alley, Dublin, cabinetmaker
1716 ,, John, Stamullin, co. Meath, tanner
1735 ,, John, Waterford, merchant
1745 ,, John, Drogheda
1755 ,, John, Dublin, glazier
1767 ,, John, Dublin, brewer
1794 ,, John
1800 ,, John James, Clonlyon, co. Gal-way, esq.
1805 ,, John, Palmerstown, co. Dubl.
1760 ,, Margaret, Cork, widow
1753 ,, Martha, Charleville, co. Cork, widow
1808 ,, Mary
1801 ,, Mathew, Ballgeen, co. Meath, farmer
1797 ,, Michael
1801 ,, Nicholas, town of Cavan
1787 ,, Paul, Waterford city (Copy)
1780 ,, Peter, New-row-on-Poddle, Dublin
1791 ,, Peter, Painstown, co. Meath, farmer
1777 ,, Richard, Parliament-st.,Dubl., merchant
1798 ,, Richard, King-street, Dublin, gent.
1745 ,, Robert, Dublin, linen draper
1659 ,, Rose, widow of Connell Farrell, Bellavauter, co. Roscom-mon, gent. **[VII.** 22
1764 ,, Rose, Dublin, spinster
1770 ,, Sylvester, Bride-street, Dublin, ale seller
1728 ,, Thomas, Dublin
1751 ,, Thos., Clonmel, co. Tipperary, farmer
1759 ,, Thomas, Dowth, co. Meath
1762 ,, Thomas, Dublin, merchant
1809 ,, Timothy, Lower Digges-street, Dublin, coach broker
1741 ,, William,Braithwaite-st.,Dubl., sheerman
1749 ,, William, Dublin, gent.

1788 **Farrell**, William, Tullamore, King's co., merchant
1806 ,, William, late of Ballsbridge, co. Dublin
[See FARRELLY, FERRALL, FERRELL.]
1806 **Farrelly**, Bryan, Claughwallybegg, co. Cavan
1769 ,, Daniel,Rathendrick,co. Meath, farmer
[See FARLEY.]
1732 **Farrer**, Ann, *alias* **Goof**, *alias* **Ward**, Rahins, co. Mayo, widow
[See FERRER.]
1721 **Farrie**, Paul, Limerick, burgess
1807 **Farrington**, William, N. E. Lib. of Cork
1751 **Farthing**, Elizabeth, Cork, spin.
1738 ,, Robert, Cork
1804 **Faucett**, James, Rathdrum, co. Wicklow
1778 ,, John, Dublin, merchant
1798 ,, John,Mullyard,co. Fermanagh, gent.
1804 ,, Joseph, Dublin city
1792 ,, Robert, Harolds Cross, Dublin, householder
[See FAWCETT.]
1775 **Fauchey**, Stephen, Dublin, gent.
1801 **Faucitt**, Paul, Ballintogher, King's co.
[See FAWCET.]
1672 **Faulconer**, David, Merchants'-quay, Dublin
1642 ,, William, London, draper (Copy)
1775 **Faulker**, George, Dublin, alder-man
1795 **Faulkiner**, Samuel, Dublin, esq.
1808 **Faulkner**, Frederick, Charlemont-street, Dublin, esq.
1757 ,, Sarah, Stoneybatter, co. Dubl., widow
1753 ,, Thomas, Dublin, merchant
1718 **Faure**, John, Portarlington,Queen's co., gent.
1770 ,, Sarah, Dublin, spinster
1785 **Faussett**, John, Coolarkin, co. Fermanagh, gent.
[See FAWCETT.]
1722 **Faussill**, De la Renatus, Sligo, esq.
1749 **Favier**, John, Dublin, esq.
1755 **De Faviere**, Ann, Dublin, widow
1752 **Fawcett**, Edward, Dublin, linen-draper
1787 ,, Edward, Waterford city
1761 ,, John, Dublin, glass grinder
[See FACITT, FAUCETT, FAUCITT, FAUSSETT.]

1682 **Fay**, Alice, *alias* **Plunkett**, Dubl., widow
1777 ,, George, Richmond, co. Dublin, gent.
1805 ,, Jane, Navan, co. Meath
1764 ,, Laurence, Finglestown, co. Meath, farmer
1629 ,, Myler, Bellaughmoon, co. Kildare, esq.
1687 ,, Stephen, Gartlestown, co. Westmeath, clerk
1799 ,, William, Annsborough, co. Kildare, miller
1752 **Faye**, Francis, Robinstown, co. Meath
1629 ,, Myler,Commerstown,co.Meath, (Copy)
1759 **Fayle**, Benjamin, Court Duffe, co. Kildare
1777 ,, John, Killonan, co. Limerick city, gent.
1770 ,, Richard, Killmoney, co. Kild.
1758 ,, Robert, Killone, King's co., farmer
1800 ,, Samuel, Dublin, tobacconist
1806 ,, Samuel, Circular-road, Dublin, esq.
1791 ,, Thomas, Dublin, merchant
1807 ,, Thomas, Waterford city
1808 ,, Thomas, Thomas-st., Dublin, merchant
1770 ,, William, Ballymullmore, co. Meath
1639 **Feabales**, John, Balladown, King's co., gent.
1720 **Fearne**, James, par. St. James, Westminster, Middlesex, Com. Chanr. (Copy)
1720 ,, Margaret, par. St. James, Middlesex, widow (Copy)
1713 **Fearnes**, Tobertynan, co. Meath
1769 **Fearon**,Lancelot, Bailieborough,co. Cavan [See FARRAN.]
1799 **Feely**, Darby, Elphin, co. Roscommon, dealer
1787 ,, Daniel, Dublin, gent.
1714 **Feild**, Mathew, Dublin, presser [See FIELD.]
1769 **Felan**, Patrick, Kilcoleman, co. Limerick, gent.
1787 ,, Sarah, Belville, co. Limerick, widow
1792 **Fell**, Nicholas, Clonmel, co. Tip., gent.
1787 ,, Robert Edward, hamlet of Clitha, co. Monaghan, esq. (Copy)
1798 ,, rev. Hans Thomas, Waterford, clerk

1781 **Fellows**, Charles, Leixlip, co. Kildare, smith
1742 **Felster**, George, Dublin, merchant
1716 **Feltham**, Owen, Dublin, gent.
1776 ,, Salisbury, Dublin, widow
1711 **Feltoe**, Jeremiah, lieut. in brigadier Newtown's regt.
1809 **Fenlon**, Rose, Merrion, co. Dublin, widow
1729 **Fenn**, Edward, Cork, brewer
1767 ,, John, Johnstown, co. Carlow, gent.
1725 ,, Joseph, Cork
1732 ,, William, Cork, sugar baker [See FINN.]
1801 **Fennel**, Robert, Garryroan, co. Tip.
1747 **Fennell**, Anthony, Birr, King's co., innholder
1806 ,, Charlotte, Caher, Abbeyville, co. Tipperary
1665 ,, Gerald, Dublin, M.D.
1736 ,, Hester, widow
1760 ,, James, Scarravahane, co. Lim.
1688 ,, John, Windy House, co. Kilkenny, gent.
1733 ,, John,Ballymorely,co.Limerick, gent.
1764 ,, John,Kilcommon,co.Tipperary
1766 ,, John, Shangunah, Queen's co., gent.
1807 ,, John, Cork city, chandler
1809 ,, John, Naas, co. Kildare, shopkeeper
1724 ,, Joseph,Dungan,co. Tipperary, gent.
1764 ,, Joshua, Kilcommonmore
1803 ,, Joshua, Caher Abbey, co. Tipperary, esq.
1666 ,, Jowan Fitz James, wid. of John Butler
1804 ,, Paul, Landscape, co. Cork, esq.
1606 ,, Richard,Coleigh, co. Tipperary
1775 ,, William, Shrurebank, co. Tipperary
1808 ,, William, Cloughreen, co. Tipperary
1801 **Fenner**, Alexander
1737 ,, Richard, Dublin, gent.
1754 ,, William, Dublin, esq.
1779 ,, William, Dublin, attorney
1768 **Fensley**, Henry
1733 **Fensom**, Richard, Dublin, gent.
1804 **Fenton**, Benjamin, Strabane, co. Tyrone
1608 ,, sir Geffrey, Dublin, knt.
1786 ,, John, Dublin, esq.
1664 ,, sir Maurice, Mitchelstown, co. Cork, bt.
1741 ,, Patrick, Dublin, gent.
1773 ,, Percy, Dublin, merchant

1660 **Fenton,** Reignold, Inchgrane, co. Antrim, gent.
1757 ,, Richard, Knockinargin, co. Wicklow, gent.
1769 ,, Richard, Shelton, co. Wicklow, gent.
1788 ,, Thomas, Dromore, co. Sligo
1671 ,, sir William, Mitchelstown, co. Cork, knt.
1671 ,, sir William, bart., son of sir Maur.Fenton, Mitchelstown, co. Cork, bart., decd.
1786 **Fenwick,** Margaret
1667 **Fenwicke,** John, Clonmore, co. Catherlogh, esq.
1665 ,, Joshua, Clonmore, co. Catherlogh
1675 ,, Ralph, Mahoony, co. Cork, esq.
1782 **Ferae,** Joseph Lewis, Dublin, esq.
1657 **Fercher,** George, minister in the parish of Kilburron
[VI. 238
1758 **Fergus,** Hugh, Galway, M.D.
1761 ,, John, Dublin, M.D.
1799 ,, Marine
1769 ,, Mary, Dublin, widow
1801 ,, Mary, Galway town, widow
1780 ,, Patrick, Galway town, gent.
1764 ,, Thady, Gobulane, co. Leitrim, merchant
1797 ,, Wm., Tuam, co. Galway, M.D. [See FERGUSON.]
1766 **Ferguson,** Andrew, Coleraine, co. Derry, merchant
1769 ,, Andrew, Strabane, co. Tyrone, gent.
1808 ,, sir Andrew, Londonderry city
1769 ,, Henrietta, Portadown, co. Armagh, widow
1747 ,, John, Belfast, apothecary
1750 ,, John, Strabane, co. Tyrone
1798 ,, John, Limerick city, merchant
1775 ,, Margaret, spinster
1803 ,, Margt., formerly of Drogheda, but late of Dublin, widow
1736 ,, Mary, *alias* **Ellis,** *alias* **Jackson,** widow
1724 ,, Samuel, Dromore, co. Down, gent.
1793 ,, Samuel, Belfast, co. Antrim, merchant
1794 ,, Saml., Markethill, co. Armagh, gent.
1729 ,, Victor, Belfast, M.D.
1763 ,, Victor, dissenting minister of Strabane
1772 ,, Victor, Newry, co. Down
1734 ,, Wm., capt. in col. Anstruther's regt. of foot
1760 **Fergusson,** John, Mourne, co. Down

1798 **Feriss,** Charlotte
1770 ,, Joseph, Dublin, merchant
1635 **Fermoy,** David, viscount (Copy)
1694 **Ferne,** William, Dublin, clk.
1673 **Ferneley,** Philip, Dublin, esq.
1732 ,, rev. Philip, Monasterevan, co. Kildare, clk.
1699 **Fernelly,** Henry, St. Kevan's-street, Dublin, esq.
1736 **Fernely,** Mary, Dublin, widow
1724 ,, Phineas, Finglas, co. Dublin, esq.
1634 **Fernes & Leighlin,** Thomas Ram, bp. of
1721 ,, Bartholomew Vigors, bp. of
1772 ,, Dr. Edward Young, bp. of
1787 ,, Dr.Walter Cope, bp. of (Large will)
1789 ,, Dr. William Preston, bp. of
1669 **Ferral,** Richard, Baron, co. Longford, esq. (Copy)
1742 **Ferrall,** Ambrose, Dublin, gent.
1808 ,, Ambrose, city of Execter (Exeter ?), esq.
1802 ,, Andrew, Athlone, co. Rosc.
1720 ,, Bryan, Narramore, co. Kildare, popish priest
1744 ,, Bryan, James'-street, Dublin
1809 ,, Charles, formerly of Dublin, late of Madeira, mercht.
1769 ,, Danl., Multifarnham, co.Westmeath
1786 ,, Daniel, Corker, co. Rosc.
1787 ,, Edwd., Booterstown, co. Dubl., esq.
1675 ,, Faghny, Newtown, co.Longford
1741 ,, Fergus, Ardanragh, co. Longford, gent.
1738 ,, Fras., Lanesborough, co. Longford, merchant
1766 ,, James, Clonburg, co. Sligo, esq.
1782 ,, James, Thomas-street, Dublin, grocer
1806 ,, James, Johnstown, co. Dublin
1767 ,, John, Rainsford-street,Dublin, gent.
1779 ,, John, Dublin, M.D.
1800 ,, John, Lanesborough, co. Longford, gent.
1689 ,, Marcus, Tinillke, co. Longford, esq.
1768 ,, Mary, Dublin, widow
1808 ,, Mathew, Clara, King's co.
1787 ,, Mathias, planter, Island St. Croix, West Indies (Copy)
1699 ,, Morgan, Ballyglass, co. Roscommon, gent.
1798 ,, Patk., Philipstown, King's co.
1722 ,, Richard, Dublin, brewer
1741 ,, Richard, Dublin, esq.

1790 **Ferrall,** Richard, Ballina, co. Kildare, esq.
1799 ,, Richard, Corker, co. Roscommon, esq.
1634 ,, Robert, Bawen, co. Longford, esq.
1736 ,, Robert, Dublin, brewer
1807 ,, Robert, Dublin city
[See FARRELL.]
1720 **Ferrand,** Nicholas, formerly captain in La Michlonier's regt.
Ferrar, John
[See FERRER, FERRERS.]
1731 **Ferrard,** Henry, lord baron
1731 **Ferre,** Michael, Dublin, gent.
1759 **Ferrell,** Anne, Dublin, widow
1769 ,, Daniel, Multifarnham, co. Westmeath
1723 ,, James, London, esq. (Copy)
[See FARRELL.]
1700 **Ferrer,** John, Dublin, esq.
1658 ,, William, Dromore, co. Down, esq.
[See FARRER, FERRERS.]
1701 **Ferrers,** Charles, Wicklow, late of Hertford, Hertfordshire, esq.
1754 **Ferress,** John, Mawkin, co. Cavan, gent.
1786 **Ferris,** Elisha, Cork city, gent.
[See FRY.]
1731 **Ferriter,** Redmond, Ballymanhig, co. Kerry, gent.
1712 **Feryes,** William, Whitehaven, Cumberland, mercht. (Copy)
1728 **Fetherston,** Cuthbert, Dardistown, co. Meath
1766 ,, Eliz., Whiterock, co. Longford, widow
1748 ,, Francis, Whiterock, co. Longford, gent.
1757 ,, Francis, student in Trinity College, Dublin
1788 ,, Gertrude, Dublin, widow
1764 ,, v. rev. John, dean of Leighlin, co. Catherlow
1776 ,, John, Dardistown, co. Westmeath
1810 ,, Mary, Mosstown, co. Westmeath
1780 ,, sir Ralph, Ardagh, co. Longford, bart.
1794 ,, Richard, Dublin, gent.
1779 ,, Robert, Dublin, esq.
1728 ,, Thomas, Castlekearan, co. Meath
1749 ,, Thomas, Ardagh, co. Longford
1772 ,, Thos., Carrick, co. Westmeath, esq.
1776 ,, Thomas, Bracklin, co. Westmeath

1790 **Fetherston,** Thomas, Killiney, co. Dublin, esq.
1771 ,, William, Carrick, co. West meath, esq. (Large will)
1742 **Fiddis,** Alexander, Tullycreevy, co. Fermanagh, gent.
1660 **Fidge,** John, Dublin, merchant [**VIII.** 144
1758 **Field,** Anne, Dublin
1803 ,, Anne, Drogheda, widow
1794 ,, Dominick, Galway town, farmer
1762 ,, Elizabeth, Dublin, widow
1784 ,, Elizabeth, Dublin, widow
1624 ,, James, Dublin, M.D.
1758 ,, Jas., Combe, Dublin, ale seller
1785 ,, John, Dublin, clk.
1758 ,, Joseph, Waterford, formerly a glover
1768 ,, Judith, Dublin
1761 ,, Michael, Sycamore-alley, Dub., ale seller
1629 ,, Thomas, Dublin, merchant
1782 ,, rev. Thomas, Fieldmount, co. Armagh, clk.
[See FEILD.]
1792 **Fielding,** Ann, Peppard's Castle, co. Wexford, widow
1722 ,, sir Charles, Dublin, knt.
1804 ,, Frances, Dublin city, spr.
1701 ,, Henry, major in sir John Hammer's regiment
1785 ,, Mark, Dublin, heraldic painter
1794 ,, Mary, Ranelagh-road, Dublin, widow
1781 ,, Stopford, Ballygarrett, co. Wexford, esq.
1733 ,, William, Dublin, coachmaker
1743 **Fieragh,** Maurice, Dublin, carpenter
1652 **Fifield,** John, Dundalk (Copy)
1772 **Filgate,** Alexander, Lisrenny, co. Louth, gent.
1659 ,, Saml., Dubl., weaver [**VII.** 166
1787 ,, Steph., Ardee, co. Louth, gent.
1673 ,, Thomas, Oxmanstown, near Dublin, innkeeper
1785 ,, Thomas, Ardee, co. Louth, esq.
1721 ,, Wm., Lisrenny, co. Louth, gent.
1670 **Finaghty,** Elinor, *alias* **Fabruck,** Turnins, co. Kildare
1726 **Finch,** Edwd., Kilcoleman, co. Tipperary, gent.
1806 ,, Elizabeth, Birr, King's co.
1738 ,, Margaret, Dublin, widow
1803 ,, Potter, Birr, King's co.
1685 ,, Ralph, Chester, gent.
1638 ,, Rebecca, Dublin, widow
1669 ,, Richard, Dublin, gent.
1789 ,, Roger, Birr, King's co., gent.
1686 ,, Symon, Kilcoleman, co. Tipp., esq.

1778 **Finch**, Symon, esq.
1673 ,, Wm., London, mercht. (Copy)
1779 ,, William, Cork, esq.
1631 **Finche**, John, Dub., gent., attorney
    of the Court of Chancery
1792 **Findlay**, Catherine, Dublin, widow
1784 **Findley**, John, the elder, Dublin,
    staymaker
1762 **Finegan**, Bryan, Drogheda, tanner
1719 ,, John, Dunfert, co. Kild., gent.
1809 ,, Thomas, Parkgate-st., Dublin,
    gent.
    [See FINIGAN.]
1723 **Finemore**, Isaac, Ratoath, co.
    Meath, gent.
    [See FINNEMORE.]
1743 **Finey**, George, Celbridge, co. Kil-
    dare, gent.
1686 **Fingal**, Lukus, earl of
1637 ,, Margaret, dow. countess of
1749 **Fingall**, Frances, countess of
1699 ,, Mabell, dow.countess of
1719 ,, Peter, earl of (Copy)
1739 ,, Robert Plunkett, commonly
    called earl of
1603 **Finglas**, Eliz., *alias* **Luttrel**, Dis-
    vetstown, widow
1607 ,, John, Westphalstown, co. Dubl.,
    esq.
1663 ,, Mary, *alias* **Dowde**, relict of
    col. Edward Dowde, Dublin
1640 ,, Walter, Ballycooled, Queen's
    co., gent.
    [See FINLASSE, FYNGLAS.]
1745 **Finglass**, Thomas, Dublin, mercht.
1758 **Finigan**, John, Balcarrick, co. Dub.,
    farmer
1726 ,, William, Mucklin, co. Kildare,
    gent.
    [See FINEGAN.]
1804 **Finiston**, Samuel, Breakhart, co.
    Antrim
1666 **Finlasse**, Richard, Dublin, gent.
1670 **Finlay**, James, Killashandra, co.
    Cavan, merchant
1734 ,, John, Dublin, merchant
1768 ,, John, Carnafenoge, co. Fer-
    managh, merchant
1769 ,, John, Dublin, gent.
1754 ,, Margaret, Dublin, widow
1805 ,, Mary, Dublin city, spr.
1786 ,, Sarah, Dublin, spr.
1776 ,, Thomas, Dublin, esq.
1804 ,, William Henry, Ginnetts, co.
    Meath
1772 **Finley**, Holland, Dublin, mercht.
1764 ,, John, Dublin, grocer
1763 ,, William, Donard, co. Wicklow,
    gent.
1809 **Finn**, Daniel

1777 **Finn**, Edmond, Kilkenny, printer
    and bookseller
1767 ,, George, Mountmellick, Queen's
    co., merchant
1777 ,, Luke, Colloony, co. Sligo, gent.
1748 ,, Mathew, Naul, co. Dub., farmer
    [See FENN, FYN, FYNN.]
1789 **Finnemor**, Thomas, Rathbawn, co.
    Kildare
1737 **Finnemore**, John, Ballyward, co.
    Wicklow, gent.
    [See FINEMORE.]
1762 **Finnex**, Math., Newry, co. Armagh
1810 **Finny**, Richard
1807 ,, Thomas
1762 ,, William, Dublin, carpenter
1753 **Finucane**, Andw., Ennis, co. Clare,
    gent.
1808 ,, Daniel, Ennis, co. Clare, esq.
1771 ,, Edmond, Ennis, apothecary
1792 ,, Michael, Ennis, co. Clare, M.D.
1795 **Firman**, Richard Flood, Slevoir, co.
    Tipperary
1733 **Fish**, Benjamin, Tubberogan, co.
    Kildare, esq.
1742 ,, Elizabeth, *alias* **Ashe**, widow
    of John F., esq.
1694 ,, Joseph, Kilkea, co. Kildare,
    gent.
1736 ,, Joseph, Tubberogan, co. Kil-
    dare, esq.
1763 ,, William, Kenna, co. Kildare,
    esq.
1784 **Fishbourne**, Robert, Carlow town,
    watchmaker
1796 **Fishcourne**, William, Carlow town
1637 **Fisher**, lady Alice, Dubl., widow
                   [**IV.** 280
1787 ,, Andrew, Gardiner's-row, Dubl.,
    esq.
1805 ,, Anne, Dublin city
1761 ,, Benjamin, Springhill, Queen's
    co. esq. (Large will)
1810 ,, Betty, formerly of Youghal, late
    of Cork, widow
1734 ,, Bridget, par. St. James, West-
    minster (Copy)
1751 ,, Catherine
1772 ,, Catherine, Dublin, widow
1660 ,, Edwd., Craddockstown, co.Kil-
    dare, esq.   [**VIII.** 57
1722 ,, Edward, Youghal, co. Cork,
    merchant
1806 ,, Esther, Wexford town
1765 ,, Frances, widow of rev. Robert
    F., Dublin, clk.
1655 ,, Francis, soldier   [**V.** 65
1790 ,, George, Carneville, co. Meath,
    esq.
1588 ,, Henry, Dublin, gent.

1744 **Fisher**, Henry, Dublin, merchant
1750 ,, Henry
1794 ,, Henry, Slape, co. Meath, esq.
1721 ,, Jas , Clonenagh, Queen's co., gent
1785 ,, Jane, Dublin, widow
1650 ,, John, Dublin
1809 ,, Jonathan, Great Ship-st., Dub.
1716 ,, rev. Joseph, Dublin, clk.
1750 ,, Lancellot, Aghnamallagh, co. Monaghan, gent.
1801 ,, Margt., Drogheda town, widow
1806 ,, Mary, Dublin city, widow
1672 ,, Maudlin, Naas, widow
1768 ,, Preston, Balsoon, co. Meath
1655 ,, Richard,sergeant of foot [**V.** 62
1661 ,, Richard, Fermoy, co. Cork,esq.
1679 ,, Richard, Dublin, gent.
1705 ,, Richard, Bolton, Lancashire, yeoman
1769 ,, Richard, Slane, co. Meath, clk.
1748 ,, Robert, Ballyvas, co. Kildare, gent.
1751 ,, Robert, Dublin, clerk
1808 ,, Ruben, Youghal, co. Cork, merchant
1802 ,, Samuel, Dublin, painter and paper stainer
1805 ,, Samuel, Antrim, co. Antrim
1738 ,, Sarah, Dublin, widow
1643 ,, capt. Thomas
1663 ,, Thomas, Ballyboy, co. Louth, gent.   [co., gent.
1716 ,, Thomas, Rathleague, Queen's
1739 ,, William, Dublin, merchant
1773 ,, William, Kurn, co. Londonderry, merchant
1785 ,, William, Kevin-street, Oxm., Dublin, gent.
1798 ,, William, Drogheda, tanner
1806 ,, William, Antrim
        [See FYSHER.]
1787 **Fitch**, Peter, Ballymacky, co. Mon., esq.
        [See FITZPATRICK.]
1758 **Fitton**, Richard, the elder, Cork, tanner
1760 ,, Richard, Cork, brewer
1786 ,, William, Cork city, burgess
1780 **Fitzgerald**, Alexander, Ballybrittas, Queen's co., gent.
1769 ,, Allen, Dublin, merchant
1750 ,, Andrew, Waterford, merchant
1808 ,, Ann, North King-st. Convent, spr.
1788 ,, Anna Dorothea
1808 ,, Anna Margaretta (called lady Ann Fitzgerald)
1690 ,, Anne, wife to James Fitz G., esq.

1723 **Fitzgerald**, Anne, Johnstown, co. Tipperary, spr.
1769 ,, Anne, Ballyrider, Queen's co., widow
1775 ,, Anne, Ballydavis, Queen's co., widow
1781 ,, Anne, daughter to Maurice F., Puchersgrange
1755 ,, Anstace, Waterford, widow
1792 ,, Arthur, Dublin, esq.
1707 ,, Augustine, Carrowkeal, co. Clare, esq.
1776 ,, Augustine, Sixmilebridge, co. Clare, esq.
1793 ,, Begnet Monica, Trim, co. Meath, widow
1765 ,, Bridget, Limerick, widow
1757 ,, Catherine, Dublin, widow
1786 ,, Catherine, Morett, Queen's co., widow
1750 ,, Charles, Clonshanboe, co. Kildare, gent.
1776 ,, Charles, Castlekeal, co. Clare, esq.
1782 ,, Charles, Ballyroan, Queen's co., esq.
1804 ,, Charles Augusta, Tullasee, co. Clare
1671 ,, Christopher, Dublin, esq.
1687 ,, Cisly, Geydenstown,co. Kildare, spr.
1757 ,, Colclough, Ballyrider, Queen's co., gent.
1763 ,, David, Cork, merchant
1781 ,, David, Coolnamoney, Queen's co., farmer
1584 ,, Edmond, Clondaly, par. Killyhan
1676 ,, Edmond, Inismore, co. Kerry, gent.
1724 ,, Edmond, Dublin, lace mercht.
1757 ,, Edmond, Kilgobbin, co. Limerick, gent.
1625 ,, sir Edward, Tecroghan, knt.
1731 ,, Edward, Dublin, gent.
1737 ,, Edward, Waterford, merchant
1779 ,, Edward, Dublin, esq.   [esq.
1782 ,, Edward, Inner Temple, London,
1803 ,, Edward, Coolnowle, Queen's co., gent.
1805 ,, Edward, Newpark, co. Wexford
1810 ,, Edward
1719 ,, Elinor, Ballinderry, co. Westmeath, spr.
1732 ,, Elinor, *alias* **Lynch**, Highfort, co. Galway, widow
1697 ,, Elizabeth, Cahirconlish, co. Limerick, widow
1755 ,, Elizabeth, widow of Maurice F., Dingle, esq.

1757 **Fitzgerald**, Elizabeth, King-street, Dublin, spr.
1765 ,, Elizabeth, Dublin, spr.
1769 ,, Elizabeth, Redmondstown, co. Westmeath, widow
1795 ,, Elizabeth, Woodford, co. Kerry, spr.
1630 ,, dame Ellane, widow of sir John F., Deceis, knt.
1727 ,, Ellen, Dublin, widow
1773 ,, Ellinor, Punchersgrange, co. Kildare, spr.
1731 ,, Frances, Limerick, widow
1710 ,, Francis, Corra, King's co., gt.
1796 ,, Francis
1749 ,, Gamaliel, Summerhill, Lib. of Cork, esq.
1684 ,, Garet, Blackwood, co. Kildare, esq.
1792 ,, Garrett, Shannon Grove, co. Limerick, esq.
1669 ,, George, Tecroghan, co. Meath, esq. (Ex.)
1756 ,, George, London, merchant (Copy)
1761 ,, George, Castledermot, co. Kildare, watchmaker
1764 ,, George, Margaret-st., Cavendish-square, Middlesex, esq.
1781 ,, George, par. St. James, Westminster, Middlesex, esq.
1638 ,, Gerald, archdeacon of Emly
1650 ,, Gerald, Dublin, gent. [**VI.** 40
1656 ,, Gerald Fitz Thomas, Ballymygall, co. Limerick, gent. (Copy)
1681 ,, Gerald, Ballynard, co. Limerick, esq.
1712 ,, Gerald, Dublin, vintner
1731 ,, Gerald, Rathrone, co. Westmeath, esq.
1740 ,, Gerald, Punchersgrange, co. Kildare, gent.
1743 ,, Gerald, Newtown Hartpole, Queen's co., esq.
1762 ,, Gerald, Kilfenora, co. Clare, gent.
1775 ,, Gerald, Rathrone, co. Meath, esq.
1795 ,, Gerald, Athy, co. Kildare, merchant
1808 ,, Gerald, Tipperary, gent.
1808 ,, Gerald, Dublin city, gent.
1808 ,, Gerald, Tarbert, co. Kerry
1810 ,, Gerald, Ballinvirra, co. Limk.
1616 ,, Gerrot Fitz James, Dromana, co. Waterford, esq.
1616 ,, Gerrot, Athy parish, gent.
1810 ,, Hannah, Johnstown, co. Wexford

1626 **Fitzgerald**, Henry, Carrick, co. Kildare, gent.
1716 ,, Henry, Ballinderry, co. Westmeath, tanner
1775 ,, Henry, Dublin, esq.
1786 ,, Hunt, major in 35th regt. of foot (Copy)
1602 ,, James, Kilrush, co. Kildare
1634 ,, James, Castleton Moylough, co. Westmeath [**IV.** 116
1637 ,, sir James, Ballysonan, co. Kildare, knt.
1663 ,, James, Cluony, co. Clare, gent,
1750 ,, James, Stonehall, co. Clare, esq.
1756 ,, James, Ardmullen, co. Limerick
1759 ,, James, Killylin, co. Westmeath, esq.
1768 ,, James, Milltown, co. Dublin, gent. (Large will)
1784 ,, James, Shipperton, co. Clare, farmer
1786 ,, Jas., par. Marylebone, Middlesex, esq. (Copy)
1785 ,, Jane, Cottage, co. Dublin, widow
1614 ,, John Fitzmorrice, Birton, co. Kildare, gent.
1665 ,, John, Dromana, co. Waterford, esq.
1681 ,, John, Inismore, co. Kerry, esq.
1705 ,, John, Johnstown, co. Westmeath, gent.
1722 ,, John, Lirfune, co. Tipperary, gent.
1725 ,, John, Carrigoran, co. Clare, esq.
1729 ,, John, Park Prospect, co. Cork, esq.
1735 ,, John, London, merchant
1741 ,, John, Dingle, co. Kerry, esq.
1742 ,, John, Dublin, woollendraper
1751 ,, John, Dublin, tailor
1753 ,, John, Lynefune, co. Tipperary, M.D.
1757 ,, John, Dingle, co. Kerry
1758 ,, John, Clonmel, co. Tipperary
1767 ,, John, Ballyweery, co. Limerick, gent.
1784 ,, John, Harley-street, London, esq. (Copy)
1788 ,, John
1790 ,, John, South Cumberland-street, Dublin, esq.
1795 ,, John, Dublin city
1801 ,, John, Rathkeale, co. Limerick, merchant
1806 ,, John, Newtownperry, Limerick, merchant
1735 ,, Laurence, gent.

1661	**Fitzgerald**, sir Luke, Feroghan, knt.	
1750	,,	Margaret
1805	,,	Martin, Kevin-st., co. Dublin, carpenter
1753	,,	dame Mary, Glin, co. Limk., now of Limerick city
1754	,,	Mary
1761	,,	Mary, Dublin, widow
1765	,,	Mary, par. St. George, Hanover-square, Middlesex, widow
1782	,,	Mary, Dublin, spinster
1791	,,	Mary, Glasnevin, co. Dublin, widow
1794	,,	Mary Ann, spr.
1637	,,	Maurice, Ballyfeighan, co. Meath, esq.
1639	,,	Maur., Suracston, par. Swords, co. Dublin, gent.
1657	,,	Maur., Ballyheeny, co. Waterford
1679	,,	Maurice, Castlelisshyne, co. Cork, esq.
1725	,,	Maurice, Dublin, merchant
1762	,,	Maurice, Carlow, miller
1775	,,	Maurice, mariner on board the "Intrepid"
1780	,,	Maurice, esq., Dingle, co. Kerry, commonly called the knt. of Kerry
1584	,,	sir Morrishe, Lecaghe, co. Kildare, knt.
1761	,,	Nicholas, Greensborough, co. Kilkenny, esq.
1797	,,	Nicholas, Limerick city, innholder
1628	,,	dame Onora, Cloyne, widow
1676	,,	Patk., Clane, co. Kildare, gt
1738	,,	Patrick, Kilnacarra, co. Mayo
1768	,,	Pierce, Hardwood, co. Meath, gent.
1781	,,	Pierce, Baltinoran
1581	,,	Redmond Oge, co. Kildare
1622	,,	Richd., Buallybeg, co. Kildare, gent.
1631	,,	Richard, Cardowgha, co. Longford, gent.
1632	,,	Richd., Clunycullan, co. Westmeath, gent.
1670	,,	Richard, Rathrone, co. Meath, gent.
1692	,,	Richard, Waterford, merchant
1705	,,	Richd., Scartmolego, co. Waterford, gent.
1721	,,	Richard, Mountrath-st., Dubl., gent.
1765	,,	Richard, Gurtnerely, co. Limerick, gent.
1776	,,	Richard, Kilminehy, Queen's co., esq. (Large)
1787	,,	sir Richard, bart.

1799	**Fitzgerald**, Richard, esq.	
1800	,,	Richd., Bansha, co. Tipperary, clk.
1800	,,	Richard, Castle Richard, co. Cork, esq.
1672	,,	Robert, Newtown Mahie, co. Meath, gent.
1719	,,	Robert, Lisquinlan, co. Cork, esq. (Copy)
1724	,,	Robert, Castledod, co. Cork, esq.
1778	,,	Robert Uniacke, Corkbeg, co. Cork, esq.
1782	,,	Robert, esq.
1788	,,	Robert, Coolnowle, Queen's co., esq.
1810	,,	Robert, Jervis-street, Dublin, attorney-at-law
1753	,,	Rose, Cork, spr.
1782	,,	Samuel, lieut. and qr.-mr. in 35th regt.
1805	,,	Sidney, Harcourt-street, Dubl., widow
1716	,,	Stephen, Morett, Queen's co., esq.
1771	,,	Stephen, Morett, esq.
1780	,,	Stephen, Portarlington, Queen's co.
1755	,,	Susanna, widow of Gamaliel F., Cork, esq.
1628	,,	Thomas Fitz John, Bosteillan, co. Cork, esq.
1660	,,	Thomas, Newcastle, co. Longford, esq. [**VIII.** 185
1663	,,	Thomas, Ballinabragh, co. Catherlogh, esq.
1667	,,	Thomas, Rath M'Cartie, co. Tipperary, esq., son and heir-apparent of John F., Innishmore, knt. of Kerry
1668	,,	Thos., Kilcromin, Queen's co., esq.
1719	,,	Thomas, Rowlish, Queen's co., gent.
1736	,,	Thos., Ovidstown, co. Kildare, gent.
1740	,,	Thomas, Ardagh, co. Limerick, gent.
1747	,,	Thos., Moyhinnagh, co. Mayo, esq.
1757	,,	Thomas, esq., knt. of Glin, co. Limerick [esq.
1765	,,	Thomas, Morett, Queen's co.,
1771	,,	Thomas, Dublin, esq.
1778	,,	Thomas, Cullen, co. Tipperary, gent.
1788	,,	Thos., Ballybeggan, co. Meath
1801	,,	Thos., Glin, co. Limerick, esq.
1802	,,	Thomas, Kilmeed, co. Kildare, gent.

1806 **Fitzgerald**, Thos., Kailstown, co.
   Kildare, gent.
1809 ,, Thos., Geraldine, co. Kildare
1810 ,, sir Thomas, jun., Lisheen, co.
   Tipperary   [gent.
1784 ,, Timothy, Castleyard, co. Dub.,
1771 ,, Walter, Crossonstown, co.
   Westmeath, gent.
1803 ,, Walter, Ballivagan, co. Kildare
1636 ,, William, Morrigans or Burri-
   gans, co. Limerick, gt.
1651 ., Wm., minister of God's Word
1673 ,, sir William, knt.
1700 ,, William, Cork, esq.
1722 ,, William, bp. of **Clonfert**, q. v.
1739 ,, William, Dublin, grocer
1744 ,, Wm., Baltinoran, co. Meath,
   gent.
1747 ,, Wm., Ballymaddock, Queen's
   co., esq.
1750 ,, William, Dublin [gent.
1763 ,, William, Baltinoran, co. Meath,
1775 ,, William, Ballyroan, Queen's
   co., esq.
   [See FYTZGERALD.]
1791 **Fitz Gibbon**, David, Lisbon, Portugal
1608 ,, Edmond, Mitchelstown, co.
   Cork, esq., called the White
   Knight
1786 ,, Elinor, Dublin, widow
1780 ,, John, Mountshannon, Lib. of
   Limerick, esq.
1772 ,, Thos., Dublin, esq., counsellor-
   at-law
   [See GIBBONS.]
1689 **Fitz Harris**, Barnabie, New Ross,
   merchant
1636 ,, James, Wexford, merchant
1629 ,, Marcus, Mackmayne, co. Wexford, esq.
1666 ,, Richard, Dublin, merchant
   [See FITZ HENRY.]
1772 **Fitz Henry**, Edwd., Middle Temple,
   London
1790 ,, Elizabeth, Enniscorthy, widow
1791 ,, rev. Jeremiah, Meyhill, Dublin,
   clk.
1804 ,, John, Ballymore, co. Wexford
1794 ,, Nicholas, Gobbinstown, co.
   Wexford
   [See FITZHARRIS.]
1782 **Fitz Herbert**, Andrew, Barns Common, Surrey, esq. (Copy)
1744 ,, William, Shircock, co. Cavan,
   esq.
1746 ,, William, esq.
1590 **Fitz John**, Mauri Dermot, Clo-
   nogher, dio. Emly, clk.
   (Copy)

1757 **Fitz Maurice**, hon. Catherine
1751 ,, Deborah, widow of col. the hon
   Wm. F.
1749 ,, Harman, Dublin, esq.
1790 ,, Hester (Copy)
1775 ,, John, Bail, co. Kerry, esq.
1804 ,, Katherine, Peafield, Dublin
   city, spr.
1742 ,, Maurice, Dublin, gent.
1799 ,, Michael, Cork city, livery stable
   keeper
1714 ,, Raymond, Dublin, esq.
1796 ,, hon. Thomas, Lleweney Hall,
   co. Denbigh (Large)
1680 ,, Ullicke, Lishohill, co Kerry,
   esq.
1711 ,, William, Gullane, co. Kerry,
   esq.
1782 ,, William, Lagatarrin, co. Mayo,
   esq.
   [See MORRIS.]
1761 **Fitzpatrick**, Andrew, Byneen, co.
   Galway, gent.
1755 ,, Catherine
1780 ,, Catherine, Thurles, co. Tipperary, widow
1806 ,, Christopher, formerly of Little
   Longford-street, but late of
   Ringsend, co. Dublin
1734 ,, Edmund, Rathneleng, Queen's
   co., farmer
1697 ,, Edwd., Park-place, Middlesex,
   esq. (Copy)
1616 ,, Grany, or Gryssel Inyn Theighe,
   late of Lissballyeteigh, par.
   of Upper Ossory
1786 ,, Hugh, Philipstown, King's co.
1750 ,, James, Carlow, gent.
1766 ,, James, Carrickmacross, co.
   Monaghan
1809 ,, James, Waterford city, cabinet
   maker
1761 ,, Jane, wife to Richard F., Galway, esq.
1810 ,, sir Jeremiah, knt.
1697 ,, John, Park-place, Middlesex,
   esq. (Copy)
1710 ,, John, Sellernamore, co. Galway,
   gent.
1740 ,, John, Dublin, esq.
1760 ,, John, Derrymalonge, Queen's
   co., farmer
1765 ,, John, Clonturk, near Drumcondra, co. Dublin
1784 ,, John, Ballagh, Queen's co.,
   gent.
1805 ,, John, North King-st., Dublin,
   publican
1810 ,, John, Mary's-lane, Dublin,
   slater

1613 **Fitzpatrick,** Jowan, wid. of Thos. **Purcel,** baron of Loughmoe, Tiperary, esq.

1803 ,, Laurence, Sandymount, near Dublin, farmer

1782 ,, Lucy, Drumcondra, co. Dublin, widow

1808 ,, Mary, widow

1805 ,, Michael, Lodge, co. Kilkenny, gent.

1755 ,, Nichs., Fethard, co. Tipperary

1719 ,, Patrick, Dublin, M.D.

1755 ,, Patrick, Kilkenny, gent.

1767 ,, Richard, Galway, esq.

1796 ,, hon. Richard, par. St. Geo., Middlesex

1674 ,, Thady, Dublin, M.D. (Ex.)

1700 ,, Thady, Dublin, esq.

1750 ,, Thady, Ballybooden, co. Kildare, esq.

1735 ,, Thos., Dublin, tallow chandler

1785 ,, Timothy, Ballybooden, Queen's co., esq.

1775 ,, William, Dublin, gent. [See PATRICK.]

1710 **Fitzsimon,** Christopher, Dublin, merchant

1748 ,, Thomas, Dublin, merchant

1750 ,, Thomas, Dublin, gent.

1769 **Fitzsimons,** Anne, Portmarnock, co. Dublin, widow

1797 ,, Anne, Dublin, widow [widow

1741 ,, Bridget, Clonsilla, co. Dublin,

1804 ,, Catherine, Dublin city, widow

1778 ,, Christopher, Dublin, merchant

1768 ,, Edward, Dublin, baker

1791 ,, Gerald, Copper-alley, Dublin

1805 ,, James, Barrack-street, Dublin, chandler

1770 ,, Jane, Dublin, spinster

1752 ,, John, Garradice, co. Meath, gent.

1770 ,, John, Dublin, merchant

1712 ,, Margery, *alias* **Marley,** *alias* **Delamar,** widow

1745 ,, Mark, Ballymadrogh, co. Dub., gent.

1765 ,, Maud, widow of Francis F., Dublin, grocer

1802 ,, Michael, Newtown, co. Dublin, farmer

1775 ,, Patrick, Kilcock, co. Kildare, merchant

1711 ,, Richard, Dublin, merchant

1736 ,, Richard, Clonsilla, co. Dublin, farmer

1757 ,, Richard, Simonstown, co. Meath

1805 ,, Richard, Meath-street, Dublin

1806 ,, Richard, Smithfield, Dublin, hay factor

1808 **Fitzsimons,** Richard, James's-st., Dublin, baker

1671 ,, Thomas, Dublin, gent.

1787 ,, Thomas, Patrick-street, Dubl., carpenter

1755 ,, Walter, New-street, co. Dublin, skinner

1772 ,, Walter, Seamount, co. Cork, esq. (proved in 1774)

1758 ,, William, Garradice, co. Meath, gent.

1801 ,, rev. William, Sydenham, co. Meath, clerk
[See FYTZSYMONES, SIMONS.]

1587 **Fitzsymons,** Nicholas, Dublin (Copy)

1617 ,, Robert, Dublin, merchant

1661 **FitzWilliam,** Christopher, then a sojourner in Catherlogh, gt.

1789 ,, John, genl. of His Majesty's Forces (Copy)

1591 ,, sir Thos. Minonge, co. Dubl., knt. (Copy)

1719 **FitzWilliams,** Christopher, Abbeyboyle, co. Roscommon

1719 ,, Elizabeth, Abbeyboyle, co. Roscommon, widow

1633 ,, Nicholas, Baldungan, co.Dub., gent.

1744 ,, Richard, esq., governor of the Bahama Islands

1736 ,, Thomas, Dublin, gent.

1578 ,, William, Jopston

1767 **Fivey,** Thomas, Loughbrickland, co. Down, merchant

1775 ,, William, Dublin, gent.

1800 **Flack,** Anne, widow

1776 ,, James, Dublin, gent.

1792 **Flahavan,** James, Ballynort, co. Limerick, farmer

1722 **Flaherty,** Bryan, Lemonfield, co. Galway, esq.

1764 ,, Edward, Henbury, Gloucestershire, esq. (Copy)

1800 ,, Edward, Enniskillen, co. Ferm., gent.

1793 ,, Frances, Galway town, spin.

1763 ,, Francis, Anglis, co. Tip., esq.

1768 ,, Julian, Galway, widow

1779 ,, Morgan, Tullykean, co. Galway

1743 ,, Peter, Dublin, brewer

1805 ,, Thomas Marrowbow-lane, co. Dublin city

1801 ,, William, Cork city, mason

1772 **Flahy,** John, Mountmellick, Queen's co.

1806 **Flanagan,** Anthony, Philipstown, King's co.

1723 ,, Arthur, Ballysologh, King's co., gent.

1784 **Flanagan**, Catherine, widow
1726 ,, Charles, Croghan, King's co., gent.
1799 ,, Christopher, Eyrecourt, co. Galway, merchant
1795 ,, James, Dublin city [chant
1750 ,, John, Clara, King's co., mer-
1784 ,, John, Francis-street, Dublin, smith and ironmonger
1807 ,, sir John, Augbee, co. Tip., gent.
1741 ,, Luke, Down, King's co., gent.
1761 ,, Luke, Loughane, King's co.
1796 ,, Nicholas, Enniskillen
1796 ,, Patrick, Edenderry, King's co., publican
1777 ,, Peter, Philipstown, King's co.
1769 ,, Richard, Walterstown
1782 ,, Tamasin, King-st., Oxm., wid.
1787 ,, Terence, Ballyglass, co. Roscommon, gent.
1751 ,, Thomas, Dublin, grocer
1788 ,, Thomas, Monasteroris
1760 ,, William, Rathfarnham, co. Dublin, gardener
1799 ,, William, Tullamore, victualler
[See FLANEGAN, FLANIGAN, FLANNAGAN.]
1769 **Flanary**, Thomas, Limerick
1786 **Flanegan**, Francis, the Barley Fields, Dublin, farmer
1765 **Flanigan**, Dennis, Loughtown, co. Kildare, farmer
1746 ,, William, Dublin, mealman
[See FLANAGAN.]
1775 **Flannagan**, Anthony, Clonsilla, co. Dublin, gent.
1583 **Flatsbury**, Jas., Wesphalstown, co. Dublin, gent.
1741 **Flattery**, Hugh, Ballyteghter, King's co., gent.
1804 ,, John, Attenkee, King's co.
1808 ,, John, Limerick city, mercht.
1662 **Flawne**, Jeremy, clerk, Ballymacarmount, co. Longford
1675 **Flaws**, Richard, Dublin, but now of Maryland, surgeon
1734 **Fleawry**, Amoury Philip, Dublin, clerk
1780 ,, rev. Anthony, Coalbaugher, Queen's co., clerk
1798 ,, John Charles, Dublin, M.D.
1805 ,, Mary, Arran-quay, Dublin, wid.
[See FLEURY.]
1807 **Fleeming**, Peter, Granard,co.Longford (see 1808).
[See FLEMING.]
1776 **Fleeson**, John, Athy, co. Kildare
1739 **Fleetwood**, Charles, Athy, co. Kildare, merchant

1774 **Fleetwood**, Charles, Janeville, co. Kildare
1770 ,, Francis, Ballinagar, co. Meath, gent.
1779 ,, Jane, Cottage, co. Kildare, widow
1800 ,, Robert, Parkstown, co. Meath, esq.
[See FLETEWOOD.]
1754 **Fleming**, Anne, Dublin, widow
1744 ,, Archibald, Killoran, co. Sligo gent.
1766 ,, Arthur, Belville, co. Cavan, esq.
1746 ,, Catherine, Drogheda, widow
1777 ,, Catherine, Ballinacarrow, co. Sligo
1772 ,, Christopher, commonly called lord Slane
1794 ,, rev.Christopher, St. Paul's par., Dublin
1734 ,, Edward, Dublin, gent.
1737 ,, Elizabeth, Dublin, widow
1759 ,, Garret, Carne, co. Kildare
1800 ,, George, Dublin
1755 ,, Ignatius, Waterford, goldsmith
1720 ,, James, lieut. in col. Cope's regt. of horse
1805 ,, James, Belville, co. Cavan
1757 ,, John, lieut. in col. York's regt. of foot
1759 ,, John,Ballintogher, Queen's co., farmer
1763 ,, John, Kilcrony, co. Down,gent.
1766 ,, John, Drogheda, merchant
1777 ,, John, Dunleer, co. Louth, distiller
1785 ,, John, Drogheda, stationer
1807 ,, John, Monasterevan, co. Kild.
1779 ,, Margaret, Anneborough, co. Kildare, widow
1749 ,, Mary, Dublin, widow
1784 ,, Mary, Drogheda, widow
1804 ,, Mary, Smithfield, Dublin, wid.
1733 ,, Mathew, Kilbride, co. Meath, farmer
1794 ,, Mathew, Oldrock, co. Sligo, esq.
1671 ,, Michael, esq.
1744 ,, Michael,Staholmuck,co.Meath, esq.
1806 ,, Michael, Hospital, co. Limk.
1689 ,, Patrick, Boly, co. Tipperary
[See FLEEMING, FLEMYING, FLEMYNGE.]
1642 **Fleminge**, William, Dublin, tailor
1796 **Flemyng**, Roger, Dublin, esq.
1582 **Flemynge**, Christopher, Derpatrick, co. Meath, gent.

1730 **Flemynge**, Richard, Dublin, gent.
1580 ,, Robert Fitz Thos., Drogheda, merchant
[See FLEMING.]
1805 **Flenigan**, Michael, city of Chester (Copy)
1753 **Fletcher**, Bartholomew, Dublin, linen draper
1703 ,, Benjamin, Dublin, esq.
1778 ,, rev. Edward
1722 ,, Elizabeth, Belfast, widow
1807 ,, Elizabeth, Dublin city, widow
1713 ,, rev. George, Armagh town, clk.
1725 ,, George, Dublin, butcher
1703 ,, Henry, Dublin, gent.
1782 ,, Honora, Britain-street, Dublin, widow
1764 ,, James, Dublin, gent.
1683 ,, John, Dublin, ironmonger
1700 ,, John, Lawtowns Hope, Hertfordshire, esq. (Copy)
1703 ,, John, surgeon in lord Kingston's regt. of foot
1732 ,, rev. John, Dublin, clerk
1770 ,, John, formerly of Dublin, now of Clooness, co. Roscommon, gent.
1777 ,, John, Rathfarnham, co. Dublin, gent.
1804 ,, Jone, Lisburn, co. Antrim, widow
1783 ,, Joseph, Dublin, merchant
1756 ,, Mary, *alias* **Stowell**, wife to John F., Dublin, esq.
1766 ,, v. rev. Philip, dean of Kildare (Copy)
1758 ,, Richard, Dublin, apothecary
1789 ,, Richard, Clarendon market, Dublin, grocer
1794 ,, Richard, Cahirnihiny, clk.
1686 ,, Robert, Cork, gent.
1794 ,, Robert, Pitt-st., Dublin, tailor
1761 ,, Thos., bishop of **Kildare**, q. v.
1729 ,, William, St. Andrew Moor, par. Cartmell (Copy)
1772 ,, William, LL.D., dean of Kildare (Copy)
1798 ,, William, Bally M'Loughlin, co. Meath, gent.
1632 **Fletewood**, Thos., Ballydearaven, co. Cork, esq.
[See FLEETWOOD.]
1767 **Fleury**, Charles, Waterford, gent.
[See FLEAWRY.]
1673 **Flin**, John, the Nall, co. Meath, miller
1794 ,, Laurence, Dunfurth, co. Kild.
1800 **Fling**, Daniel, Rathgormuck, co. Waterford
1714 ,, Michael, Dublin, gardener

1790 **Flinn**, Bartholomew, Oberstown, co. Meath, servant
1768 ,, Christopher, Dub., coachmaker
1747 ,, James, Dublin, linendraper
1804 ,, John, Ormond-quay (see 1803)
1771 ,, Laurence, Castle-st., Dublin, bookseller
1782 ,, Margt., Henry-st., Dublin, spr.
1786 ,, Margaret, Dublin, widow
1770 ,, Patrick, Lisefook, co. Roscommon, gent.
1804 ,, Peter, Dunforth, co. Kildare, farmer
1788 ,, Thomas, Carrick-on-Suir, co. Tipperary, glazier
[See FLIN, FLYN, FLYNN.]
1674 **Flinter**, Henry, Barnahill, co. Kildare, gent.
1763 ,, John, Kildare, carpenter
1774 ,, Nebuchadnezzar, Monasterevan, co. Kildare, gent.
1810 **Flood**, Ann, widow of Warden Flood, esq.
1784 ,, Anne, Buzzardstown, co. Dub., widow
1752 ,, Bartholomew, Clonfert, co. Kildare, farmer
1758 ,, Bridget, Dublin, spr.
1800 ,, Catherine, Clavanstown, co. Meath
1770 ,, Charles, Ballymack, co. Kilkenny, esq.
1748 ,, Edmund, Dublin, weaver
1746 ,, Edwd., Derreckrinal, surgeon
1804 ,, Edward, Middlemount, Queen's co., esq.
1763 ,, Elinor, Robertstown, co. Dubl.
1787 ,, Frances, Brunswick-st., Dubl., widow
1730 ,, Francis, Burnchurch, co. Kilkenny, esq.
1766 ,, Francis, Paulstown, co. Kilk., esq.
1771 ,, rev. George, Kilkenny, D.D.
1802 ,, Hatton, lieutenant-colonel of Hompeshe's hussars (Copy)
1791 ,, Henry, Farmley, co. Kilkenny, esq.
1775 ,, Isabella, York city, spr. (Copy)
1759 ,, James, Rathmore, co. Kildare, gent.
1767 ,, Jas., Clavanstown, co. Meath, gent.
1777 ,, Jas., Roper's Rest, near Dubl.
1767 ,, Jeremiah, Dublin, wool comber
1780 ,, Jerome, Athboy, shopkeeper
1734 ,, John, factor in the service of the Royal African Co., on the coast of Guinea (not proved)

1755 **Flood**, John, Rathkennan, co. Tip-
　　perary, esq.
1774 　,,　　John, Flood Hall, co. Kilk., esq.
1808 　,,　　John, Farmley, co. Kilkenny,
　　esq. (Large)
1764 　,,　　Joseph, Cuckolds-row, Dublin,
　　silkthrouster
1732 　,,　　Luke, Navan, co. Meath, inn-
　　keeper
1767 　,,　　Luke, Clavanstown, co. Meath
1800 　,,　　Luke, Roundwood, Queen's co.,
　　esq.
1730 　,,　　Marks, Dublin, gent.
1774 　,,　　Mary, Clonmel, co. Tipperary,
　　widow
1776 　,,　　Mary, Cherryvally, co. Meath,
　　widow
1779 　,,　　Mary, Watling-st., Dub., wid.
1808 　,,　　Mathias, Castleknock, co. Dub.
1791 　,,　　Patrick, Carlow, gent.
1803 　,,　　Peter, president of Maynooth
　　college
1603 　,,　　Richard, Dublin
1689 　,,　　Richard, Dublin, gent.
1703 　,,　　Richard, Colemine, co. Dublin,
　　gent.
1782 　,,　　Robert, Middlemount, Queen's
　　co., esq.
1673 　,,　　Thos., Newtown, co Longford
1775 　,,　　Thos., Cherryvalley, co. Meath,
　　farmer
1779 　,,　　Thos., Buzzardstown, co. Dub.,
　　gent. (Copy)
1649 　,,　　Walter, Dublin, merchant
1764 　,,　　Warden, chief justice of King's
　　Bench in Ireland
1797 　,,　　Warden, Dublin, esq.
1693 　,,　　William, Dublin, gent.
1726 　,,　　William, Dublin, merchant
　　[See FLOYD, FLOYDE.]
1564 **Floody**, Alison, Dublin, widow
1776 **Floory**, Thomas, Drogheda, gent.
1630 **Flower**, Benjamin, Knockmark, co.
　　Meath, yeoman
1718 　,,　　John, Dublin, merchant
1755 　,,　　John, Pill-lane, Dublin, ribbon
　　weaver
1700 　,,　　Thomas, Finglas, co. Dublin,
　　esq.
1681 　,,　　sir William, Finglas, co. Dubl.,
　　knt.
1742 　,,　　William, Dublin, merchant
1658 **Flowers**, David, Dublin, musician
　　　　　　　　　　　　　　[VI. 249
1803 　,,　　John, Dublin, hosier
1790 **Floyd**, Patrick, Ennis, co. Clare
1722 　,,　　Susana, Dublin, spr.
1656 **Floyde**, Henry, Cork　　　**[V.** 332
　　[See FLOOD.]
1799 **Flyn**, Denis, Flynville, co. Wat.

1765 **Flyn**, James, Lisdornan, co. Meath,
　　farmer
1762 　,,　　Patk., Ennis, co. Clare, mercht.
1774 **Flynn**, Festus, the elder, gent.
1768 　,,　　Richard, Dublin, merchant
1796 　,,　　Terence, Richmond-place, co.
　　Dublin
　　[See FLINN.]
1658 **Foard**, Henry, Youghal, innholder
　　　　　　　　　　　　　　[VII. 115
1758 **Foden**, Hannah, Dublin, widow
1735 　,,　　Hugh, Carrick, co. Tip., gent.
1756 **Fodger**, Samuel
1801 **Fogarty**, Elizabeth, Maynooth, co.
　　Kildare, widow
1801 　,,　　James, Maynooth, co. Kildare,
　　publican
1789 　,,　　Nicholas, Urlingford, co. Kilk.,
　　farmer
　　[See FOGURTY.]
1758 **Fogerty**, Thomas, Castle F. or
　　Garrenroe, co. Tip., M.D.
1785 **Fogey**, Malcolm, Portlongfield, co.
　　Cavan
1681 **Fogurty**, Wm., par. of Ensidogurty,
　　co. Tip., M.D. (Copy)
1713 **Foissons**, Marturin, Dublin
1767 **Folds**, Jane, widow of rev. Wm. F.,
　　vicar of Atherdee
1763 　,,　　Wm., Atherdee, co. Louth, clk.
1767 **Foley**, Catherine, *alias* **Burnett**
1803 　,,　　Darry, Tullamore, King's co.,
　　mason
1759 　,,　　Elizabeth, Dublin, widow
1722 　,,　　Hugh, Dublin, yeoman
1754 　,,　　Joseph, now in Dublin
1695 　,,　　Samuel, bishop of **Down**, q. v.
1804 　,,　　Thady, Ballyduffbeg, co. Clare,
　　farmer
1748 　,,　　Thomas, Dublin, druggist
1715 　,,　　William, Copper-alley, Dublin,
　　victualler
1808 　,,　　William
1752 **Folie**, Edward, Dublin, gent.
1643 **Follam**, Rose, widow ; late wife to
　　Robert **Fline**, Dublin, gent.
1614 **Follame**, William, Dublin, baker
1769 **Folliot**, Alice, Dublin, spr.
1670 　,,　　capt. Anthony, Londonderry
1672 　,,　　Francis, Boyle, co. Roscommon
1798 　,,　　Letitia, Dublin
1762 　,,　　John, Lukhill, Worcestershire,
　　col. of the Royal Irish regt.
　　of foot
1765 　,,　　John, governor of Kinsale, esq.
1746 　,,　　Robert, Holycrock, co. Sligo,
　　esq.
1805 **Folliott**, Francis, Serpentine-av.,
　　co. Dublin
1623 　,,　　sir Henry, knt.

1760 **Ford**, Catherine, Drogheda
1705 ,, Edward, Woodpark, co. Meath, esq.
1740 ,, Edward, Island Bridge, co. Dublin, esq.
1750 ,, Edward, Woodpark, co. Meath
1793 ,, Henry, parish priest of Enniskillen, co. Fermanagh
1802 ,, dame Jane Allen, widow
1789 ,, James, Dublin city
1801 ,, James, Ongerstown, co. Meath, farmer
1803 ,, James, Dundalk, co. Louth, esq.
1742 ,, John, Dublin, gent.
1767 ,, John, Sligo, merchant
1792 ,, Judith, Dawson-street, Dublin, widow
1730 ,, Letitia, Dublin, widow
1804 ,, Margaret, Temple-court, Dub., widow
1785 ,, Mary, Dublin, widow
1763 ,, Penelope, Dublin, spr.
1726 ,, Robert, Dublin, merchant
1733 ,, Robert, Dublin, merchant
1746 ,, Robert, Drogheda, widow
1719 ,, Roger, rector par. Dunboe, co. Londonderry, clk.
1757 ,, Roger, Dublin, gent.
1806 ,, Roger, Dublin city
1776 ,, Walter, Dublin, chandler [See FOORD.]
1791 **Forde**, Alice, Lurgan, co. Armagh
1768 ,, Ann, Dublin, widow
1617 ,, Clemente, Knockfergus, burgess
1676 ,, Elinor, Dublin, widow
1772 ,, Francis, Johnstown, co. Meath, esq.
1797 ,, Francis, lieut. in the navy (Copy)
1745 ,, John, Ballyronan, co. Wicklow, gent.
1806 ,, John, Dominick-street, Dublin city
1807 ,, John, Forest, co. Dublin
1773 ,, Margaret, Dublin, spinster
1791 ,, Mary, Moore-street, Dublin
1708 ,, Mathew, Coolgreany, co. Wexford, esq.
1729 ,, Mathew, Dawson-st., Dublin
1781 ,, Mathew, Dublin, esq. [esq.
1795 ,, Mathew, Seaford, co. Down,
1605 ,, Nicholas, Dublin (Copy)
1788 ,, Patrick, Dublin, merchant
1696 ,, Robert, Drogheda, alderman
1795 ,, Robert, Johnstown, co. Meath
1725 ,, William, Drogheda, alderman
1770 ,, William, Liverpool, Lancashire, mariner (Copy)

1726 **Fordice**, John, Antrim town, gent.
1625 **Forestell**, Abraham, Cullen, co. Tipperary, merchant
1724 **Forrest**, Anne, Dublin, widow
1758 ,, Anne, Dublin, widow
1730 ,, Barbara, Dublin, widow
1729 ,, Catherine, Dublin, widow
1803 ,, Charles, Dub., gent., attorney-at-law
1722 ,, Daniel, Dublin, gent.
1723 ,, Francis, Dublin, gent.
1733 ,, John, Lurgan, co. Armagh, linendraper
1794 ,, Martin, Carricktohill, co. Cork, farmer
1713 ,, William, Dublin, gent.
1801 **Forsayth**, Samuel, Dublin [See FORSYTH.]
1685 **Forside**, Wendrie, late minister of Westlemizie, Scotland
1746 **Forstall**, John, Dublin, woollendraper
1681 ,, Luke, Dublin, merchant
1682 ,, Marcus, Dublin, D.D.
1633 ,, Peter, Carrigloniny, co. Kilkenny, gent.
1802 **Forster**, Abraham, Ballymaloe, co. Cork, esq.
1786 ,, Alice, west suburbs of Galway, tanner
1748 ,, Anne, Dublin, spinster
1788 ,, sir Anthony, Tullaghan, co. Monaghan, bt.
1798 ,, Caroline, Dublin, widow
1774 ,, Charles, Dublin, gent.
1711 ,, col. Christian, Blewsworme, in Prussia, in Littowne, late of Monasteroris, King's co., esq.
1774 ,, Christian, Phrapper-lane, Dub., esq.
1582 ,, Christopher, Killeagh, co. Cork, gent.
1783 ,, Christopher, capt. in 55th regt.
1784 ,, Clement, Shanagarry, co. Cork, gent.
1776 ,, Dorothy, Dublin, widow
1785 ,, Elizabeth, Bannagher, King's co., spr.
1773 ,, Francis, Dublin, brewer
1776 ,, Francis, Fortesfield, King's co., esq.
1780 ,, Francis, Newry, co. Down, merchant
1782 ,, Francis, Knockakeeran, co. Donegal, gent.
1779 ,, George, Thomas-street, Dubl., chandler
1792 ,, George, Cork, merchant
1754 ,, Honor, Dublin, widow

N

1804 **Forster**, James, Ballyronan, co. Kildare, farmer
1767 ,, Jefry, Cork, clothier
1613 ,, John, Dublin, alderman
1687 ,, John, Folacham, co. Monaghan, esq.
1700 ,, John, the elder, Clanvoly, co. Monaghan, yeoman
1720 ,, John, Chief Justice of the Com. Pleas in Ireland
1733 ,, John, Thomas-court, Dublin, merchant
1738 ,, John, Tullaghan, co. Mon., esq.
1746 ,, John, Esker, co. Galway, gent.
1751 ,, John, Dublin, surgeon
1753 ,, John, Cavan, co. Cavan, merchant
1780 ,, John, Tullaghan, co. Mon., esq.
1788 ,, rev. John, D.D., rector of Drumragh, diocese of Derry
1790 ,, John, Esker, co. Galway, esq.
1801 ,, Margaret, Lisnagole, co. Fermanagh
1736 ,, Mary, widow
1764 ,, Mary, Dublin, spinster
1776 ,, Mary, London, spinster
1618 ,, Nicholas, Dublin, gent.
1724 ,, Nicholas, Esker, co. Galway, gent.
1743 ,, Nicholas, bp. of **Raphoe**, q. v.
1784 ,, sir Nicholas, Tullaghan, co. Monaghan, bart.
1657 ,, Richard, Baltrea, co. Dublin, clk.   **VI.** 209
1711 ,, Richard, Dublin, esq.
1799 ,, Robert, Bordeaux
1807 ,, Samuel, Kilmurry, co. Meath
1750 ,, Sarah, Dublin, widow
1798 ,, Sarah, Cork city
1657 ,, Thomas   [**VI.** 73
1775 ,, Thomas, Roristown, co. Meath, gent.
1778 ,, Thomas, Dublin, merchant
1802 ,, Thomas, Derryguile, Queen's co., farmer
1722 ,, Walter, Inner Temple, London, late of Trinity College, Dub., esq.
1763 ,, William, late of Kilmurry, now of Trim, co. Meath, gent.
1765 ,, William, Cork, clothier
1771 ,, William, lieut.-col. in genl. St. Clair's regt. of foot
1772 ,, William, Dublin
1789 ,, William, Bray, co. Wicklow, baker
        [See FOSTER.]

1742 **Forsyth**, John, Dromore, co. Down, gent.
1754 ,, John, Aughnecloy, co. Tyrone, merchant
1791 ,, John, jun., Ballinure, co. Ant., tanner
1799 ,, John, Ballinure, co. Antrim. esq.
1791 ,, William, Artikilly, co. Londonderry
        [See FORSAYTH.]
1758 **Fortescue**, Anne, Dublin
1747 ,, Chichester, Dellin, co. Louth, gent.
1757 ,, Chichester, Dublin, esq.
1780 ,, rt. hon. Dormer Fortescue Aland, lord baron
1789 ,, Eliz., Whiterath, co. Louth, widow
1741 ,, Faithful, Dublin, esq.
1786 ,, Faithful, Corderry, co. Louth, esq.
1766 ,, Francis, Achantober, co. Louth, gent.
1788 ,, Gerald, Dublin, esq.
1782 ,, right hon. James
1667 ,, John, Glenavy, co. Antrim
1761 ,, John, lieut. in genl. Adlercron's regiment
1781 ,, rev. John, Whiterath, co. Louth, clk.
1785 ,, Mathew, Dillon, co. Louth
1802 ,, Mathew, Stevenstown, co. Louth, esq.
1764 ,, Thomas, Frankfort, co. Down, esq.
1769 ,, Thos., Dillonstown, co. Louth, gent.
1780 ,, Thomas, Dublin, esq.
1734 ,, William, Newragh, co. Louth, esq.
1809 ,, William, Clare-street, Dublin, esq.
1770 **Forth**, Arthur, Dublin, esq.
1627 ,, Edward, Dublin, gent., 2nd son to sir Amb. Forth, knt., decd.
1789 ,, Eleanor, Dublin
1731 ,, James, Dublin, esq.
1680 ,, John, Redwood, King's co., esq.
1783 ,, Mary, Dublin
1748 ,, Nathaniel, lieut. in genl. Wentworth's regiment of horse
1798 ,, Neville, Dublin, esq.
1761 ,, Saml., Longford, co. Longford, esq.
1747 ,, Susanna, Dublin, spr.
1643 **Forthe**, John, Dublin, gent.
1755 **Fortick**, Tristram, Grange, co. Dublin, esq.

1789 **Fortick**, sir Wm., Belmont, co. Dublin, knt.
1712 **Fortin**, L'Abrosse, Waterford
1759 ,, Ellinor, Lismore, co. Waterford, widow
1741 ,, rev. Simon, Tubbrid, co. Tipperary, clk.
1800 **Fortune**, Terese, Elenaghouse, co. Dublin, spr.
1781 **Forward**, Isabella, city of Bath, widow
1709 ,, John, Castle F., co. Donegal, esq. (Ex.)
1766 ,, Mark, Dublin, upholder
1788 ,, Martha, Dublin
1770 ,, Wm., Castle F., co. Donegal, esq. (Copy)
1774 **Fosberry**, George, Limerick, esq.
1766 ,, William, Limerick, tanner
1779 **Foskey**, William, Beltuckburn, co. Louth
1581 **Foster**, Allen, Rathcoole
1785 ,, Anne, Dublin, widow
1779 ,, Anthony, rt. hon., Lord Chief Baron
1782 ,, Anthony, Dundalk, co. Louth, gent.
1688 ,, Arthur, Drumgoon, co. Fermanagh, gent.
1753 ,, Edward, Dublin, esq.
1771 ,, Edward, Jockey Hall, co. Galway, gent.
1762 ,, Elizabeth, Dublin, widow
1765 ,, Elizabeth, Halles-street, par. of Marylebone, widow
1800 ,, Elizabeth, *alias* **Gerald**
1721 ,, Francis, co. Galway, gent.
1801 ,, Geffry, Cresford, co. Galway, gent.
1792 ,, Hester, Beechhill, co. Galway, widow
1617 ,, John, Dublin, merchant
1703 ,, John, Dublin, gent.
1747 ,, John, Dunleer, co. Louth, esq.
1796 ,, John Thomas, Stone House, co. Louth, esq.
1809 ,, John William, Drogheda, esq., collector
1802 ,, Mary Ann, Meetinghouse yard, Dublin, widow
1760 ,, Simon, Ratorp, co. Galway
1805 ,, Susanna, city of Bath
1784 ,, Thomas, Dunleer, co. Louth, D.D.
1801 ,, Vere Hunt, surgeon to Kilkenny regt.
1797 ,, William, bp. of **Clogher**, q. v.
1803 ,, William, Dowdstown, co. Meath, esq.
[See FORSTER.]

1708 **Fotterall**, Thomas, Dublin, gent.
1591 **Fotterell**, Thomas, Roscall, farmer [See FOTTRELL.]
1691 **Fottiplace**, George, St. Clements Danes, London, merchant (Copy)
1618 **Fottrell**, Ann, Hartwell, co. Kild.
1627 ,, Anne, Hartwell, co. Kildare
1788 ,, Catherine, Dublin, spinster
1768 ,, Elinor, Flinstown, widow [gent.
1785 ,, John, Phrapper-lane, Dublin,
1582 ,, Thomas
1740 ,, Thomas, Fleenestown, co. Meath [See FOTTERALL.]
1741 **Fouace**, Lydia, widow
1791 ,, Thomas, Tyrellspass, co. Westmeath
1728 **Foukes**, Deborah, Ratoath, co. Meath, widow
1726 ,, Ellen, Monasterevan, co. Kild., gent.
1711 ,, John, Dowdstown, co. Kildare, gent.
1732 **Foulk**, Elizabeth, Strawhall, co. Cork, widow
1713 ,, rev. Francis, Ratoath, co. Meath, clerk
1763 **Foulke**, Anne, Youghal, co. Cork, widow
1783 ,, Digby, Tallow, co. Waterford, esq
1810 ,, Digby, Young Grove, co. Cork, esq.
1702 ,, Francis, Shangarry
1765 ,, Richard, Stranrahan, co. Tip., clerk
1691 ,, Robert, Carraghnehiney, co. Cork, esq.
1741 ,, Robert, Youghal, co. Cork, esq.
1760 ,, William, Dublin, merchant
[See FOOLKES, FOOUKES, FOUKES, FOULK, FOULKES, FOULKS, FOWKE, FOWKES.]
1795 **Foulkes**, Archibald Hamilton, Axmouth, Devon, esq. (Copy.)
1775 **Foulks**, Simon, Brittas, co. Kilk., gent.
1730 **Fountaine**, Henry, Fethard, co. Tipperary, gent.
1738 ,, lieut.-col. James
1690 ,, Susana, widow of Dr. James F., Dublin
1656 ,, Thomas, soldier [V. 310
1795 **Fowke**, Anne, Cork city, widow
1658 ,, John, the elder, Drogheda [VI. 289
1725 ,, John, Ballybritig, co. Cork
1757 ,, John, Dublin, esq.
1781 ,, John, Great Russell-street, Middlesex, esq. (Copy)

1780 **Fowke**, Joseph, Cork, merchant
1763 ,, Patience, Dublin, widow
1805 ,, Samuel, Cork city
1783 ,, Yelverton, Cork, gent.
1687 **Fowkes**, Hugh, Drogheda, glazier (Ex.)
1753 ,, Samuel, Waterford, clerk
1655 ,, Thomas, Dublin, stationer [**V.** 84
[See FOULKE, &c.]
1637 **Fowle**, Joseph, Mallow, co. Cork, clerk
1595 ,, Robert, Athenry
1670 ,, Thomas, the elder, Castle-sampson, co. Roscom., gent.
1780 **Fowler**, John, Montgomery-street, Dublin, gent.
1668 ,, Judith, Dublin, widow
1710 ,, Mary, par. St. James, West-minster, Middlesex, spin., (Copy)
1756 ,, William, Dublin, gent.
1747 **Fowles**, John, Dublin, gent.
1809 **Fowlue**, James, Toureen, Liberties of Limerick
1735 ,, William, Glin, co. Cork, gent.
1741 ,, William, Glin, co. Cork, gent.
1735 **Fownes**, sir Wm., Islandbridge, co. Dublin, bart.
1778 ,, sir Wm., Woodstock, co. Kil-kenny, bart.
1771 **Fox**, Anstace
1727 ,, Anthony, Gloghotanny, King's co., gent.
1801 ,, Anthony, Cloattany, King's co., gent.
1794 ,, Catherine, Camden-street, co. Dublin, widow
1741 ,, Celia, wife to Patrick Fox, Dublin, gent.
1722 ,, Charles, Foxhall, co. Longford, esq. (Ex.)
1746 ,, Charles, Foxhall, co. Longford, esq.
1797 ,, Christopher, Bow-street, Dublin
1782 ,, Daniel, Binfield, Berkshire (Copy)
1784 ,, Edward, Roscrea, co. Tip., merchant
1740 ,, Frances, *alias* **Herbert**, wife to Patrick F., Durrow, esq.
1807 ,, Francis, Athlone, co. Roscom-mon, merchant
1792 ,, George, Philipstown, King's co., gent.
1793 ,, George, Philipstown, King's co., gent. (see 1792)
1726 ,, Henry, Graigue, co. Tip., esq.
1690 ,, Hugh, Moyvore, co. Westmeath, esq. (Ex.)

1761 **Fox**, James, Killmaledy, King's co.
1709 ,, Jane, Dublin, spinster
1780 ,, Jane Mary, Clotany, King's co., spinster
1784 ,, John, the elder, Dublin, stay-maker
1689 ,, Joseph, Grainge, co. Tip., esq.
1800 ,, Margaret, Clonsagh, co. Dubl., widow
1784 ,, Mary, Rockfield, co. West-meath, spinster
1787 ,, Mary, Belnacor, co. West-meath, gentlewoman
1796 ,, Mathew, Athbane, co. Ros common, merchant
1734 ,, Patrick, Durrow, King's co., esq.
1743 ,, Patrick, Dublin, gent.
1798 ,, Patrick, Philipstown, King's co., gent.
1750 ,, Peyton, Portmahon, co. Long-ford, esq.
1788 ,, Philip, Ballybroder, co. West-meath
1755 ,, Richard, Thomas-street, Dubl., tailor
1744 ,, Rosse, Lambeth, Surrey, gent. (Copy)
1760 ,, Sarah, widow of Richard F., Coolgard, co. Wicklow, gent.
1658 ,, Terence, late of Knowth, co. Louth, yeoman [**VI.** 275
1784 ,, Thomas, Parliament-st., Dubl., laceman
1785 ,, Thomas, Chapelizod, co. Dublin, gent.
1799 ,, William, Clonsagh, co. Dublin
1803 ,, William, Chamber-street, co. Dublin, esq.
1671 **Foxall**, Abraham, Dublin, mercht. (Ex.)
1634 **Foxe**, Nathaniel, Rathreagh, co. Longford, esq.
1629 ,, Patrick, Moyvore, co. West-meath, esq.
1648 ,, Patrick, Rathreagh, co. Long., esq. (unpr.)
1698 **Foxwell**, Peter, Garrane, co. Tip., gent.
1729 **Foxwist**, Joseph Dublin, fringe-maker
1791 **Foy**, Bernard, Corrstown, co. Dubl.
1691 ,, Frauces, Dublin, spinster
1690 ,, John, Carrickmacross, co. Monaghan, jeweller
1773 ,, Thomas, Finglas, co. Dublin, merchant
1785 **Fraine**, John, Chelsea, esq. (Copy) [See FRAYNE.]

1737 **Fraly,** John, Hospital, co. Limk., innkeeper
1690 **France,** Laurence, Dublin, cloth-maker
1741 ,, Mary, native of the city of St. Martin de Rhé
1767 ,, Nathaniel, precentor of the cathedral church of Cloyne (not proved)
1793 ,, Rose, Cork, widow
1721 ,, Thomas, clerk, precentor of cathedral church of Waterford
1598 **Frances,** Allson, *alias* **Bradshaw,** Naas, widow
1742 **Francis,** Alice, Dublin, widow
1767 ,, Anne, Drogheda, widow
1721 ,, Edward, Cork, gent.
1799 ,, Elizabeth, Cork city, spr.
1719 ,, Evelyn, *alias* **Coskey,** Drinehorsny
1724 ,, v. rev. John, dean of Lismore
1795 ,, John, Dublin city, esq.
1745 ,, major Samuel, Dublin [gent.
1659 ,, Richd., Ballyvullen, co. Limk.,
1690 ,, Thomas, Dublin, cook
1665 **Franck,** John, Dublin, esq. (Copy; will delivered out)
1596 ,, Robert, London, blacksmith
1731 ,, Thomas, Frankford, King's co., esq.
[See FRANKS.]
1686 **Franckland,** Thomas, Cork, gent.
1691 **Francklin,** sir Wm., Maverne, Bedfordshire, knt. (Copy)
[See FRANKLIN.]
1798 **Francks,** Charlotte, Dublin, widow
1787 **Frank,** Mary, Summerhill, Dublin, widow
1787 **Frankland,** Agnes, Cork, widow
1734 ,, Barry, Cork, esq.
1763 ,, Richard, Cork, M.D.
1791 **Franklin,** Alexander, Limk., esq.
1786 ,, Jane, Dublin, widow
1772 ,, John, Youghal
1796 ,, sir John, Cork city, knt.
1803 ,, Luke, Dublin city, gent.
1655 ,, Ralph, Cork, surgeon [**V.** 197
1723 ,, Robert, Rathjordan, co. Limk., esq.
1759 ,, Terence, Dunany, co. Kildare, esq.
[See FRANCKLIN.]
1744 **Franklyn,** Ebenezer, Cork, widow
1802 **Franks,** Mathew Moorstown, co. Limerick, gent.
1780 ,, Thomas, Carrig, co. Cork, gent.
1787 ,, Thomas, Dubl., esq.
1805 ,, Thomas, Mallow, co. Cork
[See FRANCKS.]

1780 **Frankquefort,** Esther, Portarlington, Queen's co., widow
1733 **Franquefort,** Henry, Portarlington, Queen's co., gent.
1788 ,, Hester, Portarlington, Queen's co.
1788 ,, Jane, Portarlington, Queen's co.
1765 ,, Paula, Portarlington, Queen's co., spr.
1755 ,, Peter, Portarlington, Queen's co., esq.
1806 **Fraser,** Charles, Dublin city
1749 ,, Claud, Gracedieu, Liberty of Waterford, esq.
1801 ,, George, Birr, King's co.
1749 ,, James, Lib. of Carrickfergus
[See FRAZER.]
1801 **Fraven,** Francis, Gardenhill, co. Limerick
1723 **Frayne,** Christopher, Dublin, M.D.
1774 ,, George, Dublin, grocer
1743 ,, Ignatius, Joristown, co. Westmeath, gent.
1761 ,, Michael, Ballymahon
1709 ,, Nicholas, Dublin, merchant
1745 ,, Nicholas, Dublin, gent.
1789 ,, Richard, Dublin, mariner
[See FRAINE.]
1787 **Frazer,** Anne, Edgeworthstown, co. Longlord, spr.
1807 ,, Anne, Dublin city, widow
1787 ,, David, Finglas
1730 ,, George, Park, King's co., esq.
1759 ,, James, Dublin, tobacconist
1780 ,, James, Dublin, barrister-at-law
1780 ,, John, Bridge-st., Dubl., tobacconist
1754 ,, Robert, esq., gov. of Kinsale
[See FRASER.]
1778 **Frazier,** James, Snugborough, co. Meath
1796 **Frear,** Isaac, Carlton, Cumberland, slater
1748 **Free,** Wm., mariner on board the "Granada" sloop
[See FREEMAN.]
1768 **Freear,** Abraham, Ballykeen, Qu. co.
1701 **Freebody,** Joseph, Dublin, slater
1774 **Freeman,** Anne, Youghal, co. Cork, spinster
1744 ,, Danl,, Raplagh, co. Tipperary
1807 ,, David, Castletownsend
1808 ,, Eliza Ann, Castletownsend, co. Cork
1741 ,, Henry, Freemount, co. Cork, esq.
1807 ,, James, Ballivak, co. Tip., esq.
1783 ,, Jane, Cork, widow
1786 ,, Jane Dorothy

1705 **Freeman**, John, Dublin, surgeon
1727 ,, John, Kappanagoute, co. Cork, gent.
1744 ,, John, Ballinguile
1766 ,, John, Dublin [gent.
1807 ,, John, Freemount, co. Wicklow,
1780 ,, Joseph, Youghal, co. Cork, esq.
1789 ,, Mary, Dublin, widow
1775 ,, Mathew, Castlecor, co. Cork, esq.
1785 ,, Patrick, Holstons-st., Dublin, coach broker
1786 ,, Phebe, Nenagh, co. Tip., wid.
1718 ,, Richard, Ballinguile, co. Cork, gent.
1739 ,, Robert, Dublin, periwigmaker
1759 ,, Robt., Tomdaragh, co. Wick.
1779 ,, Robert, Ballinguile, co. Cork, gent.
1790 ,, Robt., Harold's Cross, co. Dub.
1741 ,, Samuel, Waterford, esq.
1804 ,, Simon, Freehall, co. Dublin
1766 ,, Susanna
1668 ,, Thomas, Dublin, merchant
1733 ,, Thos., Esker, Queen's co., esq.
1736 ,, Thomas, Antigua, America (Copy)
1788 ,, Thos., Tomdaragh, co. Wick., gent.
1732 ,, Wm., Castlecor, co. Cork, esq.
1765 ,, William, Castlecor
   [See FREE.]
1656 **Freind**, Robert, Dundrum [V. 306
   [See FREND.]
1782 **Freke**, hon. Grace, city of Bath, widow (Copy)
1764 ,, sir John, Castle F., co. Cork, bart.
1777 ,, sir John, Castle Freke, bart.
1707 ,, Percy, Wesbilney, Norfolk, esq. (Copy)
1728 ,, sir Percy, bart.
1717 ,, sir Ralph, Rathbarry, co. Cork, bart.
1794 **Fremantle**, lieut.-col. Stephen
1802 **French**, Agnes
1778 ,, Agnus, *alias* **Darcy**, Flaskagh, co. Galway, widow
1593 ,, Alexander, Galway, merchant
1757 ,, Andre, Fitz Peter, Galway, mariner
1801 ,, Andrew, Camberwell, Surrey
1756 ,, Anne, Frenchpark, co. Roscommon, widow
1806 ,, Anne, Cork city, widow
1807 ,, Anne, Galway town, widow
1765 ,, Anthony, Mitchelstown, co. Cork, gent.
1776 ,, Anthony, Colemanstown, co. Galway, gent.

1780 **French**, rev. Anthony, Maryborough, Queen's co., clk.
1786 ,, Anthony Fitz Gregory, Galway, esq.
1795 ,, Anthony Dominick, Galw. town
1729 ,, Arthur, Clonquil, co. Roscommon, esq.
1769 ,, Arthur, Frenchpark, co. Roscommon, esq.
1779 ,, Arthur, Tuam, co. Galway, esq.
1792 ,, Arthur, Croydon, co. Dubl., esq.
1799 ,, Arthur, Frenchpark, co. Roscommon, esq.
1772 ,, Bartholomew, Ballykinknave, co. Mayo, gent.
1793 ,, Bridget, widow
1793 ,, Broderick, the sheds of Clontarf
1544 ,, Catherine, Dublin
1799 ,, Catherine, Ballinakill, Queen's co., widow
1800 ,, Catherine, Dublin, widow
1761 ,, Charles, Greethill, co. Galway, gent.
1784 ,, sir Chas., Castle F., co. Galw.
1720 ,, Christopher, Tyrone, co. Galw., esq.
1797 ,, Christopher, formerly lieut.-col. 52nd regt.
1804 ,, Christopher, Brook Lodge, co. Galway
1772 ,, Cicily, Loughrea, co. Galway, widow
1801 ,, Darcy Hall, Corgery, co. Galway, esq.
1670 ,, Dominick, Dungar, co. Roscommon, esq.
1752 ,, Dominick, Galway, merchant
1771 ,, Dominick, Loughrea, co. Galw., merchant
1793 ,, Dominick, Dublin, merchant
1746 ,, Edmond, Dublin, merchant
1761 ,, Edmond, Esker, co. Galway, gent.
1787 ,, Edmond, co. Galway
1668 ,, Elizabeth, St. Finbarries, widow
1808 ,, Elizabeth, Dorset-street, Dub., widow
1799 ,, Francis, Cottage, co. Mayo
1805 ,, Francis, George's-hill, Dublin, merchant
1809 ,, Francis, Ballinvilla, co. Mayo, esq.
1770 ,, George, Innfield, co. Roscommon, esq.
1712 ,, Gregory Fitz Robuck, co. Galway
1808 ,, Gregory Anthony, Galway town
1789 ,, Helen, Portcarren, co. Galway, widow
1681 ,, Henry, Dublin, gent. (Ex.)

1768	**French,** Henry, Drimharsna, co. Galway, esq.
1788	,,	rev. Humphrey, Dunshaughlin, co. Meath, D.D.
1748	,,	Hyacyncth, Clogballymore, co. Galway, esq.
1758	,,	Ignatius, Carrarea, co. Galway, esq.
1805	,,	Ignatius, Carrarea, co. Galway, esq
1718	,,	Isabella, widow of Daniel F., Belturbet, co. Cavan
1659	,,	James, Sligo, esq. **[VIII.** 1
1711	,,	James, Cork, alderman
1746	,,	James, Dublin, merchant
1747	,,	Jas., ensign in genl. Howard's regt.
1757	,,	James Fitz Robert, Galway, mariner
1757	,,	James, Lodge, co. Cork, esq.
1760	,,	James, Portcarrin, esq.
1762	,,	James, Cork, merchant
1754	,,	Jane, wife to John French
1776	,,	Jane, Dublin, widow
1754	,,	Jeffry, Middle Temple, London, esq.
1750	,,	Joan, *alias* **Lynch,** Galway (prob. from Tuam dio., 1749; Copy)
1633	,,	John Fitzvallentine, Galway, burgess (Copy)
1734	,,	John, Park, co. Roscommon
1754	,,	John, Middle Temple, London, gent.
1756	,,	John, Highlake, co. Roscommon, esq.
1769	,,	John, Dublin, merchant
1769	,,	John, Dublin, merchant
1771	,,	John, Dublin, chandler
1776	,,	John, New Ross, co. Wexford, gent.
1778	,,	John Fitz Andrew, Galway, merchant
1789	,,	John
1789	,,	John Fitz Joseph, Galway town, gent.
1800	,,	John, Dublin
1786	,,	Julia
1723	,,	Marcus, Rahassane, co. Galway, esq.
1771	,,	Marcus, Rahassane, co. Galway, esq.
1775	,,	Mark Mathew, Galway, mercht.
1795	,,	Mark FitzPeter, Galway, merchant
1801	,,	Martin, Frenchgrove, co. Mayo, esq.
1685	,,	dame Marie, widow of sir Peter F., Galway, knt.
1784	,,	Mary, Williams Gate, Galway

1794	**French,** Mary, *alias* **Marshal,** *alias* **Lynch,** Frenchcrook, co. Mayo
1691	,,	Mathew, Belturbet, co. Cavan, esq.
1714	,,	Mathew, Cork, but in Isle of Man, esq. (Copy)
1722	,,	rev. Mathew, preby. of Kilcroot, dio. of Connor
1755	,,	Mathew, Dublin, merchant
1759	,,	Nicholas, Clogh, co. Galway, gent.
1769	,,	Nicholas, Carrowreagh, co Galway, gent.
1782	,,	Nicholas, Cottage, co. Roscommon
1794	,,	Nicholas John Patrick, Ballinasloe, co. Galway
1618	,,	Patrick, Monivea, co. Galway, merchant
1708	,,	Patk., Duras, co. Galway, esq.
1744	,,	Patrick, esq.
1748	,,	Patrick, Peterwell, co. Galway, esq.
1771	,,	Patrick, Dungar, co. Roscommon, merchant
1774	,,	Patrick, Galway, merchant
1784	,,	Patrick, Cloghballymore, co. Galway, esq.
1786	,,	Patrick, Duras, co. Galway, esq.
1799	,,	Patrick, Colemanstown, co. Galway
1584	,,	Peter Fitz John, Galway, alderman
1636	,,	sir Peter, Galway, knt.
1765	,,	Peter, Moycullen, esq.
1733	,,	Philip, Cork, alderman
1638	,,	Richard, Belturbet, co. Cavan, merchant
1686	,,	Richard, Dublin, merchant
1779	,,	Richard, Dublin, alderman
1782	,,	Richard, Baltinglass, co. Wicklow, merchant
1750	,,	Robt., Rahassane, co. Galway, esq.
1772	,,	Robert, late one of the Justices of the Com. Pleas
1774	,,	Robert Fitz James, Galway, merchant
1779	,,	Robert, Monivea, co. Galway, esq.
1789	,,	Robert, Rahassane, co. Galway, esq.
1804	,,	Robert, lieut. in an independent company of foot
1799	,,	Rose, spinster
1770	,,	Sampson Towgood, Cork, esq. (Not proved)
1803	,,	Sarah, widow

1770 **French**, Savage, Cork
1781 ,, Shepherd, New Ross, co. Wexford, tallow chandler
1732 ,, Susanna, *alias* **Osburne**, *alias* **Brunning**, Monoon, co. Galway
1782 ,, Temple, Limerick city
1753 ,, Thomas, Youghal, co. Cork, gent.
1785 ,, Thomas, Moycullen, co. Galway, esq.
1808 ,, Thomas, Abbey-street, Dublin
1638 ,, Walter, Galway, gent.
1658 ,, Walter, Kinsale, merchant
                                    [**VII**. 148
1724 ,, William, Dublin, alderman
1766 ,, William, Loughrea, co. Galway, merchant
1785 ,, William, dean of Ardagh
1602 **Frenche**, Robucke Fitz John, Galway, alderman
1721 **Frend**, Benjamin, Ballyrehy, King's co., esq.
1742 ,, Bridget, Ballyrehy, King's co., widow   [co., spinster
1742 ,, Catherine, Ballyrehy, King's
1777 ,, George, Creville
1675 ,, John, Carrickareely, co. Limerick, esq. (Ex.)
1749 ,, John, Dublin, esq.
1671 ,, Jonathan, Kilmurry, co. Kilkenny, gent.
1683 ,, Samuel, Carrickereely, co. Limerick, gent.
1719 ,, Samuel, Carrigareely, co. Limerick, esq.
1650 ,, Thomas, Dunsink, farmer
                [See **FREIND, FRIEND**.]
1779 **Fresearode**, Magdalen Bauldry, Rotterdam (Copy)
1730 **Fresneau**, Francis, Cashel, mercht.
1806 **Friend**, Richard, Fairview
                [See **FREND**.]
1701 **Frith**, Samuel, Waterford, mercht.
1806 ,, Thomas, Kinsale, co. Cork, attorney
1655 **Frizall**, John, Dublin, soldier
                                    [**V**. 100
1755 **Frizell**, John, Strand-street, Dubl., ale seller
1806 ,, Richard, Rathfarm, co. Dublin, esq.
1788 **Frood**, James, Dublin, merchant (Large)
1789 **Frost**, Catherine, Wicklow town, spinster
1780 ,, Edward, Wicklow town, gent.
1697 ,, John, Dublin, gent.
1756 ,, Leonard, Grange, co. Meath, gent.

1787 **Fry**, Benjamin, Mountmellick, Queen's co.
1776 ,, Edward, Dublin, druggist
1788 ,, Henry, Frybrook, co. Roscommon, esq. (Large)
1802 ,, Joanna, Kilmollog, King's co.
1796 ,, John, Boyle, co. Roscommon, esq.
1797 ,, Martha
1803 ,, William, Nicholas-st., Dublin, lace merchant
                [See **FERRIS**.]
1668 **Frye**, George, Liverpool, Lancashire, merchant (Copy)
1763 **Fudge**, Garret, Youghal, co. Cork
1781 ,, George, Youghal, clothier
1774 ,, Susanna, Youghal, co. Cork, spr.
1772 ,, Thomas, Youghal, co. Cork, gent.
1774 ,, Thomas, Youghal, co. Cork
1674 **Fugill**, Alice, Dundalk, widow
1808 **Fulham**, Michael Joseph, Cork city, merchant
1795 **Fullam**, Catherine, Dublin, spinster
1761 ,, George, Ballyfermot, co. Dubl., farmer
1751 ,, John, New-st., Dublin, farmer
1793 ,, John, Bridge-street, Dublin
1660 ,, Laurence, Francis-st., gent.
                                    [**VIII**. 199
1618 ,, Symon, Ninche, co. Meath, farmer
1718 **Fuller**, Abraham, Lahinch, King's co., farmer
1740 ,, Abraham, Kinnegad, co. Westmeath, farmer
1769 ,, Abraham, Cork, linendraper
1800 ,, Bartholomew, Belfast, co. Antrim, surgeon
1728 ,, Elizabeth, Lahinch, King's co., widow
1752 ,, Elizabeth, Limerick, widow
1741 ,, Henry, Ballitore, co. Kildare, farmer
1733 ,, Jacob, Waterstown, co. Westmeath, farmer
1772 ,, John, formerly of Woodfield, King's co., now of Violet Hill, co. Dublin, gent.
1784 ,, John, Ballitore, co. Kildare
1805 ,, John, Bandon, co. Cork
1783 ,, Joseph, Violet Hill, co. Dublin, esq.
1737 ,, Mary, Meath-street, Dublin, widow
1736 ,, Samuel, Dublin, bookseller
1802 ,, Sarah, Dublin, widow
1791 ,, Thomas, Sundayswell, Liberty of Cork, gent.

1775 **Fuller**, William, Church-lane, clk.
1778 ,, William, Dublin, esq.
1803 **Fullerton**, Allen
1669 ,, Elinor, Wicklow, widow
1628 **Fullwood**, Lewis of London, turner; Dublin, merchant
1774 **Fulton**, Elizabeth, Dublin, widow
1803 ,, John, Coleraine, co. Londonderry
1804 ,, Samuel, Dorset-street, Dublin, merchant
1771 ,, William, Kilkenny, gent.
1748 **Funican**, Elizabeth, Ballingley, co. Wexford, widow
1803 **Funicane**, Benjamin, Ballyscanlan, co. Waterford, gent.
1800 **Funston**, John, Dublin, esq.
1738 **Funucan**, Edith, *alias* **Perry**, Newtown, Ardcath, co. Meath, widow
1809 **Funycan**, John, Newtown, co. Meath, gent.
1763 **Furey**, Jeremiah, Sligo, esq.
1807 ,, Peter, Castlebar, merchant
[See FURY.]
1744 **Furlong**, James, Hawkins-quay, Dublin, ale seller
1616 ,, Patrick Fitzpatrick, Wexford, gent.
1795 ,, Susana, Patrick-street, Dublin, widow
1762 **Furnace**, Francis, Dublin, widow
1790 **Furnell**, Michael, Ballycahane, co. Limerick, esq.
1750 ,, Patrick, esq.
1710 **Furroe**, Mary Anne, Carlow, widow
1710 ,, Stephen, Carlow, gent.
1804 **Fury**, Christopher, Clonshanny, King's co., farmer
1804 ,, Jeremiah, Sligo town, esq.
[See FUREY.]
1755 **Furzer**, Daniel, Kinsale
1759 **Fyan**, Dorothy, widow of John F., Drogheda, gent.
1584 ,, Richard, Dublin, alderman
[**I.** 51
1650 ,, Richard, Dublin, apothecary
1734 **Fyans**, Francis, Dowestown, co. Meath, gent.
1806 ,, Thos., Dunleer, co. Louth, gt.
1557 **Fyn**, Patrick, Dublin
[See FINN.]
1586 **Fynglas**, John, Ballcadden, co. Dublin
[See FINGLAS.]
1752 **Fynn**, Edward
1804 ,, John, Lucan, co. Dublin
[See FINN.]
1632 **Fysher**, sir Edward, Prospect, co. Wexford, knt.
[See FISHER.]

1558 **Fytzgerald**, Christopher, Deswellis town
[See FITZGERALD.]
1575 **FytzSymones**, Edward
[See FITZSIMONS.]

—G—

1733 **Gabally**, John, Dublin, merchant
1773 **Gabb**, Mary, *alias* **Brady**, Drogheda, widow
1765 **Gabbet**, John, Limerick, gent.
1741 ,, Joseph, Ballyvorneen, co. Lim., esq.
1744 **Gabbett**, James, Killonan, co. Limk. city, gent.
1797 ,, Joseph, lieut.-gen. of the forces
1801 ,, Joseph, Dublin city, esq.
1713 ,, Wm., Ballyvorneen, co. Limk., gent.
1729 ,, Wm., Caherline, co. Limerick, esq.
1801 **Gabbit**, Joseph Spiers, capt.-lieut. in His Majesty's regt. of foot (Copy)
1796 **Gabbott**, Thos. Spiers, Rochelle, South Lib. Cork, esq.
1809 **Gabell**, Anne, widow
1739 **Gadbury**, Thomas, Carter's-alley, Dublin, yeoman
1763 **Gaddis**, John, Dublin, shoemaker
1796 ,, John, Lurgan, co. Armagh, innholder
1769 **Gaffaney**, Marks, George's-quay, Dublin, pilot
1734 **Gaffie**, Thady
1805 **Gaffney**, Mary, widow
1591 ,, Robert, chaplain of Kilkenny
1732 **Gaffny**, Darby, Fleet-st., Dublin
1742 ,, Michael, Fleet-st., Dubl., cakeman
1784 ,, Patrick, Milltown, co. Meath, gent.
[See GAFFANEY.]
1799 **Gaffodie**, Joseph, Dublin, gent.
1778 **Gage**, Hodgson, Bellarena, co. Derry, esq.
1697 ,, John, Mullingan, co. Londonderry, esq. (Ex.)
1763 ,, John, presbytery, Aghadowey, dioc. Derry
1764 ,, Sarah, Newtown Limavady, co. Londonderry, widow
1787 ,, Thomas, gen. of the army and col. of the 11th dragoons (Copy)
1707 ,, Wm., Garnvaghy, co. Londonderry
1739 ,, Wm., Coleraine, co. Derry, esq.

1751 **Gaggin**, Alice, Limerick, spr.
1752   ,,   Rebecca, Limerick, spr.
1758 **Gaghron**, Patk., Dublin, maltster
1811 **Gahagan**, Lewis, Kilcarner
        [See GEOGHEGAN.]
1762 **Gahan**, Catherine, Dublin, spr.
1765   ,,   Danl., Coolquill, co. Tipperary, esq.
1800   ,,   Daniel
1731   ,,   George, Coolquill, co. Tipperary, esq.
1801   ,,   Hannah
1796   ,,   John, Cork city, esq.
1717   ,,   dame Medecis
1705 **Gaich**, John, Gageborough, King's co., M.D.
1712   ,,   Ruth, relict of doctor John G.
1714 **Gaigneaur**, David, Dublin, mercht.
1780 **Galan**, Peter, Dublin, sugar baker
1800 **Galbraith**, Andrew, Cappahard, co. Galway, esq.
1739   ,,   Arthur, the Manor, Leitrim, esq.
1778   ,,   George, Tumduff, Queen's co., farmer
1803   ,,   George, Graigue, Queen's co.
1704   ,,   Hugh, Johnstown, co. Longford, gent.
1673   ,,   James, Ramorane, co. Ferm., esq. (Ex.)
1787   ,,   James, Roscarvey, co. Tyrone, esq.
1675   ,,   Jane, *alias* **Conynghame**, Dowlish, co. Donegal, wid.
1810   ,,   John, Dublin city
1739   ,,   Mary, Dublin, widow   [esq.
1712   ,,   Robt., Cloncorick, co. Leitrim,
1758   ,,   Rose, Dublin, widow
1795   ,,   Samuel, Old Derrokes, Queen's co., esq.
1799   ,,   Samuel, Everton, Queen's co.
1576 **Galders**, John, Dublin, merchant
1800 **Gale**, Peter, Dublin, esq.
1758   ,,   Saml., the Coombe, Dub., weaver
1804   ,,   Thomas, Kilrush, Queen's co., farmer
1791   ,,   William, Whitehaven, merchant (Copy)
1654 **Galey**, John, private soldier
1714 **Gallacher**, Patk., Snioge, co. Meath, farmer
1765 **Gallagher**, Chas., Dub., linendraper
1768   ,,   Charles, Carrick, co. Leitrim
1768   ,,   Charles, Carrick, co. Leitrim, gent.
1777   ,,   John, Kiltohork, co. Leitrim
1811   ,,   John, Townsend-st., Dublin
1771   ,,   Owen, Corsparrow, co. Leitrim, esq.
1805   ,,   Patrick, Manor Hamilton, co. Leitrim

1786 **Gallagher**, Richard, Castlebar, co. Mayo, gent.
1809   ,,   Thomas, Dame-lane, Dublin, dairyman
1762   ,,   William
1795   ,,   William, Rusky, co. Donegal, farmer
1808   ,,   William, Ginnetts, co. Meath, farmer
        [See GALLACHER, GALLAUGHER.]
1751 **Gallairdy**, Lewis, rector of Ardbrackan, dioc. Meath
1759 **Galland**, Elizabeth, Killowen, co. Derry, widow
1722   ,,   Margt., Gallgorme, co. Antrim, widow
1730   ,,   Wm., Greenhills, co. Antrim, esq. (Ex.)
1769 **Gallaugher**, James, Ardfarna, co. Donegal
1722 **De Galleniere**, Peter Peze, minister of the Gospel at Dublin
1636 **Gallway**, sir Geffry, bart., co. Limk.
1712 **Gallwey**, John, Cork
        [See GALWAY.]
1789 **Gallphin**, Catherine, Enniskillen, co. Fermanagh
1801 **Galt**, Chas., Coleraine, co. Londonderry
1766   ,,   Jane, Coleraine
1700   ,,   John, Coleraine, alderman
1733   ,,   John, Coleraine, co. Londonderry, merchant
1801   ,,   John, Coleraine, merchant
1776   ,,   William, Coleraine, co. Derry, merchant
1604 **Galtrym**, Walter, Dublin, mercht.
1663 **Galwan**, Nich., Youghal, alderman
1707 **Galway**, capt. Arthur, Ballynetray, co. Waterford, esq.
1747   ,,   David, Bantry, co. Cork, merchant
1794   ,,   Edmond, Cork city, esq.
1783   ,,   Edward, Dungavan, co. Wat., merchant
1766   ,,   Elinor, widow
1802   ,,   Francis, Cork, esq.
1810   ,,   Henry, Bordeaux, France, merchant (Copy)
1782   ,,   John, Carrick, co. Tip., esq.
1794   ,,   John, Lota, co. Cork city
1800   ,,   Margt., Hot Wells, Bristol, spr.
1807   ,,   Mary Anne, Lisbon, Portugal
1809   ,,   Rose, Denzille-st., Dublin, wid.
        [See GALLWAY, GALLWEY.]
1725 **Galwey**, *alias* **Cantwell**, widow
1804   ,,   Frances, Glanmire-road
1771   ,,   Margt., Castletown or Castletownsend
1706   ,,   Patrick, Cork, gent.

1733 **Galwey**, Wm., Lotabeg, co. Cork, esq.
1771 ,, Wm., Castletown, co. Cork
1707 **Galwith**, James, Wentworth-street, Middlesex, silk thrower
1796 **Gambell**, John, Letterkenny, co. Donegal
1794 ,, William, Wasford
1768 **Gamble**, Ann, Londonderry, spr.
1773 ,, Ann, Dublin, widow
1808 ,, Baptist, Graan, co. Fermanagh, gent.
1805 ,, David, Ratona, co. Fermanagh
1749 ,, Elizabeth, Cork, widow
1798 ,, Geo., Mountalto, co. Antrim, esq.
1802 ,, Henry, Lurgan, co. Armagh
1800 ,, Jane, *alias* **Goldsmith**, Dubl., widow
1707 ,, John, Strabane, co. Tyrone, merchant
1724 ,, John, Oldcourt, co. Cork, gent.
1750 ,, John, St. John's, co. Wexford
1784 ,, John, Rathrobin, King's co.
1785 ,, John, Lisnagree, esq.
1791 ,, John, the younger, Dub., esq.
1793 ,, John, Brookville, co. Dublin, esq.
1802 ,, Marianne, Camden-st., Dublin, spr.
1762 ,, Mossom, Londonderry, esq.
1733 ,, Onesiphorus, Old Court, co. Cork city
1769 ,, Onesiphorus, St. John's, co. Wexford, esq.
1733 ,, Robert, Londonderry, mercht.
1807 ,, Samuel, Dublin city, merchant
1773 ,, Thomas, Dublin, linen weaver
1775 ,, Thos., port of Dublin, mariner
1808 ,, Thomas, Ballaghmore, co. Fermanagh
1711 ,, William, Tober, co. Westmeath
1749 ,, William, Dublin, merchant
1779 ,, William, Dublin, esq.
1808 ,, William, Ballaghmore
[See **Gambell**.]
1805 **Gammon**, Laurence, Woodpark, co. Dublin
1656 ,, William, trooper [**VI**. 35
1795 **Ganly**, James, Strokestown, co. Roscommon, esq.
1806 ,, Martha, Glasnevin, co. Dublin, widow
1756 **Gannailiff**, John, Dublin, gent.
1801 **Gannon**, James, Dublin, baker
1787 ,, John, Church-street, Dublin, baker
1789 ,, John, Cornmarket, Dub., linen-draper
1808 ,, Letitia, Dublin city

1787 **Gannon**, Patrick, Walshestown, co. Kildare, farmer
1777 ,, Richard, Wardtown, co. Meath, farmer
[See **Cannon**.]
1657 **Ganny**, John, Dublin, butcher [**VI**. 102
1801 **Gard**, Richard, Garrymore, co. Cork, gent.
1732 **Garde**, Thos., Bowlmore, co. Cork, gent.
1764 ,, Thomas, Garrymore, co. Cork, gent.
1766 ,, Thomas, Deansford, co. Cork, gent.
1807 ,, Thomas, Dublin city, esq.
1793 ,, Wm., Ballinacurra, co. Cork, gent.
1765 **Gardes**, Stephen, Rathbone-place, gent. (Copy)
1791 **Gardiner**, Alexander
1758 ,, Arthur, esq., captain in the "Monmouth"
1810 ,, Caleb, Island-bridge, co. Dub., merchant
1769 ,, right hon. Charles, esq.
1783 ,, Frances, Dublin, spr.
1785 ,, Frances, Longford, co. Longford
1765 ,, George, Drumcondra, co. Dub., esq.
1601 ,, Gilbert, Dublin, gent.
1660 ,, Gilbert, ensign [**VIII**. 158
1746 ,, James, Dublin, gent.
1764 ,, James, Dublin, surgeon
1802 ,, James, Rathrohan, King's co.
1804 ,, Jeremiah, Borrisokane, co. Tipperary
1755 ,, right hon. Luke, Dublin, esq. (Large will)
1700 ,, Mary, widow of Rich'd. G., esq.
1796 ,, Mary, Townsend-street, Dubl., widow
1792 ,, Mathew, Portron, co. Roscommon, gent.
1735 ,, Oliver, Loughbrickland, co. Down, clk.
1701 ,, Richard, Dublin, esq.
1771 ,, Robert, Dublin, gent.
1774 ,, Robert, Dublin, gent.
1783 ,, Robert, Armagh, brazier
1808 ,, Robert, Dublin city, esq.
1657 ,, captain Samuel, Dublin [**VI**. 98
1695 ,, Sarah, widow of Robert G., Dublin
1796 ,, Susana, Maddenstown, co. Kildare, widow
1797 ,, Thomas, Borris-in-Ossory, Queen's co.

1800 **Gardiner**, Thomas, Dublin, gent.
1659 ,, Wm., soldier in capt. Vivyan's company [**VII.** 180
1690 ,, William, late of Dublin, now of Chester, gent.
1789 ,, William, surgeon in East Indies
1796 ,, William, Carlown, Queen's co., gent.
1808 ,, William, the elder, Youghal, co. Cork
1808 ,, William, Kells, co. Antrim, M.D. [See GARDNER.]
1738 **Gardner**, Elizabeth, Loughbrickland, co. Down, widow
1776 ,, Geo., Portron, co. Roscommon
1729 ,, Robert, Westminster, Middlesex, esq. (Copy)
1753 ,, Samuel, Youghal, co Cork, clothier
1723 ,, Thomas, late of col. Charles Otway's regt. at Portmahon [See GARDINER.]
1743 **Gareshes**, Jane, Cork, late of Dub., widow
1799 **Gargan**, John, Milltown, co. Meath, farmer
1634 **Garlick**, Charles, Dublin, gent.
1770 **Garner**, Thomas, Cuffe-st., Dublin, gent.
1783 **Garnet**, George, Dublin, barrister-at-law [gent.
1785 ,, George, Howrath, co. Meath,
1747 ,, James, Kells, co. Meath
1736 ,, John, Tipperary, gent.
1755 ,, John, Kells, co. Meath, gent.
1782 ,, John, bp. of **Clogher**, q. v.
1598 ,, Thomas (no date, Copy)
1677 **Garnett**, Bartholomew, Limerick, alderman
1751 ,, George, Dublin, merchant
1802 ,, George, Newpark, co. Dublin, esq.
1805 ,, Mary, Merrion-row, Dublin
1668 ,, Nicholas, Belfast, chandler
1623 ,, Thomas, Drogheda [gent.
1760 ,, William, Patrick-st., Kilkenny,
1811 ,, William, Kells, co. Meath
1773 **Garnou**, George, formerly of Middle Temple; now of Dub., esq.
1769 ,, Samuel, Dublin, gent.
1671 **Garold**, Mary, widow of John G., Dublin, gent.
1598 **Garrolde**, Thomas, Dub., alderman
1642 **Garrard**, John, St. Kevins-street, baker
1798 **Garratt**, Humphry, Harold's Cross, co. Dublin
1793 ,, Joseph, Cork city, chocolate maker [See GARRETT.]

1798 **Garre**, Mary, Dublin, widow
1636 **Garrett**, Anthony, Kilurd, dio. Lismore, co. Waterford, gent.
1786 ,, George, Streamstown, co. Mayo
1790 ,, Jane, Janeville, co. Carlow
1790 ,, rev. John, rector of Crossboyne, dio. Tuam
1799 ,, John, Finglas, co. Dub., dairyman
1696 ,, Sarah, Dublin, widow
1759 ,, Thomas, Killgarrin, co. Carlow, gent.
1760 ,, Thomas, Killgarrin
1783 ,, William, Clonfarta, co. Carlow, gent. [See GARRATT.]
1763 **Garrod**, Henry, Cork
1765 **Garry**, Patrick
1748 **Garskin**, Bartholomew, Dublin, gt.
1772 **Garstin**, Alithea, Dublin, wife of John G., esq.
1726 ,, Anne, Dublin, widow
1782 ,, Anthony, Braganstown, co. Louth
1778 ,, Benjamin, Dublin, merchant
1676 ,, James, Braganstown, co. Louth, esq. (Ex)
1773 ,, rev. James, rector of Moyglare, co. Meath, clk.
1733 ,, John, Dublin, esq.
1808 ,, John, Molesworth-st., Dublin, attorney-at-law
1686 ,, Martha, Glassdromon, widow
1660 ,, Symon, Drogheda, capt., esq.
1749 ,, Thomas, Dublin, gent.
1684 ,, William, Glassdromon, co. Armagh, gent.
1802 ,, William, Balbriggan, co. Dub., tallow chandler
1731 **Garth**, Thomas, Newbone-st., par. St. Geo. Martyr, gent. (Co.)
1792 **Gartley**, Hugh, Dundalk, co. Louth, maltster
1668 **Garton**, John, senior, Callybacky, co. Antrim, gent.
1769 **Gartside**, Henry, Drogheda, mercht.
1756 ,, John, Cuffe-street, Dub., gent.
1777 ,, John, Kevinsport, co. Dublin, grocer
1806 ,, John, a capt. in His Majesty's 90th regt. of foot
1726 ,, William, Drogheda, merchant
1757 **Garvan**, Francis, esq.
1762 **Garvey**, Henry, Woodfield, co. Mayo, gent.
1788 ,, John, Dublin
1744 ,, William, Cook-street, Dublin, victualler
1732 **Gascoyne**, Benjamin, Cheswick, Middlesex, esq. (Copy)

1749 **Gascoyne**, Dorothy, Dublin, spr.
1681 **Gash**, John, Castle Lyons, co. Cork, gent.
1707 ,, Richard, quar. mas. in brig. Cunningham's regt.
1724 **Gaskell**, Nicholas, Dublin, gent.
1723 ,, Thomas, Dublin, tailor
1725 ,, William, Dublin, dairyman
1777 ,, William, Malpas-street, Dub.
1785 **Gaskill**, Peter, city of Bath, gent. (Copy)
1759 **Gason**, John, Killoshalloe, co. Tipperary, gent.
1772 ,, Richard, Killoshalloe, co. Tipperary, esq.
1772 ,, Samuel, Nenagh, co. Tipperary, gent.
1736 **Gass**, John, Dublin, merchant
1713 **Gassande**, John Anthony, gent.
1809 **Gatchell**, Jonathan, Mountmellick, Queen's co.
1721 **Gates**, Ralph, Athlone, co. Roscommon, farmer
1772 ,, Ralph, Ballyteigh, co. Wicklow, gent.
1738 ,, Thomas, Greatconnell, co. Kildare, gent.
1755 ,, Thomas, Greatconnell, co. Kildare, gent.
1709 **Gaubert**, Lewis, Waterford, gent.
1764 ,, Stephen, Wexford, shopkeeper
1635 **Gaudin**, Robert, St. Patrick-street, French merchant
1731 **Gaughegan**, Francis, Dublin, gent.
1730 ,, Mary, Wood-quay, Dublin, widow
[See GEOGHEGAN.]
1636 **Gaulte**, Adam, Grange, Killdallogy, co. Derry
1758 **Gautiers**, Simon, Dubl., wine cooper
1657 **Gavan**, Christopher, Dublin
[**VI.** 32 ; **V.** 206
1762 **Gaven**, Henry, Mountjoy, co. Dub., esq.
1735 ,, Jane, Drogheda, spinster
1642 ,, John, Dublin, tanner
1737 ,, Luke, sen., Dublin, merchant
1790 ,, Luke, Dublin, esq.
1733 ,, Thomas, Dublin, merchant
1736 ,, William, Dublin, gent.
1777 ,, William, Dublin, esq.
[See GAVAN, GAVYN.]
1771 **Gavin**, John, Limerick, clothier
1729 ,, Robert, Ballyrasheen, co. Londonderry, linendraper
1617 **Gavyn**, Tristram, Archdalestown, co. Fermanagh, gent.
[See GAVEN.]
1792 **Gaw**, Patrick, Belfast, co. Antrim, merchant

1694 **Gay**, Anne, Dublin, widow
1742 ,, Grace, Mullaghtee, co. Louth, widow
1693 ,, John, Dublin city
1727 ,, John, Grangegorman-lane, co. Dublin, gent.
1780 ,, John, Redmondstown, co. Westmeath, esq.
1788 ,, John, Gaybrook, co. Westmeath, esq.
1771 ,, Joseph, par. of Clontibret, co. Monaghan
1718 ,, William, Colinstown, co. Kildare, gent.
1760 **Gayen**, Cathne., Blaris, co. Antrim
1800 **Gayer**, Edward, Derryaghy, co. Antrim, gent.
1807 ,, John, Dublin city, esq.
1755 ,, rev. Philip, vicar of Derryaghy, co. Antrim, clk.
1730 **Gayner**, James, Dublin, gent.
1765 ,, James, Leamy, co. Westmeath
1792 **Gaynor**, Elizabeth, Dublin, widow
1780 ,, Hugh, Killisherny, co. Leitrim, esq.
1770 ,, James, Dublin, grocer
1740 ,, John, Dublin [widow
1776 ,, Mary, Garrycastle, King's co.,
1696 ,, Nichs., Blackcastle, co. Westmeath, esq.
1765 ,, Peter, Leixlip, co. Kildare
1782 ,, Richard, Stackstown, co. Westmeath, farmer
1681 ,, Ross
1721 ,, Vere, Blackcastle, co. Westmeath, widow
1779 ,, William, Dublin, grocer
[See GAYNER.]
1706 **Gayton**, John, Dublin, brewer
1800 **Geagan**, John, of the ship "America," mariner
1783 **Geale**, Benjamin, Claremont, co. Dublin
1803 ,, Daniel, Dublin, merchant
1795 ,, Ebenezer, Dublin, merchant
1802 ,, Elizabeth, Dublin, spinster
1797 **Geary**, John, Limerick city, gent.
1744 **Geasly**, Roger, Tallow, co. Waterford
1768 **Geddes**, George, Dublin, hosier
1729 **Gee**, Anne, widow of Thomas G., Leap, King's co., gent.
1777 ,, Dorothy, Castletown, co. Meath, widow
1787 ,, James, Lisrow, co. Waterford, gent.
1704 ,, John, Nevoughly, co. Westmeath, farmer
1746 ,, John, Woodfield, King's co., farmer

1805 **Gee**, Mary, Liscrow, co. Waterford
1720 ,, Thos., Leap, King's co., gent.
1741 ,, Thomas, Longford, King's co.
1740 ,, Timothy, Moyvoghlagh, co. Westmeath, farmer
1788 **Geelan**, Mary, *alias* **Thompson**, Dublin, widow
1660 **Geere**, William, Allshallows, Honeylane, London (Copy)
1671 ,, William, London, esq.
1662 **Geering**, Alexander, Londonderry, gent.
1742 ,, Richard, Dublin, esq. (Large will)
1600 **Geffre**, John, Dublin
1797 **Gelling**, David, Dublin, hat manufacturer
1809 ,, John, Newmarket, co. Dublin, gent.
1791 **Gellis**, Anne, Dublin, widow
1698 **Gellius**, Isaac, Izigeac, France, at present refugiate in Dublin
1786 **Gemmell**, Robert, Greenwich, Kent (Copy)
1808 **Gemmill**, Robt., Belfast, co. Antrim, merchant
1743 **Geneste**, Lewis, Lisburn, co. Antrim
1766 **Gent**, William, Dublin, gent.
1802 **Gentleman**, Robert, Kanturk, co. Cork, gent.
1602 **Geoghe**, sir Edwd., Waterford, knt.
1628 ,, sir James, Kilmainham, co. Waterford, knt.
1592 ,, John, Dublin, alderman
1669 **Geoghegan**, Alson, *alias* **Bricerton**, widow
1741 ,, Andrew, Dublin, gent.
1789 ,, Arthur, Dublin, gent.
1776 ,, Bryan, Jamestown, co. Westmeath, gent.
1807 ,, Bryan, Rosemount, co. Westmeath, esq.
1762 ,, Charles, Dunlavin, co. Wicklow, farmer
1789 ,, Charles, Naas, co. Kildare, merchant
1737 ,, Edward, Smithfield, Dublin, saddler
1741 ,, Edwd., Philadelphia, America, merchant
1731 ,, Francis, Dublin
1767 ,, Francis, Dub., barrister-at-law
1802 ,, Francis, Curragh, co. Westmeath, esq.
1791 ,, Garrett, Dublin, gent.
1748 ,, Gerald, Portarlington, Queen's co., merchant
1797 ,, Ignatius, Soho-square, Middlesex, esq. (Copy)
1679 ,, James, Dublin

1745 **Geoghegan**, James, Dromore, co. Westmeath
1749 ,, James, Athlone, merchant
1786 ,, James, Bellville, co. Westmeath, gent.
1754 ,, John, Linally, King's co., gent.
1785 ,, John, Jamestown, co. Westmeath
1788 ,, John, Portarlington, Queen's co., gent.
1727 ,, Kedagh, Carne, co. Westmeath
1783 ,, Kedagh, Donore, co. Westmeath, esq.
1801 ,, Margaret, Donore, co. Westmeath, widow
1676 ,, Owen
1763 ,, Richard, Ballybrickoge, co. Westmeath
1797 ,, Ruth, Dublin, widow
1742 ,, Thos., Dunlavin, co. Wicklow, merchant
1750 ,, Thomas, Ballengarry
1771 ,, Thos., Portarlington, Queen's co., gent.
1778 ,, Thomas
1806 ,, Thos., Kilbeggan, co. Westmeath
1727 ,, William, Brackanagh, King's co., gent.
[See GAHAGAN, GAUGHEGAN, GOEGHEGAN.]
1806 **George**, rev. Luke, rector of Killanny
1774 ,, Samuel, Dublin, hatter
1740 ,, Simon, Babrahin, King's co.
1768 ,, Susana, Dublin, widow
1685 ,, William, Dublin, skinner (Ex.)
1779 ,, William, Dublin, hatter
[See GORGES.]
1686 **Georges**, Samuel, esq., Justice of Common Pleas
1799 **Geraghty**, James, Moate convent, Carmelite friar
1773 ,, Michael, Athlone
1808 ,, Michael, Leixlip, co. Kildare, grocer
1806 ,, Peter, Ballyneagheraghty, co. Galway, farmer
1801 ,, Thomas, Killynon Pratt. co. Westmeath, farmer
[See GIRAGHTY.]
1700 **Gerald**, Henry, Monard, co. Cork
1607 ,, James, Waterford, merchant
1691 ,, Wm., Newcastle, co. Limerick, farmer
1638 **Geraldine**, Richard, gent.
1790 **Geran**, Daniel, Mitchelstown, co. Cork
1659 **Gerard**, Jas., provost of Belturbet, **[VII.** 146

1784 **Gerard,** Mason, Belgriffin, co. Dublin, esq.
1723 ,, William, Dublin, gent.
1785 **Germain,** James, Kilcock, distiller
1674 **Gernon,** Christopher, Dublin, shoemaker
1720 ,, Edwd., Miltown, co. Louth, esq.
1735 ,, Ellinor, Dublin, spinster
1717 ,, Elizabeth, widow of Richd. G., esq.
1732 ,, Elizabeth, Dublin, spr.
1562 ,, sir James, Killincoole, co. Louth, knt.   [**I.** 65
1633 ,, James, Monaghan, merchant
1755 ,, James, Newry, esq.
1789 ,, James, Dublin, linendraper
1713 ,, John, Crooked Stone, co. Antm., gent.
1766 ,, John, Killincoole, co. Louth, esq.
1777 ,, Margaret, Back-lane, Dublin, widow
1755 ,, Mary, Dublin, spr.
1802 ,, Mary, Dublin, widow
1780 ,, Nich., Broomfield, co. Cavan
1729 ,, Patrick, Dublin, periwigmaker
1745 ,, Patrick, Killincoole, co. Louth, gent.
1755 ,, Patrick, Scurlogstown, co. Kildare, gent.
1811 ,, Patk., Drogheda town, distiller
1716 ,, Richard, Dublin, gent.
1629 ,, Thos., Molinstown, co. Louth, gent.
1561 **Gerot,** John, Rush
1803 **Gerrand,** Eliz., city of Hamburg, widow (Copy)
1804 **Gerrard,** Bartholomew, Skeigh, co. Dublin, gent.
1728 ,, Elinor, wife of Peter G., Dubl., mariner
1752 ,, Elizabeth, Dublin, widow
1723 ,, John, Dublin, goldsmith
1799 ,, John, Skeagh, co. Dubl., farmer
1742 ,, Jonathan, Dublin, brewer
1738 ,, Joseph, Trinity College, Dubl.
1750 ,, Mary, *alias* **Mason**, Dublin, widow
1750 ,, Samuel, Clangill, co. Meath
1807 ,, Sophia
1737 ,, Thomas, Drogheda, alderman
1763 ,, Thomas, Liscartan, co. Meath, gent.
1793 ,, Wm., Dormstown, co. Meath, gent.
1703 **Gerry,** John, Galway, merchant
1790 **Gervais,** ven. Henry, archdeacon of Cashel
1756 ,, Isaac, dean of Tuam
1783 ,, Mary, wife to Francis G.

1787 **Gervais,** Noah, Killmatogue, King's co., surgeon
1730 ,, Peter, Dublin, merchant
1800 ,, Peter, Armagh city, esq.
                [See JERVIS.]
1743 **Gerveran,** Isaac, Dublin, esq.
1779 **Gervereau,** Margaret, Dublin, spr.
1708 **Gethin,** Deborah, Sligo, spr.
1793 ,, John, Dublin, esq.
1808 ,, John, Cottage, co. Sligo, esq.
1778 ,, dame Margaret
1751 ,, Mary, Doneraile, co. Cork, widow of Brandolph G.
1723 ,, Percy, Sligo, co. Sligo, esq.
1779 ,, Percy, Firgrove, co. Cork, esq.
1679 ,, Richard, jun., younger son of Richard G., Ballyfenatyr, co. Cork, esq.
1709 ,, sir Richard, Dublin, bart.
1774 **Getty,** Robt., Belfast, woollendraper
1751 **Geyhin,** Lawrence, Bornessileagh, co. Tipperary, innholder
1667 **Ghest,** John, Dublin, gent.
1670 **Ghuest,** John, Kilkenny, gent.
1762 **Giball,** David, the Poddle, co. Dub.
1738 **Gibb,** William, Dublin, mariner
1768 ,, Wm., Rosleen, co. Ferm., gent.
1734 **Gibbal,** James, New-row, co. Dub., skinner
1724 **Gibbes,** Daniel, Cork, gent.
1791 **Gibbin,** Geo., Frederick-st., Dubl., esq.
1777 ,, Martha, Dublin, spr.
1799 ,, Rice, Dublin, surgeon
                [See GIBBONS.]
1781 **Gibbings,** Bartholomew, Gibbings Grove, co. Cork, esq.
1796 ,, Bartholomew, Mallow, co. Cork
1742 ,, Thos., Foremore, co. Cork, esq.
1725 **Gibbins,** John, Courtstown, co. Kildare
1686 **Gibbon,** Francis, Heathstown, co. Westmeath, esq.
1688 ,, Henry, Dublin, gent.
1739 ,, Jeffry, capt. of maj.-general Bissett's regt. of foot
1739 ,, rev. John, Loughcrew, co. Meath, clk.
1774 ,, Rice, Dublin, surgeon
1721 ,, rev. Robert, Kilworth, co. Cork, clk. (Ex.)
                [See GIBBONS, MC KIBBON.]
1757 **Gibbons,** Agnes, Dublin, milliner
1795 ,, Andrew, Dublin, tobacconist
1763 ,, Henry, Little Longford-st., Dub.
1809 ,, James, Baldoyle, co. Dublin
1633 ,, John, Dublin, alderman
1749 ,, Jno., Kindlestown, co. Wicklow
1811 ,, John, Moate, co. Westmeath, shopkeeper

1745 **Gibbons**, Mary, widow
1798 ,, Peter, Waterford city, gent.
1732 ,, rev. Richard, Dublin, clk.
1782 ,, Richard, Dublin, esq.
1796 ,, Samuel, Mountainstown, co. Meath, esq.
1777 ,, Thomas, Dublin, lace weaver
1788 ,, Thomas, Dublin, merchant
1712 ,, William, Dublin, alderman
1787 ,, William, Ballykeel, co. Down
[See GIBBIN, GIBBINS, GIBBINGS, GIBBON, FITZGIBBON.]
1747 **Gibbord**, James, mariner on board the " Pearl " man-of-war
1690 **Gibbs**, Charles, late of Norwich, now of Dublin, esq., capt. in sir Henry Bellasis' regt.
1764 ,, Danniel, Derry, co. Cork, esq.
1656 ,, Margery, wife to William Gibbs, Dublin, tailor [**V.** 246
1757 ,, Robert
1661 ,, William, Dublin, tailor
1737 **Giberne**, John, capt., at present in St. Y'polite, in Languedoc (Copy)
1716 **Gibney**, Patrick, Smithstown, co. meath, farmer
1746 **Gibson**, Anthony, Bridgefoot-street, Dublin
1745 ,, Charles, Bettystown, co. Meath, gent.
1786 ,, Elizabeth, Cork city, widow
1800 ,, Elizabeth, Dublin, spinster
1741 ,, George, Earl-street, Dublin, joiner
1784 ,, George, Whitehall, Middlesex (Copy)
1799 ,, George, Dorset-street, Dublin, gent. [farmer
1738 ,, Hugh, Scarva, co. Down,
1764 ,, John, the elder, Sligo
1794 ,, rev. John, rector of Clonmore, co. Louth
1746 ,, Joseph, Dublin, butcher
1797 ,, Joseph, Lambtons Buildings, Durhamshire (Copy)
1797 ,, Margaret, *alias* **Beere**, *alias* **M'Laughlin**, *alias* **Greg**, Dublin, widow
1795 ,, Richard Ellis, Belin, Queen's co., esq.
1756 ,, Robert, Dublin, dealer
1681 ,, Samuel, Dublin, gent.
1807 ,, Samuel
1672 ,, Seafoule, Drogheda, esq.
1811 ,, Susana, Baggot-street, Dub., widow
1701 ,, Thos., the elder, tallow chandler
1729 ,, Thomas, lieut. and adjutant in col. Pocock's regt.

1803 **Gibson**, Thomas, Dublin city, gent.
1758 ,, William, Dub., cabinet maker
1789 ,, William, Sligo town, surgeon
1791 ,, William, Marlborough-street, Dublin, esq.
1795 ,, Wood, D.D., rector of Cabra
1713 **Gibton**, Geffrey, Mill-street, Dubl., tanner
1777 ,, Jeffry, Dublin, gent.
1712 ,, John, Palmerstown, co. Dublin, brewer
1776 ,, John, Dublin, esq.
1770 ,, Margaret, Dublin, widow
1782 ,, Rebecca, Dublin, widow
1743 ,, Thomas, Dublin, lace weaver
1743 ,, Thomas, Dublin, merchant
1738 ,, William, late of Dublin, now of the Isle of Man
1810 ,, William, Wingfield, co. Wicklow, esq.
1753 **Giddings**, Robert, London, gent.
1796 **Gideon**, John, Shrubbs, co. Dublin, esq.
1773 **Gieran**, Peter, Cork, merchant
1713 **Giffard**, Duke, Castlejordan, co. Meath, esq.
1803 ,, sir Duke, Castlejordan, bart.
1772 **Gifford**, Arthur, Ahern, co. Cork, esq.
1779 ,, Catherine, Ballysop, co. Wexford, widow
1805 ,, Eleanor, Brunswick-st., Dublin
1676 ,, John, Castlejordan, co. Meath, esq.
1793 ,, Mary, Waterford town, widow
1770 ,, Nicholas, Ballysop, co. Wexford, gent.
1778 ,, Richard, Kitt Anns, co. Cork, esq.
1782 ,, rev. Richard, Boveragh, co. Londonderry, clk.
1753 ,, William, Waterford, gent.
[See GIFFARD, JEFFERS, JEFFORS.]
1735 **Gignous**, Charles, Waterford
1746 **Gilagh**, Margaret, Carlow, widow
1615 **Gilberde**, John, Woodford, Essex, gent. (Copy)
1763 **Gilbert**, Christopher
1743 ,, Claudius, divinity professor of Trin. Coll., Dublin, and rector of Ardstra, diocese Derry
1781 ,, Daniel, Platinstown, co. Wexford, farmer
1752 ,, David, Thomastown, co. Wicklow
1783 ,, Ford, Dublin, gent.
1713 ,, Gertrude, Dublin, widow
1686 ,, Jane, widow
1779 ,, Jane, *alias* **Hormidge**, widow

1784 **Gilbert**, Jane, Dublin, spr.
1659 ,, John, soldier   **[VII.** 101
1686 ,, John, Kilminshy, Queen's co., esq.
1776 ,, John, Clones, co. Wexford, gt.
1809 ,, John, Arklow town, gent.
1766 ,, Joseph, Cuffe-street, Dublin, coachmaker
1782 ,, Joseph, Corecannon, co. Wexford, farmer
1737 ,, St. Leger, Killminshy, Queen's co., esq.
1743 ,, Lydia, Humphreystown, co. Wicklow, widow
1753 ,, Martha, Dublin, spinster
1694 ,, Mary, Dublin, widow
1784 ,, Richard, Humphreystown, co. Wicklow, gent.
1643 ,, Robert, Dublin, gent.
1772 ,, Robert, formerly of Fethard, co. Tipperary, now of Ballyronan, co. Wicklow, gent.
1792 ,, Robert, Ferrybank, co. Wicklow, farmer
1658 ,, Thomas, Lackoe, Derbyshire, gent.   **[VI.** 294
1691 ,, Thos., Izaacstown, co. Meath, gent.
1597 ,, William (Copy)
1655 ,, William, Dublin   **[V.** 163
1735 ,, William, Humphreystown, co. Wicklow, gent.
1799 ,, William, Thomastown, co. Wicklow
1792 **Gildea,** James, Clonigashell, co. Mayo, esq.
1809 ,, John, Ballinrobe, co. Mayo, esq.
1791 **Giles**, Bridget, Youghal, co. Cork
1765 ,, George, Youghal, alderman
1802 ,, George, the younger, Youghal, co. Cork, esq.
1742 ,, Isaac, Annagh, co. Cork
1797 ,, James, Youghal, co. Cork
1748 ,, Nicholas Cullen, Dublin, gent.
1785 ,, Nicholas, Youghal, co. Cork, esq.
1727 ,, Richard, Youghal, co. Cork, alderman
1768 ,, Richard, Youghal, esq.
1811 ,, Sarah, wife to Richard Giles, Dublin city
1786 ,, Susana, Youghal, co. Cork
1767 ,, Ursula, *alias* **Green**, widow of George Giles, esq.
1799 ,, rev. Walter, Youghal, co. Cork, clk.
1806 ,, William, Montpelier-hill, co. Dublin
   [See GYLES.]

1751 **Gilesnan,** John, Williamstown, co. meath, gent.
1761 ,, Philip, Kilpatrick, co. Westmeath
1777 **Gilker**, Eneas, Ballyvarry, co. Mayo, gent.
1789 **Gilkison**, Alexander, Tullybegg, co. Donegal
1677 **Gill**, Alexander, Lurgan Clanbrazil, co. Armagh, gent.
1721 ,, Catherine, widow of John G., Lurgan Clanbrazil, co. Armagh
1754 ,, Elizabeth, Dublin, widow of Joseph G., timber mercht.
1757 ,, Elizabeth, Dublin, widow
1692 ,, Grace, Dublin, widow
1761 ,, Henry, Carrickfergus, co. Antrim, alderman
1738 ,, John, rector of Anamullin
1742 ,, Joseph, Dublin, merchant
1770 ,, Mary, Dublin, widow
1800 ,, Michael, Dublin city
1797 ,, Laurence, Rosan, co. Meath
1655 ,, Thomas, Dublin, shoemaker   **[V.** 235
1627 ,, Walter, Athare (Athea, Newcastle, ?) co. Limerick, gent.
1745 ,, William, Dub., timber mercht.
1773 **Gillaspy**, John, stationer
   [See GILLESPY.]
1735 **Gillegan**, Danl., Athlone, co. Westmeath, merchant
1789 **Gillelan**, John, Holestone, co. Antrim, gent.
1787 **Gilleland**, James, Taltarg, co. Antrim, gent.
1804 **Gillen**, John, Praughduff, co. Antrim
1677 **Gillet**, Dennis Frenchman, Cule, Londonderry
1774 ,, John, Youghal, co. Cork, esq.
1681 ,, William, Waterford, gent.
1808 **Gillespie**, Clements, Newry, co. Armagh, merchant
1761 ,, Elizabeth, wife to Robert G., Cumber, co. Down, gent.
1796 ,, John, Dublin city
1735 ,, Robt., Parsonstown, King's co.
1771 **Gillespy**, Charles, Dublin, watchmaker
1741 ,, James, Gortalowry, co. Tyrone
1787 ,, Margaret, Dublin, widow
1788 ,, William, Cumber, co. Down
   [See GILLASPY, GILLESPIE.]
1772 **Gillgan**, Peter, Thomas-st., Dublin, grocer
   [See GILLIGAN.]
1792 **Gillhuly**, Peter, Taish, co. Leitrim, farmer
1811 **Gilliard**, Elinor, Chapel Izod, widow

1802 **Gilliard**, Richard, Chapel Izod, co. Dublin, gent.
1808 **Gilligan**, Edward
[See GILLGAN.]
1628 **Gilliott**, Job, Dublin, esq.
1793 **Gillman**, George Massy, late capt. 27th regt. of foot
1732 ,, Hayward, St. Finbary's, Cork, gent.
1658 ,, Henry, Caragoohan, co. Cork city
1765 ,, Herbert, Shanacloyne, co. Cork, gent.
1746 ,, John, Curriheen, Lib. of Cork, gent.
1758 ,, St. Leger Hayward, Curriheen, Lib. of Cork, gent.
1740 ,, Stephen, Curriheen, Sth. Lib. of Cork
1763 **Gillmer**, Richard, ensign in general Braggs' regt.
1778 **Gillmore**, John, Boghead, co. Antrim
[See GILMORE.]
1762 **Gills**, John, Cluncollogue, King's co.
1796 **Gilsinan**, John, Clunmore
[See GILSENANE.]
1810 **Gilman**, Herbert, the elder, Oldpark, co. Cork
1789 **Gilmer**, Anne, Dublin, but of Bath
1779 ,, John, Dublin, esq.
1756 **Gilmore**, James, Dublin, mariner
1699 ,, Patrick, Wolverhampton, Staffordshire, gent. (Copy)
1753 ,, Tobias, Dublin, servant to Ben Burton
[See GILLMER, GILLMORE, GILMER.]
1734 **Gilpin**, John, Whitehaven, Cumberland, merchant
1725 **Gilsenane**, John, senr., Williamstown, co. Meath, farmer
[See GILLSINAN.]
1803 **Giltrap**, Robert, Deerpark, Baltinglass, farmer
1762 **Giraghty**, Edward, Roscommon, gent.
1722 ,, Elinor, Dublin, spinster
1774 ,, Mary, Killyon, co. Kildare, widow
1770 ,, Owen, Shepin, co. Westmeath, dealer
[See GERAGHTY.]
1699 **Girard**, Jane, native of Bergerac, in Perigord, refugee
1766 **Girattry**, Owen
1751 **Gird**, William, Royal Hospital, gt.
1617 **Giriaght**, Richard, Philipstown, King's co., merchant
1778 **Gisborne**, James, maj.-genl. of His Majesty's forces

1762 **Gitte**, Daniel, Grafton-street, Dub., merchant
1758 **Giveen**, Robert, the elder, Killowen, co. Londonderry, merchant
1807 **Given**, Catherine
1783 ,, James, Dublin, esq.
1791 ,, Mary, Kildare town, widow
1804 ,, Mary, Dublin city, widow
1690 **Glanally**, dame Susana, baroness of
1678 **Glanawly**, Hugo, lord baron of
1787 **Glannan**, John, James-street, Dub., skinner
1801 ,, Mary, Dublin, widow
1776 ,, Thomas, co. of Dublin city, skinner
1773 **Glannon**, John
1759 ,, Margaret, *alias* **Flyn**, Dublin
1751 ,, Valentine, Dublin, skinner
1691 **Glanville**, Edmond, Clonmel, merchant
1775 ,, Nicholas, Limerick
1800 **Glascock**, James, Dublin, esq.
1799 ,, Jane, *alias* **Albridge**, Dublin, widow
[See GLASSCOCK.]
1755 **Glascott**, George, Ballyfarnoge, co. Wexford, gent.
1811 ,, John, Aldertown, co. Wexford
[See GLASSCOTT.]
1677 **Glasgow**, Archibald, Rathmalton, co. Donegal, clk.
1755 **Glass** Edward, Athlone (Ex.)
1781 ,, John, Clonowen, co. Roscommon, esq.
1789 ,, Margaret, Clarendon-st., Dub., widow
1738 ,, Richard, Athlone, co. Roscommon, gent.
1745 **Glasscock**, Francis, Kilbride, co. Kildare, gent.
1799 ,, Francis Albridge, in East India Company's Service
1772 ,, Thomas, Inch, co. Tipperary
1755 ,, Walter, Dublin, esq.
[See GLASCOCK.]
1633 **Glasscoke**, William, Cork, gent.
1788 **Glasscott**, George, Ballynomona, co. Wexford
1780 ,, John, Ballynomona, co. Wexford
[See GLASCOT.]
1811 **Glassford**, John, lieut. in His Majesty's navy
1679 **Glassingham**, William, Dublin, merchant
1778 **Glatigny**, Susanna, co. Dublin, spinster
1766 **Gleadeau**, Thomas, Dublin, esq.
1768 **Gledstanes**, Albert, Dublin, esq.

1752 **Gledstanes**, Anne, widow of George G., Lisboy, co. Tyrone, esq.
1792 „ Frances, Daisyhill, co. Tyrone
1739 „ George, Lisboy, co. Tyrone, esq.
1746 „ James, Fardross, co. Tyrone, esq.
1782 „ Margt., Fardross, co. Tyrone, widow
1709 „ Mathew, Dublin, gent.
1785 „ Susana, Dublin, spr.
1778 „ Thomas, Fardross, co. Tyrone, esq.
1807 „ Whitney, Dublin city, esq.
1730 **Gledstaynes**, Thos., Dubl., mercht.
1720 **Glegg**, Henry, Dublin, merchant
1654 „ captain Robt., Nicholas-street, Dublin **[IV.** 88
1809 **Glen**, William, Maghrymenagh
1693 **Glendie**, John, dean of Cashel, and preby. of St. Michael, Dub.
1787 **Glenholme**, John, Ballymaska, co. Down, farmer
1700 **Glenn**, John, Londonderry, mercht.
1777 „ William, Cahirneman, co. Galway, gent.
1770 **Glenny**, Isaac, Savilmore, co. Down, gent.
1778 „ Isaac, Glenville, co. Down, gt.
1770 **Glerawley**, William, lord visct.
1774 **Gligson**, Murtogh, Tinnerannagh, co. Tipperary, farmer
1802 **Glison**, Elizabeth, Dublin, widow
1794 **Glissan**, Andrew Moregh, Cork, woollen draper
1786 „ Thos, Carrickabrick, co. Cork
1790 **Gloster**, Bridget, Dublin, widow
1688 **Glover**, Henry, Darrenstown, co. Limerick, gent.
1777 **Glyn**, Mary
1643 **Goads**, Roger, Schoolhouse-lane, clk.
1695 **Goatley**, Mary, wife to Senles Goatley, London, painter and stainer (Copy)
1806 **Godber**, Ricd., North-strand, Dub., gent.
1735 **Godbey**, Peter, Dublin, esq.
1736 **Goddall**, Caroline, executrix of Francis Cornwall, esq.
1756 **Goddard**, Elizabeth, Youghal, co. Cork, widow
1748 „ lieut.-col. Henry
1720 „ Holland, Cork, merchant
1800 „ rev. John, Newry, co. Down, clk.
1808 „ John, Newry, co. Down
1742 „ Rebecca, Cork, widow
1706 „ Richard, capt. in col. Lellington's regt.

1802 **Goddard**, Sarah, Kilkenny, widow
1757 „ Thomas, captain
1799 „ Wllliam, Dublin, esq.
1768 **Goddes**, George, Dublin, hosier
1757 **Godeau**, Samuel, co. Dublin, goldsmith
1774 **Godfrey**, Ann, Dublin, widow
1750 „ Anne, Dublin, widow
1730 „ Anthony, Dublin, glazier
1730 „ Arabella, par. St. Martin-in-the-fields, Middlesex, wid. (Copy)
1741 „ Benj., par. St. James, Westminster (Copy)
1755 „ Edward, lieut. of marines
1751 „ Elizabeth, Cork, widow
1735 „ Geo., Kinsale, co. Cork, gent.
1685 „ John, Dublin, merchant
1712 „ John, Bushfield, co. Kerry, gent. (Ex.)
1734 „ John, Dublin, gent.
1734 „ John, Drogheda, alderman
1782 „ John, Anna, co. Kerry, esq.
1790 „ Lawford, Birr, King's co.
1686 „ Margaret, Knockgraffan, co. Tipperary, widow
1744 „ Rowley, col. Read's reg. of foot
1725 „ Stephen, Coleraine, alderman
1771 „ Thos., Clonmel, co. Tipperary, chandler
1639 „ William, Coleraine, alderman
1696 „ Wm., Knockgraffan, co. Tipperary, esq.
1701 „ captain William (Copy)
1712 „ Wm., Coleraine, co. Londonderry, esq.
1747 „ Wm., Bushfield, co. Kerry, esq.
1763 „ Wm., lieut.-col. in the army, and major in the 28th regt. of foot
1703 **Godfry**, Sankey, capt. in lieut.-gen. Earl's regt. of foot
1753 **Godley**, Ann, Drogheda, widow
1784 „ Elizabeth, *alias* **Rogers**, *alias* **Bolton**, widow
1806 „ John, Sackville-st., Dublin city, esq.
1791 „ rev. Richd., Tullyclea, co. Ferm.
1779 „ rev. William, D.D., rector of Mullabrack
1808 „ William
1810 „ William, Congleton, Cheshire, gent. (Copy)
1676 **Godolphin**, Francis, Dublin castle, esq., priv. sec. to Arthur, earl of Essex, L.L. (Ex.)
1716 **Godsell**, Amon, Moorstown, co. Limerick, gent.
1757 „ James, Mallow, co. Cork, gent.
1716 „ Richard, Dublin, gent.

1664 **Godwin,** Alice, Dublin, widow
1669 ,, Edward, Wicklow, tanner
1674 ,, Edward, Dublin, gent.
1811 ,, John, Cork city, gent.
1642 ,, Robert, Drogheda
1664 ,, Stephen, Dublin, gent.
        [See GOODWIN.]
1679 **Goeghegan,** James, Dublin, barber-
        surgeon
1726 ,, Kidagh, Carne, co. Westmeath
1676 ,, Owen, Robinstown, co. Long-
        ford, gent.
        [See GEOGHEGAN.]
1632 **Goery,** Henry, Trim, merchant
1767 **Goff,** Eliz., Horetown, co. Wexford
1757 ,, Fade, Dublin, merchant
1752 ,, Jacob, Drumcondra, linen-
        draper
1799 ,, Jacob, Little Horetown, co.
        Wexford
1800 ,, James, Boulbawn, co. Wexford,
        farmer
1801 ,, John, Portarlington, Queen's
        co., shoemaker
1754 ,, Joseph Fade, Dublin, merchant
1753 ,, Mary, Drumcondra, co. Dubl.,
        widow
1754 ,, Richard, Dublin, merchant
1767 ,, Richard, Little Horetown, co.
        Wexford, gent.
1809 ,, Richard, Tottenham-green, co.
        Wexford
1799 ,, Robert, Bormount, co. Wex-
        ford, esq.
1801 ,, Thos., Portarlington, Queen's
        co., cooper
1762 ,, Wm., Garristown, co. Dublin,
        farmer
        [See GOUGH.]
1729 **Goffe,** Jonas, Waterford, chandler
1648 ,, Michl., Lond., mercer (Copy)
1656 ,, Thomas, soldier   [**V.** 349
1774 **Gofton,** John, Dublin, gent.
1756 **Goggin,** Anne, Meath-st., Dublin
1810 ,, Bryan, Swift's-row, Dublin city
1787 ,, Mary, Dublin, widow
1773 ,, Stephen, Limerick, gent.
1743 ,, Wm., Meath-st., Dub., clothier
1757 ,, William, Dublin, merchant
1760 ,, William, Limerick, burgess
1807 ,, Wm., Killarney, co. Kerry
1811 ,, Wm., Limerick city, printer
1804 **Going,** Andrew
1759 ,, Elizabeth, Clonmel, widow
1805 ,, James, Bellisle, co. Clare, gent.
1762 ,, Philip, Ballyphillip, co. Tip-
        perary, gent.
1780 ,, Robert, Traverstown, co. Tip-
        perary, esq.
1794 ,, Thos., Coolbay, co. Cork, esq.

1610 **Goire,** Thomas, Trim, merchant
1692 **Golborn,** John, Killinagh, co. Kil-
        dare, clk.
1720 **Golborne,** Daniel, Dublin, gent.
1730 ,, Elizabeth, Dublin, widow
1691 ,, Enock, Garrycastle, co. West-
        meath, esq.
1664 ,, Robert, Dublin, gent. [**IX.** 196
1777 **Gold,** George, Merrion-row, Dublin.
        dairyman
1745 ,, Nathaniel, London, merchant
1600 **Golding,** Elizabeth, Belgart, co.
        Dublin, widow
1757 ,, Elizabeth, Dublin, widow
1601 ,, Gilbert, Dublin, gent.
1589 ,, John, Perston Landy, gent.
        (Copy)
1699 ,, John, sen., the Strand, Dublin,
        shipwright
1704 ,, John, Dublin, gent.
        [See GOULDING.]
1792 **Goldsborough,** Wm., Mountmellick,
        Queen's co., gent.
1628 **Goldsmith,** Edwd., Kilcock, co. Kil-
        dare, gent.
1764 ,, Edwd., Limerick, esq.
1748 ,, Hester, Dublin, widow
1769 ,, Isaac, dean of Cloyne
1768 ,, Joseph, Ballyoughter, co. Ros-
        common, gent.
1794 ,, Mary, Dublin, widow
1792 ,, Maurice, Dublin, gent.
1808 **Gollock,** James, Forest, co. Cork,
        esq.
1811 ,, Rebecca, Cork city, widow
1791 ,, Thos., Shandangan, co. Cork,
        gent.
1805 **Gonan,** Persis, Limk. city, widow
1780 **Gone,** George
1784 **Gonne,** Ann
1757 ,, Geo., Brookhill, co. Mayo, clk.
1768 ,, George, Londonderry
1752 ,, Henry, Barberstown, co. Kild.,
        gent.
1785 ,, Henry, Abbey, Dublin, gent.
1792 ,, Henry, Dublin, attorney
1797 ,, Margaret, Dublin, widow
1797 ,, Margt. Elizabeth, Dublin, wid.
1785 ,, Martha, Londonderry city, spr.
1804 ,, Martha, Castlepollard co. West-
        meath, widow
1769 ,, Thos., Dublin, gent.
        [See GONE.]
1761 **Good,** Henry
1636 ,, John, Coonebeg, Queen's co.,
        gent.
1780 **Goodacre,** George, College-green,
        Dublin, glover
1669 **Goodaker,** Henry, Dublin, mercht.
1728 ,, William, Dublin

1680 **Goodall**, John, Dublin, gent.
1752 **Goodbody**, Joseph, Mullanahard, Queen's co.
1800 ,, Mark, Mountmellick, Queen's co., merchant
1726 ,, Mathew, Meath-st., Dublin, tallow chandler
1759 ,, Richard, Clonagh, Queen's co., farmer
1765 ,, Samuel, Ereckstown, co. Westmeath, gent. (Large will)
1663 **Goode**, Wm., sir Allen St. George's troop, Killenure, co. Tip.
1708 **Goodenough**, Richard, Dublin, esq. (Ex.)
1720 ,, Sarah, Kilkenny, widow
1758 **Goodfellow**, James, Belfast, gent.
1761 ,, James, Island of Madeira, last of Belfast, gent.
1771 **Goodlat**, Thomas, Dublin, esq.
1766 **Goodlatt**, Jane, Strabane, co. Tyrone, widow
1582 **Goodinge**, Mathew, Dub., mercht.
1602 **Goodman**, Geo., Oldfield, Worral, Cheshire, gent.
1576 ,, James, Damestown, co. Dubl.
1777 ,, John, Trim, co. Meath
1738 ,, Robert, Dublin, gent.
1742 **Goodricke**, Thomas, Cahirnetna, co. Limerick, gent.
1804 **Goodshaw**, Thomas, Leixlip, co. Kildare
1730 **Goodwin**, Frances, Dublin, widow
1778 ,, Garnet, Dublin, gent.
1768 ,, George, Limerick, esq.
1793 ,, George, mariner
1792 ,, James, Dublin
1735 ,, John Philip, par. St. Martin, Middlesex, esq. (Copy)
1740 ,, rev. John, Dublin, clk.
1749 ,, John, providore to the Royal Hospital
1782 ,, John, Dorset-st., Dublin, coach owner
1779 ,, Mary, Dublin, spinster
1809 ,, Mary, Limerick, co. Wexford, widow
1703 ,, Mathew, gent.
1713 ,, Peter, Royal Hospital, Dublin, gent. [gent.
1730 ,, Richd., Butterstown, co. Dub.,
1731 ,, Robert, Kennedy's-lane, Dub., gent.
1703 ,, Thomas (written in a pocketbook)
1729 ,, Timothy, abp. of **Cashel**, q.v.
1654 ,, William [**IV**. 62
1680 ,, William, Dundalk, esq.
1763 ,, William, Dublin, carpenter
1778 ,, William, Wexford town, gent.

1681 **Goodwyn**, Robert, East Grimstead, Sussex, esq.
1597 ,, captain William, esq.
1568 **Goodwyne**, Robert
1666 **Gookin**, Robert, Courtmaschery, co. Cork, esq.
1752 ,, Robert, Carrigeen, co. Cork, esq.
1692 ,, Vincent, Lincolns Inn, Middlesex, gent.
1757 **Goold**, Anne, Dublin, spr.
1745 ,, Caleb, Dublin, mercht.
1737 ,, Edmond, Dublin, mercht.
1752 ,, Elizabeth, Dublin, widow
1759 ,, Elizabeth, Rainsford-st., widow
1771 ,, Francis, Cork, merchant
1789 ,, George, Cork, merchant
1782 ,, Henry, Ballydahin, co. Cork, gent.
1781 ,, Hester, Harold's Cross, co. Dublin, widow [widow
1805 ,, Mary Catherine, Cork city,
1722 ,, Michl., Jamesbrook, co. Cork, esq.
1784 ,, Michl., Jamesbrook, co. Cork, gent.
1721 ,, Robert, Drominey, co. Cork, gent.
1658 ,, Thomas, Cork, alderman [**VII**. 41
1727 ,, Thomas, Dublin, merchant
1808 ,, Thomas, Dublin city, esq.
1734 ,, William, Cork, merchant [See GOULD.]
1773 **Goolden**, Patk., St. James's-street, Dublin
1776 **Goolding**, William, Birr, King's co. [See GOULDING.]
1656 **Goord**, Nicholas, foot soldier [**V**. 274
1758 **Gordon**, Adam, Middle Temple, London, gent. (Copy)
1691 ,, Alexander, capt. of foot, Ardandraigh, co. Longford, gent.
1766 ,, Alexander, Dublin, printer
1787 ,, Alexander, Dub., watchmaker
1800 ,, Alexander, Feltrim, co. Dublin, esq.
1786 ,, Ann, Newgrove, co. Cork, widow
1763 ,, Archibald, captain in lord Blakeny's regt.
1735 ,, Charles, Moraick, Aberdeenshire, lieut. in earl Orkney's regiment
1792 ,, Charles, Park-place, co. Dubl., esq.
1755 ,, David, Dublin, watchmaker
1772 ,, Esther, Carrickmacross, co. Monaghan, widow

1676 **Gordon**, George, Dublin, gent.
1746 ,, George, Strabane, co. Tyrone, merchant
1770 ,, George, Navery, co. Down, gent.
1755 ,, Hannah, Mackenagh, co. Tyrone
1799 ,, Henrietta, Bellmount, co. Carlow
1724 ,, Henry
1745 ,, Hugh, Dublin city, gent.
1738 ,, Jas., Mackanagh, co. Tyrone, gent.
1789 ,, James, Raphoe town
1729 ,, Jane, Dublin, widow
1723 ,, John, Athlone, co. Roscommon, gent.
1769 ,, John, Dublin, gent.
1772 ,, John, Belfast, merchant
1781 ,, John, Templebar, Dubl., paper stamper
1811 ,, John, Aughrim-street, Dublin, gent.
1763 ,, Mary, wife to Charles G., Dub., esq.
1783 ,, Patrick Simpson, Rosemount, co. Louth, gent.
1746 ,, Robert, Newry, co. Down
1784 ,, Robert, Newgrove, co. Cork, esq.
1742 ,, Samuel, Clonmel, co. Tipperary
1757 ,, Samuel, Spring-garden, co. Waterford, gent.
1775 ,, Samuel, Dundalk, co. Louth
1793 ,, Stephen, Dublin, ironmonger
1733 ,, Thomas, Dublin, esq.
1760 ,, Thomas, Dublin, gent.
1796 ,, Thomas Knox, Loyalty Lodge, co. Down, esq.
1807 ,, Thomas, Spring-garden, co. Waterford
1727 ,, William, banker in Paris
1746 ,, William, Dublin, butcher
1773 ,, William, Dublin, coachmaker
1796 **Gore**, Ann, Dublin, widow
1799 ,, Ann, Dublin, spinster
1782 ,, Annesley, Belleek, co. Mayo, esq.
1698 ,, sir Antony, Newtown Gore, co. Mayo, bart.
1730 ,, Arthur, Clonrone, co. Clare, esq.
1742 ,, sir Arthur, Newtown, co. Mayo, bart.
1744 ,. Arthur, Ballygarrett, co. Carlow, esq.
1805 ,, Arthur, Kilkenny city
1748 ,, Catherine, widow of William G., esq.
1663 ,, captain Charles

1777 **Gore**, Charles, Goresgrove, co. Kilkenny, esq.
1781 ,, Charles, Goresgrove, co. Kilkenny, esq.
1733 ,, lady Elizabeth, widow of sir Ralph G., bart.
1743 ,, dame Elizabeth, widow of sir Ralph G., Dublin, bart.
1713 ,, dame Ellinor, widow of sir Arthur Gore, bart.
1750 ,, Frances, *alias* **Ingoldsby**
1724 ,, Francis, Clonrone, co. Clare, esq.
1763 ,, Francis, St. Patrick's Close, Dub., gent.
1763 ,, Francis, late of Sligo, now of Dublin, esq.
1801 ,, Francis, Goodwood, co. Clare, esq.
1762 ,, Frederick, Dublin, esq.
1764 ,, Frederick, Dublin, esq.
1757 ,, Gertrude, daur. of Richard G., Sligo, esq.
1786 ,, Hamilton, Catherine's Grove, co. Dublin, esq.
1657 ,, lieut.-col. Henry, Magherabeg, co. Donegal   [**VII.** 20
1729 ,, Henry, Sligo, co. Sligo, esq.
1764 ,, Henry, capt. of the 25th company of marines (Copy)
1691 ,, Hugh, bp. of **Waterford**, q. v.
1787 ,, Humphrey, Dublin, gent.
1742 ,, capt. John, in America
1806 ,, John, Glasnevin-road, co. Dub.
1730 ,, Mary, Dublin, spr.
1750 ,, Mary, Ballygarrett, co. Carlow
1768 ,, Mary, wife to Dr. William G., bishop of Elphin
1629 ,, sir Prowle, Magherabeg, co. Donegal
1716 ,, Ralph, Dublin, alderman
1724 ,, Ralph, Barrowmount, co. Kilk., esq.
1733 ,, sir Ralph, Bellisle, co. Ferm., bart.; one of the Justices of Ireland
1778 ,, Ralph, Barrowmount, co. Kilk., esq.
1753 ,, Richard, Sligo, esq.
1765 ,, Richard, Sandymount, co. Wicklow, esq.
1808 ,, right hon. Richard, Clontarf, co. Dublin
1727 ,, Robt., Artarmon, co. Sligo, esq.
1768 ,, Robert, Dublin, esq.
1735 ,, Sarah, Dublin, spr.
1774 ,, Sarah
1705 ,, sir William, bart.
1730 ,, Wm., Woodford, co. Leitrim, esq. (Large will)

1737 **Gore**, Wm., Dryanleigh, co.Leitrim, gent.
1750 ,, Wm., Barrowmount, co. Kilk., esq.
1769 ,, Wm., Woodford, co.Leitrim, esq. (Large will)
1784 ,, William, bp. of **Limerick**, q. v.
1807 ,, William, Ballymacrickett, co. Antrim
1696 **Gorges**, Henry, Dublin, esq., son of J. Gorges, Derry, esq., decd.
1727 ,, Henry, Summerseat, co. Londonderry, esq.
1681 ,, Jane, Summerseat, co.Londonderry, wid. of John G., esq.
1728 ,, Jane, Dublin, widow
1728 ,, Richard, lieut.-gen.
1778 ,, Richard, Killbrew, co. Meath, esq.
[See GEORGE.]
1779 **Gorham**, Elizabeth, *alias* **Edmunds**
1785 ,, Jas., Obrenan, co. Kerry, gent.
1737 **Gormacan**, Augustin, Leighlinbridge, co. Carlow, mercht.
1807 **Gormacon**, Rose, Dublin, widow
1780 **Gorman**, David, Rarush, co. Carlow
1796 ,, Fortescue, Dublin, esq.
1787 ,, James, Ennis, co. Clare, gent.
1795 ,, Martha, Glenavy, co. Antrim, widow
1786 ,, Mary, Dublin, spr.
1755 ,, Michael, Clonmel, merchant
1800 ,, Owen, Tullamore, King's co., publican
1754 ,, Thomas, Inchiquin, co. Clare, gent.
[See GORMON.]
1602 **Gormanston**, Catherine, *alias* **Fitz Williams**
1600 ,, Chris., viscount
1788 ,, Thomasyn Preston, dow. lady viscountess. (Copy)
1788 **Gormanstown**, Anthony Preston, viscount
1629 ,, Jenico, viscount
1756 ,, Jenico Preston, commonly called lord viscount (Not proved)
1754 **Gormansway**, Anthony, Dublin
1801 **Gormley**, Mathew, Kevin's-st., co. Dublin, innkeeper
1681 **Gormlie**, Richard, Dublin, butcher
1711 **Gormly**, John, Carrig, co. Kildare, gent.
1638 **Gormogan**, Donogh, Newtown, co. Catherlogh, gent.
1787 **Gormon**, Francis, Dublin, esq.
1775 ,, Luke, Coluna, Queen's co.
1778 ,, Sylvester, Drominihy, co.Clare, gent.

1729 **Gormon**, William, Maryborough, Queen's co., apothecary
1766 ,, William, Ennis, co. Clare, gt.
1773 ,, William, Glenavy, co. Antrim gent.
[See GORMAN.]
1728 **Gornall**, William
1770 **Gorroll**, William, Lurgybrack, co. Donegal
[See CARROLL.]
1687 **Gorst**, John, Dublin, gent.
1776 ,, Thomas, Newtown, Cheshire, gent. (Copy)
1790 **Gosford**, Archibald, lord viscount (Large)
1807 ,, rt. hon. Arthur, lord visct.
1697 **Gosling**, Charles, Kilkenny, esq.
1751 **Goubrisk**, Dennis, Money, King's co., farmer
1768 **Goubuisk**, Joseph
1656 **Gouers**, Edwd., Widtown, co. Louth, gent. **[V.** 312
1642 **Gough**, Barbara, *alias* **Bath**, Clontoirke, co. Dublin, widow
1631 ,, Edward, Dublin, alderman
1750 ,, Elizabeth, Limerick, widow
1695 ,, Francis, Cork, gent.
1733 ,, James, Berilstown, co. Meath, yeoman
1785 ,, James, Cole-alley, Meath-st., Dublin
1660 ,, John, Dublin, merchant **[VIII.** 181
1781 ,, John, Dublin, alderman of Limerick
1792 ,, John, Cole-alley,Thomas-court, schoolmaster
1672 ,, Marcy, Dubl., widow of captain William Gough, Donassy, co. Clare
1785 ,, Mathew, Dublin, gent.
1627 ,, Patrick, Dublin, alderman
1639 ,, Patrick, Dublin, alderman **[VIII.** 96
1739 ,, Patrick, Dublin, gent.
1713 ,, Richd., Martinstown, co. Louth, gent.
1641 ,, Robt., chanter of St. Mary's and St. Catherine's, Limerick (Copy)
1771 ,, Samuel, Dublin, merchant
1763 ,, Thomas, Bristol, merchant
1745 ,, Warr, Limerick, gent.
1604 ,, William, Dublin, alderman
1660 ,, William, Sutton, co. Dublin, gent. **[VIII.** 99
1667 ,, William, Dunasa, co. Clare, gent.
1755 ,, William, Little Horetown, co. Wexford, gent.

1797 **Gough**, William, Dublin, clk.
1701 „ Yeoman, Dublin, currier
  [See GOFF.]
1581 **Goughe**, Patrick, Dublin, alderman
1766 **Gould**, Garrett, Knockraha, co.
  Cork, gent. [gent.
1697 „ Gerrott, Knockraha, co. Cork,
1746 „ Helen, Cork, widow
1714 „ Henry Fitzdavid, Cork, mercht.
1707 „ John, Dublin, vintner
1735 „ Laurence, Cork, merchant
1673 „ Michael, Cork, esq. (Ex.)
1681 „ Patrick Fitz Edmond, Cork,
  merchant
1686 „ Richard, Bunne, co. Cavan,
  yeoman
1752 „ Richard, Macroom
1645 „ William, Kinsale, burgess
  [See GOOLD.]
1779 **Goulding**, Alice, Paradise-row,
  Dublin, spinster
1746 „ Christopher, Dublin, printer
1758 „ Christopher, Lees-lane, Dublin,
  cooper
1709 „ Ellen, Dublin, widow
1682 „ Mary, *alias* **Luttrell**, Dublin,
  widow
1772 „ Michael, Dublin, merchant
1655 „ Thomas, soldier [**V.** 124
1769 „ William, the younger, Birr,
  King's co., merchant
1607 **Gouldinge**, Wm., Dublin, mercht.
  [See GOOLDING, GOLDING.]
1770 **Goullin**, Peter, Killart, co. Kildare,
  gent.
1804 **Gourley**, James, Sackville-street,
  Dublin
1735 **Gourney**, rev. Dr. Robert, preby. of
  Cumber, dio. Derry
1810 **Gowan**, Clotworthy, city of Bath,
  esq. (Copy)
1760 „ rev. Geo., clk., rector of Envor,
  co. Donegal
1778 „ George, Dublin, gent.
1669 **Gower**, Thomas, Dublin, gent.
1744 **Gowne**, Robert, esq.
1744 **Gowran**, Ann, dowager baroness
1676 „ John, earl of [**XI.** 259
1764 **Grace**, Catherine, New-st., Dublin,
  widow
1609 „ Edmond, Walterstown (the
  original in Irish)
1620 „ Edmond, Kilkenny, gent.
1768 „ Elizabeth, Dublin, widow
1709 „ Frances, now wife to John G.,
  Shanganah, Queen's co.
1658 „ Francis, Dublin, gent.
  [**VIII.** 35
1775 „ George, Cutpurse-row, Dublin,
  haberdasher

1782 **Grace**, George, Cullahill, Queen's co.
1614 „ Gerald, Nenagh, co. Tipperary,
  esq.
1690 „ James, Raheny, co. Dublin,
  esq. (Ex.)
1782 „ James, Dublin
1804 „ Jane, Dublin city, widow
1769 „ Johanna, Dublin, widow
1626 „ John, Enagh
1719 „ John, Borris, Queen's co.
1765 „ rev. John, Dub., clk. (cancelled
  will)
1784 „ John, formerly lieut. in the 12th
  dragoons
1790 „ John, capt. of carbineers in the
  Imperial service
1761 „ Joseph, fellow of Trinity Coll.,
  Dublin
1716 „ Laurence, Dublin, esq.
1765 „ Mary, wife to Oliver G., of
  Gracefield, Queen's co., esq.
1761 „ Michael, Sheffield, Queen's co.,
  esq.
1789 „ Michael, Dublin, gent.
1626 „ Oliver, Carny, co. Tipperary
1708 „ Oliver, Shanganah, Queen's co.,
  gent. [esq.
1735 „ Oliver, Brittas, co. Tipperary,
1753 „ Oliver, Mount Oliver, Queen's
  co., clk.
1804 „ Oliver, Cullenswood, co. Dubl.,
  esq.
1720 „ Patk., Hodgestown, co. Meath,
  farmer
1767 „ rev. Patrick, Dublin, clk.
1792 „ Patk., Skerries, co. Dub., P.P.
1773 „ Pierce, Dublin
1784 „ Richard, Dubl., revenue officer
1801 „ Richd., Southville, Queen's co.,
  esq.
1782 „ Samuel, Galway town, burgess
1746 „ Sheffield, Dublin, surgeon
1770 „ Thomas, formerly of Raheny,
  now of Dublin, esq.
1771 „ William, par. Stamullin, co.
  Meath, farmer
1778 „ William, formerly of Dub., late
  of St. Germains, in France
1784 **Grady**, Henry, par. St. James, Westminster (Copy)
1788 „ Honora
1787 „ John, New-street, Dubl., blacksmith
1808 „ Mary, Cappercullen, par. of
  Abington
1804 „ Michael, Stokestown
1773 „ Nichs., Grange, co. Limerick,
  esq.
1779 „ Standish, Lodge, co. Limerick,
  esq.

1780 **Grady,** Standish, Cahir, co. Limerick, esq.
1793 ,, Standish, Cappercullen, co. Limerick, esq.
1804 ,, rev. Theadus, Barna
1769 ,, Thomas, Killballyowen, co. Limerick, late of Dublin
1789 ,, Thomas, Harley-st., Middlesex, esq. (Copy)
1792 ,, William, Raheen, co. Limerick
1723 **Graffan,** rev. James, clk.
1554 **Grage,** William
1673 **Graham,** Alexander, Crevecallahan, co. Tyrone
1659 ,, Andw., Dromuor, co. Longford, gent.   **[VIII.** 10
1737 ,, Andrew, Convoy, co. Down
1683 ,, *alias* **Grimes,** Anthony, corporal of Trim, gent.
1790 ,, Archibald, Gledstown, co. Fermanagh
1803 ,, Archibald, Athlone, co. Westmeath, surgeon
1706 ,, Arthur, Tullygraham, co. Mon., esq.
1737 ,, Arthur, Ballyheridan, co. Armagh, gent.
1787 ,, Arthur, Dublin city
1792 ,, David, Oldtown, co. Londonderry
1666 ,, Edward, Dublin, esq.   [esq.
1798 ,, Francis, Temple-street, Dubl.,
1770 ,, Hannah, Londonderry, widow
1746 ,, Hector, Culmain, co. Mon., esq.
1808 ,, Hector, Dublin city, esq.
1714 ,, Hugh, qr.-master of col. Ross's regt. of horse
1688 ,, sir James, Drogheda, knt.
1719 ,, James, Dundalk
1768 ,, Jas., capt. in genl. Whatgrave's dragoons
1800 ,, Jas., Ballymaglave, co. Down, farmer
1661 ,, John, Balliber, Queen's co., son of Richard G., esq.
1667 ,, John, Ballinan, Queen's co., esq.
1709 ,, John, Athy, co. Kildare, tanner
1717 ,, John, Drogheda, alderman (Ex.)
1724 ,, John
1742 ,, John, Dublin, gent.
1743 ,, rev. John, Hockly, co. Antrim, clk.
1753 ,, John, Drogheda, alderman
1777 ,, John, Great George's-st., Dubl., esq.
1787 ,, John, Summerhill, co. Donegal, esq.

1791 **Graham,** John, Phibsborough, co. Dublin, tailor
1802 ,, John, late in the service of the East India Co. in Bengal (Copy)
1807 ,, John, Belfast, co. Antrim, merchant
1805 ,, Martha, Dublin city, widow (Large)
1808 ,, Mary, Cootehill, co. Cavan, spinster
1732 ,, Milicent, Athy, co. Kildare, widow
1683 ,, Pearce, Limerick, burgess
1787 ,, Percis, Cork, widow
1804 ,, Philip, Banbridge, co. Down, gent.
1762 ,, Richard, Cullmain, co. Mon., esq.
1680 ,, Robert, Balliheridon, co. Arm., gent.
1721 ,, Robert, Drogheda, esq.
1735 ,, Robert, Dublin, staymaker
1747 ,, Robert, Derry, gent.
1775 ,, Robert, Ballycoog, co. Wick., gent.
1788 ,, Robert, Netherby, Cumberland, D.D. (Copy)
1772 ,, Susana, Dublin, spinster
1710 ,, Thomas, Castle-street, Dubl., glover
1748 ,, William, Plattan, co. Meath, esq.
1748 ,, William, brig.-gen., and col. of foot
1797 ,, William, Drumgoon, co. Ferm., gent.
1806 ,, William, Carlow town, apothecary
1808 ,, William, lieut.-col., Meath militia
[See GREAME, GREHAM, GRIMES, GRYMES.]
1661 **Grahame,** major Thomas, Youghal, co. Cork
1707 **Grahan,** Daniel, Dublin, esq.
1697 **Grahme,** Renold, Munington, Yorkshire, esq. (Copy)
1736 **Grainder,** capt. Samuel de la Motte, Carlow, esq.
1698 **Granard,** Arthur, earl of
1734 ,, Arthur, earl of
1729 ,, Catherine, dow. countess of
1769 ,, George, earl of (Large will)
1784 ,, George, earl of
1778 ,, Letitia, dowager countess of
1765 **Grandison,** John, earl of
1630 **Grandisone,** sir Oliver St. John, knt., lord viscount, and lord Tregoose

1744 **Grange**, Edmond, Sallymount, co. Wicklow, esq.
1790 ,, John, Rahavill, co. Wicklow, gent.
1742 **De La Grange**, Peter, Sieur de St. Maird, Dublin, esq.
1780 ,, rev. Richard Chapel, Camden-street, Dublin
1743 ,, Thomas, Killowen, co. Wex., gent.
1784 ,, William, Kevin-street, Dublin, innkeeper
1778 **Granger**, Ellinor, Ashgrove, co. Dublin, widow
1735 ,, Hugh, par. of Carmoney, co. Antrim, mariner
1758 ,, Thomas, Ashgrove, co. Dublin, esq.
1789 **Grant**, Archibald, Manchester-sq., Middlesex (Copy)
1805 ,, Christophina
1799 ,, Donald, esq.
1699 ,, George, Ballidalagh, in Scotland, now in Skiberreen, co. Cork, esq.
1787 ,, George, Dublin, cabinetmaker
1811 ,, George, lieut. in the navy (Copy)
1800 ,, Hester, Broadstone, Dublin, widow
1792 ,, James, par. of Clare Abbey,co. Clare
1698 ,, Jasper, Grantstown, co. Wat., esq.
1752 ,, John, archdeacon of Barum and Bannon, residentiary in the cathedral of St. Peter, Oxon. (Copy)
1800 ,, John, Dublin city
1805 ,, Julian, Ballintemple, widow
1770 ,, Luke, Dublin, esq. (Large will)
1603 ,, Mary
1760 ,, Mary, Cork, widow
1604 ,, Richard, Waterford, gent.
1627 ,, Robert, Waterford, butcher
1741 ,, Stephen, Cork, victualler
1706 ,, Thomas, co. Cork
1750 ,, Thomas, Kilmurry, co. Cork, gent.
1785 ,. William, Dublin, gent.
1795 ,, William Alexander, Cork city, esq.
1809 ,, Wm., Exmouth, Great Britain, esq.
1706 **Grantham**, James, Ardmoyle, co. Tipperary, clerk
1775 ,, Richard, Dublin, esq.
1721 ,, Thomas, rector of Knockmark, co. Meath

1708 **Granville**, John, lord baron of Poteridge (Copy)
1707 **Gratan**,Patrick, Belcamp, co.Dubl , D.D.
1768 **Grattan**, Catherine, spinster
1746 ,, Charles, Enniskillen, school-master
1801 ,, David, Annagh, co. Galway, gent.
1746 ,, James, Dublin, merchant
1747 ,, James, Dublin, M.D.
1766 ,, James, Dublin, esq.
1754 ,, rev. John, minister of St. Audoen's, Dublin
1754 ,, John, Clonmeen, co. Kildare, gent.
1762 ,, John, Rabbitfield, co. Kildare, farmer
1782 ,, Katharine, Dublin, widow
1786 ,, Olivia, spinster
1772 ,, Ralph, Brookville, co. Tipp., D.D.
1736 ,, Richard, lord mayor of Dublin
1746 ,, Richard
1744 ,, Robert, Rabbitfield, co. Kildare, gent.
1802 ,, Rosana, widow
1768 ,, Samuel, Dublin, merchant
1742 ,, William, Dublin, merchant
1790 ,, William,Sylvanpark,co.Meath, esq.
1798 ,, William, Rathangan, co. Kildare, esq.
1787 **Gratton**, Arthur, Rathclonbrackan, King's co., gent.
1801 ,, Arthur, Rathville, King's co.
1772 ,, David, Rabbitfield, co. Kildare, gent.
1750 **Grave**, Andrew (nuncupative, not proved)
1743 ,, rev. Joseph, Ballycommon, King's co., clerk
1748 ,, Mary, Dublin, widow
1754 ,, Mary, Dublin, spinster
1656 **Graves**, Anthony, trooper [**VI.** 22
1791 ,, Barth., Millbank, Queen's co., gent.
1669 ,, Edmond, Drogheda, mercht.
1722 ,, Francis, Drogheda, gent.
1789 ,, Jane, *alias* **Hodgson**, widow
1795 ,, Jeffry, Drogheda, bricklayer
1809 ,, rev. John, Drogheda town
1728 ,, Samuel, Castledawson, co. Derry, yeoman
1803 ,, Samuel, one of the admirals of H.M. Navy (Copy)
1780 ,, Thomas, Castledawson, co. Derry, esq.
1682 ,, William, Ramullin, co. Meath, gent.

1767 **Graves**, William, Drogheda, esq.
1784 ,, William, Bow-st., Dublin, esq.
[See GREAVES.]
1673 **Gray**, Alexander, Bristol, mercht.
1701 ,, Anne, Ballinrobe, co. Mayo, widow
1786 ,, Anne, widow
1801 ,, Anne, Donard, co. Wicklow, widow
1804 ,, Anne, Letterkenny,co.Donegal
1696 ,, Edward, Dublin, tailor
1770 ,, Edward, Dublin, esq.
1799 ,, Francis, Cork city, esq
1655 ,, George, and six other troopers in col. Prittie's regt.
1792 ,, George, Loughadian, co. Down, linendraper
1800 ,, George, Portobello, co. Dublin
1807 ,, Geo., Graymount, co. Armagh
1741 ,, Isaac, Dublin, tallow chandler
1729 ,, James
1751 ,, John, Cork, merchant
1774 ,, Joseph, Cork, merchant
1794 ,, Joseph, Lebeg, co. Wicklow, farmer
1804 ,, Joseph, Bishop-street, Dublin
1802 ,, Martha, Portobello, Dublin, widow
1772 ,, Mary, Lisnacrieve, co. Longford
1661 ,, Nathaniel, London, esq., now of Dublin (Copy)
1791 ,, Pope, Cork city, esq.
1799 ,, Robert, Woodford, co. Galway, gent.
1763 ,, Sarah, Cork, widow
1803 ,, Sarah, par. St. James, Clerkenwell (Copy)
1771 ,, Sewell, Dublin, ironmonger
1737 ,, Stephen, Cork, merchant
1804 ,, Thomas, Rosclough, Queen's co., farmer
1808 ,, Warner Wall, Rockbrook, Queen's co., esq.
1695 ,, William, Durrow, co. Kilkenny, gent.
1723 ,, William, Cudha, Queen's co., esq.
1805 ,, William, Rutland-sq., Dublin city
[See GREY.]
1795 **Grayborne**, Mary, Cumberland, widow (Copy)
1808 **Grayburne**, Thomas, Ardee-row, Dublin, clothier
1726 **Graydon**, Alexander, ensign
1739 ,, Alexander,Killishe,co.Kildare, esq.
1736 ,, Catherine, Dublin, widow
1766 ,, Catherine, Dublin, widow

1753 **Graydon**, Erasmus,Dysart,co. Sligo (Not proved)
1771 ,, George, Killishe, co. Kildare, esq. (Large will)
1750 ,, Grizel, Elverstown, co. Dublin, widow
1673 ,, John, Barristown, co. Dublin, gent.
1790 ,, John, Cavanagarvan, co. Fermanagh, M.B.
1725 ,, Robt., Russellstown, co. Wicklow, esq.
1803 ,, Thos., Greenhills, co. Kildare
1756 **Grayson**, Abraham
1809 ,, Anthony, formerly of Dublin, late of Londonderry
1799 **Gready**, William, Rallahasna, co. Westmeath, farmer
1623 **Greame**, Geo., Monyquid, Queen's co., gent.
1628 ,, sir Ricd., Lynanstown, Queen's co., knt.
[See GRAHAM.]
1780 **Grear**, John, Cultroe, co. Down, farmer
1692 **Greatracks**, Edmund, Newaffane, co. Waterford, esq. (Ex.)
1781 **Greatrakes**, Valentine, Quarter, co. Waterford, gent.
1685 **Greatraks**, Alice, Meddop Hall, co. Wexford, widow
1684 ,, Valentine,Oldaffane,co.Waterford, esq.
1760 ,, Valentine, Quarter, co. Waterford, gent.
1686 ,, William,Newaffane,co.Waterford, esq.
1738 **Greaughan**,Laurence,Drumcondralane, victualler
1673 **Greaves**, Nicholas, D.D., dean of Dromore
[See GRAVES.]
1731 **Grecory**, Mary, *alias* **Fullerton**, widow
1724 **Green**, Abraham, Ballymaros, co. Limerick, esq.
1758 ,, Adam, Dublin, gent.
1739 ,, Alexander, in Mairns of Aberlour, North Britain
1766 ,, Ann, Dublin, spinster
1803 ,, Ann, Dublin, widow
1772 ,, Barbara, widow of William G., Usher's-quay, gent.
1733 ,, Benjamin, Dungarvan, co. Waterford
1765 ,, Benjamin, Dublin, alderman
1789 ,, Bridget
1789 ,, Catherine, Eyre Court, co. Galway, widow
1777 ,, Deborah, Limerick, spinster

1720 **Green**, Elizabeth, Dublin, widow
1765 ,, Elizabeth, Limerick, spinster
1775 ,, Elizabeth, Dublin, widow
1776 ,, Elizabeth, Clooncolloy, King's co., spinster
1805 ,, Elizabeth
1782 ,, Francis, Graigue, co. Limerick, esq. (Large will)
1759 ,, George, Abbey, co. Limerick, esq.
1760 ,, George, Abbey, co. Limerick, esq.   [chandler
1762 ,, George, Bolton-street, Dublin,
1683 ,, Godfrey, Killmanahane, co. Waterford, esq.
1768 ,, Godfrey, Dublin, merchant
1780 ,, Godfrey, Scart, Lib. of Limerick, esq.
1798 ,, Godfrey, Dublin, esq.
1731 ,, rev. Henry, Palacemore, co. Longford, clk.
1738 ,, Henry, Dublin, apothecary
1745 ,, Henry, Ballymacres, co. Limk., merchant
1741 ,, James, Rock of Dungarvan
1770 ,, James, Dublin, butcher
1807 ,, James, Cappaghmurrow, co. Tipperary
1810 ,, James, Newport-street, Dubl., shipwright
1728 ,, Jane, St. Sepulchre's, Dublin, widow
1799 ,, Jane
1711 ,, John, Ratherow, co. Carlow, gent.
1717 ,, John, Dublin, merchant
1725 ,, John, Dublin, gent.
1737 ,, John, Nether-Oldtown, Banff-shire, North B., farmer
1746 ,, John, Oldabbey, co. Limerick, esq.
1760 ,, John, Craig, co. Limerick, esq.
1762 ,, John, Cluncullogue, King's co.
1772 ,, John, Dublin, gent.
1779 ,, John, Stickillen, co. Louth, gt.
1779 ,, John, Coolroe, co. Wicklow, farmer
1794 ,, John, Corbally, co. Galway
1801 ,, John, Cappoquin, co. Waterford, gent.
1803 ,, John, Greenville, co. Kilkenny, esq.
1804 ,, John, Boherbee, East Lib. of Limerick, gent.
1757 ,, Joseph, Belfast, co. Antrim, gent.
1769 ,, Joseph, Dublin, merchant
1777 ,, Joseph, Dublin, esq.
1723 ,, rev. Lucas, rector of Bally-macky, co. Tipperary, clk.

1784 **Green**, rev. Marlborough, Eyre Court, clk.
1682 ,, Marmaduke, Drumisklin, co. Fermanagh, gent.
1756 ,, Michael, Rocksborough, co. Tipperary, esq.
1656 ,, cornet Nicholas, Dublin   [**VI**. 36
1741 ,, Nicholas, Carker, co. Cork, merchant
1769 ,, Nichs., Clahane, co. Limerick, esq.
1775 ,, Nuttall, Low Grange, co. Kilkenny, esq.
1773 ,, Philip, Tullamore, King's co., gent.
1779 ,, Priscilla, Dublin, spr.
1687 ,, Richard, Oxmantown, smith
1727 ,, Robert, Belfast, esq.
1808 ,, Robert, Greenhills, co. Galway
1760 ,, Rodolphus, Kilmanahan, co. Wexford, esq.
1804 ,, Rodolphus, Passage, co. Waterford
1710 ,, Saml., Killaghy, co. Tipperary, esq.
1774 ,, Sarah, Dundalk, co. Louth, widow
1778 ,, Sarah, Dublin, widow   [chant
1733 ,, Simon, Youghal, co. Cork, mer-
1738 ,, Stephen, Dublin, apothecary
1721 ,, Symon, Youghal, co. Cork, merchant
1742 ,, rev. Thomas, Coghellstown, co. Meath, clk.
1754 ,, Thomas, Low Grange, co. Kilkenny, esq.
1758 ,, Thomas, Dublin, silversmith
1807 ,, rev. Thomas
1811 ,, Thomas C., Hammersmith, Middlesex
1733 ,, William, Dublin, surgeon
1754 ,, William, Dublin, gent.
1768 ,, William, Rushane, co. Clare
1773 ,, Wm., Stickillen, co. Louth, esq.
1800 ,, rev. William, Glasnevin, co. Dublin
1809 ,, Wm., Kilrush, co. Dubl., esq.
1764 **Greene**, Anthony, Dublin, merchant
1769 ,, Catherine, Dublin, widow
1632 ,, Cavendish, Shannet, co. Limk., gent.
1795 ,, Dorothea, Tullamore, King's co., spr.
1677 ,, Eliah, College-green, Dublin, esq.
1736 ,, Godfrey, Moorstown, co. Tipperary, esq.
1706 ,, Hadesby, Shelly Hall, Essex, gent. (Copy)

1691 **Greene,** Henry, Drestinan, co. Fermanagh, gent.
1800 ,, Henry, Prussia-street, Dublin
1685 ,, John, or St. John, mayor of Coleraine
1784 ,, John, Lettyville, co. Tipp., esq.
1803 ,, John, Greenville, co. Kilkenny, esq.
1807 ,, John, Carrickmacross, co. Mon.
1805 ,, Mary, Dublin, widow
1625 ,, Mathew, New Ross, merchant
1795 ,, Michael, capt. in the co. Tipperary militia
1769 ,, Richard, Dublin, gent.
1752 ,, Robert, Tyrmore, co. Limerick, gent.
1786 ,, Robert, Dublin, merchant
1796 ,, rev. Robert, prebendary of Tipperary and vicar of Rathmore
1797 ,, Thomas, Gurtroche, co. Cork, gent.
1749 ,, Wm., Dungarvan, co. Waterford, gent.
1781 ,, William, Killamanaheen, co. Waterford, esq.
1781 ,, Wm., Ballymacres, co. Limk., esq.
1794 ,, William, Eastmoreland, co. of Dublin city, esq.
1808 ,, Wm., Dublin city, bookseller
1807 **Greenfield,** Angel
1788 ,, rev. Andrew, rector of Moira, co. Dublin
1740 **Greenham,** Edwd., mariner belonging to the "Salisbury"
1637 ,, John, Dublin, gent.
1744 ,, John, Dublin, silk dyer
1792 **Greenhow,** Francis, Thomastown, co. Kildare
1773 ,, Wm., Earl-st., Dubl., merchant
1794 **Greenly,** Robert, Castlereagh, co. Roscommon, merchant
1801 ,, Sarah, Dublin, spr.
1748 **Greenway,** Robert, Dublin, gent.
1723 ,, Samuel, Newry, co. Down, clothier
1746 ,, William
1757 ,, Wm., Newry, co. Down, gent.
1778 **Greenwood,** Benj., Portarlington, King's co., merchant
1778 ,, Mary, *alias* Russell, Hodgestown, co. Kildare, widow
1753 ,, Samuel, Dublin, spr.
1777 **Greer,** Henry, Lurgan, co. Armagh, merchant
1796 ,, James, Milltown, co. Tyrone, linendraper
1740 ,, John, Tullyanaghan, co. Down, draper
1782 ,, Joseph, Dungannon

1737 **Greer,** Thos., Ballinakill, Queen's co., weaver
1746 ,, Thos., Bernagh, co. Tyrone, linendraper
1803 ,, Thos., Rhonehill, co. Tyrone [See GRIER.]
1796 **Greg,** Thomas, Belfast, co. Antrim, esq.
1746 **Gregan,** James, Stonybatter, co. Dublin, dairyman
1678 **Gregan,** Thomas, Dublin, merchant
1774 **Gregg,** Abigail, Blackhorse-lane, Dublin, widow
1750 ,, David, Phinidurk (Finnydurk, co. Donegal, ?)
1789 ,, Frederick, Derry city, esq.
1785 ,, Henry, Kilkenny city, gent.
1780 ,, Jinn or Jean
1747 ,, John, Coleraine, co. Derry, formerly of Virginia, farmer
1802 ,, John
1780 ,, Patrick, Manor Hamilton, co. Leitrim
1774 ,, Richd., Mellmount, co. Tyrone, gent. [draper
1760 ,, Robert, jun., Dublin, woollen-
1714 ,, Thomas, Brouginsoken, co. Londonderry, farmer
1750 ,, Thomas, Dublin, sailor
1811 ,, Thomas, Cork city, gent.
1768 ,, William, Dublin, merchant
1782 ,, Wm., Parkmount, co. Antrim, merchant
1784 ,, William, Manor Hamilton, co. Leitrim, gent. [See GREG.]
1664 **Greggs,** James, Raheen, King's co., gent.
1672 **Gregorie,** George, Dublin, esq.
1664 **Gregorry,** Giles [XIII. 14
1751 **Gregory,** Anne, Dublin, widow
1742 ,, Benjamin, Maynooth, co. Kildare, clk.
1733 ,, George, clk., curate of par. of Down
1809 ,, Martha, Dublin city, widow
1738 ,, Mary, *alias* Dunlap, Coleraine, widow
1788 ,, Mary, Kilkenny, widow
1790 ,, Mary, Borrisokane, co. Tipperary, widow
1771 ,, Ralph, Roobrickan, co. Kildare, clk. [clk.
1757 ,, Robert, Pentower, Queen's co.,
1811 ,, Robert, Coole, co. Galway, esq. (Large)
1775 ,, Sophia, Pentower, Queen's co., widow
1726 ,, William, Dublin, tanner [See GREGORIE.]

1696 **Gregson**, Anne, widow of George G., Lisburn
1690 ,, George, Lisburn, merchant
1718 **Greham**, Ellinor, Dublin, spr.
[See GRAHAM.]
1792 **Grehan**, Thedy, Dublin, esq.
1757 ,, William, the Boot Inn, Bootlane, Dublin, innkeeper
1601 **Gren**, Andrew, Kilmainham, co. Dublin, gent.
1549 **Grenane**, John, Lusk
1782 **Grenville**, Geo., Watton Underwood, Bucks (Copy)
1733 **Gresson**, John, Augher, co. Tyrone, gent.
1783 ,, Mary, Swadlinbar, co. Cavan, widow
1709 **Gretten**, Robert, Reneghan, co. Kildare, farmer
1697 **Gretton**, Simon, Clonmeel, co. Kildare, farmer [watchmaker
1796 **Greville**, Henry, Dublin, late a
1708 ,, John, Nicholstown, co. Kildare, gent.
1802 ,, Samuel, Wells, co. Dubl., gent.
1675 **Grey**, Henry, Dublin, esq. (Ex.)
1790 ,, Richard, Nadrid, co. Cork
1747 ,, Samuel, Dublin, esq.
[See GRAY.]
1802 **Greydon**, Richard, North-strand, Dublin, esq.
1801 **Gribbin**, James, Dublin, gent.
1669 **Grice**, Richard, Transtown, co. Limerick, gent.
1779 **Grier**, Andrew, Derrymackeegan, co. Westmeath, gent.
1779 ,, Frances, Dublin, widow [gent.
1790 ,, Robert, Cooreen, co. Galway,
1784 ,, Stephen, Finea, co. Westmeath, gent.
1795 ,, William, Cabra, co. Dublin
[See GREER.]
1771 **Grierson**, Hugh Boulter Primrose, Dubl., printer and stationer
1753 ,, Geo., Essex-st., Dubl., printer
1755 ,, Geo. Abraham, printer to H. M.
1775 ,, John, Doolystown, co. Meath, gent.
1763 ,, Robert, Newtown, co. Meath
1775 ,, Robert, Dublin, gent.
1804 ,, Robert, formerly of Smithfield, salesmaster
1757 **Griesdall**, Thomas, Ringsend, gent.
1788 **Griffin**, Bridget, Galway town, wid.
1767 ,, Charles, Laggagh, co. Meath, gent.
1798 ,, Daniel, Galway town, mercht.
1807 ,, Daniel FitzGerald, lieut.-col. in the East India Co's. service (Copy)

1683 **Griffin**, Edward, Griffinstown, co. Westmeath, gent.
1773 ,, Frances, Branockstown, co. Meath, widow
1742 ,, Henry, Clonbrien, co. Kerry, esq.
1773 ,, Jane, Dublin, spinster
1735 ,, John, Londonderry, mercht.
1735 ,, Luke, Charleville, co. Cork
1793 ,, Maurice
1756 ,, rev. Michael, Elphin, co. Roscommon, clerk.
1717 ,, Mortogh, Killarney, co. Kerry
1749 ,, Thomas, Waterford, tobacconist
1763 ,, Thomas, Ballinulta, co. Wicklow, farmer
1789 **Griffith**, Acheson, Dublin, attorney
1748 ,, Anne, *alias* **Carroll**, Dublin, widow
1789 ,, Anthony, Dublin, gent.
1762 ,, Charles, Dublin, gent.
1789 ,, Christopher, Padsworth, Berkshire (Copy)
1736 ,, David, Dublin, wine cooper
1677 ,, Edward, Bunglane, co. Donegal, gent.
1711 ,, Edward, St. James', Middlesex (Copy)
1736 ,, Edward, Cloonagh, co. Sligo, gent.
1764 ,, Edward, Dublin, esq.
1711 ,, Henry, Ballyhaevan, co. Sligo, gent.   [esq.
1800 ,, Henry, Ballytivenan, co. Sligo,
1809 ,, Henry, Cuffe-street, Dublin, esq.
1725 ,, Humphrey, Ballyhunan, co. Sligo
1798 ,, James, Drum, co. Cavan, gent.
1773 ,, Jane, Portarlington, Queen's co., widow
1660 ,, Jeremiah, Ture, co. Donegal, gent.
1639 ,, John, Tadinny, co. Mon., yeoman
1671 ,, John, serjeant-major, Dublin, esq.
1799 ,, John, Charlemount-place, co. Dublin, esq.
1808 ,, Joseph, Charlemount-st., Dubl., clothier
1752 ,, Lewis, Dublin, esq.
1629 ,, sir Maurice, co. Leitrim, knt. [**II.** 157
1629 ,, sir Maurice, Drumrouske, co. Leitrim, knt. [**II.** 157
1768 ,, Peter, Kilbrush, co. Kildare, farmer
1781 ,, rev. Richard, chaplain of 17th dragoons (Copy)

1661 **Griffith,** Robert, London, gent.
  [**IX.** 50
1666 ,, Robert, Dublin, esq., serjeant-at-law
1704 ,, William
1775 ,, William, Ballytivenan, co. Sligo, esq.
1802 **Grifith,** Catherine, Padworth, Berkshire (Copy)
1744 **Grimaudet,** Jane, Dublin, widow
1702 **Grimes,** Thomas, quarter-master in brigadier Langston's regt. of horse
  [See GRAHAM.]
1735 **Grimsel,** John, Bridge-st., Dublin, silk weaver
1704 **Grimston,** Ursula, Stratford, near London
1707 **Grinaway,** Christopher, Bandon-bridge, co. Cork, esq.
1761 **Grinsell,** Joseph, Graige Cloghy, co. Tipperary, gent.
1780 **Gripenkerk,** Hartwicke, Dublin, grocer
1658 **Grist,** Robert, Youghal, maltster
  [**VII.** 81
1808 **Groaly,** John, Barrack-st., Dublin, shoemaker
1616 **Grogan,** Bryan, Magharegarry, co. Down, gent.
1721 ,, John, Johnstown, co. Wexford, esq.
1774 ,, John, Dublin, grocer
1784 ,, John, Johnstown, co. Wexford, esq. (Large will)
1762 ,, Overstreet, Dublin, mercht.
1730 **Grollier,** Esther, Drogheda, widow
1638 ,, Jacob, London, French mercht., now in Dublin
1668 ,, Timothy, Dublin, victualler
1787 **Grome,** John, Eyre Court, co. Galway, esq.
1623 **Gromell,** James, Limk., alderman
1805 **Gromwell,** Mary, Limerick city, widow
1650 **Gronna,** Joseph
1798 **Groome,** rev. Edward, Castlecomer, co. Kilkenny, clerk
1760 **Grorke,** Laurence, Carrowmanna
1789 **Grose,** Edward, par. St. Andrew, London (Copy)
1745 **Grossvenor,** Katherine, spinster, now in the service of col. Wm. Hall, of Conduit-st., Hanover-square
1789 **Grosvenor,** Thomas, Old Conaught, co. Wicklow, gent.
1726 **Grourk,** Denis, Dublin, merchant
1768 **Grove,** Arabella, Greenhills, co. Tipperary, widow

1773 **Grove,** Blenerhasset, Dublin, esq.
1796 ,, Catherine, Kilcummer, co. Cork, widow
1793 ,, Elizabeth, Dublin, spinster
1810 ,, Elizabeth, Abbey-street, Dublin, spinster
1730 ,, col. George, par. St. James, Westminster
1736 ,, Henry, par. St. George, Middlesex, of the forces (Copy)
1750 ,, Ion, Ballyhimock, co. Cork, esq.
1794 ,, Jas., Castlegrove, co. Donegal, esq.
1729 ,, Joseph, Tipperary
1682 ,, Thomas, Castle Shanachan, co. Donegal, esq.
1792 ,, Thomas, Bath city, esq.
1735 **Groves,** John, Dublin, gent.
1802 **Grubb,** Benjamin, Clonmel, co. Tip., merchant
1729 ,, John, New Ross, co. Wexford, gent.
1784 ,, John, Anner Mills, co. Tipp.
1726 ,, Rebecca, *alias* **Thresser,** Waterford, widow
1740 ,, Rebecca, Waterford, widow
1797 ,, Robert, Clonmel
1738 ,, Thomas, Waterford, mercht.
1756 **Gruby,** Agnes, Dolphin's Barn, Dublin, widow
1744 ,, William, Dublin, tanner
1798 **Grueber,** rev. Arthur, rector of Kilkeeran, diocese of Tuam
1803 ,, rev. Arthur, rector of Crossboyne, diocese of Tuam
1808 ,, John, capt. of the Louth militia
1559 **Gruffythe,** John, clerk, treasurer of Llandaff, dean of St. Asaph, and preby. of Castleknock
1793 **Grumley,** Michael, Wicklow, shopkeeper
1793 ,, Samuel, Wicklow town, shopkeeper
1808 **Grumly,** James, Patrick-st., Dublin, victualler
1731 ,, John, Dublin, broker
1638 **Grundy,** William, Dublin, saddler
  [**IV.** 346
1783 **Gruniman,** Anne, Monasterevan, Queen's co.
1746 **Gryams,** John, mariner on board the " Dublin " privateer
1709 **Grymes,** Edmond, Dublin, gent.
1745 ,, sir George, Naas, co. Kildare, bart.
  [See GRAHAM.]
1614 **Grymesdich,** George, Dublin, gent.
1606 **Grymesditch,** Ralph, Dublin, gent. (Copy, original delivered out)

1700 **Guard**, Alice, widow of Thomas Guard
1797 **Gubbins**, George Stamer, Kilfrush, co. Limerick, esq.
1759 ,, Joseph, Cork, merchant
1767 ,, Joseph, Kilfrush, co. Limk., esq.
1776 ,, Joseph, Kilfrush, co. Limk.
1809 ,, Launcellot (Copy)
1671 **Gubbon**, *or* **Gibbon**, Garrett M'Shane, Ballylopine, co. Cork
1737 **Guerin**, Peter, Dublin, gent.
1787 **Guff**, Thomas, Roscommon town
1797 **Guideon**, Sampson, Lincolns Inn Fields, Middlesex, esq. (Copy)
1714 **Guidott**, Anthony, Lincolns Inn, Middlesex (Copy)
1667 **Guilford**, Elizabeth, countess of (Copy)
1780 **Guillenan**, Margaret, Rainsford-st., Dublin
1720 **Guillevan**, Patrick, Johnstown, co. Westmeath, farmer
1787 **Guillislan**, Robert, Standing Stone, co. Antrim
1706 **Guilloneau**, John Peter, Sieur de Maison Neave, French gent.
1728 **Guinebauld**, Florent, lord of Lamilliere
1795 **Guiness**, Samuel the elder, Dublin, gent.
1807 **Guinness**, Arthur, Dublin city, brewer
1733 **Guion**, Daniel, Dublin, merchant
1754 **Guirne**, Thomas, Derry, Queen's co., farmer
1733 **Guizot**, Anthony, Dublin, merchant
1781 **Gully**, Daniel, Middleton, co. Cork
1796 **Gumbleton**, George Connor, Maisonette, Devonshire, esq.
1757 ,, Richard, the elder, Tallow, co. Waterford, gent.
1776 ,, Richard, Castlerickard, co. Waterford
1792 ,, Richard, Castlerichard, co. Waterford, esq.
1706 **Gumby**, Robert, Fort William, Bengal (Copy)
1796 **Gun**, George, Knockanagh, co. Kerry, gent.
1802 ,, George, Ballybunion, co. Kerry, esq.
1766 ,, John, Cloghbrien, co. Kerry, esq.
1615 ,, William, Limerick, clk.
1723 ,, William, Rattoo, co. Kerry, gent.
1771 ,, William, Dublin, esq.

1744 **Gunn**, George, Carrigafoyle, co. Kerry, esq.
1699 ,, William, late of Rattoo, co. Kerry, esq.
1792 **Gunnell**, Edward, Ardee, co. Louth
1658 **Gunner**, Thomas, sergt. of foot [**VI.** 251
1793 **Gunning**, Alexander, Athlone, co. Westmeath, clk.
1799 ,, Anne, Dublin, widow
1717 ,, Bryan, Castlecoote, co. Roscommon, esq.
1751 ,, George, Cluniburn, co. Roscommon, esq.
1776 ,, Jas., Ballym'william, co. Longford
1715 ,, John, Dublin, gent.
1763 ,, Mary, *alias* **Adamson**, Dublin, widow
1773 **Gunston**, John, Capel-street, Dubl., upholder
1672 **Gurley**, John, sergt. to col. Brent Moore's company
1806 **Gurly**, Michael, King-st., Oxmantown, Dublin, cordwainer
1797 ,, Thos., the elder, Carlow town, esq.
1742 **Gurnall**, Thomas, of the Plantation in co. Down, maltster
1701 **Gurraudet**, Peter, Dublin, gent.
1739 **Guthrey**, George, Dublin, mercht.
1781 **Guthrie**, John, Blarnagh, co. Clare, gent.
1676 **Guthry**, John, Dromore, co. Down, merchant
1694 **Guy**, James, St. James', Westminster, London (Copy)
1802 ,, Peter, Ballinderrin [grocer
1811 ,, Richd., Ballybott, co. Armagh,
1811 ,, William, Greenwood Park, co. Down
1754 **Guybon**, Francis, Dublin, gent.
1756 **Guyn**, John, Limerick, saddler
1772 **Guynan**, Mary, Blackpool, Lib. of Cork, widow
1788 **Guyon**, Anne, Clonmel, co. Tipp.
1771 ,, Herbert, Liverpool, Lancashire, mariner
1761 **Gwin**, captain Lewis [See GWYN.]
1700 **Gwither**, Charles, Trinity College, M.D.
1709 ,, Saml., Robertstown, co. Meath, gent.
1718 **Gwyllim**, Meredyth, Gwyllimbrook, Cavan, esq.
1681 ,, Thos., Ballyconnell, co. Cavan
1779 **Gwyn**, Jane, Bryansford, co. Down, spinster [See GWIN.]

1739 **Gyde**, John, the elder, par. of Radborough, Gloucestershire, gent. (Copy)
1701 **Gyles**, John, par. St. Giles-in-the-fields, Middlesex (Copy)
1745 ,, John, Dundalk, co. Louth, gt.
1795 ,, Ross, Castletown Coty, co. Louth, esq.
[See GILES.]

—H—

1639 **Hackat**, William, Prieststown, co. Meath, gent.
1799 ,, John Dorrington, Watterstown, co. Westmeath, esq.
1780 **Hacket**, Ann
1761 ,, Arthur, Clonmel, co. Tipperary, gent.
1673 ,, Bartholomew, son of Edmond H., Prieststown, decd.
1660 ,, James, Esgirr, co. Kilkenny, gent. [VIII. 119
1710 ,, James, Prieststown, co. Meath, gent.
1776 ,, rev. James, Newry, co. Down, clk.
1639 ,, John Fitz James, Gambonstown, co. Tipperary, gent.
1775 ,, Philip, Dublin, gent.
1627 ,, Richd. Fitz Thomas, Limerick, merchant
1627 ,, Richard, dean of Killaloe
1629 ,, Robert, Dublin, farmer
1693 ,, sir Thos., Dublin, knt. (Copy)
1767 ,, Thomas, Dublin, gent.
1792 ,, Thos., Dublin, attorney-at-law
1795 ,, Thos., Ballinamona, King's co.
1691 ,, Walter, Thurles, co. Tipperary, merchant
1810 **Hackett**, Bartholomew, Capel-st., Dublin, silver cutter
1713 ,, Catherine, Lambeg, co. Antrim, widow (Copy)
1611 ,, James Fitz Piers, Limerick, merchant
1716 ,, James, Orchardstown, co. Tipperary, gent.
1744 ,, James, Rockby, Yorkshire, now of Fethard, co. Tipperary
1803 ,, Laurence, Sportfield, co. Kilkenny
1776 ,, Patrick, Dublin, publican
1795 ,, Philip, Dublin, gent.
1583 ,, Richard, Fethard, burgess
1749 ,, Theobald, Cranahurty, co. Tipperary, gent.
1697 ,, Thomas, bp. of **Down**, q. v.
1706 ,, sir Thomas, Dublin, knt.

1707 **Hackett**, Thomas, Thurles, co. Tipperary, esq.
1713 ,, sir Thomas, Dublin, knt.
1738 ,, Thomas, College-green, Dubl., gent.
1805 ,, Thomas, formerly of Dublin, late of Enderby Hall
1737 ,, William, Westreaves, co. Dub., gent.
1750 ,, William, Isle of Wight
1763 **Haddaway**, Benjamin, Grany, co. Kildare, gent.
1750 ,, William, Grany, co. Kildare, gent.
1769 **Hadden**, James, Dublin, distiller
1769 ,, William, Dublin, shipwright
[See HADON.]
1765 **Haddock**, Benjamin, Ballinderry, co. Antrim
1658 ,, James, Malone, co. Antrim
[VII. 14
1707 ,, John, Carranbane, co. Down, gent.
1785 **Hadock**, rev. Isaac, Hillsborough, co. Down, clk.
1749 **Hadon**, John, Drogheda, alderman
[See HADDEN.]
1635 **Hadsar**, Ricd., Keppock, co. Louth, esq.
1774 **Hadsor**, Bartholomew, Prussia-st., Dublin, gent.
1795 **Haffield**, Mary, Dublin, widow
1785 **Hagan**, James, Brefoot-st., Dubl., clothier
1720 ,, Terence, Dublin, victualler
[See EGAN.]
1806 **Hagarty**, Hester, Prussia-street, co. Dublin, spinster
1763 **Haggard**, Mable, Dublin, widow
1755 **Hagherin**, Elizabeth, Waterford, widow
1744 **Hagthorpe**, Thos., Tipperary town, gent.
1762 **Hague**, Samuel, Dublin, merchant
1766 **Haighton**, Thos., Dublin, mercht.
1747 **Haines**, Christopher, Dublin, gent.
1718 ,, Edward, sen., Dublin, gent.
1694 ,, Robert, Chapel Izod, gent.
[See HYNES.]
1699 **Hairs**, William, Dublin, gent.
1801 **Halbert**, James, Wicklow, leather cutter
1679 **Halbridge**, Alexander, Newry
1726 ,, John, Dromore, co. Down, esq.
1737 **Hale**, Edward, Drogheda, apothecary
1762 ,, Elizabeth, wid. of Edward H., Drogheda, apothecary
1779 ,, John, formerly of George's-lane, coach maker

1750 **Hale,** Paul, Dublin, gent.
1747 ,, Richard, Dublin, silk dyer
1745 ,, William, Dublin, gent.
1788 **Hales,** Helen, Dublin, widow
1756 ,, Mathew, Glassaganny, co. Tipperary, gent.
1771 ,, Mathew, Forge, co. Waterford
1782 ,, rev. Saml., preby. of Kilbrittain, dio. Cork
1691 ,, Stephen, Kilkenny, esq.
1675 **Halford,** William, Cloghamon, co. Wexford
1786 **Halfpenney,** Michl., Garvey Bridge, co. Meath, farmer
1785 ,, Patrick, Summerhill, co. Dub., baker
1805 **Halfpenny,** William, co. Dublin, farmer
1785 **Hall,** Barker, Alasty, co. Kildare, gent.
1773 ,, Benjamin, Battersea, Surrey, esq. (Copy)
1784 ,, Catherine, Dublin, widow
1793 ,, Christopher, Tonagh
1659 ,, Danl., soldier in capt. Vivian's company   [VIII. 184
1800 ,, Daniel, Clonough, co. Wexford, farmer
1737 ,, David, surgeon and lieut. in genl. Bisset's regt.
1630 ,, Edwd., New Grange. co. Meath, gent.
1714 ,, Edward, Strangford, co. Down, esq.
1715 ,, Edwd., Mitchelstown, co. Cork
1794 ,, Edward, Dover, Kent, esq.
1748 ,, Elizabeth, Dublin, widow
1785 ,, Elizabeth, Dublin, widow
1798 ,, Elizabeth, Duke-st., Dublin
1805 ,, Elizabeth, Rahoboath, co. of Dublin city
1799 ,, Frances, Dublin, widow
1706 ,, Francis, Mount Hall, co. Down, esq.
1761 ,, Francis, Strangford, co. Down, esq.
1770 ,, George, Drogheda, brewer and distiller
1741 ,, Hanibal, Dublin city, surgeon
1663 ,, Henry, bp. of **Killala,** q. v.
1758 ,, James, Dublin
1772 ,, James, Ballinderry, co. Antrim, farmer
1799 ,, James, Enniskillen
1802 ,, Jane, Dublin, widow
1689 ,, Jeremie, late of Boothtown, Yorkshire, now of Dublin, M.D. (Ex.)
1713 ,, John, Dublin, merchant
1731 ,, John, Dublin, gent.

1735 **Hall,** rev. John, D.D., rector of Ardstra, co. Tyrone
1743 ,, John, Dublin, shoemaker
1758 ,, John, Dublin, merchant
1788 ,, John, Clare-st., Dublin, esq.
1728 ,, Joseph, Ballaghtobin, co. Kilkenny, gent.
1773 ,, Joseph, Dolphin's Barn, Dubl.
1777 ,, Jos., Athlone, co. Westmeath, merchant
1793 ,, Joseph, Lurgan, co. Armagh, distiller
1765 ,, Margaret, Dublin, spinster
1762 ,, Mary, wife of Wm. H., Tullamore, King's co.
1717 ,, Michael, Dublin, gent.
1804 ,, Patrick, Francis-street, Dublin, woollen draper
1712 ,, Richard, Armagh, innkeeper
1721 ,, Richard, Dublin, gent.
1778 ,, Richard, Great Britain-street, Dublin
1800 ,, Robt., Tonagh, co. Fermanagh, gent.
1797 ,, Roger, Mount Hall, co. Down, esq.
1783 ,, rev. Rowley, rector of Killyleagh, co. Down
1787 ,, Rowley, Holles-street, Dublin, esq.
1781 ,, Ruth, Dolphin's-barn, co. Dub., widow
1778 ,, Saml., Kilcanop, co. Wexford, farmer
1798 ,, Sarah, Tipperary town, widow
1799 ,, Sarah, Tipperary town, widow
1801 ,, Savage, Narrowwater House, co. Down, esq.
1784 ,, Simon, Tyraverty, co. Mon.
1801 ,, Sober, Limerick city, esq.
1753 ,, Susanna, Dublin, widow
1657 ,, Thomas   [VI. 224
1734 ,, Thomas, Dublin, silk dyer
1755 ,, Thomas, Dublin, merchant
1765 ,, Thomas, Dublin, esq.
1769 ,, Thomas, Ennis, co Clare
1734 ,, Toby, Dublin   [gent.
1720 ,, William, Clonmore, King's co.,
1755 ,, William, master and one of the governors of the Roy. Hos.
1772 ,, William, Tullamore, King's co., apothecary
1775 ,, William, Greenfield, co. Cork, gent.
1779 ,, William, Crosscool Harbour, co. Wicklow, farmer
1797 ,, William, Baggot-street, Dubl., esq.
1804 ,, William, Chamber-street, co. Dublin, dyer

1803 **Hallagan**, Thomas, Riverstown, King's co., farmer
1801 **Hallahan**, John Andrew, Tallow, co. Waterford, gent.
1712 **Hallam**, Elizabeth, Waterford, now in Great Britain
1672 ,, Henry, Dublin, gent.
1673 ,, John, Hallam Hill, King's co., gent.
1699 ,, John, Waterford, esq.
1788 ,, Robert, Limerick, alderman
1720 ,, Thomas, East Bergholt, Suffolk, gent. (Copy)
1735 ,, Thomas, East Bergholt, Suffolk, gent. (Copy)
1800 **Hallaran**, William, Castlemartyr, co. Cork, esq.
1741 **Hallean**, Mathew, Dublin, grocer
1681 **Halley**, Michael, Dublin, skinner
1802 **Halliday**, Charles, Carrick-on-Suir, gent.
1762 ,, Elizabeth, Dublin, widow
1761 ,, George, Walker's-alley, Dubl., carpenter
1779 ,, Henry, Dublin, merchant
1805 ,, John, Newry, co. Armagh
1776 ,, William, Dublin, mercht.
[See HALYDAY, HOLLIDAY.]
1803 **Halligan**, George, Dublin, hotel-keeper
1799 ,, Samuel, Glasnevin-road, co. Dublin
1779 **Halloran**, Denis, Killeerandy, co. Clare, farmer
1748 ,, Joseph, Carricnesure, co. Tip.
1774 ,, Michael, Limerick, shopkeeper
1775 **Hallowes**, Chambre, Dublin, late of Glassiwel, Derbyshire, esq.
1787 **Halluran**, James, Lahardane, co. Clare
[See HALLORAN.]
1793 **Hallwood**, Lancelott, Dublin, merchant
1637 **Halman**, *alias* **Hatton**, Jennet, Ballramston, co. Meath, widow
1770 **Halpen**, Mary, London, widow (Copy)
1708 **Halroide**, Elizabeth, Dublin, widow
[See HOLROYD.]
1636 **Halse**, Thomas, Youghal, gent. [**IV.** 295
1693 **Haltridge**, William, Dromore, co. Down, merchant (Ex.)
1792 **Haly**, Francis, Cork
1634 ,, James, Cashel, merchant
1784 ,, John, Timolin, co. Kildare, innkeeper
1790 ,, John, Macroom, co. Cork, gent.
1811 ,, John, Cork city

1772 **Haly**, Nicholas, Macroom, co. Cork, merchant
1781 ,, Patrick, Macroom, co. Cork, gent.
1800 ,, Thomas, Oakfield, co. Donegal, esq.
1811 ,, William, Cork city, mariner
1803 **Halyday**, Henry, Barrack-street, Dublin
[See HALLIDAY.]
1692 **Haman**, John, Cork
1718 ,, John, Cork, merchant
1730 ,, sir John Dickson, Woodhill, co. Cork, bart. (Ex.)
1760 ,, John, Marsham-street, Middlesex, gent. (Copy.)
1737 **Hamer**, Edward, Dublin, tallow chandler
1789 ,, Michael, Liverpool, merchant (Copy)
1716 ,, Samuel, Dublin, victualler
1754 **Hamersly**, George, Clunkeen, co. Monaghan
1745 ,, Sarah, *alias* **Mullhollon**, Tamnadease, co. Derry, widow
1689 **Hamerton**, Richard, Clonmel, co. Tipperary, esq. [esq.
1733 ,, Robert, Hamerton, co. Tipp.,
1778 ,, Robert, Kilkenny, esq.
1754 ,, Sarah, Kilkenny
1805 **Hamill**, Bridget, Camden-street, co. Dublin, widow
1755 ,, Bryan, Derryaghy
1803 ,, Francis, Dublin, merchant
1715 ,, George, Dublin, gent.
1772 ,, Hans, Ballyatwood, co. Down, esq.
1666 ,, Hugh, Ruchwood, esq.
1776 ,, Hugh, Knockanes, co. Antrim
1785 ,, Hugh, Anne-street, Dublin, merchant
1760 ,, James, Dublin, gent.
1740 **Hamilton**, Agnes, Caledon, now of Dublin, spinster
1807 ,, Agnes, Strabane, co. Tyrone, spinster
1740 ,, rev. Alexander, Moneyrea
1790 ,, Alexander, Ivorstown, co. Clare, gent.
1809 ,, Alexander, Hampton, co. Dubl., esq.
1803 ,, Ally, *alias* **Ramage**
1655 ,, Andrew, Killenewer, co. Donegal, esq. [**V.** 149
1707 ,, Andrew, Mulenard, co. Donegal, gent. (Copy)
1723 ,, Andrew, Dunboyne, co. Meath, esq.
1768 ,, Andrew, Ballymacdonnell, co. Donegal, esq.

1799 **Hamilton**, Andrew, Linashanker, co. Down
1810 ,, Andrew, Tullyowen, co. Donegal
1793 ,, Ann, Glasnevin, co. Dublin, spinster
1803 ,, Ann, Belfast, co. Antrim, wid.
1742 ,, Anne, Dublin, widow
1765 ,, Anne, Dublin, spinster
1755 ,, Anthony, Kilnacarra, co. Longford, esq.
1665 ,, Archbald, abp. of **Cashel**, q. v.
1712 ,, Archibald, lieut.-col. of lord Mountjoy's regt.
1749 ,, Archibald, lieut.-gen. of His Majesty's forces
1753 ,, Archibald, Strabane, co. Tyrone, cornet
1753 ,, Archibald, Stranocum, co. Antrim, esq.
1777 ,, Archibald, Dublin, M.D.
1802 ,, Archibald, Mulnagon, co. Tyr., esq.
1759 ,, Arthur Cecil, Castle H., co. Cavan, esq.
1667 ,, dame Beatrix, widow of sir William H., Manor Elliston, co. Tyrone
1740 ,, Catherine, widow of ven. W. H., archdeacon of Armagh
1777 ,, Catherine, Dublin, spinster
1794 ,, Catherine, Dublin city, widow
1802 ,, Catherine, *alias* **Gates**, widow
1753 ,, Charles, Dunboyne, co. Meath, esq.
1795 ,, Charles, Mullingar, gent.
1801 ,, Charles, Portglenone, esq.
1692 ,, Christian, Carnasure, co. Down, widow
1636 ,, Christopher, Kilmainham wood, gent.
1695 ,, Claud, Munterloney, co. Tyrone, esq.
1737 ,, Claud, Strabane, co. Tyrone, esq.
1782 ,, Claude, Beltrim, co. Tyrone, esq. (Large)
1666 ,, Claudius, Laragh, co. Wicklow, esq.
1739 ,, Darcy, Fahy, co. Galway, esq.
1780 ,, Dorothea, widow of hon. and rev. Francis H.
1727 ,, Edward, Galway, merchant
1743 ,, Edward, Dublin, stationer
1809 ,, Elinor, Gola, co. Monaghan, widow
1664 ,, dame Elizabeth, *alias* **Willoughby**, wife to sir Francis Hamilton, bart. (Copy, original given out)
1753 ,, Elizabeth, Ballyroney parish

1755 **Hamilton**, Elizabeth, Killyglasson, co. Cavan, widow
1757 ,, Elizabeth
1762 ,, Elizabeth, Dublin, widow
1780 ,, Elizabeth, *alias* **Rynd**, Enniskillen, co. Fermanagh
1786 ,, Elizabeth, Dublin, spinster
1795 ,, dame Elizabeth, Marlborough-street, Dublin, widow
1789 ,, Ellinor, Dublin, widow
1775 ,, Ezekial, Spau in Germany, clk.
1721 ,, Frances, *alias* **Madden**, Dublin, widow
1674 ,, sir Francis, Castle Hamilton, co. Cavan, bart.
1695 ,, Francis, Tullybrick, co. Armagh esq.
1716 ,, sir Francis, Castle H., co. Cavan, bart.
1746 ,, hon. and rev. Francis, Dunleer, co. Louth
1777 ,, Francis, Newforge, co. Down
1783 ,, rev. Francis, D.D., vicar of Dundalk
1732 ,, Frederick, Walworth, co. Londonderry, lieut.-gen. of His Majesty's forces, and Privy Councillor
1798 ,, Frederick, Greenwich, Kent, esq. (Copy)
1803 ,, Frederick (claiming to be lord viscount Boyne)
1791 ,, Galbraith, Dublin, merchant
1699 ,, Geo., co. Tyrone, gent. (Died in Hispaniola)
1772 ,, Geo., Tyrela, co. Down
1784 ,, rev. Geo. Cary, Dublin, clk.
1793 ,, George, third Baron of the Exchequer
1811 ,, Gorges, Cottage
1754 ,, Gustavus, Dublin, esq.
1795 ,, rev. Gustavus
1656 ,, Hans, Carnasure, co. Down, captain
1728 ,, Hans, Frankford, co. Armagh, esq. [esq.
1783 ,, Hans, Summerhill, co. Dublin,
1734 ,, rev. Henry, jun. fellow of Trin. College, Dublin
1743 ,, Henry, Cork, esq.
1754 ,, Henry Cary, Piedmont, co. Louth, esq.
1782 ,, sir Henry, city of Bath, bart.
1637 ,, Hugh, Lisdeving, co. Tyrone, gent.
1807 ,, Hugh, bishop of **Ossory**, q. v.
1779 ,, rev. Hutchinson, Edgeworthstown, co. Longford, LL.D.
1690 ,, Isabell, widow of James H., Clonmel, co. Tipperary

1701	**Hamilton,**	Isabell, Caledon, co. Tyrone, widow
1765	,,	Isabella, Strabane, co. Tyrone, widow
1802	,,	Isabella, spr.
1683	,,	Izabell, Kilgole, co. Donegal, widow
1652	,,	Jas., Mullaghmore, co. Antrim, gent.
1658	,,	James, Roscrea, co. Tipperary, esq. **[VII.** 107
1672	,,	James, Glasgow, student **[XIIII.** 66
1687	,,	James, Clonmel, co. Tipperary, esq. (Ex.)
1691	,,	James, Carnasure, co. Down, esq.
1700	,,	James, Tullymore, co. Down, esq. (Ex.)
1703	,,	James, Strabane, co. Tyrone, merchant
1706	,,	James, Bangor, co. Down, esq.
1710	,,	James, Courthills, co. Meath, esq.
1710	,,	James, Prieststown, co. Meath, gent.
1713	,,	James, Ballykeigle, co. Down, gent.
1719	,,	James, Derryboy, gent.
1728	,,	Jas., Ballinagarvey, co. Antrim, esq.
1730	,,	rev. Jas., Castlehill, co. Down, clk.
1730	,,	James, Ballyfatton, co. Tyrone
1735	,,	James, Dublin, esq.
1736	,,	James, Rock Hamilton, co. Down, gent.
1750	,,	James Campbell, Westminster, esq.
1755	,,	Jas., Brownhall, co. Donegal, esq.
1756	,,	James, Kilkenny, merchant
1763	,,	Jas., Mountcharles, co. Don., esq.
1763	,,	James, Dunboyne, co. Meath, esq.
1767	,,	Jas., Newry, co. Down, mercht.
1772	,,	James, Carlow, esq.
1776	,,	James, Belfast, esq.
1791	,,	James Moore, Disertereale, co. Tyrone, esq.
1796	,,	rev. James, Mount Collier
1798	,,	James, Dublin, alderman
1800	,,	James, Warrenpoint, co. Down, gent.
1800	,,	Jas., Sheephill, co. Dubl., esq.
1801	,,	James, Brushbank, co. Antrim, gent.
1801	,,	Jas., the younger, Drewstown, co. Meath

1806	**Hamilton,**	James, Brucless, co. Donegal
1811	,,	James, Antrim town
1659	,,	Jane, widow of Wm. Hamilton, merchant, Down
1741	,,	Jane, widow of rev. James H., par. of Knock, co. Down
1763	,,	Jane, Dublin, widow
1793	,,	Jane, Dublin city (Large)
1793	,,	Jane, Turrit, near Glasnevin, co. Dublin, spr.
1798	,,	Jane, Monaghan town, spr.
1690	,,	Jocelyn, Eirenagh, co. Down, esq.
1703	,,	John, Edinburgh, minister of the Gospel (Copy)
1705	,,	John, captain in brig. Gustav H.'s regt.
1706	,,	John, Brownhall, co. Donegal, esq.
1708	,,	John, Carrowbeg, co. Tyrone, gent.
1713	,,	John, Kilbride, co. Antrim, gent.
1713	,,	John, Caledon, co. Tyrone, esq.
1723	,,	John, Castledillon, co. Armagh
1742	,,	John, Donemanagh, co. Tyrone, esq. (Unproved)
1750	,,	John, Dublin, gent.
1751	,,	John, Dublin, goldsmith
1761	,,	John (Not entered)
1765	,,	John, Londonderry, gent.
1765	,,	John, Tullycullion, co. Tyrone, gent.
1767	,,	John, Newcastle, co. Limerick, clk.
1778	,,	John, Strabane, co. Tyrone, esq.
1778	,,	John, Bristol, but late of Dub., merchant
1787	,,	John, Waterford, esq.
1789	,,	John, lieut. in the 37th regt. of foot
1790	,,	John, Anglish, co. Tyrone
1793	,,	John, Carlow town, esq.
1809	,,	John, Phibsborough, co. Dublin, esq.
1811	,,	John, Brownhall, co. Donegal, esq.
1797	,,	Joseph, Dublin, public notary
1805	,,	Katharine, widow
1769	,,	Leslie, Bartlet's Buildings, Holborn, London, gent.
1761	,,	Letitia, wid. of count Archibald H., Strabane, co. Tyrone
1741	,,	Lettice, widow of col. George H., Millburn, co. Derry
1717	,,	Lucy, Caledon, co. Tyrone, wid.
1753	,,	Magdalen, Dublin, spr.
1629	,,	Malcolm, archbp. of **Cashel**, q.v.
1692	,,	Margt., Munagh, co. Donegal, widow

1723 **Hamilton**, Margt., *alias* **Forbes**, wife to Nathan H., gent.
1771 ,, Margt., Newry, co. Armagh, widow
1786 ,, Margt., Ballindreat, co. Don., widow
1791 ,, Margaret, Dublin, spr.
1802 ,, Marianne, Ayr, Ayrshire, Nth. Britain, widow
1770 ,, Mary, Dublin, widow
1806 ,, Mary, widow of capt. Hans Hamilton
1787 ,, rev. Nicholas, vicar of Donaghadee, co. Down
1770 ,, Otho, Waterford, esq., lieut.-governor of Placentia
1811 ,, Otho, Romford, Essex, esq. (Co.)
1662 ,, Patrick, Strabane, merchant
1700 ,, Patk., Granshaw, par. Cumber, co. Down, gent.
1746 ,, Patk., Fahy, co. Galway, gent.
1749 ,, rev. Patrick, Killyleagh, co. Down, clk.
1780 ,, sir Patrick, Dublin, knt.
1789 ,, Peter, Heathlawn, co. Galway, esq.
1776 ,, Philippa, Rice Hill, co. Cavan, widow
1793 ,, Rebecca, Dublin, widow
1736 ,, Richard, Dublin, esq.
1692 ,, Robert, Killyclunie, co. Tyrone, gent.
1755 ,, Robert, Mentlone, co Armagh
1764 ., Robert, Ballydorn, co. Down, gent. [esq.
1768 ,, Robert, Fairfield, co. Galway,
1777 ,, Robert, Dublin, barrister-at-law
1786 ,, Robert, Ballindreat, co. Don.
1790 ,, Robert, Dublin, esq.
1796 ,, Robert, Navan, co. Meath
1786 ,, Roger, Dublin, apothecary
1769 ,, Rose, Stonyfields, co. Tyrone, widow
1791 ,, Sarah, *alias* **Washington**, co. Kildare, widow
1796 ,, Skeffington, Dublin
1735 ,, hon. Sophia, Bangor, co. Down, widow
1748 ,, hon. Sophia, Sackville-st., par. St. James, Westminster (Copy)
1757 ,, Susanna, Lisburn, co. Antrim, wife to James H.
1709 ,, Thomas, Currenshegoe, co. Monaghan, gent.
1751 ,, Thomas, Dublin, merchant
1792 ,, Thomas, Dublin, esq.
1630 ,, Wm., Lougheaske, co. Donegal, gent.

1657 **Hamilton**, William, Downpatrick, merchant [**VI**. 78
1662 ,, sir William, Manor Ellistown, co. Tipperary, knt. [**IX**. 159
1670 ,, William, Hamilton's Bawn, co. Cavan, esq.
1679 ,, William, Liscloony, King's co., esq.
1681 ,, Wm., Ballyfatten, co. Tyrone
1683 ,, William, Cashel, clk.
1686 ,, William, Erenagh, co. Down, esq.
1686 ,, William, Caledon, co. Tyrone, esq.
1694 ,, William, Limmivallinagh, co. Antrim, esq.
1705 ,, William, Manor Elliston, co. Tyrone, esq. [esq.
1716 ,, William, Killyleagh, co. Down,
1730 ,, ven. William, clk., archdeacon of Armagh
1732 ,, William, Dublin, merchant
1737 ,, William, Dublin, surgeon
1743 ,, William, Lissagor, co. Mon.
1747 ,, William, Beltrim, co. Tyrone, esq.
1751 ,, William, Anglish, co. Tyrone, esq. (Not proved)
1738 ,, William, Londonderry, mercht.
1763 ,, William, Donemanagh, co. Tyrone
1775 ,, William, Dublin, M.D.
1779 ,, William, Newry, co. Down
1781 ,, William, Omagh, co. Tyrone, gent.
1784 ,, William, formerly of Friskill, co. Longford, late of Dublin
1793 ,, Wm., Dunnamana, co. Tyrone, esq.
1797 ,, rev William, fellow of Trinity College, Dublin
1800 ,, William, Garrison, co. Fermanagh
1802 ,, William, New Ross, co. Wexford
1806 ,, William, North King-street, attorney
1806 ,, William, Minola, co. Mayo, gent.
1657 **Hamington**, Thomas, Belfast, burgess [**VI**. 242
1707 **Hamlen**, Bartholomew, Drogheda, merchant
1590 ,, John, Smithstown, co. Meath, gent.
1749 **Hamlin**, Mary, Drogheda, widow
1661 **Hamlington**, William, Crowton, Cheshire, yeoman [**IX**. 31 & 48

1739 **Hammaker**, capt. Richard, Bangor, co. Down
1740 **Hammersley**, Thos., Anaghorish, co. Londonderry
1804 ,, William, Tipperary town, esq.
1778 **Hammersly**, Wm., Castledawson, co. Derry, distiller
1605 **Hammon**, Robert, Trim
1758 **Hammond**, Dowdall, Limerick
1647 ,, George, Dublin, gent.
1806 ,, Helena, spinster
1804 ,, John, Dublin, harpsichord maker
1748 ,, Simon, Dublin
1794 ,, William, Cottage, co. Waterford
1741 **Hamon**, Hector, Dublin, esq.
1755 ,, Isaac
1754 **Hampden**, John, par. St. George's, Hanover-square, Middlesex, esq. (Copy) [See HAMPTON.]
1731 **Hampson**, Charles Pollard, Castlepollard, co. Westmeath, esq.
1785 ,, Charles, Nonsuch, co. Westmeath
1658 ,, Thomas, Taplow, Bucks, esq. [**VI.** 282
1624 **Hampton**, Christopher, abp. of Armagh, q.v.
1663 ,, John, Isle of Wight, gent.
1642 ,, William, Dublin, goldsmith [See HAMPDEN.]
1702 **Hamson**, Ambrose, Drogheda, gt.
1699 ,, Constance, Dublin, widow
1735 ,, Letitia, *alias* **Pollard**, widow of Charles P., Castlepollard
1684 ,, Thos., Aughirevey, co. Cavan, esq.
1788 **Hanan**, William, Tallow, co. Waterford, merchant [See HANNON.]
1807 **Hanbury**, William, Galway town
1760 **Hanchet**, William, Waterford, late barrackmaster
1763 **Hancock**, Jacob, Lisburn, co. Antrim, merchant
1793 ,, Jacob, the younger, Lisburn, co. Down
1656 **Hancoke**, Richard [**VI.** 67 [See HANDCOCK.]
1742 **Hand**, Ephraim, Dub., scale maker
1758 ,, Margaret, Dublin
1771 **Handcock**, rev. Elias
1780 ,, Elizabeth, Clontarf, co. Dublin, widow
1675 ,, James, Dublin, cook
1781 ,, Jane, Dublin, spinster
1757 ,, John, Lisburn, co. Antrim, merchant

1764 **Handcock**, John, Lisburn, co. Antrim, merchant
1766 ,, John Gustavus
1793 ,, rev. John, vicar of Lowry, co. Cavan
1729 ,, Joseph, Dublin, merchant
1677 ,, Margaret, Dublin, widow
1771 ,, Mary, widow of John H., Newbridge, co. Dublin, esq.
1739 ,, ·rev. Mathew, archdeacon of Kilmore
1739 ,, Richard, Kilkenny, gent.
1791 ,, rev. Richard, Dublin, clk.
1730 ,, Robert, Carlow
1754 ,, Robert, Waterstown, co. Westmeath, esq. [meath
1796 ,, Robert, Athlone, co. West-
1803 ,, Sarah
1718 ,, Stephen, dean of Kilmacduagh
1726 ,, Thomas, Twyford, co. Westmeath, esq.
1741 ,, Thomas, Dublin, merchant
1758 ,, Tobias, Upper Court, co. Kilkenny, gent.
1706 ,, William, Dublin, esq.
1741 ,, William, Willbrook, co. Westmeath, esq.
1794 ,, William, esq. [See HANCOCK, HANCOKE.]
1706 **Handcocke**, Mary, *alias* **Burgh**, widow
1701 ,, William, Recorder of Dublin
1722 ,, William, Willbrook, co. Westmeath, esq.
1788 **Handfield**, John, late lieut.-col. 40th regt. of foot
1811 **Handlen**, Philip, Old Merrion, co. Dublin, esq.
1765 **Handy**, Hannah, Dublin, widow
1731 ,, John, Kilbeggan, co. Westmeath, gent.
1764 ,, John, Brackareagh, co. Westmeath, gent. [gent.
1759 ,, Jonathan, Johns-street, Dublin,
1766 ,, Mary, Dubl., dau. of Thos. H., merchant
1741 ,, Saml., the elder, Brackareagh, co. Westmeath, gent.
1779 ,, Samuel, Coolylogh, co. Westmeath, esq.
1754 ,, Thomas, Dublin, merchant
1777 **Hanigan**, Maurice
1702 **Hankes**, Joseph, Dublin, merchant
1751 **Hankinson**, Richard, Dublin, esq.
1788 **Hanks**, Jeremiah
1792 ,, Jeremiah, Birr, King's co., chandler
1785 **Hanlen**, Christopher, Dublin, livery stable keeper [See HANLON.]

1731 **Hanley**, John, late of Dublin, now of Tirlicken, co. Longford [See HANLY.]
1805 **Hanlon**, Bryan, Mary-street, Dubl., corn chandler
1802 ,, Jas., Mountbagnell, co. Louth, farmer
1811 ,, James, Dublin city, woollen draper
1802 ,, John, Red Cow, co. Dublin
1802 ,, John, Ballymorren, co. Wicklow, farmer
1728 ,, Phelim, Dublin, innkeeper
1656 ,, Richard, Abbottstown, co.Dubl., yeoman [**V.** 294
1750 ,, Timothy, Grangeforth, co. Carlow, farmer
[See HANDLEN, HANLEN.]
1773 **Hanly**, Bartholomew, Galway, gent.
1810 ,, Bridget, Bride's Alley, Dublin, widow
1811 ,, Edmond, Rosebank, co. Dublin
1713 ,, Edward, Shaghtebeg, co. Roscommon, gent.
1753 ,, John, Cole-alley, Dublin
1753 ,, John, Dublin, gent.
1795 ,, John, Silvermines, co. Tipp., innkeeper [common
1810 ,, Luke, Fair Valley, co. Ros-
1759 ,, Mathias, Dublin, gent.
1805 ,, Samuel, Galway town
1774 ,, Thomas, Dublin, peruke maker
1808 ,, Thomas, Bride's-alley, Dublin, carpenter
[See HANLEY, HENELY, HENLEY, HENLY.]
1640 **Hanmor**, Mary, Dublin, widow
1771 **Hanna**, James, Tamory, co. Down
1794 ,, James, quartermaster serj. 27th regt. of foot
1797 ,, John, Worbleshenny, Liberties of Londonderry [mercht.
1798 ,, Samuel, Newry, co. Armagh,
1786 ,, William, Whitehouse,co.Donegal
1807 ,, William, Grenwood-park, co. Down
[See HANNA, HANNAG, HANNAH, HANMOR.]
1698 **Hannag**, William, Dublin, tailor
1741 **Hannah**, Alexander, Ballykeel, co. Down
1810 ,, Humphry, town of Cove
1788 **Hannan**, Cornelius, Oberstown, co. Kildare, farmer
1802 ,, Patrick, Dunshaughlin, co. Meath, innholder
1668 ,, Richard, Gormanstown, co. Meath, farmer
[See HANNON.]

1766 **Hannel**, George, Wicklow, gent.
1799 **Hannell**, Elizabeth, Ringsend, co. Dublin, widow
1712 **Hannington**, Thomas, Cumber, co. Down, gent.
1749 **Hannon**, John, *alias* **Hall**, Dublin, gent.
1760 ,, Timothy, Cork, ale seller [See HANAN, HANNAN.]
1802 **Hanrahan**, Michael, late of Tourlogh, co. Tipperary
1805 ,, Pierce, Rathkeale, co. Limk., attorney
1762 **Hansard**, Elizabeth, Dublin, widow
1760 ,, Frances, widow of rev. Ralph Hansard
1758 ,, John, Dublin, esq.
1770 ,, Judith, widow of Ralph H. Baltinglass, co. Wicklow, clk.
1709 ,, Mary, subs. of Dublin, widow
1749 ,, Nicholas, Dublin, gent.
1749 ,, rev. Ralph, Baltinglass, co. Wicklow, clk.
1759 ,, rev. Ralph, vicar of Castledermot
1620 ,, sir Richard, Lifford, co. Donegal, knt.
1702 ,, Richard, Lazyhill, Dublin, esq.
1721 **Hanson**, John, Dublin, gent.
1676 **Hanway**, Richard, Dublin, alderman (Ex.)
1721 **Hanyn**, James, Iskerboy, co. Galway, esq.
1744 **Hanyngton**, capt. James, Ballyobekin, co. Down
1725 **Hara**, Laurence, Gregstown, co. Donegal, gent.
1750 ,, Laurence,Gregstown,co.Donegal, esq.
[See O'HARA.]
1599 **Harbert**, Harry, Cotlandstown, co. Kildare, gent.
1798 **Harberton**, Arthur, lord viscount
1694 **Harbord**, hon. William, Grafton Park, Northamptonshire (Copy)
1785 **Harborne**, Frances, Dublin, widow
1756 ,, Jeffry, the elder, Simonstown, co. Kildare, gent.
1733 ,, Michael, Dublin, gent.
1691 ,, William, Dublin, gent.
1733 ,, William, Dublin, merchant
1744 **Harbort**, Jeramiah, Mortlestown
1811 **Harbourne**, George, Simonstown, co. Kildare, gent.
1807 ,, John, Baltinglass, co. Wicklow [See HARBORNE.]
1712 **Hardcastle**, Rosamond, Phrumplestown

1788 **Harden**, Henry, Barrybrook, co. Armagh, esq.
1762 ,, John, Borris Hagh, co. Tipp., gent.
1763 ,, Thomas, Lurgan, merchant
1777 ,, William, Borrisoleigh, co. Tipperary
1801 **Hardiman**, Robert, Loughrea, co. Galway, esq.
1790 ,, Walter, Loughrea, co. Galway [See HARDYMAN.]
1787 **Hardin**, James, Wormwood-gate, Dublin, carder
1788 ,, Meridyth, Belfast, co. Antrim
1766 ,, Susanna, Lurgan, Armagh, widow
1785 ,, Thomas, Belfast, co. Antrim, merchant
1772 **Harding**, Ambrose, Dublin, esq.
1721 ,, Ann, *alias* **Tydd.**
1778 ,, Dominick, Macroom, co. Cork, gent.
1802 ,, Dominick, Macroom, co. Cork
1649 ,, Francis, Dublin, saddler
1779 ,, Henry, Kigh, co. Tipp., gent.
1766 ,, Hugh, Donnybrook, near Dubl., turner
1806 ,, James, Harrybrook, co. Arm., esq.
1802 ,, Jane, Cork, widow
1665 ,, John, the elder, Kilgobbin, co. Dublin
1700 ,, John, Chelworth, Wiltshire, gent. (Copy)
1758 ,, John, Cork, gent.
1786 ,, John, Cork, alderman
1793 ,, John, Channel-row, Dublin, victualler
1809 ,, John, Ballyrene, Queen's co.
1766 ,, Jonathan, Derrykeel
1772 ,, Joseph, Stoyle, co. Limerick
1785 ,, Margaret, Dublin, widow
1811 ,, Mary A., Cork city, widow
1723 ,, Peter, Barry's Great Island, co. Cork, gent.
1692 ,, Richard, the Grange, Baldoyle, farmer
1773 ,, Richard, Cork
1795 ,, Samuel, Newlawn, co. Limk.
1732 ,, Thomas, Balingohig, co. Cork, gent.
1804 ,, Thomas, Prussia-street, co. Dublin, gent.
1810 ,, Thomas, Cork city, burgess
1750 ,, Valentine, Cork, merchant
1714 ,, William, Cork, gent.
1720 ,, William, Clogadalton, co. Limk.
1763 ,, William, Cork, esq.
1777 ,, William, Clonlee, King's co., gent.

1719 **Hardman**, Margaret, Drogheda, widow
1692 ,, Robert, Drogheda, alderman [See HARMAN.]
1802 **Hardy**, Edward, Thomas-st., Dublin, ironmonger
1810 ,, Edward, Dublin city, iron merchant
1739 ,, · Francis, Ballybrack, co. Wicklow, gent.
1763 ,, Henry, Dublin, gent.
1803 ,, James, Dreemart, co. Armagh
1756 ,, John, esq.
1759 ,, John, Magheramuk, co. Antrim, farmer
1798 ,, John, Dublin, saddler
1801 ,, John, Dublin, silk mannfacturer [farmer
1723 ,, Joseph, Graigue, co. Tipperary,
1755 ,, Joseph, Dublin, merchant
1766 ,, Robert, Ballinderry
1811 ,, Samuel William, paymaster, 11th regt. of foot (Copy)
1799 ,, Thomas, Kilmacart, co. Carlow, gent.
1797 ,, William, Kilkenny city, esq.
1716 **Hardyman**, Thomas, Lyddyard Treygooze, Wiltshire, esq. (Copy) [See HARDIMAN.]
1650 **Hare**, Edward, Dublin, tailor
1787 ,, Margaret, New-street, Middlesex (Copy)
1685 ,, Michael, Monkstown, co. Dubl., esq.
1762 ,, Nicholas
1795 ,, Richd., Cork city, esq (Large)
1796 ,, Roger, Ballybrown, co. Limk., gent.
1759 ,, William, Cork, linendraper
1811 ,, William, Dubl. city, apothecary
1737 **Harfford**, John, Dublin, barber surgeon
1726 **Harford**, Elizabeth, Dublin, widow of William H., victualler
1734 ,, John, Derryrelan, co. Monaghan, gent.
1741 ,, John, Dublin, baker
1745 ,, John, New Haggard, co. Meath, farmer
1763 ,, Patk., Bride-st., Dublin, linendraper
1761 ,, Richard, Dublin, upholder
1720 ,, William, Dublin, victualler
1775 ,, William, Clare, co. Armagh [See HARTFORD.]
1793 **Hargraft**, Humphrey, Winetavern-street
1808 **Hargrave**, Abraham, Cork city, architect

1752 **Hargrave**, William, lieut.-gen. at Gibraltar
1785 **Hargrove**, Laurence, one of the State Messengers
1786 ,, Laurence, Dublin, one of the Messengers
1799 **Harkan**, Neal, Raheen
1746 **Harkness**, Wm., Dungannon, co. Tyrone, merchant
1783 **Harksen**, Conrad, Lond., merchant (Copy)
1769 **Harley**, William, Dublin, gent. [See HURLY.]
1757 **Harloe**, Jno., Rathmullen, co. Sligo, esq.
1782 ,, Mary, wife to John H., esq.
1706 ,, William, Rathmullen, co. Sligo, esq.
1796 **Harman**, Caleb Barnes, esq.
1784 ,, v. rev. Cutts, dean of Waterford
1673 ,, Edward, Derrymoyle, Queen's co., esq.
1780 ,, Edward, Dublin, esq.
1766 ,, Frances, Dublin, widow
1720 ,, Geo., Athy, co. Kildare, gent.
1691 ,, Hungerford, Benekerry, co. Carlow, gent.   [gent.
1800 ,, Luke, Old Ross, co. Wexford,
1807 ,, Ralph, Ballyhaise. co. Cavan
1809 ,, Samuel, Cork city
1668 ,, sir Thomas, Dublin, knt.
1714 ,, Wentworth, Dublin, esq.
1757 ,, Wentworth, Dublin, esq.
1758 ,, Wesley, Moyle, co. Carlow, esq.
1684 ,, Wm., Derrymoyle, co. Carlow, esq.
         [See HARDMAN].
1694 **Harmer**, John, Dunmaghan, co. Cork, esq.
1764 ,, John, Mary's-lane, Dub., blacksmith
1793 **Harnet**, Daniel, Cork, merchant
1780 ,, James, Cork city, esq. (Large will)
1794 **Harnett**, James Fuller, Aghamore, co. Kerry, esq.
1704 **Harney**, Phleyael, Knocklow, co. Wicklow, gent.
1794 ,, Silvester, Dubl., woollendraper
1701 **Harokesworth**, Abraham, Dublin, carpenter
1794 **Harold**, James, Loftus-lane, Dubl., gent.
         [See HARROLD.]
1755 **Harper**, Anne, Dublin, widow
1788 ,, Hannah, Dublin, widow
1783 ,, Helen, Dublin, spr.
1783 ,, Isabella, Cork, widow
1770 ,, James, Kilmacan, co. Cavan (Not proved)

1776 **Harper**, James, Ennis, co. Clare, super gauger
1657 ,, John, soldier   [**VI.** 197
1665 ,, John, par. Christ church, London, haberdasher (Copy)
1701 ,, John, Dublin, tinworker
1762 ,, John, Cork, mercht. (Lge. will)
1783 ,, John, Dublin, gent.
1753 ,, Samuel, Straffan
1799 ,, William, town and co. Antrim, watchmaker
         [See HARPOR, HARPUR.]
1621 **Harpole**, dame Mary, widow of sir W H., knt.
1793 ,, Robt., Shrule, Queen's co., esq.
1662 ,, William, Queen's co., esq.   [**IX.** 164
1767 **Harpor**, Geo., Clonork, King's co.
1778 ,, John, Maryborough
1810 **Harpur**, rev. Ephm., Bloomville, clk.
1685 ,, John, Dolphin's-barn, near Dublin, tanner
1753 ,, John, Mell, co. Louth, esq.
1784 ,, Rebecca, Hillbrook, co. Dubl. widow
1754 ,, William, Dublin, gent.
1786 **Harricks**, Dudley, Onagh, co. Wick.
1802 ,, Jos., Ballybrow, co. Wicklow, gent.
1808 ,, William, Onagh, co. Wicklow
1803 **Harrihill**, John, Anglesea-street, perfumer
1764 **Harrington**, Anderson, Grange Con, co. Wicklow, esq.
1663 ,, Daniel, Dublin, gent. (Copy)
1673 ,, Henry, Louth, late of Muffe, co. Londonderry, gent. (Copy)
1671 ,, James, Waltham, Holy Cross, Essex, esq.
1725 ,, James, Grange, co. Wicklow, esq.
1766 ,, John, Athy, co. Kildare, gent.
1770 ,, John, Donanstown, co. Cork, M.D.
1657 ,, Robert, Laytonstone, Essex   [**VI.** 156
1666 ,, Walter, Dublin, gent. (Ex.)
1784 ,, William, Athy, co. Kildare, gt. [See HARTY.]
1800 ,, William, Cork city, merchant
1783 **Harriot**, Mary Anne, Rahahey, co. Tyrone
1798 **Harris**, Abel, Monleen, co. Cork, esq.
1730 ,, Alexander, quartermaster of horse
1778 ,, Anne, Dublin, widow
1713 ,, Arthur, chanter of the cathedral of Connor

1638 **Harris**, sir Edward, Dublin, knt., jus. of K.B. [**IV.** 262
1689 ,, Edward, Dublin, goldsmith
1760 ,, Edward, Belfast, merchant
1665 ,, Francis, Dublin, gent.
1710 ,, Henry, Dublin, merchant
1768 ,, Hopkin, Dublin, merchant
1720 ,, Hopton, Queen's co.
1757 ,, Jas., Athy, co. Kildare, gauger
1638 ,, dame Jane, Dublin, widow [**IV.** 263
1745 ,, John, Mountrath, Queen's co., merchant
1766 ,, John, Jevenah, co. Tyrone
1769 ,, John Drury, Dublin, esq.
1776 ,, John, Dublin, shoemaker
1779 ,, John, Mountrath, Queen's co., merchant
1790 ,, John, Bandon, co. Cork
1802 ,, John, Barnahaley, co. Cork, gt.
1805 ,, John, Cork city
1723 ,, Joseph, Cork
1799 ,, Joseph, Cork city
1803 ,, Joseph, Cabra, co. Dub., farmer
1727 ,, Laugharne, Mountmellick, Queen's co., gent.
1664 ,, Nicholas, Dublin, gent.
1798 ,, Richard, Cork city, esq.
1627 ,, Robert, Trim, tailor (Copy)
1701 ,, Robert, Dublin, gent.
1740 ,, Robert, Dublin, esq.
1753 ,, Robert, Kilcullen Bridge, co. Kildare
1788 ,, Rodolph Glander, Dublin, hotel keeper
1661 ,, Samuel, Belfast, gent.
1798 ,, Sarah, Longfield, co. Westmeath, widow
1672 ,, Thos., Ballymony, co. Wicklow, yeoman [**XIV.** 68
1762 ,, Thomas, Dublin, esq.
1803 ,, Thomas, Cork city
1695 ,, Walter, Dublin, esq.
1723 ,, Walter, Dublin, esq.
1762 ,, Walter, Dublin, esq.
1790 ,, Walter, Dublin, esq.
1740 ,, William, Dublin, feltmaker
1792 ,, William, Nth. Cumberland-st., Dublin, slater
1796 ,, Wm., Charlemont-st., Dublin, gent.
1766 **Harrison,** Abraham, Clonkeel, Queen's co., farmer
1776 ,, Ann, Dublin, spinster
1666 ,, Anthony, Turlogh, co. Mayo, gent.
1807 ,, Charles, Limerick, hardware merchant
1727 ,, Christopher, capt. in brigadier Newton's reg. of foot (Copy)

1763 **Harrison,** Christopher, Dublin, merchant (Large will)
1768 ,, Christopher, vicar of Abbeylaragh, &c., co. Londondy.
1700 ,, Edward, Marlea, co. Ant., esq.
1726 ,, Francis, Dublin, esq.
1810 ,, Gertrude, Limerick city, widow
1634 ,, Hannibal, Raphoe, co. Donegal, yeoman
1760 ,, Harriott Henrietta, near Carrick, co. Tipperary, widow
1768 ,, Henry, Wexford, esq.
1809 ,, Henry, Dublin city, esq.
1776 ,, Isaac, Ormond-street, Dublin, weaver
1623 ,, John, London, merchant tailor (Copy)
1670 ,, John, Dublin, merchant
1744 ,, John, Eaghterdivie, co. Tip.
1749 ,, John, Castle Lyons, co. Cork, esq.
1781 ,, John, Dublin, merchant
1786 ,, John, Goodwill, co. Wicklow, gent.
1797 ,, John, Limerick city, burgess
1802 ,, John, North Strand, Dubl., esq.
1803 ,, John William, Garruragh, co. Clare, esq.
1810 ,, rev. John J., Naas, co Kildare
1766 ,, Joseph, Dublin, esq.
1772 ,, Joseph, Cork, gent.
1790 ,, Joseph, Bow-st., Dub., hosier
1811 ,, Jos., Cork city, woollen draper
1707 ,, Isabella, Dublin, but at the Hot Wells, Bristol
1799 ,, Margaret, Dublin [dare, esq.
1731 ,, Marsh, Castlemartin, co. Kil-
1728 ,, Mary, par. St. George, Hanover-square, London, widow, (Copy)
1792 ,, Mary, Dublin, widow
1683 ,, Michael, Marlea, co. Antrim, esq. (Ex.)
1683 ,, Michael, Marlea, co. Antrim, esq. [**XIII.** 446
1709 ,, Michael, Dublin, esq.
1785 ,, Patience, Ballyrea, co. Wex., spinster
1630 ,, Peter, Dublin, gent.
1752 ,, Philip, *alias* **Nutley**, *alias* **Venables**, widow
1811 ,, Rebecca, Limerick city, widow
1656 ,, Richard, soldier at the siege of Waterford
1656 ,, Richard, trooper at the siege of Waterford [**V.** 336
1714 ,, Richard, Dublin, gent.
1733 ,, Richd., Aghish, co. Clare, gent.
1738 ,, Robert, Fortfergus, co. Clare, esq.

1740 **Harrison**, Robert, Ballysallagh, co. Clare, gent.
1752 ,, Robert, vicar of Street, &c., dio. Armagh, clk.
1766 ,, Robert, Limerick, esq.
1769 ,, Robert, sheds of Clontarf, co. Dublin, gent.
1770 ,, Robert, Dublin, gent.
1775 ,, Robert, Dublin, gent.
1743 ,, Roger, Crecan, co. Wexford, gent.
1768 ,, Roger, esq, collector of Londonderry
1790 ,, Roger, Londonderry, esq.
1729 ,, Sarah, par. St. Martin-in-the-fields, Middx., widow (Copy)
1747 ,, Simon, mariner on board the "Hinde" sloop
1714 ,, Theophilus, rector of Killalan, co. Meath
1720 ,, Theophilus, D.D., dean of Clonmacnoise
1609 ,, Thomas, Dublin, tailor
1758 ,, Thos., St. Martin's-lane, Dub., plasterer
1770 ,, Thomas, Dublin, esq.
1736 ,, William, Dublin, esq.
1769 ,, William, Castle-street, esq.
1791 ,, William, Garryragh, co. Clare, esq.
1795 ,, William
      [See HARRIS.]
1667 **Harrisone**, Mathew, Dublin, esq.
1584 **Harrisonne**, Hadrian, Dubl., smith [**I.** 32
1806 **Harrisson**, Robert, Greatford, co. Westmeath
1725 **Harrold**, Margaret, Limk., widow
1760 ,, Mary, Newry, co. Down, widow
1602 ,, Oliver, Limerick, merchant
1673 ,, Patrick, Limerick, merchant
1747 ,, Peter, Newry, gent.
1633 ,, Piers, Limerick, alderman
1725 ,, Richard, Pennywell, East Lib., Limerick, gent.
1687 ,, Stephen FitzRichard, Limk., merchant
1664 ,, Thos., Sixmilebridge, co. Clare, merchant
      [See HAROLD.]
1733 **Harrolds**, John, Dubl., now of London, merchant (Copy)
1690 **Harsnet**, Adam, Carlow, merchant
1707 **Hart**, Anne, *alias* **Cusack**, of Glastown, co. Meath, widow
1760 ,, Anne, Dublin, widow
1794 ,, Catherine, Dublin, widow
1676 ,, Christopher, Dublin, gent.
1724 ,, Christopher, Dublin, baker
1747 ,, David, Dublin, hosier

1789 **Hart**, Edward, Cowlawley, Queen's co., farmer
1789 ,, Edward, Kilcock, Queen's co.
1762 ,, Elizabeth, Dublin, widow
1758 ,, George, Kilderry, co. Donegal, esq.
1811 ,, George, lieut.-col. of the 36th regt. of foot
1712 ,, Henry, Muff, co. Donegal, esq.
1737 ,, Henry, Londonderry, alderman
1734 ,, rev. Henry, Galway, clk.
1763 ,, Henry, Dublin, alderman
1809 ,, James, South Earl-st., Dublin, attorney
1801 ,, Jane, Dublin, widow
1758 ,, Joab, Island of Antigua, merchant (Copy)
1740 ,, John, Wardfield, Berkshire, esq. (Copy)
1755 ,, John, ensign in col. Dunbar's regt. of foot
1804 ,, John, Sackville-street, Dublin
1750 ,, Mary, *alias* **Russell**, wife to Hen. H., Dublin
1802 ,, Mary, West Arran-st., Dublin, widow
1681 ,, Merrick, Crover, co. Cavan, esq.
1810 ,, Owen, New-row, Dubl., mercht.
1642 ,, Philip, Tallow, co. Waterford, burgess (Copy)   [gent.
1705 ,, Richd., Galestown, co. Meath,
1799 ,, Robert, Watling-street, Dubl., skinner
1788 ,, Roger, a prisoner of war, St. Domingo
1780 ,, Simon, Dublin, esq.
      [See HARWOOD.]
1793 **Harte**, Easther, Rathcoole, co. Dub. widow
1742 ,, Henry, Coolruss, co. Limerick gent.
1791 ,, Percival, Coolruss, co. Limk., esq.
1662 ,, Richard, Cloghnamanagh, co. Limk., esq.
1796 ,, William
1767 **Hartford**, Andrew, Proper-lane, Dublin, merchant
1778 ,, Bibby, Kilkenny, esq.
1750 ,, James, Dublin, cooper
1774 ,, Mary, Dublin, widow
      [See HARFORD.]
1767 **Hartigan**, Edwd., Dubl., apothecary
1791 **Hartley**, Isabella, Dub., spinster
1656 ,, Major Jereh., London [**V.** 277
1709 ,, John, Dublin, merchant
1716 ,, Sarah, Dublin, widow
1780 ,, Thomas, Dublin, gent.
1781 ,, Thomas, Frederick-st., Dublin, gent.

1800 **Hartley**, Travers, Dublin, mercht.
1680 ,, William, Dublin, cordwainer
1760 **Hartlib**, Mary, Dublin, spinster
1741 ,, Michael, clk.
1803 **Harton**, John
1716 **Hartonge**, John, bishop of **Derry**, q. v.
1674 **Hartopp**, George, Dublin, esq.
1713 **Hartpole**, Dame Bridget, Shrule, Queen's co.
1795 ,, Geo., Shrule, Queen's co., esq.
1714 ,, Wm., Shrule, Queen's co., esq.
1594 **Hartpoole**, Robt., Catherlogh, esq. (Copy)
1664 **Hartshorne**, Edward, Wick, gent.
1742 ,, Richard, major of sir Robert Rich's dragoons (Copy)
1730 **Hartson**, Elizabeth, Dublin, widow
1702 ,, James, Antrim town, gent.
1781 ,, James, Carlow town, esq.
1730 ,, John, Antrim, gent.
1746 ,, rev. William, Antrim, clk.
1688 **Hartstonge**, Francis, eldest son of sir Standish H., bart. (Copy)
1797 ,, sir Henry, Bruff, co. Limerick, bart.
1803 **Hartstrong**, Ann, *alias* **Welde**
1769 ,, John, Dublin, esq. [bart.
1751 ,, sir Standish, Bruff, co. Limk.,
1682 **Harstronge**, lady Ann, wife to sir Stan. H., bart.
1705 ,, Standish, Dub., esq. (Ex.)
1706 **Hartus**, Hy., capt. in lord Mahon's regt. of foot
1698 **Hartwell**, John, senr., armourer to the train of artillery
1705 ,, Margaret, Dublin, widow
1810 **Harty**, James, Clonmel, co. Tipp. [See HARRINGTON.]
1741 **Harvey**, Anne, Ballyhacket, co. Carlow, widow
1796 ,, rev. Christopher, Templehill, co. Wexford
1795 ,, David, Derry city
1792 ,, Francis, Bargy Castle, co. Wexford, esq.
1809 ,, Francis, Cork city, merchant
1763 ,, Garret, Dublin, woollen draper
1773 ,, Geo., Mallinhall, co. Donegal, esq.
1760 ,, rev. James, Great Killiane, co. Wexford, clk.
1768 ,, Jas., Wigan, Lancashire, esq. (Copy)
1772 ,, James, Londonderry, merchant
1793 ,, James, Dublin, gent.
1810 ,, James, Dublin city
1750 ,, John, Dunmore, co. Donegal, gent.

1796 **Harvey**, John, Great Killiane, co. Wexford, esq.
1798 ,, John, Dublin, tallow chandler
1802 ,, Margaret, Dublin, widow
1802 ,, Margaret, Milltown, co. Dubl., spinster
1791 ,, Martha Cecilia, Wigan, Lancashire, spr. (Copy)
1800 ,, Martha, Killiane, co. Wexford, spinster
1666 ,, sir Peter, Dublin, knt.
1808 ,, Reuben, Pleasantfield, Lib. of Cork
1777 ,, Rose, Londonderry, widow
1758 ,, Thomas, qr.-master in general Brown's regt. of horse
1804 ,, Thomas, Youghal, co. Cork
1800 ,, Vigors, Derby, Derbyshire, esq. (Copy)
1765 ,, rev. William, Bridge of Bargy, co. Wexford, clk.
1782 ,, William, Lurgan-st., Dublin
1808 ,, William, Youghal, co. Cork, merchant
1711 **Harvy**, Thomas, Dublin
1599 **Harvye**, Robert, gent.
1721 **Harward**, Edward, Terlicken, co. Longford, gent.
1774 ,, John, Portrony, co. Roscommon, esq.
1770 ,, William, Dublin, esq.
1806 **Harwood**, rev. Edward, Millbrook, co. Waterford
1678 ,, George, soldier in Galway
1669 ,, James, Newcastle Lyons, co. Dublin, gent.
1776 ,, rev. John Dalton, Clonmel, co. Tipperary, clk.
1779 ,, Mary, Dublin, widow
1728 ,, rev. Richard, Mountmellick, Queen's co., clk.
1746 ,, Richard, Harwood's Camp, co. Wexford, esq. [See HART.]
1745 **Hasard**, Jason, Dublin, mercht.
1692 ,, Jason, Mullimisker, co. Fermanagh, esq. [See HASSARD.]
1807 **Haskett**, Saml., Tullamore, King's co.
1720 **Haskins**, James, Kilkenny, upholsterer [See HOSKINS.]
1776 **Haslam**, James, Maryborough, Queen's co., gent.
1784 ,, Richd., Ballycommon, King's co., gent.
1718 **Haslerigg**, William, Roanstown, co. Kildare, gent.
1796 **Hasleton**, James, Dublin, gent.

1807 **Haslett**, William, Cloony, co. Londonderry
1710 **Haslock**, John, Dublin, tanner
1600 **Hassall**, Richard, London, mercht.
1809 **Hassard**, Jason, Gardenhill, co. Fermanagh
1804 ,, John, Carra, co. Fermanagh, esq.
        [See HASARD, HAZARD.]
1774 **Hasset**, Martin, Limerick, broker
1803 **Hasshie**, Michael, Marinsmore, co. Clare, gent.
1809 **Hasting**, Rachel, Wexford town, widow
1797 **Hastings**, Elizabeth, Clogher, co. Tyrone
1792 ,, Frances, widow
1776 ,, James, archdeacon of Leighlin
1774 ,, John, Lisburn, co. Antrim, merchant
1791 ,, Patrick, Dublin, apothecary
1779 ,, Stephen, Limerick, apothecary
1794 ,, rev. Thomas, archdeacon of Dublin, LL.D.
1809 **Hastler**, James, New Forest, co. Tipperary
1763 **Hatch**, Henry, Dublin, esq.
1676 ,, John, the elder, Duleek, co. Meath, gent. (Ex.)
1721 ,, John, Duleek, co. Meath, clk.
1747 ,, John, Bellair, co. Meath, gent.
1787 ,, Jos., Drumbarrow, co. Meath, gent.
1710 ,, Nicholas, Duleek, co. Meath, gent.
1787 ,, Samuel, Dublin, gent.
1793 **Hatchell**, George, Wexford town, merchant
1699 **Hatchman**, Thomas, Edenderry, King's co., grazier
1774 **Hatfield**, Catherine Grace, Dublin, widow
1809 ,, sir Geo., Charleville, co. Cork
1804 ,, John, Ardagrah, co. Westmeath
1676 ,, Judith, Killinure, co. Westmeath, widow
1719 ,, Leonard, Killinure, co. Westmeath, gent.
1764 ,, Richard, Dublin, gent.
1672 ,, Ridgeley, Killinure, co. Westmeath, esq.
1746 **Hathorn**, John, Drogheda, mercht.
1772 ,, John, late of Drogheda, now of Balbriggan, co. Dublin, merchant
1782 ,, Mary, Balbriggan, co. Dublin
1789 **Hatter**, Mathew, Newtown, co. Kildare
1752 **Hattin**, Grizel, Dublin, widow
1727 ,, Jonathan, Dublin, slater

1804 **Hatton**, Bartholomew, New-row, skinner and farmer
1747 ,, Edith, Wexford, widow
1632 ,, Edward, Monaghan, clk.
1639 ,, Edward, Ballramstown, co. Meath, yeoman
1742 ,, Henry, Gorey, co. Wexford
1747 ,, Henry, Wexford, esq.
1793 ,, Henry, Gt. Clonard, co. Wexford, esq.
1637 ,, James, Knockballymore, co. Fermanagh, clk.
1742 ,, James, Cooldross, co. Wicklow
1671 ,, John, Agevy, co. Londonderry, gent.
1773 ,, John, Newbay, co Wexford, esq.   [esq.
1778 ,, John, Ballymartin, co. Wexford,
1761 ,, Richd., Tomreland, co. Wicklow
1759 ,, Robt., Gorey, co. Wexford, clk.
1689 ,, Theodosia, *alias* **Harrington**, Muff, co. Derry, widow
1689 ,, William, Dublin, printer
1810 ,, William, town of Wexford, esq.
1782 **Haugh**, Jas., Crawley's Yard, Lib. of Thomas-st., carpenter
        [See HAWES.]
1757 **Haughan**, John, Cork-hill, Dublin, grocer
1808 **Haughton**, Abigail
1778 ,, Benjamin, Mullamast, co. Kildare, gent.
1766 ,, Chas., Mountcharles, co. Wexford, esq.
1793 ,, John, Clontarf, co. Dublin
1785 ,, Jonathan, Ballyton, co. Kildare
1783 ,, Joseph, Reban, co. Kildare
1761 ,, Priscilla
1788 ,, Richard, Coolacork, co. Wicklow, farmer
1699 ,, Robt., clk., vicar of Strabannon, co. Louth
1668 ,, Thomas, Dublin, merchant
                                [XII. 69
1778 ,, William, Waterford, schoolmaster
        [See HOUGHTON, HUTTON.]
1754 **Haukes**, Nicholas, Mount Talban, co. Roscommon, gent.
1775 **Haven**, Steph., Belfast, co. Antrim, esq.
1806 ,, Steph., Somerset-st., Middlesex (Copy)
1780 **Haw**, Jas., Ballybrien, co. Carlow, farmer
1635 **Haward**, Edmond, Coleraine, alderman
1618 ,, Nicholas, Dublin, esq.
1808 **Hawarden**, right hon. Ralph, lord visct.

1622 **Hawes**, Dorothy, widow
  [See HAUGH, HAW.]
1786 **Hawker**, John, Harold's-cross, co.
  Dublin, gardener
1757 **Hawkes**, Charles, Briarfield, co.
  Roscommon, esq. (Large)
1662 ,, John, Billiluke, co. Wicklow
  (Copy)
1803 ,, John, Surmount, co. Cork, esq.
  (Large)
1804 ,, John, Cork, tallow chandler
1716 ,, Lewis, Ballynafad, co. Roscommon, esq.
  [See HAWKS.]
1719 **Hawkesworth**, Elizabeth, Dublin,
  widow
1787 **Hawkey**, Elizabeth, Dubl., widow
1794 ,, rev. John, Pullein, Kingscourt,
  co. Cavan, clk.
1670 **Hawkford**, Wm., Nechills, Staffordshire, yeoman (Copy)
1736 **Hawkins**, Anne, Cork, widow
1763 ,, Charles, Oldcastle, co. Meath,
  merchant
1777 ,, Frances, Killaloe, co. Clare,
  widow [gent.
1768 ,, Francis, Killaloe, co. Clare,
1760 ,, Henry, Dublin
1707 ,, John, Cork, merchant
1729 ,, rev. John, Royal Hospital,
  Dublin
1734 ,, John, Cork, gent.
1758 ,, John, Dublin, esq.
1798 ,, John, Enniscorthy, co. Wexford,
  attorney-at-law
1725 ,, Thomas, Dublin, merchant
1787 ,, Thomas, Dublin, upholder
1680 ,, William, Dublin, esq.
1755 ,, William, Dublin, apothecary
1787 ,, sir William, knt., Ulster King
  of Arms
1787 **Hawks**, John, Castlenode, co. Roscommon, esq.
  [See HAWKES.]
1787 **Hawkshaw**, Elizabeth
1744 ,, John, Dublin, esq., LL.D.
1792 ,, rev. John, Kilmarren, co.
  Monaghan, clk.
1811 ,, John, Anamartin, co. Fermanagh
1803 ,, Margaret, Cumberland-street,
  Dublin
1749 ,, Priscilla, Dublin, widow
1763 ,, Richd., Royal Hospital, Dubl.
1803 ,, Richard, Millbrook, co. Tipperary, esq.
1683 ,, Thomas, Oxmantown, gent.
1780 ,, Thos., Dublin, timber mercht.
1746 **Hawkshead**, Thos., Shane, Queen's
  co., esq.

1782 **Hawksley**, John, St. James's-street,
  Dublin, gent.
1808 **Hawksworth**, John, Mountrath,
  Queen's co.
  [See HOWKESWORTH.]
1715 **Hawley**, rev. Thomas, archdeacon
  of Dublin
1774 ,, or **Halley**, Vernon, Dublin,
  Dublin, gent.
1723 ,, William, Dublin
1691 **Hawse**, Thomas, London, mercht.,
  died in Dublin
1803 **Hawtenville**, Elizabeth, Dublin
1710 **Hawthorn**, George, Dubl., mercht.
1762 **Hawthorne**, James, Downpatrick,
  merchant
1753 ,, John, Downpatrick, co. Down,
  gent.
1787 ,, Richd., the elder, Downpatrick,
  co. Down
1801 ,, Sophia, Downpatrick, co. Down,
  spinster
1796 ,, Steel, Downpatrick, co. Down,
  esq.
1804 **Hawtrey**, rev. Ralph, Waterford
  city, clk.
1740 **Hay**, Albin, Dromore, co. Cork,
  gent.
1773 ,, David, Dublin, bookseller
1811 ,, David, Dublin city, esq.
1762 ,, Edward, Ballinkeel, co. Wexford, gent.
1780 ,, Edward, Dublin, seedsman
1801 ,, Harvey, Ballinkeel, co. Wexford, esq.
1659 ,, sir James, Smithfield, Scotland,
  knt. and bart. [VII. 162
1726 ,, James, Dublin, apothecary
1798 ,, John, Newcastle, co. Wexford,
  esq.
1807 ,, Mary, Dublin city, widow[gent
1735 ,, Philip, Ballinkeel, co. Wexford,
1810 ,, Phillip, New Ross, co. Wexford
1635 ,, William, Dublin, esq.
1771 **Haycock**, Michael, Dublin, gent.
  [See HEACOCK.]
1656 **Hayday**, qr.-master Wm. [VI. 2
1693 **Haydock**, Josias, Kilkenny, alderman
1726 ,, Josias, Kilkenny, esq.
1714 **Haydocke**, Adam, Kilkenny, alderman
1730 ,, Stephen, esq., mayor of Kilkenny
1806 **Haydon**, Catherine, Lr. Merrion-
  street, Dublin
1807 ,, Henry, Naas, co. Kildare, distiller
1744 ,, Thomas, Kill M'Oliver, co. Kilkenny, esq.

1737 **Haydon**, William, Kill M'Oliver, co. Kilkenny, esq.
[See HEYDON.]
1798 **Hayes**, Atwell, Cork city, esq.
1803 ,, Benjamin, Cork, attorney-at-law
1808 ,, Benjamin, Marblehill, co. Cork, esq.
1759 ,, Darby, Killuragh, co. Limerick, gent.
1760 ,, Edmond, Limerick, clothier
1721 ,, Edward, Old Forge, co. Waterford, gent.
1737 ,, Edward, Ballydowling, co. Wicklow, gent.
1778 ,, Edward, Cherrymount, co. Wicklow, merchant
1702 ,, sir Jas., Greatbegbury, Kent, knt. (Copy)
1703 ,, James, Ballyfree, co. Wicklow
1752 ,, Jeremiah, Cahirgillamore, co. Limerick, gent.
1727 ,, John, Dublin, merchant
1787 ,, John, Coureven, co. Tipperary
1793 ,, John, Gardiner's-place, co. Dublin, esq.
1808 ,, John, Baltinglass, co. Wicklow
1795 ,, Joseph, Cork, merchant
1793 ,, Kennedy, Paulavere, co. Cork, farmer
1744 ,, Mary, Dublin, widow
1803 ,, Mary, Drogheda, widow
1804 ,, Michl., Prosperous, co. Kildare, builder
1810 ,, Richard, Dublin city, mercht.
1614 ,, Robt., Ryanduffbeg, Queen's co., gent.
1795 ,, Saml., Avondale, co. Wicklow, esq.
1807 ,, sir Saml., Drumboe Castle, co. Fermanagh (Copy)
1805 ,, Thos., Lower Feakill, co. Clare, farmer
1730 ,, William, Dublin, merchant
1737 ,, William, Upper Coombe, Dubl., brewer
1790 ,, William, Dublin, gent.
[See HAYS, HEASE, HEAYS, O'HEA.]
1658 **Haylor**, Michael, Ballinacarrick, co. Cavan
1736 **Hayman**, John, Polmore, co. Cork, esq.
1770 ,, John, Youghal, co. Cork, gent.
1778 ,, John, student of physic in Edinburgh
1672 ,, Samuel, Youghal, merchant
1724 ,, Samuel, Youghal, co. Cork, alderman

1788 **Haynes**, Benjamin, Kenny Court, co. Kildare, gent.
1658 ,, John, Dubl., vintner [**VII.** 16
1736 ,, John, Kenny Court, co. Kildare, esq.
1691 **Hayns**, William, Bridge-st., Dubl., merchant
[See HYNES.]
1728 **Hays**, William, Limerick, M.D.
[See HAYES.]
1627 **Hayward**, Edward, Grange, co. Waterford, gent. [**II.** 52
[See HEYWARD.]
1661 **Hazard**, John, Youghal, merchant
[See HASSARD.]
1657 **Heacock**, Samuel, Dublin, tailor [**VI.** 101
[See HAYCOCK.]
1752 **Head**, John, Waterford
1713 ,, Joshua, London, gent. (Copy)
1760 ,, Mary, widow of Michael H., Derry, co. Tipperary
1711 ,, Michael, Waterford, alderman
1749 ,, Michael, Derry, co. Tip., esq.
1770 ,, Samuel, late Dublin, now of Bordeaux, esq.
1723 ,, Thomas, Headsgrove, co. Kilkenny, esq.
1804 **Headon**, Anth., Dub. city, carpenter
1617 ,, John, Dublin, shoemaker
1781 **Healy**, Anne, Merchant's-quay, Dublin, widow
1806 ., Anne, George's-quay, Dublin city, widow
1800 ,, Barth., Dub., silk manufacturer
1801 ,, Ellin, Cork city, spr.
1788 ,, James, Garnafelia, co. Westmeath
1774 ,, Jane, widow of Francis H., Cork, burgess
1730 ,, Patrick, Finglas, co. Dublin, mason
1757 ,, Patrick, Maynooth, co. Kildare, grocer
1772 ,, Peter, Boyle, co. Roscommon, dealer
1811 ,, Peter, Dublin city
[See HEALY, HELY.]
1801 **Heaphy**, Tottenham, Dublin, gent.
1640 **Hearb**, Phillip, par. Lismore, co. Waterford, yeoman
1768 **Heard**, Ann, Kinsale, co. Cork, wid.
1780 ,, Ann, Cork city, spr.
1780 ,, Bickford, Cork city, gent.
1775 ,, Edward, Kinsale, co. Cork, merchant
1789 ,, John, Kinsale, co. Cork, esq.
1800 ,, John, Dublin, esq.
1782 ,, William, Cork city, gent.
[See HERD, HIRD, HURD.]

1773 **Hearin**, Thos,, Callan, co. Kildare, merchant
1657 **Hearing**, Francis, soldier [**VI.** 75
1809 **Hearn**, Beverley, Ring, co. Waterford, esq.
1805 ,, James, Blackhall market, Dub.
1788 ,, Thomas, Canty, co. Waterford, gent.
1733 **Hearne**, Andrew, Hearnbrook, co. Galway, gent.
1769 ,, Daniel, archdeacon of Cashel
1783 ,, Edmond, Hearnbrook, co. Galway, gent.
1804 ,, Edm., Hearnbrook, co. Galway
1801 ,, Ellen, Galway, spr.
1771 ,, John, Cork, linendraper
1769 ,, Mark Anthony, Dublin, esq.
    [See HEARIN, HEARN.]
1726 **Hease**, Darby, Ballyhadane, co. Limerick, farmer
    [See HAYES.]
1602 **Heath**, captain Augustine
1629 ,, John, Edenreagh, co. Tyrone, esq.
1715 ,, John, Finglas, co. Dublin, gent.
1776 ,, Lydia, co. Dublin, widow
1741 ,, Saml., Kilmainham, near Dublin, tanner
1769 ,, Thos., Delf lane, Staffordshire, potter (Copy)
1785 ,, Thos., York-st., Dub., carpenter
1657 ,, William, Belfast. shoemaker
    [**VI.** 172
1784 ,, William, Mucklows, co. Wexford, wheelwright
1751 **Heathcote**, sir William, Hursley, Hants, bart. (Copy)
1705 **Heathfield**, William, surgeon in col. Stanhope's regt. of foot
1806 **Heatley**, John M., Rosemount, co. Dublin, esq.
1707 ,, William, Dublin, gent.
1802 **Heatly**, Anne, wife to William Heatley, esq.
1747 ,, Charles, Dublin, gent.
1747 ,, Henry, Dublin, merchant
1751 ,, Jane, Dublin, widow
1764 ,, rev. Michael, Dublin, clk.
1742 ,, William, Dublin, bookseller
1736 **Heaton**, Francis, Dublin, esq.
1739 ,, Grizel, spr.
1666 ,, Richard, Dublin, vintner
1666 ,, Richard, Baliskenagh, King's co., D.D., dean of Clonfert
1797 **Heavisid**, John, Dublin, merchant
1692 **Heays**, Philip, Clownish, co. Monaghan, gent.
    [See HAYES.]
1677 **Hebb**, Arthur, Dublin, gent.

1711 **Hebburn**, Arthur, Hebburn, Northumberland, esq. (Copy)
1678 **Hecklefield**, John, Lurganboy, co. Fermanagh, gent.
1581 **Hederton**, David, Dromiskin, co. Louth
    [See HETHERINGTON.]
1637 **Heely**, or **Hely**, Abraham, Bristol, ironmonger [gent.
1686 ,, Patrick, Coldwinter, co. Dubl.,
    [See HEALY.]
1791 **Heenan**, John, Birr, King's co., physician
1804 **Hegarty**, Thos., Cork city, gent.
1771 **Hegerty**, Luke, Kilcaltrin, co. Carl.
1731 **Hegley**, Patrick, Dublin, dairyman
1747 **Hehir**, James
1796 ,, John, Moylagh
1753 ,, Patrick, Rineen, co. Clare, gt.
1757 **Heighington**, major Geo., Donard, co. Wicklow
1811 **Helden**, Anne, Dublin city, widow
1810 ,, Benjamin, Dublin city, esq.
1798 ,, Cornelius
1806 **Hellen**, Dorothea, Mespill bank, co. Dublin, widow
1793 ,, Robert, one of the Justices of the Common Pleas
1793 **Helly**, Catherine, Dublin, spr.
1788 ,, Joice, Dublin, spr.
1750 **Helsham**, Arthur, Legatsrath, co. Kilkenny, esq.
1749 ,, Hester, *alias* **Cramer**, Kilkenny
1769 ,, Jane, Jervais-st., Dubl., widow
1682 ,, Nathaniel, Dublin, tanner
1738 ,, Richard, Dublin, M.D.
1756 **Hely**, Edward, Drumcondra-lane, Dublin, gardener
1789 ,, Elizabeth, Dublin, spr.
1761 ,, George, Kilkenny, esq.
1786 ,, George, Rockville, esq.
1756 ,, rev. Gorges, Kilkenny, clk.
1776 ,, Hilliard
1701 ,, sir John, Chief Justice Common Pleas in Ireland (Ex.)
1741 ,, John, major in col. Cornwall's regt. of foot (Copy)
1790 ,, John, jun., Foulkscourt, co. Kilkenny (Copy)
1762 ,, Margaret, Drumcondra-lane, Dublin, widow
1811 ,, Pierce, Rockville, co. Waterford, esq.
    [See HEALY.]
1802 **Hemming**, Joseph (generally known by the name of Henry Heming), Stavin, city of Glasgow
1810 **Hemmings**, John, Dub. city, silversmith

1770 **Hemphill**, Alexander, Downpatrick, gent.
1793 **Hemsworth**, Godfrey
1698 ,, Henry, Dublin, esq.
1735 ,, John, Dublin, druggist
1746 ,, John, Dublin, M.D.
1803 ,, John, Strokestown, co. Roscommon, gent.
1747 ,, Mary, Dublin, widow
1769 ,, Thos., the elder, Abbeville, co. Tipperary, clk.
1767 **Henchin**, James, Dublin, mealman
1736 **Henchy**, Peter, Ennis, co. Clare, gent.
1784 **Hency**, Francis, Mullingar, co. Westmeath, gent.
1659 **Henderken**, William, Back-lane, Dublin, joiner [**VIII.** 42
1763 **Henderson**, Ann, Stonybatter, wid.
1760 ,, Elizabeth, widow of Patrick B., Dublin, gent.
1776 ,, George, Ballyshannon
1783 ,, Hugh, Dublin, seed merchant
1773 ,, Isabella, Dublin, spr.
1773 ,, James, Belfast, merchant
1735 ,, John, Donoghmore, co. Donegal, esq.
1767 ,, John, late of London, now of Mountmellick, surgeon
1777 ,, Jno., Fahuran, King's co., gent.
1793 ,, John, Belfast, co. Ant., mercht.
1802 ,, John, Toomon Hall, co. Wick., farmer
1808 ,, Kennedy, Castledawson, co. Londonderry, esq.
1809 ,, Mary, city of Bath
1767 ,, Mathew, Dublin, merchant
1741 ,, Patk., Mountmellick, Queen's co., merchant
1741 ,, Robert, Cork, merchant
1789 ,, Robert Cearnes, Carrick, co. Donegal
1761 ,, Samuel, Patrick-street, Dublin, leather cutter
1776 ,, Susanna, Dublin, widow
1702 ,, Walter, Dublin, merchant
1773 ,, Warren, Stradbally Hall, Queen's co., gent.
1773 ,, rev. William, Drogheda, clk.
1783 ,, William, par. of Dromond, co. Antrim
1785 ,, William, Beresford-st., Dublin, merchant
1778 **Hendley**, Christopher, Dubl., esq.
1788 ,, Erbery, Newstown, co. Carlow, esq.
1777 ,, Roger, Heclash, co. Cork, gent.
1797 ,, Roger, Inishannon, co. Cork, esq.

1796 **Hendley**, Mathias, Mount Rivers, co. Cork, esq.
1757 **Hendrick**, Anne, Dublin, single woman
1764 ,, Charles, Dublin, merchant
1762 ,, Edwd., Dublin, woollen draper
1799 ,, Frances, Castlewarden, co. Kildare, spinster
1743 ,, John, Islandbridge, co. Dublin, brewer
1768 ,, Margaret, Dublin, spinster
1754 ,, Mary, relict of John H., Dubl., alderman
1804 **Hendy**, William, Dublin city, carpenter
1802 **Henely**, John, Mallow, co. Cork, gent.
1750 **Heney**, Frances, Dublin
1728 **Henley**, Jane, Dublin, widow
1714 **Henly**, James, Patrick's Well-lane, Dublin, grocer
1723 ,, James, Patrick's Well-lane, Dublin, gardener
1700 ,, Roger, Dublin, gent. [See HANLY.]
1806 **Henn**, Bridget, Limerick city, widow
1803 ,, Margaret, William-st., Dublin, spinster
1736 ,, Thos., Paradise-hill, co. Clare, esq.
1796 ,, William, of the King's Bench
1802 ,, Wm., Paradise, co. Clare, esq.
1797 **Hennecy**, John, Ballymacmoy, co. Cork, gent.
1810 **Hennessy**, Bryan, Cork city, butter buyer
1802 **Hennesy**, David, Dromin, co. Cork, farmer
1779 ,, Geo., Ballymacmoy, co. Cork, gent.
1800 ,, John, Kilkenny city, gent. [See HENESSY, HENNECY.]
1739 **Henning**, David, Newry, co. Down
1796 **Henry**, Alexander, Richardstown, co. Louth, gent.
1779 ,, Anne, Dublin, widow
1752 ,, Elizabeth, widow
1806 ,, Geo., Clinkirk, co. Monaghan, farmer
1744 ,, Gustavius, Abbey, co. Donegal, miller
1802 ,, Helena, Henry-street, Dublin
1744 ,, Hugh, Drogheda, gent.
1744 ,, Hugh, Dub., esq. (Large will)
1792 ,, Hugh, Dublin, carpenter
1802 ,, Hugh, Lodgepark, co. Kildare, esq. (Large will)
1767 ,, James, late of Dublin, now of Cambrai, Flanders, esq.
1804 ,, James, Donadea

1768 **Henry**, Jebez, Dublin, tailor
1772 ,, John, Ballyshannon, co. Donegal, gent.
1774 ,, John, the elder, Cloverhill, co. Antrim, esq.
1790 ,, John, Dublin, esq.
1796 ,, John, Broomfield, co. Mon., esq.
1809 ,, John, city of Richmond, Virginia (Copy)
1794 ,, Johnston, Cloverhill, co. Antrim, esq.
1796 ,, Joseph, Straffan, co. Kildare, esq. (Large)
1810 ,, Joseph, Lodge Park, co. Kildare, esq.
1803 ,, Margt., Ballymoney, co. Antrim, widow
1798 ,, Mary, Dublin, spinster
1793 ,, Michl., Trinity College, Dubl.
1804 ,, Miles, Sligo
1757 ,, Robert, Dubl., now of Knightsbridge, Middlesex, esq. (Copy)
1810 ,, rev. Robert, town of Slane, clk.
1792 ,, Trusty, Dublin, gent.
1741 ,, Walter, Abbey, co. Donegal, yeoman
1768 ,, v. rev. Wm., rector of Unry, and dean of Killaloe•
1723 **Henshall**, Daniel, Dublin, merchant
1673 **Henshaw**, Nathaniel, Dublin, M.D.
1788 **Henzell**, Bigoe, rector of Kilbrew, co. Meath, clk.
1732 **Henzey**, Bigoe, Barnagrothy, King's co., gent.
1728 ,, Joshua, Dublin, merchant
1741 **Hepburn**, Archibald, lieut. in Royal Scotch regt. of foot
1788 ,, David, Portobello, co. Dublin, esq.
1778 ,, John, Dub., professor of mathematics
1666 **Hepburne**, William, Londonderry, esq.
1806 **Hepenstall**, Benjamin, Harold's-cross, co. Dublin
1806 ,, George, Sandymount, co. Dub., esq.
1801 ,, Isabella, spinster
1792 ,, John, the elder, Cornagower, co. Wicklow, farmer
1802 ,, John, Athleague, co. Roscommon
1805 ,, Mary, Rockmount, co. Down
1716 **Hepworth**, Thomas, Dubl., butcher
1791 **Heran**, Anthony, Galway, merchant
1685 **Herault**, John, Bristol, gt. (Copy)
1808 **Herbert**, Bartholomew, Dublin city, merchant

1781 **Herbert**, Bastable, Killarney, co. Kerry, esq.
1785 ,, Catherine, Dublin, widow
1691 ,, col. Charles (Codicil only)
1629 ,, sir Edward, Durrow, King's co., knt.
1657 ,, of Chirbury, Edward, lord [**VI.** 104
1713 ,, sir Edward, Durrow, King's co., bart.
1800 ,, Edward, Muckross, co. Kerry, esq. (Copy)
1719 ,, Francis, Oakley Park, Shropshire, esq. (Copy)
1753 ,, George, Binnaghan, Holt, co. Kildare
1695 ,, of Chirbury, Henry, ld. baron
1780 ,, Jane, Tralee, co. Kerry, widow
1785 ,, John, Limerick city, tallow chandler
1796 ,, John, Castle Island, co. Kerry, esq.
1801 ,, John Otway, clk.
1780 ,, Lucy, widow of Arthur H.
1811 ,, Martha, Carrick-on-Suir, co. Tipperary
1804 ,, rev. Nicholas, Carrick, co. Tipperary, clk.
1675 ,, Philip, sergt. to sir Wm. King's company
1777 ,, rev. Robert
1779 ,, Thomas, Muckross, co. Kerry, esq.
1801 ,, Thomas, Fanninstown, co. Limerick
1733 ,, William, Carlow, gent.
1787 **Herd**, Edward, Moore-street, Dub., gent. [See HEARD.]
1735 **Herdman**, John, Aghatarra, co. Armagh
1671 **Herdum**, Robert, Corballymore, co. Waterford, gent.
1630 **Herman**, Martin, Cork, merchant
1773 ,, Mary, Dublin
1706 **Herne**, John, Dublin, gent.
1721 **Heron**, Alexander, late lieut. in col. Lucas' regt. of foot
1788 ,, Catherine, Dublin, spinster
1792 ,, Catherine, Montague-st., Dub., widow
1740 ,, Randal, Tullykeel, co. Louth, esq.
1699 ,, Samuel, St. Margaret's, Westminster (Copy)
1809 ,, Samuel, Lisburn, co. Antrim, attorney
1792 ,, William, Callan, co. Kilkenny, esq. [See HERNE.]

1798 **Herrick**, Elizabeth, Cork city, spr.
1736   ,,   Gershom, Shippool, co. Cork, esq.
1788   ,,   John, Ardackling, co. Cork, esq.
1798   ,,   Thomas, Bousfield, Shippool, co. Cork, esq.
1798 **Herries**, Robert, city of London (Copy)
1805 **Herring**, Anne, Graigue, Queen's co., widow
1807   ,,   Darby, Carlow, esq.
1712   ,,   Thomas, Dublin, gent.
1659 **Herriott**, Archibald, Dromore, co. Down, esq.   **[VIII.** 15
1801 **Hertfort**, John, Broomfield, co. Armagh, attorney
1803 **Hervey**, Frederick Augustus, bp. of **Derry**, q. v.
1803 **Hesley**, Mathew, Exchequer-street, Dublin, smith and farrier
1627 **Hetherington**, David, Ballyroan, Queen's co., gent.
1749   ,,   Geo., Thomascourt and Donore, victualler
1766   ,,   George, Derryduff, Queen's co.
1794   ,,   George, Kildare town, apothecary
1775   ,,   William, Knightstown, Queen's co.
        [See HEDERTON.]
1698 **Heveningham**, Walter, Aston, near Stone, Staffordshire, esq.
1802 **Heverin**, Francis, the elder, Ballinasloe, co. Galway
1753   ,,   John
1779   ,,   Peter, Dublin, mercht.
1746 **Hevey**, Hugh, Boggstown
1760   ,,   John, Kinnegad, co. Westmeath, mercht.
1791   ,,   Joseph, Dublin, mercht.
1774   ,,   Sylvester, Dublin, mercht.
1805 **Hevy**, Garret, Mount Hevey, co. Meath, farmer
1805   ,,   Robert, Castletowndelvin, co. Westmeath
1678 **Hewar**, John, Dublin, gent.
1748 **Hewatson**, John, Dublin, mercht.
        [See HEWETSON.]
1629 **Hewet**, Edward, Kilmainham, co. Dublin, yeoman
1633 **Hewetson**, Christopher, Dublin, treas. of Christ Church (Copy)
1754   ,,   Christopher, Thomastown, co. Kilkenny
1769   ,,   Christopher, Cloghuisk, co. Carlow, esq.
1770   ,,   Constance, *alias* **Hunt**, wife to Moses H.

1786 **Hewetson**, Eleanor, Dublin, widow
1791   ,,   Hester, co. Dublin, widow
1658   ,,   John, Kildare, esq.   **[VII.** 137
1776   ,,   John, Dublin, cutler
1744   ,,   Margery, Betaghstown, co. Kildare, widow
1730   ,,   Mary, Annaghs, co. Kilkenny, widow   [esq.
1753   ,,   Michael, Coolbeg, co. Donegal,
1721   ,,   Moses, Betaghstown, co. Kildare, gent.
1761   ,,   rev. Nicholas, Grange, co. Wexford, clerk
1783   ,,   Patrick, Betaghstown, co. Kildare, M.D.
1789   ,,   Robert, capt. in the Queen's co. regt. of dragoons
1793   ,,   Sarah, *alias* **Cridland**
1688   ,,   Thomas, Kildare, esq. (Copy)
[See HEWATSON, HEWSON, HEWISON, HEWSTON, HUSON.]
1707 **Hewett**, Catherine, Dublin, widow
1774   ,,   Easter
1782   ,,   Henry, Dublin, esq.
1699   ,,   Isaac, Dublin, gent.
1709 **Hewison**, Elizabeth, Dublin, widow
        [See HEWETSON.]
1794 **Hewit**, hon. Ambrosia, spinster
1783   ,,   John, Dublin, but of London, esq.
1629   ,,   Mary, Kilmainham, widow
1806 **Hewitt**, James, Nassau-st., Dublin, silversmith
1804   ,,   the hon. John, dean of Cloyne
1811   ,,   Thomas, Cork city, esq.
1790 **Hewson**, rev. Francis, Woodford, co. Kerry, clerk
1766   ,,   John, Rathdowney, Queen's co.
1765   ,,   Joseph, Clonakenny, co. Tipp.
1659   ,,   William, soldier in capt. Vivian's com.   **[VII.** 186
        [See HEWETSON.]
1707 **Hewston**, George, lieut. in lord Dungannon's regt. of foot
1691 **Heyden**, Alexander, Kilcoad, co. Wicklow, esq.
1742   ,,   Catherine, *alias* **Byrne**, widow
1770   ,,   Elizabeth, Enniscorthy, co. Wexford, widow
1741   ,,   Samuel, Wicklow, gent.
1807 **Heydon**, Daniel, Dublin city
1702   ,,   Elizabeth, Dublin, spinster
1659   ,,   Francis, Dublin, silk weaver   **[VIII.** 70
1743   ,,   Samuel, Dublin, esq.
1798   ,,   rev. Samuel, Ferns, co. Wexford, clerk
        [See HAYDON, HEYDEN.]
1639 **Heygate**, James, archdeacon of Clogher   **[IV.** 310

1640 **Heygate**, John, rector of Dromully, co. Fermanagh, diocese Clogher

1754 **Heylan**, Patrick, Kilbeggan, co. Westmeath, gent.

1747 **Heyland**, Dominick, Castlerow, co. Londonderry, gent.

1780 ,, Dominick, Coleraine, co. Londonderry, esq.

1802 ,, rev. Robert, rector of Coleraine, co. Londonderry

1800 ,, Rowley, Glenoak, co. Antrim, esq. (Large)

1793 **Heylin**, James, Dublin, gent.

1773 **Heyn**, Martin, Gort, co. Galway, apothecary

1659 **Heyward**, Jeremiah, Limerick, burgess **[VIII.** 13
[See HAYWARD.]

1747 **Heywood**, Ann, Drogheda, widow

1766 **Hiatt**, Samuel, Coombe, Dublin, apothecary
[See HIETT.]

1658 **Hibbart**, Joseph, Dublin, clothier **[VII.** 83

1678 ,, William, Dromore, co. Waterford, esq.

1661 **Hichcock**, Hester, London, widow (Copy)

1783 ,, William, Cork, gent.

1788 **Hickes**, Henry, Navan, co. Meath, M.D.

1707 ,, John, Kilkannan, co. Cavan, gent.
[See HICKS.]

1766 **Hickey**, Daniel, Dublin, mercht.

1756 ,, Edward, Clonmel, M.D.

1755 ,, rev. John, late of Cashel, now of Dublin, clerk

1756 ,, Martin, Dublin, tailor

1795 ,, Michael

1746 ,, rev. Morgan, Kilmore, co.Tipp., clerk

1770 ,, Nicholas, Clonkeen, near Clonbullock

1606 ,, Owen, Bolton

1677 ,, William, Dublin, M.D.

1775 ,, William, Dublin, grocer and confectioner
[See HICKIE.]

1671 **Hickford**, Thomas, London, haberdasher (Copy)

1793 **Hickie**, Bartholomew,Limerick city, gent.

1801 ,, Catherine, Callan, co. Kilkenny

1801 ,, Francis, Dublin city, gent.

1744 ,, James, Glibb, Dublin, victualler

1748 ,, John, Sixmilebridge, co. Clare, gent.

1755 ,, John, Dublin, cutler

1765 **Hickie**, John, Cappagh, co. Clare, gent.

1739 ,, Laurence, Cashel, alderman

1750 ,, Mary, Weston Favill, Northamptonshire, widow

1717 ,, Michael, Great Billing, Northamptonshire, gent. (Copy)

1811 ,, Michael, Kilelton, co. Kerry, esq.

1769 ,, Thomas, Dublin, merchant, late at Amsterdam

1810 ,, Thomas, Augher, co. Tyrone, gent.

1786 ,, William, Cork, merchant

1811 ,, William, Dublin city, gent.
[See HICKEY, HICKY.]

1764 **Hickington**, Peter, chaplain of the "Berwick" and "Culloden" ships of war (Copy)

1688 **Hickman**, Andrew, Cluneboye, co. Clare, gent. (Copy)

1710 ,, Ann, *alias* **Burgoine**, wife to Charles H., bishop of Derry (Ex.)

1713 ,, Charles, bishop of **Derry**, q.v.

1804 ,, Hannah, city of Limerick, wid.

1744 ,, Henry, Kilrush, co. Clare

1760 ,, Henry, Kilmore, co. Clare, esq.

1710 ,, John, Londonderry, esq.

1810 ,, John, Caherban, co. Clare, esq.

1753 ,, Poole

1677 ,, Thomas, Ballyhyman, co.Clare, esq.

1718 ,, Thomas, Barntick, co. Clare, esq. (Ex.)

1738 **Hicks**, Andrew, Dublin, tailor

1776 ,, George, Creghta, co. Roscommon, gent.

1780 ,, rev. George, Rushy-park, co. Roscommon, clerk

1799 ,, John, Kilmicanoge, co. Wicklow

1727 ,, Peter, Lisduff, co. Tipperary, clerk

1766 ,, Richard, Creta, co. Roscommon, gent.

1802 ,, Thomas, Creta, co. Roscommon, esq.
[See HICKS.]

1784 **Hickson**, James, Dingle, co. Kerry, surgeon

1788 ,, James, Tralee, co. Kerry, merchant

1785 ,, John, Tralee, co. Kerry, apothecary

1797 ,, Mary, Tralee, co. Kerry, wid.

1752 ,, Robert, Dingle, co. Kerry, gent.

1797 ,, Robert, junior

1800 ,, Robert, Cork city

1665 **Hicky**, Mary, wife to William Hicky, Dublin, M.D.
1668　,,　Mary, wife to William H., M.D. (Copy)
1790　,,　Mary, Dublin, spinster
1671　,,　Morish, Droym, co. Clare, gent.
　　　　[See HICKIE.]
1665 **Hieron**, Jeremiah, Great Hormead, Hertfordshire, clerk (Copy)
1780 **Hiett**, Hannah, Palmerstown, co. Dublin, spinster
1724　,,　Jos., Dublin, patten maker
　　　　[See HIATT.]
1746 **Hiffernan**, Cornelius, Dublin, stone cutter
1766　,,　James, Dublin, esq.
1795　,,　Jas. Cantillon, Castle Roberts, co. Limerick, esq.
1779　,,　John, Dublin, esq.
1786　,,　John, Kilbreedy, co. Limerick, gent.
1787　,,　John
1752　,,　Macraith, Lattin (Unproved)
1748　,,　Mary, Newcastle, co. Limk., widow
1752　,,　Michael, Tipperary town, gent.
1784　,,　Michl. Camas, co., Limk., esq.
1765　,,　Sarah, *alias* **Owens**, widow
1794　,,　Terence M'Mahon, Liskennet, co. Limerick, esq.
1733　,,　Timothy, Ennis, co. Clare
1752　,,　William, Ballynahow, co. Tipperary, gent.
1811　,,　Wm., Derk, co. Limerick, esq.
1752 **Hiffernane**, James, Dublin, gent.
1751　,,　Patrick, Tipperary, gent.
1635 **Higgens**, James, Ballykelly, co. Londonderry, gent. (Copy)
　　　　[See HIGGINS.]
1775 **Higginbotham**, Abbigail, Largy, co. Cavan, spr.
1765　,,　Andw., Nutfield, co. Cavan, gt.
1768　,,　George, Largy, co. Cavan, gt.
1789　,,　Henry, Linenhall-st., Dublin
1699　,,　John, Barnhill, co. Kildare, farmer
1781　,,　John, Bolton, co. Kildare
1765　,,　Mary, widow of Andrew H., Nutfield, co. Cavan, gent.
1799　,,　Richard, Carrabay, co. Cavan, gent.
1771　,,　rev. Robert, Laurelhill, co. Londonderry, clk.
1786　,,　Saml., Bolton, co. Kildare, gt.
1737　,,　Thomas, Tullymaglowhy, co. Cavan, gent.
1762　,,　Thomas
1780　,,　Thos., Ballintrure, co. Wicklow, farmer

1788 **Higginbotham**, Thos., Cootehill, co. Cavan, gent.
1809　,,　Thos., Drumcondra, co. Dubl., merchant
1760　,,　Wm., Clarah, co. Cavan
1789　,,　Wm., Dublin, saddler
　　　　[See HIGINBOTHAM.]
1801 **Higgins**, Ann, Ballina, co. Mayo, widow
1796　,,　Benjamin, Dublin, gent.
1741　,,　Catherine, Limerick, widow
1796　,,　Charles, Westport
1750　,,　Edwd., lieutenant and surgeon in lord Tyrawley's regt. (Copy)
1809　,,　Eneas, native of Westport, co. Mayo (Copy)
1803　,,　Frances, Cole's-lane, widow
1728　,,　ven. Francis, archdeacon of Cashel
1802　,,　Francis, Dublin
1757　,,　Geo., Silverhill, co. Dub., esq.
1770　,,　George Lyddle, Silverhills, co. Dublin, gent.
1802　,,　Henry, South Green, co. Kildare, farmer
1791　,,　Hugh, esq.
1808　,,　Hugh, Sligo town, gent.
1726　,,　James, Dublin, gent.
1802　,,　James, Dublin, innholder
1740　,,　John, Limerick, merchant
1805　,,　John, Faughny, co. Longford, gent.
1783　,,　Luke, Kinnegad, co. Westmeath, innkeeper
1790　,,　Luke, Dorset-st., Dublin
1743　,,　Maurice, Tincalla, co. Waterford, gent.
1746　,,　Paul, Dublin, merchant
1745　,,　Ralph, Bellewstown, co. Meath, farmer
1800　,,　Ralph, Trim, co. Meath
1724　,,　Robert, Dublin, mercer
1749　,,　Robert Palfrey, Dublin
1807　,,　Silvester, Crinstown, co. Kildare
1790　,,　Thomas, Kinnegad
1793　,,　Thomas, Barleyhill, co. Meath, hatter
1746　,,　Timothy, Dublin, merchant
1737　,,　Wm., Meelick, co. Clare, gent.
1752　,,　William, a quartermaster
1759　,,　Wm., late capt. in Royal Dragoons, now of Dublin
1771　,,　Wm., Bellewstown, co. Meath, farmer
1781　,,　Wm., Cork-hill, Dublin, grocer
　　　　[See HIGGENS, HUGGENS.]
1747 **Higginson**, Henry, Nappan
1670　,,　John, Dublin
1789　,,　Joseph, Grange Mellon, co. Kildare, esq.

1804 **Higginson**, Richard, Clonmel, co. Tipperary, farmer
1789 ,, rev. Thos., vicar of Ballinderry, co. Antrim
1800 **Higinbotham**, Elizabeth Anne, Summerhill, co. Dubl., wid. [See HIGGINBOTHAM.]
1785 **Higley**, Patrick, Henry-st., Dublin
1751 **Higly**, Wm., the Coombe, co. Dubl., comber
1656 **Hiknebotham**, Jno., trooper [**V**. 355
1634 **Hill**, Anna, Dame-st., Dub., widow
1716 ,, Anne, widow of John H., Dub., esq.
1780 ,, Anne, Hollyhill, Cork, widow
1665 ,, Arthur, Hillsborough, co. Down, esq.
1783 ,, Charles, St. John's, co. Wexford, esq.
1811 ,, Charles, Killmount, co. Antrim
1746 ,, Christopher, Dublin, aleseller
1772 ,, Christopher, Dublin, merchant
1758 ,, David, Dublin, tailor
1750 ,, Edmond, Oberstown, co. Kildare, esq. [esq.
1675 ,, Edward, Rathbane, co. Mayo,
1759 ,, Edward, Dublin, esq.
1764 ,, Elizabeth, Clonmel
1773 ,, Elizabeth, High-st., Dub., wid.
1788 ,, Elizabeth, Queen's co., widow
1792 ,, Eliz., Virville, co. Dublin, spr.
1792 ,, Eliz., Virville, co. Dublin, wid.
1627 ,, Francis, Drogheda, baker
1658 ,, Francis, Clonmel, victualler [**VII**. 79
1807 ,, Francis, Mullingar, co. Westmeath, victualler
1718 ,, George, Dublin, gent.
1752 ,, George, Dublin, gent.
1773 ,, rev. Hugh, Cavendish-row, Dublin, D.D.
1739 ,, James, Killowen, King's co.
1766 ,, James, Limerick, tanner
1659 ,, John, soldier in capt. Vivian's com. [**VII**. 186
1704 ,, John, Killmainham, co. Dublin, gent.
1755 ,, John, Dublin, esq.
1764 ,, John, Gorey, co. Wexford, innholder
1773 ,, John, Tatebawn, co. Louth, farmer
1794 ,, John, Drogheda-st., Dublin
1803 ,, John, Ballyloghbeg, co. Ant.
1804 ,, John G., Streamstown, co. Wesmeath, esq.
1811 ,, John, Fethard, co. Tipperary
1720 ,, Jonathan, Dublin, gent.
1788 ,, Jonathan, Mountrath, Queen's co.

1780 **Hill**, Joshua, Limerick city, tanner
1810 ,, Lancelot, Limerick city, esq.
1791 ,, Letitia, Dublin, spr.
1811 ,, Lysaght, Templeacre, liberties of Cork
1751 ,, Marcus, Goosegreen Lodge, forest of Alice-holt, Hampshire, esq.
1691 ,, Margaret, widow of Robt. Hill, Carrickmacross, esq,
1810 ,, Mary
1699 ,, Michl., Hillsborough, co. Down, esq. (Ex.)
1682 ,, Moses, Hill Hall, co. Down, esq.
1647 ,, Peter, Dub., esq., sergt.-at-arms
1659 ,, Richd., soldier in capt. Vivian's com. [**VII**. 183
1699 ,, captain Richard, sir John Hammer's regt. of foot
1723 ,, Richd., Earl-st., Dub., brewer
1737 ,, Richard, Dublin, pin maker
1688 ,, Robert, Carrickmacross, co. Monaghan, gent.
1708 ,, Robert, Dublin, brewer
1771 ,, Robert, Cloneen, co. Longford
1787 ,, Roger, Kilbride, co. Wicklow, farmer
1694 ,, Rowland, Kinerton, Cheshire, gent.
1787 ,, sir Rowland, Hawstone, Shropshire, bart. (Copy)
1739 ,, Rowley, Walworth, co. Londonderry, esq.
1694 ,, Samuel, Coleraine, esq.
1760 ,, Samuel, Strangford, co. Down, esq.
1648 ,, Thomas, Dublin, baker
1655 ,, Thomas, Newtown Limavady, trooper [**V**. 229
1672 ,, Thomas, Dublin, gent.
1673 ,, Thomas, D.D., dean of St. Canice's church, Kilkenny
1690 ,, Thomas, Skreen, co. Meath, clk.
1735 ,, Thomas, Dublin, pewterer
1750 ,, Thomas, Waterford, merchant
1789 ,, Thomas, Dublin, merchant
1809 ,, Thomas, Portarlington, Queen's co., gent.
1810 ,, Thos., Shanballyduff, co. Tipperary, esq.
1661 ,, William, Dublin, surgeon
1667 ,, William, Finglas, D.D.
1693 ,, Wm., Hillsborough, co. Down, esq.
1750 ,, William
1775 ,, William, Maryborough
1760 **Hillam**, Thomas, Newry, co. Down, carpenter

1781 **Hillary**, Caroline, Marlborough-st., Dublin, widow
1780 ,, John, Marlborough-st., Dublin, gent.
1785 ,, John, Cork city, silversmith
1746 ,, Sarah, Mountrath, Queen's co., widow
1800 **Hillas**, Malcolm, Aughnavalog, co. Down, farmer
1791 ,, Robert, the elder, Doonecoy, co. Sligo, esq.
1790 ,, Thomas, Dublin
1790 ,, Wynne, Dublin, esq.
           [See HILLIS.]
1657 **Hilliam**, John, Enniskillen, gent. [**VII**. 45
1739 **Hilliard**, Christopher, Baltigarran, co. Kerry, gent.
1678 ,, Robert, Dublin, distiller
1802 ,, Robt., Chancery-lane, Dublin, gent.
1801 ,, William, Listrim, co. Kerry
1780 **Hillis**, Alice, widow
           [See HILLAS.]
1626 **Hillman**, Thos., Coleraine, alderman
1805 **Hillyard**, Mary, Kenagh, co. Long.
           [See HILLIARD.]
1688 **Hilme**, Isaac, Dublin, clothier
1688 **Hilton**, Henry, Dublin, merchant
1714 ,, John, Newtown Stewart, co. Tyrone, gent.
1691 ,, Ralph, late of Chester, at the camp before Limerick
1699 ,, Richard, Dame-st., Dublin, brazier
1673 ,, Robt., Dublin
1651 ,, William, Dublin, esq.
1772 **Hincks**, Edward, Dublin, merchant
1792 ,, Wm., Gurteen, co. Kilkenny, farmer
1711 **Hind**, George, Castlemeaghan, co. Westmeath, esq.
1770 ,, Richd., late of Waterford, now of Dublin, gent.
1674 **Hinde**, Ann, Dublin, widow
1779 ,, Jarvis, Anadown, co. Galway, esq.
1668 ,, John, London, haberdasher (Copy)
1737 ,, John, Dublin, merchant
1729 ,, Martha, Dublin, widow
1767 ,, Richard, the elder, Waterford, gent.
1689 ,, Thos., D.D.; dean of Limerick
1690 ,, Thos., Killoy, co. Roscommon, gent.
1765 **Hindes**, Michael, Dublin, cutler
1748 **Hindman**, John, Dublin, carpenter
1805 **Hinds**, Alexander, Capel-st., Dubl.
1799 ,, Ann, Drumkeel, co. Cavan, spr.

1791 **Hinds**, John, Newgrove, co. Longford, esq.
1797 ,, Luke, Dublin, coal factor
1793 ,, Ralph, Kimmis Mill, co. Meath, esq.
1780 ,, Thomas, Cornaseer, co. Cavan, gent.
1793 ,, Thomas, Prussia-st., Dub., esq.
1811 ,, Thomas, Dublin city, gent.
1778 ,, Walter, Cuirikane, co. Cavan
1805 ,, Walter, Bruce Hall, co. Cavan, esq.
           [See HIND, HINDE, HINDES.]
1776 **Hingston**, rev. James, presbytery of Donoghmore, dio. Cloyne
1746 ,, John, Cork, merchant
1787 **Hinkson**, John, Mayfield, co. Mon.
1754 ,, Thos., Drumgury, co. Cavan
1702 **Hinton**, Edward, Kilkenny, D.D.
1743 ,, rev. Dr. John, dean of Tuam
1630 ,, Randal, Kinsale, gent.
1656 ,, Thomas, trooper   [**VI**. 49
1796 ,, Thos., Enniscorthy, merchant
1753 **Hiorne**, James, Dublin
1683 ,, John, Athy, gent.
1713 ,, John, Dublin, tailor
1730 ,, Mary, Dublin, widow
1755 **Hippisley**, William, Staunton, Wiltshire, esq. (Copy)
1729 **Hird**, Leonard
1809 ,, Thomas, Dublin city
           [See HEARD.]
1737 **Hiscox**, Joseph, London, merchant (Copy)
1770 **Hitchcock**, Daniel, Harristown, co. Meath
1798 ,, Dorothy, Dublin, widow
1771 ,, James, Harristown, co. Meath, farmer
1661 ,, Wm., London, merchant tailor (Copy)
1747 **Hiverin**, Francis, Flash, co. Rosc.
1670 **Hoare**, Abraham, Dublin, gent.
1709 ,, Edward, Cork, alderman
1741 ,, Edwd., Killcoolishkill, co. Cork, esq.
1790 ,, Edwd., the Crescent, Bath, esq. (Copy)
1724 ,, John, Coolfada, co. Cork, gent.
1730 ,, Joseph, Cork, merchant
1741 ,, Joseph, Cork, merchant
1802 ,, sir Joseph, Annabella, co. Cork, bart.
1799 ,, Mathew, Dublin, shoemaker
1635 ,, Melson or Melchor, New Ross, mercht.
1724 ,, Richard, Dublin, esq.
1764 ,, Robert, Cork, esq.
1806 ,, Robert, Factory Hill, co. Cork, esq.

1765 **Hoare**, Russell, Cork, mercht.
  [See HORE.]
1781 **Hobart**, Benjamin, Carlow town, gent.
1765 ,, Mathew, Birr, King's co., gent.
1793 ,, Mathew, Birr, King's co., gent.
1790 ,, Nathaniel, Birr, King's co., gent.
1781 ,, Samuel, Birr, King's co., merchant
1780 **Hobbs**, Ann, Waterford, widow
1786 ,, Anne, Shanrahan, co. Tipp., widow
1768 ,, Rodolphus, Tipperary, gent.
1789 ,, Thomas, Barnaboy, King's co., gent.
1810 ,, Thos., Killnegall, King's co., esq.
1745 ,, William, Tipperary town, gent.
1774 ,, William, Shanrahan, co.Tipp., clerk
1709 **Hobson**, Samuel, Wexford, co.Wexford
1628 ,, William, Kilmore, co. Armagh, yeoman
1774 **Hodder**, Francis, Cork, mercht.
1732 ,, George, Dublin, joiner
1771 ,, George, Cork, esq.
1801 ,, George, Fountainstown, co. Cork, esq.
1804 ,, Samuel, Cork city, esq.
1726 ,, Wm. Hoddersfield, co. Cork, gent.
1788 ,, Wm. Hoddersfield, co. Cork, esq.
1770 **Hoddock**, Mary, Ballygroman, co. Cork
1713 **Hodge**, Mary, *alias* **Nugent**
1709 ,, Robert, Dublin, gent.
1780 **Hodgens**, Thomas, Pill-lane, Dubl.
1755 **Hodges**, George, Shanagolden, co. Limerick, gent.
1788 ,, George, Old Abbey, co. Limk.
1680 ,, Humphrey
1802 ,, John, Sealodge, co. Clare, gent.
1797 ,, Peter, Castlewellan, co. Down, mercht.
1678 ,, Thomas, London, merchant (Copy)
1750 ,, William, Shanagolden, co. Limerick, gent.
1732 **Hodgin**, Margaret, Ballyaney, co. Armagh, widow
1716 ,, William, Elbow-lane, Dublin, weaver
1811 **Hodgins**, Patrick, of His Majesty's ship "Nereide"
  [See HODSON.]
1756 **Hodgkinson**, Roger, Lisburn, co. Antrim

1775 **Hodgkinson**, Sarah, Lisburn, co. Antrim, widow
1811 **Hodgson**, George, Dublin city, esq.
1713 ,, Henry, Dawsonbridge, co. Londonderry
1793 ,, James, Dublin, gent.
1655 ,, John, Birr, King's co., gent. [V. 86
1717 ,, John, Bovagh, co. Londonderry, gent.
1717 ,, John, the younger, Bovagh, co. Londonderry, gent.
1725 ,, Lemael, Dunshaughlin, gent.
1807 ,, Lewis, Dublin city
1774 ,, Mary, Ballynascreen, co. Londonderry, widow
1756 ,, Robert, Dublin, esq.
1767 ,, Sarah
1795 ,, Thomas, Dublin, gent.
1713 ,, William, Tuitestown, co.Westmeath, gent.
  [See HODSON.]
1764 **Hodnet**, Edmund, Derryleigh
1807 ,, Martha
1782 ,, William, rector of Mycross, Ross diocese
1810 **Hodson**, Charles, Greek-street, Dublin, vintner
1781 ,, Daniel, St. John's, co. Roscommon, esq.
1800 ,, Edward, Rathfarnham, co. Dublin, esq. (Large)
1760 ,, Elizabeth, Coolkenna,co.Wicklow, widow
1770 ,, Elizabeth, daughter of Wm.H., St. John, co. Roscommon, esq.
1770 ,, Joanna, Athlone, co. Roscommon, spinster
1686 ,, John, bishop of **Elphin**, q. v.
1749 ,, John, Clonoquin, co. Roscommon
1691 ,, Laurence, Coolkenna, co. Wicklow, esq.
1729 ,, Leonard, Ballinacor, co. Westmeath, clerk [Dublin
1789 ,, Leonard, Green Hills, co.
1792 ,, Leonard, Dublin
1744 ,, Lorenzo, Coolkenna, co. Wicklow, esq.
1770 ,, Maria, Athlone, co.Westmeath, spinster
1786 ,, Mary, Dublin, widow
1799 ,, Oliver, Grove, co. Roscommon
1797 ,, Thomas, Hodson's Bay, co. Roscommon, esq.
1700 ,, William, Tuitestown, co.Westmeath, gent.
1770 ,, William, Athlone, co. Westmeath, esq.

1779 **Hodson,** William, Athlone, co. West-
        meath, gent.
1794 ,,   William, St. John's, co. Ros-
        common, esq.
        [See HODGIN, HODGSON, HUDSON.]
1805 **Hoey,** Ann, Dublin city, widow
1795 ,,   Edward, Waterford city, shop-
        keeper
1699 ,,   Elizabeth, Melville, co. Kil-
        kenny, widow
1773 ,,   Hannah, Dublin, widow
1777 ,,   James, Dublin, printer
1789 ,,   Jane, Parliament-street, Dubl.,
        widow
1664 ,,   sir John, Cotlandstown, co. Kil-
        dare, knt.
1793 ,,   John, Raheny, co. Dublin,
        farmer
1798 ,,   John, Dundalk, co. Louth,
        plumber and glazier
1808 ,,   Michael, Castledermot, shop-
        keeper
1699 ,,   William, Dunganstown, co.
        Wicklow, esq.
1808 ,,   William Parsons, Richmond, co.
        Dublin
1809 **Hoffman,** George Godfrey, Dublin
        city, esq.
1675 **Hofford,** Thomas, Dublin, gent.
1760 **Hoffshleger,** Anne, Dublin, widow
1753 ,,   John Bernard, Dublin, mercht.
1783 **Hogan,** Darby, Ross, co. West-
        meath, farmer
1724 ,,   Charles, Ladyrath, co. Meath
1737 ,,   Cornelius, Dublin, gent.
1743 ,,   Cornelius, Carrigagown, co.
        Tipperary, gent.
1779 ,,   Daniel, Phibsborough, co.
        Dublin, esq.
1760 ,,   Edmond, Ennis, co. Clare, esq.
1793 ,,   Ellen, Longford
1742 ,,   Garret, Ballynegall, co. West-
        meath, gent.
1773 ,,   John, Balnaskeagh, lately of
        par. Castletown, co. West-
        meath
1791 ,,   John, Limerick, schoolmaster
1803 ,,   John, Limerick, woollendraper
1757 ,,   Mary, Limerick, widow of
        Francis H., gent.
1769 ,,   Michael, Geighanstown, co.
        Meath, gent.   [gent.
1747 ,,   Murtagh, Cross, co. Clare,
1789 ,,   Owen, Dublin, esq.
1752 ,,   Patrick
1767 ,,   Patrick, New Ross, co. Wexford,
        shopkeeper
1810 ,,   Patrick, Dublin city, attorney
1786 ,,   Peter, Limerick city, formerly
        a woollen draper

1741 **Hogan,** Philip, Monroe, co. Tip-
        perary, farmer
1743 ,,   Philip, Waterford, gent.
1785 ,,   Susanna, Whitehall, co. Dublin,
        widow
1730 ,,   William, Dublin, gent.
1731 ,,   William, King-street, Dublin
        [See HUGGINS.]
1781 **Hogg,** James, Lisburn, co. Antrim,
        merchant
1790 ,,   Margaret, Constitution Hill, co.
        Dublin, widow
1766 ,,   Thomas, Londonderry, mercht.
1770 ,,   William, Londonderry, alder-
        man   [merchant
1773 ,,   William, Lisburn, co. Antrim,
1797 ,,   William, Limerick, gent.
1759 **Hoggard,** Thomas, Dublin, clothier
1811 **Hoguet,** Anthony J., Dublin city,
        farmer
1675 **Hoile,** Jonathan, Kilteal, Queen's
        co., clerk
1699 **Holcroft,** Charles, Dublin, esq.
        [XVIII., 313
1700 ,,   Charles, Dublin, esq.
1702 ,,   Hamlett, lieutenant in sir John
        Hammer's regiment
        [See HOLDCROFT.]
1783 **Holdbrook,** Anne, Dublin, widow
1810 **Holdcroft,** George, Kells, co. Meath.
1770 **Holdigan,** Philip, Drogheda, gent.
1801 **Holdsworth,** John, Dublin, gent.
1692 **Holgate,** George, London, haber-
        dasher (Copy)
1678 ,,   William, London, leather seller
        (Copy)
1639 **Hollam,** Wm., Dublin, shoemaker
1766 **Holland,** Deborah, Limerick, widow
1786 ,,   Henry, lord baron of Foxley,
        Wiltshire (Copy)
1787 ,,   Henry, Limerick, burgess
1728 ,,   Hezekiah, Crossagalla, lib. of
        Limerick, alderman (Large)
        (Ex.)
1791 ,,   Joseph, Limerick, gent.
1787 ,,   Margaret, Athy, co. Kildare,
        widow
1730 ,,   Randal, Limerick, alderman
1753 ,,   Simon, Crossagalla, lib. of
        Limerick, gent. (Large will)
        (Ex.)
1742 ,,   capt. Thos., Crossagalla, lib.
        of Limerick
1788 ,,   Thomas, Bandon, co. Cork,
        shopkeeper
1630 **Hollenpriest,** John, Newtown, co.
        Dublin, gent.
1754 **Holliday,** Abraham
1788 ,,   Catherine, Philipstown, King's
        co., widow

1734 **Holliday**, John, Killgoreen, co. Galway, gent.
1779 ,, rev. John, rector of Ballyburly or Primult
1776 ,, Joseph, Carrick, co. Tipperary, clothier
[See HALLIDAY.]
1791 **Hollingsworth**, John, Ballinakill, co. Wexford, farmer
1674 **Hollington**, Josias, clk., vicar-gen. of the see of Cashel
1662 ,, Richard, *alias* **Gray**, Dublin, innholder
1747 **Hollinworth**, Thomas, New-row, Dublin, merchant
1752 **Hollister**, Thomas, par. St. Martin, Middlesex, tailor (Copy)
1802 ,, William, Castel, Dublin, gent.
1779 **Hollond**, John, Carroreagh, co. Antrim, gent.
1644 **Hollowood**, James, Big Lagore, co. Meath, farmer
1660 **Hollyman**, Charles, Croncrogh, co. Cath., yeoman
1749 **Hollywood**, Bridget, Dublin, widow
1718 ,, Christopher, Artane, co. Dubl., esq.
1643 ,, John, Hobertstown, co. Meath, gent. (Ex.)
1666 ,, John, Artaine, co. Dub., esq.
1689 ,, John, Bushe, co. Dublin, priest
1740 ,, Laurence, Artaine, co. Dublin, gent.
1741 ,, Nicholas, Dublin, merchant
1582 **Holman**, Richard, Dublin, saddler
1775 **Holmes**, Alice, par. St. George, Bloomsbury, Middlesex (Copy)
1796 ,, Ann, *alias* **Alloway**, Dorset-st., Dublin
1691 ,, Bridget, Dublin, widow
1802 ,, Catherine, Athlone, co. Westmeath, widow
1809 ,, Catherine, Granard, co. Longford, widow
1786 ,, Elizabeth, Bolyart, King's co.
1805 ,, Elizabeth, Prospect, King's co.
1779 ,, Esther, Dublin, widow
1737 ,, George, Liscloony, King's co., esq.
1690 ,, Gilbert, Ovidstown, co. Kildare, gent. [chant
1762 ,, Hugh, island of Antigua, mer-
1759 ,, Isabella, Dublin, widow
1790 ,, Isabella, Dublin, spr.
1662 ,, James, Finea, co. Westmeath, gent.
1732 ,, James, Dublin, merchant
1744 ,, Jennett, Belfast, co. Antrim, widow

1721 **Holmes**, John, Dublin, tailor
1754 ,, John, Ballintober, co. Limk., gt.
1779 ,, John, formerly of Belfast, late of Dublin, merchant
1783 ,, John, Athlone, co. Westmeath, merchant
1803 ,, John, Dublin city
1789 ,, Lancelot, Millmount, co. Rosc.
1807 ,, Martha, Prospect Hall, co. Cork, widow
1718 ,, Mary, Dublin, spr.
1675 ,, Peter, St. Mary's-lane, Oxmantown, esq.
1803 ,, Peter, Peterfield, co. Tip., esq.
1683 ,, Robert, Clongery, co. Kildare, gent.
1796 ,, Robert, Ballydam, co. Limk., esq.
1707 ,, Sampson, Crone-ne-horne, co. Wicklow, gent.
1789 ,, Samuel, Kells, co. Meath, esq.
1803 ,, Susanna
1766 ,, Thomas, Dublin, merchant
1806 ,, Wally, Watterstown, co. Meath
1754 ,, William, Cork
1760 ,, William, Belfast, merchant
1762 ,, Wm., the elder, Donoghmore, co. Tyrone
1706 **Holroide**, Isaac, Dublin, merchant
1778 **Holroyd**, Isaac, at Bath, esq.
1729 ,, John, Dublin
1741 ,, Sarah, Dublin, widow
[See HALROIDE.]
1669 **Holt**, Eliz., Drumcar, co. Louth, widow
1792 ,, Lady Frances
1730 ,, Joan, Dublin, widow
1750 ,, John, formerly of Dublin, now of Philadelphia, mariner
1786 ,, John, Ranelagh-road, co. Dublin, dyer
1637 ,, Michael, Agheenhoyly, Queen's co., gent.
1698 ,, Samuel, Dublin, gent.
1774 ,, Thomas, Dublin, gent.
1792 ,, Thomas, Haggart
1759 ,, Valentine, Dublin, merchant
[See HOULT.]
1810 **Holton**, Richard, Athlone, co. Roscommon, merchant
1660 **Holtue**, Robert, soldier, Birr garrison, King's co. [**VIII**. 107
1720 **Holworthy**, Mathew, Hackney, Middlesex, esq. (Copy)
1766 **Holy**, rev. sir Philip, Dublin, bart. (Copy)
1670 **Holywood**, Laurence, Philpotstown, co. Meath, gent.
1687 ,, Luke, Piercetown, co. Meath, gent.

1769 **Homan,** David, Drumcooley, King's co., farmer
1769 ,, Elizabeth, wife of George H., Sharock, co. Westmeath
1791 ,, Elizabeth, Moate, co. Westmeath, widow
1682 ,, John, Moate Granoge, co. Westmeath, gent. (Ex.)
1741 ,, John, Dublin, ironmonger
1793 ,, Martha, Cunaburrow, King's co.
1809 ,, Mary Anne
1767 ,, Mathew, Limerick, M.D.
1802 ,, rev. Philip, Surock, co. Westmeath
1785 ,, Richard George, Francis-st., Dublin, woollendraper
1787 ,, Richard, Moate Granoge, co. Westmeath, esq.
1802 ,, Richard, Great Ship-st., Dubl., grocer
1773 ,, William, Francis-st., Dublin
1744 **Home,** James, Dublin, esq.
1795 ,, James, the island of Jersey, esq. (Copy)
1800 **Honan,** Andrew, Kilmore, co. Roscommon, gent.
1757 ,, Jas., Ennis, co. Clare, mercht.
1772 ,, Mary, Limerick, widow
1799 **Hone,** Joseph, the elder, Dub., esq.
1803 ,, Joseph, York-st., Dublin, esq.
1743 ,, Nathaniel, Dublin, merchant
    [See OWEN.]
1808 **Honeywood,** sir John, Evington, Kent, bart. (Copy)
1785 ,, Philip, Markshall, Essex, genl. of His Majesty's forces (Copy)
1762 **Honner,** Edwd., Mountrath, Queen's co., innholder
1670 ,, John, Madame, co. Cork, esq.
1675 ,, John, Garranard, co. Cork, gent.
1678 ,, Robt., Madain, co. Cork, gent.
1809 ,, William
1706 **Honohane,** Jno., Broghill, co. Cork, esq.
1731 ,, Mary, Cork
1789 **Hood,** Daniel, Cork, stationer and bookseller
1724 ,, John, Dublin, victualler
1796 ,, Robert, Portarlington, Queen's co.
1672 **Hooke,** Thomas, Danganspidoge, co. Kilkenny, D.D.
1675 ,, Thomas, Dublin, merchant
1667 **Hooker,** Charles, Dublin, esq.
1806 **Hoolan,** Wm., Clonomohun, King's co., farmer
    [See HOULAGHAN.]

1754 **Hoole,** Anne
1768 ,, Elizabeth, Dublin, spinster
1667 ,, William, Lisburn, gent.
1737 **Hoop,** Robert, Dublin, merchant
1791 ,, Thomas, Crowhill, co. Armagh, esq.
1740 **Hoope,** John, Lurgan, co. Armagh, esq.
1676 ,, lieut.-col. George, St. Martins, Westmeath
1706 ,, Jas., Middle Temple, London, esq. (Copy)
1781 **Hoops,** Alex., Tipperary, merchant
1747 ,, John, Tipperary, gent.
1750 ,, John, Tipperary town, merchant
1753 ,, John, Tip. town, gent. (Ex.)
1692 **Hope,** Eliz., Loughkeen, co. Tip., widow
1671 ,, Jane, *alias* **Cheevers,** *alias* **Casey,** *alias* **Ducket,** widow
1743 ,, Mary, widow
1611 ,, Thomas, Dublin
1723 **Hopes,** Anthony, par. Ballinderry, co. Antrim, farmer
1803 ,, John, Dublin city, merchant
1757 **Hopkins,** Bridget, spinster
1796 ,, Elizabeth, Great Britain-street, Dublin, spinster [widow
1806 ,, Eliz., Booterstown, co. Dublin,
1792 ,, Ellinor, Cork, spinster
1690 ,, Ezekiel, bishop of **Derry,** q.v.
1776 ,, Fras., Tullow, co. Carlow, clk.
1778 ,, Francis, Darristown, co. Westmeath, gent.
1789 ,, Francis, Dublin, esq.
1763 ,, John, Mullingar, co. Westmeath
1768 ,, John, Munsborough, co. Roscommon, gent.
1797 ,, John, Shillelagh, co. Wicklow, farmer
1802 ,, John, Headstown, co. Meath
1724 ,, Joseph, Waterford, esq.
1748 ,, Joseph, Possetstown, co. Meath
1750 ,, Joseph, the younger, Possetstown
1765 ,, Richard, Oldtown
1788 ,, rev. doctor Richard, co. Dublin
1700 ,, Saml., Ramelton, co. Donegal, gent.
1811 ,, Samuel, Wheatfield, co. Kildare
1777 ,, Stephen, Cork, merchant
1669 ,, Thomas, co. Kilkenny, gent.
1766 ,, Thomas, Dublin, ribbon weaver
1783 ,, rev. Thomas, Castlerickard, co. Meath, clk.
1620 **Hoppe,** Walt., Mullingar, co. Westmeath, gent. (Copy)
1780 **Hopper,** Arthur, Ballinakill, Queen's co., gent.

1803	**Hopper**, Edward Hart, Cork, merchant	
1769	,, George, Dublin, hairdresser	
1800	**Hopson**, Ellinor, Dublin, widow	
1782	,, Martha, Dublin, widow	
1782	,, Thomas, Essex-street, Dublin, grocer	
1786	,, Thomas, Bishop-street, Dublin, carpenter	
1798	**Hopwood**, Joseph, Dublin, laceman	
1590	,, Myldrede, *alias* **Clyfford**, Dub., widow	
1775	**Horan**, Anthony, Galway, merchant	
1781	,, Daniel	
1739	,, Jas., New Grange, co. Meath, gent.	
1791	,, James, Dublin, merchant	
1805	,, John, Galway town	
1803	,, Mary, Dublin, widow	
1809	,, Mary, widow	
1771	,, Robert	
1737	**Hore**, Bartholomew, Dubl., mariner	
1794	,, Cæsar, Drury-lane, London, chandler (Copy)	
1786	,, Catherine, Prussia-st., Dublin, widow	
1793	,, Christopher, Newmarket, co. Dublin, esq.	
1681	,, James, Dungarvan, co. Waterford, merchant	
1724	,, James, Carlow, co. Car., gent.	
1602	,, John Fitzmathew, Dungarvan	
1696	,, Mathew, Shandon, co. Watd., esq.	
1591	,, Michael, Dungarvan, merchant	
1630	,, Philip, the elder, Kilsalehan, co. Dublin, gent.	
1669	,, Richard, Dublin, vintner	
1804	,, Richard, Killarney, co. Kerry	
1774	,, Thos., Prussia-st., Dub., gent.	
1636	,, Walter, Waterford, merchant	
1746	,, Wm., Harperstown, co. Wexford, esq.	
	[See HOARE.]	
1733	**Horish**, Christr., Dub., merchant	
1731	,, John, the Grange, Ballyboghill, co. Dublin, gent.	
1796	,, John, Dublin	
1763	,, Patrick, Dub., tallow chandler	
1764	,, Patrick, Baldoyle, co. Dublin, gent.	
1731	,, Paul	
1800	,, Susanna, Donnybrook, co. Dublin, widow	
1731	**Hornby**, John, Balleece, co. Wick.	
1762	,, John, Dublin, alderman	
1768	,, Mary, Deer Park, Queen's co.	
1756	,, William, Clonenaugh, Queen's co., farmer	
1788	,, William, South Carolina	

1711	**Horncastle**, Christphr., Dub., gent.	
1691	**Hornedg**, John, Colemana, co. Carlow, yeoman	
	[See HORNIDGE.]	
1775	**Horner**, Esther, Dublin, spinster	
1699	,, John, mariner in the King's Service	
1778	,, Mary, Dunlavin, co. Wicklow, widow	
1777	,, Saml., Finglas, co. Dublin, esq.	
1802	**Hornibrook**, John, Bandon, co. Cork, esq.	
1807	**Hornidge**, Cuthbert, Russelstn., co. Wicklow, esq.	
1771	,, James, Dublin, gent.	
1740	,, Rich., Russelstown, co. Wick., farmer	
1788	,, Richard, Tullfaris, co. Wick., esq. [gent.	
1710	,, Wm., Cloncorban, King's co.,	
1783	,, Wm., Russelstown, co. Wick., gent.	
	[See HORNEDG.]	
1735	**Hornsby**, Ann, Dundalk, widow	
1724	,, Joseph, Cobham Hall, Kent, gent. (Copy)	
1726	,, Nathaniel, Dublin, gent.	
	[See ORMSBY.]	
1783	**Horsbrough**, Thos., Ballycarragh, co. Antrim, farmer	
1642	**Horseley**, William, Dublin, gent.	
1800	,, George, Epsom, Surrey, gent.	
1655	,, Richard, soldier [V. 216	
1673	**Horslyn**, Alice, Dublin, widow	
1627	**Horsman**, Ingram, mayor of Carrickfergus	
1808	**Hort**, sir John, Arlington-st., Middlesex, bart.	
1754	,, Josiah, archbp. of **Tuam**, q. v.	
1786	,, Josiah George, Hortland, co. Kildare	
1800	**Horton**, Abraham Veridet, Dublin	
1741	,, Elinor, Dublin, widow	
1757	,, John, Dublin, painter	
1789	,, William, Dublin, esq.	
1725	**Horwell**, John, Dublin, gent.	
1762	**Hosea**, Mary, Dublin	
1699	**Hosier**, Isabell, of Dublin, widow	
1676	,, Richard, Dublin, clk.	
1770	**Hoskin**, Charles, Dublin, gent.	
1632	**Hoskines**, or **Hockins**, Vincent, vicar of Berenanely, &c., co. Tipperary	
1660	**Hoskins**, Henry, Ballinbarne, co. Meath, gent.	
1686	,, William, Galway, burgess	
	[See HASKINS.]	
1773	**Hosty**, Bridget, formerly of Ayr-st., par. St. James, Westminster, now of Dublin	

1799 **Hosty**, James, Dublin
1796 **Hotham**, John, bp. of **Clogher**, q. v.
1778 **Hothan**, sir Beaumont, Sth. Dalton, Yorkshire, bart. (Copy)
1778 **Hough**, Elizabeth, *alias* **Stephens**, *alias* **Biker**, widow
        [See How.]
1800 **Houghton**, Henry, Balliane, co. Wexford, esq.
1747 ,, Anne, widow of Matthew H., Dublin, merchant
1798 ,, Benjamin, Cork-street, Dublin, furniture manufacturer
1746 ,, Edward, Ash-street, Dublin
1793 ,, Edward, Hendrick-st., Dublin
1685 ,, Ellenor, widow of George H., esq.
1751 ,, Henry, Ross, co. Wexford, gent.
1773 ,, Joseph, Dublin, merchant
1772 ,, Mary, Shangannah, co. Dublin, widow
1743 ,, Mathew, Dublin, merchant
1773 ,, Ralph, St. John's, co. Wexford, esq., late capt. 69th regt.
1738 ,, Thomas, par. St. Martin-in-the-fields, Middlesex (Copy)
1744 ,, Thomas, Kilmarnock, co. Wexford, gent.
        [See HAUGHTON.]
1758 **Houlaghan**, Thomas, *alias* **Nolan**, Gaula, co. Fermanagh, gt.
        [See HOOLAN, OULAHAN.]
1746 **Houlden**, John, Diaper Hall, co. Down, gent.
1731 **Houlding**, James, Carlow
1755 ,, Robert, Dublin, gent.
1783 ,, William, Bordeaux, merchant (Copy)
1655 **Hoult**, Charles, soldier   [**V.** 103
1687 ,, Richd., par. St. Martins-in-the-Fields, Middlesex (Ex.)
        [See HOLT.]
1773 **Houragan**, Christian, Limerick, widow
1749 ,, David, Limerick, merchant
1792 ,, David, Ballyadams, co. Limk., gent.
1786 **Hourigan**, Daniel, Tantore, co. Limerick, gent.
1797 **Houssaye**, Isaac, par. St. James, Essex, gent. (Copy)
1676 **Houston**, David, Lazyhill, near Dublin, mariner
1782 ,, Elizabeth, Dorset-street, Dub., widow
1730 ,, Francis, Ashgrove, co. Roscommon, esq.
1777 ,, Francis, Tullydowey, co. Tyrone, esq.

1800 **Houston**, Henry, lieut. in East India Co.'s Service (Copy)
1704 ,, James, Dublin, merchant
1737 ,, Jane, Castle Stewart, co. Tyrone, now in Dublin, spr.
1770 ,, Jane, Belfast, widow
1728 ,, John, Castle Stewart, co. Tyrone, esq.
1737 ,, John, Castle Stewart, co. Tyrone, esq.
1773 ,, Joseph, Atherdee, co. Louth
1790 ,, Joshua, Wellington, co. Dubl., esq.
1791 ,, Mary, Dublin, widow
1725 ,, captain Robert, Knock, King's co.
1801 ,, Shean, Dublin, watchmaker
1765 ,, William, Dublin, merchant
1783 ,, William, Hartsfort, Mourne, co. Down
1685 **Houstone**, William, Graigs, co. Antrim, esq.
1772 **Houstoun**, Francis, rector of Killowen
1672 **Hoveden**, Anthony, Waterford, gent.
1720 **Hovell**, Hugh, Cork, gent.
1698 ,, William, Cork, alderman
1780 **Hovenden**, Ann, widow
1713 ,, Anthony, Bridgetown, co. Wexford, esq.
1799 ,, John, Toiererane, Queen's co., esq. (Large)
1808 ,, John Taaffe
1806 ,, Nicholas, Gurteen, Queen's co.
1612 ,, Pierce, Tankardstown, esq.
1770 ,, Richard, Ballymoyler, Queen's co., gent.
1791 ,, Richard, Ballylihane, Queen's co.
1797 ,, Richard, Dublin, esq.
1641 ,, Robert, Ballynamiatagh, co. Armagh, esq.
1754 ,, Thomas, formerly of Gurteen, Queen's co., now of Dublin, esq.
1739 **How**, Hannah, Dublin, widow
1738 ,, John, Dublin, merchant
1683 ,, Thomas, Dublin, merchant
1747 ,, Thomas, Dublin, alderman
        [See HOWE.]
1780 **Howard**, Abraham, Rathowen, co. Westmeath, esq.
1738 ,, Adam, Cortcloon, co. Westmeath, gent.
1768 ,, Adam, Cortcloon, co. Westmeath, gent.
1776 ,, Alfred, Dublin, gent.
1768 ,, Alice, Dublin, widow
1793 ,, Catherine, Essex-street, Dubl., widow

1811 **Howard**, Catherine, Redcross, co. Wicklow
1809 ,, Cornelius, Waterford city, victualler
1786 ,, Georges Edmond, Dublin, esq. (Large)
1799 ,, Hugh, Dublin, esq.
1749 ,, Jane, Dublin
1691 ,, John, Dublin, wine cooper
1747 ,, John, Dublin, M.D.
1786 ,, John, Scark, co. Wexford, gent., farmer
1807 ,, John, Waterford
1790 ,, Manus, Dundalk, co. Louth
1746 ,, Margaret, Dublin, widow
1782 ,, Michael, Courtloon, co. Westmeath
1764 ,, Patience, Dublin, widow of Robert H., late lord bishop of Elphin
1810 ,, Peter
1710 ,, Ralph, Dublin, M.D.
1788 ,, Richd., Knockrobin, co. Wicklow, farmer
1740 ,, Robert, bp. of **Elphin**, q. v.
1800 ,, Robert, Rathowen, co. Westmeath, esq.
1810 ,, Sarah, wife to Robert Howard, esq.
1664 ,, Thomas, Dublin, merchant
1798 ,, Thomas, Baronstown
1802 ,, Thomas, His Majesty's Phœnix Park
1680 ,, William, Dublin, merchant
1727 ,, William, Dublin, esq. [cook
1742 ,, William, Gowran, co. Kilkenny,
1775 ,, William, Enniskillen, co. Fermanagh
1792 ,, William, Dublin, gent.
1746 **Howe**, Phebe, Kinsale, spr.
1795 ,, Thomas, Killinure, co. Cavan, gent.
[See **How.**]
1792 **Howell**, Edward, Clonmel, co. Tipperary, saddler
1787 ,, Richard, Rath, co. Louth, farmer
1701 ,, Thomas, Dublin, merchant
1709 ,, Thomas, Dublin, joiner
1712 **Howey**, John, Kilrea, co. Londonderry, merchant
1714 ,, John, the younger, Kilrea
1783 **Howis**, Edward, Waterford, mercht.
1768 **Howison**, Charles, Dublin, mercht.
1776 ,, Elizabeth, Dublin, spinster
1783 ,, Elizabeth, Dublin, spinster
1700 ,, James, Springtown, co. Longford, esq.
1811 ,, Jas., Russell-place, co. Dubl., esq.

1745 **Howard**, John, Dublin, gent.
1810 ,, Mary, Dublin city, widow
1721 **Howkesworth**, Robert, Bristol, merchant (Copy)
[See **Hawksworth**.]
1758 **Howley**, Ann, Dublin, widow
1811 **Howlin**, Abraham J., Castle Palliser, co. Wexford
1704 **Howse**, Edward, Bandon Bridge, co. Cork, gent.
1804 ,, rev. George, Inch House, co. Wexford, clk.
1805 ,, John, Wicklow, esq.
1716 ,, Richard, Dublin, gent.
1660 **Howsigo**, Thomas, Waterford, innholder   [**VIII.** 157
1636 **Howth**, Cicily, lady, *alias* **Cusack**, dowager baroness [**IV.** 338
1627 ,, Elizabeth, lady dowager
1607 ,, Nicholas St. Laurence, knt., lord baron of
1645 ,, Nicholas, lord baron of
1649 ,, Thomas, lord baron of
1727 ,, Thomas, lord baron
1802 ,, right hon. Thomas, earl of
1671 ,, William, lord baron of
1748 ,, William, lord baron of
1769 **Howtrey**, Ralph, the elder, Waterford
1803 **Hoyland**, Anthony, Paul-st., Cork, merchant
1788 ,, Archilaus, Stacumnie, co. Kildare, carpenter
1672 **Hoyle**, Ann, Dublin, spinster
1743 ,, Anstace, Dublin, widow
1730 ,, Richard, Dublin, M.D. [farmer
1776 ,, Robert, Burgage, co. Wicklow,
1800 ,, Robert, Burgage-moyle, co. Wicklow, gent.
1743 ,, William, Dublin
1804 **Hoyne**, Nicholas, Dublin city, baker
[See **Owen.**]
1808 **Hoysted**, John, Watterstown, co. Kildare
1744 ,, Thomas, Mountophily, co. Kildare, esq.
1755 **Huate**, Joseph
1758 **Huband**, Edmond, Dubl., merchant
1795 ,, Elizbth., Waterford city, widow
1805 ,, Sir John Hayes, Dublin city
1723 **Hubblethrone**, Chas., Dubl., gent.
1757 **Hubburt**, Peter, Clare, co.
1762 ,, William, Dublin, esq.
1783 **Hubert**, Francis, par. St. James, Westminster (Copy)
1638 **Huchins**, Thos., Michelstown, co. Cork, tanner   [**IV.** 311
1734 **Huddleston**, Andrew, Dublin, carpenter
1659 ,, Anthony, soldier   [**VII.** 184

1692 **Hudleston**, Themistocles, Dublin, gent.
1803 **Hudson**, Charles, Rear Admiral in Royal Navy (Copy)
1757 ,, rev. Edward
1785 ,, Esther, Fishamble-st., Dublin, widow
1810 ,, Hannah, Cooladine, co. Wex.
1678 ,, James, Clonemy, co. Tip., esq.
1742 ,, capt. James, Lisvisgil, co. Cork
1701 ,, John, Dublin, hosier
1775 ,, John, Dublin, carver and gilder
1764 ,, Margaret, widow
1657 }
1660 } ,, Nicholas, Dublin, merchant [**VII**. 64 ; **VIII**. 66
1775 ,, Richard, Liscongill, co. Cork, gent.
1803 ,, sir Walter, Enniskillen, knight
1687 ,, Wm., London, gent. (Copy) [See **HODSON**.]
1726 **Hudspeth**, Thomas, sergeant in col. Pocock's regiment
1752 **Hues**, Martin, Munganstown, co. Westmeath [See **HUGHES**.]
1614 **Huessey**, Walter, Mulhussey, co. Meath, esq.
1775 **Huetson**, John, Dublin, carver and gilder
1797 **Huey**, John, Bellisle, co. Antrim
1686 **Hufton**, William, Dublin, joiner
1595 **Huggens**, Mistress Joan (?), gentlewoman of lord D. Russell's family
1795 **Huggins**, John, Glenard, co. Tyrone
1797 ,, Letitia, Gortnaglush, co. Tyrone
1780 ,, Robert, Dublin, gent.
1802 ,, Wm., Coal Island, co. Tyrone [See **HIGGINS, HOGAN**.]
1807 **Hughes**, Abraham, Wexford town
1774 ,, Ann, relict of Richd. H., Cork, burgess
1796 ,, Ann, Dublin, widow
1776 ,, Arthur, Newry, co. Down, mer.
1780 ,, Benj., Ballystrane, co. Dublin
1774 ,, Blackford, Dublin, esq.
1772 ,, Bridget, *alias* **Healy**, Dublin, widow
1789 ,, Bridget, the Hot Wells, Gloucestershire, spinster
1757 ,, Bryan, Dublin, grocer
1719 ,, Edmond, Athlone, merchant
1804 ,, Edward, Ballymore Eustace, co. Dublin, innkeeper
1658 ,, Elizabeth, widow of Owen H., Londonderry, vintner [**VII**. 163
1798 ,, Elizabeth, Belline, widow
1811 ,, Elizabeth, Slade, co. Wexford, widow

1804 **Hughes**, Felix, Michael's-lane, woollen draper
1775 ,, Francis Annesley, Dublin, esq.
1802 ,, Francis, Dublin, gent.
1764 ,, James, Dublin, woollen draper
1808 ,, James, Dublin city, brewer
1668 ,, John, Dublin, gent.
1747 ,, John, Kinnegad, co.Westmeath
1799 ,, John, Plymouth, Devonshire, col. in the Kingston militia (Copy)
1799 ,, Joshua, Coolkennedy, co. Tip.
1771 ,, rev. Lambert, D.D., Dublin
1794 ,, Mathew, Springhill, co. Watd.
1656 ,, Owen, Londonderry, vintner [**VI**. 52
1800 ,, Paul, Dublin, esq.
1678 ,, Peter, Dublin, gent.
1721 ,, Peter, Dublin, esq.
1754 ,, rev. Pierce, co. Wexford, clk.
1736 ,, Ralph, Tullamore, King's co.
1762 ,, Richard, Dublin, vintner
1663 ,, Robert, par. Lanvaylogg, Anglesey, gent.
1671 ,, Robert, Dublin, gent.
1809 ,, Roger, Carlow town, merchant
1694 ,, Samuel, Cashel, esq.
1766 ,, Samuel, Seskin, co. Tip., esq.
1690 ,, Thomas, Dublin, gent.
1723 ,, Thomas, Liverpool, mariner
1760 ,, Thomas, Dublin, esq.
1800 ,, Thomas [farmer
1691 ,, William, Kilnecart, co. Carlow,
1764 ,, William, steward of the ship "Othello," London
1785 ,, rev. William
1797 ,, Wm., Ballymultany, co. Sligo [See **HUES, HUGHS, HUHES**.]
1794 **Hughs**, John, Boot-lane, Dublin, cooper
1795 ,, Timothy, Cork, ironmonger
1810 **Hugo**, Thos., Dromeen, co. Wick., esq.
1791 **Hugon**, Thos., the elder, Dromeen, co. Wicklow, esq.
1791 **Huhes**, Elizabeth, Dublin, widow [See **HUGHES**.]
1713 **Huish**, Thomas, Courtnebolly, co. Wicklow, gent.
1748 **Huleat**, Jas., Cork, esq. (Not proved)
1756 ,, Samuel, Limerick, gent.
1758 **Huleatt**, Daniel, Dublin, gent.
1768 ,, Hannah, *alias* **Higgins**, Dub., widow
1765 ,, John, Dublin, gent.
1780 **Hulings**, John, Mount H., Lib. of Waterford
1705 **Hull**, Elizabeth, Cork
1640 ,, George, par. Ballyculter, co. Down, esq.

1690 **Hull**, Jennett, Lisburn, wid. of Wm. Hull
1692 ,, John, Innisbegnaclery, harbour of Baltimore, co. Cork, now residing in London (Copy)
1709 ,, John, Curranbawn, co. Down, gent.
1685 ,, Randal, Cork, merchant
1693 ,, sir Richard, Lymeon, co. Cork, knt.
1772 ,, Rd., Leithyhill Place, Surrey, esq. (Copy)
1658 ,, Wm., Cork, merchant (Copy)
1690 ,, William, Lisburn, gent.
1808 **Hully**, Elizabeth
1628 **Hulsehert**, Wm., St. Patrick's-st., near Dublin, merchant
1792 **Hulton**, John, Dublin, tape weaver
1789 **Humberstone**, Isabella, Dubl., spr.
1772 **Humble**, rev. Charles, Newtown Stewart, co. Tyrone, clk.
1719 ,, rev. John, rector of Donagh, dio. Derry
1692 **Humbles**, Thomas, Creevlegh, co. Wicklow, gent.
1750 **Hume**, lady Alice, Dublin, widow
1701 ,, dame Ann, Dublin, widow
1722 ,, Elizabeth, St. Johnstown, co. Longford
1755 ,, George, Humeswood, co. Wicklow, esq.
1731 ,, St. Gustavus, Castle Hume, co. Fermanagh, bart.
1805 ,, rev. Gristus, Downslodge, co Wicklow
1705 ,, dame Mary, Castle Irvine, co. Fermanagh, widow
1695 ,, sir John, Castle Hume, co. Fermanagh, bart. (Ex.)
1778 ,, Robert, Lisannover, co. Cavan
1789 ,, Robert, Dublin, esq.
1798 ,, Thomas, Cariga, co. Leitrim
1752 ,, William, Butterswood, co. Wicklow, esq.
1802 **Humfrey**, Almer, Dublin, carpenter
1721 ,, Catherine, Portlemon, co. Westmeath, widow
1686 ,, Edward, Clognagh, co. Carlow, gent.
1763 ,, Edward, Dublin, esq.
1782 ,, Esther, Carlow, widow
1693 ,, John, Dublin, gent.
1745 ,, John, Donode, co. Kildare, esq.
1756 ,, John, Donard, co. Wicklow, clk.
1786 ,, Richard Fenton, Carlow town, esq.
1748 ,, Roleston, Dublin, esq.
1649 ,, William, Dublin, merchant
1758 ,, William, Carlow, esq.

1794 **Humfrey**, William, Donard, co. Wicklow, esq.
1722 **Humfreys**, Evan, Rosstrevor, co. Down, gent.
[See HUMPHREY, &c.]
1604 **Humfry**, Ellinor, *alias* **Luttrell**, Dub., widow, and Margaret Luttrell, her daughter
1744 ,, Mathew, Carlow, merchant
1766 **Humphres**, Isaac, Calcutta, East Indies
1709 **Humphrey**, Henry, Portlemon, co. Westmeath, esq.
1702 ,, James, esq.
1811 ,, John, Glanstall, co. Limerick
1781 ,, rev. Richard, Northumberland-street, clk.
1703 ,, Thomas, Dromehoney, co. Fermanagh, gent.
1775 ,, Thomas, Dublin, esq.
1734 **Humphreys**, Charles, clk., LL.D., par. St. Andrew, Holborn (Copy)
1796 **Humphries**, John, Dublin, gent.
1775 **Humphry**, John, Dublin, esq.
1807 **Humphrys**, Christopher, Dublin, oil and colour merchant
1808 ,, Despard, Farmhill, co. Londonderry
1807 ,, Frances Catherine, Dublin city, widow
1796 ,, George, Newtownbarry, co. Wexford
1760 ,, Isaac, Rushall, Queen's co., gent.
1779 ,, Jane, Dublin, widow
1792 ,, Sarah, Killmilogue, King's co.
1801 ,, Walter, Cornmarket, Dublin, merchant
1788 ,, William, Cornmarket, Dublin, merchant
1787 **Hunchin**, William, Thomas-street, Dublin, publican
1787 **Hungerford**, Beecher, Cork
1802 ,, John, Burrin, co. Cork, esq.
1756 ,, Richard, The Island, co. Cork, gent.
1784 ,, Richard, The Island, co. Cork, esq.
1695 ,, Walter, Buscott, Berkshire, D.D. (Copy)
1680 **Hunloke**, Denham, Chelsea, merchant tailor (Copy)
1680 ,, Francis, London, painter and stainer (Copy)
1755 **Hunt**, Anne, Chamber-street, Dub., widow
1685 ,, Benjamin, Dublin, gent.
1802 ,, Charles, lieut. in His Majesty's Navy

1763 **Hunt,** Christopher, Jerpoint, co. Kilkenny
1808 ,, Daniel, New Garden, co. Galway, esq.
1728 ,, Edward, Dublin, esq.
1747 ,, Edwd., Dunmore, co. Kilkenny
1770 ,, Edward, Dublin, alderman
1733 ,, Frances, Dublin, widow
1594 ,, George, Athdare, co. Limerick, gent.
1796 ,, Henry, Dublin city, esq.
1684 ,, Henry, Dublin, gent.
1697 ,, Henry, Drumott, co. Tipperary, gent.
1752 ,, Henry, Friarstown, Lib. of Limerick, gent.
1629 ,, John, Dublin, merchant
1671 ,, John, Dublin, gent.
1693 ,, John, Dublin, merchant
1737 ,, John, Glangoole, co. Tipperary, esq.
1720 ,, John, Garteen, King's co., gent.
1768 ,, John, Limerick, gent.
1780 ,, rev. John, Clopook, Queen's co., clk.   [esq.
1797 ,, John, Newcastle, co. Meath,
1800 ,, John, Dublin, esq.
1761 ,, Margaret, Dubl., gentlewoman
1709 ,, Peter, Abbeyrathasel, co. Tipp.
1705 ,, Raphael, Dollarstown, co. Kildare, gent.
1788 ,, Samuel, capt. in the service of the E. India Co. (Copy)
1691 ,, Thomas, Dublin, esq.
1709 ,, Thomas, Dublin, bookseller
1746 ,, Thomas, Dublin, upholder
1762 ,, Thomas, Dublin, saddler
1775 ,, Thomas, Dublin, gent.
1787 ,, Vere, Curragh, co. Limerick
1792 ,, Vere, Cappagh, co. Tipperary, esq
1733 ,, William, Carlow, gent.
1758 ,, William, par. St. Paul, Covent Garden, Middlesex, tailor
1765 ,, William, Ennis, co. Clare
1798 **Hunter,** rev. Alex., Limerick, clk.
1752 ,, Francis, Newtown, co. Down
1715 ,, James, Ballyrogan, co. Louth, gent.
1740 ,, James, Dublin, wine cooper
1771 ,, James, Lisburn, co. Antrim, linen merchant
1789 ,, James, Sycamore-alley, Dublin, printer
1805 ,, James, Ballinderry, co. Antrim
1763 ,, Jane, Dublin, widow
1794 ,, John, Lisburn, co. Antrim, but now at Bath, esq. (Copy)
1739 ,, Margaret, Ringsend, Dublin, widow

1742 **Hunter,** Mary, Cappoquin, co. Waterford, widow
1811 ,, Nicholas, Drumcovitt, co. Londerry, esq.
1779 ,, Olivia, Dublin, widow
1790 ,, Richard, Troy, Lib. of Derry, esq.
1784 ,, Robert, Downpatrick
1788 ,, Samuel, Limerick, merchant
1804 ,, Samuel, Limerick city, mercht.
1676 ,, Thomas, Ringsend (Ex.)
1771 ,, Thos., formerly of Birr, King's co., now of Anson, N. Carolina (Copy)
1801 ,, Thomas, Limerick city, gent.
1671 ,, William, Sligo, merchant
1774 ,, William, Moyallan, co. Down, linendraper
1791 ,, Wm., Donaghadee, co. Down [See HUNT.]
1734 **Hunyngton,** Mary, Drogheda, widow
1662 **Hurd,** Fras., Lisdown, co. Kilkenny, widow of col. Hurd
1662 ,, Humphrey, Lisdowney, co. Kilkenny, esq. [See HEARD.]
1809 **Hurley,** John, Ballyclamasy, co. Cork, farmer
1628 **Hurlie,** Andrew, Kilmallock, burgess
1623 **Hurlston,** Jasper, Drogheda, alderman
1685 **Hurly,** sir Maurice, Doone, co. Galway, bart.
1637 ,, Morris, Knocklong, co. Limk., esq.
1628 ,, Randal, Kilmallock, burgess
1805 ,, Timothy, Cork city, merchant
1780 ,, Thomas, Cork city, gent.
1634 ,, William, Edendough Carrick, co. Antrim, gent.
[See HARLEY, HURLEY, HURLIE.]
1687 **Hurst,** Benjamin, Coombe, Dublin, merchant
1741 ,, James, Galway, esq.
1657 ,, John, Dublin, butcher [**VI.** 99
1772 ,, William, Dublin, merchant
1791 ,, Wm., Donnybrook, co. Dublin, gent.
1682 ,, Thomas, Dublin, gent.
1802 **Husband,** Elizabeth, Dublin, spinr.
1799 ,, Mary, *alias* **Goodwin**
1768 **Huse,** John, Summerhill, co. Meath, millwright
1682 ,, Thomas, Dublin, merchant
1720 **Huson,** rev. Benjamin, Dromiskin, co. Louth, clerk
1737 ,, rev. Nathaniel, Enniscorthy, co. Wexford, clerk

1809 **Huson**, Richard, Dublin city, esq. (Large)
1764 ,, Sarah, Templeshannon, co. Wexford, spinster
1795 ,, William, New-row, Dublin, manufacturer
[See HEWETSON.]
1669 **Hussey**, Abigail, Enniscorthy, wid.
1804 ,, Ann, Rathkenny, co. Meath, widow
1666 ,, Bartholomew, Enniscorthy, co. Wexford
1788 ,, Catherine, Thomas-st., Dubl., widow
1786 ,, Dudley, Dublin, esq.
1634 ,, Edmond, Phepotstown, co. Meath
1742 ,, Edward, Westown, co. Dublin, esq.
1761 ,, Edward, Dublin, esq.
1757 ,, Elizabeth, *alias* **Burgh**, widow of Ignatius H., Dublin, esq.
1811 ,, Elizabeth S., Foley-place, Middlesex, widow (Copy)
1788 ,, Francis, Waterford city
1629 ,, George, Rosskeen, Queen's co., gent.
1743 ,, Ignatius, Dublin, esq.
1766 ,, Ignatius, Dublin, esq.
1636 ,, James, Smarmore, co. Louth, priest
1737 ,, James, Galtrim, co. Meath, esq.
1760 ,, James, Dublin, grocer
1760 ,, James, the elder, Courtown, co. Kildare, esq.
1768 ,, James, Dublin, esq.
1787 ,, James, Dublin, esq.
1776 ,, Jane, Dublin, widow
1614 ,, Joan, Moyglare, co. Meath, widow (Copy)
1752 ,, John, Dublin, esq.
1769 ,, John, Spike Island, co. Cork, gent.
1773 ,, John, Longford-street, Dublin, gent.
1799 ,, John, Dingle, co. Kerry, esq.
1803 ,, John, Rathkenny, co. Meath, esq.
1671 ,, Luke, Westown, co. Dublin, gent.
1792 ,, Margaret, widow
1626 ,, Martin, Culmullen, co. Meath, gent.
1722 ,, Martin, Dublin, gent.
1766 ,, Mary, Mary's-lane, Dublin, spinster
1783 ,, Mary, Dublin, widow
1670 ,, Meyler, Culmullen, co. Meath, gent.

1757 **Hussey**, Myler, eldest son to John H., late of Courtown, co. Kildare, esq.
1798 ,, Nicholas, Dublin, esq.
1664 ,, Patrick, baron of Galtrim, co. Meath
1774 ,, Patrick, Ardmore, co. Kerry, gent.
1666 ,, Peter, Culmullen, co. Meath, esq.
1749 ,, Peter, Belgart, co. Kildare, gent.
1783 ,, Philip, Dublin, painter
1807 ,, Richard, Queen Ann-st., east (Copy)
1678 ,, Robert, Galtrim, co. Meath, esq.
1747 ,, Robert
1776 ,, Stafford, esq., called lord baron of Galtrim
1787 ,, Susanna, Dublin, widow
1629 ,, Thos., Mulhussey, co. Meath, esq.
1700 ,, Thomas, Culmullen, co. Meath, gent.
1752 ,, Thos. FitzEdward, Ardemore, co. Kerry, gent.
1765 ,, Thomas Dillon, Cheveaux, France
1711 **Hutcheson**, Alexander, Drumalig, co. Down
1776 ,, Alexander, Dublin, gent.
1794 ,, Barbara, Dublin, widow
1746 ,, Francis, professor in Glasgow University
1756 ,, Hans, Newry, co. Down
1766 ,, James, Athy, co. Kildare, gent.
1799 ,, James, Coleraine
1801 ,, Mary, Dublin
[See HUTCHINSON.]
1795 **Hutchins**, Daniel, Dublin, gent.
1760 ,, Noble, Dublin, butcher
1758 **Hutchinson**, Ann, widow of Dr. Francis H., bishop of Down and Connor
1799 ,, Ann Sophia, city of Bath, spinster
1676 ,, Daniel, Dublin, alderman (Ex.)
1792 ,, Deborah, Dublin, spinster
1699 ,, Edward, Knocklofty, co. Tipp., esq.
1752 ,, Edward
1671 ,, Elizabeth, Dublin, widow of Thomas H., co. Kildare, gent.
1774 ,, Elizabeth, Dublin, widow
1808 ,, dame Elizabeth, Dublin city, widow
1759 ,, Emanuel, Codrum, co. Cork, esq.

1740 **Hutchinson**, Francis, bishop of **Down**, q. v.
1768 ,, Francis, archdeacon of Down
1808 ,, sir Francis, bart.
1797 ,, Hannah, Masseytown, co. Cork, widow
1769 ,, Hartley, Dublin, esq.
1728 ,, Hugh, Bantry, co. Cork, esq.
1769 ,, Hugh, Dublin, gent.
1805 ,, Hugh, Clonea, co. Cork, esq.
1739 ,, James, Knockballymeagher, co. Tipperary
1780 ,, James, Knockballymeagher, co. Tipperary
1711 ,, John, Dublin, smith
1712 ,, John, Dublin, smith
1729 ,, John, Ballyrea, co. Armagh, gent.
1753 ,, John, Timoney, co. Tipperary
1779 ,, John, Edenderry, King's co., gent.
1794 ,, right. hon. John Hely, princ. Secretary of State
1749 ,, Jonathan, Cork, merchant
1754 ,, Joshua, Dublin, merchant
1778 ,, Magdalen, Dublin, widow
1754 ,, Margaret, New-row, Dublin, widow
1807 ,, Martha. Bandon, co. Cork
1797 ,, Mary, Dublin, spinster [esq.
1797 ,, Massy, Mount Massy, co. Cork,
1757 ,, Richard, Knocklofty, co. Tipperary, esq.
1803 ,, Richd., Stranocum, co.Antrim, esq.
1688 ,, Robert, Edenderry, King's co., gent.
1758 ,, Robert, Dublin, merchant
1773 ,, Robert, Hollyhill, co. Cork, esq.
1749 ,, Samuel, Listuder, co. Down, esq.
1752 ,, Samuel, Dublin, esq.
1773 ,, Samuel, Hollyhill, co. Cork, esq.
1780 ,, Samuel, bishop of **Killala**, q.v.
1709 ,, Sarah, London, widow (Copy)
1761 ,, Sarah, widow of Thomas H., Wicksworth, co. Derry, esq. (Copy)
1748 ,, Thomas, Wickworth, Derbyshire, gent.
[See HUTCHESON, HUTCHISON.]
1780 **Hutchison**, Elizabeth, Summerhill, co. Meath, widow
1742 ,, Frances, Dublin, widow.
1784 ,, Francis, Dublin, M.D.
1731 ,, John, Patrick-street, Dublin, victualler
1778 ,, John, Dublin, merchant
1718 ,, William, Dublin, merchant

1785 **Hutson**, John, York Buildings, co. Middlesex, tailor (Copy)
1799 **Hutton**, Francis, Red Lyons-square, Middlesex (Copy)
1808 ,, Henry, Dublin city, alderman
1708 ,, John, Dublin, innholder
1759 ,, John, Dublin, merchant
1765 ,, John, Dublin, butcher
1778 ,, Joshua
1797 ,, Maxwell, Dublin
1780 ,, Robert, Dublin, tanner and currier
1781 ,, Sarah, Dublin, widow
1781 ,, Thomas, Channel-row, Dublin, victualler
[See HOUGHTON.]
1721 **Hyde**, Arthur, Castle H., co. Cork, gent. (Ex.)
1772 ,, Arthur, Castle H., co. Cork, esq.
1733 ,, Edward, Dublin, innkeeper
1810 ,, James, Cullenswood, co. Dub., gent.
1635 ,, John, clk., chaplain of St. Nicholas-Within, and petty canon of St. Patrick's, Dubl.
1718 ,, John, Mokoile, co. Wexford, gent.
1728 ,, John, Dublin, bookseller
1768 ,, John, Cregcastle, co. Cork, esq.
1790 ,, John, Upper Clapton, co. Middlesex, merchant (Copy)
1778 ,, Mary, Belfast, widow
1798 ,, Robert, Drumart, co. Armagh
1744 ,, Samuel, Belfast, co. Antrim, merchant
1799 ,, Samuel, Belfast, co. Antrim, gent.
1750 ,, Sarah, Donnybrook, co. Dubl. widow
1699 ,, Thomas, Rosse, merchant
1723 ,, Thomas, Newtown, King's co., gent.
1791 ,, William, Templenoe, co. Cork, gent.
1658 **Hydes**, Robert, trooper [**VI.** 281
1736 **Hylan**, Catherine, widow
1747 ,, Mary, *alias* **Nowlan**, wife of Patrick H., Dublin, mercer
1811 **Hyland**, Edythia, Queen-st., Dubl., widow
1790 ,, Isabella, Kilbride, co. Kildare, widow
1808 ,, James, Tipper, co. Kildare
1787 ,, John, Church-street, Dublin, dealer
1795 ,, John, Kirkell, co. Kilkenny
1803 ,, John, formerly of Dublin, but late of High-st., London
1765 ,, William, Kilbride, co. Kildare

1763 **Hylard**, James, Currachtown, co. Meath, farmer
1678 **Hyly**, Robert, Drogheda, gent.
1754 **Hyndford**, Elizabeth, countess dow. (Copy)
1777 **Hyndman**, Archibald, Belfast, co. Antrim, merchant
1797 **Hynes**, Clare, Moyvore, co. Westmeath, widow
1801 ,, Honora, Castlebar, co. Mayo, widow
1782 ,, Jas., Aughnebaughy, co. Westmeath, gent.
1810 ,, Luke, Cork city, esq.
1711 ,, Michael, lieut. in col. Brook's regt. of foot [gent.
1771 ,, Patrick, Rathrowan, co. Mayo,
1797 ,, Philip, Duck-lane, Dubl., tripe manufacturer
[See HAINES, HAYNES.]

—I—

1743 **Ikerrin**, Margaret, lady viscountess
1673 ,, Pierce, lord visct.
1695 **Ikerryn**, James, lord visct.
1684 **Iley**, Ann, St. Nicholas' par., Dub., widow
1668 ,, Thomas, Dublin, merchant
1699 **Illingworth**, capt. Robert, Dublin (Ex.)
1616 **Ince**, Thomas, London, haberdasher
1793 **Inchiquin**, Mary, dow. countess
1674 ,, Morogh, earl of
1744 ,, William, earl of
1777 ,, William, earl of
[See INSIQUINE.]
1642 **Inge**, Thomas, Dublin, tanner
1788 **Ingham**, John, Dublin, attorney-at-law
1744 ,, Robert, Dubl., cabinet maker
1755 ,, Thomas, Dublin
1693 **Ingilfield**, John, Dublin, tallow chandler
1771 **Inglass**, rev. Richard, rector of Kilcar, dio. Raphoe
[See ENGLISH.]
1700 **Ingoldsby**, sir Henry, Dubl., bart.
1720 ,, Henry, Dublin, gent. (Ex.)
1757 ,, Henry, Carrtown, co. Kildare, esq. (Large will)
1711 ,, Richard, lieut.-genl.
1630 **Ingould**, John, London, grocer
1780 **Ingram**, Anne, *alias* **Hara**, widow
1768 ,, Claud, Ballyshannon, co. Don.
1765 ,, Elizab., Edenderry, co. Down, widow
1789 ,, George, Stonepark, co. Roscommon, gent.

1734 **Ingram**, Hannah, Limerick, widow
1774 ,, James, Strabane, co. Tyrone, clk.
1790 ,, James, Cork, merchant
1793 ,, rev. Jocelyn, co. Tyrone, clk.
1770 ,, Joseph, Castleblayney
1792 ,, Mary, Limerick city
1631 ,, Thomas, Moyne, co. Louth, gent.
1665 ,, William, Belloverum, Ireland (Copy)
1762 ,, William, Edenderry, co. Down, merchant
1637 **Inkersall**, John, Castlemoate, Queen's co., esq.
1729 **Inman**, Jos., Thomas-court, Dubl., clothier
1740 ,, Joseph, Thomas-court, Dublin, clothier
1800 ,, Joseph, Ballybrittan, King's co., gent.
1759 ,, Miriam, Ballybrittan, King's co., spinster
1784 ,, Thomas, Glandoran, co. Wexford, gent.
1804 **Innes**, Charles, Dromantine, co. Down, esq.
1762 ,, James, lieut.-col., Dubl., esq.
1768 ,, Jane, Jackson Hall, co. Louth, widow
1758 ,, major Geo., Dublin, esq.
1783 ,, Perrot, Magilligan, co. Londonderry, esq.
1764 ,, Wm., Dromantine, co. Down, esq.
1736 **Innis**, Joseph, Belfast, merchant
1685 **Insiquine**, Elizabeth, dow. countess of (Ex.)
[See INCHIQUIN.]
1706 **Irby**, Anthony, Clonmore, co. Limerick, D.D.
1736 **Iredell**, Jane, widow
1808 **Ireland**, Anna Maria, Cork city, spinster
1739 ,, Courcy, Ireland's Grove, Queen's co., esq.
1810 ,, Jane, Cork city, widow
1742 ,, Thos., Palmerstown, co. Dubl., farmer
1794 ,, Thomas
1771 ,, Wm., Ballygawley, co. Tyrone. gent.
1698 **Ireton**, Charles, Dublin, LL.D.
1637 **Irish**, John, Dublin, clk.
1637 ,, Mary, widow of John J., Rathcormick, clk.
1780 **Irvine**, rev. Andrew, curate
1727 ,, Archibald, Drumchay, co. Fermanagh, gent.
1778 ,, Charles, Gortin, co. Tyrone

1755 **Irvine**, Christopher, Castle Irvine, co. Fermanagh, esq.
1796 ,, Christopher, Johnstown, co. Fermanagh, esq.
1767 ,, Ellinor, Dublin, widow
1758 ,, Gerard, Greenhill, co. Fermanagh, esq.
1794 ,, Gerard, The Hill, co. Fermanagh
1795 ,, Gerard, Greenhill, co. Fermanagh
1808 ,, Jas. J. V., Cross, co. Galway, esq.
1716 ,, John, Cooles, co. Fermanagh, esq.
1738 ,, John, capt -lieut. in brig.-genl. Kane's regiment at Minorca (Copy)
1787 ,, John, Rockfield, co. Fermanagh, esq.
1810 ,, Martha, formerly of Johnstown late of Dublin
1810 ,, Olivia, South Frederick-street, Dublin, spinster
1766 ,, William, Dublin, merchant
1712 **Irving**, Alexander, Dub., plumber [See IRVINE.]
1742 **Irwin**, Alexander, Oran, co. Roscommon, esq.
1762 ,, Alexander, Kilmore, co. Sligo
1797 ,, Arthur, Greenmount, co. Monaghan
1803 ,, Arthur, Willowbrook, co. Sligo, esq.
1776 ,, Catherine, widow of lieut.-genl. Alexander I.
1714 ,, Christopher, Lybeg, co. Roscommon, gent.
1772 ,, Christopher, Dublin, gent.
1811 ,, David, Ferny, co. Cork, esq.
1779 ,, Deborah, Athlone, co. Roscommon, widow
1734 ,, Edward, Oran, co. Roscommon, gent.
1741 ,, dame Elizabeth, *alias* **Bunbury**
1771 ,, Elizabeth, Dublin, widow
1791 ,, George, Derrygore, co. Fermanagh, gent.
1810 ,, Greham, Jervis-street, Dublin, coachmaker
1718 ,, Henry, Ballomaghan, co. Sligo, gent.
1753 ,, Hy., Spring-garden, co. Sligo, esq.
1807 ,, Henry, Rockborough, co. Roscommon
1715 ,, James, London, gent.
1780 ,, Jane, widow of Edward Griffith Irwin, esq.
1794 ,, Jane, widow
1749 ,, John, Lisballely, co. Sligo, gt.

1752 **Irwin**, John, Sligo, esq.
1765 ,, John, Dublin, shoemaker
1770 ,, John, the elder, Carnabrock, co. Monaghan, gent.
1777 ,, John, Park-st., Dub., silkweaver
1778 ,, John, Woodhill, co. Donegal, esq.
1801 ,, John
1701 ,, Lancellot, Cooles, co. Fermanagh [widow
1779 ,, Mary, Woodpark, co. Galway,
1802 ,, Mary Anna, Dublin, widow
1767 ,, Richard, Mount I., co. Sligo, gent.
1810 ,, Robert, Emlaroryboy, co. Roscommon, gent.
1807 ,, Samuel, Kinsale, co Cork, esq.
1809 ,, Thomas, Dublin city, merchant
1755 ,, Wm., Mount I., co. Armagh, gent.
1796 ,, William, Eccles-street, Dublin, esq.
[See ERWIN.]
1747 **Irwine**, Charles, par. St. James, Westminster (Copy)
1714 ,, Christopher, Castle I., co. Fermanagh, esq.
1710 ,, Thomas, Dublin, apothecary
1718 ,, Wm., Dennilohan, co. Armagh, gent.
1783 ,, William, Kinsale, co. Cork, esq.
[See IRWIN.]
1742 **Isaac**, John, Hollywood, co. Down, esq.
1789 ,, Letitia
1789 ,, Montgomery
1694 ,, Peter, Dublin, gent.
1680 ,, Robert, Mynehead, Somersetshire, mariner
1744 ,, Simon, Ballywalter, co. Down, esq.
1802 ,, Thomas Bunbury, Hollywood, co. Down, esq.
1709 **Isaack**, Chas., Drogheda, mercht.
1749 **Isack**, Thomas, Dublin, goldsmith
1792 **Isdall**, Oliver, Conlastown, co. Westmeath, esq.
[See ESDALL.]
1809 **Isemonger**, Elizabeth, Clonmel
1629 **Iveagh**, sir Arthur Magenis, lord viscount
1744 ,, Margaret, lady viscountess
1685 **Iveer**, Peter, Dublin, hatter
1692 **Ivers**, Henry, Mount Ivers, co. Clare, esq.
[See EVERS.]
1634 **Ives**, Andrew, Galway, merchant (Copy)
[See EVES.]

1771	**Jackson,**	Robert, Aldermanbury, London, merchant (Copy)
1809	,,	Robert, Roscrea, co. Tipperary
1705	,,	Samuel, Dublin, esq.
1810	,,	Strettel, Peterboro', Liberties of Cork
1656	,,	Thomas, Dublin, gent. [**VI.** 59
1672	,,	Thomas, Ballyduff, co. Watd.
1740	,,	Thomas, Dublin, yeoman
1751	,,	Thos., Creaghstown, co. Meath, esq.
1759	,,	Thomas, glass seller
1786	,,	Thomas, Edenderry, King's co.
1796	,,	Thomas, Lisnalow, co. Meath, gent.
1798	,,	Thomas, Edenderry, King's co.
1805	,,	Thomas, Tullydoey, co. Tyrone
1809	,,	Thomas, Ballyboy, co. Monaghan, apothecary
1688	,,	William, Coleraine, esq. (Ex.)
1697	,,	William, Dublin, merchant
1707	,,	William, Bray, co. Wick., gent.
1712	,,	Wm., Coleraine, co. Londonderry, esq.
1734	,,	Wm., Clonmel, co. Tip., clk.
1735	,,	rev. William, Dublin, clk.
1746	,,	William, Coleraine, esq.
1774	,,	William, Mill-st., Dubl., tanner
1785	,,	William, Youghal, alderman
1794	,,	Wm., Mountrath, Queen's co., victualler
1795	,,	William, Limerick city, gent.
1771	,,	Zachary, Moneclenoe, Liberties of Limerick, gent.
1780	**Jacob,**	Andrew, Dublin, gent.
1808	,,	Anna Maria, Dublin city, spr.
1802	,,	Anne, Dublin, widow (Large)
1786	,,	ven. Arthur, D.D., archdeacon of Armagh
1807	,,	Bostocke Rich., Wexford town
1688	,,	Edward, Vickerstown, Queen's county, gent.
1791	,,	Hannah, Enniscorthy, widow
1761	,,	Isaac, Waterford
1753	,,	Jane, Dublin, widow
1776	,,	John, Ormond-market, Dublin, dealer
1781	,,	Joseph, Waterford city, mercht.
1775	,,	Leond., Ballymahon, co. Longford, esq.
1771	,,	Margaret, Dublin, spinster
1753	,,	Mathew, St. Johnstown, co. Tipperary, gent.
1764	,,	Mathew, Mobarnan, co. Tip., esq.
1780	,,	Mathew, Mobarnan, co. Tip., esq.
1685 .	,,	Michael, native of Spaun (Ispahan ?), in Persia, now of Dublin, merchant

1759	**Jacob,**	Walter, Faranefreny, co. Carlow
1609	,,	Walter, Dorleyston, gent.
1788	**Jaffray,**	Abbigail, Dublin, widow
1773	,,	Robert, Dublin, merchant
1606	**Jaie,**	Ralph, Dublin, glover
1734	**Jalaquiere,**	John, Southampton, a batchelor (Copy)
1789	**James,**	Fras., Dublin, wine cooper
1796	,,	Jane, Dublin, widow
1749	,,	John, Rathbeg, King's co., gent.
1802	,,	John, Brusna, King's co.
1803	,,	John, Ballychristal, co. Wexford, esq.
1806	,,	John, Brookvale, co. Monaghan, esq.
1702	,,	Joseph, Dublin, merchant
1787	,,	Joseph, Prospect, King's co., gent.
1720	,,	Nathaniel, Dublin, merchant
1808	,,	Ralph, Uselands, co. Wicklow
1795	,,	Richard, Carnew, co. Wicklow, chandler
1660	,,	William, Athlone, soldier [**VIII.** 139
1783	,,	William, Dublin, pewterer
1807	,,	William, Dublin, alderman
1774	**Jameson,**	Hugh, Cork, esq.
1749	,,	Humphrey, Belfast, merchant
1728	,,	John, Sligo
1807	,,	John, Drummond, co. Wicklow
1782	,,	Mary, Waterford, widow
1786	,,	Robert, Newry, co. Down, merchant [See JAMES.]
1593 } 1660 }	**Janes,**	Jas., Dubl., alderman [**VIII.** 58
1627	,,	Mary, *alias* **Carus,** widow of James J., Dublin, alderman
1797	**Janns,**	Arthur, Limerick city, gent.
1688	,,	Richard, Black Castle, co. Meath, esq.
1664	**Jans,**	Edward, Dublin, alderman
1763	,,	John, Dublin, surgeon
1684	,,	Michael, Maynham, co. Kildare, gent.
1713	**Jaque,**	Gideon
1779	**Jaques,**	Rachell, Limerick, widow
1787	**Jaquess,**	Joseph, Limk., clothier
1671	**Jarman,**	Jane, widow of Edward J., the elder, Conigh, co. Cork
1724	,,	Philip, Coolenarig, co. Wicklow, farmer
1739	**Jarvis,**	Charles, Cleveland court, St. James, Westminster (Copy)
1750	,,	Penelope, Somerset House, Middlesex, widow (Copy) [See JERVIS.]

1774 **Jaumard**, Grace
1752 ,, rev. John, M.A., chaplain to bishop of Waterford
1634 **Jaye**, James, Corbally, Queen's co., gent.
1667 **Jean**, David, St. Andrew's parish, Dublin, gent.
1811 **Jebb**, sir Henry, Dublin city, knt.
1767 ,, Richard, Drogheda, alderman
1771 **Jeeb**, Edward, Boyle, apothecary
1804 **Jeff**, James, Slane, co. Meath, gent.
1720 **Jeffcott**, Mathew, Toureigh, co. Kerry, gent.
1783 **Jefferies**, Frances, Limerick city, widow
1791 **Jeffers**, Mary, Drogheda
1740 **Jefferyes**, James, Blarney, co. Cork, esq.
1780 **Jefferys**, James St. John, Blarney Castle, co. Cork, esq.
1716 **Jeffors**, George, St. Audeon's par., Dublin
[See GIFFORD.]
1722 **Jeffrys**, sir James, Blarney, co. Cork, knt. banneret
[See JEFFERIES, JEFFERYS.]
1636 **Jeggin**, John, Malahide, co. Dubl., yeoman
1798 **Jellet**, Morgan, Moira, co. Down, esq.
1792 **Jellett**, John, Stafford-st., Dublin, jeweller
1811 **Jellico**, Samuel, Caher, co. Tipp., merchant
1730 **Jellous**, Robert, the elder, Moortown, co. Meath, gent.
1757 ,, Robert, clerk
1628 **Jellus**, Henry, Dublin, merchant
1811 **Jelous**, Laurence
1608 **Jenings**, John, Dublin, tanner
1792 **Jenkin**, Caleb, Dublin, alderman
1746 ,, Elizabeth, widow
1786 ,, rev. Thomas, rector of Maryborough, Queen's co.
1684 **Jenkins**, Benjamin, Cork, gent.
1729 ,, rev. David, Strabane, co. Tyrone, clerk
1734 ,, Fairfax, cornet in col. Oughton's regt.
1776 ,, rev. Heywood, Kilrubet, co. Leitrim   [ford
1783 ,, John, Gortnagloon, co. Longford
1804 ,, Ralph, Killeagar, co. Wicklow
1772 ,, William, co. Donegal, esq.
1657 **Jenkinson**, Morgan, Cornmarket, baker   [**VI**. 116
1790 ,, Richard, Monasterevan, co. Kildare, coachmaker

1772 **Jenkesson**, James, Dublin, grocer
[See JENKINS.]
1685 **Jennet**, John, Oldbridge, co. Meath, gent.
1586 ,, Nicholas, Notteslan
1736 **Jennett**, Catherine, Ardcath, co. Meath, wid.
1775 ,, Christopher, Flemingtown, co. Meath, gent.
1763 ,, James, D.D., formerly parish priest of Dunboyne
1787 ,, James, Finglas
1754 ,, John, Swords, co. Dublin
1775 ,, John, Dublin, brewer
1792 ,, Thomas, Blackrock, co., Dublin
1769 **Jenney**, Edmond, Liverpool, Lancashire
1779 ,, Elizabeth, Dublin, widow
1742 ,, ven. Henry, archdeacon of Dromore
1759 ,, Henry, D.D., rector of Armagh
1792 ,, Henry, Dublin, esq.
1785 ,, Marmaduke, Drumask, co. Armagh, esq.
1769 ,, Mary, widow of Henry J., D.D.
[See JERMY.]
1804 **Jennings**, David, par. of St. Clement Dames, Middlesex
1789 ,, Dominick, Liskeavy, co. Galway
1790 ,, Dorothy, par. St. Ann, Westminster, widow (Copy)
1761 ,, George, Castletown, co. Mayo, esq.
1769 ,, James, Milltown, co. Dublin, gent.
1748 ,, John, Ballyshannon, co. Donegal
1784 ,, Monica, Limerick, spinster
1723 ,, Penelope, Kilkenny, widow
1679 ,, Robert, Kilkea, co. Kildare, gent.
1711 ,, Samuel, Kilkenny, gent.
1794 ,, Teresa, Dublin, widow
1805 ,, Theobald, Lisline, co. Galway
1804 ,, Tobias, Drogheda town, gent.
1810 **Jenny**, Elizabeth, Dublin city, spin.
[See JENNEY.]
1786 **Jephson**, Anne E., *alias* **Butler**, wife to Wm. Jephson, esq.
1755 ,, Anthony, Mallow, co. Cork, esq. (Revoked by decree)
1756 ,, Anthony, Mallow, co. Cork, esq.
1789 ,, Deborah, Mallow, co. Cork, widow
1781 ,, Denham, the elder, Mallow, co. Cork, esq.
1693 ,, Jno., Moyalla, co. Cork, esq.

1766 **Jephson**, John, Carrick-on-Suir, co. Tipperary, esq.
1655 ,, dame Mary, widow   [**V**. 144
1693 ,, Michael, dean of St. Patrick's, Dublin
1771 ,, Osborn, Carrick-on-Suir, co. Tipperary, esq.
1803 ,, Robert, Blackrock, co. Dublin, esq.
1660 ,, William, Mallow, co. Cork, esq.   [**VIII**. 25
1720 ,, very rev. William, dean of Lismore
1779 ,, William,Innishannon,co.Cork, esq.
1783 **Jermyn**, Stephen, Ringfinin, co. Dublin
1749 **Jervis**, Bazill, Dublin
1796 ,, Esther,Great Britain-st.,Dubl., spinster
1761 ,, John, Birr, King's co., esq.
1709 ,, dame Mary, Dublin, widow
1750 ,, Mary, Dublin, widow
1719 ,, Nicholas, Dublin, gent.
1725 ,, Samuel, Droome, co. Cork, esq.
1760 ,, Thomas, Dublin, coachmaker
    [See GERVAIS, JARVIS, JERVOIS.]
1737 **Jervois**, Joseph, Currivarahane, co. Cork, esq.
1798 ,, Joseph
1750 ,, Sampson, Dublin, esq.   [esq.
1806 ,, Sampson, Bandon, co. Cork,
1787 ,, Samuel, Cork city, esq.
1795 ,, Samuel, Brade, co. Cork
    [See JERVIS.]
1735 **Jesse**, David, Farranrory, co. Tipp., gent.
1770 ,, Hen. Jessefield, co. Tipperary, esq.
1758 ,, Mary, Ballingarry, co. Tipp., spinster
1736 **Jesson**, Elizabeth, Dublin, widow
1811 ,, James, Dame-street, Dublin, merchant
1669 ,, Thomas, Dublin, innholder
1808 **Jessop**, Eary, Prussia-street, co. Dublin, gent.
1749 ,, Francis, Ballintemple, co. Longford, gent.
1775 ,, Francis, Church-street, Dublin, grocer
1785 ,, George, Kincor, King's co., gent.
1745 ,, John, Dublin, gent.
1778 ,, John, Coolfin,King's co.,farmer
1760 ,, Mary,Shrule,widow of Nicholas J., Drimnacor, co. Longford
1763 ,, Richard, Drimnacor, co. Longford, gent.

1730 **Jessop**, Robert, Drury,co. Longford, esq.
1746 ,, Robert, Ballintemple, co. Longford
1742 ,, Samuel, Carlow, clothier
1785 ,, Samuel, Coombe, Dublin, woolcomber
1778 ,, Thomas, Mount Jessop, co. Longford, esq. (1776)
1786 ,, Thomas, Carlow town, mercht.
1775 ,, William, Clontarf, co. Dublin, esq.
1792 ,, William, Ballywilliam, King's co., gent.
1784 **Jeurs**, Robert, Mount Jeurs, co. Clare, esq.
1730 **Jeuvers**, Mary, Dublin, spr.
1568 **Jevanes**, David
1699 **Jeve**, Thomas, par. Fryan, Middlesex, esq.   [**VIII**. 336
1700 ,, Thomas, Fryan Barnet, Middlesex, esq. (Copy)
1769 **Jevers**, Augustine, Great Connell, co. Kildare
1780 ,, Elizabeth, Kilgrogy, co. Tipperary, spr.
1758 ,, Henry, Mount J., co. Clare, esq.
1729 ,, John, Dublin, esq.
1771 ,, William, Fortwilliam,co. Clare, esq.
    [See EVERS.]
1701 **Jevon**, Rachell
1655 **Jewell**, serjeant Andrew, Athlone   [**V**. 132
1638 **Joanes**, Elizabeth, Dublin, widow
1789 **Jocelyn**, Elizabeth, Aungier-street, Dublin, widow
1772 ,, Frances, dow. viscountess
1762 ,, George, lieut.-genl., Carlisle, now of Leixlip, co. Dublin
1801 ,, George, esq.
1765 ,, John, St. Peter's par., Dub.
1757 ,, Robert, ld. visct., Lord High Chancellor of Ireland (Copy)
1718 **Jodrell**, Burdett, Dublin, esq.
1675 **John**, Isaac, Dublin, goldsmith
1756 ,, Michael, Dublin, gent.
1732 ,, Samuel, Dublin, gent.
1623 **Johnes**, sir Baptist, Vintnerstown, co. Derry, knt.
1638 ,, Patrick, Malahide, co. Dublin
1642 **Johns**, Abraham, Bideford, Devonshire, merchant
1611 ,, John, Athlone, merchant
1760 **Johnson**, Abigail, Dublin, widow
1786 ,, Andw., Blackpool, nth. suburbs of Cork
1732 ,, Ann, Dublin, spinster
1749 ,, Ann, Dublin, widow

1694	**Johnson,** Anthony, Edenderry, tanner		1780	**Johnson,**	John, Drumsarah, co. Londonderry
1630	,,	Arthur, Dublin, stationer	1784	,,	John, Headford, co. Galway, esq.
1771	,,	Benjamin, Dublin, gent.			
1794	,,	Benjamin, Mecklenburgh-st., Dublin	1785	,,	John, clerk of St. Thomas's par., Dublin
1743	,,	Catherine, spinster	1787	,,	John, late a capt. in 100th regt. of foot
1599	,,	Christopher, Dublin, gent.			
1628	,,	Christopher, Ballycastle, co. Wexford, husbandman	1804	,,	John, Belfast Gate-street, Lisburn, Methodist preacher
1682	,,	Christopher, Dublin, esq.	1600	,,	Justinian, Dublin, gent.
1798	,,	Clement, lieut. in the navy	1804	,,	Letitia, Tours, in Touraine, France, widow
1753	,,	David, Ballyboughlane, or Gt. B.-street, gardener			
1730	,,	Edward, par. St. James, Westminster	1784	,,	Mary, Clough, co. Down
			1811	,,	Mary, *alias* **Burnside**
1769	,,	Edward, Magherelegan, co. Down	1618	,,	Mathew, Dublin
			1804	,,	Michael, Kilcarty Lodge, co. Meath, esq.
1794	,,	Edward, Ballymullen, Queen's co., gent.	1758	,,	Noblet, Cork, merchant
1804	,,	Edwd., Kilmagig, co. Wicklow, farmer	1746	,,	Paul, Dublin, merchant
			1616	,,	Richd., Ballickwilliams, King's co., gent.
1702	,,	Elizabeth, widow of Robert J., 2nd jus. of Com. Pleas in Ireland	1686	,,	Robert, Rosmead, co. Westmeath, gent.
1735	,,	Elizabeth, Dublin, widow	1687	,,	Robert, 2nd jus. Com. Pleas
1770	,,	Elizabeth, *alias* **Quail**, Magherelegan, co. Down, gentlewoman	1731	,,	Robert, Dublin, esq.
			1734	,,	Robert, Mitchelstown, co. Cork
			1767	,,	Robert, bp. of **Cloyne**, q. v.
1774	,,	Elizabeth, Drumcondra-lane, Dublin	1787	,,	Robert, Liverpool, Lancashire, esq.
1763	,,	Ellinor, Dublin, widow	1808	,,	Robert
1728	,,	Esther, Dublin, spinster	1773	,,	Samuel, Dublin, gent.
1786	,,	Frances, Cork city, widow	1753	,,	Sarah, Dublin, spinster
1690	,,	Francis, Pettivorth, Sussex, clk.	1779	,,	Sidney, Drumcondra-lane, co. Dublin, widow
1684	,,	George, Roscrea, co. Tipperary, gent.	1665	,,	Susanna, Killurny, co. Waterford, widow
1713	,,	George, Dublin, surgeon	1658	,,	Thomas, Tullyhanon, co. Fermanagh, gent. [**VIII.** 170
1672	,,	Henry, Aghlecky, co. Limerick, gent. (Copy)	1700	,,	Thomas, Liberty of Dublin, gardener
1794	,,	Henry, Meath-street, Dublin, worsted manufacturer	1787	,,	Thomas, Dublin, watchmaker
1702	,,	James, Abbeyboyle, co. Roscommon	1804	,,	Thomas, Arran-quay, Dublin, M.D.
1783	,,	James	1627	,,	William, Huningstown, co. Fermanagh
1790	,,	James, Lisnaniska, King's co., gent.	1714	,,	Wm., Ballywillwill, co. Down, gent.
1597	,,	Jeffrey, Dublin, chief ingrosser of the Exchequer	1749	,,	William, Finglas Bridge, co. Dublin, esq.
1625	,,	John, Dublin, gent.	1770	,,	William, Lizard, co. Limerick, gent.
1694	,,	John, Chapel Izod, weaver			
1702	,,	John, Newforge, co. Antrim, gent.	1783	,,	William, King-street, Oxm., Longford
1723	,,	John, Dublin, gardener	1786	,,	William, Arklow, co. Wicklow
1736	,,	John, Coombe, weaver	1804	,,	William Henry, co. Wicklow, gent.
1739	,,	John, Dublin, innkeeper			
1751	,,	John, lieut. in col. Batterau's regiment	1747	**Johnston,**	Abigail, *alias* **Deane**
1769	,,	John, Killeigh, King's co.	1768	,,	Abraham, Meath-street, Dubl., brass founder
1774	,,	John, Killaneil, co. Monaghan, gent.			

1777	**Jolly**, David, Killinollog, King's co., cordwainer	
1747	,,	Elizabeth, Dublin, widow
1757	,,	Elizabeth, Dublin, widow
1747	,,	Ellinor, Fethard, co. Tip., wid.
1781	,,	Jacob, Dublin, grocer
1782	,,	Jacob, Dublin, grocer
1709	,,	Robt., Knockelly, co. Tipperary, gent.
1789	,,	Samuel, Readsland, co. Meath, gent.
1797	,,	William, New-row-on-Poddel, co. Dublin, gent.
1810	**Jones**, Abraham, Coollattin, co. Wicklow, esq.	
1707	,,	Adam, Dublin, butcher
1804	,,	Alice, Dublin city, widow
1679	,,	Ambrose, bp. of **Kildare**, q. v.
1697	,,	Ambrose, Cashel, esq.
1766	,,	Ambrose, Oldcastle, co. Meath, innkeeper
1767	,,	Ambrose, Lyss, co. Meath, gent.
1786	,,	Ambrose, Jonesborough, co. Meath, gent.
1757	,,	Ann, Bolton-street, Dublin, widow
1765	,,	Ann, Dublin, widow of rev. Wm. Jones (Large will)
1777	,,	Ann, Newtown-Perry, Limerick city, widow
1716	,,	Arthur, Dublin, esq.
1733	,,	Benjamin, Dublin, merchant
1782	,,	Bolton, Drumod, co. Leitrim
1733	,,	Bridget, Youghal, co. Cork, widow
1753	,,	Brook, Dublin
1671	,,	Bryan, Dublin, esq.
1741	,,	Catherine, Querrin, co. Clare, widow
1760	,,	Catherine, Dublin
1762	,,	Catherine, Waterford, widow
1765	,,	Catherine, Dublin, widow
1767	,,	rev. Charles, Dublin, D.D. (1768)
1788	,,	Charles, Kilmacurragh, co. Wicklow, farmer
1788	,,	Chas., Killincarrig, co. Wicklow, gent.
1780	,,	Christopher, Sligo town
1787	,,	Christopher, Dublin, merchant
1658	,,	Cicily, *alias* **Hill**, Dub., widow [**VII**. 31
1779	,,	Conway, Lisburn, co. Antrim, M.D.
1799	,,	Daniel, Banada, co. Sligo, esq.
1743	,,	David, Arundel Court, Dublin, yeoman
1786	,,	David, Beaupark, co. Meath
1735	,,	Edward, Wexford, esq. (Copy)
1736	**Jones**, Edward, Ballyherberry, co. Tipperary, gent.
1742	,,	Edward, Youghal, co. Cork, esq.
1748	,,	Edward, Tullow, co. Carlow, tanner
1759	,,	Edwd., Ballymoney, co. Antrim, esq.
1775	,,	Edward, Mount Pleasant, co. Cork, esq. [esq.
1787	,,	Edward, Grove, co. Meath,
1805	,,	Edward, Stowe, Shropshire (Copy)
1677	,,	Elizabeth, Dublin, widow of Dr. John J.
1753	,,	Elizabeth, Dublin, widow
1757	,,	Elizabeth, *alias* **Painter**, Dub.
1764	,,	Elizabeth, Geashill, King's co., widow
1784	,,	Elizab., Great Ship-st., Dublin, spinster
1785	,,	Elizabeth, Bensford, co. Meath
1787	,,	Elizabeth, Clontarf, co. Dubl., spinster
1797	,,	Elizabeth, Killincarrig, co. Wicklow, widow (Large)
1642	,,	Ellinor, widow of alderman George J., Dublin
1747	,,	Ellinor, Dublin, widow
1673	,,	Frances, Dublin, spinster
1785	,,	Frances, widow
1809	,,	Frances, Dublin city, spinster
1676	,,	Francis, Mullinabro, co. Kilkenny, gent.
1638	,,	George, Dublin, alderman
1650	,,	George, son to alderman Wm. George J., Dublin (Copy)
1746	,,	George, Rathconrath, co. Westmeath, esq.
1786	,,	George, Lincolns Inn, Middlesex (Copy)
1646	,,	Henry, Newtown, co. Dublin, esq. (Copy)
1681	,,	Henry, bp. of **Meath**, q. v.
1717	,,	Henry, Oldtown, co. Kildare
1760	,,	Henry, Knock, co. Westmeath
1761	,,	Humphrey, Mullinabro, co. Kilkenny, esq.
1771	,,	Humphrey, Belturbet, co. Cavan, esq.
1788	,,	Isabella, Tintern Abbey, co. Wexford, widow
1778	,,	Jas., Mullachrohan, co. Meath, gent.
1784	,,	James, Galway, burgess
1805	,,	rev. James, Cornmarket, Dubl.
1693	,,	Jane, Kilkenny, widow
1708	,,	Jane, Dublin, spinster
1719	,,	Jane, Monasterevan, co. Kildare, widow

1746	**Jones,**	Jane, Dublin, spinster
1650	,,	Jeane, Dublin, widow
1642	,,	Jeremy, Dublin, cook
1695	,,	Joane, *alias* **Howard**, widow of Walter J., Dublin, esq.
1714	,,	rev. John, Dublin, D.D.
1715	,,	John, D.D., precentor of Kildare and vicar of Donamaine
1733	,,	John, Belturbet, co. Cavan, esq.
1746	,,.	John, Dublin, gent.
1752	,,	John, Youghal, co. Cork, esq.
1755	,,	John, Dublin, merchant
1757	,,	John, Belturbet, co. Cavan, esq.
1760	,,	John, Howth, co. Dublin, mariner
1768	,,	John, Wicklow, brewer
1770	,,	John, Limerick, alderman
1784	,,	John, Coolbeg, co. Wicklow, gent.
1788	,,	John, Mullinabro, co. Kilkenny, esq.
1798	,,	John, Abbeybreny, co. Wexford, farmer
1803	,,	John, Newtown
1808	,,	John, Jones Lodge, co. Wicklow, esq.
1809	,,	John, William-street, Dublin, attorney
1646	,,	Lewis, bp. of **Killaloe**, q. v.
1661	,,	captain Lewis, Dublin
1669	,,	Lewis, Kinsale, merchant
1741	,,	Lewis, Dublin, esq.
1744	,,	Lewis, Dublin, gent.
1767	,,	Lewis, Dublin, esq.
1796	,,	Lewis, Tubberpatrick, co. Sligo, esq.
1781	,,	Loftus, Ardnaglass, co. Sligo, esq.
1800	,,	Louisa
1796	,,	Margaret, Belturbet, co. Cavan
1803	,,	Margaret Maria, Charlton, Kent (Copy)
1811	,,	Margaret, Coollattin, co. Wicklow, spinster
1782	,,	Maria, Youghal, co. Cork
1795	,,	Martha, Waterford city, widow
1742	,,	Mary, Kilmainham, co. Dublin, widow
1743	,,	dame Mary, widow
1765	,,	Mary, Dublin, widow
1780	,,	Mary, Lisburn, co. Antrim, spinster
1655	,,	Mathew, serjt. in the garrison of Rathcleen [**V.** 161
1660	,,	Michael, esq., Lieut.-Genl. of the Horse [**VIII.** 186
1749	,,	Michael, Island Bridge, co. Dublin, esq.

1786	**Jones,**	Morgan, Lesfeeny, co. Tipperary
1695	,,	Nicholas, Dublin, esq.
1737	,,	Nicholas, Donabate, co. Dubl., popish priest
1807	,,	Nicholas, George's-hill, Dubl., cooper
1664	,,	lieut.-col. Oliver
1695	,,	Oliver, esq., 2nd justice K. B. (copy; original lost in the troubles)
1789	,,	Patrick, Thomas-court, Dubl.
1811	,,	Rachel, Dublin city, widow
1725	,,	Rath, Dublin, esq.
1807	,,	Rebecca, Kingscourt, co. Cavan
1643	,,	Richard, dean of Elphin
1695	,,	Richard, Dublin, gent.
1727	,,	Richard, Tomnifinogue, co. Wicklow
1760	,,	Richd., Booterstown, co. Dub., esq.
1770	,,	Richd., George's-lane, Dublin, coachmaker
1781	,,	Richard, Bye Bridge, co. Kildare, gent.
1789	,,	Richard, Carrick-on-Shannon
1799	,,	Richard, Mallow, co. Cork, gent.
1739	,,	Robert, Mountkennedy, co. Wicklow, esq.
1746	,,	rev. Robert, Ballibea, co. Mon., clerk
1756	,,	Robert, Dublin, brewer
1764	,,	Robert, Ballynulta, co. Wicklow, farmer
1791	,,	Robert, Coombe, Dublin, shoemaker
1637	,,	sir Roger, Sligo, knt.
1676	,,	Roger, Lazyhill, co. city of Dublin, esq.
1677	,,	Roger, Dublin, esq.
1748	,,	Roger, Dollanstown, co. Meath, esq. (Large will)
1759	,,	Samuel, Dolphin's Barn, co. Dublin, dairyman
1780	,,	Samuel, Hoey's court, Dublin, gent.
1801	,,	Samuel, G. P. O., Dublin
1783	,,	Sarah, Dublin, spinster
1710	,,	Theodore, Waterford, alderman
1684	,,	sir Theodore, Osberstown, co. Kildare, knt.
1660	,,	Thomas, soldier [**VIII.** 145
1676	,,	Thomas, Dublin, alderman
1700	,,	Thomas, London, citizen and fringe weaver (Copy)
1703	,,	Thomas, Dublin, esq.
1715	,,	Thomas, Tuleneskea, co. Mon., gent.

1716 **Jones,** Thomas, Ardnaree, co. Mayo or Sligo, esq.
1720 ,, Thomas, Lisronagh, co. Tipp., gent.
1721 ,, Thomas, capt. in lord Hinchinbrook's regt.
1724 ,, Thomas, Osberstown, co. Kildare, esq.
1732 ,, Thomas, Cookstown, co. Meath, gent. [esq.
1750 ,, Thomas, Ardnarea, co. Mayo,
1762 ,, Thomas, Cork, gent.
1765 ,, Thomas, Limerick
1765 ,, Thomas, Vesingstown, co. Meath
1770 ,, Thomas, Croatenstown, co. Kildare, gent.
1777 ,, Thomas, Waterford, ironmonger
1787 ,, Thomas, Dublin, wool merchant
1796 ,, Thomas, Clarendon-st., Dublin, gent.
1797 ,, Thomas, Ballyphillip, barony of Newcastle
1798 ,, Thomas, Blackrock, co. Dublin
1804 ,, Thomas, capt. of the Sligo militia
1807 ,, Thomas, Cork city, shopkeeper
1809 ,, Thomas, Slaney Park, co. Wicklow, esq.
1693 ,, Valentine, Killmacmurearty, co. Armagh, gent.
1761 ,, Valentine, Lisburn, co. Antrim, esq.
1703 ,, William, Crossdrum, co. Meath, yeoman
1724 ,, William, Waterford, alderman
1729 ,, William, Dublin, merchant
1738 ,, Wm., the younger, Drogheda
1741 ,, William, Tipperary, gent. man
1743 ,, William, Waterford, alderman
1747 ,, rev. William, vicar of Athlone
1749 ,, William, Newtown, co. Meath, gent. (Large will)
1751 ,, William, Dublin, lately a major of general Clayton's regt.
1753 ,, rev. William, Dublin, clerk
1760 ,, William, Dublin, merchant
1771 ,, William, Killough, co. Wicklow
1796 ,, William, Dublin, gent.
1797 ,, William, Dublin city, gent.
1798 ,, William, Ballytrasna, co. Wicklow, gent.
1802 ,, Wm., cornet in His Majesty's 3rd regt. of Royal Irish Dragoons

1805 **Jones,** William, Joneslake, co. Westmeath, esq.
1807 ,, William
1809 ,, William, Summerhill, Dublin, gent.
1762 **Jonine,** Edmund, Ballinrobe, co. Mayo
1785 ,, Edmund, Lisnamoyle, co. Mayo, gent.
1758 ,, Richard, Hollymount, co. Mayo, merchant
1772 ,, Ulick, Coolmackay, farmer
1774 ,, Ulick, Rathgranaher, co. Mayo, gent.
      [See Jonyne.]
1789 **Jonston,** rev. Francis, Tullycross, co. Down
      [See Johnston.]
1797 **Jonyne,** John, Raheens, co. Mayo, gent.
      [See Jonine.]
1803 **Jordan,** Ann
1755 ,, John, Mountmellick, Queen's co., clothier
1800 ,, Nicholas, Bellewstown, co. Meath, farmer
1636 ,, Richard, Dublin, merchant [**IV.** 195
1804 ,, Thomas, Chapelizod, co. Dubl., cotton printer
1802 ,, William, Chapter-court, Dubl., scrivener
1757 **Jorden,** col. John, par. St. Mary-le-bone, Middlesex (Copy)
1761 ,, Susana, Dublin, spinster
1601 **Jordon,** Alson, Dublin, widow
1738 ,, Elizabeth, Dublin, widow
1700 ,, Frans., Gravesend, Kent, gent. (Copy)
1715 ,, Francis, Thomas-st., Dublin, innholder
1717 ,, Gabriel, Dublin, distiller
1616 ,, James, Dublin, stabler
1754 ,, Richard, Kilfenora, co. Clare, farmer
1713 ,, Robert, Crumlin, co. Dublin, gent.
1674 ,, Rose, *alias* **Warren,** Crumlin, widow
1704 ,, Symon, Pill-lane, Dublin, innkeeper
      [See Jordan, Jorden, Jourdan.]
1723 **Jouamier,** Stephen, Dublin
1758 **Jourdan,** John, Dunshaughlin, co. Meath, clerk
1789 **Joy,** Henry, Belfast, co. Antrim, printer
1785 ,, Robert, Belfast, printer
1797 **Joyce,** Ann, Loughrea, co. Galway widow

1793 **Joyce**, Catherine, Galway town, spinster
1781 ,, Gregory, Galway town
1787 ,, James, Corcullentrough, co. Armagh, gent.
1796 ,, James, Loughrea, co. Galway, merchant
1811 ,, James, Portadown
1791 ,, Margaret, Galway, spinster
1802 ,, Martin, Derrigensla
1800 ,, Mathew, Galway town, M.D.
1786 ,, Pierce, Galway town, merchant
1796 ,, Thomas, Mervue, Galway town, merchant [way, gent.
1748 ,, Walter, Lisdonough, co. Gal-
1754 ,, Walter, Galway, merchant
1794 **Joye**, James, Granny Ferry, co. Kilkenny, farmer
1805 **Joyes**, rev. John, Roman Catholic Warden of Galway [See JOYCE.]
1760 **Joynte**, Dudley, Ballinacourtney, co. Limerick, gent.
1787 ,, William, Limerick, tallow chandler
1654 **Jubbs**, Martin, officer in the army at Maryborough
1767 **Judd**, Ambrose, Roundwood, co. Wicklow, gent.
1764 ,, Hannah, Dublin, spinster
1757 ,, Peter, Dublin, tallow chandler
1763 ,, Samuel, Dubl., tallow chandler
1729 **Judge**, Arthur, Mosstown,co.Westmeath, esq.
1771 ,, Bridget, Mullingar, widow of Hugh J., M.D.
1774 ,, Jane, St. Omer, France, wid. (By decree)
1731 ,, John, Gageborough, King's co., esq.
1790 ,, John, Windgates, co. Kildare
1811 ,, John
1783 ,, Judith, Carpenterstown, co. Westmeath, spinster
1774 ,, Juliana, Dublin, widow
1764 ,, Mary, Ballincard, King's co.
1796 ,, Patrick, Dublin, baker
1747 ,, Peter, Ballysheil, King's co., esq.
1765 **Judkin**, Dorothea, Cashel city, wid.
1731 ,, Elizabeth, Greenhills, co. Tip., widow
1796 ,, John Lapp, Cashel city, esq.
1737 **Julabert**, Israel, Dublin, baker
1735 **Julian**, Allan, Dublin, gent.
1749 ,, Christopher, Listowel, co. Kerry
1798 ,, rev. Christopher, Tullamore, co. Kerry, clerk

1757 **Julian**, George, Dublin, gent.
1726 ,, James, Listowel, co. Kerry, esq.
1788 **Julien**, John, Dublin, merchant
1718 ,, Peter, native of St. John de Brueil in France, now in Dublin
1788 **Jurgens**, Charles, Dublin, grocer
1767 **Justice**, John, Ballynrudellig, co. Kerry, gent.
1778 **Justus**, William, Dublin, gent.
1672 **Juxon**, Thomas, 2nd son of John J., late of East Sheen, Surrey, esq.

——K——

1734 **Kane**, Anne, Clourish, co. Mon., widow
1776 ,, Bernard, Dublin, gent.
1774 ,, Darby, Newry, co. Down, innholder
1750 ,, Elizabeth, Dublin, widow
1739 ,, Jas., Dowlaght, co. Tipperary, farmer
1808 ,, John, Dublin city, gent.
1727 ,, Joseph, Dublin, alderman
1809 ,, Mark, Great Ship-street, Dubl.
1778 ,, Martha, Dublin, spinster
1805 ,, Martin, Dublin city
1737 ,, Mary, Dublin, widow
1699 ,, Mathew, Coombe, clothier
1757 ,, Nathaniel, Dublin, alderman
1778 ,, Redmond, Dublin, esq.
1747 ,, Thomas, Dublin, vintner [See CANE, KEAN.]
1660 **Karnesborough**, Wm., Ballycalane, co. Kildare (Inventory only)
1710 **Karns**, Chas, mariner on board Her Majesty's ship " Somerset "
1767 **Karr**, lieut. John, Belturbet, co. Cavan
1778 ,, John, Dublin, jeweller
1764 **Katherins**, Joseph, New-st., Dubl., gent.
1787 **Kathrans**, John, Butterfield-lane, co. Dublin, gent.
1780 **Kathrens**, Joseph, Dublin, gent.
1789 ,, Murray, Cottage, co. Dublin
1773 ,, Paul, Dublin, staymaker
1774 ,, Samuel, Upper Church-street, Dublin, gent.
1795 ,, Samuel, Dublin, gent.
1553 **Katly**, Donogh, par. Ardkill
1663 **Kavanagh**,Bryan,Borys, co.Cather. (Borris, co. Car.) esq. (Co.)
1730 ,, Bryan, Newtown, co. Cavan, gent.
1741 ,, Bryan, Borris, co. Carlow, esq.

1768 **Kavanagh,** Bryan, Dublin, mercht.
1783 ,, Bryan, Castledermot, co. Kilkenny, gent.
1768 ,, Charles, Rocksavage, co. Carlow
1778 ,, Charles, Kilkenny, gent.
1794 ,, Charles, Dublin, woollen draper
1632 ,, Daniel, *alias* **Spannagh,** Cloenmullen, co. Carlow, esq.
1772 ,, Daniel, Coolenemara, co. Carlow, gent.
1767 ,, Darby, Dublin, clothier
1741 ,, Denis, Castledermot, co. Kild., innkeeper
1781 ,, Denis, Poddle, co. Dubl., merchant
1804 ,, Edmond, Teira, co. Carlow
1786 ,, Elizabeth, Dublin, widow
1749 ,, Ellinor, Marley, co. Carlow, widow
1791 ,, Felix, Ballybeg, co. Carlow, gent.
1773 ,, George, Kilcrotty, co. Wexford, esq.
1791 ,, Gereld, Marley, co. Carlow, esq.
1679 ,, Griffin, Boderene, co. Wexford, gent.
1799 ,, James, Ballascarton, co. Wexford, farmer
1756 ,, John, Killabegs, co. Wexford
1671 ,, Mary, Leperstown, co. Wicklow, widow
1718 ,, Michael, New Ross, co. Wex., merchant
1779 ,, Michael, King-st., Dubl., gent.
1796 ,, Mich., Castledermot, co. Kild.
1636 ,, Morgan M'Brien, Borris, co. Carlow, esq.
1773 ,, Morgan, New Ross, co. Wex., merchant
1622 ,, or **Cavanagh,** Morrogh Backagh or Morgan, Cartigleod, co. Catherlogh, gent.
1747 ,, Murtogh, Knockduff, co. Carlow
1794 ,, Patrick, Dublin, gent.
1797 ,, Patrick, Dublin, livery stable keeper
1799 ,, Patrick
1809 ,, Patk, Bull-lane, Dublin, gent.
1809 ,, Richard, Fleet-street, Dublin, merchant
1738 ,, Thos., Rockburough, co. Wexford, esq.
1790 ,, Thos., Borris, co. Carlow, esq.
1767 ,, Timothy, Rathburrin, co. Kilkenny, farmer
1772 ,, Timothy, Dublin, gent.
1772 ,, William, Dunbrow, co. Dublin
[See CAVANAGH.]
1770 **Kaven,** Valentine, Dublin

1762 **Kavenagh,** Edmond, Ballygarret, co. Limerick, gent.
1713 **Kay,** John, Dublin, shoemaker
1765 **Keaghran,** Patrick, Dublin, gent.
1800 **Keaghry,** Cicily, Galway town, spr.
1797 ,, Michael, Galway town
1700 **Keally,** Thomas, Upper Grange, co. Kilkenny, gent.
1678 **Kealy,** John, Gowran, co. Kilkenny, esq.
1746 ,, John, Carrigleagh, co. Waterford, esq.
1781 ,, John
1699 ,, Margaret, *alias* **Raget,** widow of Thomas Kealy, Wells
1782 ,, Murtogh, green of Naas, co. Kildare, brogue maker
1697 ,, Rich., Wells, co. Carlow, gent.
1689 ,, Thomas, Kilkenny, gent.
1810 ,, Thomas, Kilenabehy, Queen's co., farmer
[See KELLY.]
1776 **Kean,** Andrew, Newry, co. Down, merchant
1726 ,, Bartholomew
1795 ,, Bartholomew, Bruff, co. Limk.
1794 ,, Charles, Bruff, co. Limerick, farmer
1757 ,, John, Limerick, esq. (Copy)
1801 ,, Joseph, Dublin, esq.
1787 ,, Michael, Ranelagh-rd., Dublin, shoemaker
1769 ,, Richard, Cappoquin, co.Waterford, esq.
1777 ,, Sarah, Britain-street, Dublin, widow
1768 ,, Thomas, Limerick, gent.
1771 ,, William, Clontarf, co. Dublin
1775 ,, William, Cavan, co. Down, merchant
1780 ,, William, Clontarf, co. Dublin, esq.
1792 ,, William, Newry, co. Down
1803 ,, William, formerly of Dublin, late of Bath
[See CANE, KEANE, KEENE, KENE, &c.]
1729 **Keanan,** James
1811 **Keane,** Elizabeth, Nenagh, co. Tipperary, spinster
1756 ,, John, Cappoquin, co. Waterford, esq.
1597 ,, Patrick, Mellifont (No date)
1802 **Kearin,** Alice, Donony, co. Wexford, widow
1763 ,, John
1802 ,, Mogue, Donony, co. Wexford, farmer
1783 **Kearnan,** Peter, Gorey, co. Wexford
[See KIERNAN.]

1780 **Keating**, Thomas, Dublin, gent.
1780 ,, Valentine, city of Poictiers, France, esq.
1811 ,, Walter, Kells, co. Meath
1719 ,, William, Dublin, gent.
1741 ,, William, Dublin, esq.
1754 ,, William, Crana, co. Tipperary, gent.
1761 ,, Wm., Montpelier, co. Limerick, gent.
1771 ,, William, Colotore, co. Westmeath, farmer
1780 ,, William, gent.
1795 ,, William, Dublin, gent.
1809 ,, William, Waterford city, merchant
1740 **Keatinge**, Rachell
1750 **Keats**, Ellinor, Dublin, widow
1639 **Keatting**, Edmond, Possextown, co. Meath, gent.
1734 ,, Jeffery, Clonmel, co. Tipperary, gent.
1679 ,, John, Gurteen, co. Waterford, gent.
1680 ,, Oliver, Ballynunnery, co. Carlow, esq.
1715 ,, William, Dublin, merchant
1735 ,, Wm., Clocully, co. Tipperary, gent.
[See KEATING.]
1811 **Keays**, Christopher, S. Liberties of Cork, merchant
[See KEYS.]
1792 **Keef**, Andrew, Bramblestown, co. Kilkenny
1771 **Keefe**, Arthur, merchant .
1746 ,, Daniel, Laravalty, co. Cork, gent.
1803 ,, Daniel, Cork, butter merchant
1811 ,, Daniel, Tankardstown, Queen's co.
1743 ,, Edmond, Carramaney, co. Carlow, gent.
1805 ,, John, Newtown Stewart, co. Tyrone
1803 ,, Michael, Dublin city
1795 ,, Richd., Rathangan, co. Kildare, flour miller
1789 ,, Thomas, Kinsale, clk.
1809 ,, Thos., Rathangan, co. Kildare, miller
1795 **Keegan**, Bernard, Boyne-street, Dublin
1626 ,, John, Dublin, linendraper
1791 ,, John, Dublin, apothecary
1800 ,, Phanton, Clonagh, Queen's co., farmer
1629 ,, Robt., Castlejordan, co. Meath
1809 ,, Robt., Castlejordan, co. Meath, farmer

1783 **Keegan**, William
1786 ,, William, Oldcastle, co. Meath
[See KEGGAN.]
1807 **Keeghan**, Michael, Pintown, co. Tipperary, farmer
1804 **Keeling**, Robert, co. Dublin
[See KELLY.]
1797 **Keely**, Edward, Dublin, paper stainer
1794 ,, Mary, Portarlington, Queen's co.
[See KELLY.]
1752 **Keen**, Arthur, Dublin, gent.
1792 ,, Jane, Carolina, widow
1700 ,, Talbot, Dublin, gent.
1766 **Keenan**, James, Castledermot, co. Kildare, merchant
1806 ,, John, Strickleen, co. Louth, farmer
1783 ,, Peter, Heathstown, co. Louth, farmer
1753 ,, Richard, Dublin, grocer
1767 ,, Thos., Heathstown, co. Louth, farmer
1757 ,, William, Ligdoory, co. Meath, farmer
[See KENNAN.]
1749 **Keene**, Anne, Rathfarnham
1764 ,, Gilbert, esq.
1809 ,, John, Dame-street, Dub., goldsmith
1691 ,, Stephen, Cork, innkeeper
1708 ,, Talbot, Dublin, apothecary
1724 ,, rev. Talbot, Cashel, co. Tipperary, clk.
[See KEAN.]
1713 **Keeys**, Jane, *alias* **Swan**, *alias* **Stewart**, Dublin, widow
1656 **Keggan**, Cornelius, Dub., innholder
[**V.** 248
[See KEEGAN.]
1788 **Kehoe**, Ambrose, Dunlavin, co. Wicklow, brewer
1788 ,, Barneby, Kilcullen Bridge, co. Kildare, shopkeeper
1793 ,, Denis, Kilkenny, hardware merchant
1805 ,, Jane, Kilcummey, co. Carlow, widow
1778 ,, Michael, Cook-st., Dublin
1809 ,, Patrick
1688 ,, Peter, Carrick, co. Tipperary, farmer
[See KEOGH, M'KEOGH.]
1680 **Keigh**, Laughlin, Lazy-hill, Dublin, salt boiler
1794 **Keightly**, Anne, Island-bridge, Dublin
1786 ,, Thos., Island-bridge, co. Dub., esq.

1784 **Keilly**, Richd., Lismore, co. Waterford, esq. (Large)
1780 **Keily**, Edmond, Cork city, saddler
1809 ,, John, Belgrove, co. Cork, esq.
(Large)
[See COLCLOUGH.]
1802 **Keine**, Mary, Dublin, widow
1671 **Keith**, Alexander, Newtown Butler,
clk.
1777 ,, Jeremiah, Cootehill, co. Cavan,
merchant
1777 **Kelburn**, Ebenezer, Dublin, clk.
1764 **Kellan**, Patk., Drogheda, victualler
(Not proved)
1562 **Kelle**, Wm., the Grange, Ballyboghill
[See KELLY.]
1763 **Kelleher**, Mathew, Ballingrive, co.
Galway, gent.
1809 **Keller**, Letitia, Dublin city, widow
1811 **Kellet**, Ann
1772 ,, Charles, Cornasesk, co. Cavan
1786 ,, Christopher, Wexford town,
esq. [gent.
1747 ,, Edward, Cornasesk, co. Cavan,
1779 ,, Edwd., Clonmel, co. Tipperary,
esq.
1802 ,, James, Rathbane Lodge, co.
Meath, esq.
1752 ,, John, Rathenree, co. Meath
1791 ,, John, Moate, co. Westmeath,
gent.
1798 ,, John, Moate, co. Westmeath,
farmer
1792 ,, Mary, widow
1769 ,, Thomas, Channel-row, Dublin,
victualler
1797 **Kellett**, Charles, Dublin, hatter
1809 ,, James, Fordstown, co. Meath,
esq.
1806 ,, John, North King-st., Dublin
city
1792 ,, Robert
1767 ,, Wm., Clonmel, co. Tipperary,
esq.
1789 ,, William, lieut.-col. 39th regt. of
foot
1762 **Kellie**, Alexander, Dublin, tobacconist
[See KELLY.]
1747 **Kells**, Hugh, Newry, co. Down,
merchant
1798 ,, Sarah, Dublin, widow
1740 **Kelly**, Alexander, Dubl., innkeeper
1791 ,, Alice, Greenmount
1784 ,, Allen, Portarlington, Queen's
co., gent.
1758 ,, Ally, Kew Green, Surrey
1739 ,, Andrew, Francis-street, Dubl.,
mealman

1753 **Kelly**, Andrew, Stonybatter, Dublin,
gent.
1804 ,, Andrew, Dawson-st., Dublin
1749 ,, Ann, Kellybrook, co. Westmeath, gent.
1761 ,, Ann, Dublin, spinster
1712 ,, Anthony, Parcelstown, co. Westmeath, gent.
1771 ,, Anthony, Drimgriffin, co. Galway, gent.
1805 ,, Anthony, Clonagsee, co. Roscommon, gent.
1747 ,, Barnaby, Dublin, merchant
1807 ,, Bridget, Clonase, co. Roscommon
1810 ,, Bridget, Loughrea, co. Galway,
spinster
1811 ,, Bridget, Bolton-street, Dublin,
widow
1706 ,, Bryan, Bellaforen, co. Roscommon, esq.
1742 ,, Bryan, Dublin, shoemaker
1751 ,, Bryan, Aghverheney, co. Roscommon
1783 ,, Bryan, Gardenford, co. Roscommon, esq.
1800 ,, Bryan, Mulloughmore, co. Galway
1755 ,, Catherine, widow
1763 ,, Catherine, Ormond-market,
Dublin, spinster
1776 ,, Catherine, Tighe-street, Dubl.,
widow
1778 ,, Charles
1779 ,, Clare, Dublin, widow
1663 ,, Colla, Dublin, gent.
1660 ,, Danl., Carribeg, co. Roscommon
[VIII. 139
1733 ,, Daniel, Skinner-row, Dublin,
grocer
1756 ,, Daniel, Drummin, Queen's co.
1768 ,, Daniel, par. priest of Killosolan,
co. Galway
1772 ,, Daniel, Dawson's grove, co.
Armagh
1778 ,, Daniel, Dublin, gent.
1789 ,, Daniel, Cargins, co. Roscom.,
esq.
1792 ,, Danl., Clara, King's co., tallow
chandler
1794 ,, Daniel
1807 ,, Daniel, Tullamore, King's co.
1614 ,, David, Dublin, stabler [esq.
1756 ,, Denis, Kellybrook, co. Roscom.,
1757 ,, Denis, late of Jamaica, now of
Lisduffe, co. Galway, esq.
1782 ,, Denis, Lackagh, co. Kildare,
farmer
1789 ,, Denis, Loughrea, co. Galway,
gent.

1790 **Kelly**, Denis, Cuffe-street, Dublin
1804 ,, Denis, Ballyndin, Queen's co., farmer
1740 ,, Dennis, formerly of Aghsane, co. Galway, now of Dublin, esq.
1782 ,, Dennis, College-green, Dublin, publican
1795 ,, Dennis
1796 ,, Dinis, Castle Kelly, co.Galway, esq.
1695 ,, Edmond, Clongoeswood, co. Kildare, merchant
1733 ,, Edmond, Scregg, co. Roscom., esq.
1736 ,, Edmond, Castleruby, co, Roscommon, gent.
1767 ,, Edmond, Churchborough, co, Roscom., esq. (Not proved)
1781 ,, Edmond, Churchborough, co. Roscommon, esq.
1794 ,, Edmond, Prince's-st., Bedford-row, Middlesex, esq.
1803 ,, Edmond, Gortbeg, co. Galway, gent.
1806 ,, Edmond, Glinsk, co. Galway
1809 ,, Edmond, Fidane, co. Galway, esq.
1690 ,, Edward, Dublin, baker
1730 ,, Edward, Dublin, cooper
1768 ,, Edward, Ballycollin, King'sco., farmer
1771 ,, Edward, Dublin, weaver
1776 ,, Edward, Fennecross, King'sco., farmer
1790 ,, Edward, Portarlington, Queen's co.
1795 ,, Edward
1755 ,, Eleanor, Dublin, widow
1803 ,, Elinor, Loughrea, co. Galway, spinster
1749 ,, Elizabeth, Maryborough, Qu. co.
1783 ,, Elizabeth, spinster
1789 ,, Elizabeth, Dublin, widow
1793 ,, Elizabeth, Dublin, spinster
1800 ,, Elizabeth, Dublin, widow
1810 ,, Elizabeth, Churchborough, co. Roscommon, widow
1770 ,, Ellinor, Mullingar, co. Westmeath, widow
1802 ,, Ellinor, Ormond-market, Dubl., widow
1772 ,, Emanuel, Dublin, gent.
1809 ,, Festus, Dublin city, gent.
1791 ,, Frances, Knockmore, co. Roscommon, widow
1729 ,, Francis, Mary's-lane, Dublin, gent.
1758 ,, Francis, Dublin, gent.

1796 **Kelly**, Francis, Meath-row, Earl Meath's Liberties, merchant
1793 ,, Hannah, Dublin, widow
1741 ,, Henry, Dublin, linendraper
1794 ,, Henry, Dublin, gent.
1721 ,, Hubert, Cloonbane, co. Westmeath
1779 ,, Hugh, Plunket-street, Dublin, tobacconist
1697 ,, *alias* **Hurley**, Grany, Derrynaslen, co. Tipperary, widow
1753 ,, Ignatius, Mary's-lane, Dublin, stationer
1770 ,, Ignatius, Cargins, co. Roscom., esq.
1756 ,, James, Dublin, merchant
1768 ,, James, Lackan, co. Roscom.
1790 ,, James, Johnstown, co. Meath, farmer
1793 ,, James, Dublin, gent.
1798 ,, Jas., Rowlandstown, co. Meath-farmer.
1800 ,, James, Dublin, merchant
1800 ,, James, Dublin, Dr. of Music
1803 ,, James, Moon, co. Kild., farmer
1806 ,, James, Thomas-street, Dublin, china manufacturer
1784 ,, Jane, Summerhill, co. Dublin
1557 ,, John
1650 ,, John, Dromanagh, co. Dublin, yeoman
1652 ,, John, Dublin, gent.
1694 ,, John, Clonlyon, co. Galway, gent.
1713 ,, John, Tulsk, co. Roscom., esq.
1714 ,, John, Clonlyon, co. Galway, esq.
1730 ,, John, Clonraher, Queen's co., gent. [esq.
1732 ,, John, Keenagh, co. Roscom.,
1755 ,, John, Dubl., gent. (Not proved)
1758 ,, John, Clonraher, Queen's co., gent. (Not proved)
1765 ,, John, Limerick, merchant
1772 ,, John, Loughrea, co. Galway, esq.
1773 ,, John, Ballybricken, Liberties of Waterford, tanner
1777 ,, John, Lanesborough, co. Longford, gent.
1787 ,, John, Ballybane, co. Galway, gent.
1800 ,, John, Killane, co. Wex., farmer
1806 ,, John, Great Ship-street, Dubl. city, wine merchant
1809 ,, John, Drogheda, apothecary
1809 ,, John, Portarlington town, gent.
1809 ,, John, Castle-st., Dubl., gent.
1810 ,, John, Liscoffey, co. Roscom., farmer

1597 **Kelly**, William, Dublin, gent.
1719   ,,   William, Furrock, co. Roscommon, gent.
1732   ,,   William, Cork, baker
1736   ,,   William, Ballinlass, co. Galway, gent.
1742   ,,   William, Dublin, gent.
1748   ,,   William, Kells, co. Meath, merchant   [gent.
1748   ,,   William, Mucklon, co. Galway,
1762   ,,   William, Dublin, linendraper
1762   ,,   William, Brickfield, co. Roscommon, gent.
1766   ,,   William, Cloonburn, co. Roscommon, gent.
1781   ,,   William, Newry, co. Down
1792   ,,   William, Dublin, gent.
1799   ,,   William, Athlone
    [See KEALY, KEELING, KEELY, KEILLY, KELLE, KELLIE, KILLIKELLY.]
1640 **Kelsaie**, George, native of Scotland
1749 **Kelsey**, Henry, Buenos Ayres, Span. Indies, tailor
1743 **Kelsick**, Isaac, Dublin, merchant
1720 **Kelsoe**, John, Ringsend, Dublin, anchor smith
1743   ,,   John, port of Glasgow, North Britain (Ex.)
1781   ,,   John, Stormanstown, co. Dubl.
1743   ,,   Mary, *alias* **Hamilton**, widow (Ex.)
1677 **Kelson**, John, Drumbony, Limerick city, gent.
1712 **Kemeyes**, Nicholas, Dublin, esq.
1798 **Kemeys**, John, Downingstown, co. Kildare, esq.
1731   ,,   Lewis, Kilmogue, Island of Allen, co. Kildare, surgeon
1721   ,,   Mary, Dublin, widow
1809 **Kemmis**, John, Castle-street, Dub., gent.
1774   ,,   Thomas, Killeenlinah, Queen's co.
    [See KEMEYS.]
1790 **Kemp**, dame Elizabeth, Tooting, Surrey, widow (Copy)
1732   ,,   Henry, Dublin, gent.
1764   ,,   Samuel
1796   ,,   William Forster, Cork, grocer
1798 **Kempston**, Catherine, Camden-st., Dublin, spinster
1781   ,,   Elizabeth, Dublin, widow
1723   ,,   Grace, Dublin, widow
1799   ,,   Henry, Dublin city, gent.
1775   ,,   John, Clogheen, co. Tipperary, clk.
1810   ,,   John, Dublin city, confectioner
1676   ,,   Nichs., Drummurry, co. Cavan, esq.

1795 **Kempston**, Thos., Dublin city, gt.
1675 **Kemus**, John (Will wanting)
1700 **Kemyes**, Nichs., Ferns, co. Wexford, esq.
1789 **Kenagh**, William, Castlemartyr
    [See KENNA.]
1722 **Kenan**, Bryan, Dublin, merchant tailor
1580   ,,   Patrick, House of St. James
1608   ,,   William, Dublin, tanner
    [See KENNAN.]
1637 **Kendal**, Edward, Ayles, co. Cork, gent.
1734 **Kendall**, Charles, Walton's Grove, co. Kilkenny, esq. (Ex.)
1777   ,,   James, Dublin, gent.
1745   ,,   Mary, Dublin, spinster
1743   ,,   Melosina, duchess of (Copy)
1629   ,,   Robert, Cloghymover, co. Galway, gent.
1782 **Kendelan**, Francis, Thomas-street, Dublin, chandler
1670 **Kendrick**, Thomas, Newcastle, co. Tipperary, esq.
    [See KENRICK.]
1675 **Kene**, Edward, Dublin, gent.
1694   ,,   Thomas, Athy, co. Kildare, gent.
    [See KEAN.]
1803 **Kenedy**, James, Dublin city, coach owner
1803   ,,   James, Mullinahack, Dublin city, linen and woollen draper
    [See KENNEDY.]
1795 **Kenmare**, Thomas, lord viscount
1694   ,,   Valentine, lord visct. (Ex.)
1799 **Kenna**, Edmond, *alias* **M'Kenna**, Carrick-on-Suir, co. Tipperary
1760   ,,   James, Killelan, co. Kildare, innholder
    [See KENAGH.]
1772 **Kennan**, Christopher, Dubl., tanner
1791   ,,   Emelia, widow   [gent.
1759   ,,   George, Ashtown, co. Dublin,
1777   ,,   Jane, Dublin, widow
1736   ,,   John, Dublin, merchant
1789   ,,   Robert, Peamount, co. Dublin, gent.
1796   ,,   Sarah, Dundalk, co. Louth
1704   ,,   Thomas, Dublin, merchant
1741   ,,   Thos., Diswellstown, co. Dub., farmer
1769   ,,   Thomas, formerly capt. 34th regt. of foot, now of Dublin, esq.
1781   ,,   Thos., Diswellstown, co. Dubl., esq.
    [See KEENAN, KENAN.]

1736 **Kennedy**, Thomas, Carlow, esq.
1757　,,　Thomas, Dublin, linen glazier
1761　,,　Thomas, Frankford
1793　,,　Thomas, Barrack-st., Dublin, shoemaker
1802　,,　Thomas, Dublin
1808　,,　Thomas, Barrack-st., Dublin, dairyman
1672　,,　Walter, Dublin, alderman
1710　,,　Walter, Dublin, esq.
1748　,,　Walter, Dublin, esq.
1726　,,　William, Dublin, one of the Yeomen of the Guards of the Castle of Dublin
1744　,,　Wm., Mullo, co. Longford, esq.
1777　,,　Wm., Knockagoney, co. Down, farmer
1786　,,　Wm., Knockagoney, co. Down
1796　,,　rev.Wm., Ballylevin, King's co.
1809　,,　William, Kilkenny city
　　　　　[See KENEDY.]
1767 **Kenelley**, Henry, Dublin, merchant
1747　,,　Joyce, Dublin, widow
1787 **Kenney**, Anne, *alias* **Rogers**, widow
1776　,,　Christopher, Ballinlough, Lib. of Cork, gent.
1779　,,　Courtney, Ballinrobe, co.Mayo, gent.
1811　,,　Courtney, Ballinrobe, co.Mayo, esq.
1751　,,　Henry, Wexford, esq.
1791　,,　Honora, Galway, spinster
1788　,,　James, King-st., Oxm., Dublin, saddler
1790　,,　Jane, Galway town, spinster
1774　,,　John, Dublin, salesman
1794　,,　John, Mullow, co. Longford, gt.
1802　,,　John, Brierfield, co. Galway, gent.
1794　,,　Mary, *alias* **Kennedy**, widow
1745　,,　Miles, Clonegall, co. Carlow, gent.
1788　,,　Patrick, prebendary of Clonmethan, dio. Dublin
1772　,,　Robert, Rosetown, co. Kildare, gent.
1759　,,　Terence, Dublin, gent.
1708　,,　Thomas, capt. of His Majesty's ship "Falmouth" (Copy)
1807 **Kenny**, Alex., Dublin city, gent.
1808　,,　Denis, Hartwell Mills, co. Kild.
1684　,,　Edward, Cullen, co. Cork, gent.
1757　,,　James, Dublin, merchant
1809　,,　James, Kilbride
1809　,,　James, city of Dublin, sugar baker
1804　,,　Neal, Phibsborough, co. Dublin
1682　,,　Richard, Wexford, esq. (Ex.)
1806　,,　Simon, Mountmellick, merchant

1811 **Kenny**, Thomas, Glasnevin-road, co. Dublin, cabinetmaker
　　　　　[See KENNEY, KILKENNY, KILLKENNEY.]
1736 **Kenrick**, Elizabeth, Clonmel, co. Tipperary, widow
　　　　　[See KENDRICK.]
1743 **Kent**, Anthony, Newport-pagnell, Bucks, gent. (Copy)
1770　,,　Aquila, Greenhill, co.Tipperary
1802　,,　rev. Charles, Skreen, co. Sligo
1790　,,　Edmond, Carrick-on-Suir, co. Tipperary, innholder
1747　,,　Elizabeth, Roscrea, co. Tipperary, widow
1789　,,　Ellinor, Galway, widow
1737　,,　Francis, Ennis, co. Clare, gent.
1770　,,　Francis, Ennis, co. Clare, gent.
1791　,,　George, Arran-quay, Dublin, paper stainer
1715　,,　John, Waterford, esq.
1796　,,　John, Roscrea, co. Tip., esq.
1597　,,　Robert, Daneston, co. Meath, esq. (No date.)
1664　,,　Thomas, Daneston, co. Meath, esq.
1763 **Keogh**, Darby, Cornmarket, Dublin, merchant
1791　,,　Edmond, Shalea, co. Roscommon, gent.
1806　,,　Francis, Ballyderry, co. Galway, gent.
1809　,,　George, Chilcomb, co. Kilkenny
1788　,,　John, M.D.
1790　,,　John, Fade-street, Dubl., gent.
1803　,,　John, Eccles-st., co. Dublin, esq. (Large)
1769　,,　Laughlin, Feakill, co. Roscommon, gent.
1804　,,　Laurence, Keoghville, co. Roscommon, esq.
1768　,,　Mary, Kilkenny, widow
1805　,,　Mary, servant
1795　,,　Patrick, Dublin city
1779　,,　Peter, Feakill, co. Rosc., gent.
1807　,,　Thos., New Ross, co. Wexford, esq.
1792 **Keoghoe**, Catherine, Minmaud, co. Carlow, widow
1652　,,　Maurice, Ginginstown
　　　　　[See KEHOE, KEOGHOE, KEOUGH, KEUGH.]
1756 **Keon**, Ambrose, Dublin, gent.
1809　,,　Ambrose, Newbrook, co. Leitrim, gent.
1793　,,　Anne, Dublin, gent.
1811　,,　John, M.D.
1769　,,　Mary, Ballinamore, co. Leitrim, widow
1794　,,　Robert, Dublin, gent.

1801 **Keon**, William, Dublin, gent.
　　　[See KEONS, KEOWEN.]
1809 **Keonan**, rev. Patk., P.P. of Kilbrew
1718 　,, Peter, Balrath, farmer
1811 **Keons**, Myles, Keonsbrook, co.
　　　Leitrim, esq.
1786 **Keough**, Laurence, Fade-st., Dub.,
　　　trader
1749 　,, Mathew, Kilkenny, chandler
1777 　,, Michael, Athlone, co. Ros-
　　　common, gent.
1783 　,, Thomas, Kilcullen bridge, co.
　　　Kildare, butcher
　　　[See KEOGH.]
1754 **Keowen**, John, Follymor, co. Down,
1781 　,, William, Murlogh, co. Down,
　　　farmer
1723 **Ker**, Alexander, Dublin, glazier
1767 　,, Andrew, Portatrave, co. Mon.,
　　　esq.
1723 　,, Elizabeth, widow
1781 　,, Hugh, Dublin, merchant
1797 　,, John, Summerhill, Dublin
1718 　,, Margt., Flowerfield, co. London-
　　　derry, widow
1797 　,, Margaret, Dublin, spinster
1744 　,, Peter, late lieut.-colonel of
　　　dragoons　　　[gent.
1781 　,, William, Newcastle, co. Meath,
1810 **Keran**, Patk., Rough Grange, co.
　　　Meath
　　　[See KERIN.]
1755 **Kerby**, James, Garricktagurt, co.
　　　Cork
1783 　,, Maurice, Glanogra, co. Limk.,
　　　farmer
　　　[See KIRBY.]
1671 **Kerdiff**, John, Rollestown, co.
　　　Meath, gent.
1671 　,, John, D.D., rector of Navan
1734 　,, Wm., St. Margaret's, co. Dubl.
1702 **Kerdiffe**, John, Kerdiffstown, co.
　　　Kildare, esq.
1641 　,, Simon, Dublin, merchant
1597 **Kerdyff**, Christopher, Dilletston, co.
　　　Dublin, gent. (No date)
1675 **Keresforth**, Mary, Dublin, spr.
1673 　,, Robert, Dublin, esq.
1791 **Kergan**, John, Galway town
1688 **Kerin**, Daniel, Esker, Queen's co.,
　　　esq.
1756 　,, Edmond, Dublin, merchant
1752 　,, Mary, widow of Thomas K.,
　　　Pimlico, Dublin, dyer
1804 　,, Mary, Ennis, co. Clare, widow
1733 　,, Nathaniel, Esker, Queen's co.,
　　　gent.
1785 　,, Patk., Corrofin, co. Clare, gent.
1810 　,, Peter, Skikanagh, co. Clare,
　　　farmer

1780 **Kerin**, Terence, Dublin, gent.
1745 　,, Thomas, Pimlico, co. Dublin,
　　　dyer
　　　[See KEARIN, KEARNAN, KERAN,
　　　KIERAN.]
1799 **Kernan**, Patrick, Dublin, gent.
　　　[See KIERNAN.]
1582 **Kerowan**, Edmond, Galway
1725 **Kerr**, Andw., Newcastle, co. Meath,
　　　gent.
1753 　,, Andrew, Portatrave, co. Mon.,
　　　esq. (Ex.)
1810 　,, Anna H., Linenhall-st., Dublin
1779 　,, David, Catetallon-st., London,
　　　merchant, but at Wanstead,
　　　Essex (Copy)
1768 　,, Elizabeth, wid. of Thomas K.,
　　　Waterford, seedsman
1765 　,, Esther
1771 　,, George, capt. in the East India
　　　Company's service (Not
　　　proved)
1794 　,, Hannah, Dublin, widow
1793 　,, Henry
1749 　,, Hugh, Dublin, baker
1749 　,, James, Tullydraw, co. Tyrone,
　　　surgeon
1720 　,, John, par. St. James, Clerken-
　　　well, Middlesex, gt. (Copy)
1728 　,, hon. John, commonly called
　　　lord John Kerr (Copy)
1748 　,, John, Dublin, gent.
1759 　,, John, Martinstown, co. West-
　　　meath, gent.
1800 　,, Margery, Summerhill, Dublin,
　　　widow
1804 　,, Mary, Cork city, widow
1679 　,, Robert, Ballyaghrane, co. Lon-
　　　donderry, gent.
1792 　,, Robert, Newry, co. Down,
　　　merchant
1756 　,, William, Ballymena, co. Ant.,
　　　merchant
1723 **Kerraghan**, Thady, Athlone, co.
　　　Westmeath
1746 **Kerrin**, Patrick, the Glebb, co.
　　　Dublin, wigmaker (Not
　　　proved)
1799 **Kerry**, Anastatia, countess of
1684 　,, Honora, dow. countess of
1776 　,, Mary, Cherry-lane, Dublin
1660 　,, and **Lixnaw**, Patk., lord baron
　　　of (Ex.)
1742 　,, Thomas, earl of
1697 　,, and **Lixnaw**, Wm., lord baron
　　　of
1747 　,, William, earl of
1597 **Kerwan**, Murtagh, Tavelagh Cot-
　　　tier (No date)
　　　[See KIRWAN.]

1758 **Kesterson**, William, Cork, gent.
1665 **Kett**, John, Dublin, merchant
1771 **Kettlewell**, Abraham, Drogheda, gent.
1763 ,, Chas., Callaghtown, co. Meath, gent.   [gent.
1703 ,, John, Callaghtown, co. Meath,
1735 ,, Thos., Thomastown, co. Meath, farmer
1811 **Keugh**, Wm., Wexford town, esq.
      [See KEOGH.]
1553 **Kewan**, Katherine, Dublin
1701 **Keyes**, Thomas, Blackchurch, co. Kildare, gent.
1792 **Keys**, Charles, Dublin, gent.
1788 ,, Frances, Cavanacor, co. Don., widow
1775 ,, Hugh, Cloolaness, co. Ferm.
1794 ,, John, Killynoogan, co. Fermanagh, gent.
1800 ,, Nathaniel, Cavanacor, co. Donegal, esq.
      [See KEAYS.]
1597 **Keysar**, Joan, St. Werburgh's par., Dublin, spr. (No date)
1654 **Kid**, John, Dublin, soldier   [**V**. 42
1737 **Kidd**, David, Dublin, tailor
1736 **Kidwell**, Wm., Dublin, stonecutter
1791 **Kieran**, Anthony, Collon, co. Louth, gent.
1741 ,, Hugh, Owencullmaden, co. Fermanagh, gent.
1675 ,, John, New-row, Thomas-court, brewer   [gent.
1694 ,, Thomas, New-row, near Dubl.,
      [See KERIN.]
1802 **Kiernan**, Bryan, Aughalough, co. Leitrim, gent.
1797 ,, Elizabeth, Dublin, widow
1795 ,, Francis, Dublin, merchant
1809 ,, Francis, Dublin city, esq.
1811 ,, George, Henry-street, Dublin, apothecary   [ford
1757 ,, Hugh, Derrycassin, co. Long-
1709 ,, James, Dublin, gent.
1806 ,, John, Rihiboth, co. Dublin
1807 ,, John, Granard, co. Long., gent.
1807 ,, Judith, Aughavoe, co. Cavan
1753 ,, Richard, Crebay, co. Meath farmer
1802 ,, Richard, Dublin, M.D.
1787 ,, William, Dublin, esq.
      [See KEARNAN, KERNAN.]
1620 **Kierry** and **Lyksnawe**, Thos., lord baron of
      [See KERRY.]
1743 **Kiest**, Mary, Dublin, widow
1640 **Kighoe**, Joan, Culmine, co. Dublin, widow
1797 **Kilby**, William, Dublin, merchant

1679 **Kildare**, Ambrose Jones, bp. of
1761 ,, Dr. Thomas Fletcher, bp. of
1790 ,, right rev. Chas. Lindsay, lord bishop of (Copy)
1666 ,, Elizabeth, countess of
1758 ,, Elizabeth, dow. countess of, par. St. George, Hanover-square (Copy)
1586 ,, Gerald, earl of
1708 ,, John, earl of (Copy)
1608 ,, Mabel, dow. countess of
1780 ,, Marie, dow. countess of
1743 ,, Robert, earl of
1787 **Kiles**, William, Dublin, esq.
1792 ,, Wm., Waterford, watchmaker
1791 **Kilkenny**, Edward, Dublin
      [See KENNY.]
1663 **Killala** and **Achonry**, Henry Hall, bishop of
1751 ,, and **Achonry**, Mordecai Cary, bishop of
1780 ,, rt. rev. Dr. Saml. Hutchinson, bishop of
1646 **Killaloe**, Lewis Jones, bishop of
1650 ,, Ed. Parry, D.D., bishop of
1670 ,, Edward Worth, bishop of
1675 ,, Daniel Wittar, bishop of
1692 ,, John Roane, bishop of
1696 ,, Henry Ryder, bishop of
1739 ,, rt. rev. Dr. Chas. Carr, bp. of
1771 ,, rt. rev. Dr. Nichs. Synge, bishop of (and Kilfenora)
1810 **Killen**, Ann, Cardenstown, co. Meath
1800 ,, Robert, Strabane, co. Tyrone
1755 **Killikelly**, Bryan, Muniscrebeg, co. Galway, gent.
1768 ,, Fergus, Carrownamandra at the Windmill, co. Galway
1735 ,, Luke
1746 ,, Martin, Dublin, merchant
      [See KELLY.]
1789 **Killin**, rev. John, D.D.
      [See KILLEN.]
1789 **Killkenney**, Jas., Emla, co. Roscommon
1788 ,, Mathew, Cleen, co. Roscommon, gent.
      [See KENNY.]
1794 **Killmain**, John, lord baron
1720 **Killpatrick**, Charles, Dubl., painter
1780 ,, John, Corville, co. Tip., esq.
      [See KIRKPATRICK.]
1798 **Kilmaine**, rt. hon. lady Alicia, dow. countess of
1797 **Kilmartin**, Luke, Aughrenagiltha, co. Roscommon
1687 **Kilmore**, Danl., *alias* M'**Kilmore**, Capanagh, co. Galway, yeoman

1656 **Kilmore,** William Bedel, bp. of [VI. 24
1672 ,, Robert Maxwell, bp. of (Ex.)
1698 ,, and **Ardagh,** Wm. Smith, bishop of
1713 ,, Ed. Wethamhall or Wetenhall, bishop of
1775 ,, Dr. Dennison Cumberland, bishop of
1709 **Kilpatrick,** Jane, Dublin, widow [See KILLPATRICK.]
1803 **Kilwarden,** rt. hon. Arthur lord viscount
1766 **Kilworth,** Stephen Moore, lord baron, afterwards lord viscount Mountcashell
1787 **Kimberly,** Edward, Dublin, stonecutter
1789 ,, Margaret, Drogheda, spinster
1745 ,, Sarah, Drogheda, widow
1787 **Kinane,** Paul, Galway, fisherman
1634 **Kinastin,** Edwd., Saule, co. Down, esq.
1634 ,, Francis, Saule, co. Down, esq.
1809 **Kinch,** Edward, Tomnahealy, co. Wexford, farmer
1797 ,, James, Cumstown, co. Wicklow, gent.
1747 **Kindelan,** Bryan, Dublin, shopkeeper
1724 ,, Celia, Lyons Den, co. Meath, widow
1787 ,, Michael, Thomas-st., Dublin, chandler
1755 ,, Peter, Drogheda, tanner
1740 **Kindellan,** Patrick, Ballnekade, co. Meath
1805 ,, Samuel, Dorset-street, Dublin
1797 ,, Robert, Dublin, gent.
1807 **Kine,** Bryan, Creggs, co. Galway, gent.
1805 ,, Peter, Crosswell, co. Galway
1762 **King,** Alexander, Durrow, co. Kildare, gent.
1760 ,, Andrew, Dublin, gent.
1789 ,, rev. Andrew, Dublin, clerk
1786 ,, Anna, Durrow, co. Kilkenny, widow
1700 ,, Anne, *alias* **Humphrys,** wife to Chas. K., Bishopscourt, co. Down
1754 ,, Anne, Dublin, widow
1809 ,, Anne, Ballynahruck, co. Galway, widow
1787 ,, sir Anthony, Dublin, knt. and alderman
1797 ,, Anthony, Dublin, barrister-at-law
1791 ,, Bryan, Gt. George's-st. Dubl., baker

1694 **King,** Catherine, wife to Chas. King, and late wife and executrix to Chas. **Ward,** Killough, co. Down, esq.
1799 ,, Catherine, Dublin, widow
1699 ,, Charles, Dublin, esq.
1714 ,, Charles, Dublin, gent.
1773 ,, Charles, Sligo, merchant
1790 ,, Charles, Dublin, cardmaker
1800 ,, Conolly, Dublin, widow
1738 ,, David, Dublin, goldsmith
1772 ,, David, Dublin, woollen draper
1744 ,, Denis, New-row, co. Dublin, brewer
1774 ,, Dorothea, Dublin, widow
1639 ,, Edward, bishop of **Elphin,** q. v.
1801 ,, Edward, Phibsborough, co. Dublin, gent.
1802 ,, Edward, Gt. Britain-st., Dubl., gent.
1735 ,, Elizabeth, Dublin, widow
1747 ,, Elizabeth, wife to John King
1764 ,, Ellinor, Dublin, widow
1795 ,, Frances, Sackville-st., Dublin
1665 ,, Francis, Radoony, co. Sligo, esq.
1722 ,, Geo., Kilpeacon, co. Limerick, esq.
1771 ,, George, Dublin, currier
1749 ,, alderman Gilbert
1788 ,, Gilbert, Drogheda, esq.
1795 ,, Gilbert, Gloucester-st., Dublin, gent.
1811 ,, Gilbert, formerly major in the 7th Dragoons
1741 ,, rt. hon. sir Henry, Rockingham, co. Roscommon, bart
1741 ,, Henry, Sligo
1787 ,, Henry, Ringsend, co. Dublin, shipwright
1776 ,, Hugh, Lurg, co. Cavan
1765 ,, Isabella
1687 ,, James, Charlestown, co. Roscommon, esq. (Ex.)
1727 ,, James, Dublin, merchant
1756 ,, James, Gola, co. Fermanagh
1772 ,, James, Dublin, esq.
1789 ,, James, Corcraff, co. Cavan
1795 ,, v. rev. James, D.D., dean of Raphoe [esq.
1798 ,, James, Eustace-street, Dublin,
1767 ,, Jane, Kingswell, co. Tipperary, widow
1801 ,, Jane, Dublin, spinster
1788 ,, rev. Jeremiah, Mackmine, co. Wexford, clk.
1640 ,, John Sobiesky, Dublin, mercht.
1668 ,, John, London, draper (Copy)
1673 ,, John, Boyle, co. Roscommon, gent.

1682 **King**, John
1699 ,, John, Wicklow, gent.
1722 ,, sir John, Rockingham, co. Roscommon, bart.
1728 ,, John, co. Dublin, brewer
1736 ,, John, Charlestown, co. Roscommon, esq.
1737 ,, John, Tobberbyan, co. Tipperary, gent.
1743 ,, John, gent., commission officer in col. Rose's regt.
1763 ,, John
1769 ,, John, Dublin, esq.
1778 ,, John, Ballylin, King's co., esq.
1779 ,, John, Brownstown, co. Kildare
1784 ,, John, Waterford, merchant
1785 ,, John, Clondalkin, co. Dublin, gent.
1786 ,, John, Carlow town, mercht.
1806 ,, John, Dublin city, woollen-draper
1810 ,, John, Dublin city, brazier
1811 ,, John, Prospect Hall, co. Limerick, esq.
1774 ,, Laurence
1759 ,, Maccarrell, Dublin, gent.
1755 ,, Margaret, widow
1795 ,, Margt., Fardross, co. Tyrone
1731 ,, Marion, Dublin, widow
1748 ,, Mary, Field Court, Gray's Inn, Middlesex, widow
1803 ,, Mary, Werburgh-st., Dublin
1734 ,, Mathew, par. St. Giles, Middlesex, gent. (Copy)
1771 ,, Myhill, Mackmine, co. Wexford, gent.
1690 ,, Nathaniel, Ballinecarrog, co. Cath., gent.
1696 ,, Nathl., Bennekerry, co. Cath., esq.
1783 ,, Nicholas, Fraigh, co. Wexford, esq.
1790 ,, sir Patrick, Dublin, knt.
1666 ,, Ralph, LL.D., recorder of Derry
1753 ,, Richard, Athy, co. Kildare
1771 ,, Richard, Carlow, merchant
1784 ,, Richard, Upper Dorset-st., co. Dublin, measr.
1657 ,, sir Robert, Boyle, co. Roscommon, knt.		(**VI**. 137
1708 ,, sir Robert, Rockingham, co. Roscommon, bart.
1711 ,, Robert, Dublin, esq.
1732 ,, Robert, Dublin, saddler
1749 ,, Robert, Dublin, cutler
1760 ,, Robert, Prospect Point, co. Dublin, esq.
1773 ,, Robert, Dublin, alderman
1787 ,, Robert, LL.D., dean of Kildare
1808 ,, Robert, Dublin city

1777 **King**, Samuel, Baltinglass, co. Wicklow, brewer
1801 ,, Simon, Dublin, esq.
1789 ,, Sobeisky, Dublin, merchant
1781 ,, Susana, *alias* **Laurence**, Dub., widow
1684 ,, Thomas, Carrickfergus, mercht.
1742 ,, Thomas, Dublin, weaver
1767 ,, Thomas
1771 ,, Thomas, Dublin, merchant
1775 ,, Thomas, Dublin, merchant
1800 ,, Thomas, Dublin, esq.
1811 ,, Thos., Kingsfort, co. Wicklow, esq.
1703 ,, William, Bishop's Court, co. Down, gent.
1715 ,, William, Ballinafad, co. Sligo, gent.
1722 ,, William, Charleville, co. Cork, gent.
1729 ,, William, abp. of **Dublin**, q. v.
1734 ,, William, Dublin, gent.
1748 ,, William, Kingsborough, co. Sligo, gent.
1756 ,, William, Redcross, co. Wicklow
1803 ,, William, Baltinglass, co. Wicklow, esq.
1747 **Kingbarry**, Thomas, Dublin, M.D.
1705 **Kingdom**, Mary, par. St. Andrew, Holborn, Middlesex
1628 **Kinge**, John, Dublin, esq.
1630 ,, Dublin, gent.
1632 ,, George, the elder, Clontarf, co. Dublin, esq.
1637 ,, sir John, Close of the Cathedral of Litchfield, Staffordshire, knt.
1706 ,, sir William, Kilpeacon, co. Limerick, knt.
1755 **Kingoare**, Jonathan, Ballyboes, co. Donegal
1755 **Kingsborough**, Robert, ld. baron of
1790 **Kingsbury**, Elizabeth, St. Ann's par., Dublin, spinster
1763 ,, Esther, Dublin, widow
1805 ,, Thomas, Dublin city, LL.D.
1800 **Kingsland**, George, ld. visct.
1691 ,, Henry, ld. visct. (Ex.)
1740 ,, Mary, lady viscountess
1663 ,, Nicholas, ld. visct.
1727 ,, Nicholas, ld. visct.
1796 **Kingsley**, Pincke, Dublin
1802 ,, Wm., Rockford, co. Tipperary, gent,
		[See KINSLEY.]
1796 **Kingsmill**, Edward, Belfast, co. Antrim, esq.
1705 ,, Hannah, Cork, widow
1703 ,, Thomas, Cork, merchant
1774 ,, Thomas

1798 **Kingston,** Arabella, Bandon, co. Cork, widow
1804 ,, Danl.,townofEnnistyne,revenue officer
1797 ,, Delany
1798 ,, Edward, earl of
1757 ,, James, Ballycateen, co. Cork, gent.
1764 ,, James, lord baron of (Large will)
1676 ,, John, lord
1731 ,, John, lord baron (Copy)
1803 ,, John, Dublin, gent.
1810 ,, Julia, city of Bath
1693 ,, Robert, lord **[XVII.**
1799 ,, Robert, earl of
1779 ,, Samuel, Bandon, co. Cork, gt.
1761 ,, Thomas, Coonaderrig, King's co., farmer
1806 **Kinin,** John, Dublin city, gent.
1661 **Kinkead,** capt. Alexander, Dublin, gent.
1793 ,, Alexander, Dublin, revenue officer
1762 ,, Moses, Hillsborough, co. Down
1707 ,, Wm., Aughastrike, co. Down, linen draper
1785 ,, William, Condry, co. Cavan
1811 **Kinna,** John, Birr, King's co.
1804 ,, Owen, Birr, King's co.
1806 **Kinnane,** James, Ennis, co. Clare, merchant
1771 **Kinneen,** Michael, Galway, distiller (Not proved)
1725 **Kinneer,** James, Waterford, gent.
1720 ,, rev. William, Fiddown, co. Kilkenny, clk.
1794 **Kinross,** Joseph, Limerick city, esq.
1761 **Kinsale,** Gerald De Courcy, lord baron of
1784 **Kinselagh,** Bartholomew, Mount-townland, co. Meath
1749 ,, Edmond, Dunleckney, co. Carlow
[See KINSILAUGH.]
1807 **Kinsey,** Henry, Clontarf, co. Dublin, gent.
1794 **Kinshela,** John, Kilkenny, mercht.
1745 **Kinsilaugh,** Michael, co. Dublin, gardener
1811 **Kinsley,** Morgan, Enniscorthy, co. Wexford
1805 ,, Michael, Exchequer-st., Dubl., brewer
1807 ,, Thomas, Capel-street, Dublin
[See KINGSLEY.]
1802 **Kippax,** Charles Berkly
1806 **Kirby,** Caroline Elizabeth, Dublin city, widow

1770 **Kirby,**James, Limerick, shopkeeper
1768 ,, John, Tallow Bridge, co.Waterford, M.D.
1776 ,, Margaret, Dublin, widow
1799 ,, Mary, Youghal, co. Cork, wid.
1720 ,, Nicholas, Callas, co. Cork
1781 ,, Patrick, Bohernedelane, co. Limerick, farmer
1772 ,, Richard, Dublin, butcher
1792 ,, Timothy, Tallow Bridge, co. Waterford, esq.
[See KERBY, KIRKBY.]
1800 **Kirchhoffer,** John, Dublin, cabinet maker
1676 **Kirdiffe,** William, Kerdiffstown, co. Kildare, gent.
1806 **Kirk,** Anne, Londonderry city
1766 ,, Bryan, Dublin, gent.
1739 ,, Dorothy, par. St. Andrew, Holborn, Middlesex, wid. (Copy)
1779 ,, Henry, Dublin, peruke maker
1740 ,, John, Birr, King's co. victualler
1799 ,, Martha, Londonderry
1799 ,, Martha, Coleraine, co. Londonderry, widow
1711 **Kirkby,** Roger, Tralee, co. Kerry, esq.
1768 ,, Roger, Dublin, esq.
[See KIRBY.]
1806 **Kirker,** James, Belfast, tanner and currier
1795 **Kirkland,** John, Dromin, co. Longford, esq.
1791 **Kirkpatrick,** Alexander, Drumcondra, co. Dublin, esq.
1758 ,, Francis, Dublin, painter and stationer
1737 ,, Robert, Dublin, hosier
1636 ,, Thomas, native of Scotland
1742 ,, William, Cork, merchant
[See KILLPATRICK.]
1729 **Kirkwood,** Andrew, Killala, co. Mayo, gent.
1736 ,, Andrew
1804 ,, Andrew, Newcourt, co. Wicklow, esq.
1800 ,, James, Arklow town
1765 ,, Samuel, Killala, co. Mayo, gent.
1765 ,, William, Killcummin,co.Mayo, gent.
1800 ,, William, Killala, co. Mayo, gent.
1559 **Kirowan,** David, Galway
1636 ,, Robert Fitzpatrick, Galway, merchant
1641 **Kirrin,** John, Youghal **[VI.** 186
1790 **Kirwan,** Alice, Church-street, Dublin, widow

1777 **Kirwan**, Annabell, Galway town, widow

1640 ,, Andrew, Fitzpatrick, Galway, alderman

1773 ,, Andrew, Galway

1786 ,, Andrew Fitzwilliam

1802 ,, Andrew, Miltown

1780 ,, Bridget, widow of Ambrose K.

1790 ,, Bridget, Galway town, widow

1811 ,, Bridget, Frenchgrove, co. Mayo, widow

1807 ,, Edmond, Dalgin, co. Galway, esq.

1787 ,, Elizabeth, Galway, widow

1800 ,, Hyacinth, major in Galway militia

1781 ,, John, formerly of Castlehacket, now of Dublin, esq.

1794 ,, John Anthony, Galway town, merchant

1791 ,, Julian, Galway, spinster

1809 ,, Margery, Castletown, widow (Copy)

1759 ,, Mark, Galway, gent.

1755 ,, Martin, Dalgin, co. Mayo, esq.

1807 ,, Martin, Frenchgrove, co. Mayo, esq.

1789 ,, Mary, Dublin, widow

1795 ,, Mary, Hillsbrook, co. Galway, widow

1802 ,, Mary, Milltown, co. Mayo, wid.

1754 ,, Patrick FitzThomas, Galway, merchant

1758 ,, Patrick, Cregg, co. Galway, esq.

1766 ,, Patrick, Tuam, co. Galway, gent.

1770 ,, Patrick, Fitzpierce, Tuam, co. Galway, merchant

1794 ,, rev. Patrick, Dublin, clerk

1795 ,, Patrick, Claremont, co. Mayo

1798 ,, rev. Patrick, Galway town

1797 ,, Peter, formerly par. priest, Izon, in France

1759 ,, Richard, Currastoonmoore, co. Roscommon, gent.

1779 ,, Richard, Woodfield, co. Galway, esq.

1776 ,, Robert, titular bishop of Achonry, co. Sligo

1794 ,, Sophia Hamilton, Dublin, wid.

1733 ,, Thomas Fitzpatrick, Galway, merchant

1797 ,, Thomas, Galway town, esq.

1810 ,, Thomas, Isle of Man (Copy) [See KERWAN.]

1774 **Kirwin**, John, Dublin, esq.

1748 ,, Nicholas Fitzrobuck, Galway, merchant

1676 **Kirwood**, William, All-Hallows, Lombard-street, silkman

1804 **Kissane**, William, Scallihene, co. Tipperary

1660 **Kitching**, Richard, Dublin, gardener   [VIII. 71

1640 **Kitchinman**, Thomas, London, mercer (Copy)

1767 **Kittrick**, Walter, Dublin, publican

1781 **Kittson**, George, Prussia-st., Dubl., gent.

1794 ,, Richard, surgeon's mate of 28th regt. of foot

1766 **Knabbs**, John

1787 **Knapp**, Bridget, Dublin, widow

1791 ,, Edmond, Cork, alderman

1762 **Knapton**, John, lord baron

1724 **Knaresborough**, Michael, Waterford, merchant

1796 ,, Michael, Kilkenny city, esq.

1735 ,, Oliver, Dublin, merchant

1789 ,, Robert, Dungarvan, co. Waterford, gent.

1785 ,, William, Kilkenny city, gent.

1635 **Knatchbull**, Vincent, Killahie, co. Kilkenny, esq.

1736 **Knauge**, Mathew, Flesstown, co. Roscommon, esq.

1784 **Knight**, Andrew, Corcummins, co. Monaghan, gent.

1794 ,, Ann, Broomfield, co. Cavan, spinster

1736 ,, Bulstrode Peachy, par. St. Ann, esq.

1728 ,, Christopher, Ballynoe, co. Cork, gent.

1782 ,, Christopher, Charleville, co. Cork, gent.

1799 ,, Christopher Henry, Brickfield, co. Limerick

1805 ,, sir Christopher, Limerick city, knt.

1789 ,, Edmond, Castlebar, co. Mayo, merchant   [co.

1740 ,, Francis, Maryborough, Queen's

1773 ,, Henry, Maryborough, Queen's co., gent.

1691 ,, James, Dublin, gent.

1726 ,, James, Dublin, gent.

1740 ,, James, Dublin, glazier

1767 ,, Jas., D.D., rector of Drumragh, co. Tyrone

1700 ,, John, Cork, mariner

1720 ,, Joseph, Chiswick, Middlesex, esq. (Copy)

1775 ,, Mary, Dublin, widow

1742 ,, lieut. Richard, Donegal, co. Donegal

1772 ,, Richard, Leigh, King's co., farmer

1777 ,, Richard, Knightsgrove, co. Longford

1710 **Knox,** William, Ashmoyn, co. Donegal, gent.
1770 ,, William, Ennis, co. Clare, gt.
1783 ,, William, St. Mary's-abbey, Dublin, esq.
1806 ,, William, Cleghen, co. Donegal
1809 ,, William, Cork city
1629 **Knoyle,** Leonard, Ballygally, co. Waterford, gent.
1732 **De Knuydt,** Mary, widow of Thomas Vanson De K. (Copy)
1714 **Kyan,** Adam, Castledermot, co. Kildare, glazier
1792 ,, Andrew, Dublin, merchant
1698 ,, Anne, Oberstown, co. Kildare, widow
1799 ,, Bellew, Dublin, spinster
1800 ,, Catherine, Dublin, spinster
1766 ,, Howard, Mt. Howard, co. Wexford, gent.
1682 ,, James, Casinstown, clk.
1801 ,, John Howard, Douglas, Isle of Man, esq.
1588 **Kyfte,** Nicholas, an Irishman then in Portugal, and proved then
1723 **Kyle,** Hugh, Dublin, merchant
1765 ,, Samuel, Dublin, gent.

—L—

1739 **Labarte,** Bartholomew, Clonmel, co. Tipperary, merchant
1781 ,, Frances, Clonmel, co. Tipperary, widow [gent.
1767 ,, John, Clonmel, co. Tipperary,
1809 ,, Joseph M., Clonmel town, atty.
1726 **La Baslme,** Gaspard
1728 **Labat,** Andrew
1763 ,, Susanna, Dublin
1721 **De Laboissiere,** John, Portarlington, esq.
1762 **Laborde,** John, par. of Lea, Queen's co., esq. (Copy)
1734 **Labrousse,** John Poisson, Portarlington, esq.
1786 **Lacelles,** Frances, Dublin, widow [See LASCELLES.]
1759 **Lachappel,** Mary
1703 **De La Cherois,** Nicholas, major in ld. Lifford's regt. of foot
1806 **Lackey,** John, commander of the "St. Vincent" cutter (Copy)
1707 ,, Robert, Ballykealy, co. Carlow, farmer [See LECKY.]
1780 **Lacky,** John, Kilkenny city, esq.
1805 ,, Michael, 10th regt. of foot
1733 ,, Thos., Clonmel, co. Tipperary, gent.

1783 **Lacour,** Mary, Rathvilly, co. Carlow, shopkeeper
1735 **Lacy,** Andrew, Crooked Staff, Dubl., clothier
1773 ,, Bridget
1802 ,, David, Fortmoy, co. Tipperary, gent.
1766 ,, Francis, Dublin, gent.
1773 ,, James, Cornmarket, Dublin, hosier
1801 ,, Margaret, city of Limerick, widow
1733 ,, Mary, *alias* **Comerford,** relict of capt. John L., co. Limerick
1755 ,, Mathew, Dublin, merchant
1735 ,, Michl., Ballinderry, co. Meath, gent.
1742 ,, Michael, suburbs of Dublin, weaver
1804 ,, Nicholas, Bride-street, Dubl., grocer [gent.
1741 ,, Patrick, Rathcahill, co. Limk.,
1786 ,, Patk., Newport, co. Tipperary, land surveyor
1750 ,, William, Lissurelin, co. Limk.
1787 **Ladavize,** Theresa, Dublin city
1672 **Ladd,** Ellinor, Fatleg, co. Waterford, spinster
1675 ,, Henry, Dublin, gent.
1771 **Ladeveze,** Anthony, late a lieut.-col. of foot
1804 **Ladevieze,** John, Dublin city, esq.
1809 **Ladley,** Dorcus, Bridgefoot-street, Dublin, spinster
1811 ,, Thomas, Bridgefoot-st., Dubl., publican
1800 **Ladly,** William, Dublin, fish dealer
1686 **Ladyman,** John, Swallowfield, Berkshire, gent.
1800 ,, Mary
1665 ,, Richard, Dublin, late of London, linendraper
1684 ,, Samuel, D.D., vicar of Clonmel, and archdeacon of Limerick
1614 **Laffan,** Edward, Ballythomas, co. Tipperary, gent.
1607 ,, Jas., Graystown, co. Tipperary, esq.
1662 ,, Richard, Newtown, co. Tip., esq.
1777 ,, Thomas, Kilkenny, gent.
1729 **Lafite,** Mathew, Dublin, esq.
1723 **Lafortelle,** Cæsar, Dublin, gent.
1779 **Lafranchina,** Philip
1805 **Lahey,** Valentine, Cashel city
1779 **Lahy,** Henry, Ahakellmore, co. Cavan, gent.
1767 ,, John, Tircullen, co. Cavan
1800 ,, John, Williamstown, co. Westmeath, gent.

1771 **Lahy,** Joseph, quarter-master of the 14th regt. dragoons
1803 ,, Richard, Kilkenny, linen and woollen draper [See LEAHY.]
1787 **Laidman,** Mark, Dubl., stonecutter
1786 **Laird,** Francis, Dublin, merchant
1787 ,, Jas., Newtownards, co. Down, innkeeper
1648 **Lake,** Edward, Dublin, alderman
1648 ,, Elizabeth, Chester, widow of alderman Edward Lake
1727 ,, Ezekiel, Holycross, co. Tip., gent.
1721 ,, Francis, Dublin, esq.
1697 ,, James, London, gent.
1685 ,, Peter, Dublin, gent.
1713 ,, Thomas, London, esq. (Copy)
1789 **Laleman,** Peter, Dublin, esq.
1792 **Lally,** Bartholomew, Galway, baker
1782 ,, James, Conagher, co. Galway
1809 **Lalor,** Alice, Cork city, widow
1709 ,, Darby, Killough, co. Tipperary, gent.
1673 ,, Denis, Dublin, gent.
1729 ,, Elizabeth, wife to Thomas L., Dublin, barber surgeon
1804 ,, James, St. Stephen's-green, Dublin, esq.
1807 ,, Jas., Clonnemuckoge, co. Tip., esq.
1728 ,, John, Munny, Queen's co., farmer
1773 ,, John, Ballinure, co. Wicklow, farmer [esq.
1785 ,, John, Long Orchard, co. Tip., esq.
1802 ,, John, formerly of Oldcastle, co. Tipperary, but late of Dublin, gent.
1809 ,, John, lieut. in the 73rd regt. of foot (Ex.)
1810 ,, John, Mount Landscape, co. Dublin, attorney
1774 ,, Mary, widow of Mathias L., Killough, co. Tipperary, esq.
1774 ,, Mary, Dublin, widow
1796 ,, Mathias, Killough, co. Tipper., gent.
1798 ,, Nicholas, Ballyragget, co. Kilkenny
1779 ,, Patrick, Forrest, Queen's co., farmer
1799 ,, Peter, Mountrath, Queen's co.
1658 ,, Teighe, Tully, co. Down [VII. 113
1783 ,, William, Clonsoughy, Queen's co., farmer
1784 ,, William Digby, Maryborough, Queen's co. [See LAWLER, LAWLOR.]

1733 **Lamalquiere,** Lewis, Portarlington, esq.
1733 **Lamaria,** Anthony, Mount Aaron, co. Carlow, esq.
1803 **Lamb,** Edward, Naas, co. Kildare
1805 ,, Francis, Maynooth, co. Kildare
1801 ,, Hall, Dublin city, esq.
1780 ,, James, Dublin, merchant
1749 ,, Jane, Dublin, widow
1703 ,, John, Waterford, alderman
1715 ,, John, Dublin, mariner
1803 ,, John, Ballingarry, co. Tipper., gent.
1794 ,, Maria
1701 ,, Thomas, formerly of Jamaica, now of London, merchant (Copy)
1810 ,, Timothy, Castlebar, co. Mayo
1724 ,, Wm., Willow Grove, co. Wicklow, esq.
1737 ,, William, Dublin, chandler
1764 ,, William, Dublin
1804 ,, William F., Leeson-st., Dublin, esq.
1626 **Lamballs,** John, Dublin
1735 **Lambart,** Ellinor, Dublin, spinster
1783 ,, Gustavus, Beaupark, co. Meath, esq.
1786 ,, Mary, spinster
1762 ,, Ralph, Dublin, esq.
1796 ,, Richard, major of 3rd regt. of foot
1798 ,, Sophia, Dublin, spinster [See LAMBERT.]
1698 **Lambe,** Benjamin, Waterford
1788 ,, Elizabeth, widow
1765 ,, John, Dublin, esq.
1738 ,, Margaret, spinster
1716 ,, Richard, Dublin, chandler and merchant
1800 **Lambermont,** John, Dublin, shoemaker
1734 **Lambert,** Anne, Dublin, widow
1748 ,, Arran, gent.
1660 ,, Chas., earl of Cavan [VIII. 120
1786 ,, Charles, Cregclare, co. Galway, esq. [esq.
1786 ,, Charles, Beaupark, co. Meath,
1689 ,, Elizabeth, St. Werburgh's par., Dublin, widow
1754 ,, Emilia, Painstown, co. Meath, spinster
1715 ,, Francis, Ballyclare, King's co., gent.
1723 ,, Geo., Downpatrick, co. Down, esq.
1775 ,, Hamilton (Proved in 1789)
1789 ,, Hamilton, lieut.-gen.
1789 ,, Henry, Grafton-street, Dublin, hosier

1700 **Lambert**, James, Carnagh, co.Wexford, gent.
1799 ,, Jas., Narrow-water, co. Down
1688 ,, John, Ross, co. Wexford
1714 ,, John, Athy, co. Kildare, gent.
1749 ,, John, Kilcroney, co. Wicklow, gent.
1784 ,, John, one of the Town Clerks of Dublin
1796 ,, John, Millfort, co. Galway, esq.
1799 ,, sir John, Duke-st., Manchester-square, bart. (Copy)
1781 ,, Lewes Jones, Dublin, esq.
1745 ,, Margaret, Dublin, widow
1740 ,, Montague, Dublin, esq.
1711 ,, Oliver, Painstown, co. Meath, esq.
1730 ,, Patrick, Carnagh, co. Wexford, gent.
1808 ,, Patrick, Carnagh, co. Wexford, esq.
1763 ,, Peter, Dublin, merchant
1777 ,, Richard, Rathdrum, co. Wicklow, gent.
1751 ,, Robt., Dunlady, co. Down, esq.
1782 ,, Robert, Stafford-street, Dublin, gent.
1661 ,, Thomas, Dromiskin, co. Louth, clerk
1770 ,, Thomas, Kevin-street,co.Dubl., linendraper   [esq.
1797 ,, Thos., Summerhill, co. Galway,
1810 ,, Thomas, Callan, co. Kilkenny
1780 ,, Walter, Cregclare, co. Galway, esq.
1808 ,, William, Ballyhack, co. Wexford
       [See LAMBART, LAMPORT.]
1607 **Lambine**, Thomas, Shian, Queen's co., gent. (Copy)
1735 **Lamenes**, Peter, Dublin, gent.
1808 **Lamie**, John, Edendork, co.Tyrone, esq.
1700 **DeLamisecle**, John Favar-suir, native of Peulawienrens in France
1698 **Lamly**, John, Athy, gent.
1737 **Lamolliere**, lieut. Stephen, Dublin
1774 **Lamprey**, George, Dublin, cutler
1796 ,, Jane, Dublin, widow
1790 ,, Richard, Dublin, gent.
1747 **Lamport**, John, Dublin, mariner
1650 ,, Patrick, Dublin
       [See LAMBERT.]
1633 **Lamporte**, Thomas, Wexford, merchant
1800 **Lanauze**, George, Kill, co. Cavan, esq.
1729 **Lancaster**, Charles, par. of Hawkhurst, Kent, gent.

1632 **Lancaster**, John, clerk, precentor of Lismore (Copy)
1579 ,, Josias, Drogheda
1585 ,, Thos., archbp. of **Armagh**, q.v.
1768 ,, rev. Thomas, Suckville, co. Roscommon, clerk
1691 **Lance**, col. Thomas, Dunboe, co. Londonderry
1763 **Land**, Charles
1658 **Landen**, Edward, Clare, esq. [VIII. 60
1783 **Lander**, John, Youghal, co. Cork
1767 **Landers**, Robert, Dublin, hatter
1738 **Landey**, Elias, capt. in genl. Dormer's regt. of foot
1798 ,, Frances, Inch, co. Dublin, widow
1758 **Landre**, Elizabeth, widow of Mr. Peter L.
1767 ,, John, par. St. Giles, Middlesex, statuary (Copy)
1747 ,, Peter, Dublin, gardener
1791 ,, Susanna, Merrion-row, Dublin, spinster
1725 **Landrean**, Peter, Dublin, esq.
1741 **Landy**, John,Thurles, co.Tipperary, merchant
1795 ,, Thomas, Balbriggan, co.Dubl., publican and dealer
1788 **Lane**, Abraham, Cork, clothier
1783 ,, Alice, *alias* **Jones**
1725 ,, Ambrose, Lane's-park, co. Tipperary, esq.
1783 ,, Ambrose, Lanesborough, co. Tipperary, gent.
1790 ,, Ann, Drogheda, widow
1791 ,, Ann, Cork, widow
1780 ,, Dorothea, Dublin, widow
1657 ,, Elizabeth, widow [VI. 110
1706 ,, Francis, capt. in lieut.-gen. Langston's regt. of horse
1810 ,, Freeman,capt. in the 30th regt. of foot
1732 ,, Gawen, Cork, merchant
1758 ,, George, Ballylackin, co. Cork, gent.
1792 ,, James, Dublin, esq.
1695 ,, John, Cork, clothworker
1750 ,, John, Rathline, co. Longford, esq.
1786 ,, John, par. St. Paul, Covent Garden, gent. (Copy)
1810 ,, Martin, Galway town
1784 ,, Mary, widow
1774 ,, Mathew, Rosbercon, co. Kilkenny, gent.
1807 ,, Nicholas F., Dublin, attorney-at-law
1790 ,, Richard, Ballyscanlan, co. Limerick, esq.

1774 **Lane**, Robert, Cork, esq.
1786 ,, Sarah (Copy)
1667 ,, Thomas, Cloghonane,co.Tipp., gent.
1700 ,, Thomas, Dromagh, co. Cork, esq.
1673 ,, William, Cattiganstown, co. Tipperary, gent.
1754 ,, William, Cork, merchant
1777 ,, William, Drogheda, esq.
1778 ,, William, Dublin, attorney-at-law
1799 ,, William, Cork city, burgess
1805 ,, William, Cork city, attorney
1628 **Lanes**, Ann, Kilcorr, King's co., widow
1735 **Lanesborough**, Brinsley, lord viscount
1780 ,, Brinsley, earl of
1760 ,, Catherine, dow. viscountess
1721 ,, Frances, dow. viscountess (Copy)
1683 ,, George, lord viscount. (Ex.)
1768 ,, Humphrey, earl of
1724 ,, James, lord viscount (Copy)
1738 ,, Mary, dow. viscountess (Copy)
1806 ,, the rt. hon. Robert Herbert, earl of
1788 **Lang**, Alexander, Dublin, mercht.
1790 ,, George, Eccles-street, Dublin, merchant
1793 ,, Hugh, Carnmeen, co. Down
1788 ,, James, Dublin
1683 ,, John, Ballygillgane, co. Sligo, gent.
[See LAYNG.]
1788 **Langan**, Andrew, Church-street, Dublin, tallow chandler
1745 ,, James, Dublin, merchant
1804 ,, James, Church-street, Dublin
1766 ,, John, Ballykeel, co. Kilkenny
1810 ,, John, Maynooth, co. Kildare
1794 ,, Judith, Dublin, widow
1755 ,, Nicholas, Rudder, co. Meath
1750 ,, Patrick, Dublin, cooper
1758 ,, Patrick, Dublin
1802 ,, Patrick, Rath, co. Meath, farmer
1604 ,, Robert, Dublin, tailor
1697 **Langdale**, John, Dublin, haber-dasher
1657 **Langdall**, Christopher, Drumboe, co. Donegal, esq. **[VI.** 135
1741 **Lange**, George, Derrydrumuck, co. Down
1671 **Langer**, John, Youghal, alderman
1798 **Langford**, Anne, Tullaha, co. Lim., spinster
1716 ,, sir Arthur, Summerhill, co. Meath, bart.

1768 **Langford**, Elizabeth, Kells, co. Limerick, widow
1639 ,, sir Hercules,Carrickfergus,knt.
1683 ,, sir Hercules, Summerhill, co. Meath, bart.
1798 ,, Hercules, lord viscount
1755 ,, John, Kells, co. Limerick
1782 ,, John, Castleconway, co. Kerry
1692 ,, dame Mary, widow of sir H. L., Summerhill, bart.
1787 ,, Richard, Kilkenny city, apoth-ecary
1738 ,, Robert, Banemore, co. Limk., gent.
1726 ,, Susana, par. St. Paul, Covent Garden, spinster (Copy)
1713 ,, Theophilus, Kinsale, esq.
1719 ,, William,Gardenfield,co.Limk., esq.
1708 **Langham**, Ann, St. Bridget's par., Dublin, widow
1701 ,, Joseph, Dublin, victualler
1697 **Langharne**, James, Pentoden,Pem-brokeshire, gent. (Copy)
1693 ,, John, the elder, Pontevaughan, Pembrokeshire (Copy)
1793 **Langhelt**, John, Summerhill, Dublin
1733 **Langley**, Anne, Rathmacon, co. Kilkenny, spinster
1723 ,, Charles, Lisnabrook, co. Tipp., esq.
1793 ,, Charles, Lisnamrock, co.Tipp., esq.
1724 ,, Daniel, student in Trin. College, Dublin
1793 ,, Dorcas, Dublin, spr.
1793 ,, Edmond, Dublin, surgeon
1666 ,, Henry, Kilmaninge, co. Water-ford, esq.
1679 ,, Henry, Dublin, gent.
1761 ,, Herbert, Dublin, gent.
1759 ,, James, Dublin, merchant
1739 ,, John, Kilkenny, gent.
1748 ,, John, Dublin, merchant
1731 ,, Mary, Bolehall, Warwickshire, widow
1803 ,, Roger, Fort Lewis, co. Cork, gent.
1738 ,, Saml., Bolehall, Warwickshire (Copy)
1803 ,, Sophias, Brittas
1770 **Langrish**, Robt., Knocktopher, co. Kilkenny, esq.
1741 **Langrishe**, Anne, Waterford, wid.
1803 ,, dame Hannah
1811 ,, sir Hercules, Dublin city, bart.
1717 **Langston**, lieut.-gen. Francis, par. St. James, Westminster (Copy)

1794 **Langton,** Ann, Birr, King's co.
1660 ,, James, Kilkenny, merchant [**VIII.** 120
1723 ,, John Fitz Robert, Kilkenny, merchant
1750 ,, John, Dublin, esq.
1761 ,, John, Waterford, gent.
1709 ,, Michael, Durrow, co. Kilkenny, ·merchant
1737 ,, Michael, Kilkenny, merchant
1799 ,, Philip, Birr, King's co.
1765 **Langwell,** Mathew, Killowen par., co. Londonderry, farmer (Copy)
1805 **Lanigan,** Valentine, Charlestown, co. Kilkenny [See LANGAN.]
1808 **Lanphiere,** Sarah, wife to Thomas L., Cashel
1702 **Lansden,** Charles, Dublin, butcher
1712 **Lantilhae,** Henry, Portarlington, Queen's co., esq.
1744 **Lanty,** Richard, Monasterevan, co. Kildare
1737 ,, Thomas, Coolnefeeragh, co. Kildare, innkeeper
1625 **Lany,** John, Dublin, alderman
1794 **Lapham,** Henry, Chambers-street, Dublin
1724 **La Piere,** Stephen, Dublin, mercht.; native of Languedoc
1765 **Lapierre,** George, Dublin, mercht.
1785 **Laplant,** Moses, Cork city, surgeon (Copy)
1714 **Lapp,** John, Waterford, merchant
1732 ,, Stephen, Waterford, esq.
1782 **Laracey,** John, Ballysallagh, co. Kilkenny
1648 **Larcan,** Laurence, Duncannon, gt.
1634 ,, Peter, Dublin, mercht. [**IV.** 112 [See LARKIN.]
1804 **Large,** Ellinor, Newport, co. Tipperary, widow
1678 ,, Thomas, Ballynamoe, co. Tipperary, gent.
1782 **Largon,** John, Carlow town, carpenter
1792 **Lark,** Robert, Kilcoony, King's co., farmer
1767 ,, Thos., Birr, King's co., farmer
1772 **Larkan,** Catherine, Dublin, widow
1634 **Larke,** Thos., Dublin, gent., Messenger of the Council Table, and one of the Pursuivants
1661 **Larkin,** John, London, fishmonger
1797 ,, John, parish of Coolock
1803 ,, John, Dublin, chandler
1805 ,, Mary, Dublin city
1801 ,, William, Dublin, poulterer [See LARCAN.]

1768 **Larkon,** William, Enniscorthy, co. Wexford, victualler
1753 **Larn,** Daniel, Cork, tallow chandler
1702 **Larquier,** James Bord, a lieut.-col., pensioned (Copy)
1744 **Lartigue,** Sarah, Dublin
1797 **Lascelles,** Rowley, Hammersmith, Middlesex, esq. [See LACELLES.]
1768 **Lassell,** Isaac, Dublin, merchant
1742 **Lassere,** Elias, Cork, merchant
1799 **Latande,** Angelica Henrietta, Portarlington
1780 **Latchford,** Michael, Nicholas-st., Dublin, currier
1769 ,, Thomas, Kilcock, co. Kildare
1600 **Laten,** John, Naas, co. Kildare, gt.
1796 **Lateurnell,** John, Turveyhill, co. Dublin
1746 **Latham,** James, Dublin, spinner
1806 ,, John, Cork city, esq. [esq.
1738 ,, William, Brookend, co. Tyrone, [See LEATHAM, LETHUM.]
1766 **Latimer,** David, Birr, King's co., merchant
1665 ,, Hugh, Pagestown, co. Meath, gent.
1550 **Latnar,** Christopher, Bankeworth, Wiltshire
1745 **Latouche,** David Digge, Dublin, banker
1785 ,, David, Dublin, banker
1810 **La Touche,** John, Harristown, co. Kildare, esq.
1804 ,, Wm. Diggs, Dublin city, esq.
1763 **Latouches,** James Diggs, Dublin, merchant
1781 **La Trobe,** Henry, Dublin, gent.
1735 **Lattin,** Alice, Dublin, spinster
1788 ,, Ambrose, formerly of Dublin, but at Zell, in Germany
1800 ,, Catherine, widow
1785 ,, Geo., Morristown, co. Kildare
1790 ,, John, Multifarnham, co. Westmeath, land surveyor
1700 **Latton,** dame Dorothy, wife to Geo. L., Berkshire, esq. (Copy)
1598 **Latware,** Richard, D.D. (No date)
1790 **Lauder,** Margaret, Dublin, widow
1740 ,, Robert, Moyclare, King's co., gent.
1698 ,, William, Drumalaigue, co. Leitrim, esq. [See LAWDER.]
1728 **Laueaute,** John, Dame-st., sub. of Dublin, wigmaker
1742 **Laughlin,** Anne, widow of captain Thomas L.
1807 ,, Arthur, Dublin, shoemaker (Copy)

1790 **Laughlin**, Bryan, Terenure, co. Dublin, publican
1749 ,, Brewster, Dublin, esq.
1771 ,, Catherine, Dublin, widow
1656 ,, George, soldier [**VI.** 34
1774 ,, Jacob, Dublin, lace weaver
[See LOGHLAN, LOUGLIN.]
1730 **Launders**, Edward, Clonmel, co. Tipperary, gent.
1757 ,, Jane, Clonmel, co. Tipp., spr.
1570 **Laundy**, Thomas
1808 **Laurenson**, Edward, lieut. in the 89th regt. of foot
1794 ,, Robert, Rathmoyle, Queen's co., esq.
[See LAWRENSON.]
1769 **Laurent**, John, Dublin, merchant
[See LAWRENT.]
1723 **Lautan**, Tristan, Dublin, gent.
[See LAWTON.]
1666 **Lavallen**, Patrick, Cork, alderman
1681 **Lavallin**, James, Waterstown, co. Cork, esq. (Ex.)
1725 ,, Melichor, Waterstown, co. Cork, esq.
1751 ,, Melshor, Coolowen, North Lib. of Cork, esq.
1686 ,, Patrick, Waterstown, co. Cork, esq.
1789 ,, Peter, Waterstown, co. Cork, esq.
1771 ,, Phillip, Waterpark, co. Cork, esq.
1709 **La Vally**, James, captain in brig. Brooks' regt. of foot
1734 **Laveaute**, Elizabeth, Booterstown, co. Dublin, widow
1716 **Lavender**, Richard, Dublin, currier
1763 **Laverock**, Thomas, Ballyboughlin, King's co., gent.
1811 **Laverton**, Henry, Naas town, shopkeeper
1735 **Lavery**, Eugene, Dublin, gent.
1745 ,, Henry, Lib. of Limerick, linendraper
[See LAVORY.]
1768 **Lavill**, Bernard, Dublin, tailor
1728 **Lavit**, Joseph, Cork, merchant
1770 ,, Nathaniel, Cork, gent.
1758 ,, Walter, Cork, esq.
1779 **Lavitt**, Christiana, Cork, spr.
1780 **Lavory**, Elizb. *alias* **Blenerhasset**, Riddlestown, co. Limerick, widow
[See LAVERY.]
1762 **Laurdy**, Edward
1798 **Law**, Aughry, Castlewellan
1797 ,, Elizabeth, Belfast, co. Antrim, widow
1808 ,, Francis, Cork city, clk.

1765 **Law**, George, Dublin, gent.
1802 ,, George, Banville, co. Down, gent.
1795 ,, James, Edenderry, co. Down
1810 ,, John, bishop of **Elphin**, q.v.
1790 ,, Michael, Raphoe, co. Don., M.D.
1801 ,, Richard, Dublin
1789 ,, Robert, Dublin, D.D.
1793 ,, rev. William, rector of Killea, co. Donegal
[See LAWE.]
1657 **Lawcock**, Chris., trooper [**VI.** 184
1775 **Lawder**, Angel, Dublin, spinster
1767 ,, David, Ballysheen, co. Kerry, esq.
1759 ,, Dorcas, Dublin, wid. (see 1761)
1737 ,, Elizabeth, widow
1801 ,, Frederick, Mough, co. Leitrim
1750 ,, James, Kilmore, co. Roscommon, esq.
1779 ,, James, Kilmore, co. Roscommon, esq.
1790 ,, Jane, Dublin, widow
1797 ,, Lancellot, Clover Hill, co. Leitrim, esq.
1803 ,, Phebe, Charlestown, spinister
1801 ,, Townley, Dublin city
1715 ,, William, Bonybeg, co. Leitrim, esq.
[See LAUDER, LOWTHER.]
1786 **Lawe**, Robert, Dublin, esq.
[See LAW.]
1780 **Lawellin**, rev. Joshua, Dublin
1794 **Lawler**, Dennis, Back-lane, Dublin, gent.
1740 ,, John, Dublin, linendraper
1808 ,, John
1791 ,, Luke, Timolin, co. Kildare
1807 ,, Terence, Garrane, co. Waterford, esq.
[See LALOR.]
1596 **Lawles**, John, vicar of Balscadden
1726 ,, Mary, *alias* **Burke**, Kilkenny, widow
1686 ,, Major Patrick, Kinsale, of col. Justin M'Carty's regt.
1779 ,, Patrick, Dublin, banker
1663 ,, Richard, Talbot's Inch, co. city Kilkenny
1799 ,, Richard, Dublin, esq.
1627 ,, Walter, Kilkenny, alderman
1738 **Lawless**, James, Shankill, co. Dub., gent.
1795 ,, John, Dublin city, woollen draper
1783 ,, Luke, Eccles-street, co. Dub., gent.
1744 ,, Mary, Shankill, co. Dub., wid.
1776 ,, Michael, Dublin, brewer

1778 **Lawless**, Richard, Dublin, currier
1779 ,, Robert, Dublin, esq.
1772 **Lawlor**, James, Killarney, co. Kerry, M.D.
[See LALOR.]
1697 **Lawndy**, Agnes, wid. of Edward L., Youghal, ald.
1686 ,, Edward, Youghal, merchant
1730 ,, Edward, Muckeridge, co. Cork, esq.
1798 **Lawrance**, Alexander, Coleraine, merchant
1721 ,, Esther, Dublin, widow
1737 **Lawrence**, Catherine, Dublin, wid.
1782 ,, Charles, Ballycraig, co. Antrim
1734 ,, Dorothy, . Whitefriar-street, Dublin, widow [meath
1734 ,, Dorothy, Rossmead, co. West-
1694 ,, Elizabeth, London, spinster
1768 ,, Frances, *alias* **M'Naughton**, widow of Thomas Worsop L., late capt. in Handasyde's regt.
1721 ,, Henry, Woodfield, co. West-meath, gent.
1781 ,, Henry, Waringstown, co. Down
1725 ,, George, Whitehaven, Cumber-land, mariner (Copy)
1707 ,, James, Lazyhill, Dub., mariner
1804 ,, John, Carrigacrow, co. Wick-low, farmer
1747 ,, Nicholas, mariner
1709 ,, Peter, Dublin, bookseller
1759 ,, admiral Peter, Woodfield, co. Galway
1684 ,, Richard, Dublin, esq.
1691 ,, Richard, junior, Dublin, gent. (Copy)
1757 ,, Robert, Dublin, cordwainer
1786 ,, Samuel, Back-lane, Dublin, dealer [cooper
1796 ,, Samuel, Tucker's-row, Dublin,
1721 ,, Thomas, Lazyhill, Dublin, mariner
1762 ,, Thomas Worsopp, Warings-town, co. Down, esq.
1809 ,, Thomas D., Lawrencetown, co. Down, esq.
[See LAWRANCE.]
1799 **Lawrenson**, Alice, spinster
1810 ,, Anna, or Joanna, Stradbally, Queen's co.
1797 ,, Edward, Rathmoyle, Queen's co., gent
1766 ,, Lawrence, Dublin, gent.
1794 ,, Richard, Archerstown, Queen's co.
1807 ,, William, Rosebrook, Queen's county, esq.
[See LAURENSON.]

1767 **Lawrent**, Lewis, Dublin, merchant
[See LAURENT.]
1795 **Lawson**, Anne, Dublin widow
1784 ,, Endymion, Dublin, gent.
1719 ,, Epaphroditus, Drumin, co. Cavan, gent.
1734 ,, Henry, esq. capt. His Majy's. ship the "Dublin" yacht
1759 ,, John, D.D., senior fellow of Trin. Coll., Dub.
1738 ,, Joseph, Dublin, carpenter
1803 ,, Mary, Newry, co. Down, spr.
1787 ,, Roger, Newry, co. Down, tallow chandler
1726 **Lawton**, Hugh, Ballybeg, co. Cork, farmer
1788 ,, Hugh, Castlejane, Liberties of Cork, esq.
1670 ,, John, Birr, King's county
1773 ,, John, Cork, merchant
1809 ,, Leslie, Dublin city, gent.
1804 ,, Richard, Cork city, merchant
1758 ,, Treyer, Cork, merchant
[See LAUTAN.]
1712 **Layng**, Henry, Coola, co. Sligo, gent.
1756 ,, James, Gartmarderos, gent.
1677 ,, John, Killashandra, co. Cavan, clk.
[See LANG.]
1758 **Laynge**, Henry, Clones, co. Mon.
1774 **Layngue**, Margaret, Dublin, wid.
1629 **Lea**, Humfrye, par. Erigle, co. Tyrone, gent. [gent.
1780 ,, John, Philipsburgh, co. Dublin,
1752 ,, Mary, *alias* **Thomas**, wife to John L., Cashel, gent.
1598 ,, Nicholas FitzNicholas, Water-ford, merchant [I. 92
1805 ,, Patrick, Blackrath, co. Kildare, farmer
1781 ,, Ruth, Dublin, widow
1598 ,, Thomas, St. Patrick's-st., joiner
1672 ,, Thomas, esq., keeper of the Council Chamber
[See LEE.]
1656 **Leadbeater**, Robert, Dublin, gent.
[VI. 58
1727 ,, William, Dublin, cardmaker
[See LEDBETTER.]
1768 **Leader**, Edward, Mt. L., co. Cork, gent.
1738 ,, Henry, Tullig, co. Cork, gent.
1771 ,, Henry, Tullig, co. Cork, esq.
1809 ,, Henry, Tullig, co. Cork, esq.
1731 ,, John, Mt. L., co. Cork, esq.
1766 ,, John, Keal, co. Cork
1801 ,, John, Baggot-st., Dublin, esq.
1802 ,, William, Bedford-row, Middle-sex, coachmaker (Copy)

1793 **Leahy**, David, Bettyville, co. Limk. farmer
[See LAHY.]
1752 **Leake**, Elizabeth, *alias* **Newhouse**, Cloughjordan, co. Tipperary, gentlewoman
1805 ,, George, Rathkeale Abbey, co. Limerick, esq.
1740 ,, John, Queensborough, co. Louth, tide waiter
1743 ,, John, Dublin, merchant
1727 ,, Pierce, Newcastle, co. Limk., gent.
1804 ,, Richard, Rathmines, co. Dubl., attorney
1808 **Leakin**, Jane, Thomas-st., Dublin city
1731 **Leane**, Timothy, Dublin, gabbard owner
1810 **Leany**, Christr., barony of Ratoath, co. Meath
1672 **Leary**, Cornelius
1799 ,, Lucius, Kinsale, co. Cork, gent.
1788 ,, Thomas, Kinsale, co. Cork, gent.
1790 **Leatham**, Bossell, Manor Waterhouse, co. Fermanagh esq.
1783 ,, William
[See LATHAM.]
1767 **Leathem**, Hugh, Dublin, merchant
1738 **Leathes**, Margaret, Hillsborough, co. Down, widow
1746 ,, Robert, Dundalk, co. Louth, gent.
1743 ,, Thomas, Waterford
1730 ,, William, par. St. George, Westminster, Middlesex, esq. (Copy)
1790 **Leathley**, Elizabeth
1757 ,, Joseph, Dublin, bookseller
1770 ,, Joseph
1810 ,, Joseph, Dublin city, esq.
1766 ,, Joshua, Dublin, woollen draper
1634 **Leatt**, Nichls., London, ironmonger
[**IV.** 47
1804 **Leavens**, Robert, Churchtown, co. Louth
1791 **Leavy**, Bryan, Killore, co. Westmeath, farmer
1763 **Leazenby**, Thomas, Dublin, shoemaker
1810 **Lecale**, rt. hon. Charles, lord baron
1741 **Leckey**, Joyce, Kilmeany, co. Carlow, widow
1800 **Leckly**, Sally
1774 **Lecky**, Catherine, Londonderry, widow
1790 ,, Holland, Armagh city, esq.
1809 ,, Holland
1796 ,, Hugh, Agwy, co. Londonderry

1794 **Lecky**, James, Drumcondra-road, co. Dublin, merchant
1796 ,, James, Killrork, co. Carlow
1797 ,, John, Ballykealy, co. Carlow
1793 ,, Thomas, Derry city, esq.
1776 ,, William, Kilmarney, co. Carlow
[See LACKEY.]
1773 **Lecock**, Margaret, *alias* **Gaggin**, *alias* **Patten**, Limerick
1790 **LeCouf**, Peter, Ballygall, co. Dubl., gent.
1788 **Ledbetter**, Joseph, Bandon, esq.
1793 ,, Joseph, Bandon, co. Cork
[See LEADBEATER.]
1787 **Le Despenser**, rt. hon. Francis lord (Copy)
1768 **Ledger**, Richard, Whitehaven, Cumberland, merchant
1754 ,, Wm., Derrinaslin, co. Tipp.
1768 ,, William, Dubl., coal merchant
1793 **Ledlie**, John, Corglasson, co. Tyrone
1806 **Ledsam**, John, Dublin, esq.
1804 ,, Sarah, Dublin city, widow
1782 **Ledwich**, Edward, LL.D., Dean of Kildare
1590 ,, John, Drogheda, merchant
1633 ,, John, Kenles, merchant
1794 ,, John, Dublin, esq.
1805 ,, Matthew, Scholarstown, co. Dublin
1797 ,, Susana, Dublin, widow
1804 ,, Thos., Old Court, co. Wicklow
1804 ,, rev. William
1810 ,, rev. Wm., P.P., Rathfarnham
[See LUTWITCH.]
1676 **Ledwiche**, Pierce, Corregarrowe or Potlelare, co. Roscommon, gent.
1801 **Ledwidge**, Dennis, Killarney, co. Wicklow, farmer
1766 ,, Edmund, the Coombe, Dublin, grocer
1767 ,, James
1801 ,, Thomas, Trim, co. Meath
1733 **Ledwitch**, James, New-row, co. Dublin, shoemaker
1651 **Ledwitche**, Thomas, Gaffrice, co. Meath
1733 **Ledwith**, Alice, Dublin, widow
1796 ,, Arthur, the 108th regiment of foot
1752 ,, Lawrence, Athboy, gent.
1709 **Ledwitt**, Redmond, Dublin, gent.
1805 **Lee**, Alexander, Ardee, co. Louth
1768 ,, Anthony, Dublin, gent.
1745 ,, Benjamin, Merrion, co. Dublin, gent.
1786 ,, Benjamin, Merrion-st., but late of Bath

1801	**Lee**, Catherine, Dublin, spinster
1726	,,	Edward, Barnarusacully, co. Tipperary, gent.
1730	,,	Francis, Dublin, gent.
1778	,,	Garrett, Cootehill, co. Cavan, gent.
1772	,,	George, Newry, co. Down, gent.
1713	,,	Henry, Dublin, merchant
1692	,,	James, Cadiz, merchant, native of Waterford (Copy)
1737	,,	James, Chequer-lane, Dublin
1767	,,	John, par. St. Bridget, Dublin
1779	,,	John, Barnadown, co.Wexford, farmer
1787	,,	John, Navan, co. Meath, farmer
1790	,,	John, Newry, co. Armagh, gent.
1806	,,	John, Philipsburgh-lane, co. Dublin, gent.
1808	,,	John
1682	,,	Margaret, *alias* **Power**, *alias* **Strange**, widow
1746	,,	Margaret, Dublin, esq.
1763	,,	Margaret, Dublin, widow
1791	,,	Michael, Cootehill, co. Cavan
1623	,,	Nicholas Fitzjohn, Waterford, gent.
1804	,,	Phillip, Lattaglochan, co. Cavan, gent.
1708	,,	Richd., Clanderelaw, co. Clare, esq.
1759	,,	Richard, surveyor of excise at Coleraine, co. Derry
1694	,,	Samuel, Dublin, printer
1779	,,	Samuel, Dame-street, gent.
1673	,,	Thomas, Dublin, cook [**XIV**. 150
1720	,,	Thomas, Newmarket, co. Dubl., weaver
1731	,,	Thomas, Dublin, gent.
1756	,,	Thomas, Kilteel co. Kildare, farmer
1795	,,	Thomas, Dublin, gent.
1797	,,	Thomas, Dublin, apothecary
1804	,,	Thos., Tralee, co. Kerry, M.D.
1808	,,	Thos., Dublin city, linen draper
1810	,,	Thos., Springmount, co. Kilk.
1718	,,	William, esq., capt. in brig. Bor's regiment
1763	,,	Wm.,Tanderagee, co. Armagh, linen merchant
1792	,,	rev. William, vicar of Innismagree, co. Leitrim
1802	,,	William, Doneymooney, co. Londonderry [See **Lea**, **Leigh**.]
1801	**Leear**, George, Dublin city, mercht.
1765	,,	John, Glasnevin, late of Dublin, silkweaver

1712	**Leece**, George, Dublin, tailor
1809	**Leech**, Allen, Rosebrook, Queen's co.
1803	,,	Anna Maria, spinster
1754	,,	Thomas, Allestock, co. Palatinate of West Chester, now of Dublin, skinner
1754	,,	Thomas, Dublin, Battleaxe Guards
1680	,,	Walter, Dublin, gent.
1753	,,	Walter, Christchurch-lane, Dublin, felt maker
1701	,,	Wm., Dungannon, co. Tyrone, gent.
1796	,,	William Copperthwaite, Dublin
1708	**Leeds**, Michael, Dublin, merchant
1618	**Leene**, Thomas, Rathmore, dio. of Dublin
1811	**Lees**, sir John, Blackrock, bart.
1719	**Leeson**, rev. Hugh, Dublin, clk.
1811	,,	John, Newcastle, co. Wicklow, publican
1741	,,	Joseph, Dublin, esq.
1802	,,	Joseph, Roundlane, co. Dublin, esq.
1742	,,	Margaret, Dublin, spinster
1784	,,	Michael, Portobello, co. Dubl., merchant
1762	,,	Robert, Dublin, gent.
1690	,,	William, Dublin, merchant
1751	,,	William, counsellor-at-law
1806	,,	William, Newgrove, co. Galway
1798	**Leet**, Ambrose, Dublin, esq.
1808	,,	Rebecca, Dublin city, linen draper
1721	**Le Evique**, Stephen, Dublin
1743	**Lefanu**, Philip, Dublin, esq.
1795	,,	rev. Phil., D.D.
1809	,,	Rebecca, Dublin city, widow
1797	,,	William, Dublin, esq. (Large)
1732	**Le Gaigneur**, David, Dub., mercht.
1778	**Legg**, Alexander, Malone, co. Antrim
1774	,,	Joseph, of the Scotch quarter in Carrickfergus
1770	,,	Robert, Belfast, gent.
1691	**Legge**, Francis, late of Cappagh, co. Tipperary, esq.
1670	,,	William, par. Little Minories, London, esq. (Copy)
1802	**Legh**, Peter, Dublin city
1793	**Legrand**, Catherine
1709	**Le Gras**, Peter, Portarlington, Queen's co.
1629	**Legross**, Thomas, Croswaite, Norfolk, esq. (Copy)
1697	**Lehunt**, George, St. Martin's, town of Haverford West, Pembrokeshire, esq. (Copy)
1688	,,	Mary, Cashel, widow

1772 **Lehunte,** Cathеrine, wife of Thomas L., Dublin, esq.
1799 ,, George, Artramont, co. Wex.ford, esq.
1708 **Le Hunte,** Richard, Kilmacow, co. Kilkenny, gent.
1753 ,, Richard, Lanryan, Pembrokeshire, esq.
1783 ,, Richard, Artramont, co. Wexford, esq.
1775 ,, Thomas, Dublin, esq.
1756 **Leiburn,** Catherine, widow
1743 **Leicester,** sir Frans., Nethortabbey, Cheshire, bart. (Copy)
[See LYSTER.]
1706 **Leigh,** Andrew, Friarstown, co. Kildare, gent.
1810 ,, Arabella, Dublin city, widow
1638 ,, sir Arthur, Fentenagh, co. Tyrone, knt. and bart.
1657 ,, David   [VI. 228
1759 ,, Edward, D.D., treasurer of St. Patrick's, Dublin
1692 ,, Francis, Cullenmore, co. Westmeath, esq.
1727 ,, Francis, Robert, Dublin, esq.
1778 ,, Francis, Drogheda, esq.
1696 ,, Humphrey, Killarney, co. Westmeath, clk.
1729 ,, James, Waterstown, co. Louth, esq.
1733 ,, John, Drogheda, alderman
1738 ,, John, Greenhills, co. Louth, esq.
1758 ,, John, Rosgarland, co. Wexford, esq.
1810 ,, John, Dublin city, esq.
1700 ,, Judith, Dublin, spinster
1788 ,, Judith, Dublin, spinster
1789 ,, Mary, Dublin, widow
1772 ,, Michael, Cullenmore, co. Westmeath
1751 ,, Richard, Cullenmore, co. Westmeath, esq.
1739 ,, Robert
1784 ,, Robert, Dublin, gent.
1803 ,, Robert, Rosgarland, co. Wexford, esq.
1767 ,, Sarah, widow of John L., Greenhills, co. Louth, esq.
1727 ,, rev. Thomas, rector of Haynestown, co. Louth
1737 ,, Thomas, Cullenmore, co. Westmeath, gent.
1796 ,, Thos., Ranelagh-rd., co. Dub., esq. (Copy)
[See LEE.]
1597 **Leighlin,** Richard Merydith, bp. of
1805 **Leighton,** Elizabeth, Bishop-street, Dublin, widow

1685 **Leighton,** sir Ellis, knt., St. Andrew's par., Holborn, London (Copy)
[See LIGHTON.]
1773 **Leinster,** James, duke of
1804 ,, the most noble Wm., duke of
1734 **Leisly,** David, cornet of col. Nevill's dragoons (Copy)
1739 **Leister,** Rachell, Dublin, widow
1804 **Leitrim,** the right hon. Robert, earl of
1786 **Leland,** Henry, Drogheda, alderman
1767 ,, John, Dublin, D.D.
1808 ,, John, Hanover-square, Middlesex (Copy)
1759 ,, Margaret, Dublin, widow
1760 ,, Mary, Drogheda, widow
1743 ,, Ralph, Dublin, glass grinder
1768 ,, Ralph, Branganstown, co. Kildare
1757 ,, Robert, Dublin, glass seller
1708 **Le Large,** Robert, Dublin, mercht.
1773 **Lely,** Edward, Finglas, co. Dublin, esq.   [maker
1765 **Le Maister,** William, Dub., cabinet
1791 **Le Maistre,** Elizabeth, Dublin, spinster
1797 **Lemmon,** Richard, Baltimore town, America (Copy)
1638 **Lemon,** Alice, Dublin, widow
1691 ,, Charles, Dublin, gent.
1637 ,, Henry, Dublin, merchant
1803 ,, Joseph, Lemongrove, co. Westmeath, gent.
1650 ,, Thomas, Dublin, gent.
1628 **Lenagh,** Richard, Clonmel, mercht.
1792 **Lenaghan,** John, Dunfert, co. Kildare
1767 ,, Walter, Dublin, chandler
1797 **Lenahan,** John, Cork-street, Dubl., tanner
1806 **Lendrick,** James, Dublin city, esq.
1780 ,, John, Fort William, co. Antrim
1763 **Lendrum,** George, Cruise, co. Tyrone, esq.
1787 ,, John, capt. in infantry in E. Indies (Copy)
1759 **Lenechan,** William, Beverstown, co. Dublin, farmer
1772 **Lenehan,** John, Calfstown, par. of Carbury, co. Kildare
1746 **Lenim,** Margaret, Dublin, widow
1670 **Lenis,** Christopher, Rathbeggan, co. Meath, farmer
1658 **Lennan,** John, Cahirdangan, co. Galway, gent.
1597 ,, William, Dublin
1795 **Lennergain,** Morgan, Newtown
1662 **Lenning,** Arthur, Downabrasalagh, co. Donegal, gent.

1768 **Lennon**, Anthony, Athlone, co. Roscommon, gent.
1801 ,, Catherine, spinster
1761 ,, Chas., Walshstown, co. Westmeath, gent.
1756 ,, Daniel, Ballinrig, co. Meath
1782 ,, Elizabeth, Mullingar, co. Westmeath, widow
1794 ,, Elizabeth, widow
1748 ,, George, Doonis, co. Westmeath, gent.
1805 ,, James, Laurencetown, co. Galway
1591 ,, John, Dublin, alderman
1742 ,, John, Mullingar, co. Westmeath, gent.
1767 ,, John, Dromerue, co. Monaghan
1803 ,, John, Carlow, gent.
1809 ,, Marcella, Montgomery-street, Dublin
1801 ,, Mathew, R. C. bishop
1553 ,, Patrick, Damaston, co. Dublin
1804 ,, Robert, Kildare, co. Kildare
1784 ,, Rose, Dublin, spinster
1770 ,, Sabina, *alias* **Pierce**, Athlone, widow
1776 ,, Sandys, Liscormuck, co. Longford
1744 ,, Thomas, Cloncullen, co. Roscommon, gent.
1799 ,, Thomas Bunbury, Carlow town
1741 ,, William, Newtown, co. Westmeath, gent.
1798 ,, Wm., Great Downs, co. Westmeath, gent.
1810 ,, William H., ensign in the P.W. regt.
     [See LERMAN.]
1756 **Lennox**, Boyle, Dublin, esq.
1733 ,, Robert, Belfast, merchant
1780 ,, Robert, par. St Paul, Covent Garden, Middlesex, esq. (Copy)
1801 ,, Susanna, Dublin, spinster
1797 **Lenoutre**, Francis, *alias* **Dumullin**
1675 **Lenox**, Wm., the elder, Woohead, Derry
1682 **Lenthall**, Thomas, London, fish merchant
1732 ,, William, Dublin, esq.
1623 **Lenton**, Edward, Kilmainham, esq.
1640 **Leonard**, Alex., Waterford, gent.
1770 ,, Alexander
1778 ,, Arthur, Moren, co. Down
1630 ,, Catherine, *alias* **Ley**, Kilkenny, widow
1785 ,, Christopher, Dublin, baker
1747 ,, Job, Farnees, co. Wicklow
1594 ,, John, Waterford, alderman
1746 ,, John, Carha, co. Galway, gent.

1777 **Leonard**, John, Brownstown, co Kildare, esq.
1786 ,, Manwaring, Castledermot, co. Kildare, gent.
1692 ,, Margt., *alias* **Lee**, Waterford, widow
1805 ,, Margt., Man of War, co. Dublin
1800 ,, Mary, Dublin, spinster
1801 ,, Maurice, Man of War, co. Dubl.
1774 ,, Nicholas, Fordoms-alley, Dubl., weaver
1808 ,, Patrick, Dublin city, gent.
1640 ,, Robert, Waterford, merchant
1791 ,, Stephen, Cloonkall, co.Galway, gent.
1723 **Leplant**, Mary, Dublin, widow
1669 **Lepper**, Andrew, Stranorlar, co. Donegal, gent.
1806 **Lerwe**, Henry
1727 **Lesac**, Peter, Dublin, merchant
1762 **Leslie**, Alex., Aghnaloe, co. Fermanagh, clk.
1794 ,, Alexander
1759 ,, Charles, Dublin, goldsmith
1793 ,, Charles, Cork, esq.
1800 ,, Charles Powell, Dublin, esq.
1790 ,, Edmond, archdeacon of Down
1733 ,, Elizabeth, Castlecoole, co. Fermanagh, widow
1754 ,, rev. Dr. George, Ballyconnell, co. Carlow
1661 ,, Henry, bishop of **Meath**, q. v.
1733 ,, ven. Henry, archdn. of Down
1745 ,, Henry, Markethill, co.Armagh, esq.   [esq.
1786 ,, Henry, Nutfield, co.Fermanagh,
1803 ,, rev. Henry, Tanderagee, co. Armagh, D.D.
1724 ,, James, Tarbat, co. Kerry, esq.
1811 ,, James, Kilbride, co. Dublin
1672 ,, Jane, widow of Henry, late bp. of Meath
1669 ,, John, the elder, par. Donakadie, co. Tyrone
1692 ,, John, the elder, Tukevraghan, co. Tyrone, gent.
1721 ,, v. rev. John, dean of Dromore
1739 ,, John, Strabane, co. Tyrone, esq.
1778 ,, John
1780 ,, Joyce, widow
1765 ,, Julia Henrietta, Henry-street, Dublin, widow
1792 ,, Mary, Kevans port, Dublin, widow
1805 ,, Mathew, Calcutta, in the East Indies
1780 ,, Moses, Dublin, gent.
1773 ,, rev. Peter, Ahoghill, co. Antrim, D.D.

1793 **Leslie,** Peter, Lincoln's Inn, esq. (Copy)
1672 ,, Robert, bishop of **Clogher,** q.v.
1744 ,, Robt., Castle L., co.Monaghan, esq.
1704 **Lesone,** George, Corindolly, co Galway, esq.
1729 **L'Establere,** Rene de la Doupe, Dublin, gent.
1806 **Lester,** Charles, Dorset-st., Dublin
1657 ,, Randall, Dublin, merchant [VI. 160
1783 ,, Samuel [See LYSTER.]
1730 **Lestrange,** Charles, Colemoneen, Queen's co., gent.
1793 ,, Christopher, Dublin
1666 ,, Henry, Moystown, King's co., esq.
1777 **L'Estrange,** Edmund, Keoltown
1774 ,, Henry, Dublin, esq.
1773 ,, John, Keoltown, co. Westmeath, esq.
1810 ,, rev. John, curate of St. Werburgh's par.
1603 ,, dame Margaret, widow of sir Thomas L., knt.
1581 ,, sir Nicholas, knt.
1743 ,, Richard, Frankbrook, co.Westmeath
1747 ,, rev. Robert, Castlepollard, co. Westmeath
1807 ,, Samuel, Larkfield
1762 ,, Susanna, Mullingar, co. Westmeath, spinster
1589 ,, sir Thomas, knight (Dated at Galway)
1655 ,, Thomas, Castle Strange, co. Roscommon, esq. [V. 115
1802 ,, Thomas, Drogheda-st., Dublin
1677 ,, William, Castle Cuffe, Queen's county, esq. (Ex.)
1780 **Letablere,** Blanch
1775 ,, very rev. Daniel, D.D., dean of Tuam
1754 **Letablier,** John, Dublin, goldsmith
1784 **Letch,** rev. Henry, assistant-curate of St. Paul's par., Dublin
1779 **Letherbarrow,** Jane, Drogheda, spinster and merchant
1743 **Lethieullier,** William, Dublin, esq.
1725 **Lethem,** Thomas, Cork, gent. [See LATHAM.]
1770 **Letournell,** Allen, Dublin, gent.
1811 **Lett,** Joshua, Lower Killalagain, co. Wexford
1747 ,, Stephen, Newcastle, gent.
1810 ,, Thomas, Dublin city, widow
1638 **Leveislie,** Thos., St. Mary's Abbey, Dublin, carpenter

1649 **Leventhorpe,** Ralph, late of Dublin, esq. (Copy)
1618 **Leverett,** Wm, Athlone pursuivant of arms
1808 **Leverty,** James, Cuffe-st., Dublin, shopkeeper
1809 **Levesley,** Susanna, Ballyphilip, co. Wicklow
1748 **Levi,** Isaac, Inns-quay, Dublin, merchant
1766 **Levinge,** sir Charles, Waterford, bt.
1802 ,, Elizabeth, Dublin, spinster
1724 ,, sir Richard, bart., Ch. Justice, Common Pleas
1747 ,, sir Richd., Highpark, co. Westmeath, bart.
1783 ,, Richard, Dublin, esq.
1786 ,, sir Richd., High Park, co.Westmeath, bart.
1762 **Levings,** James, Dublin, cooper
1800 **Levingstown,** Alexander, Dublin, accountant
1788 **Levins,** John, Glasmahonogue, co. Dublin, landholder
1810 ,, Thos., Hampstead, co. Dublin, farmer
1749 **Levy,** Abraham, Dublin, merchant
1789 ,, Bartholomew, Dublin, grocer
1721 ,, John, Longford, co. Longford, merchant
1569 **Lewcas,** John, Dublin, alderman [See LUCAS.]
1783 **Lewellin,** Robert, Silvermines, co. Tipperary, esq.
1785 **Lewers,** John, Castleblayney, co. Monaghan
1603 **Lewes,** John, Dublin, merchant
1615 ,, Patrick, Dublin, butcher
1714 **Lewin,** Joseph, Cloghans, co.Mayo, esq.
1810 ,, Robert, Longacre, Middlesex (Ex.)
1797 ,, Thomas, Cloghans, co. Mayo, esq.
1747 **Lewis,** Catherine, Braithwaite-st., Dublin, widow
1718 ,, David, Waterford, alderman
1754 ,, David, Waterford, alderman
1673 ,, Elizabeth, Dublin, widow
1747 ,, Ellinor, wife to Henry L., gent.
1777 ,, Foulkes, Callan, co. Kilkenny, gent.
1729 ,, George, clerk, archdeacon of Meath
1791 ,, George, Galway, burgess
1764 ,, Henry, Aughmacart, Queen's co.
1784 ,, James, Belfast, merchant
1745 ,, John, Dublin, butcher

1784 **Lewis**, John, Hammond-lane, Dublin, glazier
1789 ,, John, Bowbridge, co. Dublin, gent.
1790 ,, John, dean of Ossory (Copy)
1800 ,, John, Donord, co. Wicklow, farmer
1646 ,, Luke, Carlow, maltster
1772 ,, Marcus, Waterford, mercht.
1741 ,, Martha, Dublin, widow
1769 ,, Mary, *alias* **Burne**, *alias* **Saul**, Athy, co. Kildare, widow
1785 ,, Mary, Castleblake, co. Tipp., widow
1748 ., Michael, Tullygorey, co. Kildare, esq.
1791 ,, Michael, Myrtle grove, King's co., esq.
1793 ,, Michael, Clonmel, co. Tipp., saddler
1691 ,, Richard, Lismore, co. Cavan, esq. (Ex.)
1758 ,, Richard, Dublin, gent.
1657 ,, Robert, Moyallow, co. Cork, gent.   [**VI.** 202
1704 ,, Roger, par. St. Margaret, Westminster, barrister (Copy)
1730 ,, Sarah, Waterford, widow
1771 ,, Theobald, Clonmel, co. Tipp., esq.
1709 ,, Thomas, lieut. Delorain's regt. of foot
1727 ,, Thomas, senior, Aughmacart, Queen's co., gent. [gent.
1767 ,, Thomas, Balcarra, co. Mayo,
1730 ,, Tobias, Dublin, gent.
1714 ,, William, Tullygorey, co. Kildare, gent.
1718 ,, William, Tullygorey, co. Kildare, gent.
1756 ,, Wm., Winetavern-street, Dubl., plumber
1763 ,, ven. archdeacon William
1767 ,, ven. archdeacon William
1767 ,, Wm., Castletogher, co. Galway, gent.
1678 **Lewys**, sir John, London, knt. and bt. (Copy)
1581 **Ley**, John, Dublin, butcher
1674 ,, John, Drogheda, merchant
1589 ,, Nicholas, Waterford, alderman   [**I.** 36
1609 ,, Patrick, Dunshaughlin, co. Meath, gent.
1536 **Leyath**, Nicholas, par. of Castleknock, co. Dublin
1684 **Leycester**, John, Kilcarmick, Queen's co. esq. (Ex.) [See **Lyster**.]

1803 **Leyden**, Sarah, Temple Bar, Dubl., widow
1678 **Leyland**, John, Dublin, gent.
1700 ,, Sarah, widow
1655 **Leynagh**, Pierse, Castlejordan, co. Meath   [**V.** 172
1706 **Leyne**, Alson, Dublin, widow
1801 ,, Gerald, Tramore
1700 **Leynerit**, James, a ship captain, a refugee in Dublin on account of religion
1715 **Leynes**, Gerald, Tromon, co. Meath, gent.
1760 **Leyns**, Christopher, Kilballyporter, co. Meath, farmer (the contents established by decree)
1759 **Lhoyd**, Elizabeth, *alias* **Ledger**
1786 ,, Elizabeth, Dublin, widow
1769 ,, Rice, Killaloe, co. Clare, clk., LL.D.
1758 ,, Thomas, Dublin, M.D. [See **Lloyd**.]
1721 **Liddell**, Richard, Bakenstown, co. Kildare, farmer
1768 **Lidwell**, George, Lissanure, co. Tipperary, gent.
1790 ,, Robert, Lissanure, co. Tipp., esq.
1809 **Lidwill**, Thomas, Carlow town, esq.
1722 **Liffesly**, Joseph, Dublin, mercht.
1789 **Lifford**, James, lord viscount, lord chancellor of Ireland (Large)
1708 **Liffsley**, John, Dublin, carpenter
1742 ,, Lydia, Dublin, widow
1632 **Liford**, John, Sherby hundred in Virginia, clk.
1706 **Lifsley**, James, Dublin, merchant
1649 **Light**, Nicholas, butcher
1748 **Lightburn**, rev. Wm., rector of Langfield, dio. Derry
1797 **Lightburne**, Harcourt, Dublin, esq.
1782 ,, Mary, *alias* **Robins**, wife of Willoughby L.
1697 ,, Stafford, Trim, esq.
1762 ,, rev. Stafford, Trim, co. Meath, clk.
1762 ,, Stafford, the younger, vicar of Rathgraffe, dio. Meath
1671 ,, Dr. Wm., Chanter of Christ Church, Dublin
1803 ,, Willoughby, one of the aldermen of Dublin
1806 **Lighton**, sir Thomas, Dublin city, bart. (Large) [See **Leighton**.]
1737 **Ligo**, Thomas, Hacketstown, co. Dublin, esq.
1802 **Lill**, Carey, Dublin, widow
1791 ,, rev. Edward, D.D.

1786 **Lill**, Elizabeth, Dublin, widow
1783 ,, Godfrey, 2nd justice of the Common Pleas
1791 ,, James, Cork, esq.
1793 ,, Mary, Cork, widow
1765 ,, Rebecca, Dublin, widow
1804 ,, Robert, Gaulstown, co. Westmeath, esq.
1761 ,, Thomas, Dublin, esq.
1775 ,, rev. William, LL.D., Drogheda
1776 **Lillies**, John, Drumboe, co. Roscommon, gent. [common
1801 ,, Philip, Drumboe, co. Roscommon, gent.
1790 **Lilly**, Alexander, Dublin, jeweller
1784 ,, Daniel, Belfast, co. Antrim
1626 **Limbirie**, John, Cork, mariner
1703 **Limerick**, Mary, dow. countess of
1755 ,, Paul, clk.
1722 ,, Thomas, earl of (Copy)
1694 ,, Nathaniel Wilson, bishop of
1725 ,, Thomas Smyth, bishop of (Ex.)
1755 ,, William Burscough, bishop of
1784 ,, rt. rev. Dr.Wm. Gore, bishop of
1794 ,, rt. rev. Wm. Cecil Pery, lord bishop, baron Glentworth
1786 **Linam**, Charles, Dublin, builder [See LYNAM.]
1632 **Linch**, Geffery FitzDominick, Galway, merchant [**IV.** 17 [See LYNCH.]
1656 **Lincoll**, Garrett, Waterford, merchant
1603 ,, Patrick, Dublin
1782 **Lincoln**, Mary, Chapelizod, co. Dublin, widow
1750 ,, Nicholas, Dublin, gent.
1763 ,, Richard, Dublin, gent.
1637 **Lincolne**, Bartholomew, Waterford, merchant [**IV.** 169
1670 ,, James, Dublin, merchant
1702 ,, Michael, Dublin, merchant
1677 **Lincorne**, Catherine, *alias* **Tancard**, Dublin, widow (Copy)
1786 **Lindamire**, Teresa, Abbey-street, Dublin, widow
1761 **Lindesay**, John, Laughry, co. Tipp., esq. [See LYNDSAY.]
1736 **Lindon**, Jane
1797 ,, Thomas, Youghal, co. Cork, revenue officer [See LYNDON.]
1757 **Lindsay**, Alexander, Kilmore, co. Monaghan, clk.
1700 ,, Andw., Ballyaderlan, co. Donegal, gent.
1765 ,, Ann, Dublin, widow
1790 ,, Charles, bp. of **Kildare**, q.v.
1683 ,, Fergus, Ballym'Richard, co. Antrim, tanner

1745 **Lindsay**, George, Cork
1758 ,, John, Karrareagh, co. Down, farmer
1766 ,, John, Dublin, gent.
1802 ,, John, Lindville, sth. Liberties, city of Cork, esq.
1765 ,, Joseph, Lazers-hill, Dub., gent.
1742 ,, Robert, one of the judges of the Com. Pleas
1776 ,, rev. Samuel, late rector of Enniskillen
1749 ,, Sarah, Newry, co. Down, widow
1724 ,, Thomas, abp. of **Armagh**, q.v.
1748 ,, Thomas, Dublin, distiller
1797 ,, Thomas Bucknell, Turin Castle, co. Mayo, esq.
1751 ,, William, Newry, co. Down, now of Newcastle-upon-Tyne
1805 **Lindsey**, Owen, Dublin city, esq.
1811 ,, Thomas, the younger, Hollymount, co. Mayo
1708 **Linegan**, John, Dunbrow, co. Dubl., esq.
1659 **Lingard**, Richd., Workinton, Cumberland, clk.
1671 ,, Richard, D.D.
1752 **Lingen**, Joseph, rear-admiral in His Majesty's Navy
1749 ,, William, Dublin, esq.
1750 **Linihan**, Daniel, Clonmel, co. Tipperary, gent.
1804 **Linn**, Anne, Caledon, co. Tyrone, widow
1659 ,, Marmaduke, Dubl., cordwainer [**VIII.** 15 [See LYNNE.]
1721 **Linnard**, Patrick, Kilmacow, co. Cork, tanner
1796 **Linnell**, John, Nottinghill, Middlesex (Copy)
1778 **Linney**, John, Acton, co. Armagh
1657 **Linnington**, John, Fox-and-Green, co. Dublin, farmer [**VI.** 229
1703 **Linscomb**, Richard, Cork, innholder
1563 **Liomes**, Richard
1713 **Liron**, John De La Rouirere, Sligo, esq.
1691 **Lisburn**, Adam, lord visct. (Copy)
1739 **Lisle**, Catherine, Dublin, spr.
1789 ,, Elizabeth, dowager lady
1781 ,, John, lord baron of Mountnorth, co. Cork
1798 ,, rt. hon. John, lord baron [See LYLE, LYSLE.]
1797 **Lismore**, Cornelius, lord baron
1791 **Lisward**, Edward, Dublin, gent.
1805 **Litchfield**, John, Cork city, mercht.
1745 ,, Joshua, Dublin, pewterer

1778 **Litchfield**, William, Dunlavin, co. Wicklow, gent.
1677 **Littell**, Francis, Dublin, esq. (Ex.)
1657 ,, William, gent., belonging to the Lord Protector's Troop [**VI**. 161
1746 ,, William, Carrick, co. Leitrim, innholder
1803 **Little**, rev. Andrew, Longford, clk.
1754 ,, Christopher, corpl. in genl. Ligoniere's regt. of horse
1669 ,, Elizabeth, Dublin, widow
1768 ,, George, Lisnanaugh, co. Longford
1792 ,, James, Kilcotrim, co. Carlow
1726 ,, John, Lisnanaugh, co. Longford
1768 ,, John, Carterstown, co. Louth
1791 ,, John, Carrick-on-Shannon, co. Leitrim
1732 ,, Robert, Rathfriland, co. Down, gent.
1741 ,, Simon, Lisnanaugh, co. Longford, gent.
1791 ,, Thomas, Raheendara, co. Carlow, farmer
1752 ,, William, Carragulan, co. Down
1762 ,, William, Lurgan Green, co. Louth, farmer and miller
[See LYTTLE, PETTIT.]
1755 **Littleford**, Dutifull, Mullingar, co. Westmeath, spinster
1794 **Littlehales**, Baker, John (Copy)
1802 ,, Baker, John (Copy)
1811 ,, the rev. Storer C., vicar of Kill
1764 **Litton**, Benjamin
1808 ,, Edward, Dublin city, esq.
1698 ,, Henry, Newmarket, Dublin, clothier
1773 ,, Joseph, Dublin, woollendraper
1741 ,, Thomas, Dublin, esq.
1784 ,, Thomas, Oldtown, co. Kildare, esq.
1803 ,, Thomas, Dublin city, gent.
1715 ,, William, lower Combe, Dublin, clothier
1779 **Livesby**, Robert, Tinnahinch, co. Wicklow, innholder
1754 **Livesey**, Edward, Donmore, co. Galway, gent.
1730 **Livesley**, Robert, Ballycoyle, co. Wicklow, gent.
1808 ,, Samuel, Ballyphillip, co. Wicklow, farmer
1735 **Lively**, Anne, Ballycoyle, co. Wicklow
1806 ,, Henry, Ballyshillas, co. Wickl.
1741 **Livingston**, Alexander, Armagh, maltster

1757 **Lloyd**, Christopher, Dublin, D.D.
1675 ,, sir Edward, Borthllyoyd, Montgomeryshire, knt. (Copy)
1702 ,, Edward, Dublin, alderman
1811 ,, Erasmus, par. of St. Peter, Worcestershire (Copy)
1765 ,, Evan, Dublin, ropemaker
1764 ,, George, curate, Arklow, co. Wicklow
1774 ,, George, Clonmel, co. Tipperary, merchant
1768 ,, Guy, Beylough, Norfolk, now at Paris, esq.
1674 ,, John, Lloydiarth, Anglesey
1695 ,, John, Waterford, merchant
1758 ,, John, Tullaghan, co. Roscommon, gent.
1764 ,, John, Ballynakill, co. Tip., gt.
1769 ,, John, Croghan, co. Roscommon, gent.
1804 ,, John
1809 ,, John, Rosanna, co. Tip., esq.
1682 ,, Joseph, Killoskihane, co. Tipperary, gent.
1801 ,, Mary, widow
1665 ,, Owen, Abbeyboyle, co. Roscommon, esq.
1800 ,, Richard, Tamnamore, co. Tyrone
1811 ,, Richard, Bawdeswell, Norfolk (Large)
1767 ,, Robert, Cullenmore, co. Louth, officer of excise
1794 ,, Robert, Dublin, merchant
1802 ,, Robert, Dublin
1794 ,, Stephen, Glasshagad, King's co.
1698 ,, Thomas, Croghan, co. Roscommon, esq.
1802 ,, Thomas, Athlone
1809 ,, rev. Thomas, Castle Lloyd, co. Limerick
1811 ,, Thomas, Mount Fresco, co. Tipperary, esq.
1536 ,, William
1719 ,, William, Trin. Coll. Dub., D.D.
1766 ,, William, Croghan, co. Roscommon
1773 ,, William, Dublin city, M.D.
1798 ,, William, Smith Hill, co. Roscommon, esq.
1807 ,, William
1798 ,, Yeeden, Annesville, co. Roscommon, esq.
[See LHOYD, LOYD.]
1784 **Loane**, John, Charleville, co. Cork, gent.
1672 **Lochard**, Peter, Pimlico, near Dublin, esq.
1789 **Lock**, Anne, Newcastle, co. Limerick, widow (Copy)

1690 **Lock**, Anthony, Downpatrick, gent.
1703 ,, Patrick, Colmanstown, co. Dublin, gent.
1720 ,, Richard, Dublin, esq.
1787 ,, rev. Thomas, rector, Newcastle, dio. Limerick
[See LOCKHART, &c.]
1734 **Lockard**, Arthur, Christianstown, co. Kildare
1628 **Locke**, Patrick, Dundalk, gent.
1636 ,, Patrick, Colmanstown, co. Dublin, gent.
1694 ,, Robert, Dublin, gent.
1779 **Locker**, John, Knockananig, co. Cork, gent.
1810 **Lockhart**, Richard, Boyle, co. Roscommon, gent.
[See LOCK.]
1671 **Lockhead**, James, late of Glasgow, now of Dublin, merchant
1686 **Lockington**, Richard
1808 ,, William
1742 **Lockinton**, John, Lisleagh, co. Tipperary, farmer
1756 ,, William, Chequer-lane, Dublin
1565 **Lockwode**, Thomas, dean of St. Patrick's, Dublin
1783 **Lockwood**, Benjamin, Cashel, co. Tipperary, esq.
1799 ,, William, Clerahan, co. Tipperary, esq.
1655 **Loder**, John, Kells, co. Meath
1639 **Lodge**, Alice, Clonfaddoe, co.Clare, widow
1740 ,, Anne (not proved)
1769 ,, Elizabeth, Dublin
1763 ,, Francis, Dublin, esq.
1782 ,, Francis, Bakerstown, co. Tipperary, esq.
1807 ,, Francis, Kilkenny, alderman
1800 ,, Jane, Dublin city
1679 ,, Mary, *alias* **Groves**, widow
1617 ,, Thomas, St. Michan's par., Dublin
1638 ,, Thomas, Killaloe, archdeacon
1769 **Loe**, Thos., Derryduff, Queen's co.
1688 ,, Thomas, Dublin, gent.
1605 **Loftus**, Adam, archbishop of **Dublin**, q.v.
1769 ,, Alice
1709 ,, Anne, Loftus Hall, co. Wexford, widow
1666 ,, Sir Arthur, Dublin, knt.
1725 ,, of Ely, Arthur, lord viscount
1781 ,, Arthur, esq.
1667 ,, dame Cecilia, Dublin
1792 ,, Diana, Dublin
1648 ,, sir Dudley, Castle-street, Dublin, knt.

1694 **Loftus**, Dudley, Dublin, LL.D., judge of the Prerogative Court
1714 ,, Dudley, Killyon, co. Meath, esq.
1772 ,, Dudley
1808 ,, Dudley, Killyon, co. Meath,esq.
1680 ,, of Ely, Edward, lord viscount
1737 ,, Edward, Grange, co. Kildare, esq.
1800 ,, Francis, Loughrea, co. Galway, widow
1672 ,, Grissel, daur. of sir Adam Loftus, knt.
1762 ,, Hannah, wid. of lieut.-col. Simon L.
1707 ,, Henry, Loftus Hall, co. Wexford, esq.
1684 ,, of Ely, Jane, dow. viscountess
1684 ,, John, Fethard, co. Wexford, gt.
1758 ,, John, Nutgrove, co. Galway,gt.
1765 ,, Lettice, dow. lady viscountess
1668 ,, Nicholas, Fethard, co. Wexford, esq.
1767 ,, Nicholas, lord viscount (Large will)
1639 ,, Richard, Tessarin, King's co., gent.
1640 ,, sir Robert, Mellifont, co. Louth, knt.
1739 ,, Robt.,Capperoe,King'sco.,esq.
1650 ,, of Ely, Sarah, dowager lady viscountess
1773 ,, Sarah
1782 ,, rev. Smyth
1636 ,, sir Thomas, Tymochoe, Queen's co., knt.
1769 ,, Thos., Killyon, co. Meath, esq.
1806 ,, Thomas, esq.
1746 **Logan**, David, mariner
1786 ,, Geo., Nutgrove, co. Down, gt.
1791 ,, Jacob, Coleraine, co. Londonderry, tanner
1728 ,, Jane, par. St. Clement Danes, Middlesex (Copy)
1798 ,, John, Ballymena, co. Antrim, esq.
1747 ,, Sidney, Dublin, widow
1802 ,, Susanna, Coleraine,co.Londonderry, widow
1715 ,, William, Dublin, apothecary
1659 **Loggan**, Matthew, Carrickfergus
1598 **Loghan**, Laurence, Rush, co. Dublin, mariner (No date)
1741 **Loghlan**, Morgan, Limerick, merchant
1721 ,, Terence, co. Roscommon, gent.
[See LAUGHLIN.]
1729 **Loghlin**, Michael, Carrick, co. Tipperary, gent.
1626 **Lomax**, Thomas, Dublin

1762 **Lombard**, Edward, Dublin, gent.
1749 „ George, the younger, Cork, merchant
1769 „ George, Cork, merchant
1685 „ James, Gortvolire, co. Cork, gent.
1769 „ James, formerly of Lombards-town, co. Cork, now of Cork city, esq.
1783 „ James, Cork, merchant
1764 „ John, Gortmalyre, co. Cork, gt.
1773 „ rev. Peter, Dublin, clk.
1718 „ William, Cork, esq. (Ex.)
1754 „ William, Cork, merchant
        [See LUMBARD.]
1799 **Lombord**, rev. Edmund, Lombards-town, co. Cork, clk.
1735 **Londonderry**, Lucy, dow. countess (Copy)
1757 „ Thomas Pitt, earl of (Copy)
1808 **Lonergan**, Bryan, Newcastle, co. Tipperary, gent.
1802 „ Francis
1784 „ Maurice, Whitesforth, co. Wat.
1805 „ rev. William, Carrickbeg, co. Waterford
1781 **Long**, Ann, Rathmines, co. Dublin, widow
1612 „ Bartholomew, Dearre, co. Kil-dare, gent.
1730 „ Edward, Curraglass, co. Cork, gent.
1769 „ Eliz., the younger, Withum, Essex, spr. (Copy)
1773 „ Elizabeth, widow
1799 „ Elizabeth, Clonmel, co. Tipp., widow
1806 „ Elizabeth, Cahir, co. Tip., spr.
1785 „ Geo., Braithwaite-st., Dublin, clothier
1705 „ Henry, Londonderry, alderman
1802 „ Henry, Iron Hill
1618 „ James, Dublin, gent.
1737 „ John, Clothworkers-sq., Dubl., weaver
1763 „ John, Derrymasera, Queen's co., farmer
1785 „ John, Kildare town, innholder
1791 „ John, Paradise-row, Dublin
1807 „ John, Drogheda town, vintner
1808 „ Jos., Duncrum, co. Londonderry
1806 „ Jonathan
1794 „ Mary, Braithwaites-st., Dublin, widow
1806 „ Mary, Dublin, widow
1713 „ Mathew, Tulloghphelan, co. Carlow, gent.
1810 „ Moses, Marlborough-st., Dub., pawnbroker
1792 „ Nichs., Templetown, co. Louth

1716 **Long**, Oliver, Dublin, esq.
1808 „ Phebe, Limerick city, widow
1797 „ Rachel, par. St. Mary, Middle-sex, spr. (Copy)
1614 „ Richard, Dublin, gent.
1768 „ Robert, Omagh
1774 „ Robert, Ballina, co. Mayo, gent.
1798 „ Robert, captain in East India Co.'s service (Copy)
1748 „ Roger, the Two Chimneys, co Dublin, farmer
1772 „ Samuel
1810 „ Stephen, Limerick city, esq.
1766 „ Thos., Mitre-court, Cheapside (Copy)
1790 „ Thomas, Dublin, gent.
1791 „ Thomas, Monasterevan, co. Kildare, cooper
1605 „ William, Dublin
1768 „ William, Stillorgan, co. Dublin (Not proved)
1787 „ William, Melksham, Wiltshire, esq. (Copy)
        [See LONGE.]
1787 **Longan**, Robert, Ballincourty, co. Waterford
1762 **Longbottom**, Alice, Dublin, widow
1745 **Longchamp**, Paul de (Copy)
1605 **Longe**, George, Dublin, tanner
1671 „ Patrick, Clondarath, co. Long-ford, esq.
1697 „ Richard, Killinbrack, co. West-meath, gent.
        [See LONG.]
1601 **Longet**, Laur., Sauventry, farmer
1723 **Longfield**, Catherine, Kilbride, co. Meath, widow
1740 „ Hawnby, Ballynascarty, co. Cork
1730 „ Jno., Castlemarry, co. Cork, esq.
1765 „ John, Longueville, co. Cork, esq.
1751 „ Mary, Kilmacow, co. Cork, wid.
1711 „ Robert, Kilbride, co. Meath
1765 „ Robert, Castlemarry, co. Cork, esq.
1784 „ Robert, Dublin, esq.
1790 „ Robert, Dublin, esq.
1704 **Longford**, Ambrose, earl of
1639 „ dame Ann, widow of said sir Hercules
1794 „ Chas., Dublin, chip hat presser
1793 „ Edwd. Michael, lord baron
1794 „ Elizabeth, dowager countess
1700 „ Francis, earl of
1734 „ Gertrude, Doneraile, co. Cork, widow
1666 „ Henry, Enniskillen, co. Fer-managh, gent.
1766 „ Thomas, lord baron

1811 **Longueville,** right hon. Richard, lord viscount
1777 **Longworth,** Elizabeth, Dubl., wid.
1751 ,, Fras., Creggan, co. Westmeath, gent.
1803 ,, Fras., Creggan, co. Westmeath, esq.
1779 ,, Geo., Athlone, co. Westmeath, esq.
1784 ,, Henry, Tubbrid, co. Westmeath
1760 ,, John, Athlone, co. Westmeath
1782 ,, Mary, Athlone, co. Westmeath, widow
1762 ,, Sarah, Creggan
1772 **Lookup,** George, late par. Covent Garden, Middlesex, now at The Hague, esq. (Copy)
1767 **Lopdell,** Charles, Galway, burgess
1801 ,, Christopher, Derryowen, co. Clare, esq.
1731 ,, John, Millpit, co. Galway, esq.
1775 ,, John, the elder, Athenry, co. Galway, gent.
1717 **Lorcan,** Bryan, Daggin, co. Galw., gent.
1728 **Lord,** Edward, Dublin, apothecary
1791 ,, Edward, Dublin city
1791 ,, Edward, Bermuda, co. of Dublin city
1774 ,, Francis, Dublin, gunmaker
1775 ,, John, Dublin, esq.
1804 ,, rev. John, rector of Ballintemple
1801 ,, Princilla, Bandon, co. Cork, widow (Copy)
1765 ,, Thos., cornet in the 5th regt. of dragoons
1799 ,, Thomas, Dublin, dealer
1777 ,, William, Dunleary, co. Dublin
1797 **Lorinan,** Mathew, Ardee, co. Louth
1725 **Loron,** De Tharot Gabriel, esq. (Copy)
1736 **Lorte,** Margaret, Kenagh
1722 **De Lorthe,** Isaac, Dublin, esq.
1641 **Losse,** Ambrose, esq., Dublin
1727 **Lostau,** Bernard, col. Hawley's reg. of foot
1610 **Lott,** John
1699 **Lough,** John, Carrick M'Cosker, co. Ferm., gent. **[XVIII.** 254
1700 ,, John, Carrick M'Cosker, co. Fermanagh, gent.
1779 **Loughlin,** Christian, Dublin, lace weaver
1766 ,, James, surgeon's mate to royal regt. of Ireland [See LAUGHLIN.]
1737 **Louis,** Susana, Dublin, widow
1608 **Louth,** Oliver, lord baron of [See LOWTH.]
1804 **Lovary,** Peter, Oldtown, co. Kildare

1715 **Love,** Abraham, Cork, gent.
1790 ,, Eliz., *alias* **Allen,** Cloughboy, co. Tyrone, widow
1750 ,, John, Castlesaffron, co. Cork, esq.
1728 ,, Joseph, Dublin, gent.
1797 ,, Patrick
1690 ,, Richard, Killarney, co. Kerry, gent.
1768 ,, Robert, Cloughboy, co. Tyrone
1810 ,, William, Clare, co. Cavan
1773 **Lovelace,** Arthur, Galway, esq.
1696 ,, Thos., Roscommon, esq. (Ex.)
1597 **Lovell,** Francis (Copy)
1707 ,, rev. George, Tullymore, co. Antrim, clk.
1749 ,, George, esq., reformed capt. in gen. Irwin's regt.
1706 ,, Jane, London, widow
1755 **Lovelock,** Charles, Musicfield, co. Galway, gent.
1679 **Lovett,** Christopher, Dublin, gent.
1732 ,, Frances, Dublin, widow
1777 ,, Clotilda
1681 ,, John, Dublin, esq., marshal of the town courts
1710 ,, John, Dublin, esq.
1770 ,, Jonathan, Kingswell, co. Tip., esq.
1651 ,, Thomas, Maynooth, gent.
1780 ,, William, esq.
1709 **Low,** Adrian, St. Martin's Le Grand, London, founder (Copy)
1730 ,, Ann, Dublin widow
1748 ,, Ann, widow
1800 ,, Ann, Newtown, co. Westmeath, widow
1794 ,, Barecah, Newtown, co. Westmeath, esq.
1735 ,, Barekah, Newtown, co. Westmeath, esq.
1690 ,, Ebenezer, Newtown, co. Westmeath, esq.
1742 ,, Edmond, mariner
1763 ,, Edward
1777 ,, Eusebius, Dublin, esq.
1681 ,, Geo., Knock, co. Westmeath, gent.
1723 ,, George, Ballylacken, King's co., esq.
1752 ,, John, Fairfield, co. Westmeath, gent.
1758 ,, John, Fairfield, co. Westmeath. gent.
1784 ,, rev. Lancellot, Newpark, co. Westmeath, D.D.
1807 ,, Nathaniel, Lowville, co. Galway, esq.
1770 ,, Richard, Newtown, co. Westmeath, gent.

1742 **Low**, Robt., Brookhill, co. Tipperary, esq.
1778 　,,　 Robert, Fethard, co. Tipperary, esq.
1803 　,,　 Saml., Conahir, co. Westmeath
1808 　,,　 Simon, Cork city, merchant
1725 　,,　 Thomas, Donomoney
1731 　,,　 Thomas, Kilcornan, co. Westmeath, farmer
1734 　,,　 Thomas, Waterford, distiller
1678 　,,　 William, Newtown, co. Westmeath, esq.
　　　　　　[See LOWE.]
1659 **Lowans** or **Lawnes**, James, soldier
　　　　　　　　　　　[VII. 182
1786 **Lowcay**, Anthony, Roestown, co. Wexford, esq.
1734 　,,　 Mary, Roestown, co. Wexford, widow
1714 　,,　 rev. Robert, Rowestown, co. Wexford, clk.
1793 **Lowder**, James, Waterford, gent.
1725 **Lowe**, Anne, widow
1809 　,,　 Charles, Cork city
1730 　,,　 David, Fethard, co. Tipperary, esq. (Large will)
1767 　,,　 David, Brookhill, co. Tipperary, gent.
1790 　,,　 Elizabeth, Dublin, spinster
1770 　,,　 Hamilton, Roesgreen, co. Tip., esq. (Large will)
1807 　,,　 James, Sallypark, co. Cork
1631 　,,　 John, Cantrellstown, co. Dubl., farmer
1635 　,,　 John, Dublin, baker
1790 　,,　 John, Dublin, apothecary
1807 　,,　 Lucy, Newtown, co. Westmeath, spinster
1684 　,,　 Robert, Knockally, co. Tip., esq. (Ex.)
1750 　,,　 Robert, Mallardstown, co. Kilkenny, esq.
1710 　,,　 Samuel, Clonerill, King's co., esq.
1629 　,,　 Thomas, clk., Dublin
1789 　,,　 Thomas, Dublin, gent.
　　　　　　[See LOW.]
1711 **Lownde**, Elizabeth, Old Castle, co. Meath, spinster
1799 **Lowndes**, Francis, Cravelstown, co. Meath, gent.
1809 　,,　 Mary, Kells, co. Meath, widow
1800 　,,　 Nathaniel, Cravelstown, co. Meath, grazier
1778 **Lowry**, Galbraith, Aughenis, co. Tyrone, esq. (Large will)
1787 　,,　 rev. Jas., Tullybog, co. Tyrone (Large)
1790 　,,　 James, Brookdale, co. Tyrone, clk.

1692 **Lowry**, John, Aghenis, co. Tyrone, gent.
1698 　,,　 Captain John, Atherdee
1731 　,,　 John, Dublin, tailor
1729 　,,　 Robert, Aughenis, co. Tyrone, esq.
1775 　,,　 Robert, Ballyboy, King's co., gent.
1745 　,,　 Thomas, Kilcock, co. Kildare
1629 **Lowth**, Mathew, lord baron of
1689 　,,　 Mathew, lord baron of
1725 　,,　 Ann, dow. baroness, widow of John L., of East India
　　　　　　[See LOUTH.]
1788 **Lowther**, Anne, Staffordstown, co. Meath, widow
1767 　,,　 Edward, par. St. Martin-in-the-Fields, Middlesex, gent.
1716 　,,　 George, Kilrue, co. Meath, esq.
1734 　,,　 George, Hurlestown, co. Meath, gent.
1809 　,,　 George, Newcomen-place, co. Dublin, esq.
1792 　,,　 Georges, Kilrue, co. Meath, esq.
1624 　,,　 sir Gerard, knt., Jus. Common Pleas
1660 　,,　 sir Gerard, knt., Ch. Jus. Com. Pleas　　　　　[VIII. 73
1733 　,,　 James, Dublin, gent.
1782 　,,　 John, Staffordstown, co. Meath, esq.
1722 　,,　 William, Moate Granogue, co. Westmeath, merchant
　　　　　　[See LAWDER.]
1649 **Lowton**, John, Kevins-street, Dub., butcher
1734 **Loyd**, Andrew, Dublin, esq.
1790 　,,　 Catherine, *alias* **Philpot**
1723 　,,　 David, Dublin, esq.
1748 　,,　 Edward, Cashel city, gent.
1785 　,,　 Edward, Ballincollig, co. Cork, esq.
1670 　,,　 Elizabeth, *alias* **Chambers**, widow
1746 　,,　 Elizabeth, Kilduff, co. Tipper., widow
1793 　,,　 Frances, widow
1754 　,,　 Gabriel, Dublin, carpenter
1737 　,,　 George, Trin. Coll., Dublin, B.D.
1790 　,,　 Griffith, Dublin, merchant
1798 　,,　 Hugh, Kildromin, co. Limerick, esq.
1658 　,,　 John, Rhulas, Denbighshire, gent.　　　　　[VII. 75
1746 　,,　 John, Fresco, co. Tip., gent.
1749 　,,　 John, Carnarvon, Wales, esq. (Copy)
1784 　,,　 John, Cronagh, co. Tipperary esq.

1796 **Loyd**, John Thomas, Rockville, co. Roscommon
1791 ,, Mary, Dublin, spinster
1778 ,, Owen, Rockville, co. Roscommon, esq.
1793 ,, Owen, Rockville, co. Roscom.
1791 ,, Plunket, Dublin, M.D.
1778 ,, Rickard, Castle Lake, co. Tip., esq.
1657 ,, Thomas, rector of Bodforry, Flintshire [**VI.** 214
1746 ,, Thos., Chanter of the Catholic Church of Limerick
1753 ,, Thos., Clonmore, co. Tipperary, gent. [esq.
1747 ,, Trevor, Gloucester, King's co.,
1716 ,, William, lord bishop of Killala and Achonry
[See LLOYD.]
1784 **Lube**, Dennis, Corcoranstown, co. Kildare, glazier
1745 ,, Thomas, Corcoranstown, co. Kildare, farmer
1799 **Lucan**, Charles, earl of
1757 **Lucas**, Abagail, Castle Shane, co. Monaghan, widow
1727 ,, Benj., Ballingaddy, co. Clare, gent.
1771 ,, Charles, Dublin, M.D.
1798 ,, Charles, Carnarvon, Wales
1664 ,, Edward, Dublin, gent.
1757 ,, Edwd., the elder, Castle Shane, co. Monaghan, esq.
1775 ,, Edwd., Castle Shane, co. Monaghan, esq.
1796 ,, Edwd., Newgrove, co. Armagh, esq.
1811 ,, Elizabeth, Cork city, widow
1657 ,, cornet Francis, Castle Shane, co. Monaghan
1746 ,, Francis, Dublin, esq.
1759 ,, Fras., Greenon, co. Monaghan, esq.
1770 ,, rev. Francis, Drumgoon, co. Cavan, clk.
1798 ,, Francis, Mount Lucas, co. Wicklow
1689 **Lucas**, Gilbert, Drogheda, tanner
1710 ,, Jasper, Youghal, co. Cork, esq.
1811 ,, Jasper, Cork city, merchant
1704 ,, John, Rathdaniel, co. Carlow, gent.
1764 ,, John, Ballymacooda, co. Clare, gent.
1747 ,, Mary, Castle Shane, widow of Francis L., esq.
1782 ,, Mary, Glaslough, co. Monaghan, widow
1750 ,, Mathew, Rathdaniel, co. Carlow, esq.

1734 **Lucas**, Moore, Dublin, merchant
1767 ,, Samuel esq.
1649 ,, sir Thomas, Colchester, Essex, knt. (Copy) [gent.
1718 ,, Thomas, Parkhall, Lancashire,
1727 ,, Thomas, Castle Shane, co. Monaghan, esq.
1764 ,, Thomas, Ennis, co. Clare, mercht.
1723 ,, William, Berryfield, Northamptonshire, grazier (Copy)
1751 ,, William, Drogheda, alderman
1755 ,, William, captain in earl of Homes' reg. of foot
1668 **Luce**, Luke, St. Cath. Colman's par., Lon., mercht.
1782 **Lucey**, Maurice, Cork city, mercht.
1770 ,, Thomas, Cork, mercht. tailor
1742 **Lucy**, Helen, Desart, co. Kilkenny, widow
1694 **Ludford**, Francis, Osberstown, co. Kildare, gent.
1713 **Ludlaw**, Duglas, Dublin, widow
1750 ,, Peter, Ardsalla, co. Meath, esq.
1724 ,, Stephen, Dublin, esq.
1778 ,, Thomas, Atherdee, merchant
1769 ,, William, Dublin, esq.
1713 **Ludlowe**, Thomas, Ealing, Middlesex, gent. (Copy)
1766 **Luffingham**, Benjamin, Fishamble-street, Dublin
1739 **Lugg**, Elizabeth, *alias* **Felkis**, Cork, widow
1724 ,, Samuel, Cork, merchant
1591 **Lumbard**, Francis, Waterford
1581 ,, Margaret, widow
[See LOMBARD.]
1730 **Lumley**, Henry, Cork, gent.
1755 ,, Hugh, Ballymaloe, co. Cork, gent.
1708 **Lumm**, Dorothy, Dublin, widow
1717 ,, Dorothy, Dublin, spinster
1708 ,, Elnathan, Dublin, banker
1756 ,, Sarah, widow
1731 ,, Susanna, Dublin, spinster
1744 ,, Thomas, Lummville, King's co. esq.
1742 **Lundgren**, John, of the company of Battle Axe Guards, Dublin
1798 **Lundres**, William, Lucan, co. Dublin, miller
1811 **Lunell**, George, North Great George's-street, Dublin, esq.
1774 ,, William, Dublin, merchant
1748 **Luneman**, Simon, Dublin, gent.
1794 **Lunn**, Henry, Dublin, merchant
1801 ,, Mary, Henrietta, widow
1801 **Lupton**, Henry, Longford, Queen's co. farmer

1786 **Lushington**, William, Dublin, esq.
1769 **Lusk**, Thomas, Attybleny, King's co.
1791 **Luther**, Bridget, Dublin, widow
1763 ,, Edward, Lismoyney, co. Westmeath, esq. (Not proved)
1697 ,, John, Youghal, merchant
1765 ,, John, Ballyboy, King's co. esq.
1795 ,, Richard, Clonmel, co. Tipperary, merchant
1604 **Luttereel**, John, Dublin, stabler
1577 ,, Simon, Russardstown, co. Dublin
1772 **Luttrell**, Alice, Dublin, spinster
1794 ,, James, capt. in His Majesty's Navy (Copy)
1620 ,, John, Killeigh, co. Dublin, gent.
1803 ,, John, Ashtown, co. Kildare, farmer
1754 ,, Margrett, Phœnix-street, spinster (the original transmitted to the delegates in England in 1742)
1567 ,, Nicholas, Clonsilla, co. Dublin, gent.
1610 ,, Nicholas, Luttrellstown, co. Dublin, gent.
1634 ,, Richard, Dublin
1595 ,, Robert, Dublin, baker
1730 ,, Robert, Luttrellstown, co. Dublin, esq.
1597 ,, Simon, Luttrellstown, co. Dublin, esq.
1540 ,, Symon, Dublin, merchant
1634 ,, Thomas, Luttrellstown, co. Dublin, esq.
1673 ,, Thomas, Ranoghern, co. Westmeath, esq.
1757 ,, Thomas, Dublin, merchant
1676 ,, William, Schoolhouse-lane, Dublin, gent.
1732 ,, William, Belgard, co. Kildare, gent.
[See LUTTERELL.]
1717 **Luttrill**, Henry, Dublin, esq.
1741 **Lutwidge**, Jas., Whitehaven, Cumberland, mariner (Copy)
1747 ,, Thomas, merchant (Copy)
1750 **Lutwitch**, Andrew, Dub., perfumer
[See LEDWICH.]
1552 **Luz**, Bartholomew, par. Newcastle, co. Dublin
1688 **Lydall**, William, Dublin, gent.
1810 **Lydon**, Luke, Galway town, mercht.
1610 **Lye**, John, Rathbride, co. Kildare, gent.
1598 ,, Richard, Tassagard, husbandman (No date)
1602 ,, Simon, Waterford, merchant

1630 **Lye**, Thomas, Kilkenny, alderman
1631 **Lyelly**, Isabella, Crossendane, Queen's co., widow [**II.** 285
1659 **Lyghoe**, John, soldier in capt. Vivian's co. [**VII.** 181
1766 **Lyle**, Ellinor, Coleraine, co. Londonderry, widow
1778 ,, Hugh, Coleraine, co. Londonderry, esq.
[See LISLE.]
1797 **Lymberry**, Bridget, Waterford city, widow
1650 **Lynager**, Daniel, Oxmantown
1677 **Lynagerr**, John, Dub., esq. (Ex.)
1768 **Lynam**, Charles
1793 ,, John, Dublin, woollen draper
1799 ,, Joseph, Dublin, banker
1760 ,, Richard, Coleraine, co. Londonderry, clk.
1739 ,, Sarah, Coleraine, co. Londonderry, widow
1792 ,, Sarah, Dublin, widow
1776 ,, William, Croydon, co. Dublin, mercht.
[See LINAM.]
1553 **Lyname**, Nicholas, Dublin
1578 **Lynane**, Bill
1802 **Lynar**, Alexander, Capel-street, Dublin
1783 ,, David, Dublin, woollen draper
1782 ,, David, Syon, co. Kildare, farmer
1770 **Lynch**, Alexander, Galway, gent.
1794 ,, Alexander, Ballinasloe, co. Galway, esq.
1791 ,, Anne, Ballybought, co. Dublin, widow
1791 ,, Anne
1733 ,, Anstace, Kilquan, co. Galway, widow
1638 ,, Anthony Fitz James, Galway, alderman
1781 ,, Anthony, Dublin, merchant
1751 ,, Arthur, Galway town
1783 ,, Arthur, Beaghmore, co. Galway, gent.
1778 ,, Bridget, Galway, widow
1789 ,, Bridget, *alias* **French**, Galway, widow
1784 ,, Catherine, Drogheda, widow
1800 ,, Charles, Petersborough Castle, co. Galway, esq.
1752 ,, Christopher, Barrack-street, Dublin, merchant
1771 ,, Christopher, Cakestown, co. Meath, gent.
1783 ,, Christopher, Church-street, Dublin, pinmaker
1785 ,, Christopher, Cook-street, Dublin, breeches maker

1805 **Lynch**, Patrick, Exchange-street, Dublin, publican
1602 ,, Peter Fitzmarcus, Galway, alderman
1810 ,, Peter, Moate, co. Mayo, esq.
1721 ,, Philip, par. St. James, Westminster, Middlesex, esq. (Copy)
1782 ,, Pierce, Rathvilladoon, co. Galway, gent.
1809 ,, Richd., Swanlinbar, co. Cavan
1583 ,, Robt. Fitzharris, Galway, alderman
1734 ,, Sarah, Cork, widow
1635 ,, Stephen, Galway, merchant
1637 ,, Stephen, Galway, merchant [**IV**. 238 & 282
1637 ,, Stephen, Galway, esq.
1679 ,, Father Stephen
1791 ,, Surna, Cloghballymore, co. Galway, widow
1765 ,, Terence, Dublin, writing clerk
1758 ,, Thomas, late of Cadiz, in Spain, now of Galway, merchant
1768 ,, Thomas, Pall Mall, Mid., tailor (Copy)
1771 ,, Thomas, Killeen, co. Meath, farmer [gent.
1771 ,, Thomas, Rockfield, co. Mayo,
1773 ,, Thomas, Galway, esq.
1780 ,, Thos., Ballybought, co. Dubl., gent.
1787 ,, Thomas, Pall Mall, Middlesex, tailor (Copy)
1793 ,, Thomas, Lavally, co. Galway, gent.
1802 ,, Thomas, Lowberry, co. Roscommon, esq.
1811 ,, Thomas, Shannon Bridge, co. Roscommon
1728 ,, William, Keilticona, King's co.
1758 ,, William, Lydican
1766 ,, William, Dublin, bricklayer
1793 ,, William, Charleville, Queen's co., gent.
1798 ,, William, Dublin, esq. [See LINCH.]
1595 **Lyncoll**, William Fitz James, Waterford
1783 **Lynd**, Grace, *alias* **Bell**, Coleraine, co. Derry, widow
1765 **Lyndon**, Alice, widow of rev. Roger L.
1727 ,, Edward, Dublin, esq.
1769 ,, Elizabeth, Dublin, widow
1757 ,, George, Dublin, gent.
1699 ,, sir John, Dublin, knt., Justice of K. B.
1740 ,, John, Glasnevin, co. Dublin, esq.

1758 **Lyndon**, John, Dublin, wine mercht.
1783 ,, Margaret, Dublin, esq.
1753 ,, rev. Roger, Little Cuffe-street, Dublin, clk.
1804 ,, Roger, Tomduff, co. Wexford, esq. [See LINDON.]
1750 **Lyndsay**, David, par. of Killowen, co. Derry, merchant
1699 ,, Hellen, Ballindarlin, co. Donegal, widow
1785 ,, Mary, *alias* **Ingram**
1749 ,, Robert, Belleek, co. Mayo
1759 ,, Saml., Belfast, co. Antrim (late of Newry)
1754 ,, Thomás, Turin, co. Mayo, esq.
1758 ,, William, Dublin, merchant
1763 ,, William, Island of Antigua [See LINDESAY.]
1684 **Lyndsey**, James, Dublin, gent.
1792 **Lyneall**, Benjamin, Cork-st., Dub., esq.
1751 **Lynehaghan**, John, Sligo, mercht.
1619 **Lynett**, James, Waterford, mercht.
1656 **Lynge**, Michael, Dundalk [**V**. 334
1788 **Lynham**, Henry, Dublin, stonecutter
1721 ,, John, Dublin, gent.
1780 **Lynn**, John, Dungulph, co. Wexford, esq.
1649 **Lynne**, Marmaduke, Dublin, gent.
1625 ,, William, Londonderry, gent.
1672 ,, Wm., Cloghagall, co. Tyrone, gent. [See LINN.]
1746 **Lynott**, Hubert, Ballinhane, co. Mayo
1808 ,, Ulick, Galway town
1781 **Lyon**, Benjamin, par. St. Catherine, Jamaica
1743 ,, Charles, Dublin, merchant
1799 ,, Charles Wilson, lieut.-genl.
1690 ., Edmond, Kilbride, co. Carlow, gent.
1751 ,, Esther, Dublin, widow
1777 ,, John, Waterford, alderman
1790 ,, John, D.D., minister of St. Bride's par., Dublin
1779 ,, Mary, Waterford, widow
1747 ,, Mitchel, son of Charles L., Dublin, merchant
1780 ,, Susana Arabella, wife of col. Charles W. Lyon
1627 ,, William, bishop of **Cork**, q. v.
1758 ,, William, Moron, co. Down, court officer
1786 **Lyons**, Ann, North Anne-street, Dublin, widow
1803 ,, Charles, Kinnegad, co. Westmeath, shopkeeper
1772 ,, David, Belfast, linendraper

1777 **Lyons**, Denis, Croom, co. Limerick, farmer
1809 ,, Denis, Croom, co. Limerick, esq.
1807 ,, Elizabeth, Grafton-st., Dublin, widow
1804 ,, Hannah, Dublin city, widow
1783 ,, Henry, River Lyons, King's co., esq.
1793 ,, James, Newcastle, co. Dublin, farmer
1784 ,, Jeremiah, Rainsford-st., Dubl., grocer
1703 ,, John, Kinnegad, co. Westmeath, gent.
1743 ,, John, Ladestown, co. Westmeath, esq.
1798 ,, John, Dublin, silk mercer
1804 ,, John, Ladestown, co. Westmeath, esq.
1756 ,, Mark, Dublin, merchant
1764 ,, Patrick, Old Graig, co. Meath, farmer
1782 ,, Philip, Dublin, esq.
1811 ,, Redmond, Kilkenny city
1803 ,, Samuel, Watling-street, Dubl., tanner and skinner
1806 ,, Samuel, Canwick, co. of the city of Lincoln, esq.
1742 ,, Susanna, Dublin, widow
1741 ,, Thomas, Dublin, alderman
1808 ,, Thomas, Old Park, co. Antrim
1799 **Lysaght**, Andrew, Gurtreen M'Nemara, co. Clare
1808 ,, Andrew, Ballyvorda, co. Clare
1783 ,, Anthony, Summerville, co. Clare, esq.
1754 ,, Charles, Ballybreen, co. Clare, gent.
1782 ,, Daniel, Ennis, co. Clare, gent.
1792 ,, hon. Elizabeth
1806 ,, Francis, Moy Castle, co. Clare
1764 ,, John, Monah, co. Clare, gent.
1799 ,, hon. Joseph, city of Cork
1801 ,, hon. James, city of Cork
1725 ,, Nicholas, Brickfield, co. Limk., esq.
1735 ,, Nicholas, Brickfield, co. Limk., esq.
1680 ,, Thomas, Pallas Greane, co. Tipperary, merchant
1762 ,, Thomas, Ballykeal
1811 ,, Thomas, Ennis, co. Clare, esq.
1783 ,, William, Moanreel, co. Clare, gent.
1798 ,, William, Cork city, esq.
1803 ,, William, Mount North, co. Cork, esq.
1694 **Lysle**, Gerald, Dublin, surgeon
[See LISLE.]

1745 **Lyster**, Anthony, Athlone, co. Roscommon, esq.
1754 ,, Anthony, Newpark, co. Roscommon, esq.
1800 ,, Anthony, Grange, co. Roscommon
1806 ,, Anthony, Newpark, co. Roscommon
1800 ,, Christopher, Dublin city, esq.
1790 ,, Elizabeth, Dublin, spinster
1803 ,, Fielding, esq.
1804 ,, Mary
1761 ,, Mathew, esq., counsellor-at-law
1800 ,, Mathew, Newpark, co. Roscommon, esq.
1799 ,, Richard Rumbold, Dublin, esq.
1798 ,, Thomas, Grange, co. Roscommon, esq.
1799 ,, Thomas, ensign in the 39th regt.
1808 ,, rev. Thomas, Coldblow-lane, Dublin, D.D.
1722 ,, William, Castlecoote, co. Roscommon, esq.
1788 ,, William
1790 ,, William, *alias* O'Dwyer, Dubl., esq.
[See LEICESTER, LESTER, LEYCESTER, MCALESTER, ST. LEGER.]
1786 **Lyston**, Edmond, Dirty-lane, Dubl., carpenter
1805 **Lyttle**, rev. Joseph, Letterkenny, co. Donegal
[See LITTLE.]

—M—

1703 **Mabe**, Jas., Cappagh, co. Kildare
1749 **Macabe**, John, Dublin, gent.
1779 ,, Susanna, Waterford
[See M'CABE.]
1700 **M'Adam**, Philip, St. Thomas Island, co. Clare, fisherman
1729 ,, Philip, Gortalogher, co. Clare, gent.
1658 **M'Adame**, lieut. John, Liskitle, co. Tyrone, or Youghal (Copy)
[See M'CADAM.]
1737 **M'Alester**, John, Kilkenny, gent.
[See LYSTER.]
1795 **M'Alister**, Anne, Eccles-st., Dubl., widow
1788 ,, Archibald, Dub., cabinetmaker
1723 ,, Eneas, Dublin, gent.
1798 ,, William, Coleraine, co. Derry, whitener of linen
[See LYSTER.]

1720 **M'Alexander**, John, Cootehill, co. Cavan, merchant
1721 ,, John, Cootehill, co. Cavan, merchant
1788 **M'Allen**, Eliz., Athy, co. Kildare
1755 ,, John, Dublin, esq.
1791 ,, John, Athy, co. Kildare, esq.
1796 **M'Alley**, Thos., Dublin, musician
1808 **M'Allister**, Jane
1794 ,, John, Dundalk, co. Louth, publican
1808 **Macan**, Robt., Carriff, co. Armagh [See M'CANN.]
1792 **M'Annelly**, Sarah, Omagh, co. Tyrone, maid servant
1793 **M'Ardell**, Edward, Dundalk, co. Louth, publican
1788 ,, Owen, Dundalk, co. Louth, chapman
1777 ,, Philip, Dorset-street, Dublin, heraldic painter
1768 **M'Ardle**, Henry, Thomas-st., Dublin, dealer
1773 **Macartan**, Philemon, Drominacoil, co. Down, gent.
1740 **Macarthy**, Dermod, Dublin, gent. [See M'CARTHY.]
1800 **Macartney**, Alicia, Dublin, widow
1755 ,, Catherine, *alias* **Johnston**, Dublin, widow
1789 ,, Catherine, Richmond, Surrey, spinster
1803 ,, Catherine, Dublin, widow
1759 ,, Charles, Dublin, esq.
1757 ,, George, Dublin, esq.
1779 ,, George, Dublin, esq.
1788 ,, Geo., Belfast, co. Antrim, esq.
1790 ,, James, Armagh
1795 ,, James, Brookborough, co. Fermanagh
1728 ,, John, Belfast, merchant
1793 ,, William, Marlough, co. Down, esq. [See M'CARTNEY.]
1767 **M'Aulay**, Alexander, Dublin, esq.
1758 ,, Silvester, Skerries, co. Dublin, innholder
1807 **M'Auley**, Bernard, Drumdirig, co. Antrim
1804 ,, Hugh, Dromoney, co. Antrim [See M'AWLEY, MAGAWLEY, M'GAULY.]
1805 **M'Auliffe**, John, High-st., co. Cork
1778 **M'Awee**, William, par. Lifford, co. Donegal
1730 **M'Aweey**, James, Dubl., gardener
1770 **M'Awley**, Stephen, Dublin, coachmaker
1792 **M'Bride**, Darcus, Dublin, widow
1779 ,, David, Dublin, M.D.

1782 **M'Bride**, William, Belfast, co. Antrim, nailer
1659 **M'Brinne**, John, Monimore, co. Derry, merchant
1722 **M'Bryan**, Patrick, Big Riverstown, co. Meath, farmer
1811 **M'Cabe**, Edward, Kimmage, co. Dublin, farmer
1741 ,, Henry, Price's-lane, Dublin
1775 ,, Henry, Spittlefields, Dublin, timber merchant
1800 ,, John, Eaghter, co. Cavan
1763 ,, Mary, Dublin, widow
1771 ,, Mary, Dublin, widow
1770 ,, Patrick, Dublin, merchant [See MACABE.]
1770 **M'Cadam**, George, Belfast, co. Antrim, merchant [See M'ADAM.]
1733 **M'Caffery**, Patrick
1771 **M'Caffry**, Margaret
1800 **M'Calby**, John, Dublin, musician
1721 **M'Call**, John, Lurgan, co. Antrim, apothecary
1723 ,, Murdock, Deraghy, co. Antrim, tanner
1803 ,, Samuel, Limerick city, mercht.
1807 ,, Samuel, Glyntown, co. Cork, esq.
1788 ,, William, Cork-st., Dublin, silk manufacturer
1780 **M'Calla**, John
1733 **Maccallester**, John, Sandywell, Gloucestershire, gent.
1733 **M'Calley**, Wm., Dublin, victualler
1769 **M'Cally**, Mary, *alias* **Bradstreet**, Willsbrook, co. Longford, widow
1733 ,, Patrick, Ballyboy, co. Longford, gent.
1764 ,, Robert, Robinstown, co. Longford, gent.
1766 ,, Simon, Bradstreet, Willsbrook, co. Longford, esq.
1768 **M'Calpin**, James, Belfast, co. Antrim, merchant
1772 **M'Camon**, Fras., Newtown Hamilton, co. Armagh
1760 ,, John, Newry, co. Down, merchant
1788 ,, Jno., Derrycughan, co. Armagh
1772 ,, Moses, Newry, co. Down, merchant
1810 **M'Can**, David, Summerhill, co. Down
1701 ,, Geo., Richmount, co. Armagh
1757 ,, John, Dublin, linendraper
1776 ,, Peter, Athy, co. Kildare
1754 ,, Samuel, Dublin, merchant
1795 ,, Thomas, Armagh city, esq.

1807 **M'Cance**, John, Upperfalls, co. Antrim, linen merchant
1780 **M'Candles**, James, Scarva, co. Down
1719 **M'Cane**, George, lieutenant in col. Sydney's reg. of dragoons
1801 **M'Cann**, Andrew, Ormond-market, Dublin, victualler
1748 ,, Arthur, belonging to the "Angliana" man-of-war
1706 ,, James, James's-st., Dublin, leather dresser
1810 ,, James, Dublin city
1801 ,, John, Armagh, gent.
1810 ,, Nicholas, Little Kilrue, co. Meath
1790 ,, Robt., Cabb-st., par. St. Mary, Middlesex, chandler
[See MACAN, M'CAN.]
1794 **M'Canna**, Cicely, Watling-street, Dublin, widow
1802 ,, Michael, Mannanstown, co. Meath
1756 **M'Cannon**, George, Dublin, tailor
1758 ,, William, Dublin, tailor
1722 **M'Cants**, John, Dublin, gent.
1691 **M'Carrell**, Allen, Monacree, co. Armagh, farmer
[See M'KERRALL.]
1757 **Maccarrell**, Jno., Dublin, alderman
1773 **M'Cartan**, John, Newry, co. Down, shopkeeper
1769 **M'Carter**, Samuel, Drummill, co. Monaghan
1713 **M'Carthy**, Ann, *alias* **Bamber**, wife of Francis M'C. of Dub., gent.
1758 ,, Bartholomew, Dublin, chandler
1704 ,, Chas., Cloghroe, co. Cork, esq.
1714 ,, Charles, Lisnaboy, gent.
1728 ,, Charles, Dublin, merchant
1748 ,, Charles, Lagganstown
1770 ,, **More**, Charles, Pallas, co. Kerry
1781 ,, Charles, Kilkenny city, gent.
1801 ,, Charles, South Lib. of Cork, gent.
1785 ,, Clare, Galway town
1774 ,, Cormick, Thurles, co. Tipperary, shopkeeper
1781 ,, Dalton, Dublin, esq.
1760 ,, Daniel, Branganstown, diocese of Kildare, gent.
1802 ,, Daniel, Lakeville, Lib. of Cork
1761 ,, Denis, Doneen, co. Cork, gent.
1762 ,, Denis, Springhouse, co. Tipperary, gent.
1810 ,, Denis, Travers-st., Cork city
1713 ,, Dennis, Springhouse, co. Tipperary, gent.

1788 **M'Carthy**, Dennis, Shangarry, co. Cork, farmer
1763 ,, Ellen
1747 ,, Eugene, mariner
1769 ,, Florence, Ballycorginny, co. Cork, gent.
1811 ,, Helen, *alias* **O'Leary**
1800 ,, James, Tralee, co. Kerry, merchant
1750 ,, Jane, Inchiguise, co. Kildare, widow
1756 ,, Justin, Springhouse, co. Tipperary, gent.
1811 ,, Justin, Newcastle, co. Limerick
1809 ,, Lewis W., Galway, attorney
1799 ,, Marcum, Ballyvoug, co. Cork
1714 ,, hon. Margaret, par. St. Ann, Westminster, spr.
1784 ,, Michael, Cork, pub. not.
1809 ,, Michl., Dublin city, boot maker
1761 ,, Owen, Irish town, Bandon, co. Cork, innkeeper
1771 ,, Patrick, Thomas-street, Dubl., grocer
1810 ,, St. George, Dublin city, gent.
1749 ,, Timothy, mariner
[See MACARTHY.]
1758 **M'Cartie**, Charles, Cork, esq.
1761 ,, Charles, Cork, esq.
1764 ,, Daniel, Carricknavar, co. Cork, esq.
1809 ,, Denis, Rhaduane, co. Cork, esq.
1693 **M'Cartney**, Chichester, Belfast, merchant
1691 ,, George, Belfast, esq.
1702 ,, George, Belfast, co. Antrim, merchant
1775 ,, Henrietta, par. St. George, Westminster, widow
1738 ,, Isaac, Belfast, esq.
1692 ,, James, Belfast, esq., lieut. in col. St. John's regt. of foot
1727 ,, James, the elder, Dublin, but in London, esq.
1734 ,, John, Calestown, co. Meath, farmer
1776 ,, Margaret, Dublin, spinster
1796 ,, Mary, Enniskillen, co. Fermanagh
1717 ,, William, Callstown, co. Meath, gent.
[See MACARTNEY.]
1788 **M'Carty**, Anne, Dublin, widow
1720 ,, Charles, Cloughroe, co. Cork, esq.
1712 ,, Denis, Kinnegad, co. Westmeath, gent.
1792 ,, Elinor, Donnybrook, co. Dubl., widow

1792 **M'Conchy**, William, Antrim town, gent.
[See MACHONCHY.]
1752 **M'Conehey**, William, Antrim, shop-keeper
1784 **M'Connel**, Jannett, Lustikell, co. Donegal
1763 **M'Connell**, John, Anderson's-court, Dublin, tailor
1766 **M'Coppin**, Jas., Newtown-Forbes, co. Longford, merchant
1805 **M'Cormack**, Joseph, Meath-street, co. city Dublin
1725 **M'Cormick**, Anne, Dublin, spinster
1789 ,, Dennis, Monaghan, dealer
1722 ,, John, Mell, co. Louth, gent.
1800 ,, Jos., Simonstown, co. Meath, farmer
1808 ,, Lettice, Jervais-st., co. Dublin, widow
1774 ,, Michael, Church-street, Dubl., cornchandler
1800 ,, Murtagh, Newmarket, co. Dublin, farmer
1773 ,, Robert, Rostrevor, co. Down, merchant
1802 ,, William, Dublin, slater
1804 ,, William, Harold's Cross
1672 **M'Cowey**, Donnough, Avolly, co. Wicklow, farmer
1754 **M'Coy**, Patrick, Dublin, gardener
1808 **M'Cracken**, Bernard, Dublin city, hair dresser
1780 **M'Cragh**, *alias* **Kirwan**, Bridget, Galway town
1769 **M'Craight**, James, Cloonwille, co. Fermanagh
1728 **M'Craith**, John, Hammamtown, co. Limerick, farmer
1771 ,, Robert, Loughloher, co. Tipperary, gent. (Large will, not proved till 1812)
1782 ,, Thomas, Knocknagapagh, co. Cork, farmer
[See MAGRATH.]
1771 **M'Crakan**, Samuel, Roundwood, co. Wicklow
1769 **M'Craken**, Samuel, Roundwood, co. Wicklow, gent.
1746 ,, William, co. of Dublin city, carpenter
1743 **M'Crath**, Terence, Dubl., victualler
[See MAGRATH.]
1750 **M'Crea**, Seneca, par. St. John, Dublin, tailor
1777 ,, Archibald, Argry, co. Donegal
1764 **M'Creary**, Jane
1811 **M'Credy**, William, Bride-st., Dub., upholsterer

1801 **M'Creery**, Anne, Dublin, widow
1808 ,, James, High-street, Dublin, merchant
1791 ,, Michael, Kilkenny city, coach-maker
1750 ,, Robt., Moate, co. Meath, gent.
1796 ,, Thomas, Dublin, merchant
[See M'CREARY.]
1785 **M'Creight**, Andrew, Banvale, co. Down, linen merchant
1772 ,, John, Blarney, co. Cork, linen manufacturer
1787 ,, William, Coolmorine, co. Cork
1730 **M'Cright**, John, Dublin, mariner
1773 **M'Croarey**, Hugh, Carmagram, co. Antrim
1787 **M'Cullagh**, John, Clady, co. Arm., linendraper
1741 ,, Nicholas, Broadstone, carman
[See MACULLA, M'CULLOCH.]
1728 **M'Culloch**, Henry, Fewghoge, co. Antrim, esq.
1789 ,, John, Antrim town, surgeon and apothecary
1682 ,, Wm., Raneldstown, co. Antrim, esq.
1800 ,, William, Camoley, co. Armagh
1797 **M'Cullock**, Anne, Dublin, spinster
1725 ,, James, barony of Tome, co. Antrim, gent.
1743 ,, William, Piedmont, co. Antrim, esq.
1747 **M'Cullom**, John, Dremnalery, co. Antrim, esq.
1791 **M'Cullough**, Alexander, Claymore, co. Armagh
1772 ,, John, Parkgate, Cheshire, mariner
1793 **M'Cullum**, Hugh, Limnarely, co. Antrim, esq.
1770 **M'Curdy**, rev. James, Cornark, co. Antrim, clk.
1804 ,, Jenny, Corvally, co. Antrim
1801 **M'Cutchen**, Andrew, Groskeen, co. Longford, gent.
1718 **M'Cutchion**, Adam, Belfast, merchant
1755 **M'Danell**, Anthony, Dublin, timber merchant
1734 ,, Daniel, Charlemont, co. Mon.
1752 ,, James, Francis-street, Dublin, meatman
1796 **M'Daniel**, Catherine, Dublin, widow
1763 ,, Charles, Bellisle, co. Antrim, esq. (Not proved)
1770 ,, Charles, Baytown, co. Meath
1773 ,, Cornelius, Charlesland, co. Wicklow, farmer
1762 ,, Dominick, Dublin, merchant
1765 ,, Elizabeth, Dublin, widow

1792 **M'Daniel**, James, Esker, Queen's co., farmer
1728 ,, Mary, Coombe, Dublin, widow
1763 ,, Mary, widow of Dominick M'D., William-st., Dub., mercht.
1723 ,, Mathew, Dublin, grocer
1763 ,, Michael, Polestown, co. Kilkenny, farmer
1789 ,, Patrick, Booterstown, co. Dub., gardener
1796 ,, Richard, Dublin, brazier
1758 ,, William, Ballintlea, Queen's co., farmer
1798 **M'Daniell**, Constantine, Raheenduff, Queen's co., esq.
1732 **M'Dermot**, Michael, Castlemihane, co. Roscommon, gent.
1758 **M'Dermotroe**, Terence, Knockranhue, co. Roscommon, gent.
1786 **M'Dermott**, Anthony, Dublin, merchant
1804 ,, Bartholomew, Phibsborough, co. Dublin
1802 ,, Bridget, Dundalk, co. Louth, widow
1744 ,, Bryan, Lissoseeny, co. Sligo, gent.
1785 ,, Bryan, Courtduff, co. Kildare, farmer
1702 ,, Cormack, Ardconry, co. Roscommon, gent.
1765 ,, Dominick, Thomastown, co. Louth, gent.
1778 ,, Edmond, Emla, co. Roscommon, esq.
1803 ,, Elizabeth, Cork, widow
1789 ,, Francis, Dublin, gent.
1804 ,, Henry, Ballimore, co. Meath
1809 ,, James, Aughamore, co. Leitrim
1811 ,, James, Roscommon
1724 ,, Jane, widow
1800 ,, Jane, Dublin, widow
1721 ,, John, Dublin, apothecary
1795 ,, John, Dublin, merchant
1801 ,, John, Dublin, attorney
1808 ,, John, city of Dub., linen draper
1773 ,, Mary, Dublin, spinster
1776 ,, Mary, Dublin, widow
1786 ,, Mary, Cootehill, co. Roscommon
1784 ,, Michael, Cork, goldsmith
1807 ,, Michael, Roscommon
1768 ,, Owen, Ballyglass, co. Roscommon, esq.
1787 ,, Owen, Usher's-quay, Dublin, esq.
1796 ,, Owen, Drumsna, co. Leitrim
1793 ,, Peter, Dublin, esq.
1797 ,, Philip, city of Dublin
1811 ,, Roger, teacher of music

1790 **M'Dermott**, Terence, ensign in 35th regt. of foot [See DARBY.]
1770 **M'Dermotteroe**, Elizab., Loughan, co. Westmeath, gentlewoman
1728 **M'Dermottroe**, Bryan, Castletehyn, co. Roscommon, gent.
1736 ,, Roger, Knockranny, co. Roscommon, gent.
1794 **M'Donagh**, Mathew, Dunmore, co. Galway
1724 ,, Patrick, Dublin, merchant [See M'DONOGH.]
1788 **M'Donald**, Angus, Wicklow town, shopkeeper [widow
1766 ,, Ann, Lurgan, co. Armagh,
1790 ,, Edmond
1762 ,, Hy., Drumcondra-lane, Dubl., gardener
1784 ,, Henry, Dorset-street, Dublin, gardener
1808 ,, James, Clondoolisk, King's co.
1804 ,, John, sergt. in 64th regt.
1811 ,, John, Sligo, merchant
1810 ,, Patrick, North King-st., Dub., victualler
1735 ,, Randal, Dublin [See M'DONNELL.]
1808 **M'Donall**, Miles, Cloonmore, co. Mayo [See M'DONNELL.]
1782 **M'Donaugh**, Richard, Kevin-street, Dublin, grocer [See M'DONOGH.]
1679 **M'Donell**, Alexander, Tate, co. Armagh, gent.
1780 ,, Alexander, Dublin, merchant
1779 ,, David, Capel-street, Dublin, whipmaker
1759 ,, Farah, Derouil, co. Mayo
1725 ,, Hy., Drumcondra-lane, Dublin, gardener
1739 ,, Mary, *alias* **Kelly**, *alias* **King**, *alias* **Harris**, wife to John M'D., Dublin, gent.
1743 ,, Randall, late of Barbadoes, now of Dublin, merchant
1594 ,, Teigh, Leslwaine (Copy from Cork)
1700 ,, William, lieut. in sir Hen. Bellassis' regt. of foot
1801 **M'Donnell**, Agnes, Castlebar, co. Mayo, widow
1701 ,, Alexander, *alias* **M'Greygoyer**, Dromusna, co. Leitrim, esq.
1775 ,, Alexander, Ballymagara, co. Antrim
1803 ,, Catherine, New Sackville-st., Dublin

1742 **M'Donnell**, Charles, Kilkee, co. Clare, esq.
1792 ,, Charles, Newhall, co. Clare, esq.
1802 ,, Charles, Terenure, co. Dublin, carpenter
1803 ,, Darby, Killeen, co. Dub., paper manufacturer
1738 ,, Elizabeth, Limerick, widow
1804 ,, Elizabeth, widow
1791 ,, Ellinor, Dublin, widow
1744 ,, Eneas, Dublin, brewer
1777 ,, Fardy, Newry, co. Down, merchant
1770 ,, Francis, Mucline, co. Mayo, gent.
1728 ,, dame Hannah, widow of sir Randal M., bart.
1787 ,, Henry, esq.
1738 ,, James, Kilkee, co. Clare, esq.
1738 ,, James, Cloncullen, co. Clare, gent.   [gent.
1771 ,, James, Taunagh, co. Mayo,
1784 ,, James, Adderig, co. Dublin, gent.
1790 ,, James Martin
1790 ,, James, Newmarket-on-the-Coomb, brewer
1807 ,, Jas., Dolphin's Barn, co. Dub.
1776 ,, Jeremy, Castlebar, co. Mayo, gent.
1797 ,, John, Dublin, merchant
1806 ,, John, Charleville
1790 ,, Mary, Dublin, widow
1792 ,, Mary, Limerick, widow
1730 ,, Michael, Castlebar, co. Mayo, merchant
1759 ,, Patrick, Castlebar, co. Mayo, gent.
1786 ,, Patrick Randall, Liberty Hall, co. Mayo, esq.
1770 ,, Randal, Carrickmacross, co. Monaghan, tanner
1777 ,, Randal, Rossbeg, co. Mayo, gent.
1738 ,, Randall, Kilbrickan, co. Clare, esq.
1741 ,, Randall, commonly called sir Randal M'D., bart.
1810 ,, Rose, Hanover-st., Dubl., wid.
1788 ,, Sarah, Newport, co. Mayo
1793 ,, Thomas, Lurgan-st., Dublin, merchant
1809 ,, Thomas, Essex-st., Dublin, painter
1736 ,, Walter, Dublin, commander of the ship "Randal"
1777 ,, William, Dublin, grocer
    [See M'DONALD, M'DONALL, O'DONNEL.]

1810 **M'Donogh**, Andrew, Tuam, co. Galway, merchant
1777 ,, Anne
1761 ,, Anthony, Hillsborough, co. Clare, gent.
1783 ,, Augustine, Monasterevan, co. Kildare, innkeeper
1799 ,, Charles, Ennis, co. Clare, esq., M.D.
1741 ,, Edmond, Limerick, merchant
1738 ,, Ellinor, widow of Terence M'D., now of Belnagaw
1752 ,, Ellinor, Townagh, co. Clare, widow
1739 ,, Farrell, Dublin, tailor
1788 ,, Francis, Sligo, gent.
1789 ,, Frederick, Dublin, farmer
1738 ,, John, Cahirmaguily, co. Clare
1748 ,, Michael, Dublin
1758 ,, Michael, Dublin, linendraper
1755 ,, Miles, Back-lane, Dubl., linendraper
1796 ,, Miles, the elder, Trabane, co. Galway, gent.
1751 ,, Nicholas, Beaghagh, co. Clare, gent.
1752 ,, Patrick, Ennis, co. Clare, gent.
1755 ,, Patk., Frearghan, co. Londonderry, gent.
1771 ,, Patrick, Dublin, gent.
1801 ,, Peter, Londonderry city, atty.-at-law
1713 ,, Terence, Dublin, esq.
    [See M'DONAGH, M'DONAUGH.]
1789 **M'Donough**, Charles, Plunket-st., Dublin, broker
1796 ,, Laughlin, Huntsfield
1801 **M'Dougall**, Andrew, city of Waterford
1748 **M'Dougle**, Hugh, mariner
    [See M'DOWELL.]
1706 **M'Dowal**, David, sen., Arging, co. Monaghan
1795 **M'Dowall**, Andrew, Killybegs, co. Donegal
1728 **M'Dowell**, Benjamin, Rathmore, co. Antrim, linendraper
1802 ,, Frances
1804 ,, Henry, Killybegs, esq.
1748 ,, Hugh, Donaghadee, co. Down, gent.
1798 ,, James, lieut. in 89th regiment of foot
1749 ,, John, Ballitrust, co. Cavan, gent.
1749 ,, John, Carrickfergus, esq.
1762 ,, John, Drogheda, land surveyor
1811 ,, John, Lisburn, co. Antrim, tobacconist

1772 **M'Dowell**, Samuel, Newry
1801 ,, Willdridge, Aughnacloy, co. Tyrone, shopkeeper
1658 ,, Withrid, Ballymaconnell, co. Down, gent. **[VIII.** 3
1594 **M'Edmond**, Molmoreny, Raheen, Queen's co., one of the captains of Her Majesty's Gallowglasses
1788 **M'Egan**, Darby, Birr, King's co.
1733 ,, John, Shanagh, co. Tipperary, gent.
1668 ,, Stephen, Lisliogh, co. Tipperary, gent.
1797 **M'Ellheenny**, James, Prospect, co. Tyrone
1809 **M'Ennery**, James, Thomastown, co. Kilkenny
1772 ,, Richard, Callan, co. Kilkenny
1807 ,, Thomas, Dawson-st., perfumer
1763 **M'Enroe**, Edmond
1748 **M'Evers**, Nicodemus, Dublin, merchant
1809 **M'Evoy**, Danl., Mountrath, Queen's co.
1789 ,, Dennis, Dublin, silk dyer
1808 ,, Francis, Abbey-st., Dublin, surgeon
1740 ,, George, Dublin, gent.
1775 ,, James, Dublin, gent.
1770 ,, John, Lib. of Dublin, farmer
1791 ,, Thomas, Drogheda, linen merchant
1800 ,, Thomas, Drogheda, merchant
1808 ,, Timothy, Townsend-st., Dubl., carpenter
1788 ,, Wm., Longford town, farmer
1744 **M'Farlan**, Giles, Dublin
1808 **M'Farland**, James, Strabane, co. Tyrone
1810 ,, Patrick, Leardan
1789 **M'Farran**, Hugh, Dublin, gent.
1790 ,, John, solr.-gen. in the Carribee Islands (Copy)
1788 ,, Margaret, Nassau-st., Dublin, gentlewoman
1763 **M'Farren**, James, Dublin, gent.
1711 **M'Farsan**, James, Dublin, mariner
1771 **M'Gachin**, rev. Stephen, Ardillas, King's co.
1778 ,, Susanna, *alias* **Lewis**
1753 **M'Gaghan**, Mathew, Drumcondra-lane, gardener
1799 **M'Garr**, John, Dolphin's Barn, co. Dublin, gent.
1771 " Nicholas, Walshestown
1811 **M'Garry**, Charles, Poyntz's Pass, co. Armagh
1808 ,, Owen, Johnson's-court, Dubl., shoemaker

1796 **M'Garvey**, Gilbert, Maynooth, co. Kildare
1783 **M'Gauly**, James, Copper-alley, Dublin, gent. [See M'AULEY.]
1763 **M'Gauran**, Edward, Dublin, M.D.
1811 ,, Michael, Clonbockoge, co. Cavan
1787 **M'Gawley**, Anne, Newry, spinster
1772 ,, Bartholomew, Ardee, co. Louth [See M'AULEY.]
1742 **M'Gee**, Charles, Ballymoney, co. Antrim
1776 ,, James, Glasnevin-road, co. Dublin, merchant
1808 ,, Thomas, Clondolesk, King's co., farmer
1756 **M'Geough**, Joshua, Drumsill, co. Armagh, gent.
1678 **Macghee**, David, Loghmonie, co. Tyrone
1752 ,, George, Strabane, co. Tyrone [See MAGEE.]
1767 **M'Ghee**, Rebecca, Dublin, widow
1727 ,, Theobald, Port M'Ghee, co. Kerry
1745 ,, Theobald, Dingle, co. Kerry [See MAGEE.]
1690 **M'Gill**, Hugh, Kirkstown, co. Down, esq. (Ex.)
1683 ,, James, Ballymonestragh, co. Down, esq. (Ex.)
1723 ,, Thomas, Dublin, innholder [See MAGILL.]
1721 **M'Gilldoney**, Edmond, Towernacroune, co. Antrim, gent.
1684 **M'Ginn**, Catherine, *alias* **M'Donell**, widow
1777 **M'Ginnis**, Honora, Galway town, widow
1767 ,, Owen, Galway
1787 **M'Glathry**, Thomas, Foughart, co. Louth, farmer
1791 **M'Gough**, William, Armagh
1807 **M'Gowan**, Anne, Harold's-cross, co. Dublin, widow
1804 ,, Robert, Dublin, atty.-at-law
1759 **M'Gown**, Alexander, lieut. in col. Lambton's regt. of foot
1747 ,, Wm., Donaghadee, co. Down, merchant
1780 **M'Gowran**, Joanna, Blackhorse-lane, Dublin, widow [See MAGAURAN.]
1760 **M'Grah**, John, Dublin, innholder [See MAGRATH.]
1775 **M'Graigor**, Christopher, Drumall, co. Fermanagh
1764 **M'Grane**, Thomas [See MAGRANE.]

1803 **M'Grath**, Daniel, Charleville, co. Cork, publican
1705 ,, Margt., *alias* **Creagh**, Limk., widow
1804 ,, Thomas, Belfast, co. Antrim, gent.
1777 ,, Wm., Ballymacart, co. Waterford, gent.
   [See MAGRATH.]
1780 **M'Grean**, Michael, Baltrasna, co. Meath, farmer
1807 **M'Gregor**, John, Limerick, tallow chandler
1760 ,, Patrick
1780 **M'Grinn**, Daniel, Clondavin, co. Meath
1746 **M'Guier**, James, mariner belonging to the "Suffolk" man-of-war
1795 **M'Guire**, Andrew, Knowth, co. Meath, grazier
1810 ,, Arthur, Dawson-st., Dublin, esq.
1741 ,, Constantine, Dublin, victualler
1800 ,, Constantine, Drumcliff, co. Clare
1789 ,, Elizabeth, Dublin, widow
1808 ,, Elizabeth, Drogheda, widow
1799 ,, Francis, Dublin, esq.
1766 ,, James, Watling-street, Dublin, skinner
1773 ,, John, Killartry, co. Louth
1778 ,, John, Lisnagderry, co. Fermanagh
1794 ,, Joseph, Dublin city
1793 ,, Margaret, Fishamble-st., Dublin, widow   [farmer
1710 ,, Patk., Moorchurch, co. Meath,
1781 ,, Patrick, par. St. Mary, Dublin, manufacturer
1727 ,, Richard, Dublin, banker
1754 ,, Thomas, Clunimore, co. Meath, farmer
1786 ,, William, par. St. George, Hanover-square, esq.
   [See MAGUIRE.]
1798 **M'Guirk**, Arthur, Dolphin's Barn, timber merchant
1795 **M'Gusty**, Daniel, Dublin city, esq.
1811 ,, Robert, Navan, co. Meath
1780 **M'Gwire**, Jas., Dublin, merchant
1700 **M'Gwyre**, Bryan, Carrickmagriffin, co. Tipperary, gent.
1578 **M'Gye**, Edmond, par. Balscaden
1711 **M'Hallam**, David, Athlone, mercht.
1737 **Machan**, Wm., capt. in earl Effingham Howard's regt.
1793 **Macharron**, Moses, London, mercht.
1733 **Machel**, Hugh, surveyor of the port of Strangford

1738 **Machel**, Jane, Dublin
1657 **Machen**, John, trooper   **[VI**. 94
   [See MACHAN.]
1679 **Machlie**, William, Dublin, gent.
1779 ,, William, Dublin, gent.
1720 **M'Holm**, James, Galway, merchant
1780 **Machonchy**, George, Dublin, M.D.
1806 ,, George, esq.
1799 ,, John, Cloghog, co. Antrim, gent.
   [See M'CONCHY.]
1798 **M'Hugh**, Edwd., Dublin, clergyman
1793 ,, Ellinor, Headfort
1787 ,, Mary, Knockageehan, co. Fermanagh, widow
1804 ,, Michael, Lodge, co. Galway
1763 ,, Patrick, Kilmain, co. Mayo
1809 **M'Hugo**, Walter, Grousehill, co. Galway, esq.
1743 **M'Ilroth**, Thomas, Ballyrenny, co. Down
1777 **M'Ilwain**, Thomas, Belfast, co Antrim, merchant
1811 **M'Ilwaine**, James, Newtown Limavady, co. Londonderry
1732 **M'Inerheny**, Michael, Limerick, merchant
1804 **M'Ininch**, John, Liverpool, mariner
1785 **M'Intire**, Robert, lieut. in the 100th regt. of foot
1808 **M'Intosh**, Alexander, Powerscourt, co. Wicklow, gent.
1810 **M'Kane**, Sarah, city of Dublin, esq.
1627 **M'Keallegh**, Teigh, Kilbalintalone, Queen's co., gent.
1743 **M'Kedy**, James, Ballymena, co. Antrim, merchant
1753 ,, Wm., Ballymena, co. Antrim, merchant
1807 **M'Keever**, Mary, Keeverstown, co. Louth, widow
1781 **M'Keney**, Jno., Galway, shopkeeper
1801 **M'Kenly**, John, Kilmainham, co. Dublin, gent.
1803 ,, Townly, Dublin, carpenter
1791 **M'Kenna**, Francis, Dundalk, co. Louth, gent.
1762 ,, James, Dublin, gent.
1795 ,, James, Dundalk, co. Louth, merchant
1790 ,, John, par. priest of Donnymore and Kilbride
1808 ,, John, Carrick-on-Suir, co. Tipperary, R.M.C.
1791 ,, Mathew
1794 ,, Patrick
1809 ,, Theobald, Dublin, barrister
1765 ,, Thomas
1782 **M'Kenny**, Jas., Stephen-st., Dubl., hosier

1790 **M'Kenny**, Thomas, the Royal Hospital, sergt.-major
1787 **M'Kensie**, Samuel, the younger, Caledon Manor, co. Tyrone
1796 **M'Keogh**, Stephen, Dunlow, co. Galway
1809 **M'Keon**, John, Dublin city, chandler
1768 ,, Owen, Drimdoo, co. Leitrim, gent.
[See M'KONE, M'OWEN.]
1762 **M'Keough**, John
[See KEHOE, M'KEOGH.]
1701 **M'Kerrall**, Robert, Dublin, mercht.
[See M'CARRELL.]
1749 **M'Kibbon**, Joseph, Hillsborough, co. Down
[See GIBBON.]
1787 **M'Kieran**, Bryan, Cornmarket, Dublin, linendraper
1766 **M'Kiernan**, Bryan, Ned, co. Cavan
1765 ,, Frances, Stomulley, co. Longford
1761 ,, John Philip, Derrycassan, co. Longford, M.D.
1764 **M'Killip**, Neil, Coleraine, mercht.
1758 **M'Kinlie**, Nathaniel, Ballinasloe, co. Galway, esq.
1764 **M'Kinly**, Alexander, Altnacarney, co. Tyrone
1721 **M'Kinsie**, Ann, widow of Alexander M'K., Belfast, mariner
1783 ,, John, Cloondaharrow, co. Roscommon
1806 **M'Kinson**, Thos., Trim, co Meath, publican
1792 **M'Kinstry**, John, Armagh city, attorney-at-law
1803 **M'Kippins**, John
1805 **M'Knight**, John, Limerick city, surgeon
1801 **M'Kone**, Arthur, Belrobin, co. Louth, farmer
1791 ,, Nicholas, Ardglass
[See M'KEON.]
1773 **M'Laughlin**, Cornelius, Drogheda, merchant
1769 ,, John, Dublin, merchant
1790 ,, Margt., Watling-st., Dublin, widow
1795 ,, Martha, Abbeytown, co. Roscommon, widow
1804 ,, Patrick, Dublin city, esq. [esq.
1670 ,,. Richd., Ballydowney, co. Kerry,
1758 ,, William, Dublin, merchant
[See M'LOGHLIN, M'LOUGHLIN, MELLAUGHLIN.]
1782 **M'Lean**, John, Drumcondra, co. Dublin, vintner
1807 ,, John, Dublin city, watchmaker
[See M'CLEAN.]

1736 **M'Leanhan**, John, Conway, co. Donegal (This will declared void)
1722 **M'Lelan**, John, Dublin, gent.
1773 **M'Leland**, Thomas, Lisnaree, co. Down
[See M'CLELLAND.]
1811 **M'Leod**, Margaret, *alias* **Daniel**, Dublin city, widow
1721 **M'Leroy**, Samuel, Lazers-hill, Dublin, shipwright
1685 **M'Loghlin**, John, Dublin, gent.
[See M'LAUGHLIN.]
1785 **M'Lorinan**, Hugh, Temple-st., Dublin, esq.
1810 ,, James, Cornmarket, Dublin, linendraper
1697 ,, Margaret, *alias* **Morris**, widow of Patrick Moder M'L., Aghadrimdirige, co. Tyrone
1720 ,, Math., Moneymore, co. Derry, gent.   [gent.
1728 ,, Math., Moneymore, co. Derry,
1747 ,, Patrick, Pill-lane, Dublin, victualler
1769 ,, Thos., Annaghbrish, co. Derry, gent.
1756 **M'Loughlan**, Philip, Cork, mariner
1765 ,, Terence, Anglesey-st., Dublin
1793 **M'Loughlin**, Hugh, Shrove, co. Donegal
1810 ,, James, Borahan, co. Kildare
1811 ,, Thos., Bannagher, King's co.
[See M'LAUGHLIN.]
1794 **M'Mahon**, Ann, Summerhill, co. Dublin
1775 ,, Anne, Dublin, widow
1806 ,, Arthur, Queen's co., shopkeeper
1773 ,, Bryan, Coolgreany, co. Wexford, innkeeper
1794 ,, Catherine, Cork, spr.
1805 ,, Cath., Ballyglass, co. Clare, widow
1724 ,, Coll, Belletreane, co. Monaghan, gent.
1787 ,, Donatt, Clenagh, co. Clare, esq.
1759 ,, Donnell, Querin, co. Clare, gent.
1706 ,, Francis, Dublin, merchant
1754 ,, Glasney, Dublin, brewer
1754 ,, Henry, Clenagh, co. Clare
1797 ,, Henry, Limerick city, gent.
1738 ,, Hugh, Armagh, sometimes residing in Drogheda
1793 ,, Hugh, Glasnevin, co. Dublin, surgeon
1775 ,, James, Hollywood, co. Galway
1804 ,, James, Aghaglass, co. Monaghan

1773 **M'Neale**, Daniel, Navan, co. Louth, esq.
1763 ,, Hellen, widow of lieut. Rochford M'Neale
1802 ,, James, Newry, co. Armagh
1769 ,, John, Lower Faughart, co. Louth, esq.
1783 ,, Malcolm, Ballymascanlan, co. Louth, esq.
1707 ,, Robert, Dublin, gent.
1745 ,, Robt., Bombay, mariner (Copy)
1783 ,, Robert, Ballymascanlan, esq.
1737 ,, Rochfort, Dublin, gent.
1743 ,, Sarah, Caleresaken, co. Antrim, widow
1709 **M'Neil**, Danl., Binian, co. Donegal, esq.
1765 ,, Eliz., Dublin, widow
1731 ,, Henry, Ballymascanlan, co. Louth, esq.
1729 ,, Hugh
1800 ,, Hugh, Mullingar, co. Westmeath
1738 ,, Neil, Belfast, co. Antrim
1800 **M'Neill**, Alexander, Drimnakell, co. Antrim
1758 ,, Ann, *alias* **Montgomery**, wid. of Hector M'Neill, Dunseverick, co. Antrim, esq.
1756 ,, Archibald, Belfast, gent.
1765 ,, Daniel, Coleraine, co. Derry, esq.
1788 ,, Daniel, Monaghan town, M.D.
1803 ,, Gordon, Dublin city
1802 ,, John, Dublin, gent.
1801 ,, Lyndon, Dublin, spinster
1788 ,, Mary, Drumlumph Wallace, co. Derry
1788 ,, Roger, Dublin, esq.
1795 ,, William, Culbane, co. Londonderry, gent.
[See M'NEALE.]
1798 **M'Neilly**, Mary, Dublin, widow
1749 **M'Nemara**, Bridget, Cork, widow
1740 ,, Francis, Ardagh, King's co., esq.
1760 ,, George, Cong, co. Mayo, esq. (Not proved)
1684 ,, James, Ennis, co. Clare, gent.
1785 ,, James, Ayle, co. Clare, esq.
1708 ,, John, Limerick, merchant
1742 ,, John, Limerick, merchant
1748 ,, Jno., Ballymarkahan, co. Clare
1783 ,, John, Limerick city
1788 ,, John, Chirinagh, co. Clare, gent.
1750 ,, Lott, Cohy, co. Clare, gent.
1808 ,, Mary, Tuam, co. Galway
1718 ,, Mathew, Oldcourt, co. Cork, farmer

1765 **M'Nemara**, Mathew, Athlone, apothecary
1774 ,, Mathew, Limerick, esq.
1794 ,, Mathew, O'Brien's Bridge, co. Clare, gent.
1747 ,, Norcott, Limerick, gent.
1779 ,, Thady, Ayle, co. Clare, esq.
1799 ,, Thady, Dublin city, gent.
1735 ,, Thomas, Cork, merchant
1740 ,, Thos., Clounfadder, co. Clare, gent.
1783 ,, Thomas, Fenloe, co. Clare, esq.
1780 ,, Timothy, Formoyle, co. Clare, esq.
1762 ,, William, Doolen, co. Clare, esq. (Proved in 1777)
1775 ,, William, Rathany, co. Limk., gent.
1777 ,, Wm., Doolen, co. Clare, esq. [See M'NAMARA.]
1764 **M'Noe**, Joseph, sen., Ballymena, co. Antrim, late capt. in col. Whiteshed's regt. of foot
1561 **M'Nolly**, Maurice, par. Castleknock
1757 **M'Owen**, John, Dublin, carrier [See M'KEON.]
1802 **M'Parlan**, Bernard, Sligo, doctor in physic
1790 **M'Peake**, Neale, the elder, Ardnagross, co. Antrim
1736 **M'Quein**, capt. in the Royal Regt. of Foot
1769 **M'Quilan**, Mary, Dublin, widow
1659 **M'Quin**, Roger, Ballycassan, co. Clare, gent. [**VII.** 167
1787 **M'Quoid**, Thomas, Downpatrick, merchant
1747 **M'Quon**, Cicily, Dublin, widow
1747 **M'Quone**, John, Dublin, poulterer
1586 **M'Robens**, George, soldier
1791 **M'Roberts**, Elizabeth, Dublin, wid.
1744 ,, Nicholas, Dublin, distiller
1807 **M'Robin**, Andrew
1755 **M'Sharry**, Abraham, Drogheda, M.D.
1810 **M'Sorly**, Michael, Bridge-st., Dub., merchant
1799 **M'Sweeny**, Bryan, Kanturk, co. Cork, gent.
1795 ,, Henry, Kanturk, co. Cork
1721 ,, Morgan, Cork, merchant (1722)
1796 **M'Swiny**, Martin, Dromtarriff, farmer
1797 ,, Morgan, Kilnaglory, co. Cork
1802 ,, Morgan, Macroom, co. Cork, farmer and shopkeeper
1639 **M'Swyny**, Dwell, Kilmore, co. Tipperary, gent.

1772 **Maddison**, Catherine, Irishtown, co. Dublin, spinster
1776 ,, Dorothea, Irishtown, co. Dubl., spinster
1754 ,, John, Dublin, gent.
1755 ,, Margt., Monkstown, co. Dubl., spinster
1788 ,, Martha, Irishtown, co. Dublin, spinster
1771 ,, Mary, Irishtown, co. Dublin, spinster
1804 **Maddock**, Frances, Waterford city, spinster
1732 ,, Hannah, Coldblow, co. Dublin, widow
1780 ,, Henry, Gilbertstown, co. Meath, gent.
1736 ,, Isaac, formerly of Dublin, now of Enniscorthy, co. Wexford, gent.
1762 ,, James, Dublin, esq.
1794 ,, John, Prussia-st., Dublin, gent.
1756 ,, Joseph, capt. in col. Stewart's regt. of foot
1782 ,, Robert, Dublin, gent.
1803 ,, Wm., Waterford city, watch-maker
[See MADOX, &c.]
1804 **Maddox**, Jane, Dublin city, widow
1594 ,, William
1658 **Madhop**, Edmond, Dublin, esq.
[VII. 36
1739 **Madock**, Isaac, Dublin, merchant
1715 ,, Joseph, Dublin, linendraper
1738 **Madocks**, John, Dublin, merchant
1739 ,, Martha, Dublin, widow
1726 ,, Samuel, Dublin, merchant
1594 **Madox**, Hugh
[See MADDOCK.]
1754 **Madras**, Anne, Cork
1774 ,, John, Cork, clk.
1808 **Maffet**, Samuel, Farranfad, co. Down, esq.
1804 **Maffit**, John, Cope-st., Dubl., tailor
1765 **Maffitt**, William, Clogh
1784 **Magaghran**, John, Corcandess, co. Cavan, gent.
[See MAGAURAN.]
1793 **Magan**, Anne, widow
1777 ,, Arthur, formerly of Togherstown, co. Westmeath, late of Clonearl, King's co., esq. (Large will)
1808 ,, Arthur, Clonearl, King's co., esq.
1754 ,, Edward, Togherstown, co. Westmeath, esq.
1805 ,, Mary, Leeson-street, Dublin
1738 ,, Morgan, Togherstown, co. Westmeath, esq.

1732 **Magan**, Richard, Unnoe, co. Westmeath, gent.
1710 ,, Thos., Togherstown, co. Westmeath
1750 ,, Thos., Togherstown, co. Westmeath, esq.
[See MANGAN.]
1806 **Magarr**, John, Anglesea-st., Dublin city
1781 **Magarry**, Bryan, Pill-lane, Dublin
1754 ,, Patrick, Balledock, co. Down
1733 **Magauran**, Daniel, Ballinrink, co. Meath, gent.
1796 ,, Edmond, Liseaughty
[See MAGAGHRAN, MAGAWRAN.]
1731 **Magauen**, David, Scurlogstown, co. Kildare, farmer
[See MAGAGHRAN, M'GOWRAN.]
1727 **Magaw**, John, Brafords-st., Dublin, clothier
1729 **Magawley**, John, Tully, co. Westmeath, gent.
1739 ,, John, Tully, co. Westmeath
1800 ,, Patk., Awley, Temora, King's co.
[See M'AULEY.]
1784 **Magawran**, Patk., Kells, co. Meath, farmer
[See MAGAURAN.]
1796 **Mageary**, Michael, Mohill, co. Leitrim, gent.
1781 **Magee**, Andrew, Waterstown, co. Meath, baker
1763 ,, Ann, Dublin, widow
1702 ,, Charles, Cavin (Dated in 1702)
1804 ,, Charles, Glendun, co. Antrim
1802 ,, Christopher
1752 ,, Henry, Carrickfergus, gent. (Dated 1752)
1753 ,, Henry, Carrickfergus, gent.
1801 ,, James, Naas, co. Kildare
1763 ,, Nicholas, formerly of Dublin, now of Lisburn, co. Antrim
1801 ,, Nicholas, Tankardstown, co. Meath
1804 ,, Owen, Cloughogh, co. Antrim
1758 ,, Patrick, Drogheda, carman
1795 ,, Robert, Dublin, merchant
1798 ,, William, conductor of Ordnance in India
1801 ,, Wm., Summerhill, co. Down
[See MACGHEE, M'GHEE, MAGHEE.]
1754 **Magenis**, Anne, widow of Daniel M., Dromentyan, co. Down, esq.
1735 ,, Arth., Calragh, co. Down, gent.
1756 ,, Arthur, Glan, co. Down, gent.
1631 ,, Bryan Oge M'Brown, Edentecullowe, co. Down, gent.
[II. 268

1726 **Magenis,** Daniel, Castlewellan, co. Down, esq.
1765 ,, Mary, widow of John M., Shanrod, co. Down, gent.
1640 ,, Hugh Fitzjohn, Newry, gent.
1808 ,, col. Hugh, Dublin city
1706 ,, Phelemy, Castlewellan, co. Down, esq.
1730 ,, Richard, Dromore, co. Down, gent.
1757 ,, Richard, Dublin, gent.
1793 ,, Roger, Bally Ely, co. Down
1751 **Mageniss,** Thomas, Naventown, co. Meath, gent.
1684 **Magenisse,** Constantine, King's Inn, Dublin, esq.
1780 **Magennis,** Arthur, Ballymecraeny, co. Down
1790 ,, Arthur, Ballsgrove, near Drogheda
1807 ,, Edward, Lisburn, co. Antrim, merchant
1782 ,, Elizabeth, Dungannon, co. Tipperary, widow
1803 ,, John, Dublin city, gent.
1804 ,, John, Ryder's-row, Dublin
1807 ,, Richard, Warringstown, co. Down, esq.
1793 **Mageough,** Joshua, Greenwood Park, co. Down
1808 ,, Shelton, Greenwood Park, co. Down, spinster
1811 **Maghan,** Frances
1771 ,, James, *alias* **Mahan,** Firalahon, co. Galway, gent.
1774 ,, Julian, Castle Taylor, co. Galway, widow
1771 ,, Martin, Drimconnert, co. Galway, gent.
1800 ,, Martin, Drimconnert, co. Galway, gent.
[See **Mahon.**]
1770 **Maghee,** Rev. George, Strabane, co. Tipperary, clerk
[See in B 1769.] [See **Magee.**]
1738 **Maghlin,** Robert, Breekhill, co. Clare, esq.
1738 **Magill,** Captain James, Bombay, East Indies
1765 ,, Henry, Dublin, gent.
1800 ,, James, L'Derry city, merchant
1718 ,, Jane, Lurgan, Armagh, widow
1677 ,, John, Gillhall, co. Down, esq. (Ex.)
1699 ,, John, Gillhall, co. Down, bart.
1780 ,, John, Dublin, formerly of the North Strand, esq.
1795 ,, John, Ballycrun, co. Down, farmer
1748 ,, Mary, Dublin, spinster

1806 **Magill,** Mary, Dublin city, widow
1789 ,, rev. Moses, curate of St. Mary's par., Dublin
1808 ,, Rachel, Dublin city, widow
1790 ,, Richard, Drumgath, co. Down
1745 ,, Robert Hawkins, Gill Hall, co. Down, esq.
1761 ,, Samuel, Ardmillan, co. Down
1798 ,, Samuel, Clintanagoolan, co. Down, farmer
[See M'Gill.]
1793 **Magiverin,** Richard, tailor
1603 **Maglanoghan,** Loghlin, co. Westmeath
1794 **Maglew,** John, Skerries, co. Dubl., mariner
1773 **Magran,** Patk., Drogheda, brewer
1782 ,, Patrick, Crow-street, Dublin, gent.
1804 **Magrane,** Edward, Baldoyle
1804 ,, Mathew, Stamullin, co. Meath yeomanry
[See M'Grane.]
1804 **Magrath,** Anne, New Ross, co. Wexford
1806 ,, Anne, New Ross, co. Wexford, widow
1737 ,, Cornelius, Clonmel, co. Tipperary, widow
1791 ,, Deborah, Dublin, spinster
1682 ,, Ellen, *alias* **Bagot,** Ballinlee, co. Limerick, widow
1785 ,, Eneas, Knockmain, co. Roscommon, esq.
1807 ,, Folliott, Dublin, esq.
1769 ,, James, Castlerea, co. Rosc.
1809 ,, James, Gal. town, shopkeeper
1730 ,, John, Derry, co. Tipperary
1741 ,, Luke, Clonybeg, co. Clare, gent.
1673 ,, Marcus, Clarina, co. Limerick, gent.
1800 ,, Mark, capt. 89th reg. of foot
1726 ,, Martin, Dublin, victualler
1775 ,, Mary, Dublin, spinster
1810 ,, Mary, Dublin city
1674 ,, Marcus, Kilkenny, co. Limerick, gent.
1734 ,, Maurice, Dublin, gent.
1624 ,, Milerius, abp. of **Cashel,** q. v.
1772 ,, Philip, Raplough, co. Tip.
1798 ,, Sarah, Lurgangreen, co. Louth, widow
1718 ,, Terence, Gurteens, co. Tipperary, esq.
1744 ,, Terence, Redmondstown, co. Tipperary, gent.
1674 ,, Thos., Kilberry, co. Lim., esq.
[See M'Craith, M'Crath, M'Grah, M'Grath.]

1810 **Maguire**, Charles, Cork city, linen-draper
1769 ,, Connor, Farkagh, co. Fermanagh, gent.
1786 ,, Connor, Dublin, grocer
1639 ,, Edmond, Leixlip, gent.
1729 ,, Dublin, gent.
1757 ,, Elizabeth, Barnekilley, co. Dublin, gidow
1792 ,, Frances, Dublin, widow
1749 ,, Hugh
1766 ,, Hugh, Castle Nugent, co. Longford, esq.
1777 ,, Ignatius, Strand-st., Dublin, wine merchant
1719 ,, James, Dublin, esq.
1767 ,, Margaret, Dublin, widow
1783 ,, Michael
1801 ,, Michael, Dublin city
1734 ,, Morgan, Murphystown, co. Dublin, farmer
1780 ,, Morgan, Dublin, ribbon weaver
1807 ,, Patrick, Dublin city, M.D.
1775 ,, Philip, Dresoge, co. Meath, farmer
1790 ,, Philip, Dublin, esq.
1807 ,, Philip, Enniskillen, co. Ferm.
1801 ,, Richard, Cork, apothecary
1785 ,, Thomas, Drogheda, farmer
      [See MACGUIRE, M'GUIRE.]
1808 **Maher**, Daniel, Ballinasloe, co. Galway, gent.
1800 ,, Elizabeth, Eden Hall, co. Kilkenny, widow
1800 ,, James, Dublin, apothecary
1788 ,, John, Dublin, apothecary
1810 ,, Nicholas, Dublin city
1809 ,, Patrick, Kilrush, co Kildare, farmer
1803 ,, Timothy, Pill-lane, Dublin
      [See MEAGHER.]
1810 ,, Timothy, Nicholas-st., Dublin
1788 **Mahon**, Arthur, Cavetown, co. Rosc.
1686 ,, Barnaby, Dublin, gent.
1747 ,, Catherine, *alias* **Archer**, *alias* **Bugell**
1727 ,, Charles, Back-lane, Dublin, linen draper
1776 ,, Charles, Strokestown, co. Roscommon, merchant
1770 ,, Dominick, Dublin, merchant
1794 ,, Edmund, Cragleigh, co. Clare, esq.
1803 ,, Elizabeth, Dublin city, spinster
1739 ,, Ellinor, spinster
1743 ,, Ellinor, hon., Aughnamallagh, co. Monaghan, widow
1735 ,, Francis, Hanover-square, liberty of Donore, merchant
1744 ,, James, Killurin, K. co., farmer

1771 **Mahon**, James, *alias* **Maghan**, Firalahon, co. Galway, gent.
1783 ,, James, Ennis, co. Clare, esq.
1777 ,, John, Dolphin's Barn, co. Dubl., innholder
1785 ,, John, Castlegar, co. Gal., esq.
1794 ,, Lawrence, Limerick
1792 ,, Mary, Dublin, widow
1777 ,, Michl., Raheen, co. Galway, gent.
1759 ,, Murtogh, Ennis, merchant
1681 ,, Nicholas, Ballenemully, co. Roscommon, esq. (Ex.)
1778 ,, Nicholas, Limerick, merchant
1785 ,, Patrick, Strokestown, co. Roscommon, merchant
1785 ,, Patrick, Dublin
1788 ,, Paul, Dublin, merchant
1768 ,, very rev. Peter, Dean of Elphin
1767 ,, Ross, Castlegar, co. Galway, esq.   [esq.
1788 ,, Ross, Castlegar, co. Galway,
1801 ,, Susanna, Dublin city, spinster
1755 ,, Thomas, Dublin, ribbon weaver
1763 ,, Thomas, Dublin, merchant
1766 ,, Thomas, Ennis
1811 ,, rev. Thomas, Arenaduff, co. Leitrim
1788 ,, Timothy, Dublin, esq.
1733 ,, William, Dublin, gent.
      [See MAGHAN, MAUGHAN.]
1800 **Mahony**, Andrew, Cork city, gent.
1749 ,, Cornelius, Knockbrack, co. Kerry
1753 ,, Cornelius Lawrence, Cork
1790 ,, Dennis, Dromore, co. Kerry
1807 ,, Florence, Cullinagh, co. Kerry
1779 ,, John, Tralee, co. Kerry, mercht.
1807 ,, Kean, Cullinagh, co. Kerry, gent.
1753 ,, Mary, Cork, widow
1801 ,, Robert, Charleville, co. Cork
1658 ,, Teighe, in the army
1639 ,, Terlagh, Ardfert, co. Kerry, esq.
1783 ,, Timothy, Blackpool liberty, Cork, clothier
1743 ,, William, Cork, esq.
1799 ,, William, Carrigrohan, South Liberties of Cork
1805 ,, William, Rocksand quay, Cork, maltster
1604 **Maighey**, Robert, Dublin, baker
1763 **Maignon**, Peter, Dubl., sugar boiler
1726 **Mainaduc**, Alcide Bonniot, refugee, Cork city
1673 **Maine**, William, Dublin, carpenter
      [See MAYNE.]
1808 **Mainwaring**, John, riding master of the 17th light dragoons

1744 **Mainwarning**, Mary, widow
1593 ,, Richard, soldier under captain George Bingham
[See MAYNWARNING, &c.]
1749 **Maire**, Anne, Eyrecourt, co. Galway, widow
1583 ,, John, merchant, born in Edinburgh
[See MEARES.]
1720 **Maitland**, Adam, Hillsborough, co. Down
1783 ,, Adam, Newry, co. Down, merchant
1792 **Maitley**, John, Dublin, merchant
1745 **Major**, Charity of Carlingford, co. Louth, widow
1807 ,, Elizabeth, Charlemont-street, co. Dublin, widow
1752 ,, Henry, Camlin, co. Donegal
1798 ,, Henry, Ballyshannon, co. Donegal
1775 ,, rev. John, Camlin, co. Donegal, clerk
1808 ,, John, Killinacriddar, co. Donegal
1788 ,, Sarah, Muff, co. Derry
1580 ,, Wm., Dublin, tallow chandler
1725 ,, Wm., Acton, co. Armagh, clk.
1792 ,, rev. William, Erigle, co. Monaghan, clerk
1780 **Makilwaine**, Andrew, Derry, atty.
[See M'ILWAINE.]
1698 **Maklelan**, Alex., Dublin, merchant
1596 **Malbie**, dame Thomasin, widow of sir Nicholas M., knt.
1584 **Malby**, sir Nicholas, knt., gov. of Connaught and Thomond
1789 **Malcom**, Wm., Mt. Alexander, co. Down, gent.
1791 **Malcomson**, Rachel, Lurgan, co. Armagh, widow
1563 **Maledye**, Thos., par. Mallafrydred
1735 **Malet**, Abraham, Dublin, merchant
1756 **Maley**, Ann, *alias* **Brangan**, wife to Mathias M., Dublin, hosier
1740 ,, Daniel, Dublin, tailor
1744 ,, Thomas, Limerick, innholder
[See MALIE, MALLY.]
1748 **Malide**, Paul, major - general DeGrange's reg. of dragoons
1779 **Malie**, Andrew, Dublin, gent.
[See MALEY.]
1712 **Malkin**, Thomas, Dublin, victualler
1804 **Mallet**, Robert, Capel-st., Dublin, cabinetmaker
1637 **Mallone**, James, Trim, merchant
1758 **Mallows**, Chas., Dubl., embroiderer
1709 **Mally**, James, Knockmastre, co. Meath, farmer
[See MALEY.]

1658 **Malone**, Anne, Trim, wid. [**VII.** 33
1793 ,, Anne, Dublin, widow
1770 ,, Anthony, Ballinahowna, co. Westmeath, clerk
1776 ,, Anthony, Privy Councillor (Large will)
1793 ,, Catherine, Dublin, widow
1735 ,, Daniel, Dublin, gent.
1767 ,, David, Ballinahowna, co. Westmeath, esq.
1635 ,, Edmond, Dublin, alderman, [**IV.** 137
1736 ,, Edmond, Dublin, esq.
1758 ,, Edmond, Ballinahowna, co. Westmeath, esq.
1774 ,, Edmond, one of the Justices of the Common Pleas
1771 ,, Francis, Mecklenburgh-street, Dublin, esq.
1739 ,, Henry, Litter, King's co., esq.
1584 ,, James, Dublin, merchant
1721 ,, James, Dublin, bookseller
1743 ,, James, Winetavern-st., Dubl., ale seller
1781 ,, James, Ballyragan, co. Kildare, farmer
1791 ,, James, Clonmel, co. Tipperary, shopkeeper
1756 ,, Jane, Dublin, spinster
1597 ,, Jesper (No date)
1592 ,, John, Dublin, alderman
1657 ,, John, Dublin, maltster [**VI.** 87
1733 ,, John, Curtrons, co. Westmeath, esq.
1756 ,, John, Dublin, gent.
1799 ,, Joseph, Ballynagarig, co. Kild.
1765 ,, Letitia, Dublin, spinster
1644 ,, Margaret, Dublin, widow
1795 ,, Margaret, Dublin
1808 ,, Mary, Dublin city, wid. (Large)
1715 ,, Richard, Dublin, merchant
1717 ,, Richard, Ballynahowna, co. Westmeath, esq.
1758 ,, Richard, Dublin, gent.
1762 ,, Richard, Dublin, esq.
1783 ,, Richard, Elmgreen, co. Dublin, esq.
1806 ,, Richard, Dublin city
1783 ,, Ruth, Ballinahowna, co. Westmeath, widow
1757 ,, Thomas, col. Hopson's regt. of foot
1806 ,, Thomas, Ballinglen, co. Wick.
1666 ,, William, late of Lismullin, co. Meath, esq., Dubl., alderm.
1737 ,, William, Kilkenny, gent.
1788 **Malony**, John, Long-lane, Newstreet, Dublin
[See MOLONY.]
1767 **Malory**, Anne, Dublin, widow

1691 **Malrosse**, Alexander, Dusoge, co. Down, innkeeper
1655 **Man**, John, Dublin, upholsterer [**V.** 221
1678 ,, William, Dublin, upholsterer
1741 **Manby**, rev. George, chanter of Elphin
1796 **Manders**, John, Blackpool, North Lib. of Cork, clothier
1786 ,, Jonathan, Cork, merchant
1740 **Mandeville**, Catherine, Cappagh, co. Tipperary, widow
1749 ,, Catherine, Clonmel, widow
1769 ,, Edmond, Waterford, merchant
1790 ,, Edmond, Dublin, esq.
1776 ,, Edward, Raheen, co. Waterford, M.D.
1761 ,, Francis, Hamerton, co. Tipperary, gent.
1751 ,, Jas., Ballydine, co. Tipperary
1771 ,, John, Ballynahinnose, co. Tipperary, gent.
1765 ,, Thos., Ballydine, co. Tip., esq.
1809 **Mangan**, Alice, Mary-st., Dublin, widow
1740 ,, Christopher, Dublin, gent.
1726 ,, Ellinor, Legacurrin, Queen's co., widow
1749 ,, John, Dublin, butcher
1750 ,, John, Legacurrin, Queen's co., gent. [gent.
1777 ,, John, Piercetown, co. Kildare,
1809 ,, Michael, High-street, Dublin, woollen draper
1721 ,, Richard, Legacurrin, Queen's co., gent.
1769 ,, Richard
1779 ,, Richard, Dowdingstown, co. Kildare, gent.
1800 ,, Thomas, Dublin, gent. [See MAGAN, MANNING, MANNION.]
1769 **Mangham**, John, Dublin, grocer
1802 **Mangin**, Alexander, Dublin, esq.
1797 ,, Paul, formerly captain in 46th regt. of foot
1798 ,, Samuel Henry, Dublin, esq. [See MANGAN.]
1756 **Manifold**, Benjamin, Kilbride, co. Wicklow, farmer
1799 ,, Benj., Ferrybank, co. Wicklow, farmer
1735 **Manley**, Isaac, Dublin, esq.
1744 ,, John, Sedcop, Kent, esq.
1808 ,, Orlando, major-genl. of His Majesty's forces
1677 ,, Thomas, Ballyroan, Queen's co., minister of God's word
1803 **Manliff**, Josiah, Rooske, King's co., farmer

1803 **Manly**, Jos., Tullamore, King's co.
1805 ,, Joshua, Dublin city, merchant
1793 **Mann**, Charles, Moy, co. Tyrone
1789 ,, Isaac, bp. of **Cork**, q.v.
1607 **Manne** or **Manbe**, James, Atherdee, merchant
1811 **Mannen**, Charles, capt. in the 71st regiment
1810 **Mannin**, Anthony, Lismorta, co. Tipperary, esq.
1809 **Manning**, Archibald, Dublin city, gent. [farmer
1790 ,, George, Corballis, co. Wicklow,
1756 ,, John, Cork-st., Dubl., breeches maker
1788 ,, Nathaniel, Drakestown, co. Louth, gent.
1802 ,, Patrick, Dublin, innkeeper
1765 ,, Thomas, Clara, King's co., farmer
1811 ,, William [See MANGAN.]
1811 **Mannion**, Thomas, Bannagher, King's co. [See MANGAN.]
1771 **Mannix**, Geo., Youghal, co. Cork, alderman
1808 ,, William, Cork city, gent.
1673 **Manrasine**, Anth., Dublin, mercht.
1739 **Mansell**, Jane, Dublin, spr.
1711 ,, Thomas, Anarosty, co. Limk., gent. [See MAUNSELL.]
1688 **Mansergh**, Bryan, Ballyburr, co. Kilkenny, esq.
1725 ,, Danl., Macrony, co. Cork, esq.
1786 ,, Elizabeth, Cashel city, co. Tipperary, widow
1705 ,, James, Macrony, co. Cork, esq. (Large)
1774 ,, James, Macrony, co. Cork, esq. (Large will)
1768 ,, Nicholas, Greenane, co. Tipperary, esq.
1777 ,, Richd., Ballyboulter, co. Dublin, paper manufacturer
1754 ,, Sarah, *alias* **Wemys**, widow of George M. Coolgrange, co. Kilkenny
1707 ,, Wm., par. St. Clement Danes, Middlesex, gent.
1636 **Manseur**, Margett, Inch, Queen's co., widow
1796 **Mansfield**, Elizabeth, Lodge House, co. Waterford
1807 ,, Patrick, Dublin, leather seller
1798 ,, rev. Ralph, Letterkenny, co. Donegal
1770 ,, Rhoda, Lifford, co. Donegal, spinster

1776 **Mansfield,** Wm., Hamond's-marsh, Cork
1794 ,, William, earl of
[See MAUNSELL.]
1747 **Manson,** James, Fairview, co. Armagh, esq.
1702 ,, capt. Theophilus
1721 **Manus,** Catherine, widow of Patk. M., Adamstown
1607 **Manve** or **Marme,** James, Atherdee, merchant
1737 **Manwaring,** Charles, capt. in gen. Sutton's regiment [gent.
1807 ,, James, Gregg's-lane, Dublin,
1760 ,, Mary, Dublin
1732 ,, Thomas, Bristol
1736 ,, Thomas, Dublin, cooper
1727 ,, William, Maynooth, co. Kildare, gent.
1763 ,, William, Dublin, musician
1669 **Manwood,** col. Jerome, Woolwich, Kent (Copy)
1781 **Manypenny,** Hannah, Dublin, chandler
1802 ,, Thos., Pimlico, Dub., woollen manufacturer
1652 **Mapas,** Ignatius, Dublin, gent.
1756 ,, John, Dublin, esq. [esq.
1793 ,, John, Rochestown, co. Dublin,
1800 ,, John Folie, Dublin, esq.
1637 ,, Patrick, Dublin, alderman
[IV. 213, 1666-92
1762 **Maple,** William, Dublin, esq.
1809 **Mapletoft,** rev. Nathaniel, clerk
1779 **Maguay,** George, Dublin, mercht.
1800 ,, Susanna, Dublin, widow
1763 **Mara,** Francis, Charter House, Middlesex, pensioner
1803 ,, James, Newry, co. Armagh
1803 ,, Richd., Roscrea, co. Tipperary
[See MEARA.]
1778 **Marcell,** Lewis, Waterford, esq.
1782 ,, Magdalen, Waterford, widow
1767 **Marchant,** Eliz., *alias* **Hammond,** Waterford
1715 **DeMarchinville,** Abel Armeneaulet, Portarlington
1652 **Marckom,** Elizabeth, widow
[See MARKHAM.]
1796 **Margaret,** Margt., Dublin, spr.
1743 ,, Peter, capt. in gen. Bisset's regt. of foot
1745 ,, Peter, late capt. in col. Huske's regt. of foot
1768 **Margas,** John, Dublin, optician
1685 **Margetson,** Anne, Dublin, widow
1679 ,, James, archbishop of **Armagh,** q. v.
1690 ,, John, Dublin, esq., major in earl of Kingston's reg. of foot

1805 **Margisson,** Jane, Limerick city, merchant
1793 **Marguerin,** John, Ballyhaise, co. Cavan, gent.
1794 **Mark,** Elizabeth, Dublin, widow
1748 ,, Hugh, mariner on board the "Salisbury" man-of-war
1802 ,, Mary, Dublin, widow
1787 ,, Thomas, Limerick, merchant
1676 **Markes,** Nathaniel, Clare Hill, Queen's co., esq.
1794 **Markey,** Anne, Ninch, co. Meath, spinster
1782 ,, Jas., Ninch, co. Meath, farmer
1783 ,, James, Bellhill, co. Down
1775 ,, John, Dublin, cooper
1781 ,, John, Dublin, baker
1787 ,, Nicholas, Glaspistol, co. Louth, farmer
1770 ,, Thomas, Dunleer, co. Louth, brewer
1769 **Marky,** Thomas, Hungry Hall, co. Meath, carman
[See MARK.]
1750 **Markham,** George, Newabbey, co. Tipperary, gent.
1794 ,, John, Clonacody, co. Tipperary
1693 ,, Moses, Dublin, weaver
1694 ,, Stephen, Tuitestown, co. Westmeath, gent.
1743 ,, Susanna, Dublin, widow
1671 ,, Wm., Tuitestown, co. Westmeath
1744 ,, William, Dublin, late of Ashtown, co. Kilkenny, esq.
1780 ,, William, NewAbbey, co. Tipp., gent.
[See MARCKOM.]
1784 **Marklin,** rev. Gerard, Dublin, clk.
1781 **Marland,** John, Dub., sugar boiler
1795 ,, Paul, co. Wexford
1763 **Marlay,** Geo., bp. of **Dromore,** q. v.
1803 ,, Richd., bp. of **Waterford,** q. v.
1756 ,, Thomas, Lord Chief Justice of the King's Bench [esq.
1784 ,, Thos., Celbridge, co. Kildare,
[See MORLEY.]
1713 **DeMarlemont,** Rachel Texter, Portarlington, spinster
1732 **Marley,** Isabella, Dublin, widow
1657 ,, Symon, Portan, co. Meath
[VI. 232
[See MORLEY.]
1757 **Marlow,** Wm., Dublin, merchant
1733 **Marmion,** rev. Abel, Killevally, co. Westmeath, clk.
1798 ,, Anthony, Dundalk, co. Louth, baker
1796 ,, Henry, Lisburn, co. Antrim, gent.

1781 **Marmion**, Nicholas, Louth, co. Louth
1724 ,, Stephen, Dundalk, co. Louth, gent.
[See MERRYMAN, MARYMAN.]
1685 **Marnel**, Thomas, Ballyquin, co. Waterford, farmer
1687 **Marnell**, Edmond, Garryclohy, co. Tipperary, gent.
1796 ,, Edmond, Marnel's grove, co. Galway, esq.
1784 **Marner**, Henry, Ormond-quay, Dublin, grocer
1734 **Marney**, John, Dublin, merchant
1721 **Maroney**, Jas., Clonmel, merchant
1660 **Marow**, col. John, Chester, esq.
1728 **Marple**, Richd., Meath-st., Dublin
1659 **Marriot**, Thomas, gentleman-at-arms in capt. Vivian's company [VII. 181
1735 **Marriott**, Joseph, Dublin, gent.
1661 **Marris**, John, south Elmsaul, Yorkshire, gent. (Copy)
1800 **Marron**, Owen, Dublin, slater
1807 ,, Patk, Drogheda town, mercht.
1804 **Marsden**, Eleanor, Dublin city, wid.
1801 ,, John, Virvale, co. Wicklow
1668 ,, Josiah, Gallencoobelly, or Gallencrobelly, co. Wat., gent.
1737 ,, Margaret, Dublin, widow
1702 ,, Mary, *alias* **Loftus**, Athlone, widow
1754 **Marsh**, Anne, Dublin, widow
1752 ,, Barbara, Dublin, widow
1802 ,, Elizabeth, Camden-st., Dublin, spinster
1719 ,, Epaphroditus, Fethard, co. Tipperary, esq.
1713 ,, Francis, abp. of **Dublin**, q. v.
1771 ,, Francis, Dublin, esq.
1749 ,, Henry, Moyalley, K. co. esq.
1796 ,, Isaac, Dublin, attorney-at-law
1734 ,, v. rev. Jeremiah, D.D., dean of Kilmore
1790 ,, rev. Jeremy, rector of Athenry, diocese of Tuam
1753 ,, Judith, widow of v. rev. dean Jeremy Marsh
1695 ,, Mary, Dublin, widow
1713 ,, Narcissus,abp. of **Armagh**,q.v.
1737 ,, Peter, the elder, Moyalley, co. Westmeath, gent.
1740 ,, Peter, Moyalley, K. co., esq.
1804 ,, Peter, Ballynaminton, K. co.
1810 ,, Peter, Moate, co. Westmeath
1781 ,, Samuel, Knockmaroon, co. Dublin, gent.
1762 ,, Warburton, Moyalley, K. co.
1779 ,, William, Moyalley, K. co., esq.

1758 **Marshal**, Andrew, Ardsalla, co. Meath, gardener
1782 ,, Andrew, Ringclare, co. Down
1695 ,, Alex., Dublin, merchant
1773 ,, Anthony
1749 ,, Gregory, Gowran, co. Kilkenny
1805 ,, Jas., Analore, co. Monaghan, gent.
1806 ,, Jane
1806 ,, Jane, Armagh, spinster
1743 ,, John, par. Shankill, co. Arm., linendraper
1781 ,, John, Tuam, co. Galway, gent.
1782 ,, John, Gorteenroe,co.Cork, esq.
1746 ,, Lawrence, Timolin, co. Limk., esq.
1777 ,, Mary, Dominick-st., Dublin, widow
1770 ,, Ralph, Ballymacadam, co. Kerry, gent.
1745 ,, Robert, Cloghala,co. Kilkenny, gent.
1774 ,, Robert, Dublin, esq.
1790 ,, Rosanna, *alias* **Hamill**, Ferrybank, co. Waterford
1784 ,, Simeon, collector of Galway
1799 ,, Thomas, Dublin, merchant
1719 ,, Timothy, Dublin, gent.
1773 ,, William, Tuam, Galway, gent.
1791 ,, Wm., Drinadally, co. Meath, esq.
1699 **Marshall**, Humphrey, Dame-st., Dublin, distiller
1713 ,, James, Kilkenny, soap boiler
1736 ,, James, Armagh, merchant
1730 ,, John, Aynsome, Lancashire, yeoman
1802 ,, John, Armagh, gent.
1808 ,, John, Birr, King's co., mercht.
1810 ,, Ralph, Calnaferry, co. Kerry
1807 ,, Richd., Drummartin, Scotland
1675 ,, Robert, Dublin, gent.
1802 ,, Robert
1761 ,, Sarah, *alias* **Bond**, *alias* **Hodder**, widow
1649 ,, Thos., clk. in Trin. Coll., Dub.
1763 ,, Vincentia, relict of John M.
1765 ,, Wm., the elder, Dublin, esq.
1770 ,, William, Dublin, esq.
1786 ,, Wm.,Ferrybank,Lib. of Waterford
1779 **Marston**, Anne, Dublin, spinster
1793 ,, Daniel, Dublin, merchant
1782 ,, Paicilla, Dublin, spinster
1783 ,, Phebe, Dublin, spinster
1781 ,, Sarah, Dublin, spinster
1804 **Martell**, Geo., Waterf. city, mercht.
1796 ,, John, Killmalock, co. Galway
1766 **Marten**, Henry, son of Henry M., Dublin, gent.

1752	**Marten,** Jas., Knockingin, co. Dublin	
1730	,, rev. Thomas, Kilkenny, clk. [See MARTIN.]	
1758	**Marthe,** Frederick	
1777	**Martin,** Abraham, Sligo	
1671	,, Adam, Blackcosway,co. Down, esq.	
1758	,, Alex., Cork, cordwainer	
1786	,, Alex., Bandon, co. Cork	
1786	,, Alice	
1651	,, Anthony, bp. of **Meath,** q. v.	
1772	,, Austin, Drogheda, cabinetmkr.	
1667	,, Catherine, wid. of John Martin, esq.	
1768	,, Charles, Sligo, merchant	
1788	,, Christopher, Ralieastown, co. Dublin, farmer	
1725	,, Cornelius, Limerick, gent.	
1732	,, Cornelius, Dublin, victualler	
1652	,, Daniel, Kilkenny, burgess	
1742	,, Dugall, of the "Severn" man-of-war	
1666	,, Edward, Drogheda, alderman	
1720	,, Edward, Dublin, gent.	
1767	,, Edward, Dublin, esq.	
1770	,, Edward, Greenville, co. Sligo	
1788	,, Edward, Greenville, co. Sligo, gent.	
1747	,, Elizabeth, Mile End, Middlesex	
1762	,, Elizabeth, Cork, widow	
1603	,, Francis FitzThomas, Galway, alderman (Copy)	
1723	,, Francis, son of Robert M., Dublin, gent.	
1775	,, Francis, Ballymanagh, W. sub. of Galway	
1784	,, Frederick, town of Sligo	
1679	,, Fulke, Lurgan Clanbrasil, co. Armagh, esq.	
1681	,, Geo., Newton, par. Garristown	
1755	,, George, Dublin, M.D.	
1811	,, George, Dublin city, esq.	
1671	,, Henry, the younger, Dublin, gent. (Ex.)	
1727	,, Henry, Knockingin,co. Dublin, gent.	
1791	,, Henry, Balbriggan, co. Dublin, gent.	
1779	,, Isabella, Dublin, spinster	
1776	,, Jacob, Grafton-street, Dublin, glover	
1707	,, James, St. Francis-st., Dublin, butcher	
1717	,, James, Dublin, gent.	
1745	,, James, Monaghan	
1783	,, James, Dublin, hatter	
1786	,, James, Sweetmount, co. Dublin	
1754	,, Jane, *alias* **Corner,** Dublin, widow	

1656	**Martin,** John, Lurgan, co. Armagh, esq. **[V.** 250	
1688	,, John, Coleraine, gent.	
1745	,, John, St. Angelo, co. Fermanagh, gent.	
1748	,, John, Dublin, merchant	
1750	,, John, Balrath, co. Meath	
1752	,, John, Ennis, co. Clare, vintner	
1760	,, John, Dublin, mercht. (Large will)	
1786	,, John, Limerick city, M.D.	
1790	,, John, Knockingin, co. Dublin	
1800	,, John, Sligo, esq.	
1808	,, John, Dublin city, atty.-at-law	
1808	,, John, Dundalk, co. Louth, merchant	
1806	,, Joseph, Ardbrin, co. Down, farmer	
1806	,, Judith, Castlebar, co. Mayo	
1770	,, Lewis, Mullingar, co. Westmeath, merchant	
1759	,, Margaret, Galway, spinster	
1713	,, Mary, *alias* **Sarrazin,** Dublin, widow	
1767	,, Mary, *alias* **Taylor,** Gort, co. Galway, widow	
1798	,, Mary, Dublin, widow	
1804	,, Mary, Sandymount, co. Dubl., spinster	
1772	,, Mathias, Drogheda, tanner	
1803	,, Michael, Dublin, gent.	
1735	,, Miles, Cork, gent.	
1811	,, Nicholas, Ross, co. Galway	
1779	,, Patrick, Park-st., Dub., presser	
1744	,, Patrick, Blackhorse-lane, Dublin, innkeeper	
1745	,, Peter, Dublin, mealman	
1799	,, Peter, Dublin, ironmonger	
1738	,, Philip, Pimlico, Dubl., clothier	
1754	,, Richard, Dublin, esq.	
1769	,, Richard, Naas, co. Kildare, grocer	
1594	,, Robag, Galway, merchant	
1715	,, Robert, Rakeragh, co. Tyrone, gent.	
1717	,, Robert, Dublin, gent.	
1796	,, rev. Robert, clk.	
1811	,, rev. Robert, Lower Gardiner-st., Dublin	
1720	,, Samuel, Dublin, gent.	
1755	,, Standish, Dublin, esq.	
1797	,, Thady, Usher's-quay, livery stable keeper	
1659	,, Thomas, Dublin, carpenter **[VIII.** 44	
1660	,, Thos., Clonmel, gent. **[VIII.** 83	
1681	,, Thomas, the elder, Newragh, co. Wicklow, yeoman	
1764	,, Thomas, Knockatubber, co. Louth, farmer	

1806 **Martin**, Thos., Island-bridge, co. Dublin, gent.
1800 ,, Timothy, James-street, co. Middlesex [co.
1752 ,, Wm., Mountmellick, Queen's
1767 ,, William, Dorset-st., Dublin
1775 ,, William, Cork
1787 ,, rev. William, D.D., rector of Killashandra
1780 ,, Willis, Cootehill, co. Cavan, gt.
1789 ,, Young, Inns-quay, Dub., watch and clock maker
[See MARTEN, MARTYN.]
1593 **Martine**, Wm., Galway, alderman
1807 **Martley**, Wm., Newtown Ballyfallen, co. Meath
1808 **Martyn**, Andrew, Blanemore, co. Mayo
1789 ,, Catherine, Galway, spinster
1691 ,, Clement, Dublin, gent.
1657 ,, Dominick Fitz Thomas, Galway, merchant [VI. 117
1733 ,, Elizabeth, Dublin, widow
1800 ,, Frances, city of Bath, widow
1804 ,, Mary, Curramore, co. Mayo, widow
1787 ,, Oliver, city of Bath, esq.
1807 ,, Oliver, town of Galway, M.D.
1797 ,, Peter, Castlebar, co. Mayo
1788 ,, Richd., Tuam, co. Galway, gt.
1722 ,, Sarah, Dublin, spinster
[See MARTIN.]
1811 **Marum**, Daniel, Kilkenny city
1799 **Maryman**, John, Dublin city, gent.
1770 ,, Martin, Cook-st., Dublin
1767 ,, Thomas, Dublin, merchant
[See MARMION.]
1714 **De Maseres**, Abraham, a refugee in London
1707 **Maslin**, Wm., Lisburn, co. Antrim, innkeeper
1789 **Mason**, Anne, widow
1769 ,, Caleb, Roscrea, co. Tipperary
1703 ,, Christopher, Curra, co. Galway, gent.
1771 ,, Frances, Roscrea, co. Tipperary, widow
1748 ,, Henry, Nymph Hall, co. Wexford, esq.
1795 ,, Henry Mark, Dublin, esq.
1685 ,, John, Castledermott, gent.
1738 ,, John, Waterford, esq.
1784 ,, John, vicar-choral of Christ's Church and St. Patrick's
1809 ,, right hon. John Monk
1773 ,, Isaac, Dublin, cardmaker
1708 ,, Joseph, Collinstown, co. Kildare, yeoman
1640 ,, Mark, Dublin, chandler (An account of his effects)

1808 **Mason**, Muriella, Philipstown, King's co., widow
1796 ,, Nich., Ballyboghill, co. Dublin, farmer
1783 ,, Olivia, Knock, King's co., spinster
1744 ,, Patrick, Capel-street, Dublin, victualler
1766 ,, Peter, Moyra, co. Down, gent.
1734 ,, Richard, Kevin-street, Dublin
1701 ,, Robert, Dublin, chandler
1719 ,, Robert, Masonsbrook, co. Galway, esq.
1728 ,, Robert, Dublin, gent.
1771 ,, Stanhope, late of Liverpool, now of Moira, co. Down
1657 ,, Thomas, Patrick-st., Dublin
1691 ,, Thomas, Dublin, merchant
1758 ,, Thomas, Dublin, gent.
1759 ,, Thomas, Dolphin's Barn-lane, Dublin, gent.
1803 ,, Thomas, Limerick, clothier
1765 ,, William, Moyalley, King's co., gent.
1765 ,, William, Bridgefoot-st., Dubl.
1771 ,, William, Coolen, co. Limerick, gent.
1757 **Massa**, Sebastian, Dublin, gent.
1627 **Massam**, William, Dublin [II. 35
1675 ,, *alias* **Massy**, Robt., upholsterer, son of Robt. M., Cowedwen, Denbighshire, upr., decd.
1805 **Massareene**, rt. hon. Anne, dow. countess
1731 ,, Rachel, dow. viscountess
1699 **De Massas**, Stephen, Dublin, esq.
1811 **Massereene**, rt. hon. Henry, earl of
1665 ,, John, lord viscount (Ex.)
1695 ,, John, lord viscount (Ex.)
1686 ,, Margt., dow. viscountess (Ex.)
1798 **Massey**, Charles, Tiverton, Devonshire, esq.
1803 ,, Charles, Griston, co. Limerick, esq.
1804 ,, Dorothy, Templecarrig, co. Wicklow
1764 ,, Eliz., Ballyveir, co. Tip., widow
1810 ,, sir George, knt.
1808 ,, sir Hugh Dillon, city of Bath, bart.
1756 ,, Jas., Templecarrig, co. Wicklow, farmer
1709 ,, Samuel, Dublin, M.D.
1674 **Massie**, sir Edward, Abbeyleix, Queen's co., knt.
1693 ,, Samuel, Dubl., mercht. (Copy proved at Chester)
1751 **Massilos**, Eliz., *alias* **Pettetrean**, wid. of capt. John M., Dubl.
1738 **De Massilos**, John, Dublin, esq.

1746 **Massiot**, James, Cork, merchant
1766 **Massy**, very rev. Charles, dean of Limerick
1798 ,, Eliz., Maryville, co. Limerick, widow
1782 ,, rev. Geo., Elm, co. Limkerick, clk.
1770 ,, Godfrey, Tenncrana, co. Clare, clk.
1701 ,, Hugh, Dontreleague, co. Limk., esq.
1758 ,, Hugh, Dontreleague, co. Limk., esq. (Not proved)
1760 ,, Hugh, esq. (Not proved)
1774 ,, Hugh Ingoldsby, Newgarden, co. Limerick, esq.
1788 ,, Hugh, lord baron (Large will)
1790 ,, Hugh, lord baron
1805 ,, Hugh Ingoldsby, Rockstown, co. Limerick
1712 ,, Humphrey, Killmihill, co. Limerick, esq.
1759 ,, Humphrey, Kilnegurteen, co. Cork, esq.
1675 ,, or **Massam**, Robert, upholsterer, son of Robert M., Cowedwen, Denbighshire, upholsterer, deceased
1784 ,, Thomas, Dublin, shoemaker
1761 ,, Wm., Kilnepark, co. Wicklow, farmer
1777 ,, William, Dublin, merchant
1677 **Master**, John, Phepotstown, co. Meath, gent.
1779 ,, Peter, Dublin, gent.
1804 **Masters**, Elizabeth, Amthill, Bedfordshire, widow
1788 ,, Margaret, spinster
1808 **Masterson**, Elizabeth
1726 ,, Ellinor, *alias* **York**
1794 ,, Jane, Castletobbett, spinster
1754 ,, John, Dublin, gent.
1764 ,, John, Castletown, co. Waterford, esq.
1797 ,, John, Dublin, merchant
1784 ,, Luke, Ballyduff, co. Kilkenny
1680 ,, Roger, Moneyseed, co. Wex., esq.
1781 ,, Roger, Moneyseed, co. Wex., esq.
1718 **Matersin**, Thomasin, Moneyseed, co. Waterford, widow
1732 **Materson**, John, Kilk., apothecary
1630 ,, Rowland, Barrashannon, co. Wexford, gent.
1766 **Mather**, Elinor, wife to Henry M., Felagh, co. Kildare
1642 ,, Griffith, St. Michan's par., Oxmantown, gent.
[See MATHEW.]

1791 **Mathers**, Henry, Fealough, co. Kild.
1722 ,, John, Drumgor, co. Armagh, gent.
1730 ,, John, Monreverty, co. Armagh, gent.
1798 ,, John, Croneskagh, co. Carlow, gent.
1803 ,, John, Belfast, co. Antrim
1729 ,, Thos., Ballynaghy, co. Armagh, clk.
1717 ,, William, Lylo, co. Armagh, gent.
[See MATHEWS.]
1742 **Mathew**, Catherine, Dublin, widow
1783 ,, Catherine, Arran-quay, Dublin, spinster
1744 ,, Charles, Dublin, gent.
1653 ,, col. Edmond
1774 ,, Edmond, Thomastown (Not proved)
1754 ,, Elizabeth, London, spinster
1670 ,, Frances, Thurles
1734 ,, George, Thurles, co. Tip., esq.
1760 ,, George, Thomastown, co. Tipperary, esq.
1765 ,, rev. Henry, Athy, co. Kild., clk.
1735 ,, Honora, widow of Thomas M., Anfield, co. Tipperary, esq.
1667 ,, John, Dublin, clerk
1771 ,, Mary, Dublin
1778 ,, Mary
1687 ,, Pricilla, *alias* **Briten**, widow
1759 ,, Richard, Dublin
1774 ,, Robt., Drimragreagh, co. Ant.
1711 ,, Theobald, Thomastown, co. Tipperary, esq.
1720 ,, Theobald, Thomastown, co. Tipperary, esq.
1736 ,, Theobald, Thomastown, co. Tipperary, esq.
1781 ,, Thomas, Thurles Castle, co. Tipperary, esq.
1770 ,, William, the elder
1660 **Mathewes**, quarter-master John, Francis-st., Dublin, gent.
1660 ,, Margaret, widow of quartermaster John, Francis-st.
1805 **Mathews**, Benjamin, Angel-alley, Dublin
1774 ,, Catherine, Dublin, widow
1803 ,, Catherine, Usher's-quay, Dubl.
1735 ,, Constantine, Dublin, maltster
1743 ,, Cornelius, Dublin, gent.
1747 ,, David, Dublin, merchant
1755 ,, rev. Edwd., precentor of Down
1757 ,, Edward, Dublin, esq.
1769 ,, Elizabeth, Dublin, linendraper
1779 ,, Francis, Galway, gent.
1794 ,, Fras., Marrowbone-lane, Dub., land surveyor

1752 **Mathews**, George, Springvale, co. Down, gent.
1731 ,, Humphrey, Fennypark, co. Wicklow (Unproved)
1743 ,, . Jas., Haggartstown, co. Louth
1809 ,, James, Great Strand-st., Dubl., painter   [gent.
1597 ,, John, Athlone, co. Westmeath,
1660 ,, John, Bonnetstown, co. Kilkenny, esq.
1700 ,, John, Dublin
1733 ,, rev. Jno., Newcastle, co. Down, clerk
1791 ,, John, Fleet-st., Dublin, slater
1805 ,, John, Killare, Westmeath, gt.
1807 ,, John, Loughrea
1796 ,, Joseph, Bonnetstown, Liberties of Kilkenny
1769 ,, Margaret, Dublin
1787 ,, Mary, Mary's-lane, Dublin
1692 ,, Nathaniel, Dublin, druggist
1750 ,, Owen, Clarendon-st., Dublin, coachman
1785 ,, Patrick, Drogheda, brewer
1787 ,, Patrick, Dublin, merchant
1800 ,, Patrick, Stillorgan, co. Dublin
1687 ,, Peter, Rosmacka, co. Louth, gent.
1677 ,, Philip, Cork, alderman
1796 ,, Richard, Newbridge, co. Westmeath, gent.
1803 ,, Richd., Dorset-st., Dubl., gent.
1692 ,, Samuel, Bonnetstown, co. Kilk. city, esq.
1759 ,, Samuel, Bonnetstown, Kilkenny, gent.
1776 ,, Sarah, Dublin, widow
1799 ,, Solomon, Killare, co. Westmeath, gent.
1703 ,, Theobald, Annfield, co. Tipp.
1804 ,, Thomas, Drogheda, esq.
1698 ,, Wm., Templelyon, co. Wicklow, esq.
1732 ,, William, Blanchfieldstown, co. Kilkenny, esq.
1788 ,, Wm., Charlesland, co. Wicklow, farmer
1801 ,, Wm., Rodney, Cumberland
   [See MATHER, &c.]
1807 **Mathewson**, Joseph, Moss-st., Dublin, gent.
1804 **Matson**, Esther, Summerhill, co. Meath, widow
1548 **Matterdall**, Thomas, Tallaght
1778 **Maturin**, rev. Charles, Dublin, clk.
1766 ,, Jane, *alias* **Cudmore**
1732 ,, Rachel Garrigue, Dublin, wid.
1749 ,, Sarah, Dublin, widow
1802 **Maud**, Henry, Harold's-cross, co. Dublin, gent. (Large)

1704 **Maude**, Ann, Dublin, spinster
1713 ,, Anthony, capt. in lord Dungannon's regt. of foot
1685 ,, Robert, Kilkenny, esq.
1750 ,, sir Robert, Dundrum, co. Tipperary, bart.
1788 ,, sir Thomas, Dundrum, co. Tipperary, bart.
1689 **Maudesly**, rev. Jas., Drogheda, clk
1741 **Maudsley**, lieut. John, Killeigh King's co.
1737 **Maughan**, Jonathan, Dubl., apothecary
   [See MAHON.]
1767 **Maugher**, Peter, Cullalag, co. Wick.
1723 **Maule**, Charles, Dublin, esq.
1787 ,, Dorcas, Dublin, spinster
1758 ,, Henry, bishop of **Meath**, q. v.
1750 ,, Hester, Dublin, spr.
1673 ,, Thomas, St. Andrew's par., Dublin, esq.
1752 **Mauleverer**, Bellingham, rector of Maghera, co. Londonderry
1804 ,, Mary, co. Dublin, widow
1791 ,, James, Dublin, esq.
1803 **Maume**, Garrett, Charleville, co. Cork, merchant
1658 **Maunder**, William, Galway butcher
        [**VII.** 84
1705 **Maunsel**, Boyle, Gaulstown, co. Kilkenny, gent.
1794 ,, Catherine, widow
1672 ,, John, London, leather seller (Copy)
1805 ,, rev. Wm., Limerick city, D.D.
1779 **Maunsell**, Cath., *alias* **Roberts**, *alias* **Ridgate**, widow
1765 ,, Edward, Rockborogh, co. Dublin
1685 ,, John, Ballybornane, co. Limk., esq.
1752 ,, John, Cork, merchant
1802 ,, John, Dublin, attorney-at-law
1758 ,, Joseph, the elder, Caragh, co. Galway, gent.
1767 ,, Richard, Limerick, esq.
1791 ,, Richard, Limerick, clk.
1687 ,, Thomas, the elder, of Macollop, co. Waterford, gent.
1692 ,, Thomas, late of Maccollop, co. Waterford, now at Chester
1744 ,, Thomas, Thorp-Malsor, Northamptonshire, esq.
1768 ,, Thomas, Limerick, esq. (Large will)
  [See MANSELL, MANSFIELD, MONSELL.]
1755 **Maurice**, Alice
1758 ,, Edward, bp. of **Ossory**, q. v.
1807 ,, Mary, Dublin city, widow

1691 **Maurice**, Peter, Kelfenhir, Denbighshire, clk. (Copy)	1790 **Maxwell**, John, lieut.-col. in the army
1731 ,, rev. Theo., archdeacon of Tuam [See FITZMAURICE, MORRIS.]	1803 ,, John Waring, Finnebrogue, co. Down, esq.
1791 **Maurik**, Joseph, Dundalk, co. Louth, gent.	1685 ,, Margaret, Collegehall, co. Armagh, widow
1720 **Mauson**, Wm., Magheralyn, co. Down, gent.	1715 ,, Margaret, Mullaghtanny, co. Armagh, widow
1808 **Mauvillain**, Sarah, White Hall, Middlesex	1758 ,, dame Margaret, Armagh, wid.
1664 **Maw**, Robert, Dublin, cutler	1712 ,, Margery, Dublin, widow
1754 ,, rev. Robert, Wexford, clk.	1791 ,, Mary, Pill-lane, Dublin, widow
1699 **Mawdsley**, Elizab., Dublin, widow	1805 ,, Matt., Tannybrack, co. Antrim
1798 **Mawm**, Garrett, Charleville, co. Cork, merchant	1683 ,, Phebe, Farnham, co. Cavan, spinster
1735 **Mawman**, Margaret, widow	1776 ,, Richard, Pill-lane, Dublin, merchant
1810 **Max**, Edward Engh., of Clonmel, co. Tipperary	1672 ,, Robert, bp. of **Kilmore**, q. v.
1769 ,, John, Killough, co. Tipp., esq.	1709 ,, Robert, Dublin, mariner
1733 ,, Simon, Gaile, co. Tipp., gent.	1737 ,, Robert, Fellows Hall, co. Arm., D.D.
1777 ,, Thos., Killough, co. Tipp., esq.	
1773 **Maxwell**, Albert, Roscrea	1750 ,, Robert, Falkland, co. Mon,, esq.
1740 ,, Ann, Fellowshall, co. Arm., wid.	1755 ,, Robert, Moynalty, co. Meath
1776 ,, Ann, Finnebrogue, co. Down, widow	1769 ,, Robt,, Finnebrogue, co. Down, esq.
1782 ,, Ann, Dublin, spinster	1772 ,, Robert, Kilkenny, esq.
1791 ,, Ann, Dublin	1779 ,, Robt., Killyfaddy, co. Londonderry
1720 ,, Arthur, Drumbeg, co. Down, esq.	1801 ,, Robert, esq.
1754 ,, Arthur Rainey, Castlehill, co. Down, esq.	1793 ,, Thomas, Dublin, merchant
	1709 ,, William, Strabane, co. Tyrone, merchant
1784 ,, Charles, Denzille-st., Dublin	
1766 ,, Cole, Riversfield, co. Limerick, gent.	1789 ,, William, Birdstown, co. Donegal, esq.
1792 ,, Edward, Finnebrogue, co. Down	1801 ,, Zachariah, Dundalk, co. Louth, esq.
1734 ,, Elizabeth, Dublin, widow	
1798 ,, Francis, Lr. Brook-street, London, widow	1704 **May**, sir Algernon, par. East Greenwich, Kent, knt.
1759 ,, capt. Geo., Finglas, co. Dublin	1738 ,, Andrew, Mayfield, co. Waterford, gent.
1803 ,, Grace, Dublin city, spinster	
1757 ,, Hamilton, Drumbeg, co. Down, esq.	1808 ,, Denis, Dublin city
	1710 ,, Edward, Dublin, esq.
1709 ,, rev. Henry, College Hall, co. Armagh, clk.	1729 ,, Edward, Mayfield, co. Waterford, esq.
1798 ,, Henry, bp. of **Meath**, q. v.	1742 ,, Edward, Mayfield, co. Waterford, esq.
1803 ,, Henry, Croven, co. Cavan, esq.	
1729 ,, Hugh, Rooban co. Down, esq.	1711 ,, Elizabeth
1682 ,, James, Drumbeg, co. Down, gent.	1722 ,, Humphrey, Dublin, esq.
	1767 ,, Mary, Dublin, widow
1772 ,, James, the elder, Omagh, co. Tyrone	1795 ,, Michael, Sligo town, cordwainer
1799 ,, James, Dublin, clk.	1771 ,, William, Newport, co. Dublin, merchant
1714 ,, John, Farnham, co. Cavan, esq.	1678 **Mayart**, John, Loughenny, or Rincelia, co. Down, esq. (Ex.)
1750 ,, John	
1754 ,, capt. John, the younger, of Cardines	1809 **Mayberry**, William Stephenson, lieut. in the Royal Navy
1763 ,, rev. John, Faganstown, co. Meath, clk.	1776 **Mayers**, John, a mariner on board the "Prudent"
1784 ,, ven. John, D.D., Archdeacon of Clogher	1802 **Mayfield**, James, Capel-st., Dubl., corn chandler

Y

1742 **Maylor**, Paul, Cork, cooper
1765 **Maynard**, Anne, Limerick, widow
     of capt. Thomas M.
1751 ,, Barry, Ballyvelley, co. Kerry
1690 ,, sir Boyle, Curryglass, co. Cork,
     knt. (Ex.)
1632 ,, Mary, widow of Mr. John M.,
     of Dublin
1669 ,, dame Mary, London, widow
     (Copy)
1712 ,, Samuel, Curryglass, co. Cork,
     esq.
1630 ,, sir William, Curryglass, co.
     Cork, knt. (Copy)
1734 ,, William, Curryglass, co. Cork,
     esq.
1686 **Mayne**, Benjamin, Charleville, co.
     Cork, clk.
1780 ,, Charles, Dyon, co. Monaghan,
     esq.
1733 ,, Jane, Waterford, widow
1805 ,, Joseph, Goland, co. Fermanagh
1807 ,, Joseph, Dublin city, attorney-
     at-law
1711 ,, Richard, Waterford, merchant
1805 ,, Sarah, Stafford-st., Dubl., wid.
     [See MAINE.]
1666 **Maynwaringe**, Dudley, Dubl., esq.
1665 ,, Magdalen, wid. of M'Nath M.
1636 **Maynwarning**, Henry, Kilk., esq.
1647 ,, Mathew, esq., Constable of
     Dublin Castle
     [See MAINWARNING, &C.]
1693 **Mayo**, Ellinor, lady viscountess
1753 ,, John, lieut. in gen. St. Clair's
     regt. of foot
1767 ,, John, lord viscount
1790 ,, John, earl of (Large will)
1771 ,, Margaret, viscountess
1797 **Mayson**, Peter, Froomselwood,
     Somersetshire, clk.
1788 **De la Maziere**, Andrew, Fleet-st.,
     Dublin
1761 ,, Jane, Dublin
1789 **Maziere**, Peter, Dubl., wollendraper
1791 **Meacham**, William, lieut. in 28th
     regt. of foot
1718 **Mead**, Dominick, Tullyheady, co.
     Tipperary, esq.
1740 ,, Henry, Carricknasure, co. Tip-
     perary, gent.
1771 ,, James, Birdhill, co. Meath,
     gent.
1595 ,, John, *alias* **Myaghe**, Cork, esq.
1732 ,, Patrick
1734 ,, Patrick, Cork, apothecary
1744 ,, sir Richard, Ballintober, co.
     Cork, bart.
1728 **Meade**, Andrew, Newcastle, co.
     Limerick, gent.

1797 **Mead**, Anne, Carrigafoyle, co.
     Kerry, widow
1780 ,, Charles, Carrickmacross, co.
     Monaghan, merchant
1756 ,, Christopher, Kilrush, co. Clare,
     gent.
1782 ,, David, Kinsale, co. Cork, esq.
1765 ,, Edward, Drogheda, alderman
1773 ,, Edward, Clonbertin, co. Louth,
     farmer
1763 ,, Ellinor, Kinsale, co. Cork, wid.
1784 ,, Fras., Carrigafoyle, co. Kerry,
     esq.
1767 ,, George, Limerick, merchant
1811 ,, Grace, Bandon, co. Cork
1741 ,, James, Cork, apothecary
1742 ,, James, Dublin, mariner
1766 ,, James, Dublin, esq.
1777 ,, Jane, Cavendish-row, Dublin,
     spinster
1704 ,, John, Cork, M.D.
1707 ,, sir John, Ballintober, co. Cork,
     bart.
1718 ,, John, London, goldsmith
1778 ,, Jno., Carrickmacross, co. Mon.,
     merchant
1800 ,, rev. John, Ballymartle, co.
     Cork, clk.
1738 ,, Margaret, Clonmel, co. Tipp.
1747 ,, Margaret, Ballyheale, co. Kil-
     dare, widow
1737 ,, Mary, widow
1744 ,, Mary, Clonina, co. Clare, wid.
1738 ,, Peter, Cork, merchant
1810 ,, Peter, Waterford city, gent.
1745 ,, Richard, Kinsale, co. Cork, gt.
1778 ,, Richard, Charleville, co. Cork,
     gent.
1677 ,, Robert, Dublin, brewer
1753 ,, Robt., Dubl., carpenter (Dated
     1753)
1799 ,, Robert, Dublin city, formerly
     of Kinsale
1788 ,, rev. Samuel   [gent.
1709 ,, Thos., Clonmel, co. Tipperary,
1773 ,, Thomas, Dublin, esq.
1791 ,, Thomas, Limerick city, gent.
1805 ,, Thos., Drumcondra, co. Meath,
     gent.
1764 ,, William, dean of Cork
1797 **Meadows**, Arthur, Wexford town
1800 ,, Joseph, Newbay, co. Wexford,
     gent.
1723 **Meagh**, Henry, Ballyhale, co. Kil-
     kenny, gent.
1636 ,, John Fitz Stephen, Cork, mer-
     chant   [**IV.** 194
1675 ,, John, Seskin, co. Kilk., gent.
1623 ,, Nicholas Fitz John, Kilmallock,
     burgess

1640 **Meagh**, Robt., Fitz David, Cork, alderman
1635 ,, Stephen FitzGarret, Cork, gent.
1623 ,, William, Limerick, alderman
1786 **Meaghan**, Patk., Thomas-st., Dub., tobacconist
[See MEIGHAN.]
1751 **Meagher**, Chas., Thurles, co. Tipp.
1734 ,, Dorothy, Dublin, widow
1802 ,, Edmond, Castletown, Queen's co., farmer
1811 ,, Edmond, Thurles, co. Tipp.
1757 ,, Elizabeth, Dublin
1791 ,, Henry, Doran, co. Tipperary, farmer
1753 ,, James, Kilkenny, innholder
1760 ,, Jas., Kill, co. Kildare, farmer
1684 ,, John, Clonelne, co. Tip., gent.
1758 ,, John, Toomivara
1761 ,, John, Tullamacjames, co. Tipperary, gent.
1800 ,, John, Ballymorris, co. Tipperary, esq.
1805 ,, John, Castletown, Queen's co., gent.
1807 ,, John, Castletown, Queen's co., farmer
1784 ,, Luke, Kilkenny city, gent.
1810 ,, Michael, Cloneen, co. Tipp.
1729 ,, Nicholas, Golden Bridge, co. Tipperary, shoemaker
1715 ,, Thomas, Kilkenny, merchant
1796 ,, Wm., Corville, co. Tipperary, farmer
[See MAHER.]
1793 **Meakins**, John, chandler
1784 **Mealy**, Edmond, Ballybough, co. Dublin, carpenter
1785 **Meany**, John, Pennywell, Lib. of Limerick
1811 ,, John, Donaghmore, co. Cork, farmer
1757 **Meara**, Cornelius, Blackrock, co. Dublin
1681 ,, Edmond, Dublin, M.D.
1769 ,, Thady, Nenagh, co. Tipperary, merchant
1810 ,, Wm., Whiteford, King's co.
[See MARA.]
1779 **Meares**, Anne, Annsgrove, co. Westmeath, widow
1775 ,, Charles, Dalestown, co. Westmeath
1795 ,, rev. Chas., Prospect, co. Dubl., clk.
1773 ,, Edward, Dublin, merchant
1774 ,, Elizabeth, Dublin, widow
1804 ,. Eliz., Ballybeg, co. Wicklow
1768 ,, Francis, Limerick
1778 ,, George, Dublin, esq.

1745 **Meares**, John, Saltacre, co. Westmeath, gent.
1790 ,, John, Mearescourt, co. Westmeath
1699 ,, Lewis, Mearescourt, co. Westmeath, esq. (Ex.)
1752 ,, Lewis, Dublin, esq.
1765 ,, Lewis, Stafford-street, Dublin, wine merchant
1799 ,, Richard, Doughill, King's co., farmer
1738 ,, Robert, Almoritia, co. Westmeath, esq.
1775 ,, Samuel, Drumavail, co. Mon.
1763 ,, Thomas, Ballyhane, co. Westmeath
1808 ,, Thomas, Rath, co. Westmeath
1738 ,, Wm., Curtson, co. Westmeath
1753 ,, Wm., Killinboy, co. Westmeath
1774 ,, Wm., Sandhills, co. Monaghan (Not proved)
[See MAIRS.]
1790 **Meath**, Anthony, earl of (Large will)
1715 ,, Chambre, earl of (Copy)
1763 ,, Chaworth, earl of
1675 ,, sir Edwd. Brabazon, knt., earl of
1708 ,, Edward, earl of
1772 ,, Edward, earl of
1584 ,, *alias* **O'Moore**, James
1621 ,, and **Clogher**, George Montgomery, bp. of
1651 ,, Anthony Martin, bp. of, and provost of Trin. Coll., Dubl.
1661 ,, Henry Leslie, bp. of
1681 ,, Henry Jones, bp. of
1697 ,, Anthony Dopping, bp. of
1705 ,, right rev. Dr. Richd. Tennison, bp. of
1715 ,, Dr. William Moreton, bp. of
1723 ,, rt. rev. Dr. John Evans, bp. of
1733 ,, rt. rev. Dr. Welbore Ellis, bp. of
1758 ,, rt. rev. Dr. Henry Maule, bp. of
1766 ,, rt. rev. Dr. Richard Pocock, bp. of (In will Ossory)
1798 ,, rt. rev. Henry Maxwell, lord bp.
1652 ,, William, earl of
1685 ,, William, earl of
1797 ,, William Brabazon, earl of
[See METHE.]
1798 **Mecham**, Geo., Athlone, co. Westmeath, esq.
1779 ,, Robt., Athlone, co. Westmeath, farmer
1798 **Mecredy**, rev. Alexander, Tullynakill, co. Down
1722 **Mecum**, Danl., Coleraine, co. Derry
1810 ,, Frances, Dublin city, widow
1780 ,, James, Dublin, flax dresser
1769 **Medcalf**, Ann, Dublin, widow

1791 **Medcalf**, Catherine, wipow
1789 ,, Francis, Gurteen, co. Kildare, farmer
1721 ,, rev. John, clk.
1737 ,, Joseph, Gurteen, co. Kildare, farmer
1810 ,, Susanna, widow
1750 ,, William, Dubl., ribbon weaver
     [See METCALF.]
1749 **Medcalfe**, Sarah, Dublin, widow
1729 ,, Thomas, Dublin, shoemaker
1767 ,, Wm., Drogheda, marshalsea keeper
1758 **Medd**, John, councillor-at-law (Ex.)
1797 **Medlicot**, Frances Phillipa, Dalkey Lodge, co. Dublin, spinster
1730 ,, George, esq.
1793 ,, John, Moortown, co. Kild., gent.
1729 **Medlicott**, Eliz., widow of Geo. M., Tully, co. Kildare, esq.
1808 ,, Eliz., Charlemont-st., co. Dub., spinster
1790 ,, Esther Carolina, widow
1760 ,, George, Grange Gorman-lane, Dublin, gent.
1771 ,, James, Tullow, co. Carlow, clk.
1771 ,, James, Ardscol, co. Kild., esq.
1757 ,, John, Grangebeg, co. Kildare, esq.
1762 ,, Joseph, Dublin, esq.
1739 ,, Mary, Tully, co. Kild., widow
1737 ,, Samuel, Dunmurry, co. Kildare, esq.
1738 ,, Thomas, Dublin, esq. (Copy)
1743 ,, Thomas, Dublin, gent.
1795 **Mee**, Alice, Leixlip
1799 ,, Elizabeth, Dublin, widow
1691 ,, Giles, Dublin, alderman
1799 ,, Isaac, Cork city, merchant
1789 ,, John, Armagh city
1809 ,, Susanna, Templeville, co. of Cork city
1736 ,, Temperence, Cork, widow
1736 ,, Thomas, Cork, cordwainer
1656 ,, William, Kilrush, co. Westmeath   [VI. 27
1563 **Meed**, Patrick, Kinsale, merchant and alderman
1743 **Meeke**, Thomas, Londonderry
1778 **Megahan**, Margaret, Atherdee, co. Louth, widow
1760 **Meggs**, Henry, Limerick
1778 **Meheux**, Bryan, Dublin, gent.
1781 **Meighan**, Michael, Navan, co. Meath, gent.
1771 ,, Patk., Cabra, co. Cavan, mcht.
1791 ,, Patrick, Conagher, co. Carlow, farmer
     [See MEAGHAN.]
1768 **Meissonnier**, Pauline, Dublin, wid.

1790 **Melaghlin**, Mary, Mullingar, co. Westmeath
1766 **Meldrum**, King, Winetavern-street, Dublin
1807 **Melefont**, David, lieut.-col. of the 10th regt. of foot
1658 **Mellaghlin**, James, Rathew, co. Westmeath, clk. [VII. 123
1739 **Mellaughlin**, James, Tripiloe, co. of the city of Dublin, clothier
1738 ,, Thomas, Dublin, M.D.
     [See M'LAUGHLIN.]
1789 **Mellefont**, David, esq.
1754 ,, Gilbert, Dunmanway, co. Cork, esq.
1778 ,, Richd., Downemark, co. Cork, esq.
1802 ,, William, esq.
1772 **Melling**, John, Liverpool, Lancashire, merchant (Copy)
1777 **Mellor**, Ebenezor, Edenderry, King's co., merchant
1772 **Menagh**, John, Fanaghmore, co. Armagh
1804 **Mendip**, rt. hon. Anne, lady (Copy)
1803 ,, rt. hon. Welbore, lord
1536 **Melor**, Patrick
1719 **Melton**, Thomas, Rathmore, King's co., butcher
1789 **Melville**, David, Dublin, merchant
     [See MITCHELL.]
1795 **Melvin**, George, Dublin, attorney
1690 ,, James, Athlone, co. Westmeath, merchant
1749 ,, John, of His Majesty's ship "Medway"
1734 **DeMelyer**, Casca, Portarlington, Queen's co., esq.
1661 **Mephain**, Robert
1794 **Mercer**, Alex., Crumlin, co. Dublin
1721 ,, Bryan, Hillsborough, co. Down, gent.
1799 ,, Deborah
1702 ,, John, Dublin, gent.
1781 ,, Luke, Dublin, esq.
1702 ,, Mary, Dubl., wid. of Dr. Geo. M.
1735 ,, Mary, Dublin, spinster
1784 ,, Mounser, collector of Dundalk
1787 ,, Richard, Dublin, esq.
1810 ,, Richard, formerly of Ireland, late of Edinburgh
1806 ,, Robert
1783 ,, Simons, Leighlin Bridge, co. Carlow
1801 ,, Thomas, Dublin
1759 ,, William, Dublin, esq.
1772 ,, William, Dublin, esq.
1760 **Mercier**, Charles, Portarlington, Queen's co., esq.
1811 ,, Charlotte, Portarlington, sptr.

1706 **Mercier**, Claud, Fiddown, co. Kilk., gent.
1809 ,, Dinah, Dub. city, mantua mkr.
1786 ,, Esther, Portarlington, Queen's co., widow
1719 ,, Francis, Dublin, esq.
1809 ,, Francis
1769 ,, rev. Henry, sen. fellow of Trin. Coll. Dub.
1804 ,, John, Portarlington, Queen's co. esq.
1724 ,, Peter, Dublin, gent.
1669 **Meredeth**, sir Amos, Ballinakill, Queen's co., bart.
1788 **Meredith**, John, Templeraney, co. Wicklow, farmer
1802 ,, sir John, Gardiner's-place, co. Dublin, bart.   [esq.
1783 ,, Joshua, Clonegown, King's co.,
1801 ,, Rice, Clonegark, Queen's co., gent.
1597 ,, Richard, bp. of **Leighlin**, q. v.
1778 ,, Richard, Shrowland, co. Kild.
1785 ,, Richd., Rathnalogh, co. Kerry, esq.
1668 ,, sir Robert, Dublin, knt.
1789 ,, Susanna, Dublin, widow
1677 ,, sir Thomas, Dublin, knt. (Ex.)
1729 ,, Thomas, Dublin, confectioner
1753 ,, Wm., Blackhorse-lane, Dubl., gent.
1732 **Meredyth**, Arth., Dollardstown, co. Meath, esq.
1701 ,, sir Chas., par. St. Ann's, Soho, Middlesex, knt.
1710 ,, Chas., Newtown, co. Meath
1769 ,, rev. Chas., Newtown, co. Meath, dean of Ardfert
1793 ,, Chas., Glasnevin, co. Dublin, cabinetmaker
1787 ,, Deborah, *alias* **Simpson**
1773 ,, Elizabeth, Dublin, spinster
1798 ,, Frances, Dublin, widow
1797 ,, Helen, Dublin
1789 ,, Henry, Dublin, esq.
1755 ,, Jane, Dublin, spinster
1685 ,, Lettice, lady
1791 ,, Mary, Delleville, co. Dub., wid.
1794 ,, Mathew, Rerymore, Queen's co., gent.
1743 ,, Richard, Dublin, esq.
1747 ,, Robert, Shroland, co. Kildare, esq.
1769 ,, Sarah, Dublin, widow
1719 ,, Thomas, lieut.-gen. of His Majesty's Forces
1731 ,, Thomas, Dublin, esq.
1773 ,, Thos., Newtown, co. Meath, esq.
1665 ,, sir Wm., par. of Kilcullen, co. Kildare, bart.

1726 **Merefield**, Ellinor, Dublin, spinster
1724 ,, Thomas, Castle-street, Dublin
1663 **Mericke**, William, Dublin, gent.
1676 **Meridith**, Catherine, Dubl., widow
1729 ,, Jane, par. of Cumber, co. Down, widow
1711 **Meriton**, George, Dublin, esq.
1680 **Meriwether**, capt. John, Cork
1780 ,, capt. John, Cork
1790 **Merle**, John, Ranelagh, co. Dublin, gent.
1744 **Mernyne**, Garret, Youghal, co. Cork, merchant
1678 **Merony**, Pierce, Cloneigh, co. Clare, gent.
1771 **Merrfield**, Robert, the elder, of Drogheda
1799 **Merrick**, Garret, Drumcondra, co. Dublin, esq.
1786 ,, Rosanna, Dublin, widow
1784 ,, Wm., sen., Greagan, co. Mayo, gent.
1738 **Merrifield**, Michael, Dublin, gent.
1791 **Merrit**, Bartholomew, Dublin
1804 **Merritt**, John, Dub., silk manufac.
1707 **Merrony**, Margaret, *alias* **Creagh**, widow
1793 **Merry**, Patk., Wood-street, Dublin, grocer
1639 ,, Thos., *alias* **Halligan**, Callan, co. Kilkenny, burgess
1646 **Merryman**, William, Dubl., brewer [See MARMION.]
1676 **Mervin**, sir Audley, Dublin, knt.
1634 ,, Edmond, Dublin, esq.
1783 **Mervyn**, Anne, Dublin, widow
1776 ,, Arthur, Naul, co. Meath, esq.
1716 ,, Audley, Naul, co. Meath, esq.
1767 ,, Eliz., Mullingar, co. Westmeath, wife to Arthur M.
1701 ,, Henry, Dublin, esq.
1748 ,, Henry, Trillick, co. Tyrone, esq. [See 1765.]
1765 ,, Henry, Trillick, co. Tyrone, esq.
1728 ,, Hugh, Baldwinstown, co. Dub., esq.
1753 ,, James, Castlehill, co. Tyrone, esq. (Large will)
1757 ,, James, Dublin, gardener
1771 ,, Jane, wife to Arthur M., Naul, co. Meath, esq.
1720 ,, Olivia, Naul, co. Meath, wid.
1680 **Merydeth**, Dorothy (Copy)
1781 **Merydith**, Dorothy
1597 ,, Richard, bp. of **Leighlin**, q. v.
1681 **Meskell**, David Fitz David, Cork, merchant (Copy)
1752 **Mestayer**, Charles, Dublin, mercht.
1774 **Metcalf**, Ann, Dublin, spinster

1758 **Metcalf**, Edward, Dublin, merchant
1807 ,, Jas., Drogheda town, alderman
1750 ,, Mathew, Mountrath, Queen's co.
1774 ,, Susanna, Dublin, milliner [See MEDCALF.]
1751 **Metcalfe**, John, Cunagh, co. Meath, gent.
1751 ,, William, Newry, co. Down, gent.
1735 **Metge**, Peter, Navan, co. Meath, gent.
1777 ,, Peter, Athlumney, co. Meath, esq.
1809 ,, Peter, Athlumney, co. Meath, esq.
1583 **Methe**, Hugh, lord bishop of
1800 **Methold**, Francis, Bath city (Copy)
1749 **Meulh**, James, sergt. in colonel Battereaus' regt.
1799 **Mewlds**, Thomas, Rathmines-road, co. Dublin, gent.
1557 **Mey**, James, Chapellysott (Chapelizod ?)
1773 **Meyler**, Elizabeth, Dublin, widow
1759 ,, Mathew, Dublin, carpenter
1660 ,, Nicholas, Shelebeggan, gent. [**VIII.** 109
1707 ,, Nicholas, Dublin, gent.
1762 ,, Patrick, Sallymount, co. Kildare, esq.
1765 ,, Stephen, Kildare, gent.
1799 ,, Thos., Dubl. city, glass manufacturer
1678 **Meylor**, Geo., Dublin, gent. (native of Drogheda)
1743 ,, James, Sallymount, co. Kildare, gent.
1675 **Meyrick**, John, Carrickfergus, gent.
1748 **Mezerac**, Mark Anthony, Kilmellog, King's co.
1634 **Miagh**, Pierse, Youghal, alderman
1625 **Miannaghane**, John Oge, Cork, merchant
1729 **Michel**, James, Carlow
1770 ,, James, London, watchmaker
1684 ,, John, Dublin, esq., also called major John M.
1761 **Michell**, Abraham, Carlow, tanner
1808 ,, Peter, Great Britain-st., Dubl. [See MITCHELL.]
1779 **Mickle**, Joseph, Thomastown, co. Kildare
1758 ,, Samuel, Timahoe, co. Kildare, farmer
1766 **Midleton**, George, lord viscount
1765 ,, Margaret, *alias* **Fitz Gerald**, Plunket-street
1774 ,, rev. Midleton Comyn, Santry, Dublin diocese

1765 **Middleton**, Nich., Dublin, mercht.
1674 ,, Peter, St. Johnstone, co. Longford, carpenter
1655 **Middlebrooke**, Thomas [**V.** 222
1747 **Middleton**, Alan, lord visc. (Copy)
1728 ,, Allan, lord viscount
1747 ,, Ann, dow. lady viscountess
1694 ,, Anna, wife to Mark M., Arm., esq.
1742 ,, Barnaby, Dublin, merchant
1705 ,, sir Hugh, bart.
1780 ,, Rebecca, Dublin, widow
1800 ,, Thomas, Balomona, co. Wexford, farmer
1792 ,, William, Harold's-cross, co. Dublin, gent.
1664 **Miechelburn**, Abraham, Kilcrandra, co. Wicklow, gent.
1733 **Miffant**, dame Mary, widow of Peter **Dupuy**, esq., lieut. de Bruneval
1629 **Might**, Henry, Dublin, gent.
1789 **Miles**, John, Rochestown, co. Tipperary, esq.
1791 ,, Lawford, Dublin, gent.
1811 ,, Lawford, Rochestown, co. Tip.
1768 ,, Thomas, Waterford, goldsmith
1766 ,, William, Ballywilliam, co. Tip. [See MYLES.]
1802 **Miley**, Roger, parish priest of Blessington
1802 ,, Roger, priest of the parish of Blessington and Rathmore
1790 ,, Wm., Ballymore Eustace, co. Dublin, brewer
1802 **Milikin**, William, Dublin, gent.
1765 **Millar**, Douglas, Ballinrobe, widow of rev. James M.
1741 ,, Peter, Dublin, gent. [See MILLER.]
1782 **Millard**, Mary, Dublin castle
1744 **Millbank**, Samuel, Raheen, Kilkenny, gent.
1785 ,, William, Dublin
1809 **Millea**, Catherine, Kilkenny city, widow
1807 ,, John, Ross-lane, Dubl., tailor
1774 ,, Lawrence, Limerick, mercer
1795 ,, Margaret, Limerick city, silk mercer
1803 **Miller**, Alexander, Castlebar, co. Mayo
1781 ,, Anne, Portaferry, co. Down, widow
1810 ,, Charles, Milford, co. Tipperary
1801 ,, Crosdaile, esq.
1802 ,, Edward, Coagh, co. Tyrone, architect
1811 ,, George, lieutenant-col. in His Majesty's Service

1809 **Miller**, Hannah, Dublin city, chandler
1671 ,, Hugh, Coleraine, burgess
1726 ,, James, Milford, co. Mayo, esq.
1767 ,, rev. James, Ballinrobe, co. Mayo, clk.
1768 ,, James, Dublin, gent.
1774 ,, Jas., Dub., joiner and cabinet-maker
1739 ,, Jane, Timaho, co. Kildare, widow
1656 ,, John, late of Dublin, now of Bristol, merchant [**V.** 238
1661 ,, John, late Dub., now of Bristol, merchant
1732 ,, John, Ballyfin, Queen's co
1740 ,, Jno., Ballycasey, co. Clare, esq.
1763 ,, John, Dublin, merchant
1797 ,, John, formerly of the island Tobago, West Indies, esq. (Copy)
1803 ,, John, James-st., Dublin, gent.
1807 ,, John, Stratford-on-Slaney, co. Wicklow
1808 ,, John, Granby-row, Dublin, gt.
1658 ,, Joseph, Rossgarland, co. Wexford, gent. [**VI.** 273
1791 ,, Joseph, Wexford, clk.
1776 ,, Martha, Dublin, widow
1786 ,, Mercia, Dublin
1809 ,, rev. Oliver, Prospect, co. Dub., clk.
1650 ,, Ralph
1726 ,, Robert, Milford, co. Mayo, esq.
1747 ,, Robert, Milford, co. Mayo, esq.
1759 ,, Robert, lieut. of His Majesty's Fleet
1703 ,, Samuel, Dublin, gent.
1729 ,, Stephen, Kilrea, capt. in col. Michel's regt.
1807 ,, Stephen, Dublin city, merchant
1795 ,, Susanna, Monkstown, widow
1687 ,, Thomas, Limerick, alderman (Copy)
1654 ,, Wm., capt. of a troop of horse in col. Ingoldsby's regiment [**V.** 14
1756 ,, Wm., the elder, Lurgan, co. Armagh, shopkeeper
1779 ,, William, Lurgan, co. Armagh
1798 **Milles**, Jeremiah, Harley-st., Middlesex, esq. (Copy)
1785 **Millet**, John, Prospect Hall, co. Tip., esq.
1769 **Millett**, Mathew, Kyle, co. Tip., gent.
1760 **Milley**, John, Johnville, co. Kilk., clerk
1748 ,, rev. Nicholas, Graiguenamanagh, co. Kilkenny, clk.

1729 **De Milliere**, Sepus,, Dublin, esq.
1806 **Millikin**, John
1789 ,, Robert, Cork, gent.
1799 **Milling**, Nathaniel, Ardee, co. Louth, esq.
1790 ,, Oliver, Ardee, co. Louth, M.D.
1662 **Millington**, Richd., Dub., mercht.
1804 **Millner**, Thomas
1804 **Mills**, Alice, Boyle, co. Roscom.
1718 **Millthorpe**, Elizabeth, Dublin, wid.
1717 ,, John, Little Gennets, co. Meath
1807 **Milltown**, rt. hon. Brice, earl of
1783 ,, Joseph, earl of (Large will)
1788 **Millwood**, Thomas, Dublin, gent.
1805 **Mills**, Alice, Boyle. co. Roscom.
1763 ,, rev. Anthony, Galway, clk.
1793 ,, Anthony, Mount Prospect, co. Roscommon, esq.
1779 ,, Daniel, Rathdrum, co. Wick., apothecary
1753 ,, Edward, Dublin, esq.
1791 ,, Elizabeth, Athy, co. Kildare, widow (Ex.)
1698 ,, George, Dublin, tailor
1800 ,, sir George, Dublin, gent.
1784 ,, Hill, surgeon to 58th regt. foot
1662 ,, Humphrey, Dublin
1743 ,, James, Killmague, co. Kildare, gent.
1762 ,, James, Mayfield, co. Kildare, gent.
1784 ,, James, Bolton-street, Dublin, surgeon
1792 ,, James, Brideswell, co. Westmeath, linen manufacturer
1796 ,, Jane, Sligo
1697 ,, John, Dublin, merchant
1737 ,, John, Youghal, co. Cork, mcht.
1761 ,, John, Fairhill, co. Mayo, mcht.
1764 ,, John, Killinmore, King's co., farmer
1765 ,, Joseph, Leperstown, co. Dubl., farmer
1770 ,, Mark, Collony, co. Sligo
1720 ,, Mary, Limerick, spinster
1743 ,, Oliver, Knockhall,co. Roscommon, gent.
1810 ,, Oliver, Knockhall, co. Roscom.
1757 ,, Rathburn, Dublin
1719 ,, Richard, Dublin, gent.
1700 ,, Robert, Dublin, merchant
1764 ,, Samuel, Turnings, co. Kildare, esq.
1787 ,, Samuel, Turnings, co. Kildare, esq.
1804 ,, Sarah, Lisnaree, co. Down
1699 ,, Thos., Ballybeg, co. Cork (Ex.)
1740 ,, Thos., bp. of **Waterford**, q. v.
1761 ,, Thos., Dublin, gent.
1802 ,, William, Dublin, jeweller

1758 **Milne**, John, Stonybatter, co. Dubl.
1701 **Milner**, James, Dublin, bookseller
1789 ,, Sarah, Bandon, co. Cork, wid.
1703 **De Milton**, John
1810 **Milton**, Dorothea, Digges-street, Dublin, widow
1786 ,, Mary, widow
1799 ,, Mary, Dublin city, spinster
1800 ,, Mary Ann
1734 ,, Sarah, Dublin, widow
1721 ,, William, Dublin, merchant
1755 ,, Wm., the elder, Blackwood, now of Dublin
1788 ,, Wm., Cottage, co. Kild., esq.
1802 **Miltown**, rt. hon. Joseph, earl of (Copy)
1737 **Milvin**, Sarah, Coleraine, co. Derry, widow
1696 **Milward**, Clement, Enniscorthy, co. Wexford, gent.
1709 ,, Clement, Dublin, merchant
1759 ,, Henry, Limerick
1731 ,, Thomas, Ballyhagaghan, co. Wexford, gent.
1681 **Minchin**, Chas., Moneygall, King's co., gent.
1804 ,, Dorothy, Green Hills, co. Tip., widow
1780 ,, Francis, Dublin, merchant
1788 ,, Francis, Dublin, woollen draper
1776 ,, Hannah, Dublin, widow
1805 ,, Hugh, Erina, co. Clare
1733 ,, Humphrey, Busherstown, King's co., esq.
1748 ,, Humphrey, Inchmore, co. Kilkenny, gent.
1777 ,, Humphrey, Dublin, esq.
1796 ,, Humphrey, Gt. George's-street, Hanover-sq., esq. (Copy)
1682 ,, John, St. Paul's, Covent-garden, Middlesex, baker (Copy)
1734 ,, John, Inchmore, co. Kilk., esq.
1746 ,, John, Kilkenny, gent.
1764 ,, Paul, Bough, co. Carlow, esq.
1739 ,, Penelope, Dublin, widow
1686 ,, Thomas, Busherstown, King's co., esq. (Ex.)
1763 ,, Walcott, Dublin, merchant
1721 ,, William, Busherstown, King's co., esq.
1759 ,, William, Dublin, gent.
1763 **Minis**, Edwd., Toberdaly, King's co.
1807 **Miniss**, Bristow, Belfast, co. Antrim
1722 **De Minnett**, Cosme, Dublin, esq.
1788 **Minnitt**, Joshua, Annaghbeg, co. Tipperary, esq.
1792 ,, Paul, Blackfort, co. Tip., esq.
1709 ,, Robert, Knigh, co. Tip., gent.
1773 ,, Robert, Blackfort, co. Tip., gt.

1737 **Minnitt**, Thomas, Smock-alley, Dublin, cooper
1802 **Mintou**, John, Beechmont, co.Cork, esq.
1811 ,, John, Cork city, vintner
1761 **Miott**, Alexander, Dublin, merchant
1738 **Mirfield**, Thomas, Dublin, gent.
1766 **Misler**, capt. Elias Peter, George's-quay, Dublin
1792 **Misset**, Elizabeth, Piercestown, co-Kildare, widow
1627 ,, James, Dublin, merchant
1769 ,, Jas., Dowdingstown, co. Kild., gent.
1681 ,, Jane, *alias* **Jones**, widow (Ex.)
1784 ,, Joseph, Leitrim, King's co.
1771 ,, Laurence, Naas, co. Kild., gt.
1790 ,, Mary, Dublin, widow
1740 ,, Patrick, Dublin, woollendraper
1668 ,, Richard, Dublin, merchant (Letter of Athy)
1762 **Missett**, Andw., Corbally, co. Kild., gent.
1749 **Mitchel**, Adam, Rathgibbon, King's co., farmer
1743 ,, rev. Andrew, Enniskillen, co. Fermanagh, clk.
1790 ,, Andw., Boolenarag, King's co.
1784 ,, rev. Coote, vicar of Rathdrum, co. Wicklow
1774 ,, Dodsworth, Cork, gent.
1749 ,, Elizabeth, Rathgibbon, King's co., widow
1761 ,, George, Ballykealy, King's co., gent.
1772 ,, George, Dublin, tobacconist
1789 ,, George, Belfast, co. Antrim
1803 ,, George, M.D. (late deceased)
1768 ,, Henry, Dublin, gent.
1798 ,, Henry, Mitchelsfort, co. Cork, esq.
1767 ,, James, Tuninvinrey, co. Mon.
1774 ,, James, Carlow, gent.
1788 ,, James, Dublin, merchant
1791 ,, Jane, Dublin, spinster
1682 ,, John, Dublin, linendraper
1735 ,, John, Dublin, gent.
1769 ,, John, Sunnyhill, co. Kildare, yeoman
1746 ,, Mary, *alias* **Fetherston**, Ballin-torley, co. Roscommon
1749 ,, Mary, Dublin, widow
1779 ,, Mary, *alias* **Webber** Glas-nevin, co. Dublin, widow
1762 ,, Nathaniel, Stradbally, Queen's co., esq.
1750 ,, Patk., the younger, Big Butter-lane, Dubl., esq.
1750 ,, Patrick, Dublin, M.D.
1787 ,, Samuel, Dubl., attorney-at-law

1796 **Mitchel,** Samuel, Belfast, co. Antrim, merchant
1797 ,, Susanna, spinster
1691 ,, Thomas, late of Cork, now of London, merchant (Copy)
1799 ,, Thos., Castlestrange, co. Roscommon, esq.
1764 ,, Topham, Newtown, co. Dublin, esq.
1774 ,, Topham, Dublin, esq.
1730 ,, Wm., London, mercht. (Copy)
1748 ,, Wm., Dickstown, co. Antrim
1774 ,, William, Newry, co. Down
1790 ,, William, Pine-hill, co. Down
1719 **Mitchelburn,** Richd., Dublin, gent.
1807 **Mitchell,** Abraham, Athy, co. Kild.
1723 ,, Caleb, Dublin, carpenter
1744 ,, Dublin, spinster
1809 ,, Ellen, Mitchelsfort, co. Cork, widow
1700 ,, Gillies, Ballinrobe, co. Mayo, merchant
1720 ,, Hugh, London, mercht. (Copy)
1757 ,, Hugh, Dublin, merchant
1764 ,, Israel, Stradbally, Queen's co., esq.
1674 ,, John, Burris-lane, co. Tipperary, merchant
1801 ,, John, Frolick, co. Roscommon, esq.
1807 ,, John, Cork city, coal factor
1802 ,, Mary, Dublin, widow
1809 ,, Nathaniel, Clonmel, co. Tipperary, esq.
1738 ,, Samuel, par. St. Martin-in-the-fields, tailor
1721 ,, Thomas, Aghada, co. Cork, gt.
1755 ,, lieut. Thomas, Cork
1807 ,, Thomas, Ballybryan, co. Galway, farmer
1808 ,, Thomas, Ballintopin, co. Mon.
[See MELVILLE, MICHELL, MULVIHILL.]
1752 **Mithel,** Thomas, Ballykenly, King's co., gent.
1742 **Moat,** John, Kilgreel, co. Antrim, linendraper
1808 **Mocher,** Flower, Enfield, Middlesex, lieut.-general
1787 **Mockler,** Edward, Phibsborough, co. Dublin
1789 ,, rev. James, rector of Tipperary, diocese of Cashel
1796 ,, Joanna, Gortmore, co. Cork, widow
1796 ,, Mary, Phibsborough, co. Dubl.
1612 **Mocler,** Edward, Moclerstown, dio. Cashel, gent.
1679 **Moderwell,** John, Strabane, mercht.
1779 ,, John, Strabane, merchant

1799 **Moderwell,** Robert
1791 **Moffat,** Patrick, Garryricken, co. Kilkenny
1705 **Moffet,** John, Letterboy, co. Fermanagh, gent.
1750 **Moffit,** John, Hazelhatch, co. Dubl., gent.
[See MOFFAT.]
1680 **Mogg,** John, Dublin, tailor
1781 ,, John, Dublin, tailor
1795 **Mogles,** James, Cutpurse-row, Dublin, laceman
1750 **Moir,** Rachel, *alias* **Dunn,** Aberdeen, Scotland, wid. (Copy)
1793 **Moira,** John, earl of
1676 **Moland,** John, Ballymacarnon, co. Meath, gent.
1736 ,, John, Dublin, esq.
1795 ,, John, Warwick, Bucks, in America (Copy)
1717 ,, Joseph, Dublin, gent.
1740 ,, Lettice, Dublin, widow
1799 ,, Richard (Copy)
1747 ,, Robert, Dublin, esq.
1735 ,, rev. Samuel, Dublin, clk.
1737 ,, Thomas, Dublin, gent.
1720 **Molegan,** Thomas, Firrbane, King's co., farmer
1804 **Molesworth,** Arthur, Clifton, Gloucestershire, esq. (Copy)
1786 ,, Bourchier, Clitterhouse farm, co. Middlesex
1779 ,, Bysse, Dublin, esq.
1769 ,, Edwd., Bueno Retiro, co. Dublin, esq.
1726 ,, John, lord viscount
1803 ,, John, Ealing, Middlesex, esq.
1763 ,, Mary Jenny, viscountess
1806 ,, Ponsonby, Charlemont-st., co. Dublin, esq.
1760 ,, Richard, lord viscount
1803 ,, Whitched, Dublin
1770 ,, William, Bath, Somersetshire, esq. (Copy)
1775 ,, hon. Wm., Bath, Somersetshire, esq. (Copy)
1803 ,, Wm., Holles-st., Dubl., gent.
[See MAULSWORTH, MOLSWORTH.]
1715 **Moline,** Patrick, Limerick, clk.
1781 **Molineaux,** Dorothy, Dublin, spr.
[See MOLYNEAUX.]
1810 **Moller,** Andrew, York-st., Dublin, merchant
1781 ,, rev. Cliffe, Poolbeg-st., Dublin
1726 **Mollineaux,** John, London, citizen and draper (Copy)
[See MOLYNEAUX.]
1773 **Mollowney,** Edward, Killena, co. Kildare, farmer
1794 **Molloy,** Arthur, Killyon, King's co.

1697	**Molloy,** Bryan, Donore, co. Kildare, gent.	
1764	,,	Bryan, Gragwaller, Queen's co., gent.
1665	,,	Chas., Rathlyhen, King's co., esq.
1679	,,	Chas., Raligh, King's co., gt.
1685	,,	Charles, Cartrons, King's co., gent.
1779	,,	Charles, Coolnahiley
1803	,,	Constantine
1808	,,	Constantine John, Moate, co. Westmeath
1654	,,	Cosny, Derryalny, King's co., gent.
1760	,,	Daniel, Kilcleagh, co. Westmeath, gent.
1777	,,	Daniel, Frankford, King's co., gent.
1768	,,	David, Narrowbeg, co. Kildare, farmer
1753	,,	Dominick, Dublin, merchant
1790	,,	Dorothy, Mountbolas, King's co., spinster
1788	,,	Edmond, Frankford, King's co.
1745	,,	Edward, Gullerstown, co. Dub., farmer
1807	,,	Edward, Dovehill, King's co.
1763	,,	Ellenor, John-st., Dublin (Not proved)
1801	,,	Ellinor, Dublin
1740	,,	Elizabeth, Grangegorman-lane, Dublin, widow
1795	,,	Elizabeth, Dublin, widow
1753	,,	Francis, Dublin, gent.
1804	,,	Francis, Frankford, King's co., gent.
1636	,,	Hugh, Ballyduffe (Copy)
1774	,,	John, Dublin, wine cooper
1801	,,	John, co. Dublin, farmer
1803	,,	John, Clombelia, King's co., gent.
1805	,,	Josh, Rathrobin, King's co., farmer
1804	,,	Michael, Trenane, farmer
1801	,,	Paul, Dublin, attorney
1798	,,	Peter, Ormond-quay
1810	,,	Philip, Ormond-quay, Dublin, merchant
1773	,,	Thady, Frankford, King's co., gent.
1668	,,	William, Dublin, gent.
1770	,,	William, Doughill, King's co., gent.
1777	,,	Wm., Streamstown, King's co.
1810	,,	William, Dublin city, esq. [See MULLOY.]
1753	**Mollyneaux,** Elizabeth, widow of John M., Dublin, gent. [See MOLYNEAUX.]	

1538	**Molon,** Richard	
1776	**Molony,** Ann, *alias* **Connor**	
1746	,,	Barthw., Limerick, merchant
1785	,,	Denis, Lackarugh, co. Clare, farmer
1809	,,	Eleanor, Williams-lane, co. Dublin, widow
1810	,,	Fras., Cork city, butter buyer
1733	,,	James, Ballynahiney, co. Clare, gent.
1794	,,	James, Abbey of Athy, co. Kildare, esq.
1808	,,	James, Limerick city, grocer
1809	,,	John, Limerick city, gent.
1769	,,	Michael, Acres, co. Clare, gt.
1806	,,	Miles, Borrisokane, co. Tipp. [See MALONY, MULLOWNEY.]
1725	**Molsworth,** Robert, lord baron Philipston, and visc. Swords [See MOLESWORTH.]	
1804	**Molton,** Esther, Killeagh, co. Cork, widow	
1674	**Molyneaux,** Adam, Ballymuloy, co. Longford, esq.	
1797	,,	sir Capel, Castledillon, co. Armagh, bart. (Large)
1739	,,	Catherine, Dublin, spinster
1636	,,	Daniel, Newland, co. Dub., esq.
1739	,,	sir Daniel, Dublin, bart.
1752	,,	Daniel, Dublin, ironmonger
1801	,,	Elizabeth, of the city of Bath, widow of sir Capel M.
1719	,,	Francis, London, citizen and tallow chandler
1806	,,	George William
1735	,,	John, Dublin, ironmonger
1738	,,	Patk., Galway, merchant
1772	,,	Pooley, Richmond, Surrey, esq.
1801	,,	Robert, Castledermot, co. Kild.
1692	,,	Samuel, Dublin, esq.
1728	,,	Samuel, par. St. Martin, Middlesex, sec. to His Royal Highness the Prince of Wales (Copy)
1733	,,	sir Thomas, Dublin, bart. (Large will)
1790	,,	Wilhelmina, Dublin, spinster
1699	,,	William, Dublin, esq.
1774	,,	William, Dublin, merchant [See MOLINEAUX, MOLLINEAUX, MOLLYNEAUX.]
1592	**Molynex,** Thos., Chancellor of the Exchequer	
1743	**Monaghan,** James, Mullingar, co. Westmeath, shoemaker	
1788	,,	Patrick, Castletown, par. Kilbarry
1799	,,	Patrick, Dublin, chandler
1794	,,	Richard, Liscartan, co. Meath, farmer

1765 **Monahan,** Patrick, Dublin, brewer
1783 ,, Wm., Bow Bridge, Dublin, skinner
[See MONAGHAN.]
1730 **De Moncal,** Andrew, Dublin, esq.
1742 **Moncal,** rev. Chas., chaplain of general Otway's regt.
1700 **De Moncant,** John, Dublin, gent.
1802 **Monch,** rt. hon. Chas. Stanly, lord viscount (Large)
1783 ,, Henry Percey, Dublin, esq.
1785 ,, ven. John Stanley, LL.D., archd. of Derry
1786 ,, Laurence, Dublin, farmer
1715 ,, Sarah, Dublin, widow
[See MONCK.]
1802 **Monchton,** Miles, Killmihill, co. Limerick
1752 **Monck,** Charles, Grangegorman, Dublin, esq.
1805 ,, George Paul, city of Bath
1710 ,, Henry, Dublin, esq.
1788 ,, Henry, Dublin, esq.
1737 ,, Manley, Dublin, esq.
1786 ,, Mary, Coleraine, widow
1800 ,, Rose, Dublin, widow
[See MONCH, MONKS, &c.]
1798 **Moncrieffe,** Richd., Dubl., alderm.
1804 **Mondet,** Abraham, Pinnor, Middlesex
1769 ,, Jane, Dublin, widow
1762 ,, Lodowyck, Dublin, gent.
1804 ,, Wm., Gt. Fitchfield-st., Middlesex (Copy)
1781 **Mondett,** William, Dublin, gent.
1702 **Moneypenney,** Henry, Galla, co. Meath, clk.
[See MONYPENNY.]
1795 **Monfort,** Frances, Corry, co. Longford, widow
1783 ,, Lewis, Glackstown, co. Westmeath, esq.
1663 **Mongomerie,** Hugh, lord viscount of the Great Ardes
[See MONTGOMERY.]
1764 **Mongrand,** Lewes, Dublin, mercht.
1726 **Monk,** George, Dublin, esq.
1656 **Monkes,** John, trooper [**VI.** 2
1810 **Monks,** Richard, Dorset-street, co. Dublin
1810 ,, Wm., Huntstown, co. Dublin, gent.
[See MONCK.]
1694 **Monro,** Andrew, Cherryvalley, co. Down, esq.
1776 ,, Benjamin, Ranelagh-road, co. Dublin
1809 ,, Rev. George
1792 ,, Henry, Bombay, in the East Indies (Copy)

1748 **Monro,** Hugh, Lib. of Westminster, gent. (Copy)
1759 **Monroe,** George, lt.-col. in gen. Otway's rgt.
1741 ,, Henry, Matherforth, co. Down, linen draper
1773 **Monsel,** Henry, *alias* **Conyngham,** Dublin, widow
1761 **Monsell,** Sainborne
1752 ,, Wm., Donogroge, co. Clare, esq.
1788 ,, Wm., Firvoe, Lib. of Limerick, esq.
[See MAUNSELL.]
1807 **Montague,** Richard, Tullamore, King's co., publican
1749 **Montandre,** Francis De la Rochefoucaut, marquis of (Copy)
1698 **Monteage,** Stepn., All Hallows on the Wall, London, mercht., (Copy)
[See MONTAGUE.]
1753 **Montford,** Ellinor, Dublin, widow
1776 ,, Henry, Bawn, co. Longford, esq.
1744 ,, capt. Peter
1803 ,, Peter, Prussia-st., Dubl., esq.
1801 **Montfort,** Margaret, Dublin, widow
1602 **Montgarret,** Edmond Butler, lord viscount
[See MOUNTGARRET.]
1764 **Montgomerie,** Geo., Ballynure, co. Monaghan, esq.
1651 ,, lt.-col. Hew, par. of Ayr, Argyleshire, Scotland
1663 ,, Hugh, lord visct. of the Ardes
1669 ,, Hugh, Ballyhanwood, esq.
1695 ,, Hugh, Drogheda, esq.
1741 ,, Hugh, capt. in sir John Cope's dragoons
1746 ,, Hugh, Shancracken, co. Arm.
1661 ,, sir James, Rosemount, knt.
1811 ,, Leslie, co. of Dublin city
1716 ,, Sir Thomas, knt. (Copy)
1779 ,, Wesly, Dublin, merchant
1679 ,, Worsley, Dublin, merchant
1722 **Montgomery,** Alex., Ballilock, co. Monaghan, esq.
1729 ,, Alex., Dubl., esq. (Large will)
1767 ,, Alex., Dublin, merchant
1785 ,, Alex., Rosefield, co. Mon., esq.
1796 ,, Alex., Dublin, attorney
1796 ,, Alex., Mt. Charles, co. Donegal, esq.
1800 ,, Alex., Convoy, Donegal, esq.
1807 ,, Alex., Donegal
1808 ,, Alex., Bessmount, co. Mon., esq.
1802 ,, Alice
1791 ,, Anne, Prussia-st., Dublin, wid.
1788 ,, Arch. M'Neill, Dublin, esq.

1770 **Montgomery**, Eliz., Dublin, widow
1789   ,,   Elizabeth, Moore-st., Dublin, widow
1804   ,,   Elizabeth, Dorset-st., Dublin, widow
1761   ,,   Geo., Drumrollogh, co. Fermanagh, esq.
1777   ,,   George, Shillee, co. Cork, esq.
1787   ,,   George, Ballyconnell House, co. Cavan, esq.
1801   ,,   Grizel, Dublin, esq.
1805   ,,   Grizelda, Dublin city, esq.
1800   ,,   Hannah, Edenderry
1791   ,,   Henry, Rushin, co. Fer., gent.
1636   ,,   Hugh, lord visct. of the Great Ardes
1723   ,,   Hugh, Derrygonnelly, co. Fermanagh, gent.
1749   ,,   Hugh, Willoughby, Carrow, co. Fermanagh, esq.
1792   ,,   Hugh Lyons, Drogheda, esq.
1797   ,,   Hugh, Castle Hume, co. Fermanagh, esq.
1807   ,,   Hugh, in the East Indies, lieut.-col.
1699   ,,   James, Lisse, co. Tip., gent.
1787   ,,   James, Dublin, apothecary
1791   ,,   James, Carree, co. Fermanagh
1797   ,,   rt. rev. James, abp. of Raphoe
1798   ,,   James, Belfast, co. Antr., esq.
1735   ,,   Jane, Newry, co. Down, widow
1743   ,,   Jane, widow of Hercules M., of Ballylessam, esq.
1679   ,,   John, Croghan, co. Donegal, gent.
1779   ,,   John, Croghan, co. Donegal, gent.
1783   ,,   John, Lisdrumgullion, co. Armagh, merchant
1797   ,,   John, Ballyleck, co. Monaghan
1803   ,,   John, Oldtown, co. Kild., esq.
1808   ,,   Joseph, Ivey Lodge, co. Down
1763   ,,   Mary, Dublin, wife to Thomas M., Dublin, merchant
1793   ,,   Mathew, Dunmuckrum, co. Donegal, gent.
1810   ,,   Mathew, Dublin city
1772   ,,   Richard, Dublin, merchant
1770   ,,   Robert, Dublin, esq.
1799   ,,   Robert Alexander, major of 54th regiment
1811   ,,   Robt., Ballyrush, co. Down, gt.
1786   ,,   Salisbury Wilhelmina, *alias* **Tipping**
1804   ,,   Samuel, Londonderrry city, merchant
1797   ,,   Susana, Rosemount, co. Down
1761   ,,   Thos., Kildare-st., Dublin, esq.
1793   ,,   Thomas, Donegal town
1798   ,,   Vaughan, Dublin, esq.

1683 **Montgomery**, William, Bellisceogh or Barlisberry, co. Dub., gt.
1737   ,,   William, Dublin, merchant
1743   ,,   William, Templeoge, co. Dubl.
1744   ,,   William, Dublin, esq.
1799   ,,   Wm., Hillsborough, co. Down, esq.
1801   ,,   William, Dorset-st., Dublin
      [See Montgomerie, Mountgomery.]
1709 **Montrath**, Charles, earl of (Copy)
1715   ,,   Charles, earl of (Copy)
1721   ,,   Henry, earl of (Copy)
      [See Mountrath.]
1658 **Monypenny**, Arthur
1791   ,,   Hyrick, Dundalk, co. Louth, gt.
      [See Moneypenney.]
1639 **Moodie**, John, Armagh, merchant
1718 **Moody**, John, Clonmel, co. Tipperary (Copy)
1747   ,,   John, Lisrah, co. Armagh
1761   ,,   John, Newtown Limavady, co. Derry, linendraper
1773   ,,   Margaret, wife to William M., Lisraw, co. Armagh
1726   ,,   Robert, Dublin, gardener
1715   ,,   Thomas, Ipswich, Suffolk, gent. (Copy)
1797 **Moonan**, Patk., Drogheda, butcher
1781 **Moondy**, James, dissenting minister of Newry
1638 **Moone**, Henry, Athedowy, co. Londonderry, gent.
1769 **Mooney**, Catherine, Limerick, wid.
1766   ,,   Elizabeth, Dublin, widow
1674   ,,   James, Kildare, gent.
1783   ,,   James, Queen-street, Dublin, dairyman
1809   ,,   James, New-st., Dublin, grocer
1756   ,,   Jane, Dublin, widow
1796   ,,   Johana, Borris, co. Carlow, wid.
1663   ,,   John, Corracollin, King's co., gent.
1753   ,,   Jno., Newcrane-lane, Rainsford st., innkeeper
1780   ,,   John, Dublin, baker
1779   ,,   Jonach, Ballylee, co. Galw., esq.
1805   ,,   Laurence, Galway town, miller
1801   ,,   Margaret, Dublin, spinster
1746   ,,   Mary, Bow-lane, Dublin, wid.
1802   ,,   Mary, Athlone, co. Roscommon, widow
1798   ,,   Maurice, Dublin city
1748   ,,   Michael, Kevins-st., Dublin, blacksmith
1775   ,,   Miles, Dublin, gent.
1755   ,,   Owen, Doone, King's co., esq.
1802   ,,   Patrick, Waterford, merchant
1638   ,,   Thomas, Trim, gent.
1796   ,,   Thomas, Commons of Ratoath
1753   ,,   William, Dublin, vintner

1764 **Moore**, Wm., Lackaghbeg, King's co. gent.
1811 ,, Wm. H., Grange Mooney, co. Meath, esq.
1800 **Moony**, Mark, Dublin
1791 ,, Patrick, Arran-quay, Dublin, cooper
1762 ,, Ter., High-st., Dub., merchant
1771 ,, Walter, Carnalway, co. Kildare, gent.
1724 **Moor**, John, Mountmellick, Queen's co., merchant
1726 ,, Trevor, Parsonstown, King's co., gent.
1642 ,, Wm., St. Thomas-court, near Dublin, gent.
1730 **Moorcroft**, Elizabeth, Kells, co. Meath, widow
1732 **Moore**, Abigail, *alias* **Morgin**, Moinhall, co. Cavan, widow
1792 ,, Acheson, Coldrum, co. Tyrone
1636 ,, Adam, Croghan, King's co., gent.
1666 ,, Adam, esq., younger son of Chas., late visc. Moore
1741 ,, Alen, Kearne, co. Antrim
1717 ,, Alexander, Magherafelt, co. Londonderry, gent.
1740 ,, Alice, Boley, co. Wexford, wid.
1634 ,, Allan, Caldroome, co. Tyrone
1657 ,, Ann, sometimes of Londonderry, late of Carnarvon, spr. [**VI**. 142
1729 ,, Ann, *alias* **Archer**, Kilkenny, widow
1777 ,, Ann, Cork, widow
1801 ,, Ann, Belfast, co. Antrim, wid.
1754 ,, Anne, *alias* **Leister**, widow of Thomas M., bookseller
1650 ,, Anthony
1670 ,, Archibald, Drogheda, gent.
1756 ,, Archibald, City-quay, Dublin
1778 ,, Archibald, Newry, co. Down
1805 ,, Archibald, Newtown, co. Dubl.
1780 ,, rev. Arthur, Ravenfield, co. Cavan, clk.
1706 ,, Barry, Shenton, Leicestershire, esq.
1742 ,, Boyle, Dublin, esq.
1726 ,, Brabazon, Mount Ferrable, co. Monaghan
1782 ,, Brent, Milltown-road, Dublin suburbs, esq.
1750 ,, Catherine, Desertcreat, co. Tyrone, widow
1755 ,, Catherine, Raheenduff, Queen's co., widow
1745 ,, Charles, Corbit, co. Down
1754 ,, sir Charles, Dublin, bart.
1797 ,, Charles, Cranfield, co. Down

1796 **Moore**, Chidly, Ardmoyle, co. Tipp., esq.
1787 ,, Christian, Eccles-st., Dublin, widow
1747 ,, Christopher, Carlingford, co. Louth
1751 ,, Clothworthy, Cherryvalley, co. Antrim
1799 ,, hon. Colville, Kilberry, co. Cork, esq.
1769 ,, Daniel, Roskelton, Queen's co.
1783 ,, David, Montague-st., Dublin
1798 ,, David, Charlemont, co. Arm., gauger
1809 ,, Deborah, widow
1793 ,, Dorcas, Fatham, co. Armagh, spinster
1618 ,, sir Edwd., Mellifont, co. Louth, knt.
1671 ,, Edward, Lisburn, gent.
1722 ,, Edward, Knockorden, co. Tipperary, gent.
1781 ,, Edwd., Blackmoor-yard, tailor
1781 ,, ven. Dr. Edward, archdeacon of Emly
1787 ,, Edwd., Mountbrown, co. Dublin, brewer
1804 ,, Edward, Mooresfort, co. Tipperary, esq.
1733 ,, Elizabeth, Parsonstown, King's co., widow
1762 ,, Eliz., Mooremount, co. Louth, widow [widow
1771 ,, Elizabeth, Tullyvin, co. Cavan,
1798 ,, Eliz., Magherafelt, co. Derry, widow
1804 ,, Elizabeth
1788 ,, Ellen, Dublin, widow
1727 ,, Ellin, Tullamore, King's co., widow
1692 ,, sir Emanuel, Roscarbarrie, co. Cork, bart.
1733 ,, sir Emanuel, Donmore, co. Cork, bart.
1795 ,, sir Emanuel, Cove, co. Cork
1770 ,, Frances, Ballinasloe, co. Galway, spinster
1662 ,, Francis, esq., Mellifont, co. Louth
1730 ,, rev. Fras., Raheenduff, Queen's co., clk.
1771 ,, Fras., Corduff, co. Dublin, esq.
1797 ,, Fras., Julianstown, co. Meath, farmer
1705 ,, Garnett, Moate, co. Mayo, esq.
1665 ,, Garret, 2nd son of Chas., late viscount Moore, Drogheda [**IX**. 214
1628 ,, sir Garrett, lord viscount, Drogheda (Copy)

1723 **Moore,** Garrett, Balla, co. Mayo, esq.
1778 ,, Geo., Moore-st., Dublin, gent.
1800 ,, George, Ashbrook, co. Mayo
1742 ,, Guy, Abbey, co. Tip., esq.
1762 ,, Henry Wm., Drumbanagher, co. Antrim, esq.
1771 ,, Henry, Cork, merchant [gent.
1787 ,, Henry, Ballyaglisle, co. Limk.,
1794 ,, Henry, Peter-st., Dublin, esq.
1785 ,, Hester, Dublin, spinster
1720 ,, Howard, Julianstown, co. Meath, gent.
1751 ,, Hugh, Ballyhalaghan, co. Tyr.
1728 ,, Ignatius, Ballintry, co, Meath, gent.
1658 ,, James, Ballyhalaghan, gent. [**VII.** 61
1700 ,, James, Bellisle, co. Antrim
1703 ,, rev. Jas., Athy, co. Kild., clk.
1722 ,, James, Drogheda, merchant
1724 ,, James, Deserteragh, co.Tyrone, esq.
1728 ,, Jas., Ballenacreemor, par. Ballymoney
1737 ,, Jas., Knocknolosset, co. Cavan
1755 ,, James, Tillyown, co. Donegal
1752 ,, James, Tullyvin,co. Cavan, esq.
1763 ,, James, Dublin, clerk
1766 ,, Jas., Newport, co. Mayo, esq.
1773 ,, James
1779 ,, Jas., Ballina, co. Kildare, esq.
1784 ,, James, Ballidivity, co. Antrim, esq.
1784 ,, James, Boate-street, Newry
1802 ,, James, Dorset-street, Dublin, merchant
1803 ,, Jas., lieut.in Her Majesty's 19th regt. of foot
1803 ,, James, College-green, Dublin
1806 ,, James, Nutgrove, Queen's co.
1767 ,, Jane, Drumsilla, co. Cavan
1784 ,, Jane, Newry, co. Down
1633 ,, sir John, Croghan, King's co., knight
1656 ,, John [**V.** 238
1659 ,, John, drummer [**VII.** 187
1671 ,, John, Dublin, mercht. (Admon. granted in 1681-1688)
1682 ,, John, Croghan, King's co., esq.
1694 ,, John, Belfast, merchant
1699 ,, John, lieut. and adjutant in Brig. Ingoldsby's regt.
1701 ,, John, Glenhoyes, co. Tyrone, gent.
1732 ,, John, Dunlavin, co. Wicklow, merchant
1733 ,, rev. John, Limerick, clk.
1750 ,, John, Barybor, Queen's co., gt. (dated 1750)

1751 **Moore,** John, Dublin, merchant
1752 ,, John, Drumbanagher, co. Armagh, esq.
1756 ,, John, Ballintaffy, co. Mayo, gt.
1767 ,, John, Dublin, breeches maker
1768 ,, John, Dublin, goldsmith
1771 ,, John, Ballymoney, co. Antrim, gent.
1778 ,, John, Drumon, co. Tyrone
1780 ,, John, Dublin, M.D.
1791 ,, John, Ballantry, co. Meath, farmer
1797 ,, John, Carrickbeg, co. Waterf., merchant
1799 ,, John, Dublin, dep. registrar of deeds
1801 ,, John, Clogh, co. Down
1811 ,, John, the elder, Drumbanagher, co. Armagh
1779 ,, Joseph, Cloghan, King's co., esq.
1800 ,, Joseph, Clonmel, co. Tip., clk.
1735 ,, lady Mary, *alias* **Burke**
1779 ,, Loughlin, Roskelton, Queen's co.
1618 ,, Lawrence, Drogheda, merchant
1771 ,, Letitia, *alias* **Kelly**, Cloghan, King's co., widow
1804 ,, Letitia, Lismore, co. Galway, widow
1779 ,, Lettice, Dublin, widow
1746 ,, Lewis, Creemorgan, Queen's co., esq.
1776 ,, Lewis, Creemorgan, esq
1777 ,, Lewis, Dublin, gent. [esq.
1804 ,, Lorenzo, Merrion-sq., Dublin,
1783 ,, Lucy, Dublin, widow
1784 ,, Mable, Mooregrove, co. Antrim, widow
1691 ,, Margaret, Clonmel, widow
1752 ,, Margaret, *alias* **Smith**
1770 ,, Margaret, Graigue, Queen's co., widow
1788 ,, Margaret, King-street, Dublin, spinster
1746 ,, Margaretta
1805 ,, Martha, French-street, Dublin
1751 ,, Mary, relict of rev. Richard M.
1771 ,, Mary, Salestown, co. Meath, widow
1787 ,, Mary, Dublin
1795 ,, Mary, Dublin, spinster
1805 ,, Mary, Glasnevin, co. Dublin
1787 ,, Mathew, Blackrock, co. Dubl., esq.
1737 ,, Michael, Drogheda, merchant
1743 ,, Michael, Cloncoran, co. Roscommon, esq.
1658 ,, Murtogh, Hurlingford, co. Kilkenny, gent. [**VII.** 96

1673 **Moore**, Nicholas, Ardaghstown, co. Louth, esq. (Ex.)
1756 ,, Nicholas, Mooremount, co. Louth, esq.
1792 ,, Nicholas, Cork, gent.
1757 ,, Oliver
1784 ,, Oliver, Dublin, esq.
1762 ,, rev. Patrick, clk.
1798 ,, Patrick, P.P. of Drogheda
1623 ,, Peter, Drogheda, saddler
1808 ,, Peter, Grafton-st., Dubl., bookseller
1722 ,, Philip, Moor Park, King's co., esq.
1746 ,, Pierce, Loran, Queen's co., gt.
1746 ,, Randal, Mounterrible, co. Monaghan, esq.
1668 ,, Richard, formerly of Coventry, now of Youghal, merchant
1690 ,, Richard, Clonmel, esq.
1693 ,, Richard, Enniskillen, gent.
1699 ,, Richard, Cashel, esq.
1739 ,, Richard, Kilworth, co. Cork, worsted comber
1757 ,, Richard, Dublin
1769 ,, Richard, Capel-st., Dublin
1771 ,, Richard, Dublin, gent.
1784 ,, Richard, Tullamore, King's co., gent.
1804 ,, Richard, Tullamore, King's co.
1807 ,, Richard, Clongee, esq.
1809 ,, Richard, Rathdowney, Queen's co.
1723 ,, Robert, Ballyrony, co. Down, farmer
1776 ,, Robert, Dublin, distiller
1779 ,, sir Robert, Holystone, Northumberland, bart.
1788 ,, Robert, Dublin, glazier
1684 ,, Roger, Dublin, esq.
1748 ,, Roger
1795 ,, Ross, Carlingford, co. Down, esq.
1804 ,, Ross B., Carlingford, co. Louth, esq.
1775 ,, Sampson, Moore Lodge, co. Antrim, esq.
1783 ,, Samuel, Bray, co. Wicklow, apothecary
1751 ,, Sarah, Antrim, widow
1799 ,, Sarah, Dublin, spinster
1703 ,, Stephen, Kilworth, co. Cork, esq.
1750 ,, Stephen, Clonmel, esq.. commonly called Col. M.
1777 ,, Stephen, Chancellorstown, co. Tipperary, esq.
1737 ,, Susanna, Dublin, widow
1767 ,, Thady, Cappanamorogue, Qu. co., gent.

1638 **Moore**, Thomas, Croghan, King's co., esq.
1650 ,, Thomas, late of Carlow, now of Cabragh, near Dublin, gent.
1660 ,, Thomas, Graigue, Queen's co., maltster [**VIII.** 105
1702 ,, Thomas, Chancellorstown, co. Tipperary, esq.
1752 ,, Thomas, Marlefield, co. Tipp., esq.
1756 ,, Thomas, Barretstown
1772 ,, Thos., Londonderry, merchant
1781 ,, Thomas, Bain, co. Tipp., esq.
1781 ,, Thos. Chidly, Clonmel, co. Tipperary, esq.
1783 ,, Thos., junior, Cork, merchant
1797 ,, Thomas, Elbow-lane, sub. of Dublin, tape weaver
1798 ,, Thomas, Cork city, merchant
1799 ,, Thomas, Cork city, esq.
1800 ,, Thomas, Rathganey, co. Westmeath [esq.
1808 ,, Thos., Mooresbrook, co. Mayo,.
1559 ,, William, Dublin, merchant
1658 ,, Wm., Glaneterston, Scotland,. gent. [**VII.** 92
1672 ,, William, par. Penderin, dio. St.. David's (Copy)
1692 ,, William, Salestown, co. Meath, esq.
1693 ,, sir William, Rosscarberrie, co. Cork, bart. (Ex.)
1715 ,, William, lieut. in brig. Tyffin's regiment
1735 ,, William, Atherdee and Moore Hall, co. Louth, esq.
1736 ,, William, Dublin, esq.
1748 ,, William, Cootehill, co. Cavan,. esq.
1749 ,, William, Drumon, co. Tyrone
1752 ,, William, Ballymacreemore, co. Antrim, gent.
1752 ,, William, Cork, surgeon
1756 ,, William, Timahan, co. Wexford
1761 ,, William, Salestown, co. Kildare, esq.
1762 ,, hon. William, ensign in genl. Cornwallis's regiment
1767 ,, William
1770 ,, William, Ahoghill, co. Antrim,. gent.
1774 ,, William, Waterford, clk.
1776 ,, William, Dublin, tobacconist
1783 ,, William, Moore Lodge, co. Antrim, esq.
1784 ,, sir William, bart., capt. in 61st regiment of foot
1787 ,, William, Ballyhaise, co. Cavan
1788 ,, William, Drumont, co. Tyrone,. esq.

1803 **Moore**, William Maxwell, Dublin
1803 ,, William, Tullyvin, co. Cavan, esq.
1811 ,, rev. William, Kingscourt, co. Cavan
[See MOOR, MORE.]
1771 **Moorehead**, John, Dunmurry, co. Antrim
1775 **Moorhead**, James, Milltown, co. Down, linendraper
1788 ,, James, Moate, co. Westmeath
1802 **Moran**, Anne, *alias* **Lyons**
1786 ,, Bryan, Sligo town, merchant
1760 ,, Daniel, Leitrim, co. Leitrim, gent.
1791 ,, Daniel, Roscrea, co. Tipperary
1789 ,, Jacob, Dublin, merchant
1752 ,, James, Dublin, merchant
1753 ,, James, Kilcock, co. Kildare, farmer
1682 ,, Juan, *alias* **Nowlan**, widow of Patrick M., porter, Dublin
1755 ,, Michael, Ennis, co. Clare, M.D.
1772 ,, Michael, Dublin, tailor
1782 ,, Michael, Roscrea, co. Tipperary, gent.
1790 ,, Michl., Pill-lane, Dubl., tallow chandler
1790 ,, Moage, New Ross, co. Wexford, tanner   [farmer
1796 ,, Peter, Ratoath, co. Meath,
1751 ,, Philip, Dublin, victualler
1785 ,, Roger, Prumplestown, co. Kildare, farmer
1764 ,, Thomas, Dublin, par. St. Ann's
1794 ,, Thomas, Dublin, merchant
1803 ,, Thos., Ardbrackan, co. Westmeath
[See MORIN.]
1784 **Mordaunt**, sir John, knt. of the Bath (Copy)
1682 **Morden**, John, Longsutton, Lincolnshire, clk. (Copy)
1604 **More**, Edward, Dublin, clk.
1589 ,, Jennett, wife to Luke Ralifort M., Clunycavan, co. Meath
1707 ,, John, Dublin, merchant
1584 ,, Owene, Mariner-stone, county Meath, esq.
[See MOORE.]
1734 **Morecroft**, Elizabeth, Dublin, spr.
1723 ,, James, D.D., archdeacon of Meath
1774 ,, James, Dublin, clk.
1769 ,, Susanna, Dublin
1713 **Morell**, Daniel, Kilkenny, esq.
1749 ,, Philip, Dublin, esq.
1805 **Moreton**, Johnston, Liscarbin, co. Leitrim, esq.
1715 ,, William, bp. of **Meath**, q. v.

1624 **Morfphye**, Wm., Kilkenny, burgess
1753 **Morgan**, Ambrose, Howth, co. Dublin, vintner
1745 ,, Andrew, Dublin, merchant
1761 ,, Andrew, Milltown, co. Dublin, gent.
1779 ,, Andw., Charles-st., Dub., dyer
1796 ,, Anne, Carrickeeny, co. Arm., widow
1681 ,, sir Anthony, knt.
1752 ,, Anthony, Dublin, esq.
1685 ,, Bridget, Dublin, widow
1780 ,, Brunton, Kilmore, co. Dublin
1738 ,, Charles, Dublin, esq.
1771 ,, Chadleigh, Kilkenny, esq.
1790 ,, Columb, Dublin, esq.
1769 ,, David, Dublin, gent.
1776 ,, David, New-row, Dub., needlemaker
1751 ,, Edward, Dublin, carpenter
1729 ,, Elizabeth, Dublin, spinster
1795 ,, Elizabeth, Caranutta, co. Cork, widow
1763 ,, Ellinor, Dublin, spinster
1761 ,, Francis, Cork-st., Dublin, gent.
1771 ,, Francis, Dublin, gent.
1752 ,, George, Roundwood
1801 ,, George, Duhig, Cork city, esq.
1729 ,, Henry, Dublin, tailor
1721 ,, Hugh, Cottlestown, co. Sligo, esq.
1763 ,, Hugh, lieut.-col. 90th regt.
1768 ,, James, Naventown, co. Meath, farmer
1773 ,, James, Dublin, gent.
1779 ,, James, the Coombe, Dublin, dealer
1790 ,, James, Dublin, merchant
1760 ,, Jane, Coleraine, co. Londonderry
1788 ,, Jane, Cork city, widow
1775 ,, John, Galway, alderman
1775 ,, John, Kilcolgan, co. Galway, esq.
1794 ,, John, Dunmoylan, co. Limk., gent.
1808 ,, Joseph, Lurgan Green
1738 ,, Judith, Waterford, widow
1789 ,, Laurence, Primatestown, co. Meath, farmer
1767 ,, Mary, Dublin, widow
1762 ,, M'Nemara, Dublin, esq.
1742 ,, Morgan, Yerboston, Pembrokeshire, gent. (Copy)
1742 ,, Morgan, Yerboston, Pembrokeshire, gent.
1594 ,, Patk., Enagh, co. Clare, gent.
1733 ,, Penelope, Dublin, spinster
1807 ,, Peter, Bridestown, co. Cork, esq.

1780	**Morgan**, Redmond, Rathcoffey, co. Kildare (Copy)	
1752	,, Richard, Dublin, esq.	
1765	,, Richard, Dublin, stonecutter	
1804	,, Richard, Longford-st., Dublin, esq.	
1637	,, Robt., Dromorhire, co. Leitrim, gent.	
1681	,, Robert, Castletown, co. Sligo, esq. (Ex.)	
1760	,, Robert, Crumlinstown, co. Kildare, esq. [esq.	
1781	,, Robert, Castletown, co. Sligo,	
1800	,, Rosanna, Dublin	
1766	,, Samuel, Dawson-st., Dublin, gent.	
1676	,, Temperence, *alias* **Coulston**, widow of alderman J. M.	
1656	,, Thomas, Cork [**VI.** 27	
1743	,, Thomas, Dublin, tailor	
1756	,, Thomas, Dublin, esq.	
1767	,, Thomas, Raheen, co. Waterford, esq.	
1782	,, Thomas, Dublin, esq.	
1803	,, Thomas, Blanchardstown, co. Dublin, publican	
1691	,, William, vicar of Arnargher, co. Westmeath, clk.	
1743	,, William, Waterford, alderman	
1784	,, William, Polboy	
1786	,, Wm., Waterford city, alderman	
1788	,, William, Dublin, confectioner	
1756	,, Worthington, Dublin, esq.	
1795	**Morgell**, Crosbie, Mount Morgell, co. Limerick, esq.	
1738	,, Philip, Dingle, co. Kerry (Ex.)	
1810	,, Robert H., Oughterard	
1810	,, Thomas, Kill, co. Kildare, barrister-at-law	
1580	**Morgho**, Gormell, Killdroght	
1694	**Morgill**, Phillip, Ballyneclogh, co. Clare, gent.	
1781	**Moriarty**, Blase, Dingle, merchant	
1739	,, Thos., Dingle, co. Kerry, mcht.	
1785	,, Thos., Dingle, co. Kerry, gent.	
1659	**Morice**, Robert, soldier [**VII.** 186	
	[See MORRIS.]	
1781	**Morin**, John James, Dublin, sugarbaker	
	[See MORAN.]	
1791	**Morine**, Mary, Dublin, widow	
1794	**Morisy**, Wm., Coolhest, co. Waterford, gent.	
1672	**Morley**, Cuthbert, London, gent.	
1723	,, George, Tuitestown, co. Westmeath	
1770	,, George, Richmond, co. Westmeath	
1705	,, Henry, Farthingstown, co. Westmeath, gent.	

1736	**Morley**, John, Cork, esq.	
1790	,, John, Dublin, heraldic painter	
1796	,, Joseph, Dublin	
1808	,, Joseph, sergt. in the 88th regt.	
1726	,, Martin, Clonfad, co. Westmeath, gent.	
1741	,, Miriam, Cork, widow	
1741	,, Richard, Gillerstown, co. Westmeath, gent.	
1770	,, William, Richmond, co. Westmeath, gent.	
1811	,, William, CherryGarden, King's co., esq.	
1657	**Morly**, John, soldier in captain Camby's company	
	[See MARLAY, MARLEY.]	
1781	**Mornington**, Garret, earl of	
1758	,, Richard, Lord Baron	
1774	**Morony**, Andrew, Dunaha, co. Clare, esq.	
1783	,, Blanch, Limerick, widow	
1778	,, Edmond, Parteen, co. Clare, esq.	
1741	,, John, Dunaha, co. Clare, gent.	
1758	,, John, Limerick, merchant	
1785	,, Joseph, Dublin, gent.	
1793	,, Mary, Cork city, widow	
1603	**Morphe**, John, Dublin, alderman	
1672	,, Don John, col. of the Irish regt. in Spain	
1698	,, John, Waterford, merchant	
1686	**Morphy**, Ann, Dublin, widow	
1808	,, Denis, Cork city, gent.	
1784	,, Edmond, Kilkenny city, gent.	
1763	,, Garrett, Ballinakill, Queen's co., esq.	
1702	,, Hugh, Cork, merchant	
1728	,, Jane, Dublin, widow	
1673	,, John, Swords, co. Dublin, gent.	
1683	,, John, Dublin, LL.D.	
1799	,, John, Mt. Prospect, co. Kerry, esq.	
1730	,, Richard, Dublin, gent	
1776	,, Stephen, Mt. Desart, co. of Cork city, farmer	
	[See MURPHY.]	
1805	**Morpie**, Thos., Dublin, truss-maker	
1729	**Morres**, Andrew, Dublin, gent.	
1754	,, Edmond, Thurles, co. Tipperary	
1721	,, dame Ellen, widow of sir John M., of Knockagh, co. Tipp., bart.	
1742	,, Francis, Kilkreen, Kilkenny city, esq.	
1777	,, sir Haydock Evans, bart.	
1793	,, Isabella, Dublin, spinster	
1718	,, James, Rossestown, co. Tipp., esq.	
1644 / 1647	,, sir John, Knockagh, co. Tipp., bart. (put together)	

z

1720 **Morres**, sir John, Knockagh, co. Tipperary, bart.
1744 ,, John, Malahide, co. Dubl., esq.
1739 ,, Mary, Dublin, widow (stated 1739, not proved)
1753 ,, Mary, Ballymurreen, co. Tipp., spinster
1765 ,, dame Mary
1742 ,, Nicholas, Latragh, co. Tipp., gent.
1624 ,, Redmond, Templemore, co. Tipperary, esq.
1740 ,, sir Redmond, bart.
1757 ,, Susanna, widow of Nicholas M., esq.
1785 ,, William, Dublin, butcher
1762 **Morress**, James, Lazershill, Dublin, bricklayer
1720 **Morrin**, Nicholas, Clonagh, co. Kildare, farmer
1804 ,, Patrick, Usher's-quay, Dublin, vintner
1811 ,, Richard, Kennedy's-lane, Dub.
1722 **Morris**, Abraham, Cork, merchant
1674 ,, Alice, *alias* **Roberts**, widow of Thomas M., of Kannarchy-dall, near the Welsh-poole, Montgomeryshire, gent.
1794 ,, Alice, Rathdown, co. Wicklow, spinster
1780 ,, Andrew, west suburbs of Galw., gent.
1750 ,, Anne, New Ross, co. Wexford, widow
1783 ,, Apollos, Clonkeen, co. Cork
1741 ,, Benjamin, Waterford, esq.
1767 ,, Benjamin, Waterford
1797 ,, Benjamin, Gracedieu
1811 ,, Benjamin, Waterford city, esq.
1772 ,, Edmond, Dublin, merchant
1717 ,, Edward, Old Court, co. Dublin, gent.
1718 ,, Edward, Mullagha, co. Meath
1794 ,, Edward, Richmond, co. Dublin, esq.
1790 ,, Elizabeth, Tralee, co. Kerry, spinster
1789 ,, Ellen, Aungier-st., Dubl., wid.
1747 ,, Henry, Dublin, grocer
1786 ,, Henry, Eustace-street, Dublin, surgeon
1788 ,, Isabella, Dublin, widow
1727 ,, James, Castlemartin, co. Kild., gent.
1687 ,, Jane, Dublin, spinster
1730 ,, Jane, Dubl., widow of John M., gent.
1686 ,, John, London, esq. and alderman (Copy)
1705 ,, John, Dublin, mariner

1712 **Morris**, John, Dublin, gabbar manufacturer
1741 ,, John, mariner on board the "Ripon" man-of-war
1753 ,, John, Dromrecomond, co. Antrim (dated 1753)
1764 ,, John, Mullagha, co. Meath, gt
1765 ,, John, Waterford, merchant
1769 ,, John, Cork, maltster
1775 ,, John, Cork, maltster
1788 ,, John, Dorset-st., Dublin, esq.
1806 ,, John, Tubberabonny, co. Dubl.
1736 ,, Jonas, Cork, esq.
1742 ,, Joseph, Ballynavin, co. Waterf
1758 ,, Joseph, Tankardstown, co. Meath, gent.
1743 ,, Mary, Waterford, widow
1783 ,, Mary, Galway, spinster
1793 ,, Mary, Cork, widow
1800 ,, Nicholas, Gortroe, co. Galway
1735 ,, Patk., Silverwood, co. Armagh gent.
1768 ,, Patk., Dublin, dancing-master
1777 ,, Patrick, Galway town
1794 ,, Quire, Mountrath, Queen's co. gent.
1765 ,, Rachel, Limerick, widow
1780 ,, Rachel, Littleton, co. Kerry spinster
1780 ,, Redmond, Dublin, gent.
1784 ,, Redmond, Dublin, esq.
1692 ,, Richard, Waterford, merchant
1705 } ,, Richard, Ballyfarnam, co. Dubl. esq.
1720 } ,, col. Richard, quarter-master and barrack-master-general
1774 ,, Richard, Rathdown, co. Wicklow, farmer
1810 ,, Richard, Mullins, co. Wicklow
1763 ,, Roger
1694 ,, Samuel, Ballybeggan, co. Kerry esq.
1804 ,, rev. Samuel, Glebe Lodge, co. Tyrone, clerk
1806 ,, Solomon, Gortin, co. Tyrone
1715 ,, Theophilus, Cork, merchant
1717 ,, Theophilus, Cork, merchant
1738 ,, Thos., New Ross, co. Wexford
1771 ,, Thomas, Dublin
1797 ,, Thos., Lisburn, co. Antrim, esq
1724 ,, Wm., Dublin, barrister-at-law
1764 ,, Wm., Castle Salem, co. Cork gent.
1785 ,, William, Waterford, esq.
1791 ,, William, Waterford city, counsellor-at-law
1807 ,, William, Meath-street, Dublin grocer

[See FITZMAURICE, MAURICE, MORICE.]

1750 **Mottley**, Sarah, Dublin, widow
1725 ,, Thomas, Dublin, skinner
1703 ,, Walter, Dublin, alderman
1769 ,, Walter, Moon, co. Kildare, esq.
           (not proved)
1744 **Mottly**, Joseph, Dublin, weaver
1740 **Mouat**, dame Elizabeth
1749 ,, Florah, Waterford, widow
1766 ,, Jane, Waterford, spinster
1759 **Mouls**, John, Dublin, clothier
1656 **Moulsworth**, Robert, Dublin, mrct.
                            [**V**. 330
       [See MOLESWORTH.]
1675 **Mounckton**, Nicholas, Knockanny,
           or Knockawny, co. Dublin,
           gent.
1735 **Mounier**, John, London, merchant
1659 **Mounke**, William, soldier in capt.
           Vivian's comp.   [**VII**. 181
1638 **Mounsell**, John, London, saltster
           and merchant adventurer,
           of England, late of Court
           Brown Castle, co. Limerick
1806 **Mountain**, Dianna, Dublin city,
           widow
1675 **Mountalexander**, Catherine, dow.
           countess of
1718 ,, Hugh, earl of
1744 ,, Hugh, earl of
1771 ,, Mary Angelica, countess of
1757 ,, Thomas, earl of
1790 **Mount Cashel**, Stephen, earl of
1779 **Mountgarret**, Edmond, lord visct.
1780 ,, Edmond, lord viscount
1787 ,, John, mariner on board the
           "Orpheus"
1764 ,, Margaret, viscountess
1736 ,, Richard, viscount
       [See MONTGARRET.]
1679 **Mountgarrett**, Edmond, lord visct.
1793 ,, Edmond, lord viscount
1739 ,, Katherine, dowager viscountess
1782 **Mountgomery**, Wm., New York,
           in America
1798 **Mountjoy**, rt. hon. Luke, lord visct.
1693 ,, William, lord viscount
1728 ,, William, lord viscount (Copy)
1766 **Mountmorres**, Harvey, lord baron
           of Castle M., co. Kilkenny
1798 ,, Harvey Redmond, lord viscount
           (Copy)
1780 ,, Mary, dowager viscountess
1698 **Mountrath**, Ales, countess of
1744 ,, Algernon, earl of (Copy)
1672 ,, Charles, earl of
1802 ,, rt. hon. Chas. Henry, earl of
           (Copy)
       [See MONTRATH.]
1719 **Mountray**, James, Aghamoyles,
           co. Tyrone, esq.

1700 **Mourilliard**, John, Amsterdam, but
           late of Dublin, merchant
1809 **Mouritze**, Stafford, Mt. Bailee, co.
           Louth
1649 **Mourphye**, Patrick, Kilkenny, mct.
       [See MURPHY.]
1742 **Moutray**, Anketell, of col. Gueses'
           regt. of foot
1802 ,, rev. Anketell, Favour Royal,
           co. Tyrone, clk.
1778 ,, James, Killybrick, co. Tyr., esq.
1779 ,, John, Favour Royal, co. Tyr.,
           esq.
1778 ,, Leslie, Killybrick, co. Tyr., esq.
1804 ,, Mary, Belturbet, co. Cavan
1773 ,, Rebecca, Dublin
1783 **Mowlds**, Wm., Oldtown, co Wick.
1676 **Moxon**, Nathaniel, Dublin, mercht.
1685 **Moyer**, Lawrence, Lowlayton, Essex,
           esq. (Copy)
1775 **Moylan**, David, Cork, merchant
1773 ,, Dennis, Cork, merchant
1799 ,, John, Cork city, merchant
1748 **Moyle**, Bryan, Donnamore, co.
           Meath
1751 ,, Godfrey, Jameston, co. Leitr.
1686 ,, John, Dublin, gent.
1724 **Moylen**, William, Liss, gent.
1757 ,, Wm., Lisnasiky, co. Galway,
           gent.
1650 **Moynes**, Abraham, an architect
           employed in the army
1785 **Moynham**, Michael, Clonenkenny,
           co. Tipp.
1775 ,, Robert, Limerick, dancing
           master
1756 **Mukins**, Elizabeth, Kilkenny, wid.
1706 ,, Isaac, Kilkenny, alderman
1810 **Mulcahy**, Patrick, Dromore, co.
           Waterford
1774 **Mulcall**, Wm., Ballymurragh, co.
           Kilkenny, esq.
1747 **Muldoon**, Andrew, Dublin
1756 ,, Mary, the Coombe, dealer
1753 **Muldun**, Nicholas, Foore, co. West-
           meath
1764 **Muledy**, Daniel, Carrickfergus, co.
           Antrim, gent.
1759 ,, John, Gartlony, co. Meath, gt.
1772 **Mulhallen**, Robert, Kilkenny, esq.
1805 **Mulhern**, Ralph, Gardiner's-street,
           Dublin
1671 **Mulhollan**, John, Conaghie, co.
           Monaghan, gent.
1805 ,, Robert, Malcolm Ville, co.
           Carlow
1713 **Mulkeran**, Thomas, Waterford, gt.
1803 **Mullally**, Maria Teresa, George's-
           hill, Dublin, spinster
1719 ,, Martin, Kill, co. Kildare, farmer

1759 **Mullan**, John, Newry, co. Down, shoemaker
    [See MULLIN.]
1808 **Mullarky**, Augustin
1805 ,, Patrick, Colga, co. Sligo
1801 **Mullay**, James, Dublin city, gent.
1809 ,, Judith, Dublin city, widow
1745 **Mullcail**, John, Clone, co. Kilkenny, gent.
1802 **Mullcaile**, James Philip, George's hill, Dublin
1788 **Mullcaill**, Elizabeth, Kilkenny, wid.
1785 **Mulldoon**, John, Braithwaite-street, Dublin, clothier
1689 **Mulledy**, John, Dublin, gent.
1781 ,, Patrick, Ballinakill, M.D.
1792 **Mullegan**, Francis, Dublin, widow
1749 ,, Francis, Athlone, merchant
1757 ,, James
1794 ,, Mary, Dublin, widow
1785 ,, Patk., Dublin, attorney-at-law
1761 ,, Thomas, Firbane, King's co., merchant
1796 **Mullen**, Catherine, Dublin, widow
1736 ,, James, Dublin, gent.
1805 ,, John, Dublin city
1791 ,, Mary, Boyle, co. Roscommon
    [See MULLIN.]
1809 **Mullhall**, Patrick, Ballycommon, King's co.
1799 ,, Thos., Cavan-st., Dublin, baker
1781 **Mullhallon**, John, the younger, esq.
1794 **Mullhollan**, Patk., High-st., Dublin
1702 **Mullhollon**, Toby, Dublin, gent.
1785 **Mulligan**, Cornelius, Magstown, co. Dublin, farmer
1778 ,, Robt., Rathvilly, co. Carlow, gt.
1770 **Mullin**, Catherine, *alias* **Donnelly**, Aclare, co. Meath
1751 ,, Isabella, Dublin, widow
1790 ,, John, Mary's-abbey, Dublin, silk dyer
1747 ,, Nicholas, suburbs of Dublin, victualler   [publican
1810 ,, Thos., Thomas-street, Dublin, [See MULLAN, MULLEN.]
1806 **Mullock**, Sarah
1794 **Mullowney**, Andrew, Francis-st., Dublin, tailor
1717 ,, Walter, Kilmore, co. Kildare, farmer
1807 **Mullowny**, Catherine, Waterford city, widow
1788 ,, Daniel, Tullamore, King's co. [See MOLONY.]
1796 **Mulloy**, Coote, Hughstown, co. Roscommon, gent.
1779 ,, Lawrence, Carroroe, co. Galway
1805 ,, Wm., New Ross, co. Wexford [See MOLLOY.]

1801 **Mulock**, John, Bellair, King's co., clerk   [gent.
1791 ,, Robert, Banagher, King's co.,
1777 ,, Thomas, Dublin, public notary
1807 **Mulvany**, Jas., Dublin city, carrier
1756 **Mulvey**, John, Dublin, shoemaker
1784 ,, Mary, Thomas-st., Dub., widow
    [See MULVANEY.]
1784 **Mulvihill**, Laurence, Knockanera, co. Clare, gent.
    [See MITCHELL.]
1809 **Mulvogue**, John, Boyle, co. Rosc.
1779 **Mulys**, Daniel, Channel-row, Dub., surgeon
1729 ,, John, Dublin, merchant
1783 **Mumford**, Wm., St. Omers, Prov. of Artois, gent. (Copy)
1762 **Mun**, Daniel, Dublin
1742 **Munday**, Mathew, Castleblayney, co. Monaghan, innkeeper
1675 **Mundy**, George, Castlejordan, co. Meath, clk.
1688 **Munier**, John, Dublin, practitioner in physic
1769 **Munkittrick**, Alex., Dublin, carrier
1775 ,, Alex., Dublin
1807 ,, Alex., Ardee, co. Louth, baker
1783 ,, Robert, Atherdee, co. Louth, baker
1756 **Munns**, Edward, vicar of Drumcliff
1711 **Munson**, Grace, George's-lane, Dublin, widow
1734 **Muony**, Richard, Limerick, mariner
1655 **Murcett**, John   [V. 167
1775 **Murdoch**, James, Belfast, merchant
    [See MURTACH, MURTAGH.]
1670 **Murdock**, Joseph, Youghal, merct.
1709 ,, Margaret, *alias* **Keeth**, wife of John M., Newry
1727 ,, Robt., Newry, co. Down, mcht.
1787 **Murphy**, Andrew, Drogheda, mcht.
1807 ,, Andrew, Dublin city, attorney-at-law
1686 ,, Aney, Lisalican, co. Carlow, widow
1754 ,, Ann, Dublin, spinster
1761 ,, Ann, Dublin, widow
1811 ,, Anne, Dublin city, widow
1767 ,, Arthur, Smythstown, co. Meath, farmer
1787 ,, Arthur Odell, Limerick city
1810 ,, Arthur, Oulartleagh, co. Wexford, esq.
1810 ,, Arthur, Outerleigh. co. Wexford, esq.
1741 ,, Barnaby, Irishtown, Kilkenny, merchant
1754 ,, Barnard
1762 ,, Bryan, Sportsfield, co. Kilkenny, gent.

1754	**Murphy**, Richard, Dublin, dyer	
1793	,, Richard, Haggartsgreen, co. Kilkenny	
1788	,, Robert, Templeoge, co. Dublin, esq.	
1738	,, Thomas, Maynooth, co. Kildare, farmer	
1790	,, Thomas, Newtown, co. Dublin, gent.	
1802	,, Thomas, Leinster mill, co. Kildare	
1803	,, Thos., Inistioge, co. Kilkenny	
1757	,, William, Dublin, shipwright	
1759	,, William, London	
1766	,, Wm., Mitchelstown, co. Cork, gent.	
1793	,, William, co. of Dublin city	
1807	,, Wm., Knockmore, co. Carlow	
1774	,, Martin, Waterford, merchant [See MORPHY, MOURPHYE.]	
1701	**Murray**, Alexander, D.D., dean of Killala	
1771	,, Alexander, Dublin, esq.	
1799	,, Alexander, Mountmurray, co. Westmeath, esq.	
1756	,, Andrew, Fannet, co. Donegal, esq.	
1772	,, Andrew, Henry-st., Dublin, gt.	
1771	,, Ann, Dublin, spinster	
1766	,, Anne, Dublin, spinster	
1799	,, Archibold, Ballyshannon, co. Donegal, merchant	
1790	,, Bridget, *alias* **Shore**, Dublin, furrier	
1788	,, Bryan, Lishoy, co. Westmeath, gent.	
1789	,, Catherine, Richmond, co. Dublin, spinster	
1744	,, Charles, Dublin, gent. [See 1792.]	
1781	,, Creagh, Stratford, Aungier-st., Dublin, esq.	
1782	,, David, Dublin, furrier	
1792	,, David, Gorey, co. Wexford, shopkeeper	
1769	,, Edward, Wexford, esq.	
1803	,, Emanuel, Kilkenny city, mchr.	
1799	,, Florinda, widow	
1761	,, George, Dublin	
1789	,, George, Belfast	
1810	,, Geo., Mecklenburgh-st., Dublin, gent.	
1778	,, Isaac, Ballintra, co. Donegal, gent.	
1752	,, James, Killybegs, co. Donegal	
1793	,, James, Brocka, co. Wicklow, farmer	
1806	,, Jane, Camden-st., shopkeeper	
1699	,, John, Ballyhogodan, Queen's co., clerk	

1767	**Murray**, John, Warringstown, co. Down	
1769	,, John, Waterford, mercht.	
1769	,, John, formerly surgeon to earl Rothes' regt.	
1788	,, John, Meath-st., Dublin, hatter	
1792	,, John, Monaghan, esq.	
1800	,, John	
1804	,, John, Grafton-st., Dub., haberdasher	
1770	,, Marcella, Dublin, widow	
1790	,, Margt., Rainsford-st., Dublin, widow	
1746	,, Michael, Ballymaconnolly, co. Louth, smith and farrier	
1805	,, Nathaniel, Dublin, goldsmith	
1751	,, Patrick, Coolcor, co. Meath, farmer	
1758	,, Philip, Brayfoot-street, Dublin, clothier	
1780	,, Richard, Dublin, glover	
1696	,, Walter, Ravilly, co. Catherlough, gent. **[XVII.** 186	
1792	,, Walter, Rath, Queen's co., farmer [gent.	
1696	,, Wm., Ravilly, co. Catherlogh,	
1765	,, Wm., St. Thomas-st., Dublin, innkeeper	
1774	,, William, Glenevy, co. Antrim, linendraper	
1776	,, William, Feikanaughan, co. Tyrone, esq.	
1781	,, Wm., Lifford, co. Donegal, esq.	
1788	,, Wm., Drumilihue, co. Down	
1677	**Murren**, Denys, Towlerton, Queen's co.	
1703	**Murrey**, David, Douglas, in the Isle of Man	
1700	,, John, par. of St. Martin-in-the fields, Middlesex, gt. (Copy)	
1761	,, Thos., Braithwaite-st., Dublin, widow	
1730	**Murry**, Bryan, Dublin, gent.	
1786	,, Jas., Newtowndally, co. Dub., farmer	
1664	,, John, Harbourstown, co. Meath, gent.	
1761	,, John, Dublin, woollendraper	
1790	,, John, Little Mary-st., Dublin	
1776	,, Robert, Dublin, coachmaker [See MURRAY.]	
1788	**Murtach**, Richard, Pilltown. co. Meath, weaver	
1775	**Murtagh**, John, College-gr., Dublin [See MURDOCH.]	
1720	**Murth**, Richard, Haverford West, Pembrokesh., mcht. (Copy)	
1700	**Muschamp**, Denny, late of Pall Mall, Middlesex, esq. (Copy)	

1665 **Muscry**, Charles, lord viscount
1788 **Musgrave**, Christopher, Ballyin, co. Waterford, esq.
1800 ,, John, Ballyin, co. Waterford
1741 ,, Richd., Lismore, co. Waterford
1788 ,, Richard, Salterbridge., co. Waterford
1677 ,, Thomas, St. Patrick's, Dublin, brewer
1780 **Mussen**, John, Lisburn, co. Antrim, apothecary
1763 **Mussenden**, Daniel, Belfast, mcht.
1799 ,, Frances
1786 ,, Hariot, Dublin, spinster
1690 ,, Isabella, widow of Francis M., Hillsborough, co. Down
1792 ,, Isabella, Dublin
1736 ,, Jane, Dublin, widow
1784 ,, Jane, Dublin
1786 ,, Jane, Dublin, spinster
1780 ,, William, Belfast, co. Antrim, esq.
1750 **Musson**, Wm., Ringsend, Dublin, tide waiter
1756 **Muston**, John, Farranthinton (Copy)
1765 **Mutlow**, Elizabeth, Woodstown, co. Waterford, widow
1687 ,, John, par. Chiswick, Middlesex, esq.
1694 ,, Mary, par. St. Martin-in-the-fields, Middlesex, wid.(Copy)
1671 **Myagh**, David FitzJames, Cork, esq.
1657 **Myaghe**, John, Kinsale, merchant
1597 ,, Stephen (no date)
1729 **Myddleton**, James, Lanesborough, co. Longford, esq.
1789 **Myers**, Christopher, Monkstown, co. Dublin, architect
1736 ,, Jeremiah, Dublin, grocer
1805 ,, Randle, brigade-major of the co. Wicklow
1789 ,, Richard, Crownelea, co. Wick.
1801 ,, Graham, Dublin, esq.
1727 **Myhill**, Jane, Dublin, widow
1782 ,, Jane, Dublin, widow
1691 ,, John, Ballysop, co. Wexford,gt.
1772 **Myles**, Oliver, Youghal, co. Cork, clothier
1675 ,, Rodulph, Clondalkin, co. Dub., gent.
1799 ,, Thos., Ballydrennan, co. Tipp., gent.
[See MILES.]
1790 **Mylne**, William, Dublin, esq.
1595 **Mynce**, Joshua, co. Meath
1584 **Mynne**, Thomas, Dublin, gent.
1767 **Mynshall**, Elizabeth, Louisa, *alias* Turner, *alias* **Brown**
1732 **Myre**, Robert, Dublin, esq.

——N——

1707 **Naghten,** Bartholomew, Loughboy, near Dublin, gent.
1803 ,, Catherine, Roscommon, spinst.
1784 ,, Ellinor, Athlone, co. Roscommon, spinster
1796 ,, Jas., Killeen, co. Roscommon
1751 ,, Laughlin, Killeen, co. Roscom.
1757 ,, Loughlin, Thomastown, co. Roscommon, esq.
1788 ,, Mable, Athlone, widow
1794 ,, Mathias, Galway, chandler
1786 ,, Thomas, Thomastown, co. Roscommon, esq.
1808 ,, Timothy, Castlerea, co. Roscommon, M.D.
[See NORTON.]
1784 **Nagle**, Athanasius, Ballylegan, co. Cork
1796 ,, Edmd., Clogher, co. Cork, esq.
1796 ,, Elizabeth, Cork city, widow
1805 ,, Garrott, Ballinamore, co. Cork, esq.
1793 ,, Honora
1710 ,, Jas., Garranevelley, co. Tipp., gent.
1800 ,, Jas., Annakisy, co. Cork, gent.
1774 ,, Jane, Monkstown,co.Cork, spr.
1745 ,, Peter, Dublin, mariner
1719 ,, Richd., Fethard, co. Tip., esq.
1764 ,, Richd., Mount N., co. Cork, gt.
1681 ,, Susanna, Youghal, spinster
1805 **Nail**, John, Blackhall, co. Kildare
[See NEALE.]
1757 **Nairac**, John, the elder, Dubl., mct.
1796 ,, John, Dublin, merchant
1806 ,, Rebecca, Dublin city
1751 **Naizon**, col. Peter, Gt. Marlborough-st., Middlesex (Copy)
1741 **Najac**, Anthony, Dublin, esq.
1811 **Nally**, Anthony, Galway
1801 ,, John, Dalgin, co. Galway
1669 ,, William, Robuck, co. Dublin, farmer
1729 ,, William, Dublin, merchant
1759 **Nalty**, Henry, Limerick, co. Wexford, farmer
1664 **Nangle**, Arthur, Kilbixy, co. Westmeath, gent.
1777 ,, Catherine, Maghera, co. Derry, spinster
1752 ,, Christopher, Dublin, gent.
1751 ,, Dudley, Silliot Hill, co. Kildare, gent. [gent.
1610 ,, Edmond, Dowlka,co. Longford,
1771 ,, Edward, Kildaulkey, co.Meath, esq.

1758 **Nangle**, Ellinor, Dublin, widow
1721 ,, George, Laraghs, co. Kildare, gent.
1743 ,, James, Tenemoney, co. Wexford, gent.
1809 ,, John, Dublin city, gent.
1723 ,, Margery, *alias* **Fitzsimons**, Kill, co. Dublin, widow
1802 ,, Maria, Dublin, widow
1789 ,, Patrick, Church-street, Dublin, vintner
1758 ,, Peter, Dublin, grocer
1615 ,, Robert, Ballysax, co. Kildare, esq.
1733 ,, Walter, Tyrrellspass, co. Westmeath, farmer
1762 ,, Walter, Kildalky, co. Meath, esq.
1776 **Naper**, Anne, par. of St. George, Middlesex, widow (Copy)
1692 ,, Dorothy, Loughcrew, co. Meath, widow (Copy)
1738 ,, Gerrard, quarter-mast. in gen. Naper's regt. of horse
1676 ,, James, Loughcrew, co. Meath, esq.
1718 ,, James, Loughcrew, co. Westmeath
1740 ,, Robert, esq., lieut.-gen. of His Majesty's Forces
1741 ,, Wm., Hillsborough, co. Meath, esq.
1802 ,, William, Littletown, co. Westmeath, esq.
1805 **Napier**, George, the hon. col.
1802 ,, Patrick
1733 **Napper**, Henry, New Ross, co. Wexford, esq.
1789 **Narney**, John, Biddeford, co. Kildare, esq.
1746 **Narton**, Mary, Merchants'-quay, Dublin, gentlewoman
1737 **Nary**, Cornelius, Dubl., R. C. priest [See NEARY.]
1768 **Nash**, Andrew, Dublin, gent.
1800 ,, Andrew, Ballygalan, co. Waterford, esq.
1751 ,, Catherine, Mallow
1809 ,, Charles, Carn, co. Mayo, esq.
1769 ,, Christian, *alias* **Stackpole**, Limerick, widow
1748 ,, David, Killmichael, co. Limer.
1669 ,, Edmond, Ballyteige, co. Limerick, gent.
1774 ,, Henrietta, Dublin, widow
1790 ,, James, Limerick
1793 ,, Jane, Limerick, spinster
1802 ,, John, Ballymacooley, co. Cork, gent.
1794 ,, Lewellin, Cork, esq.

1805 **Nash**, Lewellin, South Liberties of Cork, esq.
1800 ,, Mathew, capt. in Royal Irish artillery
1804 ,, Michael, Dublin city, gent.
1746 ,, Nicholas, Dublin, esq.
1725 ,, Richd., Ardtagit, co. Clare, gt.
1794 ,, Richard, Limerick, esq.
1780 ,, Thomas, Ballyscanlan, co. Limerick, gent.
1770 ,, rev. Wm., Farrihy, co. Cork, clk.
1741 **Nasmyth**, Thomas, Dublin, gent.
1804 **Nason**, Elizab., Newtown, co. Cork
1776 ,, John, Ballyscrerloge, co. Cork
1740 ,, William, Cork, merchant
1743 **Naughten**, Stephen, Dublin
1794 **Naughton**, Bridget, Mullinahack, Dublin, spinster
1636 ,, Neale, Dublin, merchant
    [IV. 177
    [See NORTON.]
1734 **Nayler**, Anne, widow of Jonathan N., Rathmoon, co. Wicklow
1716 ,, Jonathan, Rathmoon, co. Wicklow, gent.
1680 ,, Samuel, Dublin, surgeon
1688 **Naylor**, Andrew, Carrowgeen, co. Kildare, farmer
1804 ,, rev. Charles, of the town and county Carlow, clk.
1758 ,, Wm., Rathmoon, co. Wicklow, esq.
1803 **Neail**, Jas., Killawilly, co. Cavan [See NEALE.]
1794 **Nealan**, Elizabeth, Youghal, co. Cork, widow
1807 **Neale**, Anne, Tullamore, King's co.
1725 ,, Arthur
1741 ,, ven. Benjamin, Mount N., co. Carlow, archd. of Leighlin
1692 ,, Constantine, Wexford, esq.
1791 ,, John, Dublin, surgeon
1811 ,, John, Mountmellick, Queen's co.
1691 ,, Mary, Dublin, widow
1743 ,, Mary, widow
1687 ,, Nathaniel, Dubl., coachmaker
1767 ,, Samuel, Christianstown, co. Kildare, farmer
1792 ,, Samuel, Springmount, North Lib. of Cork, merchant
1681 ,, Wm., Loughstown, co. Dublin, yeoman
1732 ,, Wm., Dublin, weaver
    [See NAIL, NEILL, NIELL.]
1678 **Neall**, Robert, Dublin, butcher
1809 **Neary**, Christopher, Dublin city [See NARY.]
1701 **Neatby**, Fras., lieut. in brig. Langston's regt. of horse

1775 **Neate**, Wm., London, esq., mercht.
(Copy)
1698 **Neau**, Martin, Mairenes, in Sain-
tonge, an inhabitant in St.
Anns, Soho, London
1714 **Neave**, William, co. Longford, esq.
1793 **Necomen**, Catherine, Stephen's-
green
1697 ,, sir Thos, Sutton, co. Dubl., knt.
1762 **Nedham**, Robt., Newry, co. Down;
now at Berkenham, Kent,
esq. (Large will, Copy)
1766 **Needham**, Andrew, Dublin, mercht.
1792 ,, Mary, Dublin, spinster
1781 ,, Ruth, Paulville, co. Carlow, spr.
1784 ,, Richd., Turbert, co. Kerry, gt.
1664 } ,, Symon, Ballycarroll, Queen's
1683 }   co., esq.   [**XIII.** 4
1718 ,, Thomas, Dublin, gent.
1729 ,, Thomas, Crownehorne, co.
Wicklow, gent.
1806 ,, Thomas, Dublin city, banker
1695 ,, William, Hydebrook, co. Westmeath, esq.
1740 **Neesham**, John, Tatlow-bridge, co.
Waterford, tanner
1728 **Neigans**, Henry, Belfast, sugar
baker
1803 **Neil**, John, Grand Canal Harbour
[See NEALE.]
1784 **Neilan**, Margaret, Limerick, spr.
[See NEYLAN.]
1735 **Neile**, Amo, Dublin, merchant
1786 **Neill**, Elizabeth, Dublin, widow
1802 ,, Hugh, Naptown, co. Dublin,
farmer
1793 ,, James
1759 ,, Mary, Dublin, widow
[See NEALE.]
1696 **Neilon**, Edward, Kilcarhah, co.
Clare, gent.
1811 **Neilson**, Hugh, Inchreboy, co.
Derry, farmer
1704 ,, Robert, Belfast, co. Antrim,
apothecary
[See NELSON.]
1788 **Nelan**, Maurice, Cork, merchant
1754 **Neligan**, Maurice, Moydow, clk.
1761 ,, rev. Michael, Granard, clk.
1758 **Nelligan**, Eliz., Longford town, wid.
1735 **Nellson**, Thomas, late of Milltown,
co. Monaghan, now of Dub.,
gent.
1686 **Nelmes**, Anthony, Dublin, gent.
1637 **Nelson**, Constance, Dublin, widow
[**IV.** 255
1627 ,, John, Dublin, cook
1808 ,, John, Dublin city
1784 ,, Mary, *alias* **Malone**
1775 ,, Oliver, Dublin, stationer

1772 **Nelson**, Richard, Dublin, esq.
1800 ,, Rose, Dublin, spinster
1739 ,, Samuel, Dublin, turner
1807 ,, Thomas, Arran-quay, Dublin,
merchant
1699 ,, Wm., Ballinrath, King's co.,
clerk
1758 ,, Wm., Armagh town, merchant
[See NEILSON.]
1732 **Nelsonn**, Mary, Dublin, spinster
1697 **Nelthorpe**, Henry, Dublin, jeweller
1757 ,, James, Lynford, Norfolk, esq.
(Copy)
1700 **Neper**, Edwd., Belturbet, co. Cavan
1809 **Nerhiney**, Hugh, Slata, co. Roscommon
1770 **Nesbit**, rev. Andrew, Killybegs, co.
Donegal
1784 ,, Andrew, Dublin, esq.
1795 ,, Anne, Dublin, widow
1797 ,, Anne, Greenhills, co. Donegal,
widow
1771 ,, Charles, Dublin, tailor
1791 ,, Cosby, Lismore, co. Cavan, esq.
1798 ,, Ezekial, Bath city, M.D.
1783 ,, Gifford, Tubberdaly, King's co.,
esq.
1766 ,, James, Greenhill, co. Donegal,
esq.
1767 ,, James, Tubberdaly, King's co.
1793 ,, John, Kinnaghan, co. Meath,
gent.
1762 ,, Margery, Dublin, widow
1774 ,, Sarah, widow of Gifford N.,
Tubberdaly, King's co., esq.
1757 ,, Thomas, Strabane, co. Tyrone,
merchant
1789 ,, William, Milltown, co. Meath,
gent.
1799 ,, rev. William, Drogheda
1721 **Nesbitt**, capt. Albert
1753 ,, Albert, London, esq. (Copy)
1777 ,, Albert, London, esq. (Copy)
1755 ,, Alexander, Kilmacredan, co.
Donegal, gent.
1778 ,, Alexander, Dublin, esq.
1708 ,, Andrew, Brentor, co. Donegal
1808 ,, Andrew, Carrickaagoe, co.
Donegal
1742 ,, Anne, Dublin, widow
1811 ,, Anne, Gloucester-st., Dublin
1758 ,, Cairncross, Aughamore, co.
Londonderry (Large will)
1805 ,, Catherine, Dublin city, widow
1786 ,, Charles, Greenhills, co. Donegal, esq.
1806 ,, Coote, Aughry, co. Leitrim,
esq.
1766 ,, Francis, Carrygone, co. Longford, gent.

1773 **Nesbitt,** Gifford, formerly of Tubberdaly, King's co., esq., now of Bloomsbury-square, London

1744 ,, Hugh, Tullydonnell, co. Don.

1766 ,, Hugh, Tullydonnell, co. Donegal, gent.

1750 ,, James, Greenhills, co. Donegal, esq.

1764 ,, James, Croghan, King's co., gent.

1805 ,, James, Lisconbane, co. Tipperary, clk.

1765 ,, Jane, widow of Alexander N., Kilmacredan, co. Donegal

1803 ,, Jane, Athlone, co. Westmeath, widow

1780 ,, John, Aughry, co. Leitrim, esq.

1808 ,, Joshua, Lifford, co. Donegal

1803 ,, Louisa, late deceased

1752 ,, Thomas, Lismore, co. Cavan, esq.

1802 ,, Thos., Kilmacredan, co. Donegal, esq.

1740 ,, Wm., Athy, co. Kildare, clk.

1744 ,, William, Drumalee, co. Cavan [See NISBIT.]

1801 **Nessfield,** Saml., James's-st., city of Dublin, tanner

1663 **Nest,** Francis, Maynooth, gent.

1766 **Nethercoat,** Edward, Callan, co. Kilkenny, gent.

1768 **Netterfield,** Thomas, Swanlinbar, co. Cavan

1741 **Netterville,** Catherine, Dublin, wid.

1792 ,, Catherine, Dublin, spr.

1610 ,, Christopher, Blackcastle, co. Dublin

1744 ,, Edmond, surveyor of the port of Sligo

1777 ,, Edmond, Longford, co. Galway. esq.

1769 ,, Edward, Dublin, esq., M.D.

1811 ,, Edward, Dublin city

1721 ,, dame Frances, Mohober, co. Tipperary, widow

1663 ,, John, lord viscount

1742 ,, Luke, Stateen, co. Meath, esq.

1802 ,, Margt., Brunswick-st., Dublin, widow

1799 ,, Mary, Dublin, spinster

1689 ,, Nicholas, lord viscount

1716 ,, Nicholas, Cruiserath, co. Meath, esq.

1719 ,, Nicholas, Lecarrow, co. Galway, esq.

1763 ,, Nich., Hollymount, co. Meath, now of Dublin, esq.

1676 ,, Patrick, Lecarrow, co. Galway, esq.

1734 **Netterville,** Patrick, Longford, co. Galway, esq. (Not proved)

1607 ,, Richard, Corballis, co. Dublin, esq.

1791 ,, Robert, Cruiserath, co. Meath, esq.

1799 ,, Thomas, Marlay, co. Meath

1709 ,, William, Dublin, gent.

1757 ,, Wm , Donnecarney, co. Dublin, esq.

1790 ,, William, Snugsborough, co. Meath, esq.

1801 ,, William, Dublin city, esq.

1793 **Nettles,** Jane, *alias* **Drew**

1681 ,, John, Foureen, co. Waterford, esq. (Ex.)

1715 ,, John, Foureen, co. Waterford, gent.

1728 ,, John, Foureen, co. Waterford, esq.

1786 ,, John Ryves, Nettleville, co. Cork, esq.

1727 ,, Martha, widow

1712 ,, Robt., Maghalavagh, co. Cork, esq.

1640 **Nettleton,** George, the Castle, Dublin, gent.

1634 **Neuce,** capt. Samuel, Clare, gent.
[IV. 42

1749 **Neve,** Thomas, Ballyneill, co. Londonderry, gent.

1637 **Nevell,** John, New Ross, co. Wexford, merchant

1636 ,, Thos. Fitzwalter, Wexford, mt.

1742 **Nevett,** Sarah, wife to Caleb Nevett

1771 **Nevill,** Arthur Jones, Furnace, co. Kildare, esq.

1653 ,, Beaumont

1759 ,, Elizabeth, Dublin, spinster

1727 ,, Francis, Belturbet, co. Cavan, esq.

1737 ,, Garrett, Dublin, merchant

1721 ,, Henry, Bunnavalley, co. Westmeath, gent.

1756 ,, Henry, Barretstown, co. Kildare, gent.

1735 ,, John, Newcastle, co. Dub., esq.

1703 ,, Margaret, wid. of Richard N., esq.

1682 ,, Richard, Gt. Fornaghts, co. Kildare, esq.

1720 ,, Richard, esq.

1750 ,, captain Richard, Furnace, co. Kildare

1688 ,, Robert, Great Fornaghts, co. Kildare, gent.

1778 ,, Sabina, Dublin, widow

1745 ,, Timothy, Limerick, gent.

1752 ,, Wm., Mountmellick, Queen's co., clothier

1744 **Neville**, Clement, lieut.-gen. of the Forces
1737 ,, Elizab., Dunmore, co. Galway, widow
1719 ,, Walter, Ballyraheen, co. Wicklow, gent.
1799 **Nevin**, Agnes, Dublin, widow
1764 ,, Daniel, the Glibb, Dublin, victualler
1659 ,, Hugh, Ballycotland, minister [**VI.** 54
1783 ,, Hugh, Tullyglishoglade, co. Armagh
1804 ,, Hugh, Tullyclear, co. Fermanagh, clk.
1754 ,, Jane, Donaghadee, co. Down
1780 ,, Jane, wife to James N., esq.
1777 ,, John, Graigboy, co. Down, gt.
1784 ,, John, Dublin, merchant
1725 ,, Margery, relict of Cowel N.
1811 ,, Patk., Old Kilcullen, co. Kild.
1775 ,, Sarah, Dublin, widow
1655 ,, Thomas, the elder, Munkreddinge, Scotland, esq. [**V.** 260
1754 ,, Thos., Marlborough, co. Down
1767 ,, Wm., son of Sarah N., Dublin, widow
1784 ,, Wm., Downpatrick, dissenting minister
1791 **Nevins**, Anne, Dublin, spinster
1774 ,, Rachel, formerly of Kinglass, now of Edenderry, King's co., widow
1751 **Nevinson**, Jas., Sellerna, co. Galway, grocer
1741 **Nevitt**, Caleb, Dublin, ironmonger
1810 **Newbold**, Ambrose, lieut. in 29th regt. of foot
1762 ,, Mary, Clonmel, co. Tipp., wid.
1693 **Newburgh**, Anne, Dundalk, widow
1750 ,, Anne, Bath, Gt. Britain
1675 ,, Arthur, esq.
1762 ,, Arthur, Kildalky, co. Meath, esq.
1741 ,, Brockhill, Ballyhaise, co. Cavan, esq. [esq.
1798 ,, Broghill, Ballyhaise, co. Cavan,
1804 ,, Elizab. Marianne, Camac, wid.
1728 ,, Henry, Raheck, co. Cav., esq.
1660 ,, Thomas, Lifford, co. Donegal, esq.
1693 ,, Thos., Castlefyn, co. Donegal, esq.
1702 ,, Thomas, Ballyhaise, co. Cavan, gent.
1776 ,, Thomas, Ballyhaise, co. Cavan, esq.
1777 ,, William, Drumcarn
1790 ,, Wm. Perrot, Ballyhaise, co. Cavan, esq.

1671 **Newcom**, John, Dublin, merchant [See NEWCOMEN.]
1712 **Newcomb**, John, Aughenville, King's co., gent.
1764 ,, Wm., the elder, Ballychristial, King's co., esq.
1783 ,, Wm., Tullamore, King's co., esq.
1789 **Newcombe**, Arthur, of Wilson's Hospital, co. W.Meath, clk.
1792 ,, Elizabeth, Seapoint, co. Dublin, spinster
1792 ,, Frances, Dublin, spinster
1772 ,, John, Dublin, merchant
1800 **Newcome**, Wm., abp. of **Armagh**, q. v.
1802 **Newcomen**, Arabella, Dub., spinst.
1761 ,, sir Arthur, Mosstown, co. Longford, bart.
1766 ,, Brabazon, Galliahtown, co. Longford, esq. (Large will)
1710 ,, Bridget, Dublin, widow (Ex.)
1807 ,, Catherine, Stephen's-gr., Dub., widow [esq.
1732 ,, Chas., Droming, co. Longford,
1687 ,, Elizabeth, Dublin, widow
1797 ,, Frances
1740 ,, lady Jane, Dublin, widow
1668 ,, sir Robert, Dublin, knt.
1670 ,, Robert, Dublin, gent. [**XII.**183
1736 ,, sir Robt., Mosstown, co. Longford, bart.
1809 ,, Sarah, Stephen's-gr., Dublin, spinster
1737 ,, Thos., Dovehill, co. Tipp., esq.
1782 ,, Thos., Droming, co. Long., esq.
1789 ,, sir Thos., Mosstown, co. Longford, bart.
1766 ,, William, Dublin, esq.
1807 ,, sir Wm., Gleadowe, Dublin, bt. [See NEWCOM, NEWCOMB.]
1784 **Newel**, Andrew, Castle Wellan, co. Down, merchant
1694 **Newell**, John, Dublin, gent. [See NEWILL.]
1793 **Newenham**, Geo., Cork, merchant
1749 ,, Hannah, Cork
1706 ,, John, Cork, esq.
1735 ,, John, Cork, clothier
1787 ,, John, Maryborough, South Lib. of Cork, esq.
1759 ,, Richard, Cork, merchant
1725 ,, Thos., Cork, esq.
1766 ,, Thos., co. Cork, esq.
1736 ,, William, Cork, esq.
1760 **Newett**, John, Dublin, weaver
1744 **Newland**, Felix, Rathcomane, co. Cork, farmer
1713 ,, George, Meath-street, Dublin, clothier

1760 **Newland**, Martin, Dublin, tailor
1789 **Newman**, Adam, Newberry, co. Cork, esq.
1808 ,, Adam, Kingsale, co. Cork, esq.
1790 ,, Catherine, Newberry, co. Cork, widow
1731 ,, Chas., Kilshanig, co. Cork, gt.
1799 ,, Chas., Cork city, surgeon
1788 ,, Christopher, Gardenrath, co. Meath, farmer
1739 ,, Dillon, Dromineen, co. Cork, esq.
1754 ,, Edward, Irishtown, co. Dublin, farmer
1717 ,, Elizabeth, Cork, widow
1793 ,, Grace, Greenfort, co. Cork, spr.
1801 ,, rev. Henry, Newberry, co. Cork
1787 ,, Hugh, Killbaliver, co. Meath, farmer
1634 ,, Jacob, Dublin, gent.
1668 ,, Jane, widow of John N., Dubl., esq. [**XII**. 12
1659 ,, John, soldier [**VII**. 184
1797 ,, Mary, Cork city, widow
1784 ,, Patrick, the Coombe, co. Dublin, baker
1693 ,, Richard, Cork, esq.
1773 ,, Richard, Newberry, co. Cork, esq.
1728 ,, Roger, Corballis, co. Dublin, farmer
1744 ,, William, mariner
1806 ,, Wm., Kinsale, co. Cork, mcht.
1730 **Newport**, John
1784 ,, Samuel, Waterford, merchant
1750 ,, Simon, Waterford, merchant
1649 **Newsam**, Christopher, Dublin, mct.
1651 ,, Ellen, Dublin, widow
1791 **Newsom**, George, Cork, merchant
1770 ,, John, Cork, merchant
1810 ,, John, the elder, Cork city
1785 ,, Sarah, Cork city, widow
1726 **Newstead**, Catherine, Dublin, wid.
1810 ,, Eliz., Liscormick, co. Longford
1723 ,, Richd., Cannerstown, co. Westmeath, esq.
1755 ,, Wm., Belgrove, Queen's co., esq.
1784 **Newton**, Barth., Carlow town, esq.
1736 ,, Christian, Drogheda, widow
1795 ,, Cromwell, Clovenedan, co. Arm., gent.
1745 ,, Edmond Umrigar, co. Wicklow, clerk
1754 ,, Frances, wid. of Bartholomew N., gent.
1771 ,, George, Dublin, merchant
1797 ,, Henry, Killowen, co. Londonderry
1780 ,, James, Dublin, gent.

1602 **Newton**, Jn., Corrofin, co. Galway, gent.
1714 ,, John, major-general
1763 ,, Margt., Flowerhill, co. Antrim, widow
1699 ,, Marmaduke, Carrickfergus, gt.
1788 ,, Pierce, Ballinahallin, co. Wex.
1771 ,, Rebecca, *alias* **Hamilton**, Umrigar, co. Wicklow, wid.
1609 ,, Richard, Carrickfergus, ald.
1753 ,, Robt., co. Waterford, victualler
1776 ,, Sarah, Dublin, widow
1810 ,, Susanna, Elmfield, co. Carlow, spinster
1696 ,, Thomas, Drogheda, alderman
1754 ,, William, Dublin, merchant
1724 **Newtown-Butler**, Theophilus, lord baron
1734 **Neylan**, William, Ballygownane, co. Clare, gent.
[See NEILAN.]
1786 **Neynoe**, Barbara, Grafton-st., Dublin, widow
1776 ,, John, Newport, Dublin, esq.
1775 ,, William, London, esq., mercht.
1679 **Nicholas**, Eliz., widow, Youghal
1695 ,, John, Lazyhill, near Dublin, esq. (Ex.)
1746 ,, John, Waterford, gent.
[See NICOLAS.]
1630 **Nicholet**, Richard, Tallow, co. Waterford, gent.
1736 **Nicholls**, Geo., Losset, co. Cavan, gent.
1763 ,, Hannah, Drogheda, widow
1795 ,, Jno., Chelsea, Middlesex (Copy)
1759 ,, Jonathan, Drogheda, alderman
[See NICHOLSON, NICOLLS.]
1692 **Nichols**, John, par. Kilbolane, co. Cork, esq.
1793 **Nicholson**, Anna Maria, Balrath, co. Meath
1780 ,, Anne, Ballykeelykeenan, Qu. co., widow
1801 ,, Anne, widow
1811 ,, Anne, wife to Joshua Nicholson, esq.
1777 ,, Catherine, Maghera, co. Derry, spinster
1809 ,, Catherine, Summerhill, Dublin city, widow
1730 ,, Charles, lieut. and adjutant in Royal Regt. of Ireland
1775 ,, Christopher, Balrath, co. Meath, esq.
1800 ,, Christopher, Balrath, co. Meath, gent.
1731 ,, Edward, Castlerea, co. Roscommon, clk.
1780 ,, Edward, Dublin, esq.

1649 **Nicholson**, Elizabeth, Dublin, wid.
1789 ,, Eliz., Aungier-st., Dubl., widow
1802 ,, George, Drogheda
1805 ,, Hampden, Cottage, co. town of Drogheda, esq.
1800 ,, Henrietta, widow
1676 ,, Henry, Rathcoole, co. Dublin, gent.
1754 ,, Henry, Dublin, merchant
1676 ,, Jas., St. Michael's par., Dublin, gent.
1779 ,, Jas., Rockcorry, co. Monaghan
1789 ,, Jas., Royal Hospital, esq.
1757 ,, Jane, Dublin, widow
1781 ,, John, Ballymacaret, co. Down, gent.
1782 ,, John, Balrath, co. Meath, esq.
1785 ,, John, Furtalla, co. Tipp., gt.
1716 ,, Joseph, Richardstown, co. Tipperary, gent.
1794 ,, Lydia, Waterford city, spr.
1754 ,, Margaret, Dublin, widow
1793 ,, Mary
1796 ,, Mary, Wilmar, co. Tipperary, spinster
1802 ,, Penelope, Summerhill
1766 ,, Richard, Ballykeen, Queen's co., farmer
1737 ,, Rose, Dublin, widow
1754 ,, Saml., Castleconnor, co. Sligo, gent.
1716 ,, Thos., Balrath, co. Meath, esq.
1784 ,, Thomas, Bath, Somersetshire, esq.
1794 ,, Thomas, Dublin, merchant
1800 ,, Thomas
1705 ,, William, Richardstown, co. Tyrone, gent.
1727 ,, William, abp. of **Cashel**, q. v.
1756 ,, William, Gt. Britain-st., Dubl., gardener
1773 ,, Wm., Wilmar, co. Tip., esq.
1794 ,, William, Sligo town, esq.
[See NICHOLLS.]
1739 **Nickols**, Edward, par. Kilmore, co. Meath
1720 **Nickson**, Abraham, Coolattin, co. Wicklow, esq.
1759 ,, Abraham, co. Wicklow, esq.
1798 ,, Abraham Augustus, Munny, co. Wicklow [widow
1751 ,, Isabella, Killmure, co. Wickl.,
1765 ,, John, Gibraltar
1806 ,, Lorenzo, Chapel Izod, co. Kilkenny, esq.
1748 ,, Lydia, Munny, co. Wicklow, relict of Abraham N., Coolattin, esq.
1783 ,, Timothy, Ballymurphy, co. Carlow, gent.

1806 **Nickson**, Wm., Mullaghduff, co. Fermanagh
[See NIXON.]
1726 **Nicolas**, Charles, Dublin, gent.
1754 ,, Charlotte, Dublin, widow
[See NICHOLAS.]
1705 **Nicolls**, Henry, Drogheda, ald.
1784 ,, Simon, Shancorr, co. Cavan, gent.
[See NICHOLLS.]
1767 **Nicolson**, Elizabeth, Killough, co. Down, widow
1802 ,, John, Cork, gent.
[See NICHOLSON.]
1786 **Nihell**, Anastasia, Limerick city, widow
1733 ,, James David, Limk., merchant
1798 ,, Margaret, Limerick city, widow
1703 ,, Patrick, Glaslowen, co. Clare, gent.
1766 **Nihill**, Alice, Rylane, co. Clare, widow
1800 ,, Anne, Dublin city, widow
1776 ,, Ignatius, Limerick, merchant
1810 **Nilan**, James, Nth. King-street, Dublin, linendraper
1771 **Nisbet**, James, Kinsale, co. Cork, surgeon
1782 **Nisbit**, Fras., Portarlington, King's co., esq.
1789 ,, Henry, Aghmore, co. Longford, bart.
1730 ,, John, Drumod, co. Leitrim, esq.
[See NESBITT.]
1762 **Nisbitt**, Florinda, Aghamore, co. Longford, spr.
1713 ,, John, Shankhill, co. Down, gt.
1765 **Nix**, Elizabeth, Dublin, widow
1769 ,, John, Killenny, co. Meath, gt.
1770 ,, Mary, Nenagh
1745 ,, Richard, Grange Clare, co. Kildare
1742 ,, Stephen, Thomas-st., Dublin, cutler
1775 ,, Stephen, Grange Clare, co. Kildare, gent.
1688 ,, Swift, Dublin, gent.
1719 ,, Thomas, Drumcolley, King's co., farmer
1767 **Nixon**, Adam, Clontubrid, co. Monaghan, clk.
1791 ,, Alexander, Nixon Hall, co. Fermanagh, esq.
1774 ,, rev. Andrew, Belturbet, co. Cavan, clk.
1677 ,, Anthony, Dublin, gent.
1703 ,, Anthony, Dublin, esq.
1767 ,, Arabella, late of Dublin, now of Bath, widow
1758 ,, Catherine, Dublin, spinster

1759 **Nixon**, David, Dublin, esq.
1811 ,, Elizabeth, Rathmines, co. Dub.
1764 ,, Geo., Newtown, co. Wexford, esq.
1766 ,, Henry, Athy, co. Kildare, esq.
1811 ,, Humphrey, Nixon Lodge, co. Cavan
1791 ,, Jacob, surgeon of 4th regt. dragoon guards
1737 ,, James, Aughufadda, co. Mon.
1800 ,, rev. James, Philipstown, King's co.
1773 ,, John, Redmills, co. Dubl., gt.
1800 ,, rev. John, Wheathill, co. Fermanagh
1764 ,, Leonard, Innishhugh, co. Mayo
1777 ,, Mary Anne, Belturbet, co. Cavan, widow
1800 ,, Mathew, Ballyhaise, co. Cavan
1713 ,, Richd.,Sheetstown,co.Kildare, gent.
1750 ,, Robert, Dublin, gent.
1786 ,, Robert, Dublin, gent.
1797 ,, Thos., capt. in 56th regt.
1760 ,, William, one of the vicars of Galway
1788 ,, William, Mullichiff, co. Fermanagh, gent.
[See NICKSON.]
1794 **Noal**, George, Killavally, co. Cavan
1760 **Nobileau**, Chas., Dublin, merchant
1793 **Noble**, Adam, Longfield, co. Mon., esq.
1776 ,, Brabazon,Donamoine,co.Mon., esq.
1746 ,, Edward, Kilbalam, co. Wicklow, farmer [esq.
1790 ,, Fras., Raheens, co.Monaghan,
1637 ,, Henry, Urney, co. Tyrone, clk. [**IV.** 256
1771 ,, Jas., Clenteverin, co. Fermanagh
1784 ,, Jerome, Summerhill, co. Dubl., esq.
1704 ,, John
1602 ,, Magdalyn, Kilkenny
1777 ,, Margaret, Donamoine, co. Monaghan, widow
1794 ,, rev. Mark, Portora, co. Fermanagh, clk.
1791 ,, Mary, widow
1797 ,, Mary, Dublin, widow
1805 ,, Mary, Dublin city, widow
1754 ,, Mungo, Glassdrumond, co. Fermanagh
1750 ,, Thomas, Dublin, gent.
1780 ,, Thomas, Summerhill, co. Ferm.
1666 **Noell**, sir Martin, Dublin, knt.
1670 ,, sir Martin, Ballyhinch, co. Kilkenny, knt. (Ex.)

1690 **Noise**, Richard, Dublin, vintner
1792 **Nolan**, Cicily, Galway town
1760 ,, Clare, Galway, spinster
1773 ,, Gerald, Dublin, gent.
1721 ,, Gregory, par. St. Giles, Middlesex, gent. (Copy)
1775 ,, John, Dublin, esq.
1802 ,, Joseph Edmond, Clonalis, co. Roscommon
1806 ,, Mary,Watling-st., Dublin, wid.
1786 ,, Michael, Galway town, mchnt.
1802 ,, Oliver, Curry, co. Galway, esq.
1791 ,, Patrick
1629 ,, Thomas, Ballinrobe, co. Mayo,. esq., or of Clonkerky
1696 ,, Thomas, Dublin, maltster
1697 ,, William, Dublin, maltster
[See NOWLAN.]
1599 **Nolane**, Christoph., Tredith (Copy)
1783 **Noon**, John, Kildare
[See NUN.]
1678 **Noone**, John, Cork, sergt. to capt. Wacham St. Leger's comp.
1699 **Norbury**, John, Brampton, Huntingdonshire, esq. (Copy)
1786 **Norcliffe**, Wm., Glasnevin,co. Dub.
1758 **Norcott**, Arthur, Waterhouse, co. Cork, gent.
1764 ,, Hugh, Springfield, co. Cork, gt
1792 ,, Jas., Springfield, co. Cork, esq.
1792 ,, William, Springfield, co. Cork, esq.
1627 **Nore**, Alice, St. Catherine's par.,. London, widow (Copy)
1754 **Norgate**, Margery, widow of capt., lieut. Mathew N., of Hargrave's regt.
1731 **Norman**, Charles, Kilshanig, co. Cork, gent. [esq.
1800 ,, Charles, Gardiner-st., Dublin,
1776 ,, Edward, Drogheda, alderman
1726 ,, Elizabeth, Londonderry, widow
1741 ,, Henry, Dublin, gent.
1807 ,, Izak, Drogheda, esq.
1741 ,, Mary, Drogheda, widow
1781 ,, Richard, house steward to lady Bowley
1743 ,, Robert, Dublin, esq.
1692 ,, Samuel, Londonderry, alderm.
1750 ,, Sarah, Lagore, co. Meath, wid.
1804 ,, Sarah, Cortlee, co. Donegal
1794 ,, rev. Thos., Lagore, co. Meath,. clk. (Large)
1705 ,. William, Dublin, bookseller
1721 ,, William, Drogheda, alderman
1809 **Normanton**, rt. hon. Chas. Agar,. earl of
1680 **Norrice**, Alice, Newcastle, co.Down
1679 ,, Thomas, Newcastle, co. Down,. gent.

1768 **Norrington**, Anne, Waterf., widow
1752 ,, George, Waterford, victualler
1767 **Norris**, Anne, Dublin, widow
1774 ,, Catherine, Strangford, co. Down, widow
1792 ,, Catherine, Strangford
1763 ,, Chas, Ballyloughlin, co. Down, clk.
1774 ,, Cicily, Strangford, co. Down, widow
1783 ,, Edward, Oberstown, co.˙Louth, farmer
1764 ,, Elizabeth, Ballyloughan, co. Down
1755 ,, Jas., major in gen. Hamilton's dragoons
1774 ,, James, the elder, Caledon, co. Tyrone
1783 ,, John, New Church-st., Dublin, brazier
1793 ,, John, Limerick city, merchant
1769 ,, Patk., Oberstown, co. Louth, farmer
1792 ,, Patk., Carnacop, co. Meath, gt.
1719 ,, Ralph, Dublin, merchant
1789 ,, rev. Richard, D.D.
1792 ,, Robert, Glasnevin
1798 ,, Samuel, Strangford, co. Down, gent.
1660 ,, Thomas, Dublin, saddler
1745 ,, capt. Toby, Dublin, esq.
1727 ,, William, Dublin, esq.
1781 ,, William, Dublin, brassfounder
1784 ,, William, Old Court, co. of Dublin city
1801 **Norry**, John, Commons of Cashel
1678 **North**, Edwd, Donard, co. Wicklow, gent.
1805 ,, Edwd., Broomfield, co. Dublin, esq.
1776 ,, Eleanor, Dublin, widow
1738 ,, Francis, Dublin, esq.
1745 ,, Henry, Kilkenny, esq.
1726 ,, John, Dublin, Earl-st., ribband maker
1757 ,, John, Tyrrelspass, co. Westmeath, gent.
1663 ,, Joseph, Dublin, gent., belonging to the army
1729 ,, Joseph, Newcastle, co. Westmeath, gent.
1786 ,, Joseph, Brackland, King's co., gent.
1792 ,, Joseph, Garrynahane, co. Galway, gent.
1803 ,, Mary, Newport, co. Tipp., wid.
1739 ,, Patrick, the Coombe, Dublin, dealer
1772 ,, Philip, Tubberbonny, co. Dub., gent.

1801 **North**, Rachel, Cool, King's co., landholder
1789 ,, Richard, Dublin
1766 ,, Roger, Newcastle, co. Westmeath, gent.
1791 ,, Roger, Guilford, co. Westmeath, gent.
1758 ,, Thomas, Ballysolough, King's co.
1773 ,, Thurgood, Tinoe, co. Tipp.
1660 ,, William, soldier [**VIII**. 109
1722 ,, Wm., Lawrencestown, King's co.
1775 ,, William, Cool, King's co., farmer
1783 ,, William, Kilbride, co. Westmeath, gent.
1800 ,, William, Clonfad, co. Westmeath, esq.
1660 **Northcott**, Frances, Westmeath, widow [**VIII**. 64
1660 ,, captain Lewis, Westmeath [**VIII**. 62
1787 **Northey**, Edward, Epsom, Surrey, esq. (Copy)
1787 ,, William, Ballynaten, co.Wicklow, farmer (Copy)
1678 **Norton**, Alexander, Dublin, shoemaker
1744 ,, Anne, Dublin, widow
1765 ,, Brett, Dublin, esq.
1724 ,, Charles, Dublin, goldsmith
1737 ,, Daniel, *alias* **Naughton**, Dubl., glazier
1698 ,, Ephraim, Carleton, co.Wexford, farmer
1770 ,, Henry, Dublin, merchant
1677 ,, Michael, Dublin, wigmaker
1743 ,, Richard, Dublin, merchant
1737 ,, Robert, Clough, co. Wexford, esq.
1778 ,, Robert, Dublin, gent.
1628 ,, Samuel, Clare, gent. [**II**. 85
1732 ,, Samuel, Dublin, merchant
1784 ,, Sarah, High-street, Dublin, widow
[See NAGHTEN, NAUGHTON.]
1599 **Nott**, James, Dublin (no date, not proved, about the year)
1677 ,, Roger, London, merchant tailor (Copy)
[See KNOTT, NUTT.]
1635 **Notte**, Thomas, Aghadown, co.Cork, esq. [**IV**. 162
1750 **Nottingham**, Francis, Kilmatalway, co. Dublin, gent.
1784 ,, Peter, Fairfield, co. Galway, gent.
1690 **Nowlan**, Charles, Ballykealy, co. Catherlogh, gent.

1794	**Nowlan**, Daniel, Mount Pleasant, co. Carlow	1624	**Nugent**, sir Christopher, Moyrath, co. Meath, knt.
1757	,, Dennis, Lee's-lane, Dublin	1626	,, Christopher, Corbetstown, esq.
1791	,, Dennis, George's-quay, Dublin, grocer	1794	,, Clare, Dublin, widow
1764	,, Edward, Carlow, merchant	1623	,, Edmond, Rockoienell, co. Westmeath, gent.
1690	,, Elizabeth, Dublin, widow	1803	,, Edmond, Borheenclough, Lib. of Waterford
1752	,, Felix, Cork, tallow chandler		
1807	,, James, Back-lane, Dubl., merchant	1769	,, Edward, Fiermore, now of Athlone, gent.
1808	,, Jane, Golden-lane, Dubl., wid.	1752	,, Elizabeth, Finglas, co. Dublin, widow
1790	,, John, Loughrea, co. Galway, gent.	1659	,, Ellinor, *alias* **Plunket**, Stonehall, co. Westmeath, widow
1800	,, John, Kilcullen Bridge, co. Kildare, shopkeeper		[**VIII.** 7
1772	,, Laurence, Whiteswall, co. Kilkenny, esq. [baker	1780	,, Ellinor, widow
		1793	,, Ellinor, widow
1789	,, Laurence, Pill-lane, Dublin,	1796	,, Ellinor, North Great George's-street, Dublin, spinster
1779	,, Margaret, Dublin, merchant		
1804	,, Margaret	1686	,, Francis, Dardistown, co. Westmeath, esq.
1811	,, Margaret, Townsend-st., Dubl., spinster	1753	,, Geo., Castlerickard, co. Meath, esq.
1725	,, Mark, Dublin, gent.		
1799	,, Mary, Gormanstown, co. Meath, widow	1800	,, George, Nurney, co. Kildare, gent.
1781	,, Michael, Dublin, esq.	1758	,, Hannah, Dublin, spinster
1794	,, Philip, Francis-street, Dublin, innholder	1744	,, Haytor, Dublin, esq.
		1738	,, Hyacynth Richard, esq., commonly called lord Riverston
1692	,, Roger, Dublin, shoemaker		
1764	,, Thomas, Dublin, merchant	1671	,, Ignatius, esq., son of the late earl of Westmeath
1698	,, William, Dublin, merchant		
1791	,, William, Dublin, merchant [See NOLAN.]	1721	,, sir Ignatius, knt. (Copy)
		1747	,, Ismay, Dublin
1742	**Nowland**, Charles, Black-pits, Dublin	1626	,, James, Clonlost, co. Westmeath, esq.
1779	**Noy**, Edward, Newbrook, co. Dubl., esq.	1669	,, James, Dublin, esq.
		1701	,, James, Newtown, Queen's co., gent.
1746	,, William, Island-bridge, co. Dublin, esq.	1795	,, sir James, Donore, co. Westmeath, bart.
1778	,, William Stearne, Chapelizod, co. Dublin, esq.	1808	,, James, Mornington, co. Westmeath
1722	**Noyret**, John, Dublin, merchant		
1736	**Nugent**, hon. Alice, Dublin, wid.	1737	,, Jane, Derrymore, co. Westmeath, widow
1798	,, Alicia		
1804	,, Alicia, *alias* **Barnwall**, Ballinacon	1757	,, Jane, Clonlost, co. Westmeath, widow
1801	,, Andrew, Dysert, co. Westmeath, esq.	1689	,, John, Donower, co. Westmeath, esq.
1726	,, dame Anne, widow of sir Thos. N., bart.	1756	,, John, Killasonna, co. Longford, esq.
1775	,, Anne, Athboy, widow of Packenham N., esq.	1762	,, John, Enagh, co. Cavan, esq.
		1774	,, John, Johnstown, co. Westmeath, gent.
1777	,, Anne, Mullingar, co. Westmeath	1776	,, John, Queen-street, Dublin
1758	,, Catherine, *alias* **Royn**, *alias* **Farrelly**, Dublin	1778	,, John, Arran-quay, Dublin, merchant
1759	,, Catherine, Dublin, widow	1788	,, John, Ballnacarrow, co. Westmeath, esq.
1790	,, Catherine, Dublin, spinster		
1790	,, Catherine, Johnstown, co. Westmeath, widow	1802	,, John, Dublin, saddler
		1804	,, John, Johnstown

1811 **Nugent**, John, Dysart, co. Westmeath, esq.
1740 „ dame Joyce, *alias* **Netterville**
1757 „ Lavallin, Dublin, gent.
1795 „ Margaret, Constitution-hill,
Dublin, widow
1650 „ Mary, *alias* **Barnewall**, Dunfert, co. Kildare, wid.
1757 „ Mary, Britain-street, Dublin
1787 „ Mary, spinster
1797 „ Mary, Dublin, widow
1770 „ Mathias
1739 „ Michael, Carlinstown,co.West-
meath, esq.
1754 „ Michael, Ballnacarrow, co.
Westmeath
1797 „ Michael, Eliza Vale, co. Dublin,
esq.
1684 „ Oliver, Correlstown, co. Westmeath
1771 „ Patrick, Dublin, carpenter
1799 „ sir Peter, Donore, co. Westmeath, bart.
1739 „ Pierce, Tulla, co. Tipperary,
gent.
1609 „ Piers, Drogheda, alderman
1728 „ Robt., Carlanstown, co. Westmeath, esq.
1770 „ Robert, Bobsgrove, co. Cavan,
esq.
1773 „ Robert, Mabestown, co. Westmeath, esq.
1809 „ Robt., Multifarnham, co.West-
meath
1720 „ Rose, Calbinstown, widow of
Robert N., esq.
1789 „ Sarah, Sallymount, co. Westmeath, widow
1763 „ Susanna Catherine, commonly
called lady Riverston
1586 „ Thomas, Moyrath, co. Meath,
esq.
1635 „ Thomas, Dunfert, co. Kildare,
esq.   [**IV.** 42
1712 „ Thomas, Cushenstown, co.
Westmeath, esq.
1765 „ Thomas, Gneeve, co. Cavan,
gent.
1767 „ Thomas, Drogheda, aleseller
1768 „ Thomas, Mullaboden, co. Kildare, gent.
1774 „ Thomas Herbert, Kilcormuck,
King's co., esq.
1781 „ Thomas, Kilwater, co. Westmeath, gent.
1804 „ Thomas, Smithfield, Dublin,
saddler
1811 „ Thomas
1609 „ Walter, Drogheda, major
1723 „ Walter, Dublin, gent.

1728 **Nugent**, Walter, Carpenterstown,
co. Westmeath, esq.
1781 „ Walter, Carpenterstown, co.
Westmeath, esq.
1572 „ William Fitz Thomas, Abbey of
Larray, co. Longford
1614 „ William, Newhaggard, near
Trim, esq.
1754 „ William, co. Dublin, esq.
1776 **Nun**, Benj., Dublin, paper manufacturer
1782 „ Ebenezer, formerly of Calcutta,
late of Dublin, gent.
1786 „ Richard, mariner (Copy)
[See NOON, NUNN.]
1798 **Nunan**, David, Cork, butter mercht.
1800 „ Eugene, Glashyoman, co. Kerry,
gent.
1754 **Nunn**, Hannah, widow of Richard
N., Hill Castle, gent.
1800 „ Jane, Wexford, widow
1790 „ rev. Joshua, Enniscorthy
1802 „ rev. Joshua, Enniscorthy, co.
Wexford, clk.
[See NUN.]
1729 **Nutley**, Richard, Dublin, esq.
1749 **Nutt**, John, Dublin, carpenter
1727 **Nuttal**, Charles, Boolybeg, co. Kildare, esq.
1736 „ Richard, Dublin, gent.
1773 **Nuttall**, John, Mountnebo
1746 „ Joseph, Dublin, alderman
1713 „ Richard, Dublin, gent.
1804 **Nuzum**, Jas., Ballyellan, co. Wexford, farmer

—O—

1796 **Oakes**, Medicis, Dublin, widow
1763 „ Theophilus, Brown-st., Dublin,
handkerchief stamper
1768 **Oakman**, Robert, Cork, linendraper
1705 **Oates**, Joseph, Dublin, merchant
1728 „ Thomas, Lisburn, co. Antrim,
surgeon and apothecary
1772 **Oatfield**, John, Bullardstown, co.
Dublin, gent.
1597 **O'Beaghan**, John, or Shan, Rath-
fernon
1768 **Obeirn**, Sarah, *alias* **Jones**, wife to
Wm. O'B., Drumcliff, co.
Sligo
1749 **O'Beirne**, Connell, Cloonfadda, co.
Roscommon, gent.
1801 „ Connell, Cloonfadda, co. Roscommon, esq.
1796 „ Margaret, *alias* **Burke**
1798 „ William, Sligo town, esq.
[See BYRNE.]

1754 **Obins**, Anthony, Portadown, co. Armagh, esq.
1756 ,, Anthony, Portadown, co. Armagh
1755 ,, Deborah, wife to rev. John O., D.D.
1788 ,, Hamlet, Bellview, co. Armagh
1775 ,, rev. John, D.D., rector of Raie, co. Donegal
1786 ,, Margaret, Clare-street, Dublin, spinster
1762 ,, Mary, *alias* **Burleigh**, *alias* **Jackson**, Portadown, co. Armagh, widow
1766 ,, Mary, Portadown, co. Armagh, widow (1765 Lib.)
1784 ,, rev. Michael, rector of Drumcliff, dio. Elphin [magh
1798 ,, Michael, Castleobins, co. Armagh,
1731 ,, Wm., Portadown, co. Armagh, gent.
1759 **O'Birney**, Daniel, Lowries Holme, co. Derry, gent.
1765 **O'Boyle**, Phelim, Ballyshannon, co. Donegal, farmer
1790 **Obre**, Edward, Lisburn, co. Antrim, esq.
1758 ,, Fras., Clantelew, co. Armagh, gent.
1810 **O'Brien**, Alice, Castle Connor, co. Sligo, spinster
1778 ,, Anne, Limerick, widow
1791 ,, Barbara, widow
1796 ,, Barbara
1770 ,, Bartholomew, Kilmainham Wood, co. Westmeath, gt.
1801 ,, Benjamin, master of the works, House of Industry
1744 ,, Brien, Roskill, co. Limerick, gent.
1763 ,, Bryan, Garahill, co. Carlow
1742 ,, Catherine, Dublin, widow
1803 ,, Catherine, Portobello, co. Dub., spinster
1789 ,, Charles, Killure, co. Galway, esq.
1634 ,, Crogher M'Thomas, Liffunshion, co. Tipperary
1757 ,, Cornelius, Clonfadda, co. Clare
1807 ,, Cornelius, Nenagh, co. Tipperary, esq.
1665 ,, Cuogher, Coylnocorry, co. Cork, gent.
1737 ,, Daniel, James-street, Dublin, brewer
1791 ,, Daniel, Dublin, hosier
1799 ,, Daniel, Reyninch, co. Tipperary, farmer
1805 ,, Daniel, Boherboy, Limerick city

1801 **O'Brien**, rev. David, Vicarfield, co. Longford
1697 ,, Dermott, Gortmore, co. Tipperary, gent. (Copy)
1796 ,, Digby, Cork city, gent.
1717 ,, sir Donat, Dromclane, co. Clare, bart. (Ex.)
1778 ,, Donatus, Batherwick, Northamptonshire, esq.
1767 ,, sir Edward, Dromoland, King's co., farmer
1787 ,, Edward, Ballynaclanough, co. Westmeath
1801 ,, Edward, Rostellan Castle, co. Cork, esq.
1806 ,, Elizabeth, Blackall-row, Dub.
1764 ,, Ellinor, Clonfadda, co. Clare, gent. [torney
1797 ,, Fitzgerald, Limerick city, attorney
1791 ,, Francis, Essex-street, Dublin
1811 ,, Henry, Blatherwick, Northamptonshire (Copy)
1777 ,, James, Pill-lane, Dublin, innkeeper
1778 ,, James, Newcastle, co. Limk.
1788 ,, James, Ennis, co. Clare, esq.
1799 ,, James, Werburgh-st., Dublin esq.
1806 ,, James, Limerick city, mercht.
1811 ,, rev. James, F.R.M.P.
1703 ,, John, Dungullane, co. Cork, gent.
1763 ,, John, Gernonstown
1792 ,, John, Limerick, merchant
1792 ,, John, Francis-street, Dublin
1792 ,, John, Drumrahin, co. Leitrim, esq.
1803 ,, John, Tobergregan, co. Dublin, farmer
1811 ,, John, Carrigoon, co. Cork, gent.
1771 ,, Julia, Dublin, widow
1798 ,, sir Lucius, Dromoland, co. Clare, bart.
1729 ,, Margaret, Carrickfergus, wid.
1772 ,, Margaret, Ballyglass, co. Clare (not proved)
1797 ,, Margaret, Dublin, widow
1805 ,, Margaret, Charleville, co. Cork, widow
1808 ,, Margaret, Ballyglass, co. Clare
1774 ,, Mathew, Limerick, victualler
1780 ,, Mathew, Tarmons, co. Kerry, M.D.
1749 ,, Michael, Mary-street, Dublin, aleseller (not proved)
1758 ,, Michael, Dublin, gent.
1783 ,, Michael, Dubl., woollendraper
1793 ,, Michael, Wyestown, co. Dubl., farmer

1797 **O'Brien**, Michael, Cork city, gent.
1633 ,, Morgan, Glanduffe, co. Tipp., gent (Copy)
1631 ,, Morogh, Cahirnagown, co. Clare, gent.
1758 ,, Patrick, Dublin, distiller
1784 ,, Patrick, Dublin, merchant
1767 ,, Richard, Ballineclonagh, gent.
1794 ,, Robert, Waterford, merchant
1802 ,, Robert, Drumholla, co. Leitrim, esq.
1810 ,, Robert, Church-street, Dublin, gent.
1791 ,, Sarah, widow
1781 ,, Simon, Timolin, co. Kildare, innholder
1795 ,, Stafford, Ballyanny, co. Tipp., esq.
1761 ,, Terence, Cross, co. Clare, gent.
1789 ,, Terence, Ennis, co., Clare, clothier
1807 ,, rev. Terence, Liffey-st, Dublin
1626 ,, sir Terlogh, Castlearra, co. Tipp., knt. and bart. [II. 8
1743 ,, Terlogh, Knockdrom, co. Clare, gent.   [gent.
1781 ,, Timothy, Roskill, co. Limerick,
1788 ,, Timothy, Grangebeg, farmer
1782 ,, Thomas, Tabouraheeny, co. Tipperary, gent.
1802 ,, Thomas, Lower Merrion-street, Dublin, grocer
1719 ,, William, Skarbarry, co. Cork, gent.
1752 ,, rev. William, Blatherwick, Northamptonshire, clerk
1763 ,, William, Dublin, shoemaker
1768 ,, William, Boherlorde, co. Limk., gent.
1796 ,, Wm., Donavilly, co. Leitrim, gent.
1798 ,, William, King's co.
1803 ,, William, Limerick, merchant
1759 **O'Bryan**, Christopher, Ballinlug, co. Meath, farmer
1765 ,, Christopher, Instymon, co. Clare, esq.
1802 ,, Donoughe, Cratloe, co. Clare, esq.
1724 ,, Henry, Blatherwick, Northamptonshire, esq.
1790 ,, John, Waterford, gauger
1803 ,, Teresa
1712 ,, Timothy, Dublin, linen weaver
1804 ,, Timothy, Charleville, co. Cork, esq.
1707 ,, William, Kilmacahill, co. Cork, gent.
1677 **O'Bryen**, Danl., Kilmurry, co. Limk. gent.

1784 **O'Bryen**, Helena, Moyvanine, co. Limerick, spinster
1709 ,, John, Newhall, co. Clare, esq.
1626 ,, sir Terrelagh, Castle Arra, co. Tipperary, knt. and bart.
1640 ,, Wm., Coylnacurra, co. Cork, gent.
1751 ,, Wm., Mitchellstown, co. Cork, gent.
1764 **O'Bryne**, John, Ballaney, co. Meath, gent.
1769 **O'Bryon**, Gertrude, Cork, widow [See O'BRIEN, &c.]
1780 **O'Callaghan**, Alicia, Dublin, wid.
1796 ,, Callaghan, Coolancollig, co. Cork, farmer
1732 ,, Catherine, Loughmore, co. Tipperary, widow
1638 ,, Choghor, abbey of Odorney, co. Kerry, gent.
1737 ,, Cornelius, the younger, Bantyre, co. Cork, gent.
1739 ,, Cornelius, the elder, co. Cork, gent.
1740 ,, Cornelius, Dublin, esq.
1748 ,, Cornelius, Drunsheky, co. Cork
1772 ,, Cornelius, Bantyre, co. Cork, esq.
1781 ,, Cornelius, Shanbally, co. Tipp., esq.   [esq.
1800 ,, Cornelius, Ashgrove, co. Cork,
1772 ,, Daniel, Killgorey, co. Clare, esq.
1672 ,, Donogh, Cloonlunnan, co. Louth, farmer
1794 ,, Mary, Dublin, spinster
1803 ,, Owen, Cooleville, co. Armagh, esq.
1761 ,, Robert, Stranbally, co. Tipp., esq.
1778 ,, Robert, Clonmeen, co. Cork, esq.
1747 ,, Roger, Dirgallon, co. Cork, gent.
1759 ,, Timothy, Bregogue, co. Cork, esq.
1680 **O'Callaghane**, Cahir, Curra, co. Cork, gent.
1799 **O'Callagher**, Felix, Dubl., alderman
1770 **O'Carroll**, Thady, Dublin, gent.
1767 **O'Coner**, Denis, Sligo, esq. [See O'CONNOR.]
1788 **O'Connell**, Connell, M.D.
1641 ,, Cormocke or Charles, co. Cork, physician
1722 ,, Daniel, Cork, gent.
1727 ,, Maurice, Newtown
1600 ,, Owen
1786 ,, Thomas, Rathkeal, co. Limk., M.D.

1804 **O'Conner**, Dennis, Belanagane, co. Roscommon, esq.
1791 **O'Connor**, Andrew, Rosc. town, merchant
1795 ,, Bridget, Dublin, widow
1810 ,, Catherine
1758 ,, Charles, Knockadoe, co. Sligo
1795 ,, Dominick, commonly called O'Connor Don, Clonallis, co. Roscommon, esq.
1800 ,, Dominick, Island-bridge, co. Dublin, vintner
1609 ,, sir Donogh, knt., Sligo
1806 ,, Dorothea, Clondra, co. Longford, widow
1809 ,, Edmond, Mallow, co. Cork, M.D.
1789 ,, Frances, Milltown, co. Rosc.
1791 ,, George, Ardlonan, co. Meath, esq.
1639 ,, John, Carrigfoyle, co. Kerry, esq.
1751 ,, John
1778 ,, John, Timona, co. Roscommon, esq.
1793 ,, John, Skibbereen, co. Cork
1803 ,, rev. John, Drogheda
1804 ,, rev. John, Drogheda
1811 ,, John, city of London, esq. (Copy)
1626 ,, Lysagh, Leixlip, co. Kildare, esq.
1810 ,, Margaret, Galway, widow
1799 ,, Mary, Dublin, widow
1808 ,, Patrick, Ross-lane, Dublin, tailor
1808 ,, Roger, Castle, co. Longford
1808 ,, Roger, Galway, merchant
1803 ,, Thomas, Bolton-street, Dublin, esq.
1807 ,, Wm., Dubl. city, innkeeper
[See O'CONER.]
1610 **O'Corcrane**, Teigh M'Shane, or Corcrane, Ardcollum, co. Tipperary, gent.
1791 **O'Dea**, Henry, Dublin, shoemaker
1806 ,, Thady, Lisbane, co. Clare, farmer
1656 **Odell**, Christopher, lieut. [**V.** 265
1725 ,, John, Ballingarry, co. Limerick, esq.
1761 ,, John, Bealdurogy, co. Limerick, esq.
1783 ,, John, Odell Lodge, co. Waterford
1790 ,, John, Ballynarugie, co. Limerick, esq.
1807 ,, John, Southpark, co. Waterford
1763 ,, Thomas, Shannon Grove, co. Limerick, esq.

1762 **Odle**, Ellinor, widow of Fitzmaurice O. esq.
1700 ,, John, the elder, Ballingarry, co. Limerick, esq.
1735 **Odlum**, Edward, Capineur, King's co., farmer
1775 ,, Edwd., Little Longford, King's co., farmer
1770 ,, Ellinor, Ballychristal, King's co.
1739 ,, Henry, Geashill, King's co., farmer
1771 ,, Henry, Aughanvilla, King's co., gent.
1781 ,, Henry
1802 ,, Henry, Kilmurry, King's co.
1803 ,, Henry, Cappincur, King's co., esq.
1767 ,, Richard, Ballydowran, King's co., farmer
1770 ,, Richard, Kilmurry, King's co., gent.
1780 ,, Richard, Ballaghmoony, gent.
1809 ,, Thomas, Mountrath, Queen's co., quartermaster
1801 ,, William, Malahide, co. Dublin
1797 **O'Doherty**, rev. Henry, Derry, co. Monaghan
[See 'ODOUGHERTY.]
1794 **O'Donell**, Manus, Newcastle, co. Mayo, esq.
1618 **O'Donilane**, Donnille, Stacornnie
1681 **O'Donill**, Marcus, Cantwell's-court, co. Kilkenny, gent.
1758 **O'Donnell**, Alice, Dublin, widow
1788 ,, Ann, widow
1770 ,, Charles, Newcastle, co. Mayo, esq.
1774 ,, Con, Larkfield, co. Leitrim
1764 ,, Connell, Newport, co. Mayo
1793 ,, rev. Dominick, Largyreagh, co. Donegal
1762 ,, Hugh, Newport, co. Mayo, esq.
1801 ,, James Moore, esq.
1773 ,, John, Egmont, co. Cork, gent.
1802 ,, John, ensign in 110th regt. of foot
1767 ,, Marcus, Newport, co. Mayo, esq.
1774 ,, Richard, Maganstown, co. Tipperary, esq.
1809 ,, Richard, Dunmore Castle, co. Clare, esq.
1780 ,, Simon, Limerick, merchant
1788 ,, William, Clonmonny, co. Clare, gent.
1804 ,, William, Meatmarket-lane, Limerick, victualler
1585 ,, Terence, dean of Armagh
[See M'DONNELL.]

1678 **O'Donnoghue**, Geffry, Glanfleckle, co. Kerry, gent.
1804 **O'Donoghue**, Daniel, Killarney, co. Kerry, esq.
1790 ,, Jeffrey, Cork, esq.
1808 ,, Patrick, Killarney, co. Kerry
1808 ,, Robert, Cork city
1630 **O'Donovane**, Daniel, Rahine, or Castle Donovane, co. Cork, gent.   [gent.
1806 **O'Dougherty**, Michael, Cork city, [See O'DOHERTY.]
1797 **O'Dowd**, James, prisoner in the Four Courts Marshalsea
1798 **O'Dowda**, Letitia, Dublin, widow
1628 **O'Doweley**, William M'Donoghe, Biallaragged, co. Kildare, farmer
1781 **O'Driscoll**, Teresa, Annakessy, co. Cork
1627 **O'Duloghry**, John, Dunmoylane, co. Limerick, gent.
1619 **O'Dwyer**, Morogh M'Conagher, Ballyolaghan, co. Tipperary, farmer
1629 **O'Dwyere**, Darby, Milltown, co. Tipperary, esq.
1610 **O'Dwyre**, Gillane neaff, Kilboy, co. Tipperary, gent. (Copy)
1776 **O'Fallon**, Redmond, Athlone
1629 **O'Farrall**, Cornelius, Dublin, gent.
1708 **O'Farrell**, Francis Fergus, Dublin, esq., major-general
1811 ,, Gerald, Dublin city, esq.
1776 ,, Jane, Kilkenny, widow
1798 ,, Michael, Limerick, R. C. priest
1757 ,, Richard, major-genl. of His Majesty's Forces (Copy)
1808 ,, Roger, Lissard, co. Longford
1765 ,, Theobold
1803 **O'Ferrall**, Anne
1803 ,, John, the elder, Sligo, esq.
1593 **O'Fferreshe**, Dowagh M'Edmond M'Donell Duffe, Grange, co. Carlow
1725 **Offey**, John, Bloomsbury-square, Middlesex, esq. (Copy)
1786 ,, John, par. St. James, Westminster, esq. (Copy)
1801 **Offlaherty**, Catherine, Galway town, spinster
1594 **O'Flaerty**, sir Morough ne doe, Aghnemedle, co. Galway, knt.
1763 **O'Flaherty**, Edmond, Aglish, co. Waterford, gent.
1808 ,, Edmond, Lettermore, co. Galway, gent.
1792 ,, John, Gananina, co. Galway, gent.

1778 **O'Flaherty**, Thomas, Clare-street, Dublin, esq.
1804 **O'Flangan**, Jos., Tullamore, King's co., distiller
1803 **O'Flinn**, or **Flinn**, John, Ormond-quay, Dublin, grocer
1805 ,, John, Carrick-on-Suir, co. Tipperary
1788 **O'Flyn**, Dorothy, Galway town, widow
1746 **O'Flynn**, Edmond, Forlogh, co. Galway, esq.
1601 **O'Fullny**, Edmond, Athlone, parochianus
1777 **O'Gara**, Farrell, Carrowmacteer, co. Mayo, gent.
1778 ,, Farrell, Carrow Macker, co. Mayo, gent.
1742 **O'Garra**, Mary, widow of Oliver O'G., esq.
1609 **O'Gary**, Manus, Ballycheever, dio. Dublin
1715 **Ogden**, Isaac, Black Pitts, Dublin, brewer
1652 ,, John, Dublin, gent.
1772 **Ogilby**, Alexander, Newtown Limavady, co. Derry
1807 ,, Mary, Newtown Limavady, co. Derry
1740 **Ogle**, Ann, wife to James Ogle, Lurgan, linendraper
1699 ,, Elizabeth, *alias* **Smith**, London, widow (Copy)
1765 ,, Frances, Dublin, widow
1781 ,, George, Newry, merchant
1712 ,, Henry, Drogheda, alderman
1803 ,, Henry, Newry, co. Armagh, merchant
1748 ,, James, Lurgan, co. Armagh, linendraper
1797 ,, James, Newry, co. Down, linendraper
1728 ,, John, Dublin, innkeeper
1773 ,, John, Drogheda, esq.
1778 ,, John, Waringstown, co. Down
1799 ,, John, Newry, merchant
1735 ,, Luke, Newcastle, Northumberland, gent.
1802 ,, Mary, Dublin, widow
1791 ,, Robert, Dysart Lodge, esq.
1719 ,, Samuel, Dublin, esq.
1743 ,, Susanna, Killaloe, co. Clare, widow
1729 ,, Thomas, Christchurch Yard, Dublin, merchant
1740 ,, Thomas, of lord George Sackville's troop at Thurles
1780 ,, William, Drogheda, alderman
1794 ,, rev. William, Spencerhill, co. Louth, clk.

1811 **Ogle**, William M., Drogheda, esq.
1705 **Oglethorpe**, William, par. St. Anne, Westminster, widow
1810 **O'Grady**, Darby, Dublin, esq.
1737 ,, John, Killballyowen, co. Limerick, gent.
1802 ,, Joseph Patrick
1717 **O'Hagan**, Arthur, Ardboe, co. Tyr., esq.
1800 **O'Halloran**, Joseph, Dublin, priest
1809 ,, Sylvester, Limerick city, esq.
1799 ,, Thady, Ballycuneen, co. Clare, esq.
1802 **O'Hallorane**, Charles, Limerick
1808 **O'Hanlon**, Hugh, Newry, co. Down, gent.
1700 ,, John, Ballyinlessin, co. Arm., gent.
1688 **O'Hara**, Adam, Arderee, co. Sligo, esq.
1773 ,, Anne, Dublin, widow
1728 ,, Arthur, Straw, co. Londonderry
1783 ,, Barnett, Clogherly, co. Antrim
1698 ,, Charles, par. St. Martin-in-the-fields, Middlesex
1740 ,, Charles, Kinsaley, co. Dublin, esq.
1760 ,, Charles, Killeen, co. Longford, gent.
1729 ,, Cormick, Drumully, co. Cavan
1769 ,, Cormick, Dublin, surgeon
1733 ,, Ellinor, Dublin, widow
1731 ,, Francis, Dublin, tailor
1745 ,, Henry, Crebilly, co. Antrim, esq.
1763 ,, Henry, Dorset-st., Dublin, esq.
1763 ,, Henry Hutchinson, Crebilly, co. Antrim, esq. (Large will)
1768 ,, Henry, Mountcolwill, co. Ant.
1774 ,, Hugh, Dublin
1796 ,, Jeffrey, Westlodge, co. town of Galway, esq.
1795 ,, John, Tamnachacherty, co. Antrim, farmer
1719 ,, Kane, Templehouse, co. Sligo, esq.
1786 ,, Laurence, Behy, co. Sligo, gt.
1759 ,, hon. Mary
1810 ,, Tobias, Castletown, co. Galway, gent.
1799 ,, William, Ballitore, co. Kildare
[See HARA.]
1757 **O'Hare**, Daniel, Newry, co. Down, merchant
1800 ,, Danl., Ballinhattina, co. Louth, farmer
1789 ,, Henry, Glyn, co. Down
1774 ,, Philip, Newry, co. Down
1607 **O'Hayer**, Donoght, Primestown, co. Dublin, yeoman

1720 **O'Hea**, James, Kilkeiran, co. Cork, gent.
[See HAYES.]
1617 **O'Heyden**, Donnoghe, Norroghbeg, dio. Dublin
1783 **O'Hirlihy**, Timothy, Macroom
1808 **Ohman**, Mary
1632 **O'Hose**, Shane, co. Meath, or near Kilbride, farmer
1806 **O'Kearny**, Francis, Cashel city, esq.
1792 **O'Keefe**, Anne, Dublin, widow
1798 ,, Arthur, Newmarket, co. Cork
1803 ,, Chas., Mount Keefe, co. Cork, esq.
1737 ,, Cornelius, Limerick, doctor
1780 ,, Cornelius, barrister-at-law
1789 ,, Dennis, esq.
1758 ,, Manus
1780 **O'Kelly**, Elizabeth, *alias* **Reily**, wife to sir Geo. O'Kelly
1802 ,, sir George, Dublin, knt.
1802 ,, Mary, wife to sir Geo. O'Kelly, knight
1636 ,, Mulmore, Dunmurry, county Cavan, gent.
1782 **O'Kennedy**, James, Woodfort, co. Galway, gent.
1607 **O'Lalor**, Teigh M'Mortagh Oge, Buaile, Queen's co.
1795 **Oldfield**, Edward, Kilkenny city
1778 **Oldham**, Thomas, Mecklenburgh-street, Dublin, stonecutter, carver, and gilder
1639 **Oldinge**, Catherine, widow of James O., Lismore, co. Waterford, gent.
1760 **Oldman**, Patrick, Dublin
1806 **O'Leary**, Bridget, Charleville, co. Cork, widow
1793 ,, Florence, Bandon-road, Cork, grocer
1604 **O'Lenaghan**, Connor, Sawcerton, cottier
1678 **O'Leyne**, Dennis, Portaferry, gent.
1758 **Olford**, Thomas, Maddenstown, co. Kildare, gent.
1793 **Oliver**, Andrew, Enniskillen, co. Fermanagh, clerk
1690 ,, Christopher, Cork, ald. (Ex.)
1732 ,, John, Dublin, wigmaker
1779 ,, rev. John, Coolmore, co. Cork, clerk
1799 ,, right hon. Oliver
1679 ,, Robert, Cloughanodfoy, county Limerick, esq.
1739 ,, Robert, Clonodfoy, co. Limk., esq.
1761 ,, Stephen, Tattykeel, co. Tyrone
1758 ,, Susanna, Dublin, widow
1799 ,, Thomas, Cork city, esq.

1699 **Oliver,** Valentine, Cashel, widow
1746 **Ollaghan,** James Montagu, Man of War, co. Dublin
1784 **O'Loughlen,** Coleman, Clonroad, co. Clare, priest
1665 **Olphert,** John, Lisburn or Lisnagarvey, quartermaster to major Geo. Rawdon's troop
1789 **Olpherts,** Richard, Armagh city, esq.
1695 ,, Wibrant, Ballynas, co. Donnegal, gent.
1770 ,, Wybrants, Ballyconell, county Donegal, esq. (Large will)
1778 **Olyff,** rev. John, Clounduglass
1639 **O'Macken,** Murtough, Corryolly, co. Roscommon, yeoman
1804 **O'Maley,** Martin, Killeen, co. Galw.
1804 ,, Patrick
1797 **O'Malley,** Patrick, Dublin, gent.
       [See MEALY.]
1639 **O'Manning,** *alias* **Manley, Corn,** or **Connor,** gent., native of Minlagh Castle, near the abbey of Kilconnell, co. Gal.
1783 **O'Mara,** John, Dublin
       [See O'MEARA.]
1802 **O'Meally,** John, Ballina, co. Mayo
1805 **O'Mealy,** James, Waterford city
       [See O'MALLEY.]
1802 **O'Meara,** Cornelius, Sallee, Coughlane, gent.
1760 ,, Morgan, Lissanisky, co. Tipperary, esq.
1797 ,, Stephen, Thavies Inn, Middlesex, merchant
1789 ,, Thos., Castle Otway, co. Tipperary, esq.
       [See O'MARA.]
1627 **O'Meigher,** Teigh Geankagh, Ballynenane, co. Tipperary, gent.
1636 **O'Molloy,** Hugh, Ballyduffe, co. Cork
1641 **O'Morrane,** John, Ballyuroghane, co. Clare, gent.
1759 **O'Mullane,** Andrew, Coolowen, Lib. of Cork, gent.
1766 ,, John, Cork, gent.
1806 ,, John, Cork city
1723 **O'Neale,** Thomas, Rathascar, co. Kildare, farmer
1753 **O'Neill,** Ambrose, Dublin, esq.
1784 ,, Anne, Abbey-st., Dubl., widow
1786 ,, rev. Arthur, Dublin city, clk.
1811 ,, Arthur, Hanover-lane, Dublin
1798 ,, Bernard, Dublin city, esq.
1670 ,, sir Bryan, Backistown, co. Dublin, knt. and bart.
1804 ,, Bryan, Ardnaree, co. Sligo

1768 **O'Neill,** Charles, Shane Castle, co. Antrim, esq. (Large will)
1778 ,, Charles, Dublin, gent.
1788 ,, Charles, Drumcondra, co. Dublin, clk.
1793 ,, Charles, Dublin, esq.
1750 ,, Clotworthy, Gortpole, co. Ant., esq.
1711 ,, Con, Lackan, co. Mon., esq.
1779 ,, Con, Rathcarron, co. Meath, gent.
1799 ,, Con, Rathcarron, co. Meath, gent.
1808 ,, Edward, Trooperstown, county Wicklow, farmer
1808 ,, *alias* **Jones,** Elizabeth, South Great George's-st., Dublin
1740 ,, Francis, Dublin
1738 ,, Henry, Church-street, Dublin, merchant
1758 ,, Henry, Dublin, gent.
1778 ,, Henry, Reynolds-court, Dublin, worsted weaver
1796 ,, Henry, Dub., earthenware man
1790 ,, Hugh, Donnybrook, co. Dublin, gent.
1727 ,, James, Mullagh, co. Cavan
1756 ,, James, Dundalk, co. Louth, gent.
1756 ,, James, Waterford, merchant
1807 ,, James, Usher-street, Dublin
1808 ,, James, Ballinclay, co. Wicklow
1724 ,, John, Fardromin, co. Longford, esq.
1739 ,, John, Edenduffcarrick, co. Antrim, esq.
1765 ,, John, Glane, co. Meath
1766 ,, John, Mary's-lane, Dubl.,tailor
1766 ,, John, Dublin, gent.
1770 ,, John, Dublin, merchant
1775 ,, John, Mount Neill, co. Kilkenny
1787 ,, John, Clohoge, co. Wicklow, farmer
1798 ,, John, lord viscount (Large)
1807 ,, John, Frederick-street, Dublin, gent.
1782 ,, Mark Kerr, Flowerfield, co. Londonderry, esq.
1699 ,, dame Mary, widow of James Wolferston O'N., Killorgan, co. Dublin, esq.
1761 ,, Mary, Dublin, widow
1771 ,, Mary, Dundalk, co. Louth, spinster
1791 ,, Mary, Dublin, widow
1808 ,, Mathew, Usher's-quay, Dublin
1728 ,, Neal, Tauriaghmore East, co. Antrim, gent.
1747 ,, Owen, Dublin, upholder

1740 **Ormsby**, Frances, Dublin, widow
1751 ,,   Francis, Willybrook, co. Sligo, esq.
1680 ,,   George, Loughmask, co. Mayo, esq.
1749 ,,   George, Tobervaddy, co. Roscommon, esq.
1757 ,,   George, Dublin
1788 ,,   George, Robsgrove, co. Roscommon, esq.
1799 ,,   Gilbert, Athlone, co. Westmeath
1758 ,,   Hannah, Cummin, co. Sligo, widow
1694 ,,   Henry, Rathlee, co. Sligo, esq.
1809 ,,   James
1694 ,,   dame Jane, Richmond, Surrey, widow (Copy)
1714 ,,   Jane, Belanamore, co. Mayo, widow
1755 ,,   Jane, Dublin, widow
1634 ,,   John, Armagh, gent.
1711 ,,   John, Alaca, co. Limerick, esq.
1721 ,,   John, Dublin, esq.   [esq.
1727 ,,   John, Athlacca, co. Limerick,
1745 ,,   John, Cloghan, co. Mayo, esq.
1799 ,,   John, Cummin, co. Sligo, esq.
1808 ,,   John, Gortudrabby, co. Mayo
1734 ,,   Lettice, Dublin, spinster
1754 ,,   Lewis, Tobervaddy, co. Roscommon, esq.
1681 ,,   Mary, spinster
1740 ,,   Mary, *alias* **Geraghty**, Dublin, widow
1759 ,,   Mary, spinster
1759 ,,   Mary Butler, widow of the hon. col. Thomas B.
1797 ,,   Mary, St. Canice, Kilkenny
1741 ,,   Mathew, Dublin, gent.
1739 ,,   Peter, capt.
1694 ,,   Philip, Sligo, esq.
1767 ,,   Rebecca, Dublin, spinster
1714 ..   Robt., Cloghan, co. Mayo, esq.
1771 ,,   Robt,, Rocksavage, co. Roscommon, esq.
1775 ,,   Robert, Sligo town, esq.
1790 ,,   Robert, Robsgrove, co. Roscommon, esq.
1799 ,,   Robert, Dublin, esq.
1716 ,,   Sarah, widow of Stephen O., Castledargan, co. Sligo
1702 ,,   Stephen, Castle Dargan, co. Sligo, gent.
1720 ,,   Theophilus, Johnston Bridge, co. Kildare, esq.
1776 ,,   Thos., Mendon, co. Dubl., esq.
1811 ,,   Thos., Castle Dargan, co.Sligo, gent.
1739 ,,   Wm., Willybrook, co. Sligo, esq.

1763 **Ormsby**, Wm., Naas, co. Kildare, gent.
1784 ,,   Wm., Castledargan, co. Sligo, esq.
1791 ,,   William, Dublin, gent.
1805 ,,   William, Dublin city, esq. [See HORNSBY.]
1662 **Ormsbye**, lieut. Thos., Comyn, co. Sligo, esq.
1802 **Ormston**, Jean (Copy)
1782 **O'Rorke**, Andrew, Creevy, co. Leitrim, gent.
1761 ,,   Farrell, Carrow Crum
1790 ,,   Hugh, Creevagh, co. Sligo, esq.
1783 ,,   Hyacinth, Ballycurry, co.Sligo, esq.
1797 ,,   Mary, Toome, co. Antrim, wid.
1809 **O'Rourke**, Fras., Carrowerin, co. Leitrim, gent.
1781 ,,   Hugh, Creevagh, co. Sligo.
1794 **Orpen**, George
1740 ,,   Richd., Ardtully, co. Kerry, gt.
1770 ,,   Richard, Valentia, co. Kerry
1810 ,,   Richard, Ardtully, co. Kerry, esq.
1768 ,,   Thos., Killowen, co. Kerry, clk.
1805 **Orpin**, Fras., Douglass, Cork city, clk.
1722 ,,   John, Dublin, gent.
1752 ,,   John, Dublin, glazier
1727 ,,   Thos., Carrickfergus, glazier
1739 **Orr**, Alex., Belfast, co. Antrim, mct.
1773 ,,   rev. Alex., now resident in Bath
1811 ,,   Alex., Belfast, co. Antrim, gent.
1805 ,,   Chas., Lisnafeffry, co. Down, farmer   [gent.
1808 ,,   Jas., Gorton, co. Londonderry,
1699 ,,   John, Letterkenny, merchant
1771 ,,   John, Killyncather, co. Down, gent. (Large will)
1780 ,,   John, Ballybritain, co. Londonderry, merchant
1807 ,,   rev. John, rector of Magherafelt, co. Londonderry
1811 ,,   Rebecca, Harborne, Staffordshire
1757 ,,   William, Ballybeen
1658 **Orred**, Edward, soldier   **[VII.** 181
1731 **Orrery**, Charles, earl of
1696 ,,   Margaret, dow. countess of Roger, late earl (Copy)
1682 ,,   Roger, earl of
1693 **Orson**, Henry, Dublin, merchant
1760 ,,   John, Millextown, co. Louth, gent.
1794 ,,   John, Millextown, co. Louth, esq.
1743 ,,   Mary, Dublin, widow
1774 ,,   Wm., Summerhill, co. Meath, gent.

1640 **Osbaldeston,** sir Richard, Dublin, knt., attorney-gen.
1696 **Osbern,** Nicholas, Cappagh, co. Waterford
1744 **Osborn,** Elizabeth, Cashel, widow
1793 ,, dame Elizabeth
1703 ,, Francis, Stackallan, co. Meath, esq.
1708 ,, Henry, Dardistown, co. Meath, esq. (Ex.)
1743 ,, Henry, Dardistown, co. Meath, esq.
1744 ,, sir John, Newtown, co. Tipp., bart.
1752 ,, Margaret, Dublin, widow
1786 ,, Patrick, Ardee, co. Louth, tobacconist
1779 ,, Samuel, Dardistown, co. Meath, esq.
1766 ,, Simon, Heronstown, co. Meath, gent.
1794 ,, Simon, Annsborough, co. Kilkenny, esq.
1711 ,, Thos., Drominchin, co. Meath, gent.
1776 ,, Thos., Smithstown, co. Meath, gent.
1783 ,, Timothy, Dublin, esq.
1793 ,, rev. William
1723 **Osborne,** Ann, widow of John O., Drogheda, esq. [army
1691 ,, Edwd., capt. in King William's
1730 ,, Elizabeth, Carrickmacross, co. Monaghan
1811 ,, Henry, Cork city, M.D.
1695 ,, John, Dublin, esq. (Copy)
1713 ,, sir John, Taylorstown (co. Waterford, bart. (Ex.)
1719 ,, John, Drogheda, esq.
1726 ,, John, Grangegorman - lane, Dublin, gent.
1757 ,, John, capt. of an Independant Comp. of Invalids
1690 ,, Joseph, Waterford, merchant
1802 ,, Margaret, Triton Lodge, widow
1778 ,, Mary, Waterford, widow
1718 ,, sir Nicholas, bart.
1688 ,, Peter, Dublin, gent. (Ex.)
1680 ,, Roger, esq., collector (Ex.)
1660 ,, Thomas, Waterford, merchant
1717 ,, sir Thos., Tickincor, co. Waterford, knt.
1762 ,, Thos., Waterford, apothecary
1807 ,, Thomas H., of Annfield, co. Kilkenny
1681 ,, Wm., senr., Youghal, mercht.
1783 ,, sir William, bart.
1757 **Osburn,** Hugh, Ballymacreety, co. Down
1750 ,, Quintin, Cork, surgeon

1676 **Osburne,** Henrie, Londonderry, alderman
[See OSBORNE, &c.]
1798 **O'Seary,** Thomas, Dublin, peruke maker
1673 **O'Shaugnussie,** sir Dermot, Gortnisegorye, co. Galway, knt.
1636 **O'Shea,** John M'William, Glanaseagh, co. Tipp., farmer
1616 **Osheanachan,** Donnough Oge, Castlegar, co. Galway, clk.
1727 **Ossett,** George, Dublin, brazier
1640 **Ossory,** Jonas Wheeler, bishop of
1672 ,, Griffith Williams, bishop of
1677 ,, John Parry, bishop of
1693 ,, Thomas Otway, bishop of
1739 ,, rt. rev. Dr. Edward Tennison, bishop of (Ex.)
1742 ,, rt. rev. Dr. Anthony Dopping, bishop of
1758 ,, rt. rev. Dr. Edward Maurice, bishop of
1807 ,, rt. rev. Hugh Hamilton, lord bishop of
1754 **Osterwald,** Lewis, pastor of the French Church, Dublin
1805 **O'Sullivan,** Annast. Theresa Maria, Dublin, spinster
1780 ,, Catherine, Dublin
1790 ,, John, Cooleck, co. Cork, gent.
1800 ,, or **Sullivan,** John, Cravagh, co. Roscommon, esq. (See letter **S.**)
1743 ,, Owen, Kilcummin par., popish priest
1744 ,, Timothy, Dublin, formerly a vintner
1780 **Oswald,** John, bp. of **Raphoe,** q. v.
1806 **Ottey,** Elizabeth, Usher's-st., Dub., spinster
1734 **Ottiwell,** John, Killcullenbridge, co. Kildare, innkeeper
1769 ,, Mathew, Mallow, co. Cork, gt.
1696 **Otway,** sir John, Ingmer Hall, Yorkshire, knt.
1730 ,, Adam, Clareen, co. Tipp., esq.
1725 ,, Cæsar, Killduff, co. Tipp., esq.
1782 ,, Cæsar, Nenagh, co. Tipperary
1801 ,, Cooke, Castle Otway, co. Tip., esq.
1807 ,, Elizabeth
1805 ,, George
1737 ,, Henry, Castle Otway, co. Tipperary, esq.
1763 ,, James, Rapla
1722 ,, John, Cloghenan, co. Tipperary, gent.
1777 ,, Loftus, Lissenhall, co. Tipperary, esq.
1789 ,, Loftus, Nenagh, co. Tipperary

1715 **Otway**, Mary, Castle Otway, co. Tipperary, widow
1693 ,, Thomas, bp. of **Ossory**, q. v.
1724 ,, Thomas, Lissenhall, co. Tipperary, esq.
1789 ,, Thomas, Castle Otway, co. Tipperary, esq.
1765 **Ouchterlony**, James, Castleculfield, co. Tyrone, gent.
1725 ,, Sarah, Kilmore, co. Armagh, widow
1753 ,, Hugh, Dublin, gent.
1742 **Oughterlony**, William, par. Richmond, Surrey (Copy)
1753 ,, William, Richmond, Surrey (Copy)
1791 **Ould**, Catherine
1790 ,, sir Fielding, Dublin, knt.
1810 **Oullahan**, Elizabeth, George-quay, Dublin, widow
1782 ,, William, Luke-street, Dublin, butcher
[See HOULIGAN.]
1797 **Oulton**, Charles, Camden-street, Dublin, gent.
1806 ,, Rachel
1774 ,, Walby, Dublin, merchant
1581 **Oure**, sir John, clk. [**V. I.** p. 10
1758 **Ousley**, Jasper, Killecackley, co. Galway, gent.
1803 ,, Jasper, Dublin, gent.
1761 ,, Richard, Lisiconor, co. Galway, gent.
1767 ,, William, Northumberland-st., Dublin, gent.
1805 ,, William, Rushbrook, co. Mayo
1772 **Outram**, John, Dublin, saddler
1714 **Overend**, Anne, Dublin, widow
1758 ,, John, Portadown, co. Armagh, merchant
1809 ,, John, Edenderry, co. Armagh
1795 ,, Richard, Lurgan, co. Armagh, gent.
1709 ,, Thomas, Dublin, innholder
1657 **Overstreet**, John, St. Catherine's, near the Tower, London
[**VI.** 117
1673 **Owen**, Andrew, Crutched Friars, London, gent.
1675 ,, David, Waterford, distiller
1692 ,, Elizabeth, Rathmoyle, Queen's co., widow
1806 ,, Elizabeth, Finglas, co. Dublin, widow
1730 ,, Ephraim, gent.
1739 ,, Henry, Ballindrumney, co. Meath, esq.
1778 ,, Henry, Ballindrumney, co. Meath, esq.
1696 ,, John, Dublin, gent.

1762 **Owen**, rev. John, minister of Swords, co. Dublin, clk.
1802 ,, John, Rahalton, co. Fermanagh
1803 ,, John, town of Monaghan
1806 ,, John, Tildarg, co. Antrim
1765 ,, Mary, widow of capt. Henry O.
1793 ,, Mary, Dublin, widow
1761 ,, Nicholas, Rathconnell, co. Monaghan, gent.
1746 ,, Patrick, Balmadrough, co. Dublin, dairyman
1747 ,, Robert, Dublin, merchant
1785 ,, Rowland, Dublin, merchant
1689 ,, Thos., St. Olaves par., London, esq.
1654 ,, William, col. Henry Prettie's troop [**V.** 5
1713 ,, rev. William, clk.
[See HONE, HOYNE.]
1749 **Owens**, David, Bridge-st., Dublin, shopkeeper
1662 ,, Edward, trooper, late in Earl of Meath's troop
1809 ,, Edward, White House, co. Antrim
1767 ,, Elizabeth, *alias* **Bradly**, Dub., widow
1783 ,, Frances, Dublin, widow
1772 ,, Francis, Bridge-street, Dublin, weaver
1808 ,, George, Stephenstown, co. Meath, gent.
1794 ,, Hugh, St. Catherine's, co. Fermanagh
1787 ,, Jane, Dublin, widow
1779 ,, John, Savoy, co. Middlesex (Copy)
1656 ,, major Lewis, Dundalk
1700 ,, Mark, Carrigduff, co. Carlow, gent.
1748 ,, Mary, *alias* **Hacket**, Swords, co. Dublin
1804 ,, Mary, Dublin city, widow
1747 ,, Patrick, Francis-street, Dublin, clothier
1791 ,, Patrick, Dublin
1678 ,, Richard, Dublin, innholder
1781 ,, Samuel, Dundermott, co. Roscommon, esq. [gent.
1766 ,, Simon, Heronstown, co. Meath,
1777 ,, Terence, Balbriggan, co. Dubl.
1766 ,, Thomas, Aclare, co. Louth, gent.
1781 ,, Thomas, Kill, co. Kildare, farmer
1784 ,, Thomas, Mary-street, Dublin, gent.
1734 ,, William, Dandermott, co. Roscommon, gent.
[See OWEN.]

1596 **Owgan**, Margaret, widow, late wife to Wm. O., Fanacklorie
1808 **Oxford**, Rose, Carrickmacross, co. Monaghan
1771 **Ozier**, Francis, Dublin, silkweaver

—P—

1793 **Pack**, Mary, Kilkenny, widow
1795 ,, v. rev. Thomas, dean of St. Canice, Kilkenny
1691 **Packenham**, Henry, Tullynally, co. Westmeath, esq.
 [See PAKENHAM.]
1691 **Packer**, Phillip, Groombridge, Kent, esq.
1787 **Packinham**, Abigail, Dubl., widow
1640 **Padge**, John, Newhall, co. Kildare, gent.
1682 **Page**, Edward, Dublin, merchant
1719 ,, Edward, Trim, co. Meath, gt.
1801 ,, Frederick, Kilmalogue, King's co., esq.
1733 ,, John, Dublin, alderman
1799 ,, John, Dundalk, co. Louth, tanner
1759 ,, Mary, Clonmel, co. Tipperary, widow
1677 ,, Patrick, Little Turnoght, co. Kildare, gent.
1632 ,, Peter, Dublin, gent.
1692 ,, Thomas, Burresillea, co. Tipperary, gent.
1724 **Pageitt**, Richard, Dublin, gent.
1729 ,, William, Dublin, gent.
1787 **Pagett**, James, Milltown, co. Dub., gent.
1768 ,, John, Dublin
1765 ,, Robert, Clonmel, co. Tipperary, surveyor of excise
1721 **De Pagez**, Gilbert, Carlow
1671 **Pain**, John, Dublin, esq.
1811 ,, John D., Bride-street, Dublin, attorney-at-law
1779 **Paine**, Anne, *alias* **Rouse**, Annbrook, co. Meath
1792 ,, Caleb, Dublin, merchant
1784 ,, Christian, wife to John Paine, esq.
1717 ,, Dominick, Dublin, merchant
1808 ,, Elizabeth, Tinahely, co. Wicklow, widow
1795 ,, George, Dublin, merchant
1690 ,, Herbert, Dublin, linendraper
1805 ,, Jack, Graigue, Queen's co., gent.
1793 ,, John, Archhall, esq.
 [See PAYNE.]

1762 **Paine**, Joseph, Monaughrum, co. Carlow, esq.
1761 ,, Judith, Dublin
1749 ,, Laurence, Clongill, co. Meath, esq.
1782 ,, Richard, Dublin, silk dyer
1736 ,, Thos., Oberstown, co. Meath, gent.
1715 ,, Wm., Killenure, co. Wicklow
1721 ,, William, Clongill, co. Meath, gent.
1766 ,, William, rector of Kilberry, dio. Meath, clk.
1792 ,, William, Coldblow-lane, co. Dublin, gent
1711 **Painter**, William, Dublin, gent.
1732 **Pairobe**, Francis, Dublin, capt. on half pay
1708 **Pakenham**, Anne, Bracklin, co. Westmeath, widow
1683 ,, Phillip, Dublin, gent.
1703 ,, Robert, Bracklin, co. Westmeath
1757 ,, rev. Robert, Kilbeggan, co. Westmeath
1760 ,, Theophilus, Dublin, victualler (not proved)
 [See PACKENHAM, PACKINHAM.]
1703 **Palfrey**, Anna Maria, widow of Henry P., Galway
1667 ,, Richard, Dublin, esq.
1751 ,, Stephen, Kildare, esq.
1783 ,, Stephen, Ballintampin, co. Longford, gent.
1726 **Palin**, John, Christchurch-yard, Dublin, late of co. Kildare, farmer
1768 ,, Joshua, Hyde-park, co. Westmeath, gent.
1773 ,, Mathew, Kevans Port, esq.
1605 **Palles**, Alexander, Dub., alderman
1661 ,, Andrew, Dublin, gent.
1739 ,, Christopher, Dublin, gent.
1747 ,, Mary, Garryrobuck, co. Cavan, widow
1661 ,, William, Dublin, gent.
1772 **Pallin**, Grace, Dublin, widow
1772 ,, John, Dublin, mercer
1805 ,, Thomas, Harold's Cross, co. Dublin, clothier
1790 **Palliser**, Catherine, Wexford town
1769 ,, John, formerly **Bury**, Cork, esq.
1797 ,, Mary, Rathfarnham, co. Dub., widow
1784 ,, Phillip, Castletown, co. Wexford, esq.
1756 ,, Thomas, Portobello, co. Wexford, esq.
1726 ,, William, abp. of **Cashel**, q. v.

1769 **Palliser**, Wm., Rathfarnham, co. Dublin, esq.
1789 ,, Wray, Derryluskan, co. Tipp., esq.
1795 **Pallisier**, rev. John, Rathfarnham, co. Dublin, D.D. [See PELLISIER.]
1764 **Pallister**, Richard, Dublin, esq.
1758 ,, Thomas, Great Island, co. Wexford, esq.
1806 **Palmer**, Amos, Derry, King's co. esq.
1690 ,, Cassandra, Dublin, widow
1806 ,, Charles, Rahin, co. Wicklow
1807 ,, Charles, Birr, King's co.
1796 ,, rev. Edmond, Clonmaken, Lib. of Limerick
1796 ,, Edward, Hollypark, King's co., esq.
1796 ,, Elizabeth, Blackrock
1721 ,, Francis, Farrow, co. Mayo, esq.
1801 ,, Francis, Dublin
1729 ,, Henry, the elder, Parsonstown, King's co., gent.
1789 ,, Henry, Birr, King's co., esq.
1801 ,, ven. Henry, archdeacon of Ossory
1777 ,, Humphrey, Rathdowney, Queen's co., esq.
1751 ,, Jas., Killballyshea, King's co.
1777 ,, James, Ballykilleen, King's co., gent.
1776 ,, Jane, Castle Bellingham, co. Louth, widow
1743 ,, John, Walton-upon-Thames, Surrey, esq. (Copy)
1788 ,, John, Cornmarket, Dublin, hosier
1797 ,, John, Grange, co. Tipperary, esq.
1801 ,, John, Kentishtown, Middlesex, gent.
1741 ,, Joseph, farmer
1761 ,, Joseph, Nenagh
1772 ,, Joseph, Dublin, ironmonger
1789 ,, Joseph, Glanacurragh, King's co., gent.
1771 ,, Mary, Dublin, widow
1808 ,, Mary, Shinrone, King's co.
1776 ,, Patrick, Dublin, esq.
1804 ,, Robert, Shraugh, Queen's co., esq.
1724 ,, Roger, Palmerstown, co. Mayo, esq.
1770 ,, Roger, Palmerstown, co. Mayo, esq.
1794 ,, sir Roger, Ballyshannon, co. Kildare, bart.
1739 ,, Rose, Portadown

1772 **Palmer**, Samuel, rector of Loughrea
1781 ,, Sarah, Dublin, spinster
1667 ,, Stephen, Dublin, vintner
1689 ,, Thomas, Dublin, scrivener
1692 ,, Thos., Clannacurragh, King's co., yeoman
1729 ,, Thos., Carrowmore, co. Mayo, esq.
1738 ,, rev. Thomas, clerk
1740 ,, Thos., Castlelackan, co. Mayo, esq.
1774 ,, rev. Thomas, Glanmore, co. Longford, clk.
1786 ,, Thomas, Tarra, co. Mayo, esq.
1790 ,, Thos., Snugborough, King's co.
1793 ,, Thomas, Cahir-Daven, Lib. of Limerick
1810 ,, Thomas, Birr, King's co.
1655 ,, Valentine, Callan, co. Tipp., [V. 156
1727 ,, William, Dublin, gent.
1767 ,, William, Dublin, esq.
1776 ,, William, Johnstown, Queen's co. gent.
1782 ,, William, Lazers Hill, Dublin, gent.
1791 ,, William, Fownes's-street, Dubl.
1803 **Palmerstown**, rt. hon. Henry, lord viscount (Copy)
1740 **Palmes**, Stephen, Dublin, esq.
1719 **Paly**, James, Shanachan, co. Down, farmer [gent.
1738 **Pandin**, Gaspard Duchail, Dublin,
1777 **Pane**, Sarah, Coolgreany, co. Wexford, shopkeeper
1645 **Pankeart**, Frederick, a Dutchman, Dublin, merchant
1749 **Pannell**, Alexander, Dublin, gent.
1630 ,, Robert, Brownstown, co. Dubl., gent.
1614 **Panting**, Richard, Dublin, mercht.
1698 **Parence**, Silans, Dublin, widow
1687 **Pargiter**, Henry, London, gent.
1663 **Paris**, Henry, late of Ardmayle, co. Tipperary, esq.
1771 **Parish**, Henry, rector of Valentia, co. Kerry
1788 **Park**, James, Belfast, co. Antrim, merchant
1767 ,, Mary, Lichfin, co. Tipp., wid.
1809 ,, Nathaniel, Bellaghan, co. Donegal
1759 ,, Robert, Maynard, co. Tipperary, esq.
1698 ,, Wm., St. Martin-in-the-fields, Middlesex, tailor [See PARKS.]
1806 **Parke**, Andrew, Sligo.
1722 ,, Charles, Magherycarny Cash, co. Sligo, gent.

1750	**Parke**,	Charles, Saught, co. Donegal, gent.
1808	,,	George, E. Arran-street, Dubl., gent.
1797	,,	Jane, Dublin, widow
1671	,,	capt. Robert, Sligo
1726	,,	Roger, Dunally, co. Sligo, esq.
1749	,,	Sarah, Ballagan, co. Louth, spinster
1758	,,	William, Drummons
1740	**Parker**,	Abbney, Fermoyle, co. Longford, esq.
1785	,,	Anthony, Castlelough, co. Tipp., esq.
1800	,,	Anthony, Castlelough, co. Tipperary, esq.
1802	,,	Catherine, widow
1766	,,	Christopher, Henry-st., Dublin
1796	,,	Christopher, Dublin
1762	,,	David, Limerick, clothier
1658	,,	Edward, Dublin, chandler [**VI**. 267
1727	,,	Elizabeth, wife to Harding P., Cork, gent.
1811	,,	Farmer, Ballyhamlist, co Wat.
1756	,,	Francis, Newtown, co. Tipp.
1802	,,	Henry, Coote, co. Tipperary
1733	,,	Howlet, Newtown, co. Tipperary, esq.
1756	,,	Isaac, Dublin, goldsmith
1798	,,	Jacob, Savelbeg, co. Down, gt.
1778	,,	James, Dublin, printer
1750	,,	Jervas, Lieut.-General of the Forces
1640	,,	John, par. Sego, dio. Dromore, co. Armagh, yeoman
1681	,,	John, archbishop of **Dublin**, q.v.
1696	,,	sir John, Fermoyle, co. Longford, knt.
1700	,,	John, the elder, Pernkip, co. Limerick, esq.
1753	,,	John, Gortroe, co. Cork, esq.
1754	,,	John, Gortroe, esq.
1808	,,	John, Astle, Cheshire, clerk (Copy)
1806	,,	Kath., Youghal, co. Cork, wid.
1802	,,	Margaret, Cork, widow
1792	,,	Michael, Sligo town, printer
1810	,,	Michael Edward, surgeon to His Majesty
1657	,,	Nathaniel, Rathtoe, co. Meath, gent. [**VI**. 168
1681	,,	Nicholas, master of the ship called the " John," of Dublin
1747	,,	Patk., Tullybrugh, co. Armagh, mill foreman
1776	,,	Richard, Kilkenny city, gent.
1787	,,	Richd., Youghal, co. Cork, esq.
1716	,,	Robert, Gortaroe, co. Cork, gt.
1747	,,	Robert, Shanrah, co. Kildare

1756	**Parker**,	Robert, Savelbeg, co. Down
1726	,,	Roger, Dublin, gent.
1738	,,	Rowland, Glasnevin, co. Dublin, gent.
1808	,,	Samuel, Dowdstown, co. Kild.
1778	,,	Thos., Inchygagan, South Lib. of Cork
1706	,,	Vernon
1760	,,	Walter, Limerick, alderman
1758	,,	William, Coolgariff, co. Wexford, gent.
1800	,,	William, Lavilbeg, co. Down, gent.
1638	**Parkhurst**,	sir Robert, London, knight and alderman [**IV**. 352 and **V**. 107, 1655.
1677	,,	sir Robt., Burford, Surrey, knt. (Ex.)
1691	,,	Robt., Burford, Surrey, esq.
1591	**Parkins**,	Henry, Dublin, gent.
1786	**Parkinson**,	Bernard, Lr. Ormondquay, Dublin, gent.
1721	,,	rev. Edward, vicar of Ardee, co. Louth
1747	,,	Edward, Drumshee, par. Dromore, linendraper
1783	,,	James, Drumcondra-lane, Dublin, carpenter
1790	,,	James, Dublin, carpenter
1744	,,	Margaret, Dublin, widow [esq.
1761	,,	Robert, Atherdee, co. Louth,
1743	,,	William, Chamber-st., Dublin, clothier
1773	**Parkison**,	Robert, Strabane, co. Tyrone
1755	**Parks**,	Hugh, Ballagan, co. Louth, gent.
1746	,,	James, Newry, co. Down
1796	,,	James, Dublin, coal dealer
1733	,,	John, Ballagan, co. Louth, gt.
1750	,,	John, Cork, clothier
1765	,,	John, Ballagan, co. Louth
1782	,,	John, Dublin city
1775	,,	Richard, Lismore, co. Waterford, gent.
1749	,,	Samuel, Dublin, surgeon
1710	,,	William, ensign and adjutant in col. Price's regt.
1775	,,	William, Cork, esq. [See PARK.]
1627	**Parkyns**,	Richard, Athboy, co. Meath, esq.
1737	**Parme**,	William, Cork, baker
1709	**Parnell**,	Anne, Dubl., widow (Ex.)
1727	,,	John, one of the Justices of the K. B.
1782	,,	sir John, Dublin, bart.
1802	,,	rt. hon. sir John, Rathleague, Queen's co., bart.

1768 **Parnell**, Mary, Dublin, widow
1736 ,, Theobald, Dublin, esq.
1685 ,, Thomas, Dublin, gent.
1793 **Parr**, Frances, Beaumaris, Anglesey, widow (Copy)
1739 ,, Henry, Dingle, co. Kerry, esq.
1765 ,, John, Cabra-lane, Dublin, esq.
1633 **Parret**, Thomas, Croghantegle, Queen's co., gent.
1618 **Parrie**, Reis, Newry, merchant
1626 **Parry**, Arthur, Newry
1735 ,, Benjamin, Dublin, esq.
1690 ,, David, Tiltown, co. Meath, esq.
1679 ,, Eliz., widow of Benjamin, bp. of Ossory
1657 ,, George, LL.D. [**VI.** 150
1694 ,, George, Trinity College, near Dublin
1660 ,, Henry, Dublin, gent. [**VIII.** 92
1762 ,, Howard, Dublin, gent.
1677 ,, John, bishop of **Ossory**, q. v.
1686 ,, Lucy, Dublin, spinster
1790 ,, Martha, Dublin
1705 ,, Philadelphia, Dublin, widow
1736 ,, Philip, Dublin, esq.
1771 ,, Silence, Dublin, spinster
1593 ,, William, gent. (To be buried in Moyne abbey)
1741 ,, William, Dublin, gent.
1616 **Parsiner**, Robt., the Ring, co. Dublin, farmer
1808 **Parson**, John, Clonfaddin, co. Wicklow, farmer
1804 ,, Laurence, Parsonstown, King's co., esq.
1673 ,, Thomas, Dublin, gent.
1760 **Parsons**, Adam, Pembrokestown, co. Cork, esq. (Lge. will)
1644 ,, lady Anne, late of Birr
1709 ,, Anne, Dublin, widow
1775 ,, dame Anne, Dublin, widow
1777 ,, rt. hon. lady Elizabeth
1668 ,, Francis, Garadice, co. Leitrim, esq.
1619 ,, Gerald, Ballencroen, co. Wick.
1782 ,, John, Hawkins-street, Dublin, shopkeeper
1674 ,, Joseph, Dublin, gent.
1629 ,, sir Law., knt., 2nd Baron of Exchequer
1673 ,, Lowther, 2nd son of William P., Birr, esq.
1699 ,, Michael, Tomduff, co. Wexford (Ex.)
1633 ,, Nicholas, the elder, Limerick, gent.
1751 ,, Richard, Blackrock, co. Dubl., gent.
1774 ,, Richard, Carrige O'Gunnell, co. Limerick, gent.

1751 **Parsons**, Thomas, lieut. in lord Bury's regiment
1794 ,, Wentworth, Birr, King's co., esq.
1653 ,, William, Parsonstown or Birr, King's co., esq.
1657 ,, sir Wm., Dublin, bart. [**VI.** 90
1658 ,, sir William, Bellamount, co. Dublin, bart. [**VII.** 94
1693 ,, William, Dublin, gent.
1741 ,, sir Wm., Parsonstown, King's co., bart.
1771 ,, William, Birr, King's co.
1791 ,, sir William, Parsonstown
1809 ,, Wm., Athlone, co. Roscommon
1739 **Partinton**, Mary, Dublin, widow
1724 ,, Peter, Dublin, gent. (Large will)
1725 ,, William, Dublin, surgeon
1722 **Partridge**, Joseph, Maryborough, Queen's co., gent.
1777 ,, Richard, Dublin, gent.
1774 ,, rev. Samuel
1655 ,, Thomas, soldier [**V.** 122
1782 ,, William, Dublin, glass-seller and gilder
1784 **Parvin**, Benj., Moate, co. Westmeath
1769 ,, John, Ballykirroe, co. Westmeath
1807 ,, Mary, Clarendon-st., Dublin
1804 **Parvisol**, Francis, Ranelagh-road, co. Dublin, esq.
1809 ,, George, Booterstown, co. Dublin, esq.
1806 ,, Marianthea, Wicklow, widow
1803 ,, William
1761 **Pascal**, John, Dublin, cordwainer
1805 **Pasley**, Ellinor, widow
1797 ,, John, Kildare
1707 ,, Jonathan, Dublin, merchant
1731 ,, Jonathan, Rosetown, co. Kildare, gent.
1787 ,, Jonathan, Dublin, haberdasher
1783 ,, rev. Joseph
1737 ,, Joshua, Irishtown, Kilkenny, gent.
1796 ,, Samuel Hiatt, Dollymount, co. Dublin, esq.
1799 ,, Thomas, Kildare, gent.
1742 ,, William, Barretstown, co. Kildare, gent.
1604 **Paslowe**, Richard, Drogheda, merchant
1811 **Pasmore**, George, French-street, Dublin, gent.
1729 **Passley**, James, Stradbally, Queen's co., joiner
1807 **Passmore**, Christopher, Killougher, co. Dublin

1807 **Passmore**, Thomas, Coolock, co. Dublin, farmer
1637 **Pater**, Thomas, Waterford, mercht. [**IV.** 215
1753 **Paterson**, Clement, lieut. in genl. Otway's regiment of foot
1762 „ Elizabeth, *alias* **Whight**, Kilkenny, widow
1738 „ James, par. St. James, Westmeath, lieut.-col. (Copy)
1761 „ James, Cumber, co. Down, gent. [gent.
1704 „ John, Ramalton, co. Donegal,
1725 „ John, Benagh, co. Down, linendraper
1691 „ Josias, Dublin, now in Glasgow, surgeon
1753 „ Josias, Dublin, late capt. in lord Tyrawley's regiment
1787 „ rt. hon. Marcus, Ch. Jus. of the Common Pleas
1747 „ Mary, Benagh, co. Down
1763 „ Mary, Dublin, widow
1777 „ Robert, Benagh, co. Down, linendraper
1754 „ Sarah, Dublin, widow
[See PATTERSON, PATTISON.]
1703 **Patrick**, Robert, Coleraine, mercht.
1768 „ Robert, Dublin, merchant [See FITZPATRICK.]
1793 **Patrickson**, Foliott, Killegan, co. Wicklow, gent.
1691 „ George, Barnadown, co. Wexford, gent.
1803 „ Hester, Fleet-street, Dublin, spinster
1778 „ Samuel, Little Hill, co. Wicklow, esq.
1691 „ Thomas, Fellow of Trinity College, near Dublin
1711 „ William, the Monastery, co. Wicklow, gent.
1741 „ William, Kilbride, co. Wicklow, esq.
1797 „ Wm., Ballybrew, co. Wicklow
1805 „ William, Blessington, co. Wicklow
1802 **Patten**, Andrew, Springfield, co. Donegal, esq.
1762 „ Lassaigne, Cork, merchant
1792 „ Lydia, Dublin, widow
1773 „ Robert, Dublin, merchant
1801 „ Thomas, Whitehill, co. Donegal
1766 „ Townley, Drogheda, alderman
1710 „ William, Drogheda, alderman
1759 „ rev. William, co. Dublin, clerk
1770 „ William, Dublin, M.D. [See PEYTON.]

1684 **Patterson**, Hanibal, Ballycoleman, co. Tyrone, gent.
1661 „ John, Bangor, merchant
1808 „ Margery, Cavan, spinster
1784 „ Mary, Mill-street, Dublin
1785 „ Rosanna, Ture, co. Cavan, widow
1808 „ Thomas, Doneraile, co. Cork
1783 „ William, Foxhall, co. Donegal [See PATERSON.]
1807 **Pattin**, Thomas, paymaster of the 7th dragoon guards [See PEYTON.]
1793 **Pattinson**, John, Maryborough, Queen's co., gent.
1759 **Pattison**, Thomas, Dublin, hosier [See PATERSON.]
1782 **Patton**, John, Ballynecle
1803 „ Marcus, Belfast, co. Antrim, merchant [See PEYTON.]
1768 **Pattoun**, Robert, Adregoolebeg, co. Galway
1744 **Pattyson**, James, Castletor, co. Meath, pedler
1749 **Paul**, lady Anne, Dublin, widow
1802 „ Anne, Glasnevin, co. Dublin, widow
1701 „ Cadwallader, Stapletown, co. Carlow, gent.
1741 „ Elizabeth, widow
1798 „ rev. Francis, LL.D., rector of St. Thomas, Dublin
1720 „ Jeffrey, Ballyraggon, co. Kildare, esq. [esq.
1729 „ Jeffrey, Rathmore, co. Carlow,
1801 „ John, Dublin city, gent.
1799 „ sir Joshua, Paul-ville, co. Cavan, bart.
1707 „ Mehetable, Rathmore, co. Carlow, widow
1790 „ Samuel, Dublin, joiner
1733 „ William, Moyhill, co. Carlow, esq.
1799 „ William, Waterford city, alderman
1800 **Paulett**, Anne, Albemarle-street, Westminster (Copy)
1800 „ Susanna, Albemarle-street, Westminster (Copy) [See PAWLETT, POWLETT.]
1690 **Paull**, Jeffry, Ballyraggon, co. Kildare, gent.
1810 **Paumier**, Elizabeth, Douglas, Isle of Man
1780 „ Peter, Dublin, but at Bath, esq.
1709 **Pavey**, Adam, Mountrath, Queen's co., gent.
1679 „ sir John, knt., Ch. Jus. Com. P. [**X.** 115

1726 **Pavey**, John, Strahert, co. Wexford, gent.
1768 ,, Joseph, Mountrath, Queen's co., merchant
1778 **Pavy**, William, Ballinamore, co. Leitrim
1752 **Pawlett**, sir Charles Armand, knt. of the Bath (Copy) [See PAULETT.]
1767 **Payne**, Anne, College-st., Dublin, widow
1808 ,, Caleb, Collinstown, co. Kildare
1720 ,, Edward, Kill Garrane, co. Carlow, gent.
1738 ,, Elizabeth, Bow-street, Dublin, widow
1563 ,, Hugh, Dublin
1724 ,, John, Bow-street, Dublin, gent.
1765 ,, John, Athlone, co. Westmeath, dealer
1785 ,, rev. John, rector of Castle Rickard, dio. of Meath
1784 ,, William, Tralee, co. Kerry, gent. [See PAINE.]
1731 **Paynter**, James, Ringwood, Hampshire, gent. (Copy)
1594 ,, Robert, Dublin
1723 **Paysant**, John, French refugee and glazier, Dublin
1726 **Payzant**, Lewis, Dublin, gent.
1768 **Peacall**, Edward, Dublin, weaver
1771 ,, Jane, Dublin, widow
1774 **Peacock**, Dorothy, Tinnepark, King's co., spinster
1735 ,, Elisha, Lower Coombe, Dublin, weaver
1776 ,, George, Barntick, co. Clare, esq.
1792 ,, George, Fortetna, co. Limerick, esq.
1782 ,, Mary, Ballyboughlan, King's co., widow
1756 ,, Rebecca, Dublin, widow
1636 ,, Richard, Dublin, gent.
1809 ,, rev. Robert, Ross, co. Tipp., clk.
1772 ,, Thomas, Tinnemuck, King's co.
1744 ,, Upton, Dublin, widow [See PECOCKE.]
1575 **Peacocke**, Anthony, St. Michan's par. Dublin, wheelwright
1692 ,, Richard, Graigue, co. Limerick, esq., merchant (Copy)
1811 **Peacon**, Thomas, Clonmel, co. Tipp., gent.
1734 **Pearce**, sir Edward Lovett, Dublin, knt.
1775 ,, Richard, Lisnagry, Lib. of Limerick, esq.

1754 **Pearce**, Samuel, Limerick, gent.
1779 ,, Sarah, Limerick, widow
1724 ,, Thos., Limk., apothecary
1738 ,, Thomas, lieut.-genl. of the Forces
1669 ,, William, Dublin, merchant [See PIERS.]
1799 **Pearde**, Harrison, Carrigeen, co. Cork, esq.
1805 ,, Henry, Mountpleasant, co. Cork
1785 ,, John, Ballyclough, co. Cork, esq.
1716 ,, Richard, Castlelyons, co. Cork
1772 ,, Richard, Carrigeen, co. Cork, esq.
1794 ,, Robert, Cottage, co. Roscommon, gent.
1656 **Pearne**, John, trooper [**V.** 345
1727 **Pearse**, Daniel, Cork, alderman
1665 ,, James, Galway, esq. [See PIERS.]
1776 **Pearson**, Anne, Dublin, widow
1772 ,, George, Dowdstown, co. Meath
1809 ,, Henry, Arbour Hill, co. Dubl.
1807 ,, James, Jamestown, co. Dublin, surgeon
1749 ,, Jane, Beamore, co. Meath, widow
1787 ,, John, Dulane, co. Meath, gent.
1791 ,, John, Golden-lane, Dublin, merchant
1795 ,, Joseph, Kinnefad, King's co., farmer
1782 ,, Launcellot, Kells, co. Meath, farmer
1804 ,, Laurence, Golden-lane, Dubl., gent.
1660 ,, Mathew, St. Patrick's Close, Dublin
1724 ,, Mathew, Dublin, alderman
1800 ,, Mathew, Finglas, co. Dublin, widower
1749 ,, Nathaniel, Dublin, alderman
1731 ,, Phillip, Dublin, alderman
1724 ,, Richard, Newtown, co. Kildare, farmer
1806 ,, Richard, James-street, Dublin, esq.
1760 ,, Robert, Kildare, co. Kildare
1761 ,, Robert, Athy, co. Kildare
1767 ,, Samuel, Clonin, King's co., farmer
1736 ,, Thomas, Beamore, co. Meath, esq.
1765 ,, Thomas, Drehett, co. Kildare, farmer
1766 ,, William [See PEIRSON, PIERSON.]
1725 **Pease**, Robert, Amsterdam in Holland, merchant (Copy)

1725 **Pebberd**, James, Dublin, esq.
1782 **Pechel**, Samuel (Copy)
1750 **Pechell**, Jacob, Dublin, esq.
1660 **Peckham**, Symon, soldier at Dunstafnyth Castle, Scotland
1560 **Pecocke**, Seth, Kinsale
[See PEACOCK.]
1795 **Pedder**, Arthur Norcott, Clontarf, co. Dublin, barrister
1769 ,, Belcher, Cork.
1793 ,, Dorcas, Cork, widow
1745 ,, Elizabeth, widow of capt. And. P.
1804 ,, Elizabeth, Clontarf, co. Dublin, widow
1805 ,, John, Cork city
1799 ,, Mary, Clonmel,co.Tipp.,widow
1779 **Peebles**, Ilans, Hamilton's Bawn, co. Armagh
1805 ,, Robert, Hamilton's Bawn
1784 **Peek**, John, Dublin, gent.
1663 **Peers**, Anne, Dublin, widow.
1716 ,, Edward, Lisburn, co. Antrim, esq.
1789 ,, Edward, Lisburn, co. Antrim, brewer
1701 ,, John, Lisburn, co. Antrim, gent.
1781 ,, John, Lisburn
[See PIERS.]
1763 **Peery**, John, Naas, co. Kildare, farmer
1771 **Peet**, George, Limerick, clothier
1787 ,, Nathan,Mountrath,Queen's co.
1785 **Pegus**, Rachel, Dublin, widow
1791 **Peirs**, William, lieut.-col.
[See PIERS.]
1724 **Peirson**, Richard, Selby, Yorkshire, gent.
1707 ,, Thomas, London, gent. (Copy)
[See PEARSON.]
1764 **Peiry**, Robert, Crampton-quay, Dublin, letter founder
1638 **Peisly**, Bartholomew, Dublin, esq.
1640 ,, capt. Bartholomew, resident at Gullabby, co. Cork
1662 ,, Elizabeth, *alias* **Gough**, Cork, widow
1667 ,, sir Francis, Roscrea, co. Tipp., knt.
1642 ,, Joseph, Dublin, gent.
1773 ,, Moses, Mountmellick, Queen's co.
1755 ,, Peter, Paddock, Queen's co.
1642 ,, Robert, Dublin, gent.
1777 **Pelin**, Henry, Ballindrum, co. Kildare, gent.
1688 **Pell**, John, Dublin, gent.
1797 **Pelley**, John, Kill, co. Galway, esq.
1727 **Pellesier**, Abel, Dublin, esq.

1777 **Pellisier**, Alex., Dublin, merchant
1781 ,, rev. John, D.D., rector of Ardstra
1756 ,, Mary
[See PALLISIER.]
1803 **Peltier**, Francis, Dublin, gent.
1721 ,, James, Dublin, esq.
1799 **Pemberton**, Benjamin, Park-place, Dublin city
1747 ,, Henry, Dublin, merchant
1659 ,, John, minister, St. John Bap. par., Chester [VII. 168
1811 ,, John, Mount Olive, co. Dublin, esq.
1797 ,, Joseph, Dublin, cutler
1756 ,, Sarah, Dublin, widow
1811 ,, Wm. Mountjoy-sq., co. Dublin
1755 **Pembroke**, Thomas, Cork, esq.
1799 ,, William, Cork, gent.
1637 **Pen**, Wm., Dub., gent., practr. in physic [IV. 186
1777 **Pender**, Edward, Ballymona, co. Kildare, farmer
1741 ,, George, Killylease, co. Wicklow, esq.
1778 ,, John, Pimlico, co. Dubl., dyer
1777 ,, Wm., Pimlico, co. Dubl., dyer
1796 ,, Wm., Kilcrow, co. Kild., farmer
[See PRENDERGAST.]
1747 **Pendred**, Elizabeth, Ballygannon, co. Wicklow, widow
1771 ,, Letitia, Gt. Cuffe-st., Dub. spr.
1788 ,, Martha, Kindlestown,co.Wicklow, spr.
1800 ,, Sarah, Ballygannon, co. Wicklow, spr.
1736 ,, William, Broughillstown, co. Carlow, esq.
1762 ,, William, Broughillstown, co. Carlow, gent.
1784 **Penefather**, Elizabeth, Bason-lane, Dublin, spinster
1788 ,, John, Clonmel, co. Tipp., esq.
[See PENNEFATHER.]
1730 **Penington**, Mary, Cork, widow
1744 **Penn**, Springet, Shanagarry, co. Cork, esq.
1766 ,, Springett, Shanagarry, co.Cork, esq.
1671 ,, sir Wm. of London, merchant tailor (Copy)
1747 ,, William, Shanagarry, co. Cork, esq.
1671 **Pennant**, Hugh, Brynshane, Flintshire (Copy)
1776 **Pennefather**, Mary, Dubl., spinster
1788 ,, Mary, Cork, widow
1768 ,, Thomas, Island-bridge, co. Dublin, esq.
[See PENEFATHER.]

1756 **Pennefether**, Catherine, Dubl., wid.
1774 ,, Frances, widow, of Thomas P., of Island-bridge, co. Dublin, esq.
1733 ,, Matthew, Dublin, gent.
1806 **Pennell**, Elizabeth, Wicklow
1780 ,, Wm., Wicklow, co. Wicklow
1667 **Pennington**, John, St. James-st., Dublin, maltster
1675 ,, John, Dublin, victualler
1759 **Penny**, Thomas, Dublin
1744 **Pennyfether**, Levinia, Glasnevin, co. Dublin, spinster
1787 **Penrose**, Anne, *alias* **Cooper**, wid.
1741 ,, Daniel, Ballycane, co. Wicklow, esq.
1775 ,, Francis, Waterford, merchant
1805 ,, Francis, Ballykeane, co. Wicklow, gent. [ford
1797 ,, George, Brooklodge, co. Water-
1737 ,, Richard, Little Brittas, co. Wicklow, gent.
1801 ,, Richd., Waterford city, mercht.
1806 ,, Susanna, Ballykeane, co. Wick.
1792 ,, Thomas, Dublin, esq.
1747 ,, Wm., Waterford, merchant
1783 ,, William, High-st., Dub., linen-draper
1797 ,, Wm., Newtown, Lib. of Watfd.
1799 ,, Wm., Waterford city, merchant
1731 **Penteney**, Wm., Rath, co. Dublin, tanner
1811 **Penthony**, Augustine, Dublin city, gent.
1800 **Pentland**, John, Drogheda, mercht.
1808 ,, John, Dublin city, gent.
1809 ,, John, Strandville, co. Wicklow
1792 ,, Thomas, Springfield, co. Dubl., widower
1779 ,, rev. Wm.
1810 ,, Wm., Letterkenny, co. Donegal.
1792 **Penton**, Geo., Basingstoke, Hampshire, gent. (Copy)
1792 **Pentony**, Christopher, Drogheda, merchant
1774 ,, Christopher, Gormanstown, co. Meath, farmer
1771 **Peppar**, Henrietta, Dublin, widow
1770 ,, Thomas, Cookstown, co. Louth, esq.
1623 **Peppard**, Geo., Drogheda, aldmn.
1760 ,, Jane, *alias* **Bickerton**, Milestown, co. Louth
1766 **Pepper**, Alexander, Cookstown, co. Louth, gent.
1804 ,, Elizabeth, Cookstown, co. Louth
1704 ,, Geo., Ballygarth, co. Meath, esq.
1751 ,, Geo., Ballygarth, co. Meath, esq.

1791 **Pepper**, George, Knockalton, co. Tipperary, esq.
1795 ,, James, Dromleck, co. Louth
1725 ,, John, par. St. George, Hanover-square, major-gen. of Forces (Copy)
1795 ,, John, Mullanstown, co. Louth, farmer.
1776 ,, Lambert, Mata, co. Tipperary, esq.
1777 ,, Lydia, Mola, co. Tipperary, widow
1684 ,, Martin, Drogheda, merchant
1777 ,, Parke, Milltown-road, co. Dub., esq. [esq.
1701 ,, Simeon, Ballygarth, co. Meath,
1800 ,, Thomas, Ballygarth, co. Meath
1629 **Pepperd**, Anthonie, Glascarrick, co. Wexford, gent. (Copy)
1698 ,, Robert, Dublin, esq. (Large will, Ex.)
1726 ,, Robert, Kerdiffstown, co. Kildare, esq.
[See PEPPARD.]
1557 **Pepyat**, Catherine
1713 **Pepys**, Arthur, captain in general Langston's regiment of horse
1720 ,, John, quarter-master of Athy
1750 ,, Mary, widow of capt. Arthur P.
1659 ,, Richd., esq., Ch. Jus. of Ireland [VII. 191
1688 **Peradice**, Richd., Youghal, mercht.
1799 **Perce**, John, Dub., attorney-at-law [See PIERS.]
1779 **Perceval**, Anne, Dublin, widow
1795 ,, Charles, rector of Bruhenny, dio. Cloyne
1656 ,, Elizabeth, widow [VI. 29
1754 ,, John, Templehouse, co. Sligo, esq.
1774 ,, rev. Keene, D.D., prebendary of Castleknock, dio. Dublin
1663 ,, sir Philip of Dub., knt. [IX. 153
1800 ,, rev. Philip, Templehouse, co. Sligo (Large)
1718 **Percevall**, John, Knightsbrook, co. Meath, esq.
1686 **Percival**, Catherine, Lady Kinsale, widow (Large will, Ex.)
1713 ,, Charles, Callan, co. Kilk., esq.
1785 ,, rev. Chas., Kilmakoe, co. Cork.
1772 ,, Edward, Garrigibbon, co. Wexford, gent.
1809 ,, Edward, Wexford, esq.
1801 ,, Elizabeth, Dublin, widow.
1791 ,, James, Kilkenny city, alderman
1807 ,, James, Kilkenny city, esq.
1772 ,, Jane, Dublin, widow
1686 ,, sir John, Burton, co. Cork, bart. (Large will, Ex.)

1737 **Percival**, John, Wexford, co. Wexf.
1745 ,, Martha, widow
1786 ,, Martha, Dublin, spinster
1783 ,, Mary
1756 ,, Robert, the younger, Knightsbrook, co. Meath, esq
1703 ,, Thomas, Drogheda, alderman
1734 ,, Wm., dean of Emly, and preb.
of St. Michan's, Dublin
1784 ,, William, Dublin, esq.
1786 ,, Wm., town and co. Wex., esq.
1794 ,, Wm., Stradbally, Qu. co., esq.
1681 **Percivall**, Dame Catherine, widow
of sir Phillip P., knt.
1737 ,, rev. Edward, Clonkeen, co.
Louth, clk.
1675 ,, George, Drogheda, alderman
1683 ,, Hugh, Gortadrommough, co.
Clare, gent.
1747 ,, rev. William, rector of Aghan-
low, co. Derry, clk.
[See PERCYVALL.]
1703 **Percy**, sir Anthony, Dublin, knt.
1744 ,, Francis, Garden-lane, Dublin,
hosier
1769 ,, George, Limerick, gent.
1725 ,, Henry, Seskin, co. Wicklow,
esq.
1768 ,, Jane, Cloneraken, co. Tipp.,
widow
1777 ,, Joanna, Limerick, widow
1682 ,, Joseph, Dublin, glover
1745 ,, Sarah, spinster, daughter of
Francis P., of Ballintemple,
King's co., gent
1795 ,, rev. William, Esker, co. Dubl.,
clk.
[See PIERS.]
1629 **Percyvall**, John, sen., Dublin
See PERCIVAL.]
1783 **Perdrian**, Daniel, Cork, merchant
1789 **Perdrisat**, Rachell, Dublin, wid.
1792 **Peree**, Thomas, Dublin, attorney-
at-law
1741 **Perg**, Dymphna, Tipperary
1763 **Perkins**, John, Dublin, gent.
1781 ,, John, Ballintraine, co. Carlow,
esq. (Large)
1787 ,, John, Ballybroony, co. Mayo,
esq.
1794 ,, Theophilus, Dublin, esq.
1658 ,, William, London, merchant
[**VI.** 252
1671 ,, William, London, merchant
1801 ,, William, Grangebeg, co. Kildare, carpenter
1737 **Perrier**, John, Dublin, wine merchant and gent.
1775 **Perrin**, Arthur, Dublin, apothecary
1787 ,, Arthur, Dublin, esq.

1810 **Perrin**, Foden, Stephen's-green,
Dublin, apothecary
1731 ,, Stephen, Gowran, co. Kilkenny,
esq.
1710 **De Perrinett**, Gasparde, Marquise
of Arcelliers, at Geneva
1749 **Perro**, Anne, Dublin, widow
1665 **Perrott**, Abraham, St. Olave's par.,
Hart-street, London (Copy)
1715 ,, Conyers, Drumshome, co. Carlow, esq. (Ex.)
1695 ,, Elizabeth, Ballyhayes, co.
Cavan, widow
1688 ,, Humphrey, Dromhom, co.
Cavan, esq.
1778 **Perry**, Alexander, Edgeworthstown,
co. Longford, esq.
1802 ,, Anne, Dublin, widow
1770 ,, Anthony, Dublin, cardmaker
1798 ,, Anthony, Perrymount, co.Wex-
ford, esq.   [law
1800 ,, Arthur, Dublin, barrister-at-
1678 ,, Benjamin, Dublin, gent.
1810 ,, Catherine, North Cumberland-
street, Dublin
1730 ,, Edward, Corr, co. Tyrone, gent.
1770 ,, Edward, Moorfield, co. Tyrone
1803 ,, Elizabeth, Palmer's Hill,
Queen's co., spinster
1794 ,, Francis, Dublin, esq.
1771 ,, Geo., Perrymount, co. Tyrone,
gent.
1801 ,, George, the elder, Cappantan-
vally, co. Clare
1795 ,, Hugh, capt. in the 14th regt.
of foot
1756 ,, James, Perrymount, co. Down
1780 ,, James, Enniskillen, co. Fermanagh
1809 ,, Joana, Aungier-st., Dubl., wid.
1710 ,, John, Woodroofe, co. Tipp.
1737 ,, John, Newtown, co. Meath,
gent.
1759 ,, John, Woodroofe, co. Tipp.,
gent.
1771 ,, John, Carlow, haberdasher
1751 ,, Margaret, Dunshaughlin, co.
Meath, widow
1785 ,, Mary, Limerick city, spinster
1799 ,, Richard, Cork city
1730 ,, Samuel, Mullaghmore, co.
Tyrone, gent.
1774 ,, Samuel, Mullaghmore, co.
Tyrone, esq.
1739 ,, rev. Stackpole, Limerick, gent.
1633 ,, William, Limerick, gent.
1792 ,, William, Woodroofe, co. Tipp.,
esq.
1802 ,, Wm., Gambonstown, co. Tipp.,
esq.

1809 **Perry,** William, capt. and adjut. of Clare militia
[See PERY.]
1801 **Perse,** Patrick, the elder, Loughrea, co. Galway, esq.
1737 **Persse,** Henry, Rocksborough, co. Galway, esq.
1805 ,, Henry, paymaster of the Galway regiment
1781 ,, Robert, Roxborough, co. Galway, esq.
[See PIERS.]
1737 **Pervin,** Benjamin, Moate Granoge, co. Westmeath, chandler
1718 **Pery,** Edmond, Stackpole Court, co. Clare, esq.
1806 ,, Edward, rt. hon. lord viscount
1690 ,, Hugh, Dublin, dyer
1794 ,, Wm. Cecil, bp. of **Limk.**, q. v.
[See PERRY.]
1746 **Peter,** Rebecca, Dublin, spinster
1742 ,, Walter, Dublin, merchant
1790 ,, Walter, Edge's-court, Dublin, esq.
1650 **Peters,** Richard, The Inns, Dublin, gent.   [gent.
1805 ,, Robert, Donnycarny, co. Dubl.,
1746 ,, Wm., Petersville, co. Meath, esq.
1680 **Peterson,** John, Oxmantown, Dub., merchant
1737 **DuPetitbose,** Daniel Le Grand, Portarlington, esq.
1762 **DuPetit Bosse,** Charles, Dublin, esq.
1786 **Petrie,** James, Drogheda, surgeon
1730 **Petry,** Jane, Dublin, widow
1723 ,, John, lieut.-col. of Carbineers
1756 ,, John, Dublin, gent.
1788 **Petten,** Saml., Lurgan, co. Armagh
1760 **Petticrew,** Hannah, Belfast, co. Antrim, widow
1742 ,, Hugh, Belfast, merchant
1744 ,, James, Dublin, merchant
1790 ,, Robert, Dublin, merchant
1790 ,, William, Crolly, co. Tyrone
1802 **Pettigrew,** Hannah, Dublin, spin.
1759 ,, James, Crolley, co. Tyrone
1787 ,, Mary, Dublin, widow
1743 **Pettit,** Christopher, Dubl., mercht.
1808 ,, Clement, Wexford
1799 ,, John, Athlone, co. Westmeath, gent.
[See LITTLE.]
1722 **Petty,** George Speeke, capt. in col. Groves' regiment.
1672 ,, John, Dublin, gent.
1688 ,, sir William, St. James, par. Westminster, knt. (Copy)
[See PETTIT.]

1712 **Pevey,** John, the elder, Mountrath, Queen's co. gent.
1599 **Peyne,** Margery, Dublin, widow
1614 **Peyton,** Chris., Dublin, merchant
1699 ,, Geo., Streamstown, co. Westmeath, esq.
1793 ,, Isaac, Coombe, silk weaver
1720 ,, sir John, Gt. Britain-st., Dubl., bart.
1730 ,, Rebecca, lady, wid. of sir John P., Dublin, bart.
1796 ,, Toby, Lagheen, co. Leitrim, esq.
[See PATTEN, PATTIN, PATTON.]
1762 **Phaire,** Aldworth, St. John's, co. Wexford, esq.   [esq.
1785 ,, Aldworth, Gar, co. Wexford,
1797 ,, Aldworth, lieut. in the 35th regt. of foot
1800 ,, Elizabeth, *alias* **Hardum,** Wat., widow
1772 ,, Frances, Enniscorthy, co. Wexford, widow
1757 ,, Onisiphorous, Templeshannon, co. Wexford, esq.
1807 ,, rt. hon. Richard, Dublin
1682 ,, Robert, Grange, co. Cork, esq.
1712 ,, Robert, Grange, co. Cork, esq.
1786 ,, Robert, Daphne, co. Wexford
1716 ,, Thomas, Mount Pleasant, co. Cork, gent.
1800 **Phealton,** John, Ballyvarrow, co. Kilkenny
1783 **Phelan,** Barnaby, Cashel city, gent.
1808 ,, David, Butler's Wood, co. Kilkenny
1792 ,, Francis, R. C. priest
1705 ,, James, Kilkenny
1805 ,, James, Audoen's-arch, Dubl., distiller
1811 ,, James, Audoen's-arch, Dubl., distiller
1803 ,, Jeremiah, Castletown, Queen's co., shopkeeper
1765 ,, John, Dublin, merchant
1780 ,, John, Largh, Queen's co.
1788 ,, John, Christchurch-lane, Dub.
1806 ,, John, Ballyragget, co. Kilk.
1743 ,, Mary, Ballinakill, Queen's co., widow
1723 ,, Murtogh, Ballinakill, Queen's co., farmer
1800 ,, Patrick, Jamaica, West Indies
1777 ,, Thomas, Kilmacshane, co. Kilkenny, farmer
1752 ,, Timothy, Tullaroan, co. Kilkenny, gent.
1742 ,, William, Waterford, merchant
1701 **Phelips,** John, Kilpatrick, but in London, deceased (Copy)

1679 **Phelpes**, Thomas, the elder, par. St. Martin - in - the - Fields, Middlesex, coachmaker (Copy)
1698 ,, Thomas, Limerick, merchant
1788 **Phelps**, Joseph, Moyallen, co. Down
1669 ,, Robert, Arklow, co. Wicklow, mariner
1810 ,, Thomas, Moyallen, co. Down
1731 **Phenney**, John, Dublin, gent.
1798 **Phepoe**, Elizabeth, city of Bristol
1777 ,, Richard, Dublin, esq.
1733 ,, Thos., Kells, co. Meath, gent.
1796 **Phibbs**, Abigail, Athlone, co. Westmeath, widow
1769 ,, Fleming, Dunnamurry, co. Sligo, now of the Coombe, Dublin
1749 ,, John, Kingsfort, co. Sligo, esq.
1803 ,, John, Lisconny, co. Sligo, esq. (Large)
1738 ,, Mathew, Rockbrook, co. Sligo, esq.
1769 ,, Mathew, Sligo, gent.
1784 ,, Mathew, Sligo, esq.
1799 ,, Richard, Dublin city, esq.
1750 ,, William, Usna, co. Rosc., gt.
1775 ,, William, the elder, Rockbrook, co. Sligo
1785 ,, rev. Wm., Abbeyville, co. Sligo, clerk
1802 ,, Wm., Hollybrook, co. Sligo, esq.
1806 **Philbin**, Thomas, Dublin
1777 **Philips**, rev. Charles, rector of Magourney, diocese of Cloyne
1793 ,, Editha, spinster
1715 ,, George, Dublin
1808 ,, Geo., Killinardin, co. Dublin, farmer
1743 ,, rev. James, preb. of Killinard, diocese of Raphoe
1793 ,, James, Kill, Limerick, apothecary
1809 ,, Jane, Dublin city, widow
1779 ,, John, surgeon to the train of artillery
1804 ,, Mary, Dublin city, spinster
1802 ,, Michael, Ashgreen, co. Meath, esq.
1790 ,, Philip, master-gunner of Chester Castle
1796 ,, Ralph, Sligo, esq.
1807 ,, Richard, Dublin city, esq.
1766 ,, Robert, Ballindoe, co. Mayo, gent.
1809 ,, Samuel, Lincoln's Inn, Middlesex (Copy)
1805 ,, Stumbles, Mount Philips, co. Tipperary, esq.

1718 **Philips**, Thos., Kilkenny, alderman
1731 ,, Thomas, Dublin, esq.
1798 ,, Thomas, Clonmore, co. Mayo, esq.
1798 ,, Wm., Wicklow town, shoemkr.
1585 **Phillipe**, Thomas, Athlone [I. 31
1671 **Phillips**, Dame Alles, Dublin, wid.
1737 ,, Benjamin, Cregg, co. Cork, gt.
1722 ,, Charles, Dublin, brewer
1787 ,, Charles, Parliament-row, Dublin, weaver
1728 ,, Chichester, Dublin, esq.
1712 ,, Christopher, Nenagh, co Tipperary, barrack-master
1724 ,, David, Begglisrenny, co. Louth, gent.
1772 ,, Edward, Clonmore, co. Mayo, gent.
1790 ,, rev. George, Donoghmore, co. Wicklow, clerk
1650 ,, Griffith, St. Thomas
1661 ,, Hugh, Commingstown, co. Tipperary, gent.
1678 ,, Rees, Dublin, vintner
1804 ,, Samuel, Dublin city, attorney-at-law
1636 ,, sir Thomas, Hammersmith, Middlesex, knt. (Copy)
1753 ,, Thomas, Dublin, gent.
1765 ,, Walter, Limerick, apothecary
1629 ,, Wm., clk., M.A., Ardmullin, co. Meath
1666 ,, Wm., St. Thomas-st., Dublin
1780 ,, Wm. Fredk., Margaret's Court, Bath
1790 ,, Wm., Charlemount-street, esq. (Large)
1738 **Phillis**, John, Meath-st., Dublin, wire dyer
1765 ,, Robert, Meath-street, Dublin, wire drawer
1793 ,, Susanna, Meath-street, Dublin, spinster
1759 **Philpot**, Catherine, Dromagh, co. Cork, widow
1669 ,, Edward, Belturbet, co. Cavan, esq.
1802 ,, Jane, Cork, widow
1712 ,, John, lieut. and adjutant in lord Inchiquin's regt.
1801 ,, Mathew, Ballinrobe, co. Mayo, esq.
1729 ,, Nicholas, Scarteen, co. Cork, gent.
1635 ,, Phillip, Dublin, gent.
1741 ,, Spencer, Scarteen, co. Cork, gt.
1787 ,, Usher, Cork, esq.
1733 ,, William, Dublin, merchant
1756 ,, William, Dromagh, co. Cork, gent.

1765 **Philpot**, William, ensign in gen.
Murray's regt.
1805 ,, Wm., Ferrybank, co. Wicklow,
gent.
1682 **Phippes**, Benjamin, Dublin, clk.,
dean of Ferns
1759 **Phipps**, John, Dublin, gent.
1790 ,, George, Cork city, esq.
1745 ,, Samuel, Dublin, linendraper
1810 ,, Wm., Clontarf, co. Dub., gent.
1733 **Picard**, Peter, Dublin, gent.
1768 **Pick**, Ellinor, Cork, widow
1740 ,, John, Cork, merchant
1726 **Pickeaver**, Joseph, Dublin, periwigmaker
1753 **Picken**, James, Dublin, gent.
1808 **Pickering**, David, Pill-lane, Dub.,
smith
1760 ,, Samuel, Sligo, merchant
1737 ,, Wm., Drogheda, carpenter
1662 **Pickersgill**, Jno.,Lowburton, Yorkshire, gent. (Copy)
1752 **Pickett**, Thomas, Monee, co. Cork,
gent.
[See PIGOTT.]
1643 **Pickinan**, Jane, St. Patrick's-close,
Dublin, widow
1695 **Pickirall**, Mary, Leestowne, co.
Dublin, widow
1726 **Pickirey**, Joseph, Dublin, sawyer
1671 **Pidcocke**, Thomas, an adventurer
in Ireland, Newington-
green, Middlesex, gent.
(and another will in 1772)
1713 **Piddock**, Richard, Dublin, gent.
1780 **Pidgeon**, John, New-row, Dublin,
farmer
1808 ,, Martha, Charlemont-st., Dubl.,
widow
1804 ,, Peter, Castlegrange, co. Wicklow, gent.
[See PIGEON.]
1746 **Pierce**, Bridget, Dublin, widow
1794 ,, Garrett, Limerick, apothecary
1785 ,, Henry, Askenviller, co. Wexf.
1772 ,, Richard, Tralee, co. Kerry,esq.
1719 ,, Robert, Ballywalter, co. Down,
gent.
[See PIERS.]
1784 **Piercy**, George, Cork, esq.
1764 ,, James, Cork, merchant (Large
will)
1796 ,, Jeffrey, Cork, merchant
1790 ,, Paul, Cork, esq.
[See PIERS.]
1656 **Piers**, capt. Edward, Salestown, co.
Meath   [**V.** 252
1742 ,, Edward, Cork, merchant
1753 ,, Edward, Tyfarnan, co. Westmeath, gent.

1808 **Piers**, Edward
1734 ,, Elizabeth, Dublin, widow
1780 ,, Elizabeth, Lislougher, co.
Meath
1788 ,, Ellinor, Dublin, widow
1768 ,, Fletcher, clk., rector of Killashee, co. Longford
1780 ,, Frances, Dublin, widow
1768 ,, George Frederick Nassau,
Dublin
1623 ,, Henry, Fristernagh, co. Westmeath, esq.
1691 ,, sir Henry, Fristernagh, co.
Westmeath, bart.
1705 ,, Henry, Low Baskin, co. Westmeath, esq.
1734 ,, sir Henry, Fristernagh, co.
Westmeath, bart.
1710 ,, dame Honoria, Dublin, widow
1730 ,, John, Kilmacoo, co. Westmeath, gent.
1747 ,, sir John, Fristernagh, co.West-
meath, bart.
1768 ,, John, Dublin, gent.
1700 ,, dame Martha, *alias* **Martin**,
Fristernagh, co. Westmeath
1754 ,, Mary, Portarlington, Queen's
co., widow
1728 ,, Thomas, Dublin, gent. (Copy)
1753 ,, Thomas, Lislogher
1603 ,, capt. William, Fristernagh, co.
Westmeath, esq.
1638 ,, sir William, Fristernagh, co.
Westmeath, knt.
1751 ,, William, Portarlington,Queen's
co.
1767 ,, lieut. Wm., Islington (Copy)
1796 ,, William,Drumgilra,co.Leitrim,
clk.
1798 ,, sir Pigott William,Fristernagh,
co.Westmeath, bart.
[See PEARCE, PEARSE, PEERS, PEIRS,
PERCE, PERCY, PERSSE, PIERCE,
PIERCY.]
1748 **Pierse**, James, Dublin, esq.
1763 ,, Jane, Dublin, widow
1787 ,, Mary, Cork, widow
1732 ,, Richard, Ballinagaragh, co.
Kerry, gent.
1761 ,, Richard, Foxall, co. Limerick,
gent.
1734 ,, Thomas, Ballinagaragh, co.
Kerry, gent.
1739 **Pierson**, Eleazor, Dublin, esq.
1809 ,, Isaac, Clonfaddin,co. Wicklow
1740 ,, John, Chelsea, Middlesex, esq.
1748 ,, Martha, Dunleary, co. Dublin,
widow
1701 ,, Samuel, Killinsoukin, co.West-
meath, gent.

1754 **Pierson**, Thomas, Stoneyford, co. Westmeath, esq.
[See PEARSON.]
1721 **Pigeon**, Henry, Geashill, King's co., gent.
1768 ,, Henry, Geashill, King's co., gent.
1767 ,, Thomas, Geashill, King's co. [See PIDGEON.]
1776 **Piggott**, Thomas, vicar of St. James, Dublin
1788 ,, William, Slevoy, co. Wexford, esq.
1591 **Pighot**, William, Dublin, alderman [**I.** 51
1711 **Pigot**, John, Kilcrum, Queen's co.
1681 **Pigott**, Alexander, Inishonan, co. Cork, esq.
1779 ,, Anne, wife to Colclough Pigott, esq.
1726 ,, Benjamin, mariner
1779 ,, Colclough, Cappard, Queen's co., esq.
1789 ,, Dowdall, Cappard, Queen's co., esq.
1773 ,, George, Cork, esq.
1789 ,, Hannah, *alias* **Clibborn,** *alias* **Goff,** Slevoy, co. Wexford
1809 ,, Jane, *alias* **Hogg,** *alias* **Piers,** widow
1654 ,, major John, Grangebeg, Queen's co. (Copy)
1728 ,, John, Brockley, Somersetshire, esq. (Copy)
1730 ,, John, Brockley, Somersetshire, esq. (Copy)
1785 ,, Mary, Dublin, widow
1797 ,, Mary, widow of archdeacon Pigott
1719 ,, Nicholas, surveyor of excise in Dublin
1643 ,, sir Robert, Dysart, Queen's co., knt.
1730 ,, Robert, Dysart, Queen's co., esq.
1756 ,, Southwell, Cappard, Queen's co. esq. (Copy)
1673 ,, Thomas, Longashton, Somersetshire, esq. (Copy)
1729 ,, Thomas, Bannahery, Queen's co., esq.
1793 ,, Thomas, Knapton, Queen's co.
1790 ,, ven. William, archdeacon of Clonfert [See PICKETT.]
1760 **Pigou,** Paul, Wexford, esq.
1695 **Pigoux**, David, Licurde la grand Noué, minister of the Gos.
1808 **Pike,** Anne, widow of Ebenezer Pike, Cork

1774 **Pike,** Benjamin, Sundays Wells, near Cork
1760 ,, Deborah, Cork, widow
1785 ,, Ebenezer, Cork city, banker
1797 ,, Elizabeth, Rathangan, co. Kildare, widow
1729 ,, Joseph, Cork, merchant
1793 ,, Joseph, Rathangan, co. Kildare
1768 ,, Richard, Cork, merchant
1811 ,, Richard, Cork city, banker
1724 ,, Robert, Kilballyheniken
1660 ,, Roger, Castlekaile, co. Kilkenny, gent. [**VIII.** 95
1797 ,, Samuel, Cork city
1801 ,, Wright, Dublin city, merchant
1800 ,, William, Dublin, plumber
1749 **Pilkington**, Alice, Dublin, widow
1790 ,, Barbara, widow
1720 ,, Daniel, Waterford, merchant
1744 ,, Edward, Dublin, gent.
1759 ,, Elizabeth, Dublin, widow
1744 ,, Mary, widow of baron P.
1763 ,, Mary, Dublin, widow
1753 ,, Richard, Sligo, esq.
1680 ,, Stephen, The Inns, gent.
1740 ,, Thomas, Rathnure, co. Westmeath, gent.
1785 **Pilkinton,** Anne, Dublin
1791 ,, John, Harold's Cross, co. Dubl., gent.
1778 ,, Michael, Skaghanagh, co. Clare, farmer
1711 ,, Richard, Rathgarret, co. Westmeath, esq.
1792 **Pilley,** Peter, Kill, co. Galway, esq.
1624 **Pillin,** Thomas, St. Patrick's, Dublin
1779 **Pillsworth**, Benjamin, Exchequer-street, Dublin, bookbinder
1744 ,, Francis, Ballintemple, King's co., gent.
1744 ,, Francis, Lackan, co. Westmeath
1761 **Pilot,** John, Allenstown
1723 ,, Joshua, Tyrecoger, Queen's co. gent.
1772 ,, Joshua, Portarlington, M.D.
1792 **Pilsworth,** George, Rosenallis, Queen's co., gent.
1804 ,, Godwin, Dame-street, Dublin, woollen draper
1796 ,, Ponsonby, Fonstown, co. Kildare
1800 ,, William, Milltown, co. Kildare
1780 **Pim,** Catherine, relict of John Pim
1771 ,, Charles, Mountrath, Queen's co.
1802 ,, Elizabeth, Armer Mills, near Clonmel

1762 **Pim**, James, Rushin, Queen's co., farmer
1750 ,, John, the younger, Dublin, merchant
1752 ,, John, Edenderry, King's co., merchant
1773 ,, John, Nurney, co. Kildare
1777 ,, John, Lacka, Queen's co., gent.
1811 ,, John, Waterford city
1806 ,, Joseph, Ballinmurrinmore, co. Wicklow
1749 ,, Joshua, Mountrath, Queen's co.
1749 ,, Mary, Rushin, Queen's co., widow
1788 ,, Mary, Ballitore, co. Kildare, spinster
1801 ,, Mary, Mountrath, Queen's co.
1801 ,, Moses, Lacka, Queen's co.
1787 ,, Robert, Mountmellick, Queen's co., merchant
1764 ,, Samuel, Cork, clothier (Large will)
1786 ,, Saml., Waterford city, mercht.
1769 ,, Thomas, Tullylost, co. Kildare
1758 ,, Tobias, Rushin, Queen's co.
1734 ,, William, Edenderry, King's co. clothier
1800 ,, William, Rathangan
1809 **Pimm**, James, Rushin, Queen's co., farmer
1729 ,, Tobias, Edenderry, King's co., clothier
1723 **Pince**, Ages, par. St. Giles, Middlesex
1788 **Pinchin**, John, Limerick, woollen-draper
1787 ,, Michael, Limerick, clothier
1799 ,, Michael, Fort, Lib. of Limerick, gent.
1788 ,, Sarah, Limerick, widow
1767 **Pinckney**, Abigail, Kevin-street, Dublin, widow
1636 ,, Tobias, Brocurra, co. Wexford, farmer
1636 **Pincknsy**, Tobias, Brocurra, co. Wexford, farmer
1767 **Pindar**, Nathaniel, Birr, King's co., merchant
1681 **Pine**, Owen, Dublin, merchant
1742 **Pineau**, Benjamin, Dublin, gent.
1705 ,, Peter, Dublin, gent.
1749 **Pinsent**, Elizabeth, widow
1694 ,, John, clk., treas. of the diocese of Leighlin
1732 ,, Robert, Athy, co. Kildare, esq.
1787 ,, sir Robert, bart.
1689 **Pinsion**, Robert, Dublin, gent.

1636 **Pippard**, Christopher, Drogheda, merchant
1736 ,, Christopher, Drogheda, mercht.
1675 ,, George, Drogheda, alderman
1758 ,, Simon
1640 ,, Thomas, Drogheda, alderman
1660 **Pitchforke**, Nichls., Sligo, trooper,
1803 **Pitman**, Elizabeth   [**VIII**. 157
1794 **Pittman**, Andrew, Dublin, whip-maker
1792 ,, Elizabeth
1738 ,, Wm., Andrawmore, co. Cork (dated 1738)
1706 **Pitts**, Charles, Dublin, gent.
1786 ,, Chris. master of the Charter School, Castledermot
1751 ,, Edward, Dublin
1787 ,, Edward, Bola, co. Wicklow
1790 ,, Mary, mistress of Arklow Charter School
1666 ,, Thomas, Stokestown, mercht.
1735 **LaPlacette**, Catherine, Dubl., spr.
1747 **Plafay**, Claudius, Dublin
1757 **Plaince**, John, Dublin, brewer
1791 **Plaistow**, Richard, lieut.-general (Copy)
1800 **Plant**, James, Castleray, black-smith
1658 ,, Samuel, Dublin, currier   [**VII**. 78
1793 ,, Samuel, Coombe, co. Dublin
1808 ,, Thomas, Athlone, co. Rosc.
1811 **Pleasance**, Joseph, Dame-court, Dublin, tavern keeper
1771 **Pleasants**, Alice, Coolnamony, Queen's co., widow
1778 ,, Charles, Dublin, gent.
1762 ,, Joseph, Maryborough, Queen's co., gent.
1729 ,, Thomas, Dublin, alderman
1772 ,, William, Gt. Britain-st, Dubl., esq.
1708 **Pleydel**, William, Dublin, gent.
1643 **Pleydell**, sir Charles, Midgehall, Wiltshire, knt.
1810 ,, Jonathan M., Wilton House, Somersetshire (Copy)
1672 ,, Oliver, Tankardstown, co. Carlow, gent.
1656 **Plomer**, Edward, Liverpool, gent.   [**V**. 270
1766 **Plowman**, William, Grangebeg, co. Kildare   [gent.
1798 ,, William, Newtown, co. Kildare,
1723 **Plukenet**, Brook, esq.
1758 ,, major John, Coldblow, co. Dub.
1756 **Plumer** or **Plimer**, Elizabeth, Clontarf, co. Dublin, widow
1659 ,, Ellinor, Dublin, widow   [**VII**. 168

1801 **Plumer,** James, Dublin city, gent.
1809 ,, Mary, Stanhope - street, co. Dublin, widow
1728 **Plummer,** Daniel, Castlequin, co. Limerick, gent.
1759 ,, Gilbert, Clontarf, co. Dublin, bricklayer
1680 ,, John, archdeacon of Leighlin
1746 ,, John, Athlone, co. Roscommon, innkeeper
1749 ,, John, Dublin, bricklayer
1793 ,, John, Ballyrankin, co. Wexford, farmer
1768 ,, Richard, Clontarf, co. Dublin
1790 ,, Richard Gilbert, Clontarf, co. Dublin, gent.
1795 ,, Wm., Ballyrankin, co. Wexford, farmer
1673 **Plunket,** Alexander, Gibstown, co. Meath, gent.
1640 ,, Animett, *alias* **Bathe,** Drogheda, widow
1583 ,, dame Anne, wife to sir Chris. Creever [**I.** 49
1775 ,, Bart., Mantua, co. Kerry, gent.
1740 ,, Bridget, par. St. James, Westminster, widow (Copy)
1720 ,, Christopher, Lurganboy, co. Cavan, gent.
1599 ,, Edward, Lagore, co. Meath, gent. [farmer
1715 ,, Edward, Clonturk, co. Dublin,
1729 ,, Elizabeth, Dillonstown, co. Louth, widow
1659 ,, Ellinor, Portmarnock, co. Dublin, widow [**VIII.** 6
1681 ,, Ellinor, *alias* **Bermingham,** widow
1720 ,, Frances, Dublin, widow
1639 ,, Francis, Clonguffin, co. Meath, gent.
1605 ,, Gerald, Grange, co. Dublin
1784 ,, Henry, Dublin, woollendraper
1688 ,, Ignatius, Derpatrick, co. Meath, esq.
1583 ,, sir John, Dunsaghly, co. Dubl., knt. [**I.** 17
1588 ,, John, Loughcrew, co Meath, gent. (Copy from Meath)
1696 ,, John, Lurganboy, co. Cavan, gent. [**XVII.** 242
1738 ,, John, Coolglassny, co. Roscommon, gent.
1774 ,, John, Navan
1801 ,, John, Dublin, silk dyer
1635 ,, Jowan, *alias* **Long,** widow of Thomas P., Dublin, ald.
1636 ,, Luke, Dublin, merchant
1683 ,, Luke, Portmarnock, co. Dubl., gent.

1788 **Plunket,** Mary Anne, Tullaghanstown, co. Meath
1691 ,, Mathew, one of lord Louth's family, died abroad
1680 ,, sir Nicholas, Dublin, knt.
1745 ,, Oliver, Kinardmore, co. Roscommon, gent.
1780 ,, Oliver, Dublin, merchant
1708 ,, Patrick, Drogheda, merchant
1712 ,, Patrick, Rentstown, co. Meath, gent.
1774 ,, Penelope, spinster
1785 ,, Randal, Dublin, esq.
1626 ,, Thomas, Dublin, alderman
1669 ,, Thomas, Raestown, co. Meath, gent.
1728 ,, Thomas, Portmarnock, co. Dublin, gent.
1732 ,, hon. Thomas, Drogheda, esq.
1746 ,, Thomas, Dublin, peruke maker
1702 ,, sir Walter, Rathbeal, co. Dubl., knt.
1804 **Plunkett,** Alex., Gormanstown, co. Meath, gent.
1767 ,, Alice, Dublin, widow
1779 ,, Alice, Dublin, widow
1794 ,, Alice, Duffield, Derbyshire (Copy)
1736 ,, Andrew, Athboy, co. Meath, surgeon
1795 ,, Anne, Longwood, co. Meath, shopkeeper
1808 ,, Barnaby, Dublin city, gent.
1769 ,, Bridget, called lady Dunsanny
1726 ,, Catherine, Dublin, spinster
1750 ,, Catherine, Britain-st., Dublin, widow
1767 ,, Elinor, widow of Nathaniel P., Oxhill, co. Roscommon
1698 ,, Ellinor, Dirr Patrick, co. Meath, widow
1639 ,, Francis, Clonguffin, co. Meath, gent
1682 ,, Fras., Moate, co. Meath, gent.
1680 ,, Garret, Kinsale, merchant
1643 ,, George, Dublin, gent.
1749 ,, Henry, Dublin, merchant
1760 ,, Henry, Dublin, esq.
1765 ,, James, Dublin, gent.
1808 ,, James, Knocksavage, co. Monaghan, esq.
1736 ,, Jane, *alias* **Wallis,** Dub., spr.
1803 ,, honble. Jane, Dublin, spinster
1807 ,, Jane, wife to Jas. Plunkett, esq.
1675 ,, John, Knocklagh, co. Meath, gent.
1675 ,, John, Londonderry, alderman
1809 ,, John, Naas, co. Kildare, victualler
1772 ,, Joseph, Rocksavage, co. Mon

1755 **Plunkett**, Luke, Portmarnock, co. Dublin, gent.
1799 ,, Luke, Knowle, Warwickshire
1811 ,, Luke, Usher's-quay, Dublin
1768 ,, Mabella, Louth Hall, co. Louth, spinster
1806 ,, Mary, Harold's-cross, co. Dub.
1754 ,, Mathew, esq., commonly called Lord Louth
1796 ,, Hon. Mathew, Balbriggan, co. Dublin
1752 ,, Michael, Thomas-st., Dub., apothecary
1764 ,, Michael, Oxhill, co. Roscommon, gent.
1792 ,, Michael, Usher's-quay, Dublin, woollen draper
1795 ,, Michael, Longwood, co.'Meath, farmer
1705 ,, Nicholas, Dublin, esq.
1751 ,, Nicholas, Dunsaghly, co. Dub., esq.
1679 ,, Patrick, Terfeckan, co. Louth, gent.
1696 ,, Patrick, Tankrath, co. Meath, gent.
1734 ,, Patrick, Dublin, apothecary
1762 ,, Patrick, Knockrow, co. Rosc.
1809 ,, Patrick, Elmpark, co. Rosc.
1809 ,, Patrick, Dublin city, M.D.
1789 ,, Peter, Keeloges, co. Roscommon, gent.
1736 ,, Randal, commonly called Lord Dunsanny
1767 ,, Susanna, commonly called Dowager Lady Louth
1788 ,, Susanna, Arthurstown, co. Louth, spinster
1699 ,, Thomas, son of Robert P., Rathmore, co. Meath, esq.
1774 ,, Thomas, Donowen, co. Cavan
1650 ,, Wm., Dublin, esq.
1770 ,, Wm., Portmarnock, co. Dublin, gent.
1744 **Pocklington**, Edward, Dubl., gent.
1804 **Pockrick**, John, Derrylusk, co. Monaghan, gent.
1766 **Pocock**, Richd., bp. of **Meath**, q.v.
1699 **Podmore**, Arthur, Dublin, gent.
1767 ,, Arthur, Dublin
1722 ,, John, Dublin, esq.
1773 ,, Mary, Dublin, widow
1778 **Poe**, Elizabeth, Atherdee, co. Louth, spinster
1679 ,, Emanuel, Glankeily, co. Tipperary, gent.
1801 ,, Emanuel, Moyroe, co. Tip., gent.
1739 ,, James, Rosneharley, co. Tipperary, esq.

1756 **Poe**, James, Rosneharley, co. Tipperary, esq.
1768 ,, James, Drumgooldstown, co. Louth, esq.
1784 ,, James, Salborough, co. Tipperary, esq.
1745 ,, Mary, Dublin, widow.
1790 ,, Mary, Dublin, widow
1795 ,, Mary, widow
1751 ,, Purefoy, Rosneharley, co. Tipperary, esq.
1700 ,, Thomas, Clonmaghane, King's co., gent.
1682 ,, William, Manor Poe, co. Fermanagh, esq. (Ex.)
1709 **Poictenin**, James, Portarlington, King's co., gent.
1726 **Poirier**, Lewis, Dublin, gent.
1702 **Polden**, Hugh, Cork, merchant
1785 **Pole**, Charles, of the 3rd regiment of guards (Copy)
1763 ,, Edward, Parkhall, Derbyshire, lieut.-general (Copy)
1685 ,, Nathaniel, Geraldstown, co. Meath, esq.
1788 ,, Olivia, widow of lieut.-gen. Pole
1744 ,, Sarah, Dublin, spinster
1782 ,, William, Ballyfin, Queen's co., esq. (Large)
[See POOLE.]
1637 **Polexfen**, John, Dubl., esq.
[IV., 233
[See POLLEXFIN.]
1763 **Pollard**, Anna Maria, Dub., widow
1740 ,, Dillon, Castlepollard, co. Westmeath, esq.
1804 ,, Dillon, Castlepollard, co. Westmeath, esq.
1799 ,, John, Archerstown, co. Westmeath, esq.
1700 ,, rev. Thomas, Dublin, clerk
1722 ,, Thomas, co. Longford, clerk
1718 ,, Walter, Castlepollard, co. Westmeath
1729 ,, Wm., Royal Hospital, Dublin
1796 ,, Wm., Castlepollard, co. Westmeath
1663 **Pollexfin**, James, Dublin, gent.
[See POLEXFEN.]
1781 **Pollock**, James, the elder, Newry, co. Down, merchant
1724 ,, John, Dublin, innholder
1785 ,, John, Newry, co. Down, mercht.
1742 ,, Rbt., Newry, co. Down, mercht.
1748 **Pollox**, John, gent.
[See POLLOCK.]
1724 **Pomeroy**, John, archdn. of Cork
1790 ,, John, lieutenant-general of His Majesty's Forces
1703 ,, Samuel, Pallis, co. Cork, gent.

1707 **Pomeroy**, Mary, par. St. Martin, Middlesex, widow (Copy)
1802 **Pommorrett**, Abraham, Dublin city
1765 **Pomore**, Sam., Waterford, merchant
1764 **Ponsonby**, Chambre Brabazon, Ashgrove, co. Kilkenny, esq.
1706 ,, Dame Elizabeth
1796 ,, rt. hon. lady Elizabeth
1746 ,, Folliott, captain in col. Braggs' regiment
1751 ,, Lady Frances
1770 ,, lady Frances, widow of major-general Henry P.
1681 ,, Henry, Garryna, co. Kerry, esq.
1691 ,, sir Henry, Hillsborough, co. Down, knt.
1745 ,, Henry, brigadier-general
1679 ,, sir John, knt. (Ex.)
1797 ,, John, Dublin, esq.
1793 ,, Margaret
1764 ,, Richard, Crollagh, or Crotto, co. Kerry, esq.
1800 ,, Richard, kingdom of Ireland
1717 ,, Thomas, Garrinea, co. Kerry, esq.
1782 ,, William, Carrigue, Cloghers, co. Kerry, esq.
1764 **Ponty**, James, Dublin, brazier
1636 **Pooely**, Wm., Rathcoole, co. Dubl.
1773 **Poole**, Ann, Carlow, widow
1656 ,, Dan., Belfast, mercht. [**V**. 295
1657 ,, captain Hugh. [**VI**. 219
1764 ,, Jacob, Black Pitts, co. Dublin, brewer
1804 ,, Jacob, Dublin city, alderman
1807 ,, Jas, Dame-st., Dub., jeweller
1750 ,, Mary, Ballyanker, co. Waterford, widow
1767 ,, Michael, Dublin, carpenter
1704 ,, Periam, Ballyfin, esq.
1714 ,, Richard, Dublin, gent.
1752 ,, Richard, Carlow
1789 ,, Samuel, Clonkeen, farmer
1808 ,, Sarah, Dublin city
1746 ,, Thomas, Ballyanker, co. Waterford, gent.
1772 ,, Thomas, Dub., tinplate worker
1784 ,, Thomas, Tallow, co. Waterford, gent.
[See POLE, POWELL.]
1767 **Pooler**, William
1712 **Pooley**, rt. rev. John, bp. of Raphoe
1643 ,, Thomas, Dundalk, gent., lieutenant in garrison there
1722 ,, Thomas, Dublin, esq.
1798 **Poor**, Richard, English Harbour, Antigua (Copy)
1667 **Poore**, Nicholas, trumpeter to earl Drogheda's troop of horse

1616 **Poore**, Richard, Ballyfermot, co. Dublin, husbandman [See POWER.]
1701 **Pope**, Edward, Dublin, esq.
1591 ,, Roger, Dublin, gent.
1766 ,, Sarah, Dublin, widow
1780 ,, Sarah, Bristol city, widow (Copy)
1775 ,, Thomas, lieut.-col of the 2nd horse
1718 ,, William, Cork, brewer
1738 ,, William, Cork, merchant
1741 ,, William, Cork, merchant
1801 **Popham**, Thomas, Dublin
1553 **Popingay**, Edmond
1737 **Portall**, John, Dublin, gent.
1795 ,, Magdalene, Dublin, spinster
1799 **Portarlington**, John, earl of
1807 **Portavine**, Remon, Ringsend, Dublin
1736 **Porter**, Anne, Dublin, spinster
1743 ,, Arabella, Dublin, widow
1795 ,, Frederick, Strabane
1781 ,, James, Strabane, co. Tyrone, merchant
1739 ,, John, Dublin, alderman
1789 ,, John, St. Martin-in-the-Fields, Middlesex
1727 ,, Mary Anne, Dublin, spinster
1729 ,, Mary, Dublin, widow
1774 ,, Mary, Redcross, co. Wicklow, farmer
1654 ,, Richard, Rathcoole, co.Dublin, yeoman
1799 ,, Richard, Milltown, co.Donegal, farmer
1678 ,, Robert, Dublin, gent.
1723 ,, Robert, Dublin, gent.
1734 ,, Robt., Farganstown, co.Meath, gent.
1746 ,, Simon, Carrinchagain, co. Cavan, esq.
1775 ,, Thomas, par. Ballintogher, King's co., late commander of the "Viper" sloop of war
1782 ,, Thomas, Waterford, esq.
1638 ,, William, Oldbridge, co. Meath, gent.
1700 ,, William, Liverpool, Lancashire, merchant
1742 ,, William, Birt, co. Donegal, merchant
1778 ,, William, Dunnabore, co. Armagh
1790 ,, William, Digges-street, Dublin
1781 **Porteus**, Thomas, Smithfield, Dubl., saddler
1630 **Portingal**, Jasper, Youghal, merchant

1761 **Portis**, George, Belfast, esq.
1799 ,, rev. George Macartney, Carlingford, co. Louth
1630 **Portle**, David FitzNicholas,Cashel, burgess (Copy)
1739 **Portlock**, James, Ormond-market, Dublin, butcher
1769 **Pott**, Elizabeth, Castle-st., par. St. Mary's-le-Bone, Middlesex
1765 **Potter**, Alexander, Ballow, co. Down
1706 ,, Allin, Dublin, distiller
1800 ,, Dorothea Josepha
1762 ,, Edmond, Ballygaddy, King's co., gent.
1771 ,, Frances, Kevin's Port, Dublin, spinster
1802 ,, Francis, Old Castle, co. Cork, esq.
1749 ,, John, Killinchy, co. Down, merchant
1754 ,, John, Ardmullin, co. Down
1802 ,, John, Downpatrick
1810 ,, John, Fort Union, co. Limerick, esq.
1802 ,, Samuel, Camden-street, co. Dublin, esq.
1803 ,, Thomas, Ballymacaveon, co. Down, esq.
1666 ,, William, Dublin, gent.
1738 **Potterton**, John, Rathcormick, co. Meath, gent.
1756 ,, Thomas, Rathcormick, co. Meath, gent.
1723 **Potts**, Anne, Drogheda, widow
1800 ,, Elizabeth, Dublin, widow
1796 ,, James, Dublin, printer and stationer
1804 ,, Jane, Athlone, co. Roscommon
1591 ,, John, Waterford, physician
[I. 80
1626 ,, John, Cannycourt, co. Kildare, gent.
1738 ,, John, Athlone, merchant
1760 ,, John, Belfast, co. Antrim, merchant
1717 ,, rev. Lawrence, Staplestown,co. Carlow, clk.
1670 ,, Richard, Priclure in Scotland, gent.
1771 ,, Samuel, Tenemuck, King's co., gent.
1742 ,, Thomas, Dublin, merchant
1800 ,, William, Athlone, co. Westmeath, gent.
1781 **Poujade**, Jane, Dublin, widow
1695 **Poulter**, Anthony, Bolton, co. Kildare, gent.
1746 ,, Jane, *alias* **Bingham**, Dublin, widow

1789 **Poulter**, rev. Joseph, Dunkitt, co. Kilkenny, clk.
1794 **Pounden**, Francis Joshua John
1799 ,, Jane Maria, Enniscorthy, co. Wexford, widow
1802 ,, John, Daphne, co. Wexford
1805 ,, Joshua, Dublin city, mercht
1786 ,, Mary, Enniscorthy, co. Wexford, merchant
1774 ,, Richard, Ennsicorthy, co. Wexford
1810 ,, Robert, Chamber-st., Dublin
1771 **Pountney**, William, Nangor, co. Dublin, clk.
1666 **Pourfield**, Christian, *alias* **Warren**, widow of James P., of the Wade, co. Dublin, farmer
1725 **Pourguiere**, Theodore, Clonmel, co. Tipperary, vintner
1679 **Povey**, Elizabeth, spinster
1742 ,, Richard, Dublin, esq.
1778 ,, Sarah, Dublin, spinster
1801 **Powel**, lady Anne, Dublin
1746 ,, Charles, Dublin, linendraper
1751 ,, Elizabeth, Cashel, co. Tipp., widow
1692 ,, Cornet Giles, Quilterro, co. Tipperary
1801 ,, Judith, Dublin
1801 ,, Mary Anne, Dublin, spinster
1747 ,, Richard,Newgarden,co. Limk., esq.
1774 ,, Richard, Elmgrove,King's co., esq.
1742 ,, Robert, Cloghwiller, co. Limk., esq.
1775 ,, Samuel, Dublin, printer
1741 ,, Thomas, Glasnevin, co. Dublin staymaker
1751 ,, William, Dublin, merchant
1765 **Powell**, Adam, Kilmakeon, co. Sligo, gent.
1683 ,, Benjamin, Waterford, mercht.
1794 ,, Caleb, Dublin city, esq.
1797 ,, Caleb, Newtownperry, Limk., esq.
1715 ,, Charles, Shankill,co. Kilkenny, gent.
1684 ,, Elizabeth, Mitchelstown, co. Limerick, widow
1729 ,, Elizabeth, Dublin, widow
1774 ,, Eyre Evans, Prospect, co. Limerick, esq.
1800 ,, Eyre Burton, Dublin, esq.
1763 ,, Francis, Knockballymore, co. Fermanagh, yeoman
1784 ,, George
1733 ,, Giles, Glintary, co. Limerick, esq.
1804 ,, Giles, Cork city, gent.

1701 **Powell,** Hugh, capt. in sir John Hammer's regt.
1778 ,, Isaac, Fortwilliam, co. Sligo, gent.
1810 ,, James, Kellyville, Queen's co.
1811 ,, James, Powelsborough
1755 ,, John, Dublin
1763 ,, John, Templeogue, co. Dublin, gent.
1766 ,, John, Cork, woollen draper
1790 ,, rev. John, Dublin, clk.
1785 ,, Judith, Dublin, widow
1658 ,, Richard, Limerick, apothecary [VII. 34
1684 ,, Robert, St. Francis-st., Dubl., chandler and soap boiler
1761 ,, Robert, Southern, co. Meath, esq.
1769 ,, Robert, Bandon town, pewterer
1783 ,, Robert, Limerick, gent.
1787 ,, Robert, Limerick, gent.
1672 ,, Samuel, Goffaye, Denbighshire, esq.
1730 ,, Sarah, Drombee, co. Armagh
1805 ,, Sarah, widow
1759 ,, Stratford
1799 ,, Thomas, Dublin, gent.
1662 ,, William, trooper [IX. 74
1677 ,, William, Dublin, gent.
1762 ,, William, Dublin, apothecary (Large will)
1792 ,, William, Usher's-court, pawnbroker [See POOLE.]
1805 **Power,** Alex., Ballygallane, co. Waterford, M.D.
1776 ,, Ambrose, Barretstown, co. Tipperary, esq.
1751 ,, Anthony, Rathruddy, co. Galway, gent.
1769 ,, Anthony, Dublin, merchant
1758 ,, Anne, *alias* **Wall**, Waterford, widow
1740 ,, Arthur, Fermoy, co. Cork, innholder
1703 ,, Bridget, *alias* **Thorington**, widow
1785 ,, Catherine, Georgetown, co. Waterford
1698 ,, David, Ballinegrave, co. Galway, esq. [ford
1780 ,, David, Knockaderry, co. Water-
1803 ,, David, Merrion-sq., Dub., esq.
1788 ,, Dominick, Loughrea, co. Galway, gent.
1738 ,, Edmond, Cahir Creagh, co. Galway, gent.
1772 ,, Edmond, Carrick, co. Tipp.
1789 ,, Edmond, Garnavelly, co. Tipperary, esq.

1807 **Power,** Edmond, Mayor's-walk, Waterford
1723 ,, Edward, Waterford, merchant
1757 ,, Edward, Dublin, merchant
1784 ,, Edward, Dorset-st., Dubl., esq.
1802 ,, Edwd., Knockaderry, co. Waterford
1804 ,, Edward, Waterpark, co. Clare, gent.
1734 ,, Elizabeth, Ballygarron, co. Waterford, widow
1747 ,, Elizabeth, Dublin, widow
1805 ,, Elizabeth, Nenagh, co. Tipp.
1805 ,, Ellinor, Loughrea, co. Galway, widow
1720 ,, Francis, Dublin, esq.
1755 ,, Francis, Roskeen, co. Cork, gt.
1799 ,, Francis, Maynooth, co. Kildare, esq.
1775 ,, Hodder, Ballea, co. Cork, gent.
1790 ,, Hugh, Seafield, co. Waterford
1796 ,, rev. James, parish priest of St. Michael's, co. Waterford
1802 ,, James, par. St. Martin, city of Westminister (Copy)
1806 ,, James, Youghal, co. Cork
1735 ,, Jane, Kilkenny, widow
1670 ,, Jeffrey, Meelick, co. Clare, gent.
1675 ,, John, Clonmel, merchant
1686 ,, John, Clashmore, co. Waterford, esq. (Ex.)
1694 ,, John, Inishane, co. Waterford, gent.
1740 ,, John, Clashmore
1743 ,, John, Barretstown, co. Tipperary, esq.
1746 ,, John, Dublin, gent.
1749 ,, John, Waterford (dated 1749, revoked)
1754 ,, John, Clashmore, co. Waterford, gent.
1764 ,, John, Dublin, brewer
1770 ,, John, capt. of the ship " Rump and Dozen "
1789 ,, John, Graigue, co. Kilkenny
1806 ,, John, Rosheen, co. Cork, esq.
1810 ,, John, Clogheen, co. Waterford
1765 ,, Joseph, Loughrea, co. Galway, esq.
1799 ,, Joseph, Ennis, co. Clare, gent.
1777 ,, Laurence, Bolindesert, co. Waterford, gent.
1807 ,, Margaret, Kilworth, co. Cork
1679 ,, Mary, widow of Alex. P. FitzGerald, Coolmore, co. Tipperary, bart.
1769 ,, Mary, Dublin
1771 ,, Mary, widow of Francis P., Roskeen, co. Cork, gent.

1772 **Power**, Mary, Ennis, co. Clare, widow
1802 ,, Mary, Ennis, co. Clare, widow
1775 ,, Maurice, Tyroe, co. Waterford, gent.
1679 ,, Milo, Kilkenny, esq.
1657 ,, Nicholas, Kilballykiltie, co. Waterford, esq. [**VI.** 163
1754 ,, Nicholas, Magehy, co. Waterterford, gent.
1788 ,, Nicholas, Rathgormuck, co. Waterford, esq.
1795 ,, Nicholas, Ballymakill, co. Waterford, esq.
1809 ,, Patrick, Dublin city, M.D.
1809 ,, Patrick, Lisready, co. Limerick, gent.
1749 ,, Paul, Ardapadin, co. Waterford, gent.
1673 ,, Peter, Loughrea, co. Galway, merchant
1695 ,, Pierce, Knocklaher, co. Waterford, esq.
1717 ,, Pierce, Glassy, co. Waterford, gent.
1769 ,, Pierce, Kingfarmer, co. Cork
1790 ,, Pierse, Roskeen, co. Cork, gt.
1684 ,, Richard, Carrigline, co. Cork, gent.
1706 ,, Richard, Ballindrummy, co. Galway, esq.
1731 ,, Richd., Cork-street, Dublin, gt.
1752 ,, Richard, Dublin, merchant
1755 ,, Richard, Limerick, mariner
1765 ,, Richard, Queen's-st., Dublin, innholder
1793 ,, Richard, 2nd baron of the Exchequer
1798 ,, Richard, Ferrybank, Lib. of Waterford
1798 ,, Richard, Clonkerdan
1741 ,, Robert, Aston's-quay, Dublin, merchant
1758 ,, Robert, Usher's-quay, Dublin, merchant
1795 ,, Robert, Powersgrove, co. Kildare, esq.
1803 ,, Robert, Waterford, merchant
1808 ,, Robert John, Waterford city
1634 ,, Thomas Fitz Edmond, Waterford, gent.
1688 ,, Thomas, Parke Drumbaney, Limerick city, counsellor-at-law
1734 ,, Thomas, Gaveanmorris, co. Waterford, gent.
1753 ,, Thomas, Carrick, co. Tipp., clothier
1779 ,, Thomas, Ennis, co. Clare, gent.
1799 ,, Thomas, Kilworth, co. Cork

1811 **Power**, Thomas, Waterford city
1688 ,, Valentine, Clashmore, co. Waterford, gent.
1639 ,, William, Dublin, blacksmith
1677 ,, William, Ballynegilkie, co. Waterford, esq.
1755 ,, William, Gurteen, co. Waterford, gent.
1762 ,, William, Limerick, clothier
1808 ,, William, Cloyne, co. Cork [See POORE.]
1765 **Powerscourt**, Edward, lord visct.
1722 ,, Folliott, lord viscount
1632 ,, sir Richd. Wingfield, knt., lord viscount (and his declaration) [**IV.** 82
1751 ,, Richard, lord viscount
1788 ,, right hon. Richard, lord visct.
1809 ,, right hon. Richard, lord visct.
1805 **Powis**, right hon. George Edward Henry Arthur, earl of
1742 **Powlett**, sir Nassau, knight of the Bath, commonly called lord Nass. P. (Copy) [See PAULETT.]
1733 **Poynton**, John, Dublin, cordwainer
1776 ,, John, Ballymahony, co. Longford
1685 **Poyntz**, sir John, Acton, Gloucestershire, knt. (Copy)
1708 ,, Lucas, Acton, co. Armagh, gt.
1772 **Pratt**, Anne, Dublin, widow
1706 ,, Benj., Aherpallice, co. Meath, esq.
1721 ,, Dr. Benjamin, dean of Down
1771 ,, Benjamin, Agher Palace, co. Meath, esq.
1778 ,, Edward, Workington, Cumberland, tailor
1804 ,, James, Castlemartyr, co. Cork, esq.
1733 ,, Jonah, Castlemartyr, co. Cork, merchant
1701 ,, Joseph, Dublin, esq.
1705 ,, Joseph, Cabra, co. Cavan, esq.
1793 ,, Joseph, Cabra Castle, co. Cavan, clk.
1811 ,, Luke, Newmarket, co. Kilk., gt.
1751 ,, Mervyn, Cabra, co. Cavan, esq.
1798 ,, Mervyn, Cabra Castle, co. Cavan, esq.
1793 ,, Robert, portreeve of Castlemartyn
1754 ,, Rupert, lieut. in Royal Regiment of Fusiliers
1803 ,, Sarah, Hermitage, co. Cork
1770 ,, v. rev. William, dean of Cloyne
1771 **Prendergast**, dame Anne, *alias* **William**, wife to Terence Prendergast (Copy)

1788 **Prendergast**, Edmond, Cahir, co. Tipperary, gent.
1801 ,, Edmond, Irgloony, co. Galway, gent.
1659 ,, Geffrey, Kilkenny, apothecary
1771 ,, Henry, lieut. in the 4th regt. of horse
1770 ,, James, Lackan, co. Tipperary, gent.
1792 ,, James, Dublin, gent.
1736 ,, Jeffry, Croane, co. Tipperary, esq.
1747 ,, Jeffry, Mullagh, co. Tipperary, esq.
1717 ,, John, Rathmore, co. Galway, gent.
1752 ,, John
1787 ,, John, Dublin, merchant
1803 ,, John, Castlebar, co. Mayo, M.D.
1776 ,, Lucy, Youghal, co. Cork, wid.
1772 ,, Mary, Ballomasney, co. Tipp., widow
1768 ,, Patrick, Ballynastandford, co. Mayo, M.D.
1746 ,, Penelope, lady, widow
1793 ,, Richard, Tuam, co. Galway
1805 ,, Sarah, Dublin city, widow
1627 ,, Thos. FitzGeffry, Newcastle, co. Tipperary, esq.
1709 ,, sir Thomas, Dublin, bart.
1760 ,, sir Thomas, bart., and Privy Councillor
1804 ,, Thomas, Dublin city, esq.
1754 ,, Valentine, Cullinagh, co, Cork
1691 ,, Walter, Dublin, apothecary
1722 ,, William, Dublin, baker
1746 ,, William, Dublin, gent.
 [See PENDER.]
1787 **Prentice**, Daniel, Rathmines, co. Dublin, gent.
1772 ,, Francis, Dublin, gent.
1749 ,, Robert, Dublin, merchant
1747 **Prescott**, Richard, North Clonmore, co. Tipperary, esq.
1625 ,, William, Drogheda, innholder
1777 **Presly**, John, Dublin, farmer
1771 ,, Paul, Dublin, widow
1693 **Pressick**, John, Kilbrican, co. Kilkenny, gent.
1737 **Preston**, Alice, Dublin, widow
1778 ,, Alice, Dublin, widow
1722 ,, Anthony, commonly called lord viscount Gormanstown
1788 ,, Arthur, esq.
1791 ,, Catherine
1770 ,, Elizabeth, Dublin, spinster
1756 ,, Frances, city of Bath, widow
1751 ,, Henry, Rathdown, co. Wicklow, gent.

1801 **Preston**, rev. Hy. Thos., Treffans, co. Meath
1674 ,, sir James, knt.
1805 ,, James, Londonderry city, woollendraper
1800 ,, Jane, Wexford town
1686 ,, John, Dublin, alderman
1703 ,, John, Ardsallagh, co. Meath, esq.
1753 ,, John, Lazer's-hill, Dublin, grocer
1758 ,, John, Ballinter, co. Meath, esq.
1754 ,, Joseph, esq.
1639 ,, Margaret, daughter to Jenico, late viscount Gormanstown
1802 ,, Margaret (Copy)
1704 ,, Mary, Dublin, widow
1758 ,, Mary, Gormanstown, co. Meath (not proved)
1757 ,, Nathaniel, Dublin, esq. (not proved)
1760 ,, Nathaniel, Swainstown, co. Meath, esq.
1796 ,, Nathaniel, Swainstown, co. Meath, clk.
1788 ,, rev. Plunkett, Castlerea, co. Limerick, clk.
1578 ,, Robert, Balmaddon par., co. Meath
1736 ,, Robert, Dublin, brewer
1795 ,, rev. Samuel, Clonegath, co. Kildare, clk.
1807 ,, Sarah
1654 ,, Thomas, co. of Dublin city, merchant
1732 ,, Thomas, Dublin, gent.
1785 ,, Thomas, Dublin
1792 ,, Thomas, Dublin, esq.
1599 ,, William, St. Patrick's-street, Dublin, butcher
1618 ,, Wm., Rogerstown, co. Meath, gent.
1789 ,, William, bp. of **Ferns**, q. v.
1738 **Prettie**, Henry, Kilboy, co. Tipperary, esq.
1740 **Preyse**, Walter, mariner
1764 **Price**, Andrew, Woodfarm, co. Wicklow, gent.
1673 ,, Anne, widow of John P., lately deceased
1752 ,, Arthur, abp. of **Cashel**, q. v.
1638 ,, Bartholomew, clk., prebendary of Mullogh Inonagh, co. Tipperary
1735 ,, Danett, Oundell, Northamptonshire, silk merchant (Copy)
1756 ,, David, Ballilehane, Queen's co., esq.
1778 ,, rev. David, vicar of Ballyshehan, diocese of Cashel

1691 **Prior**, Thos., Rathdowney, Queen's county, esq. (Ex.)
1751 ,, Thomas, Dublin, esq.
1780 **Pritchet**, Catherine, Dubl., spinster
1782 ,, Walter, Frankford, King's county, gent.
1789 **Pritchett**, Francis, Killyon, King's county
1765 ,, Symon, Killyon, King's county, gent.
1656 ,, Thomas, waggoner to the train of artillery [**VI.** 44
1754 ,, William, Dublin, mariner
1794 **Prittie**, Deborah, Cloughjordan, co. Tipperary, widow
1702 ,, Elizabeth, Kilboy, co. Tipp., widow
1768 ,, Hy., Kilboy, co. Tipperary, esq.
1726 **Proby**, rev. Charles, Damastown, co. Dublin, clk.
1730 ,, Thomas, Dublin, surgeon
1671 **Procter**, Thomas, Clare, co. Armagh, gent.
1744 ,, Thomas
1724 **Proctor**, Bryan, St. Luke's par., Dublin, locksmith
1648 ,, captain Thomas
1702 ,, Thomas, Symonds-court, co. Dublin, gent.
1748 ,, Thomas
1776 ,, Thomas, Dublin, cooper
1787 ,, Thomas, Clonraney, co. Wexford, farmer
1776 **Prossor**, Elizabeth, Nunstown, co. Kerry, widow
1754 ,, James, Carlow
1709 ,, Phil., Finglas, co. Dub., brewer
1802 ,, Sarah, Ballyfermott Castle, co. Dublin
1808 ,, Wm. O., Ballyfermott Castle, co. Dublin
1748 **Prothero**, Elizabeth, Dublin
1686 **Proud**, Alice, Ashfield, co. Meath, widow
1692 ,, George, vicar of Trim
1669 ,, Nicholas, D.D., co. Meath
1719 ,, Richard, York-st., Dub., gent.
1634 **Proudfoot**, John, Proudfootstown
1655 ,, Margaret, *alias* **Talbot**, widow of John P. [**V.** 189
1675 ,, Mary, Dublin, spinster
1725 ,, Robert, Earl-st., Dublin, woolcomber
1747 **Provand**, Elizabeth, Dublin, widow
1757 ,, Robert, Dublin, gent.
1776 **Pryoe**, John, Nyoddfaith, Montgomeryshire, esq.
[See **Price.**]
1672 **Puckle**, John, New Ross, co. Wexford, esq.

1760 **Pue**, James, William-st., Dublin
1762 ,, James, Dublin, printer
1657 ,, John, Dub., alderman [**VI.** 123
1758 ,, Richard, Dublin, painter
1809 ,, Robt., Shraheen, co. Mayo, esq.
1727 **Pugh**, Hugh, Dublin, merchant
1701 **Puisar**, Lewis James Le Vascur Congues, Dublin, esq.
1730 **Pujose**, Peter, Limerick, merchant
1753 **Pullatt**, Elizabeth, widow
1667 **Pullein**, Samuel, archbishop of **Tuam**, q. v.
1784 ,, rev. Samuel
1715 ,, Tobias, bishop of **Dromore**, q.v.
1668 ,, William, Bolclare, Tuam, esq.
1721 ,, Wm., Treasurer of the Chapter of Dromore
1769 **Pulleine**, Jane, widow of rev. Dr. Joshua P.
1778 ,, John
1787 ,, rev. Joshua, rector of Clonallen, co. Down
1670 **Pullin**, Richard, Ballyrahin, co. Wicklow, cooper
1727 **Pullman**, Thomas, Dublin, tallow chandler
1766 **Pumphrey**, John, Cork, woollendraper
1711 **Purcel**, captain John, esq., Conihy (see 1775)
1782 ,, Redmond, Kilkenny city, gent.
1777 ,, Richard, Templemary, co. Cork, esq.
1597 ,, Thomas, Waterford
1597 ,, Thomas Baron, Loughmore, co. Tipperary
1758 **Purcell**, Amy, Cork, esq.
1805 ,, Andrew, Clonfad, co. Westmeath, farmer
1800 ,, Catherine, Glandmore, co. Cork, widow
1790 ,, Elinor, Roscommon town, wid.
1622 ,, Ellan, Widdingstown, co. Tipperary, widow
1738 ,, Ellis, Loughmore, co. Tipperary, widow
1733 ,, Frances, Dublin, spinster
1779 ,, Frances, heretofore of Crumlin, late of Dublin, spinster
1789 ,, Goodwin, Kanturk, co. Cork
1793 ,, Ignatius, Usher's Island, Dub., esq.
1752 ,, James, Waterford, merchant
1799 ,, James, Dublin, publican
1809 ,, James, Altamont, Liberties of Kilkenny
1810 ,, rev. James, parish priest of Maycoomb
1687 ,, John, Cloghtea, co. Kilkenny, M.D.

1704 **Purcell**, John, Dublin, merchant
1706 ,, captain John, Conohy (not proved)
1747 ,, John, High-st., Dubl., woollen-draper
1770 ,, John, Templemary, co. Cork, gent.
1779 ,, John, Roscommon
1793 ,, John, Kilkenny city, merchant
1717 ,, Margaret, Dublin, widow
1742 ,, Mary, Cork, spinster
1767 ,, Mary, Knockroe, co. Kilk., spr.
1801 ,, Mary, Templemary, co. Cork, widow
1616 ,, Nicholas, Dublin, tanner
1810 ,, Nicholas, Kilkenny city, esq.
1714 ,, Philip, Kilcock
1802 ,, Pierce, Altemora, co. Cork, esq.
1753 ,, Redmond, Grove, co. Kilkenny, gent.
1711 ,, Richard, Dublin, brewer
1799 ,, Richard, clk.
1683 ,, Robert, Dublin, gent.
1692 ,, Robert, Croagh, co. Limerick, esq.
1719 ,, Rose, Dublin, widow
1623 ,, Thomas, Ballymore Eustace, co. Dublin, freeholder
1774 ,, Thomas, Ballybritt, King's co., farmer
1802 ,, Thomas, Cork, clothier
1752 ,, Toby, Archersgrove, co. Kilkenny, gent.
1788 ,, Toby, Aston's-quay, Dublin, surveyor
1679 ,, William, Crumlin, co. Dub., gt.
1728 ,, William, Kanturk
1749 **Purcy**, Thomas, Dublin, brazier
1724 **Purdon**, Bartholomew, Ballyclogh, co. Cork, esq.
1762 ,, Bartholomew, Ballyclogh, co. Cork, esq.
1790 ,, Charles, Lisnabin, co. Westmeath
1787 ,, Edward, Lisnabin, co. Westmeath, esq.
1755 ,, George, Dysert, co. Cork, esq.
1745 ,, Helena, widow (not proved)
1790 ,, Helena, co. Dublin
1738 ,, Henry, Little Island, co. Cork, esq.
1783 ,, Henry, Rockspring, co. Cork, farmer
1802 ,, Henry, Carristown, co. Westmeath, esq.
1801 ,, John, Charlemont, co. Dublin
1802 ,, Mary Anne, widow
1702 ,, Nicholas, Dysart, co. Cork, gt.
1749 ,, Simon, Bulkelly, co. Clare, esq.

1792 **Purdon,** Simon, New Garden, co. Limerick, esq.
1720 ,, Symon, Tinnerana, co. Clare, gent.
1777 ,, William, Finglas, co. Dublin
1658 **Purdue**, Cornet John, par. Ballynoe, co. Cork, gent.
1699 **Purefoy**, Brazill, Dublin, gent. (Ex.) (Large will)
1707 ,, Gamebel, Clanbullock or Purefoy's-place, King's co., esq.
1725 ,, James, Gortnakelly, co. Galway, esq.
1800 ,, James, Woodfield, co. Galway
1701 ,, John, Dublin, merchant
1790 ,, Thomasan, Dublin
1699 ,, William, Purefoy's-pl., King's co., esq.
1737 ,, William, Dublin, esq.
1797 ,, William, Cork city, esq. [See PURFOY.]
1749 **Purey**, Thomas, Dublin, brazier
1606 **Purfel**, Wm., Kilshane, co. Dublin, farmer
1699 **Purfield**, Andrew, Kilshane, co. Dublin, farmer
1801 ,, Esther, Dublin, widow
1775 ,, Thomas, Dublin, baker
1800 ,, Thomas, Dublin, gent.
1793 ,, William, Summerfield, Dublin, measurer
1673 **Purfoy**, Arthur, Shreene, co. Meath, esq. (Ex.) [See PUREFOY.]
1715 **Purnell**, Abagail, Castle of Antrim, widow
1694 **Purves**, John, London, surgeon
1758 **Putland**, George, Fulham parish, Middlesex (Copy)
1800 ,, Jane, Dublin city, spinster
1772 ,, John, Dublin, esq.
1810 ,, John, Durham-place, Surrey, esq.
1790 ,, Martha, Fulham parish, Middlesex, spinster (Copy)
1738 ,, Sisson, Little Barkamstead, Hertfordshire, esq (Copy)
1721 ,, Thomas, Dublin, esq.
1723 ,, Thomas, late of Dublin, merchant, now at Chelsea, esq. (Copy)
1749 **Puxley**, Henry, Beerhaven, co. Cork, esq.
1805 ,, Henry, Crosshaven, co. Cork, esq.
1755 ,, John, Beerhayen, co. Cork, gt.
1657 **Pyatt**, Richard, par. Kildrumfarten, co. Cavan   [**VI.** 144
1722 **Pyers**, Roger, Kilpipe, co. Wicklow, gent.

1682 **Pyke,** John, senior, Woodenstown, co. Tipperary, gent.
1714 ,, John, Waddington, co. Tipperary, esq.
1738 ,, John, Ashpark, co. Tipp., gent.
1657 **Pyman,** John, Belturbet, co. Cavan, gent.
1803 **Pyne,** Cornelius, Clonmel, co. Tipperary, merchant
1796 ,, Elizab., Dunmanway, co. Cork
1674 ,, Henry, Ballyneglass, co. Cork gent. **[XIV.** 209
1713 ,, Henry, Waterford, co. Cork
1811 ,, John, Lisgoold, co. Cork
1604 ,, Nicholas
1711 ,, Richard, knt.
1807 ,, Richard, Ballyvolan, co. Cork, esq. (Copy)
1634 **Pynney,** Thomas, Kilcleagh, par. Clogher, co. Fermanagh, gt.
1788 **Pynsent,** sir Robert, bart.
1738 **Pyatt,** Richd., Streethay, Staffordshire, esq.
1610 **Pypho,** Robert, St. Mary's Abbey, co. Dublin, esq.

—Q—

1779 **Quaile,** Michael, Swords, co. Dubl., innkeeper
1709 **Quale,** Richard, mariner on board the "Seaford" man-of-war [See QUAYLE.]
1752 **Quane,** Richard, Dublin, merchant [See COANE.]
1616 **Quarrellus,** Jonas, Cantrelstown
1779 **Quarry,** John, Johnstown, co. Waterford, esq.
1656 **Quatermas,** Roose, Greenoke, co. Meath, spinister
1751 **Quatermass,** Patk., Birr, King's co.
1735 **Quayle,** Wm., Dublin, alderman [See QUALE.]
1742 **Quaytrod,** rev. Nicholas, Kilcanaway, co. Cork, clk.
1803 **Queade,** the hon. Grace, Dublin
1693 **Quelsh,** capt. John, Dublin, gent.
1694 ,, Mary, Dublin, widow
1743 **Questebrune,** Benjamin (Copy)
1728 **Questerbrune,** rev. John, vicar of Burnchurch, dio. Ossory
1796 **Quick,** James, Dublin, coachmaker
1610 ,, Michael, Dublin, merchant
1589 ,, Robert, Drogheda **[I.** 60
1697 **Quigley,** Garrett, Carlow, gent.
1794 ,, James, Park-street, Dublin
1806 ,, John, Rathcoffey, co. Kildare
1789 **Quin,** Agnes, *alias* **French,** Beagh, co. Galway, widow

1796 **Quin,** Alice, Tramore, co. Watfd., spinster
1650 ,, Alson, Dublin, spinster
1737 ,, Anna Maria, Dublin, spinster
1789 ,, Anne, Dublin
1743 ,, Catherine, Limerick, widow
1773 ,, Christopher, Dublin, merchant
1786 ,, Christopher, Kilcock, co. Kildare, maltster
1742 ,, Daniel, Dublin, carpenter
1656 ,, Dennis, Dublin, merchant **[V.** 322
1732 ,, Dominick, Quinsborough, co. Kildare, gent.
1754 ,, Edmond, Cork, merchant
1748 ,, Edward, mariner of the "Deptford" man-of-war
1803 ,, Edwd., Molesworth-lane, Dubl.
1728 ,, Francis, Dublin, bricklayer
1791 ,, Geo., Quinsborough, co. Clare, esq.
1805 ,, hon. George, Dublin city
1788 ,, James, Malpas-st., Dublin, ribbon weaver
1790 ,, James, Galway, merchant
1639 ,, John, Dublin, merchant
1662 ,, John, Dubl., merchant (original in office) **[IX.** 62
1667 ,, John, Dublin, gent.
1734 ,, John, Bulford, co. Wicklow
1738 ,, John, Rosbrien, co. Limerick
1762 ,, John, Cahir, co. Tipperary, cordwainer
1786 ,, John, Birr, King's co., excise officer
1789 ,, John, Dublin, cooper
1806 ,, John, Ballsbridge, Dublin
1807 ,, John, Laragh, co. Westmeath
1732 ,, Mary, *alias* **Stritch,** Limerick, widow
1763 ,, Mary, Adare, co. Limer., wid.
1803 ,, Michael, Rutland-place, Dubl., coach owner
1794 ,, Patrick, Kilcock, co. Kildare, distiller
1800 ,, Patrick, Tighe-st., Dublin, gt.
1777 ,, Richard, Kilcock, co. Kildare, maltster
1784 ,, Robert, Dublin, seedsman
1714 ,, Terence, Ballykelly, co. Kildare, gent.
1793 ,, Terence, Francis-st., Dublin, grocer
1725 ,, Thady, Limerick, esq.
1751 ,, Thomas
1767 ,, Thomas, Dublin, apothecary
1812 ,, Thomas, Kilmalogue, co. Tipperary, esq.
1744 ,, Valentine, Adare, co. Limerick, esq.

1694 **Quin**, Wm., Ballycarran, co. Meath, gent.
1740 ,, Wm., Rathmore, co. Kildare, farmer
1789 ,, Wydenham, Adare, co. Limerick, esq.
        [See QUINN.]
1792 **Quinan**, Michael, Dublin, M.D.
1656 **Quine**, Richard, Dublin, joiner
        [V. 342
1803 **Quinlan**, James, Springmount, co. Tipperary
1809 **Quinn**, Jas., Cherryfield, co. Kildare
1808 ,, John, Crowe-street, Dublin, hotelkeeper
        [See QUIN.]
1758 **Quinton**, George, Dublin, gent.
1780 **Quire**, Fras., Dublin, dry cooper
1795 ,, Martha, Dublin, spinster
1795 **Quirk**, Clara, Banff, co. Limerick
1781 ,, John
1793 **Quitermass**, John, Swords, co. Dublin, dealer
1726 **Quockly**, Martin, Dublin, merchant
1734 **Quocly**, Lucy, Dublin, widow
1716 **Quy**, James, Dublin, felt-maker

——R——

1732 **Raamburgh**, Mary, *alias* **Cuyleman**, Amsterdam
1747 **Rabbitt**, Thomas, Dublin, gent.
1705 **Rabesnieres**, Theophilus, par. St. Martin, London
1734 **Raboteau**, Mary Esther, Dublin, spinster
1782 **Raby**, Richard
1729 **Racine**, Anne, Dublin, widow
1675 ,, Benjamin, Dublin, gent.
1724 ,, Benjamin, Dublin, jeweller
1809 **Radcliff**, John, capt. of the 17th regt. of foot
1793 **Radcliffe**, Mary, Dublin
1793 ,, Stephen, Dublin, LL.D.
1679 ,, Thomas, Overthorpe, Yorkshire, esq. (Ex.)
1776 ,, Thomas, Dublin, LL.D.
1692 ,, William, Tallow, co. Wat., and Branstry, Cumberland, clk.
        [See RATCLIFF.]
1786 **Radford**, Elizabeth, Dublin, linen-draper
1788 ,, Elizabeth, Wexford, widow
1766 ,, Nathaniel, Cullinstown, co. Wexford, gent.
1702 ,, William, Great Gurteens, co. Wexford, gent.
1805 **Rafferty**, Christopher, Ballardan, co. Meath, farmer

1806 **Rafferty**, Christopher, Finglas, co. Dublin
1744 **Rafter**, William, Dublin, tailor
1726 ,, Ignatius, Kilkenny, late of Dublin, gent.
1750 **Rainbelt**, John, late of Simpston, Pembrokeshire, now of Ballyroan, co. Dublin
1803 **Rainey**, Arthur, Island of Barbadoes, merchant
1746 ,, Daniel, Belfast, late minister of the English Church
1783 ,, Daniel, Dublin, M.D.
1708 ,, Hugh, Magherafelt, co. Derry, gent.
1773 ,, James, Newry, co. Down, apothecary
1793 ,, John, Greenville, co. Down
1799 ,, Thomas, Dublin, gent.
1725 ,, William, Belfast, merchant
1789 ,, William, Bellvue, co. Down
        [See RAINY.]
1752 **Rainsford**, Henry, Hanover-lane, Dublin, weaver
1790 ,, James, Dublin, goldsmith
1810 ,, Joseph Michael, Dublin city
1781 ,, Martin, Knockearne, co. Wicklow, farmer
        [See RANSFORD.]
1736 **Rainy**, Robert, Newry, co. Down
        [See RAINEY.]
1748 **Rakestrow**, John, Newry, co. Down, distiller
1746 **Ralph**, Gabriel, Cuckold's-row, Dublin, formerly a shoemaker
1801 ,, John, Dublin city
        [See RELPH.]
1787 **Ralphson**, William, Kells, co. Meath
1767 **Ralston**, Samuel, Ballymoney, co. Antrim, innkeeper
        [See ROLLESTON.]
1691 **Ram**, sir Abel, Dublin, knt.
1740 ,, Abel, Ramsfort, co. Wexford, esq.
1778 ,, Abel, Ramsfort, co. Wexford, esq.
1699 ,, Andrew, Dublin, esq.
1793 ,, Andrew, Clonatin, co. Wexford, esq.
1800 ,, Mary, Dublin, widow
1799 ,, Rebecca, Dublin, widow
1034 ,, Thomas, bishop of **Ferns**. q. v.
1803 **Ramadge**, Smith, Granby-row, Dublin, merchant (Large)
1775 ,, William, Mullans, co. Antrim, gent.
1803 **Ramage**, Elizabeth, Whitehill, co. Longford
1792 ,, Hugh, Dublin, merchant

1794 **Ramage**, James, Londonderry city, esq.
1746 ,, John, Dublin, cordwainer
1807 ,, Thomas
1778 **Rammage**, Anne, Dorset-st.,Dubl., widow
1773 **Ramsay**, Charles, Church-hill, co. Tyrone
1780 ,, Elizabeth, Dublin, widow
1735 ,, James, Dublin, gent.
1773 ,, James, Church-hill, co. Tyrone
1753 ,, Philip, Dublin, gent.
[See RUMSEY.]
1677 **Ramsey**, Archibald, Stranorlar, co. Donegal, gent.
1680 ,, Edward, Dublin, gent.
1768 ,, James, Livery
1718 ,, Mary, Foxward, co. Mayo, wife to rev. John Ramsey
1673 ,, Robert, Mountmartins-in-the-Fields,Middlesex,esq.(Copy)
1769 ,, Thomas, Ballincurra, co. Limerick, farmer
1771 **Rand**, Thomas, Gormanstown, co. Wicklow, gent.
1791 **Randal**, George, Waterford, merchant
1786 **Randall**, Elizabeth, Waterford city, widow [gent.
1693 ,, Francis, Deeps, co. Wexford,
1692 ,, Henry, College-green, near Dublin, gent.
1670 **Ranelagh**, Arthur, lord viscount
1797 ,, rt. hon. Charles, lord viscount
1712 ,, Richard, earl of (Copy)
1644 ,, Roger, lord viscount
1810 **Ranken**, David, Heathfield, co. Londonderry
1801 **Rankin**, Geo., the elder, Chamber-street, Dublin, clothier
1811 ,, James, Dublin city, gent.
1740 ,, John, Staraghan, co. Fermanagh, gent.
1772 ,, Moses, Philadelphia, master of the "Hercules"
1756 ,, Samuel, Corncamon, co. Donegal, clk.
1782 ,, Thomas, Ballee,co.Antrim,esq.
1794 ,, Thomas, Carrick-on-Suir, co. Tipp., clk.
1764 ,, William, Dublin, mariner
1669 **Rankine**,James, Londonderry, mer.
1744 **Ransford**, Edward, Dublin, esq.
1789 ,, Edward, Richmond, co.Dublin, esq.
1709 ,, sir Mark, knt., alderman of Dublin
1720 ,, Mark, Dublin, gent.
1795 ,, Mark, Portarlington, Queen's co., esq.

1756 **Ransford**, Michael, Dublin, goldsmith
1808 ,, Thomas, Rathcoole, co.Dublin, gent.
[See RAINSFORD.]
1761 **Ranson**, William, Dublin, gent.
1783 ,, William, Dublin, stationer
1784 **Raper**, John, Forrestown,co.Meath, farmer
1808 ,, John, Essex-quay, Dublin
1786 ,, Richard, Lower Exchequer-st., Dublin, glazier
1791 ,, Thomas, Dublin, carpenter
1701 **Raphoe**, Alexander Carnecross, bishop of
1743 ,, Dr. Nicholas Forster, bishop of (Large will)
1763 ,, Dr. Robert Downes, bishop of
1780 ,, John Oswald, lord bishop of
1733 **Raphson**, John, Dublin, formerly of Middle Temple, London,esq.
1708 **Rasby**, Susanna, Sheffield, Yorkshire, widow (Copy)
1711 **Rasen**, Edward, Dublin, victualler
1736 **Ratcliff**, Abraham, Newmarket-lane, Dublin, cloth worker
[See RADCLIFFE.]
1763 **Rath**, James, Irishtown
1742 **Rathborne**, Catherine, Clontarf, co. Dublin, widow
1734 ,, John, Dublin, merchant
1631 ,, Lawrence, Camelwood, co. Londonderry
1779 ,, William, Dublin, wax chandler
1810 ,, William, Belvedere-place, co. Dublin, esq.
1778 **Rathbyrne**, Jane, Dublin, widow
[See RATHBORNE.]
1787 **Ratigan**, Patrick, Dublin, timber merchant
1660 **Raughter**, Walter, Littlebirrtown, co. Kildare, gent. (Copy)
1713 **Ravan**, William, Dublin, esq.
1670 **Raven**, Constantine,Dublin, saddler
1767 **Ravenhill**, Edward, Pallace, co. Westmeath, farmer
1770 ,, Mary, Pallisboy,co.Westmeath
1790 ,, William, Tyrellspass, co.Westmeath, gauger
1792 **Ravenscroff**, Elizabeth,Ballinderry, co. Antrim
1804 **Ravenscroft**, Richard, Harcourt-place, Dublin, gent.
1638 **Ravyn**, Thomas, Dublin, gent.
1717 **Rawdon**, Brilliana, Dublin, spinster
1737 ,, Dorothy, Dublin, spinster
1684 ,, sir George,Lisburn, co. Antrim, bart. (Large will)
1724 ,, sir John, Moira, co. Down, bart.
1713 ,, Lydia, Dublin, widow

1725 **Rawleigh**, Walter, Mitchelstown, co. Cork, gent.
See ROWLEY.]
1615 **Rawley**, Richard, Fitzdavid, Ballynacarrigg, co. Limk, gent. (Copy)
1675 **Rawline**, John, Timoge, Queen's co., LL.D.
1696 **Rawlins**, John, Rathangan, co. Kildare, esq.
1789 ,, John, Dublin, esq.
1681 ,, Thomas, Dublin, gent.
1686 ,, Thomas, Dublin, gent.
1777 ,, William, Vicar-street, Dublin, timber merchant
1809 ,, William, Cavendish-row, Dubl., esq.
[See ROWLANDS, ROWLINSON.]
1725 **Rawlinson**, John, Comb, Hampshire, esq. (Copy)
1697 **Raworth**, Catherine, wife to Robt. R., esq., deceased (Copy)
1697 ,, Robert, Gray's Inn, Middlesex, esq. (Copy)
1674 **Rawson**, Catherine, widow of Gilbert R., Donoghmore, Queen's co., esq.
1675 ,, Geo., Donoughmore, Queen's co., esq. [esq.
1796 ,, George, Belmont, co. Wicklow,
1636 ,, James, Dublin, esq.
1762 ,, James, Gray Abbey, co. Kildare
1609 ,, John, Dublin
1650 ,, Luke, Petersham, Surrey, gent. (Copy)
1753 ,, Martha, Dublin, widow
1791 ,, Richard, Baltinglass, co. Wicklow, gent.
1721 **Ray**, Catherine, *alias* **Hore**, Youghal, co. Cork, widow
1716 ,, Charles, Youghal, co. Cork
1792 ,, rev. Charles
1713 ,, Elizabeth, Dublin, widow
1708 ,, Joseph, Dublin, bookseller
1729 ,, Mary, Dublin, spinster
[See REA.]
1796 **Raye**, Michael, Dorset-st., Dublin
1748 **Raymer**, Robert, Tobertynan, co. Meath, gent.
1702 **Raymond**, Anthony, Garrane, co. Cork, esq.
1726 ,, rev. Anthony, Trim, co. Meath
1800 ,, Dennis, Wyanstown, co. Dubl., gent.
1732 ,, Edward, Carraughcumna, co. Cork, gent.
1742 ,, Elizabeth, Dublin, widow
1628 ,, Ezekial, Drogheda, gent.
1758 ,, rev. Gibson, Rawn, Queen's co., clerk

1780 **Raymond**, Honora, Dromin, co. Kerry, widow
1732 ,, James, Ballyegan, co. Kerry, gent.
1771 ,, Jas., Dromin, co. Kerry, gent.
1649 ,, Joane, *alias* **Bird**, Dubl., wid.
1697 ,, Philip, Cork, merchant
1692 ,, Robt., Ballydulogher, co. Cork, gent.
1806 ,, Samuel, Riversdale, co. Kerry
1650 **Raynalds**, Paul, Killyleagh, co. Down, esq.
[See REYNOLDS.]
1749 **Rayner**, Catherine, Dublin, spinster
1756 ,, John, Tobertynan, co. Meath, gent.
1753 ,, Joseph, Dublin, mercer
1696 ,, Robert, Dublin, apothecary
[See REYNER.]
1717 **Rea**, Adam, Dublin, tailor
1760 ,, Arthur, Ruskey, co. Londonderry
1719 ,, Catherine, Waterford, widow
1792 ,, George, Strabane
1740 ,, Joan, Dublin
1704 ,, John, soldier in lord Charlemont's regiment
1747 ,, John, Newry, co. Down, tanner
1749 ,, John, Newry, co. Down, merchant
1796 ,, John, Youghal, co. Cork, gent.
1741 ,, Joseph, Waterford, gent.
1808 ,, Joseph C., Christendom, Liberties of Waterford
1673 ,, Patrick, Dublin, gent.
1692 ,, Robert, Dublin, ironmonger
1771 ,, Thomas, Monaghan
[See RAY, REAY, WRAY.]
1717 **Read**, Adam, rector of Desertegnie, co. Donegal, clk.
1685 ,, Alexander, Dublin, gent.
1749 ,, Alexander, Dublin, maltster
1750 ,, Andrew, Lurgan
1767 ,, Bernard, Dublin, revenue officer
1701 ,, Christopher, Ballinakill, co. Kildare, farmer [gent.
1752 ,, Christopher, Vicar-st., Dublin,
1808 ,, Denis, Drogheda, gent.
1663 ,, Edmond, Dublin, merchant
1803 ,, Elizabeth, late deceased
1731 ,, George, the elder, Rossenarra, co. Kilkenny, gent.
1762 ,, George, Snugsborough, co. Kilkenny, esq.
1791 ,, George, Coleraine, co. Derry
1792 ,, George, Wexford town, esq.
1798 ,, George, Snugsborough, co. Kilkenny, esq.
1809 ,, George, Three Bridges, co. Kilkenny

1705 **Read**, Henry, Woolwich, Kent, mariner (Copy)
1785 ,, Isaac, Dundalk, co. Louth
1690 ,, James, Belfast, merchant
1694 ,, James, Readrest, Surrey, gent. (Copy)
1716 ,, James, Newry, co. Down, merchant
1720 ,, James, Newry, merchant
1727 ,, James, Tolloghin, co. Down, gent.
1737 ,, James, Ballygowan, co. Down
1749 ,, rev. James, Ashroe, co. Limk., clk.
1791 ,, James, Courtown, co. Kildare, gent.
1791 ,, James, Marymount, Belfast, co. Down, farmer
1703 ,, John, rector of Killagh, co. Westmeath, clk.
1734 ,, John, Dublin, merchant
1779 ,, John, Summerhill, co. Dublin, esq.
1791 ,, John, Dublin, gent.
1783 ,, Joseph, Mountpleasant, co. Kilkenny, gent.
1805 ,, Margaret, Union-street, Dub., spinster
1756 ,, Martha, Waterside, Lib. of Derry, widow
1754 ,, Mary, Dublin, spinster
1799 ,, Mary, Dublin, widow
1791 ,, Mathew, Derrycock, co. Cavan, linen draper
1723 ,, Nicholas, Dunboyne, co. Meath, esq.
1766 ,, Patrick, Urney, King's co.
1743 ,, rev. Paul, rector of Leepatrick, co. Tyrone
1747 ,, Paul, D.D., jun. Fellow of Trinity College, Dublin
1733 ,, Philip, Woodtown West, co. Meath, gent.
1781 ,, Philip, Woodtown, co. Meath, LL.D.
1742 ,, Richard, Rossenarra, co. Kilkenny, esq.
1752 ,, Richard, Back-lane, Dublin, dealer
1788 ,, Richard, Smithfield, Dublin, labourer
1805 ,, Richard, Dublin city, esq.
1786 ,, Rose, Brown-street, Dublin, widow
1737 ,, Thomas, Modeshill, co. Tipperary, esq.
1753 ,, Thomas, Tullanacross, co. Down
1779 ,, Thos., Linenhall-street, Dubl., merchant

1803 **Read**, Thos., Parliament-st., Dubl., cutler
1777 ,, William, Vicar-street, Dublin, timber merchant
1789 ,, William, Dublin, grocer [See REED, REID.]
1682 **Reade**, Alleyn, London, merchant tailor (Copy)
1796 ,, Anne, Camden-street, Dublin, widow
1762 ,, George, Kilkenny, esq.
1806 ,, Henry, Silver Spring, co. Kilk.
1800 ,, John, Ballyseskin, co. Wexford, gent.
1751 ,, Joseph, Kells, co. Kilkenny, clk.
1751 ,, Mathew, Courtown, co. Kildare, gent.
1755 ,, Richard, formerly of Mahubber, co. Tipperary, now of London
1661 ,, William, soldier of foot in Gowran, gent.
1659 **Reader**, Enoch, Dublin, alderman
1718 ,, Magdalen, Dublin, spinster
1754 ,, Mary, Grangegorman - lane, Dublin, widow
1770 ,, Thomas, Dublin, surgeon
1726 ,, William, Dublin, apothecary
1774 ,, ven. William, archdeacon of Cork
1763 **Reading**, Begnet, Dublin, spinster
1771 ,, Benjamin, Lilletstown, co. Dublin, esq.
1721 ,, Charles, Ballycommon, King's co. gent.
1784 ,, Dymphna, Portarlington, Queen's co., spinster
1711 ,, Elizabeth, Dublin, widow
1758 ,, Ellinor, widow of John R., Readingstown, King's co., esq.
1749 ,, James, mariner on board the "Suffolk" man-of-war
1691 ,, John, Rachane, King's co., gent.
1699 ,, John, Dublin, esq.
1747 ,, John, Clonegown. King's co., esq.
1758 ,, Margaret, Cuffe-street, Dublin, spinster
1725 ,, Nicholas, Borrisoleigh, co. Tipperary, gent.
1727 ,, Otway, Borrisoleigh, co. Tipp., gent.
1789 ,, Patrick, Dublin, gent.
1764 ,, Robert, Dublin, esq.
1780 ,, Sarah, Dublin, spinster
1807 **Readshaw**, Benjamin, Athy, co. Kildare (unproved)

1767 **Ready**, Mary, *alias* **Bean**, Cow-
lane, Dublin
[See REDDY.]
1811 **Reaf**, James, Grafton-street, Dubl.,
toyman
1800 **Really**, Hugh, Drumbae, co. Fermanagh, farmer
1650 **Reard**, Ephrim, cornet to sir John
Borlase's troop
1789 **Reardan**, Edward, Tipperary town,
esq.
1770 ,, Mary, Gurrane, co. Cork, wid.
[See REREDAN, RIERDAN, RIORDAN.]
1792 **Reardane**, John, Marybrook, co.
Cork, gent.
1768 **Reardon**. John, Gurrane, co. Cork
1787 **Reay**, Margaret, Halfmoon-street,
Westmeath, spinster
[See REA.]
1660 **Reayllin**, Edmond, Dublin, yeoman
1739 **Reddich**, Anne, Clonmel, co. Tipperary, widow
1807 **Reddie**, Mathew, Ballyhadie, co.
Kildare
[See REDDY.]
1808 **Reddington**, Nicholas, Mirefield,
co. Galway, esq.
1726 **Reddrop**, Dorothy, Dublin, widow
1746 **Reddy**, Elizabeth, Dublin
1761 ,, John
1754 ,, Patrick, Dublin, merchant
1784 ,, Philip, rector of Beauville,
Lower Normandy
1723 ,, Richard, Branganstown, co.
Kildare, gent.
[See READY, REDDIE.]
1685 **Reding**, John, the elder, Raghan,
King's co., esq.
1781 **Redington**, Thomas, Kilcoman, co.
Galway
1671 **Redman**, Abagaile, Ballylinch, co.
Kilkenny, widow
1675 ,, Daniel, Ballylinch, co. Kilkenny, esq.
1793 **Redmond**, Charles, Dublin, woollen
draper
1802 ,, Eugene, Balbriggan
1804 ,, Francis, Derrykillen
1796 ,, George, Hollyfoot, co. Wexford, gent.
1807 ,, James, Smithfield, Dublin city
1785 ,, John, Dublin, mariner and
merchant
1802 ,, John, Charles-street, Dublin,
gent.
1789 ,, Mary, widow
1746 ,, Mathew, Dublin, merchant
1780 ,, Mathew, Newtown
1793 ,, Michael, Coal-quay, Dublin,
coal merchant

1805 **Redmond**, Murtagh, Rosspoyle,
co. Wexford
1684 ,, Patrick, Dublin, merchant
1704 ,, William, Dublin, distiller
1775 **Reed**, Archibald, Derrygortrevy, co.
Tyrone, farmer
1797 ,, Caleb, Frescati, co. Dublin,
gent.
1802 ,, Elizabeth, Gardiner's-place, co.
Dublin, widow
1798 ,, Ellinor, Dublin, widow
1786 ,, James, Brown-street, Dublin,
linen weaver
1772 ,, Jane, Carrickfergus
1753 ,, John, Dublin, brewer
1767 ,, John, Dublin, plumber
1761 ,, Patrick, Marlborough-street,
Dublin, linen draper
1739 ,, Penelope, Dublin, widow
1774 ,, Philip, Disart, co. Kildare,
gent.
1794 ,, Richard, Lib. of Thomas-court
and Donore, grocer
1787 ,, Thomas, Dublin, linen manufacturer
1710 ,, Wm., Ballinakill, Queen's co.
1750 ,, William, Dublin, gent.
[See READ.]
1703 **Reeve**, Mary, Dublin, widow
1777 **Reeves**, Anne, Clogah, co. Kilkenny, widow
1771 ,, Barbara, Youghal, widow
1794 ,, Boles
1811 ,, Edward H., Cork city, esq.
1613 ,, George, St. Michan's par.,
Dublin, vintner   [gent.
1764 ,, John, Danesford, co. Cork,
1780 ,, Joseph, Peter-street, Dublin
1799 ,, Mary, *alias* **Devonshire**
1742 ,, Michael, Charleville, co. Cork,
tanner
1740 ,, Robert, Isle of Man, merchant
(Copy)
1806 ,, Robert, Cork city
[See RYVES.]
1760 **Reford**, Lewis, Antrim, linen merchant
1736 **Regnaut**, Noah, Glasnevin, co.
Dublin, esq.
1685 **Regnols**, Jane, widow of Richard
R., Clonlogher, co. Clare
1790 **Reid**, Frances, Dublin, widow
1799 ,, James, Middleton, co. Cork,
clk.
1761 ,, John, Ballygallum, co. Down,
farmer   [gent.
1804 ,, John, Portaferry, co. Down,
1802 ,, William, formerly of Limerick,
late of Dublin
[See READ.]

1760	**Reigney**, Martin, Linenhall-street, Dublin, merchant	
1629	**Reignoldes**, Henry, Dublin, esq.	
1678	**Reignolds**, John, Rostrevor, co. Down, esq. (Ex.) [See REYNOLDS.]	
1745	**Reilly**, Alexander, Ballinrink, co. Meath, gent.	
1748	,, Alice, Dublin, spinster	
1755	,, Alice Mary, Dublin, spinster	
1778	,, Alice, Dublin, widow	
1732	,, Anne, *alias* **Delane**, wife to Richard R., Dublin, weaver	
1748	,, Anne, Derbyhaven, Isle of Man (Copy)	
1763	,, Anne, *alias* **Thompson**, Dubl., widow	
1790	,, Anne, Eccles-st., Dublin, wid.	
1803	,, Anne, Grenville-street, Dublin, widow	
1723	,, Bryan, Chamberlainstown, co. Meath, gent.	
1745	,, Bryan, Dundalk, co. Louth, wine merchant	
1747	,, Bryan, Ryefield, co. Cavan	
1755	,, Bryan, Grennan, co. Meath	
1785	,, Bryan, Coughilltown, co. Meath, glazier	
1793	,, Bryan, Smithfield, Dublin, salesmaster	
1799	,, Bryan, Dublin, gent.	
1741	,, Catherine, Catherinestown, co. Kildare, widow	
1746	,, Catherine, Roustown, co. Meath, widow	
1756	,, Catherine, Dublin, widow	
1779	,, Catherine, *alias* **Ford**, Dublin, widow	
1721	,, Charles, Abbeylara, co. Longford, gent.	
1722	,, Charles, Lurgan, co. Armagh, gent.	
1729	,, Charles, *alias* **Cahire**, Aghuwee, co. Cavan, gent.	
1764	,, Charles, Dublin, surgeon	
1767	,, Charles, Meadoton, co. Meath, esq.	
1767	,, Charles, Garricross, co. Cavan, gent.	
1778	,, Charles, the elder, Biglagore, co. Meath, gent.	
1780	,, Charles, Castlejordan, co. Meath, gent.	
1785	,, Charles, Mount Reilly, co. Louth, farmer	
1786	,, Charles, Dublin, gent.	
1788	,, Charles, Geighanstown, co. Meath	
1762	,, Connor, Ballinrink, co. Meath, gent.	

1768	**Reilly**, Christopher, Dubl., maltster	
1793	,, Daniel, Bachelor's-walk, Dubl.	
1723	,, Edmond, Dublin, merchant	
1780	,, Edmond, Dublin, esq.	
1720	,, Edward, Dublin, gent.	
1743	,, Edward, Ballinlough, co. Meath	
1762	,, Edward, Usher's-quay, Dublin	
1770	,, Edwd., Cullenreagh, co. Cavan, gent.	
1777	,, Edward, Dolphinsbarn-lane, tanner	
1777	,, Edward, Island-bridge, co. Dublin, gent.	
1801	,, Edward, Glasnevin-road, co. Dublin, esq.	
1803	,, Edward, Drumcondra, co. Dublin, gardener	
1796	,, Elizabeth, town of Drogheda, spinster	
1800	,, Ellinor, living with dowager lady Erne	
1756	,, Farrell, Waterstown, co. Meath, gent.	
1771	,, Frances, Cavan, widow	
1764	,, Francis, Alhame, co. Meath	
1796	,, Francis, Bailieborough, co. Cavan, shopkeeper	
1764	,, Garrett, Little Ballinlough, co. Meath	
1808	,, George, Dublin city	
1751	,, Gerald, Dublin, victualler	
1784	,, Hannah, Dublin, spinster	
1803	,, Henry Stephens, Prussia-street, co. Dublin, esq. (Large)	
1760	,, Honor, *alias* **Taylor**	
1721	,, Hugh, Curraghtown, co. Meath, gent.	
1741	,, Hugh, Drimgoone, co. Cavan, gent.	
1762	,, Hugh, Friar's Park, co. Meath, gent.	
1766	,, Hugh, Dublin, gent.	
1769	,, Hugh, Miltown, co. Meath, gent.	
1772	,, Hugh, Emper, co. Westmeath, gent.	
1787	,, Hugh, Newgrove, co. Meath, esq.	
1791	,, Hugh, Mount Reilly, co. Louth, farmer	
1793	,, Hugh, Hartstown, co. Meath, gent.	
1802	,, Hugh, Dublin, woollen draper	
1704	,, James, Bachelor's-walk, Dubl.	
1722	,, James, Ballinlough, co. Westmeath, esq.	
1733	,, James, Dublin, esq.	
1747	,, James, Carrick, co. Tipperary, merchant	
1758	,, James, Laragh, co. Kildare	

1741 **Reilly**, William, Hayestown, co. Meath, farmer
1791 ,, William, Theatre Royal, comedian
1811 ,, Wm., Fosterstown, co. Meath, gent.
[See RELLY.]
1768 **Reily**, Charles, Grenane, co. Meath, dealer
1784 ,, James, Bachelor's-walk, Dubl., cooper
1806 ,, John, Kells, co. Meath
1775 ,, Philip, Hayestown, co. Meath (set aside by decree)
1721 ,, Rose, Dublin, widow
1699 **Reinolds**, John, Dublin, esq. [See REYNOLDS.]
1617 **Relick**, Symon, Dublin, tanner
1638 **Relly**, Barnaby, Timon, co. Dublin
1637 ,, John, Killmore, co. Cavan, esq. [See REILLY.]
1631 **Relph**, John, Dublin, tailor [See RALPH.]
1674 **Remus**, John, trumpeter to col. Vere Cromwell's company
1708 **Render**, William, Davidstown, co. Louth, esq.
1724 **Renolds**, John, Clonross, co. Meath, farmer
1664 ,, William, Curloughan, co. Kilkenny, gent. [See REYNOLDS.]
1763 **Renourd**, lieut.-col. Peter, Staffordstreet, Dublin
1784 **Reredon**, Margaret, North Kingstreet, Dublin [See REARDAN.]
1791 **Rest**, Walter, Limerick, gent.
1720 **Reuden**, Thomas, capt. in brigadier Napier's regt. of horse
1796 **Reuel**, Thomas, Dublin
1756 **Revell**, Elizabeth, *alias* **Nash**
1758 ,, John, Ballymoney, co. Wicklow
1782 ,, John, Finknock, co. Wicklow, farmer
1797 ,, John, Ballygillard, co. Wicklow, farmer
1805 ,, John, Ballymoney, co. Wicklow, esq.
1788 ,, Martha, French-street, Dublin, widow
1747 ,, Wm., the elder, Dubl., mariner
1768 ,, Wm., Poolbeg-street, Dublin
1787 ,, Wm., Ardoyne, co. Wicklow, gent.
1798 **Revett**, Dorothy, Galway town, spinster
1707 ,, Thomas, Galway, alderman
1665 **Rewe**, John, Castell Dilling, co. Kildare, gent.

1737 **Reyley**, John, Dublin, maltster
1745 **Reymes**, Ellinor, widow of Wm. R., Kinsale, co. Cork, gent.
1685 ,, Wm., Parkneshoge, co. Wexford, gent.
1721 ,, Wm., Kinsale, co. Cork, gent.
1664 **Reynalds**, Theodonis [See REYNOLDS.]
1735 **Reynell**, Arthur, Castle R., co. Westmeath, esq.
1744 ,, Carew, bishop of **Derry**, q. v.
1776 ,, Dorcas, Dublin
1698 ,, Edmond, Dublin, gent.
1767 ,, Edmond, Castle R., co. Westmeath, esq.
1788 ,, Edward, Killynan, co. Westmeath, clk.
1765 ,, Elizabeth, Dublin, spinster
1766 ,, Frances, *alias* **Brush**, Killough
1744 ,, Henry, London, esq. (Copy)
1792 ,, John, Castle R., co. Cork, gent.
1804 ,, John, Balnalack, co. Westmeath, esq.
1767 ,, Nicholas, Reynella, co. Westmeath, esq.
1701 ,, sir Richd., knt. and bart. (Copy)
1736 ,, Richd., par. St.George, Bloomsbury, Middlesex, esq.
1768 ,, Richard, Killagh, esq.
1807 ,, Richard, Reynella, co. Westmeath, esq.
1794 ,, Robert, Dublin city, esq.
1790 **Reyner**, Mehetable, spinster [See RAYNER.]
1721 **Reynett**, James, Waterford, M.D.
1788 **Reynolds**, Andrew, Park-st., Dubl., merchant
1796 ,, Anne, Cornell's-court, co. Dublin, spinster
1636 ,, Charles, Laghan, co. Leitrim, esq.
1788 ,, Charles
1804 ,, Charles, Maws
1775 ,, Dorothy, *alias* **Ellis**, Ward House, co. Leitrim, widow
1770 ,, Edwin Sandys, Durham, co. Rosc., esq. (Not proved)
1795 ,, Elizabeth, Dublin, widow
1784 ,, Ellinor, *alias* **Kelly**
1790 ,, Ellinor, Pill-lane, Dublin, wid.
1768 ,, George, Grange, co. Leitrim, esq.
1772 ,, George, Dublin, alderman
1741 ,, Jane, Dublin spinster
1759 ,, Joan, Dublin, widow
1680 ,, John, Clogher, co. Tyrone, gt.
1711 ,, John, Carlow, gent.
1757 ,, John, Drumholm, co. Donegal
1768 ,, John, Doghs, co. Londonderry, farmer

1776 **Reynolds**, John, Crumlin, co. Dubl., gent.
1777 ,, John, Drumcommon, co. Leitrim, esq.
1777 ,, John, lieut. in 45th regt. of foot
1789 ,, John, Coolbeg, co. Donegal, esq.
1761 ,, Letitia, Magherychar, co. Donegal, widow
1766 ,, Margaret, Dublin, widow
1724 ,, Mathew, Dublin, esq.
1786 ,, Michael, New Market, co. Dublin, clothier
1807 ,, Michael, Cabra-lane, co. Dubl., dairyman
1809 ,, Michael, Summer-hill, Dublin, carpenter
1811 ,, Michael, surgeon in the Donegal militia
1768 ,, Nicholas, Sweeny-lane, Dublin, dyer
1767 ,, Patrick, Plunkett-street, Dublin, carpenter
1788 ,, Patrick, Coombe, co. Dublin
1796 ,, Patrick, The Manse, co. Kildare, farmer
1798 ,, Patrick, Dublin city
1806 ,, Patrick, Birr, King's co.
1799 ,, Peter, Prosper-hill, co. Dublin, farmer
1809 ,, Peter, Duke-st., Dublin, gent.
1797 ,, Richard
1721 ,, Samuel, Gt. Britain-st., Dublin, gent.
1783 ,, Stephen, Aghamore, co. Leitrim, gent.   [esq.
1632 ,, Thomas, Cluinties, co. Leitrim,
1782 ,, Thomas, Ash-st., Dublin, silk manufacturer
1768 ,, Timothy, Drumluhill, co. Leitrim, gent.
1775 ,, Wm., Dulwich, Surrey, esq., formerly of Arbour-hill, Dub.
1800 ,, Wm., the elder, Cork, gent.
[See RAYNALDS, REIGNOLDS, REINOLDS, RENOLDS, REYNALDS.]
1727 **Reyson**, John, Dublin, alderman
1795 **Rhames**, Elizabeth, Exchange-st., Dublin, widow
1809 ,, Frederick, Dublin city
1793 ,, John, Dublin
1756 ,, Margaret, Dublin, widow
1803 ,, Sarah, widow
1753 **Rhodes**, Margaret, Dublin
1745 ,, Roger, Ardrass, co. Kildare, gt.
1774 **Rial**, Mary, Clonmel, co. Tipperary, gent.
1781 ,, Wm., Clonmel, co. Tipperary, banker
[See RYALL.]

1758 **Ribton**, Anne, Sillouge, co. Dublin, widow
1773 ,, David, Dublin, esq.
1762 ,, sir Geo., the Grove, co. Dublin, bart.
1806 ,, sir Geo., Landscape, co. Dublin, bart.
1774 ,, Wm., Westforest, co. Dublin, esq.
1720 **Rice**, Edward, Mountrice, co. Kildare, esq.
1759 ,, Edward, Dingle, co. Kerry, gt.
1750 ,, Eleanor, Dublin, widow
1778 ,, Eleanor, *alias* **Murphy**, wife to Richard Rice
1698 ,, Francis, Dublin, gent.
1748 ,, George, Dingle, co. Kerry
1637 ,, James Fitz Stephen, Dinglycush, co. Kerry, gent.
1705 ,, James, Dublin, gent.
1734 ,, James, Mountrice, co. Kildare, esq.
1742 ,, James, Dublin, gent.
1768 ,, James, formerly of Mount R., co. Kildare, now of par. St. Martin-in-the-fields, Middlesex
1807 ,, James, Coleraine, co. Londonderry
1774 ,, Jane, Ennis, co. Clare, widow
1685 ,, John, Grange, co. Waterford, gent.
1751 ,, John, Ennis, co. Clare, mercht.
1756 ,, John, Dublin, merchant
1760 ,, John, Aghree, co. Wexford, gent.
1780 ,, John, Dullargy, co. Louth
1688 ,, Laurence, Trough, co. Clare
1741 ,, Luke, Pimlico, Dublin, clothie
1764 ,, Marcus, Dublin, merchant
1726 ,, dame Mary, widow of sir Stephen R., knt.
1737 ,, Mary, Cork, widow
1773 ,, Mary
1780 ,, Mary, Dublin, spinster
1711 ,, Nicholas, Tulla, co. Clare, esq.
1768 ,, Nicholas, Barbadoes
1771 ,, Patrick, Attatins, co. Kilkenny, farmer
1730 ,, Pierce, Dublin, merchant
1808 ,, Richard Stephen, Mt. Rice, co. Kildare, esq.
1640 ,, Robert, Dingle, gent.
1787 ,, Robert, West Court, co. Kilkenny, farmer
1802 ,, Robert, Coleraine, co. Londonderry, merchant
1715 ,, sir Stephen, Dublin, knt.
1748 ,, Stephen, Dublin, merchant
1786 ,, Stephen, esq.

1790	**Rice,** Stephen, Carrickfergus, co. Antrim, esq.	
1634	,, Thomas, Dinglycouche, co. Kerry, burgess	
1733	,, Thomas Fitzmarcus, Cork, merchant	
1777	,, Thos., Dingle, co. Kerry, esq.	
1806	,, Thomas, Adair Farm, co. Limerick, esq.	
1780	,, William	
1784	,, Wm., Ennis, co. Clare, gent. [See ROYCE, ROYSE.]	
1593	**Rich,** Richard, London, haberdasher	
1668	,, Stephen, Wexford, gent.	
1766	**Richard,** William, Dublin [See RICKARD.]	
1758	**Richards,** Catherine, Raheen, co. Wexford, widow	
1765	,, Edward, Enniscorthy, co. Wexford, gent.	
1798	,, Edward, captain lieutenant 55th regiment, at St. Lucia	
1729	,, Elizabeth, Dublin, widow	
1811	,, Fitzhubert, Marboro' Building, Bath	
1799	,, Frances, Old Leighlin, co. Carlow	
1795	,, Goddart, Grange, co. Wexford, esq.	
1714	,, Godfrey, Dublin, esq.	
1763	,, John, Askinvillar, co. Wexford, esq.	
1788	,, John, Dublin, gent.	
1788	,, John	
1805	,, Joseph	
1763	,, Richard, minister of Killany	
1732	,, Samuel, London, merchant	
1784	,, Solomon, Salsborough, co. Wexford, esq.	
1785	,, Thomas, Rathaspick, co. Wexford, esq. (Large) [See RICKARDS.]	
1788	**Richardson,** Archibald, Dublin, esq.	
1788	,, Aughmuty, Cooleshall, co. Longford, esq.	
1739	,, Catherine, Dreemore, co. Tyr.	
1784	,, Catherine, Belgriffin, co. Dub., widow	
1807	,, Catherine, Belgriffin, co. Dub., spinster	
1745	,, Charles, Castleroe, co. Derry	
1772	,, David, Newry, co. Down	
1797	,, David, Drum, co. Tyrone	
1769	,, Edward	
1800	,, Edward, Newry, co. Armagh, gent.	
1809	,, rev. Edward, Moorstown, co. Kildare	

1740	**Richardson,** Elizabeth, Dublin, wid,	
1801	,, Elizabeth, Lurgan, co. Armagh	
1780	,, rev. Galbraithe, Richtown, co. Tyrone, clk.	
1739	,, George, Earl-st.	
1768	,, Hannah, Dublin, widow	
1730	,, Henry, Ballycenlar, co. Down, esq.	
1786	,, Henry, Dublin, gent.	
1728	,, rev. James, Londonderry, clk.	
1771	,, James, rector of Magherafelt, co. Derry, clk.	
1777	,, Jas., Donaghmore, co. Tyrone	
1634	,, John, clerk, Levalleglishe, co. Armagh	
1655	,, John, bishop of **Ardagh,** q. v.	
1778	,, John, St. Audoen's par., Dublin, merchant	
1791	,, John, Mullingar, co. Westmeath, apothecary	
1801	,, John, the elder, Somerset, co. Derry, esq.	
1806	,, John, Athy, co. Kildare	
1806	,, John, Somerset, co. Londonderry	
1803	,, Joseph, Stramore, co. Down, linendraper	
1753	,, Lawrence, Dublin, gent.	
1752	,, Lemynge, lieutenant in colonel Ligoniere's regiment of horse (Copy)	
1784	,, Mark, Kilmacrea, co. Wicklow, farmer	
1746	,, Martha, North Strand, co. Dublin, widow	
1801	,, Martin, Dublin city, gent.	
1735	,, Mary, *alias* **Gibbons,** Ballykenlar, co. Down, widow	
1789	,, Nathaniel, Charlemont, co. Armagh, merchant	
1699	,, Nichs., par. clk., St. Bridget's, Dublin	
1807	,, Penelope, Dublin city, widow	
1793	,, Rebecca, Arbor-hill, Dub., wid.	
1789	,, Richard, Dublin, butcher	
1809	,, Richard, Montpelier-hill, Dub., grazier	
1660	,, Samuel, Drumanon	
1668	,, Thomas, Dublin, esq.	
1710	,, Thos., Caradogan, co. Tyrone, esq.	
1724	,, Thomas, Dublin, gent.	
1700	,, William, Dublin, gent.	
1742	,, Wm., Derrygalley, co. Tyrone	
1753	,, William, Dublin, merchant	
1755	,, William, Somerset, co. Londonderry, esq.	
1758	,, William, Limerick, apothecary	
1772	,, William, Belgriffin, co. Dub., esq.	

1787 **Richardson**, Wm., Dublin, mercht.
1796 ,, William, Lurgan, co. Armagh, brewer
1802 ,, William, Kilmacray, co. Wicklow, farmer
1808 ,, Wm., Hollyville, co. Dub., esq.
1757 **Richbell**, Edward, major-general of His Majesty's Forces
1663 **Richesson**, Frances, *alias* Gilbert, Tallough, co. Dublin, widow
1730 **Richey**, James, Dublin, victualler
1737 **Richison**, Abel, Dublin, weaver
1799 **Richisson**, Martin, Ballinrobe, co. Mayo
1788 **Richmond**, Margt., Dub. city, wid.
1807 ,, Thomas, Cork city, gent.
1807 **Rickard**, Jos., Dublin city, publican
1805 ,, Thomas
        [See RICHARD.]
1693 **Rickards**, Andw., Danganspidogie, co. Kilkenny, esq. (Large will ; Ex.)
        [See RICHARDS.]
1773 **Rickeaby**, George, Dub., carpenter
1645 **Rickeseys**, capt. Abraham, Dublin
1761 **Rickesies**, Rebecca, Dub., spinster
1745 **Rickett**, William, Cork, merchant
1716 **Rickson**, James, Ballinteer, co. Dublin, gent.
1759 **Ricky**, Alex., Chamber-st., Dublin, clothier
1803 ,, John, Brown-st., Lib. of Thomascourt, and Donore, co. Dub., gent.
1760 **Riddell**, Cathne., *alias* **Gledstane**, widow of rev. John R.
1707 ,, John, Newry, co. Down, merchant
1730 ,, John, Crosshill, co. Antrim (Not proved)
1758 **Riddery**, Charles, Garry Edmond, co. Mayo, gent.
1703 ,, Thos., citizen and merchant tailor (Copy)
1759 **Riddock**, Blunt, Kilkenny, gent.
1759 **Rider**, Peter, Cournellane, co. Carlow
1722 ,, Ralph, Newry, co. Down, gent.
1781 ,, Richd., Blainrow, co. Wicklow, farmer
        [See RYDER.]
1750 **Ridgate**, Grace, Dublin, widow
1685 ,, Hugh, Dublin, esq.
1745 ,, Philip, Dublin, esq.
1673 ,, William, Dublin, gent.
1807 **Ridge**, Catherine, Breda, co. Galway, widow
1808 ,, Catherine, widow
1647 ,, John, Abbeytown, co. Roscommon, esq.

1772 **Ridge**, Robert, Breda, co. Galway, esq.
1787 **Ridgeley**, Thomas, Booterstown, co. Dublin
1793 **Ridgely**, Thomas, Blackrock, co. Dublin, carpenter
1672 **Ridges**, William, London, skinner (Copy)
1796 **Ridgeway**, John, Ballydermot, King's co.
1635 **Ridgewell**, John, clk., Ballymacwilliam, King's co.
1627 **Ridgway**, Catherine, Dubl., widow of George R., esq.
1691 ,, Henry, College-green, near Dublin, gent.
1763 ,, Henry, Mountmellick, Queen's co.
1748 ,, John, Ballycarroll, Queen's co.
1768 ,, Joshua, Ballycarroll, Queen's co., gent.
1745 ,, Samuel, Dublin, shag-weaver
1702 ,, William, Ballycarroll, Queen's co., farmer
1796 **Ridley**, Ellinor, Tullamore, King's co., widow
1782 ,, Francis, Tullamore, King's co., merchant
1628 **Ridworth**, John, Armagh, burgess
1803 **Rierdan**, Simon, Whitehall, farmer
        [See REARDAN.]
1719 **Rieusset**, David, Dublin, vintner
1726 **Rieutort**, Wm., Chelsea, Middlesex, esq. (Copy)
1773 **Rigaile**, Mariana, Dublin, joiner
1737 **Rigandie**, Elizabeth, Dublin, widow
1786 **Rigby**, Alex., Dublin, gent.
1711 ,, Edward, par. St. Andrew, Holborn, esq. (Copy)
1784 ,, Mary, Spellanstown, King's co., widow
1669 **Rigg**, Abraham, Dublin, skinner
1803 ,, Amelia Josepha, Merrion-st., Dublin, spinster
1810 ,, Elenor, Bride's-alley, Dublin, widow
1737 ,, Elizabeth, Savile-green, Yorkshire, spinster (Copy)
1803 ,, Mathias, Bride's-alley, Dublin, cabinet-maker
1808 ,, Samuel, Clonmel, co. Tipperary, tanner
1750 **Rigge**, Thomas, Clonmel
1778 ,, Thomas
1716 **Riggs**, Allen, Dunmanway, co. Cork, esq.
1769 ,, Anne, widow of Edward R., Dublin, esq.
1702 ,, Edward, Riggsdale, co. Cork, esq.

1741 **Riggs,** Edward, Dublin, esq.
1743 ,, Edward, Middle Temple, Lond.
1634 ,, George, Dublin, carpenter
1721 ,, Geo., Milltown, co. Limerick, gent.
1739 ,, Geo., Middle Temple, London
1756 ,, sir John Webb, Riggsdale, co. Cork, esq.
1782 ,, John, Killucan, co. Westmeath, farmer
1811 ,, John, Leinster-street, Dublin, cabinetmaker
1667 **Right,** Robert, par. Amwell, Hertfordshire (Copy)
1747 **Rigmaiden,** Anne, *alias* **Wilmot,** wife to Robert R., Meath-st.
1783 ,, Robt., Rathmaiden, co. Meath, esq.
1784 ,, Robt., Rathmaiden, co. Meath, esq.
1774 **Rigney,** Catherine, Dublin, widow
1796 **Riky,** Arthur, Airfield, co. Dublin, gent.
1805 ,, Mary, Brown-st., Dublin, wid.
1804 ,, Robert, Brown-street, co. Dubl.
1727 **La Rimbilier,** James, Dublin, esq.
1780 **Ringland.** Martha, Carmin, co. Monaghan
1747 **Ringrose,** John, Moyne, co. Clare, esq.
1795 ,, Mary, widow (Will delivered out to Registry of Killaloe)
1783 ,, Sylvester, Clonusher, co. Clare, gent.
1768 **Ringwood,** Grace, Closeland, Queen's co., widow
1757 ,, Thomas, Tinnoran, co. Wicklow, farmer
1791 ,, Wm., Dublin, painter
1794 ,, Wm., Johnstown, co. Kilkenny, gent.
1808 **Rinkle,** Thomas, Dublin city, silk-dyer
1766 **Rinn,** James, Cornmarket, Dublin, woollen draper
1806 **Riordan,** Jas., Killarney, co. Kerry
1798 ,, Timothy, Macroom, co. Cork, housekeeper
[See REARDAN.]
1741 **Riordane,** Margaret, North Suburbs of Cork, widow
1798 **Risk,** Wm., Sandymount, co. Dublin
1747 **De La Rivaliere,** Theophilus, a capt. in His Majesty's Service (Copy)
1753 **Rivers,** Bartholomew
1809 ,, Bartholomew, Tramore, co. Waterford
1798 ,, Richard, Clonmel, co. Tipperary, merchant

1811 **Riversdale,** right hon. Rose, lady baroness
1788 ,, right hon. Wm., lord baron
1790 **Roach,** Domnk., Drogheda, coachowner
[See ROCHE.]
1677 **Roades,** John, Ballinruddy, Queen's co. (Copy)
1798 **Roan,** Thos., Kildare town, mercht.
1692 **Roane,** John, bp of **Killaloe,** q. v.
1719 **Robberts,** Hodder, Cork, gent.
1749 ,, Sarah, widow
1791 **Robbins,** Edward, Stephen's-gr., Dublin, stucco man
1780 ,, Esther, Dublin, spinster
1693 ,, Geo., New Ross, co. Wexford, gent.
1769 ,, John, Ballyduff, co. Kilkenny, esq.
1725 ,, Joseph, Ballyduff, co. Kilkenny, esq.
1761 ,, Joseph, Ballyduff, co. Tipp., esq. (Large will)
1740 ,, Martha, Ballyduff, co. Kilkenny, spinster
1697 ,, Nathaniel, Derryclony, co. Tipperary, gent.
1739 ,, Nathaniel, Dublin, esq.
1768 ,, Nathaniel, Hymenstown, co. Tipperary, gent
1770 ,, Richard, Dublin, esq.
1739 ,, Sarah, spinster
[See ROBINSON.]
1667 **Robert,** William, Dublin, gent.
1754 **Roberts,** Arth., Stradbally, Queen's co., innholder
1795 ,, Bridget, *alias* **Norris,** Ardmore, co. Cork
1770 ,, Catherine, Cork, widow
1804 ,, Charles, Rose Hill, co. Meath, clerk
1740 ,, David, lieut. in col. Johnston's regt. of foot
1749 ,, Edward, Cloverhill, co. Cavan, gent.
1801 ,, Elizabeth, Dublin city, widow
1635 ,, Ellen, Dublin, widow
1747 ,, Ellinor, Dublin, widow
1781 ,, Geo., Kile, Queen's co., gent.
1761 ,, Giles, Dublin, goldsmith
1756 ,, Hellen, Cloverhill, co. Cavan, widow
1680 ,, Hugh, Dublin, gent.
1736 ,, Jas., Athlone, co. Roscommon
1723 ,, John, Dublin, victualler
1725 ,, John, Dublin, esq.
1757 ,, John, Cragbrien, co. Clare, gardener
1778 ,, John, capt. in 65th regt. of foot
1797 ,, John, Park, co. Cork, esq.

1726 **Roberts,** Lewis, Dublin, esq.
1771 ,, Lewis, Dubl., esq. (Not proved)
1742 ,, Michael, Glanworth, co. Cork
1807 ,, Big Philip, of the town of Buckingham, clk.
1719 ,, Randal, Bridgetown, co. Cork, esq.
1753 ,, Randall, Glanworth, co. Cork, clerk
1707 ,, Richard, Dublin, gent.
1737 ,, rev. Robert, vicar of Killmadaly, dio. Clonfert
1741 ,, Robt., Mountrath, Queen's co.
1758 ,, Robert, Monkstown, esq.
1732 ,, Thomas, Dublin, carpenter
1745 ,, Thomas, Britfieldstown, co. Cork, esq.
1785 ,, Thomas, Limerick city, mercht.
1801 ,, Thomas, Cork city, banker
1678 ,, Walter, Dublin, gent.
1727 ,, William, Dublin, merchant
1742 ,, William, Dublin, LL.D.
    [See ROBBERTS.]
1794 **Robertson,** Cather., Upper Ground, Surrey, widow
1810 ,, Catherine, Ormond-quay, Dub., widow
1810 ,, Elizabeth, par. Dunboe, co. Derry
1807 ,, James, Dorset-street, Dublin, coach proprietor
1734 ,, John, Belfast, gardener
1732 ,, Margaret, Donard, co. Wicklow, widow
1768 ,, Margaret, Dublin, widow
1729 ,, Moab, Dublin, linendraper
1722 ,, Samuel, Rathkeale, co. Limk., gent.
1732 **Robin,** Francis de Portereau, esq. (Copy)
1807 **Robinett,** William, Cork city, merchant
1775 **Robins,** Anne, New Ross, co. Wexford, widow
1754 ,, George, New Ross, formerly of Ballyduff, co. Kilkenny, esq.
1799 ,, Mary, Dublin
1737 ,, Thomas, Rathfarnham, co. Dublin
1750 **Robinson,** Abraham, Dublin, merchant
1804 ,, Alex., Dublin city, merchant
1747 ,, Alice, Dublin, widow
1768 ,, Andrew, Gurteen, co. Tipp., farmer
1742 ,, Anne, Dublin, widow
1744 ,, Anne, Dublin, widow
1750 ,, Anne, Dublin, widow
1650 ,, Anthony, Dublin, vintner
1754 ,, Bryan, Dublin, M.D.

1754 **Robinson,** Christr., Dubl., pewterer
1787 ,, Christopher, 2nd Justice of the King's Bench
1747 ,, Dorothy, Armagh, wife to Dr. Arthur R.
1679 ,, Edward, Dublin, girdler
1741 ,, Elizabeth, Dublin
1788 ,, Elizabeth, Dublin, widow
1793 ,, Elizabeth
1769 ,, George, Grange, co. Leitrim, esq.
1774 ,, George, Dublin, esq.
1782 ,, George, Tripollo, Dubl., gent.
1789 ,, George, Cavanaca, co. Armagh
1804 ,, George, Baltinagarby, co. Westmeath, farmer
1763 ,, Henry, Dublin, coachmaker
1804 ,, Henry, Ballyconnell, co. Westmeath, gent.
1810 ,, Henry, Crossakiel, co. Meath
1794 ,, Isabella, Dublin, shipbroker
1810 ,, Jane, North Strand, Dublin, widow
1752 ,, John, New Grove, co. Meath, esq.
1758 ,, John, Dublin, brazier
1769 ,, John, Barcony, co. Cavan
1790 ,, John, Dublin, attorney
1792 ,, John, York-street, Dublin, merchant
1795 ,, John, Lisglassoge, co. Longford, esq.
1803 ,, John, Dublin, public notary
1805 ,, Joseph, Birr, King's co.
1742 ,, Mary, Lismoyney, co. Westmeath
1793 ,, Mary, *alias* **Montgomery**
1808 ,, Maxwell, Bagnio Slip, Dublin
1742 ,, Philip, Lisburn, co. Antrim, merchant
1805 ,, Rebecca, Kevin-street, Dublin, widow
1716 ,, Richard, Monaghan, gent.
1795 ,, Richard, abp. of **Armagh,** q. v.
1770 ,, Robert, Dublin, M.D.
1801 ,, Robert, Kilbeggan, co. Westmeath
1797 ,, Samuel, Beggarsbush, Dublin, bleacher
1809 ,, Samuel, Cloonrogeen, co. Sligo, esq.
1797 ,, Sidney, Dublin, widow
1743 ,, Susanna, Dublin, spinster
1619 ,, Thomas, dean of Kilmore
1672 ,, Thomas, Rathcoole, co. Dubl., gent.
1762 ,, Thomas, Carone, co. Cork, gent.
1675 ,, Wm., Hammersmith, Middlesex, esq.

1725 **Robinson**, sir Wm., par. St. Martin, Middlesex, knt. (Copy)
1748 ,, William, A.M., rector of Kilbragan, dio. Cork
1757 ,, William, Dublin, linen weaver
1785 ,, sir William, par. St. George, Middlesex, bart.
1787 ,, William, Bermondsey, Surrey, sailmaker (Copy)
1800 ,, William, Coolmine, co. Dublin, farmer
1801 ,, William, town of Wexford, esq.
[See ROBBINS, ROBIN.]
1796 **Robison**, David, capt. in the Invalid Company of Irish Artillery
1690 ,, Robert, rector of Belturbet, co. Cavan (Ex.)
1758 ,, Susanna, Dublin, widow
1723 ,, Thomas, Camphire, co. Waterford, yeoman
1798 **Robnett**, John, Armagh city, gent.
1801 ,, Peter, Dublin city
1655 **Robsart**, Ambrose, soldier in the Protector's regt. of foot
1768 **Robson**, John, Antrim, gent.
1741 ,, Mathew, Clonmel, co. Tipp., innkeeper
1590 **Robyns**, Arthur, Robyne-Roche or Pleurtue, co. Cork, esq.
1793 **Roch**, Catherine, Carrick-on-Suir, co. Tipp., widow
1750 ,, Edmond, Cork, esq.
1786 ,, Henry, Dublin, professor of midwifery
1744 ,, James, Dungarvan, co. Waterford, esq.
1793 ,, James, Odell Lodge, co. Waterford, esq.
1713 ,, Murtogh, Dublin, linendraper
1754 ,, William, Lissahane, co. Kerry
1763 **Roche**, Anna Maria, called viscountess Fermoy
1781 ,, Anne, Limerick, widow
1768 ,, Anthony, Ennis, co. Clare, merchant
1801 ,, Benjamin, Fonthill, co. Carlow, esq.
1786 ,, Blanch, Limerick city, widow
1794 ,, Blanch, Limerick, spinster
1807 ,, sir Boyle, Eccles-street, Dubl., bart.
1785 ,, Catherine, Limerick city, wid.
1797 ,, David, senr., Limerick city, esq.
1797 ,, David, Pill-lane, Dublin, gent.
1630 ,, Edmond, Kinsale, burgess (Copy)
1714 ,, Edmond, Ringabelly, co. Cork, esq. (sentence for his will)

1747 **Roche**, Elizabeth, widow of Thos. R., Dublin, merchant
1804 ,, Elizabeth, Kilkenny city, wid.
1668 ,, Francis FitzEdward, late of Cork, esq.
1754 ,, Francis, Cork, coachmaker
1795 ,, Hugh, town of Cove, mariner
1723 ,, James, Glynn, co. Waterford, esq.
1755 ,, James, Waterford, merchant
1768 ,, James, Dublin, gent.
1787 ,, James, Droumanaragill, co. Cork, gent.
1799 ,, James, Tibraghney, co. Kilkenny, farmer
1736 ,, John, Dublin, esq.
1760 ,, John, senior, Limerick, mercht.
1789 ,, John Philip, Limerick city, esq.
1800 ,, John, the elder, town of Cove
1804 ,, John Stephen, Limerick city
1595 ,, Jordan, Limerick, alderman
1788 ,, Luke, Kilkenny, esq.
1798 ,, Margaret, Limerick city, wid.
1655 ,, Morrish Fitz Edward, Cork, merchant
1605 ,, Philip, Limerick, merchant
1658 ,, Philip, Kinsale
1664 ,, Philip, Kinsale, esq.
1759 ,, Philip, Ballinluge, co. Cork, gent.
1797 ,, Philip John, Limerick city, merchant
1713 ,, Philips, Dublin, merchant
1730 ,, Richard, Dublin, esq.
1769 ,, Richard, Limerick, linendraper
1788 ,, Sarah Anne, Dublin, widow
1787 ,, Stephen, Limerick, surgeon
1744 ,, Thomas, Dublin, merchant
1776 ,, Thomas, Dublin, esq.
1733 ,, Ulicke, commonly called lord viscount Fermoy
1595 ,, Walter, New Ross, gent.
1754 ,, rev. William, prebendary of Killedy, dio. of Limk., clk.
1798 ,, William, Youghal, co. Cork
[See ROACH, ROCH.]
1733 **DeRochebrune**, Brunet, Dubl., esq.
1723 **Rochery**, Mary
1726 **Rochett**, Lewis, Lisburn, co. Antrim, merchant
1728 **Rochford**, David, Cork, merchant
1630 ,, Wm., Brenanstown, co. Dubl.
1679 ,, William, Laragh, co. Kildare, gent.
1770 **Rochfort**, Alice
1768 ,, Anne, *alias* **Malone**, widow
1811 ,, Charles, Tyrell's-pass, co. Westmeath
1733 ,, David, Cork, merchant
1811 ,, David, Cork city, esq.

1771 **Rochfort**, Emilia, *alias* **Wilson**
1732 ,, Hannah, widow
1784 ,, Henrietta, Dublin, widow
1665 ,, Henry, Kilbride, co. Meath, esq.
1730 ,, George, Callstown, co. Westmeath, esq.
1786 ,, George, Side Brook, co. Westmeath, esq.
1639 ,, James, Rathdrum, co. Wicklow, gent.
1662 ,, Jenico, Kilbride, co. Meath, esq.
1771 ,, John, Dublin, esq.
1809 ,, Mark, Balbriggan, co. Dublin, esq.
1811 ,, Martha
1809 ,, Michael, Limk. city, merchant
1764 ,, Richard, Jamestown, Queen's co., gent.
1727 ,, Robert, Dublin, esq.
1801 ,, Robert
1772 ,, William, Clontarf, co. Dubl., esq.
1702 **Rochforte**, James, Laragh, co. Kildare, esq.
[See ROCHFORD.]
1735 **Rock**, Owen, Killadreeny, co. Wicklow, farmer
1784 **Rockingham**, the Most Noble Charles, Marquis of (Copy)
1751 ,, Thomas, Marquis of (Copy)
1628 **Rockold**, John, Dublin, merchant
1749 **Roddy**, Edmond, par. Street, co. Westmeath, farmer
1739 ,, John, Dublin, merchant
1802 **Roden**, rt. hon. Anne, dowager countess of
1798 ,, Robert, earl of
1774 **Roderick**, Martin, Dungarvan, co. Waterford, esq.
1781 **Rodgers**, John, surgeon's mate, 32nd regt. of foot
1735 ,, Thomas, Annacray, co. Monaghan, gent.
[See ROGERS.]
1742 **Rodwell**, Tobias, Fouldon, Norfolk, yeoman (Copy)
1723 **Roe**, Alice, Drogheda, spinster
1747 ,, Alice, Dublin, widow
1713 ,, Andrew, Tipperary town, gent. (Large will)
1751 ,, Andrew, Mountbrins, co. Tipp., esq.
1808 ,, Andrew, Belview, co. Tipperary, esq.
1751 ,, Charles, Dublin
1774 ,, Charles, Dublin
1807 ,, Christiana, Dublin city, widow
1622 ,, sir Francis, Mountjoy, knt.

1765 **Roe**, Geo., Roesborough, co. Tipp., esq.
1783 ,, George Castle, Upper Ormondquay, gent.
1791 ,, Hanover, Rosanna, co. Tipp.
1756 ,, Henry, the Grange, Ballycoolen, co. Dublin, farmer
1761 ,, James, Roesborough, co. Tipp., esq.
1668 ,, John, Dublin, gent.
1673 ,, John, Bandon Bridge, co. Cork, gent.
1713 ,, John, par. St. Mary, Drogheda, gent.
1717 ,, John, Island of Antigua, in America, gent. (Copy)
1774 ,, John, Dublin, printer
1780 ,, John, Cork, esq.
1782 ,, John, Cootehill, co. Cavan, gent.
1809 ,, John, Rath
1784 ,, Joseph, Birr, King's co., cordwainer
1796 ,, Mary, Aughrim-street, Dublin, widow.
1719 ,, Patrick, Warrenstown, co. Meath, gent.
1749 ,, Patrick, Dublin, grocer
1771 ,, Richard, Dion, co. Monaghan, gent.
1799 ,, Richard, Pimlico, Dublin, distiller
1790 ,, Robert, Ranelagh, co. Dublin, gent.
1793 ,, Robert, Ringsend, Dublin
1770 ,, Thomas, Limerick, esq.
1781 ,, Thos., Mountroe, co. Armagh, esq.
1803 ,, Thomas, Dublin, labourer
1744 ,, William, Roesgreen, co. Tipp., esq.
[See ROWE.]
1725 **Roffen**, rev. Richard, Rossmore, clk.
1784 **Rogers**, Adam, the elder, Boderam, co. Wexford, esq.
1745 ,, Agnes Rochelle, South Lib. of Cork, widow
1779 ,, Allen, Dublin, victualler
1786 ,, Bayley, Cork city, esq.
1750 ,, Bignell, Dublin, gent.
1740 ,, Christopher, Lotamore, co. Cork city, esq.
1797 ,, Daniel, Ballynavin, co. Tipperary, esq.
1797 ,, David, Ballynavin, co. Tipperary, esq.
1787 ,, Edward, Bessmount, co. Wexford, esq.
1804 ,, Eleanor, widow

1768 **Rogers,** Elizabeth, Dublin, widow
1811 ,, Elizabeth, Bessmount, co.Wexford, widow
1721 ,, George, Lota, co. Cork, esq.
1799 ,, George, Dublin, pawnbroker
1728 ,, Hannah, Cork, widow
1726 ,, Henry, Kill, co. Kildare, innkeeper
1774 ,, Henry, Cork, esq.
1675 ,, Humphrey, organist of St. Mary's Church, Limerick
1808 ,, James, Thomas-court, Dublin
1807 ,, Joanna, Cork city, widow
1656 ,, John, Youghal, tailor
1691 ,, John, Urnston, Lancashire, gent.
1758 ,, John, Cork, merchant
1767 ,, John, Ashgrove, co. Cork, esq.
1776 ,, John, Monaghan, gent.
1781 ,, John, Dublin, gent.
1808 ,, John, clerk
1760 ,, Jonathan, D.D., rector of Loughgall
1757 ,, Joseph, Cork, esq.
1791 ,, Joseph, New Ross, co. Wexford, esq.
1801 ,, Joseph, Cork city, esq.
1810 ,, Joseph,' captain on half-pay of the 85th regiment
1729 ,, Linegar, Dublin, widow
1743 ,, Luke, Carraghdobbin, co. Waterford, gent.
1735 ,, Mary, Finglas, co. Dublin, wid.
1770 ,, Mary, *alias* **Perryman,** widow of Edward R., esq.
1792 ,, Mary, Sunday's Well, co. Cork
1773 ,, Neal, Dublin, merchant
1780 ,, Noblett, Cork city
1804 ,, Patrick, Upper Church-street
1797 ,, Pierce, Portlaw, co. Waterford, gent.
1788 ,, Quinton
1701 ,, Richard, Dublin, cook
1726 ,, Richard, Balgeen, co. Meath, gent.
1751 ,, Richard, Balgeen, co. Meath, gent.
1718 ,, Robert, Lota, co. Cork city, esq.
1787 ,, Robert, Lota, North Liberties of Cork, esq.
1800 ,, Robert, Cork, esq.
1787 ,, Simon, Magheracloney, co. Monaghan
1784 ,, Thomas, Killure, co. Waterford, gent.
1787 ,, Thos., Monaghan town, gent.
1787 ,, Thomas, Dublin, merchant
1808 ,, Thomas, master of the ship " Charlotte "

1764 **Rogers,** Tobias, Moira, co. Down, gt.
1788 ,, rev. Wm., Prussia-st., Dublin, clk.
1799 ,, William, Grange-Geeth, co. Meath, gent.
1800 ,, William, Cork, esq.
1807 ,, William, Dublin city [See RODGERS.]
1758 **Rogerson,** Bridget, Dublin
1724 ,, sir John, Dublin, knt.
1741 ,, John, Lord Chief Justice of King's Bench
1785 ,, John, Bettyville, co. Carlow, esq.
1735 ,, Susanna, Dublin, spinster
1726 **Roiffey,** John, Dublin, surgeon
1789 **Role,** Edward, Clonsagh, co. Dub., farmer
1698 **Rolle,** Samuel, Castletown, King's county, esq.
1713 ,, Saml., Ballyfin, co. Cork, gent.
1747 ,, Samuel, late of Ballyfin, co. Cork, clk.
1790 **Rolleston,** Catherine, Charleville, co. Cork, widow
1694 ,, Francis, Tomlogh, co. Tipperary, esq.
1779 ,, Howard, Charleville, co. Cork, gent.
1803 ,, Jas. Franck, Frankford, King's county, esq.
1780 ,, rev. Stephen, Bride Park, co. Cork, clk. [See RALSTON, ROULSTON.]
1811 **Rolston,** Henry, Barrack-st., Dub.
1783 **Rolt,** John, Cork, cooper
1800 ,, John, Cork city, cooper
1744 **Romain,** Nicholas, Dublin, esq.
1662 **Ronaine,** *alias* **Rice,** Margaret, widow of James Ronaine, and now wife to Barth. Rice [See RONAYNE.]
1662 **Ronan,** James, Limerick, merchant
1740 ,, John, mariner
1662 ,, Nicholas, Limerick, merchant
1719 **Ronane,** Dominick, Turcullen, co. Waterford, gent.
1788 **Ronayne,** Dominick, Fin Knock, co. Waterford, gent.
1762 ,, Edmond, Rochestown, co. Cork, gent.
1791 ,, Grace, Dublin, spinster
1787 ,, Jas., Dlaughlane, co. Waterford, esq.
1793 ,, Margaret, Cloughtane, co. Wexford, widow
1746 ,, Maurice, Dlaughlane, co. Waterford, gent.
1783 ,, Patk., Dlaughlane, co. Waterford, gent.

1802 **Ronayne**, Patrick, Ballynacrushy, co. Cork, gent.
1753 ,, Philip, Hodnetswood, co. Cork, gent.
1787 ,, Silvester, Youghal, co. Cork, gent.
1800 ,, Thomas, Judd-place, Middlesex, esq.
1773 ,, Wm., Cappoquin, co. Waterford, merchant
1804 ,, Uniacke, College-green, co. Waterford, gent.
[See RONAINE.]
1741 **Rone**, Anne, Dublin, widow
1722 ,, Bartholomew, Dublin, mercht.
1784 **Roney**, Edward, Thomas-street, Dublin, merchant
[See ROONEY.]
1704 **Ronsele**, Opitius Adrian Danes, lord baron
1639 **Rookby**, Ellynor, College-green, near Dublin, widow
1787 **Rooke**, Henry, Dublin, gent.
1808 ,, Thomas, Dublin city, barrister-at-law
1810 ,, Wm., Youghal, co. Cork, esq.
1805 **Rooney**, Christopher, Garristown, co. Dublin, farmer
1760 ,, Cusack, Dublin, surgeon
1808 ,, Jane, Sth. Gt. George's-st., Dublin
1754 ,, John, Rush, co. Dub., fisherman
1780 ,, John, Dublin, distiller
1759 ,, Margaret, Dublin, widow
1807 ,, Mathias, Trevet, co. Meath, gent.
1718 ,, Patrick, Tobergragan, co. Dublin, farmer
1782 ,, Patrick, Dublin, smith
1791 ,, Patrick, Dirty-lane, Dublin, timber merchant
1810 ,, Walter, Newmarket, co. Dub., brewer
1756 **Roony**, James, Dublin, gent.
1749 ,, Patrick, Navan, co. Meath, merchant
1793 ,, Roger, Glasnevin-road, co. Dublin
[See RONEY.]
1687 **Rooth**, Charles, Surlogstown, co. Kildare, gent.
1687 ,, Frances, *alias* **Craven**, Surlogstown, co. Kildare, widow
1805 **Roper**, Abigail, Roscommon, spr.
1737 ,, John, late captain in General Bisset's regiment of foot
1802 ,, Robert, Rosc., apothecary
1753 **Roquiere**, Moses, the elder, Dublin, gent.

1763 **Rork**, Elizbth., Pill-lane, Dub., wid.
1716 ,, Ternon, Creevy, co. Leitrim, gent.
1771 **Rorke**, Anne, Clogher, co. Roscommon, wid. (Not proved)
1768 ,, Bryan, Drumsna, co. Leitrim, gent.
1773 ,, Elenor, Dublin, widow
1803 ,, John, Morristown Lattin, co. Kildare, farmer
1773 ,, Margaret, Edgeworthstown, co. Longford
1792 ,, Mark, Dublin, surgeon
1797 ,, Peter, Gray's Inn, Middlesex, gent. (Copy)
1798 ,, Peter, Meath-st., Dublin, merchant, late of Maynooth
1768 ,, Roger, Dublin, gent.
[See ROURKE.]
1804 **Rosborough**, John, Newtown-Butler, co. Fermanagh, esq.
[See ROSSBROUGH.]
1699 **Roscarrock**, Edward, Rathmines, co. Dublin, esq.
1718 **Rosco**, Jeremiah, Dublin, gent.
1653 **Roscommon**, Anne, dowager countess
1694 ,, Carey, earl of (Copy from Dio. Chester)
1748 ,, James, earl of
1605 ,, Wentworth, earl of
1751 **Rose**, Cathne., par. St. Martin, Middlesex, widow
1631 ,, Edmond, St. Bride's par., Dub.
1693 ,, Edward, Dublin, merchant
1785 ,, George, Mount Pleasant, co. Limerick, esq.
1742 ,, Henry, one of the Justices of Common Pleas
1794 ,, James Fredk., Limerick, gent.
1772 ,, John, Dublin, merchant
1720 ,, Joshua, Sheffield, Yorkshire, cutler
1746 ,, Rand, Coleshall, co. Wexford, gent.
1762 ,, Richard, Limerick, gent.
1629 ,, Thomas, Cork, gent.
1680 ,, William, Rose Island, Scotland, esq.
1780 **Roseingrave**, William, Salthill, co. Dublin, esq.
1802 **Rosingrave**, Jane, Dublin, widow
1802 **Roslewin**, Ann Maria
1802 ,, Susanna
1802 ,, William
1747 **Ross**, Andrew, capt.-lieut. in col. Gardener's dragoons
1768 ,, Andrew, Dublin, saddler
1781 ,, Andrew, Robertstown, co. Kildare, gent.

1806 **Ross,** Ann, Beaufort Lodge, co. Londonderry
1748 ,, Christian Jane, Portavoe, co. Down, spinster (Copy)
1725 ,, David, Carrickfergus, carpenter
1798 ,, Edmond, Burgess, co. Tipp., gent.
1791 ,, Elizabeth, Tullamore, King's co., widow
1723 ,, Ferdinando, Dublin, gent.
1800 ,, Frances
1781 ,, Honora, Cork, widow
1696 ,, James, Portavoe, co. Down, esq. (Ex.)
1721 ,, James, Taulatokill, co. Antrim, farmer
1726 ,, James, mariner, master of the "Speedwell"
1734 ,, James, Portavoe, co. Down, esq.
1755 ,, James, Portavoe, co. Down
1757 ,, James, an officer in the Royal Hosp., near Kilmainham
1765 ,, James, Belfast, co. Antrim, merchant
1719 ,, John, Ballintogher, co. Sligo, esq.
1772 ,, John, Killoon, co. Tyrone
1791 ,, John, Garrymore, co. Tipp., gent.
1799 ,, John, Dublin, whiskey and malt factor
1810 ,, John, Burgess, co. Tipperary
1807 ,, rt. hon. Laurence Harman, earl of (Copy)
1786 ,, Margaret, Belfast
1802 ,, rt. hon. Ralph, earl of
1764 ,, Richard, earl of
1693 ,, Robert, Corean, rector of Annaduff, co. Leitrim
1750 ,, Robert, the elder, Rosstrevor, co. Down, esq.
1773 ,, Robert, Cork, vintner
1799 ,, Robert, Rosstrevor, co. Down, rt. hon.
1754 ,, Thomas, Limerick, merchant
1782 ,, Thomas, par. of Kingston, Jamaica, mariner (Copy)
1736 ,, William, Marykirk, co. Galway, gent.
1782 ,, William, Oldtore, co. Galway, esq.
1784 ,, William, Headfort, co. Galway, gent.
1788 ,, William, Derry city, esq.
1794 ,, William, Newtownlimavady, co. Derry, esq.
1786 **Rossbrough,** Alexander, Dublin, gent.
[See ROSBOROUGH.]

1799 **Rosse,** Catherine, Mount Pleasant, co. Limk., wid.
1700 ,, George, Fortfergus, Clare, esq.
1702 ,, Richard, lord viscount [See ROSS.]
1765 **Rossell,** Alice, Dublin, widow
1757 ,, Anne, Henry-street, Dublin, widow
1745 ,, Charles, Dublin, merchant
1754 ,, rev. Charles, Dublin, clk.
1770 ,, Susanna, *alias* **Aston,** Hollybrook, co. Dublin, widow [See RUSSELL.]
1811 **Rosseter,** Catherine
1788 ,, Frances, par. St. Paul, Dublin, spinster
1781 ,, Ignatius, New Ross, co. Wexford, merchant
1803 ,, William, Graigue, co. Kilkenny, merchant
1774 **Rossiter,** Ignatius, Graigue, co. Kilkenny, merchant
1806 ,, Joseph, Ross, co. Wexford, clk.
1801 **Rossmore,** rt. hon. Robert, lord baron of
1736 **Roth,** Abraham, Butlersgrove, co. Kilkenny (Large will; Ex.)
1696 ,, Edward, London, merchant (Copy)
1809 ,, Elizabeth
1736 ,, Gaspard, city of Paris (Large will) (Copy)
1786 ,, George, Dublin city, esq.
1689 ,, John, Kilkenny, merchant
1790 ,, Mary, Dublin, widow
1746 ,, Michael, Butlersgrove, co. Kilkenny
1693 ,, Peter, Clonmel, gent.
1771 ,, Richard, Mountrath, co. Kilkenny, esq.
1654 **Rothe,** Peter FitzJohn, Kilkenny, esq. (Copy)
1637 ,, Richard, Kilkenny, alderman
1623 ,, Robert, Kilkenny, esq.
1809 **Rotheram,** John
1788 ,, Samuel, Croghan, King's co.
1785 ,, Thomas, Crossdrum, co Meath, gent.
1789 ,, Thos., Dublin, tallow chandler
1781 ,, William, Drewstown, co. Meath, gent.
1648 **Rotherham,** sir Thomas, Dublin, knt., R. Co.
1755 **Rothery,** Deborah, Dublin, widow
1735 ,, Elizabeth, Dublin, widow
1731 ,, Nathaniel, Dublin, glazier
1752 **Rothwell,** John, Cannonstown, co. Meath, gent.
1735 ,, Mary, Berfordstown, co. Meath, widow

1780 **Rothwell**, Mary, Berfordstown, co. Meath, widow
1802 ,, Mary, widow
1781 ,, Richard, Berfordstown, co. Meath, gent.
1803 ,, William, late deceased (Copy)
1713 **Rotton**, John, Dublin, gent.
1724 ,, John, Dublin, esq.
1793 ,, John, Templeoge, co. Dublin, esq.
1731 **Rou**, Solomon, Portarlington, Queen's co., gent.
1796 **Rouet**, Wm., Aughendinan, Dumbartonshire (Copy)
1786 **Roughley**, Thomas, Dublin, linendraper
1733 **Rougier**, Jacob, Dublin, gent.
1810 **Roulston**, Thomas, Glen, co. Donegal
   [See ROLLESTON.]
1790 **Rourke**, Barnaby, Wickstown, co. Meath, farmer
1755 ,, Bryan, Dublin, clothier
1780 ,, Deborah, Dublin, widow
1797 ,, Edmond, Dublin, merchant
1810 ,, James, Birr, tanner
1750 ,, Jasper, Limerick, merchant
1780 ,, John, Kilmartin, co. Dublin, farmer
1796 ,, John, Dublin, pinmaker
1763 ,, Margaret, Limerick, widow
1788 ,, Mathew, Milltown-road, co. Dublin, farmer
   [See RORKE.]
1676 **Rous**, Anne, Dublin, widow
1729 ,, Joseph, Dublin, merchant
1808 **Rouse**, John, Bridetree, co. Dublin, farmer
1731 **Rousseliere**, Peter, Dublin, gent.
1711 **Roussell**, John Baptist, Bruges in Flanders (Copy)
1761 **Roussliere**, Francis Hector, Dublin, gent.
1705 **Row**, Anthony, par. St. Martin-in-the-Fields, Middlesex, esq. (Copy)
1734 **Rowan**, Alice, wife of Alexander R., Laggan, co. Down
1775 ,, Elizabeth, Dublin, widow
1794 ,, James, Ballyarnanallan, co. Down
1728 ,, rev. John, Ballynagappog, co. Down, clk.
1799 ,, Letitia, Dublin, widow   [co.
1809 ,, Margaret, Stradbally, Queen's
1772 ,, Mathew, Ballynascreen, co. Londonderry
1735 ,, Robert, Dublin, gent.
1742 ,, rev. Robt., Mullins, co. Antrim, clk. (Ex.)

1764 **Rowan**, Robert, Dublin, esq.
1768 ,, William, Richmond, Surrey, esq.
1672 **Rowe**, Dorothy, wife to Mr. Jas. R.
1707 ,, Henry, par. St. Martin,Middlesex, esq. (Copy)
1748 ,, James, mariner on board the "Syme" man-of-war
1581 ,, John, Navan, merchant
1708 ,, John, Rathmore, co. Meath, gent.
1780 ,, John, Liverpool, Lancashire, hairdresser
1807 ,, Mary, Cook-st., Dublin, widow
1769 ,, Richard, Ballyharty, co. Wexford, esq.
1731 ,, rev. Simon, rector of Ballynascreen, co. Londonderry
1810 ,, Wm., Rathmines, co. Dublin, artist
   [See ROE.]
1735 **Rowland**, Anne, Dublin, widow
1788 ,, David, Flood-street, Dublin, yeoman
1803 ,, Edward, major in Cork city royal regt. of militia
1780 ,, Joseph, Goat-alley, Dublin, distiller
1803 ,, sir Samuel, Cork, knt.
1764 ,, William, Bandon
1743 **Rowlands**, Edward, Dublin, gent. (Copy)
   [See RAWLINS.]
1684 **Rowles**, Fortescue, Dublin, esq.
1683 ,, Wm., Dunganstown, co. Wexford, gent.
1636 **Rowley**, Anne, Coleraine, widow
1748 ,, Catherine, Dublin, spinster
1781 ,, hon. Clotworthy
1805 ,, Clotworthy, Ravenswell, co. Dublin
1711 ,, George, Maberath, co. Meath, farmer
1742 ,, Henry, Maberath, co. Meath, esq.
1744 ,, Hercules, Summerhill, co. Meath, esq.
1701 ,, Hugh, Callmore, co. Londonderry, esq.
1791 ,, James, Dublin, slater
1767 ,, Letitia, Dublin, widow
1720 ,, Mary, Dublin, widow
1809 ,, Patrick, Carrick-on-Suir, co. Tipperary
1774 ,, Peter,Ballyshannon,co.Kildare
1669 ,, Seth, Shrewsbury, Shropshire, gent. (Copy)
1768 ,, sir Wm., K.C.B., Admiral of the Fleet (Copy)
   [See RAWLEIGH.]

1732 **Rowlinson**, Anne, par. St. James, Westminster, widow (Copy) [See RAWLINS.]

1800 **Royce**, Thomas Henry, Nantenan, co. Limerick, esq. [See RICE.]

1773 **Roycroft**, John, Bracklooney, co. Cavan

1789 ,, Wm., Hollymount, co. Mayo, merchant

1675 **Roydon**, Mathew, Dubl., esq. (Ex.)

1735 **Royne**, Christopher, Huntstown, co. Dublin, gent.

1801 **Royse**, Anne, co. Limerk. city, wid.

1793 ,, Henry, Kilcornan, co. Limerick, clerk

1811 ,, Nicholas F., Nantenan, co. Limerick, esq.

1768 ,, Vere, Limerick, esq. [See RICE.]

1808 **Rubie**, John, Coolmana, co. Cork, farmer

1806 **Ruckley**, Mary, Camden-st., Dubl., widow

1719 **Ruckman**, Richard, Cork-street, Dublin, gardener

1637 **Ruckston**, Jno.,Shanboe,co.Meath, farmer

1758 **Rudd**, Benjamin, Dublin, carpenter

1809 ,, Richard, Clone, co. Wexford, gent.

1790 ,, Stephen, Dublin, builder

1597 ,, Thomas, London, haberdasher (Copy)

1806 **Ruddell**, George, Knockrummer, co. Armagh

1808 **Ruddock**, Bridget, Kinsale

1733 ,, Wm., lieut. in lord Tyrawley's regt.

1762 **Rudkin**, Anne, Wells, co. Carlow

1760 ,, Bernard, Tinnegarney, co. Carlow, gent.

1722 ,, Mark, Coreys, co. Carlow, gt.

1794 ,, Mary, Carlow town

1719 **Rudyerd**, Sarah, wife to John R., London, mercer

1708 **Ruerke**, Edmond, Dublin, vintner

1733 ,, Elizabeth, Kilkenny, widow

1671 **Rugge**, Henry, clk., dean of St. Colman, Cloyne

1744 **Ruisset**, David

1744 **Rule**, Jane, wid. of rev. Dr. Ralph R.

1737 **Rulland**, Andrew, Dublin, mercht.

1755 ,, John, Temple-bar, Dublin, gt.

1751 ,, Sarah, Dublin, widow

1712 **Rumsey**, William, Dublin, gent. [See RAMSAY.]

1743 **Rundle**, Thomas, bishop of **Derry**, q. v.

1780 **Rush**, Mathew, Tuam, co. Galway, gent.

1675 **Rushworth**, Thomas, Athy, mchnt.

1785 **Russel**, Henry, Dublin, wine cooper

1787 ,, John, Essex-street, Dublin

1786 ,, Nicholas

1734 ,, Thomas, Bride-street, Dublin, merchant

1781 ,, Thos., Mountmellick, Queen's co., shopkeeper

1811 **Russell**, Abraham, Limerick city, merchant

1759 ,, Anne, Dublin, widow

1660 ,, Barthol., Waterford, maltster

1776 ,, Bryan, Ennis, co. Clare, M.D.

1739 ,, Charles, Portaferry, co. Down, gent.

1755 ,, Christopher, Dublin, surgeon

1790 ,, Christopher, Dublin, woollen draper

1811 ,, Christopher, Hardwick-street, Dublin, carpenter

1639 ,, Edmund, Tallow, co. Waterford

1775 ,, Elizabeth, Dublin, widow

1790 ,, Elizabeth, Dublin, widow

1750 ,, Francis, Dublin, merchant

1768 ,, Francis, Dublin, merchant

1800 ,, Francis, Limerick city, burgess

1805 ,, Francis, Roscrea, co. Tipp., shopkeeper

1790 ,, Garrett [date]

1597 ,, Gilbert, Seton, co. Dublin (No date)

1764 ,, Henry, Boleck, co. Galway,esq.

1790 ,, Hugh, Dublin

1720 ,, James, Dublin, gent.

1728 ,, James, Dublin, gent.

1780 ,, James, Tipperary town, gent.

1785 ,, James, Brampton, near London

1802 ,, James, Moate, co. Westmeath

1811 ,, Jas., Ratheragan, King's co., farmer

1809 ,, Jane, Harold's Cross, co. Dublin, widow

1583 ,, John, Surgotstown, co. Dublin, gent.

1687 ,, John, Emly, co. Tipperary, gt.

1724 ,, John, Ballybeg, Queen's co.

1729 ,, John, Rutland, co. Carlow, gt.

1729 ,, John, Ballydavid, co. Tipp.

1737 ,, John, Tallow, co. Waterford, gent.

1794 ,, John, Mabbot-street, Dublin, merchant

1800 ,, John, Cork city, merchant

1774 ,, Joseph, Ballinamuda,co. Westmeath, farmer

1805 ,, Joseph, Licenode, co. Westmeath, farmer (Copy)

1678 ,, Mary, *alias* **Askin**, Headfort, co. Galway, widow

1721	**Russell**, Mary, *alias* **Redmon**, *alias* **Galbally**, Dublin	
1761	,,	Mary, *alias* **Kirksha**, widow of Bernard R., Dublin, gent.
1793	,,	Mary, Limerick city
1799	,,	Mary, Dublin, spinster
1741	,,	Nuthaniel, Dublin, shoemaker
1759	,,	Patk., Dundalk, co. Louth, gt.
1794	,,	Patrick, Dublin
1763	,,	Phillip, Limerick, gent.
1729	,,	Richd., Currihills, co. Kildare, gent.
1667	,,	Robert, Birr, King's co., gent.
1688	,,	Robert, Usk, co. Kildare
1769	,,	Samuel, Upper Coombe, Dubl., clothier
1803	,,	Samuel, Coombe, Dub., clothier
1791	,,	Sarah, Dublin, widow
1778	,,	Sidney, Mt. Norris, co. Armagh, widow
1700	,,	Theodore, Dublin, esq. (Ex.)
1714	,,	Thomas, Athlone, gent.
1745	,,	ven. Thomas, archd. of Cork
1786	,,	Thomas, Dundalk, co. Louth, merchant
1735	,,	Valentine, Rathcurr, co. Louth, gent.
1582	,,	Walter, Drogheda, merchant
1780	,,	Wm., Tipperary town, gent.
1795	,,	Wm., Limerick, merchant [See ROSSELL.]
1750	**Ruth**, Andrew, Dublin, merchant	
1774	,,	James, Portumna, co. Galway, merchant
1748	,,	John, mariner on board the '' Terrible ''
1752	,,	Thomas, Birr, merchant
1809	**Rutherford**, John, Dublin city, mason	
1732	**Rutledge**, Anne, widow of capt. Simon	
1725	,,	Edward, Athy, co. Kildare, gent.
1809	,,	Elizabeth
1775	,,	Francis, Tuniecarrow, co. Roscommon, gent.
1718	,,	John, Grove, co. Kilk., gent.
1784	,,	Nicholas, Killeens, co. Sligo, gent.
1768	,,	Peter, Carrowkillen, co. Mayo, gent.
1800	,,	Peter, Cornfield, co. Mayo
1811	,,	Richard, Moore-street, Dublin, gent.
1757	,,	Thomas, Cloonameighin, co. Sligo, gent.
1792	,,	Thomas, Dublin, shoemaker
1805	,,	Thomas, Bushfield, co. Mayo, esq.
1760	,,	William, Corrymore, co. Rosc.

1800	**Rutledge**, Wm., Foxford, co. Mayo, esq.	
1671	**Ruttledge**, George, Griffinrath, co. Kildare, gent.	
1683	**Ruxton**, Henry, Bective, co. Meath, gent.	
1785	,,	John, Atherdee, co. Louth, esq.
1795	,,	rev. John, chaplain of 56th regt. of foot
1791	,,	Letitia, Dublin, widow
1767	,,	Mary, Atherdee, co. Louth, widow
1758	,,	Rendr., Dublin, joiner
1674	,,	Wm., Clonecurry, co. Meath, gent.
1751	,,	William, Ardee, co. Louth
1807	**Ryall**, Charles, Carrahtemple, co. Tipperary	
1797	,,	Phineas, Clonmel, co. Tipperary, esq. [See RIAL.]
1764	**Ryan**, Andrew, Commune, co. Tipperary, gent.	
1791	,,	Andrew, Gortkelly, co. Tipperary, gent.
1736	,,	Anthony, Dublin, victualler
1755	,,	Anthony, Dublin, apothecary
1772	,,	Anthony, Derryleagh, co. Tipperary, gent.
1810	,,	Beaumont, Baughillstown, co. Carlow
1811	,,	Charles, Church-steet, Dublin, apothecary
1630	,,	Daniel FitzWilliam, Cashel, gent.
1753	,,	Daniel, Carrick-on-Suir, co. Tipperary, gent.
1773	,,	Daniel, Inch, co. Tipperary, esq.
1798	,,	Daniel Frederick, Dublin, surgeon
1804	,,	Daniel, Limerick city, esq.
1682	,,	Darby, Castlemartyn, co. Cork, gent. (Copy)
1737	,,	Darby, Liverpool, Lancashire, merchant
1760	,,	Darby, Clogher, co. Tipperary, gent.
1803	,,	David, formerly of Barnhill, co. Carlow, but late a prisoner in the Four Court Marshall-sea
1773	,,	Dephina, Clane, co. Kildare
1811	,,	Denis, Clonmel, co. Tipperary, merchant
1735	,,	Dominick, Dublin, apothecary
1686	,,	Edmond, Ullard, co. Kilkenny, gent.
1741	,,	Edmond, Dublin, gent.
1779	,,	Edmond, Dublin, esq.

1697 **Ryves**, Wm., Cranmore, co.Carlow, esq.
1768 ,, William, Upper Court, co. Kilkenny, esq.
1783 ,, William, Castle Jane, co. Lim., esq.
1797 ,, Wm., Whitestown, co. Wicklow, esq.
   [See REEVES.]

——S——

1759 **Sabine**, Joseph, lieutenant-general of the forces (Copy)
1775 **Sacheverell**, rev. Thomas, vicar of Donaghmore
1780 **Sackville**, George, lord viscount (Copy)
1752 **Sadleir**, Bridget, Sopwell, co. Tipperary, spinster
1730 ,, Charles, Castletown, co. Tipperary, esq.
1772 ,, Clement, Shronehill, co. Tip.
1803 ,, Clement, Cork, master cooper
1718 ,, Ellenor, Dublin, widow
1798 ,, Francis, Sopwell Hall, co. Tipperary, esq. (Large)
1788 ,, Margaret, widow
1692 ,, Mary, Sopwell Hall, or Kilnelaha, co. Tipperary, widow
1725 ,, Thomas, Killnalough, co. Tipperary, esq.
1746 **Sadlir**, Robert, Brookfield, co. Tipperary, esq.
1776 **Saffeary**, John, Northumberland-st., Dublin, carpenter
1748 **Sailly**, Isaac, capt. in Gen. Bragg's regiment
1806 **Saint**, Joseph, Sir John Rogerson's-quay, Dublin
1726 **St. Agnam**, Alexander
1809 **St. Albans**, rt. hon. Aubrey, duke of
1757 **St. Aubyn**, Christian, Watfd., wid.
1739 **St. Clair**, lieutenant John
1733 ,, Mary, Clonmel, co. Tip., wid.
   [See SINCLAIR.]
1784 **St. Claire**, John, paymaster of 17th light dragoons
1762 **St. Clare**, James, Oldcastle, co. Meath, gent.
1702 **St. George**, Arthur, Athlone, co. Roscommon, esq.
1772 ,, Arthur, dean of Ross
1749 ,, Edward, Kinsale, co. Cork, gt.
1662 ,, sir George, Drumrusk, co. Leitrim, knt.
1711 ,, sir Geo., Dunmore, co. Galway, knt. (Large will)

1737 **St. George**, lord George
1724 ,, Henry, the younger, Athlone, co. Roscommon, esq.
1726 ,, Henry, the elder, Athlone, co. Roscommon, esq.
1763 ,, Henry, Tully, co. Rosc., esq.
1747 ,, Mary, par. St. George, Hanover-square, widow (Copy)
1695 ,, sir Oliver, Dublin, knt.and bart. (Ex.)
1731 ,, Oliver, par. St. George, Hanover-square, Middlesex, esq.
1726 ,, Richd., Dunmore, co. Galway, esq.
1755 ,, Richd., lieut.-gen. of the forces
1757 ,, Richard, Carrick-on-Shannon, co. Leitrim, esq.
1768 ,, Richd., Kilrush, co. Kilkenny, esq.
1789 ,, sir Richard, Woodgift, co. Kilkenny, bart.
1798 ,, Richard St. George Mansergh, Headfort, co. Galway
1785 ,, Thomas, esq.
1775 ,, lord baron Usher
1668 ,, William, Birr, King's county, gent. (Exemp.)
1739 **Saintipolite**, Lewis de Montilieu, baron of (Copy)
1772 **St. John**, Andrew, Churchhill Hall, co. Clare, gent.
1790 ,, Anna, Dublin
1681 ,, Catherine, Ballymore, co. Armagh, widow of Henry St. J., esq. (Ex.)
1750 ,, Mary, Carrick, co. Tip., widow
1808 ,, Mary, Limerick, widow
1715 ,, Oliver,Tanderagee,co.Armagh, esq.
1760 ,, Pawlet, Pollardstown, co. Carlow, esq.
1687 ,, Pierce, Culedaniel, co. Cork, gent.
1670 ,, Piers, St. Johnstown, co.Tipperary, gent. (Copy)
1717 ,, Thomas, Ballymulcashel, esq.
1641 **St. Laurence**, Charles, Drogheda, alderman
1778 ,, Gregory, King-st., Oxmantown, grocer
1638 ,, John, Cruisetown, co. Louth, esq.
1741 ,, John Henry, Howth, co. Dubl., esq.
1767 ,, Luke, Donaghadee, co. Down, gent.
1660 ,, Richard (son to sir Nicolas, baron of Howth)
1633 ,, Rowland, Drogheda, merchant
1634 ,, Thomas, Drogheda, merchant

1805 **St. Lawrance**, Thomas, bp. of **Cork**, q.v.
1647 **St. Lawrence**, capt. Thos., Howth
1731 **St. Leger**, Andrew, Ballyvoholane, co. Cork, gent.
1688 ,, Hayward, Cork, esq.
1799 ,, Hayward, Cork city, esq.
1684 ,, Heyward, Heywardshill House, co. Cork, esq.
1797 ,, Jane, Danesfort, co. Cork, spr.
1730 ,, John, Cork, esq.
1738 ,, John, Kilkenny, gent.
1743 ,, sir John, knt., second baron of Exchequer
1793 ,, Mary, *alias* **Butler**, widow
1738 ,, Robert, Newtown, co. city Kilkenny, gent.
1736 ,, Thomas, Dublin, grocer
1758 ,, Thomas, Strand-st., Dublin
1599 ,, sir Warham, knt. (Copy)
1784 ,, Warham, Cork city, esq.
1741 ,. William, Cork, merchant
1753 ,, William, Kilmurry, co. Limrk. [See LYSTER.]
1722 **St. Philbert**, James Mauclerc, Dublin, esq.
1715 **St. Tour**, Mary, Dublin, widow
1771 **Sale**, Catherine, co. Dublin, widow
1760 ,, Edward, co. Dublin, esq.
1744 ,, Elizabeth, Dublin, widow
1753 ,, Samuel, Coolcor, co. Kildare, farmer
1760 ,, Thomas, Clonkeen, Queen's county, gent.
1789 ,, Thomas, Coolcor, co. Kildare, farmer
1741 ,, William, co. Dublin, gent.
1680 **Salisbury**, Victoria, Chester, widow (Copy)
[See SALSBURY, SALUSBURY.]
1743 **Salkeld**, rev. John, Dublin, clerk
1753 ,, Thomas, Dublin, gent.
1810 ,, Thomas, London city (Copy)
1699 **Sall**, John Fitz-Walter, Cashel, gent.
1778 ,, William, Dublin, gent.
1780 **Sallery**, John, Little Ship-street, Dublin, locksmith
1799 ,, Joseph, Dublin city, smith
1782 ,, Robert, Little Ship-st., Dublin, ironmonger
1771 ,, Thos., Mentrim, co. Meath, gent.
1764 ,, William, Greenhills, co. Meath
1640 **Salmon**, Alice, par. Kilfaughnagh, co. Cork, widow
1775 ,, Anne, Tara, King's county
1811 ,, Catherine, Dublin city, spinster
1736 ,, Christopher, Clonmel, co. Tipperary, gent.

1765 **Salmon**, Daniel, St. Mary's par., Dublin
1747 ,, Francis, Johnstown, co. Westmeath, gent.
1762 ,, Fras., Tara, King's co., gent.
1717 ,, Hen., Meath-st., Dublin, gent.
1634 ,, James Suffolk, Castlehaven, co. Cork, esq.
1706 ,, James, Clonmel, co. Tipperary, esq.
1750 ,, Marcella, Johnstown, co. Westmeath, widow
1708 ,, Thos., Clonmel, co. Tip., gent.
1759 ,, rt. rev. Dr. Thomas, bishop of Leighlin and Ferns
1668 ,, William, co. Meath, gent.
1799 ,, William, Shinglis, co. Westmeath, gent.
[See SAMON.]
1810 **Salsbury**, Richard, North Strand, Dublin, painter
[See SALISBURY.]
1802 **Salt**, Ann, Dublin, widow
1770 ,, Thomas, Maws, co. Kildare
1695 ,, William, Charleville, co. Cork, gent.
1755 **Salter**, Gregory, Youghal, co. Cork, alderman
1671 **Saltonstall**, Saml., Dublin, mercht.
1724 **Salusbury**, Martha, *alias* **Howard**, Tugwin, Denbighshire
[See SALISBURY.]
1628 **Sam**, or **Sames**, Fras., Dub., gent.
1690 ,, Robert, senior, Dromnacor, co. Longford, gent.
1736 **Sambee**, Robert, par. St. Martin-in-the Fields, Middlesex, esq. (Copy)
1681 **Samborne**, Thomas, Kinsale, gent.
1696 **Samms**, Robert, St. Thomas-street, Dublin, merchant
1626 **Samon**, Paule, Shrivenham, Berkshire, yeoman
[See SALMON.]
1797 **Sampson**, Anne, Carrickfergus, co. Antrim
1781 ,, rev. Arthur, Londonderry, clk.
1734 ,, Edward, clk.
1769 ,, Ellinor, Isle of Man, widow
1764 ,, Jane, Dublin, widow
1785 ,, Jane, Newtown, co. Meath
1690 ,, Michael, Rinduffcarrick, co. Donegal, esq. (Ex.)
1719 ,, Michael, Dublin, esq.
1736 ,, Michael, Dublin, merchant
1763 ,, Ralph, Dublin, esq.
1764 ,, Robert, Hillbrook, co. Dublin, esq.
1732 ,, Wm., Inch, co. Donegal, esq.
1722 **Sampy**, Chas., Ross, co. Sligo, gt.

1712 **Samuel**, Lewis, Dublin, smith
1787 **Sanders**, Catherine
1811 ,,   Christoph., Sander's Park, co.
         Cork, esq.
1804 ,,   Edwin, Dublin city, esq.
1675 ,,   Erasmus, Dublin, esq.
1781 ,,   Mark, the elder, Brabazon's-
         row, par. St. Luke, Dublin
1667 ,,   Wm., late of Sutton Courtney,
         Berkshire, now of Dublin, gt.
1706 **Sanderson**, Alex., Drumkeevill, co.
         Cavan, esq.
1726 ,,   Alex., Castle S., co. Cavan,
         esq.
1768 ,,   Alex., The Lodge, Queen's co.,
         esq.
1787 ,,   Alex., Cloverhill, co. Cavan,
         esq.
1732 ,,   Frances, Kilkenny, widow
1680 ,,   James, Castlesanderson, co.
         Cavan, esq.
1787 ,,   Jas., Drumcassidy, co. Cavan
1696 ,,   Robt., Ballymacall, co. Tyrone,
         gent.
1725 ,,   Robert, Castle S., co. Cavan,
         esq.
1765 ,,   Robert, Drumkeen, co. Cavan,
         esq.
1801 ,,   Robert, Drumcarn, co. Cavan
1780 ,,   William, Redhills, co. Cavan
         [See SAUNDERSON, SAUNDERS.]
1741 **Sandes**, Edward, Dublin, glover
1757 ,,   Elizabeth, Kilcavan, Queen's
         co., widow
1761 ,,   Henry
1669 ,,   Lancelot, Rockesborough or
         Carrigafoyle, co. Kerry, esq.
1729 ,,   Lancelot, Kilcavan, Queen's
         co., esq.
1763 ,,   Lancelot
1788 ,,   Lancelot, Kilcavan, Queen's
         co., esq.
1801 ,,   Letitia, Dublin, widow
1807 ,,   Mary, Portarlington, Queen's
         co.
1687 ,,   sir Wm., Dublin, bart. (Large
         will; Ex.)
         [See SANDYS.]
1710 **Sandford**, Blayney, Knocktopher,
         co. Kilkenny, esq. (Copy)
1758 ,,   George, dean of Ardagh
1733 ,,   Henry, Dublin, esq.
1741 ,,   Henry, Coleraine, co. London-
         derry, esq.
1796 ,,   Henry, Castlerea, co. Roscom-
         mon, but at Bath, esq.
1756 ,,   James, Sligo, esq.
1719 ,,   Jane, Dublin, widow
1811 ,,   hon. lady Rachel, Noiding,
         Devonshire

1777 **Sandford**, Robert, Granetfield, co.
         Dublin, esq.
1793 ,,   Robert, esq.
1668 ,,   Theo., Moyglare, co. Meath,
         esq.
1741 ,,   Theophilus, major in gen. Mor-
         ley's regt. of foot
1679 ,,   Thomas, Malahide, co. Dublin,
         esq. (Ex.)
1759 ,,   William, Dublin, esq.
1810 ,,   rev. Wm., Castlerea, co. Ros-
         common
1722 **Sandham**, Rachel, Ballybeg, co.
         Wicklow, widow
1714 ,,   Richd., Rossacoose, co. Wick-
         low, gent.
1804 **Sandiford**, James, Cork city
1739 ,,   Thomas, Drogheda, alderman
1734 **Sandoz**, Abraham, Waterford, gent.
1792 ,,   Mary, *alias* **Jones**, *alias* **Morris**
1768 **Sands**, Edward, Dublin, merchant
1714 ,,   dame Grace, Dublin, widow
         [See SANDYS.]
1728 **Sandwith**, Jeremiah, Aughfad, co.
         Wexford, farmer
1740 ,,   Wm., Ballynecarrig, co. Wex-
         ford, gent.
1748 **Sandys**, Anne, Dublin, widow
1722 ,,   lady Charity, Dublin, widow
1708 ,,   Edwin, Dublin, engraver
1748 ,,   Elizab., widow of col. Robt. S.
1788 ,,   Elizabeth, Drogheda town
1795 ,,   Francis, Dublin, architect
1767 ,,   Hester, wid. of rev. Abraham S.
1802 ,,   Nehemiah, Sandfield, co. Ros-
         common, esq.
1755 ,,   Patrick, Dublin, esq.
1770 ,,   Patrick, Dublin, innkeeper
1684 ,,   col. Robert, Roscommon
1741 ,,   Simon, Dublin, gent.
1757 ,,   William, Dublin, esq.
1774 ,,   Wm., Creaghvamore, co. Long-
         ford, esq.
         [See SANDES, SANDS.]
1795 **Sanford**, rev. Daniel, Dublin, LL.D.
1745 ,,   John, Dublin, esq.
1775 **Sankey**, Abney Parker, Dublin,
         esq.
1811 ,,   Chas., lieut. in the 63rd regt.
         of foot
1687 ,,   Dorothy, Dublin, widow
1787 ,,   Edward, Dublin, alderman
1675 ,,   capt. Henry, Tenelick, co.
         Longford, esq.
1784 ,,   Jacob, Coolmore, co. Tip., esq.
1768 ,,   John, New Park, co. Longford,
         esq.
1780 ,,   John, Dublin, gent.
1646 ,,   Luke, Dublin, apothecary
1808 ,,   Mary Eliza

1801 **Savage**, Edward, Dublin, coach-maker
1799 ,, Elizabeth, Kilcarn, co. Meath, widow
1795 ,, Ellinor,Cawekeany, co.Armagh
1770 ,, Francis, Ardkeen, co. Down, esq.
1770 ,, Francis,Frederick-street,Dubl., esq.
1808 ,, Francis, Glastry, co. Down
1655 ,, Henry, Arkin, co. Down, esq.
1797 ,, Henry, Rocksavage, co. Down, esq.
1723 ,, Hugh, Ardkeen, co. Down, esq.
1732 ,, Hugh, Downpatrick, co. Down, gent.
1619 ,, *alias* **Jones**, James, Balleodan, co. Down, gent.
1749 ,, James, Ballymanish, co. Down, esq.
1751 ,, James, Finglas Wood, co. Dublin, tanner
1754 ,, James, Portaferry, co. Down
1766 ,, James, Dublin, gent.
1673 ,, John, Dublin, carpenter
1736 ,, John, Portaferry, co. Down, esq.
1773 ,, John, Dunturk, co. Down
1776 ,, John, Dublin, upholder
1793 ,, John, Ballyvally, co. Down, gent.
1803 ,, John, Knocksedon, co. Dublin
1804 ,, John, Knocksedon, co. Dublin
1755 ,, Lucas, Lissize, co. Down, gent.
1751 ,, Lucy, Dublin, widow
1784 ,, Luke,Parliament-street,Dublin, hatter
1784 ,, Margaret, *alias* **Green**, Dublin
1767 ,, Marmion, Dublin, druggist
1791 ,, Mary,North King-street, Dubl., spinster
1798 ,, Mary, Dublin, widow
1777 ,, Michael, Dublin, publican
1643 ,, Patrick, Portaferry
1647 ,, Patrick, Portaferry, co. Down, esq.
1725 ,, Patrick, Gorgery, co. Down
1732 ,, Patrick, Magherneheeley, co. Armagh, gent.
1771 ,, Patrick, Dublin, gent.
1784 ,, Patrick, Dublin, one of the attorneys
1795 ,, Patrick, Cloghern, co. Dublin, farmer
1755 ,, Peter, Dublin, butcher
1717 ,, Philip, Chancellor of the Exchequer in Ireland
1751 ,, Philip, Dungulph, co. Wexford, esq.

1781 **Savage**, Philip, Rocksavage, co. Down, esq.
1782 ,, Philip, Barrhall, co. Down, gent.
1743 ,, Robert, Dublin, gent.
1640 ,, Rowland,Ballygalget,co.Down, gent.
1725 ,, Rowland, Portaferry, co. Down, esq. (Ex.)
1790 ,, Rowland, Ballyvarly, co. Down
1770 ,, Susanna, Kilkenny, widow
1748 ,, Thomas, Portaferry, co. Down
1768 ,, Thomas, Dublin, apothecary
1811 ,, Thomas, Dublin city, esq.
1733 ,, William, Kirkistown,co. Down, esq. (Not proved)
1755 ,, William, Dunturk, co. Down
1741 **Savary,** John, the elder, East Greenwich, esq. (Copy)
1663 **Savile**, Gilbert, Greatland, Yorkshire, gent.
1680 ,, John, Greatland, Yorkshire, gent. (Copy)
1717 ,, Mary, Dublin, widow
1651 ,, Robert, late of Dublin, now of Greatland, Yorkshire, esq.
1713 **Savill**, Daniel, Roddanstown, clk.
1744 **Saville**, sir George, Rufford, Nottinghamshire, bart.
1687 **Sawbridge**, Hanna, London, widow of George S., London, esq. (Copy)
1788 **Sawer**, Thos., lieut.-col. of the 5th regt. of dragoons (Copy) [See SAYERS.]
1733 **Sawle**, Francis, par. St. Mary's Le Strand, Middlesex, woollen-draper (Copy) [See SAULE.]
1682 **Say**, George, Castlecue, co. Kilkenny, esq.
1796 ,, Margaret, Dublin
1698 ,, Richard, Waterford, mercht.
1705 **Sayer**, Thomas, Dublin, merchant
1803 **Sayers**, Andrew, Castlefin, co. Donegal
1810 ,, Edward, Limerick city, M.D.
1808 ,, John, London city, esq. [See SAWER, SYER.]
1747 **Scaife**, Hannah, *alias* **Fude**, Dubl.
1749 ,, Thomas,Finglas,co.Dublin,esq.
1775 **Scales**, Patrick, Clonmel, co. Tipp., merchant
1794 **Scallan**, John, Dublin, grocer
1791 **Scanlan**, Anne, Temple-street, Dublin, widow
1759 ,, Bartholomew, Feenaugh, co. Limk., gent.
1762 ,, Cornelius, Maine, co. Limerick, gent.

1778 **Scanlan**, Edward, Aughnacloy, co. Tyrone
1789 ,, Edward, Wardtown, co. Donegal, esq.
1791 ,, Ellinor, Leixlip, widow
1754 ,, James, Dublin, gent.
1765 ,, James, Ballyshannon, co. Donegal, gent.
1805 ,, John, Custom House, Dublin, esq.
1753 ,, Mathew, Duckstown, co. Limk., gent.
1803 ,, Matt Lane
1759 ,, Michael, Mein, co. Limerick, gent.
1775 ,, Michael, Ballylin, co. Limerick
1801 ,, Michael, Ballynatra, co. Limk., esq.
1742 **Scardevile**, Elizabeth, Dublin, spinster
1704 **Scardeville**, rev. Henry, clk.
1807 **Schaw**, Frederick B., Weston, Surrey (Copy)
1670 ,, Hugh, Kilbright, co. Down, esq.
1710 ,, William, Ballygonway, co. Down, esq.
1758 **Schoales**, Edmund, Drogheda, alderman
1799 ,, George, Drogheda, alderman [See SCOLES.]
1753 **Schofield**, Henry, Dublin, Baptist preacher and teacher [See SCOLFIELD.]
1804 **Schomberg**, sir Alexander, knt., capt. in His Majesty's Navy
1758 **Schoolding**, Grace, Dublin, widow
1810 **Schoole**, Michael, LL.D., T.C.D.
1760 **Schuldam**, Elizabeth, Dubl., widow
1723 **Schuldham**, Edmund, Dublin, gent.
1758 ,, Elizabeth, Dublin, wid. (Not proved)
1745 ,, Francis, Dublin, gent.
1746 **DeScissac**, Alex. Guibert, lieut.-gen. of the King of Sardinia's forces, and col. of a Swiss regt. (Copy)
1661 **Scoles**, John, Caurin, co. Cavan, yeoman (Exemp.) [See SCHOALES.]
1746 **Scolfield**, rev. Nicholas, Dunmanway, co. Cork, clk. [See SCHOFIELD.]
1764 **Scott**, Abraham, Dublin, chandler
1762 ,, Alexander, Lisbane, co. Down
1790 ,, Alexander, James-street, Bedford-row, esq.
1756 ,, Angel, Cahiracon, co. Clare, gent.
1791 ,, Ann, Limerick, widow
1809 ,, Anne, Kilkenny city, widow

1780 **Scott**, rev. Barlow, Dublin, clk.
1733 ,, Edward, Dublin, merchant
1696 ,, George, Boagh, co. Monaghan, gent.
1781 ,, George, Cork city, gent.
1811 ,, George, Tullyquilly, co. Down
1753 ,, James, lieut. in the Royal Irish Dragoons
1787 ,, James, Cole-alley, Dublin, tailor
1793 ,, James, Cardy, co. Down
1804 ,, James, Loughbrickland, co. Down, gent.
1733 ,, John, Caronary, co. Cavan, gent.
1757 ,, John, Hawkins-street, Dublin, surveyor
1767 ,, John, Ballygannon, co. Wicklow, gent.
1793 ,, John Pendred, Ballygannon, co. Wicklow, esq.
1795 ,, John, Walerughy, co. Cavan, gent.
1805 ,, John, Dublin city, esq.
1809 ,, John, Cahiracon, co. Clare
1811 ,, John, Williamstown-avenue, co. Dublin
1691 ,, Joseph, late of Drogheda, now of London, gent. (Copy)
1673 ,, Mary, St. Patrick's par., near Dublin, widow
1757 ,, Mary, Aungier-street, Dublin, spinster
1757 ,, Mary, Kishawny, co. Kildare, widow
1796 ,, Mary, Limerick city, spinster
1742 ,, Mathew, Dub., ship carpenter
1799 ,, Mathias, Dublin, esq.
1778 ,, Michael, Scottsborough, co. Kilkenny
1788 ,, Michael, Rushey Park, Middlesex (Copy)
1806 ,, Moses, Pill-lane, Dublin city
1768 ,, Patrick, Drogheda
1638 ,, sir Richard, Dublin, knt.
1667 ,, Richard, Carlisle, Cumberland, merchant (Copy)
1778 ,, Richard, Finglas, co. Dublin, farmer
1801 ,, Richard, Cork city, gent.
1711 ,, Robert, Dublin, gent.
1774 ,, Robert, Newry, co. Down, esq.
1808 ,, Robert, Dublin city, M.D.
1688 ,, Thomas, Newbay, co. Wexford, esq.
1760 ,, Thomas, Dublin, merchant
1770 ,, Thos., Kirkcubbin, co. Down, minister of the Gospel
1777 ,, Walter, Dublin, merchant
1642 ,, William, Dublin, esq.

1733 **Scott,** William, lieut. in Dublin barrack
1733 ,, William, Fisherstown, Queen's co., gent.
1757 ,, William, Fisherstown, Queen's co., gent.
1776 ,, William, 2nd Baron of the Exchequer
1785 ,, William, London city, surg.
1793 ,, William, Londonderry city, merchant
1797 ,, William, Dublin, carpenter
1802 ,, William, Sugar Island, co. Armagh, esq.
1794 **Scriven,** Edward, Dublin, esq.
1769 ,, Jacob, Dublin, esq.
1715 ,, Margaret, Dublin, widow
1701 ,, William, Dublin, joiner
1712 ,, William, Dublin, merchant
1742 ,, William, Dublin, gent.
1742 **Scroder,** Christopher, Waterford, blacksmith
1686 **Scroupe,** Russell, gent.
1679 **Scudamore,** Richard, Gill Abbey, near Cork, esq.
1696 ,, Thomas, Dublin, esq., sometime clk. of the office of Com. Pleas in the Exchequer
1775 **Sculdam,** Lemuel, Dublin, esq.
1785 ,, Rebecca, Grafton-street, Dubl., spinster
1778 **Sculley,** James, Cournagour, co. Wicklow, farmer
1807 **Scully,** Daniel, Mountmellick, Queen's co., gent.
1808 ,, Darby, Silverfort, co. Tipperary, esq.
1806 ,, Edmond, Cashel city, esq.
1798 ,, Edward, Naas, co. Kildare, innholder
1783 ,, Roger, Cashel, co. Tipperary
1768 ,, Timothy, Galbertstown, co. Tipperary, gent.
1755 **Scurlog,** Gregory
1700 ,, John, Rathnemanagh, Queen's co., gent. [gent.
1599 ,, Martin, Rathcredan, co. Dubl.,
1758 ,, Thomas, Baldonnell, co. Dubl., gent.
1692 **Scurloge,** Martha, *alias* **Hartpole,** *alias* **Walsh,** Ballynegawle, Queen's co., widow
1632 **Scurlok,** Robert, Trim, gent.
1756 **Scutt,** James, Sligo, esq.
1713 **Seacome,** Elizabeth, *alias* **Cooke,** Liverpool, widow
1698 ,, Richard, Dublin, gent.
1757 **Seage,** Thos., Dublin, coachmaker
1790 **Seal,** Christopher, Strand-street, Dublin, yeoman

1809 **Seale,** Edward, Clonkeen, Queen's co., farmer
1800 **Sealy,** Elizabeth, Firgrove, co. Cork, widow
1720 ,, John, Cork, esq. (Copy)
1777 ,, John, Bandon, co. Cork, M.D.
1799 ,, John, Moyglass, co. Kerry, esq.
1759 ,, Robert, Waterford, merchant
1768 ,, Samuel, Maugh, co. Kerry, gent.
1797 ,, Uri, Maugh, co. Kerry
[See SEELY.]
1807 **Searle,** Anne, Carlow
1747 **Searson,** Robert, Castle Dawson, co. Londonderry
1785 **Seaton,** Anne, Dublin, spinster
1737 ,, Charles, gent.
1787 ,, Charles, Crowpark, co. Meath, gent.
1755 ,, Elizabeth, late of Drogheda, now of Dublin, widow
1786 ,, Ellinor, *alias* **O'Neill,** par. of Ardstra, co. Tyrone
1742 ,, James, Drogheda, merchant
1790 **Seaver,** Bridget, *alias* **Patterson,** Dublin, widow
1790 ,, rev. Charles
1775 ,, Jeremiah, Dublin, clk.
1766 ,, Jonathan, mariner on board the "Foudroyant"
1784 ,, Patrick, Rogerstown, co. Dubl., farmer
[See SEYMOUR.]
1783 **Seavers,** John, Bridge-street, Dub., weaver
1795 ,, Mary, Harold's Cross, co. Dublin, widow
1807 ,, Patrick, Rogerstown, co. Dubl.
1810 **Seawright,** rev. Abraham, Presbyterian minister of Limerick
1740 **Sebatier,** John, Mountmellick, Queen's co., gent.
1784 ,, Thos., Summer Grove, Queen's co., esq.
1673 **Sebby,** Chas., Clonduff, co. Kildare, gent.
1767 ,, Elizabeth, Clonduff, co. Kildare, widow
1598 **Sedgrave,** Richard, Killeglan, 2nd Baron of Exchequer
1777 **Sedgwick,** Anthony, Moira, co. Down, apothecary
[See CHADWICK.]
1747 **Seed,** Mary, Belfast, co. Antrim, widow of W.S. [gent.
1785 ,, Thomas, Lisburn, co. Antrim,
1747 ,, William, Belfast, merchant
1755 **Seeds,** Stephen, Belfast, co. Antrim, merchant

1753 **Seeley**, John, Shine, co. Leitrim
1779 **Seely**, Anne, Dublin
1795 ,, Henry, Grouse Lodge, co. Leitrim, esq.
1745 ,, James, Castlefore, co. Leitrim, gent.
1807 ,, rev. Nesbitt, vicar of Ennismagrath
1760 ,, Rebecca
[See SEALY.]
1801 **Seery**, Edwd., Ballyhue, King's co.
1686 **Segar**, John, Dublin, goldsmith
1683 ,, Richard, rector of Clonenagh and Cloneheen, Queen's co.
1768 **Segerson**, John, Ballinskelligs
1801 **Segrave**, Barbara, Dublin, spinster
1656 ,, Charles, Lisgool, co. Ferm., esq.
1790 ,, Frances, Dunsoghly, widow
1794 ,, Frances, Dublin, spinster
1707 ,, Francis, Dublin, esq. (Ex.)
1662 ,, Henry, Little Cabra, co. Dublin, esq.
1739 ,, Henry, Cabra, co. Dub., esq.
1807 ,, James, Newbarn, co. Dublin
1720 ,, John, lieut. in general Sibourg's regiment of horse
1728 ,, Mary, widow of Francis S., of Dublin, esq.
1777 ,, Neal, Cabra, co. Dublin, esq.
1789 ,, Patrick, Pill-lane, Dublin, silk manufacturer
1765 **Seguin**, Paul, Dublin, merchant
1809 **Seix**, Richd. F., North Strand, Dub.
1761 **Selby**, Joseph, Dublin, grocer
1739 **Sellery**, James, Dublin, gent.
1791 **Sells**, Letitia, Dublin, widow
1668 **Selwin**, Penelope, wid. of Francis S., Triston, Sussex, esq. (Copy)
1664 **Sempell**, James, Dublin, gent.
1778 ,, Martha, Letterkenny, co. Donegal
1777 **Sempill**, Florinda, Letterkenny
1806 ,, Jas., Waterford city, esq.
1788 ,, Saml., Castlecavan, co. Wicklow, esq.
1644 ,, sir William, Letterkenny, co. Donegal, knt.
1785 ,, Willoughby, Donaghadee, co. Down
1730 **Semple**, Elizabeth, Dublin, widow
1782 ,, George, Dublin, gent.
1725 ,, Grissel, lady
1743 ,, Jane, widow
1784 ,, John, Abbey-st., Dublin, gent.
1803 ,, Patk., Summerhill, Dub., gent.
1767 ,, Ralph, Monaghan, gent.
1761 **Senior**, Joseph, Maryborough, Queen's county, farmer

1791 **Senior**, Richard, Moorfield, Queen's county, gent.
1736 ,, William, Drumnah, co. Dublin, farmer
1728 **Sequela**, Stephen, Kilkenny, esq.
1680 **Sergeant**, Wm., Dublin, merchant
[See **Sargent**.]
1642 **Sergier**, Richard, Dub., stationer
1756 **Seright**, James, Newry, co. Down, merchant
1669 **Serle**, Jane, Limerick, widow of col. Thos. S. (Ex.)
1700 **Settle**, James, Dublin, skinner
1697 ,, John, Finglas-bridge, co. Dub., farmer
1759 ,, John, Finglas-bridge, co. Dub., esq.
1757 ,, Sarah, Finglas-bridge, co. Dublin, spinster
1707 **Sevell**, George, Dublin, yeoman
1677 **Severn**, Roger, Lyme House, near London, esq.
1769 **Seward**, John, Royal Hos., Dublin, gent.
1774 ,, Thomas, Cork, gent.
1714 **Sewell**, Jonathan, Westminster, esq. (Copy)
[See SHUELL.]
1670 **Sexten**, Edmond, Limerick, esq. (Ex.)
1777 ,, James, Limerick
1784 **Sexton**, Catherine, Limerick, wid.
1773 ,, Edmond, Limerick, merchant
1631 ,, sir George, Dublin, knt.
1802 ,, Joseph, Ballyclough, Liberties of Limerick, gent.
1809 ,, Mary, Limerick city, widow
1742 ,, Patrick Fitz James, Limerick, merchant
1737 ,, Thomas, Ennis, co. Clare, merchant
1760 **Seymor**, Frances, Dublin, widow
1701 ,, John, Ballyknockan, King's county, esq.
1745 ,, Walter, Limerick, saddler
1768 **Seymour**, Charles, Crows Nest, co. Galway, gent.
1811 ,, Hannah, Lisnacody, co. Galway, widow
1796 ,, rev. John, Limerick, clk.
1801 ,, Jos., Kilmore, co. Galway, gent.
1779 ,, Randolph, Newtown, King's county, farmer
1795 ,, Simon, Summerset, barony of Longford, gent.
[See SEAVER.]
1805 **Shackleton**, Elizabeth, Ballitore, co. Kildare
1710 ,, John, Dublin, looking-glass maker

1793 **Shackleton**, Richard, Ballitore, co. Kildare
[See SHEKLETON.]
1787 **Shadwell**, dame Ann, par. St. Mary-le-Bone, Middlesex (Copy)
1771 ,, rev. Edwd., Kilfenora, co. Clare, clk.
1757 ,, Elizabeth, Lambeth, Surrey (Copy)
1802 ,, Geo., Ballinasloe, co. Galway
1761 ,, John, Cork, merchant
1787 ,, Jonah, Eyreville, co. Galway, esq.
1801 ,, Philip, Cloughjordan, co. Tipperary, esq.
1769 ,, Thomas, Stockwell, Surrey (Copy)
1676 **Shaem**, Edward, Ballymore, co. Westmeath, gent.
1725 **Shaen**, sir Arthur, bart.
1687 **Shaftesbury**, Anthony, earl of (Copy)
1806 **Shafton**, Benjamin, M.D.
1778 **Shaghnessy**, John, Crusheen, co. Clare, farmer
[See SHAUGHNESSY.]
1704 **Shaklady**, Robert, Grangegorman, co. Dublin, gardener
1687 **Shaldway**, James, Oldbrayston, co. Meath, farmer
1712 **Shallcross**, Samuel, esq.
1729 **Shallcrosse**, James, co. Kerry
1743 **Shalvey**, John, Dublin
1724 **Shamborg**, Elizbth., Dublin, widow
1762 **Shanaghan**, Edward Nugent
1695 **Shanaghane**, Mathew, Rathmoy, co. Tipperary, gent.
1783 **Shanahan**, Darby, par. priest of Castle Island, co. Kerry
1622 **Shane**, dame Mary, *alias* **Geoghegan**, widow
1650 ,, Patk., Mullogh, co. Down, esq.
[See SHEEHAN.]
1805 **Shanessy**, Patrick, Charleville, co. Kerry
[See SHAUGHNESSY.]
1774 **Shanks**, Andw., Lisburn, co. Antrim, merchant
1784 **Shanley**, Anne, Dublin, widow
1762 ,, Michael, Cargaugh, co. Westmeath, farmer
1776 **Shanly**, Anne
1752 ,, Bryan, Crosshea, co. Longford, gent.
1762 ,, Eneas, Banecrigh, co. Westmeath
1741 ,, Jeffry, Aughamore, co. Leitrim, gent.
1785 ,, Michael, Glasson, co. Westmeath, gent.

1782 **Shanly**, Patrick, Aughnecranagh, co. Longford, gent.
1753 ,, Thomas, Dublin, gent.
1781 ,, Thomas, Ballymahon, co. Longford, gauger
1765 ,, William, Strokestown, co. Roscommon, gent.
1806 ,, William, Tighe-st., Dublin, shoemaker
1758 **Shannon**, Joseph, Tullamore, King's county [tailor
1783 ,, Daniel, Werburgh-st., Dublin,
1699 ,, Francis, lord viscount
1765 ,, Henry, Limerick, clerk
1769 ,, Hugh, Londonderry, gent.
1767 ,, Jas., Tanderagee, co. Armagh, gent.
1785 ,, Oliver, Kilmainham, co. Dublin, tanner
1741 ,, Richard, lord viscount (Copy)
1807 ,, rt. hon. Richard, earl of
1807 ,, Wm., Mountmellick, Queen's county, brewer
1739 **Shanogle**, Sebastine, Dublin, shipwright
1727 **Shapland**, Ellen, Wexford, widow
1704 ,, John, Wexford, esq.
1799 **Sharkey**, Mary, Back-lane, Dublin, widow
1783 ,, Thomas, Back-lane, Dublin, linendraper
1806 **Sharky**, John, Fedemoyle, co Wicklow
1795 **Sharman**, Ambrose, Cornmarket, Dublin, gent.
1746 ,, John, Grange, co. Antrim
1748 ,, John, Dublin, gent.
1763 ,, Michael, Dublin, shoemaker
1806 ,, Robert, Grange, co. Kilkenny
1775 ,, Wm., Dublin, esq.
1755 **Sharp**, Ambrose, Drogheda, mariner
1781 ,, Anthony, Roundwood, Queen's co., esq. (Large will)
1787 ,, George, Clonbrone, King's co., gent.
1735 ,, Isaac, Dublin, gent.
1803 ,, Robert Anthony F., Dubl., esq.
1582 ,, Simon, Dublin, gent.
1706 **Sharpe**, Anthony, Dublin, clothier
1612 ,, George, Stockgrove, gent.
1705 ,, John, Dublin, merchant
1733 **Sharpless**, John, Roosk, King's co., farmer
1782 **Sharpley**, Adam, Church, Dublin, innkeeper
1755 **Sharply**, David, Dublin, cooper
1809 **Shaughnessy**, Jas., Bray, apothecary
1802 ,, John, Moyne, co. Mayo, gent.
[See SHAGNESSY, SHANESSY.]

1663 **Shee**, Ellen, *alias* **Dobbyn**, widow of Thomas S., Freinstown, co. Kildare, esq.
1731 ,, Henry, Derrynahinch, co. Kilkenny, gent.
1798 ,, James, Dublin, gent.
1800 ,, James, Galway, esq.
1760 ,, Joanna, Dublin, spinster
1719 ,, John, Sheeptown, co. Kilkenny, gent.
1749 ,, Marcus, Sheeptown, co. Kilkenny, esq.
1639 ,, dame Margaret, *alias* **Fagan**, widow of sir Richard S., knt.
1794 ,, Margaret, Dublin, spinster
1794 ,, Martin, Dublin
1766 ,, Mary, widow of Geo. S., Castlebar, co. Mayo, merchant
1767 ,, Mary, Dublin, spinster
1723 ,, Patrick FitzPierce, Kilkenny, merchant
1657 ,, Richard, Thomastown, mercht.
1687 ,, Richd., Wases Sheis or Sheeptown, co. Kilkenny, esq.
1735 ,, Richd., Outrath, co. Kilkenny, gent.
1739 ,, Richard, Clorane, co. Tipp., gent.
1748 ,, Richd., Sheeptown, co Kilkenny, esq. (Not proved)
1774 ,, Richd., Castle Dermot, co. Kildare, gent.
1722 ,, *alias* **Shaw**, Stephen, Dublin, merchant
1745 ,, Theobald, Waterford, shipmaster
1743 ,, Thomas, Lib. Thomas-court and Donore, weaver
1774 ,, Thomas, Dublin, gent.
1754 ,, Urith, Dublin, widow
[See SHEA.]
1797 **Sheehan**, Anthony, Ennis, co. Clare, merchant
1756 ,, David, Dublin, stonecutter
1790 ,, David, Blarney-lane, publican and tobacconist
1781 ,, Jeremiah, Cork, nurseryman
1767 ,, Mary, Limerick, widow
1793 ,, Mordecai, Dublin, stonecutter
1758 ,, Thomas, Limerick, gent.
[See SHANE, SHEAN, SHEEN.]
1786 **Sheehy**, Bryan, Gardenfield, co. Limerick, gent.
1808 ,, Bryan, Cork city, esq.
1728 ,, Catherine, widow of Peter S., Dublin, gent.
1756 ,, James, Ballycar, co. Clare, farmer
1792 ,, James, Ballyporeen, co. Tipp.
1803 ,, James, Tralee, co. Kerry, M.D.

1796 **Sheehy**, Roger, Ballintobber, co. Limerick, gent.
1797 ,, Roger, Cork city, esq. (Large)
1783 ,, William, Cork, merchant
1779 **Sheen**, John, late of the Custom House, Dublin, esq.
[See SHEEHAN.]
1716 **Sheene**, Francis, Cherryvalley, co. Antrim, gent.
1803 **Sheerin**, Anthony, Dublin
1762 ,, Bryan, Cumminstown, co. Westmeath, gent.
1804 ,, Patrick, Rathlany, co. Limk., gent.
1676 **Sheffeild**, Edmund, Kensington, Middlesex, esq. (Copy)
1808 **Shegog**, James, Loughbrickland
1805 ,, John, Loughbrickland, co. Down, gent.
1724 **Sheidow**, William, Dublin, mercht.
1806 **Sheil**, Philippa, Shrewsbury, England
1761 **Sheilds**, Margaret, widow of Wm. S., Dublin, silversmith
1744 ,, Robert, Wainstown, co. Meath, esq.
1662 **Sheile**, Toby, Portlewis-beyond-sea, merchant
1633 **Sheill**, James, Milltown, co. Dubl., farmer
1775 ,, Laurence, Dublin, tailor
1769 **Sheils**, George, Dublin, merchant
1809 ,, Henry, Newtown Darver, co. Louth
1801 ,, William, Newtown Darver, co. Louth, esq.
1802 **Shekleton**, John, Drogheda, gent.
[See SHACKLETON.]
1711 **Shelburne**, Elizabeth, lady baroness
1751 ,, Henry, earl of (Copy)
1762 ,, John Petty, earl of (Copy)
1781 ,, Mary, dowager countess
1711 **Sheldon**, Ann, Dublin, widow
1758 ,, Benjamin, Roscrea, co. Tipp., merchant
1752 ,, Catherine, wife to John S. (Copy)
1738 ,, Eleazer
1752 ,, John, Mitcham, Surrey, esq. (Copy)
1732 **Shelley**, Anne, Dublin, widow
1738 ,, Hannah, Dublin, widow
1693 ,, John, Ratoath, co. Meath, gent.
1759 ,, Richard, par. St. George, Hanover-square, esq. (Copy)
1759 ,, Sarah, par. St. George, Hanover-sq., Middlesex (Copy)
1807 **Shelly**, Anne, Leixlip, co. Kildare, widow

1762 **Sherlock**, Richard, Sherlockstown, co. Kildare, esq.
1799 ,, Richard, Dublin, esq.
1634 ,, Robert FitzEdward, Naas, merchant
1770 ,, Thomas, Irishtown, co. Kildare, esq.
1780 ,, Thomas, Dublin, merchant
1780 ,, Thomas, Dublin, woollendraper
1796 ,, Thomas, Rock Abbey, co. Cork, esq.
1802 ,, Thomas, Salsborough, co. Kilkenny
1716 ,, William, gent.
1775 ,, William, late of Wexford town, gent.
1793 ,, William, Ardee-street, Dublin, brewer
1583 **Sherlocke**, James FitzThomas, Waterford, alderman
1601 ,, James FitzJohn, Waterford, alderman
1629 ,, John FitzGeorge, Leitrim, esq., co. Waterford
1650 ,, Margaret, *alias* **Landers**, Dublin, widow
1602 ,, Patrick - FitzPeter, Waterford, merchant
1623 ,, Paul
1635 ,, Paul FitzPiers, Waterford, merchant
1667 ,, Richard, Donamore, co. Meath, farmer
1694 ,, Robert, Dublin, merchant
1808 ,, Robert, town of Glanworth
1631 **Sherman**, William, Dublin, knt.
1766 **Sherrard**, Benjamin, Dublin, weaver
1786 ,, David, Coombe, co. Dublin, merchant
1737 ,, Robert, Dublin, gent.
1747 ,, Thomas, Hanover-street, Dubl., weaver
1652 **Sherring**, John, Dublin, gent.
1780 **Sherry**, Alice, Dublin, widow
1803 ,, Arthur, Kilmurry, co. Monaghan, farmer
1802 ,, Patrick Kelly, Dublin, gent.
1810 ,, William, Dunboyne, co. Meath
1676 **Sherwin**, Edmund, Lancan, Cheshire, gent. (Copy)
1662 ,, John, Lemington, Huntingdonshire, gent. (Copy)
1670 ,, Philip, Dublin, ironmonger
1782 **Sherwood**, John, Denzille-st., Dubl., gent.
1741 ,, Joseph, Dublin, gent.
1724 ,, Robt., Athlone, co. Roscommon, esq.
1786 ,, Robt., Athlone. co. Roscommon, gent.

1775 **Sherwood**, Thos., Dublin, plumber
1773 **Shettick**, John, Kanturk, co. Cork
1797 ,, John, Kanturk, co. Clare
1759 **Shew**, John, Shanganhill, co. Dubl., farmer
1791 ,, John, Finglas, co. Dublin, gent.
1778 ,, Richard, Finglas, co. Dublin, farmer
1792 ,, Richard, Finglas, co. Dublin, farmer
1776 **Shewbridge**, Joseph, Armagh, surgeon
1799 ,, Peter Eyre, lieut. in 30th regt. of foot
1777 ,, rev. Wm., D.D., vicar of Kilcolgan, dio. Clonfert
1811 ,, Wm., Heathlawn, co. Galway, esq.
1739 **Sheyne**, William, capt. in general Moyles' regt. of foot
1792 **Shiel**, James, Dublin, alderman
1767 ,, Jane, daughter of William S., Dublin, esq.
1754 ,, John, Oxpark, co. Meath
1784 ,, John, Dublin, tailor
1798 ,, rev. Osborne, Loughbrickland, co. Down
1788 ,, William, Ballinaston, co. Wicklow, esq.
1798 **Shields**, Elizabeth, Woodpark, co. Meath, widow
1762 **Shiell**, Amelia, daughter of Wm. S., Dublin, esq.
1765 ,, Ann, daughter of William S., Dublin, esq.
1731 ,, Edmund, Mill-street, Dublin, brewer
1676 ,, Hugh, Athlone, gent.
1749 ,, Hugh, Clown, co. Westmeath, gent.
1778 ,, Jas., Ross-lane, Dublin, livery lace weaver
1703 ,, John, Dublin, shoemaker
1740 ,, John, Dublin, merchant
1809 ,, John, Mahonstown, co. Westmeath
1709 ,, Margaret, Grange, co. Westmeath, spinster
1776 ,, Mercy, Dublin, widow
1729 ,, Patk., Brendrum, co. Mayo, M.D.
1703 ,, Roger, Galtrim, co. Meath, gent.
1782 ,, Roger, Claremont, co. Mayo, esq.
1713 ,, Wm., Grenan, co. Westmeath, gent.
1760 ,, William, Dublin, esq.
1778 ,, William, Tully, King's co., esq.
1804 **Shiels**, William, Ballanaclose, co. Meath, gent.
[See SHIELDS, &c.]

1742 **Shimin,** Nicholas, Dublin, cord-wainer
1673 **Shinton,** Alex., Proudfootstown, co. Louth, gent.
1720 ,, John, Cooloney
1772 ,, Lancelot, Pranstown, co. Meath, gent.
1721 ,, Richd., Garretstown, co. Meath, esq.
1745 ,, Richard, capt. in gen. St. George's Dragoons
1808 **Shipley,** George, Castle Dermott, co. Kildare, farmer
1791 **Shippey,** John, Rockfield, co. Dubl., esq.
1611 **Shipwarde,** John, the elder, Castle Mauhowne, co. Cork, gent.
1668 **Shirley,** sir George, knt., Ch. Jus. K. B. (Copy)
1793 ,, Henrietta, Dorset-st., Dublin, widow
1793 ,, John, Croan, co. Kilkenny
1811 ,, John, Croan, co. Kilk., esq.
1686 ,, Philip, Limk., gent.
1786 ,, hon. and rev. Walter, of par. St. Mary, Dublin, clk. [See SHURLEY.]
1729 **Shollcross,** Thomas, Bishop's Court, co. Kildare
1807 **Shone,** Samuel, Galway town, gent.
1802 ,, Thos., Harbour Hill, co. Clare, farmer
1754 **Shorcliffe,** Martha, Ballincurrig, co. Cork, spinster
1760 **Shore,** John, Dublin, farrier
1772 ,, Margarett, Dublin, spinster
1741 ,, Robert, Rathmore, co. Long., gent.
1799 ,, Robert, Clony Cowan, co. Meath, gent.
1799 ,, Robert, Rathmore, co. Long., esq.
1782 ,, Samuel, Crookstown, co. Kild.
1723 **Short,** Alice, Grange, Queen's co., widow
1747 ,, Charles, Strabane, co. Tyrone
1775 ,, Edward, Greenhedge, King's co., gent.
1810 ,, Elizabeth, Gt. Longford-street, Dublin, clk.
1795 ,, Francis
1802 ,, Francis, Annfield, Queen's co., esq.
1668 ,, John, Kildillige, Queen's co., esq.
1723 ,, John, Grange, Queen's co. esq.
1768 ,, John, Wingfield, co. Tipperary, gent.
1770 ,, John, Gurteen, co. Wexford, farmer

1791 **Short,** John, Dublin, grocer
1703 ,, Jonathan, Gurteen, co. Tipp., gent.
1682 ,, Peter, London, merchant tailor (Copy)
1787 ,, Thomas, Coolcor, King's co. gent.
1787 ,, Thomas, Springhill, Queen's co. esq.
1781 ,, William, Cashilrone
1808 ,, William, Coolville, King's co.
1591 **Shortall,** Patrick, Rathardmore, gent.
1651 ,, Pierce, Fitzleonard, Inch, co. Kilkenny
1738 ,, Thomas, Waterford, merchant
1692 **Shorte,** John, Athlone, gent.
1808 **Shoueling,** Thomas, Exchequer-st., Dublin, vintner
1785 **Showell,** Thomas, Odorney, co. Kerry, gent.
1670 **Shrawbridge,** Robert, Lisanduff, co. Antrim, gent.
1591 **Shrawley,** Kenelme, Lond., skinner
1739 **Shubridge,** Wm., Dublin, merchant
1687 **Shuckburgh,** Richard, Borton, Warwickshire, esq. (Copy)
1746 **Shudall,** Charles, Dublin, tailor
1732 **Shueff,** Arthur, Channel Rock, co. Louth, esq.
1737 **Shuekmell,** Michael, Dublin, mcht.
1666 **Shuel,** Edward, Ardfert, co. Kerry, esq. [See SEWELL.]
1793 **Shuldam,** Pooley, Dublin, esq.
1667 **Shurley,** Arthur, Isfield, Sussex, esq. (Copy and large will)
1668 ,, dame Mary, widow of sir Geo. S., Chief Justice K. B. [See SHIRLEY.]
1761 **Shurlock,** Samuel, Dublin, founder
1674 **Shute,** Richard or Robert, Limerick, alderman (Ex.)
1799 **Shutter,** Joseph Robert, Collinstown, co. Dublin
1802 **Shuttleworth,** Peter, Sligo, mercht.
1672 ,, Richard, Gawthrapp, co. Lancaster, esq.
1726 **Sibbald,** Comfort, Mullymeaghan, co. Westmeath, widow
1711 ,, Henry, Mullymeaghan, co. Westmeath, gent.
1771 **Sibley,** Hannah, Dublin, widow
1757 ,, James, Dublin, silkweaver
1776 **Sibthorp,** Stephen, Drogheda, esq. [See SIPTHORPE.]
1632 **Sibthorpe,** sir Christopher, Dublin, knt., Jus. K. B.
1758 **Sican,** Ann, Dublin, spinster
1679 ,, Elizabeth, Dublin, widow

1758 **Sican**, Elizabeth, Dublin, widow
1777 ,, James, Dublin, esq.
1675 ,, John, Ballykelly or Kellistown, co. Kildare, gent.
1758 ,, John, Dublin, merchant
1766 ,, Richard, Dublin, gent.
1749 **Sidebotham**, Joseph, Dublin, merchant (Large will)
1763 ,, Samuel, Drogheda
1787 **Siggins**, Elizabeth, Kindlestown, co.
Wicklow, widow
1712 **De La Sigounier**, Charles, Clonmel, esq.
1786 **Sikes**, Elizabeth, Carlow town
1792 ,, Mary, Capinrush, co. Westmeath, spinster
1765 **Silcock**, Thos., Skinner-row, Dubl.,
printseller
1802 **Silk**, Joseph, Dublin city, brewer
1734 **Silland**, Bernard, Dublin, harnessmaker
1810 **Sillery**, Charles D., Dubl., captain
1727 **Sillk**, John, Dublin, gent.
1760 **Silver**, Joan, Dublin, widow
1724 ,, John, Fountain, co. Waterford,
esq.
1628 ,, Maurice, Ballyhander, co. Waterford, gent.
1688 ,, Owen, Youghal, esq. (Ex.)
1737 **Silvester**, Geo., Dublin, merchant
1756 ,, Wm., lieut. in gen. Handasyd's regt. (Copy)
1769 **Simcocks**, Elizab., Galway, widow
1735 ,, John, Galway, merchant
1810 ,, Samuel, Galway town
1808 ,, rev. Thomas, Dublin city, clk.
1687 **Simcoe**, John, senior, Birmingham,
Warwickshire, cutler (Copy)
1771 **Simm**, James, Belfast, merchant
1802 **Simmons**, Abigail, Wm.-st., Dubl.,
widow
1758 ,, Hannah, Mountrath, Queen's
co., spinster
1792 ,, Isaac, Cork
1743 ,, Oliver, Rathdrum, co. Tipp.,
farmer
1783 ,, Samuel, Capel-street, Dublin,
saddler
1775 ,, Thomas, Meath-street, Dublin,
merchant
1774 **Simon**, Isaac, Dublin, a native of
France
1749 **Simons**, Henry, Dublin, gent.
1786 ,, Ellis Conliff, Carlow town, attorney-at-law
1745 ,, Isaac, Mountrath, Queen's co.
1746 ,, Oliver, Rathdrum, co. Tiperary,
gent.
1666 ,, Richard, Dublin, mariner
[See FITZSIMONS, SYMONS.]

1782 **Simpson**, Anne, Clogher
1780 ,, Benjamin, Moneyhill, co. Mon.
1788 ,, Catherine, Dublin, widow
1788 ,, Daniel, Tullynamelly, co. Armagh
1674 ,, Edward, Dublin, merchant
1760 ,, Edward, Mount Campbell, co.
Leitrim, innholder
1679 ,, Francis, Dublin, gent.
1721 ,, George, Cork, gent.
1727 ,, George, Wicklow, merchant
1738 ,, George, Dublin
1779 ,, George, Dublin, esq.
1688 ,, James, Londonderry, merchant
1783 ,, James, Lisduff, King's co.
1730 ,, John, Meath-st., Dub., clothier
1732 ,, John, Dublin, carpenter
1783 ,, John, Portglenone, co. Antrim,
merchant
1788 ,, John, Ballyards, co. Armagh,
gent.
1795 ,, John, Derremeen, co. Tyrone,
gent.
1785 ,, Margaret, Dublin, widow
1755 ,, Martha, Dublin, widow
1680 ,, Mathew, Castlereagh, co. Roscommon, esq.
1752 ,, Richard, Dublin, merchant
1762 ,, Richard, Hurtle, co, Meath,
farmer
1797 ,, Richard Annesley, Dubl., esq.
1797 ,, Robert, Boyle, co. Roscommon
1783 ,, Samuel, Dublin, esq.
1693 ,, rev. Thos., Palmerstown, co.
Dublin, gardener
1737 ,, rev. Thomas, Oatfield, co. Galway, clk.
1737 ,, Thomas, Clonbrin, King's co.,
gent.
1723 ,, Wm., Dublin, merchant
1802 ,, William, Green-street, Dublin,
gent.
[See SIMSON.]
1762 **Sims**, Edwd., Spittlefield, co. Westmeath
1804 ,, Edwd., Springfield, co. Westmeath, esq.
1780 ,, Robert, Belfast
[See SYMES.]
1673 **Simson**, Anthony, Dublin
1691 ,, Jane, Wicklow, widow
1756 ,, Wm., Dublin, brazier
[See SIMPSON.]
1728 **Sinclair**, Anne, Strabane, co. Tyr.,
widow
1797 ,, Catherine, Dublin, spinster
1703 ,, rev. John, rect. of Leckpatrick,
co. Tyrone, clk.
1771 ,, John, Hollyhill, co. Tyrone,
esq.

1776 **Sinclair,** John, Ballybegh, co. Kilkenny, gent.
1764 ,, William, Bearney
1764 ,, William, Greenhills, co. Meath
1780 ,, Wm., Dublin, jeweller
       [See ST. CLAIR, SINKLER.]
1804 **Sinclaire,** George, Hollyhill, co. Tyrone
1799 ,, Thomas, Belfast, co. Antrim, merchant
1767 **Sinclare,** John, Belfast, linendraper
1734 ,, Patrick, Dublin, merchant
1746 ,, Rebecca, Drumcondra, co. Dublin, widow
1758 ,, Richard, Church-st., Dublin, merchant
1771 **Sinderbee,** Richard, Cork, mercht.
1710 **Singleton,** Edwd., Drogheda, aldn.
1726 ,, Edwd., Drogheda, alderman
1745 ,, Elizabeth, widow of rev. Rowland S.
1780 ,, Hannah, Dublin, widow
1760 ,, Henry, Privy Councillor and Master of the Rolls (Large will)
1736 ,, John, Dunleer, co. Louth, clk.
1797 ,, John, Ballygeneen, co. Clare, esq. (Large)
1741 ,, Rowland, Terfeckan, co. Louth, clk.
1726 ,, Samuel, Dublin, M.D.
1801 ,, Sydenham, Great Quebec-st., Middlesex, esq. (Large will)
1742 ,, Thomas, Singletons Grove, co. Monaghan, esq.
1801 ,, Thomas, Coolroe, co. Carlow, farmer
1710 **Sinkler,** Robert, par. Kilcronagh, co. Londonderry
1740 ,, Robert, Moneyshanare
       [See SINCLAIR.]
1792 **Sinnick,** Michael, Cahirlogue, co. Cork, clk.
1694 **Sinnot,** Dominick, Waterford, merchant
1791 ,, James, James's-street, Dublin, tanner
1745 ,, Joanna, Dublin, widow
1711 ,, Peter, Waterford, merchant
       [See SYNNOT.]
1708 **Sinnott,** Ellen, Waterford, widow
1803 ,, Nicholas, Daventry, Northamptonshire, physician
1726 ,, Thomas, Dublin, esq.
1602 **Sinott,** John
1792 **Sipthorpe,** Robert, Dunany, co. Louth, esq.
       [See SIBTHORP.]
1809 **Siree,** Charles M., Summerhill, co. Dublin, esq.

1786 **Siree,** John, Mecklenburgh-street, Dublin, gent.
1714 **De Sisoll,** Peter Vigne, lieut. of horse
1731 **Sisson,** Anne, widow of Thomas S., Dublin, Pub. Not.
1719 ,, Jonathan, Dublin, merchant
1786 ,, Jonathan, Dublin, esq.
1724 ,, Robert, Dublin, surgeon
1716 ,, Thomas, Dublin, gent.
1793 ,, William, Lucan, but at Chester
1804 **Sittered,** Patrick, Ennis, co. Clare
1639 **Skaldwell,** John, Dubl., shoemaker
1750 **Skeat,** Martha, Belfast, widow
1747 **Skeffington,** Arthur, Dublin, esq.
1796 ,, Catherine, Dublin
1758 ,, Frances Diana, Dublin
1737 ,, Hugh, Cornehough, co. Down, surgeon
1803 ,, hon. Hugh
1742 ,, John, Antrim
1777 ,, Jonathan, Newry, co. Down
1811 ,, hon. William John
1767 **Skellern,** Catherine, Dublin, wid.
1729 ,, Hugh, rector of Killashandra, co. Cavan, clk.
1712 ,, Richard, Dublin, ironmonger
1769 **Skelly,** Francis, Drogheda, tobacconist
1770 ,, Jane, *alias* **Nealan**
1758 ,, John, Killineer, Drogheda, farmer
1775 ,, Michl., Barnattan, Lib. Drogheda, farmer
1722 ,, Robert, Killineer, Lib. Drogheda, farmer
1758 **Skelton,** Catherine, Dublin, widow
1695 ,, Ichabud, Swanlinbar, co. Cavan, gent.   [gent.
1728 ,, John, Loughill, co. Kilkenny,
1767 ,, John, Dundalk, co. Louth, clk.
1808 ,, John, Dundalk, gent.
1787 ,, rev. Phillip, rector of Dunacavey, dio. Clogher
1737 ,, Walter, Dublin, gent.
1664 ,, Wm., Robertstown, co. Meath, gent.
1721 **Skeolan,** John, Kilbreedy, co Lim., merchant
1699 **Skerne,** Mary, widow of J. Skerne, Christchurch-yd., Dublin
1709 **Skerret,** Francis FitzPatrick, Galway, merchant
1709 ,, John, Drumod, co. Leitrim, gent.
1791 ,, rev. Marcus
1780 ,, Mary Fitz Nicholas, Galway, spinster
1789 ,, Mary, *alias* **Lynch,** Poolrenooma, Lib. Galway

1804 **Skerret**, Mary, Middle-st., Galway town
1752 ,, Thos., Loughrea, co. Galway, gent.
1761 ,, William, Tinnavarra, co. Clare, gent.
1807 **Skerrett**, Bridgett, Eyrecourt, co. Galway, spinster
1803 ,, Dominick, Ballinduff, co. Galway
1805 ,, Edmond, Ardskeabeg, co. Galway
1738 ,, Jas., Moate, co. Galway, gent.
1796 ,, James, Newcastle, co. town of Galway
1789 **Skeys**, Abraham, Dublin, mercht.
1757 ,, John, Cork, merchant
1787 ,, William, Dublin, merchant
1726 **Skiddy**, Francis, Dublin, esq.
1751 ,, Francis, Mountmellick, Queen's co.
1631 ,, Roger, Dublin, gent.
1794 **Skinner**, George, Dublin, gent.
1702 ,, Martin, Dublin, gent.
1681 ,, Cornet Thomas, Dundalk
1784 **Skipton**, George, Dublin, esq.
1797 ,, Salley, Prussia-street, Dublin, widow
1729 **Skollan**, Edmond, Limerick, gent.
1806 **Skottowe**, Deborah, Dublin city, widow
1771 ,, John, Waterford
1537 **Skylton**, John
1771 **Slack**, Randal, Lakefield, co. Leitrim, gent.
1776 ,, Wm., Portarlington, Queen's co., gent.
1809 ,, Wm., Kiltubrid, co. Leitrim
1784 **Slacke**, Benjamin, Slacksgrove, co. Monaghan
1674 **Slade**, Anne, Dublin, widow
1676 **Slane**, Randall, lord baron of
1771 **Slater**, Alexander, Whitehill, co. Longford, esq.
1759 ,, Jas., Munskallon, co. Longford
1803 ,, Jane, Tullamore, King's co., spinster
1761 ,, John, Dublin, watchmaker
1803 ,, John, Coolrain, King's co., gent.
1791 ,, Mathew, Coolfaney, co. Wicklow, farmer
1745 ,, Sarah, Limerick, widow
[See SLEATER.]
1741 **Slaterie**, John, Dublin, esq.
1771 **Slator**, Anne, Dublin, widow
1811 ,, Bevan, Tonyn, co. Longford, esq.
1767 ,, John, Tonyn, co. Longford, farmer

1782 **Slator**, Joseph, Stonybatter, Dublin, tallow chandler
1767 ,, Thomas, Dublin, esq.
1787 ,, Thomas, Dublin, paper manufacturer
1802 ,, William Henry, Whitehill, esq.
1773 **Sleater**, Mathew, Dublin, gent.
1789 ,, William, Dublin, printer
1801 ,, William, Dublin, printer
1810 ,, Winifred, Temple-st., Dublin, spinster
[See SLATER, &c.]
1712 **Slee**, Emanuel, New Market, Lib. Donore, Dublin
1721 ,, Rebecca, Dublin, spinster
1683 **Sleigh**, Joseph, Dublin, tanner
1802 ,, Joseph Fenn, Cork, M.D. (See will 1774)
1808 **Slevin**, John, Lestuff
1752 **Slicer**, Edward, Dublin, goldsmith
1760 ,, Elizabeth, Baldwinstown, co. Dublin, widow
1756 ,, Saml., Rathfarnham, co. Dubl., esq.
1809 **Sligo**, the most noble John Denis, marquis of (Copy)
1697 **Slingesby**, sir Henry, Kilmore or Newtown, co. Cork, knt.
1747 ,, Simon, Dublin, merchant
1678 **Slingsby**, Francis, St. Martin's-in-the-fields, London, esq. (Copy)
1788 ,, Francis, Bath city, esq. (Copy)
1652 **Slingsbye**, sir Francis, knt.
1741 **Sloan**, Alexander, Aughreagh, co. Monaghan, farmer
1753 ,, James, Lisburn
1790 ,, James, Drum, co. Monaghan
1793 ,, Samuel, dissenting minister of Markethill, co. Armagh
1796 **Sloane**, John, Lisabuck, co. Monaghan
1728 ,, Wm., par. St. James, Westminster, Middlesex, esq. (Copy)
1803 **Sloper**, Constantine, Castlebar, gent.
1743 ,, William, Westwoodhay, Berkshire, esq. (Copy)
1746 **Slothard**, Adam, Drumbane, co. Down, esq.
1756 ,, Elizabeth, Drumbane, co. Down, spinster
1747 ,, Robert, Drumbane, co. Down
1789 **Small**, Thomas, Genl. Post Office, gent.
1673 **Smallbroke**, John, Wolvey, Warwickshire, gent. (Copy)
1729 **Smalle**, Caleb, Dublin, merchant
1739 ,, Jane, Dublin, widow

1797 **Smalley**, Anne
1726 ,, Benjamin, Dublin, merchant
1751 ,, John, Shanganagh, co. Dublin, farmer
1741 **Smallhorn**, John, Ballychristoll, King's county, farmer
1702 **Smallman**, Robert, Dub., merchant
1759 **Smart**, Barbara, Ringsend, widow
1667 ,, Jas., Newtown, merchant
1769 ,, James, Killyleagh, co. Down, gent.
1760 ,, John, Balnegor, co. Antrim, gent.
1683 ,, William, Cork, gent.
1780 ,, William, Dublin, gent.
1652 **De Smidt**, Peter, Dublin, apothecary
1700 **Smith**, Abraham, Waterford, merchant
1662 ,, Alex., Dublin, gent.
1747 ,, Alex., Dublin, mariner
1669 ,, Alice, Walsham-in-the-Willows, Suffolk, widow (Copy)
1772 ,, Alice, Dublin, spinster
1700 ,, Andrew, Dublin
1740 ,, Anne, Dublin, widow
1784 ,, Arthur, Griffinstown, co. Westmeath, esq.
1707 ,, Benjamin, Dunlavin, co. Wicklow, merchant
1758 ,, Benjamin, Shronehill, co. Tipperary, clk.
1809 ,, Benjamin, Violetstown, co. Westmeath
1768 ,, Beracah, Corbally, co. Tipp.
1807 ,, Boys, Maryboro', Queen's co.
1793 ,, Carew, Baldoyle, co. Dublin, esq.
1803 ,, Catherine, Dublin, widow
1807 ,, Catherine, Dublin city
1808 ,, Catherine, Longfield, co. Cavan, widow
1808 ,, Catherine, Roscrea, co. Tipp.
1715 ,, Charles, co. Westmeath, gent.
1734 ,, Charles, Dublin, tailor
1747 ,, Charles, Dublin, clockmaker
1758 ,, Charles, Ballymoney, co. Wexford
1782 ,, Chas., Poles, co. Cavan, gent.
1792 ,, Charles, Castlepark, Limerick, esq.
1794 ,, Charles, Mullestachon, co. Meath, farmer
1806 ,, Charlotte, Dublin city, widow
1735 ,, Christopher, Dublin, gent.
1742 ,, Cuthbert, Sligo, esq.
1770 ,, Cuthbert, Sligo, gent.
1777 ,, Cuthbert, Charteville, co. Cork, esq.
1716 ,, Deborah, Coolcock, co. Westmeath, widow

1805 **Smith**, Donald, surgeon in the Breadalbane infantry
1746 ,, Dorcas, Violetstown, co. Westmeath, widow
1793 ,, Eccles, Cookstown, co. Tyrone, captain in 77th regiment
1684 ,, Edward, par. Lambeth, Surrey, esq. (Copy)
1696 ,, Edwd., New Ross, co. Wexford, merchant
1717 ,, Edward, Clonelough, co. Monaghan, gent.
1720 ,, Edward, bishop of **Down**, q.v.
1743 ,, Edward, Dover, Kent (Copy)
1747 ,, Edward, Dublin, gent.
1711 ,, Elizabeth, Haverford-West, Wales, widow
1740 ,, Elizabeth, Dublin, widow
1763 ,, Elizabeth, widow of John S. of Dublin, shipbuilder
1784 ,, Elizabeth, Dublin, widow
1788 ,, Elizabeth, Bath city, widow
1789 ,, Elizabeth, Worcester city, wid. (Copy)
1807 ,, Elizabeth
1733 ,, Ellenor, Tuitestown, co. Westmeath, widow
1691 ,, Erasmus, St. John's Court, Middlesex, esq. (Copy)
1757 ,, Esther, widow of Henry S.
1798 ,, Frances, Dublin, brewer
1766 ,, Francis, Dublin, grocer
1785 ,, Francis, Dublin, esq.
1791 ,, Fras., Arklow, co. Wick., gent.
1779 ,, Furlong, Newcastle, co. Limk., esq.
1808 ,, Furlong, Cork city, merchant
1748 ,, Gilbert, Shinrone [gent.
1765 ,, Hamilton, Mount H., co. Louth,
1766 ,, Harry, Dublin, esq.
1706 ,, Henry, lieut. in lord Donegall's regiment
1731 ,, Henry, Dublin, merchant
1742 ,, rev. Henry, Churchtown, co. Louth, clk.
1746 ,, Henry, Belvaddock, co. Meath, farmer
1756 ,, Hy., Marrowbone-lane, Dublin, dyer
1804 ,, Henry, Ballycreagh, co. Dublin, farmer
1721 ,, Hugh, Danceford, co. Down
1730 ,, Hugh, Newry, co. Down
1731 ,, Hugh, Dublin, hatter
1770 ,, . Hugh, Dublin, shipwright
1763 ,, Isaac, Anneville, co. Westmeath, esq.
1802 ,, Isabella, Dublin, spinster
1650 ,, Jas., St. Michan's parish, Dub., gent.

1686 **Smith**, James, Dublin, merchant
1699 ,, James, Londonderry, merchant
1722 ,, Jas., Raphoe, co. Don., mercht.
1774 ,, James, Moyvore, co. Westmeath, esq.
1779 ,, James, Maynooth, co. Kildare, gent.
1783 ,, Jas., Harold's Cross, co. Dubl.
1794 ,, James, Dublin, esq.
1736 ,, Jeremiah, Drogheda, esq.
1650 ,, John, Dublin, sutler
1655 ,, John, a trooper
1663 ,, John, St. Patrick's-st., shoemaker
1684 ,, John, par. Lambeth, Surrey, gent. (Copy)
1690 ,, John, Templeshannon, co. Wexford, gent., blacksmith
1690 ,, John, Belragan, co. Louth,gent.
1703 ,, John, Dublin, alderman
1717 ,, John, Boystown, co. Wicklow, gent.
1718 ,, John, Tullogh, co. Carlow, esq.
1724 ,, John, Inishtown, co. Meath, farmer
1725 ,, John, Dublin, surgeon
1731 ,, John, Dublin
1733 ,, John, Vilanstown, co. Westmeath, gent.
1737 ,, John, Corbally, co. Tip., gent.
1738 ,, rev. John, Galtrim, co. Meath, clk.
1741 ,, John, Boystown, co. Wick., esq.
1751 ,, John, Kiltoom, Westmeath
1756 ,, John, Dublin, esq. King's counsel
1762 ,, John, Griffinstown, co. Westmeath, gent.
1762 ,, John, Waterford, gent.
1765 ,, John, Cornecarron, co. Cavan, linendraper
1766 ,, John, Dublin, merchant
1769 ,, John, Dublin, gent.
1772 ,, John, Violetstown, co. Westmeath
1775 ,, John, Cork, esq.
1777 ,, John, Cork, cooper
1779 ,, John, Kildare town
1783 ,, John, late a sergeant in 49th regiment of foot
1785 ,, John, Moorsides, co. Meath, farmer
1785 ,, John, Corcreagh, co. Louth, gt.
1789 ,, John, Carlow town, shopkeeper
1791 ,, John, Baltyboys, co. Wicklow, esq.
1805 ,, John, New-street, co. Dublin, gent.
1810 ,, John, Frankford, King's co.,gt.
1811 ,, John, Mallow, co. Cork, mcht.

1738 **Smith**, Joseph, Ballybarny, co. Kildare, gent.
1780 ,, Joseph, Pithfordstown, co. Kildare, gent.
1793 ,, Joseph, city of Bath (Copy)
1805 ,, Joseph, Nenagh, co. Tipp., gt.
1702 ,, Josias, Dublin, gent.
1803 ,, Lancellot, Booterstown, co. Dublin, gardener
1789 ,, Luke, Brunswick-st., Dubl., gt.
1805 ,, Marcus, esq.
1793 ,, Margaret, Roxmastraw, co. Wicklow
1796 ,, Margaret, *alias* **Warren**, *alias* **Bathorn**
1703 ,, Mary, wife to William Smith, Waterford, alderman
1724 ,, Mary, Dublin, widow
1771 ,, Mary, Dirty-lane, spinster
1781 ,, Mary, par. St. Mary, Drogheda, widow
1802 ,, Mary, Exchequer-st., Dublin, widow
1810 ,, dame Mary Blake
1721 ,, Mathew, Tuitestown, co. Westmeath, gent.
1718 ,, Michael, Drogheda, alderman
1747 ,, Michael Wilkinson, Ballynaskea, co. Meath
1805 ,, Michael, Stonybatter, Dublin city
1809 ,, sir Michl., Newtown, King's co.
1767 ,, Muriel, Mountmellick, Queen's co.
1777 ,, Nathaniel, Roscrea, co. Tipp., gent.
1792 ,, Nathaniel Nesbit, Dublin
1639 ,, Nicholas, Portshamnanoe, co. Meath, clerk
1717 ,, Nicholas, Dublin, merchant
1789 ,, Nicholas, Castlepark, near Limerick, esq.
1807 ,, Nicholas, Castletown, Kilberry, co. Meath
1649 ,, Oliver, Crayheel, co. Cavan, yeoman
1750 ,, Pakenham, Stonetown, co. Louth, gent.
1735 ,, Patrick, Dublin, saddler
1752 ,, Patrick
1779 ,, Paul, St. Mary's par., Dublin
1757 ,, capt. Peter, Sligo, esq.
1777 ,, Peter, Dorset-st., Dublin, mct.
1766 ,, Philip, Dublin, periwigmaker
1804 ,, Philip, Moynalty, co. Meath, esq.
1690 ,, Ralph, Ballymacash, co. Antrim, gent. (Ex.)
1698 ,, lieut. Richard, of maj.-gen. William Stewart's regt.

1700 **Soubiras**, Peter, lieut. in colonel De Cambon's regt. of foot
1741 **Souch**, Wm., Dublin, gent.
1723 **South**, Henry, Bellastown
1683 **Southaick**, George, Dublin, watchmaker
1739 **Southby**, Hannah, Dublin, widow
1687 **Southcott**, Otho, Dublin, esq. (Ex.)
1809 **Southern**, Wm., Ballyduff, King's co.
1747 **Southwell**, Agnes, widow
1657 ,, Anne, London, widow (Copy)
1796 ,, Bowen, Southville, Queen's co., esq.
1731 ,, Edward, Kings Weston, Gloucestershire, Sec. of State in Ireland (Copy)
1736 ,, Edwd., Portarlington, esq.
1755 ,, rt. hon. Edward, Kingweston, Gloucestershire (Large will)
1787 ,, Elizabeth
1765 ,, hon. Henry, Danesfort, co. Limerick, esq.
1632 ,, John, Dublin, gent.
1736 ,, John, Inishcoush, co. Limerick, esq.
1804 ,, Juliana, the Glen, co. Dublin, widow
1733 ,, Lucy, Dublin, widow
1802 ,, rt. hon. Margaret, dow. visct.
1735 ,, Meliora, dowager baroness
1640 ,, sir Richard, Singleland, near Limerick, knt.
1784 ,, rev. Richard, Castlemartyr, co. Cork
1677 ,, Robert, Kinsale, esq. (Ex. Large will)
1668 ,, Thomas, Dublin, esq.
1681 ,, sir Thomas, Castlemartyr, co. Limerick, bart.
1720 ,, Thomas, lord baron of Castlemartyr
1776 ,, Thomas, Dublin, M.D.
1780 ,, Thomas George, lord viscount
1796 ,, rt. hon. Thomas Arthur, lord viscount
1720 ,, William, Dublin
1802 ,, William, Glen, co. Dublin, esq.
1793 **Sowdon**, Elizabeth, par. Kenton, Devonshire, spinster (Copy)
1756 **Sowton**, Stephen, Dungarvan, co. Waterford, esq.
1770 **Spaight**, George, Carrickfergus, alderman
1765 ,, Grace, widow of Thomas S., esq.
1721 ,, James, Carrickfergus, gent.
1766 ,, James, Riverstown, co. Westmeath, gent.

1743 **Spaight**, Mary, widow of James Spaight, Carrickfergus
1698 ,, Thos., Burane, co. Clare, esq.
1775 ,, Thos., Kinsale, co. Cork, esq.
1806 ,, William, Corbally, co. Clare [See **SPEGHT**, **SPIGHT**.]
1718 **Span**, rev. Benjamin, Templemichael, co. Longford, clk.
1746 ,, Benjamin, Castleforbes, gent.
1784 ,, Benjamin, Dublin, esq.
1727 ,, Richard, Dublin, esq.
1761 ,, rev. Samuel, Newtown Forbes, co. Longford, clk.
1763 ,, Thomas, capt. in His Majesty's army at New York (See 1768)
1768 ,, Thomas, capt. in His Majesty's army at New York
1752 ,, William, Ballynacool, co. Donegal, clk.
1780 ,, William, Milltown, co. Roscommon, esq.
1791 ,, William, Dublin, esq.
1781 **Spann**, Catherine, widow
1778 ,, Celia, *alias* **Wogan**, Celbridge, co. Kildare, widow
1781 ,, George Frederick Augustus, lieut. in 28th regt. of foot
1792 ,, Lucinda, Drumsna, co. Leitrim, widow
1616 **Spark**, Robert, Ennis, co. Clare, gent.
1623 **Sparke**, sir William, knt., justice of K. B.
1778 **Sparks**, George, attorney in the Exchequer
1808 ,, Frederick, James-street, Dubl. city
1774 ,, Michl., Jamestown, co. Leitrim, merchant
1744 ,, Samuel, Dublin, anchor smith
1790 **Sparow**, Alexander, Dublin, gent.
1662 **Sparrow**, Edward, Waterstown, co. Carlow, gent.
1800 ,, John, Enniscorthy, co. Wexford, gent.
1786 ,, Joseph, Lower Ormond-quay, Dublin, merchant
1808 ,, Joseph, the younger, Enniscorthy, co. Wexford, gent.
1808 ,, Jos., Enniscorthy, co. Wexford
1809 ,, Joseph, Tomsallagh, co. Wexford, farmer
1788 ,, Mary, *alias* **Alloway**, Dublin, widow
1794 ,, Simmons, Clonmel
1636 **Sparrowe**, Henry, Dublin, gent.
1763 **Spear**, James, capt. in service of the East India Company
1810 ,, Richard, Dublin city

1794 **Speer**, Alexander, Dublin, attorney-at-law
1789 ,, Geo., Warrenpoint, co. Down, innholder
1781 ,, Joseph, Lisburn, co. Antrim, merchant
1745 ,, Robert, Stewartstown, co. Tyrone
1794 ,, Robert, Ardee, co. Louth, apothecary
1679 **Speght**, Thomas, Dublin, merchant [See SPAIGHT.]
1783 **Speight**, Jane, Dublin, widow
1660 **Spell**, Lucy, Drogheda, widow
1796 **Spellman**, Dorothea, Dublin, wid.
1738 **Spence**, Abraham, Crookedstaff, Dublin, brewer
1787 ,, Alice, Kellymard par., spinster
1808 ,, Andrew, Queen-st., Dublin, gent.
1647 ,, Anthony, Dublin, gent.
1749 ,, Ellenor, Strabane, widow of Robert S., Donegal
1708 ,, George, Upper Coombe, Dubl., brewer
1773 ,, John, Magheragall, co. Antrim
1779 ,, John, Newry, co. Down, gent.
1783 ,, Nathaniel, Rathmelton, co. Donegal, esq.
1676 ,, Peter, Dublin, tailor
1724 ,, Robert, Donegal, esq. (Not proved, see 1791)
1791 ,, Robert, town of Donegal, esq.
1804 ,, Rose, Dublin city
1788 ,, Sarah, Dublin, widow
1772 ,, William, Magheragall, co. Antrim, linendraper
1781 **Spencer**, Alexander, Dolphin's Barn, tanner
1742 ,, Benjamin, Broadkilbeg, co. Wicklow, gent. [esq.
1756 ,, Boyle, Rathangan, co. Kildare,
1772 ,, Brent, Bath city, esq.
1775 ,, Catherine, Dublin, spinster
1678 ,, Elizabeth, St. Christopher's par., London, wid. (Copy)
1686 ,, capt. Henry, Fromrah, co. Antrim
1711 ,, Henry, lieut. in major-genl. Wade's regt.
1784 ,, Henry, lieut. of the "Cato" man-of-war
1745 ,, Humphry, Borklebeg, co. Wicklow, farmer
1797 ,, James, Rathangan, co. Kildare, esq.
1690 ,, John, Youghal, merchant
1677 ,, Margaret, St. Thomas-street, Dublin, widow
1787 ,, Mary

1796 **Spencer**, Mary, Dublin, widow
1806 ,, Mary, James-st., Dubl., widow
1682 ,, Mathew, Youghal, alderman
1734 ,, Nathaniel, Rinny, co. Cork, esq.
1768 ,, Paul, Muff, co. Londonderry
1792 ,, Pullein, Fort St. George, East Indies, esq, (Copy)
1711 ,, Quartus, Brambly Grange, Yorkshire, esq.
1726 ,, Richard, Dublin, sword cutler
1673 ,, William, par. St. Paul, Covent Garden, Middlesex, tailor (Copy)
1795 **Spenser**, Samuel, Cork city, mercht.
1797 **Spier**, Rose, Dublin
1717 ,, Thomas, Rathcannon, co. Limerick, gent.
1800 **Spiers**, William
1725 **Spight**, Wm., Riverstown, co. Westmeath, farmer [See SPAIGHT.]
1662 **Spikeman**, William, Dublin, gent.
1700 **Spiller**, Henry, captain in sir John Hammer's regiment
1767 **Spinage**, Anne, *alias* **Cuffe**
1766 **Spital**, John, major in 47th regiment
1811 **Splaine**, James, Garrane, co. Cork, esq.
1811 **Splane**, Philip, Lisnegat, co. Cork, gent.
1733 **Sporcken**, Cawlina, wife to Aug. Fredk., baron De Sporcken (Copy)
1673 **Spottiswood**, James, bp. of Clogher, q.v.
1745 **Spottswood**, John, Ballyaghy, co. Londonderry, clerk
1741 **Spragg**, Marcia, Dublin, widow
1697 **Spranger**, Charles, Dublin, brewer
1698 ,, Henry, Dublin, merchant
1725 ,. John, Dublin, esq.
1723 ,, Lucretia, Dublin, spinster
1790 **Spratt**, Christiana, Youghal, co. Cork, widow
1687 ,, Devereux, Tipperary, clk.
1801 **Spread**, Elizabeth, Macroom, co. Cork, widow
1745 ,, John, Ballycannon, co. city Cork, esq.
1792 ,, John, Forest, co. Cork
1758 ,, Melian, Cork, spinster
1792 ,, Robert, Killard, gent.
1772 ,, Thomas, Mount Prospect, co. Limerick, gent.
1710 ,, William, Ballycannon, co. Cork, esq. (Ex.)
1735 **Sprigge**, Wm., Cloonivoe, King's county, esq.
1791 ,, rev. William, Newcastle, co. Limerick, clerk

1649 **Spring**, capt. Edmond, Dub., brewer
1794 ,, Elizabeth, Leixlip, co. Kildare, spinster
1795 ,, Francis, Blackhorse-lane, Dublin, gent.
1783 ,, George, Dublin, upholder
1787 ,, Hannah, Dublin, widow
1723 ,, Henry, Dublin, glassmaker
1798 ,, John, Leeson-st., Dub., gent.
1725 ,, Joseph, Dublin, gent.
1750 ,, Richard, Westminster city, gent.
1680 **Springham**, Anne, *alias* **Eaton**, widow, Dublin
1679 ,, James, Dublin, esq.
1671 ,, John, Dublin, merchant
1668 ,, Thomas, Dublin, gent.
1672 ,, Thomas, Dublin, merchant
1696 ,, Thomas, Dublin, gent.
1650 ,, Walter, New-row, co. Dublin, tanner
1799 **Sproule**, Andrew, Curragh-milkin, co. Tyrone
1806 ,, George, Athlone
1787 ,, John, Strabane
1794 ,, John, Monkstown, co. Dublin
1791 ,, Oliver
1807 ,, Robert, Parkerswell, Devon, esq. (Copy)
1798 ,, Samuel, Dublin, painter and plasterer
1806 ,, Wm., Athlone, co. Roscommon
1715 **Spry**, William, Dublin, esq.
1759 **Spunner**, Charles, Milltown, King's county, gent.
1774 ,, Margaret, *alias* **Newstead**, *alias* **Cornwill-Kent**, Knockanroe, co. Tipperary
1787 ,, Reginald, Knockanroe, co. Tipperary, esq.
1793 ,, Robt., Ballaghan, co.Tip., gent.
1796 ,, Thomas, Milltown, King's co.
1754 ,, Wm.,Loughkeen, co.Tip.,gent.
1788 **Squire**, Anne, Dublin, spinster
1809 ,, Catherine, Roscolbin, co. Ferm.
1802 **Stables**, James
1730 **Stacey**, Thomas, Carrickfergus
1788 **Stack**, Anne, widow
1785 ,, Jas.,Ennis, co. Clare, merchant
1804 ,, Mary, widow
1666 **Stacke**, Edmond, Dublin, gent.
1716 **Stackpole**, Philip, British, co. Antrim, gent.
1721 ,, Philip, Limerick, merchant
1623 **Stackpoll**, Nicholas, Limerick, merchant
1775 **Stackpoole**, Geo., formerly of Antigua, now of Dublin, gent.
1811 ,, John, Carrulagere, co. Clare, gent.

1799 **Stackpoole**, Lucinda, Hot Wells, Bristol, spinster
1799 ,, Philip, Mt. Cashell, co. Clare,
1771 **Stacpole**, Philip, Cork, merchant
1734 **Stafford**, Anne, Brownstown, co. Meath, widow
1758 ,, Arthur, par. St. Geo., Hanover-sq., Middlesex, esq. (Copy)
1713 ,, Edmund, Brownstown, co. Meath, esq.
1786 ,, Hannah, Spencer Hill, co.Louth
1783 ,, Hugh, Maine, co. Louth, esq.
1788 ,, Hugh, Elphin, co. Roscommon, apothecary
1797 ,, James, Back-lane, Dublin
1733 ,, John, Dublin, gent.
1782 ,, John, Longford town, apothecary
1786 ,, John, Kevin-st., Dub.,merchant
1787 ,, John, Kevin-st., Dub., mercht.
1803 ,, John, Luke-st., Dub., merchant
1768 ,, Kennedy, Ballesh, co. Londonderry, esq.
1761 ,, Mary, widow of Kennedy S., Ballyleas, co. Derry
1770 ,, Mathew, Dublin, surgeon
1778 ,, Patk., Four Court Marshalsea
1624 ,, Richard, Wexford, esq.
1791 ,, Robt., Dublin, public notary
1782 ,, Sidney, Dublin, widow
1743 ,, Susanna (Copy)
1745 ,, Susanna Maria, Dublin, widow
1760 ,, Thomas, Dublin, gent.
1803 ,, Ursulla, New Ross, co. Wexford, widow
1782 ,, Wm., Crampton-court, Dublin, jeweller
1717 **Stakes**, Henry, Dublin, cardmaker
1707 **Stamer**, George, Carnelly, co.Clare, esq.
1779 ,, Geo., Carnelly, co. Clare, esq.
1766 ,, Henry, colonel of horse
1783 ,, Thomas, Ennis, co. Clare, esq.
1740 ,, William, Carnelly, co. Clare, esq. (Not proved)
1785 ,, Wm., Carnelly, co. Clare, esq.
1775 **Stancliffe**, Wm., par. Eland, Yorks.
1791 **Standish**, Deacon, Dublin, esq.
1698 ,, Hannah, par. St. Andrew, Holborn, Middlesex., widow (Copy)
1741 ,, Henry, Dublin, merchant
1695 ,, James, Hatton Garden, Middlesex, esq. (Copy)
1776 ,, rev.John, Banbridge, co.Down, clk.
1801 ,, Sarah, widow
1635 ,, sir Thos., Bruff, co. Limk., knt.
1789 **Standly**, William, Gurteen, King's county, farmer

1740 **Standring,** Jeremiah, Dublin, tallow chandler
1638 **Stanes,** Henry, Jenkinstown, co. Kilkenny, esq.
1755 **Stanford,** Ann, widow of Luke S., Belturbet, merchant
1776 ,, Bedel, Belturbet, co. Cavan, esq.
1788 ,, Daniel, Dublin, esq.
1798 ,, Elizabeth, Belturbet, co. Cavan, widow
1807 ,, James, lieut. in the Wicklow Militia
1733 ,, Luke, Belturbet, co. Cavan
1749 ,, Luke, Little Green, Dublin
1794 ,, Patrick, Westport, co. Mayo, gent.
1775 ,, William, Killberry Hill, co. Cavan, esq.
1635 **Stanhame,** Henry, co. Armagh, gent.
1774 **Stanhope,** Arthur, Woodfort, co. Down
1759 ,, Henry, Legmore, co. Down, gent.
1747 ,, John, late capt. in brig. genl. Otway's regt.
1728 ,, Lucy, dow. countess (Copy)
1708 ,, Thomas, Moyray, co. Down
1789 **Stanisheele,** Thomas, Moore-st., esq.
1763 **Stanley,** Edwd., the elder, Athlone
1808 ,, Edwd., Athlone, co. Westmeath
1768 ,, James, Dublin, esq.
1635 ,, John, the elder, Dubl., mercht.
1662 ,, John, Marlestown, co. Louth, esq.
1745 ,, sir John, North End, Middlesex, bart.
1790 ,, John, Cookstown, co. Wicklow, farmer
1811 ,, Luke, Bridgefoot-st., Dublin
1605 ,, Patrick, Marlestown, co. Louth, gent.
1683 ,, Richard, Clonead, King's co., gent.
1674 ,, sir Thomas, Dublin, knt.
1783 ,, Thomas, Kilmurry
1665 **Stanly,** Alson, *alias* **Malpas,** wid. of John S., Dublin, mercht.
1743 ,, Benjamin, Dublin, victualler
1801 ,, Butler, Ballinree, co. Tipp., esq.
1750 ,, James, Dundalk, co. Louth
1701 ,, John, Dublin, esq.
1733 ,, John, Drisoge, co. Meath, gent.
1725 ,, Michael, Dublin, gent.
1762 ,, Michael, Kilsaran, co. Louth, late lieut.-col. in the Queen of Hungary's service

1746 **Stanly,** Patrick, Dublin, victualler
1809 ,, Robert, Sligo, co. Sligo
1756 **Stannard,** Aldworth, Ballyhooley, co. Cork, esq.
1803 ,, Alice, Dublin, spinster
1755 ,, Eaton, Dublin, esq., prime sergt.-at-law
1762 ,, Eaton, Ballyhooley, co. Cork, esq.
1772 ,, Ellinor, Dublin, widow
1749 ,, George, Ballyhooley, co. Cork
1768 ,, John, Kells, co. Kilkenny, clk.
1793 ,, Robert, Stannard Grove, co. Cork, esq.
1742 **Stannus,** Elizabeth
1806 ,, Ephraim, Dublin city
1718 ,, William, Carlingford, co. Louth, esq.
1732 ,, Wm., Carlingford, co. Louth, esq.
1798 **Stanton,** Mathew, Cookstown, co. Meath, farmer
[See STAUNTON.]
1573 **Stanyhurst,** James, Dublin, esq.
1677 **Staper,** Richard, London, esq. (Copy)
1742 **Staples,** Abigail, lady, widow of sir Alexander S., Dublin, bart.
1672 ,, Alexander, Taughanvale, co. Londonderry, esq., bart.
1741 ,, sir Alexander, Dublin, bart.
1640 ,, Bartholomew, Drogheda, merchant
1681 ,, Elizabeth, lady
1665 ,, George, Dublin, gent.
1687 ,, Henry, Dublin, clk.
1748 ,, dame Mary, wid. of sir John S.
1714 ,, sir Robert, Lissan, co. Tyrone, bart.
1762 ,, Thos, Derrylaurin, co. Tyrone, clk.
1799 ,, William Connolly
1776 **Stapleton,** Bryan, Cork, mariner
1811 ,, Edmond, Ballyragget, co. Kilkenny, esq.
1801 ,, Michael, Mountjoy-place, co. Dublin, builder
1701 ,, Wm., London, knt. and bart. (Copy)
[See STEPLETON.]
1738 **Starat,** James, Fernegerah, co. Londonderry
1805 **Starkey,** Andrew, Mark's-alley, Dublin
1754 ,, James, Stubins Mills, co. Dub., farmer
1700 ,, John, London, gent.
1769 ,, John, Edenderry, King's co., weaver

1807 **Starks,** Kenneth, White's-lane, Dublin, pump borer
1710 **Starky,** Thos, Mountrath, Queen's co., gent.
1790 **Starr,** William, Shannon Grove, co. Limerick
1769 **Starrat,** William, Strabane, co. Tyrone, gent.
1673 **Staunton,** Edmond, Boveingdon, Hertfordshire, D.D. (Copy)
1662 ,, Francis, capt. of a Company in the services of the United Provinces
1754 ,, James, Galway, esq.
1773 ,, John, Woodpark, co. Galway, esq.
1733 ,, Thomas, Dublin, esq.
[See STANTON, STINTON.]
1795 **Stavelly,** Robt., Cork city, mercht.
1716 **Stawell,** Elizabeth, Dublin, widow
1716 ,, Jonas, Madame, co. Cork, esq.
1758 ,, Jonas, Mallow, co. Cork, gent.
1788 **Stear,** John, Ginnets, co. Meath, esq.
1742 ,, William, Ginnets, co. Meath, gent.
1700 **Stearne,** Dorothea, Dublin, widow
1745 ,, John, bp. of **Clogher,** q. v.
1660 ,, Robert, Tullinally, co. Westmeath, esq.
1732 ,, Robert, brig.-genl., governor of the Royal Hospital, near Dublin
[See STERNE.]
1783 **Steel,** Jane, Philipsburgh, co. Dubl., widow
1766 ,, John, Ardkirk, co. Monaghan
1768 ,, Mary, Mullaghboden, co. Kilkenny, widow
1774 ,, Ralph, Philipsburgh, co. Dub., gent.
1797 **Steele,** Blenerhasset, Dublin
1735 ,, Daniel, Dublin, bricklayer
1699 ,, Fabian, Dublin, gent.
1712 ,, Gilbert, Ballyboughlane, Dub., yeoman
1808 ,, Harriott, Moynalty, co. Mon.
1678 ,, John, Hampton-upon-Thames, Middlesex, late of Dover, Kent, esq. (Copy)
1740 ,, John, Belfast, apothecary
1752 ,, John, Belfast, merchant
1779 ,, John, Dublin, pin maker
1752 ,, Laurence, Rathbride, co. Kildare, esq.
1780 ,, Margarett, Dublin, spinster
1809 ,, Maria, dowager lady
1802 ,, Norman, Moynalty, co. Monaghan, gent.

1787 **Steele,** sir Parker, Ranelagh-road, bart.
1756 ,, Paul, Dublin, merchant
1782 ,, Richard, Newhouse, Queen's co., esq.
1784 ,, sir Richard, Hamstead, co. Dublin, bart. (Large)
1733 ,, Saml., Kilegorthrean, Queen's co., farmer
1776 ,, Sarah, Dublin, widow
1792 ,, Walter, Moynalty, co. Monaghan, gent.
1794 ,, William
1810 **Steephens,** Rebecca, Cootehill, Cavan, widow
1788 **Steer,** Charles, Painthorpe Yorkshire, esq. (Copy)
1686 ,, Wm., Legacorry, co. Armagh
1638 **Steeres,** Wm., bp. of **Ardfert,** q. v.
1747 **Steevens,** Grizel, Dublin, spinster
1682 ,, John, Athlone, clk.
1771 ,, Justin, co. Dublin, esq.
1746 ,, Steevens, Cabra-lane, co. Dublin, esq.
1804 **Stephens,** Alexander, Cootehill, co. Cavan
1735 ,, Anne, Kells, co. Meath, widow
1694 ,, Arabella, Dublin, spinster, granddaughter of sir John Stephens, knt.
1791 ,, Clothilda, Wicklow town, wid.
1753 ,, Edward, Rathfarnham, co. Dublin, shoemaker
1769 ,, Edward, Paulville, co. Carlow, farmer
1805 ,, Edward, Kilmuckaridge, co. Waterford
1705 ,, Frydesweed, Dublin, widow
1755 ,, George, Tomsallagh
1778 ,, Hannah, Dublin, widow
1767 ,, John, Ravenhill, co. Armagh, gent.
1794 ,, John, Passage, co. Waterford, gent.
1793 ,, Nathaniel, officer in the customs, Bristol
1696 ,, Richard, Dublin, gent. (Ex.)
1710 ,, Richard, Newcastle, co. Limk., esq.
1807 ,, Richard, Hermitage, co. Cavan
1673 ,, St. John, Dublin, carpenter
1797 ,, Samuel, Dublin, merchant
1806 ,, the rev. Thomas, Grange, co. Wexford, clk.
1744 ,, Walter, Dublin, esq. (Copy)
1746 ,, Walt.,Borris-in-Ossory,Queen's co., esq.
1692 ,, William, Leslin, co. Cavan, gent.
1757 ,, William, Wexford, minister

1760 **Stephens,** William, M.D., Fellow of
College of Physicians, Ireland
1768 ,, Wm. Henry Nassau, Stephens
Fort, co. Cavan, esq.
[See STEEPHENS, STEEVENS, STEVENS.]
1804 **Stephenson,** John, Dalystown, co.
Longford
1752 ,, William, Dublin, merchant
1777 ,, William, Dublin, bricklayer
1745 **Stepleton,** William, Duleek, co.
Meath, farmer
[See STAPLETON.]
1734 **Stepney,** George, Abington, co.
Limerick, M.B.
1801 ,, George, Portobello, co. Dublin,
esq.
1798 ,, Herbert Rawson, Abington, co.
Limerick
1725 ,, Joseph, Abington, co. Limerick,
esq.
1767 ,, Stepney Rawson, Dublin, esq.
1693 **Steppey,** Joseph, Dublin, mercht.
1799 **Sterling,** rev. Anthony, Coolfin, co.
Waterford, clk.
1763 ,, Edward, Garryross, co. Cavan,
clk.
1777 ,, Edward, Dublin, esq.
1734 ,, James, Whigborough, King's
co., esq.
1746 ,, John, Kellikeen, co. Cavan, esq.
1810 ,, rev. Joseph, Dublin city, clk.
1769 ,, Luke, Cork, esq.
1783 ,, Luke, Dublin, esq.
1776 ,, Margaret, Dublin, widow
1764 ,, Marlborough, Dublin, gent.
1661 ,, sir Robert, Atherdee, co. Louth,
knt.
1796 ,, William Parsons, Dublin, esq.
1739 **Sterne,** Elizabeth, Cork, widow
1764 ,, Peter, Powerscourt, co. Wicklow, clk.
1678 ,, Thomas, Dublin, goldsmith
[See STEARNE.]
1727 **Sternhert,** Thos., Dublin, victualler
1741 **Stertup,** Edward, Dublin, tailor
1740 **Steuart,** Charles, Dublin, esq.
1793 ,, Charles, Bailieborough House,
co. Cavan, esq.
1753 ,, Mary, Dublin, widow
1763 ,, col. John, Dublin
1665 ,, sir Robt., Kilmore, co. Donegal,
knt.
1747 ,, Robert, Castle Dawson, co.
Londonderry
1778 ,, Wm., Castle of Bailieborough,
co. Cavan, esq.
[See STEWART.]
1745 **Stevely,** Joseph, Dublin, hosier
1775 **Stevens,** Edward, Stormanstown, co.
Dublin

1706 **Stevens,** Henry, Dublin, alderman
1731 ,, John, Meath-street, Dublin
1742 ,, Mary, Carbery, spinster
1696 ,, Walter, Appleton, Berkshire
[See STEPHENS.]
1734 **Stevenson,** Anne, Dublin, widow
1789 ,, Elizabeth, Letterkenny, co.
Donegal
1769 ,, George, Dromoyle, King's co.
1775 ,, George, Newry, co. Down,
bookseller [esq.
1713 ,, Hans, Killyleagh, co. Down,
1747 ,, Hester, Stonybatter
1739 ,, James, Dublin, merchant
1747 ,, Jas., Stewartstown, co. Tyrone,
merchant
1765 ,, James, Derry, merchant
1769 ,, James, Dublin, gent.
1732 ,, John, Letterkenny, co. Donegal
1747 ,, John, Dublin, merchant
1799 ,, John, Whitehall, co. Antrim
1807 ,, John, Kilmore, co. Down
1794 ,, Sarah, wife to John Stephenson,
Newry, co. Down
1788 ,, Robert, Newry, bookseller
1666 ,, William, Dublin, saddler
1786 ,, William Hall, Shelton Castle,
Yorkshire, esq.
[See STEPHENSON.]
1630 **Stevinton,** Richard, Whiddy Island,
co. Cork, gent.
1809 **Steward,** Geo., assistant adjutant-
general on the Staff
1739 ,, John, Dublin, quay porter to
His Majesty's Customs
[See STEWART.]
1742 **Stewart,** Alexander, Ballylough, co.
Antrim, esq.
1753 ,, Alexander, Belfast, merchant
1781 ,, Alexander, Newtown, co. Down,
esq. (Large will)
1808 ,, Alexander, formerly of co. Fermanagh, late of N. Britain
(Copy)
1726 ,, Andrew, Thurles, co. Tipperary,
quarter master
1763 ,, Andrew, Dublin, gent.
1802 ,, sir Annesley, Fort Stewart, co.
Donegal, bart.
1754 ,, Archibald, Corcreagh, co.
Down
1760 ,, rev. Archibald, Ballintoy, co.
Antrim, clk.
1773 ,, Archibald, Colskee, co. Mon.,
gent.
1805 ,, Benjamin, capt. in the Royal
Tyrone regt.
1716 ,, Catherine, Belfast, widow
1720 ,, Catherine, Skeas, co. Cavan,
widow

1706 **Stewart**, Wm., Killymoon, co. Tyr. esq. (Ex.)
1708 ,, Wm., London, mercht. (Copy)
1713 ,, Wm., Fortstewart, co. Donegal, esq.
1727 ,, William, Hanover-sq., London (Copy) [esq.
1761 ,, Wm., Newtown S., co. Tyrone,
1764 ,, William, Bearny
1764 ,, William, Londonderry, esq.
1767 ,, William, Finnick, Scotland
1776 ,, Wm., Killygordan, co. Donegal
[See STEUART, STEWARD, STUART.]
1675 **Stewarte**, Jane. widow of Wm. S., Branstane, sometime of Corrogan, co. Tyrone, esq.
1673 ,, Wm., Bellilan, co. Don., esq.
1680 **Stibbins**, Edith, Bristol, wid. (Copy)
1782 **Stiles**, Henry, Navan, co. Meath
[See STYLES.]
1769 **Stillingfleet**, Edward, Dub., widow
1795 **Stinger**, Christian, Watfd., mariner
1777 **Stinson**, Catherine, St. John's par., Limerick, widow
1769 ,, James, Dublin, gent.
1798 **Stinton**, rev. Wm., Lurgan, co. Armagh
[See STAUNTON.]
1672 **Stoaker**, Joseph, jun., Dub., goldsmith
[See STOKER.]
1801 **Stock**, Anne, Dublin, widow
1778 ,, Fredk., Dublin, woollen draper
1813 ,, Joseph, bp. of **Waterford**, q.v.
1774 ,, Luke, Dublin, esq.
1791 ,, Samuel, Dublin, hosier
1800 ,, Stephen, Dub., woollendraper
1779 **Stockdale**, James, Dublin, gent.
1769 ,, Susanna, Cork, widow
1701 **Stockton**, John, Cuddington, Cheshire, esq.
1674 ,, Thomas, esq., J. of K. B.
1698 **Stoker**, John, Drogheda, alderman
1720 ,, Thomas, Drogheda, alderman
1802 ,, Wm., Maryboro', Queen's co.
[See STOAKER.]
1771 **Stokes**, Benjamin, Dub., goldsmith
1806 ,, rev. Gabriel, clerk, D.D.
1781 ,, rev. John, D.D., late senior fellow of Trin. Coll. Dublin
1805 ,, John, capt. in the 47th regt. of foot
1765 ,, Patrick, Cork, merchant
1779 ,, Robert, Cork, merchant
1806 ,, Nicholas, Dubl. city, merchant
1614 ,, Thomas, Maddenstown, co. Kildare, esq.
1641 ,, Wm., Balharry, co. Dub., gent.
1678 ,, William, Dublin, merchant
1793 ,, Wm., Dublin, gent.

1774 **Stone**, Andrew, Privygarden, Westmeath, esq. (Copy)
1804 ,, Charles, Lyncomb, near Bath, D.D., archdeacon of Meath
1763 ,, Christopher, Stonebrook, co. Kildare, esq.
1717 ,, Edmund, Armagh, merchant
1769 ,, Elizabeth
1729 ,, George, Armagh, merchant
1765 ,, Geo., archbp. of **Armagh**, q.v.
1776 ,, Geo., Toberhead, co. L.derry
1779 ,, rev. Guy, prebendary of Killroot, dio. Connor
1790 ,, Hannah, Whitehall, Middlesex, widow (Copy)
1742 ,, Herbert, Dublin, merchant
1769 ,, Jacob, Dublin, esq.
1690 ,, John, junr., Dublin, gent.
1723 ,, John, Armagh, merchant
1756 ,, John, Dublin, surgeon
1735 ,, Richard, Dublin, esq.
1765 ,, Richard, formerly of Dublin, now of par. St. Geo. Martyr, Surrey, gent (Copy)
1788 ,, Richard, Dublin, merchant
1677 ,, Robert, London, joiner (Copy)
1776 ,, Robert, par. Howth, co. Dublin
1799 ,, rev. Samuel, rector of Coolduft, co. Donegal
1787 **Stoney**, George, Grayfort, co. Tipperary
1797 **Stonstreet**, Thomas, Islington, near London, gent.
1794 **Stony**, Isaac, Frankford, King's co., attorney
1548 **Stoo**, Allsone, Killussy, widow
1795 **Stopford**, hon. Edwd., major-gen. of the Forces (1796)
1733 ,, Elizab., Mustards-garden, co. Kilkenny
1807 ,, rt. hon. lady Frances
1685 ,, Jas., Newhall, co. Meath, esq. (Large will, Ex.)
1721 ,, Jas., Courtown, co. Wexford, esq.
1759 ,, James, bp. of **Cloyne**, q.v.
1780 ,, rev. Jas., Sandville, co. Cork, D.D.
1707 ,, Joseph, lieut.-col. Gorge's regt. of foot
1756 ,, Joseph, Middletown, co. Wexford
1786 ,, Joseph, lieut.-col. of 15th regt. of foot
1801 ,, rev. Joseph, Charleville, co. Cork, clk.
1699 ,, Mary, Dublin, widow
1809 ,, hon. lady Mary
1793 ,, hon. Philip, lieut. in the Navy
1771 ,, Thomas, Dublin, esq.

1760 **Stopford,** William, Dublin, esq.
1797 ,, Wm., Down-street, Piccadilly, Middlesex, esq. (Copy)
1809 ,, rev. William, Vicardale, co. Monaghan, clk.
1790 **Stordy,** Wm., Back-lane, Dublin, starch and blue manufacturer
1683 **Storer,** Anthony, London, draper (Copy)
1639 ,, Wm., Dublin, gent. (of Dublin Castle)
1806 **Story,** Arabella Frances, widow
1696 ,, Catherine, Dublin, widow
1810 ,, rev. Edwd., Bokea, co. Cavan, clk.
1780 ,, Elizabeth, Dublin, spinster
1811 ,, Francis, Belturbet, co. Cavan, shopkeeper
1757 ,, Joseph, bishop of Kilmore
1768 ,, Joseph, archdeacon of Kilmore
1800 ,, rev. Joseph, Monaghan town
1810 ,, rev. Joseph, Bingfield, co. Cav.
1630 ,, Robert, London, esq. (Copy)
1780 ,, Thomas, Dublin, gent.
1793 ,, Thomas, Monasterevan, co. Kildare, dyer
1696 ,, Wm., Dublin, tailor
1805 **Stotesbury,** Geo., Swifte's Heath, co. Kilkenny
1711 ,, Richard, Dublin, gent.
1783 **Stothard,** Adam, lieut. in 3rd regt. of foot
1752 ,, John, Dromore, co. Down, lieut. of foot
1761 ,, John, Moyra, co. Down., esq.
1707 ,, Thomas, Cork, pewterer
     [See STUDDERT.]
1731 **Stott,** James, Castle Lumney, co. Louth, gent.
1696 **Stoughter,** George, Shanbally, co. Tipperary, gent.
1626 **Stoughton,** Anthony, Dublin, esq.
1644 ,, Anthony, Cork, esq. (Copy)
1780 ,, Anthony, Ballyhorgan, co. Kerry, esq.
1696 ,, Ellen, *alias* **Blenerhasset,** Letter, co. Kerry, widow
1689 ,, capt. Geo., Carrickfergus
1635 ,, John, Dublin, esq.
1632 ,, Margaret, Dublin, widow
1705 ,, Mary, Tullyrow, Queen's co., widow
1683 ,, Richard, Dublin
1737 **Stourton,** Anne, Gt. Pulteney-st., par. St. James, Westminster (Copy)
1703 **Stout,** Jefferd, Charleville, co Cork, gent.
1787 ,, Nicholas, Youghal, co. Cork, gent.

1694 **Stowell,** Geo., late of Dublin, now of Chester, tailor
1718 ,, John, Dublin, clothier
1701 ,, Wm., Dublin, alderman
1767 **Stoyte,** Anne, Dublin, widow
1707 ,, sir Francis, Dublin, knt.
1732 ,, Francis, Dublin, esq.
1748 ,, John, Dublin, esq.
1750 ,, John, the elder, Dublin, esq.
1802 ,, John, Royal Hospital, Dublin
1806 ,, John, Peter-place, Dub., gent.
1668 **Strabane,** George, lord baron of
1696 **Strafford,** Wm., earl of (Copy)
1809 **Strahan,** Hugh, Alerton, co. Dublin
1781 ,, James, Bristol city, linen mcht. (Copy)
1774 ,, Wm., Dublin, merchant
1786 **Strain,** Margaret, Omagh
     [See STRAHAN, STRAUGHAN.]
1767 **Straingwitch,** Hannah, Grange-lane, Oxm., Dublin
1793 **Strang,** Luke, Cooleagh, co. Tipp., esq.
1809 ,, Mary, Mayfield, co. Tipp., wid.
1586 ,, Richard Fitz Peter, Waterford, alderman
1766 ,, Walter, Coolcah, co. Tipp., gt.
1794 ,, Wm., Meldrum, co. Tipp., esq.
1601 **Strange,** Edward, Waterford, esq.
1733 ,, Ellen, *alias* **Mayne,** Waterford, widow
1701 ,, James, Barristown, co. Waterford
1757 ,, James, Curraghalane, co. Kilkenny, gent.
1617 ,, Paul, Waterford, alderman
1701 ,, Paul, Rockets Castle, co Waterford, gent.
1622 ,, Peter Fitz Paule, Limerick
1669 ,, Richd., Ballybrack, gent.
1729 ,, Richd., Waterford, merchant
1624 ,, Solomon, Waterford, gent.
1625 ,, Thomas, Waterford, gent.
1724 **Strangford,** Endymion, lord visct.
1743 **Strangman,** Joshua, Mountmellick, Queen's co., merchant
1747 ,, Joshua, Mountmellick, Queen's co.
1775 ,, Samuel, London, merchant
1787 ,, Thomas, Waterford city
1771 **Stratford,** Benj., Corbally, Queen's co., esq.
1739 ,, Edward, Belan, co. Kild., esq.
1753 ,, Eusby, Corbally, Queen's co., esq.
1738 ,, Fras., late of Madrid, in Spain, esq.
1801 ,, rt. hon. lady Hannah, Dublin city, spinster
1747 ,, Henry, Dublin

1699 **Stratford**, Robert, Baltinglass, co. Wicklow, esq.
1734 ,, Robert, Corbally, Queen's co., esq.
1785 ,, Robert, Tougher, co. Westmeath, widower
1786 ,, Wm., Freeduff, co. Cavan
1803 **Straton**, John, col. commandant of Royal Irish artillery
1809 ,, Sophia, *alias* **Thornhill** [See STRETTON.]
1693 **Straughan**, Geo., Kilnaclownagh, co. Wicklow, esq.
1758 ,, Richard, Ballyhaise [See STRAHAN.]
1776 **Strean**, Anne, Dublin, widow
1776 ,, Ellinor, Dublin, spinster
1745 ,, Joseph, Lisnagore, co. Mon., gent.
1780 ,, Thomas, Middletown, co. Armagh
1721 **Streaton**, John, Artobracka, co. Armagh, yeoman [See STRETTON.]
1753 **Street**, Mary, Garbally
1658 **Streeton**, John, trooper in captain Peter Courthorpe's troop
1591 **Stretch**, Johan Fitz Nicholas, Limerick, widow, sometime wife to Wm. **Yonge** of that city, citizen
1744 ,, Randal, Dublin, gent.
1736 ,, Stephen, Dublin, merchant
1775 ,, Thomas, Dublin, tobacconist [See STRITCH.]
1732 **Strettel**, Abel, Dublin, merchant
1769 ,, Elizabeth, Dublin, widow
1750 ,, Thomas, Dublin, merchant
1795 **Strettell**, Amos, Cork city, mercht.
1780 ,, Edward, Dublin, merchant
1743 ,, Elizabeth, Dublin, widow
1757 ,, Jonathan, Dublin, gent.
1748 **Strettle**, Abigail, Lurgan, co. Antrim
1741 **Stretton**, Thos., par. St. Giles-in the-fields, Middlesex
1751 ,, Elizabeth, Pill-lane, Dublin, spinster [See STRATON, STREATON, STREETON.]
1614 **Strich**, John Fitz Bartholomew, Limerick, alderman
1780 **Stringer**, Barry, Dublin, gent.
1754 ,, Elizabeth, Dublin, widow
1808 ,, Francis, Dublin city, esq.
1772 ,, John, Enniscorthy, co. Wexford, gent.
1784 ,, Mary, Ballinakill, Queen's co.
1787 ,, Moses, Kilmurry, co. Wicklow, widow

1774 **Stringer**, Robert, Dublin, esq.
1777 ,, Sarah, Dublin, widow
1792 ,, Sarah, Summerhill, Dublin, widow
1732 ,, Thomas, Dublin, merchant
1778 ,, Thomas, Dublin, gent.
1796 ,, Thomas, Armagh city
1790 **Stritch**, Andrew, Kanturk, co. Cork, shopkeeper
1730 ,, Bartholomew, Limk., merchant
1782 ,, Catherine, spinster
1743 ,, Christian, Limerick, spinster
1766 ,, Edward, Limerick, merchant
1794 ,, Ellinor, Limerick, widow
1732 ,, Gasper, Limerick, merchant
1747 ,, George, Cork, merchant
1807 ,, Jasper, Strandville, N. Liberties of Limerick
1757 ,, John Jasper, Limerick, mercht.
1811 ,, John, Limerick city
1795 ,, Lucy, Limerick city, widow
1794 ,, Luke, Dublin, wine merchant
1794 ,, Mary, Creville, North Lib. of Limerick, widow
1802 ,, Mary Ann, Cumberland-street, Dublin, widow
1809 ,, Mary Anne, widow
1794 ,, Mathew, Limerick, merchant
1774 ,, Michael, Limerick, merchant
1737 ,, Richard, Clonmel, co. Tipp., merchant [See STRETCH, STRYTCH.]
1763 **Strogen**, Samuel, Bellgarrif, co. Cavan, clk.
1675 **Strong**, Adrian, Francis-street, Dublin, gent.
1782 ,, Bartholomew, Kilmainham, co. Dublin, gent.
1752 ,, Charles, Dame-street, Dublin, coach harness maker
1790 ,, Charles, Dublin, esq.
1717 ,, Henry, Fassaroe, co. Wicklow, farmer
1805 ,, Henery, Jervis-street, Dublin city
1767 ,, James, Dublin, clk.
1785 ,, rev. James, Fairview, co. Armagh, clk.
1744 ,, rev. John, rector of Tynan, co. Armagh
1769 ,, John, Balrath, co. Meath
1784 ,, John, Eccles-street, Dublin
1799 ,, John, Richmond, Liverpool, Lancashire, esq. (Copy)
1807 ,, John, City-quay, Dublin
1674 ,, Martha, *alias* **Brookes**, widow of Richard S., Dublin, cordwainer
1639 ,, Nicholas, Ballycullen, co. Dub., farmer

1774 **Swanton,** Mary, Kinsale, co. Cork, widow
1675 **Swanwicke,** Arthur, Moyla, co. Mayo, esq.
1784 **Swanzy,** James, Aoclreagh, co. Monaghan
1757 **Swayne,** Daniel, Ballincurrig, co. Cork, gent.
1758 ,, Francis, Derry, co. Galway, gent.
1788 ,, Francis, Limerick, gent.
1760 ,, Hugh, Cork, merchant
1806 ,, Robert, Bantire, co. Cork
1780 **Sweeaple,** John, Dublin, publican [See SWEETAPLE.]
1785 **Sweeny,** Anne, Dublin, widow
1715 ,, George, Cloney, co. Sligo, gent.
1791 ,, George Antrobus
1778 ,, Henry, Killark, co. Monaghan
1798 ,, James, Dublin, currier and publican
1806 ,, John, York-street, Dublin
1765 ,, Michael, Dublin, Alderman (Large will)
1789 ,, Miles, Enniskillen, butcher
1788 ,, Morgan, Sligo town, merchant [See SWINY, SWYNY.]
1777 **Sweney,** Elizabeth, Dublin, spinster
1789 ,, Michael, Woodbrook, co. Dubl., esq.
1774 **Sweny,** Mary, Mill-street, widow of John S., gent.
1728 **Sweet,** Stephen, Kilkenny, esq.
1805 **Sweetaple,** Dorothea, Church-st., Dublin, widow [See SWEEAPLE.]
1617 **Sweeteman,** Nicholas, Dublin
1766 **Sweetenham,** Elizabeth, Arbor-hill, Dublin, widow
1753 ,, George, Dublin, merchant
1767 **Sweetlove,** Elizbth., Drogheda, spr.
1760 ,, Wm., Drogheda, apothecary
1752 **Sweetman,** Amelia, Rathaldron, co. Meath, widow
1767 ,, Christopher, Dublin, merchant
1794 ,, Christopher, Abbey-st., Dublin, cooper
1799 ,, Christopher, Dublin, cooper
1766 ,, George, Thomas-st., Dublin, innholder
1758 ,, Henry, Dublin, brewer
1764 ,, Henry, Dublin, brewer
1803 ,, Henry, Dublin city, gent.
1803 ,, James, Dublin, esq.
1639 ,, John, Memurdy, co. Meath, gent.
1726 ,, John, Killadowan, co. Kildare, gent.
1743 ,, John, Thomas-st., Dub., dealer
1744 ,, John, mariner

1760 **Sweetman,** John, Kilbarrick, co. Dublin, farmer
1784 ,, John, Wexford town, merchant
1739 ,, Lawrence, Dublin, grocer
1684 ,, Lyonell, Dublin, gent.
1767 ,, Margaret, Hawkins'-st., Dub., widow
1776 ,, Margaret, Dublin, wife to John Sweetman
1784 ,, Mary of the Fox, co. Dub., wid.
1788 ,, Mary, Brunswick-st., Dub., widow
1798 ,, Mary, Cathedral-lane, Dublin
1719 ,, Michael, Lissenhall, co. Dubl., farmer
1776 ,, Michael, Collopswell, co. Wexford, gent.
1771 ,, Patrick, Dublin, brewer
1793 ,, Patrick, Dublin, brewer
1793 ,, Thos., Warrenhouse, co. Dub.
1805 ,, Walter, Dublin city, esq.
1769 **Swete,** Benjamin, Pleasantfield, South Lib. of Cork, esq.
1799 ,, Benj., Kilglass, co. Cork, esq.
1690 **Swettnam,** Mathew, Kinsale, merchant
1686 **Swift,** Abraham, Dublin, merchant
1704 ,, Adam, Greencastle, co. Down, esq.
1714 ,, Dean, Castlerickard, co. Meath, gent.
1811 ,, Dean, Bolton-st., Dublin
1716 ,, Elizabeth, Dublin, widow
1739 ,, Elizabeth, *alias* **Lenthall**, wid. of Dean S., esq.
1769 ,, Elizabeth, Dublin, widow
1793 ,, Elizabeth, Dublin, widow
1604 ,, Frances, widow of William S., Dub., gent.
1739 ,, Godwin, Dublin, esq.
1770 ,, Godwin, Tidenton, co. Kilkenny, esq.
1749 ,, James, Dublin, merchant
1671 ,, John, gent.
1789 ,, John, Moore-st., Dub., publican
1746 ,, Jonathan, dean of St. Patrick's, Dublin
1788 ,, Jonathan, co. Dub., esq.
1680 ,, Mary, Dublin, widow
1740 ,, Mary, Tuitestown, relict of Mr. Michael S.
1791 ,, Mary, Gt. Britain-st., Dublin, widow
1806 ,, Mary, Sidbury, Worcestershire
1739 ,, Meade, Lynn, co. Westmeath, esq.
1737 ,, Michael, esq.
1748 ,, Michael, Lynn, co. Westmeath, gent.
1777 ,, Michael, Dublin, gent.

1763 **Swift**, Richard
1790 ,, Richard
1662 ,, Thomas, Holyhead, Anglesey, esq.
1679 ,, Thomas, Dublin
1767 ,, Thomas, Lynn, co. Westmeath
1705 ,, William, Dublin, gent.
1776 ,, William, Dublin, esq.
1715 ,, Willoughby, Hertfordshire, son to Godwin S., esq. (Copy)
1759 **Swinburn**, Grace, wife to Jonathan S., Dublin, tanner
1759 ,, Jonathan, Dublin, tanner
1794 **Swindell**, Charles, North King-st., Dublin, gent.
1703 ,, Dorothea, Dublin, spinster
1707 **Swinerton**, Richard, Lisburn, co. Antrim, gent.
1777 **Swiney**, Francis, New-row, Dublin, merchant
1758 ,, Mary, Dublin, spinster
1797 ,, rev. Shapland, Templeshannon, co. Wexford, clk.
1668 **Swinfeld**, Arthur, Milltown, co. Wicklow, gent.
1797 **Swiny**, Christina, Enniscorthy, co. Wexford, spinster
1760 ,, Christine, Dublin, widow
1779 ,, Daniel, Milltown, co. Dublin, gent.
1730 ,, Francis, Two Pot House, co. Cork
1690 ,, Miles, Wexford, clk.
1729 ,, Wm., Ballyteige, co. Wexford, esq.
[See **Sweeny**.]
1806 **Switsir**, Jas., Kilkenny city, esq.
1750 **Swords**, Christopher, Dublin, ironmonger
1794 ,, Jas., Brianstown, co. Kildare, farmer
1805 ,, Patt, Dublin city
1805 ,, Thomas, Leeson-street, Dublin, builder
1779 **Swyney**, Edmond, Dublin, esq.
1795 **Swyny**, Mathew, Chiswick, schoolmaster (Copy)
[See **Sweeny**.]
1774 **Sydney**, Alex., Dudley, lord baron (Large will)
1746 **Syer**, Catherine, *alias* **Russell**, wid.
1733 ,, William, gent.
[See **Sayers**.]
1767 **Symes**, James, Hammersmith, Middlesex, esq.
1780 ,, Jane, spinster
1788 ,, rev. Jeremiah, Ballybeg, co. Wicklow, clk.
1756 ,, John, Coolboy, co. Wicklow, gent.

1750 **Symes**, Michael, Ballybeg, co. Wicklow, clk.
1809 ,, Michael, lieut.-col. of the 76th regt. of foot
1795 ,, Mitchelburne, Coolboy, co. Wicklow, esq.
1794 ,, Rachell, Coolboy, co. Wicklow
1780 ,, Richd., Ballyarthur, co. Wicklow, esq.
1794 ,, Richd., lieut.-col. of 53rd regt. of foot
1751 ,, very rev. Sutton, D.D., dean of Achonry
1667 ,, Thomas, Dublin, esq.
1790 ,, Wm., Ballybeg, co. Wicklow, lieut. in Navy
1794 ,, Wm., Dublin, yeoman
[See **Sims**.]
1796 **Symmers**, Alex., Galway town
1637 **Symonds**, John, Armagh, clk. (rector of same)
1685 ,, Samuel, Lond., grocer (Copy)
1735 **Symons**, Thos., Roskeen, Queen's co., gent.
[See **Simons**.]
1723 **Sympson**, Richard, Cork, merchant
[See **Simpson**.]
1712 **Synge**, Barbara, widow of Edward S., bp. of Cork, Cloyne, and Ross
1678 ,, Edward, bp. of **Cork**, q. v.
1741 ,, Edward, archbp. of **Tuam**, q.v.
1762 ,, Edward, bp. of **Elphin**, q. v.
1792 ,, Edward, Syngefield, King's co., clk.
1663 ,, George, bp. of **Cloyne**, q. v.
1710 ,, Margaret, widow of Samuel S., dean of Kildare, deceased
1721 ,, lieut.-col. Michl., Cowley, Middlesex (Copy)
1771 ,, Nicholas, bp. of **Killaloe**, q. v.
1708 ,, very rev. Samuel, dean of Kildare
1799 ,, Sophia, Syngefield, King's co., widow
1727 **Synnot**, Jane, Dublin, widow
1789 ,, Mark, Drumcondra-lane, co. Dublin
1639 ,, Robert, Waterford, merchant
[See **Sinnot**.]

——T——

1718 **Taafe**, Ellinor, Dublin, widow
1752 ,, James, Dublin, wine cooper
1785 ,, Jas., Springmount, co. Meath
1787 ,, James, Killcrowney, co. Louth
1689 ,, John, Calliaghtown, co. Louth, esq.

1775 **Taafe**, John, Ballinlough, co. Sligo, esq.
1786 ,, John, Rathneety, co. Louth, gent.
1753 ,, Joseph, Skinner's-row, Dublin, goldsmith
1789 ,, Patrick, Dublin, grocer
1790 ,, Patrick, Winetavern - street, Dublin, grocer
1739 ,, Richard, Mansfieldstown, co. Louth, gent. (Not proved)
1675 ,, Stephen, Athclare, co. Louth, gent.
1756 ,, Theobold, Back-lane, Dublin, linen draper
1747 ,, William, Dublin, cork cutter
1759 ,, William, Dublin, dealer
1793 **Taaff**, Edmond, Woodfield, co. Mayo, esq.
1789 ,, John, Sligo town
1766 **Taaffe**, Bridget, Drogheda, spinster
1736 ,, Christopher, Dublin, gent.
1707 ,, Edward, Dublin, gent.
1796 ,, Elizabeth, Cambrick Green, co. Louth, gentlewoman
1724 ,, George, Ranity, co. Louth, gent.
1736 ,, George, Drogheda, M.D.
1807 ,, George, Kingsfort, co. Sligo, esq.
1809 ,, George, Dublin city, esq.
1750 ,, James, Summerhill, co. Louth, gent.
1810 ,, Jane, Hendrick-street, Dublin, widow
1754 ,, John, Atherdee, co. Louth
1769 ,, John, Stephenstown, co. Louth, esq.
1773 ,, John, formerly of Dowanstown, co. Meath, now of Leicesterfields, Middlesex, esq. (Copy)
1800 ,, Mary, Brooklawn, co. Mayo, widow
1770 ,, Nichls., count, visct. Careu, lord baron of Ballymorth, lord of the bedchamber, and field marshal to His Imperial Majesty Charles VI.
1805 ,, Patrick, Killedan, co. Mayo
1794 ,, Robert, Dublin city, esq.
1730 ,, Stephen, Dowanstown, co. Meath, esq.
1773 ,, Stephen, Dematstown, co. Meath, gent.
[See TAFFE, THAFFE.]
1707 **Tabb**, Nicholas, Limerick, currier
1738 **Tabois**, Susanna, Dublin
1704 **Tabor**, Joseph, Dublin, basket maker

1781 **Tackaberry**, Nathl., Killowen, co. Wexford, farmer
1631 **Taffe**, Ismay, lady, Drogheda, wid. (no date)
1741 ,, Richard, par. St. Mary, Dubl.
1631 ,, sir William, Smarmor, co. Louth, knt.
[See TAAFFE.]
1804 **Tagert**, Jane, Woodbrook, co. Tyrone, spinster
1802 ,, Saml., Woodbrook, co. Tyrone
1808 ,, Susanna, Woodbrook, co. Tyrone, widow
1808 **Taggart**, Thomas, Celbridge, co. Kildare
1805 ,, Ursulla, *alias* **Hussey**, widow
[See TAGERT, TEGART.]
1665 **Tailer**, Edward, Tipperstown, co. Kildare, gent.
[See TAYLOR.]
1769 **Tailford**, Jane, Boylart, King's co., widow
1802 ,, Jane
1781 ,, Joseph, Boylart, King's co., esq.
1720 ,, Michael, Ballyna, King's co.
1743 ,, Thomas, Ballyna, King's co., gent.
1762 ,, William, Boylart, King's co., gent.
1596 **Tailor**, Andrew, Chester, tailor
[See TAYLOR.]
1736 **Tait**, Mary, *alias* **Malrath**, Ballyorran, co. Down, widow
[See TATE.]
1747 **Taith**, William, Aughagalbruck, co. Cavan, gent.
1765 **Talbett**, Thomas, Cootehill, co. Cavan, merchant
1618 **Talbot**, Bartholomew, Powerstown, co. Dublin, gent.
1794 ,, Benjamin
1761 ,, Bridget, Christchurch-yard, co. Dublin, widow
1792 ,, Elizabeth, *alias* **Plunkett**, Louth Hall, co. Louth, wid.
1800 ,, Frances, spinster
1690 ,, capt. George, Dublin
1811 ,, George, Ashgrove, co. Tipp., esq.
1584 ,, Jas., Agherskeethe, co. Meath
1672 ,, Jane, Malahide, spinster
1711 ,, Jane, Dublin, spinster
1652 ,, Jenn, *alias* **Aylmer**, Dollardstown, co. Meath, widow
1671 ,, Joane, Dublin, widow
1584 ,, John, Templeogue, esq. (Cover only, will gone)
1603 ,, sir John, Castlering, co. Louth, knt.

1666 **Talbot**, John, Drogheda, gent.
1787 ,, John, Roscrea, co. Tipp., gent.
1749 ,, Joseph, Castleformin, Queen's co., gent.
1733 ,, Margaret, commonly called lady Bathe, Belgert, co. Dublin
1761 ,, Mary, Kilkenny, widow
1795 ,, Mathew, Castle Talbot, co. Wexford, esq.
1595 ,, Patrick, Malahide
1778 ,, Plunkett Henry, Dublin
1760 ,, Richard, Dublin, esq.
1787 ,, Richard, Gaffney, co. Meath, gent.
1630 ,, Robert, Dublin
1667 ,, Robert, Dublin, M.D.
1743 ,, Robert, Ballyboy, King's co., gent.
1802 ,, Samuel, Rosemount, co. Tipp., gent.
1767 ,, Sharington, major-genl. of the Forces (Copy)
1601 ,, Thomas
1754 ,, Valentine, Malahide, co. Dub., esq.
1683 ,, William, Bodder, co. Meath, gent.
1748 ,, William, Oldbridge, co. Meath
1750 ,, Wm., Talbotstown, co. Wexford, esq.
1763 ,, William, Church-street, Dubl., merchant
1772 ,, William, the elder, Loughane, King's co., esq.
    [See TOLBOT.]
1691 **Tallant**, Deborah, Dublin, spinster
1739 ,, Mary, Dublin, widow
1808 **Tallants**, Anne, Inchicore, co. Dublin, widow
1796 ,, Peter, Castletown, co. Kildare
1746 **Tallis**, Francis, Emla, co. Kerry, gent.
1735 **Tallon**, Collumb, Drogheda, tanner
1778 ,, Delphina, Dublin, widow
1747 ,, Edward, Balrobin, co. Louth
1618 ,, Ellinor, Catherlogh, widow
1747 ,, Ellinor, Swords, co. Dublin, widow
1747 ,, James, Drogheda, tanner
1784 ,, Jas., Kells, co. Meath, mercht.
1747 ,, John, Dublin, saddler
1778 ,, John, Dublin, merchant
1737 ,, Laurence, Mullingar, co. Westmeath, gent.
1800 ,, Nicholas, Dublin, grocer
1761 ,, Thomas, Drogheda, distiller
1795 **Tallont**, John, Naas, co. Kildare, gardener
1733 **Talon**, John, Dublin, esq.

1793 **Tandy**, Charles, Portobello, co. Dublin, gent.
1745 ,, Drindally, co. Meath, gent.
1798 ,, George, Lisburn
1805 ,, George, Dublin city, esq.
1784 ,, Henry, Waterford, merchant
1790 ,, James, Charlotte-street, Dubl., merchant
1741 ,, John, Drewstown, co. Meath, esq.
1785 ,, John, Dublin, esq.
1800 ,, Marian
1684 ,, Thos., Drewstown, co. Meath, gent.
1711 **Tankard**, Elizabeth, Dublin, widow
1712 ,, Lawrence, Dublin, brewer
1601 ,, Nicholas
1631 **Tankloe**, Nicholas, Irishtown, co. Meath, farmer
1805 **Tanner**, Elizabeth, Cork, native of America
1626 ,, James, Donguihie, co. Limerick, gent.
1740 ,, Jonathan, Bandon, co. Cork, merchant
1776 ,, Jonathan, Bandon, co. Cork, esq.
1785 ,, Mary, Annesville, co. Cork, widow
1688 **Tarah**, Thomas, lord viscount
1700 **Tardy**, Jas., a lieutenant, reformed, in Francis Ducambon's regt. (Copy)
1802 **Tarleton**, Edward, Spellingstown, King's co.
1779 **Tarlton**, Ann, Mountmellick, Queen's co., widow
1742 ,, Digby, Killeigh, King's co., gent.
1755 ,, Digby, Killeigh, King's co., gent.
1695 ,, Edward, Killeigh, King's co., gent.
1740 ,, Edward, Killeigh, King's co., gent.
1740 ,, Gilbert, Killeigh, King's co., gent.
1778 ,, Gilbert, Killeigh, King's co., gent.
1700 ,, John, Killeigh, King's co., gent.
1758 ,, John, Killeigh, King's co., gent.
1775 ,, Weldon, Mountmellick, Queen's co., gent.
1632 **Tarpie**, Thomas, Galway, shoemaker
1769 **Tarrin**, Elizabeth, widow of Nicholas T., Coalmanstown, co. Dubl.
1767 **Tarry**, Joseph, Dublin, merchant

1739 **Tasburgh**, Henry, par. St. Giles, Middlesex, esq. (Copy)
1745 ,, Susanna, widow, Lincolns Inn Fields, Middlesex (Copy)
1743 **Tashe**, Thomas, Dublin, gent.
1780 **Tasker**, James, Dublin, surgeon
1631 ,, Peter Longbow, string maker, London
1805 ,, Susanna Frances, Dublin, wid.
1758 **Tassell**, Charles, Kile, co. Kilkenny
1766 **Tate**, Adam, Sprucefield, co. Down, linen merchant
1714 ,, Alexander, Ballybine, co. Down, gent. [hatter
1791 ,, Alexander, Essex-street, Dubl.,
1774 ,, James, Fannenierin, co. Wicklow, gent.
1754 ,, John, Newtown, co. Down
1780 ,, John, Newport, co. Dublin, gent.
1787 ,, John, Fannenierin, co. Wicklow, esq.
1758 ,, Joseph, Ballinacur, co. Wicklow, farmer
1764 ,, Margaret, Ballinacur, co.Wicklow, widow
1810 ,, Mary, Derrygore, co. Fermanagh
1804 ,, Rachel, Dublin city, esq.
1727 ,, Samuel, Dunlady, co. Down, gent.
[See TAIT, TEATE.]
1733 **Tatterson**, Charles, Templeogue, co. Dublin, gent.
1692 **Taubman**, John, Narraghmore, co. Kildare, gent.
1735 **Tauranac**, John Lewis Bacone, Fraly
1685 **Taverner**, Edward, Rathrobin, King's co., gent.
1798 ,, John Samuel, Limerick city, burgess
1782 **Tavernor**, Catherine, Castlemarket, Dublin, widow
1791 ,, George, Castlemarket, butcher
1758 ,, John, Ballymahon, co. Down
1774 ,, William, Dublin, butcher
1752 **Tawton**, Pascoe, Nicholas-street, Dublin, weaver
1614 **Tayler**, Robert, Curraglass, co. Cork, yeoman
1707 **Taylor**, Alice, *alias* **Portarlington**, Essex-street, Dublin, widow
1687 ,, Anne, Dublin, widow
1758 ,, lady Anne, wife of Walter T., par. St. Geo., Han.-square, Middlesex, esq. (Large will; Copy)
1770 ,, Anne, Cork, widow (Not proved)

1784 **Taylor**, rt. hon. lady Anne
1789 ,, Anselm, Woodcliffe, co. Limk., esq.
1737 ,, Anthony, Galway, 2nd son to William T., esq.
1791 ,, Benjamin, Killmacudd, co. Dublin
1736 ,, Berkely, Ballynort, co. Limk., esq.
1759 ,, Bridget, late of Dublin, now of Cloghbenon, co. Wexford, widow
1785 ,, Bridget, Dublin, widow
1754 ,, Catherine, wife to John T., Dublin, gent.
1785 ,, Charles, capt. in 67th regt. of foot (Copy)
1685 ,, Christopher, Dublin, merchant
1717 ,, Christopher, Dublin, gent.
1810 ,, Daniel, William-street, Dublin, chandler
1705 ,, Edward, Loughbrickland, co. Down (Not proved)
1740 ,, Edward, Derrymullen, King's co., gent.
1741 ,, Edward, Loughbrickland, co. Down, esq.
1761 ,, Edward, Ballynort, co. Limk., esq.
1769 ,, Edward, Oxford College, esq.
1802 ,, Edward, Noan, co. Tipp., esq.
1730 ,, Elizabeth, widow
1770 ,, Elizabeth, Dublin, spinster
1784 ,, Elizabeth, Dublin, widow
1749 ,, Erasmus, Dublin, glazier
1754 ,, Ellinor, Dublin, widow
1803 ,, Frances
1663 ,, Francis, Dublin, alderman
1751 ,, Francis, Dublin, merchant
1792 ,, George, Ballywalter, co. Wexford
1797 ,, Godfrey, Noan, co. Tipp., esq.
1650 ,, Henry, an officer in the army
1691 ,, Henry,Santry, and of Billington, Cheshire, yeoman
1605 ,, James, Dublin, merchant
1686 ,, James, Dublin, clothier
1747 ,, James, Elmgrove, co. Meath, esq.
1748 ,, James, Dublin, gent.
1762 ,, James, Dublin, alderman
1767 ,, James, Ray, co. Donegal, farmer
1803 ,, James, William-street, Dublin
1804 ,, James, Dublin city, esq.
1711 ,, Jane, Killenasceare, Queen's co., gentlewoman
1762 ,, Jane, Cork, spinster
1775 ,, Jane, Monasterevan, co. Kildare, widow

1811	**Taylor**, Jane, Stephen's-street, Dublin, spinster		1583	**Taylor**, Robert, New Haggard, co. Meath, gent.		

1811 **Taylor**, Jane, Stephen's-street, Dublin, spinster
1667   ,, Jeremy, bp. of **Down**, q. v.
1678   ,, John, London, girder (Copy)
1678   ,, John, Swords, co. Dublin, gent.
1697   ,, John, Bollington, Cheshire, yeoman
1714   ,, John, par. St.Giles-in-the-fields, Middlesex, gent. (Copy)
1728   ,, John, Belfast, merchant
1732   ,, John, Marrowbone-lane, co. Dublin, brewer
1737   ,, John, St. Andrew's par., Dubl., mariner
1740   ,, John, Dublin, merchant
1741   ,, John, the elder, Swords, co. Dublin, esq.
1758   ,, John, Dublin, goldsmith
1784   ,, John, Tinahely, co. Wicklow, clothier
1796   ,, John, Swords, co. Dublin, esq.
1805   ,, John, Clonmel, co. Tipperary
1808   ,, Jonathan, Tuckmill, co. Kildare
1738   ,, Joseph, Ardnehugh, co. Carlow, gent.
1759   ,, Joseph, Ardee, co. Louth, carpenter.
1790   ,, Joseph
1725   ,, Judith, widow of Robert T., Ballynort, co. Limerick, esq.
1760   ,, Lovelace, Noan, co. Tipp., esq.
1730   ,, Lydia, *alias* **Stevens**, Dublin, widow
1808   ,, Lydia, Gloucester-street, Dubl., widow
1757   ,, capt. Marmaduke, Martin's-lane, co. Dublin
1744   ,, Mary, Rathfarnham, co. Dublin
1793   ,, Mary, Aungier-street, Dublin, widow
1800   ,, Mary, Rockabbey, co. Limerick, widow
1803   ,, Mary, Dublin, widow
1756   ,, Nathaniel, Dublin, gent.
1773   ,, Nathaniel, Kilkenny, esq.
1802   ,, Paschal, Portobello, co. Dublin, gent.
1742   ,, Peter, Dublin, merchant
1802   ,, Poole, Dublin, goldsmith
1803   ,, Rebecca, Dublin, widow
1810   ,, Rebecca, of the parish of Aughabog, co. Mon., wid.
1726   ,, Richard, co. Down
1732   ,, Richard, Hollypark, co. Limerick, esq.
1750   ,, Richd., Swords, co. Dubl., esq.
1766   ,, Richard, Hollypark, co. Limerick, esq. (Copy)
1800   ,, Richard, Rockabbey, co. Limerick, gent.

1583 **Taylor**, Robert, New Haggard, co. Meath, gent.
1705   ,, Robert, Dublin, gent.
1745   ,, rev. Robert, dean of Clonfert
1748   ,, Robert, Clogath, co. Kilkenny
1777   ,, Robert, Castlepollard, co. Westmeath, gent.
1778   ,, Robt., Finedon, Northamptonshire (Copy)
1790   ,, Robert, Dublin, gent.
1627   ,, Robertson, Tallow, co. Watfd.
1702   ,, Roger, Loughcrew, co. Meath, gent.
1730   ,, Roger, Dublin, musician
1796   ,, Roger, Portobello, co. Dublin
1740   ,, Rogers, Dublin, esq.
1728   ,, Samuel, Dublin
1752   ,, Samuel, Blackpitts, co. Dublin, brewer
1811   ,, Samuel, Coleraine, co. Londonderry, merchant
1728   ,, Sarah, Dublin, widow
1787   ,, dame Sarah
1775   ,, Susanna, Kilkenny, widow
1617   ,, Thomas, esq., Culgoodagh, co. Waterford, tanner
1638   ,, Thomas, Bandon-bridge, gent
1667   ,, Thos., Jamestown, co. Meath, gent.
1682   ,, Thomas, Dublin, esq.
1710   ,, Thos., Bolany, co. Wex., gent.
1736   ,, sir Thomas, Dub., bart, privy councillor
1747   ,, Thomas, Dublin, printer
1747   ,, Thomas, Dublin, shipwright
1749   ,, Thomas, archdeacon of Ardagh and rector of Killashee
1757   ,, rt. hon. sir Thomas, bart.
1762   ,, Thomas, Dublin, gent.
1764   ,, Thomas, Dublin, alderman
1765   ,, Thomas, par. Leixlip, dyer and linen printer
1789   ,, Thos., Glasnevin, co. Dub., esq.
1790   ,, Thomas, Limerick, innholder
1704   ,, Timothy, Dublin, gent.
1703   ,, Walter, Ballymacragh, co. Galway, esq.
1811   ,, Walter, Cookstown, co. Tyrone
1667   ,, William, Dublin, brewer
1691   ,, William, Ringsend, vintner
1712   ,, Wm., Lisaura, co. Westmeath, gent.
1713   ,, Wm., Burton, co. Cork, esq.
1729   ,, William, London, bookseller (Copy)
1741   ,, William, Boyerstown, co. Meath
1741   ,, Wm., Middlehill, Worcestershire, esq. (Copy)
1761   ,, William, Cork, esq.
1775   ,, Wm., Dub., tallow chandler

1791 **Taylor**,William, the elder, Clonmel, co. Tipperary
1792 ,, William, Castlepollard, co. Westmeath, gent.
1793 ,, William, par. St. Paul, Middlesex, tailor (Copy)
1794 ,, Wm., Charlotte-st., Dub., gent.
1805 ,, Wm., Blackhall-st., Dub., gent.
1806 ,, Wm., Limerick city, captain 28th regiment of foot
[See TAILER, TAILOR, TYLER.]
1727 **Teague**, John, Dublin, gent.
1780 **Tealford**, Robert, Mountmellick, co. Westmeath, M.D.
1773 **Teap**, William, Tallow, co. Waterford, merchant
1774 **Teare**, Margaret, Athlone, co.Westmeath, widow
1786 ,, Susanna, *alias* **Robinson**
1767 **Tearnan**, Barnaby, Essex-st., Dub., vintner
1758 **Teasdeale**, William, Love-lane, London, merchant (Copy)
1660 **Teate**, Faithfull, the elder, D.D., and minister in Drogheda
1671 ,, Joseph, Kilkenny, clk.
1673 ,, Theophilus, Fellow of Trinity College, Dublin
[See TATE.]
1811 **Tedford**, Henry, Fuiard, co. Down, paper merchant
1775 **Teeling**, Bartholomew
1810 ,, Margaret, South Earl-street, Dublin, widow
1731 ,, Michael, Dublin, gent.
1735 ,, Patrick, Dublin, merchant
1677 ,, Thomas, Mullacha, co. Meath, gent.
1636 ,, Nicholas, Sylvanstown, co. Meath, gent.
1754 **Teer**, Jane, Dublin, widow
1808 ,, John, Dublin city, bricklayer
1773 **Tegart**, Edward, Acton, co.Armagh
1720 ,, Henry, Hilltown, co. Westmeath, gent.
1806 ,, Robert, Dublin city
[See TAGGART.]
1785 **Telford**, Michael, Mount Temple, co. Westmeath, esq.
1808 **Teling**, Mary, Dublin city, widow
1650 **Tellier**, Nicholas, Dublin, merchant
1701 **Tempest**, Michael, Dublin, esq.
1772 **Temple**, Elizabeth, par. St. James, Westminster, Middlesex, widow
1792 ,, Gustavus Handcock, Waterstown
1711 ,, James, Dublin, surgeon
1677 ,, sir John, knt., Master of the Rolls

1705 **Temple**, sir John, East Sheen, Surrey, knt. (Copy)
1782 ,, Richard Grenville, earl (Copy)
1741 ,, Robert, Mount Temple, co. Westmeath, esq.
1782 ,, Robert, Allenton, co.Dub., esq.
1626 ,, sir William, knt., Provost of Trinity College, Dublin
1781 **Templeton**, Anne, Newry, co.Down, widow
1785 ,, Clotworthy, lord baron (Copy)
1792 ,, James, lieut. in 6th dragoon guards
1802 ,, James, Balgriffin, co. Dublin
1784 ,, John, Richmond, co.Dub.,gent.
1783 ,, William, Cootehill, co. Cavan, merchant
1684 **Tench**, John, Mullinderry, co. Wexford, esq.
1765 ,, Joshua, Bryanstown, co. Wexford, clk.
1717 ,, Margaret, Mullinderry, co. Wexford, widow
1713 ,, Samuel, Mullinderry, co. Wexford, esq.
1761 ,, Thomas, Dublin, esq.
1807 ,, Thomas, Dublin city, gent.
1712 **Tenison**, Elizabeth, Carrickmacross, co. Monaghan, widow
1803 ,, John, Castle Brittas, co.Tipperary, esq.
1742 ,, Margaret, Glasnevin, co. Dub., spinster
1725 ,, Richard, Thomastown, co. Louth, esq.
1758 ,, Wm., Finglas, co. Dublin, esq.
1790 **Tennant**, Charles, Dublin, merchant
1791 ,, Martha, Gregg's-lane, Dublin, widow
1674 ,, Robert, Dublin, saddler
1755 **Tennison**, Anthony, Rathmore, co. Kildare, gent.
1795 ,, Dorothy, Dublin, widow
1739 ,, Edward, bishop of **Ossory**, q.v.
1709 ,, Henry, Dillonstown, co. Louth, esq.
1784 ,, Joseph, Clonmel
1705 ,, Richard, bp. of **Meath**, q. v.
1764 ,, Thos., Finglas, co. Dub., esq.
1779 ,, Thomas, one of the Justices of the Common Pleas (Large)
1663 **Tent**, lieut. John, then of Cork
1799 **Ternan**, Edmond, Strokestown, co. Roscommon, merchant
1780 ,, Rose, Tucker's-row, Dublin
[See TIERNAN, TIERNEY.]
1798 **Terney**, Dennis, Suffolk-st., Dublin, publican
1582 **Terrall**, Alsonne, Cook-st., Dublin, widow

1721 **Terrall**, Richard, Higginstown, co. Westmeath
1681 **Terricke**, George, Leigh, Essex, gent.
1778 **Terrill**, Michael, Arklow, fisherman
1735 **Terrot**, John Charles, Dublin, esq.
1724 **Terry**, Samuel, Dublin, merchant
1746 ,, Sarah, Dublin, spinster
1692 **Terrye**, Richard, Cork, maltster
1729 **Terson**, David, Dublin, esq.
1737 ,, David, Portarlington, Queen's co., esq.
1761 ,, Francis, Portarlington, Queen's co.
1765 ,, Mary, Dublin, spinster
1716 **Terwhit**, Edmond, Bishopslough, co. Kilkenny, gent.
1730 **Testefolle**, Claudius, par. St. Paul, Covent Garden, Middlesex, esq. (Copy)
1596 **Tew**, Alson, Waterford
1686 ,, David, Phepotstown, co. Meath, farmer
1756 ,, Hester, Baddinstown, co. Meath, widow
1799 ,, Hester, Dublin, spinster
1744 ,, John, Mullhussey, co. Meath, gent.
1772 ,, John, Dublin, alderman
1736 ,, Mark, Culmullen, co. Meath, gt.
1737 ,, Mark, Mullhussey, co. Meath, gent.
1739 ,, Mark, Culmullen, co. Meath, gent.
1767 ,, Mark, Killglin, co. Meath, esq.
1716 **Teysouniere**, James, La Rouviere, Dublin, gent.
1793 **Thacker**, Barker, Ballymelish, Queen's co.
1811 ,, Barker, Dublin city, tallow chandler
1793 ,, John, Boleybeg, co. Kildare, gt.
1806 ,, John, Mountrath, Queen's co.
1782 ,, Thomas, Dublin, merchant
[See THEAKER.]
1751 **Thafe**, Mary, *alias* **M'Nemara**, Carhue, co. Clare, widow
1742 **Thaffe**, John, Carhue, co. Clare, gt.
[See TAAFFE.]
1724 **Thames**, Rachel, St. Andrew's par., Dublin, widow
1777 **Thayer**, Lucia Susana, Northampton town, widow (Copy)
1793 **Thayne**, David, Cork-hill, Dublin, saddler
1761 **Theaker**, capt. George, Belfast
1713 ,, rev. Thos., Rathmore, co. Kildare, clk.
1751 ,, Thomas, Wicklow, esq.
[See THACKER.]

1692 **Thelwall**, Mary, Hillsborough, co. Down, widow
1710 **Theroulde**, John, Dublin, merchant
1735 **Therry**, James, par. Mount Nessin, Essex, gent.
1770 ,, James, Cork, gent.
1804 ,, Nicholas, Cork city, merchant
1731 **Thetford**, Esther, Belfast, widow
1761 ,, Mary, Kilkenny, widow
1702 ,, Wm., Belfast, merchant
1655 **Thewe**, Robert, soldier in col. John Hewson's company
1765 **Thewles**, Anne, widow
1760 ,, Chas., Carrick, co. Tipp., clk.
1750 ,, Flora, *alias* **Fisher**, wife to John Lewis Thewles
1691 ,, Geo., Fellow of Trin. Coll., Dub.
1792 ,, James, Dublin
1799 ,, John, Rookwood, co. Galway, esq.
1808 ,, Thos., Cloverhill, co. Roscom.
1777 ,, Wentworth, Dublin, esq.
1712 **Thibault**, Esther, Portarlington, Queen's co.
1725 **Thibout**, Mary, Dublin, widow
1583 **Thickpenny**, John, Glassmore, co. Waterford, gent.
1661 **Thimelbee**, George, Lond., mercht. (Copy)
1788 **Thirkield**, Joseph, co. Cavan, mct.
1772 **Thirkild**, Sarah, Dundalk, co. Louth
1785 **Thode**, Anne, Dublin, widow
1780 ,, Hans, Dublin, merchant
1798 **Thomas**, Amyas, Inch, co. Carlow, esq.
1803 ,, Arthur, Dublin, gent.
1776 ,, Bartholomew, Johnstown, co. Wexford, clk.
1695 ,, Benjamin, Dublin, gent.
1732 ,, Edmond, Ballymacarny, co. Meath, gent.
1807 ,, Edward, Athy, co. Kildare
1771 ,, Edwin, Dublin, esq.
1797 ,, Elizabeth, Donnybrook-road, Dublin, widow
1799 ,, Elizabeth, Kilkenny city, widow
1655 ,, Francis, soldier in col. Sadleir's regt. of foot
1806 ,, rev. Francis, clk.
1768 ,, George, Dublin, clk.
1804 ,, George, capt. in the 8th regt. of foot
1741 ,, Henry, Rathcormack, tanner
1629 ,, John, Islington, London, Middlesex, haberdasher (Copy)
1740 ,, John, Hammersmith, Middlesex, but in Carolina (Copy)
1749 ,, John, Waterford, saddler
1764 ,, John, quarter-master in gen. Douglas' dragoons

1771	**Thomas,** John, Castletown
1801	,,	John, Donnybrook, co. Dublin, gent.
1808	,,	Letitia, formerly of Waterford, late of St. Mary's par.
1802	,,	Lewis, Dublin, esq.
1796	,,	Luke, Galway, merchant
1772	,,	Mark, Queen-st., Dublin
1737	,,	Mary, widow of Edwin T., of Athlone, co. Roscommon
1762	,,	Mary, Donnybrook, co. Dublin, widow
1765	,,	Mary, *alias* **Knott**
1777	,,	Mary, Dublin, spinster
1786	,,	Mary, Dublin, spinster
1798	,,	Mary, widow
1724	,,	Richard, Dublin
1789	,,	Richard Baldwin, Dubl., gent.
1750	,,	Samuel, Donnybrook Lib., Dublin, gardener
1757	,,	Thomas, Kevin's Port, Dublin, gardener
1744	,,	Timothy, Dublin, esq.
1624	,,	Walter, Downpatrick, co. Down, gent.
1657	,,	Walter, gent., clk. of the Peace, Clogherbine, co. Kerry
1690	,,	Walter, late of Killeen, co. Kerry, gent., of Ordnance
1722	,,	William, Athlone, co. Westmeath, farmer
1749	,,	Wm. Penn, St. Paul's, Covent Garden, Westminster, gent. (Copy)
1783	,,	William, Cork, gent.
1799	,,	Wm., Barrowmount, co. Kilkenny
1763	**Thome,** Elizabeth, Dublin, widow
1760	,,	Francis, Dublin, merchant
1672	,,	Margaret, Belfast, widow
1671	,,	Wm., Belfast, merchant
1624	**Thomond,** Donatus, earl of
1693	,,	Henry, earl of (Copy)
1742	,,	Henry, earl of
1675	,,	Mary, dow. countess of (Copy)
1718	,,	Sarah, dow. countess of (Copy)
1797	**Thompson,** Agnes, Dublin, spinster
1759	,,	Andrew, Baltony, co. Donegal
1809	,,	Andrew, Clones, co. Monaghan
1806	,,	Anthony, Stephen-st., Dublin city, esq.
1787	,,	Archibald, Douglas, Cork city, sailcloth weaver
1784	,,	Arthur, College-green, Dublin, saddler
1699	,,	Charles, Dublin, alderman
1772	,,	Chas., Middle Temple, London, student (Copy)
1795	,,	David, Banagher, King's co., esq.

1796	**Thompson,** David, Passage, co. Cork
1718	,,	Dudley, Dublin, gent.
1661	,,	Edward, Dublin, gent. (Will delivered out; Copy)
1734	,,	Edward, capt. in col. Hargrove's regt.
1734	,,	Elizab., widow of Richard T., Dublin, esq. (unproved)
1780	,,	rev. Francis, vicar of Drumcree, co. Westmeath
1790	,,	Garrett, Glasmanoge, co. Dub., dealer
1770	,,	George, Coleraine, co. Derry, M.D.
1797	,,	George, Trelick, co. Tyrone, esq.
1804	,,	George, Galway town
1800	,,	Henry, Dublin, merchant
1801	,,	Henry, Ardkill, co. Londonderry
1686	,,	James, Dublin, tailor
1793	,,	James, Dublin, gent.
1804	,,	Jas., Mortimer-st., Middlesex
1723	,,	Jane, widow of Charles T., Dublin, alderman
1750	,,	Jane, William-street, Dublin, widow
1660	,,	John, Dublin, gent.
1666	,,	John, Christchurch-yard, victualler
1675	,,	John, Dublin, gent.
1731	,,	John, Killebandrick, co. Cavan, gent.
1733	,,	John, Ringsend, near Dublin
1737	,,	John, Dublin, whipmaker
1764	,,	John
1775	,,	rev. John, vicar of Kilcock
1781	,,	John, Coleraine, co. Londonderry, esq., and alderman
1798	,,	John, Muckamore, co. Antrim, merchant
1809	,,	John, Carrick-on-Suir, co. Tipperary
1762	,,	Joshua, Rawliss, Queen's co.
1802	,,	Margaret, Rathdowney
1788	,,	Mary, Monasterevan, co. Kildare, spinster
1787	,,	Mathew, Thurles, co. Tipperary, gent.
1768	,,	Norris, Legakelly, co. Cavan
1745	,,	Parr, Cork, merchant
1803	,,	Patrick, Constitution-hill, Dub.
1719	,,	Richard, Dublin, esq.
1765	,,	Richard, the elder, Cuddah, Queen's co.
1788	,,	Richard, Ralish, Queen's co.
1801	,,	Richd., Killynader, co. Antrim
1730	,,	Robert, Coleraine, merchant
1772	,,	Robt., Mitchelstown, co. Westmeath, esq. (Large will)

1778 **Thompson**, Robert, Tomacork, co. Wicklow, gent.
1795 ,, Samuel, Island of St. Croix, planter (Copy)
1791 ,, Theophilus, Dublin, esq.
1721 ,, Thos., Rich Hill, co. Armagh, merchant
1802 ,, Thomas, Greenmount, co. Antrim
1803 ,, Thos., Dungarvan, co. Waterford, merchant
1807 ,, Thos., Milltown, co. Donegal
1795 ,, Walter, Dungannon
1737 ,, William, Newry, co. Down, merchant
1745 ,, William, Cork, merchant
1751 ,, William, Dublin, surgeon
1773 ,, William, Moneydaraghmore in Mourne, co. Down
1808 ,, William
1809 ,, William, Lurgan, co. Armagh, gent.
  [See TOMSONE.]
1673 **Thomson**, Anne, Chichester, Sussex, widow (Copy)
1674 ,, Anne, Chichester, Sussex, widow
1805 ,, Anne, Mountmellick, Queen's co.
1789 ,, Benjamin, Ravensdale, co. Louth, linendraper
1806 ,, Elleanor K., Crommore, co. Londonderry
1704 ,, Henry, ensign in col. Hamilton's regt.
1735 ,, Hugh, Dublin, merchant
1744 ,, Humphrey, Moninteen, co. Monaghan
1784 ,, Jas, Creevelough, co. Tyrone
1700 ,, John, Belfast, merchant
1779 ,, John, Cootehill, co. Cavan
1741 ,, Josias, Newtown Corry, co. Monaghan, merchant
1676 ,, Maurice, Haversham, Bucks, esq. (Copy)
1779 ,, Robert, Newry, co. Down, apothecary
1650 ,, Thomas, St. Michan's par.
1681 ,, William, St. Bride's par., Dublin, merchant
  [See THOMPSON.]
1699 **Thomsone**, John, Seven Acres, Scotland, gent. (Copy)
1636 ,, Robert, Carnemoohen, co. Antrim (N. P.)
1769 **Thorn**, James, Ormond Market, Dublin, victualler
1803 ,, Richard, Rush, co. Dublin, gent.
  [See THORNTON.]

1731 **Thornbery**, Hester, par. Chessen, Herts, spinster
1786 **Thornburgh**, Joseph, Tullamore, King's co., merchant
1737 **Thorne**, Nathaniel, Tiverton, Devon, merchant (Copy)
1749 **Thornell**, Henry, Mountrath, Queen's co.
1792 **Thornhill**, Anne, spinster
1811 ,, Charlotte, Dublin city, spinster
1800 ,, Edward, Bedham, Dublin, esq.
1800 ,, Edward, Boughlone, Queen's co.
1807 ,, Elizabeth, Boughlone, Queen's co., widow
1808 ,, Mary Bm., Dublin city, widow
1766 ,, Richard, esq.
1801 ,, Richard, lieut. in the Royal Irish Artillery
1695 ,, Robert, Dublin, esq.
1764 **Thornill**, Anne, Moystown, King's co. (Not proved)
1725 **Thornton**, Ambrose, Dublin
1717 ,, Francis, Aughevanagh, mariner
1716 ,, George, Finglas, co. Dublin
1790 ,, George, Dublin, merchant
1750 ,, Henry, Dublin, gent.
1784 ,, Henry, Sligo, esq.
1707 ,, Isaac, Aughevanagh, co. Cavan
1701 ,, Jas., Aughevanagh, co. Cavan, gent.
1777 ,, James, Grange, co. Kildare, esq.
1777 ,, James, Grenvill, co. Cavan
1767 ,, John, late of St. Giles, London, now of Drogheda
1752 ,, Leonard, Wexford, gent.
1765 ,, Patrick, Dublin, dealer
1769 ,, Richard, Drogheda, tailor
1647 ,, Robert, esq., mayor of Londonderry
1717 ,, Thomas, Ballinageery, co. Dublin, gent.
1741 ,, rev. Thomas, Kildare, clk.
1777 ,, Thomas, Copper-alley, Dublin, grocer
1733 ,, William, Finglas, co. Dublin, esq.
1760 ,, William, Coolafin, co. Derry, esq.
1792 ,, William, Armagh, esq.
  [See THORN.]
1808 **Thorp**, Mathew, co. Dublin, gent.
1792 **Thorpe**, Robert, Dublin, barrister-at-law
1744 **Thresher**, Mary, widow of Daniel T., Cork, merchant
1627 **Thring**, Tremer, Drogheda, ald.

1776 **Throckmorton**, Charles, Smarmore, co. Louth, esq.
1727 ,, Theobold, Cullyhanna, co. Armagh, esq.
1754 ,, Theobold
1768 **Throp**, Philip, Dublin, clk.
1734 ,, Sarah, Dublin, widow
1741 **Thropp**, Anne, par. St. Paul's, Dublin, spinster
1734 ,, Richard, Dublin, smith
1745 **Thurgood**, Hartup, Dub., upholder
1748 **Thurkeld**, Francis, Dublin, mercht.
1660 **Thurrold**, Wm., Kilk., gunsmith
1639 **Thursby**, Francis, Dublin, clk.
1783 **Thwaites**, Elizabeth, Dublin, wid.
1726 ,, Ephraim, Dublin, maltster
1782 ,, George, Dublin, brewer
1801 ,, Henry, Dublin, grocer
1799 ,, James, Dublin city
1715 ,, Mary
1810 ,, Richard, Dublin city, esq.
1729 ,, Sarah, Dublin, widow
1677 ,, Thomas, Dougher, co. Armagh, fuller and dyer
1704 ,, William, Oxmantown, Dublin, gent.
1729 ,, William, Dublin, gent.
1748 ,, William, Dublin, esq.
1711 **Thyrry**, David, Ardnageehy, co. Cork, gent. (Ex.)
1759 **Tibboe**, Hester, wife to Thomas T., surgeon
1675 **Tibbs**, Henry, Dub., tallow chandler
1668 **Tichborne**, Henry, Dublin, esq., ensign
1705 ,, Rysse, Dublin, gent. (Copy)
1694 ,, sir William, Bowley, co. Louth, knt.
1667 **Tichburne**, sir Henry, Dublin, knt.
1792 **Tickell**, Clotilda, widow
1740 ,, Thomas, Dublin, esq.
1808 **Tiernan**, John, Naul, co. Dublin
1773 **Tierney**, Peter, Galway, gent.
[See TERNAN.]
1629 **Tiffin**, William, Dublin, gent.
1702 ,, Zacharia, Dublin, esq.
1737 **Tige**, Duke, Dublin, upholder
1773 **Tighe**, Arabella, Brompton-road, Middlesex, widow
1791 ,, Daniel, Carrick, co. Westmeath
1801 ,, Edward
1717 ,, Mabel, widow of Richard T., Dublin, merchant
1801 ,, Margaret, Blue Bell, co. Dublin
1804 ,, Margaret, Dublin city
1681 ,, Mary, widow of alderman Richard Tighe, Dublin (1677)
1673 ,, Richard, Dublin, alderman (Long will; Ex.)

1699 **Tighe**, Richard, Dublin, gent.
1736 ,, Richard, Dublin, esq.
1753 ,, Richard, Dublin, esq.
1790 ,, Richard, Laragh, co. Roscommon
1802 ,, Robert, South Hill, co. Westmeath
1763 ,, Sterne, Dublin, esq.
1767 ,, Sterne, Summerhill, co. Dublin, esq.
1790 ,, Sterne, Rathbeggan, co. Meath, esq.
1801 ,, Thomas, Lucan
1679 ,, William, Dublin, esq.
1766 ,, Wm., Rossana, co. Wicklow
1782 ,, William, Rossana, co. Wicklow, esq.
1784 ,, William, Ballyshannon, co. Donegal
1801 ,, William, Gartlandstown, co. Westmeath
1695 **Tilbury**, Tristram, Dublin, gent.
1763 **Tilly**, John, Cabra-lane, Dublin, coachmaker
1811 ,, Susanna, wife of Ben Tilly, esq.
1762 **Tilson**, Elizabeth, Dublin, widow
1783 ,, Elizabeth Ann, Dublin, spinster
1800 ,, lady Frances, Hill-st., Berkeley-square, widow (Copy)
1785 ,, rev. George, Richmond, Surrey, clk. (Copy)
1791 ,, rev. Henry, Dublin, clk.
1764 ,, James, Bolesworth Castle, Cheshire, esq. (Copy)
1785 ,, John
1722 ,, Thomas, the elder, Dublin, esq.
1744 ,, Thomas, Dublin, gent.
1779 ,, Thomas, the elder, Dublin, esq.
1771 **Timmons**, Elizabeth, Dublin, widow
1765 ,, Wm., Monkstown, co. Dublin, gent.
1791 **Timpson**, Ralph, Gurteen, co. Kilkenny
1793 ,, Robert, Waterford, esq.
1645 **Tims**, Wm., Cullinaghomath, Queen's co., gent.
[See TYMS.]
1651 **Tindall**, Francis, Dublin
1762 ,, Hannah, Magherbeg, co. Wicklow, widow
1771 ,, James, Cork, joiner
1789 ,, Jane, Dublin, widow
1751 ,, Peter, Ardoyne, co. Wicklow, gent.
[See TYNDALL.]
1716 **Tinison**, Wm., Clonmel, co. Tipp., gent.
1737 **Tipper**, Anthony, Cloghinstown, co. Westmeath, farmer

1796 **Toler**, Daniel, Beechwood, co. Tipperary, esq.
1732 ,, Dorothea, widow
1776 ,, Eleanor, Limerick, spinster
1686 ,, Elizabeth, Clara, co. Kilkenny, spinster
1794 ,, Lettice, widow
1808 ,, Otway, Modereny, co. Tipperary, esq.
1800 ,, Rebecca, Beechwood, co. Sligo
1758 ,, Richard, Ballytore, co. Kildare, esq.
1722 **Tollet**, George, Tower of London (Copy)
1809 **Tolmie**, Kenneth, capt. in the Royal Hospital, Kilmainham
1673 **Tolpet**, John, Chichester, Sussex, gent. (Copy)
1789 **Tolsom**, Thomas, Hennington-row, Surrey (Copy)
1777 **Tom**, Henry, Queen Ann-st., Middlesex, esq. (Copy)
1773 **Tomb**, David, Magherafelt, co. Londonderry
1716 ,, James, par. and co. Antrim
1762 **Tomes**, Henry, Dublin, esq.
1740 **Tomkins**, Elizabeth, Derry
1780 ,, Elizabeth, Dublin, widow
1678 ,, John, Killean, co. Clare, esq.
1802 ,, John Alex., formerly of Limerick, but late of Dubl., esq.
1717 **Tomlinson**, Alice, wife to John T., Dublin, gent.
1705 ,, rev. Daniel, Philipstown, King's co., clk. (1706)
1708 ,, Joan, widow of Wm. Tomlinson
1750 ,, John, George's-lane, Dublin, coachmaker
1668 ,, Richard, Dublin, innkeeper
1784 ,, Robert, Dublin, carpenter
1761 ,, Susanna, Dublin, widow
1789 **Tommins**, John, Arran-quay, Dubl., shoemaker
1772 ,, Patk., Dublin, heraldic painter
1770 **Toms**, Mary, St. Margaret's, Westminster, wid. of lieut. Miles Toms (Copy)
1664 **Tomsone**, Wm., The Cavane, Donachmore par., merchant [See THOMPSON.]
1793 **Tone**, Jonathan, Cassumsize, co. Kildare, esq.
1801 **Tonge**, Dorothea, Dublin, widow
1784 ,, Edward, Summerhill, co. Dub., gent.
1766 ,, John
1787 ,, Mary, Drogheda, widow
1765 ,, Philip, Shallon, co. Meath, gt.
1781 ,, Robert, Dublin, merchant
1683 ,, Thomas, New Ross, D.D.

1780 **Tonge**, Thos., Grafton-st., Dublin
1699 ,, Wm., Wexford, gent.
1754 **Tonnard**, Mary, spinster
1737 **Tonnery**, Edward, Waterf., apothecary
1776 ,, John
1773 **Tonson**, Richard, Dunkettle, co. Cork, esq.
1669 **Tooke**, Edwd., Inner Temple, Lond., esq.
1755 **Tooker**, Barry Jas., Dubl., mercer
1631 ,, Thomas, St. Thomas parish, London, gent.
1811 **Tookey**, Catherine, Montpellier-hill, Dublin, widow
1806 ,, John, Montpellier-hill, co. Dublin
1803 **Toole**, lady Catherine, Gt. George's-street, Dublin
1768 ,, Daniel, Dublin, timber mercht.
1778 ,, Darby, Dublin, gent.
1787 ,, Denis, co. Wicklow, spinster
1762 ,, Dennis, Dublin, merchant
1789 ,, Elizabeth, spinster
1800 ,, Farrell, Dublin, yeoman
1711 ,, Francis, Colehornagh, co. Wexford, esq.
1725 ,, Garrett, Monatuber, co. Kildare, farmer (Not proved)
1781 ,, John, Church-st., Dubl., gent.
1795 ,, John, Dublin, dealer
1797 ,, John, Galway town, shoemaker
1799 ,, John, Dublin, grocer
1807 ,, John, Murragh, co. Clare
1744 ,, Laurence, Ballycullen, co. Wicklow, esq.
1761 ,, Lawrence, Wicklow, esq.
1775 ,, Patk., Trim, co. Meath, esq.
1799 ,, Patrick, Dublin, skinner
1802 ,, Patk., Clontarf Sheds, co Dublin, gent.
1806 ,, Stephen
1791 **Toone**, William, Finglas, co. Dubl., gent.
1648 **Topcliffe**, Charles, Dublin, gent.
1724 **Topham**, James, Dublin, knt.
1760 ,, sir John, Dublin, gent.
1742 **Toplady**, Elizab., Enniscorthy, co. Wexford, widow
1806 ,, Elizab., Enniscorthy, co. Wexford, widow
1732 ,, Francis, Enniscorthy, co. Wexford, esq.
1709 **Toplis**, Joseph, Dublin, cutler
1765 ,, Samuel, Clounce, co. Cork
1660 **Toppin**, Thos., Waterford, butcher
1759 ,, Thomas, Crevatt, co. Armagh
1786 ,, Thos., Crewcatt, co. Armagh
1737 **Torbett**, John, Carrickfergus, apothecary

1804 **Torkinton**, John, Cork-st., co. Dub.
1806 **Torrens**, Anne, Londonderry city, widow
1804 ,, Geo., Aughamore, co. Sligo
1810 ,, Thomas, Bristol city, gent.
1685 **Torriano**, Geo., Lond., esq., merchant tailor (Copy)
1768 **Torry**, Richard, Dublin, gent.
1767 ,, Sarah, Cork, widow
1762 **Torton**, Edward, Dublin, gent.
1769 ,, Peter, Dublin, gent.
1653 **Tothill**, Robert, Dublin
1632 **Tottenham**, Barnabas, *alias* **Hancocke**, Ballyduff, co. Waterford
1758 ,, Chas., Tottenham-green, co. Wexford, esq.
1795 ,, Chas., New Ross, co. Wexford, esq.
1773 ,, Cliffe, Cork, esq.
1712 ,, Edward, Tottenham-green, co. Wexford, esq.
1793 ,, rev. Edward, Ballinahoun, co. Wexford, clk.
1798 ,, Jane, New Ross, co. Wexford, widow
1787 ,, John, Drinagh, co. Wexford, esq.
1793 ,, Synge, Fethard, co. Wexford
1761 **Tough**, Prudence, Dublin
1656 **Tourney**, Richard, capt. Sandford's troop
1792 **Tourtellot**, Louis
1795 **Tourtellott**, Peter Joseph, Dublin
1723 **Toussaint**, Peter, surgeon in col. Geo. Groves' regt. of foot
1690 **Tovey**, James, Kilkenny, gent.
1756 **Towell**, Anne, Youghal, co. Cork
1791 ,, James, Tallow, co. Waterford, esq.
1781 **Towernor**, Catherine, Castlemarket, Dublin, widow
1794 **Towers**, Albertina, Portarlington, Queen's co., spinster
1698 ,, Anthony, Dublin, esq. (Ex.)
1739 ,, Anthony, Middle Temple, esq.
1802 ,, James, Dundrum, co. Dublin, gent.
1745 ,, John, Dolphin's Barn-lane, farmer
1752 ,, John, D.D., Preb. St. Patrick's, Dublin
1759 ,, John, Dublin, hosier
1794 ,, Richard, Tillmalogue, King's co., esq.
1727 ,, Robert, Dublin, brazier
1693 ,, Simon, Geraldstown, co.Meath, esq.
1680 ,, Thomas, Kentstown, co.Meath, esq.

1770 **Towers**, Thomas, Dublin, esq.
1800 ,, Timothy, Dublin, merchant
1717 **Towgood**, Audrian, Ballincally, co. Cork, widow
1720 ,, George, Cork, esq.
1760 ,, Sampson, Cork, esq.
1707 **Towills**, Bernard, Dublin, clothier
1709 ,, Hannah, Coventry, Warwickshire, widow
1745 **Towle**, John, Hillsborough, co. Down, gent.
1663 **Towneley**, Faithfull, Drumgool, co. Louth, esq.
1764 **Townesend**, Horatio, Bridgemount, co. Cork, esq.
[See TOWNSEND.]
1723 **Townley**, Blaney, Piedmont, co. Louth, esq.
1749 ,, Blaney, Piedmont, co. Louth, esq.
1737 ,, Fras., London, mercht. (Copy)
1691 ,, Henry, Aclare, co. Louth, esq.
1699 ,, Samuel, Drumrusk, co. Cavan, esq.
1789 ,, Samuel, the elder, Newry, co. Down
1697 ,, Sarah, St. Kevin's-street, co. Dublin, widow
1722 **Townly**, Thos., Thomas Court, co. Cavan
1741 **Townsend**, Benjamin, Powerscourt, co. Wicklow
1762 ,, Cornelius, Clougheen, co.Cork, esq.
1808 ,, Edwd. Henry, Castletownsend, co. Cork
1745 ,, Elizabeth, Castle T., co. Cork, widow (Not proved)
1745 ,, Horatio, commissioner of the "Lynor" man-of-war (Copy)
1773 ,, rev. Horatio, Knockane, Finadore, co. Cork, clk. (Large will)
1736 ,, John, Clogheen, co. Cork, esq.
1810 ,, John, Shepperton, co. Cork, merchant
1742 ,, Richard, Castletown, co. Cork, esq.
1805 ,, Richard, Pallacetown, co.Cork, esq.
1725 ,, Robt., Pill-lane,Dub., innholder
1766 ,, Samuel, Ferrybank, co. Wicklow, gent.
1786 ,, Samuel, Blackrock, co. Dublin, pastry cook
[See TOWNESEND.]
1786 **Townshend**, Bridget, Blackrock, co. Dublin, widow
1697 **Towson**, William, Dublin, mariner (Copy)

1686 **Toxteth**, Jane, St. Martin-in-the-fields, Midsex., wid. (Copy)
1737 **Toy**, Daniel, Derry Hall, co. Westmeath
1789 **Tracey**, Abigail, widow
1761 ,, Daniel, Dublin, healer
1745 ,, Edwd., Birr, King's co., merct.
1782 ,, Edward, Exchequer-st., Dublin, carpenter
1771 ,, George
1751 ,, John, Porter's-row, Dublin
1747 ,, Patrick, Dublin, baker
1758 ,, Thomas, Parsonstown, King's county, merchant
1782 **Tracton**, Jas., lord baron, Tracton Abbey
1807 **Tracy**, Catherine, Dubl. city, widow
1783 ,, Darby, Angel-alley, Dublin, aleseller
1811 ,, Francis, Frederick-st., Dublin, esq.
1738 ,, Humphrey, Ballyneil, co. Londonderry, gent.
1779 ,, James, Dublin, tailor
1765 ,, John, Cork-st., Dublin, tapeweaver
1770 ,, John, Dublin, gent.
1779 ,, John, barrister-at-law
1802 ,, John, Naas, co. Kildare, gent.
1807 ,, Pearson P., Dorset-st., Dublin, gent.
1778 ,, Richard, Prince's-street,Dubl., slater
1783 ,, Thomas, Earl-street, Dublin
1783 ,, Wm., Naas, co. Kildare, slater [See TREACY.]
1808 **Trail**, Elizabeth, Dub. city, widow
1794 ,, Hamilton, Killinchy, co. Down, clerk
1783 ,, James, bishop of **Down**, q. v.
1808 ,, James, Hadleigh, Suffolk
1805 ,, Margaret, widow (Copy)
1801 **Traile**, sir John, Island-bridge, co. Dublin, knt.
1724 ,, Patk., Elsueys in the Orkneys, North Britain, now of Ballymaghon, co. Down, mariner
1743 **Tralford**, John, Dublin, gent.
1790 **Trant**, Clare, Listowel, co. Kerry, widow
1759 ,, Dominick, Dingle, co. Kerry, gent.
1790 ,, Dominick, Dublin, esq.
1798 ,, Garrett, Gransha, co. Kerry, gent.
1729 ,, dame Hellen, widow of sir Pat. T., bart.
1775 ,, James, Dublin, esq.
1755 ,, Philip
1750 ,, Richard, Dingle, co. Kerry

1796 **Trant**, Susanna, Trantstown, co. Cork, widow
1794 ,, Thos.,Aghamurto,co.Cork,esq.
1725 ,, William, Cork, merchant
1733 **Trapaud**, John, Dublin, clerk
1744 **Trapnell**, John, Thomastown, co. Kilkenny
1759 **Travers**, rev. Boyle, Dublin, D.D.
1745 ,, Casandra, Dublin, widow
1795 ,, Cassandra, Dublin, spinster
1726 ,, Daniel, Dublin, merchant
1712 ,, John, Cork, esq.
1727 ,, rev. John, vicar of St. And., Dublin
1727 ,, John, Bandon, co. Cork, esq.
1774 ,, rev. John, Mount Temple, co. Westmeath, clerk
1787 ,, Jonas, Butlerstown, co. Cork, esq.
1664 ,, Joseph, archdeacon of Kildare
1748 ,, Michael, Dublin, esq.
1676 ,, Peter, Dublin, merchant
1798 ,, Peter, Dublin, distiller
1781 ,, Robert, Ballycurreen, South Lib., Cork, gent.
1704 ,, Samuel, Dublin, merchant
1710 **Traverse**, Thomas, Bolany, co. Wexford, gent.
1710 ,, Thos., Burgess, co. Tip., gent.
1626 **Travis**, James, Dublin, gent. (Copy)
1695 **Trayer**, Gilbert, Clonmel, merchant
1727 **Treacy**, George, Tullamore, King's county, merchant
1806 ,, George, Kilcourcy
1777 ,, Martin, timber merchant
1796 ,, Martin, Boulebane, co. Tipperary, farmer [See TRACY.]
1757 **Tredenick**, William, Kenahan, co. Fermanagh, gent.
1750 **Trehee**, Patrick, London, merchant (Copy)
1734 **Tremolet**, Susanna, Dublin, widow
1731 **Tremolett**, James, Dub., merchant
1743 **Trench**, Anne, widow of v. rev. John T., dean of Raphoe
1776 ,, Eyre, Ashford, co. Rosc., esq.
1808 ,, lieut.-general Eyre Power
1793 ,, Francis Power, Dublin, widow
1704 ,, Fredk., Garbally, co. Galway, esq.
1752 ,, Fredk., Garbally, co. Galway, esq. (Large will)
1758 ,, Frederick, Dublin, esq. (L.W.)
1798 ,, Frederick, Woodlawn, co. Galway, esq.
1731 ,, George, Dublin, gent.
1787 ,, Jane, Dublin, spinster
1720 ,, rev. John, Dublin, clk.
1726 ,, v. rev. John, dean of Raphoe

1758 **Trench**, Mary, *alias* **Geering**, wife of T. Trench, Dub., esq. (Large will)
1798 ,, Mary
1770 ,, Richard Power, Garbally, co. Galway, esq.
1799 ,, Rose, Dublin, spinster
1791 ,, William, minister of Tinough
1789 ,, Catherine, Ballycane, co. Wicklow, widow
1780 ,, Grace, wife to Patrick T., Dub., brewer
1774 ,, Jas., Keehan, co. Cavan, gent.
1787 ,, Jane, Ballycane, co. Wick, spr.
1781 ,, William, Dublin, gent.
1749 **Tresham**, Thomas, Cornmarket, Dublin, hosier
1779 ,, Thomas, Kilkenny
1810 ,, Edwd., Caroline-row,Dub., esq.
1738 **Tresher**, Daniel, Cork, merchant
1786 **Tresilian**, Mathew, Thurles, co. Tipperary, gent.
1671 **Treswell**, Catherine, lady, widow
1670 ,, sir Daniel, bart.
1672 ,, Richard Plowden, Dublin, esq.
1649 **Trevor**, sir Edward, Rosstrevor, co. Down, and now prisoner in Newry
1726 ,, Edward, Brynkinall, Denbighshire, esq. (Copy)
1789 ,, Edward, Loughbrickland, co. Down
1762 **Trewman**, John, Brackey, co. Armagh
1666 **Trewsdall**, Francis, Dublin, esq.
1748 **Trimble**, Alice, widow of John T., Ballinroddy, co. Longford, gent.
1811 ,, Elizabeth B., widow
1754 ,, Francis, clk.
1726 ,, Michael, Dublin, merchant
1809 ,, Montague, Dublin city, gent.
1763 ,, Thomas, late of Ballinroddy, now of Tinnemarch, co. Longford, gent.
1781 **Trimlestown**, Elizabeth, lady
1785 ,, Robert, lord baron
1600 **Trimlitstown**, dame Amy Tyan, dowager lady
1772 **Triquet**, John Peter, Dublin, silk dyer
1804 **Trocke**, Ann, Dublin city, spinster
1803 ,, Elizabeth, Montague-st., Dub.
1711 ,, John, Dublin, hosier
1714 ,, John, Dublin, hosier
1808 ,, Sarah, formerly of Dublin, late of the hot wells, Bristol
1799 ,, Thomas, Templeshambo, co. Wexford, clk.
1794 ,, William, Dublin, merchant

1806 **Trocke**, Wm., Abbey-street, Dubl., merchant
1668 **Trotman**, Nicholas, London, fishmonger (Copy)
1778 **Trotter**, rev. Edward, Downpatrick, D.D.
1723 ,, George, Dublin, gent.
1772 ,, John, Downpatrick, co. Down, esq.
1730 ,, Ringan, Dublin, merchant
1764 ,, Stephen, Duleek, co. Meath, esq.
1744 ,, Thomas, Magherafelt, co. Londonderry
1745 ,, Thomas, Dublin, esq., LL.D.
1802 ,, Thomas, Duleek House, co. Meath, esq.
1809 ,, Thomas, Youghal, co. Cork, merchant
1712 **Trouton**, Joseph, Dublin, tailor
1795 **Troy**, Catherine, Dublin, widow
1796 ,, Christiana, Limerick city, wid.
1785 ,, James, Porterstown, co. Dubl., gent.
1707 ,, Nathaniel, bp. of **Waterford**, q. v.
1748 ,, Thomas, Kilkenny, farmer
1699 **Trubshaw**, Thomas, Dublin, gent.
1707 **Truel**, John, carpenter belonging to the "Royal Oak" man-of-war
1802 **Trueman**, Thomas, junr., Dublin
1798 **Trulock**, Thomas, Dubl., alderman (Large will)
1673 **Truman**, John, Lorganveel, co. Down
1758 **Trumble**, Ann, Sligo, widow
1774 ,, Anne, Drogheda, widow
1774 ,, Henry, Mohill, co. Leitrim
1751 ,, Morgan, Roscribb, co. Sligo, gent.
1761 ,, rev. Roger
1753 **Trumbull**, Joseph, Dublin, woollen draper
1750 ,, Lidia, Dublin, widow
1768 **Trumperant**, John, Careen, co. Roscommon, gent.
1810 **Truston**, John, Lavallyroe, co. Mayo, farmer
1794 **Trydell**, Anne, Dublin, widow
1628 **Tuam**, William Daniel, lord abp. of
1667 ,, Samuel Pullein, abp. of
1716 ,, most rev. Dr. John **Vesey**, abp. of
1741 ,, most rev. Dr. Edward **Synge**, lord abp. of
1754 ,, most rev. Dr. Josiah **Hort**, abp., and bp. of Ardagh
1775 ,, most rev. Dr. John **Ryder**, abp. of

1782 **Tuam**, most rev.Dr. JemmettBrown, abp. (Large will)
1794 „ Joseph Deane Bourke, abp., and Earl of Mayo
1804 **Tubbs**, John, Dublin city, esq.
1757 „ Nicholas, Ballyboy, King's co., clk.
1688 **Tubman**, Mathew, Fahy, co. Galway, gent.
1781 **Tucker**, John, Dublin, alderman
1768 „ Margt., *alias* **Murphy**, Ballyamen, co. Wexford, widow
1719 „ Martin, Dublin, esq.
1795 „ Martin, Petersville, co. Meath, esq.
1742 „ rev. Thos., Monalty, co. Monaghan, clk.
1780 „ Thomas, Grafton-street, Dubl.
1755 „ Thomasin, relict of rev. Thos., T., rector of Monalty
1776 **Tuckey**, Anne, Cork, spinster
1789 „ Anne, Dublin, spinster
1792 „ Davis, Carrickduff, co. Cork, surgeon
1745 „ Francis, Cork, gent.
1767 „ Jane, Cork, spinster (Ex.)
1762 „ John, Dublin, surgeon
1735 „ Mary, Dublin, widow
1764 „ Penelope, Dublin, spinster
1767 „ Timothy, Cork, M.D. (Ex.)
1785 „ Sterne, Cork city, esq.
1737 „ Thomas, Cork, merchant (Ex.)
1766 **Tuckfield**, Anne, Dublin, widow
1782 „ Jonathan, mariner in the "Exeter" man-of-war
1598 **Tuder**, Henry, Dublin, gent.
1791 **Tudor**, Mary, Dublin
1802 „ Richard, North Frederick-st., Dublin, gent.
1601 **Tue**, Robert Fitz John, Kilkenny, (Copy)
1803 **Tufft**, Robert, Kilvergan, co. Armagh, linen draper
1800 **Tuinise**, Hans, Dublin, mariner
1592 **Tuit**, William, Tuitestown
1803 **Tuite**, Elizabeth, Dublin, widow
1715 „ Ellinor, Dublin, spinster
1765 „ sir Henry, Sonna, co. Westmeath, bart.
1805 „ sir Henry, Sonna, co. Westmeath, bart.
1666 „ James, Dublin, gent.
1734 „ James, junr., now in co. Meath, gent.
1741 „ James, Fennow, co. Meath
1766 „ James, Dublin, shoemaker
1805 „ James, North King-st., Dubl.
1810 „ James, Youghal, co. Cork, merchant
1780 „ Jasper, Drumcondra-lane, wid.

1760 **Tuite**, John, Dublin, vintner
1728 „ sir Joseph, Sonna, co. Westmeath, bart.
1749 „ dame Mary
1780 „ Mary, Dublin, shopkeeper
1782 „ Mary, Henry-street, Dublin, widow
1804 „ Patience, Dublin city, widow
1719 „ Patrick, Corvanstown, co. Kildare, gent.
1689 „ Philip, Newcastle, co. Westmeath, esq.
1778 „ Philip, Newcastle, co. Westmeath, esq.
1758 **Tuke**, Francis, Drakestown, co. Meath, gent.
1790 „ Francis, Causetown, co. Meath, esq.
1806 „ James, Dublin city
1803 „ Mary, Eccles-st., Dubl., wid.
1810 **Tullekin**, Rachel, Sundays Well, Cork, widow
1782 **Tully**, Anne, *alias* **Coffy**, Belin, co. Westmeath, gentlewoman
1740 „ Hillary, par. St. Martin, Middlesex, but in Carolina
1810 „ James, Dublin city
1757 „ John, Kilcock,co. Kildare, M.D.
1794 „ John, Loughrea, co. Galway, esq.
1706 „ Laghlen, Cormanagh, co.Westmeath, glazier
1760 „ Loughlin, Ballenamulle, co. Roscommon
1704 „ Marcus, Dublin, gent.
1742 „ Mathew, Limerick, gent.
1748 „ Mathew, Gortnagrange, co. Roscommon, glazier
1811 „ Ross, Athlone, co. Westmeath
1726 **Tumin**, John, Wespanstown, co. Dublin, surgeon
1768 **Tunnadine**, rev. John, Park, Lib. of Limerick, clk.
1766 **Tunney**, John, Goul, co. Leitrim, farmer
1785 **Tuohy**, Edward, Tralee, co. Kerry
1807 „ Peter, P.P., Islandedy, co.Mayo.
1811 **Tuomy**, Ellen, Tralee, co. Kerry, spinster
1710 **Turbridge**, Mary
1780 **Turbut**, Samuel,Belfast, co.Antrim, gent.
1803 **Turkington**, John, Dublin, apothecary
1755 **Turner**, Anne, Dublin, widow
1742 „ Deborah, Dublin, widow
1634 „ Edward, Naas, gent.
1672 „ Grace, Pimlico, Dublin, widow
1707 „ Henry, Dublin, esq.
1738 „ Jacob, Lurgan, co. Armagh

1804 **Turner**, Jacob, Turner Hill, co. Armagh, esq.
1773 ,, James, Newtown, co. Wexford, gent.
1776 ,, James, Sandymount, co. Down, gent.
1724 ,, John, Lurgan, co. Armagh, linendraper
1728 ,, John, Dublin, goldbeater
1797 ,, Jonathan, Dungannon, co. Tyrone
1747 ,, Ralph, Dublin, gent.
1808 ,, Richard, Creevagh, co. Tyrone, linendraper
1790 ,, Robert, Warrenpoint, co. Down, brewer
1769 ,, Samuel, Lurgan, co. Antrim
1785 ,, Thomas, Dublin, ale seller
1765 ,, Timothy, the elder, Dublin, ironmonger
1785 ,, Timothy, Dublin, merchant
1663 ,, William, Dublin, alderman
1741 ,, William, Limerick, burgess
1782 **Turney**, William, Dublin, painter
1801 **Turnley**, Francis, Belfast, co. Antrim
1598 **Turnor**, capt. Henry, Kells, co. Meath
1666 ,, Samuel, gent. (Copy)
1778 **Turpin**, Thomas, Dublin, china manufacturer
1739 ,, William, Dublin, hosier
1733 **Tursleton**, George, Leyar, Carnarvonshire, esq. (Copy)
1774 **Turvin**, James, Cork, gent.
1747 ,, William, Kilkenny, esq.
1808 **Tuthill**, Barbara, wife to Christopher Tuthill, Faha
1712 ,, Christopher, Kilmore, county Limerick, esq.
1745 ,, Hannah, *alias* **Lucas**, *alias* **Rule**, widow
1791 ,, rev. Hugh, rector of Fintona, dio. Clogher
[See TOTHILL.]
1697 **Twaddell**, John, Coleraine, merchant
1786 **Twamley**, James, Crownelea, co. Wicklow
1715 **Tweedy**, John, Little Hilltown, co. Meath, yeoman
1747 ,, Thomas, Dublin, printer
1684 **Twells**, Edward, Dublin, tailor
1733 ,, rev. John, Dublin, clk.
1787 **Twibill**, John, Jonesborough, co. Armagh, gent.
1784 **Twigg**, Barbara, Dublin, widow
1790 ,, Hugh, curate of par. of Drumcree
1741 ,, John, Dublin, alderman
1801 ,, Thomas, Dublin, esq.

1730 **Twigge**, Diana, Limerick, widow
1742 ,, James, Bettystown, co. Meath, esq.
1702 ,, Thomas, Dublin, esq.
1726 ,, ven. Wm., archdeacon of Limk.
1805 **Twiss**, George, Anna, co. Kerry, esq.
1800 **Twogood**, George, Cork city, tin-plate worker
1809 **Twomy**, Jeremiah, Galway, gent.
1806 **Twyford**, John, Clondalkin, co. Dublin
1653 ,, Ralph, Portlester, esq.
1799 **Tydd**, Benjamin, Tullamore, King's co.
1802 ,, Daniel, Clyduff or Anngrove, King's co., esq.
1708 ,, Elizabeth, Friarstown, co. Lmk., widow
1766 ,, Elizabeth, Barriskean
1808 ,, Ellinor, Dublin city
1702 ,, Francis, Friarstown, co. Limk.
1719 ,, Francis, Ballybritt, King's co., gent.
1741 ,, Francis, Dublin, gent.
1796 ,, Francis, Cork city, gent.
1798 ,, John, Tullamore, King's co.
1803 ,, sir John, Lamberton, Queen's co.
1743 ,, Mary, Knockearly, King's co., widow
1733 ,, Thomas, Knockearley, King's co., gent.
1775 ,, Thomas, Finglas, co. Dublin, gent.
1789 **Tyler**, Charles, Athlone, co. Westmeath, merchant
1758 ,, George, Ballybehy, co. Roscommon, gent.
1793 ,, George, Newtownlimavady, co. Derry, merchant
1740 ,, Richard, Court, co. Sligo
1728 ,, Thomas, Dublin, innholder
[See TAYLOR.]
1663 **Tyllyer**, Island of Antigua, esq. (Copy)
1670 **Tyman**, Andrew, Ballymote, co. Sligo, gent.
1803 **Tymens**, John, Riverston, co. Clare, esq.
1705 **Tyms**, John, Dublin, gent.
[See TIMS.]
1808 **Tynan**, John, Dublin city, gent.
1778 **Tyndall**, Samuel, Queen-st., Dubl., merchant
[See TINDALL.]
1761 **Tynte**, Elizabeth, *alias* **Kelly**, Dublin, widow
1661 ,, sir Henry, Ballycrenane, co. Cork, knt.

1692 **Tynte**, Henry, Ballycrenane, co. Cork, esq.
1697 ,, sir Hugh, par. of Pepperharrow, Surrey, knt.
1758 ,, James, Oldbawn, co. Dublin, esq.
1785 ,, sir James, Stratford, Tubber, co. Dublin, bart.
1680 ,, John, Chelvein, Somersetshire, esq.
1645 ,, Robert, son and heir of Robert T., Ballycrinnan, co. Cork, esq.
1661 ,, sir Robert, Ballycrinnan, co. Cork, knt.   [esq.
1761 ,, Robert, Oldbawn, co. Dublin,
1671 ,, William, Cahirmoney, co. Cork, esq.
1724 **Tyrawley**, Charles, lord baron
1733 ,, Frances, lady baroness
1809 ,, rt. hon. Mary, lady baroness
1710 **Tyrell**, Ursula, Drogheda, widow
1618 **Tyrer**, John, senr., Chester, brewer (Copy)
1730 **Tyrone**, Anne, dowager countess
1769 ,, Catherine, dowager countess
1704 ,, James, earl of
1763 ,, Marcus, earl of
1767 **Tyrrell**, Adam, Robinstown, co. Westmeath, esq.
1809 ,, Ann, Ballyonan, co. Kildare, spinster
1748 ,, Christopher, Dubl., callenderer
1731 ,, Edmond, Kildangan, co. Meath, gent.
1671 ,, Edward, priest, D.D. of the Faculty of Paris, and Chanvin of the Royal church of St. Quentin
1676 ,, Francis, Kilreany, co. Kildare, gent.
1805 ,, Garrett, Ballinderry, co. Kildare, esq.
1745 ,, George, Kilreany, co. Kildare
1776 ,, George, Carrick, King's co.
1794 ,, George, Dublin, esq.
1767 ,, James, Clonard, co. Kildare
1794 ,, Dr. James, P.P., Boyle, &c,
1795 ,, James, city of Florence, Italy, M.D. (Copy)
1809 ,, James, captain in the 15th regt. of foot
1750 ,, John, Dublin, callenderer
1756 ,, John, Dublin
1781 ,, John, Strabane, co. Tyrone, esq.
1811 ,, John, Dublin city, esq.
1783 ,, Margaret, Dublin, widow
1809 ,, Mary, Ballyonan, co. Kildare, spinster

1722 **Tyrrell**, Maurice, Kildangan, co. Meath, gent.
1755 ,, Maurice, esq.
1756 ,, Maurice, Tullamore, King's co., gent.
1808 ,, Nicholas, George's-quay, Dub.
1755 ,, Patrick, Dublin, merchant
1741 ,, Simon, Spittlefield, co. Westmeath, gent.
1777 ,, Thomas, Grange, co. Kildare, esq.
1745 ,, William, Dublin, gent.
1748 ,, Wm., Kilreany, co. Kildare, gent.
1631 **Tyrrie**, Dominick FitzJames, Cork, merchant (Copy)
1690 **Tyrry**, capt. Dominick, Cork, esq.
1629 **Tyrrye**, John FitzFrancis, Cork, merchant
1597 **Tywe**, John, Waterford, merchant

——U——

1790 **Ugon**, Geo., Arkikeagh, co. Wicklow, farmer
1692 **Umfrey**, Finch, Fawkeham, Kent, now of Mulhussey, co. Meath, esq.
1734 ,, James, Rathfarnham par., co. Dublin, gent.
[See HUMPHREY.]
1810 **Underwood**, Anne L.
1732 ,, James, Dublin, gent.
1660 ,, Richard, Naas, clk.   [**IX.** 148
1803 ,, Thos., Prussia-st., co. Dublin, esq.
1784 **Uniacke**, Anne, widow
1797 ,, Frances, Cottage
1682 ,, James, Dublin, gent.
1733 ,, Jas., Mount U., co. Cork, esq.
1730 ,, John, Curreheen, co. Cork, gt.
1794 ,, John, Cottage, co. Cork, esq.
1691 ,, Mary, Dublin, widow of James U., of do., gent.
1734 ,, Mary, Youghal, co. Cork, spr.
1727 ,, Norman, Curreheen, co. Cork, gent.
1777 ,, Norman, Castletown, co. Cork, gent.
1761 ,, Richd., formerly of Mount U., now of Youghal, co. Cork, esq.
1803 ,, Richard, Aghada, co. Cork, esq.
1802 ,, Robt., Woodhouse, co. Waterford, esq.
1734 ,, Thomas, Youghal, co. Cork, esq. (Large will; Ex.)

1676 **Unmussig**, John, Cork, M.D., native of Nassau Dillonburgh, in Germany
1808 **Unthank**, Elizabeth, Great Britainstreet, N. Lib. of Cork
1790 ,, Isaac, Limerick, M.D.
1748 ,, John, Limerick, dyer
1791 ,, Robert, Bormount, co. Wexford
1582 **Upper Ossory**, sir Barnaby Fitzpatrick, knt., baron of
1698 ,, Barnaby, baron of (Ex.)
1632 ,, dame Jane Butler, Ossory, dowager
1758 ,, John, earl of, formerly lord baron Gowran (Copy)
1794 **Uprichard**, Henry, Fairview, co. Armagh
1761 ,, John, the elder, Kilmore, co. Down, gent.
1803 **Upton**, Ambrose, Dublin, esq.
1792 ,, Anne, Cork, spinster
1706 ,, Arthur, Castle U., co. Antrim, esq.
1769 ,, Arthur, Castle U., co. Antrim, esq.
1786 ,, Francis, Limerick city
1740 ,, John, Castle U., co. Antrim, esq.
1776 ,, John, Ballynaberny, co. Limerick, gent.
1785 ,, John, Glanastare, co. Limerick, gent.
1803 ,, Margaret, widow
1749 ,, Samuel, Ballybrahir, co. Cork, gent.
1807 ,, rev. Shuckett W., co. Meath
1733 ,, Thomas, Dublin, esq.
1761 ,, Thomas, sheds of Clontarf, co. Dublin
1667 **Urian**, Edward, King's co.
1697 **Ursly**, Arthur, Corlehingh, King's co., glazier
1634 **Usher**, Amy, *alias* **Nolan**, Dublin, widow [**IV.** 52
1665 ,, Arland, Farfeaghan, co. Louth, clerk
1756 ,, Arth., Ballintaylor, co. Waterford, clk.
1768 ,, Arthur, Camphire, co. Waterford, esq.
1790 ,, Beverley, Canty, co. Waterford, esq.
1770 ,, Charles, Dublin, esq.
1706 ,, Christopher, Dublin, esq.
1764 ,, Chris., Mount U., co. Wicklow, esq.
1774 ,, Chris., Kilcarry, co. Carlow, esq.
1660 ,, Elizabeth, Sutton, co. Dublin, wife to capt. Hen. U.

1803 **Usher**, Frances, Dublin, widow
1766 ,, Fredk., rector of Clontarf, co. Dublin
1673 ,, George, Dublin, merchant
1613 ,, Henry, abp. of **Armagh**, q. v.
1760 ,, Jane, Dublin, widow
1742 ,, John, Carrick, co. Leitrim, esq.
1748 ,, John, Lismore, co. Waterford, esq.
1757 ,, John, Aghalee, co. Antrim, linendraper
1765 ,, John, Coagh, co. Tyrone, gent.
1789 ,, John, Waterford city
1796 ,, John, Eastvill, co. Galway, esq.
1732 ,, Lettice, Dublin, widow
1632 ,, Luke, archd. of Armagh [**II.** 304
1792 ,, Luke, Birr, King's co., surgeon
1698 ,, Marcus, Balsoon, co. Meath, clerk
1772 ,, Margaret, Castle Jordon
1778 ,, Martha, Clontarf, co. Dublin, widow
1662 ,, Mary, *alias* **Kennedy**, Dublin, widow
1768 ,, Montague, Phapper-lane, Dub.
1807 ,, Noble Luke, Gurteen, co. Tipperary, esq.
1790 ,, Rebecca, Dublin, widow
1800 ,, Richard, Dublin, apothecary
1704 ,, Robert, Birr, King's co., apothecary
1789 ,, Thomas, capt. in the 16th regt. of foot
1636 ,, Walter, Dublin, alderman [**IV.** 172
1639 ,, sir Wm., the elder, knt., Dubl. (Copy)
1744 ,, ven. Wm., archd. of Clonfert, and rector of Derrinoose, dio. Armagh
1774 ,, Wm., Athy, co. Kildare, M.D.
1774 ,, rev. Wm., preb. of St. Audoen's, Dublin
1794 ,, William, Creagh, King's co., gent.
1752 **Ussher**, Ann, or Jenney, wife to archd. Wm. Ussher
1757 ,, Beverley, Kilmeadon, co. Waterford, esq.
1761 ,, Henry, Dublin, esq.
1732 ,, John, Dublin, esq.
1744 ,, Mary, Clonmel, co. Tipp., wid.
1750 ,, Patrick, Dublin, butcher
1745 **Uvedale**, Edmond, lieut. of colonel Browne's regt. of horse
1790 ,, John, Cork city
1768 **Uzuld**, Edward, Limerick, gent.
1770 ,, Susanna, Limerick, widow

——V——

1715 **De Valada,** Joseph, Dublin, gent.
1609 **Vale,** Gerrott Fitz Edmond, Clonmel
1765 **Valentine,** Thomas, vicar of Frankfort, co. Sligo
1724 **Valie,** Michael
1808 **Vallance,** James, Dublin city, bookseller
1808　,,　James, Cappakeel, Queen's co.
1800　,,　William, Ballinderrin, Queen's co., wool comber
1671 **Van Bobart,** Elard Arnoldi, Dublin, esq.
1719 **Van Bobbart,** Margaret, widow of James Van B., Killeen, co. Meath, esq.
　　　[See VON BOBBART.]
1692 **Vanbrugh,** Giles, Chester, gent. (Copy)
1806 **Vance,** Charles, Harold's Cross, co. Dublin
1772　,,　James, the elder, Coagh, co. Tyrone
1808　,,　James, Dublin city, alderman
1789　,,　John, vicar of Killenway
1793　,,　William, Dublin, surgeon
1728 **Van Cruyskercken,** Henry, Limk., merchant
1713 **Vandelande,** Egbert, Dublin, tailor
1722 **Vandeleur,** Boyle, Rathlahine, co. Clare, esq.
1779　,,　Frances, Sackville-st., Dublin, widow
1701　,,　Giles, Rathlahine, co. Clare
1727　,,　rev. John, Kilrush, co. Clare, clk.
1754　,,　John, Dubl., esq. (Large will)
1777　,,　John Ormsby, Maddenstown, co. Kildare, esq.
1787　,,　Mary, Cork city, widow
1772　,,　Richard, Rutland, King's co., esq.
1775　,,　Thomas, Dublin, esq.
1768 **Vandelure,** Giles, Rathlahine, co. Clare, esq.
1757　,,　Thomas, Rathlahine, co. Clare, esq.
1753 **Vanderlure,** rev. James, Cragg, co. Clare, clk.
1735 **Vandermere,** John, Dublin, painter
1673 **Vanderpoest,** Adrian, *alias* **Poest,** London, merchant (Copy)
1665 **Vanhoegaerden,** Abraham, Limk., merchant
1703 **Van Homrigh,** Bartholomew, Dub., esq.

1715 **Van Homrigh,** Bartholomew, par. St. James, Westminster, Middlesex, gent. (Copy)
1809　,,　Bartholomew, Drogheda
1804　,,　Beaver, Drogheda, attorney-at-law
1723　,,　Esther, Dublin, spinster
1786　,,　John Partinton, Drogheda
1721　,,　Mary, Dublin, spinster
1753 **Vansevenhoven,** Theodore
1773 **Vanston,** Robert, Ballyduff, King's co., farmer
1748 **Van Wieringen,** William, Dublin, gent.
1674 **Vanwinghen,** Cornelius, Dublin, tailor
1639 **Vanwycke,** Allart Clasen, Dundalk
1728 **Varangle,** John, Dublin, gent.
1746 **Vareilles,** Anthony, Dublin, mercht.
1784　,,　James, Dublin, merchant
1709　,,　John James, London
1720 **Vatable,** Mary, Dublin, widow
1716 **Vaughan,** Anne, Dublin, widow
1694　,,　capt. Bethell, Shotton, Flintshire, gent. (Copy)
1654　,,　Edward Marshall, comp.-genl. Reynolds' regt.　**[V.** 56
1658　,,　Edward, Boncranagh, gent.
　　　　　　　　　　　　　　　　　　[VII. 38
1788　,,　Ellinor, Bath city
1799　,,　Frances, Dublin, spinster
1794　,,　George, Villa, co. Down
1795　,,　Godfrey Green, Dublin, mercht.
1710　,,　Hector, Knocknamease, Qu. co., esq.
1780　,,　Hector, Francraft, King's co.
1672　,,　Henry, Bancranagh, co. Don., esq.
1780　,,　Henry, Galway town, gent.
1764　,,　Honora, Dublin, spinster
1684　,,　James, warden of Galway
1757　,,　James, Youghal, co. Cork, burgess (Ex.)
1768　,,　James, Dublin, merchant
1683　,,　John, Youghal, merchant
1685　,,　John, par. Ottery St. Mary, Devonshire, esq.
1727　,,　John, Dublin, gent.　[clk.
1744　,,　rev. John, Dromore, co. Down,
1758　,,　John William, Dublin, mercht.
1764　,,　John, Portarlington, esq.
1770　,,　John, Tullamore, King's co., merchant
1769　,,　Martin, Dublin, tailor
1798　,,　Mary, Summerhill, co. Dublin, widow
1799　,,　Murtagh, Birchfield, co. Clare, smith
1657　,,　Nicholas, Newcastle-by-Lyons, husbandman　**[VI.** 211

1702 **Vaughan**, Perkins, Dublin
1712 ,, Richard, Dublin, plumber
1744 ,, rev. Richard, Stonybatter, co. Dublin, clk.
1664 ,, Thomas, Coed, Flintshire, esq.
1738 ,, Thomas, Youghal, co. Cork, merchant (Ex.)
1792 ,, Thomas, Summerhill, co. Dub., gent.
1796 ,, Thomas, Kanturk
1659 ,, William, Drogheda, merchant [**VIII.** 46
1699 ,, William, Clonmel, merchant
1747 ,, William Peisly, Golden Grove, King's co., esq.
1748 ,, William, Golden Grove, King's co., esq.
1719 **Vaury**, John, Waterford, esq.
1661 **Vauss**, John, Kilmacrenan, co. Donegal, clk.
1778 **Vauteau**, Peter, Fade-street, Dubl., tanner
1773 **Vavasor**, Anne, Dublin, widow
1762 ,, John, Dublin, merchant
1660 **Vawdry**, John, trooper [**VIII.** 72
1799 **Veaitch**, Edwd. Stanhope, Butler's-bridge, co. Cavan, esq.
1788 ,, Wm., Newtown Butler, co. Fermanagh, clk.
1730 **Vedel**, Anthony, Dublin, merchant
1662 **Veldon**, Gerald, Dublin, baker
1630 ,, John, Dublin, esq. [**II.** 199
1655 **Venables**, Henry, Colocke [**V.** 139
1657 ,, Thomas, Dublin, esq. [**VI.** 245
1736 **Venlewen**, John, Dublin, M.D.
1774 **Verdon**, Andrew, Dublin, gent.
1686 ,, Cath., Wexford, widow (Ex.)
1723 ,, Edward, Dublin, joiner
1781 ,, Eleonora, Dublin, widow
1736 ,, Nicholas, Kilpatrick, co.Louth, gent.
1749 ,, Wm., Dublin, merchant
1733 **Vereker**, Connell, Roxborough, co. of Limerick city (Ex.)
1692 ,, Henry, Cork, gent.
1720 **De Vergese**, James, lord Daubussargues, maj.-gen. of forces
1711 **Du Vergier**, Abraham, lord of Laroche de Monroy
1769 **Verling**, Elizabeth, Dublin, widow
1725 ,, Richard, Castletown Roche, co. Cork, clk.
1744 ,, Wm., Dublin, merchant
1720 **Vernall**, John, Cork, mariner
1683 **Verner**, Henry, Gilgavenagh, co. Antrim, gent.
1788 ,, Thos., Churchhill, co. Armagh, esq.
1757 **Verney**, Thomas, Dublin, watchmaker

1776 **Vernezobre**, Chas. Abraham, Waterford, merchant
1710 **Vernner**, William, Mulleyboy, co. Derry, tanner
1803 **Vernon**, Caroline Catherine
1773 ,, Dorothy, Clontarf, co. Dublin, widow
1796 ,, Francis Venables, Dublin, gt.
1787 ,, Geo., Clontarf, co. Dublin, esq.
1805 ,, Geo., Clontarf, co. Dublin, esq.
1730 ,, James, par. St. Anne, Westminster, esq. (Copy)
1742 ,, Jane, Twickenham Park, Middlesex, widow (Copy)
1808 ,, John, Clontarf, co. Dublin, esq. (Large)
1801 ,, Laurence, Sligo
1730 ,, Mary, par. St. Geo. the Martyr, Middlesex, spinster (Copy)
1734 ,, Thomas, Twickenham Park, Middlesex, esq. (Copy)
1798 **Vero**, Chas., Verona, co. Wexford, esq.
1808 ,, Mary, Stradbally, Queen's co., widow
1772 ,, Neptune, Dublin, surgeon
1767 ,, rev. Thos., Loughrea, co. Galway, clk.
1810 **Verpyle**, Simon, Bachelor's-walk, Dublin, gent.
1727 **Du Verrier**, Alex., Dublin, esq.
1801 **Verschoyle**, Dorothea, Marrowbone-lane, co. Dubl., widow
1734 **Vershoyle**, Henry, Cork-st., Dublin, skinner
1739 **Vesey**, Agmondisham, Lucan, co. Dublin, esq.
1746 ,, Agmondisham, Lucan, co. Dublin, esq.
1785 ,, rt. hon. Agomndisham, Lucan, co. Dublin (Large)
1789 ,, rev. Agmondisham, Newport Pratt
1811 ,, Anne, Stephen's-green, Dublin, spinster
1805 ,, Francis, Dublin city
1737 ,, rev. George, Hollymount, co. Mayo (Large will)
1774 ,, Henry, clk., warden of Galway
1745 ,, Jane, Dublin, spinster
1686 ,, John, Abbeyleix, Queen's co., clerk
1716 ,, John, abp. of **Tuam**, q. v.
1762 ,, John, Dublin, clk.
1780 ,, John, Lincolns Inn, Middlesex, esq.
1788 ,, John, Dublin, esq.
1766 ,, Mary, *alias* **Dixon**, *alias* **Ormsby**, Dublin, widow
1682 ,, Theodorus, Kinsale, clk.

1798 **Vesey**,rev. Thomas, rector of Drum-
         glass
1750   ,,   Wm., Dublin, LL.D.
1734 **Vestieu**, John, Cork, gent.
1660 **Veysey**, Wm., Dundalk, gent.
                                    [VIII. 86
1744 **Vezian**, James, lieut. in sir John
         Bruce's regt. of foot
1774 **Vicars**, Anne, Dublin, widow
1788   ,,   Daniel, Ballyedmond, Queen's
         co., gent.
1807   ,,   Laurence, Portarlington
1707   ,,   Richard, Garron M'Conly,
         Queen's co., esq.
1747   ,,   Richd., Levally, Queen's co.,
         gent.
1789   ,,   Richd., Levally, Queen's co.,
         gent.
1779   ,,   Robert, Dublin, esq.
1735   ,,   Wm., Grantstown, Queen's co.,
         esq
1785   ,,   Wm., Ballinakill, co. Carlow
1810   ,,   Wm. S., Grantstown, Queen's
         co.
         [See VICKERS, VIGORS.]
1798 **Viccars**, Elizab., Cloatany, King's
         co.
1755 **Vice**, Lettice, Dublin, spinster
1704   ,,   Wm., Dublin, merchant
1789 **Vickers**, Anne, Dublin, widow
1760   ,,   Jane
1759   ,,   Richd., Ballinakill, co. Carlow,
         esq.
1763 **Vidouse**, Peter, Dublin, merchant
1741 **Vigie**, James Robert, Galway,
         alderman
1800 **Vigne**, Jas., Dublin, jeweller
1727 **Vignoles**, Charles, Dublin, esq.
1758   ,,   Isab.,Dunshaughlin,co.Meath,
         widow
1779   ,,   James, Portarlington, Queen's
         co., esq.
1807 **Vigors**, Ann, Dublin city, widow
1721   ,,   Barthol., bp. of **Ferns**, q. v.
1797   ,,   Edward, Burgage, co. Carlow,
         clerk
1760   ,,   Elizab., *alias* **Roe**, *alias* **Har-
         vey**, Wexford, widow
1781   ,,   John, Dublin, esq.
1729   ,,   Martha, Dublin, widow
1764   ,,   Thomas, Old Leighlin, co. Car-
         low, esq.
1766   ,,   Urban, Ballyconnick, co. Wex-
         ford
         [See VICARS.]
1716 **Villeneufe**, John, Portarlington,
         Queen's co., gent.
1773 **Villeneufer**, Gabriel, Dublin, gent.
1737 **Villeneuve**, Josias, Dublin, esq
1693 **Villier**, Edward FitzGerald, esq.

1783 **Villiers**, Edward, Kilpeacon, co.
         Limerick, esq.
1745   ,,   Hannah, Waterford, widow
1716   ,,   John, Ballynaboly, co. Water-
         ford, gent.
1794   ,,   Joseph, Edmondstown, co.
         Limerick, esq.
1754   ,,   Mary, widow of John V., Bally-
         naboly, co. Kildare, esq.
1758   ,,   Richard, Kilpeacon, co. Lime-
         rick, esq.
1728 **De Villiers**, Samuel, quartermaster
         in Nevill's regiment of
         horse
1752 **Vilmot**, James, Dub., tobacconist
         [See WILMOT.]
1786 **Vincent**, Alice, *alias* **Widenham**
1761   ,,   Arthur, Limerick, alderman
1669   ,,   Elizabeth, Dublin, widow
1735   ,,   John, Limerick, alderman
1766   ,,   John, Limerick, burgess
1769   ,,   John, Portobello, Dublin, gent.
1780   ,,   John, Limerick city, esq.
1746   ,,   Magdalen, par. St. Ann, West-
         minster, Middlesex, spinster
         (Copy)
1762   ,,   Richd., Newabbey, co. Kildare,
         esq.
1764   ,,   Richard, rector of parish
         Monaghan, dio. Clogher
1788   ,,   Richard, Dublin, esq.
1750   ,,   Robert
1666   ,,   Thos., Irishtown, co. Dublin,
         esq.
1731   ,,   Thomas, Limerick, esq.
1744   ,,   Thomas, Limerick, alderman
1763   ,,   Thomas, Enniskillen
1768   ,,   Thos.,Newabbey,co.Kild., esq.
1778   ,,   Winifred, widow of Robert
         Vincent
1675 **Vinson**, John
1775 **Vipond**, Luke, Dublin, gent.
1761   ,,   Wm., Finglas, co. Dub., gent.
1811 **Vipont**, Anne, Kells, co. Meath,
         spinster
1778   ,,   Chas., Jamestown, co. Dub.,
         esq.
1811   ,,   John
1749 **De Virasel**, Daniel de Belrieu,
         baron, Dublin
1803 **Virasel**, Eliza, Portnahinch, Queen's
         county, spinster
1719   ,,   James de Belrieu, baron of
1751   ,,   Magdalen, Dublin, spinster
1757   ,,   Peter, par. St. Martin, Middle-
         sex, esq.
1751   ,,   Samuel
1768 **Virazel**, Catherine, Dublin, widow
1785   ,,   Isabella Maria, Dublin, spinster
1779   ,,   Marieanne, Sarah, Dubl., wid.

1766 **Virgin**, Arthur, Carrick-on-Suir, co. Tipperary, merchant
1809 **Viridet**, rev. Daniel, Murlogh, co. Longford, clk.
1688 ,, Moses, Dublin, clerk
1701 **Du Vivas**, Peter Archer, ensign in Lamelloniere's regiment
1707 **Vivers**, John, Dublin, whitesmith
1789 **Vize**, Joseph, Aglish, co. Cork
1783 **Vizer**, Thomas Powell, Dublin, upholder
1659 **Vnett**, Ethelbert, soldier [VII. 186
1661 **Vnyon**, Richard, ensign to captain Barrington's foot company
1771 **Vokes**, Geo., Cragbeg, co. Limerick
1743 ,, Simon, Limerick, esq.
1801 ,, Simon, Fermoy, co. Cork, gent.
1786 ,, Thomas, the elder, Limerick, merchant
1716 **Von Bobbart**, James, Killeen, co. Meath, gent.
[See VAN BOBBART.]
1766 **Voster**, Anne, Cork, widow
1761 ,, Daniel, Cork (Not proved)
1784 **Voto**, Esther Martha, Dublin, spr.
1709 **Vowell**, rev. Christopher, Garryne-granogue, co. Cork, clk.
1724 ,, Christopher, Ballyoran, co. Cork, gent.
1789 ,, rev. William, Curryglass, co. Cork, clk.
1691 **Vyner**, sir Robert, London, knt. and bart. (Copy)
1674 ,, Thomas, Hackney, Middlesex, esq. (Copy)
1718 ,, Thomas, Swakely, Middlesex, esq. (Copy)

——W——

1799 **Wachope**, Alexander, Cullenswood, co. Dublin
1742 **Waddell**, Alexander, Ballykeel, co. Down, gent.
1813 ,, Elizbth.A.,Curly, co.Down, spr.
1813 ,, Isabella, Springfield, co. Down, spinster
1798 ,, James, Springfield, co. Down, esq.
1812 ,, Jane, Springfield, co. Down
1813 ,, Margaret, Springfield co. Down, spinster
1813 ,, Mary, Newforge, co. Down, spr.
1809 ,, Richard, Newry, co. Down
1790 ,, Robert, Island Derry
1813 ,, Robert, Island Derry, co.Down, esq.
1811 ,, Wm., Lordship of Newry, co. Down

1628 **Wadding**, Richd., Waterford, gent.
1704 ,, Richd., Carrick, co. Tipperary, merchant
1638 **Waddinge**, Frances, widow of Richard W., Waterford, esq.
1632 ,, Jas., Ballyellin, co. Carlow, clk.
1675 **Waddington**, Ralph, Corbally, Queen's county, gent.
1787 **Waddy**,Elizbth.,Wexford town,wid.
1798 ,, Joseph, Dublin, gent.
1802 ,, Katherine, Parliament-street, Dublin, widow
1802 ,, Richard, Dub., attorney-at-law
1793 ,, Saml., Spa Wells, co.Wex, esq.
1786 **Wade**, Anne,Essex-quay, Dub.,wid.
1753 ,, Arabella, Dublin, spinster
1755 ,, Charles
1800 ,, Charles, New Haggard, co. Dublin, gent.
1795 ,, Chrisr.,Scanlanstown,co.Meath
1776 ,, Daniel, Dublin, innholder
1742 ,, Elizabeth, Dublin, widow
1805 ,, Ellinor,Scanlanstown,co.Meath
1741 ,, George, Dublin, cordwainer
1787 ,, George, Murns, co. Meath, esq.
1791 ,, Hamlet, Scanlanstown, co. Meath
1688 ,, Henry, Clonybreny, co. Meath, esq. (Ex.)
1805 ,, James, Harlextown, co. Meath
1745 ,, Jane, Dublin, widow
1704 ,, Joan, widow of Henry W., Clonybreny, co. Meath, esq.
1711 ,, John, Clonybreny, co. Meath, esq.
1735 ,, John, Clonybreny, co. Meath, esq. (Large will)
1735 ,, John, mariner on board the " Monmouth " m.-of-w.
1739 ,, John, Dublin, M.D.
1782 ,, John,Tamminstown, co.Dublin, farmer
1791 ,, John,Essex-quay,Dub.,jeweller
1799 ,, John, Dublin, chemist
1801 ,, John, Gardiner-st., Dubl., esq.
1808 ,, John, Constitution-hill, car-penter
1746 ,, Joseph, mariner (Not proved)
1788 ,, Judith, Dublin, widow
1807 ,, Lucretia, Cork city, spinster
1792 ,, Mary, New Haggard, co. Dublin, widow
1798 ,, Nicholas, Dublin, currier
1798 ,, Nicholas, Tomingtown, co.Dub.
1802 ,, Nicholas, Dublin city, priest;
1791 ,, Peter, Tommintown, co. Dub., farmer
1775 ,, Redmond, Dublin
1800 ,, Robert, Dublin, gent.
1799 ,, Sophia, Dublin, spinster

1746 **Wade**, Thomas, Cork, merchant
1757 ,, Wm., Kilvally, co. Westmeath
1710 **Wadeley**, Robert, Chapelizod, co. Dublin, gardener
1784 **Wadick**, James, Watling-st., Dub., skinner
1730 **Wadington**, Arthur, Kilmacthomas, co. Waterford, gent.
1692 ,, sir Hen., Clostollin, co. Galway, knt.
1673 **Wadman**, John, Carrickfergus, burgess
1628 **Wafer**, Elizabeth, *alias* **Plunkett**, Dublin, widow
1762 **Waff**, Elias, Tomduff, co. Wexford, mariner
1634 **Waffer**, Roger, Guyanstown, co. Meath, gent.
1673 **Waffre**, Francis, Ballinmoney, co. Wexford
1796 **Wagget**, Christopher, Cork city
1638 **Wagstaffe**, Edward, Dublin, gent. [**IV**. 339
1642 ,, Joan, Dublin, widow
1695 **Waight**, Bernard, Dublin, gent. [See WAITE.]
1626 **Wailshe**, Nicholas Fitz James, Waterford, merchant [See WALSH.]
1725 **Wainright**, Thos., Dub., pinmaker
1656 **Wainwright**, John, trooper [**VI**. 51
1741 ,, John, one of the Barons of the Exchequer
1813 ,, William, Malton, co. Wicklow
1802 **Waite**, Lucy, form. of Rutland-sq., Dublin, widow (Copy)
1780 ,, rt. hon. Thomas, Dublin Castle (Copy) [See WAIGHT.]
1657 **Waitman**, William [**VI**. 70
1766 **Wakefield**, Edward, Ladlane, London, mercer (Copy)
1660 ,, Thos., Dublin, aldn. [**VIII**.193
1710 **Wakeham**, Richard, Ballylegan, co. Cork
1718 ,, Wm., Little Island, co. Cork, esq.
1722 **Wakely**, Arabella, Dublin, spinster
1724 ,, Elizabeth, Dublin, widow
1713 ,, John, Ballycurly, King's co., gent.
1762 ,, Lydia, George's-hill, Dub., wid.
1751 ,, Thos., Ballyborley, King's co., esq.
1807 **Walbank**, Phœbe
1736 **Walcott**, John, Croagh, co. Limck., esq.
1753 ,, John Minchin, Croagh, co. Limerick, esq.
1797 ,, Letitia, Dublin, widow

1779 **Walcott**, Wm., lieutenant-colonel of 5th regiment of foot
1765 **Walden**, Francis, Dromlyon
1691 ,, John, Milk-st., London, fishmonger (Copy)
1597 **Walderton**, Nicholas, Colecurie, co. Westmeath, soldier under the leading of capt. Frans. Croft
1790 **Waldron**, Anne, Watersland, co. Dublin
1742 ,, Cathne.,Ballyshannon, co.Don.
1812 ,, Chas.,Drumsna,co.Leitrim,esq.
1800 ,, Francis, capt. in Roscommon militia
1781 ,, Lydia, Dublin, spinster
1795 ,, Lydia, Cork city, widow
1715 ,, Michl., Correll, co. Rosc., gent.
1737 ,, Michl., Correll, co. Rosc., gent.
1793 ,, Thos., Dominick-st., Dub., esq.
1675 ,, Wm.,Richmount, co.Arm., esq.
1750 **Wale**, Dorothy, Dublin, widow
1666 ,, Edward, Lower Butlerstown, co. Waterford, clerk [esq.
1776 ,, Edwd., Rathsilla, co. Kildare,
1671 ,, Elizabeth, Butlerstown, widow of Edward Wale of do.
1777 ,, Elizabeth, *alias* **Keating**, Waterford, widow
1613 ,, Gerat, Cowylnamuycky, (Coolnamuck ?) co. Waterford, gt.
1689 ,, Isabell, Dublin, widow
1670 ,, Jas., Kilmallock, co. Limerick, burgess
1680 ,, Jas., Woodstock, co. Kilk., esq.
1700 ,, John, Limerick, esq.
1688 ,, Luke, Kilkenny, merchant
1756 ,, Mary, Staplestown, co. Carlow, widow
1665 ,, Thomas, Dublin, gent.
1636 ,, Wm., Cuilnemocky, (Coolnamuck ?) co. Waterford, esq.
1687 ,, Wm., Derryleagh, co. Kerry
1805 **Walker**, Alexander, Virginia park
1810 ,, Alex., Tinea, co. W.meath, esq.
1702 ,, Anne, Dublin, widow
1765 ,, Anne, Dublin, widow
1789 ,, Anne, Cork, spinster
1811 ,, Balser, Shinrone, King's co., victualler
1731 ,, sir Chamberlain, Dublin, knt.
1773 ,, rev. Chamberlaine, Rosconnell, Queen's county, clerk
1788 ,, Chamberlaine, Glasnevin-road, co. Dublin, gent.
1812 ,, rev. Chamb.,Rosconnell, Qu.co.
1795 ,, Charles, Dublin city, esq.
1747 ,, Constance, widow of Hugh W., Ballywilliamreagh, King's county, farmer

1700	**Walker**, Daniel, Dublin, tailor	
1745	,,	Daniel, Dublin, esq.
1746	,,	David, Shantully, co. Arm., gent.
1738	,,	Elizabeth, Dublin, widow
1766	,,	Ellinor, *alias* **Classon**, wife to James W., Dublin, potter
1701	,,	Ellis, Drogheda, D.D.
1797	,,	Francis, Cork city, esq.
1706	,,	George, Dublin, gent.
1797	,,	George, Kells, co. Meath, surgeon and apothecary
1703	,,	Godfrey, Mullacarteen, co. Antrim, gent.
1757	,,	Henry, Dublin, merchant
1805	,,	Henry, Dublin, staymaker
1725	,,	sir Hovenden, Dublin, knt.
1736	,,	Hugh, Coolerivagh, King's co., farmer
1705	,,	Isabella, Donoughmore, co. Tyrone, widow
1800	,,	Jacob, Newry, co. Down, merct.
1705	,,	James, Dublin, gent.
1740	,,	Jas., High-st., Dub., shoemaker
1779	,,	James, Final, co. Westmeath
1784	,,	James, Camden-st., Dub., hosier
1767	,,	Jane, Dublin, widow
1795	,,	Jane, Carnarvon, Wales, spr.
1626	,,	John, Dublin, esq.
1660	,,	John, Wex., cooper [**VIII.** 111
1676	,,	John, Lillies-lane, Dub., clothier
1683	,,	John, Dublin, gent.
1700	,,	John, Dublin, clothier
1722	,,	John, Lurgan, co. Armagh, mt.
1726	,,	John, Dundalk, co. Louth, esq.
1735	,,	John, Dublin, surgeon
1739	,,	John
1739	,,	John, Smithstown, co. Meath, gent.
1748	,,	John, Dublin, silk weaver
1750	,,	John, Dublin, alderman
1752	,,	John, Gurteens, co. Kilk., esq.
1754	,,	John, Castle Lyons, co. Cork, clothier
1764	,,	John, Dublin, merchant
1795	,,	John, Newry, co. Down, merct.
1803	,,	John, Ballidirity, co. Antrim, gent.
1722	,,	Joseph, Dublin, goldsmith
1758	,,	Joseph, Dublin, upholder
1805	,,	Joseph, Mt. Pleasant, co. Dub.
1812	,,	Joseph, Argyle Buildings, Somersetshire (Copy)
1797	,,	Margaret, Donnybrook
1798	,,	Martha, Bristol city, spinster
1739	,,	Mary, Dublin, widow
1755	,,	Mary, Dublin, spinster
1771	,,	Mary, Athboy and Portlester, co. Meath, widow
1782	,,	Mary, Dublin, widow
1786	,,	Mary, Dublin, widow

1795	**Walker**, Mary, Bath city, widow (Copy)	
1778	,,	Michael, Sligo, merchant
1779	,,	Michl., Meath-st., Dub., merct.
1736	,,	Philip, Dublin, innkeeper
1737	,,	Richard, Liverpool, mariner
1760	,,	Richard, Dublin, merchant
1801	,,	Richard, Dublin, gent.
1700	,,	Robert, Dublin, brewer
1769	,,	Roger, Mooneystown, co. Meath, gent.
1773	,,	Samuel, Dublin, goldsmith
1768	,,	Sarah, Dublin, spinster
1804	,,	Solomon, Francis-st., Dublin, silk manufacturer
1700	,,	Thos., Lisledy, co. Rosc., gent.
1799	,,	Thos., Portlester, co. Meath, esq.
1813	,,	Thos., Rich Hill, co. Armagh
1678	,,	Ursula, widow of Henry Walker of Dublin
1677	,,	Wm., Tankardstown, Queen's county, esq.
1740	,,	William, Dublin, tanner
1750	,,	William, Dublin, alderman
1810	,,	William, Mountjoy-place, co. Dublin, gent.
1810	,,	William, Banagher
1698	**Walkington**, Edward, bp. of **Down**, q.v.	
1775	**Wall**, Ann, *alias* **Comyn**, Dublin, wife of Thomas W.	
1784	,,	Augus., Ballyroan, Queen's co.
1772	,,	Barnaby, Rathkeale, co. Limk.
1786	,,	Catherine, Cork city, widow
1794	,,	Catherine, Mullingar, widow
1756	,,	Edmond, Dublin, gent.
1728	,,	Francis, Dublin, merchant
1744	,,	Garrett, Wallsgrove, co. Kilkenny, esq.
1778	,,	Garrett, Derrykanan
1808	,,	Garrett, Coombe, co. Dublin, grocer
1551	,,	Gerrott, Dublin, brazier
1779	,,	Henry, Henry-st., Dublin
1745	,,	Jas., Naas, co. Kild., innkeeper
1768	,,	Jas., Knockrigg, co. Wick., esq.
1773	,,	Jas., Springfield, co. Kilk., esq.
1782	,,	James, Tipperary town, gent.
1786	,,	James, Dungarvan, co. Waterford, shopkeeper
1788	,,	John, Usher's-quay, Dublin
1811	,,	John W., Castle Inch, co. Kilk.
1792	,,	Letitia, Brook Lodge, co. Cork, widow
1792	,,	Luke, Ennis, co. Clare, esq.
1633	,,	Margaret, Lissinard, co. Galway, widow
1811	,,	Mathew, Kilkenny city, gent.
1641	,,	Patk. FitzPierce, Clonmel, tailor
1725	,,	Patrick, Dublin, gent.

1756 **Wall**, Patrick, Dublin, baker
1790 ,, Patk., Pill-lane, Dub., grocer
1803 ,, Paul,Watling-st.,Dub., skinner
1806 ,, Peter, Kilkenny city
1660 ,, Richard, Belfast, gent.
1788 ,, Richard, Drogheda, peruke maker
1790 ,, Richard, Dublin, gent.
1779 ,, Susanna, Dublin
1700 ,, Thomas, Edmondstown, co. Dublin, yeoman
1754 ,, Thomas, Ballydwilish, co. Limerick, gent.
1755 ,, Thos.,Usher's-quay,Dub.,gent.
1811 ,, Valentine, Britain-st., Dublin
1747 ,, William, Coolnamucky, co. Waterford, esq.
1755 ,, Wm., Maryboro', Qu. co., esq.
1792 ,, Wm., Putney, Surrey, LL.D. (Copy)
[See WALLE.]
1800 **Wallace**, Alex., Waterford city, esq.
1813 ,, Alexander, Newry, co. Down
1720 ,, Ann, widow of James W., Annsborough, co. Down
1800 ,, Arthur, Carlow town
1739 ,, Benjamin, Belekenny, co. Donegal, gent.
1688 ,, Elizabeth, Dublin, widow
1764 ,, Geo., Smithfield, Dublin, salesmaster
1776 ,, Hans, Waterford, merchant
1740 ,, Hugh, Dublin, carpenter
1788 ,, Hugh, Waterford city, esq.
1741 ,, Isaac, Newry, co. Down, gent.
1675 ,, Jas., Urney, co. Tyrone, clk.
1719 ,, James, Annsborough, co. Down
1736 ,, Jas., Crowbane, co. Down, esq.
1790 ,, James, Aughabrack, co. Longford, farmer
1748 ,, Jane, Dublin, widow
1804 ,, Joanna, Dublin city, spinster
1666 ,, John,Copper-alley,Dub.,merct.
1725 ,, John, Dublin, merchant
1777 ,, John, Dublin, gent.
1811 ,, John, Limerick city, esq.
1794 ,, Magill, Dublin, esq.
1797 ,, Mary, widow
1813 ,, Richard, Cappenrush, co. Westmeath
1768 ,, Robt., Aughnamullen, co.Mon.
1784 ,, Robt., Newry, co. Down, gent.
1798 ,, Robert, Limerick city, esq.
1780 ,, Samuel, Milltown-road, Dublin, gent.
1723 ,, Thos., now of par St. Clement's Danes, Middlesex
1718 ,, William, Ballyobekin, co. Down, gent.

1729 **Wallace**, Wm., Crobane, co. Down, gent.
1773 ,, William, Belfast, merchant
1793 ,, William, Newry
1807 ,, William, Marli, co. Wexford
1813 ,, Wm., Limerick city, merchant
[See WALLAS, WALLIS.]
1804 **Wallas**, Archibald, Linagunag, co. Antrim
[See WALLIS.]
1754 **Wallcott**, Blaney, Dublin esq.
1758 ,, Edwd., son of John M. Walcott, Dublin, esq.
1746 ,, Ellinor, *alias* **Bryan**, Croagh, co. Limerick, widow
1766 ,, Ellinor, Dublin, widow
1693 ,, Jane, Limerick, widow
1700 ,, Thos., Croagh, co. Limck., esq.
1641 **Walle**, Ulicke, Ballinekelly, co. Carlow, esq.
1679 ,, Walter, Ballioriskill, co. Kilkenny, gent.
[See WALL.]
1777 **Wallen**, Edwd., Killena, King'sco., gent.
1778 ,, rev. Geo., rector of Devenish, co. Fermanagh
1762 ,, Thomas, gent.
1639 **Waller**,Apollo, Carne, co.Wex., clk.
1755 ,, Blanch, Limerick, widow
1692 ,, captain Edmond, Dublin, earl Drogheda's regiment
1711 ,, Edward, Cully, co. Tipp., gent.
1807 ,, Elizabeth, Limerick city, widow
1796 ,, George, Limerick city, burgess
1702 ,, James, lieut.-governor of Kinsale and Charlesfort, esq.
1810 ,, Killner, Limerick city, esq.
1811 ,, Mary, Allenstown, co. Meath, widow
1702 ,, Richard, Cully, co. Tipp., esq.
1758 ,, Richard, Cully, co. Tipp., esq.
1805 ,, Richard, Leeson-st., Dub., esq.
1732 ,, Robert, Allenstown, co. Meath, esq.
1748 ,, Robt., Cloonanny,Qu. co.,gent.
1767 ,, Robt., Rookwood, co. Galway, esq.
1780 ,, sir Robt., Mullingar, co. Westmeath
1809 ,, Robert, Allenstown, co. Meath, esq. (Large)
1762 ,, Samuel, Cully, co. Tipp., gent., son of Richard W.
1762 ,, Samuel, Newport, co. Tip., esq.
1789 ,, Thomas, Castletown, co. Limerick, esq.
1734 ,, Wm., Cully, co. Tipperary, esq.
1796 ,, Wm., Allenstown, co. Meath, esq.

1685 **Wallis,** Andrie, Shanagarrie, co. Cork, wid. of Peter W., esq.
1766 ,, Barachia, Ballycrenan, co. Cork, esq.
1639 ,, Barbara, Kilcroghan, co. Cork, spinster
1784 ,, Edward, York city, M.D.
1767 ,, rev. Fielding, rector of Magheri-culmony, dio. Clogher
1792 ,, Gertrude, Baltinglass, co. Wicklow, widow
1749 ,, Henry, Drishane, co. Cork
1800 ,, Henry, Flintfield, co. Cork, esq.
1800 ,, James, Cork city, esq.
1702 ,, Jane, Dublin, widow
1628 ,, John, esq., St. Patrick, co. Dublin, gent.
1772 ,, John, quartermaster in 3rd regiment of horse
1787 ,, John, Renny, co. Cork
1806 ,, John, Dublin city
1810 ,, John, Westwood, co. Cork
1718 ,, Nicholas, Dublin, mariner
1630 ,, Peter, Kilcocklan, co. Cork, gent.
1679 ,, Peter, Shanagarry, co. Cork, esq. (Ex.)
1677 ,, Ralph, Dublin, esq.
1686 ,, Robert, Dublin, esq.
1725 ,, Robt., par. St. Margaret, West-minster, Middlesex (Copy)
1766 ,, Robt., Knapton, Qu. co., esq.
1776 ,, Robert, Dublin, gent.
1745 ,, Samuel, Dublin, gent.
1676 ,, Thomas, Huntingdon, single man (Copy)
1741 ,, Thomas, Cork, gent.
1746 ,, Thos., Vesingstown, co. Meath, clk.
1766 ,, Thomas, Cork, gent. [See WALLACE.]
1599 **Wallop,** sir Henry, knt., vice-Treasurer and Treasurer in Ireland
1710 **Wallplate,** Nathl., Dub., merchant
1773 **Wallpole,** Anne Smyth, Dubl., wid.
1773 ,, Anne Smyth, Dublin, widow
1673 ,, John, Athlone, merchant [**XIV.** 143
1788 ,, Joseph, Ballyduff, Qu. co., gent. [See WALPOLE.]
1721 **Wallpoole,** John, Aghavoe, Queen's county, farmer
1799 **Walls,** Elizabeth, Wicklow, widow (See prob. in 1802)
1802 ,, Elizabeth, Wicklow, wid. (Will in 1799)
1795 ,, rev. John, D.D., preby. of Wicklow
1803 **Wallscourt,** rt. hon. Joseph Henry Blake, baron

1660 **Wallworth,** Peter, Dub. [**VIII.** 91
1808 **Walmsley,** Frances, widow
1688 ,, James, Dublin, merchant
1812 ,, Jas., Tolleymore, co. Down, esq.
1795 ,, Thomas, late major of the 18th dragoons
1762 **Walpole,** Edmond, Dublin, esq.
1792 ,, Elizbth., Carrooreigh, Queen's county, widow
1797 ,, George, Carrooreigh, Queen's county, farmer
1804 ,, James, Toll, co. Tipperary
1807 ,, James, Mountrath, Queen's co., woolcomber
1761 ,, John, the younger, Coole, Qu. co.
1800 ,, John, Mountrath
1792 ,, Joseph, Mountrath, Queen's county, merchant
1797 ,, Joseph, Carroo, Qu. co., gent.
1801 ,, Lambert, Theo., colonel in His Majesty's Forces
1767 ,, Richard, Mountrath, Queen's county, woolcomber
1790 ,, Robt., Mundrehid, Qu. co., gent.
1806 ,, Robert, Thurles, co. Tipperary
1773 ,, Thomas, Dublin, esq.
1772 ,, William, Mundrehood, Queen's county, farmer
1779 ,, William, Newtown, Queen's co.
1786 ,, Wm., Mountrath, Queen's co.
1808 ,, Wm., Kilrush, co. Tipperary [See WALLPOLE.]
1663 **Walsby,** John, Dublin, innkeeper
1669 **Walsbye,** Elizabeth, Dame-street, Dublin, widow
1786 **Walsh,** Alice, Cork city, widow
1793 ,, Alice, widow
1729 ,, Ally, Ballymore, co. West-meath, widow
1768 ,, Andrew, Dublin, merchant
1791 ,, Andrew, Lacy's-lane, Dublin, dairyman
1616 ,, Ann, Waterford, widow of sir Patrick W., knt.
1783 ,, Ann, Bull-lane, Dubl., spinster
1773 ,, Anne, Ellistown, co. Kild., wid.
1791 ,, Anne, Clonmel, co. Tipp., wid.
1805 ,, Anne
1807 ,, Anne, *alias* **Murray,** widow
1808 ,, Anne, formerly of Dubl., late of Wakefield, Yorks. (Copy)
1681 ,, Anthony, Dublin, gent.
1737 ,, Anthony, Ardagh, co. Louth, gent.
1773 ,, Anthony, Kilclony, co. Cork, gent.
1777 ,, Anthony, Ardagh, co. Louth, esq.
1795 ,, Barbara, Chatham-st., Dubl., widow

1772 **Walsh**, Bartholomew, Dubl., mercht.
1784 ,, Bartholomew, Mt. Neill, co. Kilkenny, gent.
1599 ,, Beale or Bess, Waterford, wid.
1800 ,, Catherine, Snowtown, co. Meath, widow
1812 ,, Cathne., Ballyduff, co. Waterfd.
1728 ,, Chas., Derrilahan, co. Tip., esq.
1801 ,, Chas., Walsh Park, co. Tipperary, esq.
1609 ,, David, Dublin, alderman
1659 ,, David, Killileath, burgess [VII. 172
1717 ,, David, Hallohoise, co. Kildare, gent.
1781 ,, David, Dublin, merchant
1802 ,, David, Clonmel, counr.-at-law
1715 ,, Edith, Dollardstown, co. Kildare, widow of Oliver W.
1590 ,, Edmond, Cork, co. Dublin, gent. (No date)
1618 ,, sir Edmond, Abbey Ourny, co. Limerick, knt.
1771 ,, Edmond, Cork, mason (Not proved)
1801 ,, Edmond, Ballybricken, in the Libs. of Waterford, farmer
1698 ,, Edward, Connagh, co. Dublin, esq. (Ex.)
1793 ,, Edward, Cork, esq.
1734 ,, Elizbth., Clonmel, co. Tip., wid.
1794 ,, Elizabeth, Wakefield, Yorks.
1804 ,, Elizabeth, Mullingar
1812 ,, Elizabeth, widow
1769 ,, Ellen, Dublin, widow
1754 ,, Ellinor, wid. of Hunt W. Ballykilcavan, Queen's co., esq.
1784 ,, Ellinor
1805 ,, Francis, Rosemary-lane, Dubl.
1764 ,, George, major-gen. and colonel of 49th foot
1807 ,, George, Dublin city, esq.
1629 ,, Henry Fitz James, Waterford, merchant
1762 ,, Henry, Killanantick, King's co., gent. (See 1765) (Copy)
1765 ,, Henry, Killanantick, King's co., gent.
1752 ,, Hunt, Ballykilcavan, Queen's co., esq.
1795 ,, Hunt, lieut.-gen. and colonel 56th foot (Large)
1680 ,, James, Athy, gent.
1696 ,, James, Logatrine, co. Dublin, esq. (Ex.)
1737 ,, rev. James, Dublin, clk.
1753 ,, Jas., Gunoughs Bar, Dunboyne
1757 ,, James, Dublin, gent.
1770 ,, James, Ballyhagan, co. Kildare, gent.

1784 **Walsh**, James, Blessington House, co. Wicklow
1797 ,, James, Dublin, gent.
1813 ,, James, Dame-street, Dublin, breeches maker
1813 ,, James, Greek-st., Dublin, gent.
1755 ,, Jane, Christ Church yard
1810 ,, Jane, Dublin city, spinster
1789 ,, rev. Jeremy, clk.
1637 ,, John, Ballmacolly, co. Meath
1637 ,, John, Waterford, merchant
1641 ,, John, Ballymogue, co. Carlow, gent.
1662 ,, John, Ballymogue, co. Carlow, gent.
1721 ,, John, Trustemagh, co. Westmeath, farmer
1736 ,, John, Ballycullen, co. Wicklow, gent.
1745 ,, John, Dublin, brewer
1757 ,, John, Kilcooly, co. Tipp., clk.
1757 ,, John, Mylestown, co. Meath, gent.
1763 ,, John, Gerrardstown, co. Meath, gent.
1776 ,, John, Dame-street, Dublin, breeches maker
1783 ,, John, Crane-lane, Thomas-st., merchant
1794 ,, John, Glover's-alley, Dublin
1709 ,, Joseph, Sheep-Grange, co. Louth, lieut. in col. Alnut's regt., a prisoner in France
1810 ,, Joseph, quarter-master of the Waterford militia
1813 ,, Joseph, Waterford city
1718 ,, Laurence, Kilcock, priest
1799 ,, Laurence, Newtown Bellew, co. Galway
1813 ,, Lucy
1689 ,, Luke, Drumdowny, co. Kilk., esq.
1616 ,, dame Margaret, widow of aldmn. Jas. W., Waterford
1716 ,, Margaret, Ballyburne, co. Wicklow, widow
1664 ,, Martin, Dublin, linendraper
1707 ,, Martin, Waterford, maltster
1708 ,, Mary, *alias* **Bourke**, Dub., wid.
1715 ,, Mary, Kilcock, co. Kildare
1763 ,, Mary, Dublin, widow
1717 ,, Mathew, Dublin, glazier
1738 ,, Mathew, Kilcock, co. Kildare, maltster
1758 ,, Mathew, Barnaran, co. Kildare, gent.
1795 ,, rev. Mathew, Philipstown, K. co.
1804 ,, Maurice, Ram Close, co. Cork, farmer
1791 ,, Moses, Poolbeg, Dub., mariner

1615	**Walsh**,	sir Nicholas, knt. Chief Justice Common Pleas
1638	,,	Nicholas, Drogheda, alderman
1743	,,	Nicholas, Bonnarren, co. Kildare, gent.
1769	,,	Nicholas, Dublin, linendraper
1772	,,	Nicholas, Dublin, mercer
1658	,,	Oliver, Dublin, gent.
1665	,,	Oliver, Dublin, gent.
1774	,,	Patrick, Milestown, co. Meath, gent.
1784	,,	Patk., Clogheen, co. Tipperary, shopkeeper
1798	,,	Patk., Moynure, co. Rosc., esq.
1623	,,	Peter FitzThomas
1768	,,	Peter, Thos.-st., Dub., mercht.
1785	,,	Peter, Dublin, carpenter
1740	,,	rev. Philip, Blessington, clk.
1745	,,	Philip, Dublin, esq.
1811	,,	Philip, S. Liberties, Limerick
1773	,,	Ralph, par. St. Mary-le-Bon, Middlesex, esq. (Copy)
1809	,,	rev. Raphael, dean of Dromore
1736	,,	Richard, Dublin, tailor
1770	,,	Richard, Nicholstown, co. Kilkenny, gent.
1777	,,	Richard, Derrinroe, Queen's county, farmer
1792	,,	Richard, Mt. Talbot, co. Rosc.
1795	,,	Richard, Snowtown, co. Meath
1603	,,	Robert Fitz James, Dublin
1630	,,	Robert, Dublin, Hackardstown, co. Waterford, gent.
1661	,,	Robert, captain in the French army in Flanders. [**IX.** 31
1740	,,	Robert, Drumdowney, co. Kilkenny, gent.
1779	,,	Robert, Mullingar, co. Westmeath, apothecary
1789	,,	Robert, Bath city, esq. (Copy)
1808	,,	Robert, Dorset-street, Dublin, linendraper
1809	,,	Robert, Killonery, co. Kilkenny
1774	,,	Sam., Kilcooly, co. Tip., gent.
1791	,,	Sophia, Dublin, widow
1739	,,	Stephen, Dublin, widow
1634	,,	Thomas, esq., LL.D., Toulouse
1637	,,	Thos. FitzJohn, Watfd., mercht.
1788	,,	Thomas, Naul, co. Meath, flour manufacturer
1798	,,	Thomas, Killenerry, co. Kilkenny, farmer
1805	,,	Thomas, Gt. Britain-st., Dubl.
1810	,,	rev. Thomas, P.P., Clara
1812	,,	Thomas, Timolin, co. Kildare, innkeeper
1769	,,	Val., Garrane, co.Watfd., gent.
1721	,,	Walt., Lazyhill, Dub., victualler
1617	,,	Wm., Newtown, co. Wicklow, gent.
1755	**Walsh**,	Wm., Christ Church-yard, Dublin, goldsmith
1785	,,	William, esq.
1798	,,	William, Ross-lane, glazier
1807	,,	Wm.,Little Moreside, co.Meath
1811	,,	William, Swansea, Glamorganshire, esq. (Copy)

[See WAILSHE, WELCH, WELSH.]

1625	**Walshe**,	Abel, Kilkenny
1609	,,	David, Dublin, alderman
1599	,,	Edmond, Cork, co. Dub., gent. (No date)
1599	,,	Edmond Fitz-, Kilgobbin, co. Dublin (Date worn away, but entered in)
1607	,,	Edmond, Pompeston, co. Dub., gent.
1612	,,	Edmond, Prompstown, gent.
1627	,,	James, Castle Robin, gent.
1605	,,	John
1646	,,	John, clk., vicar of Castle Dermott, co. Kildare
1679	,,	John, Ballinerie, co. Tip., esq.
1600	,,	sir Patrick, knt., co. Waterford
1596	,,	Robt. Fitzpeter, co. Waterford
1613	,,	Robert Fitz John, Waterford, alderman
1790	**Walsingham**,	hon. Charlotte Boyle, Stratford-place, wid. (Copy)
1786	,,	Robt. Boyle, capt. of the "Modeste" man-of-war (Copy)
1795	**Walter**,	Daniel, Dublin, gent.
1669	,,	Deanes, Waterford, widow
1804	,,	Dorothy,Oakfield, co.Don., spr.
1796	,,	Sarah,Chapelizod,co.Dub.,wid.
1698	,,	Thomas, Youghal, alderman
1757	,,	William, Dublin, woolcomber
1668	**Walters**,	George, Whideby Island, co. Cork, esq.
1791	,,	captain George, Greenwich Hospital (Copy)
1779	**Waltham**,	dowr. lady Anne (Copy)
1766	,,	John Olmius, lord baron, Newhall, Essex (Copy)
1719	**Walton**,	Jacob, Dublin, gent.
1623	,,	John, Ballykelly, co. Londonderry, gent. (Copy)
1804	,,	Richard, Montague-street, co. Dublin, attorney
1770	,,	Thomas, Athlone
1704	,,	William, Kilturk, co. Fermanagh, gent. (Ex.)
1776	**Waltron**,	John, Grangegorman, co. Kildare, farmer
1641	**Wandesford**,	Christopher, esq., Lord Deputy of Ireland, and Master of the Rolls (Large will)
1687	,,	sir Chris., Hipswell, Yorkshire, bart. (Large, Copy)

1715 **Wandesford**, sir Christopher, Dubl., bart., afterwards lord Castle-comer
1784 ,, right hon. Elizabeth, dowager countess
1784 ,, John, earl of
1720 ,, Richard, esq.
1738 **Wanesborough**, William, Richmond, Surrey, esq. lieut.-col. of the King's Regiment Dragoons, and Governor of Royal Hospital, Dublin, (Copy)
1802 **Warbrick**, George, Liverpool, Lancashire, mercht. (Copy)
1753 **Warburton**, Anne, Dublin, widow
1731 ,, George, Dublin, esq.
1753 ,, George, Firmount, co. Kildare, esq.
1772 ,, Jane, Dublin, widow
1703 ,, John, Dublin, esq.
1806 ,, John, Garryhinch, King's co., esq.
1729 ,, Mary, Dublin, widow
1746 ,, Richard, Donnecarney, co. Dublin, esq.
1767 ,, Richard, Firmount, co. Kild., esq.
1771 ,, Richard, Garryhinch, King's eo., esq.
1736 ,, Thomas, Magherafelt, co. Armagh, clk.
1762 ,, Thomas, Britania, King's co.
1786 ,, Thomas, lieut. in the 50th regt. of foot
1760 **Ward**, Anne, Dublin, widow
1797 ,, Anne, Luke-street, Dublin, spinster
1674 ,, Arthur, Dublin, esq. (Ex.)
1730 ,, Bartholomew, Bay, co. Dublin, farmer
1784 ,, Benjamin, Draper's-court, Dublin, gent.
1770 ,, Bernard Smith, Knockballymore, co. Fermanagh, esq.
1784 ,, Bernard, precentor, Down
1770 ,, Bryan, Ballysheedy, co. Galway, farmer
1739 ,, Catherine, Dublin, spinster
1755 ,, Catherine, widow of Bartholomew W., Ferritstown
1787 ,, Catherine, Killister, co. Dubl., widow [esq.
1692 ,, Charles, Killough, co. Down,
1724 ,, Charles, Mountpanther, co. Down, clk.
1728 ,, Charles, Sandford, Shropshire, esq. (Copy)
1786 ,, Charles, Millefont, co. Antrim, esq.

1808 **Ward**, Chas., Hollymount, Queen's co., esq.
1680 ,, Cromwell, Knockballymore, co. Fermanagh, esq.
1776 ,, Edward, Castlewarden, co. Kilkenny
1813 ,, hon. Edward, Castle Ward
1756 ,, Elizabeth, Dublin, widow
1757 ,, Elizabeth, Dublin, widow
1769 ,, Elizabeth, Ballybog, widow of Richard W., esq.
1772 ,, Elizabeth, par. St. Minchin, Dublin, widow
1780 ,, Elizabeth, Dublin, widow
1667 ,, Ellinor, London, and par. Walkern, Hertfordshire, wid. (Copy)
1790 ,, Francis, Dublin, tailor
1806 ,, George, Carrickmacross
1664 ,, capt. Henry
1736 ,, rev. James, dean of Cloyne
1746 ,, James, Dublin, blacksmith
1776 ,, James, Liscub, co. Galway, gent.
1811 ,, Jane, Dublin city, widow
1738 ,, John, Wardshill, co. Dublin, brewer
1754 ,, John, Steevenstown, co. Dubl.
1765 ,, John
1775 ,, John, Bow-street, Dublin
1793 ,, John, New Ross, co. Wexford, collector
1795 ,, John, Clones, publican
1801 ,, John, Dublin, merchant
1801 ,, John, Whitestown, co. Dublin
1810 ,, John C., Dublin city, gent.
1770 ,, Joseph, Doone, co. Galway, gent.
1809 ,, Laurence, St. Dolough's, co. Dublin, farmer
1793 ,, Lewis
1749 ,, Marcella, *alias* **Curtis**, widow
1798 ,, Margaret, Kilkenny
1708 ,, Mary, Dublin, widow
1739 ,, Mary, *alias* **Finigan**, wife to Christopher W., Dublin
1799 ,, Mary, Dublin, widow
1802 ,, Mary, Temple Bar, Dublin, widow
1763 ,, Mathew, Nassau-street, Dubl. (Not proved)
1783 ,, Mathew, Bay, farmer
1733 ,, Maurice, Carrickmacross, co. Monaghan, gent.
1773 ,, Maurice, Dublin, merchant
1792 ,, Meliora, Dublin, widow
1759 ,, Michael, Judge of K. B., Ireland
1809 ,, Michael, Doone, co. Galway, esq.

1751 **Ward,** Nicholas, Knockballymore, co. Fermanagh, esq.
1775 ,, Nicholas, Ballyrider, Queen's co., gent.
1754 ,, Patrick, New-row, Dublin, shoemaker
1796 ,, Patrick, Cahertiny, co. Galway
1798 ,, Patrick, Kilkenny city
1799 ,, Patrick, Dublin city, gent.
1707 ,, Philip, Capeston, co. Palatine of Chester, gent. (Copy)
1788 ,, Ralph, Dublin, esq.
1689 ,, Richard, Dublin esq.
1692 ,, Richard, Dublin, merchant
1725 ,, Richard, Dublin, brewer
1741 ,, Richard, Marsheen, co. Wexford, merchant
1810 ,, Richard, Dublin city, watchmaker
1666 ,, Robert, Derryluskane, co. Tipperary, esq. **[XIII.** 77
1768 ,, Robert, Lisbane, co. Down, esq.
1775 ,, Samuel, New-street, Dublin, victualler
1696 ,, Thomas, dean of Connor
1750 ,, Thomas, Newtown, co. Carlow
1776 ,, Thomas, Dubl., woollen draper
1704 ,, Vere, Castleward, co. Down, esq.
1691 ,, William, a carter to the train of Artillery at Limerick
1710 ,, William, Dublin, merchant
1753 ,, William, Cullaghmore, co. Sligo
1753 ,, rev. William, Middleton, co. Cork, clk.
1767 ,, William, Ballyhealy, co. Westmeath
1770 ,, William, Dublin, gent.
1713 **Warde,** Edward, Castlewarden
1801 ,, Espine, Dublin, saddler
1638 ,, Thomas, Newbawne, co. Wexford, esq.
1724 **Wardell,** Anne, Waterford, spinster
1667 **Warden,** William, Burnchurch, co. Kilkenny, esq. **[XIII.** 246
1661 **Wardlaw,** Archibald, Drumca, co. Down, esq.
1762 ,, Charles, Moore-street, Dublin, esq.
1786 ,, Charles
1783 ,, Henry, Woodgrange, co. Down
1793 ,, Jane
1802 ,, rev. John, Glebe, near Limk.
1781 **Ware,** Anne, Dublin, widow
1805 ,, Barbara, Webbville, Liberties of Cork
1650 ,, Catherine, widow of Joseph W., late dean of Elphin

1740 **Ware,** Henry, Dublin, esq.
1778 ,, rev. Henry, Dublin, D.D.
1632 ,, sir James, Dublin, knt.
1666 ,, sir James, Dublin, knt. **[XIII.** 77
1691 ,, James, Dublin, esq., now at Chester
1764 ,, James, Dublin, esq.
1650 ,, Joseph, dean of Elphin
1697 ,, Robert, Dublin, esq.
1725 ,, Thomas, Killeneare, co. Cork, gent.
1725 ,, Thomas, Killeneare, co. Cork, gent. (Ex.)
1792 ,, Thomas, Webbville, S. Liberties of Cork
1794 **Warham,** Thomas, Staffordstown, co. Meath, gent.
1718 **Warick,** Wm., Breho, co. Longford
1662 **Waring,** Adam, par. Tullagh, co. Cork, esq. (Copy)
1803 ,, Ann, Newry, co. Down, widow
1804 ,, Elizabeth, Maralin, co. Down, widow
1769 ,, Henry, Bangor, co. Down, esq.
1759 ,, Hugh, Kilkenny, esq.
1803 ,, Isaac, Carlow, baker
1785 ,, John, Downpatrick, co. Down
1802 ,, rev. John, Coalmarket, Kilkenny city, clk.
1803 ,, John, Shipton, co. Kilkenny
1811 ,, Mary A., Pottlerath, co. Kilkenny, widow
1686 ,, Paul, Tanderagee, co. Armagh, gent.
1757 ,, Richard, par. St. James, Westminster, Middlesex, esq. (Copy)
1761 ,, Richard, Waringstown, co. Down, esq.
1692 ,, Roger, D.D., archd. of Dromore
1764 ,, Samuel, Dublin, gent.
1665 ,, Thomas, Belfast, esq.
1758 ,, Thomas, Shipton, co. Kilkenny, gent.
1777 ,, rev. Thomas, rector of Moira, co. Down
1786 ,, Thos., Newry, co. Down; esq.
1794 ,, Thos., Killeshill, Queen's co., farmer
1704 ,, Wm., Waringstown, co. Down, esq.
1752 ,, Wm., Pottlerath, co. Kilkenny, esq.
1757 ,, Wm. Ball, Thatcham, Berkshire, esq. (Copy)
1760 ,, Wm., Kilkenny, gent.
1765 ,, Wm., Kilkenny, esq.
1768 ,, Wm., Dublin, esq.
1808 ,, Wm., Downpatrick, surgeon
[See WARREN.]

1676 **Waringe**, Wm., Belfast, esq.
1784 **Warlow**, Mary, Dublin
1658 **Warneford**, lieut. Robert [**VII.** 174
1707   „   Robert, Mountmellick, Queen's
         co., esq.
1687   „   Walter, Mountmellick, esq.
1743 **Warner**, Anne, Cork, spinster
1792   „   Catherine, Dublin, widow
1748   „   Edward, Ballynakilly, co. Cork
1644   „   Elizabeth, Dublin, widow
1782   „   George, Leixlip, co. Kildare,
         gent.
1682   „   Henry, lieut.-col. to maj.-gen.
         Crawford (Copy)
1783   „   Henry, Dublin, gent.
1813   „   Henry, town of Rathkeale,
         surgeon
1791   „   John, Curraghfenoge, co. Tipp.
1691 **Warr**, Edward, Towreen, co. Lime-
         rick city, alderman (Ex.)
1784 **Warre**, Frans., Rosstrevor, co. Down
1769   „   John, Dublin, merchant
1776   „   Margaret, Dublin, widow
1651 **Warrell**, Thomas, gent. (& 1657)
         [**VI.** 124
1763 **Warren**, Abel, Lowhill, co. Kil-
         kenny, esq.
1799   „   Anna Maria
1791   „   Anne Phillip, Glasnevin, co.
         Dublin, widow
1722   „   Arthur, Pimlico, Dublin, dyer
1801   „   Charity
1739   „   Christopher, Dublin, upholder
1780   „   Crofton, Dublin, gent.
1800   „   Dorothy, Dublin
1788   „   Ebenezer, Dublin, esq.
1800   „   Ebenezer, Dublin
1614   „   Edmond, Navan, merchant
1670   „   Edward, Ballaghmoone, co.
         Kildare, gent.
1757   „   Elizabeth, Dublin, widow
1782   „   Elizabeth, Mary-street, Dublin,
         spinster
1785   „   Elizabeth, Mark's-alley, Dubl.,
         widow
1799   „   Elizabeth Maria, Dublin, widow
1735   „   Ellinor, Dublin, widow
1739   „   Ellinor, Dublin, spinster
1742   „   Ellinor, Dublin, widow
1777   „   Frances, Carrickmacross, co.
         Monaghan, widow
1699   „   Francis, ensign in earl Dro-
         gheda's regt. of foot
1800   „   Folliot, lieut. 56th regt. of foot
1709   „   Geo., Hillsborough, co. Down
1768   „   Geo., Meath-st., Dubl., hosier
1787   „   Geo., Crow-st., Dublin, gent.
1703   „   Gilbert, Gublinstown, co. Kil-
         dare, gent.
1679   „   Henry, Dublin, esq.

1684 **Warren**, Henry, Castledermot, co.
         Kildare, gent.
1723   „   Henry, Grangebeg, co. Kildare,
         esq.
1770   „   Henry, Thomastown, co. Meath,
         farmer
1756   „   Jacob Peppard, Carlow, esq.
1791   „   James, Montgomery-st., Dubl.,
         gent.
1798   „   James, Killeen, Queen's co.
1811   „   Jane, Innfield, co. Meath
1618   „   John, Navan, merchant
1639   „   John, esq., sovereign of Tallow,
         co. Waterford
1666   „   John, Dublin, tallow chandler
1694   „   John, Wells, co. Wexford, gt.
1701   „   John, Carlow, esq.
1707   „   John, Dublin, haberdasher
1729   „   John, Dublin, merchant
1765   „   John, Meath-street, Dublin
1800   „   John, Cork city, esq.
1801   „   John, Coleboy, co. Cavan,
         farmer
1793   „   rev. Joseph, rect. of Monaghan
1773   „   Joshua, Galtrim, co. Meath
1743   „   Margaret, Dublin, widow
1749   „   Margery, *alias* **Heyden**, Ath-
         boy, co. Meath
1747   „   Mark, Rathboy, co. Meath
1651   „   Mary, Londonderry, widow
         [**IX.** 131
1693   „   Mary, Dublin, spinster (Ex.)
1730   „   Mary, Dublin, spinster
1766   „   Mary, wife to Folliot W.,
         Lodge, co. Kilkenny, esq.
1768   „   Mary, Fethard, co. Tipp., spr.
1726   „   Maurice, Dublin, esq.
1799   „   Maurice Peppard, Glasnevin,
         co. Dublin (Large)
1712   „   Michael, Warrenstown, co.
         Meath, gent.
1796   „   Nathaniel, Dublin, esq.
1636   „   Nicholas, Sillock, co. Dublin,
         tanner
1713   „   Nichl., Monks Grange, Queen's
         co., gent.
1729   „   Patrick, Dubl., cloth merchant
1744   „   Patrick, Dubl., woollen draper
1752   „   sir Peter, K.C.B.
1779   „   Peter, Cullenswood, co. Dublin
1734   „   Richard, Kilgreny, co. Carlow,
         gent.
1779   „   Richard, Dubl., but at Bath, esq.
1634   „   Robert, Kilmore, gent.
1743   „   Robt., Kilbarry, co. Cork, esq.
1812   „   sir Robert
1624   „   Thomas, Seaton, co. Dublin,
         tanner
1740   „   rev. Thos., Magheross, co. Mo-
         naghan, clk.

1758 **Warren,** Thomas, Dublin, merchant
1778 ,, Thomas
1658 ,, Wm., clk., minister of Tadcaster, and rector of Donaghmore, co. Donegal [**VII.** 73
1667 ,, Wm., Grangebeg, co. Kildare, esq.
1766 ,, Wm., Cork, esq. (Proved in 1793)
1782 ,, Wm., Summerhill, co. Dublin, esq.
1793 ,, Wm., Cork, esq. (See 1766)
1797 ,, Wm., Dublin, glazier
1803 ,, rev. Wm., Bocade, co. Cavan
1654 **Warrington,** Margaret, Dunshaughly, widow [**V.** 57
1652 **Warrum,** Alice, Kilkenny, widow [**IX.** 55
1685 **Warter,** Edward, Bilboe, co. Limk., esq. (Large will; Ex.)
1681 ,, Gamaliel, Bilboe, co. Limk., esq. (Ex.)
1640 ,, William, Cullen, co. Tipperary, esq.
1679 **Washer,** Henry, Burnchurch, co. Kilkenny, gent.
1761 **Washington,** James, Kilkenny, gent.
1667 ,, Laurence, Garsdon, Wiltshire, esq. (Copy)
1801 **Waterford,** the most noble marquis of (Large)
1635 ,, Michael Boyle, bishop of
1691 ,, Hugh Gore, bishop of (Ex.)
1707 ,, and **Lismore,** rt. rev. Dr. Nathaniel Troy, bishop of
1740 ,, and **Lismore,** rt. rev. Dr. Thos. Mills, bishop of
1746 ,, and **Lismore,** rt. rev. Dr. Chas. Este, bishop of
1779 ,, and **Lismore,** Richd. Chenevix, lord bishop of (Large)
1803 ,, rt. rev. Richard Marlay, lord bishop of (Died in July, 1802)
1813 ,, rt. rev. Joseph Stock, lord bishop of
1591 **Waterhous,** sir Edward, knt. (Copy)
1666 **Waterhouse,** Anne, widow of Thos. W., Dublin, alderman
1628 ,, Anthony, Woodhouse, Yorkshire, clothier (Copy)
1668 ,, Joseph, M.D., Dublin
1580 ,, Michael, Dublin, gent.
1664 ,, Thomas, Dublin, alderman
1763 ,, rev. Thomas, chanter of St. Tynbarie's, Cork
1809 ,, Wm., Waterford city, gent.
1627 **Waterland,** Henry, Dublin, gent.

1792 **Waters,** Dominick, Cork, mercht.
1812 ,, Ellinor, Cork city, widow
1798 ,, James, Dublin, innholder
1811 ,, Jane, Cork city, spinster
1748 ,, John, Dublin, cork cutter
1762 ,, Nicholas, Dublin, coachman
1740 ,, Patrick, Cork, gent.
1637 ,, Richard, Macrony, co. Cork, gent.
1765 ,, Robert, Cortall, co. Louth
1786 ,, William, par. of Aghalee, co. Antrim [See WATTERS.]
1788 **Watkins,** Anne, widow
1660 ,, Charles [**VIII.** 138
1721 ,, Isaac, Waterpark, co. Cork, esq.
1687 ,, John, Bandon Bridge, gent.
1765 ,, John, Palacetown, co. Cork, esq.
1803 ,, John, Derrybrook, co. Fermanagh
1809 ,, Katherine
1811 ,, Richard, City-quay, Dublin, publican
1754 ,, Thos., Dublin, State trumpeter
1802 ,, Thomas, Somerset, co. Tipp., gent.
1783 ,, Westrop, Oldcourt, co. Cork, esq.
1658 **Watson,** David, rector of Kilsleavy, co. Armagh [**VII.** 48
1736 ,, Elizabeth, Newry, co. Down, widow
1758 ,, Elizabeth, Dublin, widow
1743 ,, Francis, mariner
1749 ,, Francis, Dublin, saddler
1701 ,, George, par. St. James, Westminster, esq. (Copy)
1747 ,, George, Lurgan, merchant
1790 ,, George, quar.-master of the 23rd regt. of foot
1809 ,, George, Duke-lane, Dublin, coachmaker [farmer
1754 ,, Henry, Popentree, co. Dublin,
1802 ,, Henry, Rathangan, co. Kildare, gent.
1717 ,, James, Dublin, late a mariner
1747 ,, James, Cork-street, Dublin, sheerman
1772 ,, James, Brookhill, co. Antrim
1792 ,, James, Cork-street, Dublin
1809 ,, James, Kingston Lodge, co. Roscommon
1786 ,, Jane, Rarush, co. Carlow
1787 ,, Jane
1668 ,, John, LL.D.
1705 ,, John, Dublin, feltmaker
1729 ,, John, lieut. in col. Nevill's dragoons

1752 **Watson**, John, Rathrush, co.Carlow
1754 ,, John, Lurgan, co. Armagh, maltster
1757 ,, John, Carlow
1769 ,, John, Dublin, bookseller
1771 ,, John, Glasnevin, co. Dublin, gent.
1776 ,, John,Commodore of the English East India Fleet (Not proved)
1783 ,, John, Kilconner, co. Carlow
1783 ,, John, the elder, Clonmel, co. Tipperary
1787 ,, John, Beresford-street, Dublin, dairyman
1791 ,, John, Bullock, co. Dublin, esq.
1794 ,, John, Ballydarton, co. Carlow
1812 ,, John, Portadown, co. Armagh
1777 ,, Jonathan, Lisgarvan,co.Carlow
1746 ,, Joseph, Ringsend, Dublin, gent.
1787 ,, Joseph, Capincur, King's co., gent.
1797 ,, Joseph, Bettyville, co. Dublin, esq.
1728 ,, Launcellot, Newry, co. Down, merchant
1800 ,, Margaret, Dublin
1809 ,, Mary Anne, Glasnevin, co. Dublin
1689 ,, Maurice, Dublin, gent.
1759 ,, Oliver, Edenderry, King's co., merchant
1810 ,, Rebecca, Bedford-st., Dublin, widow
1691 ,, Richard
1813 ,, Richard
1783 ,, Robert, Waterford
1796 ,, Robert, Dublin, gent.
1731 ,, Samuel, Dublin, linendraper
1764 ,, Samuel Kilconnor, co. Carlow, gent. (Large will)
1768 ,, Samuel, Tullalost, co. Kildare, farmer
1784 ,, Samuel, Lisgarvan, co. Carlow
1787 ,, Samuel, Portarlington, King's co., gent.
1800 ,, Samuel, Violet Bank, King's co.
1763 ,, Sarah, Dublin, spinster
1697 ,, Thomas, Dublin, merchant
1755 ,, Thomas, Dublin, tailor
1758 ,, Thomas, Cork-street, Dublin, clothier
1761 ,, Thomas, Derrygarren, King's co.
1772 ,, Thomas, Daltonsburntown, co. Dublin, weaver
1787 ,, Thomas, Clonmickshan, co. Carlow

1794 **Watson**, Thomas, Portaferry, co. Down, merchant
1640 ,, William, Curraglass, co. Cork, maltster
1761 ,, Elizabeth, Dublin, widow
1732 ,, George, Carlow, gent.
1773 ,, Hester
1790 ,, Jane, Dublin, widow
1733 ,, John, Beamon,co. Meath,gent.
1728 ,, Wm., Ballynamallagh, co. Kildare, farmer
1788 ,, Wm., Plunket-street, Dublin, broker
1801 ,, Wm., New-row, Dublin
1805 ,, Wm., Capel-st., Dublin, book-seller
1809 ,, Wm., Elphin
1701 **Watt**, Wm., Dublin, alderman
1785 **Watters**, James, par. of Aghnalee, co. Antrim
1781 ,, John, Kilkenny, alderman
1804 ,, John, Baltinglass, co. Wicklow
1801 ,, Lewis, Kilkenny city
1784 ,, Nicholas, Kilkenny city
1809 ,, Patrick James, co. Louth
1779 ,, Wm., Kilkenny, gent.
    [See WATERS.]
1639 **Watton**, Thomas, Drogheda, alder-man
1812 **Watts**, Anne, Mallow, co. Cork, wid.
1733 ,, Benjamin, Dublin, weaver
1749 ,, Cathne., *alias* **Roche**, Cork,wid.
1794 ,, Henry, Dublin, bookseller
1738 ,, James, Dublin, merchant
1710 ,, John, Megounagh, co. Mayo, gent.
1785 ,, John, Drogheda, supervisor of hearthmoney
1662 ,, Richard, senr., Chesterton, Cambridgeshire, clk. (Copy)
1762 ,, Richard, Skinner-row, Dublin, bookseller
1753 ,, v. rev.Robt., dean of St. Canice, Kilkenny
1801 ,, Robt.,Mt. Watts, co. Cork, esq.
1691 ,, maj. Thos., Redhill, co. Cavan, esq.
1781 ,, rev. William, minister of Fid-down, dio. Ossory
1692 **Waue**, Grace, Dublin, widow
1687 ,, Richard, Dublin, gent.
1776 **Waugh**, Isabella, Carlisle, Cumber-land (Copy)
1779 ,, James, Tullycarn, co. Down
1605 **Wawen**, James, late of Chippin, co. Waterford, soldier
1764 **Waylie**, Alexander, Royal Hospital, soldier
1725 **Waymouth**, Valentine, Ballinakill, gent.

1630 **Waynman**, Geo., Armagh, miller
1733 **Wayte**, John, Dublin, gent.
1784 **Weakly**, Mary, Greenville, co. Wex.
1746 **Wear**, James, Ballyscullan, co. Antrim, merchant [See WEIR.]
1650 **Weaver**, James, Dublin, gent.
1700 **Webb**, Anne, Harristown, co. Meath, widow
1749 ,, Anne, Limerick, widow
1654 ,, Anthony, co. Limerick [**V.** 19
1736 ,, Arthur, Irishtown, Kilk., esq.
1748 ,, Arthur, Kilkenny, esq.
1770 ,, Daniel, the elder, Ballynante, co. Limerick
1706 ,, Edward, Dublin, linendraper
1703 ,, Elizabeth, Dublin, spinster
1703 ,, George, Dublin, tailor
1720 ,, Geo., Edenderry, K. co., gent.
1680 ,, Henry, Ballylarkan, co. Kilkenny, esq.
1712 ,, Jas.,Ballyneheny, co. Limerick, gent.
1724 ,, James, Cork, merchant
1730 ,, James, Dublin, clk.
1754 ,, James, Dublin, gent.
1808 ,, James, Dame-court, Dublin, gent.
1782 ,, Jane, Hilltown, co. Westmeath
1811 ,, Jane, Frederick-st., Dub., wid.
1707 ,, John, Dublin, victualler
1728 ,, John, Cloheenmilcon, co. Cork, gent.
1780 ,, John, Kinsale, co. Cork, gent.
1796 ,, John, Cork, alderman
1796 ,, John, Croghan, King's co.
1784 ,, Joseph, Drumanwey
644 ,, Margaret, par. St. Nicholas-Within, widow
701 ,, Mary, Newcastle, co.Dub., wid.
696 ,, Noah, dean of Leighlin and vicar of Dunshaughlin
768 ,, Noah, Dunshaughlin,co.Meath
776 ,, Peter, Throgmorton-st., Lond., jeweller (Copy)
755 ,, Richard, Garranamanna, co. Limerick, gent.
807 ,, Richard Henry,Webbsborough, co. Kilkenny, esq.
804 ,, Stawell, Woodbrook, co. Dubl., esq.
769 ,, Thomas, Youghal, co. Cork
791 ,, Thos., Curraghmelagh, Queen's county, farmer
774 ,, Tobias, Ballyquirk, co. Kilkenny, gent.
668 ,, William, late of Ballymote, co. Sligo, esq.
791 ,, William Bowen, Mallow, co. Cork, gent.

1693 **Webbe**, Elizabeth, Harristown, co. Meath, spinster
1730 **Webber**, Edward, Cork, esq.
1780 ,, Elizabeth, Cork, spinster
1784 ,, Ferdinandus, Marlborough-st., organ builder
1674 ,, George, Cork, merchant
1772 ,, George, Cork
1749 ,, Michael, Cork, gent.
1742 ,, rev. Saml., Baldoyle, co. Dubl., clk.
1764 ,, Saml., Kilmurry, co. Wex., esq.
1789 **Weber**, Rachell, Prussia-st., Dubl., widow
1793 **Webster**, Anne, Harold's Cross, Dublin, widow
1805 ,, Edwd., Ballyellin, co. Wexford, farmer
1775 ,, Elizabeth, Lib. of Thomascourt and Donore, widow
1783 ,, Joseph, Dubl., mrcht. (Large)
1793 ,, Joseph, Harold's Cross, Dublin
1773 ,, Mary, *alias* **Cashin**, Dub., wid.
1677 ,, Roger, Athy, baker
1782 ,, Susanna, Cork-st., Dub., widow
1771 ,, Thomas
1682 ,, William, London, merchant
1753 **Wedgwood**, James, Downings, co. Kildare
1783 **Weekes**, Ann, Cork, widow
1783 ,, Anthony, Dublin, gent.·
1678 ,, John,St.Kevin's-st.,Dub.,gent.
1802 ,, John, Dublin, attorney-at-law
1681 ,, Mark, esq.
1772 ,, Mary, Cork, widow
1762 ,, Nicholas,Cork, esq., counsellor-at-law
1750 ,, Richard, Waterford, chandler
1768 ,, Robert, Ballikinlea, co. Dubl.
1728 ,, Sarah, Waterford. widow
1777 ,, Thos., Ashgrove, co. Cork, esq.
1670 ,, Wm.,Glonegar,co.Limk.,gent.
1716 ,, William, Waterford, merchant
1737 ,, William, Waterford, merchant
1681 **Weere**, John, Drumkerrin, co. Cavan, gent. [See WEIR.]
1764 **Weever**, Elizabeth, Dublin, spinster
1803 **Wegg**, Samuel, parish of Acton, Middlesex, esq. (Copy)
1713 **Weightman**, Johanna, Athlone, co. Roscommon, widow
1709 ,, William, Athlone, co. Rosc., gent.
1800 **Weily**, James, Newry, co. Down
1692 ,, Thomas, Clonmel, merchant
1784 **Weir**, Alexander, Monaghan, co. Fermanagh, esq.
1760 ,, Ann, widow of James W., Dub., merchant

1757 **Weir,** Henrietta
1736 ,, William, captain in the earl of Orkney's regiment
[See WEAR, WEERE, WIER, WYER.]
1800 **Welch,** Edwd., Ballycoman, King's county, gent.
1802 ,, Patrick, Carlow, esq.
[See WALSH.]
1795 **Weld,** Anne, Harold's Cross, co. Dublin, widow
1746 ,, Edmond, Harold's Cross, co. Dublin
1786 ,, Elizabeth, Dublin, widow
1799 ,, Ellen, Dublin, widow
1777 ,, Hannah, Dublin
1778 ,, Isaac, Harold's Cross, co. Dublin, D.D.
1758 ,, Joseph, Dublin, merchant
1772 ,, Mathew, Dublin, esq.
1799 ,, Mathew, Lodge Mills, co. Carl.
1722 ,, Nathaniel, Dublin, esq.
1730 ,, Nathaniel, Dublin, clk.
1755 ,, Richard, Dublin, M.D.
1786 ,, Sarah, spinster
1789 ,, Sarah, Dublin, spinster
1729 ,, Thomas, Dublin, merchant
1791 ,, Thomas, Dubl., wine merchant
1755 **Welding,** James, dio. Ossory, clk.
1810 **Weldon,** Anne, Granby-row, Dublin, widow
1801 ,, Anthony, Athy, co. Kild., clk.
1767 ,, Catherine, Dublin, widow
1766 ,, Christopher, Dublin, merchant
1800 ,, Christopher, Lissaket,co. Longford
1761 ,, Elizabeth, Dublin, widow
1732 ,, George, Carlow, gent.
1773 ,, Hester
1790 ,, Jane, Dublin, widow
1733 ,, John, Beamon, co. Meath, gent.
1687 ,, Mary, *alias* **Ailmer,** widow of Patrick W., Raffin, co. Meath
1684 ,, Patrick, Knock, co. Meath, gent.
1662 ,, Robert, St. John's, co. Kildare, esq.
1638 ,, Thomas, Rosberry, co. Kildare, gent.
1731 ,, Thomas, Kilkenny, gent.
1634 ,, Walter, St. John's Bower, co. Kildare, esq.
1773 ,, Walter, Raheen, Queen's co., esq.
1804 ,, Walter, Dublin city, gent.
1658 ,, William, Killtulloge, co. Rosc., gent.
1681 ,, Wm., Raheenderry, Queen's co., esq.
1734 ,, William, Dublin, esq.

1802 **Weldon,** William, Gravelmount, co. Meath, esq.
1808 ,, William, Clonmel, co. Tipp.
1780 **Weldone,** Christopher, Grafton-st., Dublin
1593 **Wellesley,** John, Bishop's Court, co. Kildare, esq.
1615 ,, Walter Barronett, Noaghmore, co. Kildare, esq.
[See WESLEY.]
1786 **Wells,** Anne, par. Christ Church Surrey, widow
1676 ,, Hugh, Furnivall's Inn, London (Copy)
1722 ,, Thomas, Dublin
1772 **Welsh,** Andrew, Limerick, burgess
1634 ,, Anne, widow of Thos. **Power** Waterford
1754 ,, Anne, Dublin, widow
1729 ,, Anthony, Lisburn, co. Antrim gent.
1783 ,, Anthony, Dublin, esq.
1810 ,, Edmond, Island of Malta
1770 ,, Elizabeth, Celbridge, co. Kildare, widow
1792 ,, Elizabeth, Cootehill, co. Cavan widow
1755 ,, James, Dublin, M.D.
1792 ,, James, Ballyduffbeg, co.Wat
1793 ,, James, Castledermot, co. Kildare, distiller
1762 ,, Jane, New Ross, co. Wexford widow
1661 ,, John, Dublin, tailor
1731 ,, John, Ballyhonemore, co. Armagh, farmer
1754 ,, rev. John, dean of Connor
1763 ,, John, Dublin, carpenter
1766 ,, John, Killisargo, co. Monaghan, gent.
1634 ,, Josias, minister at Temple patrick
1739 ,, Mary, Peter-street, Dubl., wid
1785 ,, Rebecca, Great George's-st. Dublin, widow
1756 ,, Robert, Killorney, co. Kilk. farmer
1760 ,, Robert, New Ross, co. Wexford, peruke maker
1667 ,, Thomas, Pilltown, co. Waterford, esq.
1727 ,, Thomas, quarter-master col. Bowles' regt. of horse
1740 ,, Thomas, Dublin, poulterer
1746 ,, Thos., servant to Mr. Sheffiel Grace
1762 ,, Thomas, Celbridge, co. Kildare, gent.
1776 ,, Thomas, Taylorstown, co Waterford, esq. (Large wil

1799 **Welsh**, Thomas, Youghal, esq.
1727 ,, William, Balraheen, co. Kildare, farmer
[See WALSH.]
1771 **Welstead**, Christian, Cork, widow
1786 **Welton**, Balthazar, Moore-street, Dublin
1773 **Wemys**, Abigail, Waterdel, co. Galway, spinster
1739 ,, Francis, Dublin, esq.
1782 ,, Francis, Coolderry, King's co., esq.
1765 ,, Jas., Danesfort, co. Kilkenny, esq.
1787 ,, Martha, Dublin, spinster
1661 ,, sir Patrick, Dublin, knt.
1762 ,, Patrick, Danesfort, co. Kilkenny, esq.
[See WEYMES.]
1748 **Wenman**, Barbara, *alias* Fowle, Dublin, widow
1780 ,, Jane, Dublin, spinster
1637 ,, sir Thomas, Dublin, knt.
[**IV.** 185
1759 **Wensley**, Catherine, Sandville, co. Tyrone, widow
1774 ,, Thomas, Sandville, co. Tyrone, gent.
1666 **Wentworth**, sir George, Wentworth Woodhouse, Yorkshire, knt. (Ex.)
1788 ,, Hugh, Leeds, Yorkshire (Copy)
1686 ,, Ruisshee, Cleeve, Isle of Thanet, Kent, esq. (Copy)
1719 ,, Sarah, Ballykerne, co. Westmeath, widow
1685 ,, Thomas, Cleeve Court, Isle of Thanet, Kent, esq. (Ex.)
1745 **Wesley**, Catherine, Dublin, widow
1682 ,, Garrett, Dangan, co. Meath, esq.
1728 ,, Garrett, Dangan, co. Meath, esq.
1603 ,, Gerald, Dangan, co. Meath, esq.
[See WELLESLEY.]
1582 **Wesly**, Piers or Peter, to be buried in Ballymaglassan, co. Meath
1772 **West**, Abraham, Kilkenny, gent.
1782 ,, Catherine, Finglas, co. Dublin
1810 ,, Christopher, Tonystick, co. Fermanagh
1813 ,, David, capt. 15th regt. of foot
1800 ,, Edward, Drogheda, esq.
1813 ,, Edwd., Gerrard-st., Middlesex
1698 ,, Elizabeth, Rock, co. Wicklow, widow of Roger W., esq.
1745 ,, Elizabeth, Dublin, widow
1779 ,, Frances, widow

1809 **West**, Francis Robert, Dublin city, gent.
1713 ,, George, Athlone, co. Westmeath, gent.
1768 ,, Hamilton, Curragh, co. Dublin, gent.
1787 ,, Henry, Ballydugan, co. Down, esq.
1788 ,, Henry, Strokestown, co. Roscommon, gent.
1726 ,, James, Cranlamore, co. Longford
1751 ,, Joan, widow of John W., esq.
1657 ,, John, St. Finbarrie's, Cork, esq.
[**VI.** 164
1701 ,, John, Monasterevan, co. Kildare, gent.
1764 ,, John, Dublin, esq.
1788 ,, John, Drumdarkin, co. Leitrim
1812 ,, John, Foxall, co. Longford, esq.
1750 ,, Joseph, Dublin, cooper
1798 ,, Mark, Dublin, gent.
1757 ,, Mary, Dublin, widow
1794 ,, Mary, Dublin, widow
1813 ,, Mary, Dublin city, spinster
1812 ,, Milburne, Bath city, esq.
1779 ,, Mordant
1758 ,, Richard, Leixlip, co. Kildare, esq.
1790 ,, Robert, Dublin, master builder
1686 ,, Roger, Rock, co. Wicklow, esq.
1791 ,, Roger, Ballydoogan, co. Down (Large will)
1698 ,, Thomas, Little Boolies, co. Meath, gent.
1713 ,, Thomas, Corleagh, co. Longford, gent.
1769 ,, Thomas, Rathowen, co. Westmeath, farmer
1773 ,, Thomas, Waterford, alderman
1788 ,, Thomas, Dauntsey, Wiltshire, esq. (Copy)
1751 ,, Tichborn, Ashwood, co. Wexford, esq.
1705 ,, William, Dublin, butcher
1748 ,, Wm., Stephen's-green, Dublin
1801 ,, William, Earl Curragh, co. Dublin, esq.
1812 ,, William, Boyle, co. Rosc.
1747 **Westberry**, William, Dublin, gent.
1755 **Westbery**, William, Dublin, gent.
1809 **Westby**, Frances, Dublin city, spinster
1775 ,, Mary, Dublin, spinster
1794 ,, Mary, Dublin, widow (Large)
1716 ,, Nicholas, Dublin, esq. (Ex.)
1801 ,, Nicholas, Dublin, esq.

1673 **Westby**, Simon, New Abbey, co. Kildare, gent.
1757 ,, William, Dublin, esq.
1769 **Westenra**, Ellinor, Dublin, widow
1719 ,, Henry, Dublin, esq.
1811 ,, Henry, Dublin city, esq.
1793 ,, lady Hester, Dublin, widow (Large)
1812 ,, Margaret, Summerhill, Dublin, spinster
1772 ,, Penelope
1693 ,, Peter, Dublin, esq. (Ex.)
1668 ,, Warner, Dublin, merchant
1772 ,, Warner, Dublin, esq.
1710 **Westgarth**, Wm., Dublin, gent.
1799 **Westlake**, John, Glasnevin, co. Dublin, esq.
1731 **Westland**, Wm., Dublin, merchant
1687 **Westly**, John, Belan, co. Kildare, LL.D.
1772 **Westman**, John, Kilmainham, co. Dublin, smith
1643 **Westmeath**, sir Richd. Nugent, knt., earl of
1684 ,, Richard, earl of
1753 ,, Thomas, earl of
1673 **Westmerland**, Mathias, Dublin, esq.
1605 **Weston**, Ellenor, daughter to John W., Drogheda, merchant, deceased
1737 ,, Geo., Sutton, co. Dublin, esq.
1617 ,, Nicholas, Dublin, alderman
1735 ,, Oliver, Dublin, gent.
1661 ,, Sarah, Dublin, widow of Samuel W., Dublin, alderman
1678 ,, Thomas, Dublin, tailor
1708 ,, Thomas, the elder, Athy, co. Kildare, miller
1594 ,, sir Wm., knt., Chief Justice Common Pleas
1802 **Westray**, James's-street, Dublin
1802 ,, Henry, James's-st., Dublin
1780 **Westrop**, John, Mayford, co. Clare, gent.
1793 ,, John, Rockfield, co. Limerick, esq.
1803 ,, Poole, Fort Ann, co. Clare, esq.
1776 ,, Robert, Fortan, co. Clare
1797 **Westropp**, Anne
1768 ,, Elizabeth, widow of Mounti-fort W., Attyflin, co. Limerick
1805 ,, Jane, Castleconnell, widow
1809 ,, Jane, Limerick city, spinster
1781 ,, John, Attyflin, co. Limerick, esq.
1698 ,, Mountyfort, Bunratty, co. Clare, esq.
1741 ,, Ralph, Carduggan, co. Cork

1772 **Westropp**, Ralph, Cork, M.D.
1744 ,, Thomas, Melon, co. Limerick, esq.
1790 ,, Thomas
1732 **Wetenhall**, Edward, Cork, esq.
1717 ,, Philippia, widow of rt. rev. Dr. Edward W., bp. of **Kilmore**, q. v. (Copy)
1742 **Wetherall**, Benj., Cork, clothier
1687 ,, Charles, Upper Coombe, near Dublin, weaver
1665 ,, Henry, Dublin, merchant
1795 ,, Isabella
1794 ,, John, Dublin, esq.
1788 ,, Joseph, Cork, alderman
1752 ,, Richard, Rathfarnham, co. Dublin, gent.
1634 ,, Robert, Roestown, co. Meatl, gent.
1750 ,, Wm., Dublin, cordwainer
1784 ,, Wm., the elder, Custom House, Dublin
1749 **Wetherby**, Anne, Dublin, widow
1749 ,, rev. John, dean of Cashel
1742 ,, Smith, Dublin, widow
1751 **Wetherelt**, Hurd, Castletown, King's co., esq.
1749 ,, Thomas, Dublin, gent.
1764 ,, Vans, Castletown, King's co., esq.
1754 **Wetherilt**, Jane, Donington, Lincolnshire, widow (Copy)
1793 ,, Maria, Dublin, widow
1790 ,, Sewel, Castletown, King's co., esq.
1797 **Wetherington**, Catherine, Dublin [See WITHERINGTON.]
1688 **Weymes**, Elizabeth, Dubl., spinster
1672 ,, sir James, Donfert, co. Kilkenny, knt. [See WEMYS.]
1738 **Whaley**, rev. Nathaniel, rector of Armagh
1769 ,, Richd. Chapel, Dublin, esq. (Large will)
1766 ,, rev. Samuel, Dublin, clk.
1742 ,, rev. Thos., Syddan, co. Meath, clk. (Ex.)
1801 ,, Thos., Kingdom of Ireland
1690 **Whalley**, John, Tipperary, gent.
1690 .,, Sarah, widow of John W., Tip., gent.
1656 ,, William, Kilkenny, esq. [**V.** 256
1691 **Whally**, John, Athenry, co. Galway, esq.
1745 **Whape**, Jas., Dublin, linendraper
1691 **Wharlow**, Jane, Dublin, spinster
1642 **Wharne**, William, Jamestown, co. Dublin, yeoman

1798 **Wharton**, John, Dublin, silk manufacturer
1736 ,, Philip James, duke of (Copy)
1792 ,, Robert, Leixlip, co. Kildare
1715 ,, Thomas, earl of (Copy)
1774 **Whatley**, Stephen, Datchett, Bucks. (Copy)
   [See WHITLEY.]
1687 **Whatton**, Dorothy, Dublin, spinster
1777 **Whealan**, Darby, Ballymanus, co. Wicklow, farmer
1791 **Whearty**, Andrew, George's-lane, Dublin, baker
1790 ,, Thomas, Sth. Gt. George's-st., Dublin, baker
1658 **Wheat**, Elizabeth, wife to Wm. W., Glymton, Oxfordshire, esq.
   [**VII.** 6
1736 **Wheatley**, Joshua, Palmerstown, co. Dublin, gent.
1760 ,, Thos., Bristol, mercht. (Copy)
1758 ,, Wm., Tullamore, King's co.
   [See WHITLEY.]
1774 **Wheddon**, Hannah, Cork, widow
1714 **Wheeler**, Catherine, Dublin, spinst.
1789 ,, Elizabeth, widow
1762 ,, Francis, Templeshannon, co. Wexford, merchant
1731 ,, George, Dublin, joiner
1697 ,, Jonah, Grennan, Queen's co., esq.
1776 ,, Jonah, Leyrath, co. Kilkenny, esq.
1624 ,, Jonas, The Grange, co. Dublin, gent.
1640 ,, Jonas, bp. of **Ossory**, q. v.
1774 ,, Joseph, Enniscorthy, co. Wexford, farmer
1758 ,, Judith, Dublin, spinster
1673 ,, Oliver, Grennan, Queen's co., esq.
1723 ,, Oliver, Dublin, esq.
1737 ,, Oliver, Grennan, Queen's co., esq.
1742 ,, rev. Oliver, Knockorden, co. Tipperary, clk.
1782 ,, rev. Oliver, Mt. Brilliant, Lib. Kilkenny, clk.
1766 ,, Sarah, Cork, widow
1752 ,, Wm., Cork, merchant
1802 ,, Wm., Kilkenny, esq.
1811 **Whelan**, Alicia, wife to the rev. Thomas Phelan
1811 ,, Anna, Dubl. city, starch manufacturer
1777 ,, Arthur, Rathvol, co. Wicklow, farmer
1789 ,, James, Porter's-size, co. Kildare
1795 ,, James, Larough, co. Carlow
1767 ,, John, Liscolman, co. Wicklow

1775 **Whelan**, John, Rathmore, Queen's co., farmer
1788 ,, Mary, Belfast, widow
1748 ,, Maurice, Francis-st., Dublin, merchant
1797 ,, Owen, Mt. Garnet, co. Kilkenny
1791 ,, Patrick, Watling-st., Dublin, skinner
1808 ,, Patrick
1766 ,, Pilsworth, Munny, co. Wicklow
1805 ,, Pilsworth, Rath, co. Wicklow
1768 ,, Thos., Rath, co. Wicklow, gt.
1768 **Wheldon**, Sarah, Drogheda, widow
1813 **Whelehan**, Thomas, Castlejordan, co. Meath, farmer
1684 **Whetcombe**, John, Sherborne, Dorsetshire, gent.
1753 ,, John, abp. of **Cashel**, q. v.
1754 **Whetcome**, Ellinor, widow of John, archbishop of Cashel
1741 **Whetham**, Thos., par. St. James, Westminster, esq.
1758 **Whetston**, Francis, Dublin, surgeon
1778 **Whetstone**, Elizab., Dublin, widow
1659 ,, Thomas, Drogheda, innkeeper
1789 **Whielaghan**, Rose, *alias* **Sharpe**, Raheenduff, King's co.
1672 **Whingates**, Robert, Downpatrick, gent.
1730 **Whinrey**, John, Dublin, mason
1750 ,, Mary, Drumcondra, co. Dublin, widow
1731 ,, Nathaniel, Dublin, stonecutter
1779 ,, Samuel, Ballyboughlan, King's co., farmer
1786 ,, Samuel, Ballyboughlan, King's co., farmer
1718 ,, William, Dublin, M.D.
1800 **Whiskin**, Bartholomew, Athlone
1715 **Whistler**, Gabriel, Combe, Hampshire, gent. (Copy)
1714 **Whiston**, Theophilus, Waterford, gent.
1589 **Whit**, Henry, Clonmel, burgess
1588 ,, Stephen, Drogheda, alderman
1671 **Whitaker**, Richard, Maynooth, gent.
1658 **Whitby**, capt. Marcus, Fermoy, co. Cork, mariner [**VII.** 134
1765 ,, Catherine, widow of Robert W., Kilcregan, co. Kilkenny
1806 ,, Elizabeth, Cloneyanah, King's co.
1718 ,, Jonathan, Kilcregan, co. Kilkenny, gent. (Copy)
1776 ,, Jonathan, Waterford, esq.
1799 ,, Jonathan, Castle Blaney, co. Monaghan, merchant
1745 ,, Robert, Kilcregan, co. Kilkenny, esq.

1786	**White**, Jane, Dublin, widow	
1786	,, Jane, par. of Finglas,co.Dubl., widow	
1810	,, Jane, Scotsrath, Queen's co.	
1619	,, Jasper, Limerick, merchant	
1715	,, Joanna, Annagh, co. Wexford, widow	
1777	,, Jocelyn, formerly a captain in the 17th regt. of foot	
1619	,, John, Kells, co. Kilkenny, gent.	
1676	,, John, Oldstone, co. Antrim, gent.	
1685	,, John, Ballyellis, co. Wexford, gent. (Ex.)	
1691	,, John, Ballymore Eustace, co. Dublin, gent.	
1710	,, John, lieut. in genl. Stewart's regt.	
1715	,, John, Castlebellingham, co. Louth, gent.	
1719	,, John, Cappagh, co. Tipperary, esq. (Ex.)	
1723	,, John, Tullyhallen, co. Louth, farmer [esq.	
1723	,, John, Ballyellis, co. Wexford,	
1741	,, John, Dublin, cooper	
1759	,, John, Newry, co. Down	
1769	,, John Jervis, Ballyellis, co. Wexford, esq.	
1770	,, John, Rahagonan, co. Limk., esq.	
1774	,, John, Ballyvologue, co. Limk., farmer	
1781	,, John, His Majesty's Ship "Pearl"	
1790	,, John, Dublin, merchant	
1794	,, John, Templebar, Dublin, hat maker	
1794	,, John, Whitesford, co. Waterford, esq.	
1799	,, John, Dublin, coach owner	
1800	,, John, Whitefield	
1813	,, John, Ballinahinch	
1790	,, Joseph, lieut. in 17th regt. of dragoons (Copy)	
1800	,, Joshua, Cork city	
1776	,, Judith, wife to Wm. White, Clonmel, gent.	
1785	,, Judith, Grafton-street, Dublin	
1666	,, Laurence,Lincoln's Inn,gent. (Copy)	
1757	,, Lionel, Roscommon, gent.	
1760	,, Magdalen, Dublin, widow	
1737	,, Margaret,*alias* **Aughlin**,North Sub. of Cork, widow	
1764	,, Margaret, Castle Bellingham, co. Louth, spinster	
1777	,, Margaret, Back-lane, Dublin, widow	

1736	**White**, Margery, Drogheda, late Dublin, widow	
1728	,, Mary, Youghal, co. Cork, widow	
1802	,, Mary, Dublin, widow	
1802	,, Mary, Dublin, widow	
1807	,, Mary, Meath-street, Dublin	
1781	,, Mathew, Dublin, merchant	
1785	,, Mathew, co. Wicklow, farmer	
1801	,, Mathew, Scarnagh, co. Wexford, esq.	
1789	,, Matthias, Mullacash, co. Kilkenny, farmer	
1624	,, Michael, Waterford, gent.	
1767	,, Michael, Naas, co. Kildare	
1759	,, rev. Newport, Kilmoylan, co. Limerick, clk.	
1780	,, Newport, Kilmoylan, co. Limerick, esq.	
1804	,, Newport, Killaderry, co. Clare, esq.	
1592	,, sir Nicholas, co. Dublin, knt., Master of the Rolls	
1618	,, Nicholas, Drogheda, merchant	
1634	,, Nicholas, Waterford, gent.	
1645	,, Nicholas, Dublin, esq.	
1727	,, Nicholas, Dublin, gent.	
1727	,, Nicholas, Dublin, gent.	
1637	,, Patrick Fitz Nicholas, Waterford, merchant	
1741	,, Patk., Clonmel, co. Tipperary, merchant	
1755	,, Patrick, Dublin, victualler	
1779	,, Patrick, Dublin, tanner	
1782	,, Patrick, Finglas, co. Dubl., gt.	
1746	,, Paul, Pill-lane, Dublin	
1763	,, Peter, Chamber-street, Dublin, clothier	
1753	,, Prisca, Dublin, spinster	
1672	,, Richard, Ballimacgarnon, co. Meath, gent.	
1702	,, sir Richd., London, knt. (Copy)	
1730	,, Richard, Dublin, tailor	
1733	,, Richd., Bantry, co. Cork, esq.	
1737	,, Richard, Scart, co. Cork, gent.	
1776	,, Richd., Bantry, co. Cork, esq.	
1800	,, Richard, Watling-st., Dublin	
1801	,, Richard, Greenhall, co. Tipp., esq.	
1650	,, Robert, esq., in the army	
1700	,, Robert, Youghal, co. Cork	
1725	,, Robert, Thurles, co. Tipp., gt.	
1740	,, Robert, Garrycottegane, co. Limerick, gent.	
1767	,, Robert, Aughentaraghan, co. Armagh	
1767	,, Robert, Kevin-st., Dublin, gt.	
1783	,, Robert, Dublin, esq.	
1790	,, Robert, Sallymount, co. Wicklow, esq.	

1802 **White**, Robert, a private in His Majesty's 12th regt. of Light Dragoons
1716 ,, Samuel, Ballysimon, Lib. Limerick
1741 ,, Samuel, Birr, King's co., esq.
1771 ,, Samuel, Raheen, Queen's co.
1810 ,, Sarah, Clonmel, co. Tipperary
1704 ,, Simon, Knocksentry, co. Limerick, gent.
1776 ,, Simon, Blackrock, co. Cork
1670 ,, Stephen, Drogheda, merchant
1692 ,, Stephen Fitz Francis, Limerick, merchant
1793 ,, Stephen, Cork, merchant
1797 ,, Stephen, Bath city, esq. (Copy)
1769 ,, Symon, Limerick, burgess
1623 ,, Thomas, Waterford, gent.
1650 ,, Thomas, Dublin, maltster
1678 ,, Thomas, Redhill, co. Cavan, esq.
1722 ,, Thomas, Cappagh, co. Tipp., esq.
1733 ,, Thomas, Ratoath, co. Meath, farmer
1738 ,, Thomas, Pembrokestown, co. Waterford, gent.
1744 ,, Thos., Chequer-lane, Dublin
1745 ,, Thomas, Belfast, merchant
1760 ,, Thomas, Capel-lane, Queen's co., farmer
1770 ,, Thomas, dean of Ardagh
1774 ,, Thomas, Ballybrophy, Queen's co., esq.
1775 ,, Thos., Watling-street, Dublin, skinner
1778 ,, Thomas, Cork, clk.
1795 ,, Thomas, Dublin, merchant
1803 ,, Thomas, Cork, stationer
1623 ,, Walter Fitz Nicholas, Limerick, merchant
1634 ,, Walter Fitz John, Cloyne, mct.
1641 ,, Walter, Dublin, esq.
1673 ,, Walter, Kilmainham, gent.
1782 ,, Walter, Dublin, merchant
1618 ,, Wm., Curragh, co. Kildare, gt.
1670 ,, Wm., Dublin, gent.
1672 ,, Wm., Waterford, merchant
1683 ,, Wm., St. Stephen's-green, gt.
1740 ,, Wm., Six-mile-Bridge, co. Clare, merchant
1756 ,, Wm., Gortnequan, co. Derry, gent.
1764 ,, Wm., Harristown, co. Meath, farmer
1765 ,, Wm., Roscrea, co. Tipperary, clothier
1784 ,, William, Upton, co. Wexford, esq.
1785 ,, Wm., New-row, Dublin

1786 **White**, Wm., Cartrons, co. Clare, gt.
1798 ,, Wm., The Pass, co. Kildare, farmer
1800 ,, Wm., Balbriggan, co. Dublin, freeholder
1802 ,, Wm., Limerick, gent.
1652 **Whitefield**, Wm., Dublin, gent.
1744 **Whitehand**, John, Kells, co. Meath, gent.
1656 **Whitehead**, Daniel, soldier [**V**. 319
1710 ,, Elizabeth, Dublin, widow
1779 ,, George, Braithwaite-st., Dubl., clothier
1660 ,, John, sergt. in capt. Charles Twigg's company
1747 ,, Richard, Dublin, hosier
1762 ,, Richard, Dublin, gent.
1635 ,, Robert, Enniskeane, co. Monaghan, esq.
      [See WHITEHEAD.]
1758 **Whitehouse**, Elizabeth
1793 ,, Joshua, James's-st., Dublin, bookseller
1670 **Whiteing**, Mary, Dublin, widow
      [See WHITING.]
1813 **Whitelaw**, rev. James, vicar of St. Catherine's par.
1809 ,, Sophia, Summerhill, co. Dubl.
1737 ,, rev. William, clk.
1776 **Whitelock**, Carleton, Priorswood, co. Dublin, esq.
1681 **Whiterow**, Jason, Ballyneclogh, co. Limerick
1738 ,, Mary, Castle Otway, co. Tipp., widow
1776 **Whiteside**, Jno., Drogheda, yeomn.
1766 ,, Thos., Belfast, ship carpenter
1753 ,, Wm., Dreemore, co. Tyrone
1806 ,, Wm., Rathmines, co. Dublin
      [See WHITSITT.]
1710 **Whitestone**, Francis, Carlow, gent.
1806 **Whiteway**, George
1802 ,, John, Dublin, esq.
1802 ,, John, Dublin, esq.
1690 **Whitfeld**, Henry, Dublin, esq.
1696 ,, Hester, Dublin, wid. of Henry W., esq.
1786 **Whitfield**, Fras., Frankford, King's co., distiller
1777 ,, Joseph, College-green, Dublin, tallow chandler
1719 ,, Robert, Dublin
1731 ,, Temple, par. Rickmersworth, Hertfordshire (Copy)
1691 ,, Thomas, Dublin, gent.
1765 ,, Thomas, Watford, Hertfordshire, esq. (Copy)
1714 **Whithead**, John, Colebay, Stonyford, co. Wicklow, esq.
      [See WHITEHEAD.]

1692 **Whiting,** John, Lazyhill, near Dublin, wheelwright
[See WHITEING.]
1802 **Whitla,** Valentine, Belfast
1635 **Whitlaw,** Robert, clk.
1791 ,, Wm., Lodge, co. Roscommon, esq.
1794 **Whitley,** Elizabeth, Maryborough, Queen's co.
1707 ,, Honora, wife to Thomas W., Dublin, esq.
1725 ,, John, Irey, Queen's co., gent.
1738 ,, John
1764 ,, John,the younger, Irey,Queen's co., gent.
1674 ,, Thomas, Castle-Geshill,King's co., yeoman
[See WHATLEY, WHEATLEY.]
1731 **Whitlock,** Edward, Dublin, merchant
1687 **Whitty,** Nicholas, Dublin, gent.
1755 **Whitmore,** Anne, Dublin, spinster
1756 ,, Elizabeth, Dublin, spinster
1756 ,, Joy, Annville, co. Dublin, gent.
1763 ,, Martha, Dublin, spinster
1794 ,, Richard Beeby
1680 ,, Thomas, Dublin, merchant
1748 ,, William, Dublin, merchant
1792 **Whitney,** Benjamin, Old Ross, co. Wexford, gent.
1758 ,, Boleyn, Dublin, esq.
1805 ,, George Boleyn, Newpass, co. Westmeath
1783 ,, John, par. of Old Ross, co.Wexford
1791 ,, Nicholas, Old Ross, co. Wexford, farmer
1711 ,, Thomas, Newpass, co. Westmeath, esq.
1741 ,, Thomas, Drogheda, esq.
1665 **Whitshed,** Esther, Dublin, widow
1736 ,, James, Dublin, esq.
1736 ,, Jane, Dublin, spinster
1728 ,, Mary, Dublin, widow (Large will)
1745 ,, Samuel Warter, brig.-genl.
1697 ,, Thomas, Dublin, esq.
1664 ,, William, Dublin, merchant
1695 **Whitsid,** William, Ballydonnaghie, co. Antrim, gent.
1778 **Whitsit,** William, Monaghan
1744 **Whitsitt,** John, Dreemore, co. Tyrone
1728 ,, Joseph, Grange, co. Tyrone, gent.
1786 ,, Robert, Glaslough, co. Mon., gent.
1788 ,, Thomas, Dublin, timber merchant
1763 ,, Wm., Kilcoran, co. Monaghan

1806 **Whitsitt,** William, Killcreen, co. Monaghan
[See WHITESIDE]
1671 **Whitson,** Richard, New Ross, merchant
1788 **Whitston,** Henry, Dublin, bookseller
1719 **Whitten,** Wm., Dohill, King's co., farmer
1597 **Whittey,** Balthazar, Waterford
1785 **Whitthorne,** Elizabeth, Milltownroad, co. Dublin, widow
1779 ,, James, Dublin, watchmaker
1743 **Whittingham,** ven. Charles, archdeacon of Dublin
1773 ,, George, Dublin, surgeon
1779 ,, rev. Michael, rector of Kilpatrick
1795 ,, Wm., Dublin city, barrister
1781 **Whittingronge,** Sarah, Capel-st., Dublin, widow
1686 **Whittle,** Francis, Dublin, mercht.
1735 ,, James, Lisburn, co. Antrim
1682 ,, John, clk., vicar of Dirrogh, dio.Ossory, and of Abbeyleix, dio. Leighlin
1788 **Whitton,** Edward, Crow-st., Dubl.
1730 ,, Wm., Moynaloy, co. Meath, farmer
1804 **Whitty,** rev. Edward, Rathvilly, co. Carlow, clk.
1763 ,, Nicholas, Castletown, co. Waterford, gent.
1804 **Whitwell,** Edward, city of Bath (Copy)
1600 ,, John, in the army at Loughfoyle [**I.** 92
1792 ,, Rose (Copy)
1680 **Whorley,** Joseph, Drogheda, alderman
1670 **Whorloe,** Bassinborne, Drogheda, merchant
1559 **Whyt,** Harrie, Drysshoge
1787 **Whyte,** Anne
1735 ,, Archibald, Dublin, gent.
1700 ,, Charles, Leixlip, co. Kildare, esq.
1782 ,, Charles, Dublin, esq.
1753 ,, Christopher, *alias* **Banan,** Glenavy, co. Antrim, gent.
1582 ,, Edward, Dublin, merchant [**I.** 57
1784 ,, Edward, Rathdrum, co. Wicklow, shopkeeper
1622 ,, Francis, Dublin, esq.
1779 ,, Francis, Redhills, co. Cavan, esq. (Large will)
1662 ,, James, Dublin, gent.
1708 ,, Jane,Dublin,spinster, daughter to Walter Whyte

1615 **Whyte**, John FitzGeffry, Clonmel, esq., and alderman
1622 ,, John, Duffryn, co. Down, esq.
1781 ,, Joseph,Whitefort, co. Wexford, esq.
1753 ,, Laurence, Dublin, gent.
1674 ,, Lorenzo, Limerick, burgess
1769 ,, Mark, Dublin, esq.
1792 ,, Mark, Loughrea, co. Galway, apothecary
1742 ,, Mary, wife to John W., Dublin, esq.
1783 ,, Nichls., Dolphin's-barn, tanner
1792 ,, Nicholas, deputy-governor of the Tower of London
1744 ,, Samuel, Dublin, esq.
1811 ,, Samuel,Grafton-street, Dublin, esq.
1752 ,, Sarah, Dublin, widow
1751 ,, Solomon, Banbridge, co.Down, esq.
1691 ,, Thomas, Redhill, co. Cavan, esq.
1741 ,, Thomas, Redhills, co. Cavan, esq.
1773 ,, Thomas, Kilcock, co. Kildare, esq.
1783 ,, Thomas, Queen-street, Dublin, esq.
1667 ,, Ursulla, lady, widow (Not proved)
1708 ,, Walter, Pilchardstown, co. Kildare, esq.
1645 ,, William, Dublin, esq.
1772 ,, William, Dublin, merchant
1783 ,, William, Pill-lane, Dublin, merchant
[See WHITE.]
1544 **Whytt**, Walter, Balbrodery
1691 **Wibrants**, Elizabeth, Dubl,, widow
[See WYBRANTS.]
1720 **Wibrow**, Richard, Punchestown, co. Kildare, esq.
1780 **Wickens**, Mary Ann, Dublin, widow
1772 **Wickham**, Ignatius, Barryncoyle, co. Wicklow, gent.
1794 ,, Susanna, Paulville, co. Carlow, widow
1754 **Wickins**,Thomas, Loughlooney, co. Longford, gent.
1807 **Wicklow**, rt. hon. Alice, countess dowager of
1789 ,, Ralph, lord viscount
1733 **Wicks**, Michael, London, gent. (Copy)
1686 **Wicksteed**, Richard, Dublin, merchant
1699 **Wicombe**, Christopher, Englishtown, co. Wicklow, gent.
1787 **Widdis**, Hannah,Clunamtick

1776 **Widdrington**,William
1719 **Widenham**, Henry,Court,co.Limk. esq.
1679 ,, John, Castletown, co. Cork esq.
1709 ,, John, Castletown Roche, co Cork, gent.
1744 ,, Mary, Court, co. Leitrim widow
1785 ,, Thomas, Millford, Lib. o Limerick, clk.
1797 ,, Walter, Limerick city, esq.
1765 ,, William, Newry, co. Down
[See WEIR.]
1800 **Wigelsworth**, Joseph, Militar Infirmary
1807 ,, Robert, Church-park, co. Ros common
1636 **Wiggett**, Richard, Dublin, alder man
1704 **Wiggin**, Samuel, Dublin, joiner
1803 **Wiggins**, Thomas, capt. of Kil mainham Hospital
1790 **Wight**, ven. Edward, D.D., arch deacon of Limerick
1759 ,, John, Cork, merchant
1795 ,, John, esq.
1771 ,, Pickmar, Limerick, woollen draper
1679 **Wightwicke**, Mary, London, wido (Copy)
1771 **Wigmore**, John, Lismore,co.Water ford, gent.
1813 ,, William, Tipperary town
1740 **Wigton**, rev. Hugh, Donegal, clk
1709 **Wilcocks**, Charles, Kilbride, co Carlow, farmer
1754 ,, Elizabeth, Dublin, widow
1693 ,, Isaachar, Dublin, merchant
1710 ,, John, Mountmellick, Queen' co., gent.
1785 ,, John, Dublin, banker
1807 ,, John, Dungannon, co. Tyrone
1785 ,, Joseph, formerly of Dubl., mc
1717 ,, Nathaniel, co. Kilkenny, gent
1711 ,, Robert,Palmerstown, co.Dubl gent. (Ex.)
1771 ,, Sarah, Timahoe, Queen's co widow
1713 ,, Thomas, Corleagh, co. Long ford, gent.
[See WILCOX, WILLCOCKS.]
1664 **Wilcox**, Joyce, Dublin, widow o Nicholas W., of Dublin, gt
1652 ,, Robert, Dublin, alderm. (Copy
1760 **Wild**,Elizabeth, Dublin, widow
1665 ,, George, bp. of **Derry**, q. v.
1656 ,, James, Dublin, tailor [V. 25
1766 ,, Michael, par. St. James, West minster, gent.

1679	**Williams**, Charles, Mundilly, co. Limerick, gent.	
1763	,, Charles, the elder, College-st., Dublin, gent.	
1763	,, Charles, West-Clandon, Surrey (Copy)	
1781	,, Chas., Cloberbrian, co. Kerry, gent.	
1724	,, Christopher, Dublin, gent.	
1717	,, David, Pepperstown, co. Louth, gent.	
1748	,, David, Dublin, cabinetmaker	
1697	,, Deborah, Dublin, widow (Ex.)	
1783	,, Dorcas, Dublin, widow	
1708	,, Edward, Dublin, gent.	
1749	,, Edward, captain in brigadier Richbell's regt.	
1737	,, Elizabeth, widow	
1794	,, Elizabeth, Gordon's-lane, co. Dublin, widow	
1658	,, Ellis, captain Nuns' troop, in gen. Ludlow's regt.	
1672	,, Griffith, bp. of **Ossory**, q. v.	
1739	,, Henry, Dublin, huckster	
1768	,, Henry, Ariodstown, co. Meath, gent.	
1787	,, James, Dame-street, Dublin, stationer	
1805	,, James, Gloucester, Dublin city	
1671	,, Jane, Stratford, Essex, widow (Copy)	
1606	,, John, London, mercer	
1631	,, John, Drumgar, co. Armagh, yeoman	
1659	,, John, Dromgore, co. Armagh, yeoman **[VIII.** 9	
1671	,, John, Clongell, co. Meath, gt.	
1704	,, John, Dublin, victualler	
1707	,, John, Talley, Carmarthenshire, esq. (Copy)	
1736	,, John, Ballygarrett, co. Waterford, gent.	
1744	,, John, Clare, co. Down	
1763	,, John, Dublin, gent.	
1771	,, John, Dublin, gent. (see 1763)	
1777	,, John, Dundalk, co. Louth, gt.	
1796	,, John, Middleton, co. Cork, apothecary	
1811	,, John, Dublin city, gent.	
1765	,, Joseph, Cole's-alley, Dublin, woolcomber	
1786	,, Joseph, Chapelizod, co. Dublin, carpenter	
1797	,, Joseph, gunner of the " Dorset" yacht	
1803	,, Joseph, Killmalone, par. Prebawne	
1807	,, Joseph, Cole-alley, Meath-st., Dublin	
1813	,, Letitia	

1786	**Williams**, Mathew, Ennis, co. Clar gent.	
1627	,, captain Michael, Waterford	
1664	,, Nathaniel, Dublin, gent.	
1713	,, Nathl., Ralory, co. Louth, gen	
1747	,, Prudence, Essex-st., Dub., wi	
1729	,, Richard, Dublin, gent.	
1771	,, Richard, Charleville, co. Cor gent.	
1772	,, Richard, Dower, co. Cork, gen	
1799	,, Richard, Dublin, gent.	
1806	,, Richard, Dublin city	
1794	,, Richardson, Dublin city, esq.	
1796	,, Rowley, Cool John, co. Meat gent.	
1795	,, Samuel, Cork, merchant	
1755	,, Sarah, *alias* **Swainson**, *alia* **Chester**, Limerick, widow	
1753	,, Simon, Edenderry, King's co woolcomber	
1783	,, Solomon, the elder, Wicklov glazier	
1689	,, Stephen, Dublin, cook	
1789	,, Theodore, Ballyronan, c Derry, gent.	
1657	,, Thos., Kinsale, brewer **[VI.** 7	
1660	,, Thomas, Clogh, co. Wexfor **[VIII.** 14	
1700	,, Thos., Lond., goldsmith (Cop	
1739	,, Thomas, Peake, co. Cork	
1772	,, Thomas, Cross-lane, Dubli coachmaker	
1795	,, Trevor, Drogheda, gent.	
1671	,, Wm., Stratford, Essex (Cop	
1690	,, William, Moughonstown, c Meath, gent.	
1691	,, William, New-st., near Dubli esq. (Large will)	
1699	,, Wm., Moyra, co. Down, gent	
1730	,, William, Dublin, gent.	
1743	,, William, Dublin, coachmake	
1783	,, William, Dublin, public notar	
1788	,, Wm., Abbey-st., Dub., glassm	
1788	,, William, Gt. Britain-st., Dub coachmaker	
1805	,, William, Coombe, co. Dubli silk manufacturer	
1792	**Williamson**, Benjamin, Greenfor co. Cork, esq.	
1804	,, Boyle, Grafton-st., Dub., print	
1803	,, Christopher, Grange, co. Wicl low, gent.	
1784	,, David, Lisgillan, co. Mona ghan, linen draper	
1696	,, Edward, Edenduffcarrick, c Antrim, gent.	
1700	,, George, Belfast, co. Antrir mariner	
1793	,, George, Mullaghmore, c Meath, gent.	

735 **Williamson,** John, Dublin, mercht.
741 ,, John, Wexford, esq.
764 ,, John, Mullaghmore, co. Meath, farmer
765 ,, John, Newry, co Down, mrcht.
745 ,, Joseph, Mt. Alexander, co. Down, gent.
744 ,, Mary, Dublin widow
800 ,, Mary, Dublin, spinster
799 ,, Mathew, Dublin, printer
798 ,, Shaw, Freemanstown, co. Antrim, gent.
773 ,, Simon, Dublin, gent.
1636 ,, Thomas, Warrington, Lancashire, chapman.   [**IV.** 185
1732 ,, Thos., Rockestown, co. Wicklow, farmer
1741 ,, Thomas, Dublin, goldsmith
1794 ,, Thos., Downpatrick, co. Down, merchant
1708 ,, Wm., Athlone, co. Rosc., merct.
1722 ,, ven. Wm., archdeacon of Glendalough
1731 ,, Wm., Ringsend, Dub., mariner
1737 ,, rev. Williams, Dublin, clk.
1782 ,, Wm., Dublin, goldsmith
1785 ,, William, Camden-st., Dublin
1627 **Willimott,** Edwd., Lond., merchant
1721 **Willington,** Charles, Ballymoney, King's co.
1760 ,, Charles, Dublin, gent.
1804 ,, Charles, Eccles-st., co. Dublin
1769 ,, Elizabeth, Lisnecody, co. Galway ; at Cree, King's co.
1731 ,, James, Killaskehan, co. Tip., gent.
1776 ,, James, Castle W., co. Tip., esq.
1659 ,, John, Killeen, Queen's co., gent.   [**VII.** 160
1767 ,, John, Killaskehan, co. Tipperary, esq.
1729 ,, King, Tentower, Queen's co.
1758 ,, Mary, Ballymoney, King's co., widow
1730 ,, Palliser, Tentower, Queen's co., esq.
1790 ,, Priscilla, Waterford, spinster
1752 ,, Thos., Ballymoney, King's co.
1724 ,, Williamite, Ballymoney, King's co., gent.
1805 **Willins,** Thomas, Colp, co. Meath, gent.
1772 **Willis,** Bernard Payn, Francis-st., Dublin, flax-dresser
1774 ,, Hannah, New-row, Dubl., wid.
1782 ,, John
1807 ,, Mary, Inns-quay, Dublin
1697 ,, Thos., Liverpool, Lancs., gent.
    [See WYLLIS.]

1809 **Willison,** Catherine, Cork city, wid.
1752 ,, Samuel
    [See WILSON.]
1811 **Willman,** George, Barrack-st., Dublin, publican
1657 **Willmott,** Charles, lord viscount, Athlone   [**V.** 70
1755 **Willock,** James, Munnyslan, co. Down, gent.
1720 ,, William, Knockbridge, co. Armagh, gent.
1733 ,, William, Dublin, gent.
1754 ,, William, Athy, co. Kildare
1797 **Willoe,** Christopher, Tralee, co. Kerry, esq.
1710 ,, Richard, Bandon-bridge, co. Cork, esq.
1801 ,, Samuel, late captain in 8th regiment of foot
1811 ,, Thos., Charlotte-st., Dub., esq.
1688 **Willoughby,** Andrew, Carrickfergus, alderman
1694 ,, Charles, Dublin, M.D.
1664 ,, sir Francis, Dublin, knt. (Co.)
1678 ,, Francis, Dublin, esq.
1699 ,, Nicholas, Carrow, co. Fermanagh, esq.   [**XII.** 99
1801 ,, Sarah
1810 ,, Wm., capt. of 50th regt. of foot
1766 ,, Wyndham, Dublin, druggist
1749 **Wills,** Caspar, Willsgrove, co. Roscommon, esq.
1778 ,, Godfrey, Dublin, esq.
1710 ,, Hannah, Annagh, co. Cork, widow
1731 ,, James, Dublin, gent.
1750 ,, Martha, Dublin, widow
1812 ,, Moses, Barrack-st., Dublin
1783 ,, Robt., Annalee, co. Cavan, esq.
1792 ,, Sarah, Dublin, widow
1741 ,, Thomas, Cork, gent.
1775 ,, Thomas, Dublin, gent.
1803 **Willson,** Benjamin, Skinner's-row, Dublin, silversmith
1811 ,, David, Ballywillan, co. L.derry
1755 ,, Elizabeth, par. St. Paul, Covent Garden (Copy)
1748 ,, John, mariner on board the "Lyme" man-of-war
    [See WILSON.]
1774 **Wilme,** William, Dublin, jeweller
1655 **Wilmer,** capt. Nathl., Cashel [**V.** 19
1787 **Wilmot,** John, Dublin city, esq. (Large)
    [See VILMOT.]
1678 **Wilmott,** William, Dublin, gent.
1811 **Wilsan,** Abraham, Scarthany, co. Cork, esq.
1770 **Wilson,** Ambrose, Cahirconlish, co. Limerick, esq.

1725 **Wilson**, Andrew, Piersefield, co. Westmeath, esq.
1760 ,, Ann, Strabane, co. Tyrone, widow (See 1769)
1739 ,, Anne, Cabra-lane, Dublin, wid.
1769 ,, Anne, Strabane, co. Tyrone, widow
1783 ,, Anne, Dublin, widow
1800 ,, Anne, Dublin, spinster
1768 ,, Benjamin, Mount W., King's co., gent.
1709 ,, Catherine, Mullingar, co. Westmeath, widow
1759 ,, Christian, Scar, co. Wexford, gent.
1735 ,, David, Dublin, gent.
1766 ,, David, lieut. in 56th regt. foot (Copy)
1800 ,, David, Lisburn
1737 ,, Edward, Dublin, victualler
1690 ,, Elizabeth, Chester, widow
1734 ,, Elizabeth, Dublin, tobacconist
1741 ,, Elizabeth, Cootehill, co. Cavan, widow
1800 ,, Elizabeth, Market Hill, co. Armagh, widow
1805 ,, Elizabeth
1791 ,, Ellinor, Derry, widow
1735 ,, Ezekiel Davys, Carrickfergus, esq.
1762 ,, Fleming, Donaghmoyne, co. Tyrone
1788 ,, Frances, widow
1743 ,, rev. Francis, D.D.
1746 ,, George, Dublin, clothier
1749 ,, George, Coolmine, co. Dublin, gent.
1753 ,, George, Dublin, druggist
1755 ,, George, Bandon, clk.
1794 ,, Geo., Stephen's-green, Dublin, gent.
1804 ,, George, Wilson's-place, co. Dublin city, slater
1800 ,, Grace, Dublin, widow
1813 ,, Hannah, formerly of co. Kildare, late of Taplow
1790 ,, Henry, Sixmilebridge, co. Clare, gent.
1773 ,, Hill, Purdisburn, co. Down, esq.
1788 ,, Hill, Dublin, gent.
1805 ,, Hugh, Collinstown, co. Dublin, barrister-at-law
1753 ,, Jacob, Dublin, tallow chandler
1689 ,, James, Calliaghstown, co. Dublin, farmer
1732 ,, James, Augher, co. Tyrone, gent.
1769 ,, James, New-row, co. Dublin, tanner

1778 **Wilson**, James, Broomhedge, co. Dublin, gent.
1780 ,, Jas., Parsonstown, co. Meath esq.
1752 ,, Jane, Man of War, co. Dublin innkeeper
1753 ,, Jane, Dublin, widow
1759 ,, Jane, Dublin, widow
1786 ,, Jane, Dublin
1636 ,, sir John, Wilson's Fort, co Donegal, knt. and bart.
1672 ,, John, Doublemills, sub. of Dub
1696 ,, John Clark, Forge of Inishrush co. Derry, gent.
1710 ,, John, Dublin, merchant tailor
1714 ,, John, Scar, co. Wexford, gent.
1725 ,, John, Glanmore, co. Longford clk.
1727 ,, John, Dublin, gent.
1728 ,, John, Killballybree, co. Westmeath, esq.
1736 ,, John, Strabane, co. Tyrone, merchant
1741 ,, John, Crookstown, co. Meath, farmer
1743 ,, rev. John, rector of Kilcarr
1749 ,, John, Dublin, butcher
1756 ,, John, Bristol, mariner
1765 ,, John, Carrick, co. Leitrim
1767 ,, John, Larne, co. Antrim, merchant
1771 ,, John, Liskittle, co. Tyrone, gent.
1771 ,, John, Newtown Ards, co. Down
1771 ,, John, Roske, co. Meath, gent.
1777 ,, John, Ballitore, co. Kildare
1778 ,, John, Frankford, King's co.
1794 ,, John
1794 ,, John, Blue Coat Hospital, Dublin, esq.
1803 ,, John, Mary-street, Dublin, hotel keeper
1807 ,, John, Abbey-street, Dublin
1721 ,, Jonathan, Ardrane, co. Galway, clk.
1745 ,, Jonathan, Dublin, gent.
1743 ,, Joseph, Lurgan, co. Armagh, tinman
1746 ,, Joseph, student in Glasgow University
1769 ,, Joseph, Lurgan, co. Armagh, gent.
1776 ,, Joseph, Feddencaile, co Wicklow, farmer
1794 ,, Joseph, Sixmilebridge, co. Clare, gent.
1804 ,, Joseph, Swift's-row, Dublin, printer
1809 ,, Joseph, Dublin city, merchant
1688 ,, Joshua, Dublin, esq. (Ex.)

1800 **Wingfield**, hon. Harriot, Dublin, spinster
1677 ,, Lewis, Scurmore, co. Sligo,esq. (Ex.)
       [See WYNGFELDE.]
1808 **Wingrove**, John, Rathdrum, shop keeper
1789 **Winn**, Anne, Summerhill, co. Dubl.
1703 ,, James, Derryvillane, co. Cork
1766 **Winnett**, Clement, Dungannon, co. Tyrone, gent.
1756 ,, John, Dublin, woollendraper (Unproved)
1728 **Winnington**, Jane, Dublin, widow
1720 **Winsloe**, Thomas, Parsonstown, King's co., merchant
1769 **Winslow**, Thomas, Drogheda, carpenter (Not proved)
1786 **Winstanley**, Ellinor, widow of John W.,Milltown-road, co. Dubl.
1786 ,, George, Dublin, esq.
1801 ,, George Frederick, Philipsburgh, co. Dublin, esq.
1676 ,, John, Dublin, gent.
1786 ,, John, Milltown-road, co. Dubl.
1777 ,, Judith, *alias* **Tisdall**, Dublin
1699 ,, Richard, Dublin, gent.
1696 **Winstanly**, John, Liverpool, gent., att.-at-law (Ex.; Copy)
1796 **Winston**, Henry, Ballyneil, co. Waterford, gent.
1790 **Winter**, Arthur, Dublin, surgeon
1803 ,, Dorcas, Dublin, widow
1684 ,, Ebenezer, gent., an officer in the army
1703 ,, Elizabeth, Borriskean, co. Tipperary, widow
1755 ,, Elizabeth, Dublin, widow
1785 ,, Eliza., Mountmellick, Queen's co., widow [esq.
1745 ,, Francis, Griffinrath,co.Kildare,
1766 ,, Paul, Dublin
1740 ,, Robert, Dublin, clothier
1669 ,, Samuel, D.D. (Copy)
1692 ,, Samuel, Dublin, esq.
1811 ,, Samuel, Augher Pallis, co. Meath, esq.
1737 ,, v. rev. Sankey, dean of Kildare
1673 ,, William, London (Copy)
1746 ,, William
1785 **Winterbottom**, Benjamin, Rathmines, co. Dublin, gent.
1638 ,, Edmund, Dublin, weaver
       [IV. 339
1721 **Winterburne**, Elizabeth, *alias* **Barrett**, Dublin, widow
1730 **Winthrop**, Benjamin, Cork, merht.
1758 **Winthropp**, Stephen, London (Co.)
1623 **Winthroppe**, John, Oughadown, co. Cork, gent. (Copy)

1633 **Wirrall**, Ellenor, *alias* **Tyrrell**, widow
1745 **Wisdom**, Jeremiah, Longford, gent.
1773 **Wise**, Ellenor, Cork, widow
1803 ,, Hy., Coldicot par., Monmouthshire (Large will; copy)
1795 ,, John, Charlestown, King's co., gent.
1695 **Wiseman**, Capel, bp. of **Dromore**, q.v.
1776 ,, James, Skin Lordship, Newry, co. Down
1804 ,, Joseph, Carrigadrohid, co. Cork, shopkeeper
1709 ,, Joshua, par. St. Martin, Middlesex, gent.
1683 ,, Mary, *alias* **Venables**, widow of Edwd. W., Wexford, esq.
1704 **Witherelt**, Wm., Castletown, Clonkeen, King's co., gent.
1718 **Witherington**, John, esq., one of His Majesty's Sergeants-at-law
       [See WETHERINGTON.]
1798 **Withers**, Elizab., Cork city, spinster
1809 ,, Humphrey,Belturbet,co.Cavan, esq.
1783 ,, James, Southwark, Newry, co. Armagh
1669 ,, John, Agherskrea, co. Meath, esq.
1773 ,, John, Southwark, co. Armagh, gent.
       [See WYTHERS.]
1702 **Withington**, John, Dublin, ironmonger
1753 **Withrington**, Margaret, Lancaster, formerly of Dublin (Large will)
1675 **Wittar**, Daniel, bp. of **Killaloe**, q.v.
1758 **Witten**, Ferdinando, Dublin, victualler
1674 ,, Wm., Dublin, brewer
1731 **Wittewrong**, sir John, Stanton, Bucks., bart. (Copy)
1783 **Woddel**, Henry, Carlow
1672 **Woders**, James, Drogheda, chapman traveller
1743 **Wogan**, John, Rathcoffy, co. Kildare, esq.
1811 ,, John, North Earl-street, Dubl., merchant
1770 ,, Nicholas, Rathcoffy
1614 ,, Thomas, the Newhall, co. Kildare, gent.
1813 **Wolfe**, Bridget, Dunshaughlin, co. Meath
1810 ,, Catherine, Loughrea, co. Galway, widow
1750 ,, Dorothy, Dublin, widow

1790 **Wolfe**, Elizabeth, Dublin, spinster
1799 ,, Matthew, Dublin
1761 ,, John, Forenaughts, co. Kildare, esq.
1786 ,, John, Bishopsland, co. Dublin
1748 ,, Levi, Dublin, jeweller
1732 ,, Richard, Barronrath, co. Kildare, gent.
1779 ,, Richard, Barronrath, co. Kildare, gent.
1786 ,, Richard, Athy, co. Kildare
1799 ,, Theobald, Blackhall, co. Kildare, esq.
1784 ,, Theobald, Dublin, esq.
1787 ,, Thomas, Blackhall,co. Kildare, esq.
1795 ,, Thomas, Dunshaughlin, co. Meath
1771 ,, major Walter
1741 ,, Wm., Dublin, merchant
1810 ,, William S., Portarlington, co. Westmeath
1770 ,, Williams, a lieut. in the Royal Navy
[See WOOLFE, WOULFE.]
1757 **Wolfenden**, John, Dunmurry, co. Antrim, gent.
1743 ,, Richard, Lambeg, co. Down, linen draper
1777 ,, Richard, Lambeg, co. Down, merchant
1668 **Wolferston**, James, Stillorgan, co. Dublin, esq.
1686 ,, James, Stillorgan, co. Dublin, esq. (Copy)
1769 ,, John, Cooldross, co. Wicklow, gent.
1630 ,, Robert, Rathbranne, co. Wicklow, gent.
1689 **Wolley**, Edward, bp. of **Clonfert**, q.v.
1778 **Wolseley**, Alice, widow of sir Richd. W., bart.
1811 ,, Clement, Clare-st., Dublin, esq.
1812 ,, Clement, Weston, co. Meath, esq.
1789 ,, dame Letitia, wid. of sir Richd. W., bart.
1697 ,, brigadier Wm., Dublin
1800 ,, Wm., rector of Tullycorbet, co. Monaghan
1723 **Wolsely**, Richard, Mount Arran, co. Carlow, esq.
1781 ,, sir Richard, Mount W., co. Carlow, bart.
1702 **Wolsesley**, col. Robert, Camolin, co. Wexford
[See WOOLSEY.]
1780 **Wolsey**, rev. Thomas, Torkhill Glebe, co. Armagh

1796 **Wolverston**, Sarah, Dublin, widow
1697 **Wood**, Alex., Caledon, co. Tyrone, gent.
1756 ,, Arthur, Markethill,co. Armagh, gent.
1784 ,, Attiwell, Dublin, esq.
1741 ,, Elizbth., Rossmead, co. Westmeath, widow
1771 ,, Gerald, Winetavern-st., Dubl., shoemaker
1800 ,, Gore,Donnybrook,co.Dub.,clk.
1793 ,, Grace,Dunshaughlin,co.Meath
1795 ,, Hannah, Cork, spinster
1792 ,, Isaac, Waterford, merchant
1794 ,, Isaac, Clonmel, co. Tip., merct.
1769 ,, Isabella, Dublin, spinster
1738 ,, sir James, Marlborough-street, St. James', bart.
1781 ,, James, the elder, Oldrock
1799 ,, Jas., Leekfield, co. Sligo, esq.
1711 ,, John, Garclony,co. Meath,gent.
1730 ,, John, Rosmead, co. Westmeath, esq.
1755 ,, John, Dublin
1761 ,, John,Dunshaughlin,co. Meath, gent.
1783 ,, John, Fairy Mount, co. Roscn.
1812 ,, Jonathan, Banagher town
1792 ,, Josiah, Clonmel, co. Tipperary
1780 ,, Margaret, Drogheda, grocer
1719 ,, Mary, Dublin, widow
1701 ,, Nathaniel, M.D.
1674 ,, Richard, Dublin, merchant
1773 ,, Richard, Grange, co. Sligo, esq.
1780 ,, Richard, Dublin, M.D.
1808 ,, Richd., Mt. Merrion, co. Dub., gent.
1778 ,, Robert, par. St. George, Hanover-sq., Middlesex (Copy)
1785 ,, Robert (Copy)
1648 ,, Rowland, Dublin, gent.
1748 ,, Russell, Cork, gent.
1765 ,, Russell, ensign in gen. Whitmore's regiment
1774 ,, Sarah, commonly called S. **Clinch**, Dunshaughlin, co. Meath
1741 ,, Thomas, Drogheda, esq.
1763 ,, Thos., Cork Hill, co.Sligo,gent.
1795 ,, Thomas, Cork city, gent.
1673 ,, Wm., Tallylyn, Anglesey, esq. (Copy)
1615 **Woodall**, Jasper, Suckley, Worcestershire
[See WOODDALL.]
1768 **Woodburn**, William, Ballymoney, co. Wicklow, farmer
1799 **Woodbyrne**, John, Bolecreen, co. Wexford, farmer

1810 **Woodcock**, Elboro', Lincoln's Inn, London, esq. (Copy)
1656   ,, John, Kilkeregan, co. Kilkenny, esq.   [**V.** 308
1685   ,, John, Dublin, clk.
1670   ,, Margerie, Kilcragan, co. Kilkenny, wid. of John W., esq.
1803   ,, Samuel, Clonmore, co. Wex. ford, farmer
1671 **Wooddall**, Wm., Dublin, gent.
       [See WOODALL.]
1614 **Woodes**, Richard, Dublin, glazier
       [See WOODS.]
1666 **Woodfall**, Henry, Dublin, tailor
1671 **Woodford**, Cave, Dublin, esq.
1656 **Woodhead**, sergeant Thos. [**V.** 313
1788 **Woodhouse**, John, Dublin, gent.
1778 **Woodifield**, Robert, Beaufort B., Midsex., wine merct. (Copy)
1736 **Woodley**, Francis, Dublin, gent.
1798   ,, Francis, Cork city, esq.
1809   ,, Joseph, Cork city, esq.
1690 **Woodlock**, Clement, Watfd., gent.
1750 **Woodman**, Jonah, Dunlavin, cooper
1801   ,, Noble, Bennetstown, co. Wexf.
1812 **Woodmass**, Anne, Dub. city, widow
1793 **Woodney**, Hugh, Newry, co. Down, merchant
1650 **Woodrofe**, Ann, Greenwich, Kent, widow (Copy)
1740 **Woodroffe**, Sarah, Cork, widow
1786 **Woodroofe**, Richard, Gorey, co. Wexford, gent.
1774 **Woods**, Andrew, Ardcame, co. Tyrone, gent.
1773   ,, Archibald, Trinsillagh, co.Don.
1754   ,, David, Ballydorn, co. Down
1803   ,, Edmond, Cork, ironmonger
1769   ,, George, Carrickmacross, co. Monaghan, miller
1781   ,, George, Dublin, esq.
1769   ,, Henry, Trinsillagh, co. Donegal, gent.
1676   ,, James, Limerick, gent.
1690   ,, John, Woodkey, Dub., mercht.
1751   ,, John, Lisnisk, co. Mon., gent.
1770   ,, John, Dublin
1792 ,; Michael, Dublin, gent.
1805   ,, Michael, Cork city, esq.
1774   ,, Robert, Ballyboughlane, Dubl., gardener
1659   ,, Thomas, Kilkenny, butcher
1678   ,, Thomas, Dublin, merchant
1680   ,, Thomas, Tullagh, co. Carlow, gent.
1746   ,, Thos., Kilmanog, co. Kildare
1756   ,, Thomas, Garbally, King's co., farmer
1702   ,, William, Ringsend, co. Dubl. gent. (Ex.)

1808 **Woods**, rev. Wm. Henry, Ardagh, co. Meath
       [See WOODES.]
1729 **Woodside**, David, Dublin, joiner
1767   ,, David, Drogheda
1781   ,, Hannah, *alias* **Knight**, Drogheda, widow
1760   ,, Hugh, Castletown, Isle of Man, formerly of Dublin
1743   ,, James, Dublin, mathematical instrument maker
1802   ,, Jas., Darnaskallen, co. L.derry
1701   ,, John, Dublin, mariner (A will of later date proved)
1702   ,, John, Dublin, ironmonger
1770   ,, Margaret, Drogheda, widow
1793 **Woodward**, rev. Charles, D.D.
1797   ,, Henry, Kilmackanlow,co.Limk,
1746   ,, John, Dublin, esq.
1747   ,, Joseph, Coghilstown, co.Meath
1752   ,, Margaret, Dublin, widow
1746   ,, Mary, Dublin, widow
1794   ,, Richard, bp. of **Cloyne**, q.v.
1768   ,, Saml., Newport, co. Dub.,gent.
1795   ,, Susanna, Dublin, widow
1812   ,, Thos., Russell-place,Dub.,esq.
1741   ,, Wm., Claghprior, co. Tip., esq.
1766 **Woodworth**, Hezekiah, Dublin
1695   ,, Michael, Kilmackenerlagh, co. Limerick, gent.
1752   ,, William, Dublin, formerly of co. Wicklow
1697 **Woolastown**, Frances, Kingston, Surrey, spinster (Ex.)
1627 **Wooldridge**, John, Crook, co. Waterford, gent.   [**II.** 54
1651 **Wooley**, John, Pimlico, near Dub., clothier
1650   ,, Joseph,Grangegorman,yeoman
1657 **Woolley**, Adam, London, merchant
       [**VI.** 212
1741   ,, Mary, par. St. Martin, Middlesex, widow (Copy)
1796   ,, Mary, spinster
1702 **Woolfe**, Anne, par. St. Giles, Middlesex, widow (Copy)
1700   ,, John, par. St. Giles', Middlesex, gent.
       [See WOLFE.]
1807 **Wooloughan**, Peter, Dublin, coal factor
1799 **Woolridge**, Hugh
1805   ,, Thos., Dubl., tallow chandler
1773 **Wools**, Stephen, Pimlico, Dublin, weaver
1740 **Woolsey**, Benjamin, Portadown, co. Armagh, gent.
1752   ,, John, Priorland, co.Louth,gent.
1751   ,, Thos., Edenderry, co. Armagh
       [See WOLSELEY.]

1662 **Wren**, Thomas, Galmoylestown, co. Meath, esq.
1793 ,, Thos., Litter, co. Kerry, esq.
1787 **Wrey**, sir Bourchier, Tawstock, Devon., bart. (Copy)
1790 **Wright**, Anne, *alias* **Classon**
1664 ,, Henry, Dublin, gent.
1749 ,, ven. Henry, archd. of Killmacduagh
1766 ,, capt.Henry,Ballybough Bridge, co. Dublin
1701 ,, Jas., Gola, co. Monaghan, gt.
1772 ,, James, Cartrons, esq.
1793 ,, James, Mary's Abbey, Dublin, cabinet maker
1775 ,, Jane, Cooke-street, Dubl., wid.
1801 ,, Jane, Dublin, widow
1686 ,, John, Cork, alderman
1691 ,, John, waggoner in the train of artillery at Limerick
1733 ,, John, Dublin, tailor
1785 ,, John
1789 ,, John, Dorset-street, Dublin, gent.
1810 ,, John, Ballinclea, co. Wexford
1750 ,, Joseph, Muff, co. Londonderry, gent.
1761 ,, Joseph, Gola, esq.
1796 ,, Joseph, Dublin, esq.
1669 ,, Joshua, clk., St. Johnstown, co. Longford
1745 ,, Margaret, Pill-lane, Dublin, gentlewoman (not proved)
1788 ,, Mary, Clontarf, co. Dublin, wid.
1743 ,, Noble, Dublin, carpenter
1788 ,, Richard, Belfast, hatter
1806 ,, Richard, Cork city, esq.
1735 ,, Samuel, Mavullen, co. Derry, gent.
1776 ,, Thomas
1786 ,, Thos., Emyvale, co.Monaghan, merchant
1786 ,, Thos., Newry, co. Down, hatter
1789 ,, Thos., Cole-alley, Dublin, gt.
1733 ,, Wm., Dublin, gent.
1768 ,, Wm., Dunnaghclony par., co. Down
1771 ,, Wm., Clontarf, co. Dubl., esq. (not proved)
1778 ,, Wm., Dorset-street, Dublin
1788 **Wrightson**, Aldborough, Dundalk, co. Louth, merchant
1803 ,, Anne, Dublin, widow
1761 ,, Cadwallader, Dublin, gent.
1790 ,, Elizabeth, Dublin, widow
1783 ,, George, Dublin, alderman
1703 ,, John, Dublin, esq.
1779 ,, lieut.-col. John, Chelsea, Middlesex
1732 ,, Mathew, Dublin, gent.

1788 **Wrixon**, Edwd., Gurtreenbatra, co. Cork, gent.
1714 ,, Henry, Ballygibbon, co. Cork, gent.
1732 ,, Henry, Glinfield, co. Cork, esq.
1778 ,, Henry, Blossomfort, co. Cork, gent.
1794 ,, Henry, Assolas, co. Cork, esq.
1744 ,, John, Blossomfort, co. Cork, gt.
1740 ,, Nicholas, Ballygibbon,co.Cork, gent.
1750 ,, Robert, Kilroe, co. Cork
1753 ,, Robert, Woodpark, co. Cork, gent.
1768 ,, Robert, Cork, esq.
1659 **Wrotham**, Cornet Symon [**VII.** 189
1673 **Wybrants** Daniel, senior, Dublin, alderman [**XIV.** 130
1740 ,, Daniel, Dublin, gent.
1808 ,, James, George's-quay, Dublin, vintner
1785 ,, Margaret, widow
1639 ,, Peter, Dublin, merchant
1680 ,, Peter Fitz Daniel, Dublin,gent.
1755 ,, Peter, rector of Ballymacky, co. Tipperary
1755 ,, Richard, Dublin, clk.
1740 ,, Robert, Dublin, gent.
1744 ,, Robert, Dublin, gent.
1810 ,, Stephen, Granby-row, Dublin, esq.
[See WIBRANTS.]
1667 **Wycomb**, Maud, *alias* **Cullen**, wid.
1784 **Wye**, Francis, Castlebellingham, co. Louth
1737 **Wyer**, Cornelius, Hallohoyse. co. Kildare, gent.
1747 ,, David, Crow-street, Dublin (unproved)
1757 ,, David, Dublin, gent.
1766 ,, Elizabeth, Dublin, spinster, daughter of David W., gent. (not proved)
1747 ,, Jane, widow of Cornelius W., Hallohoyse, co. Kildare (unproved)
1713 ,, Michael, Ballybrin, co. Kildare, gent.
[See WEIR.]
1711 **Wylde**, Anthony, Belfast, mariner
[See WILDE.]
1738 **Wylie**, John, Belfast, merchant
[See WYLY.]
1600 **Wyllis**, George, lieut. to sir Francis Stafford
[See WILLIS.]
1798 **Wyly**, Alexander, Gillstown, co. Kildare
1802 ,, Ephraim,Moate,co.Westmeath
1787 ,, Joseph

1782 **Wyly**, Samuel, Millerstown, co. Kildare, dyer
1794 ,, Sarah, Thomastown, co. Kildare
1764 ,, Robt., Thomastown, co.Kildare
1803 ,, Robert, Timahoe, co. Kildare
1718 ,, William, par. Killoan, co. Londonderry
1766 ,, William, Killeagh, co. Kildare, gent.
[See WILY, WYLIE.]
1786 **Wynch**, Alexander, Upper Harley-street, Middlesex, esq. (Copy)
1670 **Wynde**, Darby, Ardagh, co. Longford, gent.
1587 **Wyngefelde**, James, par St. Giles, London, esq. [I. 65
[See WINGFIELD.]
1752 **Wynn**, William, Drumnakerran, co. Armagh, gent.
[See M'GHEE.]
1801 **Wynne**, Ann, Portarlington, Queen's co., widow
1780 ,, Catherine, Dublin, widow
1806 ,, Charles, co. of Drogheda town
1779 ,, Cornelius, Dublin, stationer
1742 ,, David, Ruthin, Denbighshire, dyer (Copy)
1810 ,, Deborah, Portobello, co. Dubl., widow
1781 ,, Elizabeth, widow of the late col. John Wynne
1808 ,, Elizabeth, wife to the rev. Thomas Wynne
1784 ,, Folliott, Cregg, co. Sligo
1789 ,, George, Rathmines-road, co. Dublin, merchant
1711 ,, Henry, London, citizen and clockmaker (Copy)
1715 ,, Hugh, A.M., rector of Aberfraw, Anglesey (Copy)
1749 ,, James, Dublin, esq.
1668 ,, John, Killaltnagh, co. Westmeath
1758 ,, John, Tansifield, co. Rosc.
1762 ,, John, D.D., chanter of St. Patrick's, Dublin
1781 ,, rev. John, Kilkenny West, co. Westmeath
1782 ,, rev. John, D.D.
1796 ,, Mary, *alias* **Carroll**, Dublin, widow
1738 ,, Maurice, Carnarvon, esq. (Copy) [esq.
1671 ,, Owen, Lurganboy, co. Leitrim,
1737 ,, Owen, Hazelwood, co. Sligo, lieut.-genl.
1756 ,, Owen, Hazelwood, co. Sligo, esq.

1765 **Wynne**, Owen, Sligo, gent.
1790 ,, rt. hon. Owen, Hazelwood, co. Sligo
1697 ,, Robert, Dublin, esq.
1760 ,, Thomas, Dundalk, co. Louth, innkeeper
[See WINN.]
1711 **Wyse**, Francis, Ballymabin, co. Waterford, esq.
1799 ,, Francis, St. John's, Waterford
1595 ,, James, Waterford, esq.
1706 ,, John, Ballinacourty, co.Waterford, merchant
1749 ,, Margaret, Waterford, widow
1696 ,, Thomas, Ballinacourty, co. Waterford, esq. (Ex.)
1775 ,, Thos., St. John's, near Waterford, esq.
[See WISE.]
1797 **Wyth**, William, Carrickmines, co. Dublin, farmer
1679 **Wythers**, Nicholas, Dublin, distiller (Ex.)
[See WITHERS.]

——Y——

1671 **Yard**, James, Limerick, merchant
1802 **Yarde**, Robert, Kinsale, co. Cork, gent.
1681 **Yardley**, Margaret, late of Lancaster, now of New Ross, widow
1730 ,, Richard, Monasterevan, co. Kildare, gent.
1677 **Yarner**, sir Abraham, knt., mus. mas. genl. of forces in Ireland
1693 ,, Abraham, Dublin, esq., mus. master genl. of the forces (Copy)
1703 ,, Abraham, Dublin, esq.
1733 ,, Catherine, Dublin, spinster
1698 ,, Francis, Dublin, gent.
1753 ,, Jane, Church-street, Dublin, widow
1797 **Yates**, Mary, Froickinham, Middlesex
[See YEATES.]
1682 **Yeaden**, John, Boyle Abbey, Roscommon, esq. (Large Will, Copy)
1691 ,, John, Boyle Abbey, co. Roscommon, esq. (Ex.)
1757 **Yeamans**, Francis, Limerick, merchant
1759 ,, John, Cork, esq.
1780 ,, Mary, Rathkeale, co. Limerick, widow

1800 **Young**, William, Newry, co. Down, merchant
1809 ,, William, Manor-street, Dublin, gent.
[See YONGE.]
1643 **Younge**, Andrew, Athy, dyer
1714 ,, James, Dublin, gent.
1618 ,, Maude, *alias* **Manwarring**, Dublin, widow
1686 ,, Richard, Dublin, gent.
1721 ,, Simon, Ballyteige, co. Wexford, gent.
1763 ,, Simon, Brookfield, co. Tipperary, gent.

1768 **Younghusband**, Elizabeth, *alias* **Dawson**, wife to Israel Y., co. Armagh, esq.
1796 ,, Joseph, Whitehaven, Cumberland, mariner (Copy)
1802 **Yielding**, Jane, Dublin, spinster
1798 ,, John Massy, Ballyphillip co. Limerick, gent.
1771 ,, Richard, Rathkeale, co. Limk.
1804 ,, Richard, Cloghers, co. Kerry, esq.
1805 ,, Theophilus, Cahireina, co. Kerry, esq.
1708 **Ysarn**, John, Clunegown, King's co., esq.

INDEX TO ALLIANCES AND ALIASES.

THE HAWKINS COLLECTION OF WILLS,
1771–1852.

THE following list of Wills is reprinted, as a fitting adjunct to the Prerogative Wills, from the Fourteenth Report of the Deputy Keeper of the Public Record Office of Ireland. Mr. Mills, in his introductory remarks to this Index, informs us that they were marked "Private Wills, taken from Mr. Hawkins' private office after his death." Mr. Hawkins was Deputy Registrar of the Prerogative Court.

In this collection, five wills bear evidence of having been proved, although not entered in the Grant Books. Twelve appear to have been ready to be proved in the Consistorial Court. Two were registered in the Registry of Deeds Office. Four have been ascertained to be duplicates of duly proved wills ; and it is not improbable that other similar cases may be found on a more extended search.

It is difficult to explain how these wills came to remain in Mr. Hawkins' office, but Mr. Mills' conjecture that it was due to the lodgment fees not having been paid, would appear to be correct, and applicable to most cases.

1845 **Adams**, John, Newcastle, co. Limk.
1799 **Austin**, John, Knockrobbin, co. Wexford. (Apparently lodged 1802)

1828 **Baker**, Margaret Morres, late of Ballymoreen, co. Tipperary, now of Dublin city. (Not dated. Intestate Administration was granted in that year)
1844 **Blake**, Giles Eyre, of Eyrecourt, co. Galway
1832 **Bradshaw**, Richard, Ayle
1798 ,, Thomas, Correnshego, co. Monaghan. (Lodged 1807)
1821 **Brewster**, Anne, co. Wicklow
1826 **Bryan**, Thomas, Naas, co. Kildare
1827 **Burgess**, Richard, Tullow, co. Carlow, gent.
1778 **Bushell**, Edward, Ballyvaughan, co. Tipperary
1827 **Butler**, Pierce, formerly of Barrack-street, now of Bridgefoot-street
1825 **Byrne**, Murtagh, Irishtown, co. of Dublin city

1802 **Coghlan**, Francis, Whitefriar-street, Dublin, oilcloth manufacturer
1826 **Craven**, Nathaniel. (Codicil to the Will of, accompanied with a statement of affairs of)
1819 **Crawford**, John, Kilkenny
1803 **Curley**, Patrick, Galway, merchant

1823 **Darby**, Benjamin, Ballynacarrick, co. Wicklow
1800 **D'Arcy**, John, Wardenstown, co. Westmeath, esq.

1800 **Dignan**, Christopher, Inan, co. Meath, farmer. (Lodged 1815)
1827 **Dobbs**, Jane, Summer-hill, Dublin, widow
1839 **Donaldson**, Robert. (Codicil to Will of)
1821 **Donilan**, Anthony, Ballieghter, co. Galway, gent.

1817 **Ennis**, Mary, Plunket-st., Dublin, widow
1804 **Evans**, rev. George, Mullaghmore, co. Tyrone, clk. (Lodged 1807)

1811 **Fawcett**, Robert, Lower Ormond-quay, Dublin, attorney
1827 **Frewin**, Jeremiah, Barronstown
1828 **Furlong**, Laurence, Enniscorthy, merchant.

1808 **Goodbody**, Samuel, Ranelagh, co. Dublin, gent.
1827 **Gray**, Hugh, Tuffnell-pl., Islington
1800 **Grindly**, Robert, Fishamble-street
1830 **Green**, Francis, Ballyshannon, co. Donegal
1824 **Greene**, George, Powerstown, co. Tipperary, M.D.

1788 **Harold**, George
1796 **Hearin**, Patrick, Cullen, co. Kilkenny, blacksmith
1825 **Hedley**, Elizabeth, Newcastle-on-Tyne, spinster [watchmaker
1835 **Heney**, Patrick, Capel-st., Dublin,
1838 **Henn**, Poole, Mornington, co. Meath
1838 **Hoey**, Michael, Newcomen-terrace, Dublin

TABLE SHOWING THE RELATION BETWEEN THE COUNTIES AND DIOCESES OF IRELAND.

County.	Dioceses in which contained.
Antrim, ...	Connor, Derry, Down, Dromore.
Armagh, ...	Armagh, Dromore.
Carlow, ..	Leighlin.
Cavan, ...	Kilmore, Meath, Ardagh.
Clare, ...	Killaloe and Kilfenora, Limerick.
Cork, ...	Cork and Ross, Cloyne, Ardfert.
Donegal, ...	Raphoe, Derry, Clogher.
Down, ...	Down, Dromore, Connor, Newry and Mourne.
Dublin, ...	Dublin.
Fermanagh, ..	Clogher, Kilmore.
Galway, ...	Tuam, Clonfert, Kilmacduagh, Elphin, Killaloe.
Kerry, ...	Ardfert.
Kildare.	Kildare, Dublin.
Kilkenny, ...	Ossory, Leighlin.
King's County, ..	Kildare, Meath, Killaloe, Ossory, Clonfert.
Leitrim, ...	Kilmore, Ardagh.
Limerick, ...	Limerick, Cashel and Emly, Killaloe.
Londonderry, ..	Derry, Connor, Armagh.
Longford, ...	Ardagh, Meath.
Louth, ...	Drogheda, Armagh, Clogher.
Mayo, ...	Killala and Achonry, Tuam.
Meath, . ..	Meath, Kilmore, Armagh, Kildare.
Monaghan, ...	Clogher.
Queen's County, ..	Leighlin, Ossory, Kildare, Dublin.
Roscommon, ..	Elphin, Tuam, Clonfert, Ardagh.
Sligo, ...	Killala, Elphin, Ardagh.
Tipperary, ...	Cashel, Killaloe, Waterford and Lismore.
Tyrone, ...	Armagh, Derry, Clogher.
Waterford, ...	Waterford and Lismore.
Westmeath, ..	Meath, Ardagh.
Wexford, ...	Ferns, Dublin.
Wicklow, ...	Dublin, Leighlin, Ferns.